A
PAUL ROBESON
RESEARCH GUIDE

PAUL ROBESON
(1898–1976)

Photograph courtesy of the Mary O. H. Williamson Collection of the Prints and Photographs Collection of the Moorland-Spingarn Research Center of Howard University. Reprinted by permission.

A
PAUL ROBESON
RESEARCH GUIDE

A SELECTED
ANNOTATED
BIBLIOGRAPHY

Compiled by Lenwood G. Davis

GREENWOOD PRESS
Westport, Connecticut • London, England

Library of Congress Cataloging in Publication Data

Davis, Lenwood G.
  A Paul Robeson research guide.

  Bibliography: p.
  Includes index.
  1. Robeson, Paul, 1898-1976—Bibliography. I. Title.
Z8747.74.D38   1982   016.782'092'4   82-11680
[E185.97.R63]
ISBN 0-313-22864-7 (lib. bdg.)

Library of Congress Catalog Card Number: 82-11680
ISBN: 0-313-22864-7

First published in 1982

Greenwood Press
A division of Congressional Information Service, Inc.
88 Post Road West, Westport, Connecticut 06881

Printed in the United States of America

10 9 8 7 6 5 4 3 2 1

FOR
ERNEST KAISER,
A BIBLIOGRAPHER'S BIBLIOGRAPHER

Contents

Foreword

The publication of this bibliography of all of the known references on Paul Robeson is a service to scholarship and to others who wish to understand the many dimensions of the life of Paul Robeson. For a number of years Professor Lenwood G. Davis, who is one of the most able Renaissance bibliographers in the United States, has painstakingly collected materials on Paul Robeson from many sources, some of them not generally known to other scholars. When a definitive book on Paul Robeson is written, the author of such a book will have to lean very heavily on the materials collected by Professor Davis.

Before his death on January 23, 1978, writing about Paul Robeson was already a literary industry. He was one of the best known African-Americans of the twentieth century. The struggle of his people in the United States, their endurance in the midst of this struggle, and their art, music, and culture in general, was the basis of his great artistry and his commitment.

In an article written for *African Magazine* in March 1976, I have observed that Paul Robeson was indeed more than an artist, activist, and freedom fighter. The dimensions of the talent made him our Renaissance man. He was the first American artist, Black or White, to realize that the role of the artist extends far beyond the stage and the concert hall. Early in his life he became conscious of the plight of his people, stubbornly surviving in a racist society. This was his window on the world. From this vantage point he saw how the plight of his people related to the rest of humanity. He realized that the artist had the power and the responsibility to change the society in which he lived.

He was born April 9, 1898, at a time of great crisis for his people. When he died on January 23, 1976, his people were still in a crisis, partly of a different nature and partly the same crisis that they faced in the closing years of the nineteenth century when Paul Robeson was born. He was born three years after Booker T. Washington made his famous Atlanta Exposition address in 1895, and two years after the Supreme Court announced a decision in the *Plessy* versus *Ferguson* Case, in which the concept of "Separate but Equal" facilities for Black Americans became law. Of course, the separateness never produced any equalness. The time and the decision did produce some of the problems that Paul Robeson would address himself to in later years.

He grew to early manhood during the Booker T. Washington era. He made his professional debut at the Harlem YWCA in 1920, in the play "Simon The Cyrenian," by Redgely Torrence. This was the same year the Jamaican Black Nationalist, Marcus Garvey, convened the historic First UNIA International Convention of the Negro Peoples of the World at Madison Square Garden. The cry "Africa for the Africans, those at home and abroad" became part of the folklore of Black America. The convention of 1920 was a monumental achievement in Black organizations. At about the same time, the intellectual movement called The Harlem Literary Renaissance was beginning.

The circumstances of Paul Robeson's growth into manhood made him mature beyond his years by 1920. In 1930, ten years after he made his professional debut, the first of a long list of books about his life and achievements was published. The book, *Paul Robeson, Negro,* was written by his wife, Eslanda Goode Robeson. There are two other books about Paul Robeson, written by African-American women writers that are worth noting here. They are: *Paul Robeson: Citizen of the World* (1946), by Shirley Graham (later Mrs. W.E.B. DuBois), and *Paul Robeson: The Life and Times of a Free Black Man* (1974), by Virginia Hamilton. The book, *Paul Robeson*, by Marie Seton, published in London in 1958, is, in my opinion, the best book on the life of Paul Robeson written by a White person.

There is now a renaissance of literature and interest in the career of the great multi-genius, Paul Robeson. In 1978, the editors of *Freedomways* expanded the special issue of that magazine (Vol. II, No. 1, First Quarter, 1971) into a full length book, *Paul Robeson the Great Forerunner.* Among other things, this book contains an extensive bibliography of published writings by and about Paul Robeson, compiled by Ernest Kaiser. In 1981, *A Pictorial Biography of Paul Robeson, The Whole World in His Hands*, written by his granddaughter, Susan Robeson, was published.

At the time of his death January 23, 1976, a new generation was discovering Paul Robeson for the first time. An older generation was regretting that it had not made the best use of the strengths and hope that he had given to them. The writer L. Clayton Jones made this comment in the *Amsterdam News* after his death.

One watches with restrained anger as a nation of hypocrites grudgingly acknowledges the passing of a twentieth century phenomenon, Paul Robeson, All American Athlete, Shakespearean Actor, Basso Profundo, Linguist, Scholar, Lawyer, Activist. He was all these things and more.

In December 1977, an Ad Hoc Committee to End the Crimes Against Paul Robeson was formed to protest the inaccurate portrayal of Paul Robeson in a new play by Phillip Hayes Dean. Their statement read, in part:

> The essence of Paul Robeson is inseparable from his ideas—those most profoundly held artistic, philosophical and political principles which evolved from his early youth into the lifelong commitments for which he paid so dear and from which he never waivered down to his final public statement in 1975.
>
> In life, Paul Robeson sustained the greatest effort in the history of this nation to silence a single artist. He defied physical and psychological harassment and abuse without once retreating from his principles and the positions to which he dedicated his life. We believe that it is no less a continuation of the same crime to restore him, now that he is safely dead, to the pantheon of respectability on the terms of those who sought to destroy him.
>
> Robeson is the archetype of the Black American who uncompromisingly insists on total liberation. His example and his fate strike to the very heart of American racism.

In his book, *Robeson: Labor's Forgotten Champion* (Detroit: Balamp Publishing Co., 1975), Dr. Charles H. Wright states that:

> Robeson saw the struggle of the working classes of Spain in the same terms that he saw the struggles of the black man in the United States. He made this clear after he left Spain and embarked on a series of public appearances on behalf of the Republicans, both on the continent and in England. It was from the continent, probably the Spanish Embassy in Paris that he issued what became known as his Manifesto against Fascism.

The Manifesto reads as follows:

> Every artist, every scientist must decide, now, where he stands. He has no alternative. There are no impartial observers.

Through the destruction, in certain countries of man's literary heritage, through the propagation of false ideas of national and racial superiority, the artist, the scientist, the writer is challenged. This struggle invades the former cloistered halls of our universities and all her seats of learning.

The battlefront is everywhere. There is no sheltered rear. The artist elects to fight for freedom or slavery.

I have made my choice! I had no alternative!

The history of the war is characterized by the degradation of my people. Despoiled of their lands, their culture destroyed, they are denied equal opportunity of the law and deprived of their rightful place in the respect of their fellows.

Not through blind faith or through coercion, but conscious of my course, I take my place with you. I stand with you in unalterable support of the lawful government of Spain, duly and regularly chosen by its sons and daughters.

His public career started in 1920 and ended in 1975, over fifty years later. He directly influenced two generations and will influence generations still to come. He was a living symbol of the Black American struggle, and he saw very clearly that this was a part of the struggle of oppressed people throughout the world.

For the nation to confront him honestly would mean that it confronts itself—to begin at last the process of reclamation of the national soul.

John Henrik Clarke
Hunter College
New York, New York

Introduction

Let me say from the outset that this work is neither comprehensive nor definitive. It is exactly what its title indicates. It would be nearly impossible for anyone to do an exhaustive study on Paul Robeson because he traveled, spoke, and performed not only all over the United States, but also in Australia, all over Europe, and especially the British Isles, as well as Russia, Canada, New Zealand, and the British West Indies. Moreover, it would take many years and a substantial amount of money for one to travel all over the world to locate data on Paul Robeson, let alone to annotate writings by and about him. I did not deal with references in foreign countries other than England and a few others, because most were in foreign languages and unavailable to the general public. Therefore, unless one reads German, Spanish, Russian, French, or other foreign languages, he or she would find little use for data from those countries. However, one of the best ways to find information about Robeson is to consult the local newspapers in the cities in which he appeared, for the news media usually covered his appearances.

While this work is definitely not the definitive compilation on Robeson, it is nevertheless, the most complete annotated one to date. The most exhaustive compilation is found in Anatol Schlosser's unpublished doctoral dissertation, and is a sixty-nine page unannotated bibliography titled "Paul Robeson: His Career in The Theatre, in Motion Pictures and on the Concert Stage" (1970). It should be pointed out that nearly twenty-five pages of this bibliography consist of programs, handbills, transcripts, scripts, scenarios, press releases, birth certificates, business records, and unpublished manuscripts. There is also Ernest Kaiser's forty-two page partially annotated bibliography in *Paul Robeson: The Great Forerunner* (1978), compiled by the editors of *Freedomways,* the source of the original idea for this present project. Another major reference on Robeson is Phillip S. Foner's *Paul Robeson Speaks: Writings, Speeches, Interviews, 1918–1974* (1978). Most of Robeson's writings and speeches are included, as well as Notes, Selected Bibliography, and Index. Dr. Foner, however, did not include Paul Robeson's weekly columns in the *People's Voice,* a Black New York City newspaper published in the 1940s. The compiler also left out many interviews from foreign countries, especially England, as well as interviews in such major Black newspapers as the *New York Amsterdam News, Pittsburgh Courier, Baltimore Afro-American, Norfolk Journal and Guide, Chicago Defender, California Eagles, Black Dispatch,* and *New York Age.* He also omitted major interviews from the *Daily Worker, National Guardian,* and the *New York Times.* In spite of its obvious shortcomings, it is still the most complete single collection of materials on Robeson to date. There is Lamont H. Yeakey's unpublished Master's thesis, "The Early Years of Paul Robeson: Prelude to the Making of a Revolutionary, 1898-1930" (1971), which includes eighty footnotes. There is also Erwin A. Salk's *Du Bois-Robeson: Two Giants of the 20th Century. The Story of an Exhibit and a Bibliography* (1977). About half of this twenty page booklet is devoted to Paul Robeson, with a Profile, a Chronology, and a Bibliography of Robeson that includes books about him, recordings and tapes, and films and videotapes. All songs on each record album are discussed as are their distributors. The latest work on Robeson is by his granddaughter. Susan Robeson, and is entitled *Paul Robeson: A Pictorial Biography* (1981). The value of this work is in the number of rare photos it contains.

This present volume is limited specifically to the printed materials on Paul Robeson for two reasons. First, it is easily accessible to the general public. Second, most of the unpublished materials are unavailable to laymen. Most of this material is located at Howard University and is presently being processed. This nearly 50,000-piece collection is scheduled to be available to users in 1985. It consists of unpublished manuscripts, letters, business correspondences, documents, handbills, programs, scrapbooks, pamphlets, and personal papers, among other items. The Paul Robeson Archives in the German Democratic Republic also has a large collection of materials on Robeson. Most of it is in German, however, and needs to be translated into English. The Schomburg Center for Research in Black Culture has very good holdings on Paul Robeson that include books, pamphlets, programs, magazine articles, and newspaper clippings on microfiche and in folders, albums of phonograph records, and some of his personal papers. These personal papers, however, are restricted and unavailable to the public. Several other libraries that are listed in the Appendix have archival materials on Paul Robeson.

It is not necessary to recapitulate Paul Robeson's life because it is documented throughout this work. It is necessary, however, to reemphasize the fact that he was a many-faceted individual who was multitalented. Robeson was truly a "Man for All Seasons." He was an all-American athlete, attorney, scholar, actor, singer, linguist, citizen of the world, humanitarian, and political and cultural exponent of international peace. His career spanned nearly fifty years. Yet, sadly enough, most young people, both Black and White, never have heard of Paul Robeson. He has virtually been stricken from the history books. Ironically, most of the leading Black scholars do not include him in their works. And when they do, he is only discussed briefly as a singer and actor and not as a political activist. Hence, generations of young people will go through life never hearing of this genius of Black political protest and Pan-Africanism. I hope that someone will build upon this embryonic work and nurture it to its maturity, so that future generations will know more about Robeson.

It goes without saying that Paul Robeson was ahead of his time. What he advocated thirty years ago is just now coming to pass. In addition to advocating freedom and independence for the African continent, he also sought better American and Russian relationships and civil rights for Black people in the United States. He was "Mr. Civil Rights" in the 1930s and 1940s. As early as the 1930s Robeson made his choice to fight for freedom. He declared: "The artist must take sides. He must elect to fight for freedom or slavery. I have made my choice. I have no alternative. . . ." Robeson fought for the freedom of all peoples for nearly half a century. He reaffirmed his position in 1973 on his seventy-fifth birthday. There was a "Salute to Paul Robeson" at Carnegie Hall in New York City. He could not attend because of ill health, but he sent a taped message. Robeson stated, in part: "Though I have not been able to be active for several years, I want you to know that I am the same Paul, dedicated as ever to the worldwide cause of humanity for freedom, peace, and brotherhood. . . . Though ill health has compelled my retirement, you can be sure that in my heart I go on singing:

'But I keeps laughing
Instead of crying,
I must keep fighting
Until I'm dying,
And Ol' Man River
He just keeps rolling along!' "

The above lines are the essence of Paul Robeson. He kept fighting the system until the day he died. Robeson was one Black man that the system could not break. They bent him many times, but in the end they never did break him. He just kept rolling along—to the end.

This work consists of two parts. Part One discusses works by and about Paul Robeson. Part Two consists of eleven appendices. All of the works in this collection are arranged chronologically to show Paul Robeson's progression and development in his widening activities. I commented on or evaluated only a few of the articles and books, because I wanted the readers to decide the merit of the works for themselves.

Any work of this nature includes the assistance of many people. I especially would like to acknowledge a few who gave invaluable advice and assistance. Ernest Kaiser of the Schomburg Center was most helpful, not only in offering encouragement, but also in sharing with me many citations that he had in his own personal collection on Paul Robeson. He also provided the impetus that I needed to finish this project. He is a "bibliographer's bibliographer." Paul Robeson, Jr., and John Henrik Clarke also provided encouragement and leads to materials on the artist. Janet L. Sims-Wood, of Howard University's Moorland-Spingarn Research Center, shared with me some of the references that I was missing. Daniel T. Williams and Clara L. Heath, of Tuskegee Institute, sent me copies of newspaper clippings from that college's files on Paul Robeson. Dr. Philip S. Foner granted me permission to use the titles of some of Robeson's articles in *Freedom*. Brigitte Boegelsack, of the Paul Robeson Archives of the German Democratic Republic; Esme E. Bhan, of the Manuscript Division of the Moorland-Spingarn Research Center; Susan Halpert, Houghton Reading Room, Harvard University; Lisa Browar, of the Beineck Rare Book and Manuscript Library of Yale University; M.A.F. Borris, of the British Library; Kenneth A. Lohf, Librarian for Rare Books and Manuscript Library of Yale University; M.A.F. Borris, of the British Library; Kenneth A. Lohf, Librarian for Rare Books and Manuscripts, Columbia University; Lee Alexander, Archivist of Atlanta University; Tal James of the Afrikan History Club, Detroit, Michigan; Estelle Rebec, of the Bancroft Library at the University of California, Berkeley; Hilary Cummings, Southern Illinois University at Carbondale; Mardel Pacheco, Princeton University Library; Jean Currie, Detroit Public Library; Barbara Dunlap, Archives and Special Collections, City College; and R. Russell Maylone, of Northwestern Library, were all helpful in supplying needed materials from their libraries.

I am also indebted to Shelia Campbell, along with Felicia Neal, Clarise Anderson, and Rajeeyah Rahman, for typing much of the original draft of this work. Ms. Campbell also typed much of the original copy while she was out of college on her summer vacation. I would also like to thank Susan Goscinski for typing the final copy of this manuscript and for making many grammatical corrections. Janie Harris also assisted with the typing, proofreading, and indexing, and special appreciation must go to her.

Several libraries also assisted me: the Library of Congress; the Schomburg Center for Research in Black Culture; the Moorland-Spingarn Research Center; the Manuscript Division of Columbia University; the Special Collection at Southern Illinois University at Carbondale; the Paul Robeson Archives of the German Democratic Republic; Detroit Public Library; University of Tennessee Library; Wake Forest Library; North Carolina Century University Library; Winston-Salem State University Library; University of North Carolina Library at Chapel Hill; Atlanta University; Duke University Library; University of North Carolina Library at Greensboro; New York Public Library; Rutgers University Library; Yale University Library; Princeton Public Library; and Montclair State College Library.

Although many people assisted me in this endeavor, I take full responsibility for any errors or omissions, and for all of its shortcomings. I would like to point out that I included only those works that I personally read and annotated. In some cases works were cited incorrectly. For instance, it has been often repeated that Michael Meyerson wrote a Master's thesis on Paul Robeson at the University of California at Berkeley. He did not write a Master's thesis, but he did write a Senior thesis. In a number of instances I saw some references, but due to a variety of reasons, I did not see the complete work. I consulted all works that were available and attempted to give complete citation data. In a number of cases I saw only newspaper clippings of articles and not the complete newspaper. Many of the clippings did not give page numbers. Moreover, many of the papers are out of print and could not be located.

In some instances, when several newspapers carried an identical story on Paul Robeson, I did not list all the newspapers, because it would be redundant and serve no useful purpose. I would also like to point out that some of the articles in this work were untitled in their original publications—thus I have given them titles. Therefore, when the reader consults the original works, he or she should not be surprised that they appear untitled. The essential point, however, is not the titles of the articles but what is in them. In spite of these minor shortcomings, I believe that this volume is the most complete reference guide of works by and about the subject to date. To reemphasize, *this is not the definitive work on Paul Robeson*! Perhaps one day someone will do a *definitive* work on him.

Part One
A Paul Robeson
Research Guide

I
Book and Pamphlets
by Paul Robeson

. . . . The artist must take sides. He must elect to fight for freedom or slavery. I have made my choice. I have no alternative. . . .

Paul Robeson

A. BOOK

1. <u>Here I Stand</u>. New York: Othello Associates, 1958. 128 pp.
   Reprinted by Beacon Press: Boston, 1971. 121 pp.

   The author, himself, best explains what he hopes to convey to the
   reader when he declares "in these pages I have discussed what
   this fight for Negro (full) freedom means in the crisis of today
   (1958), of how it represents the decisive front in the struggle
   for democracy in our country, of how it relates to the cause of
   peace and liberation throughout the world." He continues, "in
   presenting my views on this subject - and in one way or another of
   America and much of the rest of the world is discussing it. I
   have sought to explain how I came to my viewpoint and to take the
   stand I have taken. As with other men, my views, my work, my
   life are all of one piece." Though this small book is not an
   autobiography, the author does give a brief discussion to his
   early childhood and his family background. Robeson argues: "I
   speak as an American Negro whose life is dedicated, first and
   foremost, to the winning of full freedom - and nothing less than
   full freedom - for my people in America." This work is divided
   into six parts: "I Take My Stand," "Love Will Find Out the Way,"
   "Our Right to Travel," "The Time Is Now," "The Power of Negro
   Action," and "Our Children, Our World." There is an Appendix.
   The original publication also included an Appendix: A. "My
   Brother Paul," by Rev. Benjamin C. Robeson; B. An excerpt from the
   address of Dr. Benjamin E. Mays, President of Morehouse College,
   on the occasion of the award to Mr. Robeson of the honorary
   degrees of Doctor of Humane Letters, June 1, 1943; C. "A Universal Body of Folk Music - A Technical Movement in Behalf of
   Paul Robeson"; D. "The British Movement in Behalf of Paul Robeson";
   and E. "A Note on The Council On African Affairs," by W. Alphaeus
   Hunter. Numbers D. and E. were not included in the 1971 reprinted
   edition.

B. PAMPHLETS

2. Robeson, Paul and Max Yergan. The Negro and Justice: A Plea
    for Earl Bowder. New York: Citizens' Committee to Free Earl
    Bowder, November, 1941. 12 pp. (Pamphlet).

    Robeson made a speech at a mass meeting to free Earl Bowder in
    New York City on September 29, 1941. The activist declares that
    in the long struggle against fascism there has been one voice
    raised loud and clear in those days when collective action was
    necessary to defeat fascism and it is clearer today when really
    sincere collective action will mean the death of fascism on the
    soil of the Soviet Union. Robeson asserts that he was at the
    meeting because he knew that there can be no more honest evidence
    of a sincere decision to defeat fascism along with the sending of
    tanks to the Soviet Union than the freeing of Earl Bowder, so
    that he may take his rightful place in the vanguard of the
    cohorts against fascism....

3. The Job To Be Done. New York: Council on African Affairs, 1947.
    6 pp. (Pamphlet).

    The writer of this short pamphlet discusses the work done by the
    Council on African Affairs on behalf of Africa   for its freedom.
    This work briefly comments on what the Council was doing to help
    Africa gain its independence from colonial governments.

4. For Freedom and Peace. New York: Council on African Affairs,
    1949. 16 pp. (Pamphlet).

    This is a speech that Robeson made on June 19, 1949, at a
    "Welcome Home Rally" in New York City. The singer was returning
    to the United States from a European concert tour. He states
    that he was looking for freedom, full freedom, not an inferior
    brand. That, he said, explains his attitude to different people,
    to Africa, the continent from where he came. Robeson argues:
    "I know much about Africa, and I'm not ashamed of My African
    origin. I'm proud of it. The rich culture of that continent,
    its magnificent potential, gives me plenty of cause for pride.
    This was true of the deep stirrings that took place within me
    when I visited the West Indies in January. This explains my
    feeling toward the Soviet Union, where in 1934 I for the first
    time walked this earth in complete Human dignity, a dignity
    denied me at the Columbia University of Medina, denied me every-
    where in my native land, despite all the protestations about
    freedom, equality, constitutional rights, and the sanctity of
    the individuals." The world traveler also surmises that Blacks
    can not win their struggle by being lured into any kind of war
    with their closest friends and allies throughout the world. He
    concludes: "For any kind of decent life we need, we want, and
    we demand our constitutional rights-RIGHT HERE IN AMERICA. We
    do not want to die in vain any more on foreign battlefields for
    Wall Street and the greedy supporters of domestic fascism. If
    we must die, let it be in Mississippi or Georgia! Let it be

(Robeson, Paul)

wherever we are lynched and deprived of our rights as human beings!"

5. Forge Negro-Labor Unity For Peace and Jobs. New York: Harlem Trade Union Council, 1950. 15 pp. (Pamphlet).

This was a speech delivered at a meeting of the National Labor Conference for Negro Rights that was held in Chicago on June 10, 1950. He told the gathering that their meeting as men and women of American labor is in good time because it places them in the great stream of peace-loving humanity, determined to win a world of real brotherhood. It will, he continues, enable them to place the Negro trade unionists in the front ranks of a crusade to secure at least a million signatures of Negro Americans to this Stockholm Appeal for peace. The speaker concludes: "As the Black worker takes his place upon the stage of history not for a bit part, but to play his full role with dignity in the very center of the action-a new day dawns in human affairs. The determination of the Negro workers, supported by the whole Negro people, and joined with the mass of progressive white working men and women, can save the labor movement, CIO and AFL, from the betrayals of the Murrays and the Greens, the Careys, Rieves and Dubinskys-and from the betrayals, too. Of the Townsends, the Weavers and Randolphs. The alliance can beat back the attacks against the living standards and the very lives of the Negro people. It can stop the drive toward fascism. It can halt the chariot of war in its tracks." He also surmises that it can help to bring to pass in America, and in the world the dream our fathers dreamed-of a land that's free, of a people growing in friendship, in love, in cooperation and peace. "This is history's challenge to you. I know you will not fail," asserts Robeson.

6. The Negro People and the Soviet Union. New York: New Century Publishers, 1950. 15 pp. (Pamphlet).

This was an address that Paul Robeson made at a banquet that was sponsored by the National Council of American-Soviet Friendship. The dinner was held on November 10, 1949, at the Waldorf Astoria Hotel in New York City. Robeson declares, in part, ".... I have heard some honest and sincere people say to me, "Yes, Paul we agree with you on everything you say about Jim Crow and persecution. We're with you one hundred percent on these things. But what has Russia ever done for us negroes?' And in answering this question I feel that I must go beyond my own personal feelings and put my finger on the very crux of what the Soviet Union's very existence, its example before the world of abolishing all discrimination based on color or nationality, its fight in every arena of world conflict for genuine democracy and for peace, this has given us Negroes the chance of achieving our complete liberation within our own time, within this generation. To those who dare to question my patriotism, who have the unmitigated insolence to question my love for the true America and my right to be an American--to question me, whose father and forefathers fertilized the very soil of the country with their toil and with

(Robeson, Paul)

their bodies--to such people I answer that those and only those wno work for a policy of friendship with the Soviet Union are genuine American patriots. And all others who move toward a war that would destroy civilization, whether consciously or unconsciously, are betraying the interests of this country and the American people. Finally, my friends, I want to say that I believe the great majority of the American people will come to realize their identity of interests with the people of the Soviet Union and the growing People's Democracies. In this era of change, normal trade relations and peaceful cooperation can be the only answer. I am and always will be an anti-fascist and a fighter for the freedom and dignity of all men. We anti-fascists--the true lovers of American democracy--have a tremendous responsibility. We are not a small band--we are millions who believe in peace and friendship. If we mobilize with courage, the forces of world fascism can and will be defeated--in Europe, in Africa and in the United States. Because of this, I am and always will be, a firm and true friend of the Soviet Union and of the beloved Soviet people.

7. Paul Robeson Speaks to Youth. Challenge (Magazine), 799 Broadway, New York, 10003, 1951. 21 pp. (Pamphlet).

This is an address that Paul Robeson delivered at the First National Convention of Labor Youth League, November 24, 1950. He told the crowd, in part:
> The Negro Youths must be regarded as invaluable sinews
> in the arsenals of any fighting organization of young
> Americans.... We can not win the struggle for justice
> and equality without the youths and without them fully
> and freely functioning in the membership and leadership
> of all our movements for progress; it's hard to see how
> we can lose.... I don't think they're going to keep
> the voice of any of the democratic, peace-loving people
> of this country from resounding all over Europe, Asia
> and Africa, and all up and down this land of ours.
> Like Ol' Man River, I plan to keep fighting until I am
> dying-or until my people are free. And I'm sure nothing
> will stop the Labor Youth League from strengthening its
> organization, building the solidarity of the youth, and
> fighting for a land that's really free, in which men live
> in brotherhood, in security and in peace.

II
Forewords by Paul Robeson

Oppression has kept us on the bottom rungs of the ladder, and even with the removal of all barriers, we will still have a long way to climb in order to catch up with the general standard of living. But the equal *place* to which we aspire cannot be reached without the equal *rights* we demand, and so the winning of those rights is not a maximum fulfillment but a minimum necessity, and we cannot settle for less.

Paul Robeson

A. FOREWORDS

8. Foreword to <u>Uncle Tom's Children: Four Novellas</u>, by Richard
Wright. London: Victor Gollancz, Ltd., 1939.

   Robeson suggests that we have been long waiting for a book which
   would give a true and clear picture of the coloured man in
   America, especially in the deep South, where more than two-thirds
   of this oppressed minority of the United States live. Robeson
   further asserts, in part:
   > All kinds of sentimental novels of the nostalgic South
   > and of the black people have appeared from time to time,
   > --some harmless, some consciously or unconsciously libel-
   > lous. Now comes Richard Wright, flesh of these virile,
   > hard-working, suffering, but joyous Americans of African
   > descent, to create people who every one will feel really
   > exist; characters straight out of the rich life of the
   > folk who have contributed so much to the physical and
   > cultural making of present-day America; all the humour,
   > tenderness, tragedy (not pathos) are here, and much,
   > much more. For Wright portrays the Negro as he was and
   > is, --courageous, and forever struggling to better his
   > condition; the Negro descended from Nat Turner, Sojourner
   > Truth, Veasey, Frederick Douglass, and countless others
   > who fought that Americans of African blood should also be
   > free and (in words of Lincoln) "enjoy their constitutional
   > right!" Wright is a great artist, and one of the most
   > significant American authors of his time; he is in the
   > great tradition of the American Short Story.

9. Foreword to <u>Favority Songs of the Red Army and Navy</u>, Compiled
and Edited by David J. Grunes. New York: Russian-American
Music Publishers, 1941.

   He points out, in part:
   > American Negro folk songs sprang directly out of our lives
   > --our working lives--e.g., John Henry ballads and

(Robeson, Paul)

> countless others so superbly sung by Leadbetter
> and Josh White. Songs of protest, songs of faith
> in a better world, songs slow and rhythmic, tender and
> gay. So it was not surprising to find composers
> gathering these new and old melodies ... true creations
> of and for the People--expressing their joy in the new
> life, in the new society, in a new conception of human
> liberty, of human aspiration, of human possibilities
> of achievements. These songs were sung in the factories,
> in the mines, at Youth Day celebrations, at festivals,
> and especially by the soldier--choruses of the Red Army,
> trained by a great Director--Alexandroff. I am privileged
> to have the opportunity of writing this brief forword.
> For I have long deeply admired and loved the Soviet
> people as I do my own. I sincerely hope that these
> songs will help inspire a deep understanding of, and an
> admiration for, a People who I know have the progress
> of all humanity so deeply at heart.

10. Foreword to <u>Nigeria: Why We Fight For Freedom</u>, by Amanke Okafor.
     London: n.p., 1949.

The activist declares, in part:
> The use of the vast but as yet untapped resources of
> Africa for the benefit of the African peoples, and
> indeed of all mankind, is a lofty and noble aim. But
> this can be achieved only by the Africans themselves,
> and only when they shake off the shackles of colonialism
> and are free to develop their own country. It cannot
> be achieved by foreign financial concerns, whose only
> aim is to make the greatest profit out of exploiting
> the Africans. Such development plans can bring nothing
> but untold misery for countless thousands of African
> peoples. All over the world the ordinary working people
> are challenging the entrenched positions of the privi-
> leged and are organizing and fighting to win the rights
> that have so long been withheld from them. Across
> Africa, too, a new powerful urge is sweeping. More
> men and women are becoming conscious of the need for
> freedom. There are emerging individuals who, while
> inspired by a burning love of their country and their
> people, will have nothing to do with racial and
> national hatreds, pitfalls which often trap the unwary.
> One such individual is the writer of this pamphlet,
> who has made a deep study of the potentialities of his
> country. Nigeria, Britain's largest colonial possession,
> has a great future. Immensely rich in resources, both
> human and material, it requires only freedom and govern-
> ment by its own people in order to transform it within
> a generation from a backward, undeveloped colonial
> territory into one of the leading countries of the world.
> Amanke Okafor points out in this pamphlet, which fulfills
> a long-felt want, the way forward in Nigeria to all who
> stand for progress.

11. Foreword to <u>Lift Every Voice!</u>, Irwin Siber, Editor. New York:
     A People's Artist Publication, 1953.

     The singer wrote the Foreword to this Second People's Song Book.
     He declares:
           ... When Harriet Tubman went South in the dark days to
           lead the slaves and perhaps my father by way of the
           Underground Railway to freedom, thousands of human
           beings--the "salt of the earth"--lifted their voices
           in song. And so it has been wherever these of human
           kind have surged toward the light of liberation--
           men and women of every culture, color and clime.
           They have sung-and sing-songs created by the gener-
           ations-old genius of the folk. And there can be no
           greater genius. Beautiful songs--yes--sometimes of
           quiet meditation--sometimes of momentary thunder--
           sometimes of terrifying beauty for the faint of heart.
           Songs bursting through the bar-lines, calling for love,
           for brotherhood, for sisterhood, for equality, for
           freedom. It is a great privilege to greet this mag-
           nificent richly rewarding Song Book--to greet those
           responsible, the People's Artists. This is no mere
           phrase, People's Artists--it has the deepest of over-
           tones to hundreds of millions on every continent
           throughout the world....

12. Foreword to <u>Born of the People</u>, by Luis Taruc. Bombay, India:
     People's Publishing House, Ltd., 1953.

     The leader states that with great anticipation he began to read
     the story of Luis Tarcus, the great leader of the Hukhalahap,
     and of the Philippine people. For truly, as Taruc says, this
     is the sage of the people, for <u>from</u> them is he sprung and <u>to them</u>
     is he so closely bound, states Robeson. He declares, in part:
           In this magnificent and moving autobiography we see
           Luis Taruc grow with the people, reach into the most
           basic roots of the people, embrace and become a part of
           a whole people moving swiftly and unbendingly toward
           full national liberation. In the process, Taruc and
           many, many others become new kinds of human beings,
           harbingers of the future. This is an intensely moving
           story, full of the warmth, courage, and love which is
           Taruc. Here certainly is proof that the richest humanist
           tradition is inherited and will be continuously en-
           riched by the working class acting in closest bonds
           with the peasantry and honest vanguard intelligentsia--
           intellectuals who know that they must "serve the people,
           not enemies of the people." How necessary that we
           learn the simple yet profound lessons of united action,
           based upon the deepest respect for the people's wisdom,
           understanding, and creative capacity.

III
Introduction to Book, Senior Thesis, and Book Review by Paul Robeson

. . . my father was a slave, and my people died to build this country, and I am going to stay and have a piece of it just like you. And no fascist-minded people will drive me from it. Is that clear?

Paul Robeson

A. INTRODUCTION TO BOOK

13. Introduction to <u>American Negro and the Darker World</u>, by W.E.
     Burghardt DuBois. New York: National Committee to Defend
     Negro Leadership, 1957. (Pamphlet).

     Paul Robeson states, in part:
          If only all America could have been at the 135th Street
          Branch of the New York Public Library Tuesday Evening,
          May 7, 1957! For there in the intellectual environs
          of the Gallery dedicated to the Schomburg Collection--
          a Great American of African heritage was honored. A
          beautiful peice of sculpture by William Zorach, the
          noted American sculptor, was unveiled--a bronz head
          of Dr. W.E. Burhardt DuBois. Outstanding Americans
          in many fields participated. Dr. E. Franklin Frazier,
          Van Wyck Brooks, Judge Jane Bolin, Jean Blackwell--
          and many hundreds paid sincerest tribute. In this
          pamphlet is a searching and profound analysis of con-
          temporary America, of the whole world about us with
          special reference to the Africa of our forbears.
          And the challenge to each and everyone of us is in-
          escapable. Thanks to the Committee to Defend Negro
          Leadership which provided the stirring occasion for
          the delivery of this message--and thanks for this
          pamphlet so that all may read and reflect and act.
          And go out at once and get <u>The Ordeal of Mansart</u>--
          the latest book of this Great Scholar, Poet and fighter
          for all humanity--a book, the first of a trilogy, de-
          voted to the tortured but courageous history of Americans
          of African descent. And let us all be once more deeply
          thankful that we are privileged to live in the same
          period as Dr. DuBois, privileged to be a part of the
          same struggle for the full attainment of all peoples'
          freedoms and inherent human dignity.

B. SENIOR THESIS

14. "The Fourteenth Amendment: The Sleeping Giant of the American
     Constitution." Unpublished Senior Thesis, Rutgers University,
     May 29, 1919.

     This thesis included:
     I.   History of the Amendment:
          1.   Introduction
          2.   Causes leading to the adoption of the Amendment

     II. Construction and Interpretation of the first Section of
          the Amendment
          1.   Citizenship is defined
          2.   The Phrase "Subject to the jurisdiction thereof"
          3.   The Privileges and Immunities of United States Citizen
          4.   Due Process of Law
               (a). As related to Procedure
               (b). As related to Police Power
               (c). As related to Public Callings
               (d). As related to Taxation
          5.   "The Equal Protection" of the Laws

     III. Conclusion

               In the Fourteenth Amendment we have as a heritage a
          "new Magna Charta" in the words of Justice Swayne in the
          Slaughter-House Cases. "There is today a growing tendency
          to invade the liberty of the individual and to disregard
          the rights of property, a tendency manifesting itself in
          many forms. The hope of the American people lies in the
          strength of the Fourteenth Amendment." So long as the
          Constitution of the United States continues to be observed
          as the political creed, as the embodiment of the conscience
          of the nation, we are safe. State constitutions are being
          continually changed to meet the expediency, the prejudice,
          the passion of the hour. It is the law which touches every
          fibre of the whole fabric of life which surrounds and guards
          the rights of every individual; which keeps society in
          place; which in the words of Blackstone, "is universal in
          its use and extent, accommodated to each individual, yet
          comprehending the whole community." This Amendment is a
          vital part of American Constitutional law and we hardly
          know its sphere, but its provisions must be duly ob-
          served and conscientiously interpreted so that through it,
          the "Sleeping Giant of our Constitution," the American
          people shall develop a higher sense of constitutional
          morality.

C. BOOK REVIEW

15. "An Honest Approach To Africa, Says Robeson of Du Bois Book,"
     The Worker, April 27, 1947, p. 7.

     Paul Robeson reviewed W.E.B. DuBois' book Africa and The World.
     The writer declares, in part:
          ....To me the heart of the book is the light it sheds
          on the people who inhabit this continent on the back-
          ground of African civilization, and on the change in
          the Western concept of Africa and her people. Du Bois
          points out in his early chapter that there is a twisted
          background to our whole education about Africa. He
          develops very clearly the idea that here is a great con-
          tinent tnat has been raped, and that the whole recording
          of her history and peoples has been distorted to justify
          her enslavement.... Du Bois demonstrated that the
          Africans were, at first, princes. Little by little
          they became less then men in the effort to justify the
          falsificatise of scholarship following the demands of
          imperialism. In passing I would suggest that Du Bois
          some day investigate the similar treatment of the
          Chinese people who, in the earliest stages, were re-
          garded as, a great source of enlightenment in the West.
          But when it became expedient to force opium upon the
          Chinese, Chinese culture suddenly became a very back-
          ward one.... Africa and The World is a mine of
          wonderful material on the continent, both in a technical
          and poetical sense. Du Bois is one of the most
          beautiful writers in our language and has included
          many of his own poems...of the contributions of
          various writers of African descent. Personally I find
          it a book that I will always want with me.

IV
Articles by Paul Robeson

He who is not prepared to face the battle will never lead to triumph.

Paul Robeson

1. ACTOR'S EQUITY

15a. "Plain Talk," "Actors' Equity Means What It Says," People's
Voice, August 23, 1947, p. 14.

The writer discusses the Actors' Equity Association stand on discrimination. He asserts, in part:
Actors' Equity Association has decided that its members
shall not take part in plays in the National Theatre,
Washington, D.C., as long as that theatre discriminates
against Negroes who wish to buy tickets and see plays
presented there. The entire Negro people will applaud
this gratifying and splendid fight waged by the organized
actors of the nation. These members of a profession,
where there is often unemployment, have said that they
will forfeit unemployment, if necessary, in order to
remove racism from the American theatre. I believe their
stand will make for wider theatrical employment. In
Washington and elsewhere the people will respond to this
action which reflects the actor's sense of decency and
justice and which is, in itself, good, sound and dignified Americanism. The theatre on the whole, as well
as theatrical people will gain, not lose, from this
action of Actors' Equity. So a worthy fight is on.

2. AFRICA

16. "I Want to Be African," What I Want From Life, E.G. Cousins,
Editor, London: George Allen and Unwin Publishers, 1934, pp.
71-77.

He argues that Black people had their origin in Africa. Robeson
asserts tnat in his music, his plays, his films, he would always

(Robeson, Paul)

carry this central idea: to be an African. He concludes that
"multitudes of men have died for less worthy ideals; it is even
more eminently worth living for."

17. "African Culture," African Observer, Vol. 2, No. 5, March 1935,
     pp. 19-21.

     After repeatedly searching for this article, I could not locate
     it. However, I thought that it was necessary that I bring it to
     the attention of the reader. Based on Robeson's other comments
     on African culture, this article probably states that Africa has
     a rich heritage and that Black Americans should be proud of
     Africa.

18. "Primitives: On African Languages," The New Statesman and Nation,
     Vol. 12, August 8, 1936, pp. 190-192.

     He points out that it is not a matter of whether the Negro and
     other so-called "primitive" people are incapable of becoming
     pure intellectuals, it is a matter of whether they are going
     to be unwise enough to be led down this dangerous by-way when,
     without sacrificing the sound based in which they have their
     roots, they can avail themselves of the now-materialized triumphs
     of science and proceed to use them while retaining the vital
     creative side....

19. "Plain Talk," "From B'way To South Africa," People's Voice,
     October 11, 1947, p. 14.

     The writer comments on a play on Broadway and relates it to South
     Africa, freedom and independence. He suggests, in part:
          "OUR LAN'" Theodore Ward's splendid drama of the struggle
     waged by Negro freedmen for land and freedom following the
     Civil War, is a deeply-moving play. I saw it the other
     night at the Royale Theatre where it opened on Sept. 27,
     and was struck by the remarkable parallel between the
     valiant fight of the freed slaves during Reconstruction and
     the struggles which confront all darker peoples today.
     I caught a glimpse of the bigger thing this play repre-
     sented-a glimpse of oppressed peoples in many different
     lands all over the world, peoples who shared one thing
     in common, the burning hope and belief that with our victory
     over fascism would come their liberation. To these peoples,
     the colonial slaves of Asia and the feudal serfs of Europe
     and the Americas, came the same betrayal, the same shock
     of disillusionment as to the Negro freedmen after the Civil
     War. Today the oppressed and exploited millions of the
     earth are resolved to die rather than be forced back into
     imperialist and feudal bondage. There may be temporary
     setbacks, as happened for example in the brutal Dutch
     aggression against the Indonesian Republic, but the march
     of the oppressed colonial peoples of the earth is ir-
     resistibly forward....The most explosive problem in Africa
     today are centering in the Union of South Africa where

(Robeson, Paul)

racial discrimination is the most extreme and brutal to
be found anywhere in the world. The most important consideration here is the fact that the concentration of
power and wealth and white supremacy rule in South Africa
represent a threat not only to the whole of Africa, but
to India, Asia and the entire non-white world including
Negro America....

20. "Plain Talk," "America Backs South Africa," People's Voice,
October 25, 1947, p. 14.

The writer comments on the United States' involvement in South
Africa's affairs. He argues, in part:
Last Wednesday's vote in the UN's Trusteeship Committee
on India's resolution to force the Union of South Africa
to comply with the UN's charter and the Assembly's request
to bring South-West Africa under the Trusteeship system,
was indeed revealing. The Indian resolution directed the
South African Government to submit a draft trusteeship agreement for the former German Colony which it has administered
under mandate since the end of World War I. The resolution
passed by a vote of 27 to 20. There were four absentions,
one of which was Ethiopia. I was most interested in the way
in which the countries lined up on this important issue,
particularly so in the case of our own country. I must
admit that I had no illusions whatever about the way the
U.S. delegate, John Foster Dulles, would cast his vote in
the Trusteeship Committee. He did not disappoint me. For
the United States voted with the world's major colony-
holding powers - Britain, France, Belgium, the Netherlands,
along with such dubious democracies as Argentina, Greece
and Turkey. What is important here is that the U.S. voted
to support one of the most violently anti-Negro regimes
in the world in its plan to delay surrendering control
over a territory wherein live over 300,000 Negroes. When
Dulles voted against the Indian resolution he voted for the
color bar, pass laws, peonage, super-exploitation of
native labor in the mines and farms, disfranchisement,
and legalized bigotry all of which make up the pattern of
life in South Africa today.... There ought to be a great
and ringing outcry in the land against this betrayal of the
American people's trust. There ought to be some kind of
national repudiation of Dulles and Co. who, under careful
instructions to be sure, are placing the U.S. in the vanguard
of the world reaction on all the major issues before the
UN....

21. "Here's My Story," "We Can Learn From the Struggle in South
Africa," Freedom, July 1952, pp. 1, 3.

The author comments on South African's struggle for freedom and
independence from the colonists. He argues, in part:
....These South Africans aren't afraid of baiting. They
march in thousands with raised clenched fists. They sing

(Robeson, Paul)

their songs of protest (including some of mine, I modestly
add). They clamor for an end to war preparations and
demand peace. They say quite sharply and plainly they want
their youth alive to struggle for the independence of Africa,
not dead on foreign battle fields in the interest of those
bankers and factory and mine owners who have come to South
Africa, especially from the U.S., to take away their land,
diamonds, gold and uranium. These South Africans - African,
Indian, colored, white and black workers - see no threat
from the lands of Eastern Europe, from the Soviet Union
Republics, from the people of the new Chinese Republic led
by the great Mao Tse Tung. Quite the opposite, all these
are friendly people whose struggles give hope to the
African peoples. There in South Africa it happens to be the
"Western Europeans" who came generations ago to despoil the
land and enslave the indigenous inhabitants, and who
still rule as tyrannical masters - like our Southern
Byrnes, Talmadges and Rankins. These Africans are proud
of their leaders who are making great sacrifices, leaders
of every shade of opinion. They are as proud of their
leaders who behave like our Ben Davis and others who
are not so advanced in their thinking. But they are joined,
unified for the common purpose of their full equality and
independence. How we here could learn from this - we
Americans of African descent of all groups, from whatever
lands we have come....

22.   "Here's My Story," "A Lesson From Our South African Brother and
      Sister," Freedom, September, 1952, pp. 1,2.

The activist compares what was happening to Blacks in the United
States and the Union of South Africa. He argues that Blacks in
South Africa mean to win their fight against the racist government there. The leader surmises that they are going to win
because they MEAN to win. Robeson declares, in part:
      We (American Blacks) mean to win too, but we ought to
      take a lesson from our South African brothers and
      sisters. The lesson is UNITY. It was harder for them
      in many ways but now they've gotten together - the leaders
      and the people, the blacks and the Indians and the
      "coloreds" and the Trades and Labour Council, and they
      say: "This is it! Freedom for us now!" Somehow we've
      got to get united like that and it had better be soon.
      Not after the elections, but today. And why not? We're
      united now in our insistence on civil rights, but when we
      unite all our strength - churches, NAACP, trade unionists,
      lodges, women's clubs, business and professional groups -
      and move together, well, we'll get our civil rights in
      1952. And there's something else we talked about on the
      corner along with all the rest about whips and jails.
      There are the invisible chains too - like denying me a
      passport because, as the government noted in one brief,
      Robeson "has been active politically in behalf of the
      independence of the colonial peoples of Africa." I

(Robeson, Paul)

have for a fact, and I'm still fighting for my passport
which they are still keeping from me...but the African
freedom fight just keeps rolling along. And how it must
have pained certain people down in Washington to read
in the N.Y. Times that parading black and brown men in
Johannesburg were singing "Robeson songs"! Songs of
liberation - who can lock them up? The spirit of freedom -
who can jail it? A people's unity - what lash can beat it
down? Civil rights - what doubletalk can satisfy our need?
O my brothers and sisters of the two USA's - we are going
to be free!

23. "Here's My Story," "Africa Calls - Will You Help?," Freedom,
     May 1953, pp. 1, 7.

     The world traveler declares that Africa needs the help of
     American Negroes. He asserts, in part:
          ....American Negroes have a real duty to our African
          brothers and sisters, a sacred duty (Max) Yerman calls
          it merely a "sentimental interest" but Negroes who have
          not lost all pride and dignity know that if we are at
          all serious about our full freedom here in America we
          must understand what the future of Africa means. The
          Indian people understand it. One of the leaders of
          the Kikuyu, a close associate of Kenyatta, is now in
          India and Nehru himself has spoken out about the
          necessity of supporting the African and Indian people
          in South and East Africa. Can we here in America fail
          to being pressure upon the corporations involved, not
          to sabotage the African struggle? Can we fail to
          point the finger at Malan? Should we not do all in
          our power to help the people there, speaking out in
          their behalf, raising funds to send them, letting them
          know that we are on their side?.... Not only is this
          a struggle in the interest of the African people.
          Their freedom and dignity will be of immeasurable
          assistance in our final break-through here in these
          United States. New Africa will mean in the end a new
          Alabama, a new Mississippi, Arkansas, Georgia, a new
          Washington, D.C. for us. African liberation calls for
          assistance. Our leadership is weighed in the balance.
          I'm confident it will not be found wanting.

24. "Here's My Story," "A Thousand Years? No - Now's The Time For
     African Freedom," Freedom, June 1953, pp. 1, 11.

     He discusses how he discovered Africa. He asserts, in part:
          I "discovered" Africa in London. That discovery -
          back in the twenties - profoundly influenced my life.
          Like most of Africa's children in America, I had
          known little about the land of our fathers. But
          in England, where my career as an actor and singer
          took me, I came to know many Africans. Some of
          their names are now known to the world - Azikiwe, and

(Robeson, Paul)

    Nkrumah, and Kenyatta, who has just been jailed for
his leadership of the liberation struggles in Kenya.
Many of these Africans were students, and I spent
many hours talking with them and taking part in their
activities at the West African Students Union building.
Somehow they came to think of me as one of them; they
took pride in my successes; and they made Mrs. Robeson
and me honorary members of the Union. Besides,
these students, who were mostly of princely origin,
I also came to know another class of Africans - the
seamen in the ports of London, Liverpool and Cardiff.
They too had their organizations, and much to teach
me of their lives and their various peoples. As an
artist it was most natural that my first interest in
Africa was cultural. Culture? The foreign rulers
of that continent insisted there was no culture
worthy of the name in Africa. But already musicians
and sculptors in Europe were astir with their discovery of African art. And as I plunged, with ex-
cited interest, into my studies of Africa at the London
University and elsewhere, I came to see that African
culture was indeed a treasure-store for the world....

25. "How I Discovered Africa," Fighting Talk, April, 1955.

This article was a reprint of an article that first appeared in
Freedom, June, 1953, under the title, "A Thousand Years? No -
Now's The Time For African Freedom." Since it is annotated else-
where in this work it will not be discussed here.

3. BLACK MAN'S CULTURE

26. "Riches of The Black Man's Culture," African Observer, June, 1933.

After searching for this article in several major libraries, including the Library of Congress, I was unable to find it. However, I thought that I should include it in this collection. Based
on previous remarks made by Robeson, this article probably suggests
that the Black man has a rich heritage that he can be proud of.

27. "The Culture of the Negro," The Spectator, (London), June 15, 1934,
pp. 916-917.

The artist points out that he has no desire to interpret the
vocal genius of half a dozen cultures which are really alien to
him. He argues that no matter in what part of the world you find
him, the Negro has retained his direct emotional response to outside stimuli; he is constantly aware of an external power which
guides his destiny. Robeson surmises that no wonder the Negro
is an intensely religious creature and that his artistic and

(Robeson, Paul)

cultural capacities find expression in the glorification of some
deity in song. He concludes that the American and West Indian
Negro worships the Christian God in his own particular way and
makes him the object of his supreme artistic manifestation
which is embodied in the Negro spiritual....

28.   "Here's My Story," "Negro History - History of the Whole Negro
      People," Freedom, February 1951, pp. 1, 2.

      Robeson declares, in part:
            Is the history of the Negro people in the United
            States to be measured only by the achievement of a number
            of outstanding individuals -- as important as are these
            successes? I submit that our history is exactly what the
            words say -- the history of the whole Negro people. This
            history is not individual, but collective in its essence.
            It is a history of the group. Our forefathers were herded
            into slave ships -- herded onto the Southern plantations --
            and throughout the 250-or-so years of slavery we were
            herded and oppressed as one solid mass of humanity. We
            rebelled as one group, and with our allies, we fought our
            way to Freedom as a compact and great family unit. Our
            paper, FREEDOM, certainly receiving invaluable aid from
            the experience and knowledge of the trade union and pro-
            gressive leaders among us, must root itself in the people
            of this land, especially the Negro people. It must address
            itself to the eagerly awaiting masses, must become a voice
            such as does not exist in the Negro press at this time.
            If we do this we will be fulfilling in a magnificent way
            our present historic tasks: the fight for peace, for
            liberation of the Negro people, for the dignity of the
            whole American people, for friendship with people's govern-
            ments, for close ties with the advanced sections of the
            working peoples, white and colored, all over the world.

                    4.   BLACK-JEWISH RELATIONS

29.   "Bonds of Brotherhood," Jewish Life, November, 1954, pp. 13-14.

      Robeson declares that there is a common bond between Black Ameri-
      cans and Jewish Americans. He discusses the historical relation-
      ship between Blacks and Jews and how they have supported one
      another in their struggle for human rights.

5. BRITISH WEST INDIES

30. "Plain Talk," "West Indian Federation Is A Possibility," People's
Voice, September 13, 1947, p. 14.

The writer observes the formation of the West Indian Federation.
He suggests that Negro Americans must join with their West Indian
brothers in their efforts to create a new nation. He declares,
in part:
     West Indian Federation is now more than a vague
     possibility. It is being seriously discussed this
     month by delegates of the main labor and progressive
     political groups of the Caribbean Islands at a historical
     conference in Jamaica. This conference will draw up a plan
     for a union of the West Indian colonies of Great Britain
     into a single dominion. Coming at a time when darker peoples
     all over the world are on the move toward independence and
     self-determination, this is of tremendous significance....
     I think the most important thing to recognize in the West
     Indian situation today is that a majority of the people
     want an independent country. What does this mean to
     American Negroes? At this moment in world history nothing
     could be more important than the establishment of an in-
     dependent Negro country to the south of us and the develop-
     ment of healthy diplomatic, economic, and cultural relations
     with it.

31. "Here's My Story," "A Letter From Jamaica, B.W.I.," Freedom,
February, 1953, p. 1.

Paul Robeson shares with his readers a letter that he received
from Jamaica, B.W.I. It states, in part:
     Allow me to extend to you, on behalf of the Jamaica
     Youth Movement, warmest fraternal greetings from the
     youth of Jamacia. This movement, despite the inevitable
     red smear, is undauntedly intensifying the struggle to
     win freedom, dignity and a place in the sun for the youth
     of this country. No doubt you will be interested to hear
     that we are supporting the International Conference in
     Defense of the Rights of Youth, and we have accepted the
     invitation of the World Federation of Democratic Youth
     to send a delegation. In an effort to popularize the
     conference, we are calling a second National Conference
     on youth's rights here in Kingston in conjunction with
     radio broadcasts and public meetings. As the youth of the
     world prepare for a highly important conference in Vienna,
     we may expect the State Department to do everything possible
     to prevent an adequate representation of young people from
     the United States. While we fight for the right of our
     youth to have passports for this conference, it is good to
     know that the sentiment and problems of peoples of African
     descent will also be voiced by our sturdy young friends
     of Jamacia....

6. CHINA

32.   "Here's My Story," "Conversation About The New China," Freedom,
      May, 1951, pp. 1, 2.

      Robeson discusses "New China." He surmises, in part:
          Well, there are 500 million Chinese, and for centuries
          about 499 million of them have been living just like our
          folks in the South. Every year millions of them used to
          starve to death. And right in the biggest cities of China
          where the big powers had concessions, there were hotels
          and restaurants and clubs that a Chinese couldn't go in
          unless he was a servant. Yes -- sir, that big country of
          China was a jimcrow country, just like our country. Then
          comes along a man named Sun Yat-sen and after him a man named
          Mao Tse-tung, and the first thing Mao did was put an end to
          big plantation system that was starving the Chinese to death.
          That was the first thing, and I want to tell you, brother,
          it's a pretty big thing when you fix it so that 499
          million people will be free from hunger for the rest
          of their lives and their children's lives. The second
          thing Mao did was put an end to Jim Crow. And when I
          say "an end," Jack, I mean "an end." Never again in
          China will any Englishman or American kick around a
          Chinese rickshaw driver, or put up a sign on a building
          to keep Chinese out. That's gone, brother. Well, now,
          I want to ask you a question. Just support our folks in
          the South got the land they've been tilling all these
          centuries for the big plantation owners. Support they
          got rid of Jim Crow and started governing themselves. I'm
          not asking you to imagine anything fantastic, because that's
          going to happen someday....

33.   "Here's My Story," "Happy Birthday, New China!," Freedom, October
      1952, pp. 1, 3.

      The activist comments on new China's birthday. He declares that
      China is a power for peace as it is for liberation. Robeson also
      asserts, in part:
          Our folks call it Jubilee, that longed-for time,
          that great day a-comin' when we will stomp and shout:
          Free at last. So our hearts go out to the Chinese
          people, 475 million strong, who this month are cele-
          brating their day of Jubilee which came three years
          ago. "Chieh fung La," they shout. "Put me free" -
          and now they are truly free. China for the first time
          belongs to the Chinese people; the good earth is theirs
          and all its riches. No more drivers' lash for them - oh
          no, they're in the driver's seat now. Happy birthday, new
          China! And happy is the meaning of your rising. For now
          Africa and all of the millions of colored peoples can see
          in this new star of the East a light pointing the way
          out from imperialist enslavement to independence and
          equality. China has shown the way, no argument about

(Robeson, Paul)

    that, but some people don't pay enough attention to
one of the most important facts about China's successful struggle for liberation. I mean the great truth,
proclaimed by the Chinese leaders and masses alike, that
their victory could not have been won without the strong
friendship and support of the Soviet Union.... Yes,
China is a power for peace as it is for liberation.
Today, as I write, the great Peace Congress of the Asian
and Pacific Regions is meeting in Peking, capital of the
People's Republic of China. There the representatives
of the one billion, 600 million people of those areas are
uniting against the threat of war.... My people want peace,
no doubt about that. Most Americans want peace. Eisenhower
and Stevenson -- they want peace, too....

34.   "Here's My Story," "Ho Chi Minh Is The Toussaint L'Ouverture of
Indo-China," Freedom, March 1954, pp. 1, 2.

The activist declares, in part:
    As I write these lines, the eyes of the world are
on a country inhabited by 23 million brown-skinned
people - a population one and a half times the number
of Negroes in the U.S. In size that country is equal
to the combined area of Mississippi, South Carolina,
and Alabama. It's a fertile land, rich in minerals;
but all the wealth is taken away by the foreign rulers,
and the people are poor. I'm talking about Vietnam,
and it seems to me that we Negroes have a special
reason for understanding what's going on over there.
Only recently, during Negro History Week, we recalled
the heroic exploits of Toussaint L'Ouverture who led
the people of Haiti in a victorious rebellion against the
French Empire. Well, at the same time that the French were
fighting to keep their hold on the black slaves of Haiti,
they were sending an army around to the other side of the
world to impose colonial slavery on the people of Indo-China.
And ever since then the Indo-Chinese have been struggling
to be free from French domination.... In 1946 France was
forced to recognize the Republic of Vietnam, headed by Ho
Chi Minh; but like the double-crossing Napoleon in the time
of Toussaint, the French colonial masters returned with
greater force to re-enslave the people who had liberated
themselves. The common people of France have come to hate
this struggle; they call it "the dirty war"; and their
rulers have not dared to draft Frenchmen for military service
there.... And as we think about Ho Chi Minh, the modern day
Toussaint L'Ouverture leading his people to freedom, let
us remember well the warning words of a Negro spokesman,
Charles Baylor, who wrote in the Richmond Planet a half
century ago: "The American Negro cannot become the ally
of imperialism without enslaving his own race."

7. CIVIL RIGHTS

35. "Here's My Story," "Civil Rights in '54 Depends On the Fight Against McCarthyism," Freedom, November 1953, pp. 1, 4.

The author argues that Negroes must demand their Civil Rights. Robeson declares, in part:
....Whether civil rights bills will be passed in the coming session of Congress will depend not on the oft-heralded "good intentions" of Eisenhower, or the election-year promises of Congressmen, but on the degree to which the Negro people, labor, the poor farm population, and all lovers of democracy make an ernest, united and irresistible demand. We must not forget that the whole civil rights program-for voting rights in the South, for the right of our people to work and to full opportunities for advancement through adequate federal fair employment practices legislation, for the right to full protection of our very lives in states like Florida, the scene of the Moore lynch-murders -- this program was scuttled by the Eisenhower administration in the President's successful bid for Southern support. So our demands must not be narrowed, but broadened to include the whole of the Negro people in all-inclusive immediate demands for full citizenship. And all of our demands will be most effective when they merge with the battle against the book-burning, thought control, "loyalty" purges, "spy" scares and character defamation which the Democrats started and the Republicans are carrying on to ominous lengths.... So today there is the overriding necessity to preserve our democratic heritage from the wholesale attacks of McCarthyism. McCarthyism is an American brand of fascism. If this administration, which is largely a political vehicle for the giant corporations and entrenched greed, embraces McCarthy fully as it seems prone to do, then the outlook for the Negro people, labor, the foreign born and other minorities will be gloomy indeed.

36. "Turning Point," American Dialog, Vol. 1, No. 2, October-November, 1964, p. 6.

Paul Robeson comments on Barry Goldwater running for President of the United States, and the Civil Rights of Black people in America. He argues, in part:
We Americans are now at a most important turning point in our history. To us, the Negro people, the most important point since the Emancipation Proclamation. In our struggle for civil rights, we are not only fighting for our full freedom as citizens, we are also fighting for the whole unity of the American people. The majority of our fellow-

(Robeson, Paul)

> citizens recognize this and passed the Civil Rights
> Bill. With Goldwater running for president of our
> country we have a candidate who not only refused
> to support the Civil Rights Bill, but is against it
> in principle. Goldwater also challenges the very
> basis of labor union organization and would en-
> danger the gains achieved by the struggle and
> sacrifice of our working people.... A full and
> stable peace in our country demands that Negro
> and other minority Americans achieve all their
> Civil Rights, and that the American people achieve
> the social welfare benefits which our country can
> afford....

37. "We Shall Overcome," American Dialog, Vol. 2, No. 2, May-June
     1965, p. 18.

The writer comments on a number of issues including "The March on
Washington," Martin Luther King, Jr., Civil Rights, Freedom for
Blacks, Alabama, and Black Music. He surmises, in part:
> There can be no doubt that a gallant new chapter
> in American history was written in March, 1965, by
> the thousands upon thousands of Alabama folk --
> supported by many thousands more from all across
> the land, black and white together - marching toward
> the "Great Camp Meeting in the Promised Land." And
> there is no doubt that music - music of the people, by
> the people and for the people - has been integrated
> into this history-making struggle. In Alabama the
> whole struggle of the Negro people for civil rights,
> for the right to vote, for freedom, has now reached
> a new level. There were the thousands of black
> farmers and workers from the Alabama rural communities;
> there were the great numbers of the clergy and the good
> American citizenry - white and black - who answered the
> urgent call of their fellow minister and citizen, the
> Rev. Martin Luther King. They came from far and near
> to take an active part in the early struggle in the
> streets of Selma, and again to participate in the
> historic march from Selma to Montgomery, and to
> "bear witness" at the tremendous assemblage in front
> of the Capitol, the old seat of the Confederacy.
> Truly, Alabama and other regions of the Deep South
> can never be the same again. Our country can never
> be the same again. For this young Jimmie Lee Jackson
> and Rev. James Rebb gave their lives. For this the
> brave and courageous Viola Liuzzo gave the last full
> measure of devotion. All possible sympathy and
> gratitude to the families of these ever-to-be
> remembered Freedom Fighters. One recalls the like
> sacrifice of Medgar Evers, of Bill Moore, of the
> three youhg civil rights Mississippi Project workers -
> James Chaney, Andrew Goodman and Michael Schwerner....

8. FREE SPEECH

38. "Here's My Story," "Free Speech At Swarthmore," _Freedom_, May-June, 1955, p. 1.

Mr. Robeson gave a concert at Swarthmore College in Swarthmore, Pennsylvania. In addition to singing, he also spoke on various issues. He told the crowd of more than 1,000, in part:
It is good, these days, to get out to the college campuses and see the stirring of new life among the students. The Ivy Curtain of conformity, which for a decade has shut them off from the sunlight of independent thinking, is beginning to wilt. The fresh breeze of free expression is beginning to filter into the stale atmosphere of the cold-war classrooms.... Last month at Swarthmore College it was my privilege to appear both as artist and citizen, and this is always most gratifying because for me these roles are one and inseparable. Swarthmore, to which I had been invited by the Forum for Free Speech, has an enrollment of 900; but an overflow audience of 1,000 attended. Students came from other schools in that part of Pennsylvania - from Lincoln, including some of the African students there, and from Bryn Mawr.... I sought to explain to these eager young listeners how my viewpoint - which many of them thought too radical - was the natural outgrowth of my development as a Negro artist. I recalled how love for the songs of my people, the only songs for my first five years as a singer, widened to include the songs of other peoples as I grew to know them and found in them a kindred soul, a kindred beauty. I recalled how that knowledge led to an interest in other peoples, in their history and cultures, and in their lives today. And so the talk, like the songs, seemed to move around the world, noting the epochal social changes of our times, urging an understanding of that reality, stressing the all-important need for peaceful coexistence....

9. HUMAN RIGHTS

39. "Plain Talk," "Dramatic Plan to Punish Hate," _People's Voice_, December 6, 1947, p. 14.

Robeson discusses basic human rights in the world. He argues, in part:
History was made in Geneva last Friday. The United Nations Sub-commission on Minorities and Discrimination received a proposal to make racial and religious

(Robeson, Paul)

discrimination a criminal offense. It was told that
the rights of minorities should be as inviolable as the
rights of nations; that the expression of prejudice
or chauvinism in any form should be classified as a
crime. This is historic and of deep concern not only
to the millions of darker peoples throughout the
world who are the victims of color prejudice and
"white supremacy" policies, but to the masses of
men and women in all countries who still believe
in a world of sanity, decency and justice. The mal-
treatment of colored races in America, Africa and
Asia by dominant white peoples has been one of the
main stumbling blocks to the creation of such a
world. Never before in modern history has so far-
reaching a plan to suppress anti-minority bias been
presented to an international body of nations dedicated
at least in theory, to the principle of protection of
human rights.... Basic human rights, however, have
often been overlooked in the power politics which have
too often dominated the United Nations debates.
One of the most basic of human rights is a man's
right to live without fear of abuse and contempt
because of his color, race, or religion. Throughout
most of the world this right is not guaranteed. It
is, on the contrary, not only flagrantly flouted
and ignored, but often (as in our own Deep South
and in South Africa) deliberately eliminated by law
and government policy.... Friday's dramatic proposal to outlaw discrimination was made by the
representative of the Soviet Union, A.P. Borlsov,
who pulled no punches in his attack on minority
oppression throughout the world....

10. IMPERIALISM

40. "Plain Talk," "Facts On the Food Crisis," People's Voice, October
4, 1947, p. 14.

Robeson discusses the food shortage and how it affects American
Negroes and other underdeveloped countries. He suggests, in
part:
Why are Negroes here and abroad being deliberately
ignored as victims of the current world food crisis?
This is an important question which someone should
ask President Truman who has called for a national
food conservation program to alleviate suffering in
foreign countries. There is certainly need for immediate aid to those countries facing mass starvation
but it is important for us to know why this aid is
not being extended to the one-third of our own nation

(Robeson, Paul)

that is underfed as well as the millions of Negro
and darker peoples in Africa, Asia, and Latin
America, who have been suffering from a food crisis
ever since they can remember. The Negro millions of
our own South are living well below nutritional
standards necessary to good health. The death rate
and general health standards of the Negro population
dramatically show that millions live substandard
lives right here in the richest country in the world.
They face a very real food crisis with the President
and our government conveniently choose to ignore....
It is vitally necessary that Negroes and all Americans
understand the complicated background in the proposed
program to solve the world food crisis. Let us realize
exactly what we are being asked to do. We are asked
to sacrifice in the interest not of the world's
hungry millions who are certainly entitled to whatever
subsistence that this country can give but in the
interest of certain economic forces who keep
American Negroes at second class standards and
exploit colonial peoples all over the world....

41. "Plain Talk," "U.S. Plays The Imperial Game," People's Voice,
November 15, 1947, p. 14.

The columnist discusses activities in the United Nations and the
influence that the United States had over it. Robeson argues, in
part:
Imperialism took over the United Nations last week
and had a field day.... To its great discredit, and,
I am sure, the anger of informed colonial peoples, the
General Assembly:
* Weakened a previously passed resolution calling on
the South African government to submit to trusteeship agreement for the mandated territory of South-
West Africa, by omitting any reference to the fact
that the UN's charter requires this, and timidly
expressing the "hope" that South Africa would submit
such an agreement.
* Defeated a resolution introduced by India designed
to bring all colonial territories under the UN trusteeship system.
* Voted down a resolution that would require the
colonial powers to submit to the UN information on
health, education and economic standards for comparison with similar data from the advanced countries.
* Set aside a resolution recommending that the colonial
powers include in their annual reports to the UN
information concerning "the participation of local
populations in the work of local organs of administration."
* Decided that the Special Committee to be established
by the General Assembly to examine information received on colonies should not make recommendations

(Robeson, Paul)

regarding any of the colonies concerned.
There five decisions add up to a major setback to
the aspirations of the colonial peoples for independence. They are a crushing answer to the colonial
nations' mounting demands for self-rule. The United
States can take credit for this victory of imperialism,
for U.S. delegate John Foster Dulles engineered it.

42. "Here's My Story," "Which Side Are We On?," Freedom, January 1952,
    pp. 1, 2.

The activist comments on the American Government's involvement in
various international conflicts. He states, in part:
Six months ago the truce negotiations began in
Korea. But today the bloodshed continues, and
American diplomats and top brass persist in carrying
on the most shameful war in which our country has
ever been engaged. A hundred thousand Americans
dead, wounded and missing have been listed in this
war which nobody -- not even the most cynical
politician -- bothers to call a "police action"
anymore. And more than that, we have killed,
maimed and rendered homeless a million Koreans, all
in the name of preserving western civilization.
U.S. troops have acted like beasts, as do all
aggressive, invading, imperialist armies. North
and South of the 38th parallel, they have looked
upon the Korean people with contempt, called them
filthy names, raped their women, lorded it over old
women and children, and shot prisoners in the back.
Is it any wonder that Rev. Adam Powell, N.Y. Congressman, returns from a lengthy tour of Britain,
Europe, the Near East and Africa to report that the
United States is "the most hated nation in the world?"
Yes, our government is well hated because it was forced
on the people a policy which places this nation in
deadly opposition to the liberation movements of
hundreds of millions of people in all parts of the
globe. When the Iranians took back their rich oil
fields from the British exploiters, whose side were
we on? Now that the Egyptian masses are calling
for John Bull to get out of Egypt and the Suez Canal,
what position do we take?

11.   INDIVIDUAL MEN

43. "Important American Artist," Daily Worker, February 4, 1946, p. 11.

Mr. Robeson evaluates Robert Gwathmey in this article. Mr.
Gwathmey put on a one man show at the ACA Gallery in New York
City. Mr. Robeson's estimate of the artist appeared in a

(Robeson, Paul)

Foreword to the catalogue of the art show. The singer declares,
in part:
> His paintings deal with the South, but they are not
> to be confused with another regionalist movement.
> For just as social content art dealt with the hopes
> of all people for a better life so his portrayal of
> the South shows the aspirations and contributions
> of the Negro people and the failure of our society
> to recognize them. Thus Gwathmey, a white Southerner,
> expresses his region in the democratic tradition and
> in his best fusion of esthetic and social principles.
> His color has an unusual harmony which is, in effect, the
> expression of a new social concept. The atmosphere of his
> paintings is free of mysticism or supersitition. The
> statements are made clearly and strongly. In the coming
> years, when as we all hope, true equality and the brother-
> hood of man, will be a reality, Gwathmey's paintings will
> have earned him the right to feel that he has shared in
> the shaping of a better world. "Ancestor Worship" and
> "Masks" deal with the relationship of poor Negroes
> and white supremacy. "The Farmer Wanted a Boy" is a
> biography of the dismal existence of the poor whites in
> the South. "Shelling Peas" and "Lullaby" as well as
> "Singing and Mending," show the beauty and dignity of
> the Southern Negro. "Bread and Circuses" show that in
> the South we are still in the days of Nero. All of
> Gwathmey's paintings have an architectual simplicity,
> the expression of a man who wants to show how simple and
> good the world can be.

44. "Plain Talk," "A Talk With Henry Wallace," People's Voice, August
9, 1947, p. 14.

Mr. Robeson discusses his conversations with Henry Wallace. He
writes, in essence:
> ....Following Mr. Wallace's talk, I was privileged to sing
> a few songs and make a few remarks in which I stressed the
> fact that my own people are still oppressed and terrorized
> and that the fight of the Negro is a key fight in America
> today. No people's struggle can so clearly illustrate the
> nature of present-day attempts to revive in new form, a time-
> worn imperialism, as that of the American Negro. In most
> of our land, he is still caught in the grip of surviving
> feudal forms, prejudices, and semi-serfdom. We, the Negro
> people can be of great service and help to Henry Wallace,
> the great champion of the oppressed. We can deepen this
> understanding of the nature of imperialism. We can tell him
> why we fear the rebuilding of a non-de-nazified fascist
> Germany as the hub of European economy for we know what
> fascist have done and would do to us. We can tell him of
> our suffering and frustration here in the United States,
> from direct experience. We can let him know about the un-
> speakable conditions in the Panama Canal Zone, an outpost of
> American penetration. He will understand our concern for

(Robeson, Paul)

> our brothers and sisters all over this hemisphere, in
> the West Indies, Cuba, Brazil, Mexico and our concern
> for new directions in Africa. And he will understand
> and act - just as do a great host of our real allies
> in this great struggle for liberation....

45. "Plain Talk," "Speech By Henry Wallace," People's Voice,
     September 20, 1947, p. 14.

The writer comments on a speech made by Henry Wallace at Madison
Square Garden in New York City. He declares, in part:
> It was an eloquent and incisive attack on the war-
> mongers, and a blistering blast at America's present
> disastrous foreign policy which the ex-vice president
> correctly analyzed as one which "defends reaction in
> the name of freedom." Wallace addressed himself to all
> Americans, but his words carried special meaning for
> 13,000,000 Negro Americans. The program which he pre-
> sented contained specific demands for the rights of
> Negro people. "We must work," he (Wallace) declared,
> "for the day when Negroes in the South leaving a Freedom
> Train won't step forth into the reality of Jim Crowism."
> .... Difficult times are ahead of us. We need Henry
> Wallace, his vigor and dynamic idealism. He says he
> will fight for real change and the abolition of Jimcrow
> in our nation "once and for all." We can join him in the
> fight and have no reservation. For it is our fight....

46. "Here's My Story," "Set Him Free to Labor On - A Tribute to
     W.E.B. DuBois," Freedom, March 1951, pp. 4, 8.

Robeson declares, in part:
> W.E. Bughardt Du Bois is a human being full flowered --
> of the highest intellectual training in most diverse
> fields, and with it all, so direct, so devoted to the
> finest simplicity. His is a rich life of complete de-
> dication to the advancement of his own people and of all
> the oppressed and injured. First, let us not forget that
> he is one of the great masters of our language: the
> language of Shakespeare and of Milton on the one hand;
> and, on the other, of the strange beauty of folk speech -
> the people's speech - of the American Negro. He is a
> great poet, one of whom all America is proud. In these
> days of stress and struggle I often pick up one of his
> many volumes, most frequently The Souls of Black Folk.
> How I love to give myself up to those rich cadences, to
> receive sustenance and strength from those lines so deeply
> imbedded in the folk style of our people; yet enriched
> and heightened by the artistic gift of this deep-feeling
> prophet. For Dr. DuBois gives us proof that the great
> art of the Negro has come from the inner life of the
> Afro-American people themselves (as is true of the art
> of any group) - and that the roots stretch back to the
> African land whence they came. He, like so many other

(Robeson, Paul)

> great artists, turned to the people for the deepest
> fount - like Haydn, Bach, Schubert, Dvorak, Bartok,
> Tchaikovsky, Pushkin, Moussorgsky, and Mayakovsky, the
> great poet of the Russian revolution. And by his very
> participation in the people's political and economic
> struggles, he underlines the most important fact: that
> culture comes from and belongs to the people: that one
> aspect of our struggle is the obligation to bring this
> culture back to the people....

47. "Here's My Story," "Tribute to William L. Patterson," _Freedom_,
     August, 1951, pp. 1, 7.

     Robeson pays tribute to William L. Patterson. He declares, in
     part:
> I think most of the people in the United States know
> the name of William Patterson, head of the Civil Rights
> Congress, an organization which has made a magnificent
> struggle for the Trenton 6, Willie McGee, the Martinsville
> 7.... I remember also Pat's struggles around the ILD and
> the famous Scottsboro case. It was a long struggle again
> in which this young lawyer led the way. I know as a young
> man I was tremendously inspired by his going into the South
> and fighting in that area where there is the greatest
> oppression of the Negro people, and being successful in
> that struggle many, many times.... And at this time as
> we approach the celebration of his 60th birthday, I would
> like to pay tribute to Pat for the great work he has done,
> to thank him for all the clarity he has brought not only
> to me but also to the many people with whom he has worked.
> Negro people must understand that men and women like Pat
> have got to be free to work and struggle. His case is
> coming up in the fall, like that of Dr. DuBois and other
> leaders of the Negro people, and every effort must be
> made to see that the case is won, that an injustice is
> righted and he is freed to carry on the work of his or-
> ganization. And when we speak of Pat's freedom, we have
> to speak of freedom for those other leaders of the Negro
> people - of Winston and Davis, Perry and especially that
> brave colored woman, Claudia Jones, who came from the
> West Indies to help her people here. We must understand
> in the cases of Patterson and DuBois and the other working
> class leaders that they are fighting the battles of the
> Negro people....

48. "Here's My Story," "Du Bois' Freedom Spurs Peace Fight," _Freedom_,
     December, 1951, pp. 1, 6.

     Robeson discusses Du Bois and his fight for freedom and peace.
     He states that he was in the capital city, Washington, D.C.,
     the weekend of the victorious and glorious conclusion of the
     case of Dr. W.E.B. DuBois and his colleagues. It was indeed
     wonderful to feel the underlying joy and happiness in the hearts
     of all, states Robeson. He continues to surmise that there were

(Robeson, Paul)

knowing smiles, handshakes, congratulations. For this was one of
the historic points in the Negro people's struggle.... The
sttempt to stop Dr. Du Bois from speaking for peace was at the
same time aimed to silence him in his defense of the rights of
his people to voice their grievances, to call for vast improvements and changes in their condition of second class citizenship.
Time and again one returned to the inspiring figure of Dr. Du
Bois, to some evaluation of what this victory means and can
mean.... Here was a most illuminating expression of the people's
power, of the people's will of peace, asserts Robeson.... He
concludes, in part:
>   Dr. DuBois represented in his being concrete proof
>   of the possibilities of reaching out into the great
>   stream of American life. Here was a true broadening
>   and deepening of the struggle. Let us hold the or-
>   ganizational ties linked in this noble and successful
>   endeavor. Let us advance further the organizational
>   forms created, the broadening process made possible.
>   Let us bring this same unity to bear behind the
>   American Peace Crusade for millions of signatures
>   to the Five Power Pact petition, behind the struggles
>   of labor, behind the just demands of the Negro people
>   for full equality, behind the basic fight to erase from
>   the books the modern Alien and Sedition laws - the Smith-
>   Connally Act and the Mc Carran Act.... We together with
>   Dr. Du Bois and his colleagues, are deeply thankful to
>   the wonderful counsel, the lawyers, who upheld magnificantly
>   the best traditions of their profession. We wish every-
>   thing good to all the five defendants - and to their
>   families. We thank them for their courage, sacrifice
>   and real heroism. We are all elated that Dr. Du Bois
>   can return to his labors, can continue to give us of his
>   matchless poetry and prose, to inspire, guide and counsel
>   us. Certainly he can live joyously in the knowledge
>   that he is sincerely and deeply loved by the vast millions
>   of this earth....

49. "Here's My Story," "Act Together Now to Halt the Killing of Our
     People!," Freedom, February, 1952, pp. 1, 6.

     The activist declares, in part:
>   Harry T. Moore died the death of a hero. He is a martyr
>   in the age-long struggles of the Negro people for full
>   dignity and equality. His name must never be forgotten
>   and his courageous deeds must ever be enshrined in our
>   memories. His death must be avenged! The bomb which took
>   the life of this fearless fighter for freedom, made a
>   shambles of his home at Mims, Fla., and placed his wife
>   at death's door in a hospital 40 miles away, has shaken
>   the peace and tranquility of every Negro household in
>   the United States. There can be no mistaking the meaning
>   of this event. The murder of Harry Moore was a lynching
>   of a special kind. It was a political assassination.
>   Now the dastardly assassination of Moore comes as a threat

(Robeson, Paul)

to every Negro man and woman in the land: Give up your
efforts to be full citizens! Despair in your hopes to
vote and hold office in the South! Remain a people
apart, inferior in status, despised and trampled upon -
or we will blow you all to Kingdom come! Shall we accept
this verdict of Klansmen? Shall we permit the ferocious
attack of these 20th century barbarians to blunt the edge
of our common strivings? No, we cannot! We should not
be true to ourselves, our forefathers, or the memory of
Harry Moore if we did! The need of the hour is for
thousands of Harry Moores to rise and take the place of
the fallen one.... Death to the assassins of Harry
Moore and to the lyncher-sheriff McCall who killed Samuel
Shepard in cold blood! Ban the Ku Klux Klan and smash
this odious conglomeration of un-American bandits to
smithereens!....

50. "Here's My Story," "The Brave Trumpets of Albert Einstein and
His Fellow Scientists," Freedom, November, 1952, pp. 1, 8.

The writer recollects his visit with Albert Einstein. He states,
in part:
Well, here is an "atomic blast" that is all to the good.
I mean the recent outburst of 34 of the world's leading
scientists against the passport policies of the U.S. State
Department. Headed by Dr. Albert Einstein, this group of
U.S., British, Italian, French and Mexican scholars have
jarred the big shots in Washington with the charge that
the government is stifling intellectual and political
liberty. Their protest against "America's Paper Curtain,"
published in a special issue of the Bulletin of the Atomic
Scientists, cited 26 cases in which scientists and teachers
were either not permitted to enter or not allowed to leave
the country.
"There can be no doubt," Dr. Einstein wrote, "that the
intervention of political authorities in this country in
the free exchange of knowledge between individuals has
already had significantly damaging affects." So what do
we have? A distinguished panel of scientists finds that
the federal government, denying passports and visas under
the pretext of protecting the "public interest," is itself
"traducing the principles of liberty!" Surely all demo-
cratic-minded Americans must agree with Dr. Einstein's
insistence that: "The free, unhampered exchange of ideas
and scientific conclusions is necessary for the sound
development of science as it is in all spheres of cultural
life...."

51. "Here's My Story," "An Open Letter to Jackie Robinson," <u>Freedom</u>,
     April, 1953, pp. 1, 3.

Mr. Robeson, the activist, wrote a letter to Jackie Robinson, the
first Black in the Major Leagues. Robeson states, in part:
>   I noticed in a recent issue of "Our World" magazine
>   that some folks think you're too outspoken. Certainly
>   not many of our folks share that view. They think like you
>   that the Yankees, making many a "buck" off Harlem, might
>   have had a few of our ball players just like Brooklyn.
>   In fact I know you've seen where a couple of real brave
>   fellows, the Turgerson brothers, think it's about time
>   we continued our breaking into the Southern leagues -
>   Arkansas and Mississippi included. I am happy, Jackie,
>   to have been in the fight for real democracy in sports
>   years ago. I was proud to stand with Judge Landis in
>   1946 and, at his invitation, address the major league
>   owners, demanding that the bars against Negroes in base-
>   ball be dropped. I knew from my experiences as a pro
>   football player that the fans would not only take us -
>   but like us. That's now been proven many times over.
>   Maybe these protests around you, Jackie, explain a lot
>   of things about people trying to shut up those of us who
>   speak out in many other fields....

52. "Here's My Story," "Negro Americans Have Lost A Tried and True
     Friend," <u>Freedom,</u> August, 1954, pp. 1, 3.

The writer declares that Negro Americans lost a tried and true
friend when Vito Marcantonio died in 1954. He surmises, in
part:
>   In the untimely death of Vito Marcantonio progressive
>   humanity has suffered a shocking and grievous loss. He
>   was the people's tribune, standing often alone in de-
>   fense of their rights and interests in the halls of a
>   Congress over-run by the spokesmen of big business
>   and corrupt old-party machines.... In his district -
>   the 18th Congressional District of New York - Marc
>   was revered and loved as a friend, a brother, a true
>   leader, by the scores of thousands of Puerto Rican, Italian,
>   Negro, Irish, Jewish, and Slavic families - the families
>   of the poor - whose cause he aggressively championed and
>   whose problems he tirelessly helped to solve. Perhaps no
>   group of Americans is called upon to honor his name and
>   his memory more than the Negro people, not only in East
>   Harlem, but in all parts of this vast land.... The best
>   interests of the people of the 18th Congressional Dis-
>   trict and of the working people and Negro people of this
>   country, demanded that Marc act and vote for peace and
>   against war. He did, and for this the American people
>   will honor him.
>   We have lost a tried and true friend, the foremost
>   spokesman for the rights of man the Congress of the
>   United States has produced in the 20th century. For me,
>   a special sadness comes when I think that I will no longer
>   share Marc's warm and principled friendship....

53. "The Legacy of W.E.B. DuBois," Freedomways, Vol. 5, No. 1,
     Winter 1965, pp. 36-40.

     The writer discusses DuBois and tells how he influenced his
     thinking. He points out the various movements that DuBois parti-
     cipated in over the years: NAACP, Pan African Congress, Council
     on African Affairs, Communist Party of the United States, and
     American Labor Party. Robeson concludes that his cherished
     memories of Dr. DuBois was his brilliant and practical mind, his
     intellectual courage and integrity, his awareness to the world
     and of our place in it - which helped to make us also aware. He
     also injects: "His fine influence on American thinking, and on
     Negro thinking will continue to be incalculable. We admired,
     respected, appreciated and followed him because he was clear and
     forthright, because he was militant with a fighting strength and
     courage based upon wide knowledge, great wisdom and experience.
     I remember too his deep kindness. Dr. DuBois was, and is, in the
     truest sense an American leader, a Negro leader, a world leader."

                        12. LABOR MOVEMENT

54. "Plain Talk," "NMU Holds A Hot Convention," People's Voice,
     October 18, 1947, p. 14.

     Robeson comments on the National Maritime Union's sixth annual con-
     vention that was being held in New York City. He asserts, in part:
          For the last three weeks America's merchant seamen have
          been meeting in convention here in New York attempting to
          hammer out policies for their industry and to resolve if
          possible some of the critical internal problems which be-
          set their union. The National Maritime Union's sixth con-
          cention has been a hot one, marked by violent partisanship
          and discussion from the floor in which no holds are barred.
          Tempers have frequently flared to white heat and serious
          charges have been flung back and forth. It will be said
          that such conflict is inevitable within a trade union such
          as the NMU, which is relatively young and contains so many
          diverse viewpoints. But the factional fight that has rocked
          the entire union of U.S. seamen has been in many ways un-
          fortunate both for the organization itself and for the wel-
          fare of the labor movement as a whole. I cannot help feeling
          that this kind of conflict tends to weaken a union, to
          divide its membership dangerously, and to give encourage-
          ment to those forces who have an abiding hatred of labor
          unions and seek in every way to destroy their power....
          Without Unity the maximum strength of the seamen cannot
          be brought into action to protect standards which were
          won as a result of such bitter, costly struggle. I regret
          that there exists within the National Maritime Union a
          serious cleavage of opinion. I regret that this cleavage
          has prevented the union from using all of its energies to
          fight the real enemy: the Taft-Hartley Law. The national

(Robeson, Paul)

    secretary of the union, Ferdinand C. Smith, is a Negro -
    a union leader for whom I have the highest respect....

55. "Here's My Story," "Recollections of a Trip," _Freedom_, March 1951,
    p. 1.

    The writer recalls a trip he made:
        I have just returned from a most instructive and
        deeply moving journey around the East and Middle
        West. All the cities brought back memories of
        concerts in the past to thousands -- in the Phila-
        delphia Academy of Music, with the Orchestra in
        Symphony Hall, Boston, in Orchestra Hall, Chicago,
        and the Mosque, Detroit, and the beginning of
        "Othello" at Brattle Hall, Cambridge, outside of
        Boston. Most precious of the recollections was
        Cadillac Square, Detroit, when CIO took over Ford,
        and the picket lines in Packing, Farm Equipment and
        United Electrical, and Steel in Chicago and elsewhere.
        Everywhere there was deep concern and troubled
        anxiety about our country's policies; about the open
        attacks upon honest forces of labor; deep sorrow
        and anger about attacks on the Negro people of this
        nation. A decisive change has come, as far as I
        could judge. The fight is on to bring thousands
        and thousands of the people into militant struggle
        for our rights, economic, political and social --
        and, most of all, for our very lives. This trip
        made me more than ever deeply proud and happy that
        I decided way back to give my talents and energy
        to the working masses.... I know that I, for one,
        after this trip, seeing and experiencing the col-
        lective power of my people and their true and honest
        allies -- I know that we all should and must feel
        "powerful strong," that we should and must feel
        some of the mountain-moving strength of our legendary
        John Henry. So let us get into the fight, let us
        continue steadfast, let us journey to a Mt. Zion
        right here on this American earth....

56. "Here's My Story," "National Union of Marine Cooks and Stewards
    Convention," _Freedom_, June 1951, pp. 1, 2.

    The writer discusses his recent visit to the National Union of
    Marine Cooks and Stewards Convention. He writes, in part:
        Just got back from the West Coast and an exciting
        visit with trade union leaders and rank and filers
        who are charting a new course in American labor
        history. The recent convention of the National Union
        of Marine Cooks and Stewards set a standard in labor's
        struggle for the full rights and dignity of the Negro
        people that other unions in our country might do well
        to emulate. Revels Cayton, the dynamic union leader
        who is now an organizer for the Distributive,

(Robeson, Paul)

Processing and Office Workers in New York, and George
Murphy, our general manager at FREEDOM, made the trip
with me and we all had an exciting and fruitful time.
"Rev" has his roots deep in the Coast where for many
years before coming to New York, he was the outstanding Negro labor leader in a vast area that
stretches from San Diego to Seattle. He was leader
of the MCS, and was closely associated with the
struggles of the International Longshoremen's and
Warehousemen's Union -- the men who keep the cargo
moving on the docks and in the huge warehouses of
the coastal cities and whose president, Harry Bridges,
is one of the finest union leaders of our days. For
"Rev" it was like old home week as we sat with his
old colleagues in informal bull sessions which got
to the heart of the problem at MCS and all unions
face: strengthening the bond of unity between its
Negro and white members....

57. "Here's My Story," "Ford Local 600 Picnic," Freedom, September,
1951, pp. 1, 5.

The speaker comments on his recent visit to Detroit, Michigan,
and the Ford Local 600 picnic. He recalls, in part:
I have been in Detroit many times during my work in
America. But never was there quite such an occasion
as the picnic Aug. 12 sponsored by the foundry workers
of Ford Local 600, UAW, CIO. During the recent visit
I recalled previous contacts with the auto city. As
an All-American football player just out of college,
I played there with Fritz Pollard of Akron. Great
sections of the Negro community came out, just as
they turn out to see football and baseball start
there today. I had a brother who lived in Detroit -
died there - and it was the first time he had seen
me since I was a boy. I remember going around with
him and later seeing the fellows from the fraternity.
When I began my concern career, I always insisted that
my management present me under the auspices of Miss
Nellie Watts, the fine impresario in Detroit. And
often in those days I sang in the churches of the
Negro community.... Under the leadership of Nelson
Davis, a veteran unionist who was the main organizer
of the picnic, and others, the foundry workers have
developed a unity which is the core of the progressive
militancy of the entire local. And this unity is
reflected among the general officers of the union:
Carl Stellato, president; Pat Rice, vice-president;
Bill Hood, secretary, and W.G. Grant, treasurer.
These men know that they have to work together to
defend the world's largest local against the policies
of UAW president Walter Reuther who, in his support of
the Truman war program, would tie the workers to wage
freezes, escalator clauses and other gimmicks which

(Robeson, Paul)

lead to practical starvation and depression....

58. "Here's My Story," "The UAW Should Set the Pace," Freedom, March,
     1953, pp. 1, 9.

     Robeson recollects his relationship with the UAW. He argues,
     in part:
          As a great organization of American workers, the
          United Auto Workers, prepares for its convention in
          Atlantic City this month, my mind goes back to many
          of the bitter labor battles which have made the
          union movement strong and won some measure of se-
          curity and dignity for millions of working men and
          women. Most precious of recollections is Cadillac
          Square, Detroit. It was my privilege to stand there
          and sing to thousands of auto workers, massed in a
          historic demonstration, as the CIO took over Ford's.
          These struggles have given me great strength and
          confidence, and added much to my understanding. I
          shall always consider it a major factor in the course
          which I have taken that on returning to America from
          abroad in the early days of the CIO, I plunged into
          the magnificent struggles of labor. I had learned,
          during these years, an important lesson: that the
          problems of workers the world over are much the same
          and that eventually, they must all find similar
          answers.... From the U.S. scene of the late Thirties
          and early Forties another lesson became crystal clear:
          as the union movement grew in strength and numbers, the
          fight for equal rights progressed apace. The organizing
          drives needed a strong phalanx of support from the
          whole Negro community - the church, civic fraternal
          and social organizations - in short, all organized
          expressions of 15 million oppressed citizens. (It
          is not idle to recall these days how many organizing
          committees, faced with goon squads, city officials,
          who were flunkies of Big Business, and a solid anti-
          union press, found sanctuary and their only meeting
          placed in the confines of the Negro church!)....

                         13. MOVIES

59. "Plain Talk," "Two Fine Films Hit Bigotry," People's Voice,
     November 22, 1947, p. 14.

     Robeson calls "Crossfire" and "Gentlemen's Agreement," two fine
     films. He describes the films, in part:
          ...."Crossfire" is a film that carries both meaning
          for our democratic struggle and high entertainment
          value. It boldly tackles the issue of anti-Semitism

(Robeson, Paul)

in terms of its crudest and most violent aspects.
Produced by Dore Schary, whom Rep. Parnell Thomas'
Committee has labeled "un-American," this film de-
livers thumping whacks at anti-Jewish bigotry through
a story vehicle built around the murder of a Jewish
veteran by a hate-inflamed soldier. It strikes out
with both fists at the evil of one of the worst
minority situations in the U.S. - the status of the
Jewish people.... Another splendid attack on anti-
Semitism is contained in "Gentlemen's Agreement,"
which must be seen by all Americans who value their
freedom heritage and desire a better land. Adapted
by Moss Hart from Laura Z. Hobson's novel of the same
name, this picture forcefully dramatizes the cruelty
and arrogance of socially "respectable" Jew-haters.
It is a moving emotional experience whose effectiveness
is enhanced by its ability to make audiences probe
into their own attitudes and re-examine their thinking
on this question. Moss Hart's right, well-turned
script has been brilliantly translated into cinematic
terms by Elia Kazan who directed the film. The result
is a sharp indictment of anti-Semitism that is absor-
bing and disturbing.... These two films, are, in hope,
evidence that Hollywood is turning from triteness and
distortions, toward social responsibility and truth.
Diehards who are still mouthing phrases about the
evils of "propaganda in art," receive a smashing answer
in these two films which combine an important social
message with entertainment of a high order. Let us
have more of such films from Hollywood....

14. MUSIC

60. "Plain Talk," "Concert at Lewisohn Stadium," People's Voice,
     August 2, 1947, p. 14.

The writer discusses his concert at Lewisohn Stadium in New York
City. He asserts, in part:
     As I finished my concert at Lewisohn Stadium a few
     nights ago, I was again forcibly reminded of what the
     audience can contribute to the work of the inter-
     pretative artist. Seldom have I felt such warmth,
     such friendliness, such a quality of participation.
     And beyond these, an awareness and appreciation of
     the fact that an artist must be allowed to relate
     his work to the real world about him.... Traveling
     back and forth over America in this time of crisis,
     I have found the American people basically healthy -
     conscious of their traditions as a land of the plain
     or common people, still possessing a deep belief in

(Robeson, Paul)

>opportunity for the millions and aware of the need
>to extend the full benefits of citizenship to groups
>as yet denied them. But they are also confused, by
>contradictions in our foreign policy and by the failure
>to attain some of our easily realizable goals. But
>here at the Stadium was a true expression of our
>democratic faith - for this was no Peoria, but a
>whole audience of 18,000 that seemed to be caught by
>a mood expressed almost concretely in saying:
>"We are your friends, Paul, we are with you"....
>This concert on July 17, not only strengthened my
>contact with people here in New York, but again
>proved that there is deep satisfaction and reward
>for a people's artist. For is there is anything
>that pleases me most, it is to be called an artist
>of the people. And all of us who work in different
>cultural fields, especially we Negro artists coming
>as we do from an oppressed people, must recognize
>that we serve our PEOPLE or we serve those who would
>crush them and keep them in continued serfdom....

61. "Plain Talk," "Controversy in American Jazz," People's Voice,
     November 29, 1947, p. 14.

The writer gives his opinions on the Gillespie-Parker school of
jazz and the old New Orleans style. Robeson surmises, in part:
>The American jazz world is in turmoil. It is rent
>by a great, bitter controversy over the direction
>which jazz should take, about its form and musical
>principles. The other evening I became aware of
>how heated is this new conflict which has been sweeping
>across the throbbing, fluid world of American jazz
>ever since two remarkable young musicians -- named
>John Birks "Dizzy" Gillespie and Charles "Yardbird"
>Parker - began experimenting with tones and harmonics.
>The musical style which these two unusual artists
>helped produce is known by the weird term "be bop."
>I understand it is also referred to as "re bop," but
>my "hep" friends, who are on both sides of the fence
>on the issue, tell me that the former term is more
>popular and is actually preferred by the musicians
>themselves. Gillespie and Parker are not new names
>to me. I have heard them both play on several
>occasions and have been both stimulated by their
>imaginative creations and a little astounded by their
>incredible technique and musicianship. Gillespie
>is a highly-gifted trumpeter who once played in Cab
>Calloway's brass section and barnstormed throughout
>Europe about ten years ago. Parker is considered
>the high priest and fountainhead of be bop, a veri-
>table genius of the alto saxaphone. What the
>Gillespie-Parker school has created is what we
>now know as be bop, which I think deserves serious
>attention. I am anxious to see how far this group

(Robeson, Paul)

      of inventive musicians will carry this trend, and how
much they will succeed in enlarging the scope of the
language of jazz....

62. "Plain Talk," "Infantry Chorus Is Great Group," <u>People's Voice</u>,
December 13, 1947, p. 14.

The writer points out that one of the finest male choruses in
the world is the 35 members of the Infantry Chorus. He concludes,
in part:

    One of the finest male choruses currently performing
in this country, and for that matter the world, is a
group of 35 stalwart, toughtened veterans of World
War II who are in the midst of a precedent-shattering
first concert tour on which they are winning high
critical acclaim and moving audiences from coast-to-
coast in a manner seldom achieved by an organization
of male singers. They are the 35 members of the Infantry Chorus, as polished and impassioned a singing
group as I have heard. It has been my great pleasure
to hear this extraordinatily talented group perform
several times in recent months and each time I came
away lifted up and stimulated by the power and magnificent feeling of this choral group. There are
choral groups and choral groups. Some are destined
to mediocrity by inept direction or uneven singing;
some are inconsistently good. A few, a very few,
are unreservedly splendid. The Infantry Chords
belongs to the very top of this last category. A
choral group is as good as its director, and the
Infantry Chorus significantly is guided by one of
the most talented and creative figures in the world
of choral music - Leonard de Paur. Of de Paur it can
certainly be said that he has exerted a powerful
influence on American choral singing.... When the
war ended, both de Paur and the members of the chorus
were loathe to dissolve such a fine organization, so
they decided to stick together. A USO tour took them
to Europe for seven months where they were sensational.
Upon their return they were signed by Columbia Concerts
to appear professionally in this country....

63. "Songs of My People," Soveitskaia muzyka (Soviet Music), No. 7,
     July 1949, pp. 100-104 -- Translated from the Russian by Paul A.
     Russo. Quoted in **Philip S. Foner, Editor. Paul Robeson Speaks:
     Writings, Speeches, Interviews, 1918-1974.** New York: Brunner/
     Mazel Publishers, 1978, pp. 211-217.

     The singer states that the music of the American Negro has its
     origins in the ancient culture of Africa. And yet, contends
     Robeson, this enslaved people, oppressed by the double yoke of
     cruel exploitation and racial discrimination, gave birth to
     splendid, inspiring, life-affirming songs. These songs re-
     flected a spiritual force, a people's faith in itself and a
     faith in its great calling; they reflected the wrath and protest
     against the enslavers and the aspiration of freedom and happiness,
     argues Robeson. According to the world traveler, these songs
     are striking in the noble beauty of their melodies, in the ex-
     pressiveness and resourcefulness of their intonations, in the
     startling variety of their rhythms, in the sonority of their
     harmonies, and in the unusual distinctiveness and poetical
     nature of their forms.

64. "A Song To Sing," Masses and Mainstream, Vol. 8, No. 10, October,
     1955, pp. 12-14.

     The following article was written for the forthcoming 1955 album
     of photographs and background material on Joris Ivens' latest
     documentary film "The Song of the River." The album, was issued
     by the trade union publishing house of the German Democratic
     Republic. It contains 300 stills from the film and contributions
     by the various artists, including Paul Robeson, who took part in
     the production. Mr. Robeson was asked to tell about his ex-
     periences in recording the theme song. He discusses the various
     problems he encountered in making the recordings. Robeson went
     on to declare:
          Masters of culture, champions of peace -- what a won-
          derful film-making company I had become associated
          with! And there was a warm glow of appreciation for
          the invitation they had sent me, making it possible
          despite all barriers, for a Negro American to join
          with Holland Russian and German and Frenchmen and
          all of the others in creative work for peace and
          liberation.... As yet I have not seen this film
          which carried the song from a house in Harlem to
          audiences around the world. Millions in many lands
          have seen "Song of the Rivers," and heard the com-
          mentary in Arabian, Japanese, Persian, Czech,
          Polish, English, Russian, Spanish, Chinese, French,
          and many other languages but we here in America
          have been denied that opportunity. But we know that
          films for peace shall one day soon be welcomed to
          our land, and singers of peace shall be given pass-
          ports to travel abroad. No barriers can stand against
          the mightiest river of all -- the peopels' will for
          peace and freedom now surging in floodtide through-
          out the world.

65. "Freedom Music Through the Ages," Daily Worker, November 23, 1956, p. 6.

This is a partial reprint of an article that Robeson wrote for the Jewish Life Anthology in 1954. It was entitled "Bonds of Brotherhood." Since this article appears elsewhere in this book it will not be discussed here.

66. "The Related Sound of Music," Daily World, April 7, 1973. Translated by Leonard Herman from the German Version of the Paul Robeson Archives, Berlin, German Democratic Republic.

Robeson comments on Black Music and suggests that it is in the mainstream of world music. He suggests, in part:

I read a very fine article about the Soviet composer Aram Khatchaturian by A. Medvedev. My interest was particularly aroused by the following paragraph:

"'My cradle song,' said Khatchaturian, 'comes from the east.' And the study of his music indicates that the traces which the cradle song left behind in his sensitive soul and in his hearing were inexhaustible."

This is exactly the way it is with me, a black American of African origins, with my cradle song from Africa, and the traces which it left in my sensitive soul and in my hearing were also unlimitedly deep. All my life the music of the black and African music were in my soul and in my hearing. In my childhood the music of the black churches and the music of the black community were an integral component of my consciousness. As a professional musician I had the great fortune to find an early ally in the exceptionally talented black composer and arranger, Lawrence Brown. Over the years our common interests developed into a good artistic partnership and personal friendship. It was Lawrence Brown who confirmed my instinctive concept and who showed me the simple beauty of the songs of my childhood, which I heard every Sunday at the church and in the black congregations, work songs and blues of my father's people from the plantations of North Carolina. These had to become an important part of my international concert material....

15. NEW YEAR HOPES

67. "Plain Talk," "A Glimpse At The New Year," People's Voice, January 13, 1948, p. 14.

He predicts what lies ahead for the year 1948. Robeson surmises, in part:
> The year 1948 will bring new problems, new struggles
> and new responsibilities for all of us who are con-
> cerned about the state of democracy in our land and
> in foreign countries as well. It will bring into
> sharper focus the conflicts in this country between
> Property and Progress, Big Business and the Little
> People. Throughout the world the drive toward another
> war will increase in tempo; so will, I predict, the
> movement of the peace forces to prevent such a
> catastrophe. Let us not underestimate the gravity
> of the period before us. The diplomatic "cold war"
> against the Soviet Union is gaining momentum, and the
> European Recovery Program, actually a "stop Communism"
> intervention operation, has been launched, with much
> fanfare and horn-tooting. This anti-Soviet offensive
> will ultimately cost American tax-payers millions of
> dollars and bring about a tragic deterioration in
> our relations with the Soviet Union and the countries
> of eastern Europe, to say nothing of millions in
> Western Europe who resent America's brazen plan to
> forestall political change in France, Italy, Greece
> and Germany with dollars. At home, we still face an
> increasing wave of persecution of liberals and
> progressives. The Thomas Un-American Activities
> Committee, still arrogant and contemptuous of our
> constitutional liberties, will continue its witch
> hunt. Faint hearts will tremble before it and run
> for cover. But staunch defenders of free speech
> and thought will stand up to its slanders and in-
> quisitions, defying its right to deprive Americans
> of hard-won rights.... These times call for courage
> and strength. Progress is a ... thing which must
> be fought for....

68. "My New Year Hopes," Pravada, (Moscow), January 3, 1956.

This article was reprinted in the January 5, 1956, issue of New Times. Robeson states his New Years' hopes. He declares, in part:
> First, I hope for continued strengthening of the
> people's will for peace, and that the desire of the
> American people for peace will become more and more
> assertive and become predominant in deeds as well as
> in feeling. Secondly, I hope for a continued drive
> towards freedom in the colonial lands of Asia, Africa
> and Latin America, and especially in the southern
> section of the United States. Courageous struggles
> are being waged over a vast area and I hope for

(Robeson, Paul)

important and swift gains. Thirdly, I hope for the
increasing prestige of the peace forces of the
United Nations and for the admission of China, the
Mongolian People's Republic and Japan. And I hope
that soon the emerging nations of Africa will have
their representatives in the United Nations. I
hope that there will be a real solution of the
urgent problem of prohibition of nuclear weapons
and reduction of armaments, consonant with the de-
clarations jointly issued by the Soviet Union and
India and other Asian states. I hope for the easing
of tensions so that we all can travel. My deep
affection and love to the people of the Soviet
Union. There is a new day coming. Peace will
conquer war.

16. NEW YORK

69. "What Harlem Means to Me," People's Voice, July 26, 1957, pp. 1,
14.

Robeson discusses what Harlem, New York, not only means to him,
but to the world. He states, in part:
....And today, I often walk around in Harlem's
streets sensing anew its dreams and frustrations.
I see it sparkle with joy and feel its misery and
depression. Its language remains as familiar to me
as are its sights and smells. Harlem has sheltered
some of our greatest artists. How often in the
early hours of the morning I listened awe-struck
to the deep laughter and wit of Bert Williams. How
I remember the pat on the shoulder and the words of
encouragement from that great master to a bewildered
young actor. I can still remember humming the last
strains of "Little Gal," that lovely song of Rosamond
Johnson's set to the words of Paul Lawrence Dunbar,
and then rushing from the old Plantation Room into
the subway train at 50th St. and Broadway. There
just across the aisle was dear Florence Mills, the
simple, nightingale-voiced star and how proud I was
when she too gave me a nod and a smile of recognition.
I recall with profound respect and inspiration the
evenings with James Weldon Johnson reading his fervent poems or a short, never-to-be-forgotten chat
with that great scholar and tireless fighter, W.E.B.
Du Bois, a man of whom every race must be proud. So
it is with a sense of deep humility and a feeling of
nostalgia, but also with a sense of Harlem's responsibility and the Negro people's responsibilities,
that I begin writing these pieces for PV.

70. "Here's My Story," "The Road Has Been Long," Freedom, November,
     1950, p. 1.

     He states, in part:
          The other day, as I walked the streets of Harlem,
          a well-wisher stopped to say "hello" and "good luck."
          As we chatted, he paused for a moment and then, as
          though not quite certain he was doing the right
          thing, asked, "Paul, were you born in Russia?" I
          laughed, of course, but then took the time to tell
          my friend the tale that makes up the body of this
          column. For what the question reflected was that,
          somehow, the masters of the press and radio had
          convinced at least this person that a person who
          fights for peace, for the admission of People's
          China to the UN, for friendship with the Soviet
          Union, for labor's rights and for full equality for
          Negroes now, cannot be a "real" American, must have
          been "born in Russia." These are the objectives for
          which I will be fighting for some time to come,
          and to which this column is dedicated. So this is
          probably a good time to explain how I began and how
          I have come to feel the way I do about world affairs.
          The road has been long. The road has been hard. It
          began about as tought as I ever had it - in Princeton,
          New Jersey, a college town of Southern aristocrats,
          who from Revolutionary time, transferred Georgia to
          New Jersey. My brothers couldn't go to high school
          in Princeton. They had to go to Trenton, 10 miles
          away. That's right - Trenton, of the "Trenton Six."
          My brother or I could have been one of the "Trenton
          Six."....

17. PERSONAL GOALS

71. "An Actor's Wanderings and Hopes," Messenger, Vol. 7, No. 1,
     October, 1924, p. 32.

     The actor declares his future as a singer-actor depends mostly
     upon himself. He states that he has the courage to fight what-
     ever comes and is eager to work and learn. Robeson suggests he
     realizes that he always has a few steps more to go -- perhaps
     never realizing the desired perfection - but plugging away. He
     asserts that one of the great measures of a people is its culture
     and the only true artistic contributions of America are Negro in
     origin. Robeson concludes that he approaches the future in a
     happy and rather adventuresome spirit; for it is within his
     power to make this unknown trail a somewhat beaten path....

72. "I Don't Want to Be White," Chicago Defender, January 16, 1935, p. 11.

This article was originally printed in the London Daily Herald and was sub-titled in the Chicago Defender, "Famous Artist Tells Inside Facts About Race 'Psychology'." Robeson states, in part:
Sometimes I think I am the only Negro living who would not prefer to be white. It has been said that I am to leave Europe and go back among my own people. That does not mean that I am to abandon my own people. Though I shall visit Africa, and perhaps spend months among Africans, I shall return to Europe. Where I live is not important. But I am going back to my own people in the sense that for the rest of my life, I am going to think and feel as an African -- not as a white man.... It is not as imitation Europeans but as Africans, that we have a value. Yet the brains of the best Negroes have been applied to turning themselves into imperfect imitations of white gentlemen, while it has been left to the astute white man to pick up and profit by what has been cast aside.... But the Negro will remain sterile until he recognizes his cultural affinity with the East. He must just take his technology from the West.... His immense emotional capacity is the Negro's great asset.... I shall study, and talk, and write.... In between, to remind the world that a Negro has something to offer Paul Robeson will act and sing....

73. What I Want From Life by Fifteen Actors and Actresses. London: George Allen & Unwin, 1934? Reprinted by Royal Screen Pictorial, April 1935.

Paul Robeson comments on what he expects from life. He writes, in part:
I am a Negro. The origin of the Negro is Africa. It would, therefore, seem an easy matter for me to assume African nationality. Instead, it is an extremely complicated matter, fraught with the gravest importance to me and some million of colored folk, Africa is a Dark Continent, not merely because its people are dark-skinned or by reason of its extreme impenetrability, but because its history is lost. We have an amazingly vivid reconstruction of the culture of anc.ent Egypt, but the roots of almost the whole remainder of Africa are buried in antiquity. There are, however, rediscoverable, and they will in time be rediscovered. I am confirmed in this faith by recent researches linking the culture of the Negro with that of many peoples of the East. Let us consider for a moment the problem of my people - the African Negroes in the Occident, and particularly in America. We are now fourteen million strong - though perhaps "strong" is not the apt word; for nearly two and a half centuries we were in chains, and although today we are technically free and officially labelled "American Citizens," we are

(Robeson, Paul)

at a great economic disadvantage, most trades and
many professions being practically barred to us
and social barriers inexorably raised. Consequently,
the American Negro in general suffers from an acute
inferiority complex; it has been drummed into him
that the white man is the Salt of the Earth and the
Lord of Creation, and as a perfectly natural result
his ambition is to become as nearly like a white man
as possible....

74. "Here's My Story," "An Evening in Brownsville," Freedom, May,
1952, pp. 1, 6.

Robeson suggests, in part:
The other night I was in Brownsville, a section of
Brooklyn bordering on the Bedford-Stuyvesant area.
Not far away is the church where the historic con-
ference of the African Methodist Episcopal Zion
Church takes place May 7-21. In the modest home of
a friend, a Sojourner for Truth and Justice, a fighter
for the freedom of her people, I met with 30 or more
working folk. They had come to chat about some things
I had on my mind and some matters they had on theirs....
I recounted to this little group in Brooklyn, how my
whole life has been spent close to this Zion Church.
My father built a little edifice which stands today
in Westfield, New Jersey. He daily influenced many
of the younger Zion clergymen of his area, some of
whom later became Bishops, like the present senior
Bishop W.J. Walls. I was for many years head of
the Sunday School. I studied two years for the
ministry, and later changed to the law. Often I took
the pulpit for my aging beloved "Pop." The influence
of his character, his self-sacrificing life will
never leave me. He himself, was born a slave, but
he fought his way to freedom, to an education, to a
full life in the service of his people. We must all
assume greater and greater responsibilities in the
historic battles for liberation raging in the world --
at home as well as abroad. Our friends must be
measured by a new measuring rod. In this the
church has mountainous tasks to solve, a contribution of staggering proportions to make. Unselfish,
non-partisan unity among ourselves can assure a future
of real brotherhood and human growth....

18. PLAYS

75. "Reflections on O'Neill's Plays," Opportunity, Vol. 2, No. 24, December 1924, pp. 368-370.

The actor discusses Eugene O'Neill's plays, "Emperor Jones" and "All God's Chillun." He contends, in part:
> The reactions to these two plays among Blacks point out one of the most serious drawbacks to the development of a true Black dramatic literature. "We are too self-conscious, too afraid of showing all phases of our life, especially those phases which are of greatest dramatic value. The great mass of our group discourage any member who has the courage to fight these petty prejudices." One day there will be Black playwrights of great power and he will have some part in interpreting that most interesting and must needed addition to the drama of America....

76. "Some Reflections on 'Othello' and the Nature of Our Time," American Scholar, Vol. 14, Autumn, 1945, pp. 391-392.

The actor states that he was deeply fascinated to watch how strikingly contemporary American audiences from coast to coast found Shakespeare's Othello - painfully immediate in its unfolding of evil, innocence, passion, dignity and nobility, and contemporary in its overtones of a clash of cultures, of the partial acceptance of and consequent effect upon one of a minority group. Against this background the jealousy of the protagonist becomes more credible, the blows to his pride more understandable, the final collapse of his personal, individual world more inevitable. But beyond the personal tragedy, the terrible agony of Othello, the irretrievability of his world, the complete destruction of all trusted and sacred values -- all these suggest the shattering of a universe. Certainly our influence must be upon the side of progress, not reaction; upon the side of the freedom living peoples and the forces of true liberation everywhere -- peoples and forces expressing their wills in various democratic forms, liberal, cooperative, and socialist, argues Robeson. He concludes:
> An added responsibility rests upon the liberal intellectual -- the scientist, the member of the professions, the scholar, the artist. They have an unparalleled opportunity to lead and to serve. But to fulfill our deep obligations to society we must have faith in the whole people, in our potential and realized abilities. This faith, in our new world of today, must include the complete acceptance of the assumption of positions of great power by true representatives of the whole people, the emergence into full bloom of the last estate, the vision of no high and no low, no superior and no inferior -- but equals, assigned to different tasks in the building of a new and richer human society.

19. POLITICS

77. "Plain Talk," "The American Legion Convention," <u>People's Voice</u>,
     September 6, 1947, p. 14.

     The author comments on the American Legion's 29th annual con-
     cention which was held in New York City that produced an alarming
     barrage of war talk and anti-Soviet hysteria. He concludes, in
     part:
        The Legion has now become one of the main channels
        through which our present aggressive foreign policy
        is being developed into a program for a third world
        war.... We are thus faced with the definite danger
        that America's youth may not only be involved in a
        third world war, but may actually be used to engender
        a war spirit.... It is to be hoped that the more than
        100,000 Negro members of the Legion will become a
        positive force for democracy, both inside the Legion
        and in the nation at large. They can by their actions
        demonstrate the all meaning of "Un-Americanism," a
        word that has been sorely misused by many high leaders
        of the Legion. Negro Legionnaires can remind their
        leaders that instead of whipping up a false excitement
        about democracy in foreign countries, they can well
        pay some attention to the state of democracy at home....
        It is important that Negro members of the Legion take
        part in this challenge and bring forth inside their
        organization the vital problems of their people.
        They cannot allow our youth to sign a blank check
        for their own destruction.

78. "Plain Talk," "A Committee Takes A Licking," <u>People's Voice</u>,
     November 8, 1947, p. 14.

     The author discusses the Thomas Committee on Un-American
     Activities. He asserts, in part:
        The Thomas Committee on Un-American Activities
        took a licking last week and folded up after an
        elaborate publicity buildup designed to set the
        stage for a massive smear of the movie industry.
        The adjournment of the Washington hearings was a
        definite victory for Americans who still believe
        in the Bill of Rights, and our constitutional
        liberties. It was a victory for all the people,
        big and little, rich and poor, black and white,
        whom the Committee has been seeking to persecute,
        pillory and prosecute because their views happen
        to be contrary to those of the Committee's members
        and the powerful interests they represent. The
        entire country should be grateful to the brave
        little band of Hollywood progressives, who, sub-
        peonaed to appear at this 1947 Inquisition, refused
        to be intimidated and defended their right to privacy
        of thought and freedom of expression. I felt a

(Robeson, Paul)

> particular thrill of pride when John Howard Lawson,
> one of America's most brilliant minds, carried the
> fight to Rep. Thomas with such vehemence and eloquence.
> I was proud, too, of the performances of Dalton
> Trumbo, Alvah Bessie, Herbert Biberman, Albert
> Maltz and all of the others who helped to turn
> this smear circus into a real assault on the com-
> mittee's right to exist at all.... Every Negro in
> the land must be fully aware that the Thomas Com-
> mittee represents a special threat to his existence.
> The Committee's favorite tactic is to call anybody
> whom it considers dangerous a Communist....

79.   "Here's My Story," "The Road to Real Emancipation," Freedom,
      January 1951, pp. 1, 2.

> The writer declares, in part:
> January is the month of emancipation. This season
> with its connotation of dawning freedom is close to
> me. My own father -- not my grandfather -- was a
> slave. He was born in 1843 in Eastern North Carolina
> near Rocky Mount, and escaped in 1858 over the Maryland
> border to Pennsylvania. He worked on farms, earned
> enough money and went back twice to North Carolina,
> to carry money to the mother he loved so dearly. So
> he escaped three times by the underground railroad.
> Maybe he sang "Go Down Moses" as Harriet Tubman came
> to lead fortunate ones to a northern or Canadian "Canaan."
> Maybe he knew Frederick Douglass - who castigated a
> slave land for the caricature of democracy it claimed
> to be. That father reared me -- almost alone. My
> mother died when I was barely six years old. One
> thing I learned as a youth -- poor, ragged, but
> loved and helped by my struggling aunts, uncles
> and cousins in New Jersey and in Robinsonville,
> North Carolina. I learned that Emancipation --
> Freedom -- meant freedom for all my people, not just
> for a few wealthy and fortunate Negroes, but for all
> of us. And I knew I had a right to look for Freedom
> and Emancipation. Emancipation means out of the hands
> of -- out of the hands of former masters and oppressors.
> And I've spent my life finding out how to use my own
> hands -- my own talents -- for this is a necessary
> part of the dignity of any people.... No, on this
> anniversary of emancipation we can surely not think
> of sacrificing our youth and ourselves to preserve
> these empires built on the blood of our ancestors.
> And sacrifices to what end? To the world's des-
> truction!

80. "Genocide Stalks the U.S.A.," <u>New World Review</u>, Vol. 20, No. 2, February, 1952, pp. 24-29.

The activist discusses genocide in the United States. He also compares what was happening to Negroes in America with what happened to the Jewish people of Nazi Germany. Robeson suggests, in part:

> Out of the lessons of the barbarities of Nazi Germany, the voice of outraged mankind caused the General Assembly of the United Nations to adopt a Convention on the Prevention and Punishment of the Crime of Genocide. The opening statement of this historic petition dispels the generally held misconception that the crime of genocide can be charged only when there is mass extermination of a people. As defined in the United Nations Convention, genocide includes "any of the following acts committed with intent to destroy, in whole or in part, a national, ethnic, racial or religious group, as such: (a) killing members of the group; (b) causing serious bodily or mental harm to members of the group; (c) deliberately inflicting on the group conditions of life calculated to bring about its destruction in whole or in part." It is not difficult to understand why this Convention has never been ratified by the Senate of the United States.... A determined effort has been made by white supremacy to block U.S. signature. From the openly terrorist Ku Klux Klan to the more suave spokesmen of the American Bar Association, there has been a brazenly open recognition of the applicability of the convention to the treatment of the Negro people in the United States. Let anyone review the history of the Negro people of these United States. Tens of millions sacrificed in the slave ships and on the plantations....

81. "Here's My Story," "How Not to Build Canadian-American Friendship," <u>Freedom</u>, March, 1952, pp. 1, 7.

The activist declares, in part:
> I went West this past month, to Seattle, just across from Vancouver, British Columbia, Canada. Here was a convention of the Canadian section of the Mine, Mill, and Smelter Workers, a fine union with black and white leadership - Ray Dennis, Asbury Howard, Harvey Murphy and that great leader of labor, Maurice Travis, secretary-treasurer of the union. Now no American needs a passport to go to Canada so in spite of my passport difficulties, I expected no action by the State Dept. At the border, in Blaine, Washington, there were many Canadian acquaintances and a very friendly Vancouver press. They assured me that the Canadian Government would not refuse me entry, and that Vancouver was waiting to give me a warm welcome. I have appeared in Vancouver many times in concerts, in Othello, have spoken at the university there. No

(Robeson, Paul)

city has been friendlier throughout the years. The
representative of the American State Dept. called me
in and very nervously informed me that, though no
passport was needed, a special order had come through
forbidding me to leave the country. If I did, it
might mean five years, and a fine! (I thought of my
great and good friend Ben Davis - it's about time a
major fight was launched to free Ben. People in Harlem
continuously ask, "How is Ben? We need him.") Refusal to allow me to cross the border was an act of the
American administration, not an act of the American
people. And in closing, I want to speak of my own
childhood, and my "pop" who told me when I was a little
boy: "Stand firm, son, stand firm to your principles!"
"You bet I will, Pop, as long as there's a breath in
my body."

82. "Here's My Story," "We Can't Sit Out This Election," Freedom,
August, 1952, pp. 1, 4.

Paul Robeson discusses the 1952 Presidential election. He argues,
in part:
Blacks can not afford not to vote for at least two
reasons: ....For one thing, there was a third convention in Chicago that didn't get all that ballyhoo.
I mean the Progressive Party convention that nominated
Vincent Hallinan, a fighting labor attorney, for President and one of our militant women leaders, Mrs.
Charlotta Bass, for Vice President. You'll hear more
about these candidates and their platform before this
campaign is over, and I hope that you'll come to
believe as I do that here is the only ticket for
Negroes in November. And there is another reason
for not stringing along or sitting it out, regardless
of what your politics are. When you look a little
closer at what happened in Chicago you'll see something that never showed up on the TV screen; the
fact is that civil rights for Negroes was the central
issue behind all the wringing and twisting at the big
conventions. And the fact is that it was OUR DEMAND
for those rights which made that the issue! And we've
got to keep on demanding. Sure, civil rights, FEPC
and all the rest of our needs got kicked around out
there, but brothers and sisters I'll tell you one
thing: this fight is just starting good. Truth is,
you're telling me. Wherever I go about this land
on the streets, in the churches, in the unions, I
hear what you the people say about wanting our civil
rights now. Not next year, not in some great day
a-coming, but now, this year, 1952. So all of us
together - and there's no strings on us, no gag
on us, no political boss to make us second his
motions - all of us have got some talking back to
do....

83. "Here's My Story," "Two Newspaper Clippings," Freedom, December,
     1952, pp. 1, 7.

     The writer comments on two newspaper clippings concerning the
     conditions of Negroes in the United States. He reports, in part:
              Well, here on my desk are two clippings - and
              a postcard. Both clippings are from the New
              York Times. The first is a large political
              advertisement (you may have seen it in some
              other papers, too) signed by 86 prominent
              Negroes. It appeared on Oct. 24 - before the
              elections - and it doesn't stack up so well
              next to the second clipping, a news report
              dated a month later (Nov. 21). The elections
              are over, but the struggle for equal rights
              for Negro Americans goes on - and must go on
              harder than ever before. So it is not for
              the purpose of quarreling that I look back
              at the statement of the 86 Negro Democrats.
              I just want to make clear the actual situation
              that we Negroes face, and the need for united
              action by all of us. The political advertise-
              ment boasted that, "in the past 20 years....
              Negroes, along with all other Americans
              made tremendous strides economically, socially
              and in the field of education." The 86
              signers insisted that "Negroes have jobs now....
              And like Americans generally, they're drawing
              good wages.... The Negro farmer, like all
              farmers, has made tremendous progress, too."
              But here's the other clipping, a report by
              the Senate sub-committee on Labor and Labor-
              Management Relations. Based on the figures
              of the 1950 census, the report reveals that
              family income of Negroes as compared with whites
              is more unequal than it was five years ago! In
              the words of the report: "Their average income
              was $1,869 in 1950, or 54 percent cf the average
              income of $3,445 among white families." (In
              1945 the difference was 57 percent)....

84. "Here's My Story," "The 'Big Truth' Is The Answer to the 'Big
     Lie' of McCarthy," Freedom, January, 1954, pp. 1, 4.

     Robeson comments on a number of issues, such as hospitals,
     schools, homes, roads, community centers, bridges, and dams. He
     declares that those projects would mean that tens of thousands
     and millions of people would have jobs. He continues, in
     part:
              ....Every consideration of the interests of the Negro
              people, every concern of their security, their fight
              for equality, their dignity, demands that every
              gathering of Negro Americans declare that we must
              have peace, not war! Let Mr. George Schuyler marry
              Joe McCarthy, if he wants to -- we beg to be excused
              from the ceremony. Let the decrepit Max Yergan

(Robeson, Paul)

lounge around in illusions of the 19th century imperialist omnipotence if he will -- we have other
ideas. We are convinced by everything that has
happened in this nation and abroad that the path
to Negro freedom lies in firm conjunction with the
giant strides which humanity is taking in all other
countries of the world, barring none, toward enforcing the peace and silencing the warmakers.
Now, if you preach this doctrine of peace, friendship and brotherhood among the world's peoples --
you may still run into a little trouble in the
United States. That old devil McCarthy may set
out to get you! But a lot of Americans are
waking up to the fact that to be the victim of an
attack by McCarthies may not be fatal. In fact,
the only thing fatal for the American people would
be the failure to fight the McCarthite madness.
For McCarthyism means destruction of the constitutional
rights of free speech and free press and free religion.
It means the burning of books which proclaim the
scientific truth that all men are created equal.
It means the reign of fear, intimidation and terror.
I have no doubt that we will beat back McCarthyism
and restore our traditional liberties....

85.   "Here's My Story," "Greetings to Bandung," _Freedom_, April, 1955,
pp. 1, 7.

The singer sent a message to the Bandung Conference. This was a
meeting of Asian and African States, organized by Indonesia,
Burma, Ceylon, India, and Pakistan, which met April 18-24, 1955,
in Bandung, Indonesia. Robeson declares, in part:

How I should have loved to be at Bandung! In this
Indonesian city for the week beginning April 18
the homes of mankind were centered. Of course, the
State Department still arrogantly and arbitrarily
restricts my movements to the continental United
States, so that I could not join the representatives
of more than half the world who convened in the Asian-
African Conference.... I have long had a deep and
abiding interest in the cultural relations of Asia
and Africa. Years ago I began my studies of African
and Asian languages and learned about the rich and
age-old cultures of these mother continents of human
civilization. The living evidence of the ancient
kinship of Africa and Asia is seen in the language
structures, in the arts and philosophies of the two
continents. Increased exchange of such closely
related cultures cannot help but bring into flower
a richer, more vibrant voicing of the highest aspirations of colored peoples the world over. Indeed
the fact the Asian and African nations, possessing
similar yet different cultures, having come together
to solve their common problems must stand as a

(Robeson, Paul)

> shining example to the rest of the world. Discussion
> and mutual respect are the first ingredients for the
> development of peace between nations. If other
> nations of the world follow the example set by the
> Asian-African nations, there can be developed an
> alternative to the policy of force and an end to
> the threat of H-Bomb war. The people of Asia and
> Africa have a direct interest in such a develop-
> ment since it is a well-known fact that thermo-
> nuclear weapons have been used only against the
> peoples of Asia....

86. "Here's My Story," "The Constitutional Right to Travel," _Freedom_,
     July-August, 1955, p. 1.

The singer was in San Francisco giving a concert honoring the 10th
anniversary of the United Nations in its founding city. He
writes about the United States State Department denying him the
constitutional right to travel abroad. He declares, in part:
> I was especially glad to see so many new friends out
> here who are backing me in my fight for a passport.
> It has been five years since the State Department
> arrogantly and arbitrarily refused to let me travel
> abroad to practice my craft as a singer and actor to
> earn my living wherever people wanted to hear me. I've
> been invited to sing in a dozen countries since that
> time. India and France and the Soviet Union, to name
> but a few, have invited me to sing or to act. The
> British Actors Equity has invited me to do "Othello"
> over there again and promised,in an extraordinary
> action, to make available a supporting cast including
> the best actors in England. All of England's leading
> musicians and composers joined in signing another
> invitation for me to give a concert over there. This
> included Vaughan Williams, dean of British musicians.
> Despite all these invitations, the State Department
> continued to deny me a passport, refused me my Con-
> stitutional right to go where I please and when I
> please so long as I don't break the law. The only
> reasons they gave for their refusal was that I
> criticize the United States when I go abroad; and
> that I speak up for African liberation, thereby
> interfering with U.S. foreign policy. I did speak
> up for the African people when I was abroad. I
> spoke up for my people here in America, the descendants
> of African people. And I'll speak up again. The
> answer to injustice is not to silence the critic but
> to end the injustice....

87. "Robeson Urges Government to Defend Constitution Against Racists,"
     Daily Worker, September 23, 1957, p. 5.

     The writer comments on the political situation in the United
     States. He surmises, in part:
          The events transpiring in Little Rock, Ark., con-
          stitute a bold and desperate attack upon constitutional
          government. Our national morality and the political
          integrity of the nation will be tested to the greatest
          degree in this struggle. No man or woman who loves
          this country and retains faith in the ultimate
          realization for all of the concepts of liberty that
          gave it birth can remain silent. The menacing impli-
          cations of the theories of white supremacy stand
          exposed. Little Rock is in my opinion a symptom
          of the evils of racism that go to the very foundation
          of this system of government. The logical conse-
          quences of a half century of compromise, procrasti-
          nation, passivity and uncertainty surrounding the
          constitutional rights of the Negro people and their
          dignity as human beings can now be clearly seen.
          The half-century's failure of the federal govern-
          ment to protect the lives, property and rights of
          the Negro has produced the imminent danger of bloody
          racist outbreaks against Negro citizens that cannot
          possibly be localized should one occur. It has
          jeopardized orderly constitutional procedure through-
          out the nation and threatens the solidarity of the
          Union. There is but one answer. The issues raised
          in the fight for Negro rights must be resolved in
          favor of equal democracy, equal justice, equality
          of opportunity for Negroes in every phase of national
          life. The responsibility to institute these forms
          of race relations rests upon the federal government
          and every branch of that government....

88. "Here I Stand," Afro-American, March 15, 1958, Part One,
     Magazine Section, pp. 1, 3.

     This is the first of the two chapters of Paul Robeson's book,
     Here I Stand. Here for the first time Robeson, one of the most
     talented and controbersial figures of our times (1958), talks
     back to his critics.

89. "Here I Stand," Afro-American, March 22, 1958, Part Two,
     Magazine Section, pp. 1, 3.

     This is Part Two of excerpts from Paul Robeson's book, Here I
     Stand. The telling of the struggle and victory over New Jersey
     poverty and prejudice constitute the pages in this Robeson
     series. He tells how he was motherless at 9 and was raised by
     his father, his brothers and sisters.

90. "Here I Stand," _Afro-American_, March 22, 1958, Part Three, Magazine Section, pp. 2, 4.

This is Part Three of a series of articles taken from Here I Stand by Paul Robeson. In this article Robeson discusses grade school in Westfield in 1907 and then high school in Somerville in 1910. He describes what mixed schools were like in New Jersey in the early 1900s. The writer surmises that "students and teachers were friendly and urged me to attend parties and dances." According to the author his chemistry teacher was the first to dance with him on those occasions. He also argues that his father watched his studies and went over with him page by page in his books.

91. "Here I Stand," _Afro-American_, March 29, 1958, Part Four, Magazine Section, pp. 5, 8.

This is Part Four of a series of articles taken from Robeson's book, Here I Stand. He points out several things in this section. At 17, he had no thoughts of becoming an actor. When he ranked first in the country-wide college entrance examinations, he knew two things. First he was going to Rutgers' University and secondly, equality might be denied him later in life, but he knew he was not inferior. It was also pointed out that he originally wanted to go to Lincoln (Pa.) University, but after he won a scholarship to Rutgers University he decided to go there so that his father would not be under a financial strain.

92. "Here I Stand," _Afro-American_, April 12, 1958, Part Five, Magazine Section, pp. 1, 2.

In this part of a series of articles taken from Here I Stand by Paul Robeson, the author discusses his political views. He states what he said in Paris that created such a fuss in the United States. The author tells why he refused the Republican National Committee's offer to stump the country for Alf Landon for President against Franklin D. Roosevelt. Some attention was also devoted to why he declined several movie roles in Hollywood films.

93. "Here I Stand," _Afro-American_, April 19, 1958, Part Six, Magazine Section, pp. 8, 9.

Part Six is taken from Here I Stand, by Paul Robeson. In this section Robeson discussed how he almost decided to settle permanently in London, England. He changed his mind, however, when he "discovered" Africa and became interested in its culture. Robeson learned five African languages, and foresaw the Africans' struggle for independence as early as 1934. Because of his pride in Africa, he was compelled to speak out against imperialist Africa.

94. "Here I Stand," _Afro-American_, April 26, 1958, Part Seven,
     Magazine Section, pp. 4, 6.

     In Part Seven, that was also taken from his work, _Here I Stand_,
     Robeson explains why he sent his son, Paul Jr., to school in
     Russia. He answers the question whether or not he has ever been
     involved in any international conspiracy. He declares that he
     had not been involved in any international conspiracy and that he
     was not a Communist. Robeson declares: "In 1946, at a legislative
     hearing in California, I testified under oath that I was not a
     member of the Communist Party, but since then I have refused to
     give testimony or to sign affidavits as to that fact. There is
     no mystery involved in this refusal.

95. "Here I Stand," _Afro-American_, May 3, 1958, Part Eight, Magazine
     Section, pp. 8, 9.

     This is Part Eight of a series of articles taken from _Here I Stand_
     by Paul Robeson. One of the main charges against Paul Robeson
     stems from his remarks at the World Peace Conference held in
     Paris, France, in 1949. Here is his story of that stormy
     incident.

96. "Here I Stand," _Afro-American_, May 10, 1958, Conclusion Section,
     Magazine Section, pp. 5, 6.

     In this conclusion article, taken from _Here I Stand_, Robeson dis-
     cusses the Ten Principles set up in the Bandung Conference, in
     1955. He lists the ten principles as follows:
     1. Respect for fundamental human rights and for the
     purposes and principles of the Charter of the United Nations.
     2. Respect for the sovereignity and territorial integrity
     of all nations.
     3. Recognition of the equality of all races and of the
     equality of all nations large and small.
     4. Abstention from intervention or interference in the in-
     ternal affairs of another country.
     5. Respect for the right of each nation to defend itself
     singly or collectively, in conformity with the Charter of the
     United Nations.
     6. (a) Abstention from the use of arrangements of collective
     defense to serve the particular interests of any of the big
     powers.
     (b) Abstention by any country from exerting pressures
     on other countries.
     7. Refraining from acts or threats of aggression or the use
     of force against the territorial integrity or political in-
     dependence of any country.
     8. Settlement of all international disputes by peaceful
     means, such as negotiation, conciliation, arbitration or
     judicial settlement as well as other peaceful means of the
     parties' own choice, in conformity with the Charter of the
     United Nations.
     9. Promotion of mutual interests and cooperation.
     10. Respect for justice and international obligations.

97. "The Power of Negro Action," <u>Political Affairs</u>, Vol. 46, No. 8, August, 1967, pp. 33-46.

This article is a reprint of chapter 5 of the activist's book, <u>Here I Stand</u>. The editor used the article that was written a decade ago because according to him "these perceptive and brilliant words ... are a clarion call for unity in action of the Negro People in the struggle to win freedom, equality and justice in our land." Robeson asserts: "Of course there must be negotiations made in behalf of our rights, but unless the negotiators are backed by an aroused and militant people, their earnest pleas will be of little avail. For Negro action to be effective - to be decisive, as I think it can be - it must be <u>mass</u> action. The power of the ballot can be useful only if the masses of voters are united on a common program; obviously, if half the Negro people vote one way and the other half the opposite way, not much can be achieved. The individual votes are cast and counted, but the group power is cast away and discounted. Mass action - in political life and elsewhere - is Negro power in motion; and it is the way to win...." He also argues that "To be free - to walk the good American earth as equal citizens to live, without fear, to enjoy the fruits of our toil, to give our children every opportunity in life - that dream which we have held so long in our hearts is today the destiny that we hold in our hands."

98. "The Time Is Now," <u>Political Affairs</u>, Vol. 52, No. 4, April, 1973, pp. 41-52.

This article is Chapter 4 from his book, <u>Here I Stand</u>. It is significant to restate Robeson's conclusion:
>   While pointing to the pressure from the outside,
>   I was also convinced that the pressure from the
>   Negro people themselves was also a factor that would
>   have to be reckoned with, and I said so in these
>   words: This is obviously not a race war - it turns,
>   rather, on the idea of people that are free and
>   those that are not free. The American Negro has
>   changed his temper. Now he wants his freedom.
>   Whether he is smiling at you or not, he wants his
>   freedom. The old exploitation of peoples is de-
>   finitely past. That was my viewpoint more than a
>   decade ago and that is my stand today. I have out-
>   lined in this chapter the factors which, I believe,
>   make it possible for Negro rights to be achieved at
>   this time. But, as we well know, opportunity is not
>   enough. No situation, however favorable, can solve
>   a problem.

20.   RUSSIA

99.   "On Soviet Culture," <u>Daily Worker</u>, July 24, 1944, p. 11.

This article is the same Foreword that Paul Robeson wrote for
<u>Favorite Songs for The Red Army</u>, that was published in 1944 by
the Russian-American Music Publishers, Inc., of New York. In
the Foreword he concludes: "For I have long deeply admired and
loved the Soviet people as I do my own. I sincerely hope that
these songs will help inspire a deep understanding of, and an
admiration and affection for, a people who, I know, have the
progress of all humanity so deeply at heart."

100. "Here's My Story," "Thoughts on Winning the Stalin Peace Prize,"
<u>Freedom</u>, January, 1953, pp. 1, 12.

Robeson comments on winning the Stalin Peace Prize. He asserts:
....Many friends have asked me how it feels to
have received one of the International Stalin Prizes
"For strengthening peace among peoples." Usually I
say - as most prize winners do - "It's a great honor."
But, of course, this award deserves more than just
passing acknowledgment. Through the years I have
received my share of recognition for efforts in the
fields of sports, the arts, the struggle for full
citizenship for the Negro people, labor's rights and
the fight for peace. No single award, however, involved so many people or such grave issues as this
one. The prize is truly an international award.
And the prize winners include outstanding figures
from many lands. Most important, it must be clear
that I cannot accept this award in a personal way.
In the words of an editorial written by A.A. Fadyeev
in <u>Pravda</u>: "The names of the laureates of the
International Stalin Prizes are again witnesses to
the fact that the movement for peace is continuously
growing, broadening and strengthening. In the ranks
of the active fighters against the threat of war, new
millions of people of every race and nationality are
taking their place, people of the most widely differing
political and religious convictions.... The awards to
Eliza Branco and Paul Robeson reflect the important
historical fact that broader and broader sections of
the masses of the Western Hemisphere are rising to
struggle for freedom and independence, for peace and
progress; peoples that endure the full weight of the
attempts of imperialist reaction to strangle the
movement of the masses against a new pillaging war,
being prepared by American billionaires and millionaires."

101.   "To You Beloved Comrade," New World Review, Vol. 21, No. 4,
        April, 1953, pp. 11-13.

        The activist comments on the culture and economic advancement of
        the Russian peoples. He also discusses what he saw when he was
        there is 1937 awaiting a performance of the Uzebek National
        Theater. The world traveller surmises, in part:
              ....So here one witnesses in the field of the arts -
              a culture national in form, socialist in content.
              Here was a people quite comparable to some of the
              tribal folk in Asia - quite comparable to the proud
              Yoruba or Basuto of West and East Africa, but now their
              lives flowering anew within the socialist way of life
              twenty years matured under the guidance of Lenin and
              Stalin. And in this whole area of the development of
              national minorities - of their relation to the Great
              Russians - Stalin had played and was playing a most
              decisive role.... But in the Soviet Union, Yakuts,
              Nenetses, Kirgiz, Tadzhiks - had respect and were
              helped to advance with unbelievable rapidity in
              this socialist land. No empty promises, such as
              colored folk continuously hear in these United States,
              but deeds. For example, the transforming of the
              desert in Uzbekistan into blooming acres of cotton.
              And an old friend of mine, Mr. Golden, trained under
              Carver at Tuskegee, played a prominent role in cotton
              production. In 1949, I saw his daughter, now grown
              and in the university - a proud Soviet citizen....
              They have sung -- sing now and will sing his praise --
              in song and story. Slava -- slava -- Stalin, Glory to
              Stalin. Forever will his name be honored and beloved
              in all lands. In all spheres of modern life the in-
              fluence of Stalin reaches wide and deep. From his
              last simply written but vastly discerning and com-
              prehensive document, lack through the years, his
              contributions to the science of our world society
              remain invaluable. One reverently speaks of Marx,
              Engels, Lenin and Stalin -- the shapers of humanity's
              richest present and future....

                            21. SPORTS

102.   "Review of the 1917 Football Season," Rutgers Alumni Quarterly,
        Vol. 4, No. 2, January, 1918, pp. 69-75.

        This article was written by Robeson when he was a junior at
        Rutgers. The editor of the Quarterly prefaced the article by
        declaring: "Paul Robeson .... was a member of the Rutgers team.
        He was generally recognized as the best football player seen in
        action during the past season. On the offense he played end,
        where he made many sensational runs after having received for-
        ward passes from Whitehill. When line plays were called for,

(Robeson, Paul)

he was placed beside Captain Rendall at tackle, opening holes
through which the Rutgers halfbacks plunged for certain gains.
On the defense he played fullback, supporting the line in sensational style and disgnosing opposing plays with almost uncanny
instinct. He was selected by practically every football authority
in the country as the season's leading player. Never before has
a Rutgers man achieved such athletic distinction. Robeson is a
Negro, nineteen years of age, six feet two inches in height, and
two hundred and ten pounds in weight. He is one of the leaders
of his class in scholarship, and the winner of the Edward
Livingston Barbour Prize in Declamation, and the Myron W. Smith
Memorial Prize in Oratory." Robeson did point out that the one
thing which determined most the successful season was the team-
work and team spirit. He also surmised that there was no individual brilliancy, but every man did his best for a common cause
under the leadership of one of Rutgers' greatest captains, "Thug"
Rendall.

103. "Here's My Story," "Sports Was An Important Part of My Life,"
      Freedom, November, 1951, pp. 1, 7.

      The author discusses his football days at Rutgers University when
      he was an undergraduate there. He asserts, in part:
            Sports was an important part of my life in those
            days. Football, basketball, track (discus, javelin,
            shot-put and the pentathlon - best in five events),
            baseball. I was a catcher, not as good as Campy,
            but played a little semi-pro ball and dared 'em to
            start to second base a couple of times, but I'm
            sure the pitchers were slow on the windup. I'm back
            at the Rockland Palace, at another level, having gone
            through a kind of spiral, still fighting for the
            dignity of my people, but fighting harder; saying that
            time is short, that my folks can't wait for full citi-
            zenship, that they want freedom - not for a few but for
            all, all of the 15 million of us South, North, East and
            West. We want a future for our youth of constructive
            effort. For ourselves and all of our land, and for all the
            world, we want peace and friendship. I have seen many
            peoples, sung their songs, won their friendship and love,
            not for myself but for my people - for you, for your son
            and daughter, for your grandchildren. So I challenge
            the lies of would-be warmakers, the same ones who still
            hold us in bondage and talk about their Point Four pro-
            gram to supposedly raise the standards of living of
            colonial peoples. Help us, all of you, to build this
            paper, FREEDOM. Help us to fulfill our responsibilities
            to you and to those yet to come. From the expressions of
            affection, from the encouragement that I get daily as I
            walk the streets of Harlem, I know you will. I'll be
            glad to see those of our readers who attend our Freedom
            Festival at Rockland Palace. And we'll be seeing plenty
            of each other from here on out.

22. THE SOUTH

104.   "Plain Talk," "Southerners Defy Jimcrow," People's Voice, November
        1, 1947, p. 14.

        The artist comments on his travels in the South and how he per-
        formed to large mixed audiences which were unsegregated. He
        writes, in part:
                Strength and courage are on the rise among the South's
                white liberals. I was never more aware of this fact
                than during the past three weeks when I ventured into
                Virginia, South Carolina and Maryland, singing and speaking
                to large mixed audiences which were unsegregated. These
                engagements were part of my current program - my "year
                off" which I am devoting mainly to assisting progressive
                causes and lending whatever aid I can to the fight for a
                living democracy in our land. The largest and most in-
                spiring of these audiences, which to me represent the
                New South, was in Norfolk, Virginia, where on Oct. 10
                I appeared in a concert recital at the City Auditorium
                before 7,000 persons, more than half of whom were white.
                This was a benefit for the Norfolk Community Hospital and
                the Liberty Park Nursery. It was as much a gain for demo-
                cracy locally as it was a financial success for the
                sponsoring committee.... Thus, shortly before the
                concert was scheduled to begin, the Norfolk chief of
                police approached the chairman of the concert's sponsoring
                committee and said: "You've got to have these people
                separated." The committee chairman replied: "White
                people can get their money back if they don't want to sit
                with Negroes."

105.   "Plain Talk," "On Returning to Our Roots," People's Voice,
        December 27, 1947, p. 14.

        The columnist comments on his trip to North Carolina. He writes
        about his forefathers' state. Robeson declares, in essence:
                Last week I went down into the country of my fore-
                fathers and was inspired and reinvigorated by what I saw,
                heard and felt in that atmosphere. I like to go back to
                the land of my fathers for it brings me close to my roots.
                I think it is important for all of us to get back to our
                roots every now and then. My roots are in North Carolina.
                My father worked here in slavery. My grandparents lived
                here as slaves, working land which they did not own and
                creating wealth in which they never shared. Their blood
                and sweat went into the making of the great cotton economy
                of the South and hence into the building of America into
                the greatest economic power on earth. Their contributions
                are unhonored and unsung but were nevertheless substantial.
                They helped to build the region which produced them and
                gave birth to other human beings who continued the tradition
                of building. I came from this land and these people and
                am accordingly greatful to it and to them. I have a strong

(Robeson, Paul)

> sentimental attachment to this section of North Carolina
> for it has been a part of my consciousness ever since I
> can remember. This land is rich and its people are strong
> and full of dignity and a feeling of moving forward. That
> is why I like to go back to this country every so often.
> On this last trip I met again my cousins and other distant
> relatives, and felt, for the first time, a definite feeling
> of being on my own land and among my people.... I sang
> before unsegregated audiences in the city auditorium
> of Raleigh and Charlotte, as well as in the auditoriums
> at Bennett and Livingstone colleges. This to me was a sign
> of real progress in this part of the South....

106. "Here's My Story," "Southern Negro Youth," Freedom, October, 1951,
pp. 1, 7.

The writer argues, in part:
> If any people needs its youth, it certainly is the Negro
> people in the United States. The South of his birth can
> well be proud of Roosevelt Ward. He comes from our great
> traditions. Among, many, I remember especially two journeys
> to the South, both to conferences of Southern Negro youth -
> one at Tuskegee and one at Columbia, South Carolina. Never
> have I been so proud of my heritage, never so sure of our
> future here in these United States as when I stood among
> those young men and women. Never was I so proud as then
> to be an artist of and for my people, to be able to sing
> and inspire these proud descendants of our African fore-
> bearers, standing as they were with head and shoulders
> high in the deepest South. In one voice they demanded
> land for their struggling fathers and mothers, breathing
> space and free air, the full fruits of their back-breaking
> toil, full opportunity - full freedom. That's what scares
> the powers that be in the arrogant ruling circles of
> this and other lands. That's the cause of the terror.
> Roosevelt Ward was among these Southern youth. He has
> emerged as one of the young giants of our American struggle -
> modest but assured - trained and tried in the line of
> highest duty, the fight for freedom. We need him to give
> us the help and guidance of militant youth, unafraid of
> any challenge. He is one of the builders, like the young
> labor leaders gathering at Cincinnati, of a way of life
> in which his people, the Negro people, will share fully
> of this American earth and tread thereon in concrete
> realization of the fullest human dignity.

107. "Here's My Story," "Mississippi Today - History in the Making,"
Freedom, February, 1955, pp. 1, 6.

The writer declares that history is being made and written in
Mississippi. He surmises, in part:
> ....So, today, Negroes of Mississippi, as of the whole
> South, are demanding implementation of the Supreme Court
> decision on segregation in education. And as might be

(Robeson, Paul)

expected, the Dixiecrats have responded with howls of
anguish and threats of retaliation. They have done this,
of course, all over the South. But in Mississippi their
retaliation has gone well beyond the point of threats.
The planters have organized a new Ku Klux Klan. They have
laundered it a bit, given it a face-lifting, and called it
White Citizens Councils. But no Negro in Mississippi
will be fooled. He knows the Klan when he sees it, by
whatever name it's called. The misnamed Councils have
begun to exert economic pressure on the leaders and
members of the NAACP. Are you a grocer, funeral
director, physician, small farmer? Then the likeli-
hood is that you could not function without credit.
But the credit is in the hands of the banks and
mortgage companies, dominated by the planters and
big Wall Street concerns. So, say the Citizen Councils,
since we control the credit, we'll control the Negroes!
We'll starve their leaders out. We'll draw up a new
kind of blacklist, and any Negro who supports NAACP or
calls for equality in education will have to find his
living outside of Mississippi. But the planters have
reckoned without their hosts! When Governor Hugh White
called what he thought were 100 "hand-picked" Negroes
to his office to euchre them into endorsing a statement opposing the Supreme Court decision, they voted
99 to one for integration of education. In Mississippi,
that takes courage!....

23.   YOUTH

108.   "Here's My Story," "The People of America are the Power," Freedom,
April, 1951, pp. 1, 2.

The columnist declares, in part:
....All through my youth -- in my mind and in fact --
I was a part of a large family, a family to which I was
responsible. And this family stretched out from Harlem
to Washington, Baltimore, Richmond, North Carolina,
Chinago, all across the nation -- wherever the Negro
people lived and struggled. My songs were the songs
of my people -- for five years I would sing no others.
Later, when from my travels I saw the likenesses between
songs of different peoples, I learned their languages
and began to sing the folksongs of the African, the
Welsh, the Scotch Hebridean, the Russian, Spanish,
Chinese, the Yiddish, Hebrew and others. I loved the
peoples' songs created through the ages. I felt so
much more at home with these than with so-called art
songs of individual composers. And today I choose those
individually composed songs which are rooted in and

(Robeson, Paul)

deeply remindful of the folk tradition. I searched
and searched, listened and listened. I learned that
in music, whoever the composer, the base and firm
foundation was always the people's music.... I knew
I was fighting for my people, the Negro people. Most
of them were working people like these English workers,
like the Welsh miners I knew so well. I tied all this
together. I saw the same British aristocracy oppressing
white English, Welsh and Scotch workers and African and
West Indian seamen, and the whole of my people in these
lands.... The forces of progressive liberalism have
the power, if fully united and utilized, to move the
majority of the American people to the peace and friendship which they so obviously and clearly desire....

109. "Here's My Story," "Stand Firm Son," Freedom, April, 1952, pp. 1,
5.

Robeson discusses his relationship with his father. He declares,
in part:
And father -what dignity, what restraint, but how concerned for his children; especially for me, the youngest,
the baby. How simply he gave of his life to me and
others, to the whole community. How brave he was, how
uncomplaining. I remember later in Westfield he told me
to do something. I didn't do it, and he said, "Come
here." I ran away. He ran after me. I darted across
the road. He followed, stumbled and fell. I was horrified.
I hurried back, helped Pop to his feet. He had knocked
out one of his most needed teeth. I shall never forget
my feeling. It has remained ever present. As I write,
I experience horror, shame, ingratitude, selfishness,
all over again. For I loved my Pop like no one in all
the world. I adored him, looked up to him, would have
given my life for him in a flash - and here I had hurt
him, and disobeyed him. Never in all his life (this was
in 1908 and I was ten; he died in 1919) did he ever have
to admonish me again. This incident became a source of
tremendous discipline which has lasted to this day. "What
would Pop think?" I often stop and ask the stars, the
winds. I often stretch out my arms as I used to, to put
it around Pop's shoulder and ask. "How'm I doin', Pop?"
"My Pop's influence is still present in the struggles
that face me today. I know he would say, "Stand firm,
son; stand by your beliefs, today." I know he would say
"Stand firm, son; stand by your beliefs, your principles."
You bet I will, Pop - as long as there is a breath in
my body.

V
Speeches and Addresses
by Paul Robeson

I am looking for freedom, full freedom, not an inferior brand.

Paul Robeson

1. AFRICA

110. "Anti-Imperialists Must Defend Africa." Quoted in Philip S. Foner,
      Editor. Paul Robeson Speaks: Writings, Speeches, Interviews,
      1918-1974. New York: Brunner/Mazel Publishers, 1978, pp. 168-
      171.

      This is an address that Paul Robeson made at a Madison Square
      Garden rally on June 6, 1946. It was sponsored by the Council
      on African Affairs. He declares, in part:
            The race is one - in Africa as in every part of the
            world - the race between the forces of progress and
            democracy on the one side and the forces of imper-
            ialism and reaction on the other. And Africa, with
            its immense undeveloped and unmeasured wealth of re-
            sources, is a major prize which the imperialists
            covet and which we, the anti-imperialists, must defend.
            We on the anti-imperialist side are handicapped by
            lack of money, lack of powerful organization, lack
            of influence in state and international affairs.
            But, although the enemy has all the advantages and
            has a head start in the race, it is yet possible
            for us to catch up and win. It is possible to win
            if the majority of the American people can be
            brought to see and understand in the fullest sense
            the fact that the struggle in which we are engaged
            is not a matter of here humanitarian sentiment, but
            of life and death. The only alternative to world
            freedom is world annihilation - another bloody
            holocaust - which will dwarf the two world wars
            through which we have passed.... That cry must
            be drowned out by the voice of the American people
            demanding Big Three Unity for Colonial Freedom!
            To arouse all sections of our population to the
            urgency of that demand has been the purpose of this
            meeting. But we do not in any sense regard our
            job as finished with the close of this great rally.

(Robeson, Paul)

> On the contrary, my friends, the Council on African
> Affairs regards this job as having just begun. With
> your help, with the cooperation of the organizations
> with which you associated and with the support of millions
> of like-minded peoples throughout our country and in
> other countries, we shall win the fight against the forces
> of imperialism....

111. "Africa Wants Freedom, Says Paul Robeson," Daily Worker, June 7,
      1946, p. 8.

> Paul Robeson spoke at a Madison Square Garden Rally before
> 16,000 people. He told them, in part:
>> The only alternative to world freedom is world
>> annihilation.... The imperialists' "Stop Russia"
>> cry must be drowned out by the voice of American
>> people demanding Big Three unity for colonial
>> freedom. Stop Russia means stop Europe's new
>> democracy, stop labor unions, stop Negro organi-
>> zation and voting. Africa, with its immense un-
>> developed wealth is a major prize which the
>> imperialists covet and which we, the anti-
>> imperialists, must defend....

112. "African Rally for Freedom to Robeson's Songs," Daily Worker,
      April 13, 1952, p. 2.

> Thousands of Africans marched to the voice of Robeson pouring
> from loudspeakers in the Fordsburg Square in Johannesburg,
> South Africa, led by Dr. J.S. Moroka, President of the African
> National Congress. In Harlem, New York, another rally was
> being held in support of the South Africans. Paul spoke and
> declared: "The fight in Africa is a challenge to us Negroes
> from the Africans, who are saying to us, 'How long are you going
> to take it?' If the South Africans win some freedom, we will
> win some here, too."

2.   CHINA

113. "China: Promise of a New World," Paul Robeson: Tributes and
      Selected Writings. Roberta Dent, et.al., Editors. New York:
      Paul Robeson Archives, Inc., 1976, pp. 75-77.

> This was a speech delivered at Sun Yat-sen Day tribute meeting
> in New York City on March 12, 1944. He declares, in part:
>> As a Negro I am often reminded of the parallel between
>> China and Africa. Both lands have had a glorious and
>> ancient culture. Both lands have known the oppression
>> and exploitation of aliens who spat upon culture, and
>> spread abroad the poison of racial hate and intolerance.

(Robeson, Paul)

> Today we face the promise of a new world. Today in
> Burma, Chinese, Africans and Indians are fighting
> side by side with their British and American allies
> against the Japanese enemy. Today peoples of every
> color are banded together to rid the world of the
> Hitlerite doctrine and practice of master and inferior
> races. The difference in the objectives between World
> War I and World War II can be measured by the fact that
> even in the midst of the present war, at the Moscow and
> Cairo Conferences, China's position as one of the four
> great allied powers was recognized not merely in words
> but in action, and the return of all territories stolen
> from her by Japan was guaranteed. The offensive extra-
> territoriality rights maintained by the western powers
> in China to give evidence of their superiority have been
> renounced, and we have repealed the humiliating Chinese
> Exclusion Act. At the core of all that is progressive
> in China, and at the root of her new eminence as a world
> power, are the "Three People's Principles" which China's
> great leader, Dr. Sun Yat-sen, preached and practices:
> nationalism and independence, democracy and advancement
> of the condition of the people.... China's plight is
> critical....

114. "Blockade of Chinese Red Armies Hurts U.S. War on Japan,"
      Daily Worker, March 17, 1944, p. 6.

> This is the text of a speech that Paul Robeson delivered at Sun
> Yat-sen Memorial Meeting, March 12, 1944, at the Metropolitan
> Opera House in New York City. He concludes, in part:
>> The three year's blockade against the Chinese
>> guerilla force must be lifted. The entire might
>> and strength of China's 400 millions must be united,
>> under the leadership of Generalissimo Chiang Kai-shek,
>> for the achievement of the earliest possible victory
>> over Japan.... The democratic principles of Dr. Sun
>> Yat-sen must be realized for China and for the world....

3. CIVIL RIGHTS

115. "2,000 Defy Ohio State Ban Hear Robeson," Daily Worker, April 19,
      1948, p. 1.

> According to this report two thousand students at Ohio State
> University where officials refused to let Paul Robeson talk on the
> campus, assembled outdoors at the edge of the university grounds
> and heard the great Negro leader attack the men who seek to bring
> Fascism to America. Robeson addressed the Ohio State students from
> the back of a truck parked beside the campus. University officials
> had applied a rule against political speakers to keep him off the

(Robeson, Paul)

campus. The Progressive Citizens Committee, a studeng group that
recently refused to bar Communists from membership, sponsored his
appearance. The Negro leader urged the students to investigate
American fascism. He explained that the denial of civil rights
went hand in hand with the denial of economic rights to workers,
Negroes, farmers and others. Robeson declares, in part:
> I don't blame your president or trustees for keeping
> me off your campus today. I blame the directors of
> the great corporations, the Firestones, the Girdlers
> and the Rockfellers. They are the ones who donate
> the buildings and run the universities.... Who are
> the powerful forces in your midst? They are the
> sources of potential American fascism which will be
> every bit as brutal as Germany's.... I came here
> because I was concerned with what happened in Columbus.
> We have to learn to connect things that happen around
> us with ourselves. Civil rights cannot be divided....
> I will come back if you need me....

116. "From Now On I Will Make Speeches," New York Times, April 24, 1949,
p. 37.

Speaking in Oslo, Norway, Paul Robeson declared that this would
probably be his last concert trip to Europe. The world traveler
declares:
> ....From now on I will make speeches. People can hear
> my singing on records. I will give my life for the
> colored people's right to live. I see clearly the idea
> behind the dictatorship of the proletariat. In America
> dark people are not free; in the U.S.S.R. they are free.
> My son is going to study atomic energy in the U.S.S.R.
> This is impossible for him in America.
The article also stated that Robeson declared that he foresaw the
day when his political opinions and speeches would land him in
jail; but he argued that he would henceforth devote himself to
making political speeches.

117. "Meeting in Garden Scores U.S. Court: Civil Rights Congress Rally
Protests Jailing of 4 Men in Red Trial Here," New York Times,
June 29, 1949, p. 4.

Paul Robeson spoke at Madison Square Garden in New York City at
the Civil Rights Congress. He said that all American progressives
should "stand back of the Communists now on trial." Robeson
reported on his recent trip to Europe, where he said Communism
is continuing to make gains. The activist described the Communist Party as the only one that is for peace and opposed to
war, according to the article.

118. "Robeson Announces: Non-Partisan Body Formed to Aid '12' Defense,"
      Daily Worker, July 18, 1949, pp. 1, 2.

      Robeson told the 1,300 delegates at the Bill of Rights Congress
      that a non-partisan committee to defend the rights of 12 Communist
      leaders was not being formed. He said the case of the Communist
      leaders was the key to the entire struggle for Civil Rights in
      America. Robeson urged the delegates to support this committee
      "with every ounce of energy that they have as soon as it is formed."

119. "1,500 Hail Robeson in Newark: Demand Trenton Six Be Freed,"
      Daily Worker, July 22, 1949, p. 3.

      This article stated that a mass meeting of 1,500 people cheered a
      fighting speech by Paul Robeson and demanded the immediate release
      of the Trenton Six and punishment of the Trenton officials respon-
      sible for their frameup. Meeting in the Terrace Room of the Mosque
      Theatre, the audience, composed equally of Negro and white, went
      through a tiny picket line organized by the Veterans of Foreign
      Wars, which paraded outside the meeting. Although the leaders of
      the VFW had proclaimed in advance that "hundreds" of Negroes would
      show up to picket Robeson, only three, members of Jim Crow VFW
      lodges, appeared in the picket line of 40. These three stepped
      out of the line and where nowhere to be seen when Robeson arrived
      for the rally, according to the article. Robeson's speech was pre-
      ceded by six songs by the great Negro singer, in English, Yiddish
      and German. In his talk, Robeson mocked the handful of reactionary
      pickets outside the hall, declaring that "I've been in many a
      picket line - to help workers." The antics of the Un-American Com-
      mittee in summoning Jackie Robinson before them, he charged, were
      an insult to the Negro people, who need no one to testify to their
      loyalty. "We'll be loyal. I'll be loyal to the America of Harriet
      Tubman, Frederick Douglass, Abraham Lincoln and the Abolitionists,"
      Robeson said.

120. "If We Must Sacrifice," Philadelphia Tribune, July 24, 1949, p. 1.

      This was a speech that Paul Robeson made at a meeting to free the
      "Trenton Six." It was sponsored by the Civil Rights Congress of
      Newark, New Jersey. The speaker declares that American Negroes
      must not be asked ever again to sacrifice on foreign shores. If
      we must sacrifice, asserts Robeson, let it be in Alabama and Missi-
      ssippi where his race is persecuted. He suggests that Negroes
      should fight against firms like the Metropolitan Life Insurance
      Company that incite war, so they can reap ever greater profits,
      build even taller apartments from which his people are barred and
      enslave still more Negroes on Southern plantations. Robeson con-
      cludes: "I am a radical and I am going to stay one until my people
      get free to walk the earth. Negroes just cannot wait for civil
      rights. This year it's a ball player, next year we'll have a pro-
      fessional basketball player, and that's only the beginning."

121. Lane, Betty. "Robeson Heckled On Appearance in Newark Auditorium,"
      Philadelphia Tribune, July 26, 1949, p. 1.

      Paul Robeson spoke to a gathering in the Mosque Theatre in Newark,
      New Jersey. The meeting was sponsored by the Civil Rights Con-
      gress to free the "Trenton Six." To enter the theatre, Robeson
      had to cross a 40 man picket line of Veterans of Foreign Wars,
      and other veteran organizations of Essex County. They carried
      placards denouncing the singer, who appeared to not mind at all.
      Several placards told him to "go back to Russia." The singer
      declares:
              American Negroes must not be asked ever again to
              sacrifice on foreign shores. If we must sacrifice,
              let it be in Alabama and Mississippi where my race
              is persecuted. The wealth of the USA was built on
              the backs of my people yet we are made to crawl.
              We are loyal to the America of Lincoln and the
              abolitionists, but not to those who degrade my
              people. One percent of the American population
              gets 59 percent of the national income. I am a
              radical and I am going to stay one til my people
              are free to walk the earth. Negroes just cannot
              wait for civil rights. This year it's a ball
              player, next year we'll have a professional basket-
              ball player.

122. "Will Remain Radical: Robeson Assails House Committee For
      'Insult,'" Afro-American, July 30, 1949, p. 8.

      According to this report, "I am a radical. I am going to stay one
      until my people are free to walk the earth," Paul Robeson, famed
      baritone, told 1200 persons attending a rally sponsored by the
      Civil Rights Congress at the Mosque Theatre in Newark, N.J. Re-
      ferring to Jackie Robinson's House Un-American investigating com-
      mittee testimony in Washington earlier in the week in which the
      Brooklyn Dodgers' second baseman tabbed some of Robeson's opinions
      as "silly," Robeson said:
              I have only respect for Jackie Robinson. He's en-
              titled to his opinions. But the House Un-American
              Investigating Committee had insulted Robinson, me
              and our people.... Colored Americans must not be
              asked ever again to sacrifice on foreign shores.
              If we must sacrifice, let it be in Mississippi and
              Alabama where the race is persecuted....

123. "6,000 Acclaim Paul Robeson," Afro-American, October 8, 1949, p. 1.

      Paul Robeson appeared at the Tabernacle Baptist Church in Chicago
      and told the 6,000 people that came to hear him declare, "I won't
      keep quiet until every black man in America can walk with dignity
      in his own country." Four thousand of his friends and supporters
      filled the church auditorium while 2,000 stood outside around
      loudspeakers to hear him sing "Joshua Fit the Battle of Jericho,"
      and answer those who determined to still his voice, and, if pos-
      sible, ruin him financially. They paid 55 cents each for the
      privilege and put $900 into the coffers for the Civil Rights

(Robeson, Paul)

Congress, sponsor, according to his article.

124. Raymond, Harry. "Robeson Urges Action For 25 Face Prison," The
      Worker, April 16, 1950, p. 4.

      Robeson spoke to about 3,000 men and women who came to Manhattan
      Center, in New York City, to protest the mounting cold war jailing
      and suppression of free thought and speech sweeping America. He
      declares, in part:
            I am disturbed not only for the freedom of leaders of
            the American workingclass but for the freedom of all
            American liberals. What is urgent now is the rapid
            building of a mass movement for freedom all over the
            country.... We see this so-called democratic America
            using its executive and judicial powers in an attempt
            to restore and keep fascism in power. But no McCarthys
            will solve the problems of American liberty. It is the
            radical will of the American people that will solve the
            problems of American liberty. The forces of France and
            Italy will see to it that no fascist will be able to set
            foot on their soil. But somehow in America we sit around
            and listen to talk about starting a war in a few hours....
            I don't know about you, but I think all Americans tonight
            with any sense of decency must feel very ashamed. But
            we, who are the vanguard, we who say we come from left
            of center, we should be deeply ashamed.... I assure
            you this is no time to apologize. This is a struggle of
            life and death, a struggle of the many against the few.
            Either one has the power or the other has the power....

125. "Robeson Denounces Korean Intervention," Press Release, Council
      on African Affairs, June 29, 1950.

      This was a speech that Paul Robeson made at a rally sponsored by
      the Civil Rights Congress. The rally was held at Madison Square
      Garden in New York City on June 28, 1950. He told them, in part:
            ....The meaning of the President's order that the
            lives of our airmen and sailors must be sacrificed
            for the government's despicable puppet in Korea, shall
            not be lost to the millions in the East whose day of
            freedom is not far off. And it will not be lost to
            the millions of Americans who must insist louder than
            ever for peace in the world, for real freedom every-
            where, for security and brotherhood. Least of all will
            the meaning of the President's order be lost to the
            Negro people. They will know that if we don't stop
            our armed adventure in Korea today -- tomorrow it will
            be Africa. For the maw of the warmakers is insatiable.
            They aim to rule the world or ruin it. Their slogan is
            all or none.... I have said before, and say it again,
            that the place for the Negro people to fight for their
            freedom is here at home -- in Georgia, Mississippi,
            Alabama, and Texas -- in the Chicago ghetto, and right
            here in New York's Stuyvesant Town!.... How terrible

(Robeson, Paul)

> a travesty on our democratic traditions for Negro youth
> to be called on one day to put down these brave African
> peoples! What mockery that black Americans should one
> day be drafted to protect the British interest in Nigeria
> whose proud people cannot be held in bondage for another
> ten years!
> Fail to stop the intervention in Korea, and that day
> may come!
> Fail to win our government to a policy of withdrawal
> from Indo-China, Formosa and the Philippines - a policy
> of recognition of the People's Republic of China - and
> that day may not be far off!....

126. "The Negro Artist Looks Ahead," Masses and Mainstream, January,
      1952, pp. 7-14.

This was a speech Robeson made at the Conference For Equal Rights
for Negroes in the Arts, Sciences and Professions. This meeting
was held in New York City, November 5, 1951. The speaker states
that the conferees were there to work out ways and means of
finding jobs for colored actors and colored musicians, to see
that the pictures and statues made by colored musicians, to see
that the creation of Negro writers are made available to the vast
American public. They were there also to see that colored
scientists and professionals were placed in leading schools and
universities, to open up opportunities for Negro technicians, to
see that the way was open for colored lawyers to advance to judge-
ships - yes, to the Supreme Court of these United States. The
artist concludes:

> In the end, the culture with which we deal comes
> from the people. We have an obligation to take it
> back to the people, to make them understand that in
> fighting for their culture heritage they fight for
> peace. They fight for their own rights, for the
> rights of the Negro people, for the rights of all
> in this great land. All of this is dependent so
> much upon our understanding the power of this people,
> the power of the Negro people, the power of the
> masses of Americans, of a world where we can all
> walk in complete dignity.

4. COMMUNISM

127. "Radio Help Biased on Negro Problem," New York Times, July 10,
      1949, p. 31.

Paul Robeson spoke at a conference in New York City sponsored by
the Committee for the Negro in Arts. According to this newspaper, Robeson predicted the death of American democracy if this
country did not unite with the twelve indicted leaders of the

(Robeson, Paul)

Communist party to overthrow the "guys who run this country for bucks and foster cold war hysteria." The article also states, he told the 300 Negro workers in radio, television and the theatre that they were deprived of all rights, whereas inhabitants of the Soviet Union and the "people's democracies" in Eastern Europe "are in no danger of losing any of their civil rights." He accused the State Department of deliberately stifling attempts of Negro artists to depict the struggle of his race for freedom but said that a solid Communist-Progressive front, backed by all Negroes, could stop "those who railroad the Atlantic Pact through Congress while they can't do anything on civil rights," stated the article.

5. FASCISM

128. "2,500 At Leftist Rally: Robeson Says Liberals Accept Challenge of Fascists," New York Times, June 12, 1947, p. 20.

Twenty-five hundred persons met in Manhattan Center in New York City to protest investigations by the House Committee on Un-American Activities. Paul Robeson told the audience that "forces of fascism" which he defined as wealth and special privilege, "had challenged labor and liberal forces in the world in desperation." "We pick up the challenge," he asserted. Robeson praised the speaking tours of former Vice-President Henry Wallace and pre-dicted the formation of a new political party. At first, according to this article, he added, the party would "win a triumph of opposition," but later would gain a democratic success.

129. "5,500 Hear Robeson at Detroit Rally," Daily Worker, October 12, 1949, p. 8.

Robeson made this speech before the Forest Club in Detroit on October 10, 1949. He declares that although he had spoken in Detroit on several occasions he still was the same man. The actor argues that he still spoke and fought for justice against fascism and for peace. He also reminded the audience that 12 great leaders of the American working class face going to jail because he and others had not done enough. He asserts, in part:
  I don't get scared when fascism gets near, as it did
  at Peekskill or Groveland, Fla. The spirit of Harriet
  Tubman, Sojourner Truth, Frederick Douglass fills me
  with courage and determination that every Negro boy
  and girl, yes, every white boy and girl, shall walk
  this land, free and with dignity. I stand ashamed
  before you tonight. Ashamed that 12 great leaders
  of the American working class face going to jail
  at Foley Square because we haven't done enough....

130. "Appearance of Robeson in U.S. Capital Orderly," Afro-American,
      October 29, 1949, p. 6.

      This article declared that an orderly crowd of approximately 2,500
      in Turner's Arena, heard Paul Robeson denounce fascism in this
      country and declare himself loyal to an America that will accord
      his people full freedom, while several hundred members of the Metro-
      politan Police covered the entire colored area, the article stated.
      Robeson said there is no question about him being a loyal American
      to one that gives his people full and makes him a first class
      citizen. "All I'm asking for is peace and full freedom for my
      people," he stated. He called the Peekskill riot a sign of weak-
      ness in American Fascism and a sign of desperation of race mongers.
      A scroll was presented to Robeson by Miss Lilli James, vice presi-
      dent of Local 471, Cafeteria and Restaurant Workers Union. The
      affair was sponsored by several veterns, union, fraternal and civic
      groups.

6. INDIVIDUALS

131. "Speech At Funeral of Mother Bloor," Daily World, February 14,
      1976.

      This is a reprint of a speech that Paul Robeson made on August 12,
      1951, at the funeral of Ella Reeve "Mother" Bloor. He observes,
      in part:
           ....She was in the tradition of Sojourner Truth,
           Harriet Tubman, John Brown, Lincoln, Douglass, and
           Thaddeus Stevens. She was horrified when a leader of
           our nation, one of confederate lineage, declared that
           the Congress which gave the Negro people their freedom
           and the American people new freedom was the worst
           Congress in our history. No, these people were no
           part of her America. She wanted nothing to do with
           the imperialists of 1898, swaggering across the world
           to enslave the people of the Philippines, Cuba, Puerto
           Rico, Hawaii, setting their sights on the great lands
           of the East, especially China. She hailed China's
           freedom. And she wanted nothing to do with our present
           day swaggerers and would-be conquerers with their
           callous destruction of heroic and struggling colonial
           peoples. And most of all she was devoted to her
           comrades and close co-workers. She knew them as the
           salt of the earth -- as she fought for their right to
           speak -- right to bail and their right to be free and
           continue their fight for American democracy and world
           friendship. So she hands her tasks on to us. I say
           to Mother that never was I so proud as when she told me
           I was one of her sons among her countless other sons
           who loved her and will always honor and revere her
           memory. (We) will carry on -- carry on fearlessly,
           tirelessly and courageously as she did until this land

(Robeson, Paul)

      is truly the Land of the Free and the Home of the
      Brave.

132. "Speech Delivered at the Funeral of Benjamin J. Davis," New York,
      August 27, 1964 - Paul Robeson Archives, Berlin, Germany Demo-
      cratic Republic. Quoted in Philip S. Foner, Editor. Paul Robeson
      Speaks: Writings, Speeches, Interviews, 1918-1974. New York:
      Brunner/Mazel Publishers, 1978, pp. 470-471.

      Robeson made a speech at his friend's funeral. He called Mr. Davis
      a fighter for freedom. The singer talked about his thirty-five
      year friendship with Davis. Robeson declares, in part:
          In a swiftly changing world, Ben was a courageous
          and unbending fighter for the rights of all. With
          his colleagues, he worked and fought, suffered and
          sacrificed for the sacred cause of Freedom and Peace.
          He was steadfastly loyal to this cause, to his country,
          to his people, to his Party, and to his friends. Ben
          Davis lies here tonight, mourned by his folk north and
          south, mourned by millions of people in other lands
          who have long been aware of his unrelenting struggle
          for Humankind. For me this has been a time of deep
          sorrow. For Ben Davis now goes to join another Ben I
          have lost - my beloved older brother, he also joins his
          colleague Dr. W.E.B. DuBois, one of our very great
          Americans. All my family extend deepest sympathy to
          his family. We share their loss and their sorrow....

7. LABOR MOVEMENTS

133. "Robeson Advises Negro Auto Workers Join CIO," Daily Worker,
      December 17, 1940, p. 1.

      Paul Robeson spoke in Detroit, Michigan, to the Negro workers in
      the Ford plant and other industries and advised them to join the
      CIO, United Automobile Workers Union. He declares, in part:
          ....It would be unpardonable for Negro workers to
          fail to join the CIO. I don't see how that can be
          argued. If Negroes fail to do that they classify
          themselves as scab labor. Negroes can not be part of
          American democracy except through labor unions.
          Democracy can't exist without labor movements. It
          is astounding to me that a man like (Henry) Ford and
          such a large industry as the Ford Motor Co., have
          been able to operate in a democracy and not have to
          deal with the labor movement. In the United States
          today there is a terrific effort going on to take
          away the all too few rights of labor. If that
          happens the Negroes, who have the fewest rights,
          will suffer most....

134. "Negroes Should Join the CIO," Ford Facts, December 20, 1940,
      CIO News, December 23, 1940.

      These remarks by Robeson were made during a campaign to organize
      a labor union at Ford Motor Company. He states, in part:
          I am against separate unions for Negro and white
          workers. All should belong to the same organization.
          Since the Negro problem can not be solved by a few
          Negroes getting to be doctors and lawyers, the best
          way for Black people to win justice is by sticking
          together in progressive labor unions, such as the
          CIO. There is no reason in the world why Negroes
          should not join the CIO; if they fail to do so, they
          classify themselves as scab labor Negroes and cannot
          be part of the American Democracy except through labor
          unions.... A democracy cannot exist without labor
          unions.... In the United States today there is a
          terrific effort going on to take away the all too
          few rights of labor. If that happens, the Negroes,
          who have the fewest rights, will suffer most.

135. "Speech at National Maritime Union Convention," July 8, 1941 --
      Proceedings of the Third National Convention of the National Mari-
      time Union of America, affiliated with the CIO, held in Cleveland,
      Ohio, July 7th to July 14th, inclusive, 1941, pp. 56-57.

      Robeson states that he attended this convention because he felt
      very close to the maritime unions. He declares that he knew the
      whole background of the Maritime Union and the colored people of
      this country stands among the foremost for giving complete
      equality and for the advancement of the colored peoples. The
      speaker surmises that he knows that this union with its militant
      background, will come to a decision to urge the government to give
      the Soviet Union all aid possible in its fight against fascism,
      for the Soviet Union is standing four-square for the cause and
      the rights of all the oppressed peoples of the world.

136. Haessler, C.G. "Paul Robeson Places Detroit Housing Riot in World
      War Setting," Federated Press, March, 1942.

      The writer declares that Paul Robeson was the world's most famous
      living singer. Robeson told a huge audience, in part:
          The big thing in this housing dispute is that labor
          here (Detroit) is firmly on our side. This goes beyond
          national and racial boundary lines. On our side are the
          great labor movements of the world and especially the
          Soviet Union, where you feel that all who have been op-
          pressed have their rights of freedom recognized. This
          was is for freedom, and particularly for the freedom of
          the colored races. Don't think that because the Japanese
          are colored that they are leading the fight for freedom.
          A small ruthless minority in Japan persecutes all the
          rest of the Japanese and all the colored races they can
          reach.... I sang before royalty and nobility but my
          problem was still there. I could have stayed in the Soviet
          Union where color makes no difference, but I could not

(Robeson, Paul)

> forget my people who are oppressed. I had to come
> back and help....

137. "Robeson Urges War Workers to Produce to Win," Chicago Bee, August
      8, 1945, p. 1.

According to this article stimulating the war effort in various
plants throughout the country with song and by speech, Paul
Robeson, internationally-famous baritone, made a surprise appearance at Apex Smelting Company on a program sponsored jointly
by the International Union of Mine, Mill and Smelter Workers (CIO)
and management. The article declares that Robeson, in a short
address, urged the workers to maintain high production to speedily
get the weapons of warfare into the hands of fighting men and help
bring the conflict to a satisfactory conclusion. He pointed out
the relationship of the Negro people's fight for freedom and justice
with an Allied war victory. Robeson sang "Water Boy" and "John
Henry," for the workers, concluded the article.

138. "Robeson Sounds Fighting Call," People's Voice, June 8, 1946, p. 11.

Paul Robeson spoke before the Tenth Annual Convention of the National Negro Congress in Detroit. He told the convention, in part:
> I understand full well the meaning of these times for my
> country and my people. The triumph of imperialist reaction
> in America now would bring death and mass destruction to our
> and all other countries of the world. And it would push the
> Negro people backward into a modern and highly scientific
> form of oppression far worse than our slave forefathers ever
> knew. I also understand full well the important role which
> my people can and must play in helping to save America and
> the peoples of all the world from annihilation and enslave-
> ment. Precisely as Negro patriots helped turn back the Red
> Coats at Bunker Hill, just as the struggles of over 200,000
> Negro soldiers and four million slaves turned the tide of
> victory for the Union forces in the Civil War, just as the
> Negro people have thrown their power on the side of progress
> in every other great crisis in the history of our country --
> so now, we must mobilize our full strength, in firm unity with
> all the other progressive forces of our country and the world
> to set American imperialist reaction back on its heels. The
> "gentry who own our economy" are frantic. I can well under-
> stand why. They have just seen the power of Negro and white
> workers united -- in auto, in steel, in packing, in electrical
> industries, in tobacco, in rails, in the mines, and they
> know what is coming from the seamen.... The one brief period
> of democratic liberty in the whole history of the South, the
> Reconstruction decade following the Civil War, was built by
> the fighting unity of the recently freed Negro masses and
> the progressive working people of the white South....

139. "Thousands Hear Paul Robeson Sing at Mass Meeting of Tobacco
      Union," Winston-Salem (N.C.) Journal, June 30, 1947, p. 5.

      Paul Robeson appeared in an open-air concert and sang for the Black
      workers that were attempting to organize a union at R.J. Reynolds
      Tobacco Company in Winston-Salem, North Carolina. After the con-
      cert, he addressed the crowd. The activist asserts, in part:
            If anyone wants a reason for my singing here, there's the
            reason. I'll never forget my father.... If it can happen
            to boys in Greenville (S.C.), it can happen to me anywhere
            in this country.... I am devoting two years, more if nec-
            essary, to fighting for my race. I have come back to my
            people, and I am fighting not as an artist but as one of
            you.... If fighting for the Negro people and their trade
            union brothers, if that makes me the subversive that they're
            talking about in Congress, if that makes me a Red, then So
            Be It! Our national leaders are wasting their time trying
            to break down independent nations in Europe.... There's
            nothing going to happen to Tito, nothing going to happen in
            the Balkans or in China or in the Soviet Union. Those
            people have the land in their hands, and they're not going
            to take it away from thm. We're going to build a world of
            equal men.... living in a true American democracy.

140. "Robeson Raps Taft Law at Carolina Meet," Daily Worker, July 3,
      1947, p. 1.

      Paul Robeson appeared at a rally in Winston-Salem, NC, on behalf of
      United Tobacco Workers Local 22, FIA-CIO. Attacking the Taft-
      Hartley law before the largest audience ever assembled in this city,
      Paul Robeson called upon the Negro people to recognize the organized
      labor movement at this rally, and to unite in a struggle for demo-
      cracy and progress. Robeson drew prolonged applause as he declared,
      "If fighting for democracy and the welfare of my people makes me a
      'red,' well, then, so be it!" A crowd estimated at between 12,000
      and 15,000 Negro and white people stood in the blazing Carolina
      afternoon sun to hear Robeson speak and sing, states the article.

141. "Speech at International Fur and Leather Workers Union Convention,"
      Proceeding of the International Fur and Leather Workers Union
      Convention, May 20, 1948, pp. 201-204.

      The activist at the meeting states, in part:
            ....The Negro people of this land must realize today, as they
            face a new kind of struggle, that they must have courage;
            they must have knowledge that the very primary wealth of Amer-
            ica is cotton, built upon the backs of our fathers; that cotton
            taken to the textile mills of New England; and that we don't
            have to ask for crumbs to be dropped from the few up top, but
            we have the right and the responsibility to demand in militant
            ways a better life for ourselves and for the rest of the
            oppressed. Now, this is the essence of the struggle that
            we fought under Roosevelt. No one knows it better than your
            Union. I have gone about this land in many places and every-
            where do I see the Fur and Leather Workers in the vanguard
            of progress....

142. "Remarks at Longshore, Shipclerks, Walking Bosses and Gatemen
      and Watchmen's Caucus," August 21, 1948 - Typewritten record of
      Proceedings of Caucus, International Longshoremen's and Ware-
      housemen's Union (ILWU) Archives, pp. 229-232. Quoted in **Philip
      S. Foner, Editor. Paul Robeson Speaks: Writings, Speeches, Inter-
      views, 1918-1974. New York: Brunner/Mazel Publishers, 1978,
      pp. 188-190.**

      He states, in part:
          ....And I want to repeat that I come today mainly as
          one in the Union, fighting its struggle. I shall be
          in the area for just two or three days. I shall be
          back, I hope, soon again.... I am proud to see the
          leadership that you have given to the whole labor
          movement. I want to thank your courageous leader,
          Harry Bridges, for his consistent stand. The final
          word is that as members of the ILWU, we have a tre-
          mendous responsibility. I cannot tell you how the
          labor movement throughout the country looks to you
          as an example. And so there is added responsibility
          for you to carry on the fight in the next few days,
          in the next few weeks, in the next few months. What
          you do here in this Union can very well determine
          the future of the whole labor movement in these
          United States. It can mean victory for the American
          people in these times. And I, as one who comes from
          an oppressed people, one who has identified himself
          with the whole progressive struggle, know that you
          will carry on. I want to thank you from the depths
          of my heart.

143. "Robeson Addresses the Longshore and Shipclerk's Caucus,"
      The Dispatcher, September 3, 1948, p. 1.

      Robeson addressed the Longshore and Shipclerks's Caucus on
      August 21, 1948, in San Francisco, California. He told the
      Convention, in part:
          The struggle never seems to stop. It gets sharper
          and sharper. I pick up the papers today and find
          that we and our Union have a real job to do. I have
          watched your struggle, watched the consistent stand
          you have taken, and I know that you are going to con-
          tinue to do that. Taft-Hartley means death to the
          trade union movement. The two parties have been
          playing around; and, at every moment, we see that
          Truman steps in, and uses every provision he can to
          do his part of the job. You have a real problem.
          I understand. It means that you are going to tell
          them, as you have told them before, that you want
          no part whatsoever of this kind of legislation,
          which not only would break the back of the labor
          movement but would set back the whole struggle of
          American people for generations. And I understand
          that you are going to tell them that you want no
          part of voting on what the employers have offered
          to you, that you will set the terms yourselves. That

(Robeson, Paul)

I am very proud to see. In travelling about the
country it is quite clear that the struggle for
economic rights, the struggle for higher wages, the
struggle for bread, the struggle for housing, has
become a part of a wider political struggle. They
have moved men in to high places in government; and,
today, the enemies of labor control the working
apparatus of the state. They have to be removed.
There has to be a basic change. I feel that this
can only be done by seeing that we put into power
those who represent a political party which has the
deep interests of the people at heart....

144.   Morisey, A.A. "Robeson, Speaking Here, Asks Struggle For Peace,
Dignity," Winston-Salem (N.C.) Journal, April 17, 1950, pp. 1, 4.

Paul Robeson returned to Winston-Salem, North Carolina, to attend
the funeral of Mrs. Morando S. Smith, one of the principal organizers of Local 22. He spoke at the funeral and surmises:
....My visit here is very symbolic to me. I'm coming
to a State where my people were born and reared --
where my father was a slave - where my cousins are
tobacco workers in the eastern part of the state.
It is hard to believe that this person (Mrs. Morando
Smith) who has given so much to the Negro workers is
gone. Yet there are thousands of us to carry on her
labor. Her name will remain deep in the hearts, not
(only) of Negro people, but all people. She is a
symbol of the best in the land. Winston-Salem will
give her the greatest victory. Her name will remain
a part of the city. She is a symbol of the dignity
of full expression as human beings. We must dedicate
ourselves to the struggle as she did - to see that
this will be a bounteous, peaceful world in which
all people can walk in full human dignity....

145.   "Forge Negro-Labor Unity for Peace and Jobs," Political Affairs,
Vol. 55, No. 4, April 4, 1976, pp. 32-43.

This is a reprint of a speech Paul Robeson made in 1950 at the
meeting of the National Labor Conference for Negro Rights that
was held in Chicago. In this speech the activist declares:
As the Black worker takes his place upon the stage
of history - not for a bit part, but to play his
full role with dignity in the very center of the
action - a new day dawns in human affairs. The
determination of the Negro workers, supported by the
whole Negro people, and joined with the mass of
progressive white working men and women, can save
the labor movement.... This alliance can beat back
the attacks against the living standards and the
very lives of the Negro people. It can stop the
drive toward fascism. It can halt the chariot of
war in its tracks, and it can help to bring to pass

(Robeson, Paul)

in America and in the world the dream our fathers
dreamed - of a land that's free, of a people growing
in friendship, in love, in cooperation and peace.
This is history's challenge to you. I know you will
not fail.

146.   "Toward a Democratic Earth We Helped to Build," Daily World, April
8, 1976, p. 8.

This was a speech that Robeson delivered at the National Negro
Labor Council that was held in Cincinnati, Ohio, on October 27,
1951. He declares, in part:
....As I said when I was with you in Chicago a year
ago, and as I have written in the newspaper Freedom
many times, somewhere we must see the necessity of
unity between all sections of labor in this land and
throughout the world. And especially today we must
understand the deep struggle of the Negro people in
this land for these 300 years. Already you have shown
me what I was talking about in Chicago, because I am
standing here tonight free with my shoulders back because you have said, "Come to Cincinnati, Paul, and
sing for us!" And so I can say to many Americans, "I've
been to Cincinnati - to the people of Cincinnati."
....So that the whole picture could change, so that when
one talks about struggles of Negro people, the struggle
for liberation, I see it not as isolating one Negro
leader here, one Negro leader there, one woman there,
one man here. It's a concept of realizing that all of
us are struggling for our freedom; under the same pressures, looking for freedom and some day if we are
looking right, you'll see the whole thing move - the
whole thing - four million, five million, six million,
seven million. That's the kind of strength that our
allies must see when something like the labor councils
are set up. To somewhere go into Negro communities to
win great sections, millions, to the side of the common
working class people for dignity and for a decent life.
I have - I can't tell you how proud I am to be with you
tonight and to wish you well. To forge this unity deep,
so deep that nothing can ever just even touch it a
little bit let alone any chance of breaking it....

147.   "The Battleground Is Here," Freedomways, Vol. II, No. 1, 1971,
pp. 116-119.

This is an address that Robeson made to the Annual Convention of
the National Negro Labor Council. It met in Cleveland, Ohio, on
November 21, 1952. He told the delegates, in part:
....Never to forget the days of my youth -- struggling
to get through school, working in brick yards, in hotels,
on docks and riverboats, battling prejudice and pro-
scription -- inspired and guided forward by the simple
yet grand dignity of a father who was a real minister to

(Robeson, Paul)

the needs of his poor congregation in small New
Jersey churches, and an example of human goodness.
No, I can never forget 300-odd years of slavery and
half-freedom; the long, weary and bitter years of
degradation visited upon our mothers and sisters,
the humiliation and Jim Crowing of a whole people.
I will never forget that the ultimate freedom -- and
the immediate progress of my people rests on the
sturdy backs and the unquenchable spirits of the
coal miners, carpenters, railroad workers, clerks,
domestic workers, bricklayers, sharecroppers, steel
and auto workers, cooks, stewards and longshoremen,
tenant farmers and tobacco stemmers -- the vast mass
of Negro Americans from whom all talent and achievement rise in the first place. If it were not for
the stirrings and the militant struggles among these
millions, a number of our so-called spokesmen with
fancy jobs and appointments would never be where they
are. And I happen to know that some of them will
soon be looking around for something else to do.
There's a change taking place in the country, you
know. My advice to some of this "top brass" leadership of ours would be: "You'd better get back
with the Folks - if it's not already too late."

148.   "Speech Delivered to The National Negro Labor Council Convention,"
        Freedom, December, 1953, p. 1.

This article was a partial text of a speech that Paul Robeson delivered at the Convention of The National Negro Labor Council,
Chicago, October 4, 1953. Robeson argues, in part:
Some Americans have already worked out a blueprint
for what the end will be. McCarthy, Jenner, Velde,
Byrnes, Talmadge, Shivers, see in the end a world of
rotting corpses on foreign battle fields, of darker
peoples licking the boots of a new, American "master
race," of European, Asian and Latin American nations
bowing down before the power of the Yankee dollar, of
Africa prostrate at their feet. They see fabulous
riches for the few while the masses of American workers,
black and white, yellow and brown, live on the very
edge of survival. They contend that "what's good for
General Motors is good for America." They see millions
of American workers on the iron ore range, in the mines,
in the California fruit fields, together with great
sections of our Mexican, Philippine and Puerto Rican-
American brothers and sisters. Well, I think I know
the temper of the delegates to this convention well
enough to know that we say: "That dream of yours is
out-dated gentlemen. This is the TWENTIETH century.
You've put your money on the wrong horses. You're
living in the wrong century. The dream that's about
to be realized is not yours, but humanity's - humanity's
dream of a world of brotherhood, of equality, of plenty

(Robeson, Paul)

> for All of the working masses of this land, of
> colonial liberation, of full freedom for the Negro
> people of these United States of eternal and ever-
> lasting peace!" And here at home, we, the Negro
> people, must also be partisans of peace. For 90 years
> since Emancipation our people have been playing "catch-
> up" in American life, we have been battling for equality
> in education, health, housing and jobs....

8. PARIS PEACE CONFERENCE

149. "Refuse to Reveal Names of 'Leaders' Seeking Real Probe: 6 To
Refute Paul Robeson," Afro-American, July 16, 1949, pp. 1, 2.

According to this article, the distinguished singer and actor
has denied emphatically since his return to New York City that
he told the recent communist-inspired Peace Conference in Paris
that colored people would not fight for the United States in
the event of war with Russia. He told a mixed audience of 5,000
persons at Rockland Palace, New York City, on June 19: "At the
Paris Conference, I said it was unthinkable that the colored
people of America or elsewhere in the world could be drawn into
war with the Soviet Union. I repeat it with hundredfold emphasis. They will not." Robeson said his address in Paris had
been grossly misinterpreted by the American press. The six
persons invited to refute Paul Robeson were: Dr. Charles S.
Johnson, president of Fisk University; the Rev. F. Sandy Ray,
chairman, Board of Social Agencies of the National Baptist Convention, Brooklyn, New York; Lester Granger, executive secretary,
National Urban League; Rabbi Ben Schultz, director, American
Jewish League Against Communism; Thomas W. Young, Norfolk, Va.,
Journal and Guide; and George A. Hunton of the Catholic Interracial Council, New York City. Asked his opinion of Robeson's
statement, Jackie Robinson said, "All I can say is that Paul
Robeson speaks only for himself. I'm not too familiar with
what he said, and I'll have to study it before I can comment on
it.   I'd fight my aggressor -- the Russians or any other
nation. Anybody who wants to take sway to fight for it.... I
want to fight for my child's right to live in this country,
and for any other child's."

150. "Congress in Paris Assails U.S. Policy," New York Times, April 21,
      1949, p. 6.

      Paul Robeson attended the World Congress of the Partisans of
      Peace as chief of the United States delegation. Mr. Robeson
      in an improvised address, declares, in part:
              ....We colonial peoples have contributed to the
              building of the United States Government which
              is similar to that of Hitler and of Goebbels. We
              want peace and liberty and will combat for them
              along with the Soviet Union, the democracies of
              Eastern European,China and Indonesia.
      Mr. Robeson later sang spirituals and received warm acclaim with
      "Old Man River," states the article.

                        9.   PEACE AND FREEDOM

151. "The Artist Must Elect," Paul Robeson:Tributes and Selected
      Writings. Roberta Dent, et.al., Editors. New York: Paul
      Robeson Archives, 1976, pp. 74-75.

      This was a speech that Robeson delivered at Royal Albert Hall in
      London, June 24, 1937. It was sponsored by the National Joint
      Committee for Spanish Relief in Aid of the Basque Refugee
      Children. Robeson told the audience, in part:
              ....Every artist, every scientist, every writer
              must decide now where he stands. He has no alter-
              native. There is no standing above the conflict on
              Olympian heights. There are no impartial observers.
              Through the destruction in certain countries -- of
              the greatest of man's literary heritage, through the
              propagation of false ideas of racial and national
              superiority, the artist, the scientist, the writer
              is challenged. The struggle invades the formerly
              cloistered halls of our universities and other
              seats of learning. The battle front is every-
              where. There is no sheltered rear.... The artist
              must take sides. He must elect to fight for Freedom
              or for Slavery. I have made my choice. I had no
              alternative. The history of this era is characterized
              by the degradation of my people: despoiled of their
              lands, their culture destroyed, they are in every
              country, save one, denied equal protection of the law,
              and deprived of their rightful place in the respect
              of their fellows.... Again I say, the true artist
              cannot hold himself aloof. The legacy of culture
              from our predecessors is in danger. It is the
              foundation upon which we build a still higher and
              all-embracing culture. It belongs not to us, not
              only to the present generation, it belongs to our
              posterity and must be defended to the death. May
              your meeting rally every Artist, every Scientist,

(Robeson, Paul)

> every Writer who loves Liberty and Democracy.
> May it rally every black man to the side of
> Republican Spain. May its inspiring message
> reach every man, women and child who stands for
> Freedom and Justice, because "the liberation of
> Spain from the oppression of Fascist reactionaires
> is not a private matter of the Spaniards, but the
> common cause of all advanced and progressive
> Humanity"....

152. "Paul Robeson Speaks for His People and All Humanity," Sunday
      Worker, November 14, 1937, p. 11.

Paul Robeson addressed aid to Spain Rally in Albert Hall, London.
He declares, in part:

> Friends, I am deeply happy to join with you in
> this appeal for the greatest cause which faces
> the world today. Like every true artist, I have
> longed to see my talent contributing in an un-
> mistakable clear manner to the cause of humanity.
> I feel that tonight I am doing so. Every artist,
> every scientist, must decide NOW where he stands.
> He has no alternative. There is no standing
> above the conflict on Olympian heights. There
> are no impartial observers. Through the des-
> truction -- in certain countries -- of the
> greatest of man's literary heritages, through the
> propagation of false ideas of racial, and national
> superiority, the artist, the scientist, the writer
> is challenged. The battlefront is everywhere.
> There is no sheltered rear.... The challenge must
> be taken up. Time does not wait. The course of
> history can be changed, but not halted. Fascism
> rights to destroy the culture which society has
> created; created through pain and suffering,
> through desparate toil, but with unconquerable
> will and lofty vision. Progressive and democratic
> mankind fight not alone to save this cultural
> heritage accumulated through the ages, but also
> fight today to prevent a war of unimaginable
> atrocity from engulfing the world. What matters
> a man's vocation or profession? Fascism is no
> respector of persons. The artist must take
> sides. He must elect to fight for freedom or
> slavery. I have made my choice. I had no
> alternative....

153. "The Artist Must Take Sides," <u>Daily Worker</u>, November 4, 1937.

This was a speech he made in London at the Royal Albert Hall that
was sponsored by the National Joint Committee for Spanish Relief
in aid of the Spanish Refugee Children. He states that he had no
alternative to fight for the freedom of the Spanish from fascism
because his conscious would not allow him to do otherwise.
Robeson contends that the legacy of culture from our predecessors
is in danger because it is the foundation upon which we build a
still more lofty edifice. He concludes that it belongs not
only to us, not only to the present generation -- it belongs to
posterity -- and must be defended to the death.

154. "These Words Let All Americans Remember," <u>The Worker</u>, Magazine
Section, November 28, 1943, p. 4.

This article was the text of an address Paul Robeson delivered
November 16, 1943, at the First Session of the New York Herald
Tribune Forum on Current Problems at the Waldorf-Astoria in New
York City. The title of the article refers to a speech that
President Franklin D. Roosevelt made August 14, 1942, on the
second anniversary at the Atlantic Charter. Robeson concludes
that all Americans should remember the Commander-in-Chief's words
and take hope from them. President Roosevelt concludes: "We
are determined that we shall gain total victory over our enemies,
and we recognize the fact that our enemies are not only Germany,
Italy, and Japan: they are all the forces of oppression, intolerance, insecurity and injustice which have impeded the
forward march of civilization...."

155. "Jewish Group Meets on Race Relations," <u>New York Times</u>, November 26,
1945, p. 11.

Paul Robeson spoke at a meeting of the Commission on Justice and
Peace of the Central Conference of American Rabbis. The meeting
was called to discuss the relationship of the teaching of
Judaism to race problems confronting the world. Robeson declared
that the United States "has taken over the role of Hitler and
now stands for counter-revolution all over the world." The
atomic bomb, he said, should be given to Russia because "a strong
Soviet Union would be the greatest guarantee against another
world war." He went on to say, according to this article, "that
Negroes might take a chance with dictatorship - any dictatorship
that would guarantee their rights - rather than thrust vague
promises of freedom of speech."

156. "American Crusade Ends with Anti-Lynch Decree," <u>Chicago Defender</u>,
September 28, 1946, p. 1.

Standing at the feet of Abraham Lincoln's statue, Paul Robeson,
chairman of the American Crusade to End Lynching, climaxed a day-
long rally high-lighted by a visit with the President, by reading
a new Emancipation Proclamation to thousands of assembled Negro
and white citizens. Citing the abolition of slavery nearly 100
years ago as the end of the slaveholding heritage only, Robeson
stated that oppression of the Negro never ended in fact. The

(Robeson, Paul)

proclamation pointed up the resurgence of violence
which has taken the lives of a score of men and
women since the war against fascism. It called mob
violence a threat to the democratic freedom of the
country. "We, more than 1,500 citizens assembled
in our nation's capital to inaugurate the continuing
American Crusade to End Lynching, are determined that
the duly elected government of the U.S. shall fulfill
its sacred trust by using the country's every resource to end now the growing reign of mob violence
in America," the proclamation stated. The proclamation, delivered after the President told Crusade
members that lynching is not a moral issue, ended
with a call to all Americans, regardless of race,
creed or color, to demand that the 80th Congress
pass laws to put an end to the national disgrace
of mob murder.

157. "Robeson Suggests United States Test Marxism," New York Times,
      October 8, 1946, p. 13.

Paul Robeson appeared before the Tenney Joint Legislative
Committee on Un-American Activities in Los Angeles, California.
He states: "Real racial equality is almost not an American conception. If Mr. Truman is going to raise the underprivileged
third of the nation, or the Negro one-tenth, he'd better
establish a dictatorship in the South." Robeson stated that he
was not a member of the Communist Party, but depicted himself
as a Negro, as inevitably attracted to "anti-fascist" movements.
The witness asserted that regardless of Russia's totalitarian
features, it was a country which had established equality of
peoples, whites, Black and yellow, and where derogatory use of
the word "Jew" brought a jail sentence. The actor concludes:
"....Many American Negroes would prefer the equality achieved in
Russia, with all its acknowledged lack of freedom, to the
'shadowdy' freedom of speech they have in the South."

158. "Unity for Peace," Masses & Mainstream, Vol. 4, No. 8, August,
      1951, pp. 21-24.

This was a speech Robeson made at the American Peoples Congress
for Peace that was held at Chicago, June 29, 1951. The speaker
suggests that the fight for peace-resistance against the exploiters and oppressors of mankind who want war to further their
greedy ends - the fight for peace is today the center of all
these struggles, of all the aspirations of working people,
artists, intellectuals the world over who form the world movement for peace. He concludes: "We here in America have the
central responsibility to build, as the peoples of Europe and
Asia have built, a powerful movement representative of every
section of our country, which will develop from the cease-fire
in Korea into a genuine and lasting peace - and freedom - for
all mankind."

159. Hirsch, Carl. "It Was 'Paul Robeson Day' in Chicago," The
      Worker, June 8, 1952.

      According to Mr. Hirsch Chicagoans by the thousands, Negro and
      white, jammed Washington Park on June 1st for a deeply-moving
      tribute to Paul Robeson and a fervent response to his leadership
      in the struggle for peace, democracy and the liberation of op-
      pressed peoples. The writer declared that the police estimated
      the crowd at 11,000. But from the platform where he sang and
      spoke, Robeson could see masses of people in every direction. He
      pledged to them that he will continued to fight their fights
      "as long as I have breath." He sang the workers' songs and the
      spirituals, songs of struggle from far sections of the world and
      in many languages, "Kevin Barry" and "Walter Boy," "Four Rivers"
      and "Joe Hill." And when he rose to that great climax in "Old
      Man River," which he sings, "I must keep fighting until I'm
      dying," the applause thunder-clapped across the park, stated
      the writer. Robeson was reported to have declared:
            I stand for peace and friendship among peoples for
            the unity between my people and the great masses of
            working people which can bring world peace and real
            freedom.... My right to speak has been earned not
            only by myself but by my people and my forebearers.
            The great wealth of this country was built literally
            upon the backs of my people! If Negro fraternal,
            civil, religious and social organizations joined to-
            gether, they could force the powers in Washington to
            grant full civil rights status now to the Negro
            people. I will fight to get Ben and his colleagues
            out of jail, so that they can once again return to
            give leadership to the people's struggles.

160. Singer, Michael. "Robeson Tells PP Delegates of Negroes Stake
      in '52 Vote," Daily Worker, July 8, 1952, p. 4.

      Paul Robeson was national co-chairman of the Progressive Party
      (PP) and he spoke at their convention in Chicago. He declared
      that "the people want peace, civil rights, jobs, security, pro-
      tection of their old age, and a return to the Bill of Rights for
      all our citizens, black and white, and of whatever, political
      opinions." Robeson warned the Democrats and Republicans that
      it "was dangerous" to play with vote-catching double-talk about
      civil rights. The fight for peace and civil liberties is
      "indivisible," he said, and the Progressive Party "must make it
      so." He concludes: "Today we alone in the elections of 1952
      offer a chance to vote for peace, for equality of all peoples,
      for true security, for freedom-full freedom and full human
      dignity."

161. "Voting for Peace," Masses & Mainstream, Vol. 5, No. 8, August,
      1952, pp. 9-14.

      This was an address that Paul Robeson made at the National Con-
      vention of the Progressive Party that was held in Chicago on
      the Fourth of July, 1952. The activist declares that he decided
      to retire from the concert stage in 1947 so that he could enter

(Robeson, Paul)

the day-to-day struggle of the people from whom he sprung.
Logically, he recalls, in fighting for the full civil rights and
equality of his people, he entered the struggle for peace. He
concludes:
> Blacks should vote for the Progressive Party because
> it has no vested interest in Jim Crow, because it has
> no investment in slums, because it does not own the
> railroads where Blacks have to eat in special sections
> of the dining rooms on the railroad Mr. Harriman owns.
> The Progressive Party will do more to promote Black
> equality than either the Democratic or Republican
> party.

162. "Speech At the Peace Bridge Arch," August 16, 1953 - Paul Robeson
Archives, Berlin, German Democratic Republic. Quoted in Philip S.
Foner, Editor. Paul Robeson Speaks: Writings, Speeches, Interviews, 1918-1974. New York: Brunner/Mazel Publishers, 1978,
pp. 363-366.

Excerpts of this speech was printed in the American newspapers,
including several of the Black newspapers. He discusses why he
was denied a passport as well as several other issues. The
singer asserts, in part:
> I want to just say "Thank you" and "Thank you"
> again for your very great kindness in coming here
> today. It means much to us in America - much to the
> American struggle for peace in the Northwest. Some
> of the finest people in the world are under pressure
> today, facing jail, facing hostile courts, for the
> simple fact that they are struggling for peace -
> struggling for decent America where all of us who
> have helped build that land can live in decency and
> in good will. As for myself, as I said last year, I
> remain the same Paul that you have known throughout
> all these years - the same Paul - but time has made
> it harder today to preserve the basic liberties
> guaranteed to us Americans by our Constitution....
> As I say, as an American, as Jefferson in his time
> stretched his hands across to meet the great heroes
> of the French Revolution of 1789, I stretch my hand
> across the continent to shake the hand of the brave
> Soviet people and of the new People's Democracies.
> That is my right as an American. And I know -- I
> could have sung it today -- I could sing so many
> songs -- they sing only the songs of peace there in
> tnat land, and I would have liked to have sung a
> song today, "Peace Will Conquer War," a song composed
> by Shostakovich, the great Soviet composer.... So
> there's a lot of America tnat belongs to me and to
> my people. And we have struggled too long ever to
> give it up. My people are determined in America to
> be not second-class citizens, to be full citizens --
> to be first-class citizens, and that is the rock
> upon which I stand....

163. Barry, Will. "25,000 On Canadian Border Hear Robeson," Daily
      Worker, August 20, 1953, p. 2.

      Paul Robeson was not allowed to crossover into Canada for a con-
      cert. Therefore he sang on the Canada-United States borders
      through a loudspeaker system. Over 25,000 Canadians heard him
      sing and speak. Robeson spoke briefly:
            I wish I could go on (singing) all day.... This
            gathering means much to Americans who are struggling
            for peace. There are people in the Northwest who are
            facing jail, hostile courts today, simply because
            they fight for peace, for a decent and dignified
            America.... Today in America we fight, as this truce
            is concluded, for Amnesty of these leaders who have
            been imprisoned, so that they may come back and
            lead the people in the struggle for peace....

                        10. PEEKSKILL

164. Burton, Bernard. "Emergency Parley Maps Fight to Jail Mobsters,
      Guilty Officials," Daily Worker, September 11, 1949, p. 2.

      An emergency committee of prominent progressive and labor leaders
      demanded the arrest and trial of all individuals and officials
      guilty of formenting or aiding the Peekskill Outrages. The
      committee launched a campaign to beat back the fascist violence
      heralded by the Peekskill attack, Paul Robeson announced. The
      leader addressed a crowd and told them, in part:
            We were injured, were attacked by an arm of state
            and local governments. The police who were supposed
            to protect us attacked us.... Nothing can make me
            more proud than to have been a part of the Peekskill
            demonstration for democracy.... I'm prepared for
            these dangers. I was there Sunday. I will be any-
            where that I have to be in this struggle.... We
            stood peacefully. Force and violence came from the
            other side. The rest of America should defend not
            only us, but themselves by fighting, protesting and
            demanding justice in the Peekskill outrage.

165. "Sings in Washington Without Incident as Police Patrol Area,"
      Pittsburgh Courier, December 22, 1949, p. 1.

      Paul Robeson addressed a mixed group of some 2,700 people in the
      Washington, D.C., Turner's Arena in a "Negro Freedom Rally."
      The speaker told the crowd:
            There is no question about my loyalty to the
            America I love. I love the America which was
            represented by the white and Negro people who
            came to hear me on the occasion of the infamous
            Peekskill, N.Y. riot last September, by the working
            people, by the oppressed Negro people, and by all

(Robeson, Paul)

> those who believe in justice and equality. But I
> will have nothing to do with the Coxes of Georgia,
> the Rankins of Mississippi, the DuPonts of Delaware....
> That is not my America. I hope they will give the
> same protection to every Negro boy and girl and every
> white boy and girl in Washington.... I never had so
> much attention before although I am the same man who
> has been to Washington many times before to walk the
> picket line.... I am asking for the same things now
> that I asked for then - freedom, full freedom for my
> people....

The article declared that in a combination concert and lecture,
Robeson interspersed songs in English, Yiddish, German and
Russian all through his talk as he charmed the enthusiastic
audience. Not a single incident of any kind marked the peaceful
assembly. Elaborate precautions against any such incident were
taken by the Metropolitan police of Washington who patroled a
six square block area surrounding the arena, roped off the
street on which the arena is located, and provided Robeson with
a round-the-clock escort of more than a dozen detectives and
uniformed cops. More than one hundred policemen were assigned
to duty in the area, according to the article.

166. Cooper, Ruby. "Robeson Speaks to 1,500 in Chicago," Daily Worker,
      March 17, 1950, p. 8.

Paul Robeson appeared before 1,500 cheering people in Chicago and
told them: "I won't be silenced" despite being banned from
Mrs. Eleanor Roosevelt's NBC television show. "Keeping me off
any program will not prevent the truth from becoming known."
"I shall continue to fight for a decent life for the Negro people
and all oppressed people, and for a peaceful world in which all
men can walk with full human dignity." Referring to the NBC ban,
Robeson told the audience, which included many prominent Negro
figures, that "you have given your answer tonight that I will
be able to speak." The Negro people's leader recalled his visit
here immediately after the violence at Peekskill, N.Y., when an
overflowing audience of over 5,000 turned out in a protest rally
here. He concluded: "You gave your answer then to all America
that the people were going to stand up and speak. You have done
it again tonight. I thank you from the bottom of my heart."

11. POLITICS

167. "I Stand Here Ashamed," Berlin German Democratic Republic:
Paul Robeson Archives, Quoted in Philip S. Foner, Editor. Paul
Robeson Speaks: Writings, Speeches, Interviews, 1918-1974. New
York: Brunner/Mazel Publishers, 1978, pp. 176-178.

Paul Robeson delivered this above speech over Mutual Broadcasting
System on September 23, 1946. He asserts, in part:
I stand here ashamed. Ashamed that here in the
Capitol of the world's first genuine democratic
government, it is necessary to seek redress of a
wrong that defies the most fundamental concept of
that precious thing we call democracy. Ashamed
that it is necessary in the year 1946 -- 84 years
after Abraham Lincoln signed the Emancipation Proclamation, it is necessary to rekindle the democratic
spirit that brought that document into being. Ashamed
that it is necessary to publicly expose and fight
the horrible contradiction that renders hollow our
promises to lead the people of the world to their
highest aspirations of freedom. I speak of the
wave of lynch terror, and mob assault against Negro
Americans. Since V-J Day, scores have been victims,
most of whom were veterans, and even women and
children. But I am not ashamed to stand here as
a servant of my people, as a citizen of America,
to defend and fight for the dignity and democratic
rights of Negro Americans....to fight for their
rights to live. And I am not ashamed to join with
the thousands of Americans, from all over the land,
white and black, Catholic, Jewish, Protestant,
of all political persuasions, who have come together in a national pilgrimage of the American
Crusade to End Lynching. People of America, we
appeal to you to help wipe out this inhuman
bestiality, this Ku Klux Klan hooded violence,
this....this Fascism, as we have today appealed
to the President and the Attorney-General of the
United States. Democracy is the birthright of
every Negro American.
The singer also argues that the defense of that birthright is the
defense of every American's right to join a trade union, to
practice any faith of his choice, to join any club, or fraternal
organization, to exercise his voting franchise, to enjoy the privileges of the Bill of Rights and the United States Constitution....

168. "Two Worlds - Ten Years of Struggle," Komsomolskais Pravda, June
      16, 1949. Translated by Prof. Paul A. Russo of the History De-
      partment of Lincoln University, Pennsylvania. Quoted in Philip S.
      Foner, Editor. Paul Robeson Speaks: Writings, Speeches, Inter-
      views, 1918-1974. New York: Brunner/Mazel Publishers, 1978, pp.
      486-490.

      Robeson gave a concert in Albany, New York. One of the conditions
      was that he would only sing and not make any political speeches.
      He agreed. He comments on that concert. The singer argues, in
      part:
           Both sides knew that since I had returned to America in 1939,
           whenever I performed in concert, I first turned to the audi-
           ence with a story about the Soviet Union. Since then, there
           has been no concert where I would not hold up to shame fascism
           of all hues. And here Robeson was just singing. I fulfilled
           the condition. There was no speech. And all the same I did
           make one. Before each number I made a short statement ex-
           plaining the nature of the song and its contents. Indeed,
           many of them were in languages unknown to my listeners....
           Although I agitated from the stage during every concert, this
           didn't seem enough to me. I dedicated two years exclusively
           to political struggle. Only in 1949 did I return to the
           stage. Broad strata of the American public joined with the
           Progressive Party in the struggle. During the election cam-
           paign of our party, an important event for me was a trip
           through the southern states - the citadel of conservatism.
           Shortly before my departure I received a threatening letter
           from the Ku Klux Klan. They threatened to kill me if I showed
           up in the South. Nevertheless, I decided to go. I had the
           enormous satisfaction of seeing with my own eyes how my com-
           patriots had changed. Only recently resigned to their fate,
           they were afraid of even the idea of struggle. The vision of
           lynch law fettered their plans and dreams. But now in every
           town and village they came together to protect their visiting
           guests....

169. "Robeson Again Rocks America," Pittsburgh Courier, June 25, 1949,
      pp. 1, 4.

      Robeson addressed a crowd of 3,500 persons at a welcome rally in
      New York City. He told them that the Negro people would not accept
      the public recognition of one percent of their people while the
      other 14,000,000 suffered injustice. He defied any part of an
      insolent, dominating America to challenge his Americanism.

12.   RACE RELATIONS

170. "The Future of the Negro in America and What Shall His Place Be In American Life," New Brunswick Daily Home News, October 16, 1919, p. 7.

He first stated that a comparison of the progress of the Negro with that of the white American during the past fifty years was unjust, for not only did the Negro have to concede a head start of centuries to the white, but was also forced to progress under great difficulties. He went on to list the lack of educational facilities and unjust treatment visited upon Black folk. He pointed out that Black people in spite of tremendous handicaps showed their capability and willingness to sacrifice and serve the United States dutifully in both the Civil War and World War I. He suggested that a possible solution to the racial problem in America was close cooperation between the races, "both working for the good of both."

13.   RUSSIA

171. "Robeson In Plea for Aid to USSR," Pittsburgh Courier, July 19, 1941, p. 12.

Paul Robeson was given a tumultous ovation and made an honorary member of the National Maritime Union (NMU) after he had appeared and sung before nearly 400 delegates who were meeting at the NMU convention in Cleveland, Ohio. The singer told the crowd, in part:
> Adolph Hitler and Fascism have come to grips with a power that will show no quarter.... As long as we are struggling for a better life we have one cause.... I know that the National Maritime Union with its militant background will come to a decision to urge the government to give the Soviet Union all aid possible in the fight against Fascism, for the Soviet Union is standing four-square for the cause and the rights of all opposed people of the world....

172. "Robeson Lauds Russia at Spingarn Medal Banquet," Pittsburgh Courier, October 17, 1945, pp. 1, 4.

Paul Robeson was the recipient of the Spingarn Medal that is awarded annually for outstanding achievement by the National Association for the Advancement of Colored People. The actor pointed out Russia has shown the world what it can do as a people and war in the main stream of change. He urged the creation of a world where people, whether white, Black, Red, or Brown, can live in peace and harmony, and where resources can be used for the good of all, for the advancement of mankind.

173. "No Real Minorities in U.S.S.R.," Daily Worker, November 22, 1945, p. 7.

This is the text of an address that Mr. Robeson delivered at the Madison Square Garden rally held on November 14, 1945, by the National Council of American-Soviet Friendship, on the occasion of the 12th anniversary of the U.S.-Soviet diplomatic relations. In this speech, Robeson concludes:
> If the United States and the United Nations truly
> want peace and security let them fulfill the hopes
> of common people everywhere - let them work
> together to accomplish on a worldwide scale,
> precisely the kind of democratic association
> of free people which characterizes the Soviet
> Union today.

174. "Robeson Calls Russia Second Motherhood," New York Times, June 15, 1949, p. 6.

Paul Robeson was performing in concert in Moscow, Russia, and while there was interviewed by almost every newspaper in Moscow. It was pointed out that Robeson received greater acclaim than had been given in recent years to any United States visitor. Robeson also wrote a series of articles for Pravda while he was there. They were entitled, "Two Worlds." The first installment described Mr. Robeson's first visit to the Soviet Union in 1934. He began: "Your country, dear readers, is my second Motherhood." The singer pointed out that on his first trip he felt for the first time he was an equal member of society. The actor declared: "....For the first time I could proudly straighten my shoulders, raise my head high and sing with all my soul."

175. "Love Soviet Best, Robeson Declares: At a 'Welcome-Home' Rally for Him, Singer Attacks Trial of Red Leaders Here," New York Times, June 20, 1949, p. 7.

The article states that Paul Robeson told a Welcome-Home Rally in New York City that he "loved" the Soviets "because of their suffering and sacrifices for us, the Negro people, the progressive people, the people of the future in this world." According to this report the singer asserted he wanted to love all of the United States, but he loved only part of it -- the progressive part. He added that the "burden of proof rests on America" as so far as extending his affection for it was concented. Mr. Robeson declared that if the eleven Communist leaders, who were now on trial, were not freed "all Americans can say good-by to civil liberties -- and especially the Negro people can say good-by to any attempt to secure civil liberties," stated the article.

176. "Land of Love and Happiness," New World Review, Vol. 20, No. 12, December, 1952, pp. 3-4.

This was a speech that Robeson made at a meeting of the National Council of American-Soviet Friendship to mark the 35th anniversary of the USSR and the 19th anniversary of American-Soviet relations.

(Robeson, Paul)

The meeting was held in New York City, November 13, 1952. The
actor declares that Russia is the land of socialism, love and
happiness and where MAN can walk the earth proud and free. He
also asserts that the Soviet Union rises in defense of the oppressed colonial masses, exposes and indicts the Malan fascists
and the imperialist powers who masquerade as the "Free West."
Robeson concludes: "I have been, I am, and I shall always remain,
a strong, unbending friend of the Soviet people, their wise
leaders and the Land of Socialism, Equality and Peace!"

14. SOCIAL SYSTEMS

177. "It's Good to be Back," Freedomways, Third Quarter, Summer, 1965,
pp. 373-377.

This is an excerpt from a speech that Robeson made at a reception
that Freedomways held for him on his return to America after living
in Europe for five years. The singer declares:
    Our languages, our idioms, our forms of expression may be
    different, the political, economic and social systems under
    which we love may be different, but art reflects a common
    humanity. And further, much of the contemporary art re-
    flecting our times has to do with the struggles for equality,
    human dignity, freedom, peace and mutual understanding.
    The aspirations for a better life are similar indeed all
    over the world and when expressed in art, are universally
    understood. While we become aware of great variety, we
    recognize the universality, the unity, the oneness of
    the many people in our contemporary world. In relation
    to this, in our travels we visited many peoples in Socialist
    countries. Today we know that hundreds of millions of
    people (a majority of the world's population) are living
    in Socialists countries or are moving in a Socialist
    direction. Likewise newly emancipated nations of Africa
    and Asia are seriously considering the question as to
    which economic system best fits their needs. Some of
    their most outstanding leaders agree that the best road
    to the people's goals is through a Socialist development,
    and they point to the advances made by the Soviet Union,
    the People's Republic of China, Cuba and the other
    Socialist countries as proof of their contention. The
    larger question as to which society is better for humanity
    is never settled by argument. The proof of the pudding
    is in the eating. LET THE VARIOUS SOCIAL SYSTEMS COMPETE
    WITH ONE ANOTHER UNDER CONDITIONS OF PEACEFUL COEXISTENCE,
    AND THE PEOPLE CAN DECIDE FOR THEMSELVES....

15. SOUTH

178. "We Must Come South," <u>Paul Robeson: Tributes and Selected</u>
      <u>Writings</u>. Roberta Dent, et.al., Editors. New York: Paul
      Robeson Archives, Inc., 1976, pp. 64-65.

      This speech was made before an integrated gathering in New Orleans,
      in the Booker T. Washington Auditorium on October 29, 1942. He
      declares, in part:
              I had never put a correct evaluation on the dignity
              and courage of my people of the deep South until I
              began to come south myself. I had read, of course,
              and folks had told me of strides made.... but always
              I had discounted much of it, charged much of it to
              what some people would have us believe. Deep down,
              I think, I had imagined Negroes of the South beaten,
              subservient, cowed. But I see them now courageous
              and possessors of a profound and instinctive dignity,
              a race that has come through its trials unbroken. A
              race of such magnificence of spirit that there exists
              no power on earth that could crush them. They will
              bend, but they will never break. I find that I must
              come south again and again, again and yet again. It
              is only here that I achieve absolute and utter identity
              with my people. There is no question here of where I
              stand, no need to make a decision. The redcap in the
              station, the president of your college, the man in
              the street -- they are all one with me, part of me.
              And I am proud of it, utterly proud of my people.
              We must come south to understand in their starkest
              presentation the common problem that beset us every-
              where. We must breathe the smoke of battle. We
              must taste the bitterness, see the ugliness.... we
              must expose ourselves unremittingly to the source
              of strength that makes the black South strong!

16. WORLD WAR I

179. "Loyalty and The American Negro," <u>New Brunswick Daily Home News</u>,
      May 21, 1918, p. 7.

      Robeson spoke on that topic when he won first prize in the sopho-
      more extemporaneous competition. He recalled the role that Black
      Americans played in previous wars. He surmised that Blacks have
      traditionally supported America when it was at war with foreign
      countries.

180. "The War's Effect on American Manhood," Targum, April 30, 1919,
      p. 515.

      Paul Robeson spoke on the above topic his senior year and won
      first place prize in the highly valued, very competitive, Senior
      Ann Van Nest Bussing Prize in extemporaneous speaking. In
      winning this contest Robeson completes his record of four con-
      secutive victories in public speaking contests, Freshman,
      Sophomore, Junior and Senior.

17. WORLD WAR II

181. "A Victorious War Must Free All," People's Voice, August 4, 1943,
      p. 1.

      These remarks were made at Free People's Dinner in honor of the
      actor in Berkeley, California, on July 20, 1943. He declares
      that the triumphant end of World War Two must bring a world
      where there can be no question of a colored people or a white
      people, but a question purely of human beings, a world where
      there can be no question of colonial exploitation of any kind.
      The author asserts that World War Two is every man's war; this
      is not a white man's war nor a white man's victory, nor a
      colored man's war, nor a colored man's victory. According to
      Robeson, we should make sure that the victory that follows will
      be one that assures full freedom for all people in this world re-
      gardless of race or color.

18. YOUTHS

182. "The New Idealism," The Targum, Vol. 50, No. 30, June 1919,
      pp. 570-71.

      This was an oration delivered at Rutgers graduation by Paul
      Robeson on June 10, 1919. He contends that the younger generation
      must feel a sacred call to that which lies before them. He states
      that he would go out to do his little part in helping his un-
      tutored brother. Robeson states that the future of Blacks lie
      in their own hands. The orator concludes that we know that
      neither institutions nor friends can make a race stand unless it
      has strength in its own foundation; that races like individuals
      must stand or fall by their own merit; that to fully succeed they
      must practice their virtues or self-reliance, self-respect,
      industry, perseverance and economy.

183. "Robeson Addresses Negro Youth Group at YMCA in Harlem," New York
      Times, January 29, 1949, p. 9.

      Paul Robeson told a protest meeting, called by the newly organized
      Negro Youth Builders Institute, Inc., that "the oppression of the
      Negro in the United States varies only in degree in New York, New
      Jersey, Georgia and Alabama." He told the audience that the
      public must be "aroused" to the poor school conditions in Harlem
      and Brooklyn,inadequate housing, "police brutality in the North,
      generally," which would include, he said, "the railroading to
      the electric chair of six Negro youths in New Jersey." The
      activist concluded: ".... Children in cotton fields in the
      South, children on tobacco plantations and exploited children all
      over...neglected children in the North...conditions were of the
      same pattern, evidence of a colored minority in a hostile white
      world." The meeting was held in the Y.M.C.A., 180 West 135th
      Street, New York City.

184. Cooper, Ruby. "8,000 in Chicago Hear Paul Robeson," Daily Worker,
      September 26, 1949, p. 2.

      Paul Robeson gave concerts in Chicago and was greeted by 8,000
      people. Tne concerts were seen as a fighting answer to the
      violence at Peekskill and a devastating debunking of the claim
      that Robeson lacked support among the Negro people. He told the
      mostly Negro audiences: "I say to the Negro youth of this land,
      don't bow your heads. Stand up and fight for the rights due
      our people.... Let us walk with our shoulders back in full
      equality and full human dignity...."

VI
Remarks and Statements
by Paul Robeson

I am being tried for fighting for the rights of my people, who are still second-class citizens in this United States of America. . . . I stand here struggling for the rights of my people to be full citizens in this country. And they are not.

Paul Robeson

1. AFRICA

185. Proceedings of the Conference on Africa-New Perspectives. New
     York: Council on African Affairs, Inc., 1944, pp. 10-12.

     Paul Robeson made the opening remarks at this conference. As
     Chairman of the Council on African Affairs, Robeson welcomed the
     participants. He told them, in part:
         We are gathered here for the purpose of considering
         together our relation - the relation of the American
         people and their government - to Africa's place in
         the war and in the post-war world.... Although
         Americans in the past have known little about Africa
         beyond the caricatures occasionally represented in
         American movies, most of them today are beginning
         to realize, I think, that the welfare of 150 million
         Africans and other dependent peoples who make up
         almost half of the world's population is something
         that directly concerns their own welfare. This war,
         a large part of which has been and is being fought
         in colonial areas, has brought this truth home to
         them. There has been lately an increasing volume
         of literature dealing with Africa and colonial
         territories in general.... This conference is
         dedicated to promoting such unity in the interest
         of the African people and in the interest of American
         and worldwide security.

186. "Racialism in South Africa." Berlin, German Democratic Republic:
     Paul Robeson Archives, 1949. Quoted in Philip S. Foner, Editor.
     Paul Robeson Speaks: Writings, Speeches, Interviews, 1918-1974.
     New York:Brunner/Mazel Publishers, 1978, pp. 194-197.

     He declares, in part:
         ....We are often reminded of the "cold war" said
         to exist between the two great sections of the
         world, the capitalist section led by the United

(Robeson, Paul)

> States, and the socialist section at the head
> of which stands the Soviet Union. But little
> is said of the cold war of racial hatred,
> malice and intolerance, which is being waged
> with an intensified fury in an attempt to hold
> millions of people of non-European race in per-
> manent subjection. At the head of the aggressive
> forces in this cold war, too, stands the United
> States. But occupying a prominent place by
> its side is the Union of South Africa. They
> are at once agreed in their policies of racial
> discrimination, but they differ in their
> practical approach. A Negro may be lynched in
> the Southern States of America if he attempts
> to use his vote. In South Africa he is in no
> danger, only because he has no vote....
> Only the aroused enemies of the Indian and
> African peoples can gain by the racial
> disturbances which recently took place in
> Durban. We must strengthen the forces com-
> posed of the best African, Indian and European
> elements in South Africa which are struggling
> to achieve understanding among the races and
> justice for the oppressed. Their fight is the
> concern of all progressive humanity; their's
> is but a sector of the struggle for peace
> and progress. Their friends throughout the
> world are many. Here let me pay a tribute
> from this platform to the great Soviet Union
> which constantly champions the cause of the
> African and other oppressed peoples....

187. "The Real Issue in The Case of The Council on African Affairs,"
Statement issued April 24, 1953, by Paul Robeson, Chairman,
on behalf of the Council on African Affairs, concerning the
Justice Department's order for that organization to register
under the McCarran Act - Paul Robeson Archives, Berlin, German
Democratic Republic. Quoted in Philip S. Foner, Editor. Paul
Robeson Speaks: Writings, Speeches, Interviews, 1918-1974.
New York: Brunner/Mazel Publishers, 1978, pp. 345-347.

The leader comments on why the Council on African Affairs was
labeled by the United States Government as "subversive." He
argues, in part:
> The consistent job of the Council on African
> Affairs through the years since its estab-
> lishment in 1937 has been to provide accurate
> information on the conditions and struggles
> of the peoples of Africa and to support
> their efforts toward liberation. In recent
> months the Council has endeavored
> to rally American assistance

(Robeson, Paul)

for the desperate fight of black and brown South
Africans against Malan's fascist oppression, and
for the Africans of Kenya whose struggle for land
and survival the British seek to crush with most
ruthless and inhuman punitive measures. For such
work as this the Council, I am proud to say, has
received many expressions of gratitude and appreciation from African leaders. It would appear,
therefore, that in branding the Council as "subversive" and ordering it to register under the
notorious McCarran Act, U.S. authorities are at the
same time branding as "subversive" all the millions
of Africans who are today determined to be free
of the stigma of colonialism and white supremacy
domination. This attack upon the Council represents an attempt to frighten and silence all those
Americans, particularly the Negro people, who are
in any way critical of U.S. policies in Africa....
The real issue in our case is the right of advocacy
and support for the freedom of Africa's enslaved
millions, - including the descendants of Africa
who have yet to achieve their full liberty and
rights here in the United States. The Council
on African Affairs will continue to carry forward
its work and will fight all efforts to restrict its
usefulness to the cause of African freedom by means
of the unconstitutional and un-American McCarran Act.

188.   "Paul Robeson Urges Support for Jailed Leaders and Freedom
Struggles in Kenya and South Africa," Statement issued by Paul
Robeson, Chairman of the Council on African Affairs, New York,
April 13, 1953 - Paul Robeson Archives, Berlin, German Democratic
Republic. Quoted in Philip S. Foner, Editor. Paul Robeson Speaks:
Writings, Speeches, Interviews, 1918-1974. New York: Brunner/
Mazel Publishers, 1978, pp. 344-345.

Robeson comments on Afro-American responsibility abroad, as well
as in the United States. He asserts, in part:
We Americans of African descent are fighting for
our full rights as citizens, and must keep fighting
until we achieve these rights. In this fight it
will be well to remember that as American citizens
we have interests and responsibilities abroad, as
well as at home. Our Government is very interested
and active, and very busy, in Europe, Asia and
Africa. We as black and brown people are especially
interested in what our Government is doing in Asia
and Africa, because Asians and Africans are Colored
Peoples like ourselves. In Africa our Government is
actually supporting and doing business with the white
colonialists,not the African people. It is supporting
Malan in South Africa and the British in Kenya and
Rhodesia. We Colored Americans will especially want
to support our African brothers and sisters in South

(Robeson, Paul)

> Africa who are now being jailed by the Malan
> Government for peacefully resisting segregation
> and discrimination. We will especially want to
> support our African brothers and sisters in Kenya
> who are being tried and imprisoned for insisting
> upon the return of their land.... Let us protest
> the jailing of the black leaders in Kenya. Let
> us call upon our Government this week to stop helping
> the Ku Kluxer Malan and help the South African people
> who are marching irresistably toward freedom. Let
> our voices be heard in thousands of telegrams and
> letters to the President in Washington and to Ralph
> Bunche at the United Nations in New York City....

189. "The Government's Policy and Practice of Racial Discrimination
      and Oppression in the Union of South Africa," Spotlight on
      Africa, August 13, 1953.

The activist shows how Prime Minister Malan of South Africa sponsored a number of legislative acts since 1948 that made the
apartheid policy in South Africa more rigid, circumscribed and
cruel for the non-white population there: The Asiatic Laws Act,
The Mixed Marriage Act, Amendment Registration Act, The Group
Areas Act, The Bantu Authorities Act, and The Separate Representation of Voters' Act. Robeson as Chairman of the Council
on African Affairs concludes:

> The Council on African Affairs appeals to the United
> Nations to take such measures as may be necessary to
> halt the present oppression of the ten million non-
> whites of the Union of South Africa, and to avert
> the danger to international peace and harmony arising
> from the pursuit of the South African Government's
> policy and practice of racial discrimination and
> oppression. We are confident that with the aid and
> support of the United Nations, the people of South
> Africa, white as well as non-white, will willingly
> strive to achieve equal civil liberties, equal
> political rights, equal economic opportunities, and
> equality of social status for ALL South Africans.

190. "Africa and The Commemoration of Negro History," Spotlight on
      Africa, January 1955.

Paul Robeson made the following observations on Africa and its
place in history. He delcares, in part:

> I believe the misrepresentation of the African
> and the distorted picture of the American Negro
> still so prevalent in our American culture, stemming
> as they do from the same basic cause of economic
> exploitation, can NOT be attacked or rooted out
> separately. Each myth is propped up by the other;
> both must be destroyed. When that happens, the true
> worth of the Negro -- whether in Africa or in the
> Americas -- and his place in the mainstream of the

(Robeson, Paul)

> world's culture will be properly understood. When
> that happens, no one will dare to speak of white
> supremacy or Negro inferiority.

191. "A Word About African Languages," Spotlight on Africa, February,
      1955.

Paul Robeson spoke several African languages: Swahili, Zulu,
Mende, Ashanti, Ibo, Efik, Edo, Yoruba and Egyptian. He points
our that although African languages are varied and complex, but
in structure they resemble many of the tongues of other similar
cultures: Chinese, Japanese, Mongolia and Hungarian.... "After
I reached London in the '20's and the '30's ... I met students
from Asia, the West Indies, Africa. I began to listen to them
as they talked with each other and finally, I plunged into the
learning of the languages of my ancestors...."

2. COMMUNISM

192. "Ban on Communism Step Towards Fascism," People's Voice, March 22,
      1947, p. 14.

Paul Robeson comments on Labor Secretary Lewis B. Schwellenbach's
call for the outlawing of the Communist Party. The writer argues,
in part:
> There is an ominous parallel between what happened in
> Germany under Hitler and what is happening today in
> America's Secretary of Labor Schellenbach, joining
> campaign of Big Business to hamstring American pro-
> gressives and labor, has called for outlawing a
> Communist Party. The Nazis did that, too. And
> President Truman justification of a policy of
> American intervention in Greece and Turkey on the
> grounds of saving these countries from the "totali-
> tarian" menace and guarding the security of the
> United States, is remarkably similar to the anti-
> Communist smokescreen of the fascist aggressors....

3. INDIVIDUALS

193. "On the Resignation of Hanry A. Wallace," Daily Worker,
      September 21, 1946.

Paul Robeson as Chairman of the Council on African Affairs issued
a statement on its behalf:
> We are shocked by the forced resignation of Wallace.

(Robeson, Paul)

> We join with the overwhelming majority of Americans
> who want peace and democracy for this country and
> the world, in fully supporting Wallace's criticism.
> We cannot avoid the painful conclusion that Truman's
> action represents a complete capitulation to the
> reactionary minority in our country who seek world
> domination.

4. MUSIC

194. "Some Aspects of Afro-American Music," December 1956 - Paul
      Robeson Archives, Berlin, German Democratic Republic. Quoted
      in Philip S. Foner, Editor. Paul Robeson Speaks: Writings,
      Speeches, Interviews, 1918-1974. New York: Brunner/Mazel
      Publishers, 1978, pp. 436-439.

      Paul Robeson comments on Afro-American Music. He argues, in part:
          Mr. Harold Courlander, well-known authority on folk
          lore, made an extensive field trip into the rural
          South some years ago in search of authentic Afro-
          American music. He recorded this music on the spot
          where he found it. Some of this music is now available
          in several Folkways albums of records, under the title
          Negro Folk Music of Alabama.... There is no more
          evidence that Afro-American music is based on European
          music, than that European music is based on African
          music. There is however, extensive evidence that
          nearly all music in the world today stems from an
          ancient world body of original folk music - music
          created, sung, and handed down through the ages by
          the people in all parts of the world. The people
          brought this wealth of folk music with them into the
          early Churches when they were established, and here
          it was preserved, modified and eventually formalized
          in various ways, according to the developments and
          changes which took place in the Church itself....
          This contrapuntal singing, and the characteristic
          "Fourth" or tetrachord, are not only characteristic
          of early medieval Plain Chant, but also of much of
          the modern music of Moussorgsky, Bartok, Janacek,
          Vaugh Williams, Duke Ellington, George Gershwin and
          others, and also of Chinese, Indonesian, African,
          Hebraic, Byzantine, Ethiopian music, as well as
          Scotch Hebridean, Welsh and Irish music; that is to
          say it is characteristic of Pentatonic modal music.
          It would seem then, that Afro-American music is based
          primarily upon our African heritage and has been in-
          fluenced not only by European but by many other musics
          of East and West; this is true also of Afro-Cuban,
          Afro-Haitian, Afro-Caribbean, Afro-Brazilian music

(Robeson, Paul)

and our music has also influenced other music....

195. "Thoughts on Music," Paul Robeson: Tributes and Selected Writings.
      Roberta Dent, et.al., Editors. New York: Paul Robeson Archives,
      1976, pp. 72-73.

      These thoughts were taken from Paul Robeson's handwritten notes
      that were written in 1959. He gives his thoughts on music.
      The writer argues, in part:
           Some years ago, around 1956, while still immobilized,
           my attention was directed to many of the trends in
           modern music, especially as it concerned my own music --
           religious and secular "Spirituals" and "Blues." I
           sang a lot of it -- had grown up with most of it from
           a child. Remember going up to the Savoy Ball Room
           very often to hear Count Basie, as I had often heard
           Chick Webb and Ella Fitzgerald -- downtown to hear
           Don Shirley and Bach, up to Manhattan Casino to hear
           "Charlie Parker" and get "twisted around" trying to
           dance to those "off-beat riffs," down to the "Apollo"
           to hear Dizzy Gillespie take flight, and so with many
           others. And Thelonius Monk really floored me. It
           was quite clear that every field of music, ancient
           and modern, was floating around. And of course the
           incomparable "Duke" Ellington stepped back in. The
           Modern Jazz Quartet made a lasting pact with the
           Elizabethans and the Duke himself caught up with
           Shakespeare, the Minstrel Bard. And I see that
           Bernstein points out that the "Blues" meter is
           none other than the iambic pentameter of the great
           tragedies and transports us via the "Blues" straight
           to "Dunsinane." So anything seemed likely to happen --
           in the modern music and jazz field of operations.

5. NEGRO BASEBALL PLAYERS

196. "Time to Bring Negro Baseball Players into the Major Leagues,"
      Pittsburgh Courier, December 11, 1943: Chicago Defender,
      December 11, 1943; Baltimore Afro-American, December 11, 1943;
      Daily Worker, December 4, 1943; The New York Times, December 4,
      1943.

      These are remarks made by Robeson at a meeting of Black publishers'
      delegation that met with Higher Commissioner of Baseball Kenesaw
      Mountain Landis and Major League Owners. They met at the Hotel
      Roosevelt in New York on December 3, 1943. Robeson told the
      gathering that this was an excellent time to bring about an
      entry of Negro players into organized baseball. The time has
      come, states Robeson, that the owners of the baseball teams must
      change their attitude toward Negroes and keep it consistent with

(Robeson, Paul)

the attitude of the entire country. He reminded the owners that because baseball is a national game, it is up to baseball to see that discrimination does not become the American pattern. At this meeting the club owners did agree to take steps to open the way for the immediate signing of Black players.

6. PEACE AND FREEDOM

197.   "Statement on Un-American Activities Committee," News release. Council on African Affairs, New York City, July 20, 1949 - Paul Robeson Archives, Berlin, Germany Democratic Republic. Quoted in Philip S. Foner, Editor. Paul Robeson Speaks: Writings, Speeches, and Interviews, 1918-1974. New York: Brunner/Mazel Publishers, 1978, p. 218.

Paul Robeson comments on the Un-American Activities Committee and Negroes' loyalty to America. He asserts, in part:
....The loyalty of the Negro people is not a subject for debate. I challenge the loyalty of the Un-American Activities Committee. This committee maintains an ominous silence in the face of the lynchings of Maceo Snipes, Robert Mallard, the two Negro veterans and their wives in Monroe, Georgia, and the violent and unpunished murders of scores of Negro veterans by white supremacists since V-J Day. It is not moved to investigate the attempted legal lynchings of Mrs. Rosa Lee Ingram, Negro mother of 12 living children and her two sons, now jailed for life in Georgia for protecting her honor; or of the Trenton Six, or the Martinsville Seven, or the denial of simple justice to our people in the every day life of the nation's capital. Every pro-war fascist-minded group in the country regards the Committee's silence as license to proceed against my people, unchecked by Government authorities and unchallenged by the courts. Our fight for peace in America is a fight for human dignity, and an end to ghetto life. It is the fight for the constitutional liberties, the civil and human rights of every American. This struggle is the decisive struggle with which my people are today concerned. This fight is of vital concern to all progressive Americans, white as well as Negro. For victory in this struggle, Americans need peace, not war on foreign fields....

198. "Perspectives on the Struggle for Peace in the United States in
      1954," New York, January 1, 1954 - Pravada, January 2, 1954.
      Translated by Dr. Brewster Chamberlin from the German version
      entitled, "Die Perspectiven Des Friedenskampfs in den USA in Jahr
      1954," in Paul Robeson Archives, Berlin, German Democratic
      Republic. Quoted in Philip S. Foner, Editor. Paul Robeson Speaks:
      Writings, Speeches, Interviews, 1918-1974. New York: Brunner/
      Mazel Publishers, 1978, pp. 372-375.

      The activist discusses a various number of topics including the
      role of the workers in the struggle for peace. Robeson surmises,
      in part:
            The struggle for peace in the U.S., where reaction is
            especially strong, was difficult and developed slowly
            in 1953. Nonetheless reports from all corners of
            the United States prove that new successes were won
            in the peace struggle. Many trips throughout the
            nation I undertook confirmed this conclusion. The
            peace movement in the U.S. developed in the last year
            and I am convinced that it will develop still faster
            in the new year, 1954. A short time ago I attended
            the third annual congress of the National Negro Labor
            Council which has sections throughout the land. This
            organization included the workers and trade union
            functionaries from all Negro groups, white workers of
            various nationalities and the Puerto Ricans and Mexicans
            living in the U.S. Representatives of the workers in
            the steel and iron industry, the coal miners, and the
            automobile industry, representatives of the farmers,
            the workers in the electronic industry and the rail-
            roads gathered together at this congress. Particularly
            important is the fact that many senior workers and
            trade union leaders were present.... The knowledge
            of the great importance of the peace struggle also
            characterizes the congresses of the trade unions of
            the hotel and restaurant workers, the garment workers
            and the fur and tobacco workers and the leather
            industry and other not nearly so progressive unions.
            Practically for the first time this was also the case
            at the congress of the farmers of the middle west
            and the south. The situation of the farmer has grown
            worse because of the sinking prices for farm produce
            and the accumulation of an overproduction of such
            produce. The monopolies reap super profits from this
            situation....

VII
Messages and Advertisements
by Paul Robeson

Mass action—in political life and elsewhere—is Negro power in motion; and it is the way to win.

Paul Robeson

1. ACTORS' EQUITY

199. "Message to Actors' Equity," Paul Robeson: Tributes and Selected
      Writings. Roberta Dent, et.al., Editors. New York: Paul
      Robeson Archives, 1976, p. 73.

      The activist declares, in part:
            It was deeply moving for me to learn that Actors'
            Equity has decided to establish an award in my name
            and to make me the first recipient of that honor.
            Though ill-health prevents my attendance at the pre-
            sentation ceremony, I must say I felt so very close
            to you, my brothers and sisters of the acting pro-
            fession. Although I was trained to be a lawyer, it
            was your profession that welcomed me into a lifelong
            career. Just fifty years ago this spring, in 1924,
            the Provincetown Players -- including such dear
            friends as Gene O'Neill, Jimmy Light, Eleanor
            Fitzgerald, Gig McGee and others -- drew me into their
            midst and encouraged me onto the stage in their pro-
            duction of "All God's Chillun Got Wings" and "The
            Emperor Jones." Then too it was that theater group
            which, a year later, in 1925, first presented me as
            a concert singer. So you will understand that through
            all the years - off Broadway, on Broadway, across this
            land and elsewhere in the world - I have always felt
            a close kinship with fellow actors. From my earliest
            days in the theatre, when I often heard O'Neill expound
            his belief in the "Oneness of Mankind," I have been
            blessed with the warm good fellowship of so many of
            you. It has been most gratifying to me in retirement
            to observe that the new generation that has come along
            is vigorously outspoken for peace and liberation.

(Robeson, Paul)

    .... To.all the young people, black and white,
who are so passionately concerned with making a better
world, and to all the old timers among you who have
long been involved in that struggle, I say: Right
on! On this occasion, I send my heartfelt thanks and
love to you all.

2. AFRICA

200. "Food and Freedom for Africa: A Message From Paul Robeson,"
Daily Worker, June 5, 1946, p. 5.

This was an advertisement put in the newspaper by Paul Robeson as
Chairman of the Council on African Affairs on behalf of the South
African Famine Relief. It declares, in part:
    Hunger and lack of freedom always go hand in hand.
    Even in good times the Bantu people of South Africa
    suffer chronic starvation. Robbed of their land,
    confined in "reserves" and ghettoes, and reduced to
    the most subservient level of employment by a legal
    color bar, these Africans are victims of a systematic
    oppression which can hardly be comprehended, except by
    those who have lived under fascist tyranny. The
    Council on African Affairs has been able, through the
    generous response of those reached through its cam-
    paign, to send a considerable quantity of canned food
    and money to aid these stricken people. But more, much
    more, needs to be done. We Americans, however, have
    the responsibility of providing something more than
    food for the people of Africa - the whole of Africa
    with its 150 million colonial subjects. We must see
    that their demands for freedom are heard and answered
    by America and the United Nations. For without economic
    and political freedom, there cannot be any abiding
    relief from poverty and hunger. This no mere theoretical
    obligation which rests upon America to advance African
    freedom. It is an obligation which stems from the
    millions of American dollars invested in Africa's
    gold, copper, diamonds and rubber. It is an obligation
    which stems from the position of leadership which
    America holds in World affairs today. It is our solemn
    duty as Americans, as a liberty-loving people, to join
    hands with the millions upon millions of exploited and
    oppressed colonial peoples in Africa and throughout
    the world. NOW is the time for action, if we hope to
    build a free world.

201. "A Message from the Chairman to Members and Friends of the
      Council on African Affairs," New Africa, July-August, 1949.

      Paul Robeson states that he is more determined than ever to give
      his maximum time and energies in the fight for full freedom, full
      equality, for Black people. Robeson suggests that Black rights
      in the United States is linked inseparably not only with the
      struggle of all American workers, but also with the liberation
      movements of the peoples of the Caribbean and Africa and of the
      colonial world in general. The activist concludes that he must
      have the support of the friends and members of the Council on
      African Affairs, so that the council may play its most effective
      role against their oppressors and false leaders, and in fighting
      for the rights of Negroes here and in Africa and for our common
      freedom.

202. "An Important Message from Paul Robeson," Spotlight on Africa,
      (Newsletter, Council on African Affairs), February 25, 1952.

      The leader declares that Black people must unite if they are to
      bring about changes. He surmises, in part:
              Imagine all sections of the Negro people in the United
              States, their organizational and programmatic differences
              put aside, joining together in a great and compelling
              action to put a STOP to Jim Crowism in all its forms
              everywhere in this land. Think how such an action would
              stir the whole of America, raising to a new high level
              the people's resistance to the mounting fascism which
              is bent upon wiping out the constitutional rights of
              ALL Americans, starting with the Negro people and other
              minority groups. Think how such an action would be
              supported by hundreds of millions of darker peoples
              and white enemies of racism and fascism throughout
              the world -- how it would strengthen the world-wide
              struggle for freedom and peace!.... The South African
              Government is aiding in "preserving democracy" in
              Korea by sending its Jim Crow air force to help kill
              Koreans. South Africa is a part of President Truman's
              "free world." Yes, dozens of American's biggest auto,
              oil, mining and other trusts have highly profitable
              holdings in that country. And U.S. loans have been
              made available to Prime Minister Malan in order to
              accelerate the expropriation of South Africa's rich
              resources. Hence it is clear that in raising our
              voices against the Malan regime we simultaneously
              strike a blow at the reactionary forces in our own
              land who seek to preserve here, in South Africa, and
              everywhere else the super-profits they harvest from
              racial and national oppression. United support of
              our brothers' struggle in Africa is an integral part
              of our task in achieving freedom for all Americans.

3. ANNIVERSARY OF THE GERMAN DEMOCRATIC REPUBLIC

203.   "For the Celebration of the 15th Anniversary of the Founding of
the German Democratic Republic," Mermaid Theatre, London,
October 25, 1964 - Paul Robeson Archives, Berlin, German Demo-
cratic Republic. Signed by Paul Robeson and Eslanda Robeson.
Quoted in Philip S. Foner, Editor. Paul Robeson Speaks:
Writings, Speeches, Interviews, 1918-1974. New York: Brunner/
Mazel Publishers, 1978, p. 473.

The writer congratulated the German Democratic Republic on their
15th Anniversary. They declared that the founding of the GDR
was an event of tremendous importance in the modern world because
it was based upon the welfare of all people and dedicated to
Peace and Friendship between all Nations.

4. CHRISTMAS

204.   "Christmas Message," People's Voice, December 22, 1945, pp. 1-4.

Robeson surmises that he was thankful for the opportunity of
saying Merry Christmas to the People's Voice and its readers.
He said they knew that the People's Voice was the kind of paper
that works hard all year round for the things that Christmas
stands for - peace and good will among men. The writer also
declared that he knew that the readers and friends of PV are his
friends, too. The author argues:
>   This Christmas, for the first peace-time Christmas
>   for Americans in four years has a special meaning.
>   It has a special meaning in a personal sense for
>   those whose loved ones have come home from the war.
>   But in a larger sense, for all of us who do not pay
>   mere lip-service to the idea of Christian Brotherhood....
>   It is a natural thing for us to be more concerned
>   with the things that affect us personally and
>   immediately. But if this Christmas of 1945 means
>   anything at all, it should be an occasion for realizing
>   that our racial problems, our domestic problems, and
>   our foreign problems are all inter-related and of
>   one pattern. PV has stressed this fact in many of
>   its editorials. The Council on African Affairs, with
>   which I am associated as Chairman, has also endeavored
>   to bring home the fact that the colonial peoples'
>   struggle against imperialism is also our struggle.
>   Yes, the enemy is powerful. But the war with black,
>   brown, yellow and white peoples fighting together;
>   with the peoples of the United States, Great Britain
>   and the Soviet Union marching side by side in friend-
>   ship and cooperation - we shall in fact achieve
>   peace and good will among all men. That's what

(Robeson, Paul)

I hope for when I say Merry Christmas.

5.   CIVIL RIGHTS

205.   "Robeson to President Truman -- Government Must Act Against
        Lynching or the Negroes Will," The New York Times, September 24,
        1946, p. 60.

        A national conference on lynching mapped a program aimed at curbing
        mob violence and sent a delegation which told President Truman
        that if the Government failed to do something "the Negroes will."
        Paul Robeson, a sponsor of the conference, was in the group
        calling on the President, and in telling reporters of the meeting
        said Mr. Truman had objected to parts of the program. Mr. Robeson
        read a message to Mr. Truman asking him to issue "a formal public
        statement" expressing his views on lynching, and recommending
        "a definite legislative and educational program to end the dis-
        grace of mob violence." The President, according to Mr. Robeson,
        indicated tnat political matters made it difficult to issue a
        statement of his views at this time. As to possible Federal
        legislation to curb lynching, Mr. Robeson said the President ex-
        pressed tne view that passage was a political matter in which
        timing was important. The President took exception, Mr. Robeson
        asserted, to a suggestion by the delegation that it "seemed
        inept for the United States to take the lead in the Nuremberg
        trials and fall so far behind in respect to justice to Negroes
        in this country." The Presidential view, Mr. Robeson continued,
        was that Americans should not tie domestic matters to the inter-
        national situation. Mr. Robeson also said the President termed
        America and Great Britain the last refuge of freedom in the world.
        "I disagreed with this," said Robeson. "The British Empire is
        one of the greatest enslavers of human beings." He declared that
        American and British policy today were "not supporting anti-
        fascism." Asked by a reporter if he was a Communist, Mr. Robeson
        replied that he is not, and added: "I label myself as very
        violently anti-Fascist."

206.   "Message to National Conference, Manchester, England," May 27,
        1956 - Paul Robeson Archives, Berlin, German Democratic Republic.
        Quoted in Philip S. Foner, Editor. Paul Robeson Speaks: Writings,
        Speeches, Interviews, 1918-1974. New York: Brunner/Mazel
        Publishers, 1978, pp. 411-412.

        Paul Robeson sent a message to the National Conference that was
        meeting in Manchester, England. He told them, in part:
            Since I wrote to you last, I had the great pleasure
            of a few weeks of freedom - a respite from six years
            of being a prisoner of the cold war and McCarthyism
            in America. Last February I sang in Massey Hall
            in Toronto and for the metal miners in Sudbury,

(Robeson, Paul)

> Ontario. No words can describe how deeply I was
> moved by the warmth of those audiences, their over-
> flowing spirit of love and brotherhood which reached
> out to me! Invitations came from many other Canadian
> cities, urging that I come to sing for them, too.
> And so a trans-Canada tour was planned, and last
> month I was scheduled to sing a score of concerts
> from Montreal to Vancouver - my first opportunity
> for a concert tour in many years! But then on the
> eve of my departure, the Canadian government decided
> to bar me from entering Canada. The reason given was
> that the concert agency which was sponsoring my tour
> had a "left-wing" complexion. Of course, no one
> could be fooled by that flimsy explanation, since it
> was the same agency which had previously sponsored
> my Concert in Toronto. The immediate criticism of
> this decision that was made by all sections of the
> Canadian Press was proof that Ottawa's action was
> not an expression of Canadian sentiment. It is ob-
> vious that this decision, like most of the manu-
> factured goods one sees in Canada, was "made in the
> U.S.A." Not only is my right to travel denied, but
> there has been and is a deliberate policy of attempting
> to prevent me from making a living by practicing my
> profession as an artist. It is the same policy which
> is being used by the White Citizen Councils (the new
> Ku Klux Klan) in states like Mississippi, where Negroes
> who demand their right to vote and the right of their
> children to non-segregated schooling, are subjected to
> economic reprisals.... The whole world has watched
> with admiration the courage of Autherine Lucy, and
> the militant protest of 50,000 Negroes in Montgomery,
> Alabama, against Jim Crow....

6. PEACE CONFERENCES

207. "Our People Demand Freedom," Masses and Mainstream, Vol. 4, No. 1,
      January, 1951, pp. 65-67.

   This was a message Mr. Robeson sent to Sheffield, England, to the
   Peace Congress where it was holding a meeting. He told the
   delegates:
> A century ago a great leader in the freedom struggles
> of my people, Frederick Douglass, stood in England as
> you do today and called for the support of the British
> people in the battle to overthrow slavery. He recognized
> then that the interest of his enslaved people could not
> possibly be served by any aggressive policy of the slave-
> holding Government.... The life and struggles of this
> outstanding American of the nineteenth century afford

(Robeson, Paul)

me great inspiration as I find myself separated from
you by the edict of the United States State Department.
You may be assured while I remain in the United States
a victim of the detestable program of house arrest
initiated by our government, while I cannot be in your
midst and among many friends from all parts of the
world, as has been my custom in years past, I do not
remain quietly or to live a life of ease. I remain
in the United States as Douglass returned to it, and in
his words, "for the sake of my brethren." I remain to
suffer with them, to toil with them, to endure insult
with them, to undergo outrage with them, to lift up
my voice in their behalf, to speak and work in their
vindication and struggle in their ranks for that emancipation which shall yet be achieved by the power of
truth and of principle for that oppressed people.
And do today at this World Peace Congress we move
forward in the best traditions of world democracy,
representing as we do the hundreds of millions throughout the world whose problems are much the same. We
are peoples of all faiths, all lands, all colors, of
all political beliefs, united by the common thirst
for freedom, security and peace....

208. "The People Must, If Necessary, Impose the Peace," Peace Action,
      (Sydney, Australia), December, 1960 - January, 1961.

      Paul Robeson gave this message to the Melbourne Peace Conference.
      He states, in part:
          How good that during this Conference, it is our great
          joy to be here with you in Australia. The last weeks
          have been deeply moving and inspiring ones. We have
          met so many of you who are actively engaged in making
          Peace on This Earth a reality. We certainly feel
          ourselves a part of you on this historic occasion.
          Our deepest thanks to you, here on this continent,
          for your untiring efforts, and for the deep and wide
          influence you exert upon all the people of your land.
          These very days, and the days ahead, are of utmost
          importance. In America, the people are groping,
          earnestly seeking for honest guidance in solving most
          perplexing and soul-searching problems. Again the
          Negro people, the Americans of African descent,
          struggle courageously and with fierce determination
          toward some measure of full citizenship which is
          still denied them one hundred years after the so-
          called Emancipation.... You gather today, and in
          days to come to let those in power understand that
          the human race, yes, the whole of us, Black, White,
          Brown, and Yellow, yes, all of us...are on our way
          to a victorious imposing of the peace...in the end
          final peace...Complete Disarmament...on the way to
          living in peace, friendship and understanding with
          our neighbors...no, more than neighbors...with our

(Robeson, Paul)

>sisters and brothers. Is this possible and realizable?...
>A thousand times, YES.

7. SALUTE TO PAUL ROBESON

209. "Message to 'Salute to Paul Robeson'," Daily World, April 26, 1973.

Paul Robeson was not able to attend this "Salute" to him because
of ill health. He did send a taped message that states, in part:
>Dear Friends:
>   Warmest thanks to all the many friends here and
>throughout the world who have sent me greetings on
>my 75th birthday. Though I have not been able to be
>active for several years, I want you to know that I
>am the same Paul, dedicated as ever to the world-
>wide cause of humanity for freedom, peace and
>brotherhood.
>   Here at home, my heart is with the continuing
>struggle of my own people to achieve complete
>liberation from racist domination, and to gain for
>all black Americans and the other minority groups
>not only equal rights but an equal share.
>   In the same spirit, I salute the colonial liberation
>movements of Africa, Latin America and Asia, which have
>gained new inspiration and understanding from the
>heroic example of the Vietnamese people, who have once
>again turned back an imperialist agressor....
>   Though ill health has compelled my retirement, you
>can be sure that in my heart I go on singing:
>>"But I keeps laughing
>>Instead of crying,
>>I must keep fighting
>>Until I'm dying,
>>And Ol' Man River
>>He just keeps rolling along!"

8. YOUTHS

210. "Message to People's Drama Group," Daily Worker, August 18, 1949,
p. 11.

Paul Robeson sent a personal message to the People's Drama Group.
He told them, in part:
>   I want all the cast and production staff of They
>Shall Not Die to know that I and thousands of others
>deeply honor them both for the splendid and challenging

(Robeson, Paul)

> contributions they have made to the American theatre
> and also for standing firm and fighting back against
> fascist brutality and intimidation. Carry on. The
> real America is with you. You can't lose.

211. "Message to Youth Festival in Budapest," Daily Worker, August 23,
      1949, p. 4.

This message was broadcast by a Moscow radio. The speaker declares,
in part:
> I believe that the festival will still more closely
> rally on the side of peace millions and tens of
> millions of people, including the black, yellow
> and brown peoples of east and west. In the present
> historical epoch, the tasks of the supporters of
> peace and democracy are clear -- complete
> liquidation of fascism the world over and the
> establishment of lasting peace and cooperation
> with the countries of the people's democracies
> and the peoples of the Soviet Union.

VIII
Letters and Telegrams
by Paul Robeson

Wherever and whenever we, the Negro people, claim our lawful rights with all of the earnestness, dignity and determination that we can demonstrate, the moral support of the American people will become an active force on our side.

Paul Robeson

1. AFRICA

212. "Africa - Continent in Bondage," <u>New York Herald-Tribune</u>, June 5, 1946, p. 30.

Robeson sent a letter to the <u>New York Herald-Tribune</u>. The essence of the letter was that because of the conditions of Black workers in Africa, he, as Chairman of the Council on African Affairs, called a mass meeting in Madison Square Garden to raise funds for South African relief. He states, in part:
....And while certain initial steps have been taken by some of the major powers in the direction of meeting the demands of some of the colonial peoples, notably in India, there has not been the slightest indication of any intention on the part of the European powers to declare themselves on the question of freedom for the 150,000,000 persons of the Continent of Africa. So little that is true has been written about the African people and so little real knowledge of their life and struggles has been allowed to penetrate the press, the movies, the schools that for the great majority of Americans Africa is a vast, unknown and exotic land. Africans are not people to the American. In his dreams and plans for the one free world Africa is curiously and for all purposes absent. Yet nowhere in the world is there a people more oppressed, more deeply exploited, more thoroughly enslaved. Nowhere in the world is there a people more in need of the aid of free men everywhere in their struggle for the most meager of human rights, the least of human liberties. Africa is a whole continent of people living in abject misery. Poverty, hunger, disease, illiteracy are rampant among them. Their land has been taken away from them; they are forced to labor under the most brutal conditions; the lack of schools, sanitation and medical care are unspeakable....

213. "South African Gold Mine Strike," The New York Times, September 6,
      1946, p. 20.

      This letter was sent to the New York Times by Paul Robeson. He
      declares that the owners of the South African gold mines, as is
      well known, represent a form of tyranny repugnant to decent
      practice in modern industrial employment. The conscience of the
      men of goodwill everywhere must lift their voices, argues the actor.
      He concludes:
            In the name of everything that is decent in human
            relations, I appeal to my fellow Americans to make
            known their protest against such conditions to the
            South African Ministry in Washington; to send to
            the Council on African Affairs..., an expression
            of support for these grievously oppressed workers
            in South Africa; to keep the South African situation
            in mind against the time when General Smut will come
            to the United Nations Assembly in September to demand
            the annexation of South West Africa, which means more
            Africans for him to exploit....

214. "The United Nations Position on South Africa," New Africa,
      December, 1946.

      Paul Robeson, Chairman of the Council on African Affairs, sent a
      letter to the United State Delegation to the General Assembly of
      the United Nations. He told the delegation, in part:
            The Council on African Affairs is deeply concerned
            about the position which the United States delegates...
            have taken...with regard to the question of trusteeship
            and the two items concerning South Africa.... We
            feel sure that a large section of the American public
            has been deeply disappointed in the fact that the
            United States, instead of standing with those nations
            which urged unqualified rejection of the proposal
            to annex South West Africa to the Union of South
            Africa, assumed a conciliatory role and brought about
            the adoption of a resolution which makes possible
            approval of the proposal at a later date. The same
            reaction of disappointment, we feel sure, resulted
            from the part played by the United States in supporting
            the South African and British demand for disposing
            of Indian Government's complaint regarding discrimination
            against Indians in South Africa by referring this
            matter to the International World Court, instead of
            taking an immediate and positive stand against the
            admitted violation of the Charter principles on
            racial equality.
            We also urge you to reconsider... the question of
            military bases in trust territories and other aspects
            of the trusteeship agreements. The consequences of
            the action taken on these matters are extremely grave.
            We are convinced that the United States can gain
            immeasurably in terms of the larger issue of fostering
            mutual trust and good will among the larger powers,
            as well as between ruling and subject peoples, by

(Robeson, Paul)

> adopting in these matters the course of action
> urged by several of the non-colonial powers,
> notably India and the Soviet Union....

2. INDIVIDUALS

215. "Robeson Asks Truman Action on Lynching," Daily Worker, July 29,
1946, p. 3.

Paul Robeson, Chairman of the Council on African Affairs, sent the
following telegram to President Truman on the lynching of four
Blacks in Georgia. It states, in part:
> Just a few hours before your commendable message
> to Congress endorsing the ILO provisions for
> minimum working and living standards for peoples
> of colonial countries, four Negro citizens of
> this country were lynched in cold blood. This
> is a matter of more than tragic irony. The Council
> on African Affairs demands that the Federal Govern-
> ment take immediate effective steps to apprehend and
> punish the perpetrators of this shocking crime and
> to halt the rising tide of the lynch law. Only when
> our government has taken such action toward protecting
> its own citizens can its role in aiding the progress
> of peoples of other countries be viewed with trust
> and hope.

216. "Letter to the Editor of the California Eagle Concerning National
Non-Partisan Committee for the Defense of the Rights of the 12
Communist Leaders," California Eagle, August 18, 1948.

This is a letter to Mrs. Charlotte A. Bass, Editor of this newspaper. Mr. Robeson states, in part:
> It was my good fortune to participate actively in
> the two day discussions of the Bill of Rights Con-
> ference on July 16-17, and to meet informally with
> many delegates from all parts of the country and all
> walks of life. Representing diverse political and
> religious beliefs, and exchanging a variety of ex-
> periences, the majority of us saw the case of the
> 12 Communist leaders being tried for their political
> views in Foley Square and an issue of key significance
> to the whole struggle in defense of the Bill of Rights.
> This was equally true for trade unionists and scientists,
> leaders of the Negro people and college professors,
> victims of the Loyalty Order and of the House Committee
> on Un-American Activities. I think it is no exaggeration
> to say that the multiplicity of cases brought to our
> attention in the course of the Conference involved in
> one way or another the right to freedom of political

(Robeson, Paul)

association and belief now most directly theatened
by the Foley Square attempt to outlaw the Communist
Party. In the light of the general acceptance of
this fact, I took the initiative in proposing to a
number of the leaders of the Conference the formation
of a National Non-Partisan Committee for the Defense
of the Rights of the 12 Communist Leaders.... In
the tradition so similar defense committee organized
around civil rights cases in the past, we will work
to bring to the American people the issues raised in
the case of the 12, seek to stimulate various types
of popular activity including public meetings and
appeals to organizations, publish literature, and
tour speakers....

217.   "Open Letter to President Truman," New Africa, October, 1949.

This letter was signed by Paul Robeson on October 12, 1949, as
Chairman, and the Officers of the Council on African Affairs.
The signers told President Truman that Governor Thomas E. Dewey
of New York and the responsible officials under his supervision
were, at the minimum, guilty of gross negligence in the protection of the rights, property, and lives of American citizens
at Peekskill, New York, where Blacks and their supporters were
criminally assaulted. They warned the President that the
Peekskill outrages were the product of that perverted Americanism
which brands as unAmerican those who speak out for peace, who
stand up for their constitutional rights and those of their
fellow-men, or who are concerned with freedom for colonial
peoples rather than with the raw materials that can be stolen
from their lands. They concluded: "We are convinced that the
time has come to put an end to this cold war against the American
people; the time has come to utilize the agencies of our government in actual fact toward promoting democracy at home and peace
abroad. The eyes of the world are upon you, Mr. President."

218.   "Here's My Story," "A Letter to Warren Austin, U.S. Delegate to
the U.N.," Freedom, July, 1951, pp. 1, 6.

The activist sent a letter to Mr. Warren Austin, United States
Delegate to the United Nations. He argues, in part:
Dear Mr. Austin:
I address this letter to you as an American member
of the World Council of Peace, which plans to present
specific proposals on ways to peace before the United
Nations at an early date. Your summary and dis-
courteous dismissal of the request for support of
this committee's proposals constitutes a distinct
disservice to the peace-loving people of the United
states and the world.
Dr. Frederic Joliot-Curie, chairman of the Council,
in directing a request to the United Nations for a
conference, carries out the mandate of literally
hundreds of millions of people in all parts of the

(Robeson, Paul)

world. And included in these millions are great
sections of the American people, especially women
and youth, who today are finding new courage and
strength to sign petitions for peace, participate
in the various peace polls, attend peace conferences,
and march in magnificent peace parades and caravans.
They are making it clear that they as well as the
peoples of Europe and Asia, want peace and not a
senseless war of mutual destruction.
    The governments of the United States, Western
Europe, Latin America, England and India must
harken to the voices of their people. These
population majorities say: negotiate a five-power
peace pact and give the new Chinese Republic of
475 million people its rightful seat in the United
Nations, if the world is to have a United Nations
that bears any resemblance to the intent of its
founding Charter....
    The struggle today is one of peace, not war with
anyone. The people will never lose their courage
and strength to shout for peace at the top of their
voices, to fight fascist persecution and death, to
labor diligently every moment to save themselves
and mankind for the constructive building of new
and rich cultures for the universal attaining of
full equality and full human dignity.

219. "A Letter to Charles Chaplin," The Worker, July 11, 1954, p. 8.

Robeson wrote a letter to Charles Chaplin and thanked him for his
support to restore his passport to him. The singer also congratulated Chaplin for winning the Peace Prize of the World Peace
Council. He concluded the letter by saying:
    Your affirmation of life and beauty, so poignantly
    portrayed in your classic "Limelight," unites you
    inseparably with mankind everywhere; and it is that
    common affirmation which guarantees the victory of
    peace and brings ever closer the day when human
    brotherhood shall be a passport for all.

220. "Floodtide of Peace," Masses & Mainstream, Vol. 7, No. 10, October,
      1954, pp. 6-10.

This was a letter that Paul Robeson sent to Boris Polevio, Soviet
author of the Story of a Real Man. Robeson tells Polevio what it
is like to be Black and living in the United States. He told him
that he (Robeson) felt free and equal for the first time in his
life when he visited the Soviet Union. The artist concludes:
"As a firm and devoted friend, I salute the great peoples of
the Soviet Union, who have opened a new chapter in human history
and are writing by their heroism the story of real men, of real
women, and of their children who shall inherit the unlimited
future."

3. PASSPORT CASE

221. "Letter to Committee to Restore Paul Robeson's Passport." Let
      Paul Robeson Sing Again. Brochure issued by Manchester, England,
      Committee to Restore Paul Robeson's Passport. Quoted in Philip S.
      Foner, Editor. Paul Robeson Speaks: Writings, Speeches, Inter-
      views, 1918-1974. New York: Brunner/Mazel Publishers, 1978,
      p. 409.

      Paul Robeson sent a letter to the Committee to restore his pass-
      port and thanked it for its efforts on his behalf. He states,
      in part:
            I was very pleased, and deeply grateful, to receive
            your recent letter and to hear of the plans for a
            mass meeting in Manchester in support of my right
            to travel and to practice my artistic profession....
            I have closely followed the campaign which is
            being developed throughout your country, and the
            splendid work that is being done has added to the
            deep feelings of affection I have for the British
            people through all these years, and has made me look
            forward with even greater eagerness to the time when
            I will be free to visit your country again.

4. RECORDS

222. "Robeson on Records Again," Freedom, December, 1952, p. 8.

      This was a letter announcement written by Paul Robeson. The
      letter states:
            Dear Friends:
            I am writing to you about a matter that is most im-
            portant to me as an artist.
            For the past several years a vicious effort has been
            made to destroy my career. Hall-owners, sponsors and
            even audiences have been intimidated. Recently, in
            Chicago, 15,000 persons who wanted to attend one of
            my concerts had to assemble in a park because the
            hall owner had been threatened.
            The outrageous denial of my passport bars me from
            accepting contracts to appear in England, France,
            China and many other lands.
            Although I have recorded for nearly every major
            recording company and sold millions of records both
            here and abroad, these companies refuse to produce
            any new recordings for me.
            What is the meaning of this? It is an attempt to
            gag artistic expression, to dictate whom the people
            shall hear and what they shall hear. It is an
            attempt to suppress not only me, but every artist,

(Robeson, Paul)

Negro and white, whose heart and talent are enlisted in the fight for peace and democracy.
   There is a way to explode the silence they would
impose on us. An independent record company has just
been established that will make new recordings for me.
This company will also release work by other artists
banned because of their views, and younger artists
often denied a hearing.
   My first new album is now in production.
   But the making of records is only part of the job.
The big task is to make sure that the records will
reach a mass audience in every part of the country.
To do this I need the active support of all my friends.
   The first step is to assure an advance sale of
thousands of albums....

IX
Greetings
by Paul Robeson

In the wide acquaintanceships that I have had over the years, I have never hesitated to associate with people who hold non-conformist or radical views, and this has been true since my earliest days in the American theater where I first met people who challenged the traditional order of things.

Paul Robeson

1. ENGLAND

223. "Greetings to Let Paul Robeson Sing Committee." Recorded Message
      to "Let Paul Robeson Sing" meeting, Lesser Free Trade Hall,
      Manchester, England, March 11, 1956 - Paul Robeson Archives,
      Berlin, German Democratic Republic. Quoted in Philip S. Foner,
      Editor. Paul Robeson Speaks: Writings, Speeches, Interviews,
      1918-1974. New York: Brunner/Mazel Publishers, 1978, pp. 409-
      411.

      Paul Robeson sent the following recorded message to the meeting.
      He states, in part:
            Heartfelt greetings, dear friends in Manchester!
            It is deeply moving for me to know that you and so
            many others throughout Britain are speaking out in
            behalf of my right to travel, my right to resume my
            career as an international artist which I began some
            thirty years ago. Though I must send you these words
            from afar, I can say that never have I felt closer
            to you than I do today. The warmth of your friend-
            ship reaches out across the barriers which temporarily
            separate us and kindles the memories of many happy
            years that I spent among you. Here, in my home in
            New York, I recall your own great city as another home
            to me, a place where I came so often to sing and where
            I always was inspired by the flourishing cultural life
            of Manchester - the splendid orchestras, the out-
            standing contributions to classical music and the
            other arts - and by the richness of the folk culture
            of Lancashire which has given to England and the world
            the artistry of dear Gracie Fields and so many others.
            I can never forget that it was the people of Manchester
            and of the other industrial areas of Britain who gave
            me the understanding of the oneness of people - a con-
            cept upon which I have based my career as an artist and
            citizen. I recall how a Manchester friend explained
            to me how closely together we two were bound by the

(Robeson, Paul)

web of history and human suffering and inspiration.
He told me of the life of bitter hardship and toil
which his father and grandfather knew in the mills -
those "dark satanic mills" which Blacks cried out
against the words of fire - and of how the cotton which
his forefathers wove linked them with other toilers
whose sweat and toil produced that cotton in far-away
America - the Negro slaves, my own father, my own
people....

2. NEWSPAPER

224. "Paul Robeson Sends Us His Greetings," Daily Worker, (London),
May 1, 1956.

Paul Robeson cabled a May Day message to the London Daily Worker.
He wrote, in part:
....Warmest greetings to you on this historic
anniversary of the aspiration and heroic struggles
of labour. It is a privilege to send an expression
of my deep affection and respect for the millions
in the British Isles and especially on this day for
the workers from whom I learned so much and with
whom I grew and developed over many years. We
shall find peace, friendship and mutual exchange in
many fields among all the peoples of the earth and
with your help many peoples shall gain new freedoms
and full human dignity in the African lands of my
forefathers. Thanks to you of the London Daily
Worker for your constant struggles on behalf of the
English, Scots, Irish and Welsh workers, indeed all
the people of the British Islands and of all humankind....

3. RUSSIA

225. "Their Victories For Peace Are Also Ours," New World Review,
Vol. 23, No. 10, November, 1955, pp. 16-17.

The singer sent his greetings to the Russians on the anniversary
of the October Revolution that occurred there in 1917. He asserts,
in part:
Friends of peace in every land have much to celebrate
this year, and on the occasion of the 38th anniversary
of the October Revolution it is especially fitting to
salute the peoples of the Soviet Union and their government which reflects their passionate devotion to the

(Robeson, Paul)

cause of world peace. The many Americans who have recently visited the Soviet Union -- Congressmen, farmers,
clergymen, journalists, athletes, and others -- are
unanimous in their findings that the Soviet people,
far from being hostile and warlike, are openhearted
and friendly. And the evil myth of "Soviet aggression"
has been largely shattered by the consistent efforts
of the Soviet government to remove all sources of
tensions. Those voices of discord in the world which
cried out, hypocritically, for "deeds" to match the
peaceful professions of the Soviet government, are
being drowned out by the popular acclaim which has
greeted the numerous steps taken by that government
to build a lasting peace. The Austrian treaty, the
rapprochement with Yugoslavia, the establishment of
relations with West Germany, the concessions to
Finland -- yes, the world has applauded each new
breakthrough for peaceful coexistence achieved by the
Soviet Union. And the past year, too, has witnessed
the meeting of the Big Four, advocated for so long
by the Soviet Union, and the birth in Geneva of a
hopeful new spirit in international relations....
Yes, the many millions of the colonial liberation
movement, and millions more who are part of the
world-wide movement for peace, will warmly greet
the Soviet peoples on November 7th and say:
"Happy birthday, dear brothers and sisters! Your
victories for peace and freedom are also ours!"

226. "Greetings on The Anniversary of The Great October Revolution,"
New World Review, Vol. 25, No. 10, November, 1957, p. 25.

Paul Robeson sent his warmest greetings on the anniversary of the
great October Revolution in Russia. He declares, in part:
In 1934 came the first visit of my wife Eslanda and
myself to the Soviet Union. For me it was like a
visit to another planet -- where the people had no prejudice on grounds of color -- where indeed a new land
was in being. And now in 1957 the scientists of this
socialist land -- through their collective socialist
effort -- open up the probability of an actual journey
to other planets. Through the years, we have watched
the phenomenal development of this socialist society.
We have seen the birth of the People's Republic of
China, of the New People's Democracies of East and
West, all immeasurably aided by the power and might
of the Soviet Socialist Republics, and the change in
the balance of world power between the new defenders
of the rights of peoples of all colors and the
centuries-long imperialist oppressors of the West....
Surely, in the deep need for our very survival, we
shall finally find a way to universal peace, understanding and friendship.

4. YOUTHS

227. "Here's My Story," "Greetings to World Youth Festival in Berlin,"
      <u>Freedom</u>, September, 1951, pp. 1, 5.

      Robeson sent his warm and heartfelt greetings to the World Youth
      Festival in Berlin. He told them, in part:
           You are and will be the inheritors and builders
           of a new and finer civilization than has ever been
           known to men. You, young Soviet citizens, whom I
           so deeply admire, you brave youth of new China,
           young Korean patriots and fighters of inde-
           pendence throughout Asia, you young brothers and
           sisters, engrossed in crucial struggles for self-
           determination, you youth of the West Indies and of
           the South Americas, the future of the world is
           well placed in your hands. All hail the democratic,
           peace-loving youth of all the world....

X
Interviews

The truth is: I am not and never have been involved in any international conspiracy or any other kind, and do not know anyone who is. It should be plain to everybody—and especially to Negroes—that if the government officials had a shred of evidence to back up that charge, you can bet your last dollar that they would have tried their best to put me *under* their jail!

Paul Robeson

1. AFRICA

228. Thompson, T. "Paul Robeson Speaks about Art and the Negro,"
      The Millgate (London), December, 1930, pp. 157-158.

      This is an interview by the author in Manchester, England.
      Robeson contends:
           Negro spirituals have the same value as other folk
           songs, and there are many excellent melodies amongst
           them. But they are also an expression of the
           yearnings of a child-like people to be delivered
           from bondage. There seemed to be no signs of a good
           time on this earth for the Negro, and the Bible held
           our promise of better times in the next world. But
           in Africa the Negro has a music of his own.... I
           shall come back from Africa within five years with
           a music that is as revolutionary as other phases of
           Negro art. The Negro in Africa is not tied down to
           half or quarter tones, or any European musical
           conventions....

229. "Paul Robeson Decries England's Intolerance: Noted Opera Star
      and Singer Predicts Future of African Descendants Will be
      Aligned with Peoples of the East," Washington Tribune, January 5,
      1935.

      This article states that Mr. Robeson was addressing the League of
      Colored People in London. He told them, in part:
           I am unquestionably leaving England. I refuse to
           live under the sword of Democles all of my life.
           I want to be where I can be an African and not have
           to be Mr. Robeson every hour of the day. I am not
           sure where I will go. For myself, I belong to Africa,
           if I am not there in body, I am there in spirit. My
           own father, my own brother, cannot go where I go.
           They cannot come in behind me. I do not want that
           sort of thing. It is no use telling me that I am

(Robeson, Paul)

> going to depend on the English, the French or the
> Russians. I must depend on myself.... For myself,
> I have never had a feeling that I am in any sense
> inferior. We know we are intelligent. We prove
> it every day. I do not see why we cannot place a
> higher evaluation upon ourselves. I definitely
> believe that the future of the African is tied
> up with the peoples of the East, not with those
> of the West.

230. "Paul Robeson on Negro Race," Jamaica Daily Gleaner, (British
West Indies), July 17, 1935, p. 1.

The singer points out that Negroes have not the slightest idea
of Africa, as a united continent of Negroes, ever standing against
the other races. He contends that Negroes should unite and sy-
stematically develop their own culture. The world today, states
Robeson, is full of barbarism, and he feels that this united
Negro culture could bring into the world a fresh spiritual,
humanitarian principle, a principle of human friendship and
service to the community.

231. Tazelaar, Marguerite. "Robeson Finds a Natural Link to the Songs
of African Tribes," New York Herald-Tribune, October 27, 1935,
Section 8, pp. 3-5.

This is an interview with the singer. The author declares that
he wants to live for a time in Africa, where he has his roots.
He surmises:
> I want to go back (to Africa) and become thoroughly
> acquainted with their folk songs and customs. I
> believe it would be a good thing for the American
> Negro to have more consciousness of his African
> tradition, to be proud of it. Africa has contributed
> great culture to the world, and will continue to
> do so.

232. "Robeson Sails for - He Hopes 'Last' Concert," New York Herald-
Tribune, January 12, 1936, p. 20.

On his way to England, Robeson made a number of observations.
The actor states that he had great faith in Africa. He surmises, in part:
> The people of the African continent will seek out
> their own destiny. Two hundred million people,
> armed with virility and intelligence, will not
> fail. They have been held back, it is true, but
> their educational facilities are increasing
> steadily. The Africans, basically, are no more
> savages than are the American Negroes in the South.
> The African states will be free some day. It may
> come about through partial withdrawal of European
> power, or there may be a sudden overturn. Dif-
> ferences between sections of the continent would

(Robeson, Paul)

> indicate the eventual formation of a federation
> of independent Black states, rather than a single
> great Negro republic or empire....

233. O'Flaherty, J.C. "An Exclusive Interview with Paul Robeson,"
      West African Review, August 1936, pp. 12-13.

In this interview the actor gives his opinions of African culture.
He suggests:
> It is a lie to say that the African past is a
> record of mere strife between paltry tyrants.
> In the past, African communities developed along
> their own lines, in their own way, to reach a
> point of order and stability which may well be
> the envy of the world today. I plan to visit
> Africa and I am studying Effick, an African
> language.

234. "Closeness of American Negro and Africa," Evening Standard,
      (London), November 4, 1938.

Robeson was filming "Sanders of the River," and many Africans were
used in the film. He declares:
> In the two hundred and fifty or more Africans we
> rounded up, there were some twenty different dia-
> lects. I was astonished, in listening to them,
> at the closeness of our own racial derivation.
> One day on the set I overheard one of them
> speaking his nature dialect. To my amazement,
> I was able to understand much of what he said.
> I spoke to him at once, and do you know he was from
> the Ebo tribe in Nigeria -- the very tribe and country
> from which my own father's family came. Surely I
> must have heard a word or two of this language, that
> had crept into my father's speech and that he himself
> had inherited.... A phrase I got at once from this
> African I spoke of was 'aw bong.' You can say it three
> different ways to mean as many different things. In
> fact, it is rather sung than spoken, as are all the
> dialects. Suddenly its reminiscence occurred to me --
> "Ol Boy" -- the musical phrase of the Spiritual, not
> its English title, of course. There are many other
> instances.

235. "Cecelia Ager Meets: Paul Robeson," PM, April 8, 1942.

The writer, Cecelia Ager, discusses her interview with Paul
Robeson. Mr. Robeson was quoted, in part, and surmises:
> I learned from my father always to be proud that I
> was a Negro, and I thought I was. Yet if there's
> anything that eats you, it's the realization that
> you don't quite belong. I was "taken up" in England,
> but when I came back to New York and went to a restaurant
> with a friend, the proprietor said, "He does not come

(Robeson, Paul)

> in here." Then it is that you can think maybe you
> are inferior, unless you understand your heritage.
> And so the thing that gives me at least the greatest
> pride is my association with African culture, my
> share in a part of the great Oriental-Asiatic African
> Culture. Seeing how they are all related, seeing
> for instance, the similarity between the culture of
> the early Chinese tribes and the African, gives me
> a feeling of kinship with all the peoples of the
> world. Our Negroes must see beyond their own
> suffering. They must see they're connected with
> the suffering of hundreds of millions all over the
> world. They must see that their deepest concern,
> their hope, their liberation, lies with the
> destruction of fascism throughout the world for
> evermore....

236. "Robeson Says Negro 'Wants His Freedom', Warns Against Exploitation in Africa," New York Times, April 12, 1944, p. 7.

Paul Robeson declares that the temper of the American Negro has
changed during the war and that the Negro now "wants his freedom."
The actor warned of the danger of exploitation of Africa after
the war, and asserts that we in this country must listen to
President Roosevelt's interpretation of African affairs and not
to Prime Minister Churchill's. He declares, in part:

> The problem of the Negro in this country is a very
> serious one. We in America criticize many nations.
> We know that international conscience has great in-
> fluence in spite of wars. One important part of the
> solution of the Negro problem here will be the pres-
> sure of other countries on America from the outside.
> There are 100,000 Negroes now in the Army in the English
> theatre of operations. Americans wanted their se-
> gregation, as at home. The English, however, insisted
> on their being mixed in, without segregation. This
> shows the possibility of action within the Anglo-
> Saxon world, and it also shows the power of foreign
> opinion. The United States will have much to say about
> North Africa, and the Government is responsible to the
> American people. So we shall know clearly what the
> Government plans, and we should take President Roosevelt's
> interpretation and not Mr. Churchill's. We shall have
> a tremendous lot to say about what happens in Africa.
> I have learned through conversations with English
> friends that the British conservative realizes that
> India is lost, and that now 'the gravy' is in Africa.
> The African problem is a very urgent one, and will
> come into the picture more and more. Mr. Churchill
> can fall as quickly as Mr. Chamberlain did, if he does
> not see eye to eye with the British people. This is
> obviously not a race war - it turns rather, on the
> idea of peoples that are free and those that are not
> free. The American Negro has changed his temper. Now

(Robeson, Paul)

> he wants his freedom. Whether he is smiling at
> you or not, he wants his freedom. The old ex-
> ploitation of peoples is definitely past....

237. "Never Again Can Colonialism Be What It Was," New Africa, March,
      1945.

Robeson points out that many Black people and white people in the
United States believe that Africans are inferior and they are
supposed to be savages. The vast majority of the human race is
still agricultural and herdkeeping; and these people are on the
verge of a vast development due to the impact of World War Two
on world history. Never again can colonialism be what it was,
concludes the actor.

238. "My Answer," As told to Dan Burley, New York Age, September 3,
      1945, p. 5.

Robeson devotes most of this article to the discussion of Africa
and the homeland of Black peoples. He declares:
> Suppose Africa were free and a great nation like
> China? We must learn to think for ourselves and
> also to include in intelligent thought those who
> are closest to us through ties of blood, nationality,
> common interest and mutual aspirations. We want as
> many areas in this changing world of control as we
> can get as Negro people. Suppose we won the right
> to vote plus our proper share of the economic spoils
> of the South: think of the tremendous pressure Negroes
> could being upon the United Nations to help kindred
> people in other parts of the world. There is no
> reason to change what has become very significant and
> historic facts. Certainly, any Negro in the world
> would have a deep feeling for his own people, what-
> ever they are, whatever conditioning they might be in....
> As chairman of the Council on African Affairs, I can
> truthfully say that the African people are highly
> cultured and not savage and cannibalistic as the
> newspapers, radio, book and lecture propagandists
> would make them. That is the Dixiecrat program to
> keep us fighting one another and to lead us away from
> the true paths that lead to the doorway to freedom
> from which we have been detoured over the centuries....
> I am proud of it that I have made it my work to learn
> several African languages for conversation and musical
> purposes. Mrs. Robeson has been in South Africa, in
> the Uganda and in the Belgian Congo and the French
> Cameroons. She has written a book on Africa, "African
> Journey." I expect to be in Nigeria and French West
> Africa next year. There is a tremendous liberation
> movement now underway in Nigeria of which Azikwe is
> the brilliant, capable and resourceful leader....

239. "South Africa Gold Mine Strike," New York Times, September 6, 1946,
      p. 20.

      Paul Robeson as Chairman of the Council on African Affairs comments
      on Africans working in the Gold mines of South Africa. He
      declares:
              The owners of the South African gold mines, as is
              well known, represent a form of tyranny repugnant
              to decent practice in modern industrial employment....
              In the name of everything that is decent in human
              relations I appeal to my fellow Americans to make
              known their protest against such conditions to the
              South African Ministry in Washington...to keep in
              mind the South African situation against the time
              when General Smuts will come to the United Nations
              Assembly in September to demand the annexation of
              South West Africa to the Union of South Africa,
              which means more Africans for him to exploit....

240. "Urges Support for Africans' Fight on Jimcrow," Daily Worker,
      March 12, 1952, p. 5.

      The activist declares:
              It is clear that in raising our voices against the
              Malan (Prime Minister of South Africa) regime we
              simultaneously strike a blow at the reactionary
              forces in our own land who seek to preserve here,
              in South Africa, and everywhere else the superprofits
              they harvest from racial and national oppression.
              United support for our brothers' struggle in Africa
              is an integral part of our task in achieving freedom
              for all Americans and peace for the world. I urge
              you to act.

                        2. CIVIL RIGHTS

241. "Rights Group Bars Socialist Pardon: Robeson Heads Fight on Plea
      for Restoring Liberties to Workers Party Members," New York Times,
      July 18, 1949, p. 17.

      Paul Robeson spoke at a Bill of Rights Conference in New York
      City. In speaking for denial of civil liberties to the Socialist
      Workers Party, Mr. Robeson asked the conference:
              Would you give civil rights to the Ku Klux Klan?
              These men are allies of fascism who want to destroy
              the new democracies of the world. Let's not get
              confused. They are the enemies of the working
              class.... We will fight for peace everywhere and
              the Negro people will be in the forefront of that
              struggle, whatever a few phony guys are saying....
              The Negro people will be a powerful weapon, like
              China, that will pull its weight in the fight for

(Robeson, Paul)

> freedom in this world. The final test is that I
> am here in America today, fighting for my people
> whatever the consequences may be, and here I
> intend to stay.

242. Graves, Lem Jr., "Robeson Dares Truman to Enforce FEPC,"
      Pittsburgh Courier, August 13, 1949, p. 2.

Robeson criticized President Truman and accused him of defaulting
on his civil rights pledges of enforcing the Fair Employment
Practices Commission recommendations. He along with others
marched at the head of a picket line in front of the White House.
The pickets were protesting the jim crow working conditions which
had prevailed for many years at the Bureau of Engraving and
Printing. The singer points out that although Congress had not
passed any civil rights legislation, Truman and his cabinet
could do something without waiting for Congress to act. They
could enforce the orders of the FEPC, declares Robeson.

243. "Paul Robeson Says: Fight for Civil Rights Now - Don't Wait for
      November Elections," Daily Worker, August 7, 1952, pp. 1, 5.

The activist states:
> We should not have to wait until after election to
> get civil rights, we should demand them NOW.
> Candidates should press for a special session of
> Congress "before" November for the simple purpose of
> passing Fair Employment Practice Commission legis-
> lation and The President, by Executive Order, should
> wipe out segregation in the nation's Capital. Behind
> such a program, mass meetings should be held in the
> major cities, North and South, similar to the Harlem
> mass meeting. Not more unfulfilled promises, but
> action for payment on the promises is the need of the
> hour. None of the candidates for the highest offices
> in this land take a forthright position on civil
> rights and back it up with action except the
> nominees of the Progressive Party - Vincent Hallinan
> for President, and that great and courageous Negro
> woman, Mrs. Charlotte Bass for Vice President.

3. COLLEGE CONCERTS

244. Lehman, Ross B. "Paul Robeson Gives Recital," The Daily Collegian,
      (Penn State College), December 10, 1940, p. 1.

Paul Robeson not only gave concerts and recitals in concert halls,
churches, theaters and stadiums, but also on college campuses.
In late 1940 he gave a recital at Penn State College. While at
PSC, he was interviewed by the college newspaper. He told the

(Robeson, Paul)

reporter:
> I can't stop being young. I love to sing to
> college groups, to be "natural" and sing the
> melodies I want to sing -- the songs that come
> from the Heart. Students seem to catch the spirit
> of my songs better than most people.... I know the
> youth can interpret my singing. They know my
> background....

245. Shopen, Tim. "Paul Robeson Sings, Talks, Acts - See Peace Basis
in Culture," Swarthmore Phoenix (Swarthmore College), May 3, 1955,
p. 1.

Mr. Robeson appeared at Swarthmore College in Swarthmore,
Pennsylvania. The writer recalls the concert. According to the
author, Paul Robeson sang, read from "Othello" and discussed
world problems to a near-capacity audience at Clothier under the
sponsorship of the Forum for Free Speech (of Swarthmore College).
While in his political opinions he stands in a minority in this
country, the statement he is one of America's greatest artists
should go unchallenged. April 19 marked his thirtieth year as
a concert singer all over the world. As an actor his triumphs
have been his portrayals of the Emperor Jones and Othello. The
high point of the evening was the reading of the closing speech
from "Othello," states Mr. Shopen. Mr. Robeson commented that,
as he saw the part, Othello was to the end a man of great dignity,
not one who had lost his pride but rather one of another culture
in a strange land, who felt that he had been betrayed. Robeson's
physical stature and voice coupled with his acting skill made for
a tremendously powerful Othello, states Mr. Shopen. He declares
Mr. Robeson's beautiful bass voice with its incredible fullness
and resonance was perfectly and sensitively controlled. His powerful phrasing was full of warmth and understanding. Mr. Robeson's
great interest in cultures all over the world is illustrated by
the program of songs that he sang. He sang sixteen songs, ranging
from the chorale to Bach's "Christ Lag en Todesbaden" to a Warsaw
ghetto freedom song. He sang in English, German, Russian,
Yiddish, Chinese, Persian, and an African language. The audience's
response to Mr. Robeson's artistry was very enthusiastic. The consistently warm applause which followed each of his songs was ex-
ceeded by the near ovation called forth by the Othello reading,
argues the writer. Robeson said that he has invitations from all
over the world which he can't accept because the U.S. won't give
him a passport. The British Artist Equity Association has offered
him a standing invitation to perform "Othello" with "the finest
cast British theater can afford...."

246. "Visits Campuses: Tell What He Found," Daily Worker, July 20, 1955,
p. 6.

Robeson states that it was good to get out to college campuses and
see the stirring of new life among the students. He said he had
received invitations from students to appear at various universities - Northwestern, Kansas, Wisconsin, Chicago, UCLA, and

(Robeson, Paul)

others. The singer concludes: "A ferment is growing among
America's students, both Negro and White. Many are beginning to
see that if a concern for future jobs has dictated conformity, a
concern for their very lives requires that they think of themselves."

4. COMMUNISM

247.   "Robeson Raps Ban on Peoria Concert," Daily Worker, April 21, 1947,
       p. 1.

       Robeson declares that he would return to Peoria, Illinois, and
       make a test case of his cancelled appearance at City Hall. He
       said no Peoria Minister, white or colored "had the courage" to let
       him speak from his pulpit. The singer asserts, in part:
              I've never seen anything like it since Franco's Spain.
           The guys who owned the big industries there tried to use
           this even to beat the brains out of labor. It was the com-
           plete fascist technique. Peoria was like an armed camp....
           As far as Peoria is concerned, fascism has moved in.... In
           Delaware you can't talk against capitalists.... What Americans
           must understand is that the police in Peoria were backed by
           vigilante bands of legionaires.... There are only two groups
           in the world today - fascists and anti-fascists. The Com-
           munists belong to the anti-fascists group and I label myself
           anti-fascist. The Communist Party is the legal one like the
           Republican or Democratic Party and I could belong to either.
           I could just as well think of joining the Communist Party as
           any voter. That's as far as you'll get in any definition
           from me.

248.   "Singer Decries Peioria Action," New York Times, April 25, 1947,
       p. 15.

       Paul Robeson stated that he was prevented from making any public
       appearances in Peoria, Illinois, because of "terroristic control"
       of the City Council by the City Council and "reactionary forces."
       He spoke at the Tenth Annual Rally of the Council on African Af-
       fairs of which he is the Chairman. "It is a clear case of the Com-
       munist bogey being used to break the back of the whole liberal move-
       ment," concluded Robeson.

249.   "Robeson in Honolulu Backs Wallace, Denies Community Peril,"
       Honolulu Star-Bulletin, March 22, 1948.

       This article was based on a press conference that Robeson held af-
       ter finishing his 27 appearance visit to the Hawaii islands.
       Robeson told reporters that he was supporting presidential hope-
       ful Henry A. Wallace because "if anybody continues the new deal
       traditions of Franklin Roosevelt, it is Wallace." He scoffed at

(Robeson, Paul)

the idea that Wallace is a Communist, and said he believes Wallace
is a "progressive capitalist."

250.   "Robeson Defies Quiz on Communism; Says He Prefers Prison," PM,
       June 1, 1948, p. 1.

Paul Robeson told Senate questioners he would go to jail before he
would say whether he is a Communist. Sen. E.H. Moore adopted the
idea, with the suggestion that "sometimes a year in jail cools
some of these people off." Chairman Alexander Wiley of the
Judiciary Committee said he doubted that the committee would taken
contempt action. Robeson was testifying before the Judiciary
group against the Mundt-Nixon anti-Communist bill when the dispute
arose. Sen. Homer Ferguson whose direct question Robeson refused
to answer, said the committee would decide about contempt later.
The exchange took place after Robeson told the committee he thinks
members of the Communist party "have done a magnificent job in
America." "Are you an American Communist," Ferguson asked. "I
refuse to answer that question," Robeson replied with emphatic
gestures. "This is an invasion of my right to secret ballot."
Ferguson fired back the same question a second time and a third,
and Robeson finally broke out: "Nineteen leading Americans are
going to jail for refusal to answer that question and if necessary,
I will join them." Some hisses mixed with the audience applause
greeted the singer's statement, stated the article. His reference
to 19 Americans was an allusion to the Hollywood writers and others,
charged with contempt of Congress for refusal to answer similar
questions before the House Committee on Un-American Activities.
On questions he was willing to answer, Robeson told the committee:
He has "many dear friends" who are Communists, and he is "interested in a party and a people who stand for complete equality of
the Negro people in the United States." "I walked the earth (in
Russia) for the first time with complete dignity." His son went to
school there and found complete freedom from racial prejudice concluded the article.

251.   "Mundt Bill Perils All Americans, Wallace and Robeson Warn," Daily
       Worker, June 6, 1948, p. 4.

Henry A. Wallace, Presidential candidate of the Third Party Movement and Paul Robeson testified before the Senate Judiciary
Committee on the Mundt-Nixon Bill. Robeson asserts, in part:
       ....I am tremendously interested, before approaching in
       detail this bill, to ask you just a question as to why, in
       the light of the terror that I have seen and the denial of
       rights, the lynching bill is not before the Congress at this
       time, or why it hasn't come out of committee.... This bill
       seems to me to have as its basic ideas not to help the people
       of the United States, or any other people, but actually be
       terrorizing people to stop the struggle - the struggle to get
       rights for Negro people, for workers, and for other Americans
       who haven't full citizenship. I see communism as nothing but
       an extension of public ownership of the main means of re-
       sources, like the railroad workers said the other day. And

(Robeson, Paul)

>the coal mines? If they are that important, Senator, to
>the people of the United States that every time there is a
>national emergency it is life or death to the American people,
>doesn't it occur to you that instead of beating the workers
>on the head, that the government should own the railroads and
>the coal mines? Well, this is a whole struggle, of which
>communism is a part. This is a part of the conceptions of
>the struggles of human beings for ages. And you can't rule
>communism out anywhere in the world.... Why should not the
>anti-lynching bill be on the calendar now?.... Why all this
>excitement about civil rights if they are not necessary?....
>No, I say that this is not a perfect world and there are
>many ways towards the freedoms of peoples. We do it our way.
>Other nations choose socialist or communist means. If our
>way is so much better, let us prove that. One of the first
>ways to prove it is by making my people free.

252.   Shields, Art. "Cavalcade Welcomes Robeson Home," Daily Worker,
       June 17, 1949, pp. 3, 11.

Paul Robeson flew back to the United States to fight for peace and
freedom in his homeland after a four-month tour of Europe. A cavalcade of automobiles, filled with Negro and white workers who had
come to welcome him home, escorted Robeson through Harlem, after
his arrival at La Guardia Airport. He also spoke to the crowd.
He asserts, in part:
>....Everything I said during my tour of Europe was distorted
>by the Associated Press and the United Press and other Ameri-
>can press agencies. I prefer, to give what I have to say to
>papers such as the Daily Worker. If the Communist leaders go
>to the penitentiary it means that millions of Americans lose
>their freedom with them: ....I found a very complete under-
>standing of the fact that American Big Business was trying to
>take over Europe. But the people of Europe will not let Wall
>Street take them over. And the French people will not sit
>idly by while Americans rebuild Nazi Germany....

253.   "'No Surprise,' Robeson Says of Conviction of Red Chiefs," Afro-
       American, October 22, 1949, p. 1.

Paul Robeson received news of the conviction of the 11 top Communist
leaders in New York on charges of conspiring to teach and advocate
the overthrow of the United States Government by force and violence.
"We are not surprised at this," Robeson said, speaking evidently
for himself and trade union leaders surrounding him during his two-
day visit here. "It is important when in Foley Square, NYC, they
can do the same thing they do to us in Alabama, Mississippi and
Georgia."

5. FASCISM

254. "Robeson Warns of Nazism," New York Amsterdam News, October 21,
1939, pp. 1, 3.

Paul Robeson recently returned to the United States from England
and gave his views of the War situation. He argues, in part:
In discussing the present war, distinguishing carefully
between the progressive England in whose ranks I, myself
enlisted, and that small but powerful group responsible for
the rape of Ethiopia and the destruction of democracy in
Republican Spain and democratic Austria, the aid to Fascist
aggression by the group (which we shall call the Munich Men)
was done in the name of "peace," although the only sure way
to peace (an Anglo-Russian pact) was sabotaged by these
Munich people. "Now, by some mystery, these same people of
Munich (Chamberlain and Daladier) who aided Nazi aggression
war still in power to prosecute a war waged in the name of
democracy AGAINST THE NAZIS. Did I say war? Certainly not
a war which included any real assistance to Poland. In fact,
a war of such a character that Mr. George Bernard Shaw and
Mr. Ford have labeled it a "phoney war." One of the basic
things of Nazism, is that one race must be the slaves and
serfs to another.... And so if Nazi Germany is saved, there
will survive a Western civilization non-democratic even for
the majority of its Western members as well as for the
colonized and ruled Asiatics, Russians and Africans. I feel
that the solution would be a coming into power in England
and France of truly democratic governments with which, I
think, Russia would collaborate....

255. "Robeson Says Negroes Put Winning War First," Chicago Defender,
November 27, 1943, p. 1.

According to this article Paul Robeson declared Negroes regard
winning of the war against Fascism as the first requirement for
realization of a democratic America. Representing the Council on
African Affairs, of which he is Chairman, Robeson listed three
factors which arouse the "bitterest resentment among black Americans" and at the same time represent "their greatest handicap to
full participation in the national war effort." He pointed first
to economic insecurity resulting from "continuing discrimination
in employment even now." Second, he cited the segregation and
"inferior status assigned to Negroes in the armed forces" and third
the poll tax system of the South "which operates to maintain unde-
mocratic elements in places of authority not only below the Mason-
Dixon line but in our national life as a whole." Pointing to the
election of a Negro Communist to New York City's Council and the
general trend of the Negro vote toward acceptable candidates rather
than party labels, as indications of today's militant protest of
the Negro people, Robeson states that this protest represents the
development of a clearer understanding among Negroes of their goals,
their allies and their enemies. Robeson concludes:
Negroes know that their rights can only be achieved in an

(Robeson, Paul)

America which has realized all of its democratic ideals.
They know that their own struggle is bound up with the
struggle against anti-Semitism and against injustices to all
minority groups. They know that those sections of organized
labor which have enlisted membership on a plane of strict
equality constitute the Negro people's chief allies in the
struggle for democratic rights and they know, too, that the
winning of the war against Fascism is the first and fundamental requirement toward realization of a democratic America.

256. Low, Nat. "The Story of Paul Robeson," The Worker, Magazine
Section, April 16, 1944, pp. 1-3.

The author gives a biographical overview of Robeson's life. He
called him "a symbol of human freedom." Mr. Low declares that it
is impossible to explain Paul Robeson's talents simply because one
cannot EXPLAIN genius. According to the writer, Robeson stated
that his father had the greatest speaking voice he had ever heard
and when he was four his father was already preparing him for public
speaking. Robeson agrees that it was his father who instilled in
him the desire to seek the truth, to search and fight for human
equality and freedom. "It is to this wonderful man that I owe
everything," states Robeson. Paul Robeson is quoted as saying:
    How can I describe my feelings upon crossing the Soviet
    border? All I can say is that the moment I came there I
    realized that I had found what I had been seeking all my
    life. It was a new planet - a new constellation. It fills
    me with such happiness as I have never before known in my
    life.... I cannot believe in art for art's sake. My art
    must be a weapon to fight for freedom. I must remain true to
    my conscience and my people. I must never betray them....
    Teheran is the turning point of world history. It shows the
    way to a new period of human happiness, but we must still
    fight in order to guarantee it.... I hate fascism with all
    my being and would murder it as it would murder me....
According to Mr. Low, Robeson owed the only contract in stage history which allows him to walk out on a performance if there has been
"any discrimination against or segregation of, Negroes in the
audience."

257. "Paul Robeson Says Fascism Stopped His Peoria (Ill.) Concert,"
St. Louis American, April 24, 1947, p. 1.

Paul Robeson who was barred from a public appearance in Peoria said
that he expected to run into "the Peoria problem" as he continued
his concert tour of the country. He predicted that he would encounter official opposition in some other cities "because, unbe-
known to a great many people, many of America's small cities are
being run by a handful of the business people who practically own
the town." He argues, in part:
    The Peoria affair is a problem bigger than just me. It in-
    volves this: Can a city council prevent a speaker or an
    artist from appearing in that town merely by holding a meeting
    and saying he cannot appear? I have been labeled a Communist.

(Robeson, Paul)

> If Communism means pointing out to the people that their
> lives are being dominated by a handful, I guess I'm a
> Communist....

258. "Red Bogey Raised to Hide Fascism -- Robeson," Atlanta (Ga.) Daily World, June 11, 1947, p. 1.

Paul Robeson states that three times before he had seen the "red Bogey" raised to hide Fascism and justify the perpetration of crime against humanity. Mr. Robeson referred to the red hysteria of Franco's Spain, Hitler's Germany and Mussolini's Italy. "Nowadays it is raised against any people who have any pretensions to liberal ideas," he stated. Speaking of his present and future activities in the interest of labor, the singer said that he felt the example of his own career for other Negroes to emulate was not enough and that it was more important for him to give direct participation in the labor movement to improve the lot of the Negro. "I have found the destiny of the Negro race closely inter-twined with the problems of the laboring class all over the world," declared Robeson. He was speaking at a news conference in Panama City.

259. "Robeson Says Fascist Peril Greatest in U.S.," Washington (D.C.) Post, February 7, 1948, p. 1.

According to this report Paul Robeson told more than 1000 delegates to the National Youth Assembly Against Universal Military Training that the United States is the "greatest source of Fascist danger." While Wall Streeters and Southern land owners deprive workers of the "fruits of their labor," there is "complete equality in Communist states, with no grounds of color," the noted baritone told a capacity audience at the Washington, D.C., Metropolitan Baptist Church.

260. "Gen. Clay 'Like' Hitler Says Paul Robeson," Washington Post, January 19, 1949, p. 1.

Paul Robeson was reported to have declared that General Clay and other American officials in the United States zone in Germany were "like Hitler" and "like the remains of German Fascism." Robeson, in Washington with a number of Civil Rights Congress demonstrators, told a press conference that he was in Germany in 1945 and "saw" manifestations of profascism on the part of American leaders. He was quoted as declaring:
> I'm a Negro-American and I'm going to reserve some love
> (for the United States) until I'm free and the Negro
> people are free.
He was commenting on the slaying of Isaiah Nixon Austin, Georgia Negro shot and killed last September after he voted in a primary. According to this reporter, Robeson said the Justice Department is "still trying to puzzle out" whether the slaying was murder, which is solely a State matter, or an infringement on voting rights which would give the United States authority to step in.

261. "I, Too, Am American," Reynolds News (London), February 27, 1949.

Robeson points out that he belongs to another America, other than
the one that is beginning to filter funds to Franco, that is
aiding Fascist Greece and reactionary Turkey. He concludes:
       I will not belong to Franco's world. I belong to
       the world of Republican Spain, of resistance Greece
       and the new democracies. I belong to the America
       which seeks friendship with the Soviet Union. I am
       a friend of Israel, not of the oil interests. I am
       a friend of the new China, not of a revived Fascist
       Japan. I, too, am American.

262. Morris, George. "Robeson Brands Riot as Fascist Violence: Asks
Probe by (Gov.) Dewey, FBI," Daily Worker, August 29, 1949, pp. 3,
9.

Paul Robeson comments on the riot at Peekskill. He declares, in
part:
       The Negro struggle has become the very base of the
       struggle for democracy in America. It is not from
       the 12 Communist leaders that we can expect the over-
       throw of the American government, but they'd better
       watch the fascists like those at Peekskill.... I
       was a football player of parts. I was in the struggle
       where is is tough. I was in Spain when they fought
       fascism with sticks and stones.... It is not likely
       that I will be scared away by a few Legionaires....

263. Bernard, Burton. "Robeson Demands 'Jail Mobsters, Guilty
Officials,' Emergency Parley Maps Fight on Fascist Attacks,"
Daily Worker, September 6, 1949, p. 1.

An emergency committee headed by Paul Robeson demanded the arrest
and trial of all individuals and officials guilty of formenting
or aiding the Peekskill riot. Robeson declared that the fact that
the concert was held was a tremendous victory over the forces of
fascism. He also suggested that had it not been for the cops
there would have been no violence at all.

                           6. FILMS

264. "Robeson in London," Living Age, Vol. 341, September 1931, p. 85.

This article stated that Paul Robeson, the Negro actor and singer,
has been enjoying an extraordinary success in London, where he
had appeared in "The Hairy Ape" by Eugene O'Neill. Interviewed
by a representative of the Observer, Mr. Robeson announced that
one of his ambitions was to go to Africa in the expectation of
finding "new inspiration." He has a small son who is now at
school in Germany but who will soon return to the United States
to continue his studies. The father, meanwhile, is also pursuing

(Robeson, Paul)

his own education by studying the Russian language, which he finds
surprisingly easy, stated the article. Robeson declares, in part:
        I found at once that the language and the music seem
        to suit my voice, and I think there is a psychological
        explanation. There is a kinship between the Russians
        and the negroes. They were both serfs, and in the
        music there is the same note of melancholy touched
        with mysticism. I have heard most of the great Russian
        singers on the gramophone, and have occasionally found
        whole phrases that could be matched in Negro melodies....
        I have seen a great deal of O'Neill. He is one of the
        finest of all living men, shy, so modest that he can
        hardly pluck up courage to speak to a stranger, with a
        pair of eyes that seem to penetrate right through
        people. I have never seen such wonderful eyes in
        any one else. He seems to get at the essentials of
        the people he meets at once, and I feel this is ap-
        parent in his plays. O'Neill is a man of immense
        courage; tuberculosis is only one of the things he
        has had to conquer. As a playwright he is always
        experimenting, and I think it can be said that he
        has never used the same form twice. He was the first
        man to realize the dramatic possibilities of the great
        Negro problem, and the intellectuals of my race now
        appreciate what he has done for their people, although
        at first the colored people resented "All God's Chillun"
        almost as much as the white men.

264a.   "Hollywood's Negro Films 'Hallelujah' and 'Hearts in Dixie',"
        Film Weekly, September 1, 1933.

        The actor comments on two Hollywood Negro films. He declares, in
        part:
        ....The box office insistence that the Negro shall
        figure always as a clown has spoiled the two Negro
        films which have been made in Hollywood, "Hallelujah"
        and "Hearts in Dixie." In "Hallelujah" they took
        the Negro and his church services and made them funny.
        America may have found it amusing, but to English
        audiences the burlesquing of religious matters
        appeared sheer blasphemy....

265.   "The New Pictures: 'The Empire Jones'," Time, Vol. 22, No. 13,
        September 25, 1933, pp. 31-32.

        The critic comments on Paul Robeson as "The Emperor Jones." He
        asserts that in Eugene O'Neill's play, the ones which showed
        Brutus Jones, deposed and terrified, scrambling through a forest
        made dreadful by darkness, ghosts and the drums of a pursuit.
        The elaborate hysteria that makes Jones waste the silver bullet
        he has been saving for himself and, after wandering in circles,
        come gibbering back to be riddled by the bullets of his subjects,
        seems a little implausible. This may be partly because Paul
        Robeson, playing his first cinema role with effortless honesty,

(Robeson, Paul)

has in the earlier part of the story made the Emperor Jones a
person so plainly and completely real, concluded the critic.

267. "Sanders of the River," The Observer (London,), July 29, 1934.

Robeson is reported to have declared that he was "alight with
enthusiasm over the film "Sanders of the River." He said, in
part:
> You know, this film is a very exciting thing for me.
> For the first time since I began acting, I feel that
> I've found my place in the world, that there's some-
> thing out of my own culture which I can express and
> perhaps help to preserve.... I have found out now
> that the African natives had a definite culture a
> long way beyond the culture of the Stone age....
> an integrated thing, which is still unspoilt by
> Western influence.... I think the Americans will
> be amazed to find how many of the modern dance steps
> are relics of an African heritage....

268. Poston, T.R. "Robeson To Play King Christophe in British Production, He Reveals: Actor, Here Answers Critics of 'Sanders
of the River,'" New York Amsterdam News, October 5, 1935, pp. 1, 2.

Mr. Robeson had been subjected to much criticism because of his
role in "Sanders of the River." The actor portrayed an African
chief who aided the English empire builders in bringing the
"blessings" of civilization to the benighted natives. According
to Mr. Poston, much of the objection was raised by critics of the
Left who felt that after he visited to Russia last year he would
forego such roles in the future. Robeson answered his critics,
in part:
> To expect the Negro artist to reject every role with
> which he is not idealogically in agreement, is to
> expect the Negro artist under our present scheme of
> things to give up his work entirely - unless of course,
> he is to confine himself solely to the Left theatre.
> Under such an arrangement, might as well give up my
> singing, my concert work, everything. They say that
> I had no right to appear in "Sanders of the River" is
> to say that I shouldn't have appeared in "Emperor
> Jones" - that I shouldn't accept the role in "Showboat."
> The first scenes were shot in Africa fully a year
> before I assumed the role and I thought the film was
> just another Edgar Wallace thriller. The imperialist
> part was placed in the plot during the past five days
> of shooting, when Korda (London Film Productions)
> decided to follow the lead of Hollywood and at the same
> time tie the venture up with king's jubilee. The
> picture was such a great success, financially, that
> Korda decided to film the life of King Christophe
> with me in the title role. After this picture was
> completed, I was sure that I could persuade Korda to
> present the life of Menelik II on the screen. That

(Poston, T.R.)

would really be worthwhile. And of course it would
have to be done in England Europe. Could you imagine
a Black King being treated seriously in Hollywood?

269. "Film Announcement of 'The Song of Freedom'," Film Weekly, May 23,
     1936.

This newspaper carried an announcement that was prepared by the
actor. Robeson delcares:
        I believe this is the first film to give a true
        picture of many aspects of the life of the colored
        man in the west. Hitherto, on the screen, he has been
        caricatured or presented only as a comedy character.
        This film shows him as a real man, with problems to
        be solved, difficulties to be overcome. I am sure
        the audiences will appreciate the picture as much for
        this unusual honesty of characterization as for the
        dramatic intensity of its story.

270. "Robeson Tired of Caricatures," Philadelphia Tribune, May 20, 1937.

Mr. Robeson explains his plans for doing films which would show
Blacks as having dignity, courage and loyalty. The actor asserts,
in part:
        I'm sick and tired of caricatures. My people and
        the papers had a beef coming when they criticized
        me for "Sanders of the River" and "Show Boat." In
        the first place, I know where I'm going. Each
        picture progresses towards my ultimate goal. Holly-
        wood wouldn't do anything but Showboat for me because
        the South is Hollywood's box office. "Write the South
        off," I suggested. But no, said Hollywood. And what
        could I say? I hadn't the star rating then for
        pictures and couldn't cite my own box office appeal.

271. "Paul Robeson Speaks About New Film," Detroit Tribune, May 22, 1937.

Paul Robeson was bitterly critized for his role in "Sanders of
the River." In fact, the actor was ashamed of the film and
regrets doing it. Because of that film, however, he was allowed
to make better films. He explains:
        After "Sanders of the River" I created box office in
        Europe and Australia so that I am really independent
        of America so far as pictures go and am now in position
        to dictate the sort of role I may appear in for movies.
        "Song of Freedom" indicates the progression. Its major
        theme is a pure romance between me and Elizabeth Welch,
        my wife in the story.... I want to watch my films from
        now on to see if my point of view is correct. I shall
        be willing to play "bad" Negro parts, if the story
        contains a contrast, or the cause and effect element
        of our racial life. But no more "effects" without
        the "cause."....

272. Jackson, Fay. "Noted Singer-Actor Completes Film in England,"
      New York Amsterdam News, June 5, 1937, p. 1.

      The writer surmises that recently returned from Egypt where he
      and the rest of the cast of "Jericho," Capitol film being produced
      by Walter Futter in London, Paul Robeson, world-famous singer-
      actor, expects to return to the shore of America at the end of the
      summer. And he expects to shock America with his next stage play
      in the United States. According to Jackson, Robeson declares:
            When I return to New York, I am going to scare 'em to
            death. My next play is definitely Left; it doesn't
            fit words, is definitely anti-Capitalist and will make
            "Stevedore" look very tame by comparison. I am sick
            and tired of caricatures and "uncle tommish" roles for
            which my people had great justification in their pro-
            tests. I feel that I have attained the rank of stardom
            now sufficient for me to insist on the sort of roles and
            plays I want. My roles in "Show Boat" and "Sanders of
            the River," had to be undertaken by me to build myself
            up to the point wherein I would be able to dictate my
            own roles. Having created box-office in Europe and
            Australia by virtue of my efforts, I am now more or
            less independent of America where the unwanted roles
            are offered. While in Egypt, I discovered that
            Egyptians are just another bunch of colored folk.
            They consider themselves Mediterranean people - but
            they're just like us.

273. Cole, Sidney. "Paul Robeson Tells Us Why," The Cine-Technician,
      (London), September-October, 1938, pp. 74-75.

      In this interview the actor surmises that he will not act in any
      more films until they portray Blacks in a more realist light.
      He points out that the final version of most of his films were
      distorted because of the editing of the studios. Robeson also
      points out that he wanted the price of his concerts to be low
      enough so that working people can afford to come and hear him.
      He also states that the film industry is the clearest example
      of the workings of capitalism - slumps, booms, speculation,
      over-production, etc.

274. "Robeson Tells Criticism of U.S. Friends," Chicago Defender,
      November 26, 1938, p. 1.

      According to this article Paul Robeson told a group of whites at
      a luncheon in London how his American Negro friends had criticized
      him for playing such lackey roles as "Sanders of the River." The
      occasion was the luncheon given to celebrate his first popular
      engagement at a London supper cinema. Mr. Robeson said:
            I would like to be a great mind, or something but,
            I felt I belonged there, with the people. I liked
            singing to a popular audience at popular prices, and
            I am against anything which is against my principles....
            Films make me into some cheap turn I am not interested
            in. You bet they will never let me play a part in a film
            in which a Negro is on top.

275.   "Robeson Quits: Noted Actor and Singer Will Make Independent
        Films," Chicago Defender, March 11, 1939.

        According to this article, Paul Robeson broke with the commercial
        film industry. Robeson indicated his intention to make inde-
        pendent and socially significant pictures. He said he would like
        to go to the Soviet Union to do a film with **Eisenstein, then return**
        to Hollywood, to make, independently, a picture about Oliver Law,
        the Chicago Race man, who died leading a contingent of the Inter-
        national Brigade in Spain. In explaining his break with the big
        commercial studios, Robeson said:
            I have done so because I am no longer willing to
            identify myself with an organization that has no
            regard for reality - an organization that attempts
            to nullify public intelligence, falsify life and
            entirely ignores the many dynamic forces at work
            in the world today. Within the framework of the
            commercial film industry, there is now very little
            chance for an individual to express himself or to
            do anything which is sincere or worthwhile.

276.   "Robeson Hits Hollywood: Says 'Old Plantation Tradition' Is
        Offensive to My People." New York Times, September 23, 1942, p. 28.

        Paul Robeson said he was through with Hollywood until magnates
        found some other way to portray the Negro besides the usual
        "plantation hallelujah shouters." He was particularly despondent
        over his recent return to sequence in "Tales of Manhattan."
        Robeson concludes, in part:
            I thought I could change the picture as we went along
            and I did make some headway. But in the end it turned
            out to be the same old thing - the Negro solving his
            problem by singing his way to glory. This is very
            offensive to my people. It makes the Negro child-
            like and innocent and is in the old plantation
            tradition. But Hollywood says you can't make the
            Negro in any other role because it won't be box
            office in the South. The South wants its Negroes
            in the old style.

                    7. FREEDOM AND JUSTICE

277.   "Thoughts on the Colour-Bar," The Spectator, (London), August 8,
        1931, pp. 177-178.

        In this interview Robeson discusses the deepseatedness of race
        prejudice in the United States. He gives many examples of pre-
        judice against Blacks in this country. The artist points out that
        it is not so much that Blacks are discriminated against as it is
        the atmosphere which is symptomatic of the greatest evil of the
        Colour Bar in its present stage of development. He continues to
        state that even the luckiest Black must always feel alien in the

(Robeson, Paul)

country to which he is more truly indigenous than 90 percent of
his white "compatriots." The actor concludes that the most important part the Black is qualified to play in American scene is
that of implanting cultural and spiritual values into society.
In fact, surmises Robeson, the whole of American culture is de-
riving from Negro culture those qualities which appeal most directly to the intelligent European who values a depth of native
tradition in art. These cultural actualities and potentialities
have survived years of repression, but they can develop only with
great difficulty in a hostile environment....

278. "Southern Musical Journal (Memphis) Pays Tribute to Paul Robeson,"
Pictorial History of the American Negro. Thomas O. Fuller.
Memphis, Tenn.: Pictorial History, 1933, pp. 225-226.

This was an interview with the singer that was reprinted from the
Southern Musical Journal. Robeson presented a farewell concert
in America before leaving for England, where he played the lead
in Eugene O'Neill's "The Hairy Ape." He appeared with the
Westchester Negro Choral Union as guest soloist. According to
Mr. Robeson:
    The occasion is of more than passing significance,
    since it places me on the stage with some 700 members
    of my own race, all singing spirituals. And the
    peculiar importance of this is that in effective
    organization of so large a body of Negro spiritual
    singers lies the hope of preserving the unique contri-
    bution of my race to the music of America. If the
    American Negro is to have a culture of his own he will
    have to leave America to get it, unless more such
    groups as that in Westchester arise all over the land
    to cherish and develop our old spirituals. It is
    refreshing to come back to New York to discover that
    here, within an hour of the metropolis, is a band of
    700 singers, rehearsing and training under capable
    leadership, devoting their time to the singing of
    the spirituals.... I prefer a program entirely made
    up of spirituals, because I know that therein lies our
    sound and enduring contribution. I know that in the
    concession to the music of other peoples in our Negro
    programs, magnificent and masterly though they may be,
    lies the eventual obliteration of our folk-music,
    the musical idioms of our race. By accepting the
    white man's music we are passing out of the scene as
    creators and interpreters of the finest expression and
    the loftiest we have to offer. Either we must encourage
    more groups like that in Westchester to preserve our
    folk-music, or we must leave this country, those of
    us who want to see our music preserved, and go to
    Africa, where we can develop independently and bring
    forth a new music based on old roots....

279. Bolsover, Phillip. "Paul Robeson Joins Labor Theatre," Daily
      World, November 4, 1937, p. 7.

      Paul Robeson was interviewed in London. He told the reporter,
      in part:
          When I sing "Let My People Go," I want in the future
          to mean more than it has meant before. It must ex-
          press the need for freedom not only of my own race.
          That's only part of a bigger thing. But of all the
          working class -- here, in America, all over. I was
          born of them. They are my people. They will know
          what I mean. When I step on the stage in the future,
          I go on as a representative of the working-class. I
          work with the consciousness of that in my mind. I
          share the richness they can bring to art. I approach
          the stage from that angle....

280. Davis, Ben Jr. "Victory for Allies of No Good to Race: Actor-
      Singer Back in U.S. Urges Support of Peace Efforts," Chicago
      Defender, November 4, 1939, p. 1.

      In this interview Robeson declares, in part:
          I believe that the cause of the Negro colonials as
          well as the interests of the Negro people in America
          lies with those who are fighting for peace. If peace
          is brought about it will mean that the whole struggle
          for Negro freedom can be strengthened, without so
          many of the best sons of the Negro people and the
          working class losing their lives in this useless
          slaughter. The movement for peace in England is
          much stronger than one can gather from the press
          report here. As for the Negroes, millions of whom
          are victims of the British Empire, how can they
          believe Chamberlain is fighting for them, when
          the Chamberlain government contemptuously brushes
          aside the demand of India for liberation and main-
          tains her oppressive rule in South Africa? If
          anyone is really interested in freedom of oppressed
          minorities, or in the liberation of the Negro, he
          cannot help applauding the Soviet action in freeing
          the Western Ukrainians and White Russians. If you
          disagree with this action, then you must agree with
          Nazi slavery or with the subjection of weaker peoples
          by British and French Imperialism. And if Chamberlain
          believes in democracy for small nations, why did he
          hand so many over to Hitler and Mussolini? The
          Negro people will not forget Spain, Czechoslovakia,
          Austria -- and certainly not Ethiopia. The terrible
          irony of it all is that there are about one million
          black Sengalese troops being used by Daladier now to
          help make French imperialist' richer and more ruth-
          less against the colonies....
      Paul Robeson suggests that Negro Americans have every stake in
      keeping America out of this conflict, and in battling against the
      war hysteria which now seriously threatens civil rights.

281. "Paul Robeson Makes His Choice," <u>Sunday Worker,</u> November 14, 1937,
      p. 11.

      The artist explains why he chose to fight for freedom. He sum-
      marizes his views:
            ....Like every true artist, I have longed to see my
            talent contributing in an unmistakably clear manner
            to the cause of humanity.... Every artist, every
            scientist, must decide NOW where he stands. He
            has no alternative. There is no standing above
            the conflicts on Olympian heights.... The artist
            must take sides. He must elect to fight for
            freedom or slavery. I have made my choice.
            I had no alternative....

282. Lacy, Sam. "Paul Robeson Sees Great Future for Negroes in Post-
      War," <u>Chicago Defender,</u> July 24, 1943, p. 1.

      Robeson comments on Negroes' fear that the post-war world holds no
      better fate for him than has been his lot in the past. He said
      that view was unfounded. He asserts, in part:
            I am firmly convinced, that today's war will
            go a long way toward liquidating the differences
            which exist between the races of the world,
            particularly those which obtain in this country.
            I am fully aware of the fact that anti-Negro
            elements in this country will seize the op-
            portunity to discredit Negroes wherever they
            can when the present war is over. But I am
            also aware of the fact that America cannot
            hope to be a great nation in the world as it
            shapes up after the war, unless she makes up
            her mind to do the right thing. The reason
            is that the manner in which the war is being
            fought, with so many groups of the darker races
            aligned with the United Nations, makes for a
            more sympathetic understanding between the
            peoples who in the past have been at each
            other's throats.... I most certainly do think
            a Negro delegate should be included among those
            who assemble to frame the peace at the close of
            the war. Surely, no one can question the right
            of at least one and possibly several, to be
            there. Haiti should be represented, Ethiopia,
            of a certainty, should be permitted to send a
            delegate, and Liberia has every right to a
            voice in such a parley....

283.   "Robeson Tells Truman: Do Something About Lynchings or Negroes
        Will," Philadelphia Tribune, September 24, 1946, p. 1.

        Paul Robeson, spearhead of the American Crusade to End Lynchings,
        said after a White House visit that he had told the President
        that if the Government did not do something to curb lynching,
        "the Negroes would." To this statement, Robeson said, the
        President took sharp exception. The President, he said, remarked
        that it sounded like a threat. Robeson told newspaper men he
        assured the President it was not a threat, merely a statement of
        fact about the temper of the Negro people, who comprise about 10
        percent of the population. At the head of a mixed delegation,
        Robeson asked the President to make a formal declaration of dis-
        approval of lynching within the next hundred days. Robeson ex-
        plained the next hundred days would be an appropriate time for
        the President to act, because it was on Sept. 22, 1862, that
        Lincoln issued the proclamation freeing the slaves and it was on
        Jan.1 that it became effective. The President, Robeson said, told
        the delegation that Government action against lynching was
        necessarily a political matter, and that timing was important.
        The President said, Robeson reported, that this was not the time
        for him to act. Robeson also asked the President to send a mes-
        sage when Congress reconvenes urging immediate enactment of an
        anti-lynching bill. The singer said he also pointed out what he
        considered misdirections in American foreign policy. He declared
        it was hard to see the distinction between current lynchings and
        the Nuremberg war crimes trials. He explained that he meant by
        this that the United States could not logically take the lead
        in punishing Nazis for the oppression of groups in Germany while
        the Government here permitted Negroes to be lynched and shot.
        To this he said the President objected that loyal Americans should
        not mix domestic problems like lynching with foreign policy.
        Robeson states he told the President he did not see how the two
        could be separated. When he was asked whether he was a Communist,
        Robeson described himself as "violently anti-Fascist." He said
        he had opposed Fascism in other countries and saw no reason why
        he should not oppose Fascism in the United States.

284.   "Freedom in Their Own Land," National Guardian, December 20, 1948.

        The singer had just finished a concert tour through Jamaica and
        Trinidad. It was there that he stated he felt like a human being
        and he did not have to worry about his color. In those countries,
        according to Robeson, Blacks in Jamaica and Trinidad, the dignity
        of men who could make their own mistakes, men who could cut their
        own throats or make their own world. He declares that freedom
        from fear is a new thing to American Negroes. Robeson concludes:
            I am never for one moment unaware that I live in a
            land of Jim Crow. I do not grow angry about it. I
            think I understand how we must fight it. But under-
            standing or not the realization that I am a Negro in
            a land of Jim Crow does not leave me. Nor do I think
            it can, even for a moment, leave any American Negro.

285. "My Answer...." As told to Dan Burley. <u>New York Age</u>, August 6,
      1949, p. 4.

      In this article Paul Robeson defends himself from attack by the
      press. He declares:

> I'm in the headlines and they're saying all
> manner of things about me such as "enemy" of the
> land of my birth, "traitor" to my country,
> "dangerous radical" and that I am an "ungrate-
> ful" cur. But they can't say that I am not 100
> per cent for my people. The American Press has
> acted out on its own campaign of deliberate mis-
> quotations and distortion of the things I say
> and do trying to set my people against me but
> they can't win because what I say is the un-
> adulterated truth which cannot be denied. Every-
> body is trying to explain Paul Robeson. That
> isn't hard. I'm just an ordinary guy like any-
> one else, trying to do what I can to make things
> match, to find and tie up the loose ends. I am
> asked do I think the salvation of the American
> Negro lies in complete integration - social,
> political and economic, or in a highly developed
> Negro nationalism. Let me answer it in my way.
> The whole Negro problem has its basis in the
> South - in the cotton belt where Negroes are in
> the majority. That is the only thing that explains
> me completely. The Negro upper class wants to
> know why I am out here struggling on behalf
> of the oppressed, exploited Negro of the South
> when I could isolate myself from them like they
> do and become wealthy by keeping quiet on such
> disturbing subjects. This, I have found, would
> not be true of me. What I earn doesn't help my
> people that much. I have relatives in the South
> still struggling to make a living. The other
> night in Newark, one relative of mine was in
> the audience. He is a mason and a carpenter.
> What I do personally doesn't help him. I found
> I have to think of the whole Negro problem....

286. "My Answer...." As told to Dan Burley. <u>New York Age</u>, August 13, 1949, p. 4.

In this article Robeson continues to defend himself against attacks by the press. He asserts:

It is very easy to see, as in the question of India, China, Africa and the West Indies, the future of these people in the independence of their own countries. I see the Negro's struggle as demanding great concentration on the question as to where he is going and who is leading him there. We must come together as a people, unite and close ranks and with our own unity we must try and find the right allies - those whose struggles are identical to our own. We cannot escape the fact that our struggles over the last 300 years have driven us together. Suppose that in the South, where Negroes are in the majority in the agricultural belt, we had the vote like everyone else? What would happen? Wouldn't Negroes be in Congress, be governors, judges, mayors, sheriffs, and so on? Wouldn't they be in control in the South and run things as the minority people down there are doing at this very moment? There you have your answer to that charge that I am formenting strife and plotting with a foreign government to establish a Black Republic in the South. What would happen - even tomorrow - if the Negro was allowed to vote? Without any nonsense, you would have a tremendous concentration of Negro power to the United States. Many people would object and oppose it on various grounds, principally racial and economic, but you have a concentration of Irish power in Boston, Italian power in New York, and so on. Nobody has made a major issue of that, have they? What is wrong with our struggle for our right to vote, for economic liberation for civil rights?

287. Burley, Dan. "My Answer...." As told to Dan Burley. New York
      Age, September 3, 1949, p. 1.

      The activist argues that the whole Negro problem has its basis in
      the South -- in the cotton belt where Negroes are in the majority.
      Robeson wants to help these Negroes because they are being ex-
      ploited by the imperialistic Wall Street, the bankers and the
      plantation bosses. He also states that as chairman of the
      Council on African Affairs, he could truthfully say that the
      African people are highly cultured and not savage and cannibalistic
      as the newspapers, radio, book, and lecture propagandists would
      make them. The actor points out that he was proud of his African
      heritage and made it a point to learn several African languages
      for conversation and musical purposes. He concludes:
            I will go anywhere -- North, South, East or West,
            Europe, Africa, South America, Asia or Australia --
            and fight for the freedom of the people. This
            thing (freedom) burns in me and it is not my nature
            nor inclination to be scared off....

288. Burley, Dan. "'Ain't No Chains Can Bird Me' -- Robeson,"
      New York Age, September 10, 1949, p. 2.

      The reporter declared that an aroused Paul Robeson was in the city
      this week busy mapping an ambitious program against the would-be
      lynchers who tried to break up his concert at Peekskill, N.Y.,
      Sunday afternoon with a police-assisted riot. He also declared
      that he was elevated to the status of a martyr through the dumb,
      amazing stupidity of police and other law enforcement officials.
      The Robeson campaign is shaping itself as a gigantic protest
      vehicle against the flaming injustices, violences and rigid dis-
      crimination oppressing Negroes everywhere, and now it will carry
      the internationally famous singer deep into the heart of the Dixie-
      crat Southland in the near future, stated Mr. Burley. Instead
      of squelching Robeson and laughing his program off as a crackpot
      gesture, the police were allowed to perform in the best "storm
      trooper" tradition with all the brutality overtomes thrown in,
      surmised the writer. He suggested thus pushed into the spot-
      light as the No. 1 Negro figure in the world with international
      attention focused on what he does and what is done to him.
      Robeson is as explosive now as a stick of dynamite. Because of
      the power keg propensities of the American Negro question in
      world politics, his position and personal safety have become of
      vital concern and the U.S. State Department would want no part
      of explaining to an exultant Russia, and other Iron Curtain
      countries, how come Robeson was suspended from a tree "Deep in
      the Heart of Texas." No Negro since Marcus Garvey has so projected
      himself into the eyes of the public as has Robeson during the scant
      few months he has actually been in the center of the world stage.
      If he is harmed by mobs, police, crackpots or over-zealous
      officials, or if he is even jailed, he will become greater than
      ever - the last thing those battling communism want to happen,
      stated Burley. On the other hand, if he is allowed to continue
      his course, he might single-handedly force from a harrassed
      White House or Congress the long demanded civil rights for Negroes.
      These possibilities have been created by a sleepy-eyed Governor

(Burley, Dan)

in Albany, dumb Westchester County officials and others who failed
to see the danger in allowing a mob disguised as war veterans
stage a "protest" parade in the face of Robeson followers where a
riot would be inevitable. As yet, according to the writer, the
singer has not been openly declared a Communist. He has, however,
been called everything short of one: "left winger," "Soviet
sympathizer," "Pal Joey's bed partner," "fellow traveler" and the
sort of "pink" his Caucasian foes prefix with another color
designation. Because Negroes are becoming alarmingly conscious
of what they are being subjected to and with a tremendous depression peeking around the corner at everybody, Robeson's rise
as some sort of "Savior" of the poor and oppressed, black and
white, has the "Iagos" in this version of Shakespeare's "Othello"
(Robeson starred in it on Broadway) burning the midnight oil. He
concludes:

> This is the first time since Frederick Douglass
> that Negroes have been presented a lion-hearted man
> who takes action instead of writing letters, sending
> telegrams and making speeches in their own parlors
> or kitchens. It has excited admiration in the minds
> of hundreds of thousands who can hardly pronounce the
> word 'Communist,' let alone belong to that party.
> And it all can be traced back to the dull, bull-like
> thinking of those who set out to handle "operation
> Peekskill."

289. Graves, Lem, Jr. "An Exclusive Interview: Paul Robeson Tells
His Story," <u>Pittsburgh Courier</u>, September 17, 1949, pp. 1, 5.

Here are some of the questions and answers from the interview.
What does Robeson Want? In his own words: "World peace and
racial justice." On the question of peace, Robeson refused to
even contemplate a war between the United States and the Soviet
Union. He said: "America knows she cannot fight Russia now,"
pointedly implying that America could not win a war with Russia.
Since he thinks only in terms of peace, he said, he would not dis-
cuss war with Russia. At the same time he works for peace, said
Mr. Robeson, he also works for genuine freedom for Black people
the world over. He declared that he is interested in the people
of Africa and the West Indies because he sees no hope for U.S.
Negroes so long as any Black people are enslaved or terrorized.
He believes that Negroes should have their civil rights in
America and he says he has dedicated his energies to that fight.
Does he love the Soviet Union? "Yes, I have a deep affection....
When I was there, I walked the streets with manly dignity for the
first time in my life." He denies that Soviet communism is syn-
onymous with fascist terror, oppression, and denial. Does he love
America? "I do not love and will not fight to protect the America
that is Rankin, Forestal, the Duponts, or the Peekskill mob....
I love the land, the traditions of freedom and liberty (although
we have not realized the freedom the system is supposed to offer)
and I love the people who were on my side up at Peekskill."
Projected into the international spotlight - partly by his own
design and partly by the inept and vicious tactics of New York

(Graves, Lem, Jr.)

State Police - Paul Robeson is today a figure of tremendous power
and appeal. As he closed his interview, he asked a significant
question: "Will America grant to its minorities full freedom,
civil rights, and personal dignity or will it turn to fascist
oppression as did the 'storm troopers' of Germany, Italy and
Peekskill."

290. Hicks, James L. "Paul Sees An America He Would Fight For," Afro-
American, October 15, 1949, p. 5.

    Mr. Hicks surmised that Paul Robeson stated at a press conference:
        I love and will fight for the America which I saw
        on my recent trip to the West Coast. It is im-
        portant that colored people remember the racial issue
        today is not that one colored man has become successful
        but who are never given the change. The old type
        colored leader is disappearing and in his place is
        rising the colored leader of the trade union movement
        who will refuse to play Uncle Tom. Russia has
        abolished race prejudice while the United States
        maintains it. Am I supposed to be friendly with a
        nation which has ruled out discrimination. I
        should think so.

291. Pittman, John. "Mr. Freedom Himself: Paul Robeson," Daily
Worker, April 15, 1951, Section 2, pp. 1, 6.

    In this article Robeson states "We can't win freedom without
    peace. The present war drive has brought out of the sewer all
    of our white supremacist enemies and placed them in positions
    of power. By imposing peace on the war-makers, we will strike
    a mortal blow at the racists." Robeson thought that this condition
    of Negro and White people in the United States could impose peace.
    Such is the essence of his confidence, states Pittman. The
    author recalls that the actor had received many honors; however,
    the honor that Robeson appreciates most is one,according to the
    author, given him by a Negro women who sent in a subscription
    to Freedom and declared, "I think of Paul Robeson as Old Man
    Freedom himself."

292. Paul Robeson Concert Draws Enthusiastic Thousands," California
Eagle, May 18, 1950, pp. 1, 30.

    According to this report cheers and applause that fairly raised
    the roof greeted Paul Robeson, great American leader of all the
    oppressed, when he came on the stage at the Elks auditorium in a
    concert given under the auspices of The California Eagle, and the
    14th Congressional District IPP. According to the article,
    Robeson, his eyes shining with joy at the spontaneous greeting,
    remarks:
        This is the part of America that I love. I don't like
        the Rankins or the oil interests. I won't have my boy
        die for their benefit. This is the America I love, and
        this is the America I would fight for and die for. The

(Robeson, Paul)

> reactionaries are afraid of the Negro people. They
> have reason to be. There is a deep thing stirring from
> below. Among all the people who are oppressed, among
> the hungry, the suffering, among the working people.
> The millions who have built this land are beginning to
> understand, and they will not let it be stolen from
> them to benefit only the rich. We fought and died
> for this country in Alabama, in Mississippi, in
> Tennessee. We fought for our freedom. And we are
> going to have it. We are being joined by 150,000,000
> people in Africa, who are crying out, "We, too, want
> to be free. We want to be free like China."

293. Sillen, Samuel. "No Borders For Art," Masses & Mainstream, Vol. 7,
      No. 6, June, 1954, p. 4-5.

Mr. Sillen argues that the ban on Paul Robeson's travel is not
only a grave injury to him, but a terrible dishonor to America.
And all the more so when it is combined with the denial to him
in this country of regular concert and stage engagements. He
asserts that the American people, like those everywhere, are
eager to hear the magnificent voice of Robeson that was again
evidenced last month at the University of Chicago. The student
body jammed Mandel Hall on the campus, where the singer and his
accompanist, Alan Booth, gave a concert. There was a turn-away
crowd of another thousand. And this despite the campaign of
intimidation, spearheaded by the American Legion, which sought
to keep Paul Robeson off back down.   He declared: "It is important that students make the opportunity to hear Mr. Robeson;
first, because many have never had a chance to hear him, and
second, because by doing so we refuse to accede to a policy of
suppressing those whose views are controversial." He went on to
declare that the scurrilous attacks on Paul Robeson have reached
a new low with the spreading of an invention by certain newspaper columnists, notably Leonard Lyons, that the great artist
and people's leader is "changing his views." "This fantastic
slander," as Robeson termed it, is bitterly resented by everyone
who really cares about truth and decency. It is a transparent
effort by little minds to shake the tremendous respect and love
which Robeson enjoys among millions of Americans, particularly
the Negro people. According to Mr. Sillen, in a press statement
blasting these lying provocations, Robeson said:
> ....the very essence of my life and work is loyalty
> to my convictions. I am, as I have been for many
> years, firmly and fully devoted to the struggle for
> peace and democracy throughout the world, for Negro
> liberation and colonial freedom, for friendship with
> the people of the Soviet Union, new China, and the
> people's democracies of Europe. The interest of the
> working people of every land are my guiding principles,
> and I know of no force that can make me change. As
> for those who are telling the public that I have
> changed my mind, I might ask: "How stupid can you
> get?".... The fact is, every day brings new proof

(Sillen, Samuel)

>that the great cause of peace and liberation, in
>which I am inseparably united with the vast majority
>of mankind, is invincible. The doom of imperialism
>has been sounded in all of Asia, and soon Africa and
>the other colonial lands now gaining against their
>chains will rise in might freedom. And here at home
>it's beginning to look as if those who want to "go
>it alone" into a new world war can't count on having
>the American people go with them - and everybody
>else has already said no. "Change my mind?"
>Gentlemen of the press, you'd better change yours,
>because what I believe in - is happening!

294.   "Millions of Us Who Want Peace and Friendship," Moscow News,
September 17, 1958.

The freedom fighter declares that his people, the Negro people
of North America, are not yet free citizens, but one day they
are determined to be. He continues to point out that the very
essence of loyalty to one's land means the exerting of every
effort to bring the fruits of their toil to all of its citizens.
Robeson suggests that intertwined with the struggle of hither to
colonial peoples for full liberation - in Africa, in the Near East,
in Asia, in Latin America. He concludes that he is proud, deeply
proud of his friendship with the Soviet people, and proud to
belong to that America that wants peace and human brotherhood.

8. GERMAN DEMOCRATIC REPUBLIC

295.   "Interview with Press, Berlin, German Democratic Republic,"
October 1960 - Days With Paul Robeson, published in connection
with Robeson's visit to the German Democratic Republic on the
invitation of the President of the German Peace Council and the
Vice-President of the Academy of Sciences, Berlin - Paul Robeson
Archives, Berlin, German Democratic Republic. Quoted in Philip S.
Foner, Editor. Paul Robeson Speaks: Writings, Speeches, Interviews, 1918-1974. New York: Brunner/Mazel Publishers, 1978,
pp. 464-467.

One reporter asked Robeson his impression of the German Democratic
Republic. He replied, in part:
>I am very, very happy to be here with the press of
>the socialist lands. I will be able to tell my
>people about what I have seen here in your republic.
>What warmth I have received in the name of my people.
>You want to see my people in America, in Africa,
>everywhere, able to work in full dignity. Your
>government and leaders speak of full disarmament
>and peace in the world and I am sure that we shall
>speak of these things today....

296. "Mr. Robeson Denies 'Kidnap' Report," London Times, August 27,
      1963, p. 6.

      Mr. Robeson denied that the British reports of his being "kid-
      napped" from London were "completely absurd." Mr. Robeson was
      reported to have declared:
            The fact is that I greatfully accepted the cordial
            invitation of the East German Peace Council to visit
            the German Democratic Republic for a medical examination
            and a stay in a convalescent home in the G.D.R. I
            feel considerably better and my excellent English
            doctors, my friends in Great Britain and America as
            well as my family support this journey to the G.D.R.....

                        9. HONORS

297. "'Democracy's Voice' Speaks: Robeson to Receive Honorary,"
      People's Voice, May 29, 1943, p. 11.

      This article states that Paul Robeson would receive a Doctor of
      Humane Letters from Morehouse College. The article said that he
      is the only man in the world who could turn a concert into a
      rally for the rights of minority groups. He is quoted as saying:
            I wouldn't sing to segregated audiences so I sang
            in Negro schools and white people came. I was impressed
            by a youth hungry for education. If America is to
            survive, she will have to deal with the millions of
            Negroes who will no longer be in bondage. If we
            looked at an isolated America, the picture would be
            a pessimistic one, but I can honestly tell young
            students at this time that they have nothing to be
            discouraged about.... Support of the federal govern-
            ment is of primary importance to the Negro people,
            for if the government were centralized now it would
            mean the breaking down of the autonomy of the states
            and the poll tax and anti-lynch legislation would be
            put in force by the federal government....

298. "Paul Robeson Speaks to ILWU," The Dispatcher, November 19, 1943.

      Paul Robeson and Rockwell Kent were the first two to receive
      honorary life-time membership in the ILWU. After receiving the
      membership from Harry Bridges, President of the ILWU, Robeson
      declares, in part:
            I want to tell you how proud I am to become a
            member of the ILWU and a brother of Rockwell Kent.
            I have labored and I come from laboring people. I
            have hooked many a load, taken many a tray....I

(Robeson, Paul)

know what poverty is. I am already an honorary
member of another great labor organization, the
National Maritime Union. Now, I am happy to join
the Longshoremen and Warehousemen who have done
so many things. When I walk along the Front in
San Francisco, I will be proud that I can put out
my hand and say "Hello, brother." I know what
Harry Bridges has done, and I know what the fight
for Harry Bridges means. We must not lose that
fight. This is our great responsibility....

10. HOUSE UN-AMERICAN ACTIVITIES COMMITTEE

299. Young, Jack. "Paul Robeson Defies Un-American Committee," Daily
      Worker, October 11, 1946, p. 11.

      Paul Robeson appeared before the Jack B. Tenney Un-American
      Committee in Los Angeles. State Senator Tenney declared that the
      Committee is "one of the evidence that Fascism still lives."
      Robeson appeared as Co-Chairman of the National Committee to Win
      The Peace. Robeson told the group, in part:
            The American people today must decide what they are
            going to support. I as a Negro, know fascism would
            wipe me off the face of the earth. I can't support
            it.... The democracies made a horrible mistake by
            not supporting Republican Spain and they are making
            a horrible mistake now by supporting Franco.... I
            characterize myself as anti-Fascist. I am not a
            Communist. In my association with Communist through-
            out the world I have found them to be the first people
            to die, the first to sacrifice and the first to under-
            stand fascism.... There is very great differences
            between fascism and communism. Fascism is the
            domination, economic and otherwise, of a minority
            against the interests of the great masses of people.
            There is a great difference between a thing that wipes
            out entire people and another that raises them....
            We don't need to go to war to find out which way of
            life is best. We can solve it within the frame-
            work of peace by extending democracy and freedom of
            all people....

300. Berry, Abner W. "'I'll Keep Fighting,'"Paul Robeson Vows,"
      Daily Worker, April 28, 1947, p. 4.

      The author states that Paul Robeson said the attacks on him had
      come as a result of the Un-American Committee naming him along
      with 1,000 other liberals and progressive Americans who have
      supported one organization or another termed "Un-American" by
      the Rankin Committee. Robeson further asserts, in part:

(Berry, Abner)

>Whether I am or am not a Communist or Communist
sympathizer is irrelevant. The question is whether
American citizens regardless of their political
beliefs or sympathies, may enjoy their constitutional
rights.... Do not be intimidated or frightened by
those who would destroy political and academic freedom
in our country. We cannot accomplish freedom by permitting the schemes of the American Century crowd -
that Henry Luces wants to be carried through. I
appeal to labor, to professionals, to Negroes, Jews
and people of every race and nationality and faith,
to close ranks and fight for the one thing without
which nothing else can be won. We stood together
and won the war against the Axis. That was the first
front. Now we have to open the second front - the
front against the fascists at home. The place is here.
The time is now. The stakes are life and death. Let
us march together with the will to live....

301   Jones, John Hudson. "Robeson Rips House Un-Americans: Blasts
Insults to Negro People," Daily Worker, July 21, 1949, pp. 1, 9.

Paul Robeson declares that the Un-American Committee's action in
calling Jackie Robinson and other prominent Negroes to "testify
as to their loyalty is a campaign of terror and an insult to the
entire Negro people." The activist suggests that if they want
some Negroes to testify why don't they bring up some of the
Negroes who were chased from their homes in Florida yesterday.

302.   "'Not Mad at Jackie' - Robeson Tells Press," Chicago Defender,
July 30, 1949, p. 1.

At a press conference Paul Robeson states that he was not mad at
Jackie Robinson for describing him as a "siren song in bass"
before the House Un-American Activities Committee. Robeson
asserts, in part:

>I have no argument with Jackie. This has nothing to
do with me or him. It has to do with the Negro people.
The Committee is trying to terrorize Negroes so they
won't speak out. How dare they insult the Negro
people by pulling them down to Washington to swear
allegiance to Mellon and DuPont and company? Did they
invite the Italians about their loyalty? Did DiMaggio
testify? Why don't some of these white guys attack
me? Why do they get Negroes to do it? They say I've
made so much I ought to keep my mouth shut. What
money did I make compared to the billions whites
took from the Negro people during the generations of
slavery and after in the South? Now they say my concerts will be cut off. Hell, there are hundreds of
thousands of workers I can sing to. They can't stop
me from earning dough. I just cleaned up in England,
and I'm going down to Cuba now and get a pile! I
don't claim any courage for saying what I think. I'm

(Robeson, Paul)

> not a fanatic or a martyr either. A long time ago
> I decided to speak out and I learned every language
> in the world. Me, I'm lucky. I could go north
> tomorrow and make a living singing to Eskimos - in
> their own tongue? Jackie's done as fine a job of
> helping the Negro people as anyone in our time. But
> I can't be just a singer. He can't be just a ball
> player. I never forget where I came from. Jackie
> must understand this and I never forget it - when he
> or I am down in Georgia, anything can still happen
> to us!

303.   Lautier, Louis. "I Want Protection for My People..." Afro-
        American, June 23, 1956, pp. 1, 2.

The writer states that Paul Robeson appeared before a subcommittee
of the House Un-American Activities and told them:
> The United States Government should go down to
> Mississippi and protect my people. That is what
> should happen. I stand here struggling for the
> rights of my people to be full citizens in this
> country. They are not in Mississippi; they are not
> in Montgomery. That is why I am here today. You
> want to shut up every colored person who wants to
> fight for the rights of his people.... It was un-
> thinkable to me that anybody would take up arms in
> the name of an Eastland against anybody. This
> United States government should go down to Missi-
> ssippi and protect my people. This is what should
> happen. In Russia for the first time I felt like
> a full human being; no color prejudice like in
> Mississippi.
"Why don't you stay in Russia?" asked Scherer. "Because my
father was a slave and helped build this country, and I am going
to stay here just like you, and no Fascist-minded person is
going to drive me from it."

304.   "Robeson Denounces 'Un-Americans' Faces Contempt," National
        Guardian, June 25, 1956, pp. 1, 10.

According to this report, after about an hour of Paul Robeson on
the witness stand, Rep. Francis E. Walter (D-Pa), chairman of the
House Committee on Un-American Activities, banged his gavel, mur-
mured, "I've stood about as much of this as I can," and declared
the session adjourned.
    Said Robeson: "You should adjourn this forever."
    The committee members present huddled in a corner and pro-
nounced themselves unanimous in holding Robeson in contempt of
Congress. Next day the full committee ratified the contempt citation, which now goes to the full House; if it is upheld there it
goes to the Justice Dept. for court action. Robeson was subpenaed
on June 12 in pursuance of a committee probe of what Walter calls
"the use of passports in the furtherance of the international
communist conspiracy...." In a prepared statement which he was

(Robeson, Paul)

not allowed to read but which he distributed to newsmen, he said,
in part:
> It is my firm intention to continue to speak out
> against injustices to the Negro people, and I shall
> continue to do all within my power in behalf of in-
> dependence of colonial peoples of Africa. It is for
> (Secy. of State) Dulles to explain why a Negro who
> opposes colonialism and supports the aspirations of
> Negro Americans should for those reasons be denied
> a passport. Why does Walter not investigate the
> truly "un-American" activities of (Sen. James O.)
> Eastland and his gang, to whom the constitution is
> a scrap of paper when invoked by the Negro people
> and to whom defiance of the Supreme Court is a racial
> duty?.... The Committee was trying to gag me here
> and abroad.... The Committee wants to shut up
> every Negro who stands up for his rights....

11. INDIVIDUALS

305. "A Tribute to Ben Davis," Daily Worker, Septemver 4, 1949, p. 8.

Robeson declares, in part:
> ....The annual Ben Davis Ball and Celebration takes
> place this year during his campaign for re-election
> to the New York City Council. It takes place also
> at a time of unprecedented lynching and war hysteria
> in our country. Ben Davis is a victim of this
> hysteria. He is such a victim because he has fought
> against Jim-crow, lynchings and police brutality and
> anti-Semitism. He has fought for housing instead of
> A-bombs; jobs instead of guns; peace instead of war.
> Ben Davis, who is my close personal friend, deserves
> the full and unqualified support of every democratic,
> peace-loving person in our country. I am confident
> that you will want to be among those who will
> participate in this Ben Davis Ball Journal.

306. "Robeson Urges Action to Save Life of Turkish Poet," Daily Worker,
April 16, 1950, p. 2.

Paul Robeson urged all Americans to help save the life of the
leading Turkish poet, Nazim Hikmet, who entered the seventh day of
his hunger strike for freedom. Hikmet, a Communist, had served
12 years of a 28-year sentence. The sole charge against him was
that Turkish soldiers and sailors were discovered reading his
poetry. The article stated that the last of Hikmet's poems received in this country was entitled "To Paul Robeson." Robeson
was quoted as saying:
> A great Turkish people's poet lies prostrate in a prison

(Robeson, Paul)

cell, after 12 long years in prison. He is now near
death after seven days of a hunger strike as a protest against those who would prevent him from working
and fighting in behalf of the Turkish people's struggle
for democracy and peace. We in America must do everything possible to force the Turkish government to
free him. The strength of progressive America, including the Negro people, must join the fight to free
this great voice. Our writers, artists and indeed all
who love an American people's culture must make their
voices heard in protest. He will hear us and those
who would stifle his voice will also hear. We can
save this great poet of the people for the working people
of Turkey, of America and of the world if we act now.

307. "Robeson Menuhin," National Guardian, February 15, 1960, p. 12.

Two great artists, Yehudi Menuhin and Paul Robeson, in a TV discussion produced by Associated Television in London, probed the
appeal, range and depth of Jewish and African folk music of which
Robeson remains the unchallenged interpreter today. Robeson told
Menuhin that his abiding interest in folk music is not confined
only to Negro tunes and that he is also deeply interested in
Russian folk tunes in Yiddish musical lore and in the musical
traditions of many other nations. He always tries, he said, to
sing in its original language any chant or melody he tackles.
At this point the conversation turned to Yiddish and Chassidic
melodies. Excerpts of the conversation were as follows: Menuhin:
It's quite extraordinary the way you have learned so many
languages, African languages, I believe, too. Robeson: I find
aptitude to read them and get along well with them because I
find, Yehudi, that in languages their music is in essence the
songs I sing, and the folk songs. Especially the songs of chant
are in one sense an extension of poetic speech. They are like the
Negro preacher or my own father. Perhaps most of our spirituals
could be traced to a sermon. We say:
     "... you may bury me in the East, you may bury
     me in the West, but I'll hear the trumpet sound
     in that morning.... My lord how I long to go
     forth to hear the trumpet sound in that morning."
And to hear the trumpet sound to us meant, I'm sure, the trumpet
of freedom somewhere, not only religion.... Of course, you know
that before the Emancipation, the Bible was the one book that my
ancestors were allowed to read? In a sense they became literate
on the Bible. So today you can go in our churches at home and hear
the preachers' just most beautiful uses of this imagery.
Menhuin: Your singing reminds me so much of my father. In the
early days my most vivid memories of him are of him singing his
Chassidic songs of which I believe you know quite a few.
Robeson: To me it's one of the great traditions of any music,
so I almost never do a program without them, sometimes in Yiddish,
mostly in English:
     "A good day today to thee Lord God Almighty....
     I, Isaak son of Sara from Berdychev, here am I

(Robeson, Paul)

        before thee.... What hast thou done to this
        thy people? God on High! On this earth are many
        nations. The Romans, the Persians, the Babylonians,
        the Germans of those days...."
        One of the great Chassidic songs.
Menuhin: Yes, well, he would sing them and also many of a much
lighter vein, because they rather are a gay clan. They again
believed in music and the dance as expressions of religion.
Robeson: That's true.
Menuhin: In great reaction against the more determined and tal-
mudic and academic line....
Robeson: In fact I have a volume with all of them. They almost
say syllables.
Menuhin: Exactly.
Robeson: They're just dance tunes. I've got a great number of the
niguns.... I found a great likeness in this heritage and I remember now going back to my father again....
Menuhin: He taught you Hebrew, didn't he?
Robeson: Yes, he knew Hebrew and Greek, and I remember one day
he said: "Now these are the first words of the Bible, of Moses
himself, in his language. 'And in the Beginning God created the
Heavens and the Earth - Bereishit bara Elohim et hashamyim ve et
ha'aratz....' And since then I've learned to read at least in the
language. So this is the tradition which again stretched down
into Africa to be a part of the whole tradition of many people.
We come back again to that point. I remember when you were saying
that this music is like a stream into which one river runs, and
another river, of the different nations of the world....

              12. JIM CROW IN ENGLAND

308. Whitney, L. Baynard. "Robeson, Back from England, Gives Contender
      Exclusive Story," New York State Contender, October 31, 1929, p. 1.

      Paul Robeson gave the Contender his personal version of the Jim
      Crow incident at the Hotel Savoy on the Strand in London. He
      recalls in essence:
          The report that friends of mine were to honor me at
          a special dinner at the Savoy is not true. I had
          merely stopped by there to see some friends who were
          in the grill room. As I walked in, my friends came
          toward me in greeting, and as we started back to their
          table the waiter stopped me. I was very much surprised
          and asked him what did it mean. He replied that it
          was against the rules to serve me. I then called the
          manager, who told me the Hotel Savoy did not serve
          Negroes in the grill room. Both myself and my friends
          were amazed. Such a thing had never happened to me
          in England before. In fact, my friends had told me
          that such a thing would not and could not happen to

(Whitney, L. Baynard)

>me in London. But the fact remains that it did
>happen. One of the persons I was with is a member
>of the Society of Friends and said that the matter
>would be taken up at once. What made the incident so
>surprising was the fact that I had been served in
>the Savoy grill room several times and could not at
>first understand their change of attitude.... What-
>ever influence was brought to bear surely could not
>have been English, for I had not been served at better
>and finer places everywhere in London, but many of them
>considered it an honor to have me present. My English
>friends had repeatedly told me that England would
>never stoop to such an act. Aside from lowering
>England's dignity and sense of fair play, it was a
>direct insult to me, and I think the world should
>know that it did happen....

13. LABOR MOVEMENTS

309. "Robeson Holds Press Conference," Labor Herald, September 25,
1942, p. 1.

Paul Robeson was in Los Angeles supporting the trade union movement in general and the advancement of the rights of Black workers
in particular. Speaking at a press conference Robeson was quoted
as declaring, in part:
>CIO unions throughout the country are in the fore-
>front of the fight to smash barriers of racial
>discrimination in hiring.... Everywhere I go, I
>find labor unions, particularly those in the CIO,
>leading the fight to get my people jobs. A victory
>for Hitler would be the worst thing which could
>happen to my people. It would mean we would all be
>consigned to slavery for I don't know how long.
>Therefore, the salvation of Negro people lies in
>the overthrow of fascism.... We must see that we're
>not engaged in just a struggle of the colored peoples.
>Our fight for freedom embraces the common men all
>over the world - in the Balkans, among the Welsh
>miners, in the slums of London, all oppressed peoples
>in all lands. There are those in the south who say
>that this war is being fought for a new kind of life,
>but which doesn't include the Negro. But you can't
>talk about a war for new freedoms which do not in-
>clude not only my people but the people in India and
>Africa and everywhere else. It is impossible to say
>we're fighting for a freedom that excludes the colored
>people....

310. "Union Acts To Cut Roster of Officers," New York Times, May 20,
      1948, p. 23.

      Paul Robeson spoke at the biannual convention of the United Public
      Workers. He was an honorary member of this union. The singer
      addressed the delegates during the foreign policy discussion.
      Robeson denounced "the (James) Forrestals, the (John) Dulles,
      and the Hoovers" and asserted that reactionary forces were
      seeking to establish fascism in this country.

311. McEwen, Tom. "A Canadian View of Robeson's Great Peace Arch Con-
      cert," Daily Worker, August 16, 1955, p. 6.

      Robeson appeared in concert in Vancouver, Canada before an
      audience of well over 10,000 people. He was sponsored by the
      International Union of Mine, Mill and Smelter Workers Union.
      Before he sang he addressed the crowd. He states, in essence:
          I travel as an American in the interests of peace,
          uniting the peoples for peace, and I stand always on
          the side of those who will toil and labor. As an
          artist I come to sing, but as a citizen I will always
          speak for peace, and no one can silence me in this....

312. Leeson, Bob. "I'll Be There Pledge by Robeson Birthday Message
      to DW," Daily Worker, (London), January 14, 1960.

      An interview of Paul Robeson. The Daily Worker 30th anniversary
      celebration took place in March of the same year. Robeson states
      that he felt that it was very important for him to be in London
      with the newspaper. He declares that he knew that he would not
      be in Britain today (January 13th) but for the struggle is up by
      people here, and the support of all sections. The world traveler
      suggests that he was a product of the British working-class and
      progressive movement. "I came here," he asserts, "unshaped."
      "Great parts of my working-class roots are here," he concludes.

313. "Robeson in East Berlin," National Guardian, July 18, 1960, p. 12.

      Paul Robeson paid a visit to the German Democratic Republic when
      he made a surprise appearance at the annual press festival.
      This article states that about three thousand workers applauded
      "the man many Americans regard as their best Ambassador." He
      sang a number of songs. Later at the press conference, he
      commented on a variety of issues. He declares, in part:
          ....It was a great honor to play in Shakespeare's
          birthplace (Stratford-on-Avon). It was a complete
          reply to the reaction of the State Department which
          had hoped that I would never be able to re-establish
          my career.... I will certainly go back to America
          at some point. I will not allow the reactionaires
          to take my country away from me.... From now on
          every concert I do in London will be addressed to
          the workers: the price of tickets will be gauged
          to their pockets. If others want to come, they can
          come, but they will have to come to the kind of places
          where the workers gather, trade union halls, workers'

(Robeson, Paul)

    clubs. In America, when I return home, I will sing
in churches and trade unions.... I will go to the
people now. I will become once again what I really
am, a folk singer.... The basic of folk song is the
chant. "Water Boy" is not a lyrical song: it is a
conversation. I don't sing words, I sing speech.
That's what folk music is. In speech there is truth.
The song conveys the truth of the conversation.
Great folk music, that's what jazz should be. It
came out of the heart of my people....

14. MUSIC

314. Ish-Kishor, Sulamith. "The Source of the Negro Spirituals," The
Jewish Tribune, July 22, 1927.

This is an interview that was subtitled "Paul Robeson, The Famous
Baritone, Tells of the DRAMA in the Old Testament That has Given
Birth to The Negro Songs." The subtitle tells what this article
is about. The singer points that the Bible was the only form of
literature the captive Negroes could get at, even those who could
read. He concludes that it was natural for their quick imagina-
tions to find a pathetic similarity between their conditions and
that of the enslaved Hebrews. He believes that is why the Bible
made such a tremendous appeal to the Negroes, states the writer.

315. Lenz, Frank. "When Robeson Sings," Association Men, July, 1927,
pp. 495-496.

In this article Robeson comments on his music. He declares, in
part:
    ....I feel that the music of my race is the happiest
medium of expression for what dramatic and vocal skill
I possess. In the first place, Negro music is more and
more taking its place with the music of the world.
It has its own distinctive message and philosophy. I
am not ashamed of the spirituals. They represent the
soul of my people. I am trying to get out all that's
in me.... I am not imitating Barrymore, Chaliapin or
anyone else. I am not trying to prove that I can do
what the white man does. People do not ask me to
discard my program of spirituals for light stuff or
opera. They like American Negro music. I sing the
songs without distorting them.... I put my very best
into every selection. I apporach my career earnestly
and work to give pleasure. I give my best. The
further I go the better it will be for my race....

316. "Paul Robeson Comments on His Music," Detroit Times, January 20, 1928.

　　　Paul Robeson discusses Negro Spirituals. He asserts, in part:
　　　　　The distinctive gift the Negro has made to America
　　　　　has not been from the brilliantly successful colored
　　　　　men and women who, after all, have done only what white
　　　　　people are doing. It is from the most humble of our
　　　　　people that the music now recognized as of abiding
　　　　　beauty emanated.... Some of my friends hoped that
　　　　　I would succeed in the field of law and be an honor
　　　　　to my race. But such a triumph would seem much in-
　　　　　ferior, in my eyes, to the achievement of my inter-
　　　　　preting the Negro spiritual to the American public.
　　　　　No one can hear these songs as our people sang them
　　　　　and not understand the Negro a little better....

317. "Paul Robeson and Negro Music," New York Times, April 5, 1931, Section 8, p. 9.

　　　This was an interview with Robeson just before he left for England, where he played the lead in "The Hairy Ape." He suggests that he prefers a program made up entirely of Negro spirituals, because he knows that therein lies the Negroes own sound and enduring contri- bution. The singer argues that by accepting the White man's music Negroes are passing out of the scene as creators and Inter- preters of the finest expression and the loftiest Negroes have to offer. He concludes:
　　　　　Either we must encourage more groups.... to preserve
　　　　　our folk-music, or we must leave this country, those
　　　　　of us who want to see our music preserved, and go to
　　　　　Africa, where we can develop independently and bring
　　　　　forth a new music based on old roots....

318. "Paul Robeson," Daily Mail, (London), August 4, 1931.

　　　In this interview Robeson comments on working conditions in the United States and England. He surmises, in part:
　　　　　....Over there they expect you to be working at
　　　　　the top of your form all the time. In England, if
　　　　　you are not quite so good on the stage one night the
　　　　　people say, "Oh, he's a bit off-colour. He'll be all
　　　　　right again in a day or two." They still believe in
　　　　　you, follow you.... Now here in London I do not see
　　　　　why I should not be singing as well as ever to big
　　　　　audiences when I am 63 just like Chaliapine....

319. Henderson, Rose. "Paul Robeson, Negro Singer," Southern Workman, Vol. 61, April, 1932, pp. 166-172.

　　　Robeson comments on a number of topics in this article. He argues, in part:
　　　　　If I can recreate for my audiences the great sadness
　　　　　of the Negro slave in "Sometimes I feel like a mother-
　　　　　less chile," or if I can make them know the convict of
　　　　　the chain-gang, make them feel his thirst, understand

(Henderson, Rose)

> his naive boasting about his strength, feel the
> brave gaiety and latent sadness of "Water Boy;" if
> I can express to them the simple, divine faith
> of the Negro in "Weepin' Mary," then I shall
> have increased their knowledge and understanding
> of my people. They will sense that we are moved
> by the same emotions, have the same beliefs,
> the same longings -- that we are all humans
> together. That will be something to work for,
> something worth doing.... Some members of my
> race want to forget that they are Negroes.
> But they should remember that the Negro can no
> more change his blood than the leopard his
> spots. A Negro remains a Negro. Then let him
> be one, with his ideals and energies directed
> toward the ennoblement of his race. Let him
> give it a literature of its own.... The Bible
> was the only form of literature the captive
> Negroes could get at, even those who could
> read. It was natural for their quick imagi-
> nations to find a pathetic similarity between
> their condition and that of the enslaved Hebrews.
> I believe that's why the Bible made a tremendous
> appeal to the Negroes. They saw their own
> history reflected in it, and they saw their
> own vague hopes given a sort of false glow of
> possibility. They felt that their freedom also
> would depend on some miracle happening, so
> they had to have intense faith in what they
> read, or heard, of the Old Testament. You'll
> notice, by the way, that comparatively few
> of the Negro spirituals are based on the
> New Testament....

320. "Paul Robeson Interview," Daily Gleaner (Jamaica, British West
      Indies), December 17, 1932, p. 3.

Paul Robeson discusses the music of other peoples and what
it means to him. He argues, in part:
> ....The songs of the peasants are nearest to
> my heart, no matter what the nation may be....
> In my Negro heart lies buries the memory of
> centuries of oppression. The peasants are
> my kindred, and I do believe that there is a
> spiritual community among the peasants all
> over the world and that the German or the
> Hungarian peasant could as well enjoy the
> songs of the peasants of the Province as the
> working American Negro could.... The Negro
> soul will close up before everything that is
> artificial. Isn't it strange that while I
> can interpret Moussorgsky and other great
> Russian composers so as to move a Russian
> audience to tears I never could feel and render

(Robeson, Paul)

Brahms, Wagner and Schumann....

321.   "Paul Robeson Comments on Russian Music," <u>Newark (N.J.) Evening</u>
       <u>News</u>, August 16, 1933.

       The singer saw the relationship between Russian music and
       Negro music. From the beginning of his career, Robeson in-
       cluded folk songs from Russian composers into his program.
       He declares, in part:
            ....Russians told me that there was much the
            same primitiveness in many of their songs....
            Russian music reflects much the same condition
            as Negro music does, for the Russian serfs,
            before they were freed, had much the same
            situation as the Negro slaves.... I could
            not do the same with a German or a French
            song because, going back to the deep roots
            of the whole matter, there is not the same
            tradition of origin.

322.   "Robeson Spurns Music He Doesn't Understand," <u>New York World-</u>
       <u>Telegram</u>, August 30, 1933.

       This was an interview held in London, England. Robeson said
       he would not do any music that he did not understand. The
       singer suggested that he did not understand the psychology
       or philosophy of the Frenchman, German or Italian because
       their history had nothing in common with the history of his
       slave ancestors. The singer argued that one should con-
       fine oneself to the art for which one is qualified. According
       to him, one can only be qualified by understanding, and
       this is born in one, not bred....

323.   "Paul Robeson Never to Sing in Italian, French or German Again,"
       <u>Washington Sentinel</u>, September 9, 1933.

       According to this article Paul Robeson was quoted as saying
       he has no intentions of singing in Italian, French or German,
       instead he was said to be looking for a "great Russian Opera
       or play, or some great Hebrew or Chinese work," which he
       says he would be able to render with the necessary degree of
       understanding. He declares, in part:
            I do not understand the psychology or philosophy
            of the Frenchman, German or Italian. Their history has
            nothing in common with the history of my slave-
            ancestors. So I will not sing their music, nor the
            songs of their ancestors.... The trouble with the

(Robeson, Paul)

> American Negro is that he has an inferiority complex.
> He fails to realize that he come from a great ancestry
> linked with the great of the Orient.... What he
> should do is try for "black greatness" and not an
> imitation of "white greatness." I am more than ever
> convinced that the African civilization dates back to
> the times when Oriental culture, including that from
> China, began to influence the Western world. I
> believe where the Afro-American made his mistake was
> when he began trying to mimic the West instead of
> developing the really great tendencies he inherited
> from the East. I believe the Negro can achieve his
> former greatness only if he learns to follow his
> natural tendencies, and ceases trying to master the
> greatness of the West. My own instincts are Asiatic....

324. Franklin, Mortimer. "Art in Astoria," Screenland, Vol. 27, October
      1933, p. 84.

      Paul Robeson is quoted as saying that he could best serve his
      people by interpreting "the Negro soul through Negro song -- that
      is what I've come to regard as my purpose in life." While this
      may have been Robeson's earlier mission in life for his people,
      later as he became more mature he expanded on that mission and
      included interpreting more than Negro songs, but songs from
      several other peoples, nations and cultures. Moreover, he
      campaigned for human dignity not only through songs but also
      through direct action -- speaking, lecturing, marching, protesting,
      helping organize groups, donating time and money.

325. "Mr. Paul Robeson Is Interviewed," Cambridge Daily News (England),
      March 31, 1934.

      The internationally known singer states that he is including folk
      songs of other peoples into his repertoire. He suggests that this
      would be a permanent part of all his concerts. Robeson declares,
      in part:
> ....I am convinced that I can not only retain the
> interest of the serious music-lover, but also enter-
> tain the man in the street by this means. Folk songs
> are the music of basic realities, the spontaneous
> expression by the people for the people of elemental
> emotions.... Negro songs, Russian, Hebrew, and Slavonic
> folk songs, all have a deep, underlying affinity....

326. "Paul Robeson and Negro Music," Dundee Courier (Scotland), March
      27, 1935.

      Robeson was performing in Scotland and while there he was inter-
      viewed by the Dundee Courier. He told the reporter, in part:
> ....The content of modern music -- the sort of
> suggestive songs the crooner sings --
> contributed by the same mentality that makes the
> worst films in Hollywood. Popular music is launched

(Robeson, Paul)

>by Tin Pan Alley by taking the rhythm of Negro music.
>The sentiment comes from taking pure folk-music and
>putting up a song about "Lord, you made the night
>too long," or taking the pathos of "Poor old Joe"
>and putting it into "How deep is the ocean." It
>has nothing to do with the Negro, whose great sad-
>ness it is that millions are made out of it....

327.   Dorn, Julia. "Paul Robeson Told Me," TAC (Issued by Theatre Arts
       Committee), July-August, 1939, p. 23.

In this interview the singer tells why he returned to the United
States after living abroad for ten years. He returned because he
learned that his people are not the only ones oppressed. That it
is the same for Jews or Chinese as for Negroes, and that such prejudice has no place in a democracy. He sang his songs all over
the world, and everywhere he found that some common bond makes
the people of all lands take to Negro songs, as their own.
Robeson contends that keeping close to the feelings and desires
of his audiences had a lot to do with shaping his attitude toward
the struggle of the people of the world. This attitude made him
an anti-fascist, whether the struggle was in Spain, Germany or
the United States. He concludes:

>This, in turn, has made me see the pseudo-scientific
>racial barriers which had been inculcated in me from
>cradle days upward were false.... The feeling that
>all this is wrong, a feeling which has come from
>my travel, from world events which show that all
>oppressed people cry out against their oppressors --
>these have made my loneliness vanish, have made me
>come home to sing my songs so that we will see that
>our democracy does not vanish. If I can contribute
>to this as an artist, I shall be happy.

328.   "Robeson to Sing Wherever Asked," Afro-American, September 17,
       1949, p. 12.

Paul Robeson sent a letter to hundreds of people all over the
United States asking support of the Civil Rights Congress' drive
against bigotry. He declares:

>I'm going to sing wherever the people want me to
>sing. My people won't be frightened by crosses
>burning at Peekskill or anywhere else. I'm proud
>of the way my people - colored people and white
>people - fought back the Klan and the hoodlums on
>the night of August 27 at Peekskill, N.Y., and again
>on September 4.... Law suit will have to **be brought**
>against the Peekskill officials; a test to be made
>in the Federal courts against the.... "subversive"
>list....

329. "Some Aspects of Afro-American Music," Afro-American, December 21, 1956.

The singer declares:
> There is no more evidence that Afro-American music is based on European music, than that European music is based on African music. There is however, extensive evidence that nearly all music in the world today stems from an ancient world body of original folk music - music created, sung, and handed down through the ages by the people in all parts of the world. This contrapuntal singing, and the characteristic "Fourth" of tetrachord, are not only characteristic of early medieval Plain Chant but also of much of the modern music of Moussorgsky, Bartok, Janacek, Vaughn Williams, Duke Ellington, George Gershwin and others, and also of Chinese, Indonesian, African, Hebraic, Byzantine, and Irish music; that is to say it is characteristic of Pentatonic modal music. It would seem then, that Afro-American music is based primarily upon our African heritage and has been influenced not only by Europeans but by many other musics of East and West; this is true also of Afro-Cuban, Afro-Haitian, Afro-Caribbean, Afro-Braziliar music: and our music has also influenced other music.... So today we are flowing back into the mainstream of world music, which includes the music of Asia, Africa, Europe, and the Americas, with a future potential of immense richness - all giving to and taking from each other, through this wonderful world bank of music.

15. NEGRO CULTURE

330. "Paul Robeson Says Negroes Imitate Others," Newark (N.J.) Evening News, August 16, 1933.

Paul Robeson tried to prove through his own life-style that Negroes were not inferior to any group of people. He suggests, in part:
> ....What I am trying to prove is that the Negro is not inherently an inferior form of human being. Negroes the world over have an inferiority complex because they imitate whatever culture they are in contact with instead of harking back to their own tradition.... My quarrel is not with Western Culture but with the Negro imitating it....

331. "Paul Robeson," Daily News - Chronicle (London), May 30, 1935.

Robeson comments, in part, on Negro culture:
> ....All the world knows by now that I have faith in the future of the Negro. I believe that Negro culture merits an honorable place amongst the

(Robeson, Paul)

cultures of the world. I believe that as soon as
Negroes appreciate their own culture, and confine
their interest in the European to learning his
science and mechanics, they will be on the road
to becoming one of the dominant races of the
world....

332. "I Want Negro Culture," London News Chronicle, May 30, 1935.

The actor points out that he believes that the Negro culture
merits an honourable place amongst the cultures of the world. He
declares:
As soon as Negroes appreciate their own culture
and confine their interest in the European to
learning his science and mechanics, they will be
on the road to becoming one of the dominant races
in the world. The Negroes must learn the world's
technique, but stick to their own arts. Once we
have won freedom from the domination of nature,
art-living and individual-will come singing and
flowing spontaneously of itself. It is through
the theatre that Negroes aim to win world recognition for Negro productions and help the Negro
back to self-respect....

333. "Robeson Envisions Institute to Develop Talent of Negroes,"
Washington Evening Star, June 25, 1943.

According to this article Paul Robeson, a scholar and actor as
well as one of the greatest colored singers, made his first appearance with the National Symphony Orchestra at the Water Gate
as guest artist on June 24th. Mr. Robeson arrived from New York
and told of a dream he hopes will achieve fruition in peacetime -
the establishment of an institution which will develop the operatic,
dramatic and dancing talents of the Negro race. He observes, in
part:
Such an institution, perhaps sponsored by a leading
Negro university with the aid of outstanding Negro
artists, would help reveal the Negro's contribution
to American culture. It is a dream which must be
laid aside in war. I not only sing before the
peoples of many countries but make a sincere effort
to understand and appreciate them by learning something of their language and custom. When I was in
college I prepared for the ministry by taking
Greek and Latin. That training in Greek made it
easier for me to learn Russian. Then I took up
Chinese. I made a serious study of ethnology,
languages and comparative cultures. I naturally
am greatly interested in African languages. My
wife is writing a book on Africa. I sent my son
to the Congo to help him get the feel of African
life. I would say the salient features of African
life are their form of tribal government, their

(Robeson, Paul)

> philosophy, poetry, sculpture and love of music,
> comparable with that of the Aztec civilization. All
> culture tends to achieve a level of its own. Negro
> spirituals, for example, have a close community
> with the idiom of other peoples....

16. NEW ZEALAND

334. "'N.Z. is Marvelous, I Want to Return to Its Warmth' Says Robeson,"
People's Voice (New Zealand), November 13, 1960, p. 1.

> Paul Robeson gave a concert in New Zealand and was interviewed
> by the People's Voice. He said he hoped to come back to that
> country not as a singer but to visit the working people and sing
> to them at a price they can afford. He was reported to have
> said, in part:
>> In New Zealand I have felt very close to my
>> audiences. Here I have received the warmest
>> receptions of my whole life. I believe that they
>> have been due to a number of reasons. For over
>> thirty years I have received letters from New
>> Zealanders, including some from children. Many
>> people, some of them now elderly, have been waiting
>> a long time to hear my singing. It has been obvious
>> that many working people went outside their budgets
>> to attend my concerts. I was very sensitive to the
>> warmth of these receptions, and the sympathetic
>> audiences enabled me to expand as a human being with
>> the result that my concerts here have been the best I
>> have ever done. Of special interest was my visit
>> to the Maori Centre in Auckland. I want to learn
>> Maori songs and as much as I can of the Maori language.
>> So I guess I will have to come back, and that will give
>> me a chance of meeting many of my good friends again....

17. OTHELLO

335. "Paul Robeson," Pearson's Weekly, (London), April 5, 1930.

> Robeson comments on his role as "Othello." He observes, in part:
>> ....Othello in the Venice of that time was in practically
>> the same position as a coloured man in America to-day.
>> He was a general, and while he could be valuable as
>> a fighter he was tolerated, just as a Negro who could
>> save New York from a disaster would become a great man
>> overnight.... So soon, however as Othello wanted a

(Robeson, Paul)

> white woman, Desdemona, everything was changed,
> just as New York would be indignant if their
> coloured man married a white woman....

336. "Interview of Paul Robeson," The Observer (London), May 18, 1930.

Robeson surmises:
> ....The extraordinary thing about the rehearsals of
> "Othello," is that they have really given me for the
> first time a love of the theatre. I played various
> parts in America, but I have always cared more for
> my singing. Now I want to act. Shakespeare amazes
> me. His psychology is uncannily true all the time.
> In acting Othello I find that the lines come to life
> at every point. There is no need to intellectualise
> Shakespeare; the appeal is from the heart to the heart
> of the audience....

337. "I Was Nervous," World (London), May 30, 1930.

After reading of his success as "Othello," Robeson declares:
> They seem pleased about me and I'm surprised, for
> I was nervous last night and I started off with my
> performance pitched a bit higher than I wanted it
> to be....

338. "Interview of Paul Robeson," The Era (London), May 21, 1930.

It was reported that Paul Robeson observed that a great deal has
been written about his (Shakespeare) plays and his characters,
and a number of contradictory conclusions have been come to....
it is the duty of his interpreters to come as closely as possible
to what he felt.... So anyone who approaches Othello must remember that part of him which is crude, savage, and makes him
murder his wife; his dignity, nobility and quietness as well....
The secret of understanding him, however, is to find yourself in
the character, but Shakespeare, from whose mind, experience and
observation he came, states Robeson.

339. "Robeson May Alter 'Othello' Role Here," New York Times, May 22,
1930, p. 32.

The article states that Robeson admitted that he could not play
"Othello" in New York as he was doing in London. Robeson asserts:
> I was a little disturbed when we started rehearsals
> and rumors of an objection to a colored actor playing
> with a white girl came to my notice. I felt that in
> London trouble couldn't possibly arise on racial
> grounds. People there are too broadminded for that.
> The love scenes and kissing are absolutely necessary
> to the play. People objecting to my kissing Miss
> Ashcroft must realize that she is supposed to be my
> wife. If any one does object to our love making, the
> objection almost certainly will have to come from

(Robeson, Paul)

> America. They certainly wouldn't stand in America
> for the kissing and the scene in which I use Miss
> Ashcroft roughly. I wouldn't care to play those
> scenes in some parts of the United States. The
> audience would get rough: in fact, might become very
> dangerous....

340. "Robeson Talks in London for Audience Here: Negro Actor Broad-
casts His Views on 'Othello' Which He Is Acting in England,"
New York Herald, June 9, 1930, p. 5.

This article declared that the voice of Paul Robeson was projected
across the Atlantic by radio for nine minutes to tell the people
of the United States "how it feels for an American Negro to play
'Othello' in London." Introduced by Cesar Searchinger, London
representative of the Columbia Broadcasting System, as the pos-
sessor of "the most charming masculine voice in the world today,"
the actor said he hopes to play in New York in the fall. He
argues:

> From all I hear, the present production will come to
> America. I certainly do hope to play "Othello" in the
> land of my birth, especially in New York, the scene
> of my first artistic endeavors. I am positive that
> in the enlightened sections of the United States there
> can be only one question: Is this a worthy inter-
> pretation of one of the great plays of all times? I
> sincerely trust I shall see you all in October....
> In Shakespeare's time, I feel there was no great dis-
> tinction between the Moor and the brown or black.
> Surely most of the Moors have Ethiopian blood and come
> from Africa, and to Shakespeare's mind he was called
> a black moor. Further than that, in Shakespeare's own
> time and through the Restoration, notably by Garrick,
> the part was played by a black man. It is not changed
> until the time of Edmund Kean, some time about the
> middle of the nineteenth century, about 1835 or 1840,
> (Kean died May 15, 1933) when he became brown, and I
> feel that had to do with the fact that at that time
> Africa was the slave center of the world and people
> had at the time forgotten the ancient glory of the
> Ethiopians. Further than that, in the play we have
> references to the black bosom of Othello, to his
> thick lips, to Desdemona's name being begrimed and
> black as Othello's own face. Apart from the fact
> of whether he was brown or black, I think there is no
> question that he must be of a different race in order
> to make the jealousy credible. We always hear that
> Othello's jealousy is not believable, it comes too
> quickly, but I feel that is because he is not pre-
> sented as of a different race....

341. "Robeson Hopes to Act 'Othello' Here in Fall," New York Times,
      June 9, 1930, p. 23.

      Paul Robeson talked from London into microphones that were carried
      to America by radio. He declared that from all that he could
      hear the present production of "Othello" would come to America.
      The actor argues:
            I certainly do want to play "Othello" in the land of
            my birth, especially in New York, the scene of my first
            artistic endeavors. I am positive that in the en-
            lightened sections of the United States there can be
            only one question: Is this a worthy interpretation of
            one of the great plays of all times? I sincerely
            trust, that I shall see you in October. In Shakes-
            peare's time there was no great distinction between
            the Moor and brown or black. Apart from the fact of
            whether Othello was brown or black, I think there is
            no question that he must be of a different race, in
            order to make his jealousy credible....

342. "A Black Othello," Literary Digest, Vol. 106, No. 1, July 5, 1930,
      p. 16.

      This article discusses Paul Robeson in his role as "Othello" that
      was playing in London. This article generally praised Robeson in
      his role. It also quoted some words from the actor on how it
      felt for an American Negro to play "Othello" in London. He says:
            From all I hear, the present production will come to
            America. I certainly do hope to play "Othello" in
            the land of my birth, especially in New York, the
            scene of my first artistic endeavors. I am positive
            that in the enlightened sections of the United States
            there can be only one question: Is this a worthy
            interpretation of one of the great plays of all times?
            I sincerely trust I shall see you all in October....

343. "Robeson in 'Othello' At Stratford Acclaimed by Audiences and
      Critics," The Worker, April 19, 1959.

      According to this article, Paul Robeson marked another and perhaps
      the most important milestone of his long artistic career when he
      opened the Shakespeare Memorial Theatre's 100th season with a
      performance of the title role in "Othello," that was acclaimed by
      audiences and critics alike. He was interviewed after the per-
      formance and he was quoted as saying: "I am overwhelmed by the
      reception I have been given tonight. It is the great moment of
      my life."

18. PARIS PEACE CONFERENCE

344. "Robeson Assails Stettinius," New York Times, April 21, 1949, p. 6.

Paul Robeson was the chief United States delegate to the World
Congress of the Partisans of Peace in Paris, France. He declared
at the meeting that President Truman's program for colonial development, coupled with what he called the invasion of Africa by
former Secretary of State Edward Stettinius "and his millions,"
meant new slavery for Africans. He was referring to the multi-
million-dollar development scheme for Liberia that was backed by
Mr. Stettinius. Robeson concluded: "....It is that American
Negroes would go to war on behalf of those who have oppressed us
for generations against the country which in one generation has
raised our people to the full dignity of mankind...."

345. "Paris Peace Conference," Berlin, German Democratic Republic:
Paul Robeson Archives. Quoted in Philip S. Foner, Editor.
Paul Robeson Speaks: Writings, Speeches, Interviews, 1918-1974.
New York: Brunner/Mazel Publishers, 1978, pp. 197-198.

The essence of this interview that was given on May 11, 1949, is
seen in the below statements: REPORTER: You have been quoted
as saying at the Paris Peace Congress that the Negroes would never
fight the Soviet Union. Robeson answered:
        I was referring to all the forces I have mentioned
        here, but what I said has been distorted out of all
        recognition. The night before I left for Paris I
        spoke to the Coordinating Committee of Colonial
        Peoples in London, and they authorized me to greet
        the World Peace Conference with their determination
        to fight for peace. The emphasis on what I said in
        Paris was on the struggle for peace, not on anybody
        going to war against anybody. Go ask the Negro
        workers in the cotton plantations of Alabama, the
        sugar plantations in Louisiana, the tobacco fields in
        south Arkansas, ask the workers in the banana
        plantations or the sugar workers in the West Indies,
        ask the African farmers who have been dispossessed
        of their land in the South African of Malan, ask the
        Africans wherever you find them on their continent:
        Will they fight for peace so that new ways can be
        opened up for a life of freedom for hundreds of
        millions and not just for the few; will they fight
        for peace and collaboration with the Soviet Union
        and the new democracies; will they join the forces
        of peace or be drawn into a war in the interest of
        the senators who have just fillbustered them out
        of their civil rights; will they join Malan in South
        Africa who, just like Hitler, is threatening to
        destroy eight million Africans and hundreds of
        thousands of Indians through hunger and terror....

346.   "Remarks 'Distorted': Robeson's Answer," New York Age, May 21, 1949, p. 12.

This article stated that Paul Robeson declared that his remarks made at the Paris Peace Conference on April 20 had been "distorted out of all recognition." This statement was contained in a release issued by the Council on African Affairs, of which Robeson is chairman, stated the report. Robeson was widely quoted as saying that Negroes would not go to war against the Soviet Union. The explanation offered by the Council was taken from an interview with the singer in Copenhagen, Denmark. Robeson was reported as saying: "The emphasis on what I said in Paris was on the struggle for peace, not on anybody going to war against anybody. We want peace. We want a chance to know who are our true friends. You may be certain that no false Negro leader, no one who will betray the Negro masses, can convince them of any other road." The newspaper declared that from Paris last week, Dr. W.E.B. DuBois, vice chairman of the African Council issued the following statement: "I agree with Paul Robeson absolutely, that Negroes should never willingly fight in an unjust war. I do not share his honest hope that all will not." "A certain sheep-like disposition, inevitably born of slavery, will, I am afraid, lead many of them to join America in any enterprise, provided the whites will grant them equal rights to do wrong."

347.   "Robeson Sings to Huge Throngs in Copenhagen and Stockholm," Black Dispatch, May 28, 1949, p. 1.

A full explanation of what Paul Robeson actually said and meant by the statement he made at the Paris Peace Conference on April 20, which has been the subject of wide editorial and other comment in the American press, is contained in the following excerpts from an interview given in Copenhagen, Denmark, May 3, as reported by Telepress. (In his tour of the Scandinavian countries Robeson sang to record audiences: 16,000 in the Horum Hall of Copenhagen, 40,000 at a May Day demonstration in Stockholm, and tens of thousands at an open-air concert in Oslo.) The quotations from the interview follow: Reporter: How would you describe the tasks of your people in the present situation? Robeson answers, in part:

I would say that what the whole American people can do now is very decisive for the future of the world, just as decisive as what the German people could have done in 1941 and what the French people could have done in 1939, but failed to do. We have to fight what has become a colossal concentration of reactionary forces - few in numbers, but colossal in strength and influence on world affairs. However, the great bulk of what will happen will mostly be determined by what happens in Africa and the West Indies. The Asiatic problem has taken quite a different turn with the events in China, nobody can fail to see the decisive influence of that. Obviously India is very important to the British imperialists.... But in their own words British military strategy does not rest on the Asiatics or....

(Robeson, Paul)

> India alone. They have said it and they are acting
> upon it, that the defense of the British Empire depends
> on a defense in depth in Africa, coupled with American
> help. Africa has become their basis of operations.
> What happens in the Middle East depends on Africa.
> What happens to the British and American fleets in
> the Mediterranean depends on Africa. Africa has be-
> come a very decisive point. Therefore the attitude
> of the American peoples can really determine the
> question of peace or war. When you talk about Negroes
> you mostly think about the 14 million the United States,
> but you are not to forget the 40 million colored
> people in the West Indies and Latin America, and the
> 150 million in Africa. As far as they are concerned
> everybody knows that their condition is such that a
> war in the interest of imperialism which has enslaved
> them for centuries can only return them to new serfdom....

348. Hicks, James L. "Robeson Hails Jackie for Racial Contribution,"
     Afro-American, July 30, 1949, pp. 1, 2.

     Paul Robeson praised ball player Jackie Robinson as having done
     more for his race than any colored man of modern times and refused
     to allow himself to be drawn into a personal feud with the Dodger
     second baseman. In a two-hour press conference held at the
     Theresa Hotel, Robeson thwarted every effort of a battery of news-
     men to get him to "answer" Robinson's remarks before the House
     Un-American Activities Committee by launching an attack on Jackie.
     He refused them on every turn, according to the article. Robeson
     said he was encouraged to note that Jackie had felt it his re-
     sponsibility to be more than just a ballplayer. It is not
     enough, he said, for a colored person to be merely a successful
     singer or a successful ballplayer. When colored persons attain
     positions of influence, he declared, they should not hesitate to
     use that influence in speaking for the betterment of their people.
     He said he hoped Jackie would continue to use his position of
     importance towards those ends, states Mr. Hicks. Robeson re-
     peated his denial that he had said at Paris that colored people
     would not fight in a war with Russia. But he said when it became
     obvious to him that the statement he made had been purposely dis-
     ported, he had said to himself, "okay, let it stand like that."
     But now that organizations such as the House Committee were
     attempting to use it to their advantage, he now is taking the
     attitude, "Let's put the statement back into context now,"
     concludes the author.

19. PASSPORT

349. "Ask Robeson's Silence on Oppression of Negroes As Price of Passport," Daily Worker, August 25, 1950, p. 5.

Representatives of the Passport Division of the State Department told Paul Robeson, whose passport was revoked on the eve of his departure for meetings and concerts abroad, that Robeson's condemnation of the status of American Negroes should be confined to the American scene, as this was a "family affair" and should not be aired abroad. If Robeson would refrain from speaking out against the United States abroad, he could get his passport back. The actor would not agree to such an arrangement.

350. "Robeson Quotes 'Othello'," New York Times, August 17, 1955, p. 14.

Mr. Robeson called it "rather absurd" that Soviet farmers could visit here and American Baptist preachers go to Moscow, yet he was "not allowed to travel because of my friendship, open, spoken friendship -- for the Soviet people and the peoples of all the world." Quoting from Shakespeare's "Othello," he orated:
> I have done the state some service and they know it.
> I pray you in your letters when you shall these unlucky deeds relate, speak of me as I am nothing extenuate, nor set down extenuate, nor set down ought in malice.

351. "The Real Issues Behind the Denial of Robeson's Passport," Daily Worker, October 17, 1955, p. 6.

The actor-singer states that the real issue why he was denied a passport is not because he would not sign a non-Communist affidavit which the Passport Office insisted that he sign. He declares that it is clear that along with his interest in colonial liberation for African peoples, and for world peace, his stand for Negro freedom in America is at the heart of the case. The militant concludes:
> So long as race oppression and economic exploitation exist here at home or elsewhere in the world, I shall continue to denounce these evils wherever I might be. Instead of persecuting me for criticizing the conditions of Negroes in America, the United States ought to be down in Mississippi prosecuting those who have unleashed against our people a reign of terror and bloodshed....

20. PERSONAL GOALS AND INTERESTS

352. "Paul Robeson Talks of his Possibilities," New York Herald-Tribune,
      July 6, 1924, Section VII-VIII, p. 14.

      Paul Robeson comments on his future as an actor. He declares, in
      part:
              ....When a Negro does any good work as an actor
              everyone begins to talk of Othello. Of course, I
              think about Othello, but as a sort of culmination.
              I think of other parts, too. I hope the time will
              come when a Negro actor will not be limited to Negro
              parts. The trend away from realism in the theatre
              should help here.... Incidently, if I do become a
              first-rate actor, it will do more toward giving
              people a slant on the so-called Negro problem than
              any amount of propaganda and argument....

353. "Paul Robeson, Son of Slave Parents, Reaches Pinnacle," Pittsburgh
      Courier, November 7, 1925, p. 10.

      This article stated that America has produced no more remarkable
      Negro than Paul Robeson, the genius who is now playing the part
      of the Black "Emperor" of a tropic isle to London audiences.
      Mr. Robeson, lawyer, actor and singer, gives the romantic story
      of his rapid rise from obscurity to fame. "My earliest recol-
      lections are of my old father," said Mr. Robeson to "Reynold's"
      representative. "He was one of the old liberated slaves, and as
      a youngster I used to listen to him telling of the days of his
      servitude as he sat sunning himself on the porch of our North
      Carolina home. He fought in the Civil War on the side of the
      North against the South. And what slavery meant he passed on to
      my young receptive mind." Six feet four, with the physique of a
      Hercules, Mr. Paul Robeson has soft eyes, white flashing teeth,
      and a voice like an organ, stated the article. The Negro --
      what he was, what he is, what he will become -- this is the theme
      very near the heart of this man whose ambition it is to the
      white world, declares the reporter. Robeson declares:
              When my London audiences watch me play the Emperor
              Jones, the role of a bad Negro, who captures and
              tyrannises over the primitives of a tropic isle,
              tney see a modern Negro roll up the centuries and
              reveal primeval man. One does not need a very long
              racial memory to lose oneself in such a part. As
              I act civilization falls away from me. My plight
              becomes real, the horrors terrible facts. I feel the
              terror of the slave mart, the degradation of the man
              bought and sold into slavery. Well, I am the son of
              an emancipated slave, and the stories of old father
              are vivid on the tablets of my memory.

(Robeson, Paul)

> I repeated that performance at the State University,
> and was offered a scholarship to Harvard, Yale, or
> Columbia. I took the last and, working as tutor and
> in the post office, managed to get through the Law
> Schools and afterwards to become a barrister. Negro
> opinions were all for making a lawyer of me. To a
> newly freed race the law has an especial dignity.
> My folks wanted to see me a Judge of the Supreme
> Court of the United States. At Columbia I acted first
> in amateur shows. People told me I was good. But I
> doubted myself -- the stage lured me, yet I felt that
> my folk looked to me to carve out a dignified career
> in the law courts. Eugene O'Neill really swung the
> issue. After seeing me play at the Princeton Play-
> house in "All God's Chillun Got Wings," he offered
> me the part of the Emperor Jones in his play. I
> turned that offer down, as I was engaged to be married
> and not yet through my final examinations. But it set
> the course of my life....

354. Frank, William P. "Paul Robeson and the Theatre," Every Evening,
     (Wilmington, Delaware), October 4, 1926.

The writer interviewed Paul Robeson and they discussed a number
of topics. The actor states that he knows that he can sing, but
at times wonders if his reputation as an actor is not sometimes
far ahead of his actual ability. Robeson also dreams of a great
play about Haiti, a play about Blacks, written by a Black and
acted by Blacks. He dreams of a moving drama that will have none
of the themes that offer targets for a race supremacy advocate.
There is a wealth of material in the Black man's past, and above
all, Robeson fears that stereotyped format of plays that will
imitate "Lulu Belle." He also fears the commercialization of the
Blacks' characteristics and talents, but while fearing this, he
seems to accept its coming as inevitable in the American theatre,
states Mr. Frank.

355. "Robeson in London Can't Explain his Success," London Evening
     News and African World -- Reprinted in Baltimore Afro-American,
     September 22, 1928, p. 9.

This was an interview done in London, England, while Paul Robeson
was appearing there. He discusses his life from the time he was
nine years old until 1928. The singer surmises that he goes on
training his voice and learning all he can, but always he finds
that he is guided by instinct when he gets on the platform to
sing. He declares that he will only rarely act in plays because
he feels that he can achieve more by singing one single song than
by doing his best in even a good play. He asserts: "there are
so many distractions in a play, so many influences."

356.   "Famed Artist Discusses Why He's Changing," <u>Journal and Guide</u>,
        November 20, 1930, p. 1.

        Robeson discusses the reasons why he decided to join the Unity
        Theatre, a working class theatre, in London. It was his con-
        victions that it would give him more latitude for the expression
        of his art, together with more appreciative audiences than are to
        be found in the West End theatres. The actor argues, in part:
                When I sing "Let My People Go" I want it in the
                future to mean more than it has meant before.
                It must express the need for freedom not only
                of my own race. That's only part of a bigger thing.
                But of all the working-class here, in America, all
                over. I was born of them. They are my people.
                They will know what I mean. I shan't do any more
                films after the two that are being finished now.
                Not unless I can get a cast-iron story - the kind
                that can't be twisted in the making. There's room
                for short independent films. I might try to do these.
                But for the rest, I'll just wait until the right
                story comes along, either here or abroad. I
                thought I could do something for my race on the
                films, show the truth about them - and about other
                people, too. I used to do my part, go away feeling
                satisfied. Thought everything was O.K. Well, it
                wasn't. Things were twisted and changed - distorted.
                They didn't mean the same. That made me think
                things out. It made me more conscious politically.
                One man can't face the film companies. They re-
                present about the biggest aggregate of finance
                capital in the world - that's why they make their
                films that way. So no more films for me. Joining
                the Unity Theatre means identifying myself with the
                working-class. And it gives me a chance to act in
                plays that say something I want to say about things
                that must be emphasized....

357.   "Tells Why He Will Not Star in Orthodox Operas," <u>Chicago Defender</u>,
        May 19, 1934, p. 1.

        The singer discusses why he will not star in orthodox operas. He
        declares that he hopes to reestablish African cultures through
        songs. Robeson surmises:
                Critics have often reproached me for not becoming an
                opera star and never attempting to give recitals of
                German and Italian songs as every accomplished singer
                is supposed to do. I am not an artist in the sense
                in which they want me to be an artist and of the vocal
                genius of half a dozen cultures which are really alien
                cultures to me. I have a far more important task to
                perform.... When I first started singing Negro
                spirituals for English audiences I was laughed at.
                Now spirituals are accepted by English audiences.
                These songs are to Negro culture what the works of
                the great poets are to English culture: they are the
                soul of the race made manifest. No matter in what

(Robeson, Paul)

part of the world you may find him the Negro has retained his direct emotional response to outside
stimuli; he is constantly aware of an external power
which guides his destiny. The white man has made a
fetish of intellectual and worships the god of thought,
the Negro feels rather than thinks, experiences emotions
directly rather than interpret them by roundabout and
devious abstractions, and apprehends the outside world
by means of intutive perception instead of through a
carefully built up system of logical analysis. No
wonder that the Negro is an intensely religious
creature and that his artistic and cultural capacities
find expression in the glorification of some deity
in song. It does not matter who the deity is. The
American and West Indian Negro worships the Christian
God in his own particular way and makes him the object
of his supreme artistic manifestation which is embodied
in the Negro spiritual. But, what of the African Negro?
What is the object of his strong religious sense, and
how does his artistic spirit manifest itself?

358. "Negroes - Don't Ape the Whites," Daily Herald, (London), January
5, 1935.

This interview was reprinted in the Chicago Defender, January 26,
1935, under the title "I Don't Want to be White." Robeson states
that sometimes he thinks that he is the only Negro living who
would not prefer to be White. The singer discusses the greatness
of African culture and civilization and declares that he is proud
to be a Negro. Robeson surmises that the brains of the best
Negroes have been applied to turning themselves into imperfect
imitations of white gentlemen, while it has been left to the
astute white man to pick up and profit by what has been cast aside.
The actor suggests that Blacks should take their technology from
the West....

359. Dunbar, Rudolph. "No More Big Halls - Robeson," Philadelphia
Tribune, April 29, 1937, p. 1.

According to this writer Paul Robeson was quoted as saying he
would give no more big concerts, nor would he make any more big
tours in either Europe or America. The singer declares:
I am really a drawing-room singer and I really give my
best only under drawing-room conditions. The microphone provides these conditions. Film work and
phonograph recording give me the best possible medium
for my voice. I can sing naturally into the mike - or
in the bathroom. After all, the people who hear me
have a right to my best. And as I can't carry a
bathroom around with me, I am trying to cut out the
big halls with few exceptions. Where the acoustics are
really suitable to my style. In most big halls I
have to produce my voice for the benefit of the guy

(Robeson, Paul)

> in the back row of the gallery. The microphone and
> the camera let me be natural and so I am, so far as
> possible, giving up the big concerts. The strain on
> my nerves and on my voice is terrific. My voice is
> embarrassingly delicate. I simply can't afford to
> play tricks with it....

360. "Singer-Actor Sets Self on '5-Year' Task to Develop Race Heritage,"
      <u>Philadelphia Tribune</u>, May 17, 1934.

> Paul Robeson comments on a number of topics. He states, in part:
> Critics have often reproached me for not becoming an
> opera star and never attemption to give recitals of
> German and Italian songs as every accomplished singer
> is supposed to do. I am not an artist in the sense in
> which they want me to be an artist and of which
> they could approve. I have no desire to interpret
> the vocal genius of half a dozen cultures which are
> really alien cultures to me. I have a far more im-
> portant task to perform... When I first suggested singing
> Negro spirituals for English audiences, a few years ago,
> I was laughed at. How could these utterly simple,
> indeed almost savage songs interest the most sophi-
> sticated audience in the world? I was asked. And
> yet I have found response amongst this very audience
> to the simple, direct emotional appeal of Negro
> spirituals. These songs are to Negro culture what
> the works of the great poets are to English culture:
> they are the soul of the race made manifest. No matter
> in what part of the world you may find him, the Negro
> has retained his direct emotional response aware of an
> external power which guides his destiny. The white
> man has made a fetish of intellect and worship the
> God of thought, the Negro feels rather than thinks,
> experiences emotions directly rather than interpret
> them by roundabout and devious abstractions, and
> apprehends the outside world by means of intuitive
> perception instead of through a carefully built up
> system of logical analysis. No wonder, that the
> Negro is an intensely religious creature and that
> his artistic and cultural capacities and expressions
> in the glorification of some deity in song. It does
> not matter who the deity is. The American and West
> Indian Negro worships the Christian God in his own
> particular way....

361. Jackson, Fay M. "I'm Going to Shock America When I Return -
     Robeson," California Eagle, May 21, 1937, p. 1.

     This article was based on an interview with Paul Robeson while
     Capitol Films was in London shooting the last stages of
     "Jericho," starring Robeson. The actor told the reporter,
     in part:

          I expect to return to New York, I am going to
          scare 'em to death. My next play is definitely
          left; it doesn't bit words, is anti-Capitalist
          and will make "Stevedore" look very tame in
          comparison. I'm sick and tired of caricatures.
          My people and the papers had a beef coming when
          they criticized me for "Sanders of the River"
          and "Show Boat." I'll explain that. In the
          first place, I know where I'm going. Each
          picture progresses towards my ultimate goal.
          Hollywood wouldn't do anything but Showboat
          for me because the South is Hollywood's box
          office. "Write the South off," I suggested.
          But no, said Hollywood. And what could I
          say? I hadn't the star rating then for pic-
          tures and couldn't cite my own box office
          appeal. "Show Boat" proved me to be box
          office of star value and is responsible for
          my present role and salary in "Jericho."
          I refused a fortune for "Uncle Tom's Cabin"
          after that and if I did another "Show Boat"
          I would deserve any amount of criticism from
          my race that came to me. I would do another
          "Stevedore," however. After "Sanders of
          the River" I created box office in Europe
          and Australia so that I am really independent
          of America so far as pictures go and am now
          in a position to dictate the sort of roles I
          may appear in for movies. "Song of Freedom"
          indicates the progression. Its major theme
          is pure. It also showed Christophe's troops,
          black men, driving 50,000 white troops into
          the River.

     Jackson stated that Robeson wants to make lots of African

(Jackson, Fay M.)

pictures showing the true African culture without Europeans in-
pinging upon the Africans. He would do stories of Harlem's Negro
life but not without a corresponding theme of America's life.
After Christophe, producer Walter Futter and Robeson will present
Dumas and Pushkin and other great black genuises of the world's
history. Hannibal and Othello will be screened. Robeson wasn't
talking dreamstuff. Anyone in England knows that he is unquestionably one of the most popular artists here greatly honored
and respected and loved by all classes. He realized that he is
looked upon as an example, that his success reflects honor on his
race and he is choosing and directing his work carefully,
thoughtfully, to prevent any failure. He knows where he is going
and we rejoice that he has passed the first and hardest hazards
of his journey.

362. Dunbar, Rudolph. "Paul Robeson, Noted Film Star, to Devote Life
      to Problems of the Working Class," Black Dispatch, October 29,
      1937, p. 1.

      This article reports that Paul Robeson states that he has decided
      to give up roles of high salaries and devote his talent to only
      those plays which deal with the problems of the working class
      people. He contends, in part:
            The plays that I want to do in the future can only be
            done in the Unity Theatre (in London). The plays that
            I shall do will deal with Negro and working class life.
            As an artist I must have a working-class audience. In
            the Unity Theatre I can develop my stuff.... I am
            through with doing things that I have done over and
            over again in the theatre. I could get a very high
            salary in London at the exclusive West End Theatre,
            but no plays are available dealing with the world
            today. The West End Theatre is decadent because it
            does not reflect the life and struggle of the people.
            If the West End will put on plays dealing with real
            life, then I'm ready to act in them.... Plays must
            respect real life. They must not be subjective.
            That's why I was so happy with the first part of my
            film, "Song of Freedom." There I was showing the
            real life of the people, Negro, and White, together....

363. Gordon, Eugene. "A Great Negro Artist Puts his Genius to Work
      for His People," Sunday Worker, June 4, 1939.

      In this interview the singer-actor argues that having helped on
      many fronts, he felt it was time for him to return to the place
      of his origin -- to those roots which, though imbedded in Negro
      life are essentially American and are so regarded by the people
      of most other countries. He argues:
            ....It is my business not only to tell the guy with
            the whip hand to go easy on my people, but also teach
            my people -- all the oppressed people -- how to pre-
            vent that whip hand from being used against them....
            When the screen is prepared to show the people of the

(Gordon, Eugene)

United States as PEOPLE, getting away from the love
intrigues and from preoccupations with individualist
futility and, instead, focusing on the struggles
and aspirations of the Negro masses for freedom, for
liberty, and for the right to live a democratic life --
when the film does that, it will clearly reflect the
struggles and aspirations also of the whole American
people.

364. Gordon, Eugene. "Paul Robeson: A Great Artist, Put His Genius
to Work for His Own People," Chicago Defender, June 17, 1939,
p. 12.

Robeson comments on a number of issues such as his roots, politics,
his people, and folk music. He suggests, in part:
....Certainly in my travels in many countries of
Europe, particularly in Spain, and having been close
to the struggles in China, Ethiopia and the West
Indies, I have seen and recognized the essential
unity of this international fight for democracy
against fascism. Having helped on many fronts, I
feel that it is now time for me to return to the
place of my origin - to those roots which, though
inbedded in Negro life, are essentially American and
are so regarded by the people of most countries.
I used to think of myself as a concert artist, after
the fashion, say of Marian Anderson. From years of
experience I know now that I am best as a singer
of folksongs. And when I say that, I don't mean
songs of the Negro only. It seems that today,with
things as they are, no Negro can help feeling that
he represents more than merely himself. The case of
Marian Anderson is a good illustration. She is truly
a great artist, singing, as she does in that magnificent voice, the best songs of the world. She
suddenly found herself, through circumstances over
which she has no control, representing the whole
Negro people of the United States. Her responsibility took on a decided political tinge, too - of
immense importance to the Negro people. If there is
one thing I am proud of it is that I have been able
to do something along with others, toward giving
this Negro American folk music its rightful place
in the world....

365. "Interview in PM and Paul Robeson's Reply," PM, September 12 & 15,
1943.

It was pointed out in this interview that Paul Robeson, who sent
his son to school in Russia and to England so he could live like
a "first class citizen," said yesterday that never again would
he consider leaving America:
I did a lot of thinking when the war started.
I had planned to leave the United States for good

(Robeson, Paul)

and I was living in London, shuttling over to
Russia every Summer to see my boy. I thought I
saw more tolerance for Negroes abroad than I did
here. I realized then that the Negro problem here
is a minority group problem, not one of individuals
as it is in many European countries. And I realized
that America gives her minority groups more of a
chance than just about any country on earth.... Just
because I've settled down in Connecticut, don't
think I'm going to stop criticizing the United States.
I'm going right on criticizing this country until
Negroes can live like first class citizens. I'm
acting, and I'm talking for the Negroes in the way
only Shakespeare can. This play is about the problem of minority groups. It concerns a blackmoor,
who tried to find equality among the whites. It's
right up my alley.

366. "Robeson Sees Race's Best Chance Here in America," Chicago
Defender, September 18, 1943, p. 1.

According to this article, Paul Robeson was quoted as saying that
the future of the American Negro is here in America where he has
the best chance for happiness despite racial curb. The noted
singer who has been called a "citizen of the world" by many said
that the war has convinced him never again to leave this country.
He declares:
I thought I saw more tolerance for Negroes abroad
then I did here. I realized then that the Negro
here in the United States has more of a chance than
just about any country on earth.... Besides I was
homesick -- and I decided that I wasn't helping the
Negro problem in the United States by running away
from it. Just because I've settled down in Connecticut, don't think I'm going to stop criticizing
the United States....

367. Goodman, Jack. "Robeson Quits Formal Concert Field Says He Will
Sing Only Where and What He Pleases," New York Times, March 16,
1947, Section Two, p. 9.

Paul Robeson was in concert at the University of Utah's Kingsbury
Hall when he made the announcement that he would retire from giving
formal concerts for at least two years and perhaps for longer.
He declares:
You've heard my final formal concert for at least two
years, and perhaps for many more. I'm retiring here
and now from concert work - I shall sing, from now
on, for my trade union and college friends; in other
words, only at gatherings where I can sing what I
please. I will not sing down South before audiences
where my people are segregated, therefore, I will sing
only at Negro universities where white people could
attend and sit in an audience among their Negro

(Goodman, Jack)

        neighbors. Audiences of my friends, such as campus
        groups and trade union organizations, will still hear
        me sing after I leave the concert stage, "just as
        long as this voice lasts."

368. "Paul Robeson Leaves Stages for Platform," New York Amsterdam,
      May 17, 1947, p. 1.

According to this report Paul Robeson gave his Albany concert
last Friday night, at the Philip Livingston Junior High School,
before an audience of approximately 1,200 persons after Justice
Isadore B. Bookstein, of the Supreme Court, issued an injunction
restraining the Albany Board of Education from interfering with
the concert. Before the recital Robeson told reporters that this,
his 65th concert of the season, would be his last for at least
two years. He declared he is going to devote the next two years
as a lecturer against fascism. Robeson declares:
        I have had 65 concerts and thank goodness this is
        the last. In the next 2 years I will be able to be
        in Albany or in any other city as a lecturer or
        singer, as I please. I am an anti-Fascist. In
        France, in the battle against Fascism, we got along
        extremely well with Communism, and as a result many
        American lives were saved. I am afraid that we are
        more interested in Communism in America today than
        we are in Fascism.

369. Shields, Art. "Interview with Paul Robeson," Daily Worker, July 17,
      1949.

In this interview Robeson comments on a number of topics. It was
given in New York City after a four-month tour of Europe. He
said that everything he said and did while in Europe was distorted by the Associated Press and the United Press and other
American press agencies. The singer points out that he loves
the America that he is apart of. He does not love the America of
Wall Street. "I love the America of the workingclass" surmises
Robeson. The world traveler states that he found no liking for
the Marshall Plan among the common people. He found a very complete understanding of the fact that American Big Business was
trying to take over Europe, states Mr. Shields.

370. Berry, Abner W. "They Tried to Scandalize His Name -- and Failed,"
      Daily Worker, June 20, 1954, p. 10.

The author points out that several newspapers tried to scandalize
Robeson by reporting in their newspapers that Robeson would soon
break with the political Left for pressure from his wife and son.
Robeson answered the allegations by saying: "I know of no force
on this earth that can make me retreat one-thousandth part of one
inch from my firm, well-considered, repeatedly declared and dully
openly-lived beliefs." He also points out that he gave up his
career years ago to enter the struggle for freedom at another
level.

371.   "Paul Robeson,Back in The Fight After Illness, Calls for Unity,"
       The Worker, February 19, 1956, pp. 3-5, 6-8.

       After his recovery from a major operation several months ago,
       Robeson issued the following statement:
            I am determined to be freed from the unjust re-
            strictions which have for several years barred me
            from my career as an international artist - a career
            which began some 30 years ago.... The times cry out
            for increased unity, greater militancy and more re-
            solute action on the part of the entire people.
            Surely today, when as the NAACP notes, "the White
            Citizens Councils are denouncing all and sundry as
            communistic," it is time for our people's organizations
            to unite our forces, regardless of differing political
            viewpoints, for the life-and-death struggle which faces
            us all.... I am glad to be back in full stride again
            to take my place in that great people's movement to which
            I have dedicated by life as artist and citizen - the
            fight for peace and freedom, for human brotherhood and
            dignity, in America and throughout the world....

372.   Rowan, Carl T. "Has Paul Robeson Betrayed the Negro?" Ebony,
       Vol. 12, No. 12, October, 1957, pp. 31-42.

       In this long interview Paul Robeson gives his side of the story.
       He declares, in part:
            Nobody can say that I betrayed the Negro. Every-
            thing I did I did it for the Negro, for the cause
            of his dignity and self-respect. In 1947 I gave up
            my career to enter the day-to-day fight for the
            Negro people.... I castigated a white audience in
            St. Louis because it made me sick inside that they
            would come to hear me sing, but across the street
            pickets marched around the theater where no Negro
            could enter. So I insulted white America, and that's
            what caused cancellation of my concert -- not my
            leftwing political beliefs. Suddenly, white
            America was closed to me. In St. Louis, what I
            was saying is that: "I don't need you white folks,
            because I'll never be able to explain myself to
            you...." I came to my present viewpoint between
            1938 and 1940, and not in Russia but in London.
            I first went to Russia in 1934, not as a politician
            but as an artist. In 1934 when I went to Russia
            for the first time in my life I felt like a man.
            That's a fact.... And Jackie (Robinson) -- well
            he was just spitting out words Lester Granger had
            put in his mouth. If Negroes had simply remained
            neutral, the State Department could not have im-
            prisoned me.... In fact, they did only with the
            cooperation of some top leadership.... Now my
            believing this doesn't mean that I'm part of any
            world conspiracy. It just means that I've decided
            not to take any more stuff off these crackers. If
            they want to put me on trial for treason for that,

(Rowan, Carl T.)

    fine. But I say again to the Negro masses:
    I am not a member of any international con-
    spiracy. I am a very dear friend of the Soviet
    Union. I am a great admirer of the Soviet
    people....

373.   "'I Won't Desert U.S.' -- Robeson, In London," Pittsburgh Courier,
        October 4, 1958, p. 2.

        Although Robeson was making London the center for his future
        activities, he declares:
            I am not deserting the United States, the
            country of my birth. I will make London
            my center, just as many British film stars
            make Hollywood the center of their careers....
            If I have a concert in New York, I will go
            there and return to London....

374.   Matthews, George. "My Aim - Get British and U.S. People To-
        gether," Daily Worker (London), May 5, 1959.

        Paul Robeson, in an interview with the Daily Worker made a
        strong plea for the ordinary people of Britain and the United
        States to get together, and spoke of the part he hopes to play
        in bringing this about. He asserts, in part:
            Since Mr. Dulles and Mr. Macmillan can get to-
            gether the American people ought to get to-
            gether with those in other countries. There
            is another America besides that of Mr. Dulles --
            progressive America. I am very proud to be
            part of that America. I want to play my part
            in establishing contacts between that America
            and the people of Britain.... There I came in
            contact with the struggle of the Indian people
            and those of other Colonial countries. I
            speak of these matters not as a stranger, but
            because I have loved and grown up with them.
            It is natural that, returning after nine years
            absence, I should plan to spend a good deal of
            my time working here. I have had a wonderful
            welcome in Britain, and have already done
            several concerts. I have received hundreds
            of letters, and would like to thank most
            warmly all my friends in Britain for their
            kindness. In addition, I have been able to
            appear before millions of people on television here.
            But for progressive American artists there are very

(Matthews, George)

> few opportunities to appear on television.... It
> was the most heartening experience during those years
> of difficulty to know of your(people in Britain) con-
> cern with us in America, and your readiness to help
> us....

21. PLAYS

375.   "Paul Robeson's Plans," <u>New York Telegraph</u>, November 28, 1926.

The actor comments on his future plans following the closing of
"Black Boy," in which he had the starring role. Robeson surmises,
in part:
> I don't know.... It's mighty hard to get a play to
> fit. There's one they call "Abraham's Bosom" that
> they want me to do, but I don't know. It's not happy.
> It just goes down and down and there's hardly a (note)
> of hope in it. I'm afraid it wouldn't be popular and
> I can't afford to be going into plays that are fore-
> doomed to fail. In concert works I am sure of my
> date and sure of some return....

376.   "Paul Robeson Speaks about 'Black Boy,'" <u>The Era</u> (London), June 17,
1936.

The actor was not satisified with the way the play "Black Boy" was
written. He was reporteded to have argued, in part:
> .... (It) didn't go to the lengths it might have
> done.... The Negro couldn't say in it all that he
> really lived and felt. Why, the white people in the
> audience would never stand for it. Even if you were
> to write a Negro play that is truthful and intellec-
> tually honest, the audiences   in America at least,
> would never listen to it....

377.   Dunbar, Rudolph. "He Quits Big Money: Paul Robeson Says Down
With 'Uncle Tom' Roles," <u>Philadelphia Tribune</u>, October 28, 1937.

According to Mr. Dunbar, Paul Robeson stage and film star, decided
to desert the ranks of high salaried actors to devote his talent
to only those which deal with the problem of the working class.
This announcement was made immediately after he and Mrs. Robeson
joined the Unity Theatre, which boasts such names as H.G. Wells
and Sean O'Casey. Mr. Robeson declares:
> The plays I want to do in the future can only be
> done in the Unity Theatre. The plays I shall do
> will deal with Negro and Working-class life. As
> an artist I must have a working-class audience.
> In the Unity Theatre I can develop my stuff. I am
> through "doing things" I've done before over and over

(Dunbar, Rudolph)

again in the theatre. I could get a very high
salary in London at the exclusive West End theatre,
but no plays are available dealing with the world
today. The West End theatre is decadent because it
does not reflect the life and struggles of the people.
If the West End will put on plays dealing with real
life, then I'm ready to act in them. The Negro is
never cast as an equal and most scripts sent me to
read are thrown into the wastebasket because they do
not deal with ideas of social progress. I have no
room for the Uncle Tom's Cabin type of drama....

378. "War Must Free U.S. Minorities Says Robeson," Chicago Defender,
      December 30, 1944, p. 1.

Robeson declared that there will be a lot of trouble in this
country if returning Negro servicemen are not given their rights.
Asked what effect does the continued mistreatment of minorities
have on our country's reputation among other nations, Robeson
replied:
      America's continued mistreatment of minorities in
      our country makes a lie of our whole position in the
      world. First, in the matter of winning the war and
      second, in the problems that we will face when the
      war is over. If this war means anything, it is a
      war for the freedom of all minorities. How does this
      war differ from other wars in history? The war of
      1776 in our nation was fought to free the colonies
      from the tyranny of England, but the Negro was in
      slavery. The French Revolution was fundamentally a
      middle class war. The war of 1860 in our country
      brought about the freeing of the slaves as chattel
      property, but there was little thought of giving
      him full freedom and equality. This war can and
      ought to reach a level of comparative equality for
      all citizens in this country. This means the ex-
      tension of equal privileges to all people, the
      Negro and other minorities in this country and to
      China, India and Africa....

379. "Paul Robeson As 'The Emperor Jones,'" Reynold's Illustrated News
      (London), September 20, 1952, p. 4.

The actor comments on his role in "The Emperor Jones." He
declares, in part:
      ....When my London audiences watch me play the
      Emperor Jones, the role of a bad Negro who captures
      and tyrannizes over the **primitives of a tropic isle,**
      they see a modern Negro roll up the centuries and
      reveal primeval man.... One does not need a very
      long racial memory to lose oneself in such a part....
      As I act civilization falls away from me. My
      plight becomes real, the horrors terrible facts.
      I feel the terror of the slave mart, the degradation

(Robeson, Paul)

>of the man bought and sold into slavery. Well, I
>am the son of an emancipated slave, and the stories
>of my old father are his own. He is emerging from
>centuries of oppression and prejudice....

22. RUSSIA

380. Smith, Vern. "'I am at Home,' Says Robeson at Reception in
Soviet Union," Daily Worker, January 15, 1935, p. 5.

This was an interview held in Moscow. Robeson argues that he feels
at home in Russia because of the safety and abundance and freedom
he found there. He felt more kinship to the Russian people under
their new society than he ever felt anywhere else. The singer
states that it is obvious that there is no terror in Russia, that
all the masses of every race are contended and support their
government.

381. "Paul Robeson Tells of Soviet Progress," Irish Workers' Voice
(Dublin), February 23, 1935.

This was an interview of Mr. Robeson. He gave his impressions of
Russia. The writer concludes that there can be no better judge
than Paul Robeson of freedom in the U.S.S.R. The author declared
that the many encores demanded by a tumultous audience in the
Capitol cinema had left him exhausted. Scores of autograph hunters
swarmed around America's leading singer, the most famous Negro
in the world. But when they were all dispossed of, Mr. Robeson
was glad to talk to the Irish Workers' Voice on his last visit to
the Soviet Union, from which he returned a few weeks ago, stated
the writer. Mr. Robeson gives his recollections on what he observed:
>The workers are alive. You sense it in the streets,
>everywhere. You see it in their bearing. They feel
>that they are doing something, that they are laying
>the foundations of something, that they are laying
>the foundations of something great. In the factories,
>handling the most up-to-date machines, I saw men who
>obviously had been ignorant peasants a few years ago.
>In the universities and schools were students born
>in savage tribes that up to a decade ago were still
>in the Stone Age. The theatres and opera houses
>packed every might by workers. On the trains you
>see men and women studying works on science and
>mathematics. In the Soviet Union today there is
>not only no racial question; in the minds of the
>masses there is not even the concept of a racial
>question. Black, white, yellow - all were part of
>a whole, and no one thought of the question....

382. Dorn, Julia. "I Breathe Freely," New Theatre, July 1935, p. 5.

The writer interviewed the actor in Moscow. Robeson states that
"In Soviet Russia I breathe freely for the first time in my life.
It is clear, whether a Negro is politically a Communist or not,
that of all the nations in the world, the modern Russians are our
best friends." Robeson argues that he finds that the handicraft
of certain periods of the Chinese and African cultures are almost
identical; and that the Negro is more like the Russian in tempera-
ment and character. Since he speaks Russian, Robeson was able to
talk directly with children, peasants and workers, states the
writer.

383. Davis, Ben, Jr. "U.S.S.R. -- The Land for Me," Sunday Worker,
May 10, 1936.

This was an interview with the singer. Robeson states that he
intends to live in Russia and that it is the only country in the
world where he feels at home. He said he was 100 per cent in
agreement with the Communist Party position on self-determination
for the colonies in Africa and for the Negro people in America.
The actor surmises that there seems to be some kindred feeling
between the peasants in the Soviet Union and the Negro people in
America. He agrees with the Communist position on war and fascism
and the method and necessity of preventing them both. Robeson
believes that the Soviet Union is the bulwark of civilization
against both war and fascism. He concludes: "I can see no
effective means of fighting fascism except through the policies
of the Communist Party. I am in whole-hearted agreement with the
united front based on working class leadership."

384. "When I Sing," Sunday Worker, February 7, 1937.

This article was based on a broadcast from Moscow. This was the
actor's third visit to the Soviet Union. Robeson toured the
country under the auspices of the Moscow State Philharmonic. He
asserts that all of his earlier impressions of Russia were confirmed and his understanding of the Soviet ideal has been broadened and many features of Soviet society not so well understood
by him made more clear. Robeson argues that when he sings the
"Spirituals" and work songs of the Negro people to Soviet
audiences, he feels that a tremendous bond of sympathy and mutual
understanding unites Negroes. The Russian folksongs and those
of the Soviet National Republics, which were formerly Czarist
colonies, bear a close relationship to folksongs of the Negro
people, concludes Robeson.

385. Hall, Chatwood. "Paul Robeson Leaves U.S.S.R. Following Reception Second to One Given Ira Aldridge: Odessa Citizens Leap
to Platform to Kiss Famous Negro Actor," Black Dispatch, February
13, 1937, p. 1.

According to Hall, not since the great Negro actor, Ira Aldridge,
swept through Russia in a blaze of histrionic glory in the latter
half of the 19th century has a male colored artist received such
a tremendous reception as that accorded Paul Robeson, the noted

(Hall, Chatwood)

actor-singer, on his first concert tour in Soviet Russia, just
closed. From Leningrad, hugging the Artic circle, to Moscow
not so far away, through distant Kiev and on to yet more distant
Odessa on the Black Sea -- everywhere the noted baritone and
movie star, former Rutgers football and scholastic "great," has
been profusely acclaimed by Soviet toilers of all categories --
factory workers, intelligentsia, collective farmers, etc.
Robeson states:
> The most noticeable difference between Soviet
> audiences and those in the bourgeois West is that
> it seemed to me that I had close and intimate con-
> tact with the people who are themselves still close
> to their folk traditions. In America I always feel
> that I am giving something and receiving nothing in
> return. In Soviet Russia, on the other hand, the
> audiences of toilers of all colors and nationalities
> respond and give as well as take....

Hall asserts that following the Odessa concert of Robeson, in
which the great baritone's rich, mellow and almost booming voice
held the audience enraptured and evoked ovations following each
number, a citizen, so overwhelmed with Robeson's art, mounted the
platform, kissed Robeson and pinned on his coat lapel a button
bearing a picture of Lenin, the father of the national policy of
the Soviet Union which has liberated and given self-determination
to millions of formerly oppressed national minority peoples.

386.   Hall, Chatwood. "Robeson Finds Soviet A Haven for Artists of All
        Nationalities," California Eagle, October 7, 1937, p. 1.

Paul Robeson and his family visited the Black Sea Coast in Russia
for what he called a much-needed rest. They stayed in the town
of Sochi. One of the many attractions here which struck him very
forcibly, Robeson said, was that in this region he found every
possible type of nationality and color. Within a stone's throw
the Negro-blooded Abkahzians live. This district was formerly
a hot bed of racial feuds and strife under Tsarist colonial rule.
Robeson said:
> I have never and nowhere seen so many various types
> of nationalities of such splendid sanitariums and
> rest homes. Every possible modern convenience is
> available. Indeed no such mass projects for the
> working class exist or can exist in the outside
> bourgeois world.... Here I have found, in addition
> to the great houses of rest, a first class opera
> and an excellent orchestra which perform for the
> cultural enlightenment of tens of thousands of
> Soviet workers who come and go, who are guaranteed
> the right to rest by the Soviet constitution. And
> what is more remarkable and commendable, is that
> these Soviet workers are of all nationalities and
> shades of color. In one generation, the Soviets
> have completely liquidated the race problem....

387.   Hall, Chatwood. "Robeson Vacations on Black Sea Coast," <u>Richmond</u>
       <u>Planet</u>, October 9, 1937, p. 1.

       Mr. Robeson was interviewed while he was vacationing with his
       family in Russia. He states, in part:
            At present I have my son in a Soviet school in
            an environment completely devoid of all prejudice
            or racial differences, for my present attitude was
            made possible through the teachings of Russia. But
            I do want Paul Jr., to return to America often
            enough to become familiar with its traditions as
            far as the Negro is concerned, because he is, first
            of all, an American. My reason for coming back here
            to live is that I **have realized the more I live**
            abroad, the more convinced I am that I am an
            American and this is where I belong -- my roots
            are here -- the material for my career is here....

388.   "Racial Minorities Have Best Chance in Soviets, **Litivinov Wife**
       Declares," <u>Chicago Defender</u>, September 25, 1943, p. 5.

       Mrs. Ivy Litivinov, wife of the former Soviet Ambassador to the
       United States, disagreed with Paul Robeson's reported statement
       that "America gives her minority groups more of a chance than
       just about any country on earth." Mrs. Litivinov declared: "I
       cannot feel that racial minorities in the U.S.A. have as yet won
       the fair treatment which racial minority groups enjoy in the USSR.
       After all, Moscow has no segregated districts or schools and the
       ideal of places of entertainment to which certain races could not
       find access would simply not be understood there." Robeson replied,
       in part:
            I went back and forth to Europe from 1928 to 1940.
            I spent much time in England and Russia. During that
            period there appeared various statements that I would
            remain abroad, and on several public occasions, I
            stated **that I** so contemplated. Then came the rise of
            fascism. I soon saw the connection between the pro-
            blems of all oppressed peoples, and the necessity
            for the artist to participate fully. I worked as
            much as I could for the relief of the refugees from
            Germany, Austria, etc.; for the Chinese people,
            Ethiopian people, and later went to Spain, that im-
            portant focal point in the fight against fascism.
            During the struggle I realized the need for returning
            to America to become a part of the progressive forces
            of my own land. I felt deep obligations to the
            Negro people who still suffer acutely, and realized
            that their future was bound with the future of the
            great masses of the American people, including the
            forces of labor, the Mexicans, the Chinese, the
            American Indians. It would include, certainly, the
            one-third of our Nation of which our President has
            spoken as still not enjoying the full fruits of our
            American democracy. I realized that if America
            held to its democratic traditions and resolutely
            fought fascism, elected leaders who recognized

(Robeson, Paul)

>the needs of the common struggle of the in-
>divisibility of freedom for all men, the problem
>of the colored people would be well on the way
>to solution. My decision to again make my
>home in America was taken as early as 1937.
>As I said above, during the 1934-1938 period,
>I visited the Soviet Union many times, and
>decided to send my boy there to school. There
>I found the real solution of the minority and
>racial problem, a very simple solution....

389.   Newman, Joseph. "Robeson Flies to Testify Here at Trial of
       Red: Tells Soviet Union He Loves It 'More Than Any Other';
       Fears for Negroes in U.S.," New York Herald Tribune, June 16,
       1949, p. 8.

The writer declared that Paul Robeson left for New York and
plans to testify for the defense at the trial of eleven Communist party leaders. He said:

>I had to rush back because I considered their
>defense important to the democratic movement
>in the United States. If American "warmongers
>and reactionaries" are not stopped today, they
>might turn tomorrow on the 12,000,000 Negroes
>of the South and millions of workers. The
>Soviet Union is the country "which I love
>more than any other." The Soviet Union is a
>country to which I turn for comfort and sal-
>vation from racial and other troubles I en-
>counter in capitalist states. The world must
>not be deceived by references to Marian Anderson,
>Joe Louis, Dr. Ralpha Bunche and myself as
>proof of opportunities for and fair treatment
>of Negroes in the United States. Only a small
>group of well known Negroes are tolerated in
>the United States. The Negroes of the South
>are oppressed and no Negroes, including famous
>ones, are secure from lynching. Only in the
>Soviet Union, which I first visited in 1934,
>did I feel like a man. Here I found joy and
>happiness and I strove to instill a love of
>the Soviet Union in my son....

390.   "Robeson Back Home, Assails Red's Trial," New York Times, June 17,
       1949, p. 3.

Paul Robeson returned to the United States from a four month tour
of Europe and the Soviet Union. He denounced the trial of evaders
of the Communist Party as "a type of domestic fascism." The world
traveler declared that he had been misquoted abroad. Robeson
attacked the United States foreign policy and the Marshall Plan,
praised Henry Wallace, said "the Soviets are working for peace,"

(Robeson, Paul)

called the "departure" of Gerdrart Eisler, international Communist
agent, "the greatest victory for the forces of peace in the
world," and that in the Soviet satellite states of Eastern Europe
"the people are happy and singing," stated this article.

391.   "'I Love Above All, Russia,' Robeson Says," Afro-American, June
25, 1949, p. 7.

Paul Robeson was quoted by the Moscow radio as calling Russia
the "country I love above all." The Moscow radio said Robeson,
on the eve of departure, told a Tass news agency interviewer:
    I am truly happy that I am able to travel from
    time to time to the USSR -- the country I love
    above all. I always have been, I am now and will
    always be a loyal friend of the Soviet Union. I
    am taking away with me strength newly acquired
    here. And all this will serve me as a new weapon
    in the struggle for the cause of peace. I will
    name aloud the real criminals against peace when
    I testify as a defense witness at the New York
    trial of Communist leaders....

392.   "What Robeson Really Said at Moscow," Afro-American, July 30, 1949,
p. 8.

According to this article, Paul Robeson told the Russian people
his reasons for feeling so close to them. Among other things,
he said again that it was in Russia, on his first visit to that
country, "that I really felt my human dignity for the first time."
He explained that in the United States tolerance is displayed to
only a small group of eminent colored persons and that, by con-
trast, 12 million colored persons are "downtrodden and persecuted."
The renowned singer told how he had tried to instill a love for
Russia in his only son, Paul. He revealed that his son, who recently married a white girl, expects to do postgraduate work in
electrical engineering in Russia. Calling Russia the "country
I love more than any other," he said "I always have been, I am
now and always will be a most loyal and sincere friend of the
Soviet Union." He also stated, in part:
    In Moscow I had the good fortune to hear the
    opera Prince Igor at the Bolshoi Theatre, to
    see Inspector General in the Maly Theatre. I
    was delighted by both these performances. It
    goes without saying that if the opera Prince
    Igor in the Soviet production, which for you
    Muscovites is customary, were shown in America,
    it would cause a sensation. Your people ap-
    preciate art and have a delicate perception
    of it. The welcome accorded me in Moscow moved
    me to tears. First of all I regard this heart-
    felt sincerity as being addressed to my colored
    people and to the progressive movement of fighters
    for peace and democracy, which I have the happiness
    to represent. Like the Soviet artists, I strive

(Robeson, Paul)

>to serve the people with my art, to be closely
connected with the people, to reflect their
dreams and thoughts. A true artist cannot
stand aside from the struggle of the people.
I am hurrying back to America to testify for
the defense in the trial against the leaders
of the American Communist Party. Defense
of the 12 Communist has great significance for
the whole of the progressive democratic movement
in America. If the reactionaries, the warmongers,
the stranglers of freedom, are not stopped today,
then tomorrow they may   let loose violence on
the 12,000,000 colored persons inhabiting the
Southern States and on millions of working people.
Millions of common people in America are against
the warmongers and stand for peace and freedom,
they follow with admiration the efforts of the
Soviet people in ensuring peace. I am returning
to America full of optimism, full of ardent
faith in the victory of the growing and strengthening forces of democracy. I am leaving the
USSR full of inspiration....

393. "Millions of Us Who Want Peace and Friendship," <u>Moscow News</u>,
      September 17, 1958.

Robeson comments on his stay in Moscow and his friendship with
the Soviet people. The world traveler declares, in part:
>At this moment I am in Yalta. I have had a wonder-
ful visit and rest in a beautiful sanitorium, and am
about to return to Moscow and then to London. For
years I have read about the Crimea - its beauty,
its history - and each day has had its precious moments....
How wonderful was the opportunity to visit "Artek,"
to spend hours with these children of the future.
And a great honor and pleasure to meet many friends,
among them the wise and devoted leaders of the Soviet
people, as they build their great land. And everywhere the deep desire to live in "Peace and Friendship" with all peoples. And how happy they are to
meet us who come from America, to find that there
are millions of us who want peace also and friendly
cultural exchange. Many delegates are also here
from England, Scotland, and Wales, and many friends
from India.... In 1934, on my first visit to the
Soviet Union, I felt for the first time in my life
a full human being. Here was a nation whose history
and future made clear that it would be the friend
of colonial peoples struggling for liberation. Recent events have supported fully this deep faith and
belief. So I am proud, deeply proud of my friendship with the Soviet people, and proud to belong to
that America (the real America) that wants peace and
human brotherhood....

394.   "Come and See For Yourself," Moscow News, February 24, 1960.

The activist was in the Soviet Union and he invited other Americans
to come and for them to see for themselves how the people there
live. Robeson states that he and his family are very happy and
proud to see the advances of the Soviet people. He asserts, in
part:
>   We know the power and influence of the Soviet Union
>   and the Socialist world will support the struggle
>   of people everywhere for full rights and independence.
>   The whole world knows today that the Soviet people
>   only want to share their knowledge - to help create
>   abundance for all of humanity - to create a society
>   abundant and rich materially, spiritually and cul-
>   turally. Let us in our various countries in all
>   lands - contribute our share to everlasting peace
>   and friendship between nations....

395.   "America to Blame for Hungary: Paul Robeson's Line Undeviating -
Closely Questioned by Anzac Reporters," Variety, October 16, 1960,
p. 2.

While Paul Robeson was in Sydney, Australia, he was questioned by
reporters on a variety of topics. Asked were White Americans
treating Black Americans better nowadays, he was reportedly to
have asserted that the United States must modify its Dixiecrats
ways as a political necessity of its own prestige in dealing with
African and Asian nations. Moreover the old lynching spirit
would bring world condemnation, not to mention the anger of
"another strong world power" (meaning Russia), declared Robeson.
The singer is reportedly to have asserted: "I went to Spain to
support the anti-Franco forces, and I saw the awakening of Africa,
India and the other colored peoples of the world." Further
questioned about Russian methods in the Hungarian uprising and
whether he had supported such methods, Robeson replied: "Of
course, it was not a true uprising of the people. It was inspired by America and other agents. The "Voice of America"
really started it."

396.   Shields, Art. "Robeson Greets Soviet Efforts for World Peace,"
The Worker, May 19, 1963, p. 6.

Paul Robeson was recovering from a long and serious illness in
London when he gave an interview to the newspaper Sovietskaya
Russia by telephone from London. He had been living in London
for five years. He concludes with the following words:
>   May 1, in Moscow, is unforgettable. I have been in
>   your country on May Day. I remember the joyful
>   cheering on Red Square, it is a great pity that I
>   cannot be among my Soviet friends again on this happy
>   holiday of peace and labor. That is important for
>   me, for my children and for my people. I greet all
>   my Soviet friends and embrace them. I am with you....
>   I felt the attitude of the Soviet people toward me
>   quite recently on my birthday. On my 65th anniversary

(Shields, Art)

> I received many warm greetings from the Soviet
> Union. Many acquaintances and unknown people wrote
> me. Many cables, letters, and postcards, came from
> workers and pupils from amateur groups, and individual
> artists, writers and painters. I received greetings
> from the people of Moscow. I want to embrace all
> of them and thank them very much. I can not do it
> now physically. That is why I got the Sovietskaya
> Russia to help me....

23. SPANISH DEMOCRACY

397.   "Robeson Calls for Aid to Negroes' Defending Democracy in Spain,"
        The Negro Worker, June 1937, p. 2.

Robeson donated $250.00 to initiate a fund for the relief of the
dependents of Black Americans fighting in defense of democracy
in Spain. He believed that there are hundreds of Blacks in the
theater and musical life who understand what a hunger for
equality and love of mankind impelled him to start this fund.

398.   "Artist Must Take Sides, Says Robeson," Washington Tribune,
        December 4, 1937.

Paul Robeson gave a concert in Albert Hall in London to raise
money for the Spanish Loyalists. He also spoke at the concert.
He argues, in part:

> The artist must take sides. He must elect to fight
> for freedom or slavery. I have made my choice. I
> had no alternative. The history of the capitalist
> era is characterized by the degradation of my
> people: despoiled of their lands, their women
> ravished, their culture destroyed, they are in every
> country, save one, denied equal protection of the
> law, and deprived of their rightful place in the
> respect of their fellows. Every artist, every
> scientist, must decide now where he stands. He
> has no alternative. There is no standing above
> the conflict on Olympian heights. There are no
> impartial observers. Through the destruction -
> in certain countries - of the greatest of man's
> literary heritages, through the propagation of false
> ideas of racial and national superiority, the artist,
> the scientist, the writer, is challenged. The
> battlefront is everywhere. There is no sheltered
> rear. Not through blind faith or coercion, but con-
> scious of my course, I take my place with you. I
> stand with you in unalterable support of the gov-
> ernment of Spain, duly and regularly chosen by its
> lawful sons and daughters.

399. Cunard, Nancy. "Belief in Democracy Took Paul Robeson to War-Torn Spain He Tells Cuban Poet," Black Dispatch, April 16, 1938, p. 1.

This author asserts that Paul Robeson, the greatest artist of his race and one of the world's greatest singers, recently received another Negro of fine and recognized talent, Nicolas Guillen, Cuban poet and journalist who had been in Spain for over seven months. It was in Barcelona, at the time that the Italian and German Fascist bombs gave that now martyred city a first taste of the intensity of the destruction they now have had hurled upon it, declares Miss Cunard. "What reason exactly made you come to Spain?," asked Guillen. Mr. Robeson asserts, in part:
"Because of my adherence to Democracy." As an artist I am certain that it is not a genuine nor an honorable thing to set oneself on a plane above the masses of the people. To walk by the side of the people, to share in their joys and sorrows, that is right; for all of us artists owe this to the masses, from our beginnings to our success. And not only as an artist do I support the cause of Democracy in Spain, but as a Negro. They called me Pablito! No one in Madrid thinks of defeat; none dreams of complaining, despite the danger of the daily shelling, despite all the destruction the city has suffered; despite the hardships. That is war. And each contributes his own effort to win the struggle. There is no fear here. On one of my last days I played a game of football with some of the boys in the street quite close to one of the zones that was being shelled at that moment.... A few years ago, the Negro was just a figure of fun on the American stage. When O'Neill's "Emperor Jones" was first given I saw what possibilities there were for the Negro in dramatic art. I want to play this role, first on the stage and later in a film. I must tell you that this was a starting point, a means to do more important, more profound things. It was necessary to show in such a country that the Negro has artistic capacity and talent, and that he is capable of acting and of being filmed in the same way as are white people.... I am convinced today that the big American and English companies are controlled by big capital, especially by the Steel Trust, and that they will never allow me to make a picture as I would like to make it....
Paul Robeson surmises that he was not interested in making films dealing with the question of color. Mainly, according to him, the big film makers insist on giving a ridiculous caricature of the Negro, one that is supposed to make the white audience laugh. The actor was not interested in playing their game.

400.   Guillen, Nicolas. "Paul Robeson in Spain," Mediodia (Havana, Cuba), 1938 - Reprinted in Bohemia, Havana, May 7, 1976, English translation by Katheryn Silver, Daily World, July 25, 1976.

The actor was in Spain to support the cause of democracy. Robeson states that as a Black, belonging to an oppressed race and discriminated against he could not live if Fascism triumphed in the world. He traveled in a number of countries, including England, raising funds to send to the Spanish people to help them fight for their freedom. Robeson also asserts that he is not interested in playing parts in American films that present a caricature and ridiculous image of the Black. He concludes:

> What I won't do any more is work for the big
> companies, which are headed by individuals
> who would make me a slave, like my father,
> if they could. I need to work with small
> independent producers, in short films with
> songs, until the moment comes to make some-
> thing with greater breadth and more positive
> meaning than has been possible so far. I
> would like to make a film on the life of a
> Black commander of the Lincoln Battalion in
> the International Brigades, who dies there;
> but this would be refused by the big Yankee
> movie companies.... However, I hope to get
> my wish, and bring to the screen the heroic
> atmosphere that I have breathed in Spain,
> and the great participation of men of my
> race in this struggle.

401.   "Paul Robeson 'Adopted' Children," Telegraph and Independent (Sheffield, England), March 3, 1939.

Paul Robeson went to the Foodship Council on High Street and "adopted" a hundre Spanish children. When asked why he was assuming the responsibility for the one month care of the children, Robeson answered:

> In spite of betrayal by people who ought to
> have been their friends, the Spanish people
> can fight on for a long time. If they do,
> it is the responsibility of democracies to
> see they get food and arms. Republic Spain
> has been fighting the battle of progressive
> civilization and it should be clear that
> because support was not given, many more
> Americans, Englishmen and Frenchmen will
> have to die....

24. SPORTS

402. Low, Nat. "Major League Paves Way for Negroes," <u>Daily Worker</u>,
      December 4, 1943, pp. 1, 4.

      Paul Robeson and several Negro Newspaper Publishers met with major
      league baseball team owners and urged them to allow Negro players
      to enter the major league. Robeson ended his impassioned plea
      for the immediate entrance of Negroes into baseball by declaring,
      in part:
              I urge you to decide favorably on this request and
              that action be taken this very season. I believe
              you can be assured they will reflect highest credit
              upon the game and the American people will commend
              you for this action which reflects the best in the
              American spirit...
      Robeson also commented on the statement that commissioner of
      Baseball Landis made when he declared that major league baseball
      teams could sign Negro players. Robeson asserts:
              All Americans will commend Judge Landis and the
              magnates for this step in opening the way for the
              immediate signing of Negro players. This move is
              entirely in keeping with the progress of our nation
              in this way against the axis. Its manifestations
              will be felt and heard in every part of the world....

403. "Robeson Expects Majors to Drop Racial Ban Soon," <u>Pittsburgh
      Courier</u>, January 8, 1944, p. 1.

      According to this article Paul Robeson gave a personal account
      of his plea before the winter meeting of the major league base-
      ball convention last December 3, at the Hotel Roosevelt in New
      York, in the January issue of "Spotlight," a new win-the-war
      magazine for youth. In his article, Mr. Robeson states:
              There is every reason to believe that before the
              next season starts, Negro players will be in the
              major league -- earning the plaudits of the fans
              as have Negro athletes in other sports like Joe
              Louis, Henry Armstrong, Jesse Owens, Kenny
              Washington, Brud Holland and others. Negro
              athletes are among the most popular stars in our
              country. The example of Joe Louis is an inspiration
              to all Americans. Negro football players, track stars
              and basketball players have shown that, given a chance,
              they are the equals of their white brothers....

404. Gelder, Robert Van. "Robeson Remembers -- Interview with the Star
      of 'Othello' Partly About his Past," <u>New York Times</u>, January 14,
      1944, Section 2, p. 1.

      In this interview the actor discusses mainly his football days at
      Rutgers University and how he learned to control his anger. He
      controls his anger by never raising his voice and never doing what
      he means to do, states the writer.

25. WORLD WAR II

405. Davis, Ben Jr. "The Negro People Have Nothing to Gain From the
      War," Daily Worker, October 31, 1939.

      Paul Robeson returned from Europe to the United States and ex-
      pressed the view that the European conflict is an "imperialist
      war in which the Negro people have nothing to gain no matter which
      side wins." He **continues, in part:**
              I believe that the cause of the Negro colonials
              as well as the interests of the Negro people in
              America lies with those who are fighting for peace.
              If peace is brought about it will mean that the
              whole struggle for the Negro people and the
              working class losing their lives in this useless
              slaughter.... The terrible irony of it all is
              that there are about one million black Senegalese
              troops being used by Daladier now to help make
              French imperialism richer and more ruthless against
              the colonies.... The Negro people in America have
              every stake in keeping America out of this con-
              flict, and in battling against the war hysteria
              which now seriously threatens civil rights. As
              an American Negro, I know what any threat to
              democratic liberties means. I remember the last
              world war. I knew that our energies should be
              directed toward building the labor movement -
              based on Negro and white equality and in working
              for such measures as the federal anti-lynching
              bill....

406. Davis, Ben Jr. "Victory for Allies of No Good to Races," Chicago
      Defender, November 4, 1939, p. 1.

      Paul Robeson said he was convinced that the European conflict was
      an "imperialist war in which the Negro people have nothing to
      gain no matter which side wins." He further declares, in part:
              I believe that the cause of the Negro colonials
              as well as the interests of the Negro people in
              America lies with those who are fighting for
              peace. If peace is brought about it will mean
              that the whole struggle for Negro freedom can be
              strengthened, without so many of the best sons
              of the Negro people and the working class losing
              their lives in this useless slaughter. As for the
              Negroes, millions of whom are victims of the
              British Empire, how can they believe Chamberlain
              is fighting for them when the Chamberlain govern-
              ment contemptuously brushes aside the demand of
              India for liberation and maintains her oppressive
              rule in South Africa?.... Certainly, the Negro
              people in America have every stake in keeping
              America out of this conflict, and in battling
              against the war hysteria which now seriously

(Davis, Ben Jr.)

> threatens civil rights. As an American Negro, I
> know what any threat to democratic liberties means.
> I know our energies should be directed toward
> building the labor movement - based on Negro and
> white equality - and in working for such measures
> as the federal anti-lynching bill....

407. Davis, Richard S. "World Will Never Accept Slavery, Robeson
      Asserts," Milwaukee Journal, October 20, 1941.

In this interview Paul Robeson declares that as he sees **World War**
Two, it is fundamentally a collision between conservative and
liberal forces. He also believes that the war is a clash between
those who would enslave the common man and those who would give
him freedom. In such a battle, states Robeson, the forces of
slavery can never win.

408. Lacy, Sam. "Paul Robeson Sees Great Hope for Negroes in Post-War
      World," Chicago Defender, July 24, 1943, p. 5.

The writer states that Robeson was interviewed on the way to
Chicago from Great Lakes, Illinois, where he had appeared in a
recital at the U.S. Naval Training station, declared he does not
share the view of many of his race that the present world struggle
will not offer a solution to the Negro's problem. Nor does he
agree that the colored race holds no stake in the outcome of the
war. The singer asserts:
> I am firmly convinced that today's war will go a
> long way toward liquidating the differences which
> exist between the races of the world, particularly
> those which obtain in this country. I am fully aware
> of the fact that anti-Negro elements in this country
> will seize the opportunity to discredit Negroes
> wherever and whenever they can when the present war
> is over. But I am also aware of the fact that
> America cannot hope to be a great nation in the
> world as it shapes up after the war, unless she
> makes up her mind to do the right thing.... The
> reason is the manner in which the war is being
> fought, with so many groups of the darker races
> aligned with the United Nations, makes for a more
> sympathetic understanding between the peoples who
> in the past have been at each other's throats....

XI
Major Books, Pamphlets, and Booklets About Paul Robeson

My travels abroad to sing and act and speak cannot possibly harm the American people. In the past I have won friends for the real America among the millions before whom I have performed—not for Walter, nor for Dulles, not for Eastland, not for the racists who disgrace our country's name—but friends for the American Negro, our workers, our farmers, our artists.

Paul Robeson

409.   Robeson, Eslanda Goode. Paul Robeson, Negro. New York: Harper
       & Brothers, 1930. 178 pp.

       This is a biography of Paul Robeson by his wife. Much of the dis-
       cussion is centered on Robeson's career. A great deal of the
       material also discusses the author's relationship with him as
       his wife. There are many rare photos of the actor-singer.
       Several newspaper clippings are also enclosed in this work. This
       was the first biography written on Robeson.

410.   Lundell, William. Interview with Paul Robeson.n.p.:n.p., 1933?
       11 pp. Located at Moorland-Spingarn Research Center, Howard
       University, Washington, D.C.

       Robeson was interviewed on a variety of topics. The actor states
       that he was proud of his race and that the American Negro is some-
       times weak. He is weak because he is not proud of being black,
       and because he too often imitates an alien white culture. He
       also declares that here in America he too often feels himself
       only a descendant of the slaves, but there are great cultures in
       Africa which he should remember. The singer argued that he sings
       Negro songs because they suit his voice and suit him.

411.   Miers, Earl Schenck. Big Ben: A Novel. Philadelphia: West-
       minister Press, 1942, 238 pp.

       This book deals in fictional form with Paul Robeson's years at
       Rutgers University. According to the author, Robeson looked back
       upon his four years at Rutgers and reckoned them among the
       happiest of his life. The writer says, Robeson valued highly the
       friendships which were formed there, he believes great wisdom
       came from the classes he attended. The author attempts to make
       this book to be more than Robeson's story. It is in essence,
       according to the writer, the story of every Negro boy who goes
       to college, who remembers, as Robeson does, the people who loved
       and cared for him and for whom he loves and cares first and always.
       The author concludes that he should like it to be the story of a
       struggle for a high goal in our own America - the right of a
       member of any minority to be treated with dignity which

(Miers, Earl Schenck)

God bequeathed to all men....

412. Robeson, Eslanda Goode. <u>African Journey</u>. New York: John Day Co., 1945, 154 pp.

Various references are made to Paul Robeson, her husband. Paul could not go to Africa with his wife because he had signed contracts for two years work and could not break them. The author also points out that "Paul doesn't stand the heat well, changes of climate are hard on him, changes of diet and water put him off...."

413. Graham, Shirley. <u>Paul Robeson: Citizen of the World</u>. New York: Julian Messner, 1946. 264 pp.

This is one of the earliest biographies on Robeson that was written in 1946 when he was 48 years old. None of the facts in this were given to the author by Paul Robeson. They were gleaned, according to the author, from hundreds of people, relatives and friends who had known and loved him -- from old scrapbooks, from letters, from programs and from scraps of paper, unearthed in odd corners of many strange places. The author discusses Robeson and his remarks at a birthday party that was given to him on his 46th birthday. Robeson declares: "In the present (1944) world struggle, I see my work as a social weapon, not as art for art's sake. The mainspring of my life as an artist and as a person is a responsibility to the democratic forces for which I fight." There is also a short Bibliography, and Index.

414. Brown, Lloyd L. <u>Lift Every Voice for Paul Robeson</u>. New York: Freedom Associates, 1951. 14 pp. (Pamphlet).

The author, a friend of Paul Robeson, argues that all of us, Negro and white, trade unionists, professionals, cultural workers, Jewish people and other minority groups - owe a large debt to Paul Robeson. His great art has inspired us; his strength and leadership have been given unstintingly over the years; he has encouraged and helped every progressive cause of the people. He has given all, asking nothing, states Mr. Brown. He also declares that he needs us now as we need him. The fight for his passport is our fight. Let President Truman and the State Department hear from all of us. The writer concludes: "Let our voices be raised that Robeson's great voice may once again roll and resound throughout the world, singing the Song of Man, leading the chorus of peoples in triumphant hymn for Brotherhood for Democracy for Peace."

415. Gorochov, Viktor. <u>IchSinge Amerika: E in Lebensbild Paul Robesons</u>. Berlin: Verlag Neues Leben, 1955. 190 pp.

This is a biography written in German and published in Germany of Paul Robeson. The author emphasizes Robeson's role as a freedom fighter. This work is of little value to the general researcher unless he or she reads German. Several photographs are

(Gorochov, Viktor)

included in this biography.

416. Robeson, Eslanda Goode. <u>Paul Robeson Goes to Washington</u>. Salford,
      Lancashire, National Paul Robeson Committee, 1956. **12 pp.**

      This short pamphlet discusses how Paul Robeson was summoned to
      appear before the Un-American Activities Committee on June 12,
      1956, supposedly to testify in hearings concerning passport legis-
      lation. The writer declares that while Paul Robeson was in
      Washington, D.C., he made a major contribution to his country and
      to his fellow-citizens when he boldly challenged the committee
      and stood as its accuser. Robeson went to Washington with a pre-
      pared statement summarizing his position as a United States
      citizen. She concludes: "Paul Robeson, Negro, went to Washington
      on June 12, 1956, and spoke his mind about him, his people and
      his country. I think they will remember the day. His people
      will not forget it."

417. Seton, Marie. <u>Paul Robeson</u>. London: Denis Dobson, 1958. 254 pp.

      Much of this biography discusses Paul Robeson's life in England
      and Europe. The writer points out that the Federal Bureau of In-
      vestigation forced Black churches to deny Robeson the use of them
      for his concerts. Also anyone in Government service who attended
      his concerts would lose their jobs. The British author emphasizes
      the role and love that the British people had for Robeson. Seton
      declares that Robeson has remained consistent in his fight for the
      cause of justice and equality, so that the Cold War climate of the
      United States found him faced by a campaign of denigration and
      even by the withdrawl of his means and livelihood. She concludes:
      "Because he has so much courage he has not backed down in spite
      of threats and 'smear' and he is now (1957) tacitly acknowledged
      to be one of the leaders of American liberalism."

418. Der Deutche, Friedensrat. <u>Days with Paul Robeson</u>. n.p., 1961?
      35 pp.

      Short sketches of Robeson are given throughout the book. It
      gives a short history of various facets of his career. Many
      photos are seen throughout this short book. Paul Robeson's "days"
      were spent in the German Democratic Republic. Special attention
      is devoted to Paul Robeson's visits with the working class.

419. Hoyt, Edwin P. <u>Paul Robeson: The American Othello</u>. Cleveland:
      World Publishing Co., 1967. 228 pp.

      This is a biography of Paul Robeson. The author repeatedly
      emphasizes the influence that his wife, Eslanda Goode Robeson,
      had on his political thinking. Hoyt states that she was an
      "intellectual Communist" by 1939 and that she believed deeply in
      the Soviet Union and its work, and her attitudes had then and
      would later influence to a greater degree on Paul Robeson's actions.
      The writer argues that his wife was his "political mentor." Hoyt
      surmises, erroneously, that "there might have been a time when

(Hoyt, Edwin P.)

Paul wished he had abandoned or never entered politics, when he could have stepped off into the eastern Soviet with a clean conscience, and lived a quiet life as a teacher, free, a man among equals." He concludes: "No matter what anyone said about Paul's alienation from his people, his taking of the wrong road and trying to lead them down it; these were small matters in the life of Paul Robeson." This work has no bibliography or index.

420. Geogiady, Nicholas, et.al. Paul Robeson: American Negro Actor. Milwaukee: Franklin Publishers, Inc. 1969. 16 pp. (Pamphlet).

A short biographical sketch of Paul Robeson. Much of the data has appeared elsewhere and the writers give very little new information on the actor.

421. Patterson, William L. In Honor of Paul Robeson. New York: Communist Party, U.S.A., 1969. 6 pp. (Pamphlet).

This was an address given in Chicago on the 71st birthday of Paul Robeson. The speaker gives a short overview of the actor's life. Mr. Patterson declares: "Paul was a statesman Not in the realm of politics, although he stood head and shoulders over many others in that arena. He was a statesman in the sphere of art and culture. He studied the relation of art to liberation movements. Paul was an artist of the revolution. He was a fighter for a democracy of the people. He did not believe that the other cheek should be turned to the aggressor. He was in the midst of the fight for the lives of the Scottsboro Boys, Angelo Herndon, Willie McGee, the Trenton Six, and a number of other Civil Rights victims. That distinguished him from the artist - reformer." He also argues that Paul Robeson wanted and wants not only reforms, for they can change with an administration. He wants a change in the very structure of society. He wants the concert platform and the stage to reflect the historical necessity for such a transformation. Paul became a people's artist, seeing art as a weapon for the people and his mastery of it a means of training them for the liberation struggle, concludes the speaker.

422. Symposium: Paul Robeson and the Struggle of the Afro-American People of the USA Against Imperialism. Berlin: German Democratic Republic: German Academy of Art, 1972. 69 pp.

This is a collection of speeches from a symposium on Paul Robeson that was held at the German Academy of Art on April 13-14, 1971, in Berlin, German Democratic Republic. Some of the participants included Paul Robeson, Jr., John Henrik Clarke, Angela Davis, Coretta Scott King, William L. Patterson, Lloyd L. Brown, Brigette Boegelsack, Alex La Guma, Albert Norden, Claude Lightfoot, Hilde Eisler, Diana Loeser, Gordon Sydney, Sigrid Jahn, Horst Ihde and others. All of the conferees praised Robeson and in essence said that not only did the working people of the world owe him a debt of gratitude,but humanity did also; because he did his part to bring freedom and equality to mankind all over the world.

423. Hamilton, Virginia. <u>Paul Robeson: The Life and Times of a Free Black Man</u>. New York: Harper & Row, Publishers, 1974. 220 pp.

This is another biography of the actor. Most of the data in this work is known and has appeared elsewhere. Mrs. Hamilton concludes that Paul Robeson's reinstatement to a place of honor in American society was continuing, although even now (1973) it is not yet complete. No doubt, states the writer, his country owes him a position of esteem at the least,for all the years it feared and punished him. There are Notes to the Text by Chapter, Bibliography and Index. There are also 11 photos of Paul Robeson.

424. Greenfield, Eloise. <u>Paul Robeson</u>. Illustrated by George Ford. New York: Thomas Y. Crowell Co., 1975. 34 pp.

This book was written for young people and discusses Paul Robeson from birth through his seventy-fifth birthday. There are sixteen illustrations of Robeson. The author concludes: "Paul Robeson, like his father, is determined (in 1973) to be free. He says that although Black people cannot yet sing, 'Thank God Almighty, we're free at last,' they can sing 'Thank God Almighty, we've moving!'"

425. <u>Salute to Paul Robeson: A Tribute to a Forgotten Freedom Fighter</u>. Detroit: Afrikan History Clubs, No. 2 and No. 3 MC Farland Elementary School, 1975, 16 pp. (Pamphlet).

This pamphlet is a program presented by the Afrikan History Clubs, No. 2 and No. 3 in the Mackenzie High School Auditorium on April 25, 1975. It was coordinated and sponsored by the McFarland Men's Club. This work includes a biographical sketch of Paul Robeson, sayings of Robeson, some honors received by Paul Robeson, a lesson from Paul, books by and about Paul Robeson, the Paul Robeson Journal, magazine articles, and records. There are also eight photographs of Paul Robeson. Paul Robeson, Jr., was the historical consultant for this program.

426. Wright, Charles H. <u>Robeson, Labor's Forgotten Champion</u>. Detroit, Michigan: Balamp Publishing, 1975. 171 pp.

The writer attempts to make Paul Robeson's role in the labor movement understandable. The writer focuses some light on those events leading up to and surrounding his involvement with labor. The writer argues that Robeson's move toward an identification with the laboring classes took a giant step in 1935 with the London production of the play "Stevedore." The play brought Robeson into contact with a large body of Blacks, Africans and West Indians, in a common endeavor. From 1937 until Robeson's death he began to equate the plight of the working classes,in general, with that of the Black Man in America. On numerous occasions, Robeson declared that the future of the Negro is within the ranks of labor. Robeson returned to the United States in 1939, after a twelve year exile in London. Already his work with the Welsh and Scottish miners, the mill workers in Manchester, the dock workers in London, and the laboring classes in Europe, had established his identity as a staunch friend of labor. When he

(Wright, Charles H.)

returned to the United States he lined up with the trade union movement in North America - the United States, Canada, Panama and Hawaii. The unions accepted his help with open arms as they struggled for survival in the hostile environment of the late 1930's and early 1940's. The author states that Paul Robeson's last address to an American labor union was on February 7, 1958, when the International Longshoremen's and Warehousemen's Union invited him to give their Negro History Week oration that became his valedictory. In this speech Robeson declared: "Here, too, as in all of American life, we must constantly, and urgently strive and work for full equality, equality of opportunity, the recognition of the right to join, to advance, to move by virtue of honest labor, forward and upward to eventual seniority, not restrained by ancient and worn out codes of prejudice and unscientific attitudes." There is an Appendix in this work that includes: "The Hardin Report," "The Miles Report," "Ford Facts, Editorial," "Statement of Principles Constitution (of the Negro Labor Councils),""Robeson's Peace Arch Speech." A six page Index rounds out this work.

426a. Brown, Lloyd L. Paul Robeson Rediscovered. New York: American Institute for Marxist Studies, 1976. 23 pp. (Pamphlet).

This occasion paper was delivered April 22, 1976, at the National Conference on Paul Robeson, Purdue University. The author, a personal friend of Robeson, discusses the actor's life and accomplishments. The essence of this paper is that he wants the younger Black generation to know who Paul Robeson was and what he stood for....

427. Dent, Roberta, et.al., Editors. Paul Robeson: Tributes and Selected Writings. New York: Paul Robeson Archives, Inc., 1976. 112 pp.

The title tells what this work is about. More than 130 tributes are paid to Paul Robeson in this work. Some of them came from China, Finland, Russia, England, Switzerland, Scotland, Canada and Ireland. Some of Robeson's writings were grouped under the following general topics: "Culture and Heritage," "Civil Rights and Politics," and "Labor." Most of the works have appeared elsewhere. A few were original works and have not appeared elsewhere: "Thoughts on Music" (From handwritten notes, 1959), "Statement on Appearance Before the House Un-American Activities Committee (HUAC)," (Robeson was not permitted to read this statement before HUAC), "Message to Actor's Equity" (June 1, 1974). There are also 8 photos and illustrations of Paul Robeson.

428. Gilliam, Dorothy Butler. <u>Paul Robeson: All-American</u>. Washington, D.C.: New Republic Book Co., 1976, 216 pp.

This is an "unauthorized" biography of the actor, according to the Preface. Much of the material she presents is well-known and has appeared in other works. There is one chapter that deals with Robeson's personal life that the author found the need to enclose: "A Marriage in Trouble." Mrs. Gilliam states that Paul was going to divorce his wife, Essie, and marry an English woman, but she married someone else -- a Frenchman. She also states that Robeson's newspaper, <u>Freedom</u>, became a curious anomaly - a Harlem paper that was not primarily about Harlem. The author's biography, unlike other writers on the life of Robeson, did use documents from the files of the Federal Bureau of Investigation (FBI), that it had on Paul Robeson. She obtained them under the Freedom of Information Act. There are 21 photos of Paul Robeson and his family, Bibliography, a list of Robeson's Plays and Films, Notes and Index.

429. Stuckey, Sterling. <u>I Want To Be African: Paul Robeson and the Ends of Nationalist Theory and Practice, 1919-1945</u>. Monograph VI. Los Angeles. University of California, Center for Afro-American Studies. $3.00.

This was a chapter from Dr. Stuckey's dissertation, "The Spell of Africa: The Development of Black Nationalist Theory, 1829-1945," that was written in 1973. Since it has been discussed elsewhere in this work, it will not be discussed here.

430. Salk, Erwin A. <u>Du Bois-Robeson: Two Giants of the 20th Century: The Story of An Exhibit and a Bibliography</u>. Chicago: Columbia College Press, 1977. 20 pp. (Booklet).

The title tells what this work is about. Included in this work is a Profile, a Chronology, and a Bibliography of Paul Robeson that include books about him, recordings and tapes, as well as films and videotapes. Unlike some other listings on Paul Robeson's songs and films, this booklet not only gives the album, but all songs on it and distributor of each film is given.

431. <u>To Live Like Paul Robeson</u>. New York: Young Workers Liberation, 1977, 24 pp. (Pamphlet).

William L. Patterson wrote the "Introduction" to this short work. James Steel discusses "Scaling the Heights of Mount Paul Robeson For Peace, Jobs and Equality." There are also "Paul Robeson Pledge," and a poem by Ann Sadowski, entitled "A Home in This Rock." It was pointed through this pamphlet that Paul Robeson was a friend and supporter of the working people and that he did more than anyone to help improve the plight of the working man.

432. Dean, Phillip Hayes. <u>Paul Robeson</u>. Garden City, N.Y.: Doubleday,
      1978. 81 pp.

      This is a two act play on the life and times of Paul Robeson that
      starred James Earl Jones as Robeson. "Paul Robeson" opened at
      the Booth Theatre, running on Thursday and Saturday evenings,
      and on Saturday and Sunday afternoons in alternation with "For
      Colored Girls....." "Paul Robeson"closed on April 30, 1978. Don
      Gregory presented the play at the Lunt-Fontanne. Original
      staging was by Charles Nelson Reilly; scenery was designed by
      H. A. Poindexter; lighting was by Ian Calderon; costumes were
      designed by Noel Taylor; and Lloyd Richards was the director.
      Joseph Papp produced "Paul Robeson" at the Booth as a New York
      Shakespeare Festival Production. Associate Producer was Bernard
      Gersten.

433. Department of Social Studies. <u>Paul Robeson: 1898-1976</u>. Detroit:
      Department of Social Studies, Division of Educational Services,
      Detroit Public Schools, 1978. 79 pp.

      This is a booklet that chronicles the life and times of Paul
      Robeson and it illuminates the role of the family, school and
      ethnic community played in the development of his values. This
      booklet contains suggested instructional activities and school
      observances. The compilers also hoped that the information
      and suggested activities contained in this work will help in-
      structional personnel plan meaningful lessons and programs. This
      work includes "suggestions for Classroom Activities," "Suggestions
      for All-School Activities,""Bibliography," "Discography," "Films
      and Video Tapes," and "Instructional Activities." There is also
      a "Paul Robeson Word Puzzle."

434. Editors of Freedomways. <u>Paul Robeson: The Great Forerunner</u>. New
      York: Dodd, Mead, & Co., 1978. 383 pp.

      This is a collection of essays by and about Paul Robeson. There
      are also four **selections from Robeson's writings and speeches**
      There is "Tribute in Poetry" and "Tribute in Prose," "A Chronology"
      and a 42 page Bibliography that rounds out this work. Nearly 60
      photos as well as Notes on each section and an Index are also in-
      cluded. Most of the material in this volume has appeared in
      various issues of <u>Freedomways</u> magazine. The editors included a
      quote from Paul Robeson's book, <u>Here I Stand</u>, that best sums up
      this book and Robeson: "Oppression has kept us on the bottom
      rungs of the ladder, and even with the removal of all barriers, we
      will still have a long way to climb in order to catch up with the
      general standard of living. But the equal <u>place</u> to which we aspire
      cannot be reached without the equal <u>rights</u> we demand, and so the
      winning of those rights is not a maximum fulfillment but a minimum
      necessity, and we cannot settle for less."

435. Boegelsack, Brigitee. Paul Robeson: For His 80th Birthday.
      Berlin: Academy of Arts of The German Democratic Republic, 1978.
      65 pp.

      This work includes thirty-two short articles by such people as
      John Henrik Clarke, John Pittman, Brigitte Boegelsack, Lloyd L.
      Brown, Franz Loeser, Albert Norden, Alex La Guma, Vladimir Pozner,
      etc. Many of these articles have appeared in previous publications
      that are listed throughout this bibliography. There are also
      fifteen speeches, interviews, and articles by Paul Robeson. Most
      of them have also appeared in previous publications that are
      listed throughout this work. Several of the writers in this col-
      lection are from the German Democratic Republic: Brigitte
      Boegelsack, Eberhard Bruening, Hilda Eisler, Sydney Gordon, Horst
      Ihde, Diana Loeser, Franz Loeser, Albert Norden. Igor Geyevski
      is from the Soviet Union; Juan Marinello is from Cuba. Vladimir
      Pozner is from France; Alex La Guma is from South Africa. Sydney
      Gordon is from Canada. The other fourteen (14) are from the
      United States.

435a. Clarke, John Henrik, Editor. Dimensions of the Struggle Against
      Apartheid: A Tribute to Paul Robeson, Held Under the Auspices of
      The United Nations Special Committee Againat Apartheid, April 10,
      1978. New York: African Heritage Studies Association in Cooper-
      ation with the United Nations Centre Against Apartheid, 1978.
      90 pp.

      This book is a collection of the Proceedings of a Special Meeting
      of the Special Committee Against Apartheid on the 80th Anniversary
      of the birth of Paul Robeson - April 10, 1978. The Introduction
      was written by Leslie Harriman of Nigeria. He is Chairman of the
      United Nations Special Committee Against Apartheid. Several
      speeches are included: Leslie O. Harriman, "Paul Robeson: A
      Valiant Fighter for Freedom;" Fred O'Neal, "He Worked to Establish
      The Dignity of the Individual;" Lloyd L. Brown, "A Pioneer for
      African Liberation;" Cleveland Robinson, "A Fighter for the Union
      Movement;" Rikhi Jaipal, "Paul Robeson: A Great American;"
      Esther Jackson, "He Sang for Us All;" Gil Noble, "Paul Robeson:
      The Tallest Tree in Our Forest;" Peter Florin, "Paul Robeson:
      A Relentless Fighter for Human Happiness;" Jewel Gresham, "His
      Legacy Must Be Preserved;" Mohamed Adam Osman, "An Eloquent
      Spokesman for Oppressed People Everywhere;" M.A. Ibragimov, "Out-
      standing Fighter for Humans;" Dorothy Hunton, "Paul Robeson and
      The Council on African Affairs;" Mae Foner, "They Tried to Break
      Him, But They Did Not;" Alexandre Verret, "His Voice Has Not Been
      Silenced;" Louis Gomez Anzardo, "A Tribute From Fidel Castro;"
      Karen Talbot, "An Unsurpassed Son of His People;" Mfanafuthi J.
      Makatini, "A Friend of the Oppressed South African People;"
      Paul Robeson, Jr., "A Son's Tribute;" Leslie O. Harriman,
      "Closing Remarks." There are also Appendices that include:
      "Selected Statements from the Writings and Speeches of Paul
      Robeson on 'Apartheid and the Struggle in Southern Africa';"
      "Selected Statements About Paul Robeson and the Nature of His
      Commitment to the International Struggle for Justice and Peace;"
      "A Chronology of Major Events in the Life of Paul Robeson," and
      "A Selected Bibliography of Published Writings By and About

(Clarke, John Henrik, Editor)

Paul Robeson."

436. Foner, Philip S., Editor. Paul Robeson Speaks: Writings, Speeches,
      and Interviews, 1918-1974. New York: Brunner/Mazel Publishers,
      1978. 624 pp.

The title tells what this work is about. The compiler collected
most of Paul Robeson's writings, speeches, and interviews. He
also wrote a 21 page Introduction as well as a 20 page Paul
Robeson Chronology. Dr. Foner also has extensive Notes on each
chapter, a short bibliography, some of Robeson's records and tapes,
and a comprehensive index. The editor, however, did not include
Robeson's weekly columns in the People's Voice, a Black New York
City newspaper published in the 1940s. This work is still the
most complete collection of material on Robeson -- in one place --
to date.

436a. Nazel, Joseph. Paul Robeson: Biography of a Proud Man. Los
      Angeles: Holoway House Publishing Co., 1980. 216 pp.

This is one of the latest biographies on Paul Robeson. In this
paperback work, the author states that Paul Robeson - proud,
defiant, beloved, reviled, misunderstood, idolized - was above
all a man of principle, whose deep and abiding love for his people
was the driving force in his life. By refusing to play the
stereotypical roles offered him by Hollywood, he spurned fabulous
riches available to very few of his race. By championing the
rights of Black people the world over and recognizing their roots
in Africa years before the word Afro-American was coined, he
created controversy that swirled around his head for decades,
states Nazel. By defying the infamous House on Un-American
Activities Committee, he proved the power of his principles while
dooming himself to an ever-diminishing income. Even after his
death controversy continued over his star in Hollywood's Walk of
Fame. Overcoming racial prejudice was more important to him than
material considerations, even though his life-long crusade to stamp
out racism utlimately cost him his career and his health. But
his pride remained intact until the very end. He became a legend
in his own time and remains today a hero to Black people the world
over, surmises the author. He concludes: "Paul Robeson's life
and times provide modern readers with a picture of racism in
America that serves as a timely reminder that the struggle is not
yet over, while showing us that the battles he waged were not only
important but vitally necessary to the very people who often
opposed him...."

437. Robeson, Susan. The Whole World In His Hands: A Pictorial Bio-
      graphy of Paul Robeson. New York: Citadel Press, 1981. 256 pp.

This is the latest book (1981) on Paul Robeson, and the first and
only book of its kind. It was written by his granddaughter. She
discusses his life from birth to his death, through pictures.
The compiler includes a number of rare photos. She also has Notes
on each chapter. This work is a welcome addition to what is
already published on Paul Robeson.

XII
General Books, Pamphlets, and Booklets About Paul Robeson

In my music, my plays, my films I want to carry always this central idea: to be African. Multitudes of men have died for less worthy ideas; it is even more eminently worth living for.

Paul Robeson

1. ACTOR

438. Ovington, Mary White. Portraits of Color. New York: Viking
      Press, 1927, pp. 205-217.

      The writer declares:"....Robeson makes us feel that we have many
      wonderful hours to anticipate. He has within him an immense
      reservoir of power, and he has only begun to use it. Great plays
      must be written for him, plays that will show many phases in the
      life of the black man. "Black Boy," a tawdry drama, in which he
      appeared for a few weeks in 1926, gave him some new experience.
      He refused the leading role in "In Abraham's Bosom," the Pulitzer
      Prize play, weary of depicting the frustrated Negro. But some-
      thing new will come. And in the meantime there are the songs of
      his race to interpret. With each year he will gain in technique,
      while losing nothing of his native power." She also suggests:
      "So those who believe in the genius of the Negro look with
      satisfaction at Paul Robeson, black, his strong shoulders set, his
      big,firm mouth smiling, as he comes down the path. Back of him is
      notable achievement, and ahead, unmeasured heights. To have great
      artistic and dramatic power, and the same time a clear, steady mind
      that can criticize and evaluate, is given to few artists of any
      race."

439. Johnson, James Weldon. Black Manhattan. New York: Alfred A.
      Knopf Co., 1930, pp. 192-193, 196, 206-208, 224-226, 278.

      The writer discusses Paul Robeson as an actor and the roles that
      he played. He points out that Black people did not consider
      "All God's Chillun Got Wings" as any compliment to the race, but
      regarded it as absolutely contrary to the essential truth.
      However, concludes Johnson, the play ran for several weeks, and
      Paul Robeson increased his reputation "by the restraint, sincerity,
      and dignity" with which he acted a difficult role. He also
      pointed out that because of the play, "Mr. Robeson's reputation
      was now international."

440. Garvey, Marcus. A Grand Speech of the Honorable Marcus Garvey
      at Kingsway Hall, London, Denouncing the Moving Picture Pro-
      paganda to Discredit the Negro. London: Black Man Publishing
      Co., 1939. (Pamphlet).

      The leader devotes a great deal of time to denouncing Paul
      Robeson, the leading Black actor of that period. He argues that
      Robeson's roles demeaned Black people.

441. Bond, Frederick W. The Negro and the Drama: The Direct and
      Indirect Contribution which the American Negro Has Made to Drama
      and the Legitimate Stage, With the Underlying Condition Respon-
      sible. Washington, D.C.: Associated Publishers, 1940, pp. 71-74,
      158, 159.

      The author discusses Paul Robeson in Eugene O'Neill's "All God's
      Chillun." He states that in that play the Negro had come long
      way up the dramatic ladders, demonstrating, as he came, the
      vicissitudes of his race. The writer also points out that
      Robeson had the exact qualities which O'Neill had in mind when
      he created the Jim Harris role - the role played by Robeson.

442. Richardson, Ben. Great American Negroes. New York: Thomas Y.
      Crowell Co., 1945, pp. 66-67.

      The writer calls Paul Robeson a great Negro actor. He compares
      him to other great Negro actors of his era: Charles Gilpin,
      Daniel Haynes, Frank Wilson, and Frank Silvera. Richardson
      points out that Negro actors like Robeson and others provided
      impetus to plays written by white playwriters. He mentions
      such plays as "The Emperor Jones," "All God's Chillun Got Wings,"
      and "Show Boat."

443. Fisher, Dorothy Canfield. American Portraits. New York: Henry
      Holt & Co., 1946, pp. 294-297.

      Paul Robeson is included in this collection. The author declares
      that he presented one of the most imposing figures the stage has
      ever seen. She states that Mr. Robeson's country has given him
      as many rewards as any American artist ever had. Fame, admiration,
      warm liking, and money are in profusion, declares the author.
      Mrs. Fisher concludes: "Yet not the simple right taken for
      granted by the most ignorant, most commonplace white man, to come
      and go freely and naturally in his own homeland, to buy food,
      lodging, transportation, and other basic necessities of daily life
      without running the risk of being publicly insulted."

444. Isaacs, Edith J.R. The Negro in the American Theatre. New York:
      Theatre Arts, 1947, pp. 77, 84, 116-120, 122.

      Various references are made to Paul Robeson through out this book.
      The author points out that for Robeson the theatre was a se-
      condary interest. His life's devotion was not to his art, but
      to his race. His aim was to reach out to his people - and - for
      his people - to other men through the medium which came to him
      most naturally, song.

445. Fried, Donald. The Mechanical Angel: His Adventures and Enter-
     prises in the Glittering 1920's. New York: Alfred A. Knopf, 1948,
     pp. 38-40.

     The writer, a literary agent, points out that Horace Liveright,
     publisher, bought the play, "Black Boy" as a starring vehicle for
     Paul Robeson; even then (1948) he was nationally recognized as an
     outstanding figure in the world of the theater. He suggests
     that at least three of the top (white) actresses in America were
     anxious and willing to play the female lead opposite Robeson.
     Because of social pressure the owners of the play decided to use
     a Black actress. Robeson was marvellous in the play. His leading
     lady, however, received lukewarm review and the play closed,
     states Fried.

446. Gelb, Arthur and Barbara Gelb. O'Neill. New York: Harper &
     Brothers, 1960, pp. 450, 550-556, 611, 761.

     Various references are made to Paul Robeson and Eugene O'Neill.
     Much of the discussion centers around Robeson's role "The
     Emperor Jones" and "All God's Chillun Got Wings." The writers
     quoted O'Neill as saying "I believe he can portray the character
     (Jim Harris) better than any other actor could. That's all
     there is to it. A fine actor is a fine actor. The question of
     race, prejudice cannot enter here. And it is ridiculous in the
     extreme that objection should be made to Mr. Robeson." It was
     also pointed out that not only O'Neill but Paul Robeson .... and
     others were recipients of vicious letters from the Ku Klux Klan.

447. Raleigh, John Henry. The Plays of Eugene O'Neill. Carbondale,
     Ill.: Southern Illinois University Press, 1965, pp. 109, 110.

     It was pointed out that O'Neill discovered Paul Robeson who he
     described as having "considerable experience, wonderful pre-
     sence and voice, full of ambition and a damn fine man personally
     with real brains - not a 'ham'." The playwright offered Robeson
     the role as "The Emperor Jones."

448. Coolidge, Olivaia. Eugene O'Neill. New York: Charles Scribner's
     Sons, 1966, p. 163.

     The author points out that O'Neill selected Paul Robeson to play
     the husband of a white woman in "All God's Chillun." Coolidge
     also states that O'Neill had hardly conceived the play as an
     analysis of social conditions.

449. Sergeant, Elizabeth Shepley. Fire Under the Andes: A Group of
     Literary Portraits. Port Washington, N.J.: Kennikat Press, Inc.,
     1966, pp. 193-209.

     This work was originally written in 1927. In this book the author
     states that he is a fine actor, playing the stringent dramas of
     modernity; Paul Robeson the singer, working consciously and
     lovingly in an unconscious folk art, clarifying it so that white
     men may make it - as Europeans, have made their folksongs - the
     basis of a sophisticated musical expression: he is a symbol of

(Sergeant, Elizabeth Shepley)

the New Age of the Negro, a figure of our year and hour, concludes the author. She also argues that although Eugene O'Neill has showed some of the ways in which the Negroes may not achieve happiness, Robeson has. The author declares: "But Robeson on the stage, and especially when he sings - when his voice, released from inhibition, flows up and out from some darkly crystalline spring, seems to be meeting Happiness face to face."

450. Muse, Benjamin. The American Negro Revolution: From Nonviolence to Black Power, 1963-1967. Bloomington: Indiana University Press, 1968, p. 100.

The author argues that in 1919 Negro actors began to appear in serious dramatic roles in plays of Eugene O'Neill. Paul Robeson became world-famous after his performance in "The Emperor Jones," though the prejudice he encountered in the United States turned him into an embittered expatriate, states Mr. Muse.

451. Abramson, Doris E. Negro Playwright in the American Theatre, 1925-1959. New York: Columbia University Press, 1969, pp. 70, 93, 157.

The writer mentions that perhaps the most famous, even infamous, of miscegenation plays was Eugene O'Neill's "All God's Chillun Got Wings," a disturbing distorted, but psychologically profound play about a mixed marriage, concludes the author. Paul Robeson starred in the 1924 production, which provoked bitter discussion in the press. It was also stated that Paul Robeson along with other Blacks supported the Negro Playwrights Company. The writer states that Paul Robeson's name was used to arouse interest in the play "Big White Fog." Even with his talent the play couldn't be saved.

452. Dennis, R. Ethel. The Black People of America: Illustrated History. New York: McGraw-Hill Book Co., 1970, pp. 261, 284, 316.

The writer surmises that Paul Robeson was a versatile individual and gained recognition for his performance in O'Neill's "All God's Chillun Got Wings." According to the author that performance was among the first serious stage roles opened to Blacks. It was also stated that the actor, singer, and All-American football player remained very popular until the late 1940's when his radical politics cost him public favor. Robeson openly sympathized with Communism for various periods in his career.

453. Lindenmeyer, Otto. Black History: Lost, Stolen, or Strayed. New York: Avon Books, 1970, pp. 184-185.

The writer asserts that the "Emperor Jones" is memorable both in terms of its recognition of the Black presence as a theme permeating American life, and because it featured America's most mature and commanding Black actor, Paul Robeson, in the title role as a star among white actors. Critical acclaim, however,

(Lindenmeyer, Otto)

could not make the movie a financial success. The film was
barred in the South.

454. Sheaffer, Louis. O'Neill: Son and Artist. Boston: Little,
Brown & Co., 1973, pp. 37, 135, 139-143, 182, 202, 344-345.

References are made to Paul Robeson in both of O'Neill's plays,
"All God's Chillun Got Wings," and "The Emperor Jones." The
author states that O'Neill went up to Harlem (New York) one night
with Robeson and got drunk. He recalls O'Neill offering Robeson
a part in another play. The writer declares that after Feodor
Chaliapin had proved cool to the idea of "Lazarus Laughed,"
O'Neill proposed that Paul Robeson play the role in whitefáce.
"He is the only actor who can do the laughter, that's the important point. It would be good showmanship, too, no end to the
publicity it would attract...." declared O'Neill. Needless to say,
Robeson never· played the role.

455. Richardson, Ben and William A. Fahey. Great Black Americans.
Second Revised Edition. New York: Thomas Y. Crowell Co., 1976,
pp. 60, 61-69, 182.

The authors discuss "Great Black Americans" in the following areas:
"Music," "Theater," "art," "Literature," "Education," "Science,"
and "Sports." Paul Robeson is discussed under "Theater." Most
of the biographical data on him has appeared in other sources.
The writers point out that the years following World War II
were years of tribulation for Paul Robeson. His beliefs in human
equality, his sympathetic feelings for the people of the Soviet
Union, his outspoken criticism of colonialism, war, and racism
brought down on his head the wrath of the United States House of
Representatives Committee on Un-American Activities, which was
investigating political subversion. There were trying times in
America, and Paul Robeson, like many Americans with strong convictions and the courage to speak out for them, was penalized
for his unwillingness to remain silent.

456. Williamson, Joel. New People: Miscegenation and Mulattoes in the
United States. New York: Free Press, 1980, pp. 172, 177.

The writer asserts that after 1925 Paul Robeson did much to shatter
the tradition of white portraying Blacks in plays, when he
brilliantly played the lead role in Eugene O'Neill's "Emperor
Jones." It was stated that in bitterness, in frustration, some
Negro artists and intellectuals such as W.E.B. Du Bois and Paul
Robeson turned to Marxism, Communism, and Russia for relief. The
author also declares that however, many of those who turned away
soon discovered that a White man's personal ego in its readiness
to use and abuse people of other races for its own ends. According
to the writer, in the 1940's many of those thoughtful people, disillusioned, were adrift, and a few even lost their grip on their
Blackness and melted into the white world.

2. AFRICA

457. New York Herald Tribune. Report of the New York Herald Tribune
      12th Forum on Current Problems. New York: n.p., 1944 (Pamphlet).

      Paul Robeson spoke at this forum. He discussed Blacks in World
      War II, problems of Black Americans and Africa and Africans, and
      the influence of Fascism....

458. Foner, Philip S., Editor. The Voice of Black America: Major
      Speeches by Negroes in the United States, 1797-1973. New York:
      Capricorn Books, 1975. Volume 2, pp. 217-220, 233-241, 249-250,
      499-500, 591.

      Various references are made to Paul Robeson through out the book.
      Two of his speeches, however, are included in this collection.
      They are "Anti-Imperialists Must Defend Africa," and "The Negro
      Artist Looks Ahead." The first speech was delivered in New York
      City on June 6, 1946. A mimeographed copy is in the author's
      (Foner's) possession. The second speech was delivered to the
      opening session of the Conference for Equal Rights for Negroes
      in the Arts, Sciences and Professions, held also in New York
      City, December, 1951. This speech was originally printed in the
      January, 1952, issue of Masses and Mainstream.

459. Dictionary of American History. New York: Charles Scribner's
      Sons, 1976, Vol. 1, Revised Edition, p. 21.

      Paul Robeson is mentioned under the topic that discusses
      "African-American Relations." It states that in 1937 the Council
      on African Affairs was founded under the leadership of Paul
      Robeson and Max Yergan, with the goal of influencing United
      States policy in favor of African colonials. The Council remained
      active until 1955.

460. Yearwood, Lennox S., Editor. Black Organizations: Issues on
      Survival Techniques. Lanham, Md.: University Press of America,
      Inc., 1980, pp. 91, 92.

      One article, "Pan-African Organizations in America: A Brief
      Review of Forms," by Ronald W. Walters, discusses Paul Robeson.
      The writer declares that the **first organization developed by**
      Blacks with the purpose of influencing government policy toward
      Africa was the Council on African Affairs. This organization
      was established by Paul Robeson and Dr. Max Yergan in 1937.
      Robeson was its chairman and Dr. Yergan its Executive Director.
      The Council held its first conference in New York in 1944.
      The writer suggests that Dr. Yergan sabotaged the council and
      subjected Paul Robeson and W.E.B. DuBois to the most vicious
      onslaught of McCarthyism.

3. BIOGRAPHICAL SKETCHES

461. Boris, Joseph J., Editor. Who's Who in Colored America. New York: Who's Who in Colored America Corp., 1927, Vol. 1, p. 171.

There is a long biographical sketch of Paul Robeson. It details his accomplishments up to 1926. Paul Robeson was included in every edition of Who's Who in Colored America from Vol. 1 in 1927 through the 1950's.

462. Fauset, Arthur Huff. For Freedom: A Biographical Story of the American Negro. Philadelphia: Franklin Publishing and Supply Co., 1928, pp. 193-194.

The writer points out that Paul Robeson was the most notable Negro actor at present (1928) and he was one of the finest examples of the New Negro. Fauset concludes that Robeson had become the most outstanding interpreter of Negro folk songs and the race's foremost actor. In both fields he had gained international fame. This book was written for young adults.

463. Who's Who in America, 1932-1933. Chicago: A.N. Marquis Co., 1932, p. 1958.

Short biographical sketch of Paul Robeson is included in this work.

464. Yenser, Thomas. Who's Who in Colored America. Brooklyn, New York: Who's Who in Colored America, 1938-1934-1940. Fifth Edition, p. 444.

There is a short biographical sketch of Paul Robeson. The article states that Robeson played football for 4 years, baseball 3 years, basketball 2 years, and in his third year competed in track, thus winning the coveted title of "4 letterman." It was also pointed out that in April, 1925, he and his associate, Lawrence Brown, gave the first concert of All-Negro music ever given by individual artists on the stage.

465. Ewen, David, Editor. Living Musicians. New York: H.W. Wilson Co., 1940, p. 294.

A three-quarters page biographical sketch of Paul Robeson is included in this work. The article declares: "He has been praised by critics not only for the beautiful texture and resonance of his voice but also for the 'personal charm, and deep communicativeness of his singing.' His singing has been described as full of 'vitality, sincerity and depth of understanding.'" The work concludes: "His ideal is to see the establishment of a United States of Africa, to which Negroes of the world might migrate and live together with dignity and self-respect."

466. Current Biography, 1941, pp. 716-718.

This work includes a long biographical sketch of Paul (Bustill)
Robeson. He did not appear in another biography until 1976.
There is also a photo of the actor and singer. This article
states that Robeson made "more than 300 recordings." It was
pointed out that Robeson believes that he sings at his best when
he can hear himself. He tackled the problem of providing a re-
flective surface for singers in acoustically imperfect halls. An
"acoustical envelope" was evolved, and Robeson used it in
October, 1940, for the first time.

467. Hart, James D. The Oxford Companion to American Literature.
New York: Oxford University Press, 1941, p. 644.

Paul Robeson is included in this work. The compiler stated that
he was a Negro actor and singer, whose stage career included
leading roles in "All God's Chillun Got Wings," "The Emperor
Jones," and "Show Boat."

468. Fisher, Dorothy Canfield. American Portraits. New York: Henry
Holt & Co., 1946, pp. 294-297.

Paul Robeson is included in this collection. The author declares
that he presented one of the most important figures the stage has
ever seen. She states that Mr. Robeson's country has given him
as many rewards as any American artist ever had. Fame, admiration, warm liking, and money are in profusion, declares the
author. Mrs. Fisher concludes: "Yet not the simple right taken
for granted by the most ignorant most common place white man, to
come and go freely and naturally in his own homeland, to buy food,
lodging, transportation and other basic necessities of daily
life, without running the risk of being publicly insulted."

469. Guzman, Jessie Parkhurst. Negro Year Book. Tuskegee, Ala.:
Tuskegee Institute, 1947, pp. 26, 281, 380, 423, 436, 441, 442,
448, 450, 517, 588, 596, 597, 311.

Paul Robeson is mentioned as a singer, actor, and winner of several
awards, including the NAACP's Springarn Medal in 1945, and three
honorary doctoral degrees: Hamilton College (1940), Morehouse
College (1943) and Howard University (1945). There is also a short
biography of Robeson. It was pointed out that Paul Robeson contributed his talents to USO Camp Shows during World War II and never
accepted pay for his work. Also during this time Paul Robeson
was presented by the CIO on the Red Network stations of the NBC
in a dramatic story of a Negro worker's fight to win a war job
and use his skill for victory.

470. Parker, John. Who's Who In the Theatre: A Biographical Record of
The Contemporary Stage. London: Sir Isaac Pitman & Sons, Ltd.,
1947, pp. 1215-1216.

Short biographical sketch of Paul Robeson is included in this work.
This book gives a list of all of his roles between 1921-1922 and
1945. The writer stated that his favorite parts in his plays

(Parker, John)

were "Brutus Jones," and "Jim Harris."

471.   World Biography. New York: Institute for Research in Biography,
       1948, Vol. 2, pp. 4027-4028.

       Short biography of Paul Robeson. This work stated that he
       appeared with leading orchestras in the United States, Canada,
       Great Britain, Norway, Sweden and Denmark.

472.   Fitzhugh, Harriet L. and Percy K. Fitzhugh. The Concise Bio-
       graphical Dictionary of Famous Men and Women. New York: Grosset
       and Dunlap, 1949, pp. 811-812.

       The title tells what this work is about. The writers discuss
       Paul Robeson's life and accomplishments from birth through the
       Second World War. Much attention is devoted to him as an actor
       and singer.

473.   Guzman, Jessie Parkhurst. Negro Year Book. New York: Wm. H.
       Wise and Co., 1952, p. 57.

       A short biographical sketch of Robeson is included in this work.
       It also states that he toured the United States and Europe as a
       stage and concert artist. He is equally at home in music of the
       old masters, songs of popular composers, and spirituals of the
       Negro, concludes Guzman.

474.   Blom, Eric, Editor. Grove's Dictionary of Music and Musicians.
       New York: St. Martin's Press, 1954, Vol. 7, pp. 190-191.

       Paul Robeson is included in this collection. He is described as
       a bass-baritone singer and actor. Most of the biographical data
       has appeared in other references. The editor points out that the
       power and quality of his voice, and the persuasiveness and
       authority of his interpretations made him well-known as a singer.
       It was brought out that he never appeared in opera. Blom con-
       cludes that Robeson's outspoken sympathy for the Soviet Union
       made his activities in recent years increasingly political in
       character.

475.   Funk, Charles Earle, Editor. Funk & Wagnall's New Practical
       Standard Dictionary of the English Language. New York: Funk &
       Wagnalls Co., 1954, Vol. 2, p. 1132.

       Paul Robeson is included in this work. It lists him as an American
       Negro singer and actor born in 1898.

476.   Dillard, H.B. Bio-Bibliographical Index of Musicians in the United
       States of America since Colonial Times. Washington, D.C.: Pan
       American Union, 1956, pp. 317, 434-435.

       Paul Robeson is included in this work. The data on him in this
       work was taken from Edward E. Hipsher, American Opera and Its
       Composers (1934) and Joseph W. McSpadden, Light Opera and Musical

(Dillard, H.B.)

Comedy (1936). His biography, Paul Robeson, Negro (1930), by
Eslanda Robeson is also listed.

477. Sobel, Bernard, Editor. The New Theatre Handbook and Digest of
      Plays. New York: Crown Publishers, 1959, p. 573.

      A short biographical sketch of Paul Robeson is included in this
      work. It was stated that as a concert singer his rich bass voice
      and fine interpretation of Negro spirituals soon brought him fame.

478. Lawless, Ray M. Folksingers and Folksongs in America: A Handbook
      on Biography, Bibliography, and Discography. New York: Duell,
      Sloan and Pearce, 1960, pp. 109, 234, 241, 242, 340, 564, 565.

      Various references are made to Paul Robeson throughout the book.
      The writer did not give a sketch of Paul Robeson and forty-six
      other singers because they are well-known. A list of some of
      Robeson's Spirituals and Folksongs are included in this work.

479. Thorne, J.O., Editor. Chamber's Biographical Dictionary. London:
      W. & R. Chambers, Ltd., 1961, p. 1090.

      It was stated that since the end of the Second World War his
      recital and political sympathies have somewhat embittered his
      relationship with the United States. The editor also suggested
      that to know about Paul Robeson one should read his autobio-
      graphical book, Here I Stand (1958).

480. Simmons, David. Who's Who in Music and Musicians' International
      Directory. New York: Hafner Publishing Co., 1962. Fourth
      Edition, p. 178.

      A short biographical sketch of Paul Robeson is included in this
      work. Nothing new is added on Robeson's life. All of the data
      have appeared elsewhere.

481. Bridgwater, William and Seymour Kurtz, Editors. The Columbia
      Encyclopedia. New York: Columbia University Press, 1963. Third
      Edition.

      A short biographical sketch of Paul Robeson is included in this
      work. This work states that "he became known especially for
      his rendition of 'Ol Man River' in 'Show Boat' (1928) and his
      interpretations of Negro spirituals."

482. Sandved, Kjell Block. The World of Music: An Illustrated
      Encyclopedia. New York: Abradale Press, 1963, Vol. 3, pp. 1153-
      1154.

      A short biographical sketch of Paul Robeson is presented in this
      work. It was pointed out that Eugene O'Neill became so en-
      thusiastic about Robeson's acting that he gave him the leading
      role in "All God's Chillun Got Wings" (1924). When Robeson made
      his debut as a singer in New York in 1925, the attendance was so

(Sandved, Kjell Block)

large that many people failed to get into the hall. His program
consisted entirely of Negro spirituals.

483. Sabin, Robert, Editor. The International Cyclopedia of Music and
      Musicians. New York: Dodd, Mead and Co., 1964, Ninth Edition,
      1964, p. 1814.

      A short biographical sketch is given of Paul Robeson. The editor
      delcares that his support of Communism interfered with his musical
      career in the United States.

484. Davis, John P., Editor. The American Negro Reference Book.
      Engelwood Cliffs, N.J.: Prentice Hall, 1966, pp. 688-689, 803-
      804, 833, 840-842.

      Robeson is discussed in this work as an All-American football
      player and basketball player. He is also seen as an entertainer
      as well as Chairman of the Council on African Affairs. The
      editor states that Robeson was respected by Africans.

485. Rigdon, Walter, Editor. The Biographical Encyclopedia and Who's
      Who of the American Theatre. New York: James H. Heineman, 1966,
      p. 779.

      A short biographical sketch of Paul Robeson is included in this
      work. Most of the data have appeared elsewhere. He does point
      out that Robeson liked tennis, bridge and jazz for recreation
      and that he was named honorary professor at the Moscow State Con-
      servatory of Music in 1958.

486. Lamparski, Richardson. Whatever Became of....? Second Series,
      New York: Crown Publishers, 1968, pp. 80-89.

      A short section on Paul Robeson is included in this work. Most
      of the information on him in this book has appeared in other
      publications. Very little new data are cited.

487. Bergman, Peter M. The Chronological History of The Negro in
      America. New York: Harper & Row Publishers, 1969, pp. 323, 324,
      384, 413, 464, 497, 502.

      Several references are made to Paul Robeson. They include his
      biography, him on the All-American team, roles he held, and his
      earnings.

488. De Coy, Robert H. This Is Progress: The Blue Book Manual of
      Nigritian History, American Descendants of African Origin. Los
      Angeles: Nigritian, Inc., Publishers, 1969, p. 176.

      This is a short biographical sketch of Paul Robeson. Nothing new
      is added to the life and times of this internationally famous singer
      and actor.

489. Encyclopedia International. New York: Grolier, Inc., 1969,
      Vol. 15, p. 489.

      A short biographical sketch is given of Paul Robeson. The article
      states "he has impeccable diction in several languages and is able
      to project his rich, resonant voice with commanding dramatic
      authority."

490. Henderson, Edwin B. and The Editors of Sport Magazine. New York:
      Publishers Co., 1969, pp. 31, 47, 48, 199.

      There is a short biographical sketch on Robeson. It was pointed
      out that Robeson played professional football in 1920. He made
      his debut with the Hammond Pros, transferred later in 1920 to
      Akron where he played through 1921. He starred for the Milwaukee
      Badgers in 1922. The editors conclude that although his politics
      were questioned, but in the world of sports his career will never
      be dimmed.

491. Kutsch, K.J. and Leo Riemens. A Concise Biographical Dictionary
      of Singers: From the Beginning of Recorded Sound to the Present.
      Translated from German, Expanded and Annotated by Harry Ear
      Jones. Philadelphia: Chilton Book Co., 1969, pp. 362-363.

      A short biographical sketch of Paul Robeson is included in this
      dictionary. Most of the data are generally known. The compilers
      stated that Robeson had a dark, deep bass voice and he was ad-
      mired both for his art of expression and for his vocal power;
      he was particularly noted as a singer of Negro spirituals and as
      a lieder singer.

492. Thorne, J.O., Editor. Chamber's Biographical Dictionary. New
      York: St. Martin's Press, 1969. Revised Edition, p. 1090.

      A short biographical sketch of Paul Robeson is included in this
      work. The editor states that from the end of World War II his
      racial and political sympathies somewhat embittered his relation-
      ship with the United States and from 1958 to 1963, when he re-
      tired and returned to the United States, he lived in England.

493. Ploski, Harry A., et.al. Reference Library of Black America.
      New York: Bellweather Publishing Co., 1971, Vol. 3, pp. 79-80.

      Most of the data in this short biographical sketch have appeared
      elsewhere. The editors pointed out that when he did "Othello"
      in 1943 in New York, his ovation was called "one of the most pro-
      longed and wildest ... in the history of the New York theatre."

494. Toppin, Edgar A. A Biographical History of Blacks in America
      Since 1528. New York: David Mckay Co., 1971, pp. 397-400.

      Paul Robeson is discussed in this book. The author states that he
      was at his peak in the 1940's, earning more than $100,000 a year
      as a Broadway and Hollywood actor, as a concert artist, and a re-
      cording star. But his popularity began to slip in 1947 as he
      spoke out increasingly against Jim Crow. In 1948, he campaigned

(Toppin, Edgar A.)

for Progressive Party nominee Henry Wallace and associated with
Marxist groups. When he publicly doubted whether Black Americans
would fight for racist America against what he saw as nondis-
criminatory Soviet Russia, his career was ruined. By 1950, his
recital income dwindled to less than $2,000. Moreover, the State
Department cancelled his passport, cutting him off from lucrative
European appearances, states Toppins. He argues that a comeback
in the late 1950's failed when he continued his outspoken indictment of the ills of American society. Many Black actors,
musicians, athletes, singers, and other entertainers of Robeson's
day simply bit their lips and endured insults silently, hoping
that their performances would win friends and gradually break down
prejudice. Robeson could not take that passive path even at the
cost of his career. It is to America's shame and loss that his
great talents were stifled because he refused to suffer abuse in
silence, concludes the writer.

495. Slonimsky, Nicolas. Baker's Biographical Dictionary of Musicians.
      Revised with 1971 Supplement. New York: G. Schirmer, 1971,
      p. 1353.

      Paul Robeson is included in this work. The compiled lists him as
      a Negro bass singer. Slonimsky states that in 1952 Robeson was
      awarded the International Stalin Peace Prize that was worth
      $25,000.

496. Southern, Eileen. Black Americans: A History. New York: W.W.
      Norton and Co., 1971, pp. 369, 424, 439, 489.

      The writer gives a short biographical sketch of Paul Robeson.
      She points out that by 1941 Robeson was, along with Marian
      Anderson among the top ten concert musicians in the United States.
      It was pointed out that Robeson was a member of Will Marion Cook's
      Clef Club Orchestra, that served as the core of a touring
      musical show company. Professor Southern also states that White
      composer Earl Robinson's "A Ballad for Americans," became popular
      during war (Second) times partly because of its patriotic theme,
      but primarily because of its effective presentation by Paul
      Robeson in the baritone solo role.

497. Baskin, Wade and Richard N. Runes. Dictionary of Black Culture.
      New York: Philosophy Library, 1973, p. 380.

      A short biographical sketch is included in this work. It was con-
      cluded that though he sustained financial losses, experienced
      ostracism, and suffered political persecution, he refused to com-
      promise his beliefs and continued to speak out against oppression.

498. Claghorn, Charles Eugene. Biographical Dictionary of American
      Music. West Nyack, N.Y.: Parker Publishing Co., 1973, p. 373.

      Paul Robeson is included in this collection. The editor called
      him a "noted Black bass singer." All of the data in this bio-
      graphical sketch has appeared in other works.

499. Rust, Brian. The Complete Entertainment Discography: From the Mid-1890's to 1942. New Rochelle, New York: Arlington House, 1973, pp. 551-559.

There is a biographical sketch of Paul Robeson as well as all of his recordings from 1925 through 1942. His first recording was made in Camden, N.J., July 16, 1925. Lawrence Brown accompanied him on the piano. The last recording listed in this work was done in New York City, October 1, 1941. Count Basie and his Orchestra accompanied him. The editor also states that Paul Robeson made some records for Keynote of Chinese, Russian and other songs, and some remakes of his most popular spirituals, for Columbia, after 1942.

500. Ward, John Owen, Editor. The Concise Oxford Dictionary of Music. London: Oxford University Press, 1973, p. 488.

There is a very short biographical sketch of Paul Robeson. The editor did say that Robeson was of high reputation in the U.S.A. and Britain as vocal recitalist, especially (being a Negro) as sympathetic interpreter of "Spirituals."

501. Afro-American Encyclopedia. North Miami, Fla.: Educational Book Publishers, Inc., 1974. Vol. 8, pp. 2244-2245.

There is a short biographical sketch of Paul Robeson as a singer. Most of the information has appeared in other works. Rutgers University rated Robeson as "One of the most prominent living alumni members." The article states: "He called America his home and said he saw encouraging signs that the Negro eventually would become a full American in every sense of the word."

502. Doren, Charles Van, Editor. Webster's American Biographies. Springfield, Mass.: G & C Merrian Co., Publishers, 1974, p. 880.

There is a half page biographical sketch of Paul Bustill Robeson. This article states that Robeson first refused the role as "The Emperor Jones" in 1922 when it was offered to him by Eugene O'Neill. He accepted instead a role in "Taboo." In 1923 he did accept the role in "The Emperor Jones." It was stated that the high point of his career was his rendition of "Ol Man River," in the 1926 edition of "Show Boat."

503. Kinkle, Roger D. The Columbia Encyclopedia of Popular Music and Jazz, 1900-1950. New Rochelle, N.Y.: Arlington House, Publishers, 1974, Vol. 3, pp. 1644-1645.

The author states that Paul Robeson was a bass, sometimes billed as a baritone, and specialized in spirituals and work songs. A list of 10 of his movies as well as 25 of his records are included.

504. May, Robin. A Concise Encyclopedia of the Theatre. Reading,
      Berkshire, R G 1 2 Q Z: Osprey Publishing Limited, 1974, p. 95.

      Paul Robeson is included in this collection. The article stated
      that he made his name as Jim Harris in "All God's Chillun Got
      Wings" (1924), Brutus Jones in "The Emperor Jones" (1924), Joe in
      "Show Boat" in London (1928), etc. The writer surmises that al-
      though he was a famous Othello, twice in Britain, once on Broad-
      way, some found he lacked vocal variety and the technique and
      fire which the part needed, but others were greatly moved. The
      author called him "One of the great voices of the century."

505. Webster's Biographical Dictionary. Springfield, Mass.: G. and C.
      Merriam Co., 1974, p. 1268.

      A short biographical sketch of Paul Robeson is included in this
      dictionary. There are listings of his most important stage plays.

506. Who Did What?: The Lives and Achievements of the 5000 Men and
      Women - Leaders of Nations, Saints and Sinners, Artists and
      Scientists - Who Shaped Our World. New York: Crown Publishers,
      1974, p. 276.

      A one sentence biographical sketch of Paul Robeson: "American
      negro actor and singer, famous for his performances of 'Othello'
      and his singing of negro spirituals," is included in this work.

507. Ploski, Harry A. and Warren Marr II, Editors and Compilers.
      The Negro Almanac: A Reference Work on the Afro-American.
      New York: Bellwether Co., 1975, pp. 76, 810-811, 838-839, 894.

      Various references are made to Robeson throughout the book. There
      is also a biographical sketch of him. The editors assert that
      Robeson's political affiliations have at times tended to attract
      even more publicity than his artistic career.

508. Reader's Digest. Family Encyclopedia of American History.
      Pleasantville, New York: Reader's Digest Association, Inc.,
      1975, p. 959.

      The work describes Paul Robeson as a Negro actor, singer, fore-
      most Black stage star of the 1920's-1940's and supporter of
      leftist causes. It also stated that he was acclaimed inter-
      nationally as one of the finest singers and most impressive actors
      of his generation. According to critic Brooks Atkinson he dis-
      played what he called the "cavernous roar" of his awesome, bass-
      baritone voice on the concert stage and soon became internationally
      known as an interpreter of spirituals and folk songs. This sketch
      concluded: "Long identified with the cause of Negro civil rights
      and embittered at the slow pace of progress, he devoted more and
      more time to international Socialist causes after 1934."

509. Robinson, Wilhelmena S. _Historical Afro-American Biographies_.
     New York: Publishers Co., 1975, pp. 242-243.

     There is a short biographical sketch of Paul Robeson as an actor.
     Most of the data have appeared in previous publications. The
     author concludes: "Possessing a deep sympathy for the social
     underdog and having experienced the humiliations of second-class
     citizenship in his native America, Paul Robeson went to Soviet
     Russia in the late 1940's and resided there periodically until
     the mid-1960's, when he returned to the United States."

510. Wallechinsky, David and Irving Wallace. _The People's Almanac_.
     Garden City, N.Y.: Doubleday & Co., 1975, p. 896.

     The writers give a biographical sketch of Robeson. It was stated
     that in the 1960's, after living in England for a number of years,
     Robeson returned to America and was in time to see some of the
     changes he had agitated for before the nation was ready. The
     authors also called him a professional politician, who in 1950,
     spoke out against his own country and for the ideologies of the
     U.S.S.R.

511. _Collier's Encyclopedia_. New York: Macmillan Educational Corp.,
     1976, Vol. 20, p. 110.

     There is a short biographical sketch written by William Lichten-
     wanger. Nothing new is added by the writer. All of the data on
     Robeson have appeared in other references.

512. _Current Biography_, 1976, pp. 345-348.

     A long biographical sketch is given of Paul Robeson. The article
     states: "At the peak of his celebrity, while starring in 'Othello'
     on Broadway, the immensely popular black actor, singer, and
     political activist Paul Robeson was the guest of honor of a birth-
     day party given in April, 1944, by the New York theatre world and
     an organization called the Council on African Affairs. So well-
     liked was Robeson that the celebration had to be held at the
     17th Regiment Armory on Park Avenue to accommodate the nearly
     8,000 guests. The sponsors of the tribute included some of the
     most famous names in show business as well as several prominent
     figures from the black community and the American left. By the
     end of the 1940's, with the Cold War in full swing and McCarthyism
     flourishing, such a gathering would have been highly unlikely.
     As the American political climate changed, however, Robeson
     clung to his admiration of the Soviet Union and to his denunciation
     of racial unjustice. His commitment to views then considered
     radical and even subversive cost him his passport from 1950 to
     1958, and although he later made concert tours of Australia and
     Europe, cut short his career as one of America's most eloquent
     singers and actors." The article also states: "Over the years
     Robeson has acquired many interests and many friends beyong the
     entertainment business, becoming identified - and identifying
     himself - with left-wing causes. On his trip to the Soviet
     Union in 1934, he had been greatly impressed by the social ex-
     perimentation he saw there. Revisiting that country often, he

(Current Biography)

learned the Russian language and became as well known in Moscow
as he was in London and New York. He once delcared that Russia
was the country he loved more than any other, and he sent his only
child, Paul Jr., to school there, hoping that the absence of racial
and class discrimination that Robeson believed was characteristic
of Russia's schools would be to the boy's benefit...."

513. Diccionario Enciclopedico Salvat. Duodecima Edicition. Barcelona:
      Salvat Editors, 1976, Vol. 10, p. 495.

      A short biographical sketch, in Spanish, of Paul Robeson is in-
      cluded in this work. It stated that he was a noted Negro actor
      and singer and was born in Princeton, New Jersey, in 1898. It
      stated that he won the Lenin Peace Prize in 1952. There is also
      a photo of Mr. Robeson.

514. Green, Stanley. Encyclopedia of the Musical Theatre. New York:
      Dodd, Mead and Co., 1976.

      Paul Robeson is included in this collection. The author called
      him "one of the theatre's most overpowering actors." Robeson
      made his Broadway debut in 1921, scoring successes in dramas "All
      God's Chillun Got Wings," "The Emperor Jones," and "Othello."

515. Robinson, Wilhelmena S. Historical Afro-American Biographies.
      New York: Publishers Co., 1976, pp. 242-243.

      The writer surmises that possessing a deep sympathy for the social
      underdog and having experienced the humiliations of second-class
      citizenship in his native America, Paul Robeson went to Soviet
      Russia in the late 1940s and resided there periodically until
      the mid-1960's, when he returned to the United States. She also
      states that he was listed in Who's Who in America, 1974-75.

516. Smythe, Mabel M., Editor. The Black American Reference Book.
      Englewood Cliffs, N.J.: Prentice Hall, 1976, pp. 667, 690, 695,
      697, 698, 820, 930, 934.

      Robeson is discussed as an actor, athlete, concert singer and
      Chairman of the Council on African Affairs. Much of the data on
      Paul Robeson has appeared in other works.

517. World Book Encyclopedia. Chicago: Field Enterprises Education
      Corp., 1976, Vol. 16, p. 343.

      A short biographical sketch is presented of Paul Robeson. Nothing
      new is given in this write up. This article was written by
      Mary Virginia Heinlein.

518.   Encyclopedia Americana. International Edition. New York:
       American Corp., 1977, Vol. 23, p. 574.

       A short biographical sketch is given of Paul Robeson. It was
       pointed out that Robeson made his stage debut in May, 1922, in
       New York City with Margaret Wycherly in "Taboo," later playing
       the same role in England with Mrs. Patrick Campbell. The
       article declares that "his singing of 'Ol Man River' from 'Show
       Boat' was a triumph of historic and vocal art." Gradually during
       the 1930's Robeson became deeply concerned with what he called
       the "principle of scientific socialism." He became an outspoken
       fighter for Black Civil Rights and in 1948 supported the Pro-
       gressive Party of Henry A. Wallace, according to the article.

519.   Berry, Lemuel Jr., Biographical Dictionary of Black Musicians and
       Music Educators. Gutherie, Okla.: Educational Book Publishers,
       1978, Vol. 1, p. 164.

       A short biographical sketch of Paul Robeson is included in this
       collection. The compiler called Robeson a political activist,
       athlete, baritone soloist. He states that Robeson was known for
       his skill as an athlete prior to becoming a concert artist.
       Dr. Berry states that Paul Robeson recorded more than 300 records.

520.   Wallechinsky, David and Irving Wallace. The People's Almanac #2.
       New York: William Morrow and Co., 1978, pp. 103, 1201.

       The writers state: "The gifted, versatile performer - recognized
       as 'one of the greatest artists of our generation' by almost
       every nation except his own - died half-forgotten long after being
       blacklisted as a Communist during the McCarthy era."

521.   New Encyclopedia Britannica. Chicago: Encyclopedia Britannica,
       Inc., 1979, pp. 614-615.

       The article calls him a singer, actor, and Black activist. It also
       states that he obtained a law degree in 1923, but because of the
       lack of opportunity for Blacks in the legal profession, he drifted
       to the stage making a London debut in 1922. This work declares
       that he became world-famous as Joe in the musical play "Show Boat"
       with his version of "Ol Man River."

522.   Who Was Who in the Theatre: 1912-1976. Detroit, Mich.: Gale
       Research Co., 1978, Vol. 4, p. 2047.

       There is a long biographical listing of his theatre credits, be-
       ginning with his first stage appearance at the Layette Theatre
       in 1921. He appeared in "Simon the Cyrenian." The article gives
       the names of the various theatres in which he made his appearances.

523.   Wearing, J.P. American and British Theatrical Biography: A
       Directory. Metuchen, N.J.: Scarecrow Press, 1979, p. 796.

       Paul Robeson is mentioned in this collection as an American actor
       and singer. This work also lists twelve other references to
       materials on Mr. Robeson.

524. Bronner, Edwin. The Encyclopedia of the American Theatre, 1900-
      1975. New York: A.S. Barnes & Co., 1980, pp. 20, 21, 55, 143,
      544, 566.

      The author briefly discusses the role that Paul Robeson played in
      "All God's Chillun Got Wings" (May 15, 1924), "Black Boy"
      (October 26, 1926), "The Emperor Jones" (November 1, 1920). The
      writer states that Paul Robeson made his New York stage debut in
      1922 as Jim in "Taboo."

525. Meyerhoff, Rose. Try Us 1981: National Minority Business
      Directory. Minneapolis, Minn.: National Minority Business
      Campaign, 1981, pp. 1272-1285.

      There is a short biographical insert on Paul Robeson, as an actor,
      singer, athlete, and politician. It was pointed out that because
      of his vigorous political activism for Black people, (he was
      involved in demonstrations, anti-lynching campaigns and organi-
      zation efforts to politicize Black people) the House Un-American
      Activities Committee revoked his passport from 1950 to 1958.
      This prevented him from giving concerts or acting abroad. At
      home he was blacklisted and denied employment.

                        4. CAREER

526. Redding, Saunders. The Lonesome Road: The Story of the Negro's
      Part in America. New York: Garden City, N.Y.: Doubleday &
      Co., Inc., 1958, pp. 245, 275-286, 317.

      Various references are made to Paul Robeson throughout the book.
      There is, however, one section that deals specifically with him
      entitled, "A Big Man Goes Far." The writer discusses Paul
      Robeson's law career. He states that "writing briefs for cases
      involving railroads, banks, and hundreds of thousands of dollars
      hardly seemed calculated to help Robeson fulfill the service to
      his people" of which his father had used to speak. Robeson is
      reported to have told a friend: "I want to plead the case of the
      misunderstood and oppressed peoples before the highest courts of
      the land. I want to help create laws which will guard their homes
      and children; I want to legislate those laws. I want to speak
      out so the whole world will hear!" But this was not to be. He
      began to experience real frustration and according to Redding, he
      had not developed the equipment to deal with it. The author
      points out that Robeson's wife was blindly ambitious in many
      directions, but was realistic enough to know that Paul could not
      make a decent living as a Black lawyer. Meantime she drew him
      into the fields of her intellectual and social interests ....
      where she proved with all the inquisitiveness of a scientist,
      declares the author. Redding seems to imply that Mrs. Robeson
      had a tremendous influence on her husband and persuaded him to do
      a number of things.

527. Dorbin, Arnold. <u>Voices of Joy, Voices of Freedom!</u> New York: Coward, McCann & Geoghegan, 1972, pp. 76-96.

Paul Robeson is discussed in this work that was written for young people. The author argues: "Many writers have referred to the tragedy of Paul Robeson's life and it is true that his long and stormy career has had many tragic periods. But perhaps the greatest tragedy to befall him has been the disappearance of his name and memory from recent American history." The destruction of Paul Robeson was so complete that today few young American Blacks or whites know who he is and nothing of his great work toward social reform, argues Dorbin. "It is time that we remember and reinstate Paul Robeson, pioneer, hero, a man who may have been stubborn and unyielding but who always fought for his ideals with great courage and determination. The American people, the people of the theater worlds and especially the Black people will always proudly recall Paul Robeson's unique place in history," concludes the writer.

528. Richardson, Ben and William A. Fahey. <u>Great Black Americans</u>. New York: Thomas Y. Crowell Co., 1976, pp. 60, 61-67, 182.

This work gives an overview of Paul Robeson's early childhood as well as his career. The writers did not assess Robeson's impact on humanity. They only state facts, that are already well known, about him.

5. COMMUNISM

529. Karsh, Yousuf. <u>Faces of Destiny: Portraits by Karsh</u>. Chicago: Ziff-Davis Publishing Co., 1946, pp. 122-123.

There is a portrait of Paul Robeson included in this work. He calls Robeson "mobile," "vital," and "gentle." The author declares that the experience of photographing this great artist was one of the most dilightful of his professional career. While the singer was being photographed one of the newspaper people ask him if communistic sympathies had prompted him to send his son to Russia to be educated. Robeson laughed and declared: "I'm for any experiment which promises to improve the common lot of man." Some of the other portraits include outstanding people such as Noel Coward, General Charles De Gaulle, Field Marshall Sir John Greer Dill, Rt. Honorable Anthony Eden, General Dwight Eisenhower, King George VI, John Joseph Pershing, Franklin Delano Roosevelt, George Bernard Shaw, Harry S. Truman, Frank Lloyd Wright, etc.

530.   Buck, Pearl S. with Eslanda Goode Robeson.   American Argument.
        New York: John Day Co., 1949.

        This work is basically a conversation with Robeson's wife. She
        makes various references to him as a supporter of Communism,
        singer, actor, activist and concert artist.

531.   Nolan, William A.   Communism Versus the Negro.   Chicago: Henry
        Regnery Co., 1951, pp. 87, 143, 181, 191, 192, 193, 194, 195.

        The author states that during the year of 1949, Paul Robeson put
        on two great exhibitions in behalf of "freedom and peace," as
        understood by Joseph Stalin. In the spring of that year, he went
        on a four-month singing and speaking tour of Europe, especially
        Eastern Europe, the climax of which was reached at a Soviet-
        controlled peace rally in Paris, declares Nolan. With the ar-
        rogance that has ever been the hallmark of the comrades, Robeson
        solemnly protested that fifteen million American Negroes would
        refuse to fight the Soviet Union, concludes the writer. Dr. Nolan
        surmises that Robeson had announced in Prague that 95 per cent of
        the Negro leadership in the United States is corrupt, meaning
        that it categorically rejects Paul Robeson. The article continues
        to state the accusation made by a former Communist that Robeson
        dreamed of being the "black Stalin" of the United States may not
        be as far-fetched as some people thought. At any rate, according
        to Nolan, after the second Peekskill affair, Robeson took more
        than ever to imitating the Soviet Leader's remote-controlled
        love for the working class. The author seems to imply through-
        out this work that Stalin called the tune for Robeson. He also
        appeared to be Anti-Communist and Anti-Paul Robeson.

532.   Hall, Gus.   Marxism and Negro Liberation.   New York: New Century
        Publishers, 1951, pp. 10, 11.

        The author mentions Paul Robeson in his discussion of "Capitalism
        Oppresses the Negro Nation." The writer declares that the magni-
        ficent defiant triumphs of a few individual Negroes in almost
        every field of art, culture, science and sport activities in the
        face of heartbreaking difficulties - the great Paul Robeson,
        Dr. W.E.B. DuBois, D.A. Julian, Langston Hughes, etc.

533.   Palmer, Edward E., Editor.   The Communist Problem in America: A
        Book of Readings.   New York: Thomas Y. Crowell Co., 1951, pp. 243-
        279, 288.

        This article discusses "Violence in Peekskill." Paul Robeson was
        appearing in concert at Peekskill, New York, when violence broke
        out. The book states that the concert was planned mainly for
        Communists and their followers and was not intended as a propaganda
        medium through which to influence the political thinking of the
        indigenous population. The article continues to declare that the
        impression had grown throughout the United States that Paul
        Robeson and his communist sympathizers intruded into the community
        of Peekskill. That impression was flase, concludes the author.

534. Record, Wilson. <u>The Negro and The Communist Party</u>. Chapel Hill:
      University of North Carolina Press, 1951, pp. 110, 255, 265, 280,
      313.

      The author mentions that Paul Robeson was Co-Chairman of the Pro-
      gressive Party. He also points out that Mrs. Eslanda Robeson,
      Paul's wife was nominated for Secretary of State in Connecticut
      by the Progressive Party in 1948. Dr. Record concludes: "Paul
      Robeson's irresponsible remark that 15,000,000 Negro Americans
      would not fight against the Soviet Union is a windfall for such
      race baiters. In the furor which such utterance can cause, two
      centuries of Negro loyalty to the principle of democracy can be
      momentarily obscured...."

535. Foster, William Z. <u>History of the Communist Party of the United
      States</u>. New York: International Publishers, 1952, pp. 446, 449,
      475, 536.

      The author surmises that the only real cultural vigor shown in this
      period was on the left, among the communists and others influenced
      by Marxism -- Leninism. He also mentions a few writers assertions
      that Paul Robeson was not granted a passport because of his
      support for the Soviet Union.

536. Foster, William Z. <u>The Negro People in American History</u>. New
      York: International Publishers, 1954, pp. 437, 468, 515, 524-
      525, 563.

      The author calls Robeson a great singer, orator and actor. He also
      suggests that Robeson was a left-wing and Communist leader.
      Foster argues: "The very symbol of the advancing, fighting spirit
      of the Negro people, the great cultural political leader, Paul
      Robeson, was boycotted and denied a passport, because of his
      generally militant stand and because he dared to indicate the
      American Negro people would never fight against the Soviet Union."

537. Baldwin, James. <u>Notes of A Native Son</u>. Boston: Beacon Press,
      1955, p. 61.

      Mr. Baldwin declares: "....It is personally painful to me to
      realize that so gifted and forceful a man as Robeson should have
      been tricked by his own bitterness and by a total inability to
      understand the nature of political power in general, or Communist
      aims in particular, into missing the point of his own critique,
      which is worth a great deal of thought that there are a great
      many ways of being un-American,some of them nearly as old as the
      country itself...." The author declares that Robeson feels that
      the House Un-American Activities Committee might find concepts
      and attitudes even more damaging to American life in a picture
      like "Gone With the Wind" than in a possibly equally romantic
      but far less successful "Watch on The Rhine."

538. Howe, Irving and Lewis Coser. <u>The American Communist Party: A Critical History (1919-1957)</u>. Boston: Beacon Press, 1957, pp. 394, 432, 475, 478.

It was pointed out that Paul Robeson officiated at the birth of the American Peace Mobilization in Chicago on September 2, 1948. The authors state that during World War II Paul Robeson shared the platform with Donald Nelson, head of the War Production Board and was seeking Russia's alliance. There is also some alluding to Paul Robeson and the Peekskill Incident in New York.

539. Bardolph, Richard. <u>The Negro Vanguard</u>. New York: Rinehart & Company, 1959, pp. 156, 161-163, 179-180, 191, 200, 241-243, 284-291, 306-308.

The writer points out that more honored even than Marian Anderson was Paul Robeson until the middle forties, when his racial militancy and leftist affinities cost him the bulk of his following in both races. Dr. Bardolph asserts: "Robeson repeated injuries to himself and a brooding despair over the race's plight drove him at last to the far left in the racial struggle, and - more damaging to his personal fortunes - into vigorously avoided admiration for "scientific socialism" and for the Soviet Union which had long and assiduously courted his favor."

540. Thorpe, Earl E. <u>The Mind of The Negro: An Intellectual History of Afro-Americans</u>. Baton Rouge, La.: Ortlieb Press, 1961, pp. 433, 440, 475, 491.

The writer points out that a few Afro-Americans have had trips to Russia financed for them by Communists. These trips were for the purposes of studying communism either formally or informally. According to Dr. Thrope, Paul Robeson was among such persons that had his trip paid to Russia by the Communists. It was also some mentioning of Paul Robeson supporting the Progressive Party and Henry Wallace in the 1948 presidential campaign.

541. Record, Wilson. <u>Race and Radicalism: The NAACP and the Communist Party in Conflict</u>. Ithaca, N.Y.: Cornell University Press, 1964, pp. 152, 175, 176.

The writer argues that the Communist Party "was able during that era to fasten its hold more firmly on Paul Robeson and W.E.B. Du Bois and to exploit their popularity in its 'peace' and race concerns." He states that after Robeson made a speech in Paris declaring before a "peace" rally that fifteen million American Negroes would not fight against the Soviet Union, the implication to at least a segment of the American public was that Negroes were Pro-Soviet and Pro-Communist; which was probably the effect the Communist had hoped to achieve, surmises Dr. Record. The sociologist concludes that Robeson and DuBois were only individual propagandists and they were not key leaders either in the Communist Party or in the organizations through which it attempted to reach Negroes.

542. Katz, William Loren. Eyewitness: The Negro in American History.
      New York: Pitman Publishing Corp., 1967, pp. 399, 404, 449.

      The writer states that Paul Robeson along with other Blacks
      found Communism or Socialism attractive, during the 1920's. It
      was also pointed out that Robeson's fame became worldwide when
      he starred in a London production of Shakespeare's "Othello."
      Paul Robeson along with Louis Armstrong and Lena Horne and many
      other Black entertainers toured the Army Camps with USO troups
      during World War II.

543. Davis, Benjamin J. Communist Councilman From Harlem: Autobio-
      graphical Notes Written in a Federal Pententiary. New York:
      International Publishers, 1969, pp. 111-112, 133, 199-203.

      The author points out that Paul Robeson helped him get elected to
      the City Council in New York City. Robeson spoke to the base-
      ball tycoons in New York in 1945 about hiring Black baseball
      players for the major league. They told Robeson and others that
      they had no objection in principle and they would hire the first
      qualified Negro. Paul Robeson and the author were believed by
      some as "Agents of foreign power." The author argues that writers
      did the gifted Paul Robeson a grave disservice by lumping him with
      them. Davis surmises that Robeson's deep interest in the struggle
      of Africans for liberation from colonialism had been kindled by a
      trip to Africa, where he saw at first hand the unbelievable
      brutality of imperialism. The author suggests that Robeson saw
      the connection between the plight of the American Negro and the
      African people. Davis also discusses Robeson's relationship with
      Max Yergan and the Council on African Affairs.

544. Hofstadter, Richard and Michael Wallace, Editors. American
      Violence: A Documentary History. New York: Alfred A. Knopf,
      1970, pp. 364, 366.

      There is a section in this work that deals with the Peekskill
      Riot of 1949. The Communist Party sponsored a rally and Paul
      Robeson was the feature singer. The concert went as planned but
      as the audience left it was attacked by local anti-Communist.
      The police beat in the windshield and smashed the car to get at
      Paul Robeson and other passengers.

545. Lightfoot, Claude M. Black America and The World Revolution.
      New York: New Outlook Publishers, 1970, pp. 40, 94.

      This booklet contains five speeches that the author made between
      1966 and 1970. In the lecture that the author presented at Karl
      Marx University, Leipzig, German Democratic Republic, August 13,
      1969, he argues: "The late Dr. W.E.B. Du Bois, Paul Robeson, and
      William L. Patterson went into the world and made known the
      hypocrisy of the rulers of America. They pointed out that the
      contributions of declared U.S. foreign aims could best be seen
      through the treatment of Black people. Black oppression, there-
      fore, became the means through which U.S. foreign policy could
      be seen for what it really is and what it intends for the peoples
      of the world. As a consequence of this exposure Paul Robeson was

(Lightfoot, Claude M.)

driven off a concert stage and almost killed at Peekskill, New York, in 1949. Subsequently, passports were revoked from Robeson, Du Bois, and American Communists. The United States State Department sent its agents all over the world to tell lies about how improvements were being made for U.S. Negroes and how wrong Robeson, Du Bois, and Patterson were...."

546. Bently, Eric, Editor. Thirty Years of Treason: Excerpts From Hearings Before the House Committee on Un-American Activities, 1938-1968. New York: Viking Press, 1971, pp. 768-789, 977-980.

Paul Robeson's hearing before a Subcommittee of the Committee on Un-American Activities is included in this collection. Robeson appeared before the Committee on June 12, 1956. Robeson was sub-poena by the Committee and asked to surrender his American pass-port. The committee attempted to prove that Robeson was a Communist. It did not. The activist wanted to read a prepared statement before the committee but it refused to hear it. His statement is included as appendix 3 in this book. The con-clusion of Robeson's statement gives the essence of the whole document: "By continuing the struggle at home and abroad for peace and friendship with all of the world's people, for an end to colonialism, for full citizenship for Negro Americans, for a world in which art and culture may abound, I intend to continue to win friends for the best in American life."

547. Robinson, Jackie. I Never Had It Made. New York: G.P. Putnam's Sons, 1972, pp. 94-98.

The baseball player recalls his testimony before the House Un-American Activities Committee and his reactions to the statement made by Paul Robeson declaring that Blacks would not fight Russia for America. He told the committee "if Mr. Robeson actually made that statement, it sounded very silly to me but that he had a right to his personal views. People shouldn't get scared and think that one negro among 15,000,000 of us, speaking to a Communist group in Paris, could speak for the rest of the race." The statements were made in 1949 and twenty years later, the writer argues that he had grown wiser and closer to painful truths about America's destructiveness. He concludes: "And I do have increased respect for Paul Robeson who, over the span of that twenty years, sacrificed himself, his career, and the wealth and comfort he once enjoyed because, I believe, he was sincerely trying to help his people."

548. Starobin, Joseph R. American Communism in Crisis, 1943-1957. Cambridge: Harvard University Press, 1972, pp. 211-213, 295n.

It was pointed out that the most dramatic and poignant case of the dilemma in which the American left found itself - the personi-fication of its dedication and its mistaken course - involved the most famous baritone of the generation, Paul Robeson. He was internationally acclaimed by the late twenties. During a sojourn in England he was among the most sought-after American artist. Returning to the United States, he was hailed by the leading

(Starobin, Joseph R.)

organizations of the Negro world as one "of the tallest trees in
the forest." The N.A.A.C.P. awarded him its Spingarn Medal. He
was included naturally in National Citizens' P.A.C. during the
1944 campaign, states Starobin. By 1947, he had renounced the
concert stage to devote himself to the civil rights movement.
He took an active part in the formation of the Progressive Party,
and his prestige had much to do with the support Wallace received
from a large number of Negro figures, declares the author.
Robeson moved increasingly to the left and became associated in
1948 with Dr. W.E.B. Du Bois (who had by then broken with the
N.A.A.C.P., which he had helped found fifty years earlier) to form
the Council on African Affairs. This body soon became the
operational center for the association of left-minded Negro figures.
Robeson's preoccupation had an increasingly global cast, with a
strong pan-African emphasis. His sense of world mission, stemming
from his position as a "world citizen," tended to blur the specific
situation in the United States in his own mind. It was natural
that he should appear with a predominantly left wing U.S. delegation at the first gathering of the World Committee of the
Partisans of Peace in Paris, the agency which became the vehicle
of the 1949 peace campaign, surmises the writer. Starobin concludes: "A hero to the left wing throughout the world, Robeson
stood his ground at home, virtually enchained and on increasingly narrow ground. (All this coincided with the time when he was
losing his voice.) Increasingly Robeson came to see himself as a
world citizen for the very reason that his own land, including
a large proportion of his own people, did not give him support."

549. Hambry, Alonzo L. Beyond the New Deal: Harry S. Truman and
      American Liberalism. New York: Columbia University Press, 1973,
      pp. 102, 216.

      It was pointed out that the Win-the-Peace Conference which
      assembled in Washington, D.C. in early April of 1946, was initiated
      by Paul Robeson and others. The conference demonstrated the con-
      tinuing appeal of the wartime alliances and popular Front. The
      author states that Robeson was widely considered a fellow traveler
      of Communism. The author asserts that Robeson led the National
      (Henry) Wallace -- for President Committee.

550. Fax, Elton C. Through Black Eyes. Journeys of a Black Artist to
      East Africa and Russia. New York: Dodd, Mead & Co., 1974, pp.
      128-130, 150.

      The author discusses how the Soviet citizens reacted to Paul
      Robeson and how the actor reacted to them. They accepted Robeson
      as one of them. In many of the foreign countries that he travelled,
      he became conscious of the same human warmth and sincere comrade-
      ship toward him as a Black man that Robeson had felt in the Soviet
      Union. Robeson had repeatedly delcared that the only time in his
      life that he really felt that he was a "free" man was when he
      was in the Soviet Union.

551. Fried, Richard M. Men Against McCarthy. New York: Columbia
      University Press, 1976, pp. 111, 119, 137.

      There are several references to Paul Robeson and his support for
      "radical causes." It was stated that Robeson presided at a
      Communist-oriented fund-raising dinner. The author declares that
      the 1950 campaign witnessed unusual amounts of scurrility, dis-
      tortion, and redbaiting. He also asserts that "so many Democrats
      seemingly shared the banquet platform with Paul Robeson that
      that worthy must never have enjoyed a meal in domestic solitude."

552. Dennis, Peggy. The Autobiography of An American Communist: A
      Personal View of a Political Life, 1925-1975. Westport, Conn.:
      Lawrence Hill, 1977, pp. 119, 120, 244, 255.

      The author discusses her and her husband's friendship with Paul
      Robeson and Eslands Robeson. Dennis states that strongly affected
      by what Robeson had seen on his first visit to the Soviet Union,
      powerfully moved by the Spanish Civil War and the growing show-
      down with Fascism around the world, and developing from a cul-
      tural nationalist into seeing the Negro struggle as part of the
      international socialist struggle, Paul had decided to go home,
      more activist than artist.

553. Buckley, William F., Jr. A Hymnal: The Controversial Arts.
      New York: G.P. Putnam's Sons, 1978, pp. 159-161.

      This two and one-eighth page article was entitled "Commemorating
      Paul Robeson" and was dated February 14, 1976. The writer
      argues:
            Robeson never cared for civil rights in general.
            He was prophetically right in denouncing Jim Crow.
            He said he desired civil rights for American Negroes.
            But it cannot even be assumed that there was a
            genuine purity in his attachment to black rights,
            for all his talk about his identification with
            black people everywhere in the world. Because when
            such African states as he praised - Ghana, in parti-
            cular - systematically denied civil rights to other
            black citizens, there was no protest from Robeson.
            Robeson was, quite simply, a Communist fellow-
            traveler, whose service to the Soviet Union began
            in the mid-Thirties, who took his son there to
            school in the late Thirties, who accepted a Peace
            Prize from Stalin in 1952, who denied in 1946 that
            he was a Communist but a year later invoked the
            Fifth Amendment when asked the question again; who
            was denied a passport when Dean Acheson was Secretary
            of State - Acheson being the premier anti-McCarthyite
            in government; who, even when the State Department
            authorized him to visit Canada, was denied entrance
            into Canada....

554. Caute, David. <u>The Great Fear: The Anti-Communist Purge Under
      Truman and Eisenhower.</u> New York: Simon and Schuster, 1978,
      pp. 45, 161-166, 176, 178, 247-248, 242, 397, 483, 580.

      Various references and made throughout the book to Paul Robeson
      and his relationship to Russia as well as the Communist's Party.
      There is some discussion of the "Peekskill Incident" and Robeson
      involvement in it. The author states that Paul Robeson, the focal
      point of the Peekskill riots, symbolized the convergence of two
      threats to the American Celebration: <u>le rouge et le noir.</u> Caute
      also recounts Robeson's involvement with House Committee on Un-
      American Activities. The author declares that perhaps the most
      celebrated case affecting a public entertainer and the denying of
      a United States passport by the State Department was that of Paul
      Robeson. The passport he had held since 1922 was revoked in
      August, 1950. In 1955, Robeson refused to submit a non-Communist
      affidavit. He did not get his passport back until 1958.

555. Haywood, Harry. <u>Black Bolshevik: Autobiography of an Afro-
      American Communist.</u> Chicago: Liberator Press, 1978, pp. 558,
      564-565, 581, 594, 619.

      The author states that he was able to finish the above book be-
      cause he was subsidized by Paul Robeson. He declares that
      Robeson gave him a hundred dollars a month to live on while he
      completed the manuscript. According to Mr. Haywood, Robeson was
      sympathetic to what he was doing and anxious to see the book, the
      first of its kind by a Black Marxist, in print. The writer also
      argues that Robeson's book, <u>Here I Stand,</u> was an excellent ex-
      position of his political view as a militant anti-imperialist and
      class-conscious righter....

556. Bart, Philip, Editor. <u>Highlights of a Fighting History: 60 Years
      of The Communist Party, USA.</u> New York: International Publishers,
      1979, pp. 82, 168, 205-207, 243, 254, 258, 275, 286, 292, 390.

      Various references are made to Paul Robeson and his support for
      the Communist Party. Excerpts of Robeson's speech, "American
      Negroes in the War" that was delivered in November, 1943, at the
      Twelfth Annual Herald-Tribune Forum is included in this collection.
      It was also stated that Robeson led a delegation to the office of
      the Secretary General of the United Nations in New York City in
      1951 and presented a petition for the Relief from a crime of the
      United States Government Against the Negro People.

6. FILMS

557. Garvey, Marcus. <u>A Grand Speech of Honorable Marcus Garvey at</u>
      <u>Kingsway Hall, London, Denouncing the Moving Picture Propaganda to</u>
      <u>Discredit the Negro</u>. London: Black Men Publishing Co., 1939.
      (Pamphlet).

      Garvey spent a great deal of time denouncing Paul Robeson, the
      leading black actor of the 1920's and 1930's. The leader argues
      that Robeson's roles in moving pictures demeaned Black people.

558. Nobel, Peter. <u>The Negro in Films</u>. London: Shelton Robinson, 1948,
      pp. 13, 16, 18, 23, 25, 48, 54-58, 61, 64, 69, 94, 103, 109, 111-
      125, 128, 138-147, 148, 151, 154, 157, 164, 165, 169, 173-174,
      177, 183, 184, 187, 189, 210, 220, 222, 223.

      The writer points out that "Sanders of The River," was the most
      unfortunate film Robeson ever made. The actor plays Bosambo, a
      native tool employed by the White District Commissioner to keep the
      African tribes under British dominance. Neither Robeson nor his
      critics were happy about this film. Robeson announced his in-
      tention not to make further movies of this kind. Nobel also
      states that Robeson's wife, Eslanda Robeson, appeared in three
      films with her husband: "Borderline" (1930), "Big Fella" (1937),
      and "Jericho," (1938). The author states: "An idealist, he was
      a wonderful speaker who talked eagerly of his hopes and am-
      bitions, declaring passionately, 'If I can build up the great
      tragic figure of Brutus Jones so that he becomes the basis of
      tragic importance for the audience - make him a human figure -
      then tear him down in the subsequent scene; if the audience,
      moved by his degeneration, his struggles, his fate, by his
      emotions - a Negro's emotions - admire and then pity this Negro -
      they must know then that he is human, that they are human, that
      we are all human beings together.'" Mr. Nobel argues that on
      another occasion Robeson said: "If I can make people realize
      fully the pitiful struggle of Jim Harris in 'All God's Chillun
      Got Wings' and reduce them to tears for him at the end - weeping
      because a Negro has suffered - I will have done something to make
      them realize, even if only subconsciously and for a few moments,
      that Negroes are the same kind of people they themselves are,
      suffer as they suffer, weep as they weep, that all this arbitrary
      separation because of colour is unimportant," concludes the
      author.

559. Jerome, Victor J.   <u>The Negro in Hollywood Films</u>. New York:
      Masses and Mainstream, 1950, 64 pp.

      On page 59 of this pamphlet the writer states that artists of the
      stature of Paul Robeson, Charles Gilpin and Canada Lee expressed
      the burning resentment of their people toward the Hollywood racist
      pattern by spurning roles that maligned the Negro. It was also
      suggested that Robeson and other Black actors should be allowed
      to portray characters without regard to color, like - Hamlet as
      well as Othello. "It denied to him the heritage of world culture,

(Jerome, Victor J.)

even the full treasure of our common language," concludes
Mr. Jerome.

560. Hughes, Langston and Milton Meltzer. Black Magic: A Pictorial
      History of the Negro in American Entertainment. Englewood Cliffs,
      N.J.: Prentice-Hall, Inc., 1968, pp. 107, 110, 113, 126, 131,
      140-144, 336, 285, 301, 218, 336, 339, 348.

      Various references are make to Paul Robeson throughout this book.
      The editors point out that Robeson appeared in several films in
      the 1930's, all of them made in England. His best was "Proud
      Valley," in which he played a miner in a Welsh village. In 1943,
      after the success as "Othello" on Broadway, he made "Tales of
      Manhattan" in Hollywood. Disappointed in the stereotyped out-
      come, he refused all offers to make additional American films of
      that kind.

561. Lindenmeyer, Otto. Black History: Lost, Stolen, or Strayed.
      New York: Avon Books, 1970, pp. 184-185.

      Writing on the chapter "Hollywood in Black," the author surmises
      that "The Emperor Jones," is memorable both in terms of its re-
      cognition of the Black presence as a theme permeating American
      life, and because it featured America's most mature and com-
      manding Black actor, Paul Robeson, in the title role as a star
      among White actors. Ciritical acclaim could not make the movie
      a financial success. Moreover, it was successfully barred in
      the South.

562. Manwell, Roger, et.al., Editors. The International Encyclopedia of
      Film. London: Rainbird Reference Books Limited, 1972, pp. 244,
      245, 419.

      There is mentioning of Paul Robeson appearing in London in the film
      "The Proud Valley," about Welsh miners. There is also a photo of
      Robeson in a scene from the movie that was made in 1940. A short
      biographical sketch is also given of the actor. The writer states
      that he was "notable for his massive physique and deep reverberant
      voice." It lists seven movies that he appeared in.

563. Mapp, Edward. Blacks in American Films: Today and Yesterday.
      Metuchen, N.J.: Scarecrow Press, Inc., 1972, pp. 23-24, 33-34.

      The writer argues that Paul Robeson's film recreation of his stage
      success in Eugene O'Neill's "Emperor Jones" in 1933, had been a
      landmark for the Negro in films. The part of Brutus Jones was most
      demanding, requiring rotating historionic demonstrations of
      humility, strength, suspicion and fear, argues Mapp. Negro
      cinematic progress in the thirties is actually a tale of ex-
      ceptions surmises the author. "Tales of Mahhattan" was another
      motion picture that marked a backward step for the Negro in
      American films. As though the "Jim Crow" treatment was not
      sufficiently insulting, the script required Paul Robeson and Ethel
      Waters to expend their professional talents on an incredible

(Mapp, Edward)

episode, states the author. A coat containing considerable
money is dumped from an airplane flying over some shacks inhabited by Southern Negroes. "A tasteless and naive sequence
saw such eminent artists as Paul Robeson, Ethel Waters ....
demeaning themselves by impersonating superstitious 'niggers,'
thanking the Lord for his goodness in sending them the money
from the skies, praying, kneeling, sobbing, and behaving generally
in the same old credulous, sub-human manner," concludes Mr. Mapp.

564. Vaughn, Robert. Only Victims: A Study of Show Business Black-
      listing. New York: G.P. Putnam's Sons, 1972, pp. 141, 204, 217-
      221, 234-235, 270-272.

Various references are made to Paul Robeson. Chapter VI is entitled "The Paul Robeson-Arthur Miller Passport Investigation,
1956, and the Most Recent 1957-58 Show Business Hearings." The
author discusses Robeson's appearance before the United States
Congress House Committee on Un-American Activities. Vaughn
declares that Robeson gave one of the most emotional, pro-Russia
exhortations of any entertainment figure who had ever appeared
before the Committee. He also states that honors proffered
Robeson that unquestionably gave the committee members pause were
the Stalin Peace Prize and his being named honorary professor
at the Moscow State Conservatory of Music. The writer surmises
that Robeson was in the best theatrical tradition of the Hollywood Ten, demonstrating sarcasm, irascibility, rudeness, and
generally unsavory and unacceptable behavior publicly before a
Congressional committee.

565. Bogle, Donald. Toms, Coons, Mulattoes, Mammies and Bucks: An
      Interpretive History of Blacks in American Films. New York:
      Viking Press, 1973, pp. xi, 25, 31, 33, 35, 60, 70, 94-100, 102,
      119, 129, 138, 146, 147, 156, 161, 172, 184, 220.

Various references are made to Paul Robeson throughout the book.
There is one section, "Paul Robeson: The Black Colossus," that
deals specifically with the actor. The writer argues that Paul
Robeson became the First of the controversial Black political
prisoners, the first of our great Black Artists to have his art
denied him because of his political beliefs. Because Robeson
was denied a platform on which to display his art, the legend about
him was to grow, asserts Bogle. Most of the important Paul
Robeson feature films were made abroad. He was the only Black star
of the 1930's to work in foreign pictures, where he could escape
typing - or so he thought. But like his American made films, they
also seldom met with his approval, declares Bogle. He concludes
that because Paul Robeson was one of the few Black actors to
triumph in an independently produced Black film he now serves as
a lead-in for the next great phase of Blacks in films -- the period
of Black moviemakers, when independent directors and producers
made movies to tell the world what being Black was really about.

566. Landay, Eileen. Black Film Stars. New York: Drake Publishers,
      Inc., 1973, pp. 11, 20, 38, 46, 49-52, 66, 93, 101, 189.

      Various references are made to Paul Robeson throughout this work.
      The author surmises that Lena Horne found herself blacklisted from
      television in the early 1950's because of her friendship with Paul
      Robeson and her work with the Council for African Affairs, of
      which Robeson was chairman. The author compares Black actor
      Juano Hernandez to Robeson; and states "as a man Hernandez is
      reminiscent of Robeson; as a performer, he brought his talent to
      all the roles he played. But never did the parts measure up to
      the stature of the man. Landay concludes that perhaps one day
      they'll make a movie about Bert Williams or Paul Robeson or Juano
      Hernandez that will tell the real story of Blacks in films.

567. Murray, James P. To Find An Image: Black Films From Uncle Tom
      To Super Fly. Indianapolis: Bobbs-Merrill Co., 1973, pp. ix,
      9, 10, 11, 17.

      The writer states that it was Oscar Michaux, a Black producer and
      director who first cast Paul Robeson in a film. Mr. Murray also
      states that "The Emperor Jones," which starred Paul Robeson, was
      the first film about Blacks to spark serious critical evaluation.
      Reviews on the film were divided, but nearly all were compli-
      mentary to Paul Robeson, concludes the author.

568. Leab, Daniel J. From Sambo to Superspade: The Black Experience
      in Motion Pictures. Boston: Houghton Mifflin Co., 1975, pp. 78-
      79, 93-94, 109-115, 117.

      Various references are made to Robeson throughout the book. The
      writer points out that Paul Robeson made his movie debut in a
      Oscar Micheaux film, "Body and Soul," released in 1925. It was
      stated that Robeson later regretted his involvement with Micheaux,
      a Black film producer, because the producer and the film received
      no mention by any of the biographers of Robeson. The author dis-
      cusses Robeson's various European and American films. Robeson did
      not like or want to play stereotype roles and tried to alter them,
      but with limited success. Much of the data in this book on
      Robeson have appeared in other publications dealing with Blacks
      in films.

569. Null, Gary. Black Hollywood: The Negro in Motion Pictures.
      Secaucus, N.J.: Citadel Press, 1975, pp. 43, 66-69, 76-79, 117,
      135.

      The writer surmises that it was a measure of Black Hollywood's
      progress that within a few years of the appearance of "The
      Emperor Jones," Robeson had become "the most sought-after Black
      actor in the world." "The Emperor Jones" was the first vehicle
      for a Black star whose supporting players were white, concludes
      Null. Scenes from several of Paul Robeson's films are included
      in this work.

570. Patterson, Lindsay, Compiler. Black Films and Film-Makers: A
      Comprehensive Anthology From Stereotype to Superhero. New York:
      Dodd, Mead & Co., 1975, pp. 11, 12, 13, 18, 32, 121, 129, 130,
      131.

      The article, "The Negro and The Cinema," written in 1939 surmises
      that there was nearly universal satisfaction with Mr. Paul Robeson's
      acting in the title role in the cinema version of Mr. Eugene
      O'Neill's "Emperor Jones," but it is certainly not unjust to say
      that this satisfaction was prompted by Mr. Robeson's magnetic
      personality as a singer rather than by any severely critical ap-
      praisal of his talents as an actor, states the writer. For not
      ever the cognoscenti will deny that Mr. Robeson has never been an
      "actor's actor," despite the host of imitative Hamlets who have
      endeavored to follow in the wake of his success. He is mani-
      festly not an artist so finished in his command of the technique
      of acting that he has made a genuine and lasting contribution to
      the most ephemeral of all arts.... The writer suggests that Mr.
      Robeson's acting was limited to the spontaneous impression, the
      winning acquiescence obtained by a personal idiosyncrasy, such as
      his smile. His interpretation of a role is, in no disparaging
      sense, profoundly superficial by its reduction of an attribute
      of character to the lowest common denominator; in being bereft
      of subtlety, however, it has the virtue of imparting a ready
      understanding, and this merit is not to be dispised in an age
      when many arts are ingrown, afflicted with intellectual paralysis
      and spiritual anaemia, unstimulated by any flow of common values
      commonly understood, states the writer. Mr. Robeson is not,
      therefore, in the great tradition of Negro acting, to which actors
      like the late Richard B. Harrison(the original "De Lawd" of Green
      Pastures) or the late Charles Gilpin (the earliest Emperor Jones)
      belonged, or an earlier Shakespearean actor like Ira Aldridge, who
      played Aaron the Moor and Othello in the nineteenth century.
      Whatever his ultimate evaluation as an artist, Mr. Robeson un-
      doubtedly broke new ground with his "Emperor Jones," though this
      innovation was not fully appreciated by all Negroes, concludes
      the article. It was also stated that Robeson wanted to play the
      part of Joe Louis in a film based upon his career.

571. Wynn, Neil. The Afro-American and The Second World War. New York:
      Holmes and Meier Publishers, Inc., 1975, pp. 80, 88, 96.

      The writer states that Paul Robeson along with other Black actors
      brought pressure to the film industry and refused to accept parts
      which denigrated the members of their race. Robeson did sing war
      songs during World War II. His wartime "A Ballard for Americans"
      was an enormously popular song on the subject of democracy ac-
      cording to Dr. Wynn. It was during the war years, 1943-1945, that
      Paul Robeson appeared in "Othello." This production achieved the
      longest recorded run of any Shakespearian drama.

572. Cripps, Thomas. Slow Fade to Black: The Negro in American Film,
     1900-1942. New York: Oxford University Press, 1977, pp. 95, 113,
     191-193, 209-210, 216, 220, 230, 257, 267, 293-294, 310, 315-320,
     322, 352, 376, 383-384.

     Paul Robeson made several films in Britain in hopes of portraying
     Blacks in a more positive image. That, however, did not occur in
     the films. The author states that the reason for Robeson's
     failure to touch Afro-Americans from his foreign platform can only
     be guessed. Certainly the remoteness of European racial experience
     from American and the snubs Americans exhibitors would give any
     foreign film defused his message. But other more personal problems
     lay below the surface. Even his musical and theatrical work
     frustrated him. In 1938 he announced his retirement from London's
     West End theaters in order to "be himself" and to devote himself to
     "honest roles" and "protest songs." So not only the cinema seemed
     to him off its target. Furthermore, Hollywood's product steadily
     broadened its Black dimensions. A hidden key to Robeson's
     European frustration lay in the fact that he was moving closer to
     espousal of a kind of socialist international position while at
     the same time he continued to need the applause that came to him
     as a performer. He genuinely liked living among friendly neigh-
     bors in Chelsea, states Mr. Cripps. So in the depression decade
     Hollywood's liberal drift and Robeson's ambition for racial honesty
     in European cinema were equally frustrated. If black audiences
     were to receive the rewards of a black cinema, then some third
     force would have to produce them. "Race movies," with all their
     imperfections of technique, artistic quality, and Hollywood-
     derived artifice, would revive as the hope of the thirties. Like
     all black hopes, they were threadbare. "For the 'race movies'
     could not begin to solve problems such as a suitable role for
     whites. Without whites, the requirements of dramatic construction
     created a world in which Black characters acceded to the white
     ideal of segregation, and unreal black cops, crooks, judges, and
     juries interacted in such a way as to blame Black victims for
     their social plight. Nevertheless, "race movies" could have deep
     meaning for Blacks," concludes Mr. Cripps.

573. Kreuger, Miles. Show Boat: The Story of A Classic American
     Musical. New York: Oxford University Press, 1977, pp. 20, 26,
     70-73, 100-105, 112, 113, 117, 120, 122, 124, 127, 128, 133, 134,
     143, 165, 208.

     Paul Robeson as Joe is mentioned throughout this work. There are
     many photographs of Robeson in the production of "Show Boat."
     Jerome Kern felt that Paul Robeson was the only person that could
     sing "Ol' Man River" in "Show Boat." The author states that Paul
     Robeson created a personal triumph in London in the role of Joe.

574. Sampson, Henry T. Blacks in Black and White: A Source Book on
     Black Films. Metuchen, N.J.: Scarecrow Press, 1977, pp. 124, 173,
     213, 222, 227, 234.

     Various references are made to Paul Robeson throughout this work.
     He is mentioned in his role in the movies, "Body and Soul," "The
     Emperor Jones," "Show Boat," and "Congo Raid."

575. Cripps, Thomas. Black Film as Genre. Bloomington: Indiana
      University Press, 1978, pp. 33, 34, 36, 28, 44, 66, 143-144, 148,
      150.

      Various references are made to Paul Robeson throughout this book.
      He states that by 1973, only one major performing figure, Paul
      Robeson, had been treated in a scholarly article. It was also
      pointed out that the marshalling of Black creative forces outside
      of Hollywood allow the commanding presence of Paul Robeson to come
      to the screen as "The Emperor Jones."

576. Klotman, Phyliss Rauch. Frame by Frame - A Black Filmography.
      Bloomington: Indiana University Press, 1979, pp. 43, 69, 70, 71,
      72, 163, 273, 288, 418, 447, 448, 468, 482, 513, 673.

      A description of Robeson is given in his role in films. His
      films include: "Big Fella," "Body and Soul," "Borderline,"
      "The Emperor Jones," "Jericho," "Kind Solomon's Mines," "The
      Proud Valley," "Sanders of The River," "Show Boat," "Song of
      Freedom," and "Tales of Manhattan."

                          7. LABOR MOVEMENTS

577. Marshall, Ray. The Negro and Organized Labor. New York: John
      Wiley & Sons, 1965, p. 31.

      The author states that Paul Robeson and other representatives of
      Negro organizations attacked the American Federation of Labor
      (AFL) as being against Negroes.

578. Foner, Philip S. Organized Labor and The Black Worker, 1619-1973.
      New York: Praeger Publishers, 1974, pp. 282, 294-295.

      The author points out that in the summer of 1947 Local 22 was en-
      gaged in a strike for a new agreement with R.J. Reynolds in
      Winston-Salem, North Carolina, employing 11,000 workers about
      equally divided between black and white. The House Un-American
      Activities Committee (the Dies Committee, later HUAC) began in-
      bestigating the leaders of Local 22 on the grounds that it was a
      "Communist-dominated union." The investigation made headlines
      in the Winston-Salem press, but the tobacco workers were not in-
      timidated. On July 1, Paul Robeson, the militant black performer,
      spoke and sang at a mass meeting of 12,000 in Winston-Salem at
      which the theme was "full support for Local 22." The strike was
      won, and in the agreement between Reynolds and Local 22, wages
      were increased and working hours reduced. Shortly thereafter,
      as a result of Local 22's campaign to register its members to
      vote, Winston-Salem became the first Southern city in the twen-
      tieth century to send a Black (the Reverend Kenneth Williams) to
      the City Council. In 1950, Paul Robeson attended the National
      Labor Conference for Negro Rights. He delivered a powerful
      speech in which he denounced the cold war and the anti-Communist

(Foner, Philip S.)

witch hunts for their adverse impact on the conditions of Negro
Labor, condemned imperialist aims to continue domination of
Africa, and called for a return to peaceful relations between
the United States and the socialist countries. Robeson predicted
that black labor, supported by the whole Negro people together
with progressive white working men and women, could "save the
labor movement, CIO and AF of L," from the leaders who were betraying it, concludes Dr. Foner.

8. LEADERSHIP

579. Brawley, Benjamin. The Negro Genius. New York: Dodd, Mead &
      Co., 1937, pp. 294-296, 310.

      There is one section on Paul Robeson. The author states that in
      one interview Robeson declares: "I believe there is no such thing
      in England and America as co-operation from the NAACP point of
      view. Our freedom is going to cost so many lives that we mustn't
      talk about the Scottsboro case as one of sacrifice. When we talk
      of freedom we don't discuss lives. Before the Negro is free there
      will be many Scottsboros. The Communist emphasis in that case is
      right." It thus appears that Mr. Robeson's thinking is as in-
      dependent as his singing is superb, concludes the author.

580. Himer, Charlotte. Famous in Their Twenties. New York: Associated
      Press, 1942, pp. 91-101.

      One section in this collection is entitled, "Let My People Go:
      Paul Robeson." The author discusses Robeson's childhood from
      brother's and father's recollections. It was pointed out that
      in the play "Emperor Jones," in some place, Robeson was supposed
      to whistle, and he could not. He tried singing. The producers
      decided he would have to instead. That is how Robeson's singing
      began to attract public attention, according to Miss Himer. She
      concludes: In spite of his success, and in spite of his unusual
      knowledge, Paul Robeson remains humble in his faith....   Fame
      has not made him vain, but has given him a great sense of ob-
      ligation, which he has accepted earnestly.   'The further I go,'
      he says, 'the better it will be for my race,' That is Paul's
      mission."

581. Ottley, Roi. "New World A-Coming": Inside Black America. Boston:
      Houghton Mifflin Co., 1943, pp. 61, 240-241.

      The writer states that Paul Robeson was an individual Black leader,
      who by his acts, inspired the masses to greater racial solidarity.
      He points out that one night in Kansas City, Paul Robeson inter-
      rupted his concert to deliver a spirited lecture against race se-
      gregation to a startled white audience. Said the baritone: "I
      have made it a lifelong habit to refuse to sing in Southern states

(Ottley, Roi)

or anywhere that audiences are segregated. I accepted this engagement under the guarantee that there would be no segregation.
Since many local leaders of my own race have urged me to fill this
engagement, I shall finish the concert, but I am doing so under
protest." This sort of pluck has made much of an impression on
Negroes. Later, when Robeson publicly defended the Russian invasion of Finland, the Pittsburgh Courier had this to say
editorially: "It is refreshing when a Negro of prominence dis-
dains to follow the crowd for the sake of popularity and imperils
his position for principle. Our hats are off to Paul Robeson,"
concludes the author.

582. Embree, Edwin R. 13 Against the Odds. New York: Viking Press,
      1944, pp. 243-261.

      There is one section in this work entitled "Paul Robeson Voice of
      Freedom." Mr. Embree argues that Robeson returned to the United
      States in 1939 determined to give his time and his talents to
      fighting Fascism at home as well as abroad. The author continues
      to state, that since 1939, Robeson had been speaking and singing
      at meetings through out the country stressing freedom and demo-
      cracy in all his talks.

583. Myrdal, Gunnar. An American Dilemma: The Negro Problem and
      Modern Democracy. New York: Harper & Brothers, Publishers,
      1944, pp. 734, 735, 988, 994, 1184.

      The author points out that great singers like Paul Robeson and
      others have their prestige augmented by the eager virations of
      pride and hope from the whole Negro people acting as a huge
      sounding board. He declares that when Paul Robeson and Richard
      Wright sometimes discuss general aspects of the Negro problem,
      they do so only after study and consideration. These two have
      deliberately taken up politics as a major interest, states
      Myrdal.

584. Adams, Julius J. The Challenge: A Study in Negro Leadership.
      New York: Wendall Malliet and Co., 1949, pp. 34-38.

      The writer declares that because he is dynamic and dramatic, and
      because he is able and courageous, Robeson could easily step into
      a vacuum left open by the failures of others. Even with his de-
      finite leaning toward the Soviet Union, Robeson conceivably
      could take over the leadership of the Negro in America. Adams
      suggests that whether he does will depend upon the program - or
      lack of program - offered by other Negro leaders, and the action
      and attitude of the American leadership, the public and the
      politicians. If America doesn't offer something better than it
      now does for the Negro in order that the middle-of-the-road
      Negro leader will be able both to provide hope and show progress
      in racial advancement, the nation might as well settle itself
      down and prepare to deal with Paul Robeson or others like him,
      concludes the author.

585. Berry, Brewton. Race and Ethnic Relations. Boston: Houghton
      Mifflin Co., 1951, p. 140.

      The author concludes that Paul Robeson and Langston Hughes both
      use art as a weapon of protest, but their techniques are worlds
      apart.

586. Kempton, Murray. Part of Our Time: Some Ruins and Monuments of
      the Thirties. New York: Simon and Schuster, 1955, pp. 238-260.

      The writer discusses Paul Robeson along with several other Blacks
      in the 1930's; Bessie Smith, Marcus Garvey, A. Philip Randolph,
      Benjamin Davis, Thomas T. Patterson. The author gives a dis-
      torted picture of Paul Robeson. He declares: "He (Paul Robeson)
      came to Harlem only upon special occasions, almost always for
      assemblages honoring the Negro's putative identification with
      the Soviet Union. He would arrive on the platform just before
      he was to sing; he would rumble his words about this land and our
      people, making his great entrance and his great exit, on stage
      only when the spotlight was upon him; and then he would go back
      to Connecticut." The author continues to make absurd comments
      about Robeson. Kempton argues: "Paul Robeson, of course, did
      not know the Negro. He could not have been expected to; he had
      gone far away and he had taken a return road along which very few
      American Negroes traveled. He had, in fact, almost ceased to be
      an American Negro at all (Underlining the compiler's). In the
      winter of 1949, speaking from Paris, a measure of the distance
      between him and them, he promised that the fifteen million Negroes
      of the United States would never fight against the Soviet Union."
      The writer concludes: ".... And so Paul Robeson wandered, an
      African god without votaries, an emperor without subjects.
      These was an absolute nothing between him and the people for whom
      he affected to speak."

587. Wynn, Daniel Webster. The NAACP Versus Negro Revolutionary Pro-
      test. New York: Exposition Press, 1955, pp. 14-15, 17, 30, 31,
      32, 47, 57, 59-61, 63, 66, 68, 69-74, 76-77, 78-79, 83, 84.

      The writer states that the purpose of this book is to compare the
      nature and effectiveness of the leadership in Negro protest action
      as represented by the National Association for the Advancement of
      Colored People and in Negro protest revolutionary antagonism as
      exemplified by the leadership of Paul Robeson.

588. Redding, Saunders. On Being Negro in America. New York: Bantam
      Books, 1964, p. 17.

      The author states that the radicals who take the position that
      radicalism is the highest, brightest star in the ideological
      heavens, are very proud of the caliber of Paul Robeson and others.

589. Cruse, Harold. The Crisis of the Negro Intellectual. New York: William Morrow & Co., 1967, pp. 17, 23, 27, 35-36, 106, 115, 186, 219, 225, 227-231, 235-237, 240-242, 248-249, 274, 279, 285-301, 306, 328, 340, 409-410, 418, 486, 510, 521, 540, 561.

The author attacks Paul Robeson throughout the book. Cruse states that Robeson turned out to be neither very independent nor much of a leader. He also points out that Robeson wasi not at all an original thinker. His effectiveness was hampered by a considerable idealistic neivete about racial politics in America, according to the writer. He concludes that although the inside gossip had it that the Communist were having considerable difficulty controlling him, the number of articles appearing in Freedom by and about Communists, revealed that he was in fact pretty much under their control. The writer spends a great deal of time discussing the newspaper, Freedom, that was edited by Robeson between 1951-1955. He declares that Robeson had sincere intentions of teaching the masses, through his newspaper, but there was very little printed in his newspaper that could have appealed to them.

590. Editors of Ebony. The Black Revolution. Chicago: Johnson Publishing Co., 1970, pp. 5, 66.

The writers state that no one since Paul Robeson has defied American society, except Ameer(Leroi Jones) Baraka. It was also pointed out that Paul Robeson was a symbol of Black Art and Black Liberation.

591. Loye, David. The Healing of A Nation. New York: W.W. Norton & Co., 1971, pp. 53, 125, 245, 266.

The writer suggests that few Americans have cared so deeply or suffered so greatly for the American Dream than Paul Robeson. Neither Black nor White understood how this could be true if he went about praising Russia and joining peace committies in the thirties and forties, and so he was literally hounded and driven from this country. Mr. Loye argues that today, after two decades of civil rights drives have at last forced Americans to recognize the true depth and horror of their racism, and as the development of stockpiling of universal atomic death continues unchecked, Robeson no longer seems a radical. He concludes: "He was foolish and blind at times, but it was a small weakness in a large man. In all too many ways his only crime seems to have been that he spoke too openly and too soon of what he saw in the land - of the very blind."

592. Henderson, Lenneal J., Jr., Editor. Black Political Life in The United States: A Fist As The Pendulum. San Francisco: Chandler Publishing Co., 1972, pp. 60, 125, 126.

The writer points out that Paul Robeson even, despite his unfortunate politics, is well regarded because Negroes - even conservative, Republican, middle-class, affluent Negroes regard him as having sacrificed a remunerative career out of racial anguish. It was also stated that the more militant the figure, such as Paul Robeson, Frederick Douglass, and Marcus Garvey, the less

(Henderson, Lenneal J. Jr.)

likely he is to be accorded respect from white Americans.

593. Wynn, Daniel W. The Black Protest Movement. New York: Philo-
      sophical Library, 1974, pp. 36-38, 69-98.

      Chapter Three, "Revolutionary Protest Action," discusses Paul
      Robeson. A lot of discussion is devoted to W.E.B. Du Bois'
      relationship with Robeson and both of their relationships with
      the Communist Party. The author gives Du Bois, rather than
      Robeson, credit for the philosophy of the protest revolutionary
      movement. He states that Du Bois endeavored to get his opinions
      expressed through the writing of books which especially emphasized
      the race problem; through addresses in America and abroad on the
      problem; attempts at forming organizations on peace and African
      affairs; and by active participation in organizations that he felt
      to be helpful to the cause. On the other hand, according to
      Rev. Wynn, Robeson's efforts were confined to his singing and
      addresses on the problem in America and abroad; to written contri-
      butions to pamphlets, newspapers and such media, including the
      printing of his speeches in pamphlet form; to minor efforts at
      organization, and participation in organizations that he felt to
      be helpful to the cause, asserts the writer. The author declares
      that "As far as he (Paul Robeson) was concerned, the Soviet people
      had made sacrifices for African-Americans, and for this, he loved
      them." This book has no Index.

594. Walton, Richard J. Henry Wallace, Harry Truman, and the Cold War.
      New York: Viking Press, 1978, pp. 76, 160, 192, 193, 194.

      The writer argues that Paul Robeson, the legendary singer, actor,
      and social activist who was probably the best known Black man in
      the world, supported Henry Wallace for president. According to
      Walton, Robeson was one of the extraordinary men of our times,
      worked tirelessly for racial equality and world peace but even
      his unequal fame and enormous talents were no protection against
      the Cold War hysteria. In the 1950's he became unable to work,
      unable for some years to even travel, for his passport was taken
      from him by the State Department. Mr. Walton concludes: "....
      But the days of disgrace and obscurity were not upon him in 1948,
      and throughout the campaign Robeson rested scarcely more than the
      candidate. His magnetic physical presence and his magnificent
      voice were a major attraction at progressive rallies. Someday,
      soon one hopes, there will be a resurgence of interest in Robeson,
      especially among blacks for whom he could be a supreme hero."

595. Edwards, Harry. The Struggle That Must Be: An Autobiography.
      New York: MacMillan Publishing Co., 1980, pp. 205-215, 320.

      Chapter 16 in this book is entitled, "Declaration and Disengage-
      ment: A Refuse in Reflections on (Paul) Robeson." The writer dis-
      cusses the influence that Paul Robeson had on his life. He
      declares: "The more I read about this man, the more impressed I
      become with the sheer magnitude of his integrity, intellect, and
      courage. Even when I found myself in adamant disagreement with

(Edwards, Harry)

some of his assessments of and proposed solutions to the many
crises in Black America, I stood nonetheless in awe of Robeson's
monumental capacity for dedication, reasoned struggle." He also
points out that there was so much in his life that he could i-
dentify with. Robeson became a model and a hero to him,"a source
of spiritual sustenance in the difficult and sometimes depressing
period of deceleration and disengagement from a political struggle
into wnich he had poured everything he had. He became a refuge,
an inspiration, and the very embodiment of the Black athlete's long
heritage of struggle and sacrifice in pursuit of freedom and
dignity." He asserts: "My understanding of his struggles in
sport ennanced my understanding of the forces that had molded my
own life and activities. For me, Robeson's struggles within
American sport were exemplary. He was the great forerunner.
For long before the boycotts by Black collegiate athletes, long
before the courageous stand of Tommie Smith and John Carlos, long
before Curt Flood and Muhammad Ali, long before even the legendary
Jackie Robinson, there stood Paul Robeson. His is the classic
Black American sports story, and one that has influenced tremendously my vision of the Black athletes' role and responsibilities in American society. To this day, I periodically reflect
upon his sports career as a source of inspiration and example."
Edwards concludes: "....As I surveyed Robeson's life, it became
clear that the intense frustrations I'd long experienced with
racism were inevitable, that awareness has always carried pressures born of a necessity to choose sides, to elect to struggle
for self-actualization and freedom or to languish in underdevelop-
ment and oppression. In understanding Robeson, I understood that
I too was on a collision course with America from the very first
instant that I became concerned, then angry and rebellious about
the fact that being "Colored" makes a difference in this society.
Robeson taught me that conscientious struggle demands a discip-
lined fusing of personal life, profession, and politics, a unity
that can only be created and perpetuated through development of
a broad, analytical perspective on oneself and one's work in
relation to events and circumstances in this society and the
world...."

9. MUSIC

596. Mannin, Ethel. Confessions and Impressions. New York: Doubleday Doran and Co., 1930, pp. 157-161.

Chapter Eight is entitled "Paul Robeson: Portrait of a Great
Artist." The author surmises that Paul Robeson thought that a
great many Negro people thought that because the spirituals were
conceived in slavery and suffering they should not be sung any
more, and the coloured people be allowed to forget their years of
bondage; but he himself is of the opinion that whatever its
source, a thing of artistic value must be regarded solely from

(Mannin, Ethel)

that standpoint; for him it is no question of commercialising
the sufferings of his people -- "they know that," he said --
but of expressing himself through a natural medium, the songs of
his race. But that they happen to be the songs of his race is
accidental and incidental; he is too much of an artist not to be
dispassionate where aesthetic values are concerned. He has sung
the Negro spiritual to Italian audiences who could not understand
a word of them, or realize the tradition behind them, and met with
appreciative response, states Mannin. She declares, that for
Robeson: "Art is international, independent of geographic
boundaries and of race. Art is esoteric, and when Paul Robeson
sings Negro spirituals in Milan, it is not a Negro singing the
songs of his people to Italians, but a great artist expressing
himself in a medium peculiarly his own." The writer concludes:
"He intends singing European songs, and that, I think, is a good
thing, just as it is a good thing that he should be allowed to act
a part other than a Negro part, because that he happens to be a
Negro is of considerably less importance than the fact that he is
a great artist; his voice is more beautiful than any song he will
ever sing, and his personality more vital and interesting than
any role he will ever play, I think, too great a tendency to
accept him as an interesting spectacle because of his race; that
he is a Negro is an accident of birth; the supremely important
thing is that he is a magnificent artist. It is there that I
quarrel with the title of Mrs. Robeson's book. It should be not
Paul Robeson, Negro, but Paul Robeson, Artist."

597.   Kaufman, Helen Loeb and Eva B. Hansl. Artist in Music of Today.
New York: Grosset and Dunlap, 1933, p. 87.

The editors declare that although Paul Robeson is gentle of voice
and deliberate of motion, he has talents to correspond to his
appearance, dramatic and athletic ability, a keen intellect, and
a singing voice of unusual natural quality. They go on to say
that secure of his place as actor, Paul Robeson reaches out for
other worlds to conquer. Negro apirituals were then (in the
1920's) comparatively a novelty. When Robeson sang his first
program of them in New York in 1925, the throbing fervor, wide
range, and touching sincerity of his big voice, untrained though
it was, causes him at once to be hailed as a singer, surmises
the authors. There is also drawings of Robeson as well as his
signature.

598.   Hare, Maud Cuney. Negro Musicians and Their Music. Washington,
D.C.: Associated Publishers, 1936, pp. 318, 343, 371-373.

The writer points out that of all the artists of the present (1930s)
acclaim, Paul Robeson stands in the front rank, as a singer-actor.
As a musician, according to Hare, he is known as a singer of Negro
song - pieces in the vernacular; and his artistry as a vocalist
must therefore be judged in this restricted field. The author
surmises that Robeson possesses a beautiful, natural, unforced
baritone voice of great volume and his singing of the religious
racial songs has been marked with sympathetic interpretation.

(Hare, Maud Cuney)

It was also stated: "Into his voice there comes every atom of the passionate feeling which inspired the unknown composer of these melodies."

599. Locke, Alain. The Negro and His Music. Washington, D.C.: Associates in Negro Folk Education, 1936,pp. 124, 127.

The writer contends that Paul Robeson's versatile career from star athlete to Rutgers'College scholastic honors, and from folk-song singing to recitalist, actor to movie star is a symptom of an over-widening range of ambition and recognition for Negro talent. Dr. Locke states that in the three art fields that he had successfully touched, the talisman is a bass-baritone voice of exceptional timbre and a typically racial quality that has won both a popular and academic following on an international scale. "The highest point of Mr. Robeson's art, however, still resides in the ability with which his musical career started at the Greenwich Village Theatre in 1925, when with Taylor Gordon, he sang a program of Negro spirituals and work-songs with a power and vitality that was typical and revealing. For Robeson sings the Negro folk songs in their flesh and blood reality," concludes Locke.

600. Murray, Florence. The Negro Handbook. New York: Wendell Malliet & Co., 1942, pp. 217, 224, 227, 250.

Paul Robeson sang at the annual banquet of the Phi Beta Kappa Honorary Society in February, 1940. His high point in music during the year came at the Lewisohn Stadium in New York City in July when he sang the "Ballad for Americans" accompanied by the New York Philharmonic Symphony Orchestra. Applause lasted 10 minutes. Mr. Robeson had much to do with the popularizing of this patriotic number, which he introduced on the "Pursuit of Happiness" radio program in the fall of 1939. It was also mentioned that Paul Robeson was included in the Wall of Fame Honor Roll of the 1940 World's Fair. He was included because he "made notable contributions to the nation's culture and progress."

601. Embree, Edwin R. Brown Americans: The Story of A Tenth of The Nation. New York: Viking Press, 1943, pp. 194, 198, 223-229.

The author declares that Robeson's career is a fabulous story of international fame on the concert stage, in the theater, in motion pictures, in radio, of the success that has come to a simple and great hearted man who has never lost the common touch. Embree surmises that he has used his languages and his fine brain in learning all over the world how common people act and think and feel. Robeson argues in this work: "Through my singing and acting I want to make freedom ring. But most of all I want to help my homeland realize that it will grow only as it lets all its people, do their full part in making it rich and strong."

602. Van Deusen, John G. The Black Man In White America. Washington, D.C.: Associated Publishers, Inc., 1944, pp. 11, 242, 292, 293, 294, 297.

The writer declares that when one speaks of Paul Robeson it is necessary to use superlatives because in every endeavor that he undertook he excelled. He says that Robeson's most important pictures were "The Emperor Jones" and "Jericho." Mr. Van Deusen concludes that Paul Robeson, Roland Hayes, Jules Bledsoe and Marian Anderson deserve much credit for their rendition of the Spirituals.

603. Powell, Adam Clayton, Jr. Marching Blacks: An Interpretive History of The Rise of the Black Common Man. New York: Dial Press, 1945, pp. 35, 130-131.

It was pointed out that Paul Robeson, Marian Anderson and Dorothy Maynor, three Blacks, were among the ten top money makers of the concert world. They made over $100,000 a year. There is also a quote in this work contributed to Paul Robeson. A friend of Paul Robeson's once said, "Paul, everything your people are demanding is right, but it will take a hundred years." Robeson replied, "Black men, and for that matter, white men, are not going to wait a hundred years."

604. Bontemps, Arna. Story of the Negro. New York: Alfred A. Knopf, 1948, pp. 205, 206.

The writer surmises that in Paul Robeson's rise to fame more of the circumstances seemed to be accidental, for his wonderful deep voice amazed and delighted thousands of people before it had any special training. He concludes that in each field he had reached a pinnacle by the time America had reached the point of accepting a Negro actor in the leading role of Shakespeare's "Othello," and his performance in that part made history on the Broadway stage.

605. White, Walter. A Man Called White: The Autobiography of Walter White. New York: Viking Press, 1948, pp. 92, 174, 232.

The author mentions hearing Paul Robeson sing "Go Down Moses" while he was in Paris, France. He also alludes to Paul Robeson having won the N.A.A.C.P.'s Spingarn Award. According to White Paul Robeson was active in the Emergency Committee of the Entertainment Industry.

606. Ottley, Roi. Black Odyssey: The Story of The Negro in America. London: John Murray, 1949, pp. 248-250, 256, 273, 282.

The writer argues that Paul Robeson was immediately recognized as the greatest baritone singer of Negro music, after he made his debut as a concert singer at the Greenwish Village Theatre. Ottley surmises that the controversy over a scene in which a White wife kissed the hand of her Negro (Robeson) husband, in "All God's Chillun Got Wings," brought Paul Robeson forward as a public figure. Blacks also rallied to his defense but the play

(Ottley, Roi)

was unable to survive. He concludes that Paul Robeson's performance of "Othello," opposite a white actress, Uta Hagen, was
considered a milestone in the American theater.

607. Dalin, Ebba. The Voice of America: An Anthology of American
Ideas. Uppsala, Sweden: Dreyer, 1950, pp. 139-145.

There is an article by Eslanda Goode Robeson entitled "Paul
Robeson and The Provincetown Player" that was taken from her
biography, Paul Robeson, Negro. The writer discusses how Mr.
Robeson began his acting career in Eugene O'Neill's plays
"All God's Chillun Got Wings" and "The Emperor Jones."

608. Fletcher, Tom. The Tom Fletcher Story: 100 Years of the Negro
in Show Business! New York: Burdge & Co., Ltd., 1954, pp. 268,
271.

The author states that Paul Robeson was a member of the "Clef
Club." He says after Robeson's whirl with Will Cook's "Clef Club"
Orchestra the singer teamed with Carl White and Arthur Gaines in
the "Plantation Revue" starring Florence Mills. Mr. Fletcher
asserts that he cannot make it a statement of fact but he was
almost sure that Paul Robeson got his first theater experience with
the "Clef Club" outfit under the direction of Will Marion Cook.

609. Salisbury, Harrison E. American In Russia. New York: Harper &
Brothers, 1955, pp. 257-258.

The author states that he would never forget a concert which Paul
Robeson gave in the great Tchairkousky Concert Hall in Moscow
in 1949, at the height (or depth) of the ideological drive against
jazz and Western music. According to the writer, Robeson's program consisted of a potpourri of songs from various Communist
countries - a Polish number, a Russian number, a Rumanian number,
etc. The audience, however, also wanted to hear Robeson sing
"St. Louis Blues." According to Mr. Salisbury, Robeson tried to
ignore their request. Obviously he had planned his program to
meet the current ideological demands of the Party, concludes the
author. The writer also states that Robeson did not like to sing
jazz and never sang the song, "St. Louis Blues," at any concerts.

610. Lawless, Ray M. Folksingers and Folksongs in America: A Handbook
of Biography, Bibliography, and Discography. New York: Duell,
Sloan and Pearce, 1960, pp. 109, 234, 241, 242, 340, 564, 565.

Various references are made to Paul Robeson throughout the book.
The writer did not give a sketch of Paul Robeson and forty-six
other singers because they are well-known. A list of some of
Robeson's spirituals and Folksongs are included in this work.

611.   Miers, Earl Schenck. <u>The Trouble Bush</u>. Chicago: Rand McNally &
       Co., 1966, pp. 117-118, 148-152, 300.

       The author is a white Alumni of Rutgers University. He states
       that in his generation Rutgers men, who saw Robeson as a national
       celebrity, said proudly: "I go to Paul Robeson's school." When-
       ever he sang a concert in the Rutgers gym, unless one brought a
       ticket well in advance standing room in the upper balcony re-
       mained when the big night came, surmises Miers. The writer also
       asserts: "We talked about his greatness.... but not a one of us
       understood his loneliness, his heartbreak, his growing rebellion.
       No one could guess then that a day would come when angry alumni
       would demand that his name be stricken from the rolls of the
       college." The author wrote several articles and a book on Paul
       Robeson.

612.   Rollins, Charlemae. <u>Famous Negro Entertainers of Stage, Screen,</u>
       <u>and TV</u>. New York: Dodd, Mead & Co., 1967, pp. 95-99.

       The writer suggests that the rich, communicative sound of a dis-
       tinguished Negro baritone which made itself heard around the world
       was the voice of Paul Robeson. Although he preferred folk songs to
       classical music, his rendition of English, Hebrew, Russian, and
       German folk songs, often sung in the original tongue, portrayed
       the deep sincerity that made him the most famous male singer of
       Negro spirituals of his day, declares Rollins. She quotes Paul
       Robeson as declaring: "If, with my music, I can re-create for
       an audience the great sadness of the Negro slave in, for instance,
       'Sometimes I Fell Like a Motherless Child,' or if I can make them
       know the strong, gallant convict of the chain gang, make them feel
       his thirst, understand his naive boasting about his strength,
       feel the brave gaiety and sadness of 'Water Boy,' or if I can
       explain to them the simple, divine faith of the Negro in 'Weepin'
       Mary,' then I shall increase their knowledge and understanding of
       my people. They will sense that we are moved by the same emotions,
       have the same beliefs, the same longings, that, in fact, we are
       all humans together. That will be something worth working for,
       something worth doing." She concludes: "Paul Robeson is re-
       spected because of his art, vision, and understanding. He will be
       remembered for having fought for the world's peoples with his
       songs."

613.   Thomas, Jesse O. <u>My Story in Black and White: The Autobiography</u>
       <u>of Jesse O. Thomas</u>. New York: Exposition Press, 1967, pp. 142,
       152, 155.

       The writer states that Paul Robeson sang and spoke at a rally in
       Detroit, Michigan, to help sell United States War Bonds. He
       also argues that Paul Robeson as a musician made a definite contri-
       bution to Negro music.

614. Jackson, Clyde Owen. The Songs of Our Years: A Study of Negro
      Folk Music. New York: Exposition Press, 1968, p. 35.

      The writer declares that during the 1920s a number of great
      American Negro singers such as Paul Robeson, Marian Anderson and
      Jules Bledsoe were receiving a great deal of recognition and helped
      to glorify the Negro folk song.

615. Marshall, Herbert and Mildred Stock. Ira Aldridge, The Negro
      Tragedian. Carbondale: Southern Illinois University Press, 1968,
      pp. 2, 3, 22, 135, 304, 306.

      It was pointed out that Paul Robeson studies voice and diction with
      Ira Aldridge's younger daughter, Miss Amanda Ira Aldridge.
      Robeson was also to play Ira Aldridge in a film of his life; but
      the film did not materialize, because Robeson, after returning
      to the United States in the 1950's, was not permitted to leave
      again. The author called Paul Robeson "The Ira Aldridge of
      Today" (1930).

616. Patterson, Lindsay, Compiler and Editor. The Negro in Music and
      Art. New York: Publisher Co., 1968, Vol. 5, pp. 129, 198.

      There is a photo of Paul Robeson on the section that deals with
      "Famous Singers." Robeson is also compared to other great
      American Black Singers: Roland Hayes, Dorothy Maynor, and Marian
      Anderson.

617. Acheson, Dean. Present At the Creation: My Years in the State
      Department. W.W. Norton & Co., 1969, p. 130.

      The author attended the same rally that Paul Robeson did in 1945.
      Mr. Acheson was at that time serving as Under Secretary of State.
      The rally was in mid-November of 1945, and was sponsored by the
      National Council of Soviet American Friendship. He states that
      Paul Robeson and Dean Johnson were clearly the favorite two men
      of the gathering. The writer called Paul Robeson, "the great
      Negro bass who later became a Soviet citizen." The statesman con-
      cluded: ".... Paul Robeson's magnificent voice began the low
      humble of 'Ole Man River,' that moving song of the oppressed and
      hopeless. It did not end in hopelessness and resignation as the
      singer kept on rolling along, however, but in a swelling protest,
      ending on that magnificent high note of difiance produced by a
      great voice magnified by all the power of science. The crowd
      went wild."

618. Kraft, Hy. On My Way to the Theater. New York: Macmillan, 1971,
      pp. 164-165.

      The author states that for nine years the great singer and great
      American Paul Robeson was silenced, barred from public appearances
      here and deprived of the right to travel by the State Department.
      He concludes: "If God talks, it must be with the voice of
      Robeson. In this one man you find strength, conviction, compassion,
      understanding, knowledge, love, courage - greatness. When he shakes
      your hand, a transfusion takes place; you're no longer alone. To

(Kraft, Hy)

be his friend gives your life validity and meaning...."

619. Meir, August., Elliott Rudwick, and Francis L. Broderick, Editors.
      Black Protest Thought in the Twentieth Century. Indianapolis:
      Bobbs-Merrill Co., 1971. Second edition, pp. 113, 115, 357, 358.

      The editors point out that Paul Robeson's singing is truly racial.
      It was stated in an interview with John Lewis, Chairman of the
      Student Non-Violence Coordinating Committee (SNCC), that the
      masses and the Negro academic community really feel a great deal
      of understanding and love for people like Robeson and W.E.B.
      Du Bois.

620. Mingus, Charles. Beneath the Underdog. New York: Alfred A. Knopf,
      1971, pp. 351-352.

      This Black Musician gives his account of his experience with a
      European teacher who did not believe Blacks had the talent or
      ability to play European Music well. He declares: "When I was
      learning bass with Rheinschagen he was teaching me to play classi-
      cal music. He said I was close but I'd never really get it. So
      I took some Paul Robeson and Marian Anderson records to my next
      lesson and asked him if he thought those artists had got it. He
      said they were Negroes trying to sing music that was foreign to
      them. Solid, so White society has its own traditions, let'em
      leave ours to us."

621. Lovell, John Jr. Black Song: The Forge and The Flame: The Story
      of How the Afro-American Spiritual Was Hammered Out. New York:
      Macmillan Co., 1972, pp. 398, 410, 441, 442, 500, 557, 558, 561,
      577, 580.

      The author declares that one of the most accomplished of the
      spiritual singers, in his heyday, was Paul Robeson. He gave his
      first concert as a basso interpreter of spirituals in 1925. For
      five years as a singer, Paul Robeson sang only Negro folk songs.
      Mr. Lovell concludes, in part: "Robeson has sung spirituals to
      appreciative audiences all over the world. In East and West
      Germany, Russia, England, Hungary, France and elsewhere, he has
      been almost worshipped. His physical appearance, voice range
      and control, and tremendous emotional color and variety are only a
      few of the reasons why he is spiritual singer par excellence."
      There is also a short biographical sketch of Robeson.

622. Santa Barbara County Board of Education. The Emerging Minorities
      in America. Santa Barbara, Cal.: American Bibliographical
      Center - Clio Press, 1972, p. 66.

      It was pointed out that Robeson's incomparable voice and stage
      talent made him a star of first rank until after World War II.
      It was also stated that following the war his political sym-
      pathies for his American public led to his decline.

623. Henri, Florette. Black Migration: Movement North, 1900-1920. Garden City, N.Y.: Anchor Press, 1975, pp. 192-194, 339.

The author contends that the most famous of all, singer and actor, Paul Robeson, was not widely known for his singing until after 1921. In the pre-war years, however, he was a source of pride to Blacks as a college football star. Robeson won letters four times at Rutgers University and made All-American in 1917 and 1919.

624. Motley, Mary Penick. The Invisible Solider: The Experience of the Black Soldier: World War II. Detroit: Wayne State University Press, 1975, pp. 158-159.

The writer points out that Paul Robeson performed at Berchtes-garten, Germany, and received a tremendous ovation from the sol-diers. While other entertainers were treated rudely by the soldiers when they attempted to perform, Robeson had the attention of the audience. It was also pointed out that after his per-formance, he joined the outfit and had a bottle of wine with them.

625. Wilson, Conrad. The New College Encyclopedia of Music. New York: W.W. Norton and Co., 1976, Revised Edition, p. 462.

There is a one sentence reference to Paul Robeson. It states: "U.S. Black bass, world renowed for his performance of Negro songs and spirituals."

626. Ewen, David. All the Years of American Popular Music. Englewood Cliffs, N.J.: Prentice-Hall, Inc., 1977, pp. 410, 418, 422, 456.

The writer points out that the song "Gloomy Sunday" was imported from Hungary and in 1936 it was initially circulated in perfor-mances by Paul Robeson. Mr. Ewen asserts that after Robeson sang "Ballad for Americans" over CBS radio, in 1940, so many con-gratulatory telephone calls were made to radio stations featuring that program that the switchboards were jammed for hours. The song was now recorded by three major companies; that of Paul Robeson for Victor held the top spot on the recording best-selling list for months. At the RCA Victor exhibit at the New York World's Fair in 1940, so many requests were made for this song that it was soon featured regularly three times a day, states the author.

627. Fordin, Hugh. Getting To Know Him: A Biography of Oscar Hammerstein II. New York: Random House, 1977, pp. 89-90, 115, 139, 312.

The author points out that with Paul Robeson, the show, "Show Boat" was as great a success in London as it had been in New York. Fordin states that after he heard Robeson sing "Ol' Man River," he felt for five minutes that there was no other place in the world, no other time. Fordin declares that in the film version of "Show Boat,""Paul Robeson probed to be as compelling on film as he was onstage." Hammerstein told the United States Department of State that he supported Paul Robeson's right to speak, no matter what his views.

628. Horn, David. The Literature of American Music in Books and Folk
      Music Collections: A Fully Annotated Bibliography. Metuchen, N.J.:
      Scarecrow Press, 1977, pp. 48, 682, 702, A152-A154, 156, 709-711.

      This work mentions several books that discuss Paul Robeson's
      musical career. All of them are listed elsewhere in this biblio-
      graphy: Dobrin, Embree, Graham, Eslanda Goode Robeson, Hoyt,
      Seton, Woollcott.

629. Kreuger, Miles. Show Boat: The Story of A Classic American
      Musical. New York: Oxford University Press, 1977, pp. 20, 26,
      70-73, 100-105, 112, 113, 117, 120, 122, 123, 127, 128, 133, 134,
      143, 165, 208.

      Paul Robeson as Joe is mentioned throughout this work. There are
      many photographs of Robeson in the production of "Show Boat."
      Jerome Kern felt that Paul Robeson was the only person that could
      sing "Ol' Man River" in "Show Boat." The author states that Paul
      Robeson created a personal triumph in London in the role of Joe.

630. Turner, Patricia. Afro-American Singers: An Index and Pre-
      liminary Discography of Opera, Choral Music and Song. Minneapolis,
      Minn.: Challenge Productions, Inc., 1977, pp. 58-61, 233-234.

      There are several excerpts from reviews of Paul Robeson's records
      as well as selected listings of his record albums. There is a
      selected bibliography of him from collected works and books. All
      of the references, however, have appeared elsewhere and there are
      no new materials. Turner does include obituary notices from several
      newspapers and periodicals including the major Black ones. All
      references in this work on Robeson are selective.

631. Bordman, Gerald. Jerome Kern: His Life and Music. New York:
      Oxford University Press, 1980, pp. 276-277, 293, 299, 325, 356,
      400.

      It was pointed out that Paul Robeson was not to be in the cast of
      the first production of "Show Boat." Robeson was, however, later
      signed as a member of the cast. The author argues that Oscar
      Hammerstein had in mind elevating Robeson's role of Joe to some-
      thing of a one-man Greek chorus. Both Kern and Hammerstein pre-
      pared two new songs especially for Robeson to sing in the London
      production of "Show Boat." Both songs, however, were cut out of
      the London show.

632. Williamson, Joel. New People: Miscegenation and Mulattoes in the
      United States. New York: Free Press, 1980, pp. 172, 177.

      The writer states that both Paul Robeson and Charles Gilpin did much
      to shatter the traditional role of the Black actors when they so
      brilliantly played the lead role in Eugene O'Neill's "Emperor
      Jones." He concludes that in bitterness, in frustration, some
      Negro artists and intellectuals such as Du Bois and actor Paul
      Robeson turned to Marxism, Communism, and Russia for relief from
      the injustices in America.

10. OBITUARY

633. Levy, Felice, Compiler. Obituaries on File. New York: Facts on
      File, 1979, Volume 1, p. 499.

      Short obituary of Paul Robeson is presented in this work. Compiler
      states that he was a singer, actor and Black activist who won
      world fame in the theatrical role of "Othello." He died in
      Philadelphia on January 23, 1976, at the age of 77.

11. OTHELLO

634. Rogers, Joel A. World's Great Men of Color. New York: J.A.
      Rogers Publisher, 1947, Vol. II, pp. 672-678.

      Paul Robeson is included in this work under the title "Paul
      Robeson: Intellectual, Musical and Historic Prodigy." The writer
      argues that Robeson was so remarkably gifted, physically and
      mentally that development of any one of his talents would have
      been sufficient to bring him fame. Rogers devotes a great deal of
      space to newspapers' assessments of Robeson's performance in the
      play "Othello." It was pointed out that in 1944, he received an
      award from the American Academy of Arts and Letters for excellent
      diction. The author states that in 1940 Robeson discovered a new
      sound control technique. Rogers concludes that in spite of the
      world's acclaim, Robeson is as good-natured and friendly as he was
      in the Rutgers' days....

635. Young, Stark. Immortal Shadows: A Book of Dramatic Criticism.
      New York: Charles Scribner's Sons, 1948, pp. 230, 234, 235.

      The author, a drama critic, comments on Paul Robeson's role as
      "Othello," which was performed at the Shubert Theatre, October 19,
      1943. He states that Paul Robeson lacked the instinct and phrasing
      for wearing costumes per se. Young surmises that the subtle
      values of Othello Mr. Robeson at times conveys, but as often he
      does not. The critic argues that Mr. Robeson, a singer of dis-
      tinction, with the benefit of much stage experience, still lacks
      for this role the ultimate requirement, which is a fine tragic
      method. By virtue of true feeling and intensity of soul he has
      its equivalent at times, and then he is moving and deep, asserts
      the reviewer.

636. Farjeon, Herbert. The Shakespearean Scene: Dramatic Criticism.
      London: Hutchinson, 1949, p. 165.

      The critic reviews Paul Robeson's first performance as "Othello."
      He surmises: "He seemed to me .... to (lack) command. He was the
      underdog from the start. The cares of 'Old Man River' were still
      upon him. He was a member of a subject race, still dragging the
      chains of his ancestors. He was not noble enough. He was not
      stark enough. He seemed to me a very depressed Othello. The fact
      that he was a Negro did not assist him...." Mr. Farjeon concludes:
      "Shakespeare wrote this part for a white man to play and

(Farjeon, Herbert)

Mr. Robeson is not far wrong when he says that 'Shakespeare is always right.'"

637. Dalin, Ebba D., Editor. The Voice of America: An Anthology of American Ideas. Uppsala, Sweden: Dryer, 1950, pp. 139-149.

There is one section that discusses Provincetown Players that was taken from Eslanda G. Robeson's Paul Robeson, Negro. There are also some additional data on Paul Robeson. The essence of the writer's point is that Robeson was ahead of his time and spoke up for what he believed to be right.

638. Sprague, Arthur Colby. Shakespearean Players and Performances. Cambridge: Harvard University Press, 1953, p. 1.

The writer attended the production of "Othello," starring Paul Robeson. After seeing Robeson in the play he declared: "....
I was left at the close wondering whether his performance had not approached the greatness attributed to actors in other times."

639. Webster, Margaret. Shakespeare Without Tears. Cleveland: World Publishing Co., 1955. Revised Edition, pp. 22, 236.

When speaking of Paul Robeson as "Othello," the writer asserts: "When Paul Robeson stepped onto the stage for the very first time, when he spoke his very first line immediately, by his very presence, brought an incalculable sense of reality into the entire play. Here was a great man, a man of simplicity and strength; here also was a Black man. We believed that he could command the armies of Venice; we knew that he would always be alien to its society."

640. Browne, Maure. Too Late to Lament. Bloomington: Indiana University Press, 1956, pp. 237, 323.

The writer surmises that Paul Robeson had one of the finest male speaking-voices that she had ever heard. She also states that Robeson was superb as "Othello."

641. Gassner, John. Theatre at the Crossroads: Plays and Playwrights of the Mid-Century American Stage. New York: Holt, Rinehart & Winston, 1960, p. 183.

The author declares that Paul Robeson was the most memorable Moor, in the play "Othello" of our time. Robeson brought to the role a monolithic grandeur that was sufficient for tragedy even when he did very little acting, states Gassner.

642.   Lawless, **Ray M.** Folksingers and Folksongs in America: A Handbook
       of Biography, Bibliography, and Discography. New York: Duell,
       Sloan, and Pearce, 1960, pp. 109, 234, 241, 242, 340, 564, 565.

       Various references are made to Paul Robeson throughout the book.
       The writer did not give a sketch of Paul Robeson and forty-six
       other singers because they are well known. A list of some of
       Robeson's Spirituals and Folksongs are included in this work.

643.   Rosenberg, Marvin. The Masks of "Othello": The Search for the
       Identity of Othello, Iago, and Desdemona by Three Centuries of
       Actors and Critics. Berkeley, Cal.: University of California
       Press, 1961, pp. 143, 152, 153, 189-195, 198.

       In this work Robeson comments on "Othello's"cultural pride and
       sensitivity. He was highly conscious of racial divisions. The
       actor argues, in essence: "Shakespeare meant Othello to be a
       'black moor' from Africa, an African of the highest nobility of
       heritage. From Kean on, he was made a light-skinned Moor because
       Western Europe had made Africa a slave center, and the African was
       seen as a slave. English critics seeing a black Othello - like
       my Othello - were likely to take a colonial point of view and re-
       gard him offhand as low and ignorable. But the color is essentially
       secondary - except as it emphasizes the difference in culture...."

644.   Editors of Ebony. The Negro Handbook. Chicago, Ill.: Johnson
       Publishing Co., 1966, p. 357.

       Mr. Frederick O'Neal writing on "The Negro in Today's Theatre -
       Problems and Prospects," points out that Paul Robeson's "Othello"
       holds the all-time record for the Broadway run of a Shakespeare
       play. He was emphasizing the point that "Negro Show" could be
       financially successful.

645.   Draper, John W. The "Othello" of Shakespeare's Audience. New
       York: Octagon Books, 1966, p. 11.

       The writer states that in recent times Paul Robeson has showed
       that "Othello" can be a brilliant box-office success.

646.   Mitchell, Loften. Black Drama: The Story of the American Negro
       in the Theater. New York: Hawthorn Books, Inc., 1967, pp. 82-83,
       105, 117, 118, 127, 138.

       Various references are made to Paul Robeson throughout this book.
       It was pointed out that Robeson was justifiably acclaimed the out-
       standing actor of the year (1943) for playing in "Othello."
       According to the author when it reached Broadway in 1943, it was
       instantaneously successful. The writer also discusses the riot
       that occurred in Peekskill, New York, in 1949, when Robeson
       appeared in concert.

647. Katz, William Loren. <u>Eyewitness: The Negro in American History</u>.
      New York: Pitman Publishing Corp., 1967, pp. 399, 404, 449.

      The writer states that Paul Robeson along with other Blacks found
      communism or socialism attractive during the 1920's. It was also
      pointed out that Robeson's fame became worldwide when he starred
      in a London production of Shakespeare's "Othello." Paul Robeson
      along with Louis Armstrong and Lena Horne and many other Black
      entertainers toured the army camps of USO troups during World War
      II.

648. Drotning, Phillip T. <u>A Guide to Negro History in America</u>. Garden
      City, N.Y.: Doubleday & Co., 1968, p. 138.

      It was pointed out that Paul Robeson was a "trailblazer" for Black
      entertainers, when he starred in "Othello" on the Broadway Theater.
      The writer also states that Robeson "charmed" concert audiences.

649. Cunard, Nancy, Editor. <u>Negro: An Anthology</u>. New York: Frederick
      Ungar Publishing Co., 1970.

      It was stated that Paul Robeson was a performer who was admired on
      both continents. According to this work, in Robeson's London
      performance of "Othello" his distinction was greatly manifested,
      and since his return to America his fame doubled.

650. Rosenberg, Marvin. <u>The Masks of Othello: The Search for the</u>
      <u>Identity of Othello, Iago, and Desdemona By Three Centuries of</u>
      <u>Actors and Critics</u>. Berkeley, Cal.: University of California
      Press, 1971, pp. 34, 35, 143, 151, 152, 153, 189, 190, 191, 192,
      193, 194, 195, 198, 225, 284n.

      The writer contends that Paul Robeson has been the best-remembered
      "Othello" of recent decades. By the **time of the second and third**
      of his series of performances, he had made a wide reputation for
      himself - though as a singer rather than actor. It was also
      pointed out that Robeson had the physical qualities to make the
      greatest "Othello" his generation had seen. Mr. Rosenberg pointed
      out that to Paul Robeson - and others - the matter of "Othello's"
      being <u>Negro</u> is important.

651. Hatch, James B. and Ted Shine. <u>Black Theater U.S.A.: Forty-Five</u>
      <u>Plays by Black Americans, 1847-1974</u>. New York: Free Press, 1974,
      pp. 100, 392.

      The authors state that Paul Robeson opened on Broadway in "Othello"
      in 1943 and his performance, heralded as brilliant, set a record
      of 296 performances. Yet, according to the writers, a few years
      later the same Paul Robeson and his concert audiences were
      assaulted with rocks and bottles by a racist crowd at Peekskill,
      New York, while the State Police stood by and watched. It was
      also pointed out that in 1924, the press had demanded that the
      Off'Broadway production of "All God's Chillun God Wings" be banned
      because Paul Robeson kissed the hand of the White Actress.

652. Wesley, Charles H. The Quest for Equality: From Civil War to
      Civil Rights. New York: Publishers Co., 1976, pp. 158, 203, 205,
      206, 214.

      The author surmises that Robeson's performance in "Othello" earned
      him a reputation as his race's foremost Shakespearean actor. The
      writer aruges that Paul Robeson's 1951 presentation to the UN on
      behalf of the Civil Rights Congress, charging the United States with
      racial Genocide, added the weight of world opinion to the domestic
      pressure against segregation.

                        12. PEEKSKILL INCIDENT

653. American Civil Liberties Union. Violence in Peekskill: A Report
      of the Violations of Civil Liberties at Two Paul Robeson Concerts
      Near Peekskill, N.Y., August 27th and September 4, 1949. New York:
      American Civil Liberties Union, 1949, 51 pp.

      This report points out that the hysteria whipped up against the
      "public appearance" of Paul Robeson was signalized from the outset
      by a willfully deceptive misuse of terms.

654. Westchester Peekskill Committee. Eyewitness: Peekskill, U.S.A.,
      August 27; September 4, 1949. White Plains, N.Y.: Westchester
      Committee for a Fair Inquiry into the Peekskill Violence, February,
      1950, 28 pp.

      This is a documentary report on the violence that occurred in the
      town of Peekskill, in Westchester County, New York. Violence broke
      out when it was learned that Paul Robeson would present a concert.
      Robeson was asked not to come to Peekskill because if he did
      violence would break out. His reply was: "I shall take my voice
      wherever there are those who want to hear the melody of freedom or
      the words that might inspire hope and courage in the face of des-
      pair and fear. My weapons are peaceful for it is only by peace
      that peace can be attained. The song of Freedom must prevail."

655. Fast, Howard M. Peekskill: U.S.A., A Personal Experience. New
      York: Civil Rights Congress, 1951, 127 pp.

      Various references are made to Paul Robeson and his relationship
      to the riot that occurred at Peekskill, New York. The author
      points out that various newspapers labled Robeson un-American
      because of his support for the Communists. The editors of the
      newspapers suggest that he was a "tool" of Moscow. The riot
      occurred when it was announced that Robeson would sing. Because of
      the riot he did not sing at that particular time. He did sing,
      however, at a later date without any violence occurring. There
      are two photos of Paul Robeson at Peekskill.

656. Schmidt, Karl M. <u>Henry A. Wallace: Quixotic Crusade, 1948</u>.
      Syracuse: Syracuse University Press, 1960, pp. 99, 165, 167,
      186, 218, 258, 294-297.

      A great deal of attention is devoted to Paul Robeson's involvement
      in the "Peekskill Incidents." The singer and his supporters were
      attacked by a mob. Robeson supported Wallace and the Progressive
      Party in the 1950 election.

657. Markmann, Charles Lam. <u>The Noblest Cry: A History of the American
      Civil Liberties Union</u>. New York: St. Martin's Press, 1965, pp.
      286, 287, 288, 289.

      Various references are made to Paul Robeson and the riot at Peeks-
      kill, New York. The writer called Paul Robeson, a distinguished
      Negro singer who was also a Communist.

                        13. PERSONAL FRIENDS

658. Woollcott, Alexander. <u>While Rome Burns</u>. New York: Grosset &
      Dunlap, 1934, pp. 121-131.

      There is one section entitled "Colossal Bronze" that is devoted
      to Paul Robeson. The author was a neighbor of Paul Robeson when
      he was living in England. The author points out that Robeson
      helped finance his law school fee by playing professional foot-
      ball out of town on week-ends. Mr. Woollcott suggests that some
      financiers were willing to put up a million dollars to back
      Robeson as a prospective heavyweight champion of the world; but
      he would not agree to such a deal because he did not want to be
      a prize fighter. It was also asserted that Lady Mountbatten of
      London was linked romantically with Paul Robeson. The author
      suggests that the song, "Ol' Man River," was written especially
      for Paul Robeson.

659. Kaufman, Beatrice and Joseph Hennessey, Editors. <u>The Letters of
      Alexander Woollcott</u>. New York: Viking Press, 1944, p. 330.

      Mr. Woollcott wrote a letter in 1942 to D.G. Kennedy and stated,
      in part, "Once upon a time my old friend Paul Robeson, returning
      after an absence of several years in Europe, discovered that in
      the interval I had become a celebrity. At last he found me out
      in Hollywood surrounded by autograph hunters and I still remember
      his turning to his wife and saying, 'My gaud, Aleck's a mess,
      ain't he?'"

660. Adams, Samuel Hopkins. <u>Alexander Woollcott: His Life and His World</u>. New York: Reynal & Hitchcock, 1946, pp. 134-135, 145-146, 199, 203, 250, 345.

The author points out that Alexander Woollcott and Heywood Broun along with Mrs. Robeson "talked" Paul Robeson into giving a concert for "unmusical people." Adams states that it can hardly be claimed that Woollcott and Brown were responsible for Paul Robeson's **gift** to American music; but certainly they forwarded its timely development, concludes the writer. Mr. Woollcott was quoted in this book as saying Paul Robeson's voice is "indisputable.... the finest musical instrument wrought by nature in our time."

661. Hennessey, Joseph, Editor. <u>The Portable Woollcott</u>. New York: Viking Press, 1946, pp. 159-169.

There is a section in this collection on Paul Robeson, "Colossal Bronze," that was reprinted from Woollcott's book, <u>While Rome Burns</u>. Robeson was a neighbor of Mr. Woollcott when he was living in Kent, England, in the 1930's. The author states that this is "The Story of the man for whom 'Ol' Man River' was written, as told by a neighbor who occasionally catches a glimpse of him (Robeson) towering above the crowd."

662. Ulanou, Barry. <u>Duke Ellington</u>. New York: Creative Age Press, Inc., 1946, pp. 246, 253.

The author recalls that Ellington talked to Paul Robeson about writing a show for him. It was also stated that Robeson had given Ellington great support.

663. Nizhny, Vladimir. <u>Lessons with Eisenstein</u>. London: George Allen and Unwin, Ltd., 1962, pp. 27, 58, 166, 170, 171.

It was pointed out that Sergei Eisenstein wanted to direct Paul Robeson in the film "Black Majesty." Mr. Eisenstein also wanted to direct Robeson in the "Black Consul," a film about the life of Toussaint O'Overture. Neither film materialized.

664. Buckle, Richard. <u>Jacob Epstein: Sculpture</u>. London: Faber and Faber, Ltd., 1963, pp. 158, 159, 160, 184, 187, 189.

Jacob Epstein's bust of Paul Robeson is included in this work as well as some comments on Robeson and Epstein. The author states that "Robeson's, with its upward gaze, as if the singer were about to address God in the familiar language of the negro spiritual, has a noble, aspiring quality."

665. Horne, Lena and Richard Schickel. <u>Lena</u>. Garden City, N.Y.: Doubleday & Co., 1965, p. 252.

The entertainer states that she was politically blacklisted because of her friendship with Paul Robeson and her **interest, developed** through him, in the Council on African Affairs, which got named as a Communist front organization.

666. Ferguson, Blanche E. <u>Countee Cullen and The Negro Renaissance</u>.
      New York: Dodd, Mead & Co., 1966, pp. 84, 108, 121, 190.

      Countee Cullen was a friend of the Robeson's and often visited
      them in Paris, France. The author points out that Paul Robeson
      was convinced by his wife and friends that he had acting talent;
      therefore he joined the Provincetown Players. Ferguson states that
      Robeson and others were saying in the 1930's in public that no
      individual could be really free until all were free. The writer
      concludes: "Paul Robeson, for example, was interspersing his
      concert numbers with little speeches on civil rights. Middle class
      Negroes were embarrassed by this turn of events, much as they had
      been disturbed years earlier by the race-conscious preachments of
      Marcus Garvey. But where as they could dismiss Garveyism as an
      appeal to the ignorant masses, they could not ignore Robeson so
      easily. He was a highly intelligent and talented man whose
      extreme sensitivity to the sufferings of black men had caused him
      (in the opinion of some) to go astray."

667. Hill, Herbert. "Reflections on Richard Wright: A Symposium on
      An Exiled Native Son," <u>Anger, and Beyond: The Negro Writer in
      the United States</u>, Herbert Hill, Editor. New York: Harper & Row,
      1966, p. 200.

      Saunders Redding recalls that he met Richard Wright in the Fall
      of 1943 when they were attending the McCarter Theatre in Princeton,
      New Jersey, where Paul Robeson was doing "Othello." According to
      Redding, during the course of the performance it was noticeable
      that Robeson was drooling, spitting really, in the faces of the
      other actors. At intermission the Reddings, Wrights, and others
      were standing in a group when one man criticized Robeson for
      losing saliva. Wright got very mad and said, "Don't you know
      that Othello was an epilpetic and that this is a conscious, a
      purposeful thing; this is part of the role." "I don't think his
      anger had anything to do with the fact that he and Robeson were
      both Communists at the time,"concluded Mr. Redding.

668. DuBois, W.E.B. <u>The Autobiography of W.E.B. DuBois: A Soliloguy
      on Viewing My Life from the Last Decade of Its First Century</u>.
      New York: International Publishers, 1968, pp. 11f, 344f, 368,
      371, 375, 394, 396f, 409.

      DuBois mentions Robeson and his relations with the Council on
      African Affairs. He also writes about how the singer was refused
      a passport by the United States Department of State. The author,
      who was 90 years old at the time, spoke at Paul Robeson's 60th
      birthday. The speaker declares: "The persecution of Paul Robeson
      by the government and people of the United States during the last
      nine years has been one of the most contemptible happenings in
      modern history. Robeson has done nothing to hurt or defame this
      nation.... There is no person on earth who ever heard Robeson
      slander or even attack the land of his birth." DuBois suggests
      that Robeson had reasons to despise America; yet, he did not. It
      was also stated Robeson more than any living man spread the pure
      Negro folk song over the civilized world. The author concludes that
      Robeson still has hope for America and faith in God.

669. Hoyt, Edwin P. <u>Alexander Woollcott: The Man Who Came to Dinner</u>.
     New York: Abelard-Schumann, 1968, pp. 8, 22, 172, 193, 258, 309.

     It was pointed out that Woollcott befriended Paul Robeson, the
     young Negro who was learning the art of acting in playing the
     lead in "All God's Chillun Got Wings" and "The Emperor Jones."
     The author contends that Woollcott helped Robeson get together
     with Jerome Kern, and from this came the production of "Show Boat."
     Woollcott, also, according to Hoyt, helped to secure an honorary
     degree from Hamilton College for Robeson -- then he persuaded him
     to accept it. Robeson read the Twenty-Third Psalm at Woollcott's
     funeral.

670. Moussinac, Leon. <u>Sergei Eisenstein</u>. Translated by D. Sandy
     Petrey. New York: Crown Publishers, Inc., 1970, pp. 60-61,
     207-209.

     The writer states that Mr. Eisenstein wanted to make the movie,
     "Black Majesty," starring Paul Robeson, but Mr. Robeson's ob-
     ligations abroad made the movie impossible in 1935.

671. Patterson, William L. <u>The Man Who Cried Genocide: An Auto-
     biography</u>. New York: International Publishers, 1971, pp. 11,
     65-70, 140, 142, 144, 150, 154, 155, 160, 180, 191, 196, 202,
     203, 209, 210, 213.

     The author was a long-time friend of Paul Robeson and mentions it
     throughout the book. There are also three photos of Robeson in
     this book. Patterson states that Robeson told him that while the
     door was opened for him (to be successful), "it's closed to my
     brother." The writer argues that the Black Press also recognized
     Robeson's great potential as a leader. He admired him and did not
     want him to clash seriously with the existing order. It was sur-
     mised that Robeson was one of the "staunchest" supporters of
     Abraham Lincoln School that was started by William L. Patterson.
     The school closed, however, after three years of operation. The
     author recalls that Paul Robeson and a group of Black and White
     citizens carried the genocide petition to the **office of the**
     Secretary General of the United Nations in New York the same day
     that he presented copies to the various delegations in the Human
     Rights Committee at the Palais Chaillot in Paris, France.

672. Barna, Yon. <u>Eisenstein</u>. Bloomington: Indiana University Press,
     1971, pp. 16, 189, 190, 201.

     The author states that Mr. Sergei Eisenstein wanted to make a film,
     "Black Majesty," that would star Paul Robeson. The film producer
     nicknamed Robeson "Black Mayakovsky." The film was never made.

673. DuBois, Shirley Graham. <u>His Day is Marching On: A Memoir of
     W.E.B. DuBois</u>. Philadelphia: J.B. Lippincott Co., 1971, pp. 66,
     93, 97-98, 117, 118, 144, 210, 214, 239, 241-243, 268-270, 296,
     297, 328, 367, 368.

     Dr. W.E.B. and Mrs. DuBois were friends with Paul and Eslanda
     Robeson. The writer discusses her and her husband's many meetings

(DuBois, Shirley Graham)

with the Robesons' here in the United States and in Europe. Mrs.
DuBois points out that her husband told her to have Robeson sing
"Ode to Joy" at his funeral....

674. Douglas, William O. Go East Young Man: The Early Years. New
York: Random House, 1974, pp. 138, 348.

The Supreme Court Justice makes two brief references to Paul
Robeson. In the first instance, he recalls that there were six
Blacks in his law school classes and Robeson was the most memorable.
He also states that Paul worked his way through Law School by
boxing professionally. In the second case, Douglas recalls that
a Black lady came to see him, who had come with credentials from
his old classmate, Paul Robeson.

675. O'Connor, Richard. Heywood Broun: A Biography. New York: G.P.
Putnam's Sons, 1975, p. 143.

The author states that both Heywood Broun and Alexander Woollcott
urged Paul Robeson to forget about a legal career and cultivate
his superb basso profundo. Along with Mrs. Robeson, Brown and
Woollcott persuaded Robeson to perform in a series of "concerts
for unmusical people." New York was stunned by his rendition of
"Old Man River," and his career took off like a rocket, concludes
O'Connor.

676. Aptheker, Herbert, Editor. The Correspondence of W.E.B. DuBois.
Amherst: University of Massachusetts Press, 1976, Vol. II,
"Sections, 1934-1944," pp. 121, 220, 221, 222, 223, 364n, 378,
378n, 380, 397, 401, To Paul Robeson, 378.

Du Bois states that a book designed to commemorate the abolition
of slavery in the United States should include such notables as
Paul Robeson and Countee Cullen. Dr. Du Bois wrote Paul Robeson
in 1944 and asked him to join him in conveying a "Pan Africa"
Conference. According to Aptheker, there is no record of a written
response from Robeson to this letter.

677. Swallow, Norman. Eisenstein: A Documentary Portrait. London:
George Allen & Unwin Ltd., 1976, pp. 109-110.

It was pointed out that in 1934 Paul Robeson came to Moscow, and
with Eisenstein he discussed not only the Haitian proposal, "Black
Majesty," but also an adaptation of A.K. Vinogradov's novel "The
Black Consul." Nothing came of these ideas. There is also a
photo of Mr. Robeson shaking hands in Moscow with Herbert
Marshall in 1934.

678. Teichmann, Howard. Smart Aleck: The Wit,World and Life of
     Alexander Woollcott. New York: William Morrow & Co., Inc.,
     1976, pp. 21, 87, 316.

     It was stated that Woollcott met Robeson, liked him, and after
     hearing him sing a few folk songs at a party, urged him to try
     singing professionally. Woollcott along with Heywood Broun, in-
     sisted and Robeson became one of the eminent bassos of the day.
     The author was trying to make a case for Mr. Woollcott "dis-
     covering" Paul Robeson.

679. Aptheker, Herbert, Editor. The Correspondence of W.E.B. DuBois.
     Amherst:University of Massachusetts Press, 1978, Vol. III,
     "Selections, 1944-1946," pp. 1, 112, 113, 115n, 143, 196, 205,
     206, 212, 231, 232, 235, 255, 259, 259n, 263, 269, 270, 296,
     324, 346, 347, 349, 387, 388, 434, 457, From Paul 281, Robeson
     112-113, 212, 352, To Paul Robeson, 435.

     Paul Robeson discussed a number of topics with Dr. Du Bois. In
     1946 Robeson asked Du Bois to join him in issuing a call for a
     gathering in Washington, D.C., to launch an American crusade to
     end lynching in America. Du Bois stated he would support such
     a meeting. Robeson asked Du Bois in 1948 to attend a luncheon in
     honor of Pascual Ampudia, President of Local 715, United Public
     Workers. Du Bois attended the luncheon. Du Bois also wrote
     Robeson on a number of occasions. On January 5, 1961, he sent
     Robeson a letter urging him to go to China and make a tour of
     that country. He also told him that if Kennedy refused a re-
     newal of his passport, he should take out citizenship in a
     European or African country.

680. Beckford, Ruth. Katherine Dunham: A Biography. New York: Marcel
     Dekker, Inc., 1979, p. 57.

     The writer states that Miss Dunham often wonders if her own career
     was successful due to the fact that she had been exposed to people
     in the humanities like .... Paul Robeson, the Black singer.

681. Kellner, Bruce, Editor. "Keep-A-Inchin" Along: Selected Writings
     of Carl Van Vechten About Black Art and Letters. Westport, Conn.:
     Greenwood Press, 1979, pp. 29, 36, 38, 39, 55, 59, 62, 76, 115,
     117, 130-132, 140, 154-158, 168, 181, 243, 275.

     Although Paul Robeson is mentioned throughout the book there is
     one section that deals specifically with him. It is entitled
     "Paul Robeson and Lawrence Brown." The editor points out that
     in 1925 Van Vechten organized Robeson and Brown's first public
     recital and even before it occurred he had written a program
     note for a second recital. The author declares: "To those
     who are accustomed to hear Negro Spirituals delivered in a sancti-
     monious, lugubrious manner, or yet worse, with the pseudo-refine-
     ment of the typical concert singer, the evangelical, true Negro
     rendering of Paul Robeson and Lawrence Brown will come as a
     delightful surprise." It is the avowed purpose of Paul Robeson,
     and of Lawrence Brown, as the arranger of these folksongs, to
     restore, so far as they are able, the spirit of the original

(Kellner, Bruce)

primitive start to these Spirituals. In realizing this purpose,
which apparently no other public singer has hitherto entertained,
they have been markedly successful," states the writer. "Aside
from recognizing the unquestioned artistry of the performance,
their audiences will doubtless exhibit considerable amazement over
the degree of variety that these two young Negroes have been able
to introduce into their all-Negro programs.... The beauty of
these simple songs of the Negro people is celebrated the world
over: I have listened to no other interpreters who so vividly
reveal this beauty. At the present moment, I believe I'd rather
hear Robeson and Brown sing that quaintly charming air, 'Little
David, Play on Your Harp,' than hear anyone else sing anything,"
concludes Kellner.

14. SPORTS

682. Walsh, Christy, Editor. Intercollegiate Football. New York:
      Doubleday, Doran & Co., 1934, pp. 15, 131, 134.

      Paul Robeson is included on Walter Camp's 1918 All-American Team.
      He is listed as an All-American selection at Rutgers University.
      The sportsman is also listed as a Football Letter Man while at
      Rutgers. There is a photo of Robeson in his football attire.

683. Henderson, Edwin B. The Negro in Sports. Washington: D.C.:
      Associated Publishers, 1949, pp. 110-112, 122, 160, 185.

      Writing under the title, "The Magnificent Robeson," the writer
      states: "Rutgers University will always be known for two im-
      portant happenings. Rutgers and Princeton played the first foot-
      ball game in American history, and it was at Rutgers that Paul
      Robeson won four sports letters, and helped to build one of the
      greatest teams in the history of his school. He also was elected
      by Camp and the Press to gridiron honors on the 1919 and 1918
      All-American." The writer points out: "Unfortunately Rutgers
      did not have a schedule that called for contests with many of the
      more prominent football colleges, hence, not many metropolitian
      newspapers carried the spirited comment other less deserving stars
      received. Also the war in Europe was taking a toll on athletics.
      Fewer colleges were playing in 1917 and fewer still 1918. The
      public at that time was more interested in the reports of battles
      won than in games on the gridiron. It was during these trying
      days that Robeson was in the midst of his athletic career...."

684. Young, A.S. Negro First in Sports. Chicago: Johnson Publishing
      Co., 1963, pp. 76, 77, 80, 102, 147.

      The writer argues that as a result of political events or cir-
      cumstances, Paul Robeson's name seldom graces sports pages today
      (1962). He also declares that as one reads the list of great

(Young, A.S.)

Negro players, many of whom achieved local or regional, if not
national, first of importance, one is puzzled by the fact that
after Robeson, no Negro was accorded near-universal acclaim as a
football star until Cornell's Jerome Holland soared to All-American
Fame in the late 1930's. Young also asserts that Robeson, a basketball center, was a star player in 1917, 1918, and 1919.

685. Orr, Jack. The Black Athelete: His Story in American History.
      New York: The Lion Press, 1969, pp. 83, 90, 126.

It was pointed out that Robeson was a basketball and football
player at Rutgers University before he became a world-renowned
singer and actor. Rutgers, at one time, acclaimed him as one of
its finest most priminent living alumni. Robeson also played professional football for Akron and Milwaukee before turning to the
stage.

686. Jones, Wally and Jim Washington. Black Champions Challenge
      American Sports. New York: David McKay Co., 1972, pp. 41-43.

These writers state that the second Black football immortal of
the decade was Paul Robeson, who twice (1917-1918) was named
All-American by Walter Camp. Robeson was an end on the football
team, and he also starred in basketball, baseball, and track,
and was an outstanding student. Many years later, the athletic
director at Rutgers had this to say about him: "Paul Leroy
Robeson is regarded as the greatest living All-American football
player. In the opinion of most people, he, of all the All-
Americans who have been chosen, has gained the greatest and most
merited fame since his graduation. Undoubtedly, he ranks as one
of the five most prominent living Rutgers alumni, and by many
people connected with the University as the most distinguished
alumnus now living. He is one of ten men in the University's
history who won four varsity letters as an undergraduate. He
was an outstanding debater while in college and was a member of
Phi Beta Kappa, honorary scholastic society. Strangely enough,
he never was a member of the University glee club, despite the
fact that it is his magnificent voice that has brought his
greatest fame." Paul Robeson's career as an athlete was eclipsed
only by his career as an entertainer and social philosopher.
After college, Robeson starred for the Akron professional team,
coached by Fritz Pollard, a Black man. In the 1930's, already
famous as a singer but unhappy with the way things were going
for Blacks in this country, Robeson moved to the Soviet Union,
urging others to follow him. He returned later in the decade
and soon the State Department clamped a ban on his travel privileges and refused to let him go abroad. The ban wasn't lifted
until 1958, concludes the authors.

687. Chalk, Ocania. Black College Sport. New York: Dodd, Mead & Co.,
      1976, pp. 24, 97, 98, 102, 151, 167-170, 184, 331, 332, 340.

      A great deal of discussion is devoted to Robeson's football plays
      at Rutgers University. It was brought out that Walter Camp called
      Robeson the finest end that ever trod upon a gridiron. The author
      also discusses Robeson as a basketball and baseball player.

688. Brashler, William. Josh Gibson: A Life in The Negro Leagues.
      New York: Harper & Row, Publishers, 1978, pp. 189, 190.

      The author states that Paul Robeson was an outspoken gutsy radical
      and Josh Gibson was not. Mr. Brashler surmises that Mr. Gibson
      remained a symbol of excellence to Black people, but his fans
      never lived and died with the travails of his career as they did
      with those of Paul Robeson and other Blacks. The writer declares
      that Gibson was not that of a fighter but of a victim; so many
      people prefer to remember him only as that and do not put him under
      the same scrutiny as Paul Robeson and other Black athletes and
      personalities who fought the racial fight.

            15. UN-AMERICAN ACTIVITIES COMMITTEE

689. Bentley, Eric. Are You Now or Have You Ever Been: The Investi-
      gation of Show Business By the Un-American Activities Committee,
      1947-1958. New York: Harper Colophon Books, 1973, pp. 138, 139,
      140, 142, 143, 144, 145, 146, 147, 148, 149, 150, 151, 152, 153,
      154, 155, 156, 157, 158, 159.

      During the early fifties, an attempt was made by the Government
      and the press to wipe Paul Robeson off the record. On at least
      one occasion, according to Bentley, willingness to denounce
      Robeson was made the test of a movie star's patriotism, the
      movie star, being Robeson's old friend, Jose Ferrer. Columnist
      George Sokolsky states, declared Bentley. "No one has ever de-
      nounced Paul Robeson with such accurate pinpointing of his un-
      forgivable sins against his native land as Jose Ferrer." There
      is also Paul Robeson's heaing before the Senate Un-American
      Activities Committee. This testimony has appeared in the author's
      other book, Thirty Years of Treason. There are also two photos
      of Paul Robeson included in this work.

XIII
Dissertations and Theses

. . . . The (film) industry is not prepared to permit me to portray the life or express the living interests, hopes and aspirations of the struggling people from whom I come . . . *you bet they will never let me play a part in a film which a Negro is on top.*

Paul Robeson

690.   Laibman, Erwin. "Honor and Prestige: A Study of Social Role in
        a Minority," Unpublished Honor Thesis, College of the City
        of New York, January, 1953, pp. 16-22.

        Chapter Two is entitled "Paul Robeson." The writer declares that
        Robeson was an actor, singer, lecturer and organizer and one of
        those mid-twentieth century American phenomena -- a "highly con-
        troversial figure." Mr. Laibman concludes that when Robeson added
        singing to his list of accomplishments and then captured the high
        acclaim of Europe for his performance, his high position in society
        provided a great impetus for the improvement, of the status of all
        non-whites, who thus accorded him even greater honor.

691.   Schlosser, Anatol I. "Paul Robeson: His Career in the Theatre,
        In Motion Pictures, and on the Concert Stage," Unpublished Doc-
        toral Dissertation, New York University, 1970. 480 pp.

        Although this work deals mainly with Paul Robeson in the theatre,
        motion pictures and concert stage, some attention is devoted to
        his early life. Unlike much of the other works on Robeson this
        work is different for two reasons. First, it deals mainly with
        Robeson as a performer and artist. Secondly, the writer had access
        through material made available by the Robeson family. Thereby
        giving almost a complete picture of the performing life of this
        artist was possible. These files include personal and business
        correspondence, legal and financial documents, published and un-
        published writings by Robeson, scripts, scores, scenarios, programs,
        and his large collection of scrapbooks containing published inter-
        views, articles, reviews and criticisms of his theatrical, cine-
        matic and concert performances. With these materials, as well as
        primary and secondary sources available to the public, the events
        preceding a performance, the performance itself, and the public
        and critical reactions were reconstructed as well as Robeson's
        stated thinking on a particular event and performing in general.
        The author concludes: "Robeson, in theatre and motion pictures,
        fought, on the whole successfully, the forces of prejudice, always
        trying to obtain roles which portrayed the Negro with dignity.
        It was in music that he was most successful, commanding more select
        audiences than in the theatre and cinema, and exercising more

(Schlosser, Anatol I.)

control of the content of a recital than of a play or film scenario, as well as choosing the cities and halls in which his concerts were held. Robeson brought the Negro spiritual to the
concert stage and the music of his people to the world. With
his music and his acting, he constantly placed his art and his
talents in the service not only of his own people, but of all
peoples." This is the first and only doctoral dissertation written
on Robeson and includes a 69 page exhaustive bibliography.

692.   Yeakey, Lamont H. "The Early Years of Paul Robeson: Prelude to
the Making of a Revolutionary, 1898-1930," Unpublished Master
Thesis, Columbia University, 1971. 120 pp.

The writer devotes much attention to the early years of Paul
Robeson's life. He discusses at length Robeson's college days
at Rutgers University. Yeakey points out: "It is ironic that
although the first college football game ever played was held
at Rutgers, Rutgers had never produced an All-American. It would
take Robeson to bring them national recognition. This was a
singular distinction indeed, for Robeson was the first player ever
to be named All-American in any sport at Rutgers." The author
suggests that one of the reasons why he did this particular study
of Robeson was that the artist states that his early years had a
profound effect on his later life. Robeson argues, in Here I
Stand: "All which came later, after Rutgers and Columbia Law
School -- my career as an artist in America and abroad, my
participation in public life, the views which I hold today -- all
have their roots in the early years."

693.   Stuckey, Ples Sterling. "The Spell of Africa: The Development
of Black Nationalist Theory, 1829-1945," Unpublished Doctoral
Dissertation, Northwestern University, 1973. 391 pp.

This study is an exploration of a neglected dimension of Black
nationalism, the development of a theory of Afro-American autonomy
specifically designed to free people of African ancestry in
America while giving high priority to the liberation of Africans
throughout the world. The burden of the study is that Afro-
Americans in this tradition not only produced the most relevant
brand of nationalism but displayed a profound grasp of the realities confronting Black people in America. Though "The Spell of
Africa" is not an investigation into Afro-American attitudes toward
Africa, each of its major segments, including those which address
the names controversy among Afro-Americans and their attempts to
write African history, can be read on that level. The principal
objective in attempt to reconstruct the debate over names is
to disclose the clash of the contending forces of "integrationism"
and "Black nationalism," states Dr. Stuckey. There is one chapter
entitled, "I Want to be African: Paul Robeson and the Ends of
Nationalist Theory and Practice, 1919-1945." In this 46 page
chapter Professor Stuckey concludes: "He (Paul Robeson) believed
that the day was not too distant when the most incandescent dreams,
the most daring hopes of the greatest of nationalistic movements
would achieve, however, uncertain the workings of the human will,

(Stuckey, Ples Sterling)

the tangibility of freedom. It <u>was</u>, after all, that goal, the
liberation of colonized man, to which Robeson had devoted his
life."

694.   Buxton, Keith Christian. "The Development of the Political
        Thought of Paul Robeson," Unpublished Master's Thesis, University
        of Delaware, 1979. 105 pp.

        This is one of the latest thesis on Paul Robeson. Unlike others,
        however, this one attempts to deal with his political thoughts.
        This work attempts to provide readers with a complete picture of
        the development of Robeson's political thoughts. Whereas the
        literature which preceded this thesis did not attempt to deal
        with the development of his thoughts in its entirety, this paper
        spanned his entire development. Readers should now have some
        idea of Paul Robeson's political growth and maturation as well
        as the more familiar activities of his later years. By reading
        this thesis one should have a good idea of the problems which
        plagued and continue to plague Negroes in the 20th century, states
        the writer. This thesis, however, does not add anything new to
        Robeson's political thoughts. Most of the data was taken from
        Robeson's book, <u>Here I Stand.</u>

XIV
Articles About
Paul Robeson
(1916–1981)

In 1946, at a legislative hearing in California, I testified under oath that I was not a member of the Communist Party, but since then I have refused to give testimony or sign affidavits as to that fact. . . . I have made it a matter of principle, as many others have done, to refuse to comply with any demand of legislative or departmental officials that infringes upon the Constitutional rights of all Americans.

Paul Robeson

A. 1916-1919

1. LEADERSHIP

695. "Robeson Is A Leader," Targum, June, 1919, p. 563.

The newspaper states that Paul Robeson had the ability to be "the leader of the colored race in America." It also suggests that Robeson could become a better known leader than Booker T. Wasnington.

696. "Paul Robeson," Rutgers Daily Targum, June 1919, pp. 563-566.

The 1919 graduating class prophecizes that one day Paul Robeson would be tne "Governor of New Jersey." The school newspaper de-voted quite a bit of space to Robeson when he graduated. A re-view of his accomplishments were listed in the paper. It was also pointed out, in part:

> ....With the departure of the Class of 1919 the
> Rutgers' undergraduate body loses a man who has
> been for four years an active factor in its life.
> While on campus, Paul Robeson made a name and a
> record equaled by none, and now as he fares forth
> into the world we wish him the same success....
> Yet one may combine physical and mental ability
> and still lack the most important element in one's
> character, moral stamina. If such be the rule,
> Robeson is again the exception proving it, for he
> is a man through and through. His father sent him
> to old Rutgers', and not in vain, but sad to say,
> that parent did not live to witness the culmin-
> ation of a college career surpassed by none....
> Now, Paul, as you pass from our midst, take with
> you the respect and appreciation of us who remain
> behind. May your success in life be comparable to

(<u>Rutgers</u> <u>Daily</u> <u>Targum</u>)

> that of college days. In you other members of
> your race may well find a noble example, and this
> leadership is your new duty....

2. ORATOR

697. "Robeson Wins Prize," <u>Somerset Messenger</u>, June 1, 1916.

The article states: "Paul LeRoy Robeson of Somerville, won the
first prize ... in the contest for oratorical honors of the freshman class in Rutgers College.... Robeson had won high oration
honors previously, and a year ago won the scholastic championship in the contest for high school entrants held by Rutgers."

698. "The Future of the Negro in American Life, <u>Targum</u>, Vol. 50, 1918-
1919, p. 575.

The article declares: "He (Paul Robeson) first stated (in a talk
to the YMCA, New Brunswick, New Jersey) that a comparison of the
progress of the Negro with that of the white American during the
past fifty years was unjust, for not only did the Negro have to concede a head start of centuries to the white, but was also forced
to progress under great difficulties. The unjust treatment of the
Negro in the South, and especially his lack of educational facilities, were clearly pointed out. In spite of these handicaps,
it was shown that the race had made great steps in advance and
had shown their capacity and willingness to sacrifice in both the
Civil War and the war still fresh in our memory. The needed
change or solution was closer cooperation between white and black,
both working for the good of both." The writer was referring to
World War One.

3. SPORTS

699. "Robeson Returns to the Team," <u>Newark Evening News</u>, October 18,
1916.

The paper reports: "A decided improvement was shown in the
Rutgers line yesterday afternoon with Robeson back at his old
place at tackle. The whole line seemed to stiffen as soon as he
got back."

699a. "Our Own Robey," Rutgers Daily Targum, December 19, 1917, p. 285.

This article comments on Robeson as an outstanding athlete and as
an All-American end. It declares, in part:
....Our own 'Robey.' As a football man he stands out
as the best in the country today. As a receiver of
forward passes he stood out head and shoulders above
all otners. As defensive quarter back he is in a
class by himself. His greatest compliment comes
from Coach Sanford, who says he is the greatest
player of all times. When 'Robey' hit them they
stopped coming. And there are eight teams in the
country which will tell you the same. He has been
picked as the leading player in the country and as
All American end by practically every football
authority throughout the east. As everybody knows
'Robey,' you're there....

700. "Fordham Crushed by Rutgers Power: Robeson, The Sturdy Negro End
of the Visiting Eleven, Plays a Stellar Role in the Aerial Attack,"
New York Times, October 28, 1917, Sports Section, p. 5.

This article discusses the role Paul Robeson played in helping
Rutgers University defeat Fordham University 28 to 0. The writer
asserts: "It can hardly be said that one player stood out on the
Rutgers' aggregation, unless it was Robeson, the giant Negro, at
left end. He was a tower of strength both in the offense and
defense, and it was his receiving of forward passes which shattered
any hopes of glory which might have arisen in Fordham ranks during
the game. Twice the big Rutgers Negro raced down the field after
receiving a perfect toss from Whitehill. The first time Robeson
was not downed until he had covered thirty-five yards and placed
the ball on Fordham's five-yard line. On the other occasion
Robeson raced twenty-four yards before being brought to earth
again close to the Fordham goal line. Each of these passes gave
Rutgers a chance to score, and Rutgers did not throw away the
opportunity...." The article concludes: "Both the wings of
Rutgers nave been taught an excellent offense. Robeson invariably
spilled two men and several times three or four were dropped to
the ground, even before the play was well under way. The vicious
playing of Robeson was costly to Fordham, not only in the outcome
of the game but in players, since no less than three Fordham men
were sent into the game at different times to take the place of
those who had been battered and bruised by Robeson. McGrath, the
former Exeter and Yale guard, was the first opposition placed
in front of Robeson, but he did not last long. On the first play
of the game time was taken out while McGarth recovered from the
effects of a bruised jaw and eye."

701. Taylor, Charles A. "Robeson Giant Negro Plays Leading Role for
Jersey Eleven," New York Tribune, October 28, 1917.

The reporter asserts: "A dark cloud upset the hopes of the Fordham
eleven yesterday afternoon. Its name was Robeson, and it travelled
all the way across the Jersey meadows from the banks of the old
Raritan to the Bronx. There was no semblance of a silver lining

(Taylor, Charles A.)

to this cloud, and the maroon football warriors were completely
smothered by it and its accompanying galaxy of Rutgers' stars.
The score was 28-0 in favor of the dark cloud." He continues:
"Robeson the giant Negro, appeared in the line-up as left end, but
he did not confine himself to this particular post. He played in
turn practically every position in the Rutgers team before the
battle ended. With his team on the offensive, Robeson was wont
to leap high in the air to grab forward passes wherever he saw
that a man they were intended for was in another sector of the
battle field. On the defense he was kept busy on the few
occasions when Fordham appeared likely to make a score." Robeson
was supposed to play full-back defensive, and he did, but never
did a full-back range so widely as he. If there was a gap in the
line Robeson filled it. If the Rutgers ends were the least bit
remiss in stopping the dashes of Erwig and Frisch, Robeson was on
hand to prevent any substantial progress, suggests Taylor. He
concludes: "The dark cloud was omnipresent, but he had valuable
assistance in his team-mates.... It would be wrong to say that
Robeson is the entire Rutgers team. The aggregation is too well
balanced for that, but it was this dark cloud that cut off all the
sunshine for the Fordham rooters yesterday."

702. Arms, Louis Lee. "Rutgers Blanks Navy," New York Sunday Tribune,
November 25, 1917.

The reporter states: "A tall, tapering Negro in a faded crimson
sweater, moleskins, and a pair of maroon socks ranged hither and
yon on a wind-shipped Flatbush field yesterday afternoon. He
rode on the wings of the frigid breezes; a grim, silent, and compelling figure. Whether it was Charley Barrett, of old Cornell
and All-American glory, or Gerrish or Gardner who tried to hurl
himself through a moiling gauntlet he was met and stopped by this
blaze of red and Black." He declares: "The Negro was Paul Robeson
of Rutgers College, and he is a minister's son. He is also nineteen years of age and weighs two hundred pounds. Of his football
capacity you are duly referred to 'Cupid' Black of Newport and
Yale. He can tell you. It was Robeson, a veritable Othello of
battle, who led the dashing little Rutgers eleven to a 14-0 victory over the widely heralded Newport Naval Reserves." Arms
concludes: "Among the original tactical manuevers in Rutgers'
attack is the calling in of Robeson to open holes for the back
field. He is shifted by signal from left end to whatever spot
along the line had been pre-selected. Thus considerable of Rutgers'
line drives were put upon the basis of Robeson's superiority over
Black, Schlacter, Callahan, or whomever he faced."

703. "Robeson Stars," Newark Evening News, November 26, 1917.

Rutgers played the Newport Naval Reserve football team in Brooklyn,
New York, and defeated 14-0, with the following news report:
"Robeson, the end, was active in clearing the way, charging for-
ward and cleaning up with his broad shoulders."

704. Daley, George. "Robeson Takes a Place with Elect of Football,"
      New York World, November 28, 1917.

      The reporter surmises Paul Robeson, the big Negro end of the
      Rutgers eleven, is a football genius. Two or three weeks ago
      George Foster Sanford, speaking with conviction born of long ex-
      perience in the game, said: "Robeson is the best all-around player
      on the gridiron this season and the most valuable to the team.
      After seeing him play at Ebbett's Field on Saturday against
      'Cupid' Black's Naval Reserve team the disposition is to go Sanford
      one better and say that Robeson must be ranked with such men as
      Tack Hardwick and Eddie Mahan of Harvard, Charles Barrett of
      Cornell, Jim Thorpe of the Carlisle Indians, Elmer Oliphant of
      of West Point, and Ted Coy of Yale for all-around ability in
      football,"asserts Daley. He concludes: "Opening up holes for his
      backs on line plays; providing remarkable interference for his
      backs on end runs; going down the field under punts; taking for-
      ward passes, in which, by the way, he handles the pigskin with al-
      most the same sureness as a baseball; supporting the centre of the
      line on defense, or, as some have it, playing "defensive quarter-
      back"; plugging up holes from one end of the line to the other;
      tackling here, there, and everywhere; kicking off and diagnosing.
      And the greatest perhaps of his accomplishments is accurate diag-
      nosing. His ability to size up plays and quickly get to the point
      of danger is almost uncanny. He is so rarely at fault that he is
      at the centre of practically every play, and therein lies his
      greatest value, and therein is the truest measure of his all-
      around ability."

705. "Robeson on Rutgers Football Honor Roll," Rutgers Daily Targum,
      December 19, 1917, p. 282.

      This article comments on Paul Robeson as an outstanding football
      player. He was placed on the Rutgers Football Honor Roll. The
      citation that he received asserts, in part: "Robeson is the first
      of all ends. The leading strategist were unanimous in according
      this place to 'Robey!' The New York Sun writes: "With the rise
      of Rutgers this season, Robeson with his superb strength augmented
      by a knowledge of both the theory and practice of the finer points
      of football, soon proved himself one of the best forwards in the
      country. He not only met all the requirements of a first rate
      end, but also he proved a most valuable asset to the team as a
      defensive back."

706. "Rutgers Plays the Naval Reserves, Robeson Stars," Rutgers Daily
      Targum, December 19, 1917, pp. 278-279.

      The article states the outstanding job that Robeson did in helping
      Rutgers defeat the Naval Reserves. The article asserts, in part:
              ....One cause of Newsport's undoing lay in the
          giant Robeson, at Rutgers left end. If this gentle-
          man had only been content to confine himself to the
          extreme wing of Sanford's line, much of Newport's
          troubles would have been materially modified. But
          he wandered incontinently all over the field until
          the Newport team began to believe that there were,

(Rutgers Daily Targum)

>   at least, eleven Robesons, and their entire
>   horizon was obscured by him.... When Newport had
>   the ball, Robeson's secondary defense in backing
>   up in time smeared the whole Newport attack even
>   when it seemed to have a chance....
> Robeson is also discussed as a track star: "In the same meet he
> won the discus throw, with a toss of 114 feet 10 inches. During
> the 1919 track season he was the third highest point getter for
> the team...."

707. Britt, Albert. "The Dusky Rover," Outing, January, 1918.

The editor christened Robeson "The Dusky Rover," and declares:
"Football Othellos are few and far between. But I notice when one
does appear on the map, he usually leaves an indelible impression
in his wake.... there have been mighty few better examples of grit
and judgment in the history of football than Lewis of Harvard,
Pollard of Brown, and coming down to the season just closed,
Paul Robeson of Rutgers.... Yes, Robeson is a great football
player. He may be ranked with such men as Mahan (Harvard),
Oliphant (Purdue and Army), and Coy (Yale)."

708. "Robeson Wins Four 'Rs'," Rutgers Daily Targum, June 1918, p. 729.

Although Paul Robeson was only a junior he was written about more
than other students. Even the graduating class yearbook commented
on his accomplishment. It states, in part:
>   ....For the first time in the history of athletics
>   at Rutgers, this year there were three 'four 'R' men:
>   Wittpenn, Robeson, and Breckley. All three have
>   won the coveted 'R' in football, basketball, track
>   and baseball.... 'Robey' has yet another year in
>   which to play on Rutgers' teams. Last season he
>   was the center of interest in football circles,
>   being ranked on many All American teams....

709. Baker, Clifford N. "Review of the 1918 Football Season," Rutgers
      Alumni Quarterly, January 1919, Vol. 5, No. 2, p. 153.

The writer was the quarterback of the football team and had nothing
but praise for Paul Robeson. He argues: "....'Robey' recognized
by close critics of the game as the greatest and most versatile
player of all time, possessed what is known as 'football instinct,'
and was able to fathom the attack of every opponent with
lightening-like quickness. And more than this, he won his 'R'
in every branch of varsity athletics."

710. "Men of The Month: Paul LeRoy Robeson," Crisis, Vol. 15, No. 5, March, 1919, pp. 229-231.

The author states: "Paul Robeson is an athlete and is only nineteen years old, but he is six feet, two inches high, and weighs 210 pounds. He is the son of the Rev. W.D. Robeson, a Methodist clergyman in Somerville, N.J. He was graduated from the Somerville, N.J., High School in 1915, at the head of his class. In high school he full-backed on the football team. He entered Rutgers College on a four years' scholarship, won in competitive examination, in which he made the highest average in the state. He became a member of the varsity football team in his first year at Rutgers. He came into prominence, however, only recently, when he played with his colleagues and gained the victory over the Newport Naval Reserves, a team composed of former All-American players and led by Cupid Black, captain of Yale's team last year. Mr. Robeson has since been placed on the All-American and All-Eastern teams of practically every critic!" The article concludes: "His coach, Mr. George Foster Sanford, says: 'Robeson is the best football player in the country today.' Mr. Robeson, also, has maintained a high scholastic record. He has won the class oratorical prize for two years, a feat never before accomplished in the school. He is a varsity debater, plays guard in basketball, throws weights in track, catches in baseball and is a baritone soloist." There is also a photo of Paul Robeson, holding a football, standing along side Fritz Pollard.

711. "Robeson Wins Meet," Rutgers Daily Targum, June 1919, p. 573.

Although Paul Robeson was well-known for his outstanding accomplishments in football, basketball, track and baseball, what is not too well-known is his accomplishments in other sports. He was also on the track team and excelled in that sport. It was reported in a meet against Swarthmore College: "In this contest he hurled the javelin 137 feet 5 inches, 12 feet better than his nearest competitor. The strange part is that this throw was made against a fairly strong wind. What would have happened to the javelin if 'Robey' had been throwing with the wind?"

712. "Rutgers Loses Robeson: Giant Negro was One of Greatest College Stars," New York Times, June 15, 1919, Section 2, p. 4.

The article calls Paul Robeson "one of the greatest all around athletes developed in recent years." It also declares that for the past two years he has been, perhaps, the greatest player in collegiate football, while he has won his points with the weights consistently, a match for the best in basketball and a real varsity man in baseball. Robeson graduated from Rutgers in June 1919.

713. "P.L. Robeson," Crisis, Vol. 18, No. 3, July, 1919, pp. 133, 150-151.

The article states: "At the fiftieth anniversary of Rutgers College Chapter, February 22, 1919, four undergraduates were initiated to membership in the 'Phi Beta Kappa.' Among these was Paul L. Robeson, a Negro, who leads Senior Class both in scholarship and

(Crisis)

athletics. For four years Mr. Robeson has been a member of the
Football Team, and during the season 1917-1918 he gained national
fame by being selected as All-American end by Walter Camp; he has
won his varsity letter as center on the Basketball Team, catcher
on the Baseball Team, and weight thrower on the Track Team; he
also has been a member of the Debating Team. In June, 1919, he
graduated with the degree of Bachelor of Arts; then he studied
law."

714. "Paul Robeson," The Scarlet Letter, (Rutgers University Yearbook),
1919, p. 167.

Rutgers University played Navy in football and Robeson was the
star. It was pointed out, in part: "And as a thorn in her flesh,
the tall, towering Robeson commanding Rutgers secondary, dived
under and spilled her wide oblique angle runs, turned back her
line plunges and carried the burden of the defense so splendidly
that in 44 minutes those Ex-All American backs, who are fixed
luminaries in the mythology of the gridiron, made precisely two
first downs."

B. 1924-1929

1. ACTOR

A. FILMS

715. "Beautiful Colored Film Player," Variety, Vol. 127, No. 2,
      November 26, 1924, p. 1.

      The article states that Paul Robeson, the Colored dramatic star,
      completed his first picture, "Body and Soul." The Black producer,
      Oscar Micheaux, made it in New York City. It was also pointed
      out that playing "opposite Robeson was Julia Theresa Russell,
      considered one of the most beautiful colored women in New York.

716. "Robeson Leaves for England," The Hotel Tattler, July 2, 1929.

      This article states that Paul Robeson who had just joined the (4)
      Harmony Kings was leaving for London, England, to co-star with
      Madam Patrick Campbell in the film "Taboo." The article declares
      that Mr. Robeson no doubt will be to England what (Charles)
      Gilpin was to America.

B. THEATERS

717. "Negro Actor An Athlete: Paul Robeson Attended Brown and Was on
      All-American Eleven," New York Times, February 24, 1924, Part 2,
      p. 6.

      The article states that Paul Robeson, a Negro, who is to play
      opposite Mary Blair, a white actress, in the forthcoming pro-
      duction at Provincetown Theatre of "All God's Chillun Got Wings,"
      a new play by Eugene O'Neill, was a student at Brown University
      five years ago and was chosen as an end on Walter Camp's All-
      American football team for 1919. It also states that he graduated
      from Rutgers with the highest scholastic average in the history
      of the college. It was stated that he has been a political figure

(New York Times)

in Harlem, New York. Robeson attended Rutgers University and
not Brown University.

718. Editorial. "Paul Robeson," Brooklyn Daily Eagle, March 3, 1924,
      Editorial Page.

      Tne editor surmises: ".... A storm is raised by the Provincetown
      Player's determination to produce Eugene O"Neill's 'All God's
      Chillun Got Wings,' in which the love of a black man for a white
      woman is portrayed and the stage business calls for the kissing
      of the darky hero's hand by the blond heroine. Negroes and whites
      are to be in the cast.... Interference by the K.K.K. is prog-
      nosticated.... In the last analysis, the question is how to get
      social equality without absorbion of the negro race by general
      miscegenation.... Eugene O'Neill is on the wrong track. Common
      sense and common fairness will bring the solution of the problem
      nearer and nearer as the decades go on...."

719. "'All God's Chillun' Defended by O'Neill," New York Times, March
      19, 1924, p. 19.

      This article declares that Eugene O'Neill, author of the play,
      "All God's Chillun Got Wings," denied his play of a Negro's
      marriage to white woman would cause racial ill feeling. Mr.
      O'Neill argues: "Mr. Robeson I believe can portray the character
      better than any other actor could. That is all there is to it.
      A fine actor is a fine actor. The question of race cannot enter
      here."

720. "Stars of Roseanne," Billboard, April 12, 1924.

      Paul Robeson is discussed as one of the stars of the play
      "Roseanne." He played the part of the minister. The article
      states that he is not only a talented actor, known in England and
      America, but a Phi Beta Kappa honor graduate of Rutgers and an
      All-American gridiron.

721. "Paul Robeson," Crisis, Vol. 27, No. 6, April, 1924, p. 268.

      The author asserts that Paul Robeson who has played both on the
      American and English stage, has the leading role in Eugene
      O'Neill's "All God's Chillun Got Wings," a play which is to be
      produced by the Provincetown Players some time in April. The
      cast is mixed. Mary Blair, a white, now playing in "Fashion"is
      cast opposite Mr. Robeson, concludes the article.

722. Woollcott, Alexander. "'The Emperor Jones,' Revived: Paul
      Robeson Capital in Eugene O'Neill's Masterpiece," New York Sun,
      May 8, 1924.

      He declares that Robeson adds to his extraordinary physique shrewd,
      rich understanding of the role and a voice that is unmatched in
      the American theatre. Mr. Woollcott concludes: "This dusky
      giant unleashed in a great play provides the kind of evening in

(Wollcott, Alexander)

theatre that you remember all your life...."

723. Madden, Will Anthony. "Paul Robeson Rises to Supreme Heights in
      'The Emperor Jones,'" Pittsburgh Courier, May 17, 1924, p. 8.

      The critic declares: "When Paul Robeson stepped out on the stage
      of the PROVINCETOWN PLAYHOUSE in his initial performance of the
      revival of Eugene O'Neill's drama "THE EMPEROR JONES" the audience
      must have felt that it was in for a treat. This was due to
      Robeson's dominating appearance as the "EMPEROR" and his deep
      rich magnificent voice. Although it has been said that comparisons
      are odious, still in this particular case of "THE EMPEROR JONES"
      it is next to impossible to mention, or even think of this play
      without speaking or thinking of Charles Gilpin. The reason for
      this is because Gilpin was the original "EMPEROR" with his great
      artistic success being a sensation and the talk of the theatrical
      world. Of course this is as it should be, for Gilpin was, indeed,
      a master of this part," states the writer. "However," argues
      Mr. Madden, "Robeson's interpretation of the role left nothing to
      be desired. To begin with, Robeson has the physical build that
      makes him look the part of just what the character portrays
      and with that powerful, rich voice and the ease with which he
      acts, I must say the theatre has gained a great deal by the
      addition of this sterling and promising actor to its ranks. All
      through the seven scenes he never faltered in a single line in
      the change from tragedy to comedy and back to tragedy again and
      unless I am greatly mistaken, we have in Paul Robeson, one of the
      forth-coming actors of the American Stage: not Negro actor but
      actor." He continues, "If he is given the parts to play, re-
      gardless of the Color of the casts, he will rise to the heights.
      Oh! What a Brutus or an Anthony he would make. The PROVINCE-
      TOWN THEATRE was packed to capacity and over-flowing and at the
      conclusion of the play, Robeson received four curtain calls,
      while the audience whistled, stamped its feet and canes,
      shouted and yelled "BRAVO." It was a wonderful ovation." The
      reviewer concludes: "Unquestionably Eugene O'Neill is a play-
      wright of exceptional and rare ability, but as far as the Negro
      is concerned, I am inclined to believe that he is a propagandist.
      He may not be one intentionally and as DuBois says, 'O'Neill is
      bursting through.' Therefore a certain amount of credit must be
      given him for the opportunity he is giving the Negro to appear
      in serious drama in plays of mixed racial casts. It at least,
      given the Negro the opportunity to show that he can act. Never-
      theless, the plays written so far are genius productions of subtle-
      ness of the most insidious and damaging kind."

724. "Paul Robeson is 'Ol Man River'," Morning Post (London), May 4,
      1928.

      This article discusses the play "Show Boat" and Robeson's singing
      of "Ol Man River." The critic declares: "There were many things
      that went into this splendid success of "The Show Boat".... But
      the thing that will be remembered first and last -- the thing
      that held it all together and will be on everybody's lips before

(Morning Post)

many days are over, is the song 'Old Man River.' It is there
in every form, given out gravely in the rich bass of Mr. Paul
Robeson.... jazzed for dancing, wafted in an incidental music
to each pathetic scene....plugged during the interval -- and yet,
though there are over twenty other songs, we did not have too
much of it...."

725. Pollock, Arthur. "Robeson Not Good in Play," Brooklyn Daily Eagle,
      May 18, 1924.

      This critic did not like Robeson acting in "All God's Chillun Got
      Wings." He surmises, in essence: "....impossible for us to
      join the chorus of praise of Paul Robeson, the Negro actor who
      plays the role of the colored boy who has longings he cannot
      satisfy. To us he seemed little better as an actor than an in-
      telligent college boy made uncomfortable by the necessity of
      delivering a speech before his fellow students in Public Speaking...
      Robeson pumps his words out of his system one by one.... Robeson
      has a flat voice, in which there are few shadows.... His
      gestures are stiff...."

726. Budd, A.B. "'All God's Chillun' Opens in N.Y.," Afro-American,
      May 23, 1924, Section 2, p. 5.

      The reviewer states that "All God's Chillun Got Wings" deals with
      the marriage of a white woman, who has been ruined and cast off
      by a low grade prize fighter, to a respectable colored lad, who
      is a law student. The first act deals with the events leading
      up to the intermarriage. Before the play is over the white
      wife has gone insane. "You dirty nigger," she yells at her
      husband with knife uplifted to kill him. Eventually she kisses
      his hand. Budd surmises that it is supposed that O'Neill meant
      to imply that the girl went crazy because as a member of a
      "superior" race she was wed to a colored man. But I am convinced
      that Heywood Broun, of the World, was right when he declared that
      Caucasian superiority suffered a relapse here in that Paul Robeson,
      who sings a song off stage in a voice of great beauty and richness,
      is in all the action a much finer actor than any white member in
      the cast, and that it is his acting alone in the play that gives
      it any value. He concludes: "'All God's Chillun' is a hard play
      to sit thru. To see a big, respectable and cultured character
      as the slave of a slim, depraved and silly white woman, isn't
      the kind of enjoyment calculated to make a good evening's enter-
      tainment."

727. Mantle, Burns. "Paul Robeson In, 'All God's Chillun Got Wings',"
      Pittsburgh Times, May 25, 1924.

      The writer asserts that in the play, "All God's Chillun Got Wings,"
      nothing happened. Nothing resembling a riot, at least, not even
      a good healthy protest.... Mary Blair, white heroine knelt at
      the knee of Paul Robeson, Negro leading man....mumbling in her
      madness something of the gratitude she felt for him upon the wrist.
      And nobody said a word. Not a word. Nor threw anything. Nor

(Mantle, Burns)

hissed. Nor booed. Nor smacked their lips derisively....

728. Lewisohn, Ludwig. "All God's Chillun," <u>Nation</u>, Vol. 118, No. 307,
      June 4, 1924, p. 664.

The critic suggests that the play, "All God's Chillun," by the
Provincetown Players was notably fine. He declares that Mr. Paul
Robeson was a superb actor, extraordinarily sincere and eloquent.
Miss Mary Blair was a little halting in the earlier scenes. Later
she rose to the occasion and was literally thrilling at moments,
states the writer. Mr. Lewisohn concludes: "I must not omit to
mention excellent work by Frank Wilson and Dora Cole, nor the slum
scene by Mr. Throckmorton, nor the directing of Mr. James Light.
I have seen far more beauty and intelligence and mobility than
there are in this production and this play. I have seen nothing
that so deeply gave me an emotion comparable to what the Greeks
must have felt at the dark and dreadful actions set forth by the
older Attic dramatists. And these actions, too, had their origin
in inexpugnable myth and ancient terror."

729. Parsons, Lovella C. "Paul Robeson Returning From England to
      Appear in Film, 'Black Boy'," <u>New York American</u>, June 17, 1929.

According to this writer, scores of people who have returned from
England within the past few months have spoken of the sensation
that Paul Robeson has created in vaudeville. He is the lion of
the hour in London and has been given recognition seldom accorded
any American actor. Mr. Robeson made his first hit in this
country when he appeared in "The Emperor Jones," and was awarded
the Pultizer Prize by a discerning jury that spoke of him as being
one of the stage's greatest artists, concludes Miss Parsons.

730. Stallings, Lawrence. "Robeson Brings a Genius to 'All God's
      Chillun God Wings,'" <u>New York World</u>, June 21, 1924.

This reporter declares: "Regardless of the listless things said
about the play at the Provincetown, here are a few things that
have been said about Paul Robeson. It seems that **Robeson was a**
famous athlete and a prime student at Rutgers, and that since his
college years, which he left full of glory, he has been engaged
in a number of activities. He played the role Charles Gilpin,
another Negro, had created in "The Emperor Jones." It was a
question that he was not better than even the talked-of Gilpin in
that role. In fact, a great many competent judges have said that
he rose to a power and dignity overshadowing Gilpin's.... Now,
in the present play there is no doubt of his ability. Ability
in application to Robeson's work as the Negro in 'All God's
Chillun' is a wretched word. The man brings a genius to the
piece. What other player on the American stage has his great,
taut body -- the swinging grace and litheness of the man who, with
a football under his arm, sidestepped half the broken fields of the
East? And who has a better voice for tragedy than this actor, whose
tone and resonance suggests nothing so much as the dusky, poetic
quality of a Negro spiritual, certainly the most tragic utterances

(Stalling, Lawrence)

in American life?" He continues to assert: "And if one doubts
that a haphazard Negro actor engaged for one fleeting role and at
an obscure, stuffy little hell-box of a theatre has the intellectual equipment of a great player, one has three answers....
After seeing Robeson's performance in 'All God's Chillun Got
Wings,' one can imagine that Shakespeare must have thought of
Robeson."

731.   Lewis, Theopilus. "All God's Chillun Got Wings," Messenger, Vol.
        6, No. 7, July, 1924, p. 223.

        The author reviewed the play "All God's Chillun Got Wings." He
        declared: "Paul Robeson, as Jim Harris, gave an exhibition of
        sound acting which for a few minutes in the second scene of the
        second act became brilliant. Mary Blair, as Ella Downey, was
        good,too, and so was Frank Wilson as Joe...." There is also a
        photo of Paul Robeson.

732.   Nathan, George Jean. "Review of Robeson in 'All God's Chillun',"
        American Mercury, Vol. II, No. 7, July, 1924, pp. 371-373.

        The writer declares: "The singularly fine performance of the role
        of Jim Harris that the Negro Robeson gave recently in Eugene
        O'Neill's 'All God's Chillun' brings still further positive
        testing to the theory that the black man is far better fitted
        naturally for the profession of acting than his white brothers....
        The Negro is a born actor, where the white man achieves acting.
        Robeson, with relatively little experience, and with no training
        to speak of, is one of the most thoroughly eloquent, impressive
        and convincing actors that I have looked at and listened to in the
        past twenty years of theatre-going. As to his Negro colleague,
        Gilpin here acts with all the unrestrained and terrible sincerity
        of which the white actor, save on rare occasions, is by virtue
        of his shellac of civilization just a trifle ashamed."

733.   "Eugene O'Neill on the Negro Actor," Messenger, Vol. 7, No. 1,
        January, 1925, p. 17.

        Eugene O'Neill, often called "America's Greatest Playwright" wrote
        the Editor of the Messenger. He declares: "....But I do wish to
        say - and you can quote me here, if it is of any service to you -
        that my experiences as author with actor have never been so
        fortunate as in the cases of Mr. Charles Gilpin and Mr. Robeson.
        Speaking from these experiences - (and I speak too of minor members
        of the cast) - I would say that the Negro artist on the stage is
        ideal from an author's standpoint. He interprets but he does not
        detract - and when own personality intrudes it is usually (unless
        he has learned too much rubbish in the conventional "white" school
        of acting) an enrichment of the part. I think Negroes are natural
        born actors - (speaking in generalities) - while whites have to
        learn to lose their self-consciousness before they begin to learn.
        As to voice and innate lyric quality of movement and expression,
        there is no comparison. You have it 'all over us.' I have seen
        it in my own plays and I know."

734. "Sir Alfred Butt to Produce O'Neill's 'Emperor Jones" in which Brilliant Artist Will Again Appear in Title Role," New York Amsterdam News, August 5, 1925, p. 6.

This article states that Paul Robeson, accompanied by his wife, sailed for London to play the leading role in Eugene O'Neill's "The Emperor Jones." The play was scheduled to run until January, 1926.

735. "London Likes O'Neill Play: 'The Emperor Jones' and Paul Robeson Win Applause," New York Times, September 11, 1925, p. 20.

According to this article the play, "The Emperor Jones," held a London audience spellbound. It was also pointed out that "The Emperor Jones," from all indications, will have a long run, although the applause of the audience seemed almost equally divided between the play and Paul Robeson, the American Negro, who plays the title role.

736. "Robeson Gave Fine Performance," London Daily Observer, September 13, 1925.

The article states, in part: "Mr. O'Neill abolishes rules altogether.... He is wateful, dramatic, starts his plays clumsily and extravagantly because he is too impatient to work closely on them.... Mr. Paul Robeson, a Negro actor, gave a fine performance as Jones, though, I thought, it was too intellectual.... Mr. Robeson would, I fancy, be extraordinarily impressive as Jim Harris in Mr. O'Neill's 'All God's Chillun Got Wings.' Perhaps Mr. Harwood will produce this play while Mr. Robeson is here."

737. Bott, Alan. "Through A Londoner's Window," The Sphere (London), Vol. 102, No. 1339, September 19, 1925, p. 354.

The writer discusses the problems facing Paul Robeson and other Black artists. He declares, in part:
    ....When a blackman attains distinction he does it
    by overcoming at least twice the difficulties that
    confront the ambitions of a white man. The dice of
    circumstance are loaded against him. And even when
    he does win the respect of the whites by his in-
    telligence, he is likely to be regarded as a pre-
    carious freak rather than an admirable equal.
    Mr. Paul Robeson, the black actor who plays the
    leading part in The Emperor Jones at the Ambassadors
    Theatre, is an artist to the tips of his fingers, and
    an able barrister and cultured man into the bargain.
    Yet I was told, by a colleague of otherwise sound
    judgment, that we did wrong to praise him as an
    artist, because it would provoke negroes all over
    the world into conceit....

738. Shand, John. "The Emperor Jones," New Statesman, Vol. 25,
      No. 647, September 19, 1925, pp. 628-629.

      The writer asserts that the first act of "The Emperor Jones" is
      good, and could almost stand by itself. The rest of the play is a
      monologue in a series of anti-climaxes. The author has found a
      good theme; but the play will never be a famous one because there
      are so many plays with good ideas spoilt by wrong treatment,
      states Shand. He concludes: "It is worth seeing, if only for
      the first act; but mainly you ought to see it because of Mr. Paul
      Robeson is in the leading part. I have nothing but admiration
      for his performance. Where the author was good he was magnificent.
      He failed, I think, only in those pitfalls of the author's which
      only a personality of the greatest magnetism could have o'er-
      leaped. Mr. Robeson's voice, intelligence, physique, and sense of
      the stage immediately made me want to see him in "Othello"....

739. Hamilton, Cicely. "Robeson as 'The Emperor Jones,'" Time and Tide,
      (London), Vol. 6, No. 39, September 25, 1925, pp. 938-939.

      This critic comments on Robeson's role in "The Emperor Jones."
      The writer declares that the theatre was full; and the majority
      of the audience -- the large majority -- was gripped and intent
      throughout the piece; it was obvious, however, that a certain
      minority was not intent -- it was fidgetty, puzzled and given to
      inappropriate comment. It is more than likely that a much ad-
      vertised feature, the ceaseless beating of the tom-tom was the
      cause of this minority restlessness; even when the curtain was
      down between the scenes we were allowed no respite, from its awe-
      some drumming...   This lack of respite was an artistic error,
      as well as an error of judgment ..., states the author. She con-
      cludes: "Paul Robeson's performance of the negro adventurer is
      masterly; but his producer, apparently, could not trust him to
      carry his audience from scene to scene and came to his assistance
      with a drum.... Mr. Robeson is an actor to be listened to and
      The Emperor Jones is a play to be treated with respect.... Some-
      thing of Mr. Paul Robeson's success is due, no doubt, to his per-
      sonality; to his voice, which is soft as well as resonant; to his
      racial intonation and his size. Above all to his size; there
      was pathos almost unbearable in the humbling of so mighty a man."

740. "Robeson is Sensitive Actor," Outlook, October 3, 1925.

      The article declares, in part: "Doubtless the rich melody of
      Mr. Robeson's voice, and the sensitiveness of his acting, helped
      to intensify the contrast and to make Eugene O'Neill's protracted
      soliloquy seem a braver, more successful attempt to capture the
      imagination than it actually is.... these nightmare effects, the
      visions moving and miming to the hectic beat of the tomtom and
      Jones' straining pulse, are only moderately effective. But it
      says much for the art with which Mr. Robeson sustains his part
      and for the splendor of his voice that one was never at any stage
      less than interested, if never wholly absorbed."

741. "'Black Boy,' Stars Robeson," <u>Hartford (Conn.) Daily Times</u>,
      September 21, 1926.

      Paul Robeson and "Black Boy" received mixed reviews. While the
      play itself was described as "almost inexcusably bad....awkward
      and inept in dialogue, artificial in its whipped-up dramatic moti-
      vation," Robeson was seen as the "one bright spot" in the play.
      The critic declares, in part: "Mr. Robeson's equipment for this
      role is well-nigh perfect; a physical giant with a voice so deep
      and rich and powerful, both in speech and in song, that it would
      make a dramatic appeal even without the aid of a mask of extra-
      ordinary mobility of expression. And withal, he is intelligent.
      Not in the least tragic appeal of this play into revelation of a
      talent of so greal possibilities, handicapped and hedged about
      by the mere accident of color. There is the shadow behind the
      substance, which the dramatists, no doubt, sought to reveal."

742. " Black Boy," <u>New York Sun</u>, October 7, 1926.

      The play "Black Boy" had only a short run in New York City. The
      reviewer suggests that the lusty epic of a lost prize-ringer
      is made heartily human by Paul Robeson, but says there is "some-
      thing fiercely, successfully bad about the writing of 'Black
      Boy'.... It saws the air widly with its motives; its action
      tramples heavily on all reasonableness.... Yet the snort of
      animal vigor is in its puniest line, and the fascination of a
      strange, stripped humanity in its most forced moment," states
      the writer.

743. "Fore and Aft the Footlights - Here and Overseas," <u>New York Times</u>,
      October 10, 1926, Part 8, p. 2.

      There is a large sketch of Paul Roveson on the center of the page.
      Under it, the caption stated: "Paul Robeson, the Negro **Actor Who**
      Came to the Comedy Theatre on Wednesday Night as the Star of
      'Black Boy'."

744. "Robeson is Praised by New York Critics at the Opening of New Play:
      'Black Boy'," <u>New York Amsterdam News</u>, October 13, 1926, p. 13.

      The article declares that Paul Robeson, now generally accepted as
      the Race's greatest actor, made a new hit with Metropolitan critics
      when he opened at the Comedy Theatre in "Black Boy." This article
      also discusses several local newspapers that praised Robeson in
      the play.

745. "The Theatre: Black Boy," <u>Life</u>, Vol. 8, No. 16, October 18, 1926,
      p. 18.

      The critic declares the triteness of Jim Tully's plot, exaggerated
      coarseness of language, superficiality of dialogue, are more than
      offset by two redeeming features: the authentic note (struck
      most poignantly when Actor Robeson sings the spiritual, "Sometimes
      I Feel Like A Motherless Child") of the Negro's inability to find
      himself in complicated mazes of the white world; and Mr. Robeson's
      personality. His organ-like voice croons, booms in husky, mellow

(Life)

tones filled with all the languor and ebullience of his naive
race. In the third act he appears stripped to the buff - an
Apollo in black marble, a sight for any sculptor, states the
writer. Across the footlights prejudice turns to admiration.
Black Boy, with the debased morals of the U.S. Negro, can see no
beauty in his own people. Even passion withers when his sweet-
heart is revealed a yellow girl. But Paul Robeson, personally,
shines forth unashamedly black, true to the best of his own,
concludes the article.

746.   Schuyler, George S. "Young Black Joe on Broadway: Black Boy,"
        Pittsburgh Courier, November 6, 1926, Section Two, p. 2.

The writer reviews the play "Black Boy" that was being presented
at the Comedy Theatre in New York City. The critic surmises that
the play was not good drama, but it was good propaganda both for
and against the Negro. He states that "Black Boy" was a mixture
of "Is Zat So," "All God's Chillun' Got Wings," and "White Cargo."
Mr. Schuyler asserts that without Paul Robeson's mastery as Black
Boy the play would be a flat failure. He declares that indeed,
Paul Robeson in relation to the play reminds one of Atlas bearing
the early to his shoulders.

747.   "Stillmans Sail for Visit to Paris," New York Times, April 7, 1928,
        p. 4.

This article basically discusses Mr. and Mrs. James A. Stillman
who sailed on the Olympic of the White Line for Paris. It did,
however, mention Paul Robeson who saided on the same ship for
London, where he would take part in the production of "Show
Boat."

748.   Douglas, James. "A Negro Genius in London," Daily Express,
        July 5, 1928.

Robeson appeared as Joe in "Show Boat" in the Drury Lane Theater.
Douglas, the entertainment critic declares: "He is more than a
great actor and a great singer. He is a great man, who creates
the soul of a people in bondage and shows you its true kinship
with the fettered soul of man. We became like little children
as we surrendered to his magical genius...." He concludes:
"I have heard all the great singers of our time. No voice has
ever moved me so profoundly with so many passions of thought and
emotion. The marvel is that there is no monotony in the spiritual
spell. It is effortless enchantment moving through fluctuant
states of thought and feeling...."

749.   "Robeson Contract Upheld," New York Times, October 5, 1928, p. 7.

This article states that Caroline Dudley, an American manager
alleged she had a prior contract with Paul Robeson and that he
should not be permitted to continue in the play "Show Boat" in
London. The court refused to grant an injunction sought by Miss
Dudley. According to the article for several months Robeson's

(New York Times)

singing of "Ole Man River" in "Show Boat" has been one of the
sensations of the London theatre world. If for any reason Robeson
had to leave the company, said Sir Alfred Butt, manager of the
Drury Lane Playhouse, the whole production might as well cease.

750. Roger, J.A. "'Show Boat' Pleasure-Disappointment," Pittsburgh
Courier, October 6, 1928, Section Two, p. 2.

The writer declares that "Show Boat" in short, is a white man's
play, and the colored brother, as usual, occupied the usual place.
He states that even Paul Robeson, who was always superb, and as
any other person in the cast, occupied a position well in the rear:
his role being that of the lazy, good-natured, lolling darky, a
type that exists more in white men's fancies than in reality.
Roger states, however, his singing of "Old Man River" was unforgettable and was very warmly applauded.

751. Shipp, Horace. "The Wood and The Trees," The Sackerut, Vol. 8,
No. 11, June, 1928, p. 362.

The critic saw Paul Robeson in the role of Joe in the play "Show
Boat" that was playing in London, England. The reviewer made
many comments on the actor's performance. He said, in essence:
"This comparatively new star possessed an essential quality,
important to any performing artist. With or without a name, however, his singing is a delight, and his stage personality has that
aspect of bigness which makes him a friend despite the intervening
footlights...."

752. "Paul Robeson Guest in House of Commons," New York Times, November
18, 1928, p. 24.

Paul Robeson, whose performance in "Show Boat" in London, was one
of the outstanding features of that successful musical comedy, was
entertained at a luncheon in the House of Commons by members of
the Labor Party. After the luncheon, Mr. Robeson was taken to a
seat in the Distinguished Stranger's Gallery and later took tea
with James Maxton and Miss Ellen Wilkinson. Miss Wilkinson then
took Mr. Robeson around the House and introduced him to nearly
every distinguished member.

753. "Play for Paul Robeson," New York Times, November 24, 1928, p. 14.

This article states that Edgar Wallace, author of many "thrillers"
was writing a play for Paul Robeson, whose performance in "Show
Boat" was one of London's sensations. Robeson declares: "...that
Wallace has a feeling for the theatre and could write a wonderful
play about my people, but whether or not the scene will be laid in
Africa I don't know. All I can say is that he will be stepping
out into an entirely new line of country as a playwright."

2. PERSONAL GOALS

754. Frank, William P. "Robeson in 'Black Boy,'" Every Evening
(Wilmington, Delaware), October 4, 1926.

The writer discusses Robeson's personal ambitions and the various
roles that the actor would like to play. The writer suggests:
"He dreams of a great play about Haiti, a play about Negroes,
written by a Negro, and acted by Negroes. He dreams of a moving
drama that will have none of the themes that offer targets for
race supremacy advocates. There is a wealth of material in the
Negro's past, and above all, Robeson fears the stereotyped format
of plays that will imitate "Lulu Belle" and even the play he now
appears in. He also fears the commercialism of the Negro's
characteristics and talents, but while fearing this, he seems to
accept its coming as inevitable in the American theatre.... The
actor, he said, should decide whether plays offered to him will
tend to uplift, degrade, or create wrong impressions of the
Negro...." Frank concludes: "There was one question on which he
spoke with interest: The advance of the Negro as the leading man
in good plays and the reaction of the audience to such plays. In
his estimation, it is a far cry from Uncle Tom's Cabin production
to the present type as 'Emperor Jones,' or 'All God's Chillun
Got Wings.' The ability of the Negro is being discovered by
whites, he said. The talents of the Negro are being brought to
the fore and at last, he added, the shackles of intellectual
slavery are being severed."

755. "Interview with Paul Robeson," New York Telegraph, November 28,
1926.

Robeson was asked about his future plans following "Black Boy."
He surmises: "I don't know.... It's mighty hard to get a play
to fit. There's one they call 'Abraham Bosom' that they want me
to do, but I don't know. Its not happy. It just goes down,
and down and there's hardly a (note) of hope in it. I'm afraid
it wouldn't be popular and I can't afford to be going into plays
that are foredoomed to fail. In concert works I am sure of my
date and sure of some returns."

3. RACE PREJUDICE

756. Walton, Lester A. "Art is Helping in Obliterating The Color Line,"
New York World, May 17, 1925.

The author points out that Paul Robeson and other Black artists
and Black musical shows did their share toward softening race prejudice. He also stated that outside of the concert hall and the
theatre significant incidents were taking place in the daily life
of New York City with art officiating as ambassador for the

(Walton, Lester A.)

promotion of mutual understanding, appreciation and respect. It
was also pointed out that White and Black men attended a testi-
monial dinner given by the Egellor Club for Paul Robeson and
Walter F. White. According to Walton, the most appreciative expressions of Robeson's world as a versatile artist were made by
N. William Welling and often white admirers.

757. "London Grill Bars Paul Robeson: Color Line Draws on Singer and
His Wife," New York Sun, October 23, 1929.

According to this article refusal of a prominent London grill
room to admit Paul Robeson and his wife to meet English white
friends there, despite his being their guest, has raised the race
question in London in acute form. At a meeting of the Society
of Friends (Quakers) a letter from Robeson was read, which com-
plained that he had been excluded from the grill, although the
entertainment had been planned in his honor, states the article.
James Marley, Labor M.P., who called the meeting particularly to
consider the subject cited the case of a Chicago Negro newspaper
publisher, who was refused admission to thirty London hotels last
summer. A Negro in the audience at the close of the discussion
voiced the hope Premier MacDonald would not return from the United
States with "the American prejudice" against Negroes. Marley
assured him there were ways in which even a Prime Minister could
be brought to act in such a matter, concludes the article.

4. SINGER

758. "Robeson Concert Draws Much Fire," East Tennessee News, April 6,
1924.

Paul Robeson was scheduled to give a concert at Constitution Hall
to aid China. Mrs. Gifford Pinchot, wife of the former governor
of Pennsylvania, was chairman of the group that sponsored the
concert. Mrs. Pinchot issued a statement concerning the denial
of the use of Constitution Hall and was bitter in her pronouncement against the Daughters of the American Revolution. Mrs.
Pinchot resigned the chairmanship and retired as sponsor, which
she said was also being done by Mrs. Eleanor Roosevelt and a host
of others because the concert is a joint benefit with the National
Negro Congress purporting to share in the general proceeds. Giving
as her reason the dual benefit, one for aid to China to buy
medical supplies and the other, "Jobs for Negroes," Mrs. Pinchot
said that the two are so far apart there is no connection between
the two and the benefit should be for either one or the other,
and not the two organizations. Criticism was also being levelled
at the National Negro Congress for participating in the concert
in Uline Arena, declaring that by sanctioning the concert in such
a place, the Congress was inconsistent in supporting an institution
which permits a vicious jim-crow rule to govern its maintenance.

(East Tennessee News)

Following Mrs. Pinchot's withdrawal from the committee an ad
appeared in a local daily which stated that the entire proceeds
of the concert would go without deducations to the China Aid
Council of New York City to purchase medical supplies for China.

759. Broun, Heywood. "It Seems to Me," New York World, April 18, 1925.

The critic had the following words to say about the singer: "I
have heard Paul Robeson sing many times, and I want to recommend
this concert to all those who like to hear spirituals. It seems
to me that Robeson does a little better with such a song than anyone else I know; he is closer, I think, to the fundamental spirit
of the music. Into the voice of Robeson there comes every atom
of the passionate feeling which inspired the unknown composers of
these melodies. If Lawrence Brown's arrangement of 'Joshua Fit
de Battle of Jericho' does not turn out to be of the most exciting
experiences of your life, write and tell me about it."

760. "Robeson Is Singer of Genuine Power," The Times (London), April 20,
1925.

The newspaper declares, in part: "Mr. Robeson is a singer of
genuine power. His Negro spirituals have the ring of the revi-
valist, they hold in them a world of religious experience: it is
a cry from the depths, this unusual humanism that touches the
heart. Sung by one man, they voiced the sorrows and hopes of a
people."

761. "Robeson's Voice Has all It Needs," World (London), April 20, 1925.

The newspaper declares: "All those who listened last night to the
first concert in this country made entirely of Negro music - if
one may count out the chorals from Fisk and so forth - may have
been present at a turning-point, one of those thin points of time
in which a star is born and yet visible - the first appearance
of this folk wealth to be made deference or apology. Paul Robeson's
voice is difficult to describe. It is a voice in which deep bells
ring. It has all it needs - perfect pace, beautiful enunciation."

762. "Paul Robeson in Songs: Negro Baritone's Intense Earnestness
Grips His Hearers," New York Times, April 26, 1925, p. 21.

This article declares that an unusually interesting program of
Negro music was given by the baritone Paul Robeson at the Green-
wich Village Theatre before a large and enthusiastic audience.
It was pointed out that Mr. Robeson was a singer of genuine power.
The voice is ample for his needs, mellow and soft, concludes the
reviewer.

763. "Robeson Sings Spirituals," New York World, April 20, 1925.

Robeson appeared at the Greenwich Village Theatre and presented
a program of entirely Negro music. The writer declares: "All
those who listened last night to the first concert in this country

(New York World)

made entirely of Negro music...may have been present at a turning
point, one of those thin points of time in which a star is born
and not yet visible - the first appearance of this folk wealth
to be made without deference or apology. Paul Robeson's voice is
difficult to describe. It is a voice in which deep bells ring...."

764. Brown, Edgar G. "Paul Robeson Destined to be Greater Than (Roland)
      Hayes Says Brown," New York News, April 25, 1925.

      This author asserts that Paul Robeson, the artist, scholar,
      athlete, and gentleman in his initial New York recital at the
      Greenwich Village Theatre confidently sang the songs of a hope-
      ful and divinely trusting race in tones never before breathed by
      a human tongue. He concludes that the voice of Paul Robeson is
      the embodiment of the aspiration of the New Negro who pleads best
      the races progress by adhering strictly to the true endowment of
      his ancestors. Mr. Brown also argues: "Mr. Robeson is destined
      not only to be the new American Caruso, but truly America's great
      benefactor in annihilating race falsehoods as the plough covers
      up the stubbles."

765. "Paul Robeson in Concert," The Evening Post, May 5, 1925.

      The article declares: "Last night Paul Robeson and Lawrence Brown
      gave their second concert of the season and revealed once more
      their mastery of the songs of their people. They provided this
      reporter with a thrill as exquisite as the revelation of Chaliapin
      singing Moussorgsky. For Mr. Robeson combines with a glorious
      rich and mellow voice a dramatic restraint and power that seems
      to hold untold thunder behind each song. His spirituals, sung
      with classic simplicity, have a particular flavour of encompassing
      some universal tragedy of spirit within the bounds of the naive
      form of folk song. And while Mr. Robeson offered the dramatic
      foundation of the recital, Mr. Brown's sympathetic singing and
      piano arrangements completed a concert that brought cheers from
      the Sunday night gathering."

766. "Robeson Sings with Classic Simplicity," Evening Post, May 5, 1925.

      Robeson presented his second concert on May 3, 1925, and it was
      reported by the newspaper. It declared: "Last night Paul Robeson
      and Lawrence Brown gave their second concert of the season, and
      revealed once more their mastery of the songs of their people.
      They provided this reporter with a thrill as exquisite as the
      revelation of Chaliapin singing Moussorgsky. For Mr. Robeson
      combines with a glorious rich and mellow voice a dramatic restraint
      and power that seems to hold untold thunder behind each song.
      His spirituals, sung with classic simplicity, have a particular
      flavour of encompassing some universal tragedy of spirit within
      the bounds of the naive form of folk song. And while Mr. Robeson
      offered the dramatic foundation of the recital, Mr. Brown's
      sympathetic singing and piano arrangements completed a concert
      that brought cheers from the Sunday night gathering."

767.   "Three Singers Heard in Day's Concerts," New York Times, May, 1925, p. 17.

Paul Robeson was one of the three singers that appeared in concert in the same day in New York City. The other two singers were Elizabeth Forkois and Maria Muganero. The article states that Paul Robeson appeared at the Greenwich Village Theatre and gave a remarkable demonstration of dramatic power which the Negro actor has brought to the singing both of the spirituals and secular songs of his race. The audience compelled encores to nearly all his songs, states the article.

768.   Vechten, Carl Van. "All God's Chillun Got Songs: Paul Robeson and Lawrence Brown Reveal the Wealth of Melody and Emotion of the Negro Folk-Song," Theatre Magazine, August 1925, pp. 24, 63.

The author gives a short overview of both Paul Robeson and Lawrence Brown's careers. He said that Paul Robeson is a fine artist, as fine an artist in his way as Yvette Guilbert. Mr. Vechten also declares that Lawrence Brown's versions of the Spirituals are in instances remarkable.

769.   "Paul Robeson Would Become a Singer," New York Times, September 12, 1925, p. 9.

Robeson states his real ambition was to be a singer - not of opera but of simple Negro folksongs. He declares: "I want to sing - to show the people the beauty of Negro folk songs and work songs. I will not go into opera, of course, where I would probably become one of hundreds of mediocre singers, but I will concentrate on Negro music, which has never been properly handled. I may sing a little opera in the morning, but only in the bathroom." Robeson also surmises that "there are, of course, white actors who play negro parts cleverly, but in the serious rending of Negro psychology they are not comparable to Negro Actors."

770.   "Robeson Sings Negro Spirituals," Evening News, September 15, 1925.

The newspaper declares, in part: "It will be long before any of us will forget the spectacle of this magnificently built man, seated on a stool, his white collar and his white cuffs standing out against his dark suit and his dark face; his rolling eyes directed to the cabin roof; the soft beauty of his voice. These Negro Spirituals seem so complete in their pure expressiveness. No repetition, no extra verses that outlast the mood in which the song should be sung. It was an experience to store away among many experiences."

771.   "Music," New Yorker, Vol. 1, No. 48, January 16, 1926, p. 20.

This article states that Paul Robeson seems not to be too far behind Roland Hayes in popularity.

772. "Paul Robeson to Give Soul Stirring Recital," Detroit Independent,
      Janaury 22, 1926.

      According to this article so many people have heard Negro Spirit-
      uals sung by people who have no idea of their true meaning and
      their great beauty, that it will be a matter of unusual interest
      when Paul Robeson and Lawrence Brown, the two greatest exponents
      of Negro music appear in Detroit and give a concert of the music
      of their race. The writer points out that their first concert
      given in New York this year won the highest praise of the critics.
      They also gained the support of the music-loving public, for they
      were obliged to give not only one return concert, but two, states
      the article. The audiences were amazed at the variety which these
      two artists have been able to introduce into an all-negro program.
      There was no monotony; new melodies, new themes, new rhythms
      were constantly being offered as the program developed. Added
      to the musical artistry there was also the fine dramatic inter-
      pretation of Paul Robeson, who, as an actor is known to all
      theatre-goers because of his performance in Eugene O'Neill's plays,
      "The Emperor Jones" and "All God's Chillun Got Wings." To per-
      fect singing was added a rare gift of acting; at best an unusual
      combination, concludes the writer.

773. Epstein, Clifford. "Paul Robeson," Detroit News, January 29, 1926.

      Mr. Epstein had this to say about Robeson: "....Actor though he
      may be, Robeson, when he sings, does nothing else. On the concert
      stage, at least, he is all voice. Without evincing any con-
      scious effort to be so, he is now dramatic, now lyric --....
      Trifles, when he applies his skill to them, become epics of drama
      or comedy...."

774. Gunn, Glenn Dillaid. "Paul Robeson In Concert," Chicago Herald
      Examiner, February 11, 1926.

      The writer declares: "I have just heard the finest of all Negro
      voices and one of the most beautiful in the world, and those
      fortunate ones who were present last night in Orchestra Hall,
      when Paul Robeson made his first Chicago appearance, will testify
      that I do not exaggerate. In the soft mellow resonance, in sym-
      pathetic, in its organ-like ease and power, it is distinguished
      among the great voices of the present. By quality alone it
      exercises a spell that is inescapable. Long before he had finished
      his first group of spirituals, Robeson had moved his listeners
      to tears, to laughter, and to shouted demands for repetition."
      He concludes: "His programme was limited to the music of his
      race. Such a programme might easily become monotonous, but this
      singer practices a simplicity, a sincerity, and an unconscious dig-
      nity of style that immediately wins the respectful attention of
      his listeners. After the first phrase from his magnificent voice
      they are won completely. Criticism is silent before such beauty.
      His associate, Lawrence Brown, is a gifted accompanist, a re-
      sourceful arranger of the music of his people, and at times a
      capable vocal collaborator."

775. "Robeson and Brown Sing," Chicago Evening American, February 11, 1926.

Paul Robeson gave his first Chicago concert and received good reviews. The writer referred to both Robeson and Lawrence Brown, his accompanist as "singers." The writer asserts: "These two men are genuine artists - and their singing is something more than art, while it is as well delightful and stimulating diversion. They merely sing with tremendous vitality, delicacy, and poetry; and they carry the public with them every step of the way.... Robeson's diction is so clear and intelligible that one needs no program notes, and he never mouths nor sacrifices the timbre of the tone for mere pronunciation."

776. "Paul Robeson and Lawrence Brown at Town Hall," Broad Ax, February 27, 1926, p. 3.

This article states that Paul Robeson and Lawrence Brown appeared at Town Hall in New York City and sang the Negro spirituals and folk songs with their customary success. It was also pointed out that White critics declared: "Their voices retained a natural velvety quality and vibrated with real emotion."

777. Sargeant, Elizabeth S. "The Man With His Home in a Rock: Paul Robeson," New Republic, Vol. 24, No. 587, March 3, 1926, pp. 40-44.

The writer declares: "Paul Robeson is a symbol -- a symbol of the increasing important place of the American Negro on the American stage, that you will magnify or minimize according to your prejudices and desires. It is earnestly to be hoped that the men like Paul Robeson with his evangelical tradition and Lawrence Brown with his Florida verve, who are consciously and lovingly working in an unconscious folk art are establishing a 'classic' Spiritual tradition that will long live in American music." One of the critics, writing of Robeson's first concert, suggested that if Chaliapin could be conceived as singing Negro folk songs as his own, he would sing them as Paul Robeson does. "Let us give thanks that we were not born too late to hear this Negro Chaliapin render the Spirituals reverently, with wildness and awe, like a trusting child of God," concludes Miss Sargeant.

778. Hughes, Langston. "The Negro Artist and the Racial Mountain," Nation, Vol. 10, June 26, 1926, pp. 692-694.

The writer surmises that Paul Robeson's singing "is truly racial." He also declares: "Letting Paul Robeson sing 'Water Boy'.... caused the smug Negro middle class to turn from their white, respectable, ordinary books and papers to catch a glimmer of their own beauty."

779. Warner, A.J. "Program of Negro Songs Sung by Paul Robeson," Rochester (N.Y.) Time-Union, March 23, 1927.

Paul Robeson gave a concert in Rochester, New York, at the Baptist Temple. The critic of the concert declares that Mr. Robeson's program was devoted entirely to Negro Spirituals, with the

(Warner, A.J.)

exception of one or two Negro secular songs and to their performance he brought a penetration, a sympathy and a divining power
that are the fruit of true inspiration. The writer asserts that
he sings with unerring intelligence and his command of the art of
vocalization is obviously secure.

780.   "Sing Negro Spirituals," New York Times, April 21, 1927, p. 24.

Paul Robeson and Lawrence Brown appeared in Town Hall in New York
City in a program of Negro spirituals and secular dialect. The
occasion was a benefit for the Harlem Museum of African Art, the
proceeds to be devoted to a fund for the purchase of a collection
which will form the nucleus of a permanent exhibit. The article
concludes: "Mr. Robeson, as on previous occasions, made a deep
impression in his singing of familiar spirituals. His mellow
baritone seems to have gained in smoothness and control and had
all its old emotional color in the plaintive strains of the simple
melodies."

781.   "Robeson," Crisis, Vol. 35, No. 5, July 1927, p. 166.

This article declares that Paul Robeson has come in lately for a
good deal of widely separated publicity. The Y.M.C.A. advertising
for contributions, put full-page advertisements in many of the
New York papers. The advertisement, with the picture of Robeson,
said: "Negro Harlem is struggling, growing, singing, hoping. Paul
Robeson, Roland Hayes and many other Negro artists and intellectuals are aiding that struggle, firing that hope...." The
writer declares: "If Paul Robeson ever comes to this town to
sing, be sure to hear him. He is a remarkable man. You will see
a young black fellow with a kind, strong face, more than six feet
tall, with the build of an athlete." The reporter points out:
"Paul Robeson is of pure African blood, the son of a Negro
preacher who believed in his son and stirred him to develop all
that was in him. One day Paul Robeson brought home a report card
from school with seven A marks and one B mark in his studies.
His father said,'What about that B mark? If you can get seven
A's, you can get eight.' The next term Paul did get eight A's.
When he sings he stirs the pool of tears for you. His voice is
not highly trained, it has no great range. He sings the songs
of the black man's heart," concludes the writer.

782.   "Ovation for Paul Robeson," New York Times, October 30, 1927,
       Part 2, p. 3.

Paul Robeson received an ovation when he gave a recital of Negro
Spirituals at the Salle Gaveau in the Rue de la Boetie in Paris,
France. At least 500 persons were turned away from the concert
because of lack of seating space. According to the article, the
critic accorded as much praise as did the enthusiastic audience.
They said the singer's voice, which always has been highly regarded
in America, is greatly improved in range and quality as a result
of his studies, concluded the article.

783. "Robeson and Brown Triumph in Paris," <u>New York Amsterdam News</u>,
      November 16, 1927.

      This article reports on Paul Robeson and Lawrence Brown's triumph
      in Paris, France. It states: "The opening recital in Paris by
      Robeson and Brown at the Medison Gaveau was crowned with success
      from every point of view. The two artists continued to tour all
      of the leading European countries. A few days after the announce-
      ment of their appearance almost every seat was sold and on the
      night of the performance many had to be content with standing room.
      The capacity of the Salle Gaveau was about 1,700. The applause
      that greeted the first spiritual 'Wade in the Water,' one of the
      least known on the bill, left little doubt that the rest of the
      concert was going to be a success. After each selection the
      artists were heartily applauded, and were compelled to give
      several encores. At the end of the performance, almost the entire
      audience kept its seat as if the program had not been finished,
      and it was not until the artists had given three more numbers that
      it was content to leave," states the article.

784. "Paul Robeson in Benefit," <u>New York Times</u>, May 12, 1927, p. 25.

      Paul Robeson, assisted by Lawrence Brown, gave a recital at Town
      Hall in New York City for the benefit of the American O.R.T.
      This organization carried on welfare work among Jews of central
      and Eastern Europe. A large and enthusiastic audience applauded
      the singer in a program made up largely of familiar spirituals.

785. "Mr. Robeson's Matinee," <u>The Star</u>, July 4, 1928.

      The reviewer states that he wonders how many singers there are
      who could fill Drury Lane as Mr. Robeson did at his matinee. He
      concludes that Robeson is a singer of remarkable gifts with a
      beautiful, admirably controlled voice, and perfect diction.

786. "Mr. Paul Robeson," <u>Daily News and Westminister Gazette</u>, July 4,
      1928.

      This article states that Mr. Paul Robeson had a very large audience
      at Drury Lane Theatre at his matinee of Negro spirituals and folk-
      songs. The reviewer also asserts that there are not many, if any,
      operatic artists who have such perfect diction or more beautiful
      voices.

787. Douglas, James. "A Negro Genius in London," <u>London Daily Express</u>,
      July 5, 1928.

      After discussing Robeson, the artist, the writer continues: "He
      is more than a great actor and a great singer. He is a great man,
      who creates the soul of a people in bondage and shows you its
      true kinship with the fettered soul of man. We became like little
      children as we surrendered to his magical genius.... What is the
      secret of his mastery of all our highest moods and all our holiest
      emotions?.... There are seconds when his face was alight and
      aflame with seership. We saw the rapt mysticism gathering in
      intensity until it reached the height of the mood and then it

(Douglas, James)

slowly faded like a sunset, and he locked the door on it with a
tightened, tense mouth...." Mr. Douglas concludes: "Strange that
a Negro singer out of 'Show Boat' should be able to fill a vast
theatre with a divine witchery of Bunyan and Wesley, and reveal to
astonished worldlings the world beyond their world."

788.   "Woman Sues Robeson in London: Singer Broke U.S. Contract, Says
        Manager," Chicago Tribune Sunday News, September 30, 1928.

According to this report Paul Robeson was dividing his time between singing to applauding audiences in the Drury Lane theatre
and fighting off legal moves in an attempt to take him back to
America to appear in a revue there. The trouble arises from a
contract the singer made with Caroline Dudley Reagen to appear in
a colored revue in New York. Robeson says he made an agreement in
a time of financial stress, when his wife's illness forced him to
cancel his European concert tour and return hastily to the United
States. He accepted $500 in advance and meantime went to England
to play in "Show Boat," states the article. It also surmises that
London fell heavily in love with the singer and he soon saw "Show
Boat" was due for an indefinite stay. Since then he cancelled his
contract with Miss Reagan and declined the advance, giving notice
months before the production. He also offered to pay any reasonable forfeit, suggests the reporter. The producer, however, intended building the show around Robeson's name, so went right
ahead, hoping still to bring him back to America. The woman
manager first went to the Actors' Equity, which suspended Robeson
for a month - a suspension which may become permanent unless he
explains his case. This, however, does not worry the singer,
since he does not expect to return to the stage. He plans to
devote himself to singing only. But Miss Reagan suddenly popped
up in England and filed action against Robeson, as well as against
the Drury Lane theater, for breach of contract. Robeson says
he does not think the courts have jurisdiction, but nevertheless
the battle will begin on that point Wednesday. Miss Reagan really
does not want damages. She prefers the singer's services, but
Robeson likes London, concludes the writer.

789.   Ballard, Rev. Roberton. "Paul Robeson: A Genius with a Soul,"
        Star of Zion, January 31, 1929.

The article points out that Paul Robeson was in his father's
church until he was twenty-one. He was superintendent of his
father's Sunday-school, and an active worker in the church. It
was here that he first began to sing "Negro Spirituals," which
have given him almost a world-wide reputation. Robeson talks
about his father: "When people talk about my voice, I wish they
could have heard my father preach. My father was my idea of a
perfect Christian: I have seen him when taunted by the hideous
injustices of color 'bar', but never once did I know him to cherish
a thought of bitterness or even unkindliness. Towards his fellow-
man he lived as he preached, in a way that I have never met in any
other minister.... We all went to college and had a university
education through his sacrifices for us. He gave up everything

(Ballard, Rev. Roberton)

for his children. My father wanted me to enter the ministry, and
that was originally my own desire also. I went to college with
that motive. Then circumstances led to me story law, and I finally
graduated in law at Columbia University, although I never practised."

790.   "Paul Robeson in Budapest, Hungary," Pesti Naplo (Budapest),
April 13, 1929.

This newspaper states that after the Hungarian audience heard
Robeson sing, it received a "surprise"which sprang from the
spiritual and artistic life of America. The article declares:
"He was an extremely cultured singer, technically beyond criticism;
his etheral piano tones, his refined and perfect legate reveal a
highly developed vocal art; his organ a deep and solid bass....
Its brillance and colour does not dazzle, but it warms you....
It is a genuinely virile voice...."

791.   "Paul Robeson in Budapest, Hungary," Orai Ujsag (Budapest),
April 14, 1929.

This newspaper had this to assert about Robeson: "....This time
the advance notices have not exaggerated; they have only erred.
Robeson is not a Negro Chaliapin, but a Negro Hegle Lindberg.
This fantastic religiousness, this mystic manifestation of the
soul of a race, came to tell us again last night that which had
been unknown to us before Hegle Lindberg...."

792.   "Vienna Likes Spirituals," New York Times, April 17, 1929, p. 5.

The article states that Paul Robeson got a great reception at his
first concert in Vienna. According to the article, Vienna, noted
for conservatism in musical matters, felt under the spell of the
most primitive form of American Negro Music. The concert hall
was crowded to the roof to hear Robeson sing Negro spirituals.
He had to give six encores before the audience would disperse,
surmises the article.

793.   "Triumph for Negro Vocalist: Paul Robeson's Notable Singing at
Albert Hall," Daily Chronicle, April 29, 1929.

This article declares that a success, such as a musician of his
race has seldom enjoyed, was achieved by Paul Robeson as he
appeared as the "star" artist at the Albert Hall concert. The
critic declares that Mr. Robeson's superb voice has one outstanding quality, that which is best expressed by the Italian word,
"simpatico." His singing, too, has that naturalness and simplicity, which is characteristic of great art, suggests the article.

794.   Cullen, Countee. "All God's Chillun Got A Song," Radio Times,
June 28, 1929, pp. 663, 667.

The writer comments on Negro music. He also has some words about
Paul Robeson. Mr. Cullen asserts: "Paul Robeson, a tall, big-
boned American Negro with a voice like an organ and a gentle half

(Cullen, Countee)

apologetic demeanour that seems to deprecate the transplanting of these songs from their virgin soil, gathers to a recital over eight thousand (8,000) Londoners at Albert Hall." The author concludes: "There are no arias on his programme, no French ballads, no English madrigals or German Lieder, only the sorrow-songs of his people, but encore after encore is demanded until the tired artist can only come forth and bow in happy for pleading acknowledgment."

795. Mitchel, William R. "Paul Robeson Thrills Audience," Pittsburgh (Pa.) Press, December 4, 1929, p. 34.

Paul Robeson gave a concert at the Carnegie Music Hall in Pittsburg. The critic delcares that to a SUPERLATIVE degree, Mr. Robeson had everything that goes to make the artist. His rhythm is almost uncanny in its appeal, his voice, a big, **orotund** baritone of lovely quality, unspoiled by faulty training and possessing a tremendous range, from the lowest deeps to anywhere he cares to take it in the upward reaches. And all through, it is of pure, liquid gold, concludes Mr. Mitchel.

796. Holmes, Ralph. "Paul Robeson's Cello-Like Voice Charms Audience," Detroit Evening Times, December 7, 1929.

Paul Robeson gave a concert in Detroit at Orchestra Hall. The critic declares that the cello-like tones of his voice, velvet smooth, mysteriously luminous like deep, dark water stirred the hearts of his hearers until they applauded half a dozen numbers onto a programme that already included a baker's dozen. Mr. Holmes also asserts that how much that richly resonant voice reflects the calm but powerful personality of this man, or how much that personality, poised and self-assured, but not self-assertive, colors our imagination before we ever hear the voice is perhaps not a matter that concerns us here, but certainly it is that the combined effect of voice and personality is quite irresistible.

797. "Paul Robeson Applauded," New York Times, December 15, 1929, p. 29.

The article declares that Paul Robeson, actor and baritone, gave his fourth program of Negro songs before an audience that filled the Town Hall in New York City. It points out that the audience applauded him to the echo at every pause. The versatile American artist again had limited himself to songs of his race, which he gave with native eloquence, according to the article.

798. "Ovation Given Robeson at Princeton," New York Times, December 17, 1929, p. 29.

The article states: "An ovation such as has seldom been seen in Princeton greeted Paul Robeson, Negro singer, who returned to the town of his birth this evening for a concert of Negro Music." It asserts: "The concert held in Alexander Hall, was for the benefit of a colored church here of which the singer's father was at one time the minister. Robeson was required to give a

(New York Times)

half dozen encores and the audience, largely composed of students, shouted their approval as he sang Negro folk songs."

5. STATUE

799.   "Robeson in Marble: Statue World $20,000," Pittsburgh Courier, November 20, 1926, Section Two, p. 1.

This was a photo of a statue done by Antonio Salemme of New York. Robeson posed four months and it showed him in a "kneeling" pose illustrating his famed spiritual qualities.

6. VOICE

800.   "Paul Robeson Sings His Old Favorites," New York Times, November 6, 1929, p. 28.

This article states that Paul Robeson returning from engagements abroad gave his first concert of spirituals and folk music at Carnegie Hall in New York City. It was stated that the vibrant and resonant voice of the singer held the audience in their seats after each section of the program and at the close of the concert until encores were given. Many of the arrangements were by the singer's accompanist, Lawrence Brown.

801.   Sampson, Edith S. "Thousands Acclaim Robeson in Chicago," Pittsburgh Courier, November 16, 1929, p. 3.

Paul Robeson gave his second concert in Chicago after returning from Europe. The reviewer states that Paul Robeson had a rich, colorful and magnificent voice. The audience applauded and he gave several encores. It was also stated that Mr. Robeson's enunciation was marvelous.

802.   "Robeson's Return," Time, Vol. 14, No. 21, November 18, 1929, pp. 41-42.

This article states that a big, bronze-colored man, magnificently built, scrupulously dressed, walked on the stage in Manhattan's Carnegie Hall last week and waited quietly for his audience to settle. Then he began in a voice the color of his skin "I Got a Home on a Rock, Don't You See." The singer was not Roland Hayes, although for years Hayes has been the only Negro to sell out a hall of Carnegie's size. Hayes is slight, frail-appearing. He sings spirituals artfully, in a high voice that is often reedy. The Negro who sang last week in Manhattan was as tall as Basso

(Time)

Feodor Chaliapin and brawnier. His voice was big and mellow. He sang simply. He was Paul Robeson, athlete-actor-baritone. Last week's was his first U.S. appearance after a three-year absence in Europe, concludes the article.

803. "Paul Robeson Sings Group of Spirituals," Mail and Empire (Toronto, Canada), November 22, 1929.

Mr. Robeson gave a concert in Toronto, Canada, at Massey Hall. According to this article he scored an undoubted success, and conquered the audience less by artistry than genuine sincerity and a very simple and direct appeal. He concludes that Mr. Robeson has besides his splendid stage presence, a fine, natural voice, which is basso rather than baritone, very true in pitch and of velvet texture.

804. Johnson, James Weldon. "Race Prejudice and the Negro Artist," Harper's Magazine, Vol. 157, November, 1928, pp. 769-776.

The author argues that Paul Robeson sang spirituals to large and appreciative audiences in New York and over the country, giving to those songs a fresh interpretation and a new vogue. "Paul Robeson - that most versatile of men, who has made a national reputation as athlete, singer, and actor - played in Eugene O'Neill's 'All God's Chillun' and added to his reputation on the stage, and moreover, put to the test an ancient taboo; he played the principal role opposite a white woman." Johnson also states that Robeson played the title role in a revival of "The Emperor Jones" and almost duplicated the sensational production by Charles Gilpin in the original presentation.

805. J. A. R. "Elderly Woman Calls Robeson 'The Greatest,'" New York Amsterdam News, December 4, 1929, p. 11.

The writer signed her name J.A.R. Paul Robeson gave a concert at Town Hall in New York City. The reader suggests that Robeson's singing was perhaps most remarkable: "In listening carefully to him one could fancy he was bearing a chorus, if not in volume of sound at least in richness, color, and variety of tone. His voice has such depth, mellowness, strength, and amplitude that he seems to achieve by himself alone what is possible ordinarily only for a combination of voices. His voice, as in the singing of 'Deep River,' was full of religious feeling, and while strong and resonant, was tender. At times it expanded into a rich, organ-like quality," states the author. She concludes: "Robeson is without doubt the ideal interpreter of primitive strength, of rugged sincerity, faith, and even joy that one never loses the illusion of listening in on the earliest singers and creators of these classics from humble life, so far as the above mentioned qualifies are concerned."

C. 1930-1939

1. AFRICA

806. Reagan, Richard. "Be Yourselves, Robeson's Advice to His Race,"
New York Herald Tribune, January 11, 1931, Section 8, p. 2.

The author declares that Paul Robeson believed that to stifle the
primitive emotional heritage of the Negro and to foster the
sophisticate was to destroy the most potent asset of his race.
According to Mr. Reagan, Mr. Robeson admitted that he was "almost
at the point where he feels that the only emotional strength for
the American Negro will come from Africa." The writer concludes:
"He (Paul Robeson) reiterated that he was not speaking facetiously
in his aversion of those who would make of him a sophisticate,
and that he would penetrate the bush of Africa eventually and
drink his fill of savage emotions."

807. Cooke, Marvel. "Mrs. Paul Robeson, Manager and Mate," New York
Amsterdam News, October 5, 1935, p. 9.

Various references are made to Paul Robeson throughout this
article. It was pointed out that the singer was building a
Russian and Chinese collection of books. Miss Cooke suggested
that the Robesons are convinced that there is a great similarity
between Chinese and African literature. According to Mrs.
Robeson both believe in ancestor worship, magic and religion, and
that their tribal structure is similar.

2. FILMS

808. "Paul Robeson: Portrait as Emperor Jones," Theatre Arts Monthly,
Vol. 17, October, 1933, p. 801.

There is a portrait of Paul Robeson as "The Emperor Jones." It

(Theatre Arts Monthly)

was also stated that the film version of Eugene O'Neill's play, written by Dubose Heyward, takes full advantage of Robeson's double quality as an actor and as a singer.

809. "Film Contract for Mr. Paul Robeson," London Times, June 25, 1934, p. 12.

This article reported that Mr. Paul Robeson, who recently made his first appearance on the screen in "Emperor Jones," had been engaged to play the part of a native chief in "Sanders of the River," the British film version of Mr. Edgar Wallace's novel.

810. Long, Edward. "Robeson at $30,000, Best Paid Film Star," Afro-American, January 10, 1935.

According to this article Paul Robeson completed six weeks in Hollywood, playing the role of Joe in Universal's "Showboat," and was paid $5,000. per week. He is the highest paid colored star of 1935, states Mr. Long. Next to him was Bill Robinson, who drew down $3,500 every week for pictures. They were: "Hooray for Love," by RKO, "The Big Broadcast of 1936," Paramount, "In Old Kentucky," and "The Littliest Rebel," both Twentieth Century-Fox. Louise Beavers made two pictures and received an average pay check of $750 per week. They were: "West of the Pecos," and "Annapolis Farewell." Stepin Fetchit and Clarence Muse averaged $500 each a week during the year. Both were continually busy. Fetchit is under contract to Twentieth Century-Fox but Muse is free lance, concludes the writer.

811. "Paul Robeson Seen in a New Korda Film: 'Sanders of the River,' Hailed at London Premiere," New York Times, April 3, 1935, p. 20.

The article states that Paul Robeson added still another triumph to his long list of achievements, co-starring with Leslie Banks in "Sanders of the River." According to this report from London, where the film was made, Robeson made an impressive figure as Bosambo, leader of a loyal African tribe, and his deep, rich voice never was more effective than in these native melodies. "The genuine merits of the film lie in the straight forward rapidity of its story-telling and in the brilliance of its pictures of river and forest and of native ceremonials. Robeson and Banks distinguish themselves by the unaffected strength of their action," declares the Times of London.

812. "Premiere of 'Sanders of the River,'" London Daily Sketch, April 3, 1935.

Paul Robeson and his wife, along with hundreds of others attended the premiere of his movie at the Leicester Square Theatre in London. The newspaper states: "....crowds stood outside Leicester Square Theatre to watch celebrities arriving for 'Sanders of the River' gala. An ex-Queen, Cabinet Minister, and battalions of less important people packed the foyer. What a bustling and jostling.... Queen Victoria Eugenie -- she was wearing black -- and her escort,

(<u>London Daily Sketch</u>)

Mrs. Redmond McGrath, had some difficulty in getting to the stair-
case. When the show was over, a blue-coated attendant had to come
to the aid of Commander Redmond McGrath in forcing a way through
the foyer to enable the Queen to reach the exit. Lord Carisbrooke
was with his sister.... Cabinet Minister J.H. Thomas, with his
wife, were in Sir George and Lady Sutton's party.... Lady Ravens-
dale - a tiara with a halo effect, consisting of large square
stones in different colours set in gold...."

813.   Sayers, Michael. "The Drama: A Play to be Seen," <u>The New English</u>
        <u>Weekly</u>, (London), Vol. 7, No. 5, May 16, 1935, p. 93.

        This critic called "Stevedore" episodic. He declares, in part:
        "To see him (Paul Robeson) over that wharf, below which he is
        supposed to have been skulking all day long in the mud, to hear
        his panting, and then to watch his furtive, frightened, shameful
        gestures, is to be appalled at the terrible ignominy that the
        actor by the compulsion of his imagination, is forcing us to share.
        There is not a more sincere and interesting piece of acting in
        London...."

814.   "Robeson Film Called Propaganda Justifying British Imperialism:
        Nancy Cunard Says English Picture is Pure Nordic Bunk," <u>Afro-</u>
        <u>American</u>, July 6, 1935.

        This article asserts that "Sanders of the River," a British-made
        film starring Paul Robeson and Nina Mae McKinney, was bradned by
        Nancy Cunard as the most subtle of English imperialistic pro-
        paganda. She states that "Sanders of the River," is taken from
        one of the numerous best-sellers by which Edgar Wallace so
        successfully exploited a mythical African scene. "Sanders is the
        'paternal' British administrator of two million natives in Nigeria.
        (Technically impossible, be it said, as no administrator controls
        such a number.) Sanders is the iron hand in the velvet glove,
        with his consciousness of deep responsibility, his 'affection'
        for these 'black children,'"according to Miss Cunard. She said
        that "lucky man finds a real white man's n____r in the person
        of Bosambo, played by Paul Robeson, a young chief, who fights all
        his battles and finally defeats "the Old King," who has had the
        temerity to reamin an enemy to the whites of Robeson. She asserts:
        "In Paul Robeson's handsome and expressive features there is far
        more of the Red Indian than of the African. Robeson acts well,
        Miss McKinney breathes says, and breathes out a sweet enough
        lullaby. Robeson sings the theme-song laudatory of British rule,
        in English, with a few words of "African" thrown in. Miss Cunard
        concludes: "In a word, this film is pure fire and dead, dead
        meat - the true stuff of Africa which they haven't been able to
        spoil (cut it as they have), and the lifeless, outworn slogans of
        the white man's might, the ponderously hypocritical propaganda of
        this 1935, which assures us of its paternal concern, but which is
        nothing else than one more immense effort at a justification of
        imperialistic exploitation."

815. Poston, Tom R. "Robeson to Play King Christophe in British Pro-
      duction, He Reveals: Actor, Here, Answers Critics of 'Sanders
      of the River,'" New York Amsterdam News, October 5, 1935, pp. 1,
      2.

      Robeson answers his critics concerning his role in "Sanders of the
      River." He declares: "To expect the Negro artist to reject
      every role with which he is not ideologically in agreement, is
      to expect the Negro artist under our present scheme of things to
      give up his work entirely - unless, of course, he is to confine
      himself solely to the Left theatre. Under such an arrangement,
      I might as well give up my singing, my concert work, everything.
      To say that I had no right to appear in 'Sanders of the River'
      is to say that I shouldn't have appeared in 'Emperor Jones' - that
      I shouldn't accept the role in 'Showboat.'" The much-criticized
      film, Mr. Robeson states, was not originally planned as an Empire-
      building epic. The first scenes were shot in Africa fully a year
      before he assumed his role, he said, and the film was intended
      as just another Edgar Wallace thriller. The imperialist angle was
      placed in the plot during the last five days of shooting, the
      actor reported, when Korda (London Film Productions) decided to
      follow the lead of Hollywood and at the same time tie the venture
      up with the king's jubilee. The picture was such a great success,
      financially, he revealed, that Korda has decided to film the life
      of King Christophe with Mr. Robeson in the title role. After this
      picture is completed, he said, he feels sure that he can persuade
      Korda to present the life of Menelik II on the screen. "That
      would really be worthwhile, and of course it would have to be
      done in England or Europe. Could you imagine a Black King being
      treated seriously in Hollywood?" states the author.

816. "Paul Robeson Introduces 'The Song of Freedom,'" Film Weekly,
      May 23, 1936, p. 17.

      In "The Song of Freedom" Paul Robeson portrays a prince who left
      Africa and became a world-famous concert star. He leaves the con-
      cert stage of Europe and returns to Africa to claim his rightful
      place as King of Casanga. He continues to sing and raise revenue
      to help his people. Robeson states: "'The Song of Freedom' is
      the first film to give a true picture of many aspects of the life
      of the colored man in the west....this film shows him as a real
      man, with problems to be solved, difficulities to be overcome."

817. "Paul Robeson Film Picketed for Showing in Brooklyn," New York
      Amsterdam News, September 1, 1936, p. 5.

      This article states that Paul Robeson's latest film, "The Song
      of Freedom" would run for four consecutive days in October at the
      Brooklyn (N.Y.) Regent Theatre. The reviewer gives a summary of
      the film. He concludes: "This is definitely the picture not to
      miss, if you crave good acting, a plausible story with plenty of
      action and marvelous singing of the one and only Paul Robeson."

818. "Paul Robeson in King Solomon's Mine," Film Weekly, September 19,
1936.

This article declares, in part: "Paul Robeson is willing to give
up the concert platform, ignore the stage and concentrate solely
on films. But only is he can find the right roles in the right
pictures.... Robeson has never had a role in a film with which he
was really satisfied. He is not quite sure even now just what
kind of part he is looking for. 'The Song of Freedom,' which is
on at the Plaza this week, is a kind of test piece...." The
article continues: "Early this week, 'King Solomon's Mines' went
into production at Shepherd's Bush. Robeson has been signed to
play Umpobas. He would like to make that part not just a supporting role in which he will, inevitably, sing, but a living
characterization. Not just a 'splendid savage' but a man of real
thoughts and ambitions." The writer concludes: "When he has
finished 'King Solomon's Mines,' Robeson is to make a picture for
Capitol Films....to be produced by Walter Futter and will probably
be directed by Thornton Freeland. Robeson will play the part of
an American Negro soldier who remains in Africa after the World
War, becomes a chief among the Touaregs and leads his nomadic
North African tribe in a dramatic trek across the Sahara."

819. Campbell, George. "What Paul Robeson Could Do," The Bystander,
September 30, 1936, p. 566.

The author surmises, in part: "....it's 'pathetic' that in spite
of his 'enormous personality, genuine talent'....glorious voice...
he has never made one first-class movie and it looks as if he
never will. The trouble lies in the unimaginative commerciali-
sation of the screen, the insistence that a black man is not box
office unless he be either an Uncle Tom or a dealer in hot
rhythms." Mr. Campbell suggests that producers forget that
Robeson is a Negro and let him simply portray "normal human beings
in their mingled baseness and nobility, their greed and cruelty
and sacrifices of self...."

820. "Paul Robeson and Elizabeth Welch Appear in New Film," California
Eagle, October 4, 1936, p. 3.

The article states that "Song of Freedom," a new talking picture
produced by a British film company and shown for the first time
last week with Paul Robeson and Elizabeth Welch as the stars, is
receiving wide praise by English critics who at the same time declare they want the famous singer to forget his savage roles and
appear as "a distinguished and honorable gentleman." The writer
declares: "In this film, Robeson follows his 'Emperor Jones,'
and 'Sanders of the River' tradition. The white man is always
anxious to masquerade the savage ancestry of the Negro. Indirectly,
however, the white man would like to impress the Negro that his
lineage is ancient and honorable, devoid of savagery and barbarism.
But the perpetual presentation of African voodoo and esoteric
jungle influence is becoming a bit sordid. The plot of 'Song of
Freedom' is rather weak, but that does not detract from the excellence of Robeson's acting" concludes the reviewer. It was
also stated that typical of the reviews appearing in London dailies

(California Eagle)

is one by C.A. Lejeune, noted critic of The Sunday Observer: "I
am always actuely embarrassed by the sight of Mr. Paul Robeson,
probably the world's most cultivated and erudite singer, performing the songs of native Africa with lyric and orchestra, and
a crowd of oriental extra gentlemen on either hand.... The
singing, particularly the king-song, is in Mr. Robeson's best
style, and if you are sufficiently detached to be able to shut
your eyes in a cinema, you may really be tempted to think this
a work of quality. But I wish that Mr. Robeson, who has sung in
all the more august musical haunts of Europe and America, might
be allowed, just for once, to appear on the screen in a civil
capacity as a responsible citizen. The eminent coloured singer,
one knows, is a loyal child of the people, but this constant preoccupation with the sweated torso and the wriggling witch doctor
might seem to carry the back-to-the-land movement too far," concludes the critic.

821.   "Paul Robeson and Elizabeth Welch Appear in New Film," California
       Eagle, October 9, 1936, p. 1.

       The article discusses "Song of Freedom," a new talking picture pro-
       duced by a British film company and shown for the first time last
       week with Paul Robeson and Elizabeth Welch as the stars, received
       wide praise by English critics who at the same time declare they
       want the famous singer to forget his savage roles and appear as
       "a distinguished and honorable gentleman." The critic declares
       that the perpetual presentation of African voodoo and esoteric
       jungle influence is becoming a bit sordid. The plot of "Song of
       Freedom" is rather weak, but that does not detract from the ex-
       cellence of Robeson's acting. Typical of the reviews appearing
       in London dailies is that by C.A. Lejeune, noted critic of The
       Sunday Observer: "I am always actuely embarrassed by the sight
       of Mr. Paul Robeson, probably the world's most cultivated and
       erudite singer, performing the songs of native Africa with lyric
       and orchestra, and a crowd of oriental extra gentlemen on either
       hand. Mr. Robeson, who knows more about the cognate musical
       rhythms of the Slavs, the Celts, and the Aryans than the average
       Mus. Doc., appears in the present picture as a London dock-hand
       who has some little, unfinished melody tickling his brain, and
       learns in time that it is the king-song of an obscure West African
       island tribe...." Mr. Lejeune concludes: "But I wish that Mr.
       Robeson, who has sung in all the more august musical haunts of
       Europe and America, might be allowed, just for once, to appear on
       the screen in a civil capacity as a responsible citizen. The
       eminent coloured singer, one knows, is a loyal child of the people,
       but this constant preoccupation with the sweated torso and the
       wriggling witch doctor might seem to carry the back-to-the-land
       movement too far."

822. Frank, Franklyn. "Robeson Sings: After Finishing 'King Solomon's Mines,' He Gives Song Recital to Audience of Theatre Workmen," Journal and Guide, January 9, 1937.

This author surmises that when stars finish their part in a film, they generally give presents to technicians and ordinary members of the cast. So when Paul Robeson ended his portion of the forth-coming British screen play, "King Solomon's Mines," he was worried what to give until someone suggested that he give a song recital. On a vacant setting, Paul sang "Lindy Lou," "Water Boy," "Kentucky Home," and "Ol' Man River" to an audience of electricians, car-penters, plasterers, painters, camera and sound staff, all in overalls and working clothes. After the recital the audience went to the studio restaurant and drank to Robeson's health, received a box of cigarettes each, and gave three of the heartiest cheers for the great singer ever heard in these parts, states Frank. He also asserts they already started shooting on another Robeson picture, this one entitled "Big Fella," which will also include the brown-skin songbird, Elizabeth Welch, who has leaped to fame in England through records and her part in "Song of Freedom." Special songs are being written for the production by the English team of Kennedy and Carr, concludes the writer.

823. Garvey, Marcus. "Paul Robeson and His Mission," The Black Man, Vol. II, No. V, January, 1937, pp. 2-3.

Garvey argues that Paul Robeson has appeared in motion pictures that do not reflect the dignity and credit due the Negro Race, and that he or any other Negro should only appear in motion pic-tures that do reflect dignity and credit due the Negro Race.

824. Jackson, Fay. "New Robeson Film Sets Precedent," California Eagle, March 3, 1937, p. 1.

The writer states that more than 4,000 native African warriors and their families were used in "Solomon's Mines," starring Paul Robeson, Anna Lee, Cedric Hardiwick and Roland Young. Miss Jackson points out that before the unit is sent to Africa or extras employed, a complete encampment is set up for housing and feeding the people. Native labour is employed in all construction. Native singers and instruments are used for recordings to be used as a guide for musical arrangements. Native chiefs are consulted on all matters of native culture, so that no mistakes are made and the film becomes, in this sense, an historical document. She asserts that she recalls a film about Negro life was made in Holly-wood, for which the producer carelessly consulted the studio bootblack as an authority.

825. "Star Paul Robeson in New British Film," Pittsburgh Courier, May 9, 1937, p. 19.

This article states that Paul Robeson would star in the London production of the film "Jericho."

826. Jackson, Fay M. "'King Solomon's Mines,' New Paul Robeson Film,
      Is Gigantic Production," Philadelphia Tribune, March 11, 1937.

      The writer contends that staggering, even to a former Hollywood
      motion picture correspondent, are the facts and figures relating
      to the production of the Gaumont-British film, "Solomon's Mines,"
      starring Paul Robeson, Anna Lee, Cedric Hardiwick and Roland
      Young, according to a statement given out this week by Hugh
      Findley, publicity director, in a special interview, for the
      Associated Negro Press. With wages from a guinea a day upwards,
      over 300 extras gathered through the Negzro agency, Norton Bradley,
      were used during the filming of scenes in London and 4,000 native
      African warriors and their families are being used in real African
      scenes, states Jackson. She surmises that unlike some of Holly-
      wood's pictures using large numbers of Negro players and extras,
      little, if any professional jealousy pops up, according to Findley.
      Robeson is extremely popular and beloved by the players. Injury
      fell to two of our men when their feathers caught fire and they
      were severely burnt. They requested Mr. Robeson to pay them a
      visit to the hospital. They said that was all they wanted to
      cheer them up. He graciously consented to go, concludes the
      reporter.

827. Lautier, Louis. "Paul Robeson in Story Triumph; First of Its
      Kind," Pittsburgh Courier, May 29, 1937, p. 20.

      According to this reviewer "Song of Freedom" is the finest story
      of colored folks yet brought to the screen. The writer declares
      that Paul Robeson with the leading role, gave an excellent per-
      formance. He also asserts that the picture was distinguished by
      Robeson's vocalization. This British made film differs from
      American Pictures in that it depicts Negroes in heroic roles,
      declares Lautier.

828. Jackson, Fay. "Robeson Planning Return Here, Wants to Outstrip
      'Stevedore,'" New York Amsterdam News, June 5, 1937.

      It was stated that Paul Robeson recently completed the film
      "Jericho." The movie in which Robeson starred in was filmed in
      Egypt. While in Egypt, Robeson reported, he discovered that
      Egyptians are "just another bunch of colored folk." "They consider
      themselves Mediterranean people - but they're just like us," he
      declared, adding that he has become very interested in Egyptian
      films and expects to make one for them soon with Om Kalsoun, noted
      Egyptian singer, as his female lead. While in the land of the
      Saharas he disclosed, he taught Om a little English and she taught
      him Arabic. Gifted with a flair for languages, Robeson said that
      he had learned two African dialects and had discovered that African
      Negroes had a language which compared in structure, subtlety and
      intellect with other ancient tongues such as Greek, Latin, Hebrew,
      and Chinese, stated Miss Jackson.

829. "Robeson to Act in Soviet Film," Guardian, June 12, 1937, p. 1.

According to this article Paul Robeson told the Moscow Daily News that he will definitely enter Soviet films in the near future. On his way to Kislovodsk for a four months' rest, Robeson and his wife visited their young son, a student at the Kari Liebnecht school. He said that we was uncertain what the first picture would be, but that he favors "Othello." His second choice would be some American play as "Stevedore," with more emphasis on the class conflict and less on the race theme, declared the article.

830. Cunningham, James D. "King Solomon's Mines," Commenweal, Vol. 26, No. 12, July 16, 1937, p. 307.

The reviewer surmises that Gaumont-British pictures, of London, have given Sir Rider Haggard's famous story a spectacular production, establishing one of the largest locations in recent motion picture history in Natal, South Africa, where authentic outdoor scenes were photographed over great expanses of African wilds and deserts. In this connection their effort certainly is noteworthy. But, for all of the highly commendable pictorial efforts, there is a sad lack of histrionics, with Sir Cedric Hardwicke, Roland Young, Paul Robeson, Anna Lee and John Loder contributing little or nothing to the play, possibly excepting Robeson, concluded Cunningham.

831. "Movies: 'King Solomon's Mines,'" Literary Digest, Vol. 124, No. 1, July 17, 1937, p. 34.

The reviewer asserts that the real reason for going to see "King Solomon's Mines" no matter how much 1937 has outgrown Mr. H. Rider Haggard's (the writer) naivete, is Paul Robeson. The director, Robert Stevenson, very wisely used every device in his kit to play up Robeson's possibilities. He concludes: ".... Robeson sings, with the additional comment that he is a magnificent voice.... Robeson's presence gives it (the film) a pretty terrific head start."

832. "Robeson's New Film Excites British Critics: 'King Solomon's Mines' Has Excess of Inept Songs," Pittsburgh Courier, August 14, 1937, p. 13.

The article states English critics had mixed reviews about Paul Robeson's role in "King Solomon's Mines." The London Sunday Express states that Robeson looked like a King of his people, but he was made to sing childish lyrics to dreary tunes. However, Reynold News thought "'King Solomon's Mines' was a grand film."

833. "Robeson Plays Rider Haggard's King Umbopa," Life, Vol. 3, No. 9, August 30, 1937, p. 58.

This article states that Paul Robeson played the noble savage in the Gaumont British film "King Solomon's Mines." As gigantic Umbopa, African jungle carrier, he leads a group of Britons to the lost treasures of Solomon's gold mines. Incidentally, he recovers his own throne and saves his friends from an erupting

(Life)

volcano in a picture alive with the adventure, romance and mag-
nificient hokum of Rider Haggard, concludes the article.

834.   Gordon, Eugene.   "'Dark Sands' Stars Robeson," Boston Guardian,
       August 3, 1938, p. 1.

According to the writer "Dark Sands" was not in any sense a perfect picture from the Black point of view.   He declares that the
writer and producer still struggle with the old stereotypes of
singing, dancing and crapshooting blacks and with African backgrounds and desert scenes.   But the stereotypes, this time, states
Gordon, owing to an intelligence seldom found in such films, are
so well integrated with believably life-like situations that the
film viewed as a whole has a distinctly progressive tone.   Originally titled "Jericho" after its leading character (Paul Robeson),
"Dark Sands" is the story of a Black corporal who, en route to
France with a transport loaded with Black soldiers and their white
officers, is unjustly accused of murder and escapes.   Accompanied
by a white deserter from the army, he makes his way to Africa and
the Sahara desert, where he becomes the leader of a tribe.   The
writer argues that in spite of the fact that the Black soldiers
are made to entertain themselves by crapshooting and general mon-
keyshines, the film, for a number of reasons, is superior to the
usual product dealing with the race.   In the first place, Paul
Robeson appears as a peace-loving graduate of a medical school
and all his actions are in perfect harmony with such a character.
He is an upstanding, keenly intelligent and natural leader,
whether those who follow be black or white, asserts the author.
Henry Wilcoxon plays "Jericho's" captain, who is court-martialed
and sentences to five years in Leavenworth because of the Black
corporal's escape.   Released, Captain Mack sets out to find
"Jericho" and get revenge.   The clue comes when, seated in a
London movie house, the captain sees a film travelogue of a salt
trek on the Sahara.   It is led by "Jericho," Captain Mack hastens
from the theatre for the final tracking down of his man.   Mr.
Gordon concludes: "Robeson does considerable singing, these se-
quences being among the best of the film.   The two main songs are
'My Way' and 'Deep Desert.'   The desert scenes, having been taken
actually on the Sahara with real Africans, are themselves like a
travelogue.   Most of the acting is good, but Paul Robeson easily
dominates the film, which is definitely his in more ways than one."

835.   "Paul Robeson Film Picked for Showing in Brooklyn (New York),"
       New York Amsterdam News, September 17, 1938, p. 1.

The article states that coming to the Regent Theatre, Brooklyn, for
a run of four consecutive days, October 5, 6, 7 and 8, is the
latest Paul Robeson starring film production, "The Song of Freedom."
The story is a poignant and thrilling one of a Negro who longs to
return to the birthplace of his ancestors before they were snatched
away by the slave traders centuries before.   While working as a
dock laborer, his magnificent voice is overheard by an impresario,
through whom he sky-rockets to fame, becoming one of the world's
greatest singers.   Through his good fortune he is able to return

to his long lost people, who seeing him as only another civilized
man, spurn him. How he gains the confidence of the people and
becomes their king forms a thrilling climax to the story. The
article concludes: "This is definitely the picture not to miss,
if you crave good acting, a plausible story with plenty of action
and marvelous singing of the one and only Paul Robeson."

836.   "Discards Shackles of 'Uncle Tomism,'" New York Amsterdam News,
        January 7, 1939, p. 16.

According to this article for the first time in the history of the
motion pictures, the Negro threw away the shackles of Uncle Tomism
and established himself as an artist who was able to interpret
roles of deep social significance during the past twelve months.
This was especially true of "Song of Freedom" released by British
Lion Pictures and starring the brilliant baritone, Paul Robeson.
The picture did not even have the imperialistic shading that was
so evident in his earlier "Sanders of the River." The writer
declares that a militant Robeson, who sacrificed his artistic
career to fight for the freedom of his people, dominated the film.
The actor was ably supported by Elizabeth Welch. Later in the
year, co-starring with Henry Wilcoxon, Paul Robeson received much
favorable comment for his brilliant acting in "Dark Sands,"
concludes the article.

837.   "Paul Robeson in 'Big Fella,'" West African Pilot (Lagos, Nigeria),
        January 12, 1939, p. 1.

This article declares: "In 'Big Fella,' which is a recent production featuring Paul Robeson and three really good coloured
actors and actresses, he is the leading star of the picture, and
although his assignment is the usual one depicting him as a scum
and a renegade, yet he portrays the type of virtues which any
race on earth would be glad to emulate. His love and devotion
to a white boy is the theme of this story, and the acting and
singing of Robeson, in particular, are very impressive and convincing, despite obvious flaws in the technique of the film and
the plots of the story."

838.   "Robeson Quits: Noted Actor and Singer Will Make Independent
        Films," Chicago Defender, March 11, 1939, p. 1.

According to this article Paul Robeson indicates his intention to
make independent and socially significant pictures. He says he
would like to go to the Soviet Russia to do a film with Eisenstein,
then return to Hollywood, to make, independently, a picture about
Oliver Law, the Chicago Race man, who died leading a contingent of
the International Brigade in Spain. In explaining his break with
the big commercial studios, Robeson said: "I have done so because
I am no longer willing to identify myself with an organization
that has no regard for reality -- an organization that attempts to
nullfiy public intelligence, falsify life and entirely ignores
the many dynamic forces at work in the world today." Robeson maintains that, within the framework of the commercial film industry

(Chicago Defender)

there is now very little chance for an individual to express himself or to do anything which is sincere or worthwhile.

839. "Paul Robeson in 'Proud Valley,'" Hampstead and St. John's Wood
     News and Advertiser, June 1, 1939.

     The director of "Proud Valley" had this to say about Paul Robeson's
     role in the film: "....I do not wish to stress to an audience the
     fact that Robeson is a negro or a famous singer. His role is that
     of a stoker who lands in Wales, finds himself penniless, becomes
     in turn a tramp and then a miner, and befriends a poor Welch
     family whose life he shares. It is a real life story showing
     Robeson as a simple, likeable human being, who has to take the
     rough with the smooth the same as all of us...."

840. "Better Negro Films Urged by Robeson," Washington Tribune, July 15,
     1939.

     According to this article Paul Robeson endorsed the project of the
     Greater New York Committee for Better Negro Films and said that he
     would be happy to be listed among its actors. Robeson, hero of
     numerous American and British pictures and of stage plays as
     divergent in character as O'Neill's "Emperor Jones" and Shakes-
     peare's "Othello," insisted that the situation in Hollywood re-
     garding the Negro would have to be corrected. "I feel that a lot
     of this work must be outside of Hollywood," Robeson said,
     mentioning Frontier Films' "Heart of Spain" and "People of the
     Cumberland" as typifying themes around which he would like to see
     movies done of the Negro, states the article.

                              3. HONORS

841. "Paul Robeson Wins Honorary Degree of M.A.," The Echo (Rutgers
     University), June 11, 1932.

     This article states that Paul L. Robeson, Negro singer and actor,
     who was graduated in 1919, when he was a Phi Beta Kappa, a four-
     letter man in athletics and an end on the Walter Camp's All-
     American football team, was given an honorary degree at the 116th
     commencement exercises of Rutgers University, his alma mater.
     The interpreter of "Emperor Jones," "All God's Chillun Got Wings,"
     and "Othello" was given the honorary degree of Master of Arts.
     Degrees were conferrred on 600 other students.

842. "Hamilton Will Honor Robeson," New York Times, December 21, 1939.
     p. 21.

     This article states that Hamilton College would present the honor-
     ary degree of Doctor of Humane Letters to Paul Robeson at a
     special mid-winter convocation.

843.   "Paul Robeson Achieved Success as Athlete, Singer and Screen Star,"
        Newark Herald, March 4, 1936, p. 1.

        This article states that New Jersey race citizens honored one of
        their distinguished "sons" Sunday at the closing of Negro Achieve-
        ment Week, selecting Paul Robeson as one of the three persons to
        receive an award for "outstanding achievements." The article
        gives an overview of Mr. Robeson's accomplishments from his high
        school days to his starring role in "Othello."

4. MUSIC

844.   "Mr. Paul Robeson," London Times, February 17, 1930, p. 21.

        This article states that Paul Robeson appeared at Albert Hall in
        London and sang spirituals and Negro songs. The critic asserts
        that Mr. Robeson had a fine bass voice with a touch and no more
        of the woolliness that characterized many Negro voices. His
        treatment of the spirituals was entirely simple. He allowed him-
        self one sotto voce phrase at the end of "Water Boy," the convict
        song which is one of the most striking of all Negro secular songs,
        concludes the reviewer.

845.   "The East," Crisis, Vol. 37, No. 2, February, 1930, p. 59.

        It was stated that Paul Robeson, with Lawrence Brown at the piano,
        has been singing in New York and vicinity with striking success.
        The article concludes that Robeson was especially welcomed at
        Princeton, his birthplace, where the college turned out in his
        honor.

846.   "Paul Robeson, A Myth - A Legend!" Jewish Chronicle (London),
        April 8, 1930.

        This article reports that Robeson, the great Negro artist, who has
        so sweet a compassion for the underdogs of the world, sang last
        night in the Birmingham Town Hall for the Christmas Tree Fund.
        Robeson -- literally mobbed at the station in Glasgow by auto-
        graph seekers; Robeson - in Dublin; Robeson - in Marseilles;
        Robeson - in Moscow; Robeson - arriving in Barcelona, going on to
        Madrid -- singing in the American Hospital at Villa Paz, at the
        hospital base at Bennicasime. He visited the Scandinavian count-
        ties. The article states that in Oslo, Copenhagen, Stockholm he
        received tumultuous, unprecedented receptions which became anti-
        fascist demonstrations. In Oslo, after a concert during which
        ten thousand people were outside the hall, the Nordic patriots
        fell on their knees, kissing his hands while tears ran down their
        cheeks. Robeson! A myth -- a legend!, concludes the writer.

847. Brown, Ivor. "Robeson Was a One Man Band," Manchester Guardian,
      (England), May 30, 1930.

      The reporter ended his eulogistic review with these words: "As
      far as the male side of the case was concerned this Othello was a
      one man band; but Mr. Robeson's music, with all its majesty of
      tone and sweep of power, does make that form of orchestra tre-
      mendous."

848. Robeson, Eslande Goode. "Paul Robeson Aided by Congregations on
      Road to Fame," New York Evening Journal, August 18, 1930.

      The author declares that Paul Robeson, like Harry Burleigh, Roland
      Hayes, and Marian Anderson, found the Black church congregations
      one of his important audiences. She said it was and is possible
      for a Negro musician or lecturer to make an extensive tour of
      America without appearing before a white audience at all.

849. "Paul Robeson in a Program of Classical Songs," New York Times,
      January 4, 1931, Part 8, p. 9.

      There is a photo of Paul Robeson as well as an advertisement of
      him in this section of the newspaper. Under his photo the caption
      reads "Paul Robeson, in a Program of Classical Songs and Spirit-
      uals at Carnegie Hall Saturday."

850. "Paul Robeson Wins Plaudits in Concert," New York Times, January
      11, 1931, p. 26.

      The article states that Paul Robeson, the Negro baritone, who has
      now earned laurels as Othello on the dramatic stage, in addition
      to his successes as a singer, gave a recital in Carnegie Hall that
      was attended by a very large and very responsive audience.
      According to the article, Mr. Robeson's program was principally
      of Negro music, especially the spirituals, which conceals art.
      The article concludes: "The singer's admirable enunciation, his
      sincerity and manly fervor and the natural resonance of the voice
      contributed to the excellent effect of his performances." The
      writer also declared that "singing in other languages than English
      and in other dialects than that of the Negro, Mr. Robeson did
      full justice to his text as well as music."

851. "Paul Robeson's Songs Stir 4,000 in London," New York Times,
      February 17, 1930, p. 19.

      Paul Robeson gave his only London recital of Negro spirituals and
      secular songs of this season before an enthusiastic audience of
      4,000 in Albert Hall. Many of the audience clamored for "Old
      Man River," which Mr. Robeson sang in the London production of
      "Show Boat" but the singer announced he did not yet have rights
      to sing it in public, states the article.

852. "Paul Robeson at the Music Club," Huddersfield Daily Examiner,
      March 6, 1930.

      This article declares that the Music Club had a bigger audience
      for Paul Robeson then they had for any previous recital of the
      winter. The critic declares that Mr. Robeson's voice is not
      always well controlled but on certain notes there is wonderful
      richness of tone, and on occasion also beautifully vital pianissimo.

853. Williams, R. Stephen. "Why Paul Robeson Is a Great Singer,"
      Daily Express, March 11, 1930.

      The writer contends that Paul Robeson is a great singer because of
      his specialization in Negro Spirituals. He said another thing that
      makes Robeson great was his lack of artificiality. Mr. Williams
      concludes: "It is not so much Paul Robeson singing as nature
      singing through him."

854. "Paul Robeson Sings Spirituals," New York Times, March 23, 1931,
      p. 25.

      This article asserts that Paul Robeson gave his last recital in
      Carnegie Hall, following a transcontinental concert tour. Ac-
      cording to the article Paul Robeson was the most distinguished
      singing actor of his race and was greeted by an enthusiastic house.
      It concludes: "For outstanding personality, voice and diction,
      Robeson as a singer has no match since Bert Williams, while on
      stage presence his experience as a star has given a distinction
      that is his own."

855. "Paul Robeson Made a Concert Tour," Crisis, Vol. 40, No. 7, July
      1931, p. 236.

      This article declares that between January 10th and April 16th,
      1931, Paul Robeson gave thirty-four (34) concerts in the United
      States. According to this article, it was estimated that he sang
      to one hundred thousand people.

856. "Mr. Paul Robeson," Eastern Daily Press (Norwich), August 29, 1931.

      Although Paul Robeson sang songs in many different languages it
      appears as if from the very beginning of his singing career,
      Russian songs were his most successful ones. One critic asserts,
      in part:
              In the Russian songs, Mr. Robeson revealed an insight
              and a perception of the genius of the songs which were
              essential to them. This was possible because, as he
              pointed out, there was a certain affinity between the
              idiom of one or two of them and that of the negro
              songs. The text was provided in "The Player," sung
              in Russian and rendered with such expression that
              the language presented no difficulty to its ap-
              preciation....

857. "Mr. Paul Robeson," Eastbourne Gazette (England), September 2, 1931.

Although Robeson sang Negro spirituals and folk music to foreign
audiences, he later began to include classical music by Mozart,
Gretchaninoff, Schumann, Beethoven and others. When he sang in
German, for example, the critics did not, at first, receive him
enthusiastically. One critic declared: ".... English pieces were
delivered exactly in the same tone and manner in which he sings the
Negro folk songs....he seems less in touch with the mood and the
aesthetic demands of this type of lyric.... Mr. Robeson is not a
lieder singer, and he would be better advised to confine himself
to the genre of folk music of America which he sings so admirably...."

858. "Mr. Paul Robeson's Illness," London Times, November 10, 1931, p.
12.

This article states that Mr. Paul Robeson was ill with influenza
and could not leave his home to perform at the Royal Albert Hall
in London. Therefore, his concert was cancelled and the ticket
money was refunded.

859. "Mr. Paul Robeson," London Times, December 14, 1931, p. 10.

The article asserts that Mr. Paul Robeson appeared at the Royal
Albert Hall in London and sang a number of Negro songs and
spirituals. The critic surmises that Robeson has a singularly
easy and adroit style of delivery and the effect is while inten-
sifying the naivety of words and music at the same time to create
a certain reality of effect. He also states that "Mr. Robeson's
voice was not in its best condition." The writer concludes, however, that the singer had a genuine success with the audience and
had to sing many encores.

860. "Robeson In Final Recital: London Concert His Last in England --
Coming Here for Tour," New York Times, December 14, 1931, p. 17.

Paul Robeson gave a final concert in England before returning to
the United States for a short concert tour, after which he expects
to devote himself to acting, singing only for the radio. This
article states that Robeson was reported to have declared that
concert work was too strenuous and was insufficiently remunerative
while radio work was excellently paid for short programs and also
a vast audience was reached.

861. "Paul Robeson Back from England," New York Times, January 6, 1932,
p. 24.

This article states that Paul Robeson, Negro actor and singer,
returned from England on the "Olympic" to make a tour of the
United States. He will sing at the Town Hall.

862. "Students Hail Robeson: Ovation at Rutgers to Singer, Graduate
      at Opening of New Gym," New York Times, January 15, 1932, p. 24.

      The article states that Rutgers University's $800,000 gymnasium
      was opened with a concert given by Paul Robeson, Negro singer,
      who graduated there in 1919. An audience of 2,500 jammed the new
      building to cheer Mr. Robeson,concludes the article. A reception
      was tendered him.

863. "Paul Robeson Gives Two Recitals," New York Times, January 17, 1932,
      Part 8, p. 8.

      There is a large sketch of Paul Robeson almost in the center of
      the page. Under his sketch reads the caption "Paul Robeson, Who
      Gives Two Songs Recitals This Week at Town Hall." There is also
      an advertisement about Robeson appearing at Town Hall entitled
      "Return of the Great Negro Singer Paul Robeson."

864. "Robeson Achieves Triumph," New York Times, January 18, 1932, p.
      19.

      The article states that there was not a vacant seat in Town Hall
      where Paul Robeson returned in triumph for his recital in Town
      Hall after his recent tour abroad. It was pointed out that the
      Negro baritone held his audience spellbound in a program mostly
      of spirituals, several of which were greeted with such enthus-
      iastic applause that the singer repeated them. The number of en-
      cores was almost equal to the original program and included
      the familiar "All God's Children Got Wings," concludes the article.

865. "Paul Robeson Heard Again," New York Times, January 24, 1932, p.
      28.

      This article states that Paul Robeson, singing an almost completely
      new program and wholly of Negro spirituals that his audience
      applauded at the first notes, appeared at the Town Hall for the
      second time in a week. The baritone was assisted by Ignace
      Hilsberg, the Polish pianist, in two groups of piano solos and by
      Lawrence Brown in sympathetic accompaniments to the songs.

866. "Paul Robeson at Town Hall," New York Sun, January 27, 1932.

      According to this article Paul Robeson returned to this country
      from renewed triumphs on the London stage gave his first song
      recital in New York, January 17, at the Town Hall. The program
      contained many spirituals and folk songs and in the third group
      a set of four miscellaneous songs. The article states that
      Mr. Robeson used his splendidly rich baritone voice with remark-
      able skill, and, as usual, his power to communicate to his
      hearers the content of a song was of eloquent commanding power
      and excellent range. He could have repeated every number he
      gave, and encores were numerous, concludes the writer.

867. "Paul Robeson Begins Farewells," New York Times, March 7, 1932,
      p. 20.

      The article reports that Paul Robeson, distinguished as a singing
      actor on the dramatic stage as on the concert stage and among the
      foremost of American Negro artists to win repeated hearing abroad,
      appeared at the Town Hall last night in the first of two farewell
      recitals this season. The article states that more than an echo
      of Mr. Robeson's European tours was implied in a Russian group
      of songs as if a kindred aspiration of the Slavic race had impelled
      the singing of Cul's "Hunger Song," Moussorgsky's "Silent Room,"
      and Gretchaninoff's "The Captive."

868. "Music In Review: Paul Robeson Gives Program of Negro Spirituals
      at His Season's Farewell," New York Times, March 14, 1932, p. 12.

      The article states that Paul Robeson gave his farewell concert of
      the season in Town Hall. His entire program, declares the re-
      port, was given to the Negro spirituals which he does so incom-
      parably, and upon which any comment at this late date in the
      season is superfluous. The critic concludes: "Mr. Robeson's
      singing strips them away as much, as it is possible to do so, and
      leaves the listener touched by their pathos and lifted by their
      exaltation.... Those who fear that music is in danger of dying
      up in a cerebal desert nowadays had best attend one of Mr. Robe-
      son's concerts," concludes the article.

869. "Paul Robeson, Baritone," New York Times, April 15, 1932, Part 8,
      p. 16.

      There is a picture of Paul Robeson with the caption "Paul Robeson,
      Baritone, on WABC at 8 p.m. today." Also in "Week's Outstanding
      Broadcasts," it is mentioned that Paul Robeson would appear, 8:00
      to 8:30 on WABC along with Jimmy Durante and others. Robeson
      would sing "Ol' Man River" and "Water Boy."

870. Hazlitt, Henry. "Show Boat," Nation, Vol. 134, No. 34, 9, June 8,
      1932, p. 660.

      The author states that Paul Robeson as Joe in "Show Boat" brings
      a rich sonority and even a sort of racial significance to the
      singing of "Ol' Man River."

871. "Robeson Sings at Stadium," New York Times, August 1, 1932, p. 11.

      Robeson appeared in concert at Lewisohn Stadium in New York City.
      The applause that greeted him continued after each song, and rose
      to great enthusiasm following his final selection of "Old Man
      River." The audience asked for various favorite songs, which
      continued to sing for fifteen minutes, and received a great
      ovation, stated the article.

872.   M.L.S. "Robeson Receives Ovation at the Stadium," Musical Courier, Vol. 105, No. 6, August 6, 1932, p. 12.

This article discusses Paul Robeson's concert at Lewisohn Stadium in New York. He sang only Negro music. The magnetism of his voice had "such power as to fill the stadium to the farthest seat." The singer was cheered at the end of his performance and he received a standing ovation, states the writer.

873.   Cowan, Sada. "Feature Your Own Geniuses, Scenarist Advises Race Men: Praises Robeson, Hayes, Johnson, Hughes," Pittsburgh Courier, October 15, 1932, Section 2, p. 6.

The writer asserts: "I have never subscribed to the stereotyped American concept of the Negro as a buffoon, as criminal or child-like creature.... I am fully aware of the work being done currently by Negro writers, painters, singers, actors and actresses. Any prejudice I may possibly have formed regarding members of the race were swept away long ago under the magnificent beauty of the voices of such singers as Roland Hayes or Paul Robeson, or the frequently gifted lives of Negro poets such as Countee Cullen, James Weldon Johnson or Langston Hughes...."

874.   "The Palladium," London Times, October 25, 1932, p. 12.

The reviewer declares that Mr. Paul Robeson and his audience are alike to be congratulated on the success of his first music-hall appearance, which proves that there is no need for a fine singer to play down to such surroundings. The singer was appearing at the Palladium in London. He states that Mr. Robeson was a true artist, and because of that a most persuasive propagandist. The critic concludes: "In his singing of spirituals like 'I've Got a Robe" and his famous 'Ole Man River,' from 'Show Boat,' the Negro race becomes articulate...."

875.   "Robeson Considers Boris," New York Times, January 19, 1933, p. 11.

It was reported that Paul Robeson was learning Russian preparatory to accepting an invitation to sing the title role of Boris Godunoff at the Moscow Opera House. It stated that he had been studying the score enthusiastically.

876.   Breare, W.H. "Paul Robeson's Technique," The British Musician and Musical News, Vol. 9, No. 7, July, 1933, pp. 156-158.

The author discusses Paul Robeson's voice. He states: "Robeson has a natural voice. Yet there is in art nothing more unnatural than such a voice which has not been cultivated. It is the perfection of production and technique which makes the finished voice of the artist. We hear to-day plenty of so-called 'natural' voices and 'natural' singers who are very far from cultivated. But with Paul Robeson it is quite another thing. He has an extraordinary voice, but he knows how to use it so that the tones and phrases pour forth without effort -- naturally, the full sense of the term. His tone is always lyrical, it flows like a deep river which has not a ripple on its surface." The author declares that

(Breare, W.H.)

he has a wonderful range. His low tones are full, round, mellow,
rich as velvet. There are no "splinters" or jarring elements in
that portion of his range. His entire scale is perfectly and
artistically graded. From these deep tones with their long slow
vibrations there is, in taking an upward passage, a gradual and
proportionate ascent. He moves from the lower voice to the middle
and upper so gradually and with such perfect proportion that
there is never a false element in any tone. Breare concludes:
".... It is that ability to move from one portion of the voice to
another which makes his work so beautiful. One hears almost in-
cessantly in others a beautiful tone spoilt by a sudden harsh
element introduced therein by some fault of vocal production. It
is Robeson's knowledge of the office of the breath which enables
him to achieve the emotional shades or effect which is as real as
life...."

877.   "Paul Robeson in Concert," Leicester (England) Evening Mail,
       January 17, 1934, p. 10.

       Robeson appeared in several English and Scottish towns during the
       early months of 1934. One critic declares: "Paul Robeson had the
       distinction last night of attracting the largest audience Leicester
       has seen for any of this season's Celebrity Concerts. Beecham,
       Coates and Tetrazzini apparently do not possess such faithful
       admirers...."

878.   "Paul Robeson," Hull Daily Mail (London), April 11, 1934.

       The article states: ".... Facing 2,000 people in Hull, Robeson
       comes on to the stage with smooth, long strides, stands with feet
       apart, leaning his weight on the right foot, hangs his head as
       though in thought, glances at that often-folded slip of paper,
       nods to his pianist and then throws his head back and sings.
       Slight, typical gestures emphasize the humor and force of the
       songs in an indescribable way...."

879.   "Mr. Paul Robeson: Recital at Queen's Hall," London Times, April
       18, 1934, p. 14.

       This article states that Mr. Paul Robeson gave a recital at Queen
       Hall in London and attracted a large and enthusiastic audience.
       The reviewer declares that Mr. Robeson's magnificent voice and
       his obvious sincerity make him an ideal interpreter of the
       Spirituals and other traditional songs of his race. He concludes:
       "The untutored nature of his singing and the charming modesty of
       his platform manner are further aids to his success in these un-
       sophisticated songs."

880.   "Moscow Sequel to 'Steal Away to Jesus,'" London Times, January 2,
       1935, p. 10.

       This article declares that Paul Robeson who sang "Steal Away to
       Jesus" over a Soviet radio station, was visiting Moscow. It
       also states that although the Russians banned the song from being

<u>(London Times)</u>

played, it later explained that although his songs are wrapped in
a semi-religious atmosphere, they must be interpreted by listeners
as a protest against the treatment of the Negro race under the
Capitalist regime.

881.   "Soviet Dismisses High Officials of Radio for Broadcasting of a
       Robeson 'Spiritual,'" New York Times, January 2, 1935, p. 1.

       According to this report as a result of the broadcasting by a
       powerful Comintern station at Moscow of a phonographic recording
       of the voice of Paul Robeson singing the spiritual "Steal Away to
       Jesus," six prominent Soviet wireless officials and an announcer
       were removed from their posts. The Soviet press declared that
       although Mr. Robeson's songs are wrapped in a semi-religious
       atmosphere they must be interpreted by listeners as a protest
       against the treatment of the Negro race under capitalist regime.

882.   "Paul Robeson," Liverpool (England) Express, April 6, 1935, p. 3.

       One observer comments on Robeson's selection of songs. He de-
       clares, in part: ".... It is common knowledge that Mr. Robeson is
       a keen student of Russia and Russian folk songs, so it was only
       natural that he should include in his recital such songs as
       Gretchaninoff's 'Homeland Mine,' 'The Labourer's Planet,' by
       Kopyloff, and arrangements by Rimsky-Korsakov, etc..... His
       spacious voice is adequately suited to this department of his
       repertory...."

883.   "Paul Robeson," New York Times, October 20, 1935, Section 10, p. 3.

       A photo of R.H. Hoffman is in the center of the page of this
       paper. The caption under it reads, "Paul Robeson, noted Negro
       Baritone, will bring favorite songs to the WEAF audience tonight
       at 10 o'clock when he broadcasts with a Sixty Piece Symphony
       Orchestra." The orchestra was conducted by Erno Rapee.

884.   "Paul Robeson," New York Times, October 13, 1935, Part 9, p. 7.

       A photo of Paul Robeson is at the bottom of the page of this news-
       paper. Under his picture the caption reads "Paul Robeson, Baritone,
       Appearing at Town Hall Saturday, After Three Years' Absence."

885.   "Ovation Is Given to Paul Robeson," New York Times, October 20,
       1935, p. 37.

       Paul Robeson gave a recital at the Town Hall Theatre in New York
       City. Robeson was handicapped by a severe cold, but he performed
       anyway. Despite his indisposition, Mr. Robeson's every selection
       was greeted with unroarious applause, necessitating encores in
       large numbers. The article concludes: "Obviously his popularity
       has increased to such a degree with the passing years that his mere
       presence on the stage would have evoked outbursts of handclapping
       had he merely stood and turned his beaming smile on his admirers,
       especially as this was his first recital in this country in three

(New York Times)

seasons, the first chance he had given his worshippers of hearing
him in all that time...."

886. Walker, Danton. "Paul Robeson in Good Voice at Town Hall," New
      York Daily News, October 21, 1935.

      This writer declares that Paul Robeson, who's been making quite a
      name for himself, the last three years in England, Russia and other
      faraway places, returned to Town Hall in New York City. The
      Robeson fans packed Town Hall, which was quite inadequate for the
      crowd and gave him a rousing welcome. Mr. Walker concludes:
      "Unlike most of our returning prodigal sons of music, the colored
      baritone - the Lawrence Tibbett of his race - hasn't picked up any
      foreign airs abroad. He is still his own beaming, handsome un-
      pretentious self, carrying to the platform an easy grace and a
      natural charm which captivates his listeners and immediately puts
      them at their ease."

887. Danishewsky, M. "Paul Robeson Wants to Turn Comedian," Picture-
      Goer Weekly (London), October 26, 1935, p. 28.

      Paul Robeson was not interested in singing or performing in opera.
      He was offered a singing role in the opera "Aida," but he declined.
      The singer thought if he went into opera he would "probably become
      one of the hundred of mediocre singers." He also described his
      voice as "embarrassingly delicate." Robeson was reported to have
      said that he believed that he was at his vocal best when singing
      in a large drawing room, in an intimate atmosphere. He declared:
      "I can't project my vocal to the back of a large theatre or opera
      house, and do it justice; it just isn't in me to do it."

888. "Robeson Ill, Cancels Concert," New York Times, October 26, 1935,
      p. 12.

      This article states that Paul Robeson was compelled to cancel his
      concert at the Alvin Theatre in New York City because of an attack
      of laryngitis.

889. "Week-End Concerts: Mr. Paul Robeson," London Times, January 20,
      1936, p. 20.

      The article states that Mr. Paul Robeson presented a concert at
      Albert Hall and he was not so parsimonious as he promised and
      added a number of extra trifles. It is true also that he is a
      light-weight among singers, who does not easily sustain a song
      even of the calibre of Gretchaninoff's "A Player," so that he
      was wise to concentrate on the Negro spirituals which he does
      authoritatively and well, states the author.

890.   "Paul Robeson on Negro Music," The Star (London), May 20, 1936.

Paul Robeson admired several Black singers. One of his favorite
interpreters of Black music was blues singer, Bessie Smith. He
declares: ".... Bessie sings to her own people. She sings the
real thing. She has not polished it up. And the real 'blues,'
you know are as much genuine darkie material as the negro
spirituals...."

891.   "Robeson Wins Russians," New York Times, December 17, 1936, p. 34.

The article states that Soviet workers roared and pounded their
approval of Paul Robeson at a concert in the Moscow Conservatory.
Robeson sang "Old Man River," "Old Black Joe" and "Waterboy,"
which he called the "workers song." He interspersed the songs
with a few lines in Russian, all but bringing down the house,
concludes the article.

892.   White, Lucien H. "Paul Robeson, In Initial American Concert,
Reveals Sophistication, But Evidences Real Artistic," New York Age,
January 17, 1937, p. 6.

The critic declares that the years of residence in England, with
its atmosphere of culture, seem to have brought, unconsciously
though it might be, a refining influence that makes itself apparent in Paul Robeson's renditions of the music of his race. There
is the same fluency of emission, the simple dignity of a true
artist, and withal the faithful adherence to an ideal that has
always characterized Robeson's singing, and placed him an a category of dignified lonesomeness. He is alone in his class, a sui
generis, concludes the author.

893.   "Music: Paul Robeson," Brown American, Vol. 2, No. 4, July 1937,
p. 6.

This article states that while Paul Robeson was living in London
he declared that he would not give any big concerts or make any
major tours in Europe or America. Robeson's reportedly stated
that "he is really a drawing room artist and that his best efforts
are possible under drawing room conditions." Robeson insisted
that his voice is "embarrassingly delicate," concluded the writer.

894.   "Mr. Paul Robeson," London Times, April 4, 1938, p. 20.

The article states that Mr. Paul Robeson appeared in concert at
the Albert Hall in London and sang traditional and folk songs,
English, Negro and Jewish songs. The reviewer declares that "the
natural beauty of the voice, its powerful resonance, and deep
colouring were well displayed in most of these songs." He concludes: "Mr. Robeson sang with much sincerity and the sentiment
of the words and music was usually conveyed in a broadly effective
manner which was clearly appreciated by the large audience."

895.   "Paul Robeson," London Daily Mail, April 4, 1938.

This article asserts that Robeson said that he proposed to devote
himself to the songs of all peoples, and his programme last night
ranged from the Hebrides to Kazakstan, whence he selected songs
from a folk opera by Brusilofsky. The writer concludes, in part:

> If it is true that he proposes to desert the Albert
> Hall it will be a pity, for a voice such as his de-
> mands ample space. But an occasional gruff note made
> one wonder whether he has been taking care of it, the
> sound being of the kind that usually results from
> overwork....

896.   "Robeson Believes in Freedom and Justice," Jewish Chronicle
(London), April 8, 1938.

The article declares: "A new and even deeper, more varied quality
is entering into Paul Robeson's recitals these days and last Sunday afternoon at Albert Hall that quality was very evident. He
does not confine himself to the medium in which he is superlative,
that of Spirituals, but is finding songs of other peoples which
also have meaning and point for him. Thus his first group included 'Go Down, Moses' and also a modern Soviet song 'Song of
Kazakstan,' expressive of the new spirit of Soviet Russia.... His
second group included one of the songs of the Spanish Republic.
Robeson's deep humanity and sympahty with other races coming
strongly to the forefront was further emphasized when, as the first
item of his third group, he sang Hebrew Engel's 'Kaddish.' Magnificent was his interpretation of this eloquent plea: 'Let there be
an end to all these sufferings and woes.' He closed the recital
with such a fervent and moving rendering of 'Old Man River,' such
a powerfully sincere declaration of faith 'I must keep struggling,
until I'm dying' -- that it marked the climax of a recital great
not merely in vocal achievement, but in simple, heartfelt
emotion."

897.   Dunbar, Rudolph. "Paul Robeson in Triumphant Return to London
Circles," Kansas City (Mo.) Call, April 22, 1938, p. 1.

The writer attended Mr. Robeson's first concert in Albert Hall in
1936. He said when the singer gave his concert it was a triumphant success. Mr. Dunbar declares nature had been very kind to
Robeson by the endowment of a rich sonorous voice, which he uses
to great advantage. Aside from this, Mr. Robeson was a supremely
great artist, because of his simplicity, candor, and uncompromising
fanatical honesty. The author declares: "In referring to his
simplicity I do not wish to imply the ineffable innocence shown by
children, saints and idiots; I refer to the simplicity of a man who
has devoted patience in exploring and unravelling to his own
spiritual satisfaction the complexities of life and art, and has
achieved, like all great artists, the ludicity of emotion that
contains all the wisdom of experience. He has solved his problem,
and therefore benignly wishes to elucidate ours through song....'"

898. "Tell Them We Are Rising," Negro History Bulletin, Vol. 1, No. 8, May, 1938, pp. 3-7.

The article declares that the world has always admired the race for its unusual music, and as a free people the Negroes have shown what the race can do in producing .... vocalists like Paul Robeson.... It was pointed out that Paul Robeson is noted far and wide for his dramatic ability in "Othello." There is also a photo of Paul Robeson included in this article.

899. "Mr. Paul Robeson Sings at Eton College," London Times, May 9, 1938, p. 17.

This article states that Mr. Paul Robeson gave a song recital at the School Hall at Eton College in London, when a large number of boys were present. It was reported that Mr. Robeson sang many of his best-known songs, including "Ol' Man River."

900. "Paul Robeson Gives Concert," Glasgow Scotchman, August 20, 1938.

The reporter describes Robeson concert. He asserts, in part: "When Paul Robeson appeared on the platform of the City Hall here last night he was overcome with emotion at the spontaneously warm reception of Glasgow's working class. The great artist stood with tears in his eyes while the audience rose, clapped and shouted their appreciation of his work for Spain and oppressed humanity. Before singing Robeson said he was glad to work for the things we all believe in.... Robeson sang songs of the people, of love and the struggle of the people for freedom. In the afternoon, Robeson said he had never felt more like singing, and indeed showed this because again and again he gave songs from his wide repertoire of folk music," concludes the article.

901. "Mr. Paul Robeson's Recitals," London Times, November 21, 1938, p. 12.

This article declares that Mr. Paul Robeson accepted an invitation to give a week's recital at the State Cinema, Kilburn, in England. After a week at the State Cinema Robeson was scheduled to appear for a similar period at the Trocadero Cinema, Elephant, and Castle. There was to be three performances a day, and each programme would consist of songs chosen by different audiences.

902. "Mr. Paul Robeson," Daily Mail (Lancastershire), January 14, 1939.

This writer comments on affection that the English had for the singer. He declares: "The affection people have for this man is a modern portent. He came on to the stage last night with that famous slow stride of his, followed by his pianist, Lawrence Brown, who looked like Prime Minister to an African Chief. And an audience which packed this great hall pounded applause."

903.   "News in Brief," <u>London Times</u>, March 3, 1939, p. 11.

The article states that before giving a concert at Sheffield
(England), Mr. Paul Robeson went to the depot of the Sheffield
section of the Yorkshire Food Ship Council and "adopted" 100
Spanish children for one month, and made a donation to cover the
cost of caring for them.

904.   "Paul Robeson on Tour," <u>The Herald</u> (Preston, England), March 10,
1939.

Paul Robeson appeared in concert at the New Victoria Hall in
Preston. The writer states: "The whole was splendid entertainment - and if you wanted something deeper it was there to be found:
the asethetic presentation of the statement that the common
people - black, white, yellow, Russian or English - are fundamentally alike in their common heritage, in their emotions and half-
realized aspirations. It is the function of the artist to interpret - and Robeson, because he is both a great artist and a
mentally mature and philosophically adult individual, realizes
that the folk-song is the common tongue of man. His job, and I
think he consciously accepts it, is to make us understanding
neighbours; by listening to him we become so, whether we realize
it or not."

905.   Allen, Cleveland G. "Paul Robeson Thrills Audience," <u>Star of Zion</u>,
July 13, 1939, p. 1.

Mr. Allen suggests that Mother Zion A.M.E. Church, with the Rev.
B.C. Robeson, pastor, was crowded with a large and distinguished
audience of music patrons, on Sunday afternoon, July 1, to hear
Paul Robeson the noted actor and concert singer appear in a song
recital the first since his return to America shortly before.
The announcement of the appearance of Mr. Robeson, who will return shortly to Europe, created a great deal of interest, and gave
Harlem an opportunity of hearing one of the most distinguished
artists produced by the race, asserts the writer. He was presented by the Progressive Club of Mother Zion Church, of which
Mr. Frances Cline Robeson is president, and the recital was given
for the benefit of the building fund of the church. Mr. Robeson
who is the brother of the Rev. B.C. Robeson, pastor of the church,
received a fine ovation and tribute from the large audience. Mr.
Robeson who has won renown as an actor and singer was in especially
fine form, and offered a program that was well suited to his voice,
and which he rendered in a superb manner, observed Mr. Allen. He
concludes: "His singing was remarkable for its excellent diction,
splendid shading, and fine interpretation. Paul Robeson is one
of the most gifted personalities of the race and is a man of
remarkable accomplishments.   The tribute that he received from
the audience shows the place that he has won in the hearts and
esteem of the race and the American public."

906. "Bravos," _Time_, Vol. 34, No. 21, November 20, 1939, pp. 58-59.

The writer states from the first "Pursuit of Happiness" Show,
produced by CBS, lusty Negro baritone Paul Robeson volunteered.
He sang "Ballad for Americans." After Robeson finished singing
an audience of 600 stamped, shouted, and bravoed for two minutes
while the show was on the air, and for 15 minutes after. In the
next few days bags of letters demanded words, music recording,
another time at bat for "Ballad for Americans," concludes the
article.

907. "School Honors Robeson: Philadelphia Student Group Gives Silver
Cup to Actor," _New York Times_, December 14, 1939, p. 34.

Paul Robeson appeared in the musical show "John Henry," in Philadelphia, and received a silver loving cup from the student body
of Northeast High School. More than 2,000 boys were assembled
to see the presentation, and 3,000 others heard Robeson sing over
a public address system.

908. Jovien, Harold. "Singer Gets Tumultous Ovation: CBS Swamped with
Praises for Baritone," _Journal and Guide_, December 30, 1939, p. 1.

According to this writer, Paul Robeson's singing of "Ballard for
Americans," brought a studio audience to its feet in a tumultous
ovation. Columbia Broadcasting System network received many
phone calls, telegrams and letters concerning the broadcast and
a vocal interpretation by Paul Robeson.

5. NEGRO CULTURE

909. "Mr. Paul Robeson," _Daily News-Chronicle_, (London), May 3, 1935.

Paul Robeson thought that Negroes had a rich culture and that they
should appreciate it. He argues, in part: "All the world knows
by now that I have faith in the future of the Negro. I believe
that Negro culture merits an honorable place amongst the cultures
of the world. I believe that as soon as Negroes appreciate their
own culture, and confine their interest in the European to learning
his science and mechanics, they will be on the road to becoming
one of the dominant races of the world...."

6. PERSONAL FRIENDS

910. Woollcott, Alexander. "Ol' Man River - in Person," Cosmopolitan,
      July 1933, pp. 54, 55, 101, 102, 103.

      The author, a neighbor of Paul Robeson when he was living in
      England, and a writer states that of all of the countless people
      he has known in his wanderings over the world, Robeson is one of
      the few whom he would say has greatness. He points out that it
      is an indisputable fact that he is the finest musical instrument
      wrought by nature in his time. Mr. Woollcott was speaking about
      Robeson's greatness as a person, and not as an entertainer.

911. Du Bois, W.E.B. "Beside the Still Waters," Crisis, Vol. 40, No.
      5, May, 1931, p. 169.

      He states that to Broadway the Negro was not an actor, he was a
      vaudeville turn. Du Bois suggests that because Eugene O'Neill
      forced the Negro defeatist psychology partially across the foot-
      lights, half willingly Broadway endured patronizing Paul Robeson,
      for limited periods.

912. Du Bois, W.E.B. "As the Crow Flies," Crisis, Vol. 37, No. 7,
      July, 1930, p. 221.

      The author only made one reference to Paul Robeson. He did not
      explain the following sentence: "After all, the naked manhood
      of Paul Robeson would scare Philadelphia." Mr. Du Bois was a
      personal friend of Paul Robeson.

913. McCanns, Shirley Graham. "A Day at Hampstead," Opportunity,
      Vol. 1, No. 1, January, 1931, pp. 14-15.

      The writer visited Paul Robeson and his family in Hampstead, a
      suburb of London and writes her impression of them. She points
      out that Mrs. Robeson is general manager, booking agent, secretary
      and advisor to her illustrious husband. The author declares that
      Paul Robeson has come a long way from the football field of
      Rutgers to the stages of London; yet he triumphantly covered the
      distances. Mc Canns asserts that his son, Paul Jr., and his
      wife, Eslanda, motivate Robeson's life. She concludes that he
      has genius, he has brains and he has a wife. She later become a
      friend of the Robesons.

914. "Paul Robeson Book Out in England Today," New York Times, May 19,
      1940, p. 13.

      The article states the the day on which Paul Robeson makes his
      debut as "Othello" at the Savory Theatre in London, Eslanda Goode
      Robeson's biography of her husband will be published in England
      under the title, Paul Robeson, Negro. It was stated that although
      only 32 years of age, Mr. Robeson has had a distinguished career
      as an athlete, actor, and singer. Throughout the biography are
      mentioned many personalities with whom Mr. Robeson has been in

intimate contact and were his friends including Carl Van Vachten,
Eugene O'Neill, James Light, Glenway Westcott, Walter White, Frank
Harris, Maurice Browns and others.

7. PERSONAL LIFE

915. "Mr. and Mrs. Paul Robeson (To Divorce)," Atlanta World, July 1,
1932.

According to this article it is to the credit of the Robesons that
they have decided to disband their marital union, no matter what
the cost in publicity nor what the result. When two people find
they are not suited for further companionship, the only sensible
solution is a parting. The Robesons have announced their plans
of reminaing friends. The wisdom of such a decision is obvious.
Nothing except cheap publicity and heart aches could be gained from
a heated court fight, states the writer. The woman or man who
marries a genius must be prepared for numerous liaisons. Fame
brings admirers who beat their wings in the bright glow of the
great person's popularity and public acclaim. The mate who can
overlook this must also be a genius in the knowledge and understanding of human psychology. As for Paul's future plans, they
are his business and his prospects for another marriage should
affect only him and his future bride, concludes the writer.

916. "Wife Sues Robeson: Says Ennui is Cause," New York Times, June 26,
1932, p. 5.

The article states that the eleven-year-old romance of Paul Robeson
has gone on the rocks of sheer ennui, his wife divulged. His wife
declares: "I began proceedings in New York courts about a month
ago and hope to have my divorce soon. It is all perfectly friendly
and we will keep on being friends, but we've seen so much of each
other and both are just a bit tired and want our freedom." The
Robesons' had been separated about two years before Mr. filed
for divorce.

917. Carter, Lawrence E. "Disinherited English Heiress Gives Exclusive
Interview; Denies Stories in Papers about Paul Robeson," New York
Age, May 7, 1932.

According to this article Miss Nancy Cunard denies the groundless
rumor that she had chosen the Grampion Hotel in Harlem as a
trusting place for Paul Robeson. She told the newspaper reporters:
"I am astounded at your story of myself and Paul Robeson. You
must correct this immediately. I met him once in Paris, in 1926,
at the Beeufsurale Toit cabaret, and have never seen him since.
He has said so himself, in the Evening Graphic, May 2. Good for
him. Indeed he needs no patron; he is one of your greatest singers-
everyone knows that." Miss Cunard also declared emphatically,

(Carter, Lawrence E.)

"We do not know each other." She wishes him every success.

918.   Cooke, Marvel. "Mrs. Paul Robeson, Manager and Mate," New York
        Amsterdam News, October 5, 1935, p. 9.

        This article discusses Mrs. Robeson's life and the role that she
        plays in her husband's life. At the time of the interview, the
        Robeson's were living in England. It was also stressed in this
        article that Mrs. Robeson was her husband's manager.

                              8. PLAYS

919.   "Robeson in Berlin in 'Emperor Jones,'" New York Times, April 1,
        1930, p. 10.

        For the first time in an American play, directed by an American
        and given in the English language by an American actor, was
        presented on a Berlin stage. Paul Robeson played the lead in
        "Emperor Jones." The article declares that it is noteworthy
        that whereas the dialect must certainly have been difficult for
        many members of the audience, no synopsis was included in the
        program, since Robeson's acting was graphic enough to tell the
        story vividly even if all the words were not understood.

920.   "Mr. Paul Robeson as Othello," London Times, April 3, 1930, p. 12.

        This article states that Mr. Paul Robeson, the Negro actor, would
        soon appear at the Globe Theatre as "Othello." To the British
        audiences he was best known as the singer of "Ole Man River," in
        "Show Boat" that was presented in London last year (1929) and for
        his remarkable performance in "The Emperor Jones" which was pro-
        duced in Londin in 1925.

921.   "Paul Robeson Stars in 'The Emperor Jones' in German Theatre,"
        New York News, April 5, 1930.

        According to this article Paul Robeson added to his triumphs in
        Berlin, Germany, when he gave a superb, masterly interpretation
        of Eugene O'Neill's play of a Colored-American, "Emperor Jones,"
        at the Deutsches Kuenstler Theatre, which was packed to capacity.
        It was the first time that an American production in the English
        language, played and directed by Americans, was ever presented in
        a German Theatre. With very few changes O'Neill's production was
        presented as it originally was in America. The settings were a
        bit more modern and here and there a few minor changes were made
        for the benefit of the German theatre public, states the writer.
        Despite the fact that the play was given in English, James Light,

(New York News)

formerly of the Provincetown Players, had no program synopsis or
German interpretation of the language for the audience. But
Robeson's acting was forceful enough to convey the trend of the
play to the Germans, states the article. Robeson was hailed as
one of the greatest dramatic stars of the day. He has done a
great deal to favorably impress the Germans with the ability of
Americans to contribute something other than musical comedy,
murder and mystery plays to the theatre, declares the article.

922. "Robeson is Sensation in Berlin," Pittsburgh Courier, April 12,
1930, Section Two, p. 6.

Paul Robeson played the lead in the play "The Emperor Jones" in
Berlin, Germany. This was the first time that an American play,
directed by an American and given in the English language was
presented on a Berlin stage. According to this article Robeson's
acting was graphic enough to tell the story vividly, even if
all the words were not understood.

923. Tour, Henri De La. "Robeson Getting Ready for Appearnace in
Shakespeare's Immortal 'Othello': French Writer of Central Europe
Concert Tour of Talented Artist," New York Amsterdam News, May 7,
1930, p. 3.

The title tells what this article is about. He discussed Robeson's visit to Romania, Greece, Russia, Czechoslovakia, France,
Germany and England. Mr. Tour states that Paul Robeson was rehearsing for his appearance in Shakespeare's immortal "Othello,"
which had its premiere in London in May, 1930. The writer called
Robeson a "Black Hercules."

924. "Robeson Acclaimed in 'The Hairy Ape,'" New York Times, May 12,
1931, p. 29.

The author states that Paul Robeson was acclaimed in O'Neill's
"The Hairy Ape" in London when he appeared for the first time in
the role of the stoker Yank. It was pointed out that in spite of
the giant force suggested by his powerful physique and stirring
voice, Robeson's Yank seemed a far more pathetic character than
Wolhelm (a white actor, who at one time played the part) made him,
and was endowed with somewhat less ferocity.

925. "Hairy Ape Cancelled," London Times, May 18, 1931, p. 10.

This article states that Mr. Paul Robeson, whose performance in
"The Hairy Ape" at the Ambassadors Theatre was cancelled because
of the loss of his voice.

926. "Othello Rehearsals Win Robeson to Stage," New York Times, May 18,
1930, p. 31.

According to this article Paul Robeson never had any desire to
appear in a Shakespearean role until he came to England. Robeson
declares that Shakespeare amazed him because his psychology is

(New York Times)

uncannily true all the time. He surmises: "I feel the play is
so modern for the problem is the problem of my own people. It is
a tragedy of honor, rather than of jealousy.... What I found
so wonderfully real and true and beautiful is Shakespeare's superb
sympathy for the under-dog, and of course, the extraordinary
thing is that the play was written when slave traders made the
Negroes a race problem." He concludes: "There are very few Moors
in Northern Africa without Ethiopian blood in their veins, but I
am approaching the part as Shakespeare wrote it and am playing
Othello as a man whose tragedy lay in the fact that he was sooty
black."

927. "The Hairy Ape," London Times, May 19, 1931, p. 14.

This article reported that "The Hairy Ape," starring Paul Robeson,
had been cancelled after five performances. Mr. Robeson had
been suffering from a severe attack of laryngitis and had hoped to
continue in the play, but, on medical advice, decided to end his
performance so that he would not run the rish of permanently
injuring his voice.

928. Editorial. "Robeson Is a Very Good Actor," Morning Post (London),
May 20, 1930.

The editorial states, in part: "Last night Mr. Paul Robeson
played Othello, and the occasion was one of considerable artistic
interest. The interest, however, was due not to the fact that
Mr. Robeson is a man of color and that Shakespeare gave to Othello
many characteristics that belong rather to the Negro than to the
Moor, but the fact that Mr. Robeson is a very great artist. His
success both as singer and actor has been remarkable and the
interest lay in some further discovery of the range of his remarkable talents."

929. "No Other Othello Compares to Robeson," Morning Post, (London),
May 20, 1930.

The article said, in part: "A noble performance welcomed with
tumultuous enthusiasm. No need to apologise for Mr. Robeson because he is a Negro. Though in conventional grace and some
nicities of diction we have had English Othellos from whom he might
learn, there has been no Othello on our stage, certainly for forty
years, to compare with his in dignity, simplicity and true passion.... Sybil Thorndike was splendid as Emilia.... Maurice
Browne's Iago was subtle in idea, but disappointing in character."

930. Parson, Alan. "An Elaborate 'Othello,'" The Daily Mail, May 21,
1930.

The writer declares that although he has the greatest admiration
for Robeson as an actor and as a man, and his "Othello" is undoubtedly magnificent, and especially in the passionate scenes,
yet he believes "Othello" was a Moor and not an Ethiopian. He
also asserts that he was continually moved by the dignity of his

(Parson, Alan)

bearing and the nobility of the acting, he had throughout the
play, a disquieting feeling that it was not quite right, and that
this was not the real Othello.

931. Editorial. "Paul Robeson as Othello," Times Enterprise (Thomasville, Ga.), May 27, 1930.

The editor, a white man, comments on Robeson's role in "Othello."
He states: "Robeson seems to have a little sense if he has queer
notions about art and the stage. His expression 'I would not care
to play those scenes in some parts of the United States' was too
restrictive. We doubt if he would dare do it outside of some
negro section of our big cities or in a small town where they
never had problems and do not understand. Imagine Robeson putting
that on in Atlanta or New Orelans or St. Louis or even San
Francisco. Go still further and place him in that role in towns
the size of Thomasville, Valdosta, or Albany. Well, he knows
what would happen and so do the rest of us. That is one form of
Amusement that we will not stand for now or ever. This negro has
potentialities for great harm to his race. He can do them no
good and very little harm in England. We expect that it would
be best for his Othello to stay in that country or some other
where the experience has not been so serious as well as so costly."

932. Editorial. "Ostrich Civilization," New York Amsterdam News, May
28, 1930, p. 20.

The editor comments on Paul Robeson's role as "Othello," in
London. He observes that from England comes the news that Paul
Robeson has received a tremendous ovation in his first appearance
as Othello. From Philadelphia comes the news that a bronze statue
of Paul Robeson, made by a well-known New York sculpture, has
been rejected by an art committee because of "the color problem."
London admires the colored artist in the flesh; Philadelphia cannot stand him in bronze. England does not mine him kissing a
white woman in a play, since Shakespeare wrote the lines that way;
America would say that such things are untrue to life. Even if
Othello and Desdemona are man and wife, the American convention
is that they would not kiss each other. Even with the presence
of millions of mulattoes in this country, the American convention
is that the races do not mix. Even when his head alone is buried
in the sand, with the rest of his body showing, the ostrich's con-
cention is that he is hidden, states the editor. He concludes:
"Such things partly explain why white America has produced no
great art. True art knows no racial boundaries and America knows
nothing else. 'Othello' is admittedly one of Verdi's greatest
operas; but it is very seldom seen in an American opera house.
England can produce a Shakespeare in letters and a Samuel Coleridge-
Taylor in music; America never will, that is, the America of today.
Art follows civilization, and only a thin stratum of the American
public is civilized. Possibly three cities in this country would
stand for the appearance of Robeson as Othello, Peggy Ashcroft or
Lillian Gish as Desdemona - New York, Chicago and Boston - maybe.
In all others 'Othello' would have a long run - and a fast one."

933. Bishop, G.W. "Robeson Acclaimed in 'Othello' Role," <u>New York Times</u>, May 29, 1930, p. 33.

According to Bishop, an audience at the Savory Theatre rose for Paul Robeson at the close of his first interpretation of "Othello," and the curtain was raised and lowered twenty times before the frenzy of applause subsided. The author asserts that "Robeson lives the part imaginatively and, of course, his great asset is his magnificent voice, which he uses perfectly. There is only an occasional trace of American accent in his speeches and he shows fine appreciation of the flow and rhythm of verse." The writer continues to argue that "old playgoers searching their memories can recall no such scene in the London theatre in many years. Cries for Paul Robeson came from all parts of the house the moment the last lines were spoken."

934. Ashcroft, Mary. "Robeson is a Great Artist," <u>World</u> (London), May 30, 1930.

Miss Ashcroft, a white actress, played Desdemona opposite Paul Robeson in "Othello." She declares that the color question never occurred to her: "Racial prejudices are foolish at the best of times; but I think it is positively absurd that they should even come into consideration where acting is concerned. I supposed Mr. Robeson kissed me during the play about five times. Ever so many people asked me if I didn't mind, and it seemed so silly. Of course I didn't mind. I see no difference in being kissed by any other actor. It's just necessary to the play. For myself I look on it as a real privilege to act with a great artist like Paul Robeson."

935. Swaffer, Hannen. "Robeson's Art Conquered Everything," <u>Daily Express</u> (London), May 30, 1930.

The writer says: "Paul Robeson destroyed last night the foolish idea accepted for many years that Iago is a better part than Othello. Robeson's art conquered everything. Why should a black actor be allowed to kiss a white actress? I heard a few people say beforehand. There was no protest of that kind in the theatre. T'was in the part and that was that. When his rage came it was magnificent."

936. "Robeson Praised as Othello," <u>Daily Telegraph</u>, May 30, 1930.

The author declares: "Much debate of the question as to whether Shakespeare meant Othello to be a Negro or an Arab can be left to the professors; but it is certainly true that by reason of his race Mr. Robeson was able to surmount difficulties which English actors generally find in the part of Othello without even seeming to notice that they are there."

937.   "Negroes on the Stage: Paul Robeson in the Title Role of Eugene
       O'Neill's 'Emperor Jones,'" _Time_, Vol. 15 , No. 26, June 30, 1930,
       p. 55.

       The article states that a score of encores greeted Paul Robeson
       in his London debut as "Othello." It continues to assert that
       while English critics thumbed through forty years of newspaper
       files without finding a parallel, the Savoy's most serene play-
       goers clapped and bravoed tumultuously. Robeson, who long ago
       charmed London, with his singing of "Ol' Man River" and his raging
       as "The Emperor Jones," did more than act the familiar Moor. He
       constructed, we are told, a new Othello, a Moor depicting the
       tragedy of the Negro race, concludes the writer. He continues to
       suggest that musically, he is to a large extent self-taught; yet
       his booming, melodious voice has brought him many honors. His
       latest triumph, in a Shakespearean role, carries one back to the
       days of American slavery, when, with Edmund Kean as Iago, Ira
       Aldridge, another American Negro, played the Moor before crowned
       heads of Europe, concludes the writer. He also suggests that
       Paul Robeson is in the upper brackets of the theatre and
       especially as "Othello."

938.   "Paul Robeson: Missionary," _Chicago Defender_, June 7, 1930, p. 14.

       This article declares, in part, that if Robeson,through his acting,
       can make a prejudicial world pause a moment to readjust its idea
       on certain subjects, he is doing a great service as an actor.
       If he can cause one white person to see a race question through
       the eyes of one who recognizes the ability to a dark person to
       act, he has done something of which to be proud, surmises the
       article. And so we are thankful to Paul Robeson. We wish there
       were more of him. After having to break the ice in London, we
       might send him to New York, to Philadelphia, Chicago, Los Angeles,
       Washington, and finally to Sherman, Texas. But since there is
       one of him, we had better keep him in London where he is safe,
       declared the writer.

939.   Browning, Ivan H. "Tells of Struggles of Paul Robeson in 'Othello,'"
       Pittsburgh Courier, June 14, 1930, Section Two, p. 6.

       Some whites were concerned about a Black man kissing a white woman
       in the play "Othello." Miss Peggy Ashcroft, the white actress in
       the play was quoted as saying "it seems so silly for so much fuss
       to be made or for people to even ask me if I mind being kissed by
       a colored man." She also stated that she was honored to be in the
       same play with such a fine and talented person as Mr. Robeson.
       Browning declares: "Personally Paul did not fancy kissing any
       woman other than his wife and that particular part of the play
       did not in the least excite him nor give him a thrill." He
       concludes: "Perhaps, if these facts were known to all Ofays, they
       might not be so excited over his love and kissing scenes with
       Ashcroft. However, Robeson is certainly covering him with glory
       and he has now practically reached the height of his ambition,
       which in the beginning was to appear in Shakespeare's 'Othello.'"

940. "Robeson is Toast of London," Pittsburgh Courier, June 28, 1930,
      Section Two, p. 6.

      This article states that most of the English newspapers contained
      laudatory reviews of Paul Robeson in the part of Shakespeare's
      "Othello." The newspapers listed were: London Morning Post,
      Manchester Sunday Chronicle, Daily Express, Daily Chronicle, Daily
      Telegraph, London Times, Morning Advertiser and Manchester
      Guardian.

941. Watts, Richard, Jr. "The Othello of Paul Robeson," New York
      Herald Tribune, June 29, 1930, Section 8, p. 2.

      The article declares that Paul Robeson's Othello was easily the
      outstanding event of the London theatrical season. Mr. Watts sur-
      mises that no one has succeeded in disputing the fact that the
      beauty of the Robeson voice, the sheer nobility of the Robeson
      presence and the earnest forcefulness of the Robeson acting result
      in a performance that is frightening in its pathos and heart-
      breaking in its power.

942. "Robeson as Othello," Living Age, Vol. 338, July 1, 1930, p. 563.

      This article states what the Morning Post had to say about Paul
      Robeson as "Othello." It declares that the British Press has
      greeted with the grestest enthusiasm the appearance of Paul
      Robeson in Othello. Here is what the highly unemotional Morning
      Post had to say of his performance: "There is, of course, no need
      to apologize for Mr. Robeson because he is a negro. Though in
      conventional grace and some nicities of diction we have had English
      Othellos from whom he might learn, there has been no Othello on
      our stage, certainly for forty years, to compare with his in
      dignity, simplicity, and true passion. He made the part sym-
      pathetic and appealing, not only because he was real, but also
      because together with his deep, virile voice there was a child-
      like racial simplicity that made Othello's submission to Iago's
      suggestions understandable and the 'pity of it' not only poignant
      but also logical. The slight American accent is a trouble at first,
      but one soon gets used to this. In general, from an elocutionary
      point of view, one only wishes some of our actors would take
      example from his rolling and natural response to the rhythm and
      beauty of Shakespeare's verse."

943. Du Bois, W.E.B. "Along the Color Line," Crisis, Vol. 37, No. 7,
      July, 1930, p. 236.

      This article states that at the opening of Paul Robeson's inter-
      pretation of Othello in St. Louis, Mr. Robeson received twenty
      curtain calls, which is perhaps a record number.

944. Editorial. "White U.S. Critic Attempts to Belittle Robeson in
      'Othello,'" Chicago Defender, August 9, 1930, p. 5.

      The editor declares that after the foremost ciritcs of Europe
      had acclaimed Paul Robeson as one of the outstanding Shakespearean
      actors for his superb work in the drama "Othello," it remained for

(Chicago Defender)

a white American critic to attempt to find fault with the acting
of Mr. Robeson, who is one of the most versatile performers in
the theatrical world. This critic, Burns Mantle, who formerly
wrote for the Chicago Tribune, in reviewing the drama took also
upon himself the task of attempt to force what would happen if
Mr. Robeson enacted the play on Broadway, surmises the editor.
The critic foresaw embarrassment for Mr. Robeson and the retarding
of his Race's progress. Even Mr. Mantle went so far as to see the
drama as an inspiration for mob violence and race riots, states
the writer. All of which was quite unnecessary. Othello, Mr.
Robeson, and his supporting cast, including his white Desdemona,
would be welcomed in New York City and other leading American
cities, where culture and art stand above racial intolerance. He
suggests that Mr. Robeson, without embarrassment to himself or
fear of personal harm, could carry out his part in the drama as
set forth by the great English playwright to the letter without
being disturbed; because the rabble would never attend a play of
this nature. The editor concludes: "Only one or two critics,
known for their intolerance on the race question, have made a fuss
over the fact that Mr. Robeson kissed Miss Peggy Ashcroft, the
Desdemona, and even they were forced to admit that the universe
did not tremble. Miss Ashcroft plainly stated that she did not
in the least mind being kissed by Othello and that she thought
those who permitted racial differences to interfer with their
lives and thoughts were foolish."

945.   "Mr. Paul Robeson's Programme," London Times, August 26, 1930,
       p. 10.

       The article states that Paul Robeson was giving at the Savoy
       Theatre in London the first act of "The Emperor Jones" and two
       groups of songs that begin and end the evening. The reviewer con-
       cludes: "And the merit of Mr. Robeson's performance -- a tantali-
       zingly good one that makes us eager to have more of the play...."
       He also surmises that Mr. Robeson's "singing is simple, unforced,
       without extravagance, and good to hear."

946.   Morgan, Charles. "Mr. Robeson Tries an Experiment," New York Times,
       September 14, 1930, Part 8, p. 2.

       The author contends that the success of the experiment that Paul
       Robeson is making at the Savoy Theatre is proof of his complete
       acceptance by the London public. This experiment related to
       Robeson singing two groups of Negro spirituals at the beginning
       and ending of "Emperor Jones." Morgan asserts that Negro spirit-
       uals are, as a form of art, of so little value that it is hard to
       make them sustain an evening in the sophisticated circumstances
       of a theatre. He does however, surmise that Robeson pursues them
       with an admirable tact. His voice is charming; his manner has an
       unaffected case of dignity. If the songs are to be sung at all
       in the Savoy Theatre, they could scarcely be better sung, con-
       cludes the writer. He states that Mr. Robeson, by a courageously
       varied use of his talent, has been steadily increasing not only
       his popularity but his repute among discriminating playgoers.

947. "British 'Who's Who' Lists Helen Wells: Paul Robeson is also
      Included for the First Time," New York Times, December 19, 1930,
      p. 13.

      It was stated that Paul Robeson was included in the British "Who's
      Who" because of his triumphs in England. All of his London en-
      gagements are listed ending with his recent performance of "Othello"
      whereby he won new laurels in London. It is worthy to note that
      he is not even included in his own country's "Who's Who." He was
      then (1930) living in London, states the article.

948. "Robeson to Live in London," New York Times, May 14, 1931, p. 26.

      Paul Robeson announced that he planned to live permanently in
      England because it is the country where the Negro has the fairest
      play. In London, according to the singer, "people are unprejudiced
      and fair." In London, argues the actor, every man is a potential
      friend. He also asserts that some day he hopes to open a theatre
      in London to establish the recognition of Negro art in the West.

949. "Robeson Unable to Appear," New York Times, May 17, 1931, p. 31.

      The strain on the voice of Paul Robeson prevented him from playing
      the leading role in London in "The Hairy Ape." Robeson was
      acclaimed by the London critics after the opening of the play.

950. "Portrait," Outlook, Vol. 159, August 26, 1931, p. 527.

      There is a photo of Robeson and the caption under it states: "A
      Great Negro Artist. Admired and even envied for his great talents,
      Paul Robeson was the star of Eugene O'Neill's play 'Emperor Jones.'"
      He is both actor and singer."

951. Deutsch, Helen and Stella Hanau. "The Provincetown Theatre and
      the Negro," Crisis, Vol.38, No. 11, November, 1931, pp. 373-374,
      396.

      This article points out that Augustin Duncan discovered Paul
      Robeson in an amateur production of Ridgeley Torrance's "Simon
      the Cyrenian," before he was signed to play in the Provincetown
      Theatre production of "All God's Chillun Got Wings," The writers
      state that with the bulwark of approval built by Robeson, "All God's
      Chillun Got Wings," opened on May 15th to an accompaniment of
      poison pen letters, telegrams to O'Neill threatening his life and
      the lives of his children, and an anonymous promise of a bomb in
      the cellar. Included in this article was a quote from Alexander
      Woollcott who commented on Paul Robeson as Brutus Jones: "Robe-
      son adds to his extraordinary physique a shrewd, rich understanding
      of the role and a voice that is unmatched in the American theatre."

952. "Robeson in 'Show Boat,'" New York Times, May 29, 1932, Part 8, p. 5,

      The article contends that for those who admire the art of Paul
      Robeson the revival of "Show Boat," now current provides an
      opportunity to hear him at a time when the local music season is
      entirely quiescent. It is also pointed out that Robeson sings

(New York Times)

"Old Man River" with feeling and power goes almost without saying.

953.   "Robeson to Form London Repertory," New York Times, October 28, 1932, p. 22.

Paul Robeson was appearing at the Palladium Theatre in London when he announced that he would establish a permanent repertory company in London. The singer states that the company would be formed as soon as his engagements permit. He states that he would give O'Neill plays. Robeson asserts that ultimately he hopes to take that company on a world tour.

954.   Du Bois, W.E.B. "Color Caste in The United States," Crisis, Vol. 40, No. 3, March, 1933, p. 60.

It was stated that on the stage and in literature and art, the Negro had some opportunity but his genius is limited by a public who will not endure any portrayal of a Negro except as a slave, a funmaker, a moron or criminal. The writer declares there have been some few exceptions to this but they emphasize the rule. He went on to assert that neither Paul Robeson nor Jules Bledsoe was allowed to sing the title role in "The Emperor Jones" at the Metropolitan Opera; it was given to a white whose face was painted black.

955.   "Paul Robeson Arrives," New York Times, May 11, 1933, p. 14.

Paul Robeson and Mrs. Robeson arrived from London to New York where Mr. Robeson will play the leading role in the film version of "The Emperor Jones." It was also pointed out that Robeson plans to establish a repertoire of Negro plays to be produced in London at the Embassey Theatre.

956.   "Robeson Wins Plaudits," New York Times, March 14, 1933, p. 19.

Paul Robeson appeared in London in Eugene O'Neill's tragedy, "All God's Chillun Got Wings." The article states that he scored another personal triumph. Robeson was the only Black in the cast.

957.   "Filming 'Emperor Jones,' Active Production Starts Here with Paul Robeson Starring," New York Times, May 26, 1933, p. 42.

The article states that the film version of "The Emperor Jones" went into active production at the Astoria Studios in New York City.

958.   Troy, William. "Films, Cinema Minus: 'The Emperor Jones,'" Nation, Vol. 137, No. 3562, October 11, 1933, p. 419.

The writer declares that the screen version of "The Emperor Jones" was a disappointment. He states: "Of course Mr. Robeson's Emperor is 'magnificent.'   Mr. Robeson has always been magnificent in whatever he has done - even in 'Othello.'" But this magnificence, while it makes the Krimsky-Cochran picture worth seeing at any

(Troy, William)

cost, scarcely leads one to condone its failure to satisfy so
many other legitimate expectations.

959. "The Emperor is Held Over," New York Amsterdam News, September 27,
      1933, p. 7.

      This article states that the play, "The Emperor Jones," starring
      Paul Robeson, was playing at the Roosevelt Theatre in New York
      City, and held over because of public demand. The reporter sur-
      mises that the small admission fee at the Harlem theatre served
      to keep thousands wending their way there, and by the time the
      presentation closes .... all this section of the big city will be
      fully acquainted with the fact that "The Emperor Jones" lives as
      truly today as when the drums called Brutus Jones to an untimely
      death in the swamps of a West Indian Island.

960. "The Dark Emperor - Paul Robeson," Vanity Fair, 1933, pp. 14-15.

      There is a brief discussion of Eugene O'Neill's play "The Emperor
      Jones" starring Paul Robeson. The author states that the play
      was almost a classic exposition of vanity and terror. The writer
      calls Paul Robeson a scholar and indomitable athlete, actor and
      singer of distinction.

961. "Emperor Jones," Pittsburgh Courier, January 13, 1934, Section
      Two, p. 6.

      According to this article, "Emperor Jones," Paul Robeson's starring
      vehicle which has caused no end of discussion and the many critics
      dividing their opinions as to its fairness to the race, has failed
      to be listed by any of the metropolitan dailies or trade magazines
      as one of the ten best of the season.

962. "'Emperor Jones': Paul Robeson," Black Dispatch, March 21, 1932,
      p. 1.

      The author concludes that Paul Robeson, who is the only person
      adequately endowed racially, physically, histrionically and
      temperamentally to play Brutus Jones in Eugene O'Neill's famous
      drama, "Emperor Jones," is the most renowned colored figure of this
      day. Undoubtedly his background and cultural inheritance have
      combined with his talents and personality to bring him inter-
      national fame, states the writer.

963. Downing, Henry F. "Protest Over O'Neill's Play Recalls Day of Ira
      Aldridge: Famous Black Tragedian Played Opposite White Woman in
      Many Plays in Nineteenth Century," Chicago Defender, April 26, 1934.

      This writer points out that when Eugene O'Neill's play,"All God's
      Chillun Got Wings," is given its premiere at the Provincetown
      theatre, in New York City, with Paul Robeson, a Negro, in the
      principal male part, and Mary Blair, a white actress, playing the
      part of his wife, it will not be that such a combination has
      appeared on the English-speaking stage. Mr. Downing asserts that

(Downing, Henry F.)

the records show that Ira Aldridge, Negro tragedian, played in
England for many years in the early part of the last century with
great success and with white women playing opposite him among
whom was Madge Robertson Kendall, called in his day "England's
foremost actress." Some of the plays Aldridge appeared in
included "Othello," "Macbeth," "Richard III,""Hamlet," and
"Shylock."

964. Garvey, Marcus. "The World as It Is," The Black Man, Vol. 1,
No. 7, June, 1935, pp. 7-10.

The writer argues that Paul Robeson is not dignifying his race
from the parts he plays in propaganda dramas. It is hoped that he
is making enough money for himself if so that when he retires
from the stage he may be able to square his conscience with his
race by doing something for it, declares Garvey.

965. "Show Boat Personalities and Their Qualifications," Journal and
Guide, July 25, 1936, p. 5.

This article gives a short biographical sketch of Paul Robeson who
portrayed the character of Joe in "Show Boat." When "Show Boat"
first played on the London stage, Robeson had the role of Joe.
He was cast in the same part for the film version, in which he
sings "Old Man River" and "Ah Still Suite Me." The article states
that Robeson had given concerts in 700 cities of Europe and America.
It was also pointed out that his hobby is languages and, besides
English, he speaks other languages.

966. "Europe: Paul Robeson," Crisis, Vol. 37, No. 7, July, 1937,
pp. 221, 236.

This article states that at the opening of Paul Robeson's interpretation of Othello in London, Mr. Robeson received twenty
curtain calls, which is perhaps a record number. It is also
surmised that "the naked manhood of Paul Robeson would scare
Philadelphia."

967. Bolsover, Philip. "Why I Joined Labor Theatre," Daily Worker,
(London), November 24, 1937.

The actor declares that he joined the Unity Theatre because it
meant identifying himself with the working-class. And it gave him
the chance to act in plays that said something that he wanted to
say about things that he believed must be emphasized. He also
argues that working-class people can identify with him more than
the upper class because they understand what he sings.

968. "Paul Robeson," Manchester Guardian, January 8, 1938.

According to this report Paul Robeson, internationally famous
actor-singer, actively engaged in part-authoring of a play which
will dramatize Gandhi's campaign in South Africa in 1893 on behalf
of Indians settled there. The Mahatma will be the central figure
and Robeson will play the part of a miner watching the struggle
with sympathy and the surge of a new political consciousness,
concludes the author.

969. Steichen, Edward. "Paul Robeson as Emperor Jones," U.S. Camera
Magazine, Vol. 1, No. 6, October, 1938, pp. 14-19.

There are more than 27 photos of Paul Robeson as well as a brief
discussion of him in "Emperor Jones." Robeson had on the uniform
of Emperor Jones in all but one of the photos. This article is
more of a photographic essay than anything else.

970. Hall, Chatwood. "Robeson Lauded for his Desertion of English
Plays," Black Dispatch, December 25, 1938, p. 1.

Hall points out that with complete unanimity visitors from Great
Britain to the 20th anniversary celebrations of the Great
Socialist Revolution in Moscow, U.S.S.R. approved wholeheartedly
of Paul Robeson's decision to cast his lot with the working class
theatre in England. All agreed that the bourgeois theatre in
England is decadent, that the future of theatricals belongs to
the working class theatre, and that the loss of the decrepit
bourgeois theater is a great gain for the theater of the working
class, states Hall. When interviewed at the Grand Hotel, those
who expressed full approval on Robeson's action included the
following: HAROLD HUDSON, secretary of the Shop Assistants' Union
of Margate and Ramsgate, England; ROBERT MITCHELL, general secretary of the Shop Assistants' Union of Great Britain, Glasgow,
Scotland; and EVELYN BROWN, committee for Peace and Friendship
with the U.S.S.R., London.

971. "Paul Robeson," Negro History Bulletin, Vol. 2, No. 4, January,
1939, pp. 25-28.

There is a short biography of Paul Robeson in this Special Issue
devoted to "Successes on The Stage." The article states that of
all the roles, Robeson was probably the most successful as "Ol'
Man River," in "Show Boat" and as the hero in "The Song of
Freedom."

972. "Facing the Facts to be Celebrated During Negro History Week,"
Negro History, Vol. 2, No. 5, February, 1939, p. 38.

It was pointed out that on the stage Negroes have attained distinction with .... Paul Robeson.

973. "Paul Robeson Here From Europe," New York Times, May 16, 1939, p. 27.

Paul Robeson arrived in New York City on the French liner, Nor-
mandic, for a brief visit with Oscar Hammerstein. He had a conference with Mr. Hammerstein to discuss a play in which he may
take the leading role. Robeson declares that he had been giving
concerts in Europe but that he would like to appear in a play as
he likes to "break away from concerts work every now and then."

974. "Paul Robeson: Signs for Summer Run at the Ridgeway Theatre,"
Chicago Defender, June 3, 1939, p. 1.

According to this article Paul Robeson, internationally famous
singer and actor signed for a summer's run at the Ridgeway theatre
in White Plains, N.Y. Mr. Robeson returned to the states from
Europe two weeks ago where he had starred for the past several
years in films and concert halls. He was in the states several
months ago when he made one picture in Hollywood. As an opener
Robeson will do "Emperor Jones," the play which started him on to
fame following the death of Charles Gilpin. This article said for
many months local producers had attempted to interest Robeson in
doing, "The Emperor Jones" on the stages of this country but engagements abroad have generally caused him to turn down the offer.
While the Ridgeway is not on Broadway, it is considered a "Broadway Summer Theatre," where New Yorkers enjoy their pleasures in
hot weather, states the writer. Robeson had been guaranteed a
flat sum of $750 daily for ten weeks of performance in the
Ridgeway, thus becoming the highest paid actor off Broadway.
Robeson accepted the offer after turning down one that would have
placed him on Broadway playing opposite Ethel Waters. The show
featuring Miss Waters and Paul is to be produced this fall. Perhaps never before in history have such eleborate plans for a production been made as those now in the making for the appearance
of Robeson in White Plains, concludes the writer. Paul, a former
star athlete and orator at Rutgers is extremely popular in upper
New York which surrounds the territory the Ridgeway is located
in. Already seats are selling far in advance even though the show
does not open for seven weeks yet, asserts the article.

975. "Mr. Paul Robeson's Plans," London Times, July 11, 1939, p. 12.

This article asserts that Mr. Paul Robeson arrived at Southampton
(England) and proposed to make a musical play and film, both on
the life of a legendary figure of the cotton fields. The story
is called "John Henry," which is the name of a Negro giant who was
the size of a grown man when he was born. He became King of the
cotton fields and later King of the railroad. The symbolic figure
dies when he pits his great strength in a race against the loco-
motive, the mechanical giant of the white man. The film was
scheduled to be produced in New York City toward the end of the
year, according to the article.

976. McCardle, Carl W. "Living Theater: John Henry - Paul Robeson
     Returns to Roark Bradford Music Drama," Evening Bulletin, December
     12, 1939, p. 30.

     The critic states that Paul Robeson who has been away in Europe
     for several years, came back to our stage at Erlanger in "John
     Henry," a new play with music by Roark Bradford and Jacques Wolfe.
     He burst upon the stage, really, with thunder rolling and lightning
     flashing. John Henry wouldn't accept anything less in the way of
     an entrance, even if Mr. Robeson would. For John Henry is a strong
     man of the legends, the Negroes' Paul Bunyan, asserts Mr. McCardle.
     He said that Mr. Bradford has written down the tall talk and the
     tall deeds of John Henry here, and Mr. Wolfe the music to set them
     off. It is more music than play, perhaps. Folk opera maybe. Any-
     way, it fills the Erlanger with song and color and the pageantry
     of simple lives. And Mr. Robeson and his numerous colleagues in
     it give us some of the best singing heard hereabouts in the
     theater in a long time. He concludes: "This was the premiere of
     'John Henry,' and the audience, at the end applauded so persistently
     that John Henry and his girl, Julia Anne (Ruby Elzy), had to return
     to life and take bows. These two die in the last act, and Mr.
     Robeson and Miss Elzy tried, when the lights went up finally, to
     stay in their roles. They stood away from the others, staring
     rigidly ahead, as if oblivious of what was going on. Rousing
     hand-clapping soon brought them 'to,' however, they being stage-
     folk, after all."

9. RUSSIA

977. "Robeson Going to Russia: Will Be Guest of Eisenstein -- Has
     Learned Language," New York Times, December 20, 1934, p. 31.

     Paul Robeson went to Russia at the invitation of Sergei Eisenstein,
     noted Russian film producer. It will be Robeson's first visit to
     that country. It was also stated that sometime next year Robeson
     planned to go to Africa to determine the possibilities of estab-
     lishing a Negro homeland, such as Palestine for the Jews. Robeson
     compares the position of Negroes in the United States to that of
     the Jews in Germany. The article concludes that without regarding
     himself as a political messiah, Robeson has fervently devoted him-
     self to a lifelong task of bringing about the renaissance of Negro
     Art and Culture entirely distinct from the White race.

978. Hall, Chatwood. "Robeson Called 'Comrade' by Russians," Afro-
     American, January 12, 1935.

     This article asserts that Paul Robeson's visit to Moscow was pri-
     marily to visit the theatres during the present theatrical season,
     which is now at its height. Expressing a deep and genuine interest
     in the theatre, Robeson said that he considers the Soviet theatre
     the most interesting in the world, states Mr. Hall. Not only the
     theatre in the Soviet Union, he was quick to add, but the whole

(Hall, Chatwood)

new social system - new life, new culture, new economy, new
people - has for him great interest. Aside from visiting the
theatres, he will do some radio work during his present visit.
Most likely this radio work will be done in Russian,concludes
Mr. Hall. The writer explains that Mr. Robeson states that he
expects to spend much of the rest of his life in Russia, Soviet
Asia, Africa and Soviet China. The singer was quoted as saying:
"The whole future of the colored race is tied up with conditions
in those parts of the world, especially the Chinese situation
which is much like the situation in Africa. How the national
minority problem (the American colored race is a national minority
group) has been solved there deserves the closest study, as its
solution three offers a model for the solution of the race's problems wherever they exist."

979. "Robeson in Moscow," New Theatre, July, 1935.

This report declares that in the days and nights in Moscow, Robeson sometimes rode, but more often walked about, talking with
people on tramways, in buses, on street corners and in public
buildings. He was instantly recognized as a stranger, but his
warm smile opened doors and when he spoke their tongue he became
a friend. He says: "I was rested and buoyed up by the lovely,
honest, wondering looks which did not see a Negro. When these
people looked at me, they were just happy and interested. There
were no double looks, no venom, no superiority,"states the
article.

980. "Robeson Puts Son in a Soviet School," New Times, December 21,
1936, p. 18.

The article states that Paul Robeson would place his 9 year-old
son, Paul Jr., in a Russian school instead of an American one so
the boy need not contend with discrimination because of color
until he is older and his father can be with him. Paul Jr. had
attended school in Austria and the United States. In America,
according to the article, the son had a bewildering and painful
experience. It went on to state that Mr. Robeson was immensely
liked by the Russians. He was constantly studying the Russian
language, which he found a sympathetic medium for Negro songs.
He denied current rumors that he intends to become a Soviet Citizen, saying America is his country, concludes the article.

981. "Robeson to Put Son in Soviet School to Duck Discrimination,"
Pittsburgh Courier, January 2, 1937, p. 1.

This article states that the singer Paul Robeson was sending his
son Paul Robeson, Jr., to school in Russia in order to avoid
race discrimination in America until he is older and he can be
with him. Robeson denied that he intended to become a Soviet
citizen and contended that America was his country.

982. Hall, Chatwood. "Soviet Students Gloat as Robeson, Jr. Enters
      Moscow Public School," Philadelphia Independent, February 21, 1937,
      p. 1.

      The writer declares that a Happy New Year was had by Paul Robeson,
      Jr., and his Soviet school chums at Public School No. 25 in the
      Sverdlovsk district of the Red Capital at the turn of the year.
      Hall surmises that Paul Robeson, Sr., wished his son to receive
      a Soviet education where he would not be subjected to any hint or
      form of racial prejudice or chauvinism such as exists in the
      bourgeois West, so when Robeson came to Soviet Russia for his
      recent concert tour he brought his son along and enrolled him in
      a school of the Socialist Society, according to the author. Young
      Robeson's new school mates were unboundedly happy to have him come
      to them to study, asserts Mr. Hall. According to the principal
      of the school, young Robeson is making rapid progress with the
      language and all of his studies. A few of his school chums, like
      himself, speak German and give him every assistance in his classes.
      He concludes: "No possibility of facing the race prejudice which
      his noted father experienced in American schools exists for Paul,
      Jr., in Soviet schools where Soviet pupils have no consciousness
      or conception of racial hatred or prejudices. In the school are
      pupils of Russian, Ukranian, Polish, Jewish and German descent, all
      of whom study together."

983. "Paul Robeson to Flee Europe," New York Amsterdam News, April 23,
      1938, p. 1.

      According to this report Paul Robeson, his wife, Essie, and their
      son, Paul, Jr., will flee Europe for good and return to New York
      in June, it was reliably reported to The Amsterdam News. Paul Jr.,
      who is now in school in Moscow, where he was reported to be at the
      head of his class, will leave Russia soon by way of the Baltic Sea
      for London with his grandmother, Mrs. Robeson's mother. The great
      artist is convinced that Germany will now attack Czechoslovakia and
      thereby effect a Fascist ring around Russia. Not only was Mr.
      Robeson said to be fearful of a major European war breaking out
      between Russia and Germany because of the aggressions of the latter,
      but he is said to be indignant over the Fascist government that
      now exists in England. Because of general European conditions he
      will return to America for good, it was declared.

                    10. RUTGERS UNIVERSITY

984. Lawson, Edward. "Robey Comes Homes," The Anthologist (Rutgers
      University), January, 1932, pp. 7-23.

      This article briefly describes Paul Robeson's accomplishments
      while he was a student at Rutgers University. Some attention is
      devoted to Robeson's life since he graduated from that institution.
      The essence of the article was that although Robeson was not at
      Rutgers he left a legacy. Moreover, surmises Lawson, Rutgers would

(Lawson, Edward)

always be home for Robeson. Rutgers later turned her back against
Mr. Robeson in the 1950s.

11. SPANISH LOYALISTS

985. "Robeson's Voice Halts War in Spain," Atlanta Daily World, January
      29, 1937, p. 1.

      According to this article Paul Robeson stopped the "war" in Spain,
      at least until he had finished singing an appealing song. Singing
      from the Loyalist radio station, the renown singer of spirituals
      poured forth the heart-touching song. His words boomed via loud-
      speakers across the battle lines to friend and foe alike. Following
      his singing, the Bolshevist hymn, "The Fatherland," was sung,
      asserts the reporter. Even the Rebel forces led by General Fran-
      cisco Franco paid tribute to Robeson's artistry and were stirred
      by the appeal. When Robeson had finished singing, the Madrid
      announced signed off and the battle resumed, states the writer.

986. "9,000 in London Ask Help for Loyalist," New York Times, December
      20, 1937, p. 12.

      More than 9000 members of the Labor Party filled Albert Hall in
      London and demanded "arms, food and justice for democratic Spain."
      Paul Robeson attended the meeting and sang "Ol' Man River." He
      altered the line, "I'm tired of livin' and feared of dying" to
      "I must keep on struggling until I'm dyin'."

987. "Paul Robeson Sings to Aid Spanish Loyalists," Black Dispatch,
      January 8, 1938, p. 1.

      It was stated that Paul Robeson, ordinarily one of the world's
      highest paid singers, contributed his services free last week
      by singing "Ol' Man River" at a public meeting of Spanish Loyalist
      sympathizers at Albert Hall. The audience of 8,500 recalled him
      four times, declares the article.

988. "Paul Robeson Pays Visit to Spanish Loyalists," New York Times,
      January 24, 1938, p. 4.

      Paul Robeson and his wife arrived in Barcelona, Spain, for a ten-
      day visit to Loyalist Spain. He will visit the American Hospital
      at Villa Pas and doubtless will sing to patients there as well as
      give performances here and in Madrid.

989.   "Footnotes on Headliners: On Tour," New York Times, January 30,
       1938, Section   , p. 2.

       This article states that soldiers for Loyalist Spain listened to
       the singing of American actor and singer Paul Robeson. According
       to the article, the man who was once called "the greatest defen-
       sive end that ever trod a gridiron" visited the trenches of both
       the American volunteers and Spanish Loyalists. It was pointed
       out that Robeson's reputation as an actor has grown steadily
       ever since he first played "The Emperor Jones," in 1923.

                          12. SPORTS

990.   "Robeson's Modesty," New Brunswick Sunday Times, May 22, 1932,
       p. 17.

       Robeson recalls his days at Rutgers University and declares, in
       part: ".... My friend said a lot of silly things.... You know
       this business of Negro prejudice has two sides. When people hate
       you they go crazy. But when they like you they sometimes go a
       little crazy, too. In football days I got more praise than any
       white player. And I was credited with a lot of plays I never made.
       .... So it is with many white folks when they first "discover"
       a Negro."

991.   Nance, Ed. "Negro Grid Stars, Past and Present," Opportunity,
       Vol. 17, No. 9, September, 1939, pp. 272-274.

       The author asserts that Robeson made Walter Camp's "All American"
       team in 1918, being generally regarded as one of the best ends in
       football history. But in the early days some of the Rutgers players
       had realized that Robeson was a formidable rival, and that in
       addition to losing their positions on the team, they might lose
       them to a Negro. And so they had directed scrimmages against him
       until his nose had been broken, his shoulder dislocated, and one
       finger nail taken out by the roots by a player's cleats. Paul had
       become an infuriated player, his charges through the line had taken
       on a demon ferocity, and finally he had been put on the varsity to
       save it from annihilation. From then on the names of "Robeson"
       and "Rutgers" became virtually synonymous, declares the author.
       By his senior year Robeson was being compared to and included among
       such immortals as Jim Thorpe, Ted Coy, Eddie Mahan, Tack Hardwick,
       and Elmer Oliphant. At graduation, he was "All American," Phi
       Beta Kappa, a member of Rutgers' exclusive Cap and Bones Club, and
       one of the commencement orators. Robeson's last athletic appear-
       ance for Rutgers gave him especial satisfaction. As catcher on
       the baseball nine, he was largely responsible for defeating
       Princeton, 5-1, which was all the more satisfying to him because
       Princeton didn't admit Negroes to the college departments, and
       because it marked Rutgers; first athletic conquest over Princeton
       since that November day in 1869 when Rutgers emerged victorious over
       Princeton in the nation's first inter-collegiate football game,

(Nance, Ed.)

asserts the author. Mr. Nance concludes: "In Paul Robeson the
virtues of most Negro athletes were embodied - in his love of
sports, his strong competitive instinct, his thrill at the hard
contacts of playing, his inspirational leadership, his love of
good sportmanship, his happy-go-lucky fellowship, and his willingness to fight when all strength was gone. Sidat-Singh showed the
same spirit when Syracuse's cause looked doomed; instead of giving
up the fight, he passed to an aerial victory."

992.   "A Word of Advice From Hugh Bradley to Joe Louis," Pittsburgh
Courier, July 3, 1937, p. 18.

This was an opened letter to Joe Louis who had recently become
Heavyweight Champion of the World. The writer gave Louis a word
of advice. He told him that he should look at Paul Robeson who
did not have powerful friends in high places like Louis, yet had
achieved international heights in art because he overcame the
color of his skin. Bradley also told Louis that Robeson was a
greater athlete than what he would ever be. He asserts that others
had benefitted vastly by Robeson's example. The writer concludes:
"Robeson is a great Negro, Joe. He also is a greater man and an
American. I sincerely hope you will be the same.

13. STATUE

993.   "Denies Clash Over Statue: Union League Club Says Nude of Paul
Robeson Was Not Barred," New York Times, November 18, 1930, p. 4.

This article states that reports of a controversy over the alleged
barring of a nude statue of Paul Robeson by Antonio Salemme, which
was borrowed from the Brooklyn Museum by the Union League Club,
supposedly for a four-day exhibition ended by officials of the club
who said that it had no place in the recent private showing. The
recent private showing was devoted exclusively to ecclesiastical
subjects and the Robeson statue would have been completely out of
place, states the article.

994.   "Paul Robeson's Nude Statue," Opportunity, Vol. 8, No. 6, June,
1930, pp. 168-169.

Antonio Salemme did a magnificent bronze statue of Paul Robeson
for the Art Alliance of Philadelphia. This statue would be on
exhibition in Rittenhouse Square in the City of Brotherly Love.
The statue was never displayed because it was a nude statute and
by showing it, it would contribute to the "tranquillity of that
tranquil city." Since race relations were not good in Philadelphia,
the statute of a Negro in bronze would inspired great apprehension,
concludes the writer.

D. 1940-1949

1. AFRICA

995. "Would Help Colonies: International Agency to Rule in Africa is
Proposed," New York Times, April 15, 1944, p. 5.

Paul Robeson was chairman of a Conference, the subject of which
was "Africa New Perspective." In his opening remarks Mr. Robeson
criticized recent descriptions of Africa as "the last great
frontier of the world for the white man to cross" and "the jackpot
of World War II." He said these descriptions were made-to-
order propaganda for the Japanese enemy."

996. "8,500 Attend Party for Paul Robeson, 46: Singer Predicts Improved
Trade with Africa After War," New York Times, April 17, 1944, p. 38.

A public celebration of the forty-sixth birthday of Paul Robeson,
brought a throng estimated at 8,500 persons to the 17th Regiment
Armory. Entertainment was provided by stage, cinema and radio
stars. The guest of honor spoke declaring that the war should result in improved trade facilities with Africa and greater social,
educational and political opportunities for the inhabitants.

997. "Conference on Africa Planned in Spite of Go-By," People's Voice,
April 20, 1944, p. 1.

According to this article international action for freedom for
Africans was urged at a New York conference of the Council on
African Affairs, at which time resolutions were passed calling
upon the American government to take the initiative in the establishment of such international machinery as "would guarantee the
fruits of victory should be shared equally by African and other
dependent peoples of the world." At the afternoon session of the
conference presided over by Paul Robeson, chairman of the Council,
and Max Yergan, the executive director, proposals were presented
for the establishment of an international agency, patterned on
the United Nations Relief and Rehabilitation Administration.

998. "Paul Robeson and Negro History," Black Dispatch, (Oklahoma City, Okla.), March 1, 1947.

This newspaper states that Paul Robeson had taken the same position as the newspaper when he declared that an examination of the early history of Black people would develop self-respect among people of African extraction and among all people. The writer said that it (Black History) would prove that the base of present day culture and civilization is totally Black - not white - and if there can be eliminated from the mind of the young Negro thoughts of innate inferiority that have been falsely placed there, the ground has been properly followed for growth in all fields of endeavor.

999. "Robeson Seeks S. African Aid," People's Voice, September 20, 1947, p. 7.

Paul Robeson, Chairman of the Council on African Affairs, issued an appeal for funds to be sent to South Africa to release food sent there by American Negroes. It was not realized when the food was sent that customs would be charged on the food, states the article.

1000. Padmore, George. "Robeson Songs Banned from South Africa," West African Pilot (Lagos, Nigeria), May 10, 1949, p. 1.

According to Mr. Padmore, shortly before Dr. Daniel Malan left South Africa for London to take part in the conference of British Commonwealth Prime Ministers regarding India's future relations with the British Crown, the South African leader ordered the banning of all records by Mr. Paul Robeson, as a retaliatory measure against the Afro-American singer for having criticized South Africa's treatment of coloured races, when he addressed a public meeting held in London to protest against racism in the African dominion. This article also states that many people of color in England agree with Mr. Robeson's positions. However, while they all admire Mr. Robeson and respect his political convictions, many of them have expressed the view that the Negro singer, thanks to his international prestige, could do more to advance the cause of his race by interpreting their sufferings and voicing their hopes and aspirations in song than by playing the politician, which can be done much better and more effectively by others who lack his artistic gifts, suggests the writer. Mr. Padmore concludes: "No useful purpose is served by arousing anti-Negro hostility among white folk who could otherwise be won over neutralized in the black man's uphill struggle for human rights and freedom."

2. AWARDS AND HONORS

1001. Paul Robeson Honored with Degree at Hamilton: Singer Called
Exemplar of Democracy's Greatness," New York Herald, January 22,
1940.

According to this article Paul Robeson, American Negro singer and
actor received the degree of Doctor of Humane Letters from Hamilton College in a special mid-year convocation of the college.
Dr. William Harold Cowley, president of the college, in making
the presentation, said:
> Paul Robeson, in honoring you today, we do not express
> our enthusiasm alone for your histrionic and musical
> achievements; we honor you chiefly as a man, a man of
> tremendous stature, energy and physical dexterity, a
> man of brilliant mind, whose sensitive spirit makes
> possible your penetrating interpretations, and above
> all, a man who travels across the world as an exemplar
> of the humanity and greatness of our democratic in-
> stitutions.

In accepting the degree, Mr. Robeson said, in part: "The one
thing I have noticed in my travels is that the American folk song
is much the same as other folk songs and America has great opportunity to contribute to human culture." Mr. Robeson sang "Water
Boy," Ole Man River," "I Met My Brother the Other Day," "Sometimes
I Feel Like a Motherless Child" and the English folk song, "Oh
No, John, No."

1002. "Paul Robeson Gets Hamilton Degree: College Confers Honorary
Doctorate of Humane Letter," New York Times, January 22, 1940,
p. 10.

Hamilton College presented Paul Robeson with an honorary Doctor
of Humane Letters degree. The citation declared:
> In honoring you today, we do not, however, express
> our enthusiasm for your histrionic and musical achieve-
> ments alone. We honor you chiefly as a man -- a man
> of tremendous stature, energy and physical dexterity,
> a man of brilliant mind, a man whose sensitive spirit
> makes possible your penetrating interpretations, and
> a man who above all else, travels across the world
> as an exemplar of the humanity and the greatness of
> our heritage.

Robeson accepted the degree and stated, in part: "If and when this
trouble, war-torn world were reorganized, not only Western culture,
but also that of Hindus, Africans and Chinese each would contribute to the realization of a true and lasting human culture...."

1003.   "Paul Robeson Gets Annual Lincoln Award," Afro-American, February 13, 1943.

According to this article Paul Robeson received the annual Lincoln Award by the students of the Abraham Lincoln High School in Brooklyn, New York, "in recognition of his courageous championship of good will, tolerance, and minority rights." In accepting the Lincoln Award, Mr. Robeson said, in part:
This award has a special significance for me, the son of a slave who fought in the Civil War at the time of Abraham Lincoln. The American ideal of freedom in which I have faith was shaped in high schools such as yours. In traveling around the world I have learned the folksongs of the people and from their songs learned of their struggles and their sufferings. We are all on a common road with them to bring freedom to the world and to humanize it.

1004.   "Paul Robeson Honored: Lincoln Medal Given Him by Abraham Lincoln High School," New York Times, February 11, 1943, p. 22.

The Lincoln Medal awarded annually by the students of Abraham Lincoln High School to the citizen who has rendered the most distinguished service to New York City, was presented to Paul Robeson. Mr. Robeson, to whom the award was made because of his efforts for good-will, tolerance and minority rights, accepted it orally and musically. More than 1,600 students, parents and guests attended the presentation.

1005.   "Tolerance Award Given Robeson by High School," People's Voice, February 13, 1943, p. l6.

This article states that Paul Robeson humbly accepted the annual Lincoln Award tendered him by students and faculty of the Abraham Lincoln High School in Brooklyn. The Award, a bronze medallion, was presented to the noted singer after 1152 of the 4000 students had named him for his "courageous conviction and sincerity of purpose." Irving Berlin and Governor Lehman were close seconds for the honor which is conferred yearly on an outstanding American, states the author.

1006.   "Robeson Wins Medal: To Get Academy of Arts and Letters Award for Stage Diction," New York Times, February 15, 1944, p. 17.

The American Academy of Arts and Letters announced that it would give its medal this year for good diction on the stage to Paul Robeson, the Negro singer and actor now starring in "Othello." This new honor goes to Mr. Robeson for talents he exhibited at an early age. At Rutgers University he won oratory prizes for four successive years and at his graduation was commencement orator.

1007.   "Paul Robeson Wins Diction Award," <u>Philadelphia Inquirer</u>, February
        16, 1944.

        It was stated that Paul Robeson, singer and actor, had been named
        winner of the American Academy of Arts and Letters' 1944 Medal
        for good diction on the stage. Among other winners of the award,
        which has been given only nine times, were Walter Hampden, George
        Arliss, Lawrence Tibbett and Lynn Fontanne.

1008.   "Racial Bias Here Laid to the Axis," <u>New York Times</u>, April 3, 1944,
        p. 22.

        The National Federation for Constitutional Liberties gave Paul
        Robeson an award in recognition of his contributions to racial
        and national unity; Robeson made an impassioned plea for aggressive
        action against fascism in this country as well as in Europe. He
        praised President Roosevelt as having been alert against the
        dangers of fascism and declared: "We have tremendous need to re-
        cognize fascism and strike it down. America can make or break all
        mankind. The peoples of Europe who have suffered under fascism
        are clear on that but the people here are not." He also took
        immediate action to save the Jews of Europe, saying this could
        be done even though it means "heavy sacrifice and death." George
        Marshall, chairman of the federation said of Mr. Robeson:
            As a great artist, he has broken down many racial
            barriers in his profession, and he has carried the
            message of human freedom to the peoples of many
            lands. As a citizen and anti-fascist, he has
            effectively dedicated his energy and wisdom to the
            fight to abolish racial and religious discrimination,
            and to achieve that unity of all forces essential to
            the victory of all United Nations over the Axis....

1009.   "Paul Robeson to be Honored," <u>New York Times</u>, March 31, 1944, p. 27.

        This article states that Paul Robeson, star of "Othello" would re-
        ceive a citation at the Hotel Roosevelt from the National Federation
        for Constitutional Liberties for his "outstanding contribution
        toward building international unity within our country and through-
        out the world."

1010.   "Paul Robeson: Spingarn Medalist," <u>People's Voice</u>, May 5, 1945,
        p. 1.

        This article called Paul Robeson a people's artist. It also states
        that he was awarded the 30th Spingarn Medal, it was announced last
        week by Dr. John Haynes Holmes, chairman of the award committee.
        Mr. Robeson received the award for his outstanding achievements
        in the theatre, on the concert stage and in the general field of
        racial welfare. The latest triumph in his long public career is
        his appearance in Margaret Webster's production of "Othello."
        The Spingarn Medal was instituted by the late J.E. Spingarn, for
        many years president of the NAACP, to go to the "man or woman of
        African descent and American citizenship, who shall have made the
        highest achievement during the preceding year or years in any
        honorable field of human endeavor."

1011. "Scholarship Honors Robeson," New York Times, May 8, 1944, p. 12.

It was stated that a scholarship valued at $200 annually was estab-
lished by the State, County and Municipal Workers of America,
Congress of Industrial Organizations, at the New York University
Graduate Division for training in Public Service. The grant would
be awarded for twenty years, honors Paul Robeson, actor and singer.
The scholarship was intended "to quicken the interest of Negro
students in the field of Public Administration."

1012. "Recipient of 'Art and Letters Grants' for 1944," New York Times,
May 20, 1944, p. 28.

Paul Robeson received the American Academy of Arts and Letters
award "medal for Good Diction on the Stage." There is also a
photo of Robeson and three other recipients who received awards.

1013. "Paul Robeson Receives Award," Chicago Defender, November 3, 1945,
p. 1.

According to this report Paul Robeson became the 30th American of
African descent to win the Spingarn medal, awarded annually to an
American Negro for high schievement. The award is made by the
NAACP, and Marshall Field, publisher of the Chicago Sun, made the
presentation at the Hotel Biltmore in New York.

1014. "Paul Robeson Honored: Receives Spingarn Medal for Distinguished
Achievement," New York Times, October 19, 1945, p. 21.

Paul Robeson received the thirtieth annual Spingarn Medal at a
dinner of the National Association for the Advancement of Colored
People. About 600 persons attended the dinner at the Hotel Biltmore in New York City. The award was made "for distinguished
achievement in the theatre and on the concert stage as well as
active concern for the rights of the common man of every race,
color, religion and nationality." Marshall Field III made the
presentation address, and said Mr. Robeson was "typical of the
leadership of the Negro people and its spirit of pioneering for
Negro and broadly human rights."

1015. "Carver School Names 9," New York Times, January 10, 1947, p. 19.

This article states that the names of nine persons were announced
as directors of the left-wing George Washington Carver School in
New York City. Paul Robeson was one of the nine named as a director
of the school.

1016. "Paul Robeson to Get Alpha Medal," New York Amsterdam News, May 17,
1947, p. 1.

According to this article Paul Robeson, internationally acclaimed
singer and orator, was selected by Nu Chapter, Alpha Phi Alpha
Fraternity, as the 1947 recipient of the Alpha Medallion. Robeson
was nominated because of his outstanding role as a champion of
freedom. The award was presented on the campus of Lincoln
University (Lincoln, Penn.) at 8:00 p.m., Monday evening, May 12,

in the University Chapel. The Alpha Medallion is awarded each
year to a citizen who by his career has made "an outstanding contribution to the American people." Last year's award winners
were Miss Marian Anderson and Mr. Harold L. Ickes.

1017. "Russian Peak Named Robeson," New York Times, October 2, 1949,
       p. 37.

       According to this article a mountain peak in Russia was named
       after Paul Robeson, the Communist newspaper Pravda reported.

1018. "Rumanians Honor Chaplin," New York Times, October 19, 1947, p. 42.

       Charles Chaplin and Paul Robeson were elected to the honorary pre-
       sidium of the Annual Congress of Artists, Writers and Printing
       Workers, which opened in Bucharest, Rumania.

1019. "Paul Robeson Honored at Howard (University) Rites," Washington
       Post, May 5, 1948.

       According to this article Paul Robeson, stage and screen star, was
       among four outstanding Americans to receive honorary degrees at
       commencement exercises at Howard University. The citations were
       presented by Dr. Mordecai W. Johnson, president, on the university
       campus in the presence of 3000 persons. Robeson received the
       honorary degree of doctor of letters.

1020. "Bust of Robeson Set Atop 13,000-Foot Mountain in Russia,"
       Afro-American, October 29, 1949, p. 1.

       According to this article further homage was paid Paul Robeson when
       rugged Russian climbers scaled the 13,000 foot mountain named for
       the great singer to place a bust of him atop the peak. The climb,
       a real feat, took place in sub-freezing weather. Both the bust
       and the feat were dedicated in the name of "battling solidarity
       with those millions of ordinary people of America whom Paul Robe-
       son represents." The action was hailed through Russia, states the
       article.

                    3. BILL OF RIGHTS CONFERENCE

1021. "Paul Robeson Speaks for Us," National Guardian, July 23, 1949.

       The Negro delegates to the Bill of Rights Conference that was held
       in New York City, at the Henry Hudson Hotel, July 16-17, 1949,
       issued a statement stating that Paul Robeson speaks for them in
       his fight for full democratic rights and peace. The statement
       declares, in part:
            We, the undersigned Colored American delegates to this
            Bill of Rights Conference in New York City, hereby

(National Guardian)

       declare for all the world to see, that Robeson does,
indeed, speak for us not only in his fight for full
democratic rights, but also in his fight for peace....
With the arrogance and contempt for human dignity which
only a white supremacist mentality born of ignorance, can
bring to bear, fifteen million Colored citizens of America
are being treated to the spectacle of a carefully planned
campaign of open vilification and slander against a
great leader and a great American, Paul Robeson, the
like of which has not faced the American people since
the days of the great anti-slavery fighter, Frederick
Douglass. The purpose of this campaign is to separate
Mr. Robeson and his great leadership from the Colored
people in order to break their united will to be free
in order to keep Mrs. Rosa Lee Ingram and her two sons
in jail, in order to bring death to the Trenton Six
and the Virginia seven; in order to stop civil rights
legislation from ever coming to pass; in order to stop
FEPC from coming into being and in order to maintain
thousands of our people in the ranks of the unemployed....
We colored delegates, attending this Bill of Rights Conference, declare that Paul Robeson has clarified the
issue for our people and made it clear that the fight
against war and for peace is the test by which we shall
have to judge the honesty and integrity of all who would
speak up in defense of the civil rights of our people.
We declare, unreservedly, that Paul Robeson had met
that test and that we therefore shall carry on this
fight for a peaceful America....

4. BIRTHDAY

1022. "Birthday Fete to Honor Robeson," New York Times, March 22, 1944,
p. 17.

This article announces that arrangements for a birthday party to
be given in honor of Paul Robeson had been completed by a committee
of prominent theatre people, writers, and newspaper men. The
entire proceeds would be turned over to the Council on African
Affairs, an educational research body.

1023. "Police Called to Handle Crowds at Paul Robeson Birthday Party,"
People's Voice, April 22, 1944, p. 1.

According to this report with tears streaming down his cheeks as an
audience of approximately 13,000 people sang, "Happy birthday dear
Paul, happy birthday to you." Paul Robeson, on his 46th birthday,
stood in the center of a huge stage bedecked with flags of the
United Nations and received the homage of peoples of all nations,

(New York Times)

creeds and races. The 17th Regiment Armory, in New York City,
where this unprecedented celebration took place Sunday evening,
was packed to the rafters inside, with a cordon of police stationed
outside who had been called to keep would-be spectators from being
trampled and to turn away more than 5,000 who could not be accom-
modated, states the writer. With the "March of Time" newsreel
camaras and photographers from every magazine and daily newspaper
recording the proceedings which took place on the enormous stage
built in the form of a cake, the show which included a great array
of talent and outstanding figures, went down without a hitch,
according to the author. Mr. Robeson comments on what the
celebration meant to him: "I am not so concered with the show itself as I am with the feeling behind the entire affair. Such a
show can be seen at any one of a dozen places, but perhaps never
again in my lifetime will I be privileged to witness the kind of
democratic good fellowship and brotherly love of just people for
an individual as I witnessed Sunday night.... I cannot find words
to express my heartfelt gratitude to you, my friends of all
nationalities, races and creeds. I am proud to be an American
and very proud and privileged to be a representative of the Negro
people...."

1024. Powell, Adam Clayton, Jr. "Soapbox," People's Voice, April 22,
       1944, p. 5.

       Mr. Powell comments on Paul Robeson's 46th birthday. He states:
       "Robeson is the proof that the Negro has come of age in politics,
       art and social vision and that although he was led through the dark-
       ness of yesterday...he is ready to carry his people and his
       brothers, white, brown, yellow, Jew, Gentile...with creed, dialectic
       or faith through the morass of the present and that dim mist which
       separates this age from the future. Robeson is the epitome of
       the longing, the dreams, the prayers of those who nestled along
       the cool banks of the roaring Niger...of those who toiled on the
       banks of the Dnieperstroy...of the rugged pioneers who cried "mark
       twain" as they sounded the depths of America's great rivers.
       Robeson is a creature fashioned from the spilled blood and honored
       flesh of all who have ever died to be free."

5. CHINA

1025. "Wants American Troops in China Brought Home," New York Times,
       September 6, 1946, p. 8.

       Paul Robeson along with Brig General Evans F. Carlson, announced
       that they as co-chairman of the National Committee to Win the Peace
       were calling a conference on China and the Far East in the hope of
       "crystallizing strong public opinion in the United States in favor
       of withdrawing American troops from China."

6. COMMUNISM

1026. "Rally in Garden Barred," New York Times, August 29, 1940, p. 20.

Officials of Madison Square Garden refused to rent the auditorium
to the Council on African Affairs because it was on the Attorney
General's subversive list, pending action on the Mundt-Ferguson
Communist declared Bill in Congress. The Council declared that the
main purpose of the concert-rally would have been to protest the
State Department's action denying Paul Robeson, the Council Chairman the right to travel abroad.

1027. Lautier, Louis. "Robeson Proves Ability to Handle Situation,"
Afro-American, October 5, 1946, p. 1.

The delegation from the American Crusade to End Lynching saw
President Truman at 11:30 a.m., September 23. When they came out
of the President's office, a group of reporters were waiting and
ganged up on Paul Robeson, who headed the delegation and acted as
spokesman. In quiz sessions between White House visitors and the
press, no holds are barred. That was particularly true with
Robeson. For example, Robeson was asked point-blank whether he
was a Communist. After he replied that he was a "violent anti-
fascist," he was asked whether he followed the Communist party
line. "It depends on what you mean by the Communist Party line,"
he countered. "Right now the Communist Party is against lynching.
I'm against lynching." Robeson showed that he was just as able to
take care of himself in a rough-and-tumble session with the press
as he was in playing a scene as Othello with the scene-stealing
Jose Ferrer as Iago, concludes the author.

1028. Woodson, Carter G. "Choosing the Road Through Bloodshed," Negro
History Bulletin, Vol. 10, No. 8, May, 1947, p. 177.

The writer suggests that practically all Negroes who have risen
above the Uncle Tom level, are branded as Communists, if they
advocate anti-lynching legislation, fair employment practice, the
repeal of the poll tax, and the abolition of segregation. Therefore, Paul Robeson and others...have been denounced as Communists,
states Woodson.

1029. "Robeson to Visit Greeks Rebels," New York Times, May 26, 1947, p. 5.

Paul Robeson sang in Prague, Czechoslovakia for the Communist
Party Congress and later declared he would go to visit and sing
for the Greek guerrilla forces.

1030. "Wasting Time and Money," Afro-American, November 1, 1947, p. 1.

According to this article when Rep. Richard M. Nixon (R. Calif.)
asked Screen Actor Adolph Menjou at the hearing of the House
Committee investigating Communists in Hollywood, what tests he
utilized to determine whether people are Communists or not, Menjou
answered: "Well, I would consider attendance at a meeting where

(Afro-American)

Paul Robeson is appearing, applauding him and listening to his
Communist songs would be a good one."

1031. Editorial. "Paul Robeson and Communism," Honolulu Star-Bulletin,
March 27, 1948. Editorial Page.

The editor surmises that Robeson's outright denial that he was a
Communist left some doubt of this association with them. The
writer concludes that Robeson was "a great singer, and a man whose
history and personality carry a strong appeal." It was also pointed
out that he made plain his sympathy for the workingman, and his
deep personal feeling against discrimination on account of race -
a quite understandable feeling as he is a Negro and has been the
helpless victim of such discrimination, declares the editor.

1032. Childs, Marquis. "Robeson and Russia," Des Moines (Iowa) Register,
April 4, 1948.

According to this article Paul Robeson came to Washington to
testify against the Mundt Bill to control or outlaw Communism. He
expressed himself freely in spite of heckling from members of the
senate judiciary committee. As he has done often in the past,
Robeson charged repression, discrimination and a drive to establish
a fascist state. He refused to say, in answer to repeated questions, whether he was a member of the Communist Party, states
Mr. Childs. It was also pointed out that of course, there is discrimination in the United States - and repression, too. But Paul
Robeson can denounce it. And men with lesser talents and smaller
stature can speak their minds. In that other world of Russia, no
protest of any kind is possible. The answer to even a whispered
protest is prison or death. What is so strange is that Robeson
and others like him idealize that world, declares the writer.

1033. "Yergan Backs Up on Red Sympathies," Los Angeles Tribune, April 17,
1948.

This article declares that Paul Robeson and his political sponsor
Dr. Max Yergan fell out. It was pointed out that Robeson and
Dr. Yergan, who is the head and originator of the Council on
African Affairs in which the singer is also a guiding light, "are
not seeing eye to eye as to the council's political leanings."
Bone of contention is Henry A. Wallace, it was reported. Robeson
is one of the former vice president's chief supporters for President; Yergan is quoted as saying he "will not support Wallace
because I think his candidacy will do a disservice to the Negroes.
It will break up Negro unity." A tug of war between the two looms
as Robeson allegedly had insisted that the council, to which he
has contributed heavily, will support Wallace. Yergan, who is
under scrutiny by the Justice Department as the foremost Negro
Communist in the country, has been called a Red baiter by Robeson,
according to the writer. Robeson was reported to have asserted,
in part:
        I don't care what they call me. I don't subscribe
        to the conclusion that an American is unpatriotic

(Los Angeles Tribune)

        simply because he works with Communists. The
Communist party is a legal party in this country.
It isn't easy these days for any American to stand
up and fight against great odds, but someone has
to do it. Someone has to point out that things
are not beautiful in America, in Africa and other
parts of the world. If that makes me a Communist
then I'm proud to be one....

1034.   Walsh, Robert K. "Senate Query on Communism," Washington Star,
       May 31, 1948, p. 1.

       According to Mr. Walsh, Paul Robeson refused to tell the Senate
Judiciary Committee whether he belongs to the Communist Party.
Testifying at an unusual holiday hearing on the Mundt-Nixon Bill
to regulate Communist activities, Mr. Robeson defended the American
Communist Party as "standing for complete equality of the Negro"
and as having developed "out of the social condition of the world."
The singer appeared as a surprise witness in place of Albert
Janney, who had been scheduled as spokesperson for the American
Youth for Democracy. Mr. Robeson launched into a bitter attack
of the Mundt-Nixon Bill as "part of a pattern to deny democratic
rights in the United States," and he asserts that the proposed
legislation ties in with the type of "terror and denial of rights"
which he said exists particularly in the South, according to the
reporter. Senator Ferguson, Republican, of Michigan, interrupted
him three different times to ask if he was a member of the Communist Party. The first two times, Mr. Robeson brushed aside the
question by saying he would come to it later. Finally he replied:
"Today, Senator Ferguson, that question has become the very basis
of the struggle for American democracy. I, therefore, refuse to
answer it. I expect to vote this year, and if you want to send
officers up to the polling place and take my ballot out of the box
to see how I voted, you can do it. Nineteen leading Americans are
going to jail for refusal to answer that question, and if necessary I will join them." He referred to 10 Hollywood writers and
others cited for contempt of Congress for refusing to answer similar questions put by House Committees. The hearing was interrupted by applause from about 50 spectators, some of whom said
they were affiliated with the American Youth for Democracy,
declares Mr. Walsh.

1035.   "Mr. Paul Robeson and the Mundt Bill," London Times, June 1, 1948,
       p. 3.

       This article states that Paul Robeson appeared before the Senate
Judiciary Committee as a witnesse on the Mundt-Nixon Bill. Robeson refused to state whether or not he belonged to the American
Communist Party. Robeson called the Bill "hysteria," and said he
would fight it as a piece of American Fascism if it became a law.

1036. "Robeson Defies Quiz on Communism; Says He Prefers Prison," PM, June 1, 1948, p. 1.

Paul Robeson told Senate questioners he would go to jail before he would say whether he is a Communist. Sen. E.H. Moore (R., Okla.) promptly adopted the idea, with the suggestion that "sometimes a year in jail cools some of these people off." But Chairman Alexander Wiley (R., Wis.) of the Judiciary Committee said he doubted that the committee would take contempt action. Robeson was testifying before the Judiciary group against the Mundt-Nixon anti-Communist bill when the dispute arose. Sen Homer Ferguson (R., Mich.), whose direct question Robeson refused to answer, said the committee would decide about contempt later. The exchange took place after Robeson told the committee he thinks members of the Communist party "have done a magnificent job in America." "Are you an American Communist?" Ferguson asked. "I refuse to answer that question," Robeson replied with emphatic gestures. "This is an invasion of my right of secret ballot." Ferguson fired back the same question a second time and a third, and Robeson finally broke out: "Nineteen leading Americans are going to jail for refusal to answer that question and if necessary I will join them." His reference to 19 Americans was an allusion to the Hollywood writers and others charged with contempt of Congress for refusal to answer similar questions before the House Committee on Un-American Activities, asserts the article.

1037. Editorial. "Paul Robeson's Case," Washington Evening Star. June 2, 1948.

The editor states that even though Paul Robeson may not be a Communist, he is a propagandist for them. He asserts:
....Here is a man whose father was born in slavery
in this country. Yet the son, endowed with exceptional talents, has gone far. A graduate of
Rutgers, an all-American football player, an outstanding artist -- these are achievements that not
many Americans have been able to equal. Yet Mr.
Robeson pays homage to the Communists and to Russia,
and says that Russia has produced more freedom for
the people than has the United States. In the light
of this expressed opinion what difference does it make
whether he actually is a Communist or not. He has said
enough to show that he is wholly biased and that in
his testimony before the committee he appeared, not
as a witness, but as a propagandist....

1038. "Marches Picket the White House, Swarm in Capitol," New York Times, June 3, 1948, pp. 1, 12.

Thousands marched on Washington, D.C., demanding defeat of the Mundt-Nixon Communist Control Bill and the enactment before Congress recesses of the so-called civil rights programs. Paul Robeson sang three songs and addressed the crowd. He declared: "If we can't get our liberties one way we will build a new structure to get those liberties... The struggle for peace and the kind of America we want has reached another level; we have taken the

<u>(New York Times)</u>

offensive against fascism! ....We will take the power from their
hands and through our representatives we will direct the future
destiny of our nation...."

1039.   "Either Way You Win," <u>Time</u>, Vol. 51, No. 5, June 14, 1948, pp. 18-
19.

This report asserts that Paul Robeson appeared before a Senate
Judiciary Subcommittee to denounce the Mundt-Nixon Bill. The
article also surmises two days later 5,500 men and women, mostly
from New York City, descended in Washington in three special trains,
chartered buses, private cars and planes. They had a field day.
They invaded the Senate office building, picketed the White House
and caused a disturbance in a restaurant which bans Negroes. Three
were arrested. They topped off the day with a rally at the foot
of the Washington Monument, where Paul Robeson sang "Ol' Man River"
and everyone cheered the name of Henry Wallace, according to the
writer. The demonstration so riled some Senators that they
angrily trumpeted their determination to push the Mundt-Nixon Bill
through -- although it had been headed for the shelf. That was
O.K. with the Communists. If the bill became law they would be
martyrs. If it didn't, they would chortle triumphantly that they
had killed it, concludes the article.

1040.   "Robeson to Curtail Tour to Aid Red Trial in June," <u>New York Times</u>,
March 10, 1949, p. 2.

While Paul Robeson was in Glasgow, Scotland, he announced that he
would interrupt a world concert tour at the end of May so that he
could testify for the defense in the New York trial of eleven
leading United States Communists. The actor asserts: "Marxism
is on trial. It is a way of life, a philosophy. The trial should
be very interesting. I am going to take the view that Marxism is
a cultural philosophy."

1041.   "Swedes Boo Robeson: U.S. Singer Offers <u>Communist</u> Songs in
Stockholm Concert," <u>New York Times</u>, April 22, 1949, p. 29.

Paul Robeson was booed by a capacity audience in Stockholm's concert hall because it disapproved of his Communist songs. According
to the article, Mr. Robeson finished his performance by saying that
he sang for the Soviet Union and all oppressed peoples as a representative for Henry A. Wallace's America. The audience's reaction was strong, but the singer also was heartily applauded by
many fellow-travelers.

1042.   "Lena Horne Called 'Red': Canada Lee, Paul Robeson Also Named in
Probe," <u>Afro-American</u>, June 18, 1949, p. 6.

According to this article the names of Lena Horne, Paul Robeson
and Canada Lee, three of the race's leading stage and screen stars,
were listed among those of other luminaries in probes of alleged
Un-American Activities in Washington and Sacramento, California.
The article also states that Robeson's name appeared in a report

(Afro-American)

dated July 18, 1947, which read as follows: "Confidential Informant ND 402 advised SAS William J. McCarthy and Daniel F. Grade that Lionel Berman, head of the cultural committee of the Communist Party, has been successful in using well-known Hollywood personalities to further Communist Party aims, Frederic March being one of the persons who came under his influence. The informant further advised that he was satisfied the subject, who is active in the Communist infiltration of the motion picture industry, is a Communist Party member along with Edgar G. Robinson, Paul Robeson, Dorothy Parker, Donald Ogden Stuart, Ruth McKinney, Alfred Maitz, Alah Bessie, Dalton Trumbo, Millen Brand and Micael Blankfort."

1043.   "Robeson Accepts Chinese Bid," New York Times, June 3, 1949, p. 5.

According to this article Paul Robeson, who was in Warsaw, Poland, accepted an invitation from the Chinese delegation to Czechoslovakia's Communist Party Congress to sing in Communist China later during the summer. It was also stated that Robeson would return to the United States via Mongolia and revisit the "People's Democratic Countries."

1044.   "Stars Smeared in Red Probes," Afro-American, June 18, 1949, p. 6.

There are photos of Lena Horne, Canada Lee and Paul Robeson on this page. Under the caption it was stated that they were named as Communist sympathizers in probe being conducted in Sacramento, California. It was also asserted that the names of Lee and Robeson were contained in FBI reports introduced as evidence in the trial of a former Justice Department specialist.

1045.   Cayton, Horace R. "Fear and Guilt of White America," Pittsburgh Courier, September 10, 1949, pp. 1, 5.

The writer declares that the Robeson affair was a mess and that he does not agree with Robeson's philosophy. Further he thought that Robeson was acting hysterically. But that is beside the point. Regardless of everything else, the man is one of this generation's most magnificent singers. He has the right to sing no matter who sponsors him, states Mr. Cayton. He asserts: "They say that Robeson is a Communist. I wouldn't know, never having seen his 'redcard.' But, that too, is besides the point. In this country a man has the right to his own political views - at least until the political party he belongs to is outlawed. Like Voltare, I may not like what he says, but would fight for his right to say it." "Nothing that I can remember," suggests the writer, "has stirred up as much emotion about race and race relations. Most people that I have talked to, both white and colored, feel that Robeson made a mistake in the way that he handled the press. His statements certainly created fear and hatred in the minds of thousands of whites and many Negroes have to bear retaliation. The tragic part of the entire matter is that it is not and should not be considered a racial matter. It is a question of America's attitude toward the Communist party and the Soviet Union...." concludes the

(Cayton, Horace R.)

author.

1046. Editorial. "Negro and Communism," New York Age, September 17, 1949, p. 15.

The editor argues that an aspect of the recent rioting at Peekskill, paradoxical as it may seem, highlights the main reason why one of the hardest things a Negro can do is to be a "constant" Communist. The paradox was this: Paul Robeson was the main attraction at a concert benefit for the Harlem Division of the Civil Rights Congress, but about 90 per cent of those present to hear him sing were white. The publicity and propaganda before and after would have you believe that the figures were reversed and 90 per cent of the crowd were Negro and the other 10 per cent white, states the editor. He surmises, correspondingly, those opposing the whole thing on the grounds of "True Americanism," as Westbrook Pegler would put it, were "loyal, decent Americans" who want to "foreignisms" and ideologies and who would buy one way tickets to Russia for all who seek to import those ideas. He continues: An eyewitness told us that the mob had but two or three means of identifying the Robeson supporters: (1) by their color, (2) by their attire (those in sports shirts and other summer clothes) and, (3) by their 'subversive' actions. With thousands milling and fighting at close quarters, the situation in which the Negro finds himself in similar circumstances if highlighted." The writer also asserts that color identification predominates above all else. Save by their attire or acts, the blood-thirsty mob had no way of telling who was Communist among the whites and who was not. But everyone with a dark skin was suspect, and open for a sound whipping. Negroes are the greatest "joiners" on earth. They will join any church, any lodge, any club, and any movement except one that places them on a dangerous spot such as the Communist Party. If you care to make a study, you will notice that in most of the demonstrations, disorders, strikes, outbreaks, etc., in which Communists are the accused, you will find few, if any Negroes, directly involved, even though the cause or program is apparently for the benefit or advancement of the Negro. We are not talking of the few but of the many, the great masses who might take advantage of the tempting talk of the Communists to get with those who so loudly and emphatically proclaim their sympathy with the plight of the Negro. If there were anything subversive about the Negro it will not be found in his identification with mixed organizations or movements....suggests the author.

1047. "Robeson Backed on Freedom Stand," Pittsburgh Courier, September 17, 1949, p. 5.

Neil Scott made a rebuttal to Walter Winchell's hints that Paul Robeson was aiding the Communists to start a world-wide race war. Mr. Scott declares: "We Negroes disagree violently with Paul Robeson on Russia, but endorse him when he fights lynch mobs, poll tax, segregated residential districts, police brutality, etc. It is not important how much money Robeson makes, it's how much freedom does the average American Negro enjoy. Money is important,

(Pittsburgh Courier)

but freedom is what the average Negro wants, and intends to have it any way he can get it."

1048.   North, Joseph. "Robeson Testimony in Trial of Communist Leaders Blocked," Daily Worker, September 21, 1949.

Robeson, voluntarily testified on behalf of a number of Communists who were charged with advocating the overthrow of the United States Government by force and violence. He states he knew the defendants and none of them advocated overthrowing the government. The actor argues that he came to testify because the national hysteria represented in this trial goes to the roots of civil liberties for all in America. He also expresses the point that the Communist Party had done a magnificent job on behalf of the Negro people and the working class, and on behalf of people. Robeson concludes that he is not free while the Ingram family was in prison. He declares that he can be lynched just as any other Negro could. The singer asserts: "I am not free so long as any of my people are enslaved; or any people in America, like these defendants, are persecuted. When they are free, I am free."

1049.   "Baptists Back Paul Robeson?" New York Age, October 1, 1949, p. 3.

This article states that when the National Baptist Convention closed its annual session at Wrigley Field recently, President Jemison in his annual address said in part: "...The latest technique on the part of those who would defeat us is to brand every Negro who dares speak for equality and justice as Communistic or subversive. 'Be Not Afraid.' One of the highest compliments that can come to a sincere Negro leader today is to be branded subversive.... It is not Paul Robeson, the Communist, that they fear. It is Paul Robeson, the Champion of the CAUSE of black people in America and in Africa. It is the Paul Robeson who exposes the exploitations of Italy, Great Britain, and America in Africa. The time has come when Negroes of different shades of thought must not fight each other in the presence of white people...." It should be pointed out that the National Baptist Convention was one of the largest, if not the largest organization of Blacks in the United States.

1050.   "Detroit Veterans Vote to Ignore Concert Appearance of Robeson: Express Belief that Demonstration Would Only Enhance Leader's Prestige in America," Afro-American, October 8, 1949, p. 3.

According to this report, five veterans organizations urged their members not to attend the Paul Robeson concert to be held at the Forest Club, October 9, and ordered them not to stage any form of protest demonstration against it. Veterans group leaders with the exception of those of the liberal American Veterans Committee, expressed themselves as follows about the Civil Rights Congress sponsored rally: Robert Berry, State adjutant of the Disabled American Veterans, said: "We do not want to add to Robeson's prestige," R. Gerald Barr, State Commander of the American Legion, declares: "Robeson is a star performer of the Community Party.

(Afro-American)

They are doing their level best to make a martyr out of him."
Joseph R. Sanson, State commander of Amvets, asserts: "Robeson's
visit will be scrupulously ignored.... Communist Party leaders
are sending him here to cause discussion and, if possible, riot."
Herbert Devine, State commander, Veterans of Foreign Wars, states:
"The best way to treat Robeson's appearance is to ignore it."
Phil Cantor, State commander, Jewish War Veterans, said:
"While we condemn communism and fascism, we believe in the
American right for anyone to speak or anyone to listen."

1051. "Robeson Wants Uncle to Kill Reds' Trial," New York Amsterdam News,
       October 15, 1949, pp. 1, 33.

       According to this article Paul Robeson, as a member of the National
       Non-Partisan Committee, paid a visit to the Department of Justice
       to urge the quashing of the indictments against the twelve Com-
       munist leaders. The report states that he would hold a concert
       in Washington later under the sponsorship of the Negro Freedom
       Rally Committee. The singer asserts: "I expect a successful and
       orderly rally. Since Peekskill I have appeared in Los Angeles,
       Cleveland, Chicago and Detroit, and my meetings have been the
       opposite of trouble."

7. DEATH

1052. Stafford, George B. "Paul Robeson Cheats Death in Missouri,"
       Pittsburgh Courier, February 1, 1947, pp. 1, 4.

       Paul Robeson was riding in a car near Jefferson City, Missouri,
       when a wheel came off. The owner of the car reported that he
       thought the wheel had been "tampered with." No one, however, was
       hurt.

8. FASCISM

1053. Pittman, John. "Robeson, Man of His People," Daily Worker,
       November 25, 1940, p. 7.

       The author states that Robeson's appeal is universal. London took
       him to its bosom, and workmen digging in the street would drop
       their shovels when he passed to shout a hearty "Hello Paul." To
       the African people, he is a champion of the cause of freedom. The
       Spanish will never forget that he brought cheer and hope to valiant
       Loyalist soliders at a time when Spanish democracy was Western

(Pittman, John)

Europe's bulwark against Fascism, observes Mr. Pittman. He concludes: "Beloved and honored by the world, acclaimed and revered by 'the nobodies' - such is the high rank and enviable fortune of Paul Robeson."

1054.   Hall, Chatwood, "Robeson Commended for His Stand Against Fascism," Journal and Guide, October 31, 1942, p. 17.

According to this writer having heard of the outstanding role being played by Paul Robeson in the progressive anti-fascist movement in America, the well known Jewish actress, Clara Young, in a special interview declares: "I send the great Negro artist, Robeson, my heartiest greetings for his manful, courageous and sincere activity in America in the general struggle against reaction and fascism. All the great Negro artists, such as Marian Anderson, Roland Hayes, Caterina Jarboro and others, should follow Robeson's example and give themselves wholeheartedly to the fight against the deadly fascist danger, and further arouse their people to the mortal danger of fascism." Clara Young was reared in America and like the above mentioned Negro artists, has appeared in all the leading cities of Europe and America during her career. She has settled down in Russia and is active in theatrical circles, states Mr. Hall.

1055.   "Critic Flays Robeson in Canada," Pittsburgh Courier, November 10, 1945, p. 16.

This article states that Paul Robeson was appearing in Montreal, Canada, and shocked his audience and critics by interspersing talks between songs, denouncing much of the world's Fascism. Among the subject which were treated by the singer, was a blast at the Franco regime, the capitalistic system and a number of other things which he wanted to get off his chest. The critics at the concert stated that Robeson went beyong the limits of "good taste" by his ideological remarks.

1056.   "Robeson Says Fascist Peril Greatest in U.S.," Washington Post, February 7, 1948.

This article states that Paul Robeson told more than 1000 delegates to the National Youth Assembly Against Universal Military Training that the United States is the "greatest source of Fascist danger." While Wall Streeters and Southern land owners deprived workers of the "fruits of their labor," there is "complete equality in Communist states, with no grounds of color," the noted Negro baritone told a capacity audience at the Metropolitan Baptist Church, in Washington, D.C. The two-day conference which closed yesterday attracted youths from 19 states. Their average age was 21, according to the article.

1057.   "Robeson Still Desires Chance Before U-AAC," New York Age, August 6, 1949, p. 4.

According to the article Representatives John E. Rankin and John S. Wood drew the wrath of Paul Robeson as he boarded an American Airline plane at LaGuardia Airport for Chicago. The singer said: "I would especially welcome the opportunity to see and hear Representatives Wood and Rankin defend their record against American Negroes. As an American I am interested in the core of Fascism and other forces responsible for the lynching of Negroes.... (in) Georgia and Alabama."

1058.   "Fascists Wouldn't Have Dared Without Aid, Guidance of Police," Daily Worker, September 11, 1949, p. 1.

This article suggests that irrefutable evidence that Governor Dewey's State Troopers and Westchester County police were directly responsible for the hoodlum stoning of the Robeson concert-goers evoked a tempest of protest nationally. It was also pointed out that many in Westchester - who had nothing to do with the concerts and who "opposed Robeson's politics," were outraged by the two orgies of official-inspired violence.

9. FILMS

1059.   Rowe, Billy. "Robeson Files Pay Claim Against 'John Henry': Star Seeks $5,600 for Two Payless Weeks on Road," Pittsburgh Courier, February 3, 1940, p. 21.

Paul Robeson's attorney filed a claim with Actor Equity on his behalf for $5,600 that the actor was supposed to have received for starring in "John Henry."

1060.   Bower, Anthony. "The Movies: 'Proud Valley,'" New Statesman and Nation, Vol. 19, No. 472, March 9, 1940, p. 306.

The reviewer states that "Proud Valley" was likely to prove a disappointment to those looking for social significance, an attitude towards mining conditions, an approach to the colour question or even to the mere seeker after entertainment. He said that it was impossible to comment on Mr. Robeson's performance since he is called upon only to display benignness. Mr. Bower surmises that Robeson was allowed to sing "Deep River" and one or two parts with the choir, and his talents are here hardly exploited at all.

1061.   Steward, Ollie. "'Proud Valley' Gives Paul Robeson Best Starring Role," Afro-American, May 24, 1941, p. 14.

The reviewer asserts that "Proud Valley," Paul Robeson's latest starring film vehicle, which had its American premiere at the Little Carnegie Playhouse, is a triumph for Robeson, and for the British motion picture makers as well. Hollywood should take note,

(Steward, Ollie)

for Hollywood has never produced a picture in which a colored
actor or actress has been cast as Robeson is cast in "Proud
Valley," which is Hollywood's loss, and more important, a loss to
millions of movie-goers who have been waiting to see a colored
man cast as a man, States Steward. The writer concludes: "The
part he plays in shaping the lives, loves and working opportunities
in a little poverty-stricken mining town -- his smile, his pat on
the back, his ability to take hardships -- this is Robeson's real
justification for being in the pictures leading role. And the
part, incidentally, proves to this reporter that Robeson can
really act. Not as well as he can sing, perhaps; but definitely
hold his own before a movie...."

1062. "New Pictures: Tales of Manhattan," Time, Vol. 40, No. 12,
        September 21, 1942, p. 69.

        The writer gives a review of "Tales of Manhattan," starring Paul
        Robeson: "The movie is a multiplex answer to a Hollywood pro-
        ducer's dream -- a show that telescopes parts for nine stars and
        five dramatic episodes in one over-all picture. The only con-
        tinuity is provided by a tail coat which appears in each episode
        in a hand-me-down career from the shoulders of a rich wastrel to
        a scarecrow." Its episodes included: socially conscious min-
        strel show in which Paul Robeson and Ethel Waters find $50,000 in
        the tail coat, and with the help of Jack Benny's Rochester divide
        it with the Hall Johnson Choir and other Hollywood sharecroppers.
        It was pointed out that each actor was permitted to make changes
        in the script, but the only one who bothered much was Paul Robeson.
        He piously refused to have any religious words put in his mouth,
        states the article.

1063. Reddick, Lawrence D. "Educational Programs for the Improvement
        of Race Relations: Motion Pictures, Radio, The Press, and
        Libraries," Journal of Negro Education, Vol. 7, No. 3, Summer,
        1944, pp. 367-89.

        The writer declares that the two most controversial "Negro films"
        of the 1930s were "The Emperor Jones" and "Imitation of Life."
        Paul Robeson was the star in the screen version of Eugene O'Neill's
        play. With few exceptions, critics in the daily press praised
        this as one of the best films of the year. The Negro critics were
        divided. Some praised the film and others saw him as a "lackey."
        Robeson is also mentioned in "Tales of Manhattan." Dr. Reddick
        said the film was remarkable in that a "great and progressive"
        artist like Robeson would accept such a role. The writer asserts
        that it should be added, in all fairness, that in one sequence
        Robeson does get a chance to speak brake words of security for all.
        "Some critics admitted that his role 'might have been worse.'"

1064. Weiler, A.H. "By Way of Report," New York Times, September 29,
        1946, Part 2, p. 3.

        It was pointed out that Paul Robeson, Howard Fast, author, and Leo
        Hurwitz, documentary film director, joined forces to form an

(Weiler, A.H.)

independent motion-picture production company, Freedom Road Films,
Inc. The company of which Paul Robeson is president and Fast and
Hurwitz are vice presidents, will bring to the screen Fast's
novel, "Freedom Road," with Robeson in the starring role. The
novel, set in South Carolina in the Reconstruction Era, is
centered around Gideon Jackson, an ex-slave whom becomes a member
of Congress, and the plantation community farmed in harmony by
Negroes and Whites until the withdrawal of Northern troops.

1065. "Paul Robeson Offered Role of 'King Dick' in 'Lydia Bailey,'"
       Afro-American, April 5, 1947, p. 1.

According to this article Louella O. Parsons, Hollywood columnist
and radio commentator, in commenting on Paul Robeson being offered
the role of King Dick in Twentieth Century-Fox's "Lydia Bailey,"
had this to say: "I was interested to hear that Twentieth Century-
Fox had offered the role of King Dick in 'Lydia Bailey' to Paul
Robeson. I would have thought that after 'Tales of Manhattan' it
would be too much of a risk to invite him before their cameras
again." In "Tales of Manhattan" Robeson appearently approved
the story, liked himself in the film, then some of his friends
saw it and said the portrayal was too much of an Uncle Tom version
of the character. "Then Robeson sent letters to certain newspapers, condemning the picture." She also declared: "It brought
about a boycott in a number of theatres because of the racial
furor that was raised. However, the picture did make money. It
was not actually made by Twentieth, but by Boris Morros and
S.P. Eagle, who released it through that company. "Robeson
hasn't yet said whether he will accept Twentieth's offer. He is
very intelligent but misguided, obviously in some of his ideologies
and political ideas."

1066. "Robeson Received 'Letter From Africa' Shows Need for Progressive
       Films on Negro," Daily Worker, May 6, 1949, p. 12.

Paul Robeson received a letter from Bathurst, Gambia (Africa),
requesting that the actor send advice and directions on how the
writer could get some good films with Negroes in the casts and
shorter films depicting the life and achievements of famous
Negroes. The writer states that he had seen the film "Jericho,"
starring Robeson and it was well received by the people in this
West African Colony. He said a few more films like "Jericho"
and "Proud Valley," also starring Robeson, "would be a source of
inspiration to our audience...." Mr. Robeson turned the letter
over to Contemporary Films.

1067. "Russian Plan Robeson Film," New York Times, November 27, 1949,
       p. 13.

According to this article the Russians plan to produce a film about
Paul Robeson, the Negro singer, the Soviet Literary Gazette re-
ported. The scenario will be written by Anatoli Suron, a leading
Russian playwright.

10. INDIVIDUALS

1068.   "Let Me People Go," Sunday Worker, February 11, 1940, Section 2,
        p. 7.

        According to this report Abraham Lincoln was a favorite hero of
        Marian Anderson and Paul Robeson, two outstanding representatives
        of the Negro people who have made brilliant contributions to
        American culture.

1069.   "Paul, Marian are Favorites of UCLA: Poll Taken by Student Pub-
        lication Reveals Classics Winning Out Over Swing 688-672,"
        Pittsburgh Courier, March 9, 1940, p. 2.

        According to this article in a poll taken by the Daily Bruin,
        student publication of the University of California at Los Angeles
        last week, collegians in favor of classical concerts won over the
        college jitterbugs, voting among their concert favorites, Paul
        Robeson and Marian Anderson. The poll, taken to determine the
        type music students wished to hear at the bi-monthly campus con-
        certs at Royce Hall, revealed 688 favoring classical concerts
        while 672 wanted jazz-jitterbug sessions. Other choices among
        outstanding concert stars Sergel Rachmaninoff, Gladys Swarthout
        and the Ballet Ruse.

1070.   "500 of His Friends Honor Woollcott: Paul Robeson Recites,"
        New York Times, January 29, 1943, p. 19.

        About 500 persons gathered at Columbia University to pay tribute
        to Alexander Woollcott who dies at age 56. He was a critic and
        raconteur. There were only two religious notes in the service.
        Paul Robeson read the Twenty-Third Psalm, beginning "The Lord is
        My Shepherd." The last minute of the meeting was devoted to silent
        prayer.

1071.   "Louis, Robeson the Most Popular," People's Voice, June 28, 1947,
        p. 3.

        According to this article, the Gallup Poll showed that Joe Louis
        and Paul Robeson were among the country's most popular people.

1072.   "Dr. Bunche and Mr. Robeson," New York Times, July 19, 1949, p. 28.

        This was an editorial in the New York Times, whereby the editor
        compared Ralph Bunche to Paul Robeson. The writer states that
        the approach to the American Negro problem by the two persons of
        prominence is almost diametrically opposite. Dr. Bunche pleads
        the cause of the Negro in the name of real American democracy,
        states the writer. He then goes on to declare that Mr. Robeson
        pleads for the Negro cause in the name of the "new democracies of
        the world" that is the Soviet Union and its satellites.... The
        editor concludes: "Dr. Bunche and Mr. Robeson are both right in
        insisting that there cannot be second class citizens in a real
        democracy. But Dr. Bunche is devoted to the equality that arises

(New York Times)

from freedom. Mr. Robeson has attached himself to the cause of
a country in which all men are equal because they are equally
enslaved."

11. JOURNALIST

1073. "Robeson Turns Journalist; To Turn Out Column for Harlem Weekly,"
Los Angeles Tribune, July 26, 1947.

This article states that Paul Robeson would write a weekly column
in the People's Voice, a Harlem weekly. The paper was founded
and formerly published by Congressman Adam Clayton Powell, Jr.
The newspaper called Robeson "that rarity: a genius endowed with
an exceptional social consciousness." The article surmises that
the People's Voice had a "leftist flavor."

12. LABOR MOVEMENTS

1074. "Ban on Robeson Denied," New York Times, January 8, 1944, p. 11.

The actors' Equity Association, an AFL affiliate, states that it
never suggested that Paul Robeson face suspension because he was
expected to accept an honorary membership in Local No. 1 of the
State, County and Municipal Workers Union, a CIO affiliate. Since
acceptance of an honorary membership was not regarded with
"particular seriousness" Robeson probably will not be suspended
from the actors' Equity Association.

1075. "Equity Rejects Call to Penalize Robeson," New York Times, January
12, 1944, p. 26.

Actors Equity Association rejected a request by the Central Trades
and Labor Council body of AFL that it take "appropriate action"
against Paul Robeson for his honorary membership in the CIO union.
Paul Dullzell, executive secretary of Equity told the AFL that
"Mr. Robeson is not employed in any other field of activity except
as an actor and singer in our jurisdiction, and such being the
case there is no action that we can properly take in the matter."

1076. Stark, Louis. "AFL Attacks Laws in Seven States," New York Times,
January 22, 1943, p. 14.

The writer points out that William Green, president and Chairman
of the meeting of the AFL told the press that the AFL council had
received a complaint by federation affiliates in New York City
against Paul Robeson was antagonistic to it when he appealed to

(Stark, Louis)

Negroes not to join the CIO. Mr. Green ventured the opinion that
the executive council would not feel justified in taking any
action on the complaint.

1077.   "Universal Draft Favored," New York Times, January 23, 1944, p. 18.

The National Executive Board of the State, County and Municipal
Workers of America, Congress of Industrial Organization, met at
the Hotel New Yorker and gave noted singer Paul Robeson an honorary
lifetime membership.

1078.   Gore, Russell. "Robeson Sings for Ford Local 600 UAW-CIO,"
Detroit News, March 6, 1942.

The writer announces, in part: "....What has been called the
finest musical instrument wrought by nature in our time, will be
heard at Olympia on Saturday evening. It is the voice of Negro
baritone, Paul Robeson ...."

1079.   "Robeson is in Peoria But Fails to Speak," New York Times, April
19, 1947, p. 10.

Paul Robeson came to Peoria, Illinois, to speak on behalf of the
CIO union. The city would not grant him a permit to speak and
the City Council passed a resolution aimed at keeping Mr. Robeson
out of town. It opposed the appearance of any "avowed or active
propagandist for Un-American ideology." Mr. Robeson issued a
statement saying that "I will be back."

1080.   "Robeson Gets Ovation," New York Times, June 2, 1949, p. 8.

Paul Robeson attended a National Trade Union Congress in Warsaw,
Poland. Robeson addressed the meeting in Russian and concluded:
"Long live Poland, long live President Bierut." He received a
five-minute ovation from the delegates. He said he came from
"the America of (Harry) Wallace."

1081.   Raskin, H. "Maritime Union Back Lewis Stand," New York Times, July
9, 1941, p. 15.

Paul Robeson was made an honorary member of the National Maritime
Union, after he had sung ten songs and made a brief address in
which he said he felt "awfully happy and optomistic because fascism
has at last come to grips with the power that will show it no
quarters." Robeson urged the ship union to demand that the United
States give all possible aid to Russia, but made no mention of
Great Britain, concludes the article.

1082.   "Robeson Helps to Picket White House for Printers," Afro-American,
August 13, 1949, pp. 1, 2.

Paul Robeson walked in a picket line in front of the White House
with employees of the Bureau of Engraving and Printing and citizens
supporting their efforts to retain their jobs. The employees and

(Afro-American)

citizens were picketing in an effort to make known the plight of some 1800 workers in the Bureau who were about to lose their jobs as printers' assistants. The employees were asking the President to "blanket them in" their jobs the same as is done for the white plate printers. When asked by reporters why he was on the picket line, Robeson said: "For the same reason other citizens are picketing, to try to save these women's jobs." He added that he is also picketing against segregation and discrimination in the Bureau. He revealed that he was an honorary member of the citizens' committee headed by Mrs. Therese Robinson, who is also chairman of the Elks Civil Liberties Committee, and also of the UPW-CIO Anti-Discrimination Committee headed by Thomas Richardson. Robeson carried a sign which stated: "Mr. Truman take Jim Crow Off the American Dollar."

1083.   "Robeson Sings for Strikers," New York Times, July 18, 1946, p. 12.

Paul Robeson sang for pickets at the strike-bound Chrysler Corporation plant in Windsor, Ontario (Canada). He talked briefly to the strikers, walked in their picket line carrying a banner and shook hands with every man in the line.

1084.   Dunning, Alice. "Paul Robeson and Charles Howard Join Washington Picket Line in Job Fight," Black Dispatch, August 20, 1949, p. 1.

This writer declares that the fight to abolish segregation in employment at the Bureau of Printing and Engraving took on a new significance when national and internationally known personalities from various sections of the country came to Washington purposely to participate in the picket line which has now been in front of the White House for more than three weeks. Among those who marched in the picket line were Paul Robeson, famous actor-artist of Enfield, Conn., and Charles P. Howard of Des Moines, Iowa, the Keynote speaker at the 1948 National Convention of the Progressive Party. Nation-wide attention was focused on this bureau situation when Sen. William Langer (R., N. Dak.) and Cong. Vito Marcantonio (ALP., N.Y.) introduced joint resolutions in the Senate and House last week calling for an investigation of specific charges of discrimination against Negroes at the bureau, states the writer.

1085.   "CIO Leader Says Communist May Run Robeson," Afro-American, September 17, 1949, p. 2.

According to this article if Henry Wallace, former Vice President of the United States, refuses the bid, the Communist Party plans to support Paul Robeson for U.S. Senator in the seat formerly held by Robert F. Wagner. Michael Quill, president of the International Transport Workers (CIO), asserted. An Anti-Communist, Quill made the statement during a meeting of the 10th Annual State CIO Convention. Wallace, who has been mentioned as a possible candidate on the American Labor Party ticket, seems to be reluctant to accept the Communist offer, Quill stated. He added that the top leaders of the Community Party pondered the situation last

(Afro-American)

week, concludes the article.

1086.   "Stack Set Back National Maritime Union in Election," New York
         Times, September 30, 1947, p. 51.

         The National Maritime Union held its biannual convention in New
         York City. In a special order of business, Paul Robeson, who was
         an honorary member of the union, sang several songs and spoke
         briefly before the convention. Cheered by the delegates when he
         entered the ballroom and again when he left, Mr. Robeson was intro-
         duced as "an old friend and brother of ours, a great artist and a
         great man." Mr. Robeson, according to this article, called for
         opposition to "forces attempting to change a real democratic
         America." As examples of the activities of these forces he men-
         tioned recent moves to bar him and Henry Wallace from public
         appearances.

1087.   "Robeson, Kent Honored: Receive Lifetime Memberships in Long-
         shoremen's Union," New York Times, November 13, 1943, p. 15.

         The International Longshoremen's and Warehousemen's Union con-
         ferred lifetime memberships in their union on Paul Robeson, singer
         and actor and Rockwell Kent, artist. The two men were guests of
         the Union at a luncheon at the Hotel Roosevelt in New York City.

1088.   "Rockwell Kent and Paul Robeson Received Honorary Lifetime Mem-
         bership," The Dispatcher, November 19, 1943.

         This article declares that President Harry Bridges (of ILWU) be-
         stowed honorary, life-time membership on the world famous singer
         (Paul Robeson) and the well-known American artist (Rockwell Kent)
         at a luncheon in their honor at the Hotel Roosevelt, while 50
         leaders in the fields of labor and the arts rose to their feet
         to pay tribute to the men who were being honored and to the
         organization which had singled them out in recognition of the
         good anti-Fascist fight which these two great Americans have
         fought in every way. Harry Bridges explained that honorary mem-
         bership in the ILWU was not conferred indiscriminately. It was a
         token of the respect and admiration of the whole membership. "To
         be awarded honorary membership in the ILWU," said Bridges, "one
         must receive the unanimous vote of delegates to the convention.
         Paul Robeson and Rockwell Kent, leaders for many years in the
         fight against Fascism, received that vote. They are the only
         living honorary members of the ILWU. "Their membership entitles
         them to the full support of our union. And although our union is
         small, our members make up in activity what the organization lacks
         in size," concludes the article.

1089.   Raskin, A.H. "Illinois CIO Chiefs Shun TWU Session," New York
         Times, December 4, 1948, p. 28.

         Michael J. Quill, President of the Transport Workers Union ob-
         jected to Paul Robeson being the featured speaker at TWU's annual
         convention. Robeson had been an honorary member for ten years

(Raskin, A.H.)

and had attended all previous conventions. It was pointed out
that Mr. Quill had pinned the badge, conference life membership
on Robeson's lapel. Mr. Quill was allegedly seeking to oust all
left-wingers from TWU leadership, states Raskin.

13. LECTURER

1090.   "Paul Robeson Heads a List to Lecture at Democracy School,"
        Journal & Guide, September 19, 1942, p. 1.

        According to this report, Paul Robeson led a list of distinguished
        scholars, teachers and Negro leaders listed as instructors and
        guest lecturers at the School for Democracy, during the fall term.
        Mr. Robeson would step out of the role of singer and actor for
        which he is internationally known, to lecture in the course "Life
        and Culture of the Negro People." In addition to Mr. Robeson,
        the following distinguished Negro artists and writers would lecture:
        Dr. Alain Leroy Locke, Professor of philosophy at Howard University,
        author of The New Negro and other books; W.C. Handy, the father of
        the "blues"; Langston Hughes, poet; George Murphy, former Washing-
        ton editor for the Afro-American, now national administrative
        secretary of the National Negro Congress. Also, Ferdnand C. Smith,
        National Secretary of the National-Maritime Union. The chairman
        of the course will be Gwendolyn Bennett, a member of the admini-
        strative staff of the school and former Director of the Harlem
        Community Art Center. The School for Democracy, founded in
        October, 1941, during its first year, taught more than 3,000 adult
        Negro and white students, states the article. Its statement of
        policy indicates that "it was founded to help spread that knowledge
        and foster that spirit of free inquiry upon which a democratic
        people's morale must be built." It devoted attention to courses
        in Negro history and culture and its constantly expanding group
        of Negro lectures and instructors bear out the promise of its
        name, "The School for Democracy," concludes the article. It was
        also pointed out that this was one of the few courses taught on
        Negro History in New York.

14. LETTERS TO EDITORS

1091.   Friend, Michael W. "The Death of Paul Robeson," Los Angeles Times,
        February 1, 1949, Part 8, p. 1.

        The writer states: "I commend you upon the Robeson editorial. You
        show a great empathy which I would like to hope is shared by most
        of your readers. It is unfortunate that the National Football
        Foundation's Hall of Fame did not demonstrate a broader under-

(Friend, Michael W.)

standing and a more open mind."

1092.   Mason, P. "The Death of Paul Robeson," Los Angeles Times, February
        1, 1949, Part 8, p. 1.

        Mr. Mason wrote: "I'm one of your black subscribers and have
        been for a long while. I wish to thank you for your kind words
        about Paul Robeson. My basic reason for subscribing to the Times
        is: The Times tries to understand."

1093.   J.R.S. "Chastises Paul," Pittsburgh Courier, March 16, 1940, p. 6.

        The writer declares: "Accept my congratulations on your paper's
        account of Paul Robeson's flight from Germany, Russia and England
        to escape the humiliation of social inequality. Coming from Mr.
        Robeson, brilliant, scholarly gentlemen such as he is, it shows
        very poor judgment. If he would advocate equal opportunity to
        work and live and not social equality it would be more becoming
        in a brilliant scholar like him. It would help our race."

1094.   Hammond, Bill. "Paul Robeson," Honolulu Advertiser, March 18,
        1948.

        This letter concerns Paul Robeson's concert in Honolulu. It sug-
        gests that Robeson's program included a song against war, a song
        advocating racial equality, a union song, several songs in praise
        of love, and a number of spirituals. He concludes: "Perhaps the
        most blood-thirsty moment of the concert came when Mr. Robeson
        sang that revolutionary anthem, 'Old Man River,'"

1095.   Yergan, Max. "The American Negro and Mr. Robeson," New York Herald
        Tribune, April 23, 1949, p. 14T.

        The writer, a former supporter and friend of Paul Robeson, states
        that Robeson did not speak or represent his race at the so-called
        World Peace Conference in Paris. Yergan was also formerly
        Executive Director and Co-Founder of the Council on African Affairs.
        Dr. Yergan declares that Mr. Robeson, Chairman of the Council, was
        severely and openly condemned for his disgracefully unfair and un-
        democratic action and for his slavish following of Communist
        instructions with regard to the Council. He also surmises it is
        reasonable to conclude that the Robeson statements made at Paris
        has as their purpose the vicious and cynical effort which Communists
        in America have for a long time been putting forth to drive a
        wedge between American Negroes and their fellow American citizens.

1096.   Taylor, James T. "To Secure Negro Rights," New York Times, April
        26, 1949, p. 24.

        This letter was written by a Black North Carolina College Psycho-
        logy Professor concerning statements made by Paul Robeson. He
        declares that Robeson was only stating his own personal views when
        the singer asserted that Black Americans would not fight against
        Russia. Prof. Taylor surmises: "....It should be made plain once

(Taylor, James T.)

and for all to all the nations of the world that Negroes are
American citizens and that just as we expect the full privileges
guaranteed to all Americans we also expect to and will perform
with loyalty and devotion all the duties and obligations of
American citizenship in peace and in war...."

1097.   "From A Robeson Fan," New York Age, May 14, 1949, p. 12.

This letter was written by a former tech sarge. He declares, in
part: "As a vet who put in nearly five years in our Jim Crow Army,
I say Paul Robeson spoke the truth and he certainly speaks more
for the real colored people than the Walter Whites and Adam
Powells, who found it more profitable to be a Negro than white.
First off, for the sake of decent journalism at least you should
quote Mr. Robeson truthfully. He never said any thing about
fighting Russia, nor did he say that we Negroes would not defend
the U.S.A. What he did say was that Negroes would not fight for
those who have been oppressing them. It seems to be that The Age
instead of going in for a lot of nonsense might better use its
space to demand an end to Jim Crow in the Army...demand that Mr.
Truman keep some of his promises (now so empty) on civil rights.
Or does The Age think Negro men and women ought to fight another
war for the Four Freedoms while they themselves are segregated?
I saw the U.S. bring democracy to Italy, while white officers
kept informing the Italians that the 92nd Infantry men were rapists
and apes. Well, you can tell Uncle Clifford, Uncle White and
Uncle Powell that they can take that and put it under their hand-
kerchiefs before I ever enlist again."

1098.   Drayton, Arthur L. "Letter on Courier Editorial on Robeson,"
Pittsburth Courier, May 17, 1947.

The reader argues: "Your observations expressed in a recent editorial on 'The Strange Case of Paul Robeson' seemed petty and
illogical. Strangely enough, you did not even pay lip service to
the fundamental American principle of 'free speech' in your discussion of the refusals to permit him to sing in public auditoriums."
Mr. Drayton concludes, in part:
      But if the arguments you advanced in support of these
      refusals were applied to your own newspaper, might it
      not be reasonably claimed that there are times when
      you, yourself, sometimes fall short of your readers'
      expectations? Of course, no one is compelled to buy
      your paper if he dislikes any of its features. By
      the same token, Mr. Robeson does not 'compel' people
      to come to his recitals, nor does he further 'compel'
      them to hear his views on political matters. The
      fact that his views are repugnant to some assorted
      self-appointed guardians of the status quo is cer-
      tainly no reason for bypassing the Bill of Rights....

1099. Hoard, Willard. "Letter on Courier Editorial on Robeson,"
       Pittsburgh Courier, May 17, 1947, p. 21.

       The reader argues: "In your editorial of May 3, you claim that
       Paul Robeson makes communist-front speeches. The only evidence
       you have is what the Un-American Activities Committee says ...
       and it never produces any proof; it only makes accusations! The
       Courier has joined the bally-hoo for an FEPC law, and that same
       Committee claims this law is communist-inspired, and you know such
       a law is unconstitutional. Being a Negro, I believe that fair em-
       ployment should be practiced, but I don't believe it should be
       forced."

1100. O'Neill, J.M. "Communications: Concert in Albany," Commonweal,
       May 23, 1947, p. 141.

       The writer asserts: "The report in today's Times of the endorse-
       ment by the National Federation of Catholic College Students of
       the denial of the use of a high school auditorium in Albany for
       a recital by Paul Robeson is one of the most depressing stories
       I have seen in some time -- except those with a Moscow date line.
       The Catholic students here pay the Communists the supreme compli-
       ment of imitation. Any informed Catholic must know that no
       Communist does, or can, believe in freedom of opinion of or ex-
       pression for Catholics or other opposed to Communism. The denial
       of civil liberties is...necessary foundation of all dictator-
       ships and the universal position of all Stalinists. That Mr.
       Robeson, a Negro and a distinguished artist, should be so treated
       on account of his immaturity or gullibility in political matters
       is an affront to the basic, and most important, difference between
       America and the Soviet Union. To have such action approved by
       the representatives of another minority group in America, and one
       which has prospered greatly by virtue of this same fundamental
       American doctrine, is a stupid and disgraceful performance. It
       will be worth more to all Communists, and other anti-Catholic
       propagandists, than a month's editorials in the Daily Worker...."

1101. Marchbanks, Vance H., Sr. "A Retired Soldier Reflects, Says Negro
       Will Fight," Pittsburgh Courier, July 16, 1949, p. 21.

       The reader states, in part: "...There are very few who could be
       classed with those Paul Robeson referred to in his Paris speech
       a short time ago where he is reported as having said: 'Negroes
       in the United States would refuse to fight an imperialistic war
       against Russia.' It is supposed that he means a war for ter-
       ritorial expansion? Well, my guess is, judging from past ex-
       perience, if the United States should ever engage in another
       shooting war, may God forbid, the Americans of Negro blood will
       fight on the side of other Americans as they have in the past re-
       gardless of what kind of a war it is called, or who the United
       States fights against." He concludes: "And the writer thinks
       those who are not willing to fight in the future as they have in
       the past should go to the country where their heart is, and stay
       there."

1102. Black, Mrs. Vivian. "RE Paul Robeson," <u>New York Age</u>, July 30, 1949, p. 15.

The writer declares, in part: "Before you completely crucify Paul Robeson, why don't you try to see him for what he is - a great fighter for his people? I don't think Mr. Robeson is a Communist at heart. They are the only ones who will help him to fight, so he falls in line with them. I have just read in a Long Island paper where one ex-Communist accused Mr. Robeson of being a "black Stalin" and would like to ride to power on the broken backs of Negroes who are good Americans. I wonder if Mr. Johnson, the accuser, really knows what he is talking about or if he was prompted to say those things. We need more real fighters for our race and less "Uncle Toms." Mr. Robeson wants so badly to see his people treated like human beings in the United States and for one of his own to call him a "black Stalin," is shameful and a disgrace - a blow to the whole Negro race. If more Negroes would stop trying to 'pass' and be decent and prouder of our heritage, there would be greater advantage."

1103. Newman, Mrs. W.B. "Says Robeson Has Done No Harm in Voicing the Truth," <u>Pittsburgh Courier</u>, August 6, 1949, p. 14.

The reader states if Robeson and his family were treated with respect during their stay in Russia, she doesn't see any harm he did by voicing it. She concludes: "Mr. Robeson is an asset to those that are trying to besmirch him. Take heed those of you that are always 'yes sirring,' that the black people be constrained to vomit you out of our group."

1104. Patterson, William L. "The Peekskill Concert: Whole Affair Considered Associated with the Negro's Cause," <u>New York Times</u>, October 17, 1949, p. 22.

This was a letter to the Editor of the <u>New York Times</u> from the William L. Patterson, National Executive Secretary, Civil Rights Congress. The writer comments on what A. Philip Randolph had to say about Paul Robeson and Peekskill incidents. The writer states that Mr. Randolph called Robeson a "Johnny-come-lately to the cause of the Negro." He goes on to show that Robeson has been in the vanguard of Negro freedom. Patterson concludes: "Thousands flock today to the Paul Robeson meetings. Truly this man's voice must be the voice of some people seeking freedom - else why would reaction work so desperately to still it? Who in America today in greater danger from reaction than this man?...."

15. NBC AFFAIR

1105. Editorial. "Air Not Free at NBC," <u>Afro-American</u>, March 25, 1940.

The editor comments on the banning of Paul Robeson from NBC television. He asserts, in part:

(Afro-American)

> ....In a democracy such as ours, every party should
> be permitted to have its say whether the American
> Legion agrees with it or not. Legionnaires were re-
> sponsible for most of the protests above mentioned
> against Robeson's appearing on TV. If Mr. Robeson
> had been permitted to speak he certainly would have
> had both Congressman Powell and Mr. Howard at a great
> disadvantage. It would have been impossible for
> either one of those gentle men to explain why we have
> no civil rights legislation on the books, despite the
> fact that both Republicans and Democratics are com-
> mitted to it and that the 80th Congress was predomi-
> nantly Republican and the 81st Congress predominantly
> Democrat.

1106.   "Harlem Disappointed as NBC Bars Robeson Off Mrs. FDR Program,"
        New York Age, March 18, 1949, pp. 1, 2.

This article reports that the majority of Harlem opinions on the
cancellation of Mrs. Eleanor Roosevelt's NBC television show,
Sunday, because of protests on the scheduled appearance of Paul
Robeson is one of disappointment. Robeson, vice-chairman of the
Progressive Party, Congressman A. Clayton Powell, Jr., Democrat,
and Perry Howard, Republican national committeeman from
Mississippi were to discuss "The Position of the Negro in American
Political Life." The cancellation followed what an NBC spokesman said were "between two and three hundred" objections to the
show because of Robeson and the all-out opposition of the N.Y.
Journal-American. Rep. Powell said he was "Looking forward to
refuting, by means of presenting the Americans viewpoint the
political dogma of Robeson." He expressed his disappointment over
the cancellation.

16. PARIS CONFERENCE

1107.   "Negroes Hail Fraternity," New York Times, April 25, 1949, p. 25.

It was pointed out that among other things that the National
Association for the Advancement of Colored People adopted a resolution declaring that Mr. Robeson "did not express the opinion
and viewpoint of the loyal majority of Negroes of this country
when he declared at the Paris Congress that American Negroes would
not fight against Soviet Russia."

1108.   Editorial. "Mr. Robeson Goes to Town....," Pittsburgh Courier,
        April 30, 1949, p. 10.

The editor declares, in part: "As chief of the United States delegation to the World Congress of the Partisans of Peace last week,
Paul Robeson, the widely ballhooed singer, declared that American

(Pittsburgh Courier)

Negroes never would fight the Soviet Union. This was a pathetic
statement because Mr. Robeson, who belongs to more than a half
hundred Communist-front organizations (while denying he is a
Communist) cannot conceivable speak for American Negroes. No one
has delegated him to speak for them and no one will, if we know
anything about American Negroes. The colored citizens of this
country have fought in every war waged for the defense of their
country and they will continue to do so." He went on to assert:
"There is something very saddening about Paul Robeson, for while
he has reached his high position as a result of the indulgence
and patronage of wealthy capitalists, he has devoted most of his
surplus energies toward destroying those who nutured him...."

1109. Prattis, P.L. "Robeson, Du Bois Cause Uproar at Paris Meet,"
       Pittsburgh Courier, April 30, 1949, p. 3.

       This article refers to Robeson and Du Bois'speeches at the World
       Congress of Partisans of Peace that was held in Paris, France.
       Dr. Du Bois told the delegates: "If the world is to be saved
       Africa must be saved first." Robeson was reported to have told
       the delegates that American Negroes would never fight against the
       Soviet Union in the event of war with that country. According to
       Mr. Prattis, Robeson flew to Paris the opening day of the Congress.
       He was forced to the platform by the applause of the delegates. In
       a short speech he denounced the treatment of Negroes in the United
       States and declared that he labored for their freedom. The only
       time he had ever felt like a real human being, said Robeson, was
       when he was in the Soviet Union.

1110. "We'll Fight Foe, Top Leaders Say: Robeson's Paris Note Promptly
       Repudiated," Afro-American, April 30, 1949, pp. 1, 2.

       Several top Black leaders repudiated Paul Robeson's alleged Paris
       statement that "colored Americans would never fight Russia." The
       leaders emphasized Blacks'traditional loyalty to the U.S. govern-
       ment and the democratic ideals for which it stands, despite its
       shortcomings in the area of civil rights, the leaders queried
       challenged Mr. Robeson's authority to speak for the entire race.
       Some of the leaders queried included: Walter White, Executive
       Secretary of the NAACP, Mrs. Mary McLeod Bethune, Founder-President
       of the National Council of Negro Women, Charles Houston, a nation-
       ally prominent lawyer of Washington, D.C., Mrs. Velma G. Williams,
       Member of Washington, D.C. Board of Education, and mother of three
       World War II veterans; Judge James A. Cobb, Municipal Court,
       Washington, D.C., Mrs. Maude B. Richardson, Brooklyn Republican
       leader, Perry W. Howard of Washington, D.C. lawyer, and Republican
       National Committman for Mississippi went so far as to surmise:
       "I believe Paul Robeson is mentally ill, as indicated by his outra-
       geously imprudent statement. We are Americans, and, therefore,
       nationals. We have grievances, plenty of them, but they are to
       be fought out within the framework of our laws."

1111.   "Robeson Speaks for Robeson," Crisis, Vol. 56, No. 5, May 1949,
         p. 37.

         This was an editorial in the NAACP's official publication. The
         editorial refers to the Peace Conference in Paris whereby Paul
         Robeson declared that American Negroes would not fight the Soviet
         Union if a war should break out between America and Russia. The
         editor argues: "The basic fact to remember about Mr. Robeson's
         Paris speech is that he was speaking for himself. Paul Robeson
         does not represent any American Negroes. Not even ten of them
         have held a meeting and named him as their leader and spokesman.
         For many years they have admired him as an athlete and concert
         singer, but the vase majority soured on him when he began mixing
         the Communist party line with 'Water Boy.' Today Mr. Robeson, if
         he represents any group at all, speaks for the fellow travelers
         of Communism and it is well known that those are overwhelmingly
         white." The editorial concludes:
                 So Mr. Robeson has none except sentimental roots
                 among American Negroes. He is of them, but not with
                 them. He is much closer to, say, the National Council
                 of American Soviet Friendship, than he is to Fisk
                 University, the Dallas Negro Chamber of Commerce, or
                 the Brotherhood of Sleeping Car Porters. With his
                 really tremendous talents and his great personal
                 charm, Mr. Robeson could have been an outstanding
                 leader of his people at a time when they sorely needed
                 men like him. Out of the comfortable income that
                 has been his for the past twenty years he could have
                 given substantial sums to help his people up the
                 ladder. Instead he chose a circle of international
                 intellectuals and the money he must have given here
                 and there went to organizations and causes that
                 touched the American Negro's plight only obliquely,
                 at best....

1112.   "Communists," Time, Vol 43, No. 18, May 2, 1949, p. 25.

         This article concerns Paul Robeson's speech to the World Congress
         of the Partisans of Peace in Paris. This article declares that
         most flamboyant of all the troupers at the meeting was Baritone
         Paul Robeson, who vowed that American Negroes would not fight for
         the United States in a war with the Soviet Union. Robeson de-
         clares, partly in Russian and partly in English: "It is a pleasure
         to say hello to my friends from the eastern popular democracies of
         Europe -- those democracies which are showing us how people conduct
         their own destines in the interest of mankind."

1113.   Rogers, J.A. "Rogers Says: Paul Robeson May be Wrong but His
         Speech was Food for Thought," Pittsburgh Courier, May 7, 1949, p.
         12.

         The writer surmises:
                 When Paul Robeson says (allegedly) that Negroes would
                 not fight Russia, he is certainly not speaking for the
                 majority of them. They will do any and everything
                 most American whites do. However, those leaders and

(Rogers, J.A.)

>   others who rushed to declare Robeson wrong, since
>   they themselves were not being accused of dis-
>   loyalty, showed very poor strategy. A man who is
>   despised in his country is never respected outside
>   of it. Some of the mud thrown at him at home always
>   sticks to him when he goes abroad. However, Robeson
>   only heightened the picture, he did not create
>   it....

1114. Schuyler, George S. "So Along Comes Paul Robeson with the
       Clincher," Pittsburgh Courier, May 7, 1949, p. 12.

The columnist asserts: "....Of course, Mr. Robeson has never had
any mandate to speak for colored Americans and never will have
any. Like other Americans they will fight as they have always
fought against foreign aggressors and internal foes, and will cover
themselves with glory in the process. They will do so not only
because they are patriotic Americans but because even the least
intellectual American Negro knows that he is better off in this
country under this system than anybody anywhere else, granted that
it is far from perfect and that he suffers many disabilities and
proscriptions...." He continues: "Robeson's smearing of 14,000,
000 Negroes as potential traitors played right into the hands of
our worst enemies, the Negrophobes of this country. For generations Kluxers have held up the fare of 'Ethiopian domination' as
a justification for jim-crowism and repression. Both North and
South believe in Negro segregation, like that of the aboriginal
Indians, and now they have found a Negro who thinks concentration
camps are justifiable. Certainly all of these prejudiced whites
would be glad to seize upon the charge that Negroes are treason-
able as a justification for herding them into concentration camps
with the inevitable result." He also asserts: "Of course, Negroes
join in a chorus of denunciation of people like Robeson NOW but I
wonder why they have been silent so long. Robeson has been a
leading fellow traveller for over fifteen years and has loyally
carried forward the Communist line regardless of contradictions
and switches. Nevertheless, Negroes who are articulate have been
applauding his 'greatness' and that of the other Red Negro stooges
among 'artists,' professionals, and 'intellectuals.'" The writer
concludes: "At the same time these people have carried on a
systematic campaign of criticism, smearing and denunciation of
people like this writer who sounded the warning. There were times
when I was practically alone. While I have never minded being
alone, it is good to be able to be welcomed back into the fold so
many erstwhile in no cents."

1115. McKenzie, Marjorie. "The Government Ought to Regard Robeson's
       Statement as a Signal," Pittsburgh Courier, June 25, 1949, p. 14.

Paul Robeson stated at the Paris Peace Conference that American
Negroes would refuse to fight an imperialistic war against Russia.
The writer states that the government should take note of this
supposition. She asserts that a lot of anti-Communist liberals
are not happy about the way this Congress has fouled up the civil

(McKenzie, Majorie)

rignts program. Miss McKenzie concludes: "Its inaction creates
a fertile ground of discontent and potential disloyalty, whether
overt or concealed. The Government ought to regard the exaggerated response to Paul's statement as a storm signal."

1116. "Robeson Critizec by negro Union Head," New York Times, November
7, 1949, p. 23.

A. Philip Randolph, International president of the Brotherhood of
Sleeping Car Porters, declares that Paul Robeson was merely
parroting remarks made by other leftist leaders when the singer
stated it was unthinkable that the negro people of America or
elsewhere in the world could be drawn into a war with the Soviet
Union." Mr. Randolph asserts: "Neither Robeson nor I myself,
nor any other negro has the right to speak for Negroes in America."
The labor leader went on to say that anyone who hoped to mirror
the thougnts of the Negroes must at least mingle with them and
serve them. Mr. Robeson had done neither, but had spent much of
his time with Europeans,he said, according to this article.

17. PEEKSKILL INCIDENT

1117. "Legion Scores Robeson: Peekskill Requested to Boycott There,"
New York Times, August 17, 1947, p. 55.

The Peekskill (New York) American Legion condemned the theory of
Communist it attributed to Paul Robeson and requested Peekskill
citizens not to attend a concert scheduled in the Peekskill Stadium.
The appearance of Robeson was sponsored by the Cultural division
of the Committee to Aid the South. "Paul Robeson has been re-
putedly known to be a member of the board of directors of several
Communistic front organizations," the Legion statement said.

1118. "Paul Robeson Concert," Peekskill (New York) Evening Star, August
23, 1949, p. 1.

The newspaper reports, in part that Paul Robeson, noted Negro
singer and in recent months an avowed disciple of Soviet Russia,
will make his third appearance in three years... Sponsoring the
concert is "People's Artists, Inc.," an organization listed as subversive and branded a Communist front by the California Committee
on Un-American Activities in 1948. Funds collected by sale of
tickets will be used "for benefit of the Harlem Chapter of Civil
Rights Congress," according to posters nailed to trees, bulletin
boards and telephone poles in the Crompond Colony. The "Civil
Rights Congress" has been cited as subversive by former U.S.
Attorney General Tom Clark, states the article.

1119. Mardo, Bill. "Investigate Mob, Jackie Says," Daily Worker,
       August 29, 1949, p. 1.

       Jackie Robinson bitterly blasted the riot at Peekskill. He was
       quoted: "Paul Robeson should have the right to sing, speak or do
       anything he wants to.... I think those rioters ought to be in-
       vestigated and let's find out if what they did is supposed to be
       the democtatic way of doing things.... If Mr. Robeson wants to
       believe in Communism, that's his right. I prefer not to....
       Anything progressive is called Communism."

1120. North, Joseph. "Lynch Mob Runs Amuck at Paul Robeson Concert,"
       Daily Worker, August 29, 1949', p. 1.

       The author declares that the report to Gov. Dewey from Westchester
       County's District Attorney George M. Fanelli on the Robeson con-
       cert evoked shocked comment throughout the area for its total
       exoneration of the police and its numerous misstatements of fact
       that many thousands witnessed. He also suggests that a char-
       acteristic disregard for truth was revealed in Fanelli's statement
       that "all those seeking to attend the concert gained admission with-
       out hazard, and no demonstration of any nature broke out as a re-
       sult of the parade."

1121. "The Peekskill Riot," New York News, August 29, 1949, p. 1.

       The newspaper reports in part, that "the state troopers denied
       charges that they had not arrived in time to head off the three
       hour riot in which cars were overturned, women frightened into the
       woods, and veterans and Robeson fans alike beaten with clubs,
       stones and fence-posts.... In the first place, Sergeant Johnson
       (the first sergeant of Troop K at Hawthorne) pointed out the vets
       had a legal right to parade and had obtained a permit. Besides,
       he said, no one had officially requested that troopers be on hand
       before the trouble started." "'There was no need to be there in
       advance,' he asserts. We don't play into the hands of the Commies.
       We went in when we found that a crime had been committed,'" con-
       cludes the article.

1122. Egan, Leo. "Dewey Asks Report on Robeson Battle," New York Times,
       August 30, 1949, pp. 1, 28.

       New York's Governor Thomas Dewey ordered an investigation into the
       outbreak of violence near Peekskill, New York which prevented Paul
       Robeson's concert. Many pro-Robeson followers were beaten up by
       thugs.

1123. Fast, Howard. "Eyewitness Account of Fascist Mob's Attack," Daily
       Worker, August 30, 1949, pp. 3, 9.

       This novelist was present at the concert in Peekskill and wrote a
       first hand account of what happened. This newspaper article was
       the bases for a later 124 page book by Mr. Fast entitled, Peekskill:
       U.S.A.: A Personal Experience. It was published in 1951 by the
       Civil Rights Congress.

1124.   "Governor Dewey's Action," London Times, August 30, 1949, p. 3.

This report states that Governor Dewey of New York called on the authorities in Westchester County for a full report on the fracas at Peekskill, where a local group of young ex-service men broke up a left-wing open-air gathering at which Mr. Paul Robeson was to have sung. Robeson alleged that the riot was organized with the connivance of the local police and other authorities, and that there was evidence of the hand of the Ku Klux Klan, concludes the article.

1125.   Scroog, Arnold. "Rally Tonight to Hit Terror at Robeson Concert," Daily Worker, August 30, 1949, pp. 1, 9.

A giant Harlem (New York) rally was planned to protest against the attack on Paul Robeson at Peekskill.

1126. "Hooligans, Fascists Assailed," New York Times, August 31, 1949, p. 16.

According to this special report, Paul Robeson narrowly escaped lynching by a "few thousand hooligans and fascists and the Ku Klux Klan," Trybuna Luda, organ of the United Workers (Communist) party, told its readers in a front page story about the clash at Peekskill, N.Y. According to the dispatch, which was sent by the official Polish news agency, a band of Fascists persecuted the unarmed audience for three hours, after which "they burned the stage of the concert hall and after demolishing the hall went up a hill close to the city and burned a cross there according to the custom of the Kluxers.... New York police showed up a few hours later and made no arrests."

1127.   Lewis, Theophilus. "Sticks and Stones," Interracial Review, Vol. 22, September 1949, pp. 130, 140.

The writer discusses Paul Robeson and his concert at Peekskill. He suggests that it was a propaganda triumph for the Communists, who were delighted when the citizens of Westchester foolishly "blew their collective top."

1128.   Scroog, Arnold. "Westchester DA Moves to Frame Mob Victims: Asks N.Y. Police Aid," Daily Worker, September 1, 1949, p. 3.

The writer contends that a frameup against the victims of the riot at Peekskill was in the making with Westchester County District Attorney George M. Fanelli attempting to involve the New York City Police Department in framing the victims for the hoodlum assault. Mr. Scroog declares that Mr. Fanelli made it clear that he had no intentions of investigating the mobsters, whom dozens of eye-witnesses, photographs and news accounts revealed as the ones who assaulted the audience at the concert.

1129. Scroog, Arnold. "Robeson to Sing in Peekskill This Sunday,"
       Daily Worker, September 2, 1949, pp. 1, 9.

       This article states that Paul Robeson vowed to return to Peekskill
       to give a concert within one mile of the scene of the last riot
       there when he was giving a concert.

1130. "5,000 Riot over Paul Robeson," Pittsburgh Courier, September 3,
       1949, pp. 1, 5.

       According to the article about 5,000 people rioted over Paul
       Robeson's appearance in Peekskill, New York. The riot was re-
       portedly started by white war veterans who staged the initial de-
       monstration which ended in fighting. The veterans stated that
       the concert was sponsored by a Communist-front organization --
       Civil Rights Congress.

1131. Hicks, James L. "Rioting N.Y. Vets Paul's Backers Defy: 2nd
       Meeting Held on Spot of First Bloody Brawl; Cops Allied with Mob,"
       Afro-American, September 3, 1949, pp. 1, 9.

       According to the author, the riot that occurred in Peekskill, New
       York, was between followers of singer Paul Robeson and representa-
       tives of veterans organizations who broke up a scheduled open-air
       concert by Robeson in one of the most wild and lawless outbreaks
       this sedate section has ever known. After one person had been
       seriously stabbed and eight persons had been hospitalized in the
       rioting, Robeson sympathizers boldly invaded Peekskill, 5,000
       strong, and held a rally at the home of Dr. Samuel Rosen, eye
       specialist of New York City, who had a huge country home just out-
       side Peekskill, states Hicks. Robeson himself was not involved
       in the rioting. He had appeared at the scene about an hour after
       it began. He tried to enter the area but was restrained by mem-
       bers of his party. He looked on from a distance with William L.
       Patterson, secretary of the Harlem branch of the Civil Rights
       Congress, according to the author.

1132. "Robeson Defies All...To Sing at Peekskill," New York Age,
       September 3, 1949, p. 1.

       According to this article, as soon as Paul Robeson declared Monday
       that he would make an appearance at Peekskill, N.Y., where his con-
       cert scheduled for last Saturday night was canceled when a riot
       broke out between alleged vet demonstrators and persons attending
       the benefit affair, he was "seconded" by Joan Slessinger, concert
       pianist who was to have performed on the same concert, and Hope
       Foye, concert singer, who was also to have made an appearance with
       Mr. Robeson. There is a photo of the three artists together in
       this newspaper.

1133.   Walker, Jesse H.   "Singer Maps Plans to Return to Riot Scene,"
        New York Age, September 3, 1949, p. 1.

        According to this reporter an angry but stubborn Paul Robeson de-
        clared that he is planning to give a concert in the Peekskill,
        N.Y. area "within the next ten days" and warned that when he does
        he expects adequate police protection. "They'd better not do it
        again," the singer exclaimed hotly referring to the riot. The
        battle forced canceling of his yearly concert in the area after
        1,000 alleged war veterans attacked 300 men, women and children
        attending the affair at the Lakeland Acres picnic grounds. The
        concert was scheduled as a benefit for the Harlem chapter of the
        Civil Rights Congress. Robeson held a press conference at the
        Hotel Theresa to discuss the affair. In a belligerent mood and
        angrily as he spoke, the singer announced that no one would ever
        run him out of America, states Walker. The latter was in reference
        to remarks attributed to Clyde Lewis, newly elected national com-
        mander of the Veterans of Foreign Wars, that his organization
        "would be only too happy to buy a one-way ticket to Russia for
        Paul Robeson...." The singer asserts: "I'm not saying I'm not
        loyal to America. I'm loyal to the America which freed me. I'm
        not loyal to any America seeking to enslave Negro Americans and
        Africans all over the world." Paul Robeson charged that the
        actions of the veterans groups in the small New York town are
        evidence that the "fascistic pattern spreads." He linked the in-
        cident to that of the Ku Klux Klan activities in the South and
        the Germany of Hitler. "What happened?" "Is all part of a drive
        of a few people to make a war involving our people everywhere,"
        he charged. Robeson claimed that the time has come for the govern-
        ment to investigate the American Legion and the Veterans of Foreign
        Wars. Both organizations it is said were well represented in the
        mob of stick-swinging vets who stormed the entrance to the concert
        site and attacked the mixed audience, states the writer.

1134.   North, Joseph.   "25,000 Hear Robeson at Peekskill; Hoodlums Muster
        1,000 for 'Parade,'" The Worker, September 5, 1949, pp. 1, 3.

        Paul Robeson came back to Peekskill and about 25,000 Americans
        heard him sing. At this concert there were enough state police,
        county police, and deputy sheriffs to sweep the road to the con-
        cert clear of any hoodlums had they wanted to. The applause after
        each of Robeson's songs was deafening, states Mr. North. The
        concert was a success and relatively peaceful.

1135.   "Picnic at Peekskill," Time, Vol. 54, No. 10, September 5, 1949,
        p. 15.

        This article states that it was to be an orderly, "peaceable" de-
        monstration, protesting the appearance of Communist-tuned singer
        Paul Robeson at a picnic ground outisde of Peekskill, N.Y. True,
        the veterans of Westchester County had brought along enough brass
        bands to drown out a full opera company and enough pickets to keep
        any traffic from getting through. But there was to be no rough
        stuff, the leaders promised. Then the veterans, 500 strong,
        started down the road leading to the picnic grove itself, declares
        the author. In the gathering darkness, the early arrivals among

(Time)

the audience locked arms in front of a large truck, defiantly
burst into the chorus of the old radical marching song, "We Shall
Not Be Moved." Suddenly chunks of a wooden fence railing sailed
into the ranks of the defenders. Hurling stones and brandishing
clubs, the veterans charged, according to this report. The
article concludes: "The Communist-line Civil Rights Congress,
sponsors of the concert, quickly denounced the sorry affair as an
attempt to "lynch Robeson." It was hardly that. But it was an
example of misguided patriotism and senseless hooliganism, more
useful to Communist propaganda than a dozen uninterrupted song
recitals by Paul Robeson."

1136.   "Stone-Throwing After a Robeson Concert," London Times, September
        5, 1949, p. 3.

Governor Dewey ordered 200 State Police to assist a force of about
1,000 policemen, armed for the occasion as sheriff's deputies, to
preserve order at a concert given by Paul Robeson, near Peekskill,
New York. Four ex-service organizations announced that they would
organize marches of protest against holding the concert. Mr. Dewey
described the Robeson meeting as "pro-Communist," but declared
that the "right of free speech and free assumbly must be respected
however hateful the views of some of those who abuse them."

1137.   Grutzner, Charles. "Robeson, Officials Differ on Disorder," New
        York Times, September 6, 1949, pp. 1, 23.

Paul Robeson and others were attacked by a mob as he was singing
at a concert in Peekskill, New York. According to Robeson's observers more than 200 persons were treated for injuries. The mob
was supported by veterans organizations who declared "We will
continue to demonstrate against Mr. Robeson's pseudo concerts or
any other subversive meetings. We do not want Communists in this
area, under any title or pretense." Mr. Robeson asserts that the
men among the concertgoers, who outnumbered the hostile demonstrators, had shown "tremendous self-discipline" in not fighting
back. He made clear his determination to make political capital
throughout the nation, of the Peekskill disorders, asserts Mr.
Grutzner. Robeson also states that emergency committees would be
formed "all through the United States." The activist surmises:
"This has to do with every American who has any pretense to thinking
that he still lives in a democracy." The singer argues that
"Governor Dewey sent the storm troopers. He gave the illusion
that they'd be there to defend us but they were really there to
beat our brains out...."

1138.   "138 Hurt After Concert by Mr. Robeson," London Times, September 6,
        1949, p. 3.

This article declares that though 900 law enforcement officers
managed to prevent violence while Mr. Paul Robeson was singing at
the abandoned golf course near Peekskill, New York, a survey taken
in a local hospital showed 138 people injured, four of them
seriously when bottles, and stones were thrown by demonstrators at

(London Times)

at members of the audience when leaving after the concert. It was
also brought out that 3,000 of Mr. Robeson's supporters circled
him and the audience of 15,000 people as ex-servicemen attempted
to pass through the lines.

1139. "Stoning Victims Tell of Violence: Blame Police for Peekskill
        Disturbance -- Robeson in Tears," New York Times, September 6,
        1949, p. 23.

        Paul Robeson along with other concertgoers appeared as witnesses
        before the Emergence Committee to Protest the Peekskill attacks.
        Robeson states, sometimes in tears: "What happened in Peekskill
        happened to the Negro people every day in the South. We Negroes
        owe a great debt to the Jewish people, who stood there by the
        hundreds to defend me and all of us yesterday."

1140. Editorial. "Paul Robeson and The Peekskill Affair," St. Louis
        American, September 8, 1949, Editorial Page.

        This "conservative" Black newspaper declares, in part: "But the
        plight now transcends Robeson and overshodows the press -- our
        whole American Bill of Rights, which guarantees protection 'for
        those whom we dislike and bitterly disagree with' is in danger of
        being toppled -- not by the Communists, but BY THOSE WHO CLOAK
        THEMSELVES WITH THE CRY THAT THEY ARE FIGHTING COMMUNISM AND HAVE
        A RIGHT TO ACT AS HOODLUMS, LYNCHERS, STORM TROOPERS WITH THE KU
        KLUX KLAN!.... That is also the pattern by which Hitler and his
        bunch came into power. We now seriously ask: IS IT HAPPENING
        HERE NOW?"

1141. Lauter, Bob. "How the Radio Covered Violence at Peekskill,"
        Daily Worker, September 8, 1949, p. 11.

        The author declares that Radio Station WCBS had the honor of having
        made an outstnading contribution to an understanding of what
        happened at Peekskill, where Paul Robeson was giving a concert
        and where violence broke out. WCBS presented an on the spot
        account of the happenings. This account gave listeners a clear
        picture of the character of the Peekskill gangs, states Lauter.

1142. Moscow, Warren. "Police Commended in Peekskill Fray," New York
        Times, September 8, 1949, pp. 1, 34.

        Violence broke out when Paul Robeson was giving a concert at Peek-
        skill, New York. The police did not give adequate protection to
        Paul Robeson and his followers. District Attorney George M.
        Fanelli of Westchester County states that the police and others
        concerned with law and order should be commended rather than cen-
        sured for their part in the affair. The District Attorney sent
        a full "report" of the incident to Governor Thomas Dewey of New
        York.

1143.   "Mr. Robeson and Democracy," Commonweal, Vol. 50, No. 22, September
         9, 1949, p. 524.

         The writer declares that Paul Robeson, an American singer with a
         magnificent voice, has made many statements -- often foolish, or
         distorted, or stupid -- about the failures of American democracy
         and the virtues of the Soviet states. These have infuriated some
         other Americans. Last week certain of these Americans, primarily
         veterans from Peekskill, New York, posts of the Catholic War
         Veterans, the American Legion and the Veterans of Foreign Wars, de-
         cided that because of their dislike for Mr. Robeson and what he
         says, they would prevent him from giving a concert in their neigh-
         borhood. They succeeded, states the writer. "Our objective was
         to prevent the Paul Robeson concert and I think our objective was
         reached. Anything that happened after the organized demonstration
         was dispersed was entirely up to the individual citizens and should
         not be blamed on the patriotic organizations" as one of the vet-
         eran's leaders put it. The Catholic War Veteran's Commander said
         "All the veteran groups were dispersed before 9 p.m..... It was
         regrettable that it went as far as it did...." Unfortunately it
         went as far as it did and there was a three hour fight and eight
         persons were injured, one man was stabbed, and several Ku Klux
         Klan crosses were burned, surmises the author. He concludes:
                  It is a very sad affair, for every effort by the
                  patriotic organizations 'to prevent the Paul Robeson
                  concert' -- along with the blows and the crosses --
                  added just so much truth to what Mr. Robeson has said
                  in the past and will say in the future about the
                  failures of American democracy.

1144.   Editorial. "A Full Investigation is Really in Order," Afro-Ameri-
         can, September 10, 1949, p. 4.

         The editor surmises, in part: "We hear now that the uprising among
         veterans organizations which caused a riot and postponement of a
         Paul Robeson concert at Peekskill, New York, was accidental. The
         veterans have a right to peacefully picket but everybody knows
         that the veterans actually set out to break up the Robeson con-
         cert by marching and staging a band concert of their own close to
         the place where Mr. Robeson was to sing. And, the question has
         also been raised as to whether this was a bona fide veterans or-
         ganization eager to condemn Mr. Robeson and his friends and their
         Communistic leanings or was it an attack upon and an attempt to
         intimidate all colored people." In recent years many persons have
         purchased expensive homes in the Westchester County section. Some
         of the older residents have resented their new neighbors. How
         much of this peaceful picketing was directed to Robeson and how
         much against all the other colored people who have moved into
         Westchester County is an unanswered question. Governor Dewey does
         well to make an investigation of the whole indicate and he should
         deal with it promptly, concludes the editor.

1145.   Editorial. "Robeson Rumpers," <u>Pittsburgh Courier</u>, September 10,
        1949, p. 14.

        The editor comments on the Peekskill riot. He asserts, in part:
        "The air is filled with charges and counter-charges, denunciations
        and demands for all sorts of action as a result of the deplorable
        rioting and violence in Peekskill, N.Y., a few days ago in con-
        nection with a scheduled appearance of Paul Robeson and supporting
        entertainers there...." He declares that the outrage was anti-
        Robeson and anti-Communist rather than anti-Negro, and as inex-
        cussable as it was, the fact cannot be ignored that the left-wing
        group must have anticipated just such an occurrence and was pre-
        pared for it, as evidenced by the bringing of thirty-two "guards"
        and six bus loads of sympathizers from New York who formed a large
        part of the audience of 300. The editor believes: "In view of
        the fact that some Negroes are identified with unpopular and in
        some instances with subversive movements which have aroused the
        ire of large segments of the population, we should hesitate to
        charge that every fracas in which Negroes are involved is neces-
        sarily anti-Negro...."

1146.   Hicks, James L. "Troopers Club His (Robeson's) Supporters," <u>Afro-
        American</u>, September 10, 1949, pp. 1, 6.

        Paul Robeson kept his promise and came back to Peekskill, New York,
        to sing, but he sang in the midst of a complete breakdown of law
        and order, states Hicks. According to the author the chief ac-
        companiment to his singing was the dull thud of the blows which
        New York State Troopers and the State park police rained upon the
        heads and bodies of his supporters. Robeson sang to an audience
        of 20,000 in a 27-acre meadow surrounded by 700 State Troopers,
        12 busloads of State park police, the entire police force of
        Peekskill, every available man the sheriff's office could muster
        and 300 special deputies. Robeson sang; and his booming voice,
        amplified by loudspeakers as much as possible, drowned out the
        drums, bugles and fifes and the sound of jeering and marching
        of some 2,000 veterans who paraded in protest at the entrance of
        the concert grove at Hollow Brook Golf Course. Despite the police
        protection, so many of his followers were brutally beaten that the
        Peekskill Hospital announced that it was filled to capacity two
        hours after the concert...., concludes Hicks.

1147.   "Nightmare in Peekskill," <u>Nation</u>, Vol. 169, No. 11, September 10,
        1949, pp. 243-244.

        The article states: "We hope, and have a right to expect, that
        Governor Thomas Dewey will act on that sentiment in dealing with
        the disgraceful riots near Peekskill, in which attempts were
        literally made "to beat down ideas with a club." Through the wel-
        ter of reports and statements on the affair certain plain facts
        emerged: a group of veterans' organizations, acting collectively,
        set out to stop an open-air concert to have been given by Paul
        Robeson, whose warped political views have nothing to do with his
        right to speak, much less with his right to sing. 'Our objective,"
        an American Legion commander said after the first riot, 'was to
        prevent the Paul Robeson concert, and I think our objective was

(<u>Nation</u>)

reached.' In spite of the clearest kind of advance warning that
racial and political dynamite was to be set off, the authorities
not only gave the veterans permission to picket, which was legal
enough, but, whether by design or through the grossest negligence,
failed to police the gathering or even take minimum precautions.
What followed was almost inevitable: blocking of entrances, in-
cendiary epithets, open threats, and finally a free-for-all in which
cars were wrecked, scores were injured, racial tensions flared up,
and the lynch spirit arrived in Westchester, complete down to the
burning of crosses," states the writer. The article concludes:

> Paul Robeson's recent statements have been stupid
> and uncalled for, if not deliberately inflammatory,
> but the explosion at Peekskill was not merely anti-
> Communist. It was anti-Negro and anti-Semitic as
> well, charged with indiscriminate hatred. What was
> more horrifying than the ignorance of the veterans,
> who have done a fine week's work for Joseph Stalin,
> was the revelation of Nazi-like violence in the teen-
> agers, who carried out most of the terror. That is
> something that should haunt school officials, the
> parents, indeed all the citizens of Westchester
> County long after the Robeson nightmare is for-
> gotten.

1148. Rowe, Billy. "New York Cops Join 'Vets' in Shameful Spectacle,"
<u>Pittsburgh Courier</u>, September 10, 1949, pp. 1, 4.

The writer, theatrical editor of the <u>Courier</u>, covered the Robeson
concert and reports the following story. Some 1,200 officers of the
law were ordered by Governor Thomas E. Dewey to "keep the peace"
at Paul Robeson's Sunday concert, but their flying nightsticks
wrought as much mayhem in the rioting they helped carry out as
did the stones, clubs and bottles hurled by the "veterans" who
tried - unsuccessfully - to keep Robeson from singing. The officers
openly and brazenly broke the very laws they had sworn to uphold,
states Rowe. He declares: "Yes, Paul Robeson - American - came
back to Peekskill Sunday afternoon...just as he promised... and
Paul Robeson sang just as he had promised, in spite of the mobsters!
He came back in spite of the threats that had been made against
his life! But other so-called 'Americans,' with absolute dis-
regard for the Constitution of the United States and the constitution of New York State - policemen and veterans alike - executed
perfectly every disgraceful tactic which this nation has, in the
past, called 'Communist.'" The writer concludes:

> Many of these "World War II veterans" were just about
> 17 years old, which would have made them just 12 years
> old when World War II ended five years ago. But here
> they were! These young hoodlums - men, women and
> children - were, in every respect, Nazi storm-troopers,
> exact reproductions of Mussolini's Fascist, Dixie's
> infamous Ku Klux Klan and a mixture of Captain Kidd's
> murderous pirates! They were Georgia lynchers,
> Mississippi mobsters, Chicago Capone-era gangsters and
> thugs....and their ranks were more sharply emphasized

(Rowe, Billy)

> by the "defenders of law and order,' who Sunday
> trampled law and order - and the U.S. Constitution -
> in the dust. They stooped to an amazing low in
> American infamy....

1149.   "Communists Hail Heroism of Audience," Daily Worker, September 11,
        1949, p. 1.

This article states that the National Committee and the New York
State Committee of the Communist Party hailed the victory for free
speech won at the Paul Robeson concert near Peekskill and greeted
the 25,000 members of the heroic audience whose courage and discipline made the victory possible. The article went on to declare
that the crowd had been stirred to seething indignation and anger
by the officially inspired "spontaneous" fascist attack that had
prevented the original Robeson concert from taking place. They
recognized that the attempt to silence Robeson came because he
personifies the liberation struggles of more than 14 million
Negro Americans fighting lynch-terror, Jim Crow, and social,
political and economic enslavement; because Paul Robeson had uttered
aloud and unafraid the deep yearning and eagerness of millions of
Americans for peace, concludes the article.

1150.   "Demand Truman Act on New York Civil Rights," Daily Worker,
        September 11, 1949, p. 1.

The Civil Rights Congress sent a message to President Truman declaring that Federal action was needed at once "to protect the
lives and property of citizens, particularly lives and property
of Negro people." "We charge," the CRC states, "that not only
did Gov. Dewey fail to protect the civil rights of the thousands
who came to hear Paul Robeson sing on Sept. 4, but that such
failure, in the face of nationwide warnings, can only be explained
as an attack by him on the Negro people."

1151.   "Eyewitnesses Tell of Cops' Aid to Hoodlums," Daily Worker,
        September 11, 1949, p. 1.

According to this report, countless eyewitnesses to the Peekskill
violence called and visited the Daily Worker and told their stories
of what happened to them at the Paul Robeson concert.

1152.   "How the Press Handled Peekskill," Daily Worker, September 11,
        1949, p. 1.

This article states that the profit press yesterday had to report
how mobsters attacked the Robeson concert audience, although the
papers tried to minimize the violence and absolve police of com-
plicity. An effort was made to characterize the affair as a "teen
agers" outbreak, concludes the article. The newspapers referred
to in the article were: New York Herald Tribune, New York Times,
New York Daily News, and the New York Mirror.

1153.   "Information Wanted on Peekskill Guilt," Daily Worker, September 11, 1949, p. 4.

This article wanted people to come forward and help identify hoodlums, policemen, state troopers, special deputies or public officials who had anything to do with the attacks on the audience of Paul Robeson. The Civil Rights Congress also wanted interested persons to contact them immediately so that they would record what individuals saw.

1154.   North, Joseph. "Free Speech Victory Won at Peekskill, 25,000 Hear Paul Robeson; Police-Led Fascist Rampage," Daily Worker, September 11, 1949, p. 1.

Mr. North surmises that an epic in our nation's history was written last week when Paul Robeson returned to sing to 25,000 Americans within a mile of the galley where Kluxers and Legion vigilantes ambushed his concert the previous Sunday and tried to murder him. He states that when Paul Robeson appeared, the crowd stood spontaneously to welcome him - the great leader and symbol of democracy, of the Negro people, of democratic culture.

1155.   "Robeson Ruckus," Newsweek, Vol. 34, No. 11, September 12, 1949, p. 23.

The article states at 6 a.m. buses packed with "Robeson guards" began to roll into the former Hollow Brook Country Club in Upper Westchester County, breaking the Sunday quiet. Quickly and efficiently, the 2,500 guards deployed. At strategic spots empty pop bottles were neatly stacked in "ammunition" piles. Bats and broomsticks were at the ready. Then, at 2 p.m., Paul Robeson was ready to sing his defiance of the "Fascist and Reactionaries" who broke up his Peekskill concert the previous week, states the author. In a booming baritone the pro-Communist Negro told the cheering audience: "I am here to applaud you." Then he went into his concert repertory. When he had finished, he was quietly scooted away in a car. After that, the battle began. While the 15,000 Communists and sympathizers waited for word that it was "safe" to leave, a group of demonstrators tried to break through the police lines. Repulsed, they formed some distance down the road. As cars and buses began pulling out, they were met by a shower of pebbles which quickly turned into a barrage of stones and heavy rocks. Windows were shattered and cars overturned. Before the teen-age mob could be dispersed, four persons had been seriously hurt and more than 100 others suffered minor injuries. The third finger of a young woman's hand was severed. Irving Potash, one of the defendants in the Communist conspiracy trial, was hit in the eye. Twenty-six persons were arrested. By nightfall the Peekskill area began to quiet down. With the aid of anti-Communist hotheads the Communists had won a smashing propaganda triumph, concludes the article.

1156. Hallett, Robert M. "Peekskill Combats Element that Breeds Racial
       Bias," Christian Science Monitor, September 13, 1949, p. 1.

       The author states that some resident of the Peekskill area said
       that the spark that provided the violence in Peekskill was the
       pre-concert publicity. Mr. Robeson had sung there in previous years
       without major disturbance. The residents declared the first
       Robeson concert in 1949 might have been held with little public
       stir but for an article in the Peekskill Evening Star stating that
       the concert was to be sponsored by subversive organizations. In
       an editorial on the same day of the first concert, the Star said
       in part: "....The time for tolerant silence that signifies
       approval is running out." The paper later reported preparations
       by "angry" veterans groups. Subsequently perhaps sensing that the
       protest movement might get out of hand, declares Mr. Hallet, The
       Star attempted by editorials to ally the violent feelings of the
       Community. But angry citizens once aroused, were not easily
       quieted, concludes the writer.

1157. "CIO News Denounces Peekskill Outrage," Daily Worker, September 14,
       1949, p. 4.

       This article records that a leading article in the current CIO
       News, official organ of the CIO, assailed mob action in Peekskill
       and pointed out that "nobody who believes in civil liberties can
       find any justification for the type of mob riots" which accompanied
       both Paul Robeson concerts. The Franklin D. Roosevelt Chapter of
       the American Veterans Committee and the Citizen Committee Against
       Mob Violence condemned the mob violence at Paul Robeson's Concert.

1158. North, Joseph. "Klansman Warns of More Peekskills," Daily Worker,
       September 15, 1949, p. 5.

       This article states that Edward J. Smythe sent a letter to a re-
       sident of Westchester after the Klan burned a cross at the first
       Robeson concert at Peekskill which was ambushed by vigilantes in
       an effort to murder Paul Robeson. The letter states that the
       Klan was stronger in New York State today than ever. "Some of
       your highest officials and big business executives are joining
       it," Smythe wrote.

1159. Editorial. "Paul Robeson," The Dispatcher, September 16, 1949,
       Editorial Page.

       The editor discusses the Peekskill riot. He wrote: "Two attacks
       upon peaceable assemblies have been at Peekskill, New York. In
       the first instance veterans' organizations announced that they
       would parade in protest against a concert by Paul Robeson. Ap-
       parently the veterans had been incited by false newspaper reports
       and editorials regarding statements which Paul Robeson has made.
       In the first attack the veterans and hoodlums stoned, kicked and
       beat Negroes, even including aged women. In the second instance,
       after Paul Robeson had announced that he would not be initmidated
       nor would the people who backed him be intimidated, certain dirty
       elements operating under the name of "veterans" organized another
       attack and Governor Dewey of New York supposedly ordered the State

(The Dispatcher)

police actually led the attack. We know that they guided the automobiles of concert-goers into blind alleys where they knew hoodlums were waiting for them. We know the State Troopers then broke
windshields with their billies and gave tickets to drivers with
broken windshields. Even the photographs taken by the apologetic
venal press show State Troopers grinning broadly as skulls are
cracked by misguided fascist youth...."

1160. "D.A. Denies Bias Sparked N.Y. Riot," Afro-American, September 17,
1949, p. 6.

According to this article District Attorney George M. Fanelli said
at the scene of the Robeson rioting that the happenings in and
around Peekskill had no connections whatever with racial discrimination. The D.A. also asserted that he felt the beating given the
colored men had any racial connections. Mr. Fanelli said all the
colored people in Peekskill were "100% American and are not looking
for trouble." Mr. Fanelli had just finished pointing out that
"very few colored people" have gone into the concert area when six
busloads of them arrived at that moment from Harlem. He flushed
as the buses rolled up but did not comment, concludes the article.

1161. Editorial. "Mrs. FDR Acts Like the President," Afro-American,
September 17, 1949, p. 4.

The editor argues: "Mrs. Eleanor Roosevelt last week condemned
the Peekskill riots. She said: 'This is not the thing we believe
in. If he (Robeson) wants to give a concert or speak his mind in
public, no one should prevent him from doing so. No one who dis-
agrees is obliged to stay or even to go hear him. It is disgraceful to allow this kind of lawlessness.' President Truman at his
press conference last week, when asked to comment on the Peekskill
mess, said he endorsed Mrs. Roosevelt's views, declares the
editor. Why didn't the President speak first? After all he is
the elected spolesman for all the people. The editor concludes:
"Here we have Mrs. Roosevelt acting like a President of the U.S.
and President Truman acting like an ordinary citizen.""

1162. Editorial. "Dewey Should Crack Heads," Afro-American, September
17, 1949, p. 4.

The editor asserts, in part: "Governor Dewey has spoken out
strongly agsinst the Peekskill riots, but he hasn't acted. We
think he will. Some state police and angry local county deputies
beat more heads of Robeson supporters than did the veterans. Most
of the time when rioting prevails, the police are responsible
either because they take the lead or because they turn their
backs. The cops did a beautiful job on Robeson followers. A real
investigation by Governor Dewey should bring about dismissals of
guilty police and do nothing district attorneys. The cops, chief
law-breakers, in this case, must be punished, Governor, if you
want the rest of the country to be proud of New York and of your
administration," concludes the editor.

1163. Hicks, James L. "Officials Try to Whitewash Robeson Riot,"
       Afro-American, September 17, 1949, p. 12.

       According to this newspaperman, the report handed in by District
       Attorney George M. Fanelli amounts to an official "white wash"
       of the actions of State Troopers, Park Police and special deputies
       who initiated the violence themselves. As one who stood only a
       few feet from Mr. Fanelli near the main entrance to the concert
       area for the greater portion of the day (standing near him was
       the safest place in Peekskill), the writer found it hard to believe
       that Mr. Fanelli's report to Governor Dewey was an account of the
       same incidents which both of us witnessed....

1164. "Ill-Feeling, Witch Hunts," Afro-American, September 17, 1949,
       p. 12.

       According to this article, Peekskill, New York, was not the same
       after Paul Robeson's concerts there. The concerts had wrought
       havoc with the emotions of its 18,600 residents. Racial anta-
       gonism had reached its zenith, despite reports that persons of
       minority groups have no cause to fear. The article also declares
       that all Jews were communists and they were in sympathy with
       Paul Robeson.

1165. "Nation's Dailies see Peekskill Riot as Violation of Principles
       of Democracy: Even Those which Oppose Robeson Agree Vets, Police
       Erred in Attack on Supporters," Afro-American, September 17, 1949,
       p. 12.

       According to this article with almost perfect accord, newspapers
       commenting editorially on the Peekskill riot last Sunday termed
       the actions of the veterans and other belligerents, violations of
       the American principle of fair play and democracy. Although few
       expressed sympathy for Paul Robeson and those who went to Peekskill
       to hear him sing, all admitted that the riot could not be condoned,
       even those most antagonistic to Robeson and the left-wing element
       of this country, states the article. Some of the newspapers in-
       cluded comments from the New York Times, New York World-Telegram,
       Newark Evening News, Baltimore Morning Sun, New York Daily,
       Richmond News Leader.

1166. "O'Dwyer Blasts Peekskill Mobs: Mayor Regrets Westchester's Con-
       cert Riots," New York Age, September 17, 1949, p. 1.

       Mayor William O'Dwyer spoke to the New York State Convention of
       the CIO and declares: "Paul Robeson has a right to express his
       beliefs, no matter how violently we disagree. Organized labor
       must not permit the forces of reaction to rob us of our heritage.
       This means that we must defend the right of every person to speak
       no matter how violently we disagree with the thoughts expressed...
       This means that mob violence and mob rule are outrageous and un-
       American, whether they occur in Alabama or in Peekskill."

1167. "Robeson Riot Cited as Mistrial Basis," Afro-American, September
       17, 1949, p. 6.

       According to this article Judge Harold R. Medina rejected a defense
       motion for a mistrial of the eight month-old Communist trial, based
       on the grounds that the Peekskill riot was a "Conclusive manifesti-
       tation of the prejudice existing" against the 11 defendants.
       Although he called the stoning of buses and automobiles coming
       from the Paul Robeson rally Sunday, September 4, "an outrage,"
       the judge ruled that it had no connection with the trial in Federal
       District Court. He further remarked that the motion was "without
       merit and that it was aimed primarily at disrupting the trial,"
       concludes the article.

1168. "Truman Scores Riot at Peekskill," Afro-American, September 17,
       1949, p. 3.

       President Truman last Thursday indorsed Mrs. Eleanor Roosevelt's
       view in which she condemned mob violence following the Paul
       Robeson concert at Peekskill, New York. Mrs. Roosevelt was re-
       ported to have declared: "One hundred and forty-five people were
       injured. Fifty buses were stoned, and a number of private care,
       many of which did not contain people who had been at this concert,
       were molested and damaged. This is not the type of thing that we
       believe in in the United States. If peaceful picketing leads to
       this, all the pickets do is to give the Communists good material
       for propaganda. I dislike everything that Paul Robeson is now
       saying. I am opposed to him politically and I think he is doing
       a great harm to his own people. But if he wants to give a concert
       or speak his mind in public, no one should prevent him from doing
       so."

1169. "Paul Robeson Demands Arrest of Mob Bosses," New York Age, September
       24, 1949, p. 32.

       This reporter states that following the surprise indictment of six
       persons, one the son of the chief of police, in the infamous
       Peekskill Riots, Paul Robeson, at whose two Sunday musicals the
       mob violence took place, demanded that the Westchester Summer Grand
       Jury get the "real bosses" who inspired and egged on the so-called
       veterans and others into making the event a major disturbance.
       Robeson declares:
           The real criminals in the Peekskill massacre of civil
           and human rights are still untouched. Under the over-
           whelming pressure of outraged public opinion, the in-
           dictments already passed down are but a step. The
           real criminals, the bosses - rest smugly and untouched
           in plain sight of all to see, while their stooges
           face the music. The so-called leaders who openly
           and viciously encouraged the hoodlum elements to
           attack peaceful citizens on two successive Sundays at
           Peekskill, are laughing and waiting to launch another
           fascist attack on human rights. I refer to those re-
           actionary, anti-Negro, anti-Semitic elements which
           together are posing today a threat to the whole funda-
           mental or liberty and the progress of minority groups.

1170.   "Ban on Robeson Asked: Legion Urges Bowles to Judicial Powers of
        Office," New York Times, October 1, 1949, p. 15.

        The article states that the New Haven County members of the Ameri-
        can Legion asked Gov. Chester Bowles to "exercise the judicial
        powers of your office," in preventing Paul Robeson from making a
        public appearance in Connecticut. A spokesman for the Legion
        said the move was designed to prevent "another Peekskill (N.Y.)
        incident." Ironically Mr. Robeson was a resident of Enfield,
        Connecticut.

1171.   Editorial.   "The Peekskill Blues," New York Age, October 1, 1949,
        p. 15.

        The editor contends that he does not support in any manner the so-
        called Communist line. Neither do we uphold any individual or
        group who would deny the right to free speech to anyone except by
        lawful means. Whatever the purpose of the Robeson concert at
        Peekskill, the fact remains that permits had been granted for the
        affair or at least the police knew everything there was to be
        known in advance of everything, states the writer. The permission
        granted the "veterans" to stage a counter parade smack in the
        thick of things in which the concert crowd would actually be in
        contact with an opposing element looks like a deliberate attempt
        by somebody to bring on what took place. Sure, the veterans had
        every right to a counter parade. No precedent was being set by
        the situation. That sort of thing occurs almost everywhere in
        labor picketing and protests. But here things were different.
        People had been steamed up to white hot hatred by propaganda and
        agitation on both sides and when they were finally let loose at
        one another, somebody was bound to get hurt. And hundreds were,
        the editor states. He concludes: "The supporters of Paul Robeson
        used the incident to project Robeson further into the world spot-
        light as something of a martyred version of the persecuted Negro."

1172.   "Robesonites Visit State Capitol to Protest Peekskill Riot,"
        Afro-American, October 1, 1949, p. 3.

        This is a photo of Robeson supporters. Flanked by two lines of
        Albany police about 200 marchers, from New York City, paraded to
        the State Capitol in Albany to protest the disorders in Peekskill
        when followers of Pro-Red Paul Robeson were stoned by anti-red
        hecklers.

1173.   North, Joseph.   "Peekskill, N.Y.," Worker Magazine, October 2,
        1949, Section 2, pp. 1, 2, 10.

        The writer concludes:
            The violence that occurred in Peekskill was brought
            about because of the poison of the press, the lynch
            spirit of Judge Medina's courtroom and the witch-
            hunts of the Truman administration.

1174. Hallett, Robert M. "Freedom House Offers Tips to Avoid 'Peekskill Incidents,'" Christian Science Monitor, October 10, 1949, p. 1.

Freedom House offered fifteen suggestions on how to avoid "Peekskill Incidents." Robert P. Patterson, president of Freedom House states:

> Paul Robeson and his fellow members of the Communist Party won a victory in Peekskill, N.Y. They attracted the attention of more people than they had bargained for. They disrupted lives and the customs of more people than they could have hoped for. Had their meeting been completely prevented, their victory would have been complete. Their objective is martyrdom, their technique violence. In their wake in the area surrounding Peekskill they have left the social bacteria of insecurity, anti-Semitism, fear, and hatred for the colored people. This victory elsewhere must be prevented, less to cry over yesterday's spilled milk than to cry over tomorrow's spilled blood.

1175. Perry, Pettis. "Next Stage in the Struggle for Negro Rights," Political Affairs, Vol. 35, No. 1, October, 1949, pp. 33-46.

Paul Robeson is mentioned throughout the article. The writer asserts Peekskill had created great alarm and indignation among the masses of Negro people. They see Peekskill as a real threat to their own well-being and to that of all liberty-loving people. It is not accidental that the entire Negro press from one end of the country to the other has reacted and continues to react in a very determined manner to this terror, states Perry. Ever-growing sections of the Negro people are taking a stand against it, and even though many of them are not yet ready to support Paul Robeson's advanced anti-imperialist stand, they are solidly determined that his right to be heard must be maintained at all costs. It was also surmised that there is an increasing understanding on the part of the Negro people that the reactionaries, in their attack against Robeson, are striking at the very heart of the main desires and aspirations of the Negro people.

1176. Hallett,Robert M. "ACLU Terms Peekskill Riots of Vital National Significance," Christian Science Monitor, December 8, 1949, p. 1.

This article discusses the American Civil Liberties Union's 43 page study of Violence in Peekskill. The ACLU was wholly opposed to Communist or Communist-front agencies. It declares: "But when Americans condone violence in denying them their right to hold a peaceful concert on private property, they aid Communist propaganda all over the world, which delights in claiming our boasted democracy as a sham. Further, we lower out standings to the level of the Communist police-state which denied all civil liberties to opponents."

1177. "Peekskill - Guilt is Now in the Open," Daily Worker, December 18, 1949, p. 4.

This article declares that the inquiry into the Peekskill atrocities by the American Civil Liberties Union has fully confirmed the charges of the concert-goers: underlying the violence was the ugly Hitler fact of anti-Jewish and anti-Negro hatred. "The unprovoked rioting was fostered largely by anti-semitism," concludes the reporter.

1178. Scroog, Arnold. "ACLU Survey Shows Cops Allowed Mob to Attack at Peekskill," Daily Worker, December 8, 1949, p. 1.

The American Civil Liberties Union (ACLU) charged that the West-chester County Police "permitted the assault" on the Paul Robeson concert near Peekskill. According to the reporter, by implication, the report of the ACLU also laid blame for the fascist attack on the federal government's cold war policy. "They (the mobsters) believed that in denying freedom of speech to a political minority they were following the lead of federal authorities," said the report.

1179. "Robeson, 27 Others Sue for $2,020,000 for Peekskill Damage," Daily Worker, December 16, 1949, p. 4.

This report states that Paul Robeson, Howard Fast, the Civil Rights Congress and 25 victims of the Peekskill mobsters, filed suit yes-terday in the U.S. Federal Court here asking a total of $2,020,000 for personal injuries. The complaints named officials of New York State, Westchester County and Peekskill officials as well as the leaders of the organized violence. The officials were charged - under the 14th Amendment - with conspiracy to deprive Americans of their civil rights. Robeson told the newspapermen how his own car was attacked and the driver narrowly escaped injury from the flailing club of a state trooper. He said his recent tour across the country revealed that most Americans were horrified over the Peekskill atrocities. "They understood it as a threat against all Americans," he said. He ascribed his interest in the Peeks-kill concert, where he had sung the past three years, to his desire to bring music, culture, to the masses of people. The singer spoke movingly of the concert-goers who came for music and re-ceived rocks. A number of them who were badly injured appeared at the press conference to recount their experiences, states the article.

18. POLITICS

1180. Sullivan, Ed. "Little Old New York," New York Daily News, October 31, 1943.

The columnist called the article "Saga of a Nonpareil." He dis-cusses what some of Paul Robeson's classmates at Rutgers University

(Sullivan, Ed)

were doing. Mr. Sullivan quoted George Foster Sanford, Rutgers coach, as saying that what Jim Thorpe had been to the Indian race, in athletics, Robeson had been to the Negro race, but Robeson had gone far beyond that. The coach said that in his day at Yale University he'd seen many great athletes, but that Robeson was one of those Nonpareils that come along once in an age. Mr. Sullivan asked the question, what other worlds now are left for Rutgers' Robeson to conquer? He argues that the only big role left for him to play, now, is as spokesman for his race, and this drama in which he must play a leading part:

But in this, Paul Robeson must be aware of the Iagos who murmur innuendoes that inflame the Negro and arouse the whites.... The issue must be resolved in the realm of reason, and it will require steady nerves, great courage and greater patience on the part of great Americans.... Such a man as Robeson, revered by his own race, and admired by the white race, can here achieve the most important triumph that ever had distinguished him.... If he can do this, what has gone before in his career will be success in minature.... Here, indeed, is a task for an All-American.... On both sides there are men of good will, on both sides there are men who are fiercely intolerant.... The kickoff will send these two teams crashing into each other.... Robeson has figured in many such kick-offs, and has won; he must win this one, for his country.

1181.   "Lincoln Extolled to World Audience: Robeson is a Speaker," New York Times, February 13, 1944, p. 35.

There was a celebration from New York City that was opened by Paul Robeson. He said never had the occasion seemed more fitting to him than on Lincoln's Birthday. Mr. Robeson who later introduced the Archbishop of Canterbury said: "You on the other side of the narrow Atlantic know that name - Lincoln - as we know John Milton, and Garibaldi; Lafayette and Sun Yat Sen and Lenin. The names are known - they and a hundred like them - and they live forever in the minds and hearts of men for one reason mainly: they stand for liberty."

1182.   Conrad, Earl. "Robeson Grows in Stature as Symbol of Negro People," Chicago Defender, December 12, 1944, p. 1.

Mr. Conrad argues that Paul Robeson has been called "the greatest personality of the age." He declares: "It is very possible that time - that resolver and estimator of all things - will endorse this brief clause as a correct and definitive summation of the man. Kings pass and their names are soon forgotten. Conquerors are remembered briefly and bitterly. Only the liberators are immortal - and Paul Robeson is a liberator - of the human spirit. He is a liberator of the human spirit, but equally too of men's bodies. And he is loved today, in a people's age, because he is a people's figure: and for myself I prefer to consider our times, the times

(Conrad, Earl)

of the war of survival, the times of the great Twentieth Century
as simply: Paul Robeson's Age." The writer concludes:
      Paul Robeson reminds me of only one other American,
      Benjamin Franklin. Both have a similar faculty for
      all-sideness, for many and diverse talents, for hardi-
      hood, for seeing the abstract and the concrete, for
      taking part in the daily life, each of his own times.
      He is still a young man. His main contribution will
      come in the sphere of social, political, human relations.
      His music may vanish. It will be only a legend and a
      memory. Even while we live his music must be for
      us whatever it may. But his impact on the social
      structures of our day, that will remain, affecting
      the lives of generations to come. Paul Robeson has
      dared to travel along many paths, but it is his
      pioneering into the human future that has already
      struck the national imagination. I am looking for-
      ward to what it will do to him, where it will lead
      him. I invite you to watch... and follow.

1183. "Protect Negro, Robeson's Plea," New York Daily News, September
       19, 1946.

Paul Robeson, Chairman of the American Crusade to End Lynching,
warned that unless the Department of Justice acts to protect the
Negro in the South, there will be "enough disturbance to warrant
federal intervention."

1184. "Truman Balks at Lynch Action," Chicago Defender, September 28,
       1946, p. 1.

In terms which left no doubt in the minds of the delegation from
the American Crusade to End Lynching, President Truman emphatically
refused to take the initiative to end mob violence and the spread
of terrorism in America. The delegation, led by Paul Robeson,
chairman, and Mrs. Harper Sibley, President of the United Council
of Church Women and wife of the former president of the United
States Chamber of Commerce, asked the President to make a public
statement expressing his views on lynching and to recommend a de-
finite legislative and educational program to end the disgrace of
mob violence, states the author. Despite strong urgings from
several members of the delegation, President Truman inssited that
the moment was not propitious for a forthright statement from the
Chief Executive, and that further, the whole question of lynching
and mob violence was one to be dealt with in political terms and
strategy. He stated such a strategy must be worked out by responsible political leadership and patience must attend the final
solution.... Robeson tried to show the President that the mood
of the Negro had changed. He said returning veterans are showing
signs of restiveness and indicated that they are determined to get
the justice here they had fought for abroad. Robeson warned that
this restiveness might produce an emergency situation which would
require Federal intervention. The President, shaking his fist,
stated this sounded like a threat, according to this article.

1185.   "Pioneers in the Struggle Against Segregation," Survey Graphic,
        Vol. 36, January, 1947, pp. 90-91.

        It was stated that Paul Robeson, concert singer and actor, ac-
        claimed in Europe as well as America, used his great talents to
        give voice to worldwide democratic aspirations.

1186.   Keelan, Harry.   "Voice in the Wilderness," Afro-American, February
        1, 1947, p. 5.

        Mr. Keelan reports that Paul Robeson announced that he is leaving
        the concert stage to enter politics! This is a most significant
        event, not only for Afro-America but for colored people the world
        over, states the writer. He said that for Paul Robeson is a citizen
        of the world, an internationalist. His politics rise above the
        puerile, Democratic-Republican, one-party system of the United
        States, and reach up into the mature, proclaimed right, center and
        left of world politics.... So Paul Robeson has turned to the
        political left. As a citizen of the world, he knows world history.
        He has followed the revolutions of France, Russia, Mexico, China
        and Spain, also the Rooseveltian revolution in America. He has
        seen counter-revolution in Spain and America! Because of his know-
        ledge of world politics, he will not feel the insecurity of Ameri-
        cans venturing to the left for the first time. Therefore, he will
        not waste valuable time kicking around Communists, but will save
        his blows for his real enemies, the Tafts, the Vanderbergs and
        others on the political right, according to the author. Mr.
        Keelan concludes:
            No other American in the political field, including
            the President of the United States and the Secretary
            of State, has such knowledge. It cannot be gained
            by over-the-teacup displomacy! And finally, Robeson
            is a colored man. This means that he is sensitive
            to human suffering, and moves among people who are
            more considerate of others than are the whites.
            Thus armed with more intelligence, more ability,
            more sensitivity and more knowledge than any white,
            English-speaking politician or statesman, there is
            no reason why he cannot lead Afro-Americans out of
            darkness into the light of world politics. Instead
            of always bringing up the rear in the march of
            human progress, the banner of Afro-America can be
            planted by Robeson in the vanguard beside those of
            Russia, China and India!

1187.   Editorial. "Paul Robeson," Boston Chronicle, February 8, 1947.

        The writer comments on Paul Robeson's decision to speak out against
        race hatred, prejudice, and injustices in the world and specifi-
        cally in the United States. The article, declares, in part: "The
        so-called 'ivory tower' practitioners of the arts have never been
        popular among the Negro people, who have correctly recognized the
        potency of art as a weapon in their struggle for the freedom in-
        herent in their enjoyment of democratic rights. For that reason
        their souls have warmed most ardently to those Negro artists in
        the fields of music, painting, sculpture, and literature who have

(<u>Boston Chronicle</u>)

tried to enhance better interracial relations by emphasizing the
cultural heritage of their own people. An artist with Mr. Robeson's acute perception was bound to arrive at this conclusion,
though it is surely no disparagement of him to state that he merely
reflects, with the intensity of genius, the unanimous awareness
of all Negro artists worthy of the name...."

1188.   "Paul Robeson -- Freedom Fighter," <u>People's Voice</u>, April 26, 1947,
         p. 6.

This article states that wherever men are fighting for their
freedom, there Paul Robeson is. New Yorkers will again honor
Paul this Friday when the Council on African Affairs, of which he
is chairman, holds its "Rally for African and Colonial Freedom"
at 71st Regimental Armory (34th and Park Avenue), April 25, at
8:30 p.m. Robeson will be the main speaker at the rally dedicated
to "stopping imperialist agression now."

1189.   "Connecticut Official Asks Ban on Robeson," <u>New York Times</u>, April
         24, 1947, p. 37.

Willard R. Rogers, Chairman of the States Development Commission
said he had made a formal request to State Police Commissioner
Edward J. Hickey "to keep this man out" if it developed that "there
is resentment over Robeson's return to Connecticut." Mr. Rogers
said he was "disgusted" with the remarks Mr. Robeson made at the
World Peace Congress in Paris. The political activist told the
Congress that American Negroes never would fight against Russia.
Rogers wanted to bar Robeson from Connecticut, where he had his
home in Enfield, Connecticut. It was also pointed out in the
article that Walter White, secretary of the National Association
for the Advancement of Colored People, said that Mr. Robeson's
remarks in Paris did not represent the views of the majority of
American Negroes.

1190,   "Crucifixion of Paul: Paul Blasted by Press in India," <u>Afro-</u>
         <u>American</u>, May 24, 1947.

The press in India blasted America and the American press for the
crucifixion of Paul Robeson. The <u>Hindu</u>, India's greatest newspaper
declares in an editorial:
        If Paul Robeson is un-American, so much the worse for
        America. Robeson has been to Russia where he found
        that non-white persons were treated as equals by the
        government and the people of the Soviet Union. It is
        worth noting that the colored press, which speaks for
        about one-tenth of the population in the United States,
        has always been vocal in supporting the movement of
        colonial peoples for independence. Colored Americans
        do not want a special place for themselves. They want
        political and social equality. Like Robeson, they ask
        that their progress is linked with the emergence of
        suppressed peoples in other countries, and realize that
        democracy at home will come only when nations cease to

(Afro-American)

> dabble in power politics and put their own houses
> in order.

1191. "Bans Book on Paul Robeson," New York Times, March 12, 1948, p. 21.

The West Virginia Library Commission removed Paul Robeson:
Citizen of the World from its list of books recommended for children. Members of the Commission objected to the book on the
grounds of Mr. Robeson's political views.

1192. "To Fight Poll Tax," New York Times, May 16, 1948, p. 20.

This article states that Paul Robeson, Chairman of the Council on
African Affairs, announced that a non-partisan delegation from
various sections of the country would go to Washington, D.C.,
to demand immediate enactment of anti-poll tax and anti-lynching
legislation. Mr. Robeson, a member of the National Wallace-for-
President Committee, said the planned demonstration had no affilia-
tion with the Wallace campaign.

1193. "People in the News: Paul Robeson, Negro Singer and Leader Has
Been a Star Athlete, Lawyer, Actor," Washington Post, June 1, 1948.

This article discusses how Paul Robeson got started acting and
singing. The writer states that racial discrimination and a brief
experience in amateur theatricals led him to the stage where he
took the lead in a revival of Eugene O'Neill's "Emperor Jones."
He was unkonwn as a singer then, but a jungle scene gave him what
later turned out to be his great opportunity. The script called
Brutus Jones to whistle a Negro spiritual, but since Robeson
couldn't whistle, he sang a song instead about "John Henry," the
mythical hero of the Negro race. The audience thought he was
terrific and from then on it was a rapid succession of triumphs on
stage, radio, screen and concert platforms around the globe, declared the writer. But this was not enough. "It became clear to
me while I was traveling around Europe in the pre-Hitler days that
the artist is part of the social scheme, too, and obviously cannot
live apart from the world in an ivory tower. He must concern himself with social problems if he is to be a real artist of the
people," argues Robeson. The writer asserts that in 1940 he opposed
conscription. Always he fought segregation, refusing to appear
before segregated audiences. His rich baritone, which could have
brought him a lucrative income, was channeled in 1947 into a "two
year fight on fascism" - recitals were shelved while Robeson
took up the platform cudgels for the forces he felt were right,
suggests the article.

1194. "The New Party," New Republic, Vol. 119, July 26, 1948, pp. 17-18.

The article states that Paul Robeson's greatest value to the Progressive Party is probably symbolic. His artistic position is unchallenged. To other members of the Negro race he -- the man of
education, talent and renown -- is the personification of what
they, too, can accomplish, states the author. Robeson's own

(New Republic)

political creed is broader than mere advocacy of rights for one
particular group. "Since his own people have the least freedom,
he concentrates his most fiery efforts on helping them. But his
interest in all cultures is universal and his knowledge is extraordinary," the author concludes.

1195. "The Case of Paul Robeson," New York Times, April 25, 1949, p. 22.

This was an editorial in the New York Times. The editor declares
that Paul Robeson will do himself and the cause of the American
Negro a disservice if he carries out his resolution not to sing
again but to devote his life to making speeches.... Mr. Robeson
has advanced the cause of the American Negro by being an outstanding human being. He can do nothing but harm by making himself a propagandist of a party line,states the writer. He concludes:
        ....We do not believe that making speeches of any sort
        can do as much for the American Negro as is being done
        by great American Negroes who in their own personalities
        demonstrate how hollow prejudice and how ill grounded
        is discrimination. Nothing that Mr. Robeson can say
        will be half as important as the very fact of the
        existence of Roland Hayes and Ralph Bunche, of Joe
        Louis and Jackie Robinson, of Marian Anderson and
        Dorothy Maynor; yes, and of Paul Robeson....

1196. Bibb, Joseph D. "Who Speaks for Us?" Pittsburgh Courier, May 7,
       1949, p. 12.

The writer points out that neither Paul Robeson nor Walter White
of the National Association for the Advancement of Colored People,
have been elected or chosen to voice the opinions and sentiments
of the darker minority. He concludes: "....Paul Robeson's un-
wise and untimely pronouncement, and Walter White's highly pre-
sumptive and unauthorized rebuttal open up the entire issue of
self-selected spokesmen for the race. Since the influence of
Tuskegee waxed and waned, since the yellow leaf of Du Bois and the
decline of Randolph and the passing of power of the high church-
men, there has been no recognized leadership among colored
Americans...."

1197. "Robeson Unafraid," New York Age, July 2, 1949, p. 17.

This was an editorial that appeared in the newspaper. The editor
declared: "Paul Robeson, Sr., doesn't scare easily. The husky
one-time all-American end at Rutgers seems to have gotten the jump
on his foes in the all-out battle between Communism and Capitalism.
All of this adds up to one fact: Despite lynchings, discrimination,
segregation, sharp racial hatreds, America remains the only nation
where a man can speak his piece without fear of sudden liquidation,
unless, we suppose, he's in Mississippi or Georgia. Those states
you know, are in a class by themselves. We suspect, however,
that a man of Robeson's stature and caliber, would speak his lines
with the lyncher's rope in the background."

1198. "Back Robeson Peace Stand," Daily Worker, July 18, 1949, p. 2.

All of the 1,300 delegates to the Bill of Rights Congress signed
a statement concerning Paul Robeson. It said, in part: "We the
undersigned Negro delegates to this Bill of Rights Conference
in New York City hereby declare for all the world to see that Paul
Robeson does, indeed, speak for us, not only in his fight for full
rights for Negro democratic rights, but also in his fight for
peace...."

1199. "Robeson Faces Picketings: VFW Urges All Members to Get on Line
in Newark," New York Times, July 20, 1949, p. 7.

George Stevens, Essex County (N.J.) Commander of the Veterans of
Foreign Wars urged all members of the forty-six posts under his
jurisdiction to picket the appearance of Paul Robeson denouncing
him as a Communist sympathizer. Robeson was scheduled to attend
a rally in Newark sponsored by the Civil Rights Congress. Mr.
Robeson was expected to urge Governor Alfred E. Driscoll "to
dismiss the frame-up indictments of the Trenton six," Negroes
were awaiting a new trial after reversal of their conviction on a
murder charge.

1200. Matthews, Ralph. "Paul Robeson: Patriot or Traitor?" Afro-
American, August 20, 1949, p. 7.

According to Mr. Matthews, there is nothing really wrong with Paul
Robeson. He is quite sane and purposeful. If there is anything
enigmatic about the socio-political situation revolving around
this man, it exists in the minds of those who are trying to figure
him out. When you talk with him awhile and listen to his hearty
laughter as rich as his booming baritone voice, watch his use of
histrionics as he illustrates a point, see him relaxed and calm
as he spreads his huge hulk of a body out in an easy chair, you
cannot help but ask why does America which once took him to her
bosom, now find him dangerous and menacing, states Matthews. The
writer asserts Robeson knows that the things whereof he speaks
and the things in which he believes are understood better and appreciated more by the great inarticulate mass who feel the things
he talks about, but have neither the statue or the wit to say them.
When Robeson says that "it is unthinkable that the colored people
would fight to defend those who have oppressed them for generations," he is translating into words the inner resentments of a
race. And when a few Americans of color raise their voices in
repudiation, they are not talking in the same language. Robeson,
a great scholar, a world traveler, a great artist and financially
independent, is talking to men of other races as an equal not as
a vassal, declares the writer. He speaks as an emancipated individual, not as one circumscribed and enmeshed in provincialism.
According to the author:
    He speaks not for the insignificant 15 million
    Americans struggling for crumbs in a predominantly
    white America where they will always be a minority,
    but he speaks for the hundreds of millions of black
    people in Africa and other sections of the world with
    whom he feels a kinship. Robeson knows that attacks

(Matthews, Ralph)

> on him are not at Robeson, the individual, but
> at Robeson the symbol of black emergence which has
> the audacity to stand up and talk back to the white
> man. Robeson knows that to destroy and discredit
> him as an individual will destroy a segment of the
> world revolution which is challenging the status quo.
> He knows that all the attempts to create the im-
> pression that he loves or is loyal to Russia are in
> fact an attempt to reduce the narrow naturalistic
> margins and broad ideological concept. If there is
> any mystery to Paul Robeson it is this: "By singing
> spirituals he can be popular and wealthy; by fighting
> for his beliefs, he becomes despised and doors closed
> against him." For the answer as to why he made this
> choice, you will have to search the deep recesses of
> his soul.

1201. "Robeson Applauded: Rightist Turns Leftist, Retracts Condemnations
of Singer After Plays are Denied to Negroes," Pittsburgh Courier,
September 10, 1949, p. 11.

According to the article Paul Robeson was applauded by a Houstonian
who lashed a series of plays being sponsored by Eddie Dowling for
1949-50 for calling to welcome Negroes in the audience. Robert
S. Browne wrote a letter to Mr. Dowling declaring that he was re-
tracting "any condemnation" that he had made against Robeson after
his "faith" in democracy was shaken. He applauded Robeson for
risking so much for the democratic spirit which our forefathers
meant to America.

1202. "The Robeson Plight," Atlanta Daily World, September 30, 1949.

This article declares that Paul Robeson and his family were beginning to feel the sting of rebuff, which the American public is
exercising against them in one way or another.... The writer
also asserts in Connecticut, at the Robesons' home, Mrs. Eslanda
Robeson is reported to have said: "I've decided that if anyone
makes any attempts to attack me, I will kill him." Living out of
the life of that sort of philosophy, Mrs. Robeson, the reporter
says, keeps all the doors locked in the big house and sleeps with
a business-looking hunting knife next to her pillow, as well as a
Beau automatic alarm. The author points out: "That's a tense and
singularly unfortunate sort of life to live in busy America. For
the great achievements of Mr. Robeson and his wife, too, we have
great esteem. But somehow, it is difficult to work up much genuine
sympathy for their public pronouncements against the country which
gave them the opportunities they now enjoy and against which they
speak so boldly, even with the services of local police to protect
them in their speeches and rantings."

1203. Editorial. "Ignore Him That's All," <u>Detroit News</u>, October 7, 1949, Editorial Page.

Paul Robeson was appearing in Detroit, Michigan, and this news-paper advised that all should ignore him. The editorial surmises, in part:
IGNORE HIM THAT'S ALL.... It would be hard to discover any evidence of persecution in the past of one so widely admired and acclaimed, in other times, as Paul Robeson has been. Veterans and other good citizens are wise to abstain from actions calculated to add color to the great singer's current delusion....

1204. "Facts in Our Times," <u>Michigan Chronicle</u>, October 8, 1949.

Rev. Horace White of the Detroit's Plymouth Congregational Church challenged Paul Robeson to a public debate. Rev. White states:
What I think is wrong and must be challenged is the feeling that in order to correct our inequitable situation, Negroes must find themselves into the position of error or by design of siding with Russia. Mr. Robeson, has allowed himself to be placed in the vortex of international trickery; but more than that he gives the impression to trying to drag the American Negro population with him. In so doing he is trying to remove the ground from under our feet, the very ground on which we must stand if we are to really fight for civil rights in this country. Robeson or any other Negro who hopes to really contribute to the betterment of the American Negro's lot must seek to make that contribution on the basis of the De-claration of Independence and the Constitution of the United States.

1205. "Robeson Won't Speak in Dixie," <u>New York Amsterdam News</u>, October 8, 1949, pp. 1, 34.

The article contends that Paul Robeson states that he would not make a singing-speaking tour through the Dixie states, particularly until the elections. According to this report Robeson compares his concerts in Peekskill, New York, and those held in Chicago and on the West Coast and declares that the Police in the latter two places maintained excellent order and protected him personally against any would-be attempts of violence. Robeson's West Coast concert was held in Los Angeles and was sponsored by the <u>California Eagle</u>, the oldest Negro newspaper in the West.

1206. Strout, Richard L. "Robeson Fails to Rally Any Incident at Washing-ton Meeting," <u>Christian Science Monitor</u>, October 14, 1949, p. 1.

This article states that Paul Robeson addressed an audience of 3,000 - two-thirds Blacks - in a Washington, D.C., sporting arena, under auspices showing every evidence of fellow-travelers or out-right Communist direction, states Mr. Strout. According to the writer for those seeing Mr. Robeson for the first time, it was an impressive sight. Between songs and harangues, he told something

(Strout, Richard L.)

of his life. He told how a sense of responsibility to the Negro
race had made him at college, after a day at football, throw himself after a few hours of sleep into his studies, to show that a
member of his race could meet Anglo-Saxons on equal ground.
Robeson states how at the height of his fame in 1944, he had
decided the time had come for him to step down to aid "the struggle
of my people." Mr. Strout concludes:

> The feeling grew as one listened of a tremendous
> new force unleashed among American Negroes by the
> presence of this powerful personality. The dis-
> heartening fact emerged that this great new power
> was running on a transmission belt from Moscow.
> Mr. Robeson did not speak with inclusive bitter-
> ness, but with a certain massive magnanimity
> regarding injustices to this race. He spoke, he
> insisted, not as a Negro but as an American...
> There was no disturbance at the Washington meeting.
> But that the 15,000,000 members of the Negro race
> are to be tempted by a radical leader of extra-
> ordinary power and persuasiveness there could be
> no doubt.

1207.   "'Impeach,' Says Robeson," New York Times, October 15, 1949, p. 3.

Paul Robeson told a cheering audience of several thousand in
Philadelphia that he would seek the impeachment of Federal Judge
Harold R. Medina, who presided over the trial of eleven top-
ranking Communists convicted in New York City. In addressing the
"freedom rally," he declares: "I shall go back to New York tomorrow to begin impeachment proceedings against the judge. It is
the course which American people, deprived of their rights under
the constitution, took in the days of Thomas Jefferson, and it is
the course we shall take today."

1208.   May, Benjamin E. "Whether Robeson Should or Should Not Wake Up,"
Pittsburgh Courier, October 15, 1949, p. 15.

The writer declares that up to now he had said nothing in print
about the recent controversy over the activities of Paul Robeson.
Robeson had been the object of attack ever since the reported
Paris speech and the Peekskill incident simply highlighted a
situation which was already in the making. He argues:

> Robeson is symbolic of something. His rise to fame
> in song and on the stage is symbolic of what is pos-
> sible for an extraordinary Negro to achieve in our
> country. But this behavior now is also symbolic of
> the discrimination, segregation, and injustice which
> the Negro Americans must endure in this country.
> Negroes may or may not agree with what Robeson is
> doing. Nevertheless, every sane, honest Negro must
> admit that Robeson is fighting against racial injustice
> and exploitation which every American who believes in
> justice and democracy should be fighting against....
> I believe Robeson is sincere. I believe he loves his

(May, Benjamin E.)

> people. I believe he has identified himself with
> suffering humanity everywhere. I think America should
> so radically amend her ways on the question of race
> that it would become increasingly impossible for
> Robeson, or any other Negro, to feel the necessity of
> doing what he is doing. Simply to damn Robeson is to
> deal with symptoms and not the disease. Let America
> eradicate the disease.

19. PROGRESSIVE PARTY

1209. "Committee Named for Wallace Race," New York Times, January 29,
1948, p. 8.

This article announced the formation of a National (Henry A.)
Wallace For President Committee. Paul Robeson along with Rexford
Tugwell and Jo Davidson were co-chairmen of the Committee.

1210. "The Baffling Mr. Wallace," New York Times, February 8, 1948,
Part 6, p. 47.

Paul Robeson attended a Chicago convention that was supporting
Henry A. Wallace for President of the United States. Robeson was
endorsing Mr. Wallace because: "I want to destroy fascism, and
to do it I'm prepared to accept the opposite form of dictatorship;
the brittle sophistry of the official pronouncements that highlighted all the weaknesses of American democracy and ascribed their
existence to such subjective villains as 'Wall Street Profiters'
and 'warmongers.'"

1211. "Robeson to be Honored by Conn. Progressives," Afro-American,
September 17, 1949, p. 12.

The Rev. Dudley H.W. Burr, state chairman of the Progressive Party,
announced at the party's local headquarters that Paul Robeson has
been invited to be the guest of honor at a State-wide party outing
on October 9. The outing-site, for which was not specified, will
make the start of the party's campaign for elections to be held
in some Connecticut cities in November. The Progressive Party
polled 13,700 votes during the Presidential elections last year,
according to this article.

20. RACIAL DISCRIMINATION

1212. "Robeson Pickets Theatre," Pittsburgh Courier, February 8, 1947,
p. 2.

Paul Robeson joined the picket line in front of the American
Theatre in St. Louis, Missouri, in protest over the discriminatory
policy of the management seating of Negro patrons.

1213. "Robeson Charges Ban," New York Times, November 16, 1940, p. 32.

Paul Robeson and eight other men and women, including three Negroes,
filed suit for $22,500 against Vanessle's Restuarant at North
Beach, California,changing racial discrimination in alleged refusal
of service to Mr. Robeson and his party. The management of
Vanessle's contended that the restaurant already was full when the
party arrived.

21. RUSSIA

1214. Middleton, Drew. "Pravda Calls Rise in U.S. Friends Soviet
Blessing on Eve of May Day," New York Times, May 1, 1947, p. 12.

Pravda, the Communist Party newspaper in the Soviet Union, published an article stating that the growth of friendship between
Russia and the United States was the result of Moscow's courageous
and consistent struggle for durable democratic peace against the
new warmongers. The article also stated that a number of Americans
look to Moscow as "bulwark of democracy." According to the article
Paul Robeson was one of those Americans. He was also considered
a "sincere friend" of the Russian people.

1215. "Count Us Out," New York Age, May 7, 1949, p. 12.

This editorial declares, in part:
Paul Robeson, the eminent singer and actor, has been
talking pretty freely in Europe, according to the
press accounts, about the abysmal failings of this
country, his native land, and about the unbounded
glories of Soviet Russia. As an American, this is
one of Mr. Robeson's precious privileges. He is
free to speak his mind, to denounce his country and
to praise any other land he may wish to. This is
one of the freedoms accorded Americans. And like any
other freedom, it is subject to abuse. We have no
quarrel with Mr. Robeson for expressing his views,
however much we may disagree with him. But we do
object - and strenuously - to his misrepresenting the
Negro race. He is quoted as having said that, in
the event of a war between this country and the

(New York Age)

> Soviet Union, Negroes would refuse to participate in
> defense of the United States. If Mr. Robeson has taken
> a poll of Negro opinion on this issue, he has kept it a
> well guarded secret. We were never queried, nor do we
> know of anyone who was so polled. We know of no
> authority for Mr. Robeson's fantastic and presump-
> tous statement. Certainly, he was never authorized to
> speak for us.... With full realization of the short-
> comings of this country we do not share Mr. Robeson's
> view that the Soviet Union is a perfect paradise. We
> do not wish to live under a regime which considers all
> opposition as treason punishable by death. We do not
> cherish the idea of being penalized for our opinions
> any more than for our color. Mr. Robeson may thrive
> under such a police state regime. As for us, count
> us out. We will stay here where we can continue to
> carry on our fight above ground.

1216. "Robeson Arrives in Moscow," New York Times, June 5, 1949, p. 19.

It was stated that Paul Robeson arrived in Moscow by air for the
celebration of the 150th anniversary of the birth of the Russian
poet, Alexander Pushkin.

1217. "Pushkin is Hailed," New York Times, June 7, 1949, p. 3.

Paul Robeson was in Moscow, Russia, to attend a conclave celebrating
the 150th anniversary of Alexander Pushkin's birthday. It was reported that Paul Robeson said before the meeting that it was
"wonderful" to be back in the Soviet Union. It was also stated
that he planned to give three concerts in Russia before returning
to New York City to testify at the trial of the eleven Communist
leaders.

1218. "Paul Robeson Stirs a Moscow Audience," New York Times, June 9,
1949, p. 34.

Paul Robeson told a thunderously applauding audience in Russia
that the old words to the song "Old Man River," now should be
changed. In the words of the song, "man was tired of living and
afraid to die"; in the new words, he told the audience, were:
"We must fight to death for peace and freedom." He also introduced
a song, "Scandalize My Name," which he said, according to this
article, was dedicated to the international bourgeois press on the
basis of his experience since coming to Europe for the April Conference of Partisans for Peace in Paris. The refrain of the song
is "I gave my brother my hand - he scandalized my name - you call
that brother - no - no - no."

1219.   "Burden of Proof," Time, Vol. 43, No. 26, June 27, 1949, p. 36.

The article points out that Robeson was returning to America after
a four-month tour of eight European countries, including a visit
to the U.S.S.R. He declares: "I love this Soviet people more
than I love any other nation, because of their suffering and
sacrifices for us, the Negro people, the people of the future in
this world.... I am born and bred in this America of ours. I
want to love it. I love a part of it. But it's up to the rest
of America when I shall love it with the same intensity that I
love....suffering people the world over, in the way that I deeply
and intensely love the Soviet people. That burden of proof rests
upon America," concludes the world traveler.

1220.   "Robeson's View is Cited: It Needs Democratic Antidotes Clauson
Tells Rhodes Class," New York Times, July 1, 1949, p. 4.

Address G. Clauson, Jr., Richmond member of the Board of Education,
told the graduating students of the Rhodes School in New York
City, that Paul Robeson's "rejection" of the American way "should
make us resolve to strengthen our democracy where it is weak."
Speaking at this private school, Clauson said: "Why did this man,
gifted as a singer, an actor, an athlete and a scholar prefer the
restrictive regime of Russia to the democracy of his native land?
All members of democratic community must be admitted to full
participation as citizens. It is not enough to look after our
own welfare. We must secure the same rights and privileges for
others that we would have for ourselves."

1221.   "Robeson's Concert Proved Friendship, Russians Said," Afro-
American, July 30, 1949, p. 8.

According to this article when Paul Robeson appeared in Moscow on
the occasion of the 150th anniversary of Alexander Pushkin, he
gave several concerts in some of Russia's most famous concert halls.
Among them were the Palace of Culture of the Stalin Auto Plant and
the Green Theatre of the Gorky Central Parke of Culture and Rest.
The Russian's paper, Izvestia, proclaimed his appearance with the
following criticism:
          The inspired rendition, simplicity, penetration into
          the wisdom of folks, make Robeson's singing extremely
          moving and thrilling. Robeson renders Soviet songs
          with particular warmth and emotion. The "Song of the
          Motherland," in his rendition, sounds like a hymn
          of joy. Paul Robeson, the artist, realist, and
          political fighter, regards this art as a means of
          serving the colored people, a means of struggle for
          peace and freedom.
Following a concert at the Moscow Conservatory, Robeson was guest
of honor at the Central Artists' Club. Moscow's leading actors
and actresses, painters, composers and musicians, gave him a long
ovation. Then he was greeted by the writer Ilya Ehrenburg and
Yuri Zavadsky, People's Artist of the USSR, who hailed him as
"a faithful son of the American people and fighter for their
happiness."

1222. "Robeson Is Blamed for Dixie Feud," Pittsburgh Courier, August 1949, p. 3.

This article reports the story of two Black men who refused to give up their bus seats in Knoxville, Tenn. When they were told by the bus driver to move out of their seats, they were quoted as saying "By God, we must be in Russia." They were arrested by two white policemen who reportedly told them: "You're like Paul Robeson. You need to be in Russia."

1223. Editorial. "Negroes Are Americans," Life, August 1, 1949, p. 22.

The editor states that although Paul Robeson was an All-American end, a letter man in baseball, basketball and track, his honors as athlete, student, singer, actor never endeared America to him. The writer concludes that Robeson has long preferred Russia and Communism, and he surprised nobody when he said in Paris that U.S. Negroes would not fight for their "oppressors" against the Soviet Union.

1224. Hicks, James L. "Robeson A Stick of Dynamite: Trend of Leadership Shifts to Red Line," Afro-American, September 10, 1949, pp. 1, 9.

According to Mr. Hicks, Paul Robeson today is a 200-pound stick of leaded dynamite swinging like a pendulum between two burning flames and no one in America can say when, or which flame, will ignite him. The writer states:
    Every trained observer of the Robeson story will
    admit that the dynamite is getting ever closer to
    the flame and will further admit that if an explosion
    occurs it will be heard around the world. The flame
    on the right is the American status quo burning more
    strongly than ever to keep the country as it always
    has been with its high standards of living, its
    Horatio Alger opportunities, its world leadership
    and its white supremacy and suppression of the
    colored man. This is the dominant flame but it
    well may be the one to ignite the dynamite. The
    flame on the left is a weaker, smoldering fire faith-
    fully nursed by the Communist Party with its still
    pitifully small colored membership but at times
    fanned into dangerous dimensions by a wave of op-
    pression, discrimination and injustice from the fire
    on the right. This flame is still weak and under-
    nourished -- but it actually takes only one match to
    start a big fire.... In short, the Communists make
    their program so broad that colored leaders are
    finding it difficult to repudiate it. Soon they
    flirt with it and each flirtation inspires a few of
    their own followers to embrace it. If and when the
    Communist Party gains enough colored support, the
    Robeson dynamite may be exploded from the flame on
    the left.

1225. Schuyler, George S. "Paul Robeson For President in 1952!,"
       Pittsburgh Courier, September 17, 1949, p. 12.

       The writer asked, why not Paul Robeson for President in 1952?....
       He surmises: "....I want my man (Paul Robeson) to head some
       ticket and I doubt that he can get the backing of the 'reactionary'
       G.O.P. or of the Democrats (who have so many former Klansmen in
       high offices). The Progressive might nominate him and he might
       poll more votes than Henry Wallace did (who couldn't?), but he
       would need real mass support which the Progressives cannot secure."
       He concludes: "So if Dr. Robeson, to whom the NAACP gave its
       1945 Spingarn Medal for distinguished service (without mentioning
       his service to Russia) is to get into the White House, the only
       party he can head is the Communist Party. I therefore beseech the
       Politburo of the Communist Party to take time off from the treason
       trial in New York's Federal Court and give my hero an honorary
       membership in the party so we can get the 1952 campaign under way
       NOW. Wouldn't it be wonderful to have a President-elect sing his
       inaugural address?"

22. SINGER

1226. Bradford, Roark. "Paul Robeson is John Henry," Collier, January
       13, 1940, pp. 15. 45.

       The author declares that Paul Robeson is America's Number One
       Negro entertainer. His performance in "Emperor Jones" fixed him
       in that position as a dramatic actor; his performance in "Show
       Boat" settled the matter of his place as a singing actor. Mean-
       while, concert audiences had named him their favorite male Negro
       singer, asserts Bradford. There have been, since, great Negro
       actors and singers who have sat upon the pinnacle for a brief mo-
       ment. But when the final curtain falls upon a show in which
       some colored actor has achieved stardom, or when a concert artist
       has rounded the circuit and the electric thrill of the final note
       has died, there is still Paul Robeson, concludes the author.

1227. "Paul Robeson Sings 'Ballad for Americans,'" Lewisohn Stadium
       Concerts Review, Vol. 23, No. 2, January 24-26, 1940, p. 10.

       This article states that after Paul Robeson sang "Ballad for
       Americans" over the Columbia Broadcasting System program, within
       a week over two hundred American colleges, high schools,and choral
       societies requested permission to perform the song.

1228. "'Ballad for Americans' on Victor Records: A Thrilling Performance
       by Paul Robeson and the American People's Chorus and the Victor
       Symphony Orchestra," New York Daily News, May 14, 1940. p. 8.

       This is a full-page advertisement for a record, "Ballad for Ameri-
       cans" by Paul Robeson. It states that after Robeson first sang the
       song on radio, he was besieged with telephone calls, letters, and

(New York Daily News)

telegrams congratulating him on his performance, and demanding
a recording of this marvelous composition. The album was supple-
mented by an informative text that tells the complete story of
the composition and gives a summary of Mr. Robeson's career as a
concert singer, and as an actor on stage and screen, both here and
abroad.

1229.   "Paul Robeson to Appear as Soloist," Atlanta Daily World, June 8,
        1940, p. 7.

        It was stated that Paul Robeson would appear as a soloist at the
        Lewisohn Stadium in New York. He was scheduled to sing the
        "Ballad for Americans," for which he was so widely praised after
        it was heard on the "Pursuit of Happiness" radio program.

1230.   "Music of the Times: New and Current Comment," New York Times,
        June 23, 1940, Section   , p. 5.

        It was stated that Paul Robeson, soloist, would sing "Ballad for
        Americans" and other music at the Lewisohn Stadium.

1231.   Diton, Carl. "Robeson Steals N.Y. Concert," Chicago Defender,
        July 13, 1940, p. 21.

        The writer asserts that last Tuesday evening was the scene of a
        unique interracial concert given by the New York Philharmonic
        Orchestra in the Lewisohn Stadium, one of a series given annually
        throughout the summer months. He declared that Paul Robeson,
        singer-actor, was easily the dominant attraction, assisted by a
        white 50-voiced mixed chorus selected from Hugh Ross' Schola
        Cantorum, a Negro mixed chorus of 45 voices from Wen Talbert's
        singing group, and Louise Burge.... The writer asserts that the
        toying of the orchestra with Weinberger's harmonious Variations
        and Fugue on the old English tune "Under the Spreading Chestnut
        Tree" put the large audience in a splendid mood for Paul Robeson's
        ovation. He concludes: "Mr. Robeson added 'Water Boy' and 'Some-
        times I Feel Like a Motherless Child' assisted by his accompanist,
        Lawrence Brown, and the very profitable evening came to an end with
        a new version of Jerome Kern's "Ole Man River." Mark Warnow con-
        ducted this version as well as "Ballad for Americans."

1232.   "Robeson May Play Negro Exposition," Pittsburgh Courier, July 13,
        1940, p. 21.

        According to this article, with plans all but completed for his
        first national tour of America in many years, Paul Robeson, world-
        renowned bass-baritone, was considering an offer to appear in a
        concert for the American Negro Exposition in Chicago in early
        August. This report states that in regards to his first tour in
        this country in four seasons, the great singer-actor will start
        in New York City, October 6th at Carnegie Hall, after which he
        will sing at many universities. Included among them will be his
        own alma mater, Rutgers, at New Brunswick, N.J.; Colgage, at
        Hamilton, N.Y.; Northwestern, at Evanston, Ill.; Penn State, at

(Pittsburgh Courier)

State College, Pa.; Brigham Young, at Provo, Utah; Columbia, in
New York; and at the Universities of Minnesota, Washington, Oregon
and North Dakota. Mr. Robeson will be soloist in four performances of the Philadelphia Symphony orchestra in December, including
a second showing at Carnegie Hall the same month in addition to
an appearance in Town Hall during the Endowment Fund series and
at the Institute of Arts and Sciences, McMillen Theater, Columbia
University, November 7th. The pending tour will be under the
direction of the Metropolitan Musical Bureau, concludes the
article.

1233. Morris, Earl J. "Robeson Thrills 23,000," Pittsburgh Courier,
        August 3, 1940, p. 1.

        According to Mr. Morris more than 23,000 people jammed into Holly-
        wood Bowl early July 23, to thrill to the stirring music as rendered
        by Paul Robeson, assisted by the Hall Johnson Choir and Phil-
        harmonic Orchestra of Los Angeles conducted by David Broeckman.
        Mr. Robeson was accompanied during his singing of spirituals by
        Lawrence Brown. The concert of the internationally famous bari-
        tone was held on the first night of the third week in the 19th
        season of "symphonies under the stars." This was the largest
        gathering to attend the outdoor concerts this season. It was
        estimated that 25,000 people heard and saw the recital. More than
        23,000 people paid from 75 cents to two and one half dollars.
        Another thousand or so crashed the gates and fled to the hills and
        remained unmolested. The huge crowd began to stream into the
        beautiful bowl like a human Niagara as early as 6:30 p.m. and it
        was nearly 9 p.m. when they were all seated, standing in aisles
        and perched on hill tops, concludes the writer.

1234. "Paul Robeson will Sing in MGM Film," Washington Tribune, August
        3, 1940.

        According to this article Paul Robeson was selected to sing "Ballad
        for Americans" for the forthcoming Metro-Goldwyn-Mayer picture,
        "Babes on Broadway." The great American baritone has been inactive
        in pictures in recent years because of his dislike of the type of
        roles usually assigned to Negro artists, states the article.

1235. "Playwrights to Hear Robeson," Afro-American, August 3, 1940, p.14.

        This article reports that the Harlem Playwrights' Company selected
        a play by George Norford, "Big White Fog," as its first production,
        to be given by the group on September 6, at which time Paul
        Robeson would sing a group of songs and Richard Wright, author of
        "Native Son," will deliver an address. Both men are associate
        members of the company.

1236. Editorial. "Paul Robeson," <u>Chicago Defender</u>, August 10, 1940,
       p. 14.

       The editor states that Paul Robeson recaptured Chicago. He took
       it by storm again after an absence of five years. More than
       165,000 Chicagoans of every nationality, color and creed filled
       Grant Park and overflowed onto the surrounding lawns. A demon-
       stration of love and affection greeted the appearance of Robeson
       and his accompanist, Lawrence Brown. And how they did respond!
       They gave and gave again lavishly. They gave and always they
       were a part of their audience, not apart from it. It is easy to
       understand why Paul Robeson is the most beloved and the greatest
       of artists we have produced. Robeson is an artist-fighter for
       Negro America. He is more than an ambassador from his people.
       Robeson is more than a Negro, he is the embodiment in art of
       American democracy. He sings for freedom. There is no mistaking
       that fact when he opens his mouth, declares the writer. He con-
       cludes:
              Robeson refused to be the one or the other. He is
              neither an Uncle Tom nor buffoon. But not only does
              he refuse to play a passive part in the Negro struggles.
              He is openly against the war and American involvement.
              in it because he saw the suffering of the last war.
              Robeson has sung for the orphans of democratic Spain
              because he saw the Spanish people fighting against
              Fascism. Robeson has aided all movements that make
              for progressive movements as a means of bringing to
              the Negro artist full and complete freedom of cultural
              expression. This cannot fail to help his people, he
              believes.... The Negro artist must learn to be a
              spokesman for Negro freedom. This is what adds great-
              ness to our art. It has made Robeson the greatest of
              our living artists, the spokesman in art for complete
              equality for us in all walks of life.

1237. "Paul Robeson Stars in CBS Program," <u>Louisiana Weekly</u>, August 24,
       1940.

       According to this news release Eva Jessye and her famed Choir
       will be heard over CBS network Monday, August 26, in the "Forecast"
       production of "All God's Chillun," starring Paul Robeson, comedian
       Eddie Green, and Amamda Randolph. The program is one of a series
       of new radio ideas being tried out by Columbia. If chosen for
       sponsorship the same cast would be heard in a variety of programs
       built around legendary stories of great heroes, specially suited
       to Robeson's talents, concludes the report.

1238. "Paul Robeson Carries on Tho in Pain: Taking Medical Treatment for
       Leg Infection," <u>Journal and Guide</u>, August 25, 1940, p. 1.

       According to this article true to the tradition that the show must
       go on regardless, Paul Robeson continues his concert tour although
       he received medical treatment for an infected leg. It was re-
       ported that he kept his present disability from his public,
       electing to endure his pain in silence rather than disappoint them.
       Between his appearances, he has been going to New York for treat-

ments, states the article. Robeson, whose family was among the
early settlers in this section, is being hailed as a "home town
boy who made good." Although his application for admission to
Princeton University years ago was not accepted, his success at
Rutgers University as an athlete and a scholar and his international renown as an artist have established him as the leading
son of the City of Princeton, concludes the article.

1239. McLauchin, Russell. "Paul Robeson Sings 'Joe Hill,'" Detroit News,
       December 7, 1940.

During the early stages of his singing career Paul Robeson began
to include "militant" songs into his choice of encores. Not all
audiences received his militant songs with delight. Some out-
right did not appreciate him mixing politics with artistic en-
deavors. Mr. McLauchlin argues, in part: "Could it not be agreed
that the concert-platform and the soap-box belong as far apart
as possible? This is mentioned, not out of disrespect for
Robeson's views, but because he chose to sing a song called 'Joe
Hill' or something of the kind which, possessing a singularly un-
lyrical poem and an undistinguished air, could not have been included in the program of a great artist for any other reason but
a propaganda reason...."

1240. "Robeson Will Give Montclair (N.J.) Recital," Newark (N.J.) News,
       January 9, 1941.

This reporter states that Paul Robeson, Negro baritone and actor
who was born in Princeton and graduated from Rutgers University,
will sing at Montclair High School under auspices of the Women's
Educational Club of Montclair. The Women's Educational Club was
organized in 1935 to promote civic and social affairs in Montclair.
Each year the club gives a scholarship to the Montclair High
School boy or girl attaining the highest average among the Negro
students in the graduating class, concludes the article.

1241. "Quits Robeson Benefit," New York Times, April 15, 1941, p. 27.

Mrs. Cornelia Bryce Pinchot, wife of a former Governor of Pennsylvania, said she and Mrs. Eleanor Roosevelt had withdrawn from
sponsorship of a concert by Paul Robeson for the benefit of China.
She said the concert was organized for Chinese medical and war relief, but she learned that half of the proceeds were to go to the
National Negro Congress. Deceptive literature had been issued to
promote the concert, she said, one set of the folders saying it
was for the benefit of China and another saying it was Negroes.
She made it plain that she was not objecting to benefits for
Negroes, but took the position that all the money should go for the
purpose for which the affair was organized.

1242.   "The Music of the Times," New York Times, April 27, 1941, Part 8, p. 7.

A photo of Paul Robeson and Benny Goodman is in the center of the page. Under the caption it was stated that Robeson and Goodman would appear at the concert of the American Russian Institute at Carnegie Hall.

1243.   "Newark Concert Heard by 23,000," New York Times, June 4, 1941, p. 27.

Paul Robeson was the featured soloist at the first summer program given by Essex County Symphony. The article states that the evening was clearly Mr. Robeson's. His splendid voice came clearly through the amplifying system and he sang with the vigor, the perfect timing and the whole-heartedness for which he is famous, concludes the article. It was also pointed out that he was called again and again.

1244.   "Robeson Soloist at The Stadium: 14,000 Hear Baritone with the Philharmonic Orchestra," New York Times, June 24, 1941, p. 16.

Paul Robeson was the soloist with the New York Philharmonic-Symphony Orchestra at Lewisohn Stadium in New York City. Despite the chilly weather 14,000 persons turned out to hear him. It was recital by Robeson that the audience enjoyed most, according to the article. After he finished singing, Robeson received several ovations from the audience. The final encore, "Water Boy," sung so movingly that the crowd did not insist on another, though it continued to whistle and applaud, states the article.

1245.   "Stadium Sketch Book: Paul Robeson," Lewisohn Stadium Concerts Review, Vol. 24, No. 2, June 23-25, 1941, pp. 5, 25.

This is a short sketch of Paul Robeson and his accomplishments as a singer and actor. The article declares that Robeson's return to the United States in 1940 was signalized by one of the most exciting radio ventures of the season. He was referring to Robeson's rendition of "Ballad for Americans."

1246.   "Robeson Spotted for Big Radio Commercial," Pittsburgh Courier, June 28, 1941, p. 41.

This article states that the great dramatic baritone had signed and received $2,500 to do a Coca Cola commercial, which would be officially launched in September.

1247.   "Robeson is Heard by 14,000: Mammoth Crowd Pays $8,200 at Lewisohn Stadium," Pittsburgh Courier, July 5, 1941, p. 20.

Paul Robeson appeared in concert at the Lewisohn Stadium in New York City. The reviewer declares that the superb singer received one of the greatest ovations in the stadium's long and colorful history. In an encore, "Scandalize My Name," the audience joined him spontaneously in the chorus.

1248. "7,500 Hear Paul Robeson," <u>New York Times</u>, July 10, 1941, p. 17.

According to the article, the season's attendance record at Robin Hood Dell in Philadelphia, was broken when more than 7,500 persons jammed into the outdoor auditorium to hear Paul Robeson sing with the Philadelphia Orchestra. Mr. Robeson sang two new songs, "Invocation to Ogun," and "Tennessee Valley."

1249. "Paul Robeson Booked for Long Concert Tour: 51 Cities will Pay $125,000 for Chance to Hear Noted Singer," <u>Pittsburgh Courier</u>, July 12, 1941, p. 21.

This article states that the great dramatic and delineator of folk songs would start on a jaunt of 51 concert cities, colleges and halls. He received $2,500 per concert. It was also brought out that he was signed by the Columbia Recording Company to record a number of records for them.

1250. Diton, Carl. "Stadium Concert Features Robeson," <u>Pittsburgh Courier</u>, July 13, 1941, p. 1.

According to this writer last Tuesday evening was the scene of a unique interracial concert given by the New York Philharmonic Orchestra in the Lewisohn Stadium, one of a series given annually throughout the summer months. Paul Robeson, singing-actor, was easily the dominant attraction, assisted by a white 50-voiced mixed chorus selected from High Ross' Schola Cantorum, a Negro mixed chorus of 45 voices from Wen Talbert's singing group, and Louise Burge, contralto product of Knoxville College, Howard University and the Juillard. The program, based upon folksongs,varied as it was stirring, was in essence derived exclusively from American and English sources, states Mr. Diton. The author surmises that the toying of the orchestra with Weinberger's harmonious Variations and Fugue on the old English tune, "Under the Spreading Chestnut Tree," put the large audience in a splendid mood for Paul Robeson's ovation, who sang the baritone solo part in Earl Robinson's "Ballad for Americans," using his unerring skill to ferret out the hidden potentialities of the text. Mr. Robeson added "Water Boy" and "Sometimes I Feel Like a Motherless Child," assisted by his ac- companist, Lawrence Brown, and the very profitable evening came to an end with a new version of Jerome Kern's "Ole Man River." Mark Warnow conducted this version as well as "Ballad for Americans," concludes the writer.

1251. "Paul Robeson, Negro Singer, Will Appear in Durham, On October 6," <u>Durham Herald Sun</u>, September 28, 1941, Section 1, p. 6.

This article asserts that world-famed singer, stage artist and moving picture actor Paul Robeson was expected to draw a large crowd when he appeared in North Carolina College for Negroes, in Durham, N.C. It states that this would be the "first appearance of Robeson in the South." This article declares that Robeson was one of the nation's most colorful characters and is admired wherever he appears in person, on the stage or on the screen. "Durham is considered fortunate to have the opportunity to hear this world renowned Negro artist who ranks first in his

(Durham Herald Sun)

profession," concludes the article.

1252.   "Paul Robeson Will Sing Monday Night at Negro (North Carolina)
        College," Durham Herald Sun, October 5, 1941, Section 1, p. 11.

        The author states that Paul Robeson reputed as being the greatest
        interpreter of Negro spirituals, would appear at the North Carolina
        College for Negroes. This article declares that Robeson had no
        favorite music, but he shares the public's love for "Ole Man River,"
        the Jerome Kern song with which he will always be associated. The
        writer also discusses Robeson as an athlete, scholar, actor, and
        singer. He surmises that Paul Robeson was known throughout the
        English speaking world.

1253.   Kolodin, Irving. "The New Records: Paul Robeson Sings the Blues -
        A Pair of Christmas Carols - Singles," New York Sun, November 28,
        1941.

        This writer states that when the word circulated some weeks ago
        that Columbia had pooled the musical talents of Paul Robeson and
        Count Bassie and the literary ones of Richard Wright to produce
        a blues tribute to Joe Louis, there was some dubious headshaking
        as well as much anticipation. Projects of this sort seldom come
        off the way a casual record session can, asserts Mr. Kolodin.
        Well, seldom is still the word, but this is one of those rarities -
        a mighty piece of singing by Robeson and a high credit to every
        one involved. It proves, for one thing, that having a good voice
        is no disqualification for singing the blues, for Robeson's majestic
        tones have never rolled forth with more sonority on disks (this
        is, incidentally, his debut under the Columbia banner, though
        the label is Okeh) than it does in the stanzas of this traditional
        blues. Wright's verses are done in just the right allegorical
        folk vein, and the musical background is superb, especially the
        work of those two fine trumpet players, Buck Clayton and Harry
        Edison. Considering the quality on its two sides, OKeh 6475, at
        the usual low rate for this label is about the biggest bargain
        in this year's catalogue. And it might be mentioned too, that with
        "Joltin' Joe DiMaggio" and "King Joe" on this same plum label,
        OKeh is one of our leading sources of authentic and popular
        Americana, declares Mr. Kolodin.

1254.   "Paul Robeson to Sing," New York Times, December 28, 1941, p. 26.

        This article states that Paul Robeson would give a recital, at the
        residence of Mr. and Mrs. John Henry Hammond of New York City, in
        the interest of the Council on African Affairs. The Council of
        African Affairs studies conditions of life and work in Africa and
        in the interest of the people of Africa and prepares publications
        acquainting the public in the United States with those conditions.
        This article was in the Society section of the newspaper.

1255. "Robeson Cancels Concert," New York Times, February 18, 1942,
       p. 22.

       Paul Robeson called off a concert in Santa Fe, New Mexico, because
       a hotel there cancelled his reservation when guests objected to
       the presence of a Negro. Mr. Robeson said that the hotel later
       offered to accept the reservation, but he decided to stand by his
       first decision.

1256. Parmenter, Ross. "On American Singer and His World," New York
       Times, April 19, 1942, Part 8, p. 7.

       The author declares that Paul Robeson wants to make and touch
       people through his artistry and he is anxious to impress them
       with his sincerity so that through him they will come to respect,
       and even share his beliefs. It was pointed out that Robeson met
       Bernard Shaw and he couldn't discuss socialism because he did not
       know what it was all about. And when he appeared in the film
       "Sanders of the River," he was so absorbed in that it was not
       until afterward that he realized he had lent himself to "an im-
       perialist point of view" he did not believe it. Parmenter asserts
       that Robeson met Picasso, Brancusi, Milhaud and Stravinsky, when
       he was living in England in the 1920's. The writer concludes that
       from the folk-music of the lullabies, laments, love songs and
       battle songs of Africa, India, Hungary, the Hebrides, Czechoslo-
       vakia, Russia, Spain and China, he acquired new songs to sing.
       And they are songs he can sing with his whole heart, for through
       the sufferings of his own people he has come to know and embrace
       the sufferings and aspirations of all people. In the article
       Robeson was quoted as saying: "Everything I have done is an ex-
       tension of my feelings about my own people. I feel some way
       I've become tied up with this whole problem of human freedom. I
       have no end to my artistic horizon."

1257. "Dean Dixon Will Conduct," New York Times, June 29, 1942, p. 11.

       It was announced that Paul Robeson would appear in concert at the
       Lewisohn Stadium. It was stated that he would not sing "Battle
       Hymn," but instead he would sing "Ballad for Americans," "Lord
       God of Abraham," from Mendelassohn's Elijah, and Mussorgsky's
       "Saul."

1258. "Music of the Times: The News and Current Comment," New York Times,
       July 5, 1942, Part 1, p. 53.

       There is a large photo of Paul Robeson in the middle of the page.
       Under it, the caption reads "Paul Robeson will be the soloist at
       the Lewisohn Stadium next Saturday in 'Ballad for Americans' and
       later in the program will do a group of songs."

1259. "Robeson Soloist at the Stadium," New York Times, July 12, 1942,
       p. 33.

       The article states that one of the largest crowds of the season
       turned out at the Lewisohn Stadium in New York City to hear Paul
       Robeson as a soloist with the New York Philharmonic-Symphony

(New York Times)

Orchestra. The famous baritone was received with enthusiasm, as he sang works by Mendelssohn and Mussorgsky. Appearing in "Ballad for Americans," which Mr. Robeson helped to make popular throughout the nation, was the American Peoples Chorus, and this was its 113th appearance in the work, states the reviewer.

1260.   Taubman, Howard. "20,000 at Stadium Hear Robeson Sing," New York Times, July 2, 1943, p. 15.

A banner crowd of 20,000, the season's best, turned out to hear Paul Robeson in a guest appearance at the Lewisohn Stadium in New York City. Mr. Robeson sang encores for half an hour and the crowd still wanted more. The concert was unmistakable Paul Robeson, states Taubman. The flood of encores brought spirituals, excerpts from "Show Boat," "Porgy and Bess," "Joe Hill" and Army songs. No wonder the audience shouted as if it were old-home week, concludes the reviewer.

1261.   Bennett, Grena. "20,000 Hear Paul Robeson at Stadium," New York Journal-American, July 2, 1943.

This article states that 20,000 people heard Paul Robeson sing at Lewisohn Stadium in New York City. This was a record for the season. The author declares that Robeson sang with nobility and reverence.

1262.   "Paul Robeson Packs Lewisohn Stadium," People's Voice, July 10, 1943, p. 26.

According to this article that magnetic quality which hurtled Paul Robeson to the top most rung of the musical ladder and made him one of the greatest citizens of the world, gripped 20,000, packed into Lewisohn Stadium to hear him in New York City, tore the usual polite decorum from their manner and turned the concert in to a people's rally. They yelled. They whistled. They stomped. They cried for more even after the half-hour of encores and after the attendant lowered the top of the piano. For Robeson is truly a people's artist - truly what Joe Curran named him recently - the "greatest voice of democracy today," states the writer. He concludes that "the evening was truly his."

1263.   "Jewish Leaders, Robeson Urge Unity," People's Voice, July 17, 1943, p. 6.

This article declares that Jewish trade unions, civil, cultural and religious leaders, addressing 47,000 persons packed into the Polo Grounds to welcome Itzik Feffer and Solomon Michaels, the Soviet Union's peoples artists and ambassadors of good will. The writer asserts that Paul Robeson, who was introduced by Chairman Louis Levine as a "great singer of a great people," received overwhelming applause when, before he sang Engel's "Kadish," "To a Soviet Flyer," and "From Border Unto Border," he said:
        As a Negro and one of a long-suffering minority, it
        is more than fitting that the unity of struggle with

(<u>People's Voice</u>)

> the Jewish people should be clear. The Jewish
> people and the Negro people must stand side by
> side and fight for democracy.

1264. "Robeson Sings for Sailors," <u>People's Voice</u>, July 17, 1943, p. 6.

This article maintains that Paul Robeson was the guest artist at
a concert at the U.S. Naval Training Station in Great Lakes, Ill.
Two thousand Naval officers and enlisted personnel, including
hundreds of sailors of the singer's race, jammed the Station's
Ross Auditorium to capacity to hear him run the gamut of his
repetoire -- from Beethoven's soulful "Creation Hymn" to the jolly
English folk song of a laughing lass rebuffing an unwelcome
suitor -- but not too firmly -- "Oh, No, John, No," concludes the
writer.

1265. "Paul Robeson Stimulates War Production," <u>Pittsburgh Courier</u>,
August 7, 1943, p. 8.

According to this release a stimulus to greater production and
effort was given to the employees of the Apex Smelting Co., largest
aluminum smelter in the Chicago area, by the appearance at the
plant on Saturday, July 24, of Paul Robeson and a PRODUCTION FOR
VICTORY RALLY sponsored jointly by the management and the International Union of Mine, Mill and Smelter Workers. The MMSW
arranged for Mr. Robeson's appearance.

1266. "Baltimore Theatre 'Not Available' on Date in Negro Plea," <u>New
York Times</u>, March 26, 1944, p. 22.

Ms. Lillian Jackson, President of the Baltimore branch of the
National Association for the Advancement of Colored People, states
that the NAACP had planned a recital by Paul Robeson, but the Lyric
Theatre would not allow them to use the theatre for the concert.

1267. "Paul Robeson Sings First Time Since 'Othello' Started Its Tour,"
<u>New York Amsterdam News</u>, March 31, 1945, p. 5-B.

Paul Robeson flew down from San Francisco to Los Angeles and sang
for 6,000 persons of all races. This was his first appearance
since he began his tour of the play "Othello." Thunderous
applause followed his rendition of such favorites as "Joe Hill"
and "Ole Man River," states the reviewer.

1268. Editorial. "The Evils of Division," <u>Chicago Times</u>, May 11, 1945.

Paul Robeson appeared in concert in Chicago. While he was in the
Windy City, he addressed the working at the Wilson Meat Packing
Plant. He told them: "The same cynical minds that approved of
selling out Spain, Czechoslovakia and the rest of Europe would
like to sabotage the San Francisco Conference, but the common
people won't stand for it." These remarks led the Editor of the
<u>Chicago Times</u> to comment, in part: "....Already we are beginning
to have the war reviewed by so-called 'experts' who are rushing

(Chicago Times)

forth with demands that we Americans stand up and shout to the
Russian and British fighting forces that we darned well know that
we did more to lick the Nazis than they did. Mr. Robeson and
General (Dwight) Eisenhower are in agreement about the evils of
division...."

1269. "Paul Robeson Sang and Spoke to 1,000 Students at Swarthmore,"
Daily Worker, May 13, 1945, p. 6.

Robeson appeared at Swarthmore College in Swarthmore, Pennsylvania,
under the sponsorship of The Forum for Free Speech. In his speech
Robeson states that his long career as an athlete, scholar, and
artist have impressed upon him the fact that the freedom and
dignity of all mankind is a basic requirement for a peaceful and
happy world. "Mutual respect between peoples of different colors,
cultures and ways of life is essential," he said. The actor concludes:
     An atmosphere which recognizes the basic human rights
     of all people is an atmosphere in which the imple-
     mentation of the Supreme Court desegregation decision
     can be most quickly achieved. I have fought and will
     continue to fight for the kind of America and the
     kind of world in which such an atmosphere will
     prevail.

1270. "Paul Robeson Has Distinguished Record," Syracuse (New York) Post-
Standard, May 26, 1945.

This article states that Paul Robeson had distinguished himself
in four fields - athletics, acting, singing and education. It
went on to point out that is the record of the man who would give
a concert in the Syracuse (N.Y.) Lincoln Auditorium. The program
was under the sponsorship of the New York State Nurses' Assocation,
District 4. The writer also gave a brief biographical sketch of
Mr. Robeson's life.

1271. "Robeson Continues on Tho in Pain: Taking Medical Treatment for
Leg Infection," Journal and Guide, August 24, 1945, p. 1.

According to this article true to the tradition that the show
must go on regardless, Paul Robeson, the internationally known
artist continued his tour although he received medical treatment
for an injected leg. According to intimate friends, the artist
kept his disability from his public, electing to endure pain in
silence rather than disappoint them....

1272. "Events in the World of Music," New York Times, September 30, 1945,
Part 2, p. 4.

This article states that Paul Robeson, the distinguished baritone,
just returned from a five weeks' tour of Germany and Czechoslovakia
sponsored by USO Camp Shows. Mr. Robeson reported that his
soldier audiences like serious music, but that most request were
for Negro spirituals and "Ballad for Americans."

1273.   "Paul Robeson in Seattle (Washington) Program," Pittsburgh
        Courier, February 23, 1946, p. 17.

        This short article states that Paul Robeson would speak and sing
        in Seattle, Washington. The program was sponsored jointly by the
        Spanish Refugee Appeal and the Council on African Affairs. Pro-
        ceeds from the program would be divided equally between the two
        sponsors.

1274.   Gold, Mike. "Sing On, Paul Robeson! Your Music is Necessary in
        the Fight!," Daily Worker, February 8, 1947.

        This was a letter entitled "Dear Paul Robeson." The writer de-
        clares that Robeson should not give up his finest credentials -
        his music - to fight fascism. He argues that if there is one man
        in America upon whom the proud title of People's Artist might
        truthfully be placed, it is Paul Robeson.

1275.   Walker, Arthur. "Robeson Sings to 6,000 in Toronto Despite Gag,"
        Daily Worker, February 22, 1947, p. 1.

        According to Mr. Walker, the fact that the Toronto Police Com-
        mission had banned any speech by Robeson added zest to his concert.
        It not only gave him great publicity for all he stands for, but
        it also brought into the full light of day what the tories who
        sought to gag him, stand for. So far only Europe has seen the
        logical conclusion of that - with magic results - states the
        critic.

1276.   "Civil Liberties Union Protest Barring of Robeson Concert," PM,
        March 28, 1947, p. 1.

        This news release asserts that the American Civil Liberties Union
        requested action yesterday of Erastus Corning, Mayor of Albany, to
        lift the ban placed on Paul Robeson's Albany concert, declaring
        that "public meeting places should be available to all organizations
        without regard to race, color or political persuasion." The Union
        declares that "the political views of Mr. Robeson and not the
        musical content of the program have occasioned the ban. Albany
        officials, in short, are censoring Mr. Robeson for his political
        views." Mayor Corning had defended the action of the Albany Board
        of Education in revoling its previously granted permission to the
        Carver Cultural Society to hold a concert featuring Paul Robeson
        in a public school on the ground that the function was of a "highly
        controversial nature." In a letter to Mayor Corning signed by
        John Haynes Holmes, chairman of the board; Arthur Garfield Hays,
        general counsel; and Clifford Forster, action director, the Union
        states:
                We hold no brief for the alleged beliefs attributed to
                Mr. Robeson, but we must object to the evident attempt
                to discriminate in the use of a public auditorium be-
                cause of his political views. Your action opens the
                door to denying public halls on the basis of the purely
                personal prejudice of public officials. We shall be pre-
                pared to participate in any court action, if necessary,
                to compel the granting of permission to the Carver

(PM)

Cultural Society for the use of public school
facilities.

1277. "Robeson Raps Ban on Peoria Concert," Daily Worker, April 19,
1947.

According to this article a concert by Paul Robeson, scheduled in
Peoria, Ill., was called off because of "fascist techniques" employed by the local City Council, the noted Negro singer charged.
In a telephone statement to the Council on African Affairs,
Robeson assailed the Peoria Council which has unanimously adopted
a resolution condemning the appearance there of "any speaker or
artist who is an avowed or active propagandist for un-American
ideology." Plans for a City Hall reception by a Citizens Committee for the singer were spiked by Mayor Carl O. Tribel, who
reneged on an earlier approval of the hall's use despite the
Council resolution. The Mayor's reversal was based, he said, on
fear of "riots or disturbances." In a statement he inferred that
"Robeson is coming here for a fight," because the singer had told
the press of threats he's received. The ban on use of the City
Hall followed passage of resolutions by the local American Legion
which attacked Robeson and "communism."

1278. "Robeson Concert is Off," New York Times, April 24, 1947, p. 29.

The Albany (N.Y.) Board of Education withdrew permission for Paul
Robeson to give a song recital in a local high school. The singer
was engaged by the Carver Cultural Society, a Negro Methodist
Church group.

1279. "Albany Board of Education Bans Robeson," PM, April 27, 1947.

According to this article attorney Arthur J. Harvey announced
plans for legal action against the city after Paul Robeson was
denied permission to use Philip Livingston High School for a
scheduled concert May 9. Permission to use the school auditorium
was withdrawm by the Albany Board of Education. Mr. Harvey said
"further action to obtain use of the auditorium is contemplaced,"
and called the withdrawal an "insult to a prominent singer and a
slur on the Negro people as a whole." Robeson's scheduled appearance was sponsored by the Carver Cultural Society.

1280. "Albany Schools Barred to Robeson Concert," Daily Worker, April
25, 1947.

This article reports that the Albany School Board closed the doors
on a Paul Robeson concert scheduled for May 9 in Philip Livingston
High School. The board's action was taken after Mayor Erastus
Corning termed Robeson's concert "highly controversial." Arthur
Harvey, counsel for the Carver Society, called the School Board's
ban "an insult to the Negro people and to one of the greatest
Americans of this age." Harvey indicates legal steps are planned
against the city administration to force opening of the school
doors to the Negro singer. A group pf prominent New Yorkers issued

(Daily Worker)

the following statement through the offices of the Council on
African Affairs: "We are alarmed and outraged by this evidence
of mounting hysteria formented by the Un-American Committee in
Washington and other reactionary forces. We believe it is the
responsibility of all citizens who cherish democratic principles
and hate fascism to make this their fight." Among those signing
the statement were Dr. W.E.B. DuBois, Councilman Eugene Connolly,
Rev. B.C. Robeson, State Senator Kenneth Sherbell, Helen Hayes,
Lillian Hellman, Councilman Benjamin J. Davis, Jr., Florence
Eldridge, Frederic March, Michael J. Quill, Rabbi Edward El Klein,
John Latouche and others.

1281.   "Court Writ Issued in Ban on Robeson," New York Times, April 26,
1947, p. 15.

Supreme Court Judge Isadore Bookstein issued an order directing
the Albany (N.Y.) Board of Education to show cause why it should
not be restrained from interfering with the use of the Philip
Livingston Junior High School for a concert by Paul Robeson.

1282.   Cooper, Ruby. "3,500 Back Robeson at Chicago Meeting," Daily
Worker, April 29, 1947, p. 12.

About 3,500 persons attended Chicago's Salute to Paul Robeson at
the Civil Opera House. Lena Horne was present and paid tribute
to the singer.

1283.   "Lawyers Guild for Robeson," PM, April 29, 1947, p. 1.

This article reports that the National Lawyers Guild joined the
many groups appealing to Mayor Erastus Corning of Albany to revoke
the Albany Board of Education's ban on the concert appearance of
singer Paul Robeson in a high school auditorium there May 9. They
termed the action a "serious infringement of constitutional
rights." The statement said, in part:
        The officials of the city of Albany have no right to
        substitute their own prejudices for the laws and re-
        gulations under which Mr. Robeson was clearly entitled
        to the use of the public school. We need not comment
        on the outrageous and even ludicrous presumption in-
        volved in attempting to censor the views of a man who
        is not only a distinguished artist but one of America's
        outstanding public figures.

1284.   "N.Y. School Board Ordered to Justify Ban on Baritone," Afro-
American, April 29, 1947, p. 1.

This article asserts that following its refusal to permit Paul
Robeson to sing in a local high school auditorium on May 9, the
Albany Board of Education was directed to explain in court why
it should not be held in contempt for interfering with the recital.
The show cause order, signed by State Supreme Court Justice Isadore
Bookstein, was obtained on April 25, by the Carver Cultural Society,
which is sponsoring the recital. The board was given until

(Afro-American)

10 a.m. Friday to explain its action and show why it should be
allowed to stand. At the same time, the court issues a temporary
injunction restraining the board of education from interfering with
sale of tickets and advertising for the concert pending final ad-
judicating of the matter, states the article.

1285. "Clergy Hits Robeson Ban," New York Times, April 30, 1947, p. 27.

Thirteen clergymen asked the Mayor of Albany, New York, and the
Board of Education to reinstate permission for a recital by Paul
Robeson. The clergymen said they spoke as "individual citizens"
and that they "do not believe our democratic way of life will be
strengthened by closing our public halls to those whose view-
points may differ from our own."

1286. "Albany (N.Y.) Mayor Still Firm in His Refusal to Allow Robeson
to Sing in Public School," New York Times, May 2, 1947, p. 23.

Mayor Erastus Corning II, of Albany, New York, stood firm on his
refusal to allow the use of the Philip Livingston Junior High
School Auditorium for a concert by Paul Robeson. The Mayor said
he did not think gatherings of highly controversial nature should
be permitted in a public school building. The Mayor also said
there was no objection to the concert, if conducted in another
hall. The Albany Committee for Civil Rights declared that Mr.
Robeson will be invited to sing from the capital steps, "if
necessary."

1287. "Albany Ban on Robeson Arouses Sharp Protests," People's Voice,
May 3, 1947, p. 3.

According to this article in New York City, Kirsten Falgstad
(wartime collaborator with the Nazis, who gave a concert in New
York City) got a hall, but Mr. Robeson, who did everything he
could to win the war, is not allowed to sing in Albany," declares
Arthur J. Harvey, attorney for the Carver Cultural Society, which
had scheduled a concert for Paul Robeson at Philip Livingston High
School on May 9. The concert was cancelled by the Board of
Education in action taken April 23, an immediate furor was aroused
over the Board's action, as progressive and civic groups sprang
to arms in defense of the noted singer and liberal. Dr. John W.
Park, superintendent of schools here, initiated the action against
Robeson and assumed responsibility. Backing party was Mayor
Erastus Corning, who stated that he could see no reason for permitting Robeson to appear in a city school which is for the education of the school children and not intended for use in
controversial matters, states the article.

1288. Editorial. "Back Up Robeson!" People's Voice, May 3, 1947, p. 16.

The editor comments on Paul Robeson being barred from singing in
Peoria, Illinois, and Albany, New York. He says that the Negro
people were the ones slapped down when Paul Robeson was barred
from using public buildings for scheduled concerts in Peoria,
Ill., and Albany, N.Y.; and it is up to all of us to see that
these insults are withdrawn. Robeson was not barred because someone thinks he is a "Communist." The "Red" label was used merely
in an attempt to silence the most militant and powerful spokesman
for Negro rights in America today. He concludes:
    Just as the "Red" bogey is being used as a smoke-
    screen behind which to destroy labor and every other
    progressive movement in our country in preparation
    for war against Russia, so is it being used to beat
    back the growing struggles of the Negro people for
    full democratic rights. Even the NAACP is being called
    "Communist"! Mayor Carl O. Tribel, of Peoria, and
    Mayor Erastus Corning, of Albany, were acting for the
    forces of American fascism when they sought to ban Paul
    Robeson. They should be deluged with protests by the
    outraged democratic people of our land.

1289. Editorial. "The Strange Case of Paul Robeson," Pittsburgh
Courier, May 3, 1947, p. 6.

The Editor argues: "We refuse to be stampeded by the hysterical
protests broadcast by the Civil Rights Congress and the Council
on African Affairs over the refusal of authorities in Peoria, Ill.,
and Albany, N.Y., to permit Paul Robeson to sing in public-owned
auditoriums. Mr. Robeson virtually asked for just such a reaction by going about the country interrupting his program to
lecture on political subjects which most of his audience did not
pay to hear and in which the vast majority of them did not have
the slightest interest. An artist has no right to fool several
hundred people into an auditorium under false pretense, and when
an artist has offended on several occasions, civic authorities
have a perfect right to refuse to permit him to use public platforms maintained by the taxes of all the people." The Editor
concludes:
    Mr. Robeson is greatly in error if he thinks he is
    doing the cause of the Negro any good by these foolish
    exhibitions, and his political associates err if they
    think these barrages of phoney propaganda are going to
    convince anybody outside the lunatic fringe that
    Mr. Robeson is being "persecuted." Negroes have enough
    difficulties to face in America without going around the
    country creating them.

1290. "Back Barring of Robeson," New York Times, May 6, 1947, p. 29.

The New York region of the National Federation of Catholic College
Students approved the Albany (N.Y.) Board of Education's denial of
the use of a junior high school auditorium for a recital by Paul
Robeson.

1291.   "Ban on Robeson Studied by Court," New York Times, May 3, 1947,
        p. 10.

        The New York State Supreme Court studied the briefs in the case of
        Robeson against the Albany Board of Education for not granting
        him permission to give a recital at a local junior high school.
        Albany corporation counsel told the court that the town and Board
        will not subsidize Communism or anything having to do with
        Communism.

1292.   "Ban on Mr. Paul Robeson Overruled," London Times, May 7, 1947,
        p. 4.

        This article reports that a New York State Supreme Court Judge
        granted an injunction restraining the Albany (N.Y.) Board of
        Education from banning a recital to be given by Mr. Paul Robeson.
        The Board cancelled the permit on the grounds that Mr. Robeson
        had Communist leaning. The Court ruled that the Board had no ex-
        press power to revoke the permit once it had been given, regardless
        of the discretionary power it had in granting permission in the
        first place.

1293.   "Court Lifts Albany Ban on Paul Robeson Concert," PM, May 7, 1947,
        p. 4.

        According to this reporter a Supreme Court Justice ruled that Paul
        Robeson must be allowed to give a scheduled recital in an Albany
        school auditorium, but that the Negro baritone, allegedly a Com-
        munist sympathizer, must stick to singing. Justice Isadore Book-
        stein granted an injunction to prevent the Albany Board of
        Education from interfering with the recital. The article surmises
        that two weeks ago the board cancelled a permit for use of the
        auditorium that the Carver Cultural Society, a Negro church group,
        had obtained last September. The board had no right to rescind
        the agreement, Bookstein held. The political philosophy of the
        singer "has nothing to do with the purposes for which the permit
        was originally granted" the courts wrote. But she emphasized
        that "the permit of the Board of Education is for a 'musical con-
        cert' and nothing else. The injunction is to restrain defendant
        (school board) only from interfering with a 'musical concert,'"
        concludes the article.

1294.   "Paul Robeson Wins Injunction; To Sing in Albany School Hall,"
        The New York Times, May 7, 1947, p. 29.

        New York States'Supreme Court Justice Isadore Bookstein issued an
        injunction restraining the Albany Board of Education from inter-
        fering with a concert by Paul Robeson. The injunction restrained
        defendant only from interfering with a musucal concert which is
        the sole purpose for which the permit was issued, states the high
        court.

1295. "Robeson Wins Right to Albany (N.Y.) Hall," Daily Worker, May 7, 1947, p. 1.

Supreme Court Justice Isadore B. Bookstein ruled that the local Board of Education had no right to cancel a concert in a public school by Paul Robeson because of his political opinions. Justice Bookstein attached the proviso that the affair be confined to a musical concert since this was the "sole purpose for which the permit was issued." Arthur J. Harvey, attorney for the Carver Society, who sponsored the concert, said the society never intended anything but a musical program. Harvey also released a statement from Robeson saying he would sing his musical concert without comments or remarks. The crux of the Bookstein decision was that the artist's "philosophy or ideology, however objectionable to most Americans, has nothing to do with the purposes for which the permit was originally granted," states the article.

1296. "Blast Legion's Role in Banning Robeson Concert," California Eagle, May 8, 1947, p. 1.

According to this article the American Legion stood accused of harboring elements opposed to American constitutional methods and enamored of tactics calculated to arouse public hysteria and incite mob violence. The charge was made by Kenneth C. Kennedy, national commander of UNAVA (United Negro and Allied Veterans of America) who, in a letter to Paul H. Griffith, national commander of the American Legion, protested the recent barring of Paul Robeson, noted singer, from a scheduled concert at Peoria, Ill., on April 19. Robeson, who was to have given a concert at Peoria City Hall, was denied the use of the hall after a resolution had been passed by the city council comdemning him as "An active propagandist for Un-American ideology." The council's action followed an attack on Robeson by the Peoria post of the American Legion which charged Robeson with being a Communist. The letter states, in part:
It ill behooves an organization practicing segregation
of its Negro members to condemn as un-American a man
Paul Robeson who is using his art and his eloquence
to break down the walls of prejudice and intolerance.
Robeson made a contribution during World War II by
making his talent available to American troops overseas and war workers here at home. He helped in victory and deserves the country's gratitude and respect
for it....

1297. "Robeson Sings in Albany," New York Times, May 10, 1947, p. 15.

Paul Robeson sang to an audience of about 1,100 persons in the Philip Livingston Junior High School Auditorium. The City of Albany (N.Y.) tried to bar Robeson from using the auditorium. The State Supreme Court, however, issued an injunction against the city. The article states that Mr. Robeson's program was warmly applauded.

1298. "Art for Politics' Sake," Time, Vol. 49, No. 20, May 19, 1947, p. 24.

According to this article Paul Robeson is a great baritone, a good actor (Othello). He is also a Communist-liner. "There is no such thing as a nonpolitical artist," he explains at a rally of Communist war veterans in Washington. "Either the artist serves the people or he serves those who would throttle them," states the article. Albany's Mayor Erastus Corning, II, in effect, agrees. On that basis Corning had rules that Robeson could not sing in Philip Livingston Junior High School. A public school, said the Mayor, should not be open to an artist identified with Communism. But the New York State Supreme Court reversed Corning and, in effect, Robeson, by ruling that singing is an artistic performance "and nothing else." Robeson could appear in the high school. Lask week he sang. Some 1,100 people turned out to hear him. The songs were nonpolitical. So was the applause. At the end, Robeson made a non-political speech: "I shall remember this with great warmth and affection." But afterwards Paul Robeson rumbled to newsmen: "This is the sixty-fifth formal concert of my present season and thank goodness, my last. I'm going to devote the next two years to lecturing, speaking, and singing as I please," concludes the article.

1299. "Robeson Says He Will Play 'Othello' If Henry Wallace Will Talk Between Acts," Afro-American, May 24, 1947, p. 3.

According to this article a proposition to "appear in Othello for a year on Broadway or elsewhere," was advanced by Paul Robeson, if former Secretary of Commerce Henry A. Wallace would be permitted to speak between the acts at each performance. The singer-actor made this statement during the intermission of a concert he gave in Philip Livingston Junior High School auditorium. Between 1,000 and 1,100 crowded into the 1,250 capacity hall to hear Robeson. Gross receipts amounted to approximately $3,000, states the article. The singer's appearance in the high school auditorium was made possible by Supreme Court Justice Isadore Bookstein, who ruled that the Albany Board of Education could not interfere with his appearance, suggests the writer. Robeson spoke to the audience and told them, in part:

> In the future, audiences will have to hear me talk as well as sing. I will not be fettered. I do not care to give any more pretty programs. I have views on political, economic, labor and social questions, including discrimination and segregation, which I wish to express. If I can help draw an audience for Henry Wallace by singing, I will support Wallace's viewpoint. He has something to offer the country. It would be practical for him to speak between the acts of "Othello." There would be no breaking of the mood after all, most of the patrons go out to smoke.

1300.   "Robeson to Rest Year, Says Wife," Afro-American, June 28, 1947, p. 1.

According to this article, Mrs. Paul Robeson said her husband will retire for a year following his return from a concert tour in Panama. She said he had been working for 15 years without a rest or vacation. His health is "not too good," and he "must take an extended rest without contracts for a year," states Mrs. Robeson.

1301.   "A Short 22 Years -- As Robeson's Pianist," Daily Worker, July 17, 1947.

This article states that Mr. Lawrence Brown had been Paul Robeson's pianist for twenty-two years. Mr. Brown was quoted as saying that he was singer Roland Hayes' accompanist before he started working with Mr. Robeson. The pianist states that he first noticed Robeson's interest in social problems around the beginnings of the Spanish Civil War. He also declares that Robeson always had a great love and understanding of people, and if you know Paul he is not content to just know, he has to help. Mr. Brown wrote more than 30 songs that were published by London music houses.

1302.   Hague, Robert A. "Throng Cheers Robeson at Lewisohn Stadium," PM, July 20, 1947, p. 1.

Mr. Hague declares that undeterred by the oppressive heat, glowering clouds and distant lightening, one of the season's biggest crowds - 18,720 - filled Lewisohn Stadium to hear Paul Robeson, who was making his first appearance there in five years. During the first half of the program, the renowned American bass-baritone offered a triptych of classical arias with the Philharmonic under the baton of Alexander Smallens; and then, in the second half, after the musicians had packed up and left the stage, he sang a group of familiar Negro folk songs. The writer states that in the classical group, the great Robeson voice, though it sounded a bit tired in spots, was generally as impressive as ever....

1303.   "3,500 Hear Robeson: But Peekskill Residents Head Legion and Fein Attend," New York Times, August 24, 1947, p. 28.

This article states that the protest by the Peekskill Post of the American Legion seemed to be effective in keeping local residents from the Paul Robeson concert, but 3,500 vacationers from other communities attended. It was estimated that less than 100 persons from the Peekskill community attended.

1304.   "Robeson Demands Violence Inquiry," New York Times, August 29, 1949, pp. 19. 23.

A disturbance at the Lakeland Acres picnic ground prevented Paul Robeson from doing a concert there. Anti- and pro-Robeson followers engaged in fighting, overturning and smashing cars. After these incidents Paul Robeson requested an inquiry by the authorities.

1305. Hudlin, W.W. and H.B. Webber. "Robeson Ban Arouses East St. Louis," Pittsburgh Courier, November 22, 1947, pp. 1, 4.

Paul Robeson spoke at St. John's CME Church in East St. Louis, Illinois after he was denied use of public facilities. Several Negro groups that had originally sponsored Robeson's use of public facilities withdrew their support. Robeson was prompted to argue, in part: "Undue pressure was brought to keep Negroes from attending my concert. The so-called Negro leaders shouldn't try to knife a guy simply because they happen to disagree with him. It was the first time I have been segregated by my own people. Even in the deepest South, Negroes have insisted on my appearing in the main public halls, despite frowns by city officials...."

1306. "Robeson Sees Hope in Third Party Movement," The Call (Kansas City, Missouri), May 21, 1948, p. 1.

According to this article Paul Robeson sang and lectured in Kansas City, Missouri, at the Morning Star Baptist Church to an audience of 1,500 persons. Robeson, who through the years refused to sing or speak to a segregated audience, said that in the deep South white and Negro people are defying the laws of segregation to sit where they please at public meetings. Robeson says that America is in more danger from the "fascist right" than from the "red left." He said that the FBI could round up all the lefist groups in the country in three hours, "but how long would it take to gather up the big boys who are potential fascists?"

1307. "Paul Robeson Appears in Atlanta, Macon," Atlanta Constitution, June 21, 1948.

Paul Robeson accompanied by Henry Wallace backers and Third Party candidates, made two appearances in Georgia, officially launching the move to get the Third Party on the general election ballot. He spoke and sang at meetings in Macon and in Atlanta. Approximately 1,200 persons attended each of the meetings, both of which were held in Negro churches. Only a sprinkling of whites attended the meetings, according to the article. A total of $202 in cash and an unestimated amount in pledges was collected for the Third Party treasury following the Macon rally. The amount collected in Atlanta was not announced. In the Atlanta meeting, held at the Wheat Street Baptist Church, Robeson said he wished to answer a column by Ralph McGill which appeared recently in The Constitution. He said he wanted McGill to know "that I have no intention of leaving this country, although it might be easier to live in several foreign countries."

1308. "Robeson Denied Use of Gary School for Rally," Afro-American, January 24, 1949, p. 1.

According to this article Paul Robeson's concert was cancelled by the Gary (Ind.) School Board. The Board said that Robeson could not hold his concert in Roosevelt School. The concert was eventually held at the St. Paul's Baptist Church. More than 1,200 Blacks and Whites attended the performance. Robeson called the concert a "democratic triumph."

1309.   "Robeson May Quit Stage," Pittsburgh Courier, January 25, 1947, p. 1.

Paul Robeson announced in Detroit that he may quit giving concerts. He declares: "You in Michigan will have a lot to answer for with the pattern of fascism all around you. This concert may be a valedictory because I am returning to political activity. I shall come back to Detroit and Michigan, but perhaps not as a singer or actor."

1310.   "Recitals of the Week: Gigli and Paul Robeson," London Times, March 21, 1949, p. 7.

This article states that Paul Robeson appeared in concert in the Albert Hall in London and his admirers were numerous. The reporter declares that Robeson adds a warm and friendly personality that renders his concerts the more enjoyable. He concludes: "His voice is as rich as ever though lacking a little in the smooth polish that memory is notoriously fickle and the microphone through which he sang undoubtedly distorted something of the quality of his voice. The ease and style of his singing are controlled with undiminished skill, however, and his programme, ranging from Peri to Negro spirituals, commanded constant interest and appreciation."

1311.   Westgate, Robert. "Robeson in Britain Cheered Singing for Peace," Daily Worker, March 31, 1949, p. 1.

This writer declares that Paul Robeson brought a vital message to Britain at a vital moment. He speaks for what he calls "the other America" -- the America that wants peace and friendship with all countries and the right of the common people to enjoy the full fruits of their toil. This is the progressive America which Lenin clearly distinguished from its reactionary, imperialist counterpart. The great importance of Robeson's visit is that it has served to remind the British people - at the very moment when so much is happening to make them forget it - of the existence of this America for which the State and War Departments do not speak, states Mr. Westgate....

1312.   "Mr. Paul Robeson at Polish Embassy," London Times, April 9, 1949, p. 6.

The article states that Mr. Paul Robeson gave a recital at the Polish Embassy in London. The programme included English, French, and Russian songs and songs from the Warsaw (Poland) Ghetto. Members of the British Government and of the Diplomatic Corps were among those who attended.

1313.   "South Africa Bans Robeson Records on Air," New York Age, April 16, 1949, p. 8.

This article states that records made by Paul Robeson were banned by the South African Broadcasting Corporation. The broadcasting company was not controlled by the government but was operated as a semi-official agency. It was also pointed out that the govern-

<u>(New York Age)</u>

ment of South African had been under fire for many years for its policy of absolute racial segregation.

1314. "Robeson to Cut Admission Fees," <u>New York Times</u>, May 7, 1949, p. 11.

Paul Robeson declares in London that henceforth he would give a majority of his professional singing appearances for admission fees of 20 to 40 cents, with occasional free performances. He accepted an invitation from Konni Zilliacus, left-wing Labor member of Parliment to give the first of his "concerts for the working man" in the M.P.'s mining constituency of Gateshead. The article states that Robeson would sing in Liverpool, Manchester and Sheffield, and then visit Czechoslovakia, Poland and the Soviet Union.

1315. "How Prague Welcomed Paul Robeson," <u>Daily Worker</u>, June 8, 1949, p. 12.

According to this article a climax of Paul Robeson's five-day visit to Prague as a guest artist at the International Spring Music Festival was his people's program presented to a capacity audience of 15,000. For two hours before the program, youth groups paraded informally through the sunny streets of the decorated city, singing their welcome to Robeson on their way to the outdoor winter stadium on the banks of the Vltava. Hundreds who could not get into the stadium listened through loudspeakers on the green terrace outside. Accompanied by the well-known South African pianist Bruno Raikin, and assisted by the leading Czechoslovak student chorus and democratic student groups from China, India, Italy, Indonesia, Viet Nam, Spain, West Africa· and other colonial lands, Paul Robeson gave an impressive demonstration of his conviction that an artist belongs to the people and draws his inspiration from the people rather than from exclusive highbrow circles in concert halls of restricted capacity....

1316. "Robeson Blasts 'Ol' Man River,'" <u>New York Age</u>, June 18, 1949, pp. 1, 5.

According to this article the recent clash between Paul Robeson and songwriter Oscar Hammerstein II over what words should be used in the song, "Ol' Man River," started quite a local fuss over what the original words actually were. The T.B. Harms Co., publishers of the famous songs, assert that the song as sung now is the same as the original written by Jerome Kern and Hammerstein, some local experts with long memories swear that the first line which now reads "Colored folks work on the Mississippi," is a revision, and not in the original. The words "colored folks" used to either "n-----s" or "darkies,' they claim. T.B. Harms says "as" and there the controversy stands. The writer declares that all this began recently when Robeson told an audience in Russia that the words should be changed. He, in fact, has always changed many of the words whenever he has sung the song. On hearing of this, Hammerstein did a slow boil. "As the author of these words," he said, "I have no intention of changing them or permitting

(New York Age)

anyone else to change them. I further suggest that Paul Robeson
write his own songs and leave mind alone," concludes the reporter.

1317. Townsend, Willard. "The Siren Song of Robeson, Reynolds and
        Randolph," Chicago Defender, August 27, 1949, p. 17.

        Mr. Townsend argues that the "brave" new variations on the old
        spiritual theme, "Ain't Gonna Study War No More," is becoming a
        popular ditty, and every morning we find ourselves searching the
        newspapers to discover who else plans to carry the 15 million
        Negroes "down by the river side," to lay down their sword and
        shield. To date, the field has been dominated by the Big Three -
        Randolph, Reynolds, and Robeson. Interestingly enough, Randolph,
        the socialist, Reynolds, the Republican and Robeson, the domestic
        "big noise" of Slavic totalitarianism are perhaps the strangest
        combination of personalities ever to find themselves in bed with
        each other on a national "issue." With the accented tones of
        Philip Randolph, the high falsetto notes of Grant Reynolds and
        the keep organ-tone voice of Paul Robeson, this strange enchanting
        lullaby has lured us into a sea of false issues which for the
        past three years has succeeded in taking us partly away from our
        real course in the important period of post-war changes.... He
        concludes: "In the case of Philip Randolph, we will give the
        benefit of the doubt, but in the case of Harlem's "Slick" Reynolds
        and Moscow's lyrical Mr. Robeson, the siren song of defeatism con-
        tains some calculated overtones of using the 'Negro issue' for
        ulterior motives, and we can easily guess the nature and purpose.
        Reynolds, the preacher-Republican, and Robeson, the singing
        fellow traveller, are not too far apart in their designs. It is
        just a matter of what river the Negro will be 'sold down.'"

1318. "'We Must Free 12,' Robeson Told Cheering Rally,"Daily World,
        (Atlanta, Ga.), June 30, 1949, p. 1.

        Paul Robeson appeared at Madison Square Garden in New York City
        and sang several songs. He also told the crowd that he was "back
        here from Europe to fight for the 12 brave leaders at Foley
        Square, whom we can free and must free." Robeson spoke with
        passion and with buoyancy, too - with passion against the imperial-
        ists who would bathe the world with blood if they could, and with
        buoyance of the people fighting on our side. He decalres that a
        central job in this struggle here was the freeing of the Com-
        munist leaders. Communists are always in the vanguard of the
        fight for the people - at home and abroad, he went on. Robeson
        concludes: "I laid wreaths on monuments of anti-Nazi fighters all
        over Europe. The men honored were usually Communists. They were
        the first to fall in the fight for their people. And here in the
        United States the Communists are also in the front in the fight."

1319. "No Trouble Ahead if Robeson Sticks to Singing in L.A.," <u>Afro-American</u>, September 10, 1949, p. 3.

According to this article as long as Paul Robeson sings and does not talk, there will be no trouble in Los Angeles, the police declared. Robeson was scheduled to sing in Wrigley Field, Sept. 30, in honor of the 70th anniversary of the <u>California Eagle</u>. The article also surmises that the singer was always a great favorite here. When he introduced "Ballad for Americans" at the beginning of the war, music lovers jammed Hollywood Bowl to hear and cheer him, asserts the author. Since becoming a controversial political figure, he has not sung here.

1320. "Paul Robeson to Sing in Detroit," <u>Detroit News</u>, September 20, 1949.

This article states: "Robeson, Negro baritone and avowed Communist, will sing and speak at a public 'rally' here on October 9, 1949, according to Coleman Young, a Progressive Party official." Robeson's last appearance was in Peekskill, N.Y., on September 4, 1949, which occasioned a riot in which 54 people were hospitalized, 14 were arrested and 40 were taken into protective custody. The Detroit appearance will be sponsored by the Detroit Committee To Welcome Robeson.

1321. "Robeson on Whirlwind Cross Country Tour," <u>New York Age</u>, September 24, 1949, p. 32.

According to this article Paul Robeson, Chairman of the Council on African Affairs, will leave New York on Sept. 23 for a rapid cross country tour including the cities of Los Angeles, Chicago, Cleveland, Detroit, Washington, D.C., and Philadelphia, it was announced today by Dr. W.A. Hunton, the Council secretary. Robeson will speak and sing at meetings in these cities arranged by local sponsoring committees in cooperation with the Council on African Affairs, states the reporter. The article states that it was announced that the Council's chairman, who has spoken at several overflow meetings in New York City since his return from Europe last June, will bring to audiences in some of the major Negro urban centers across the country his views concerning the Negro peopel's fight for economic security, civil rights, and full equality and how this fight is directly linked with the struggle for world peace and the liberation of African and other colonial peoples. Mr. Robeson's tour has aroused widespread public interest and prompted editorial comment in many local newspapers of the cities he is to visit, Dr. Hunton reported, according to this article....

1322. "Robeson to Visit Detroit," <u>Michigan Chronicle</u>, October 1, 1949, p. 1.

Robeson was scheduled to sing in Detroit, Michigan. However, not all Blacks approved of his appearance. In fact, the all-Black Charles Young Post of American Legion did not approve of his visit. A spokesman for the Charles Young Post asserts, in part:
    It is the policy of our organization to wage war on
    all things which are dangerous to American welfare.

(Michigan Chronicle)

   The Communist Party, which is apparently sponsoring
   Robeson's appearance, has done everything in its power
   to overthrow our government. I believe we can best
   promote democracy by ignoring his (Robeson's) visit
   to Detroit. Legion members will be strongly urged
   to stay away from the meeting. They will be asked
   to stay out of the vicinity of the Club House.

1323. "Robeson Sings to 12,000 in Los Angeles," Daily Worker, October 4,
   1949, p. 4.

   Paul Robeson performed in Wrigley Field in Los Angeles, California,
   and more than 12,000 people heard him sing and talk. The city
   council passed a resolution asking residents to boycott the affair.
   However, few obeyed the request.

1324. "Sings in Washington Without Incident as Police Patrol Areas,"
   Pittsburgh Courier, October 22, 1949, p. 18.

   Paul Robeson gave a concert before 2,700 people who packed Turner's
   Arena in Washington, D.C. In a combination concert and lecture,
   Robeson interspersed songs in English, Yiddish, German and Russian
   all through his talk as he charmed the enthusiastic audience. Not
   a single indicent of any kind marked the peaceful assembly. Elaborate precautions against any such incident were taken by the
   Metropolitan police of Washington who patrolled a six square
   block area surrounding the arena, roped off the street on which the
   arena is located, and provided Robeson with a round-the-clock escort of more than a dozen detectives and uniformed cops. More than
   one hundred policemen were assigned to duty in the area. Police
   chief Robert Barrett personally directed the police operations
   from a spot at the entrance of the hall, states the article,
   Robeson told the crowd, in part:
       There is no question about my loyalty to the America
       I love.... But I will have nothing to do with the
       Coxes of Georgia, the Rankins of Mississippi, the
       Du-Ponts of Delaware.... That is not my America....
       I hope the police department will give the same
       protection to every Negro boy and girl and every
       white boy and girl in Washington. I never had so
       much attention before although I am the same man
       who has been to Washington many times before to walk
       the picket line.... I am asking for the same things
       now that I asked for then -- freedom, full freedom
       for my people....

1325.   "Robeson Sings in Peace to Capacity L.A. Crowd," Afro-American, October 15, 1949, p. 8.

The report states that Paul Robeson sang in Los Angeles at Wrigley Field and there was no trouble from the capacity crowd that packed the stadium. Robeson confined his remarks to a statement that he loved America, and that he will stay in America, but will continue to seek equal rights for all its citizens. Before Robeson sang, the Rev. Clayton D. Russell raised $10,000 in contributions from those present for the benefit of the California Eagle, one of the nation's oldest Negro newspapers, and co-sponor of the program. The large crowd attended the program despite the city council's 100 percent vote on a resolution asking the citizens to boycott the affair, concludes the article.

1326.   Hyman, Mark. "Thousands Hear Paul Robeson in Philly (Pa.) Metropolitan Opera," Black Dispatch, November 5, 1949, p. 1.

The reporter states that three thousand people stood and applauded for 15 minutes when Paul Robeson entered the Metropolitan Opera House in Philadelphia, the scene of the great singer's first concert. Mr. Hyman suggests that the concert was short and punchy with appropriate songs to keep the interest of the thousands gathered. In a paragraph Mr. Robeson told of his early childhood in this city; of his days at Princeton and Rutgers. He said he never stood for bigotry even then. His punch line, which brought the audience to its feet was "All America is horrified at Peekskill." He accused Thomas Dewey, "The men behind Dewey" and the New York State Police of starting the riot which under ordinary circumstances, would have been just another concert, states the writer. "Water Boy" drew tumultous applause as did a song in Hebrew which he learned from his father, a Methodist Zion minister. Robeson directed his remarks against American bigotry to the people who know "Joe Hill." He said that Negroes and interested people can get civil rights if they go to the nation's capital in great numbers and demand of Congress that Civil Rights be passed, concludes Mr. Hyman. After his speech, applause was timed at 14 minutes.

1327.   "Robeson 'Hot' Over the Air," Pittsburgh Courier, November 11, 1949, p. 1.

According to this report in a direct departure from anything that has happened before, the Columbia Broadcasting System presented Paul Robeson, America's most famous singer of folk songs, as the star of its Sunday afternoon program, "Pursuit of Happiness," leading the famous Lyn Murray Chorus of white and colored voices, so mixed for the occasion. Presented for the express purpose of introducing Earl Robinson's inspired folk oratorio, "Ballad for Americans," in its first radio presentation on the Columbia network, the great actor-singer and the Lyn Murray Mixed Chorus gave an inspired performance, lifting their well-trained voices from coast to coast, finding a way into radios throughout the country in a most thrilling fashion. It was Mr. Robeson's first radio work since he returned here to start in the Broadway scheduled version of Roark-Bradford's "John Henry." With that

(Pittsburgh Courier)

performance, the internationally-known star proved that his voice
has lost none of its mellowness, and as a baritone he is without
a peer, states the author. The reporter declares that the presentation of Earl Robinson's "Ballad for Americans," which Paul
Robeson calls a magnificent work, opens up an entirely new concept of American music with its freshness of spirit and its
modern cry against racial discrimination and prosecution of all
kinds. With the song, Mr. Robeson was able to call forth both
his superb singing and dramatic talent. His was a role and performance seldom accorded Negroes in this country, concludes the
article.

23. SPORTS

1328. Low, Nat. "Lewis, Robeson Confer Tomorrow," Daily Worker, December
       2, 1943, p. 1.

       The Commissioner of Baseball Judge Kenesaw Mountain Landis, invited
       Paul Robeson to meet with him to discuss the question of Negroes
       in major league baseball.

1329. Dexter, C.E. "Robeson Thrills Writers, Magnates at Baseball Meet,"
       Daily Worker, December 4, 1943, p. 3.

       When Paul Robeson spoke to the baseball owners, they all listened.
       He urged them to immediately allow Negro players to be hired in
       the major leagues. The speech by Robeson marked the official re-
       cognition of the pleas of millions who had urged that the "un-
       written" discriminatory bars be let down.

1330. Smith, Wendell. "(Negro) Publishers Place Case of Negro Players
       Before Big League Owners," Pittsburgh Courier, December 11, 1943,
       pp. 1, 17.

       Paul Robeson was invited by the Negro newspaper publishers to
       appear with them before 44 owners and officials of major league
       teams. They asked the owners to drop the color bar and allow
       Negro players to join major league teams. He told the group:
       "I come here as an American and former athlete. I come here because
       I feel this problem deeply." According to the writer, Robeson re-
       ceived a rousing ovation when he finished addressing the group.

1331. "Harris is Called: Owners Hear Robeson," New York Times, December
       4, 1943, p. 17.

       At a meeting with baseball owners Paul Robeson urged them to allow
       Negro players to enter organized baseball. Several delegates
       from the Negro press also attended the meeting. After the meeting,
       Robeson said, he was joining the movement because he thought
       this was an excellent time to bring about an entry of Negro players

(New York Times)

into organized baseball. Robeson also pointed out that on the
stage, a Negro in a white case long ago was considered incredible,
yet he considered his own appearance in "Othello" as the outstanding success of his career. The owners issued a statement
that declared that "each club is entirely free to employ Negro
players to any extent it pleases and the matter is solely for
each club's decision without any restrictions whatsoever."

1332.   "Leading Negro Paper Lauds Paul Robeson, Raps Jackie Robinson,"
         Daily Worker, July 14, 1949, p. 2.

This article reports that the Baltimore Afro-American, a leading
Negro newspaper in a sharply worded editorial in its current issue,
applauds Paul Robeson's fight for Negro rights and instructs
Jackie Robinson, baseball star, to stick to the game he knows
best. Robinson was "invited" to appear before the House Un-American Committee yesterday to "refute" Robeson's statement at the
Paris Peace Conference that American Negroes would not participate in an imperialist war. Robinson's appearance has been
postponed until next Monday. Pointing out that Robeson is a
"good American," the Afro-American asserts that he is thinking
about "millions of colored people in the South who cannot vote,
who are terrorized by mobs at the least provocation, and cannot
get a decent job or a decent education." A cartoon on the editorial page pictures Paul Robeson's great footsteps which Robinson
cannot fill. It is entitled, "Drop That Gun, Jackie!" The line
at the bottom of the cartoon reads, "The leading player in the
National Baseball League is only a tyro as a big-game hunter."
The Daily Worker later reprinted the Afro-American editorial on
Jackie Robinson.

1333.   Mardo, Bill. "Robeson Fought for (Jackie) Robinson," Daily Worker,
         July 19, 1949, pp. 2, 9.

The writer points out that Jackie Robinson's memory is short because it was not many years ago (six) that Paul Robeson spoke to
the baseball hierarchy and asked them to allow Negro players to
play in the major leagues. Robinson had recently appeared before
the House Un-American Activities Committee in Washington, D.C.,
and told them that Robeson does not speak for the Negro people.

1334.   Burley, Dan. "Robeson, Pollard, Slater Have Reunion in Harlem,"
         New York Age, August 13, 1949, p. 32.

This article declares that an impromptu reunion brought together
the only three living Negroes named to the lat Walter Camp's famous
All-American football teams when Paul Robeson, Sr., Frits Pollard,
Sr., and Municipal Court Judge Fred (Duke) Slater of Chicago got
together at Pollard's Sun Tan Studio, 217 West 125th Street for a
few hours. "This is the first time the three of us have been together in almost 30 years," Robeson declares, as the trio, who were
"pioneers" among Negro football players on white college and university teams as well as professional, talked back in the dim past
of Negro athletic history and compared notes once again, states

(Burley, Dan)

Mr. Burley. Pollard won his laurels at Brown University; Robeson
at Rutgers and Slater at the University of Iowa. Pollard was a
halfback whose exploits made front page headlines across the
nation in 1916-17. Robeson, an end, has been rated among the all-
time greats, the same going for Slater, who performed at tackle
for the Hawkeyes. The late William H. Lewis of Harvard, was the
fourth Camp selection.

24. THE ROBESON ESTATE

1335. "Seven Bedrooms, Five Baths in Robeson Home - The Beeches," Afro-
American, October 1, 1949, p. 2.

This article describes the Robeson's home in Enfield, Conn. It
states that "The Beeches," the Robeson estate, so named because
of the stately beech trees which rise about its rolling lawn, is
a charming setting for the classic Georgian type Colonial home.
The pillared entrances lead into a pleasant house furnished with
functional simplicity. There are balconied drawing room and
dining rooms on the main floor, as well as kitchen and two pan-
tries; five bedrooms and three baths on the second floor; two
bedrooms, two baths and a lounge on the top floor. Most of the
beds are seven feet affairs built to accommodate the towering
artist. A competent housekeeper assists in the running of the home
and a local gardener tends the lawn. There are swimming pool,
recreation house, two full-length bowling alleys, tennis and
basketball courts, showers and dressing rooms and billiard and
pool tables. A spiraling flagpole rises to the right of the
house, concludes the article.

25. THEATER

1336. "London Raves over Paul Robeson as 'Othello': American Actor Gets
Big Ovation," Chicago Defender, May 24, 1940, p. 5.

This article declares that with his magnificent voice and splendid
physique, Paul Robeson, in London at the Savoy Theater, becomes a
worthy successor to the immortal Shakespearean tragedian, Ira
Aldridge, in the drama "Othello." At the conclusion of the play
Mr. Robeson won enthusiastic applause from an audience which
packed the theater. Critics hailed his acting as a triumphant
success. Mr. Robeson was supported by one of the foremost Shakespearean actresses in England, Miss Sybil Thorndike, who enacted
the role of Emilia. Miss Peggy Ashcroft, another well known
dramatic star, was the Desdemona. One of the most interested
persons in the vast audience was Dame Madge Kendal, who played

(Chicago Defender)

Desdemona to the Othello of Mr. Aldridge 65 years ago, states the
author. The article concludes:
    The triumph of the American Monday evening in the
    difficult drama marked his first effort in a Shakes-
    spearean play. Mr. Robeson, who is recognized as
    one of the most versatile signers and actors in
    existence, only began preparations for his role of
    Othello in recent months. He returned to London
    several weeks ago after a marked success in the
    starring role of "Emperor Jones" in Berlin.

1337.   McKay, Claude. "Paul Robeson as an Actor," New Leader, January
        20, 1940.

        The author surmises that as an artist, he has increased the dig-
        nity of and respect for the Negro on the stage. He has played
        tragic roles with fine insight and his rating is as high in the
        legitimate theatre as in the concert hall. Robeson is hailed as
        a pathfinder by the large body of young educated Negroes. He is
        one of them. They see in him the iconoclast, breaking down the
        old traditions of the Negro on the stage, according to Mr. McKay.

1338.   "Voice and Dramatic Talent Blend in Production which Could be Song
        Collection," Journal and Guide, January 20, 1940, p. 16.

        This article asserts that the great Paul Robeson, who has not been
        seen on Broadway since 1932, when he appeared in a rebirth of Flo
        Ziegeld's "Showboat," made a triumphant return last week to lend
        his magnificent voice and his remarkable dramatic ability to the
        role of "John Henry" in a musical fantasy by Roark Bradfork and
        Musical Director Jacques Wolfe. Robeson belongs to the chosen
        few of the theatre who are capable of sweeping critics and audi-
        ences before them by the very force of their personality, ir-
        respective as to whether the vehicle in which they are appearing
        is good or bad material, states the writer. He argues:
            To say that Robeson scored a resounding personal tri-
            umph at last week's premiere at the Forty-fourth
            Street Theater is to put it mildly, for without the
            magic of his golden baritone and the atmosphere of
            awe which seems to radiate from his massive physique,
            "John Henry" would be nothing more than a collection
            of beautiful songs with a stingy amoung of dialogue
            to string them together....

1339.   Woodson, Carter G. "Letter to the Honorable Arthur W. Mitchell,"
        Negro History Bulletin, Vol. 3, No. 6, March, 1940, p. 87.

        The writer states that of the many persons who have undertaken to
        imitate the Negro on the stage none has as yet been able to mani-
        fest that art to take the place of the Negro in the histrionic
        sphere, although racial antagonism has often supplanted the Negro
        elsewhere. Ira Aldridge....Paul Robeson are cases in evidence,
        states Woodson.

1340. "Robeson Eyes Wright's Book, Native Son, As Next Play," Chicago Defender, April 20. 1940.

According to this article the nation-wide success of Richard Wright's novel, Native Son, as one of the best sellers has convinced several Broadway producers that with Paul Robeson in the lead role it will make an ideal play for theatre-goers. It was learned that producers Eddie Dowling and Marc Connelly have made it known that they're after the book to adapt it for a stage version. Robeson would be the proper one to take the part of Bigger Thomas, who in the book, is the main character. His magnificent physical buildup corresponds exactly with that of Thomas as Wright has pictured him. Robeson is said to have been eyeing the book as his next Broadway play since it first hit the market, states the article.

1341. Du Bois, W.E.B. "A Chronicle of Race Relations," Phylon, Vol. 3, No. 4, Fourth Quarter, 1942, p. 33.

The writer declares that during the 1942 season Paul Robeson appeared as Othello and this was the first time that the character was played by a Negro since Ira Aldridge; which despite critics, was undoubtedly the type that Shakespeare had in mind, states Dr. Du Bois. Robeson received good reviews for his role.

1342. "Marian Anderson to Sing," New York Times, May 31, 1942, p. 25.

The article states that Marian Anderson and Paul Robeson would sing at a free "inter-racial war bond rally" at the Lewisohn Stadium. The rally was being held on behalf of the Treasury Department and would dramatize the war bond appeal among all races.

1343. Bessie, Alvah. "For I Am Black," New Masses, September 8, 1942, pp. 27, 28.

The author reviewed Paul Robeson in "Othello" that enthused audiences at Princeton, New Jersey. The reviewer assets that Mr. Robeson had closed a brief engagement at the McCarter Theater on the beautiful Princeton campus. At his last matinee performance a wildly enthusiastic audience gave the artist an ovation rarely seen in the American theater. The critic declares that it is certain that Mr. Robeson as well as his director thinks of the character he is playing as a Negro, and the implications he wrings from the role are wide and deep with his understanding of the part his people have played in history, both ancient and modern. To see this does not require such obvious evidence as the way the actor reads the line, "For I am black." He has infused his understanding of his people so profoundly throughout the drama that one would have to be intellectually blind not to see the point and draw conclusions. Othello was a black man who married a white woman, and the dramatist (who never hesitated to take liberties with his source material) was aware of the problem he posed in this play, asserts Bessie....

1344.   Isaacs, Edith J.R.   "The Negro in the American Theatre: A Record
of Achievement," Theatre Arts, Vol. 26, No. 6, August, 1942, p. 503.

The author points out that in "All God's Chillun Got Wings," Paul
Robeson played a leading role, that of a young Negro intellectual
who married a White woman (Mary Blair) and with her fights a losing
fight against racial antagonism. The play was boldly written and
excellently played but it had many of O'Neill's most marked faults
and he had not yet achieved the dramatic security he was soon to
find in the longer play-form. The drama's imperfections left it
open to every form of attack and it did not survive them long.
But Robeson's acting and -- soon after -- his first concert of
spirituals and work songs established his reputation as an artist
which has grown steadily since then, concludes Isaacs.

1345.   "Robeson as 'Othello,'" New York Times, August 16, 1942, Part 8,
p. 1.

The reviewer states that Robeson occasionally got a disturbing
tremolo in his voice in the play Othello, his performance is
heroic and convincing. He makes Othello a man to command and to
command respect. You believe in him first as a great soldier.
But he has a kindly, tender side with Desdomona, he is soft
spoken, gentle, delicately deferential, and in the beginning, a
little in awe of the childlike charm...., concludes the writer.

1346.   "Tragic Handkerchief: First U.S. Appearance in Othello," Time,
Vol. 40, No. 8, August 24, 1942, pp. 66, 68.

The review states that Robeson gave a performance that even at its
worst was vivid and that at its best was shattering. The author
states that Robeson's great voice, statue, bearing, were physically
impressive. He gave a plausible impression of being just such a
towering man as was Othello himself. More important, Robeson conveyed the bigness of Othello's nature -- its warmth, poetry
(nobody in Shakespeare utters lordlier speech), simplicity, trust-
ingness: the clawing horror which seizes Othello when Iago dupes
him into thinking himself a cuckold could come only from an uttered
unjealous nature. All the same, Robeson's towering personality
unbalanced the play by dwarfing Iago. Most absolute of villains,
who hates goodness, craves power, thrives on destruction. Iago --
as somebody has said -- is the plot, since he engineers every
last detail of it, unloosing all hell with a dropped handkerchief.
A great Iago can usually steal the show. As a pretty good Iago,
Jose Ferrer could not against Robeson, even hold his own....,
concludes the article.

1347.   "Life Goes to a Performance of Othello," Life, Vol. 13, No. 9,
August 31, 1942, pp. 82-85.

It was pointed out that Robeson was the first United States Negro
to play the passionate Moor in Shakespeare's tragedy of jealousy.
The article states that Robeson gave an unusual and electrifying
presentation of "Othello." The play was presented at Harvard
and Princeton Universities. Robeson is seen in several scenes
from the play. It was stated that "Robeson brought to the part

(Life)

the giant stature and range of voice that Shakespeare intended
when he wrote it in 1621," concludes the writer.

1348. "18 Cited for Aiding Race Relations," New York Times, February 7,
       1943, p. 48.

       The Schomberg Collection of Negro Literature of the New York Public
       Library conducted a nationwide poll to determine the eighteen
       persons or institutions who had done the most for the improvement
       of race relations. Paul Robeson was included "for symbolizing and
       promoting the folk art of many lands and peoples and for his per-
       formance last summer in the leading role of Shakespeare's immortal
       play 'Othello.'"

1349. "New Haven to See 'Othello,'" New York Times, July 19, 1943, p. 13.

       The Theatre Guild announced that "Othello" with Paul Robeson
       starring would open at the Shubert in New Haven, Connecticut.
       Additional performances there completed, it would go to Boston
       for two weeks.

1350. Norton, Elliot. "Paul Robeson as Othello," Boston Sunday Post,
       September 26, 1943.

       The critic comments on Paul Robeson's role in the play of "Othello."
       He states that "Mr. Robeson doesn't seem up to it in the great
       scenes, save one." Mr. Norton did say, however, that: "There is
       command and real dignity in his voice and manner, to bear out his
       own reminder that he is 'of royal siege.' There is a great gentle-
       man's deference and gallant affection in his manner with his wife.
       In the speech before the Venetian ducal council, wherein he pleads
       that he won his wife fairly, he is more than plausible; he is down-
       right exciting.... Again, in the scene where he steps into the
       drunken brawl which costs his lieutenant Cassio his commission,
       Mr. Robeson walks with the great men of the stage. His towering
       wrath and coldly commanding presence dominate the stage.... For
       the rest of it, however, except at the very end, when he dis-
       covers that he has murdered his wife vainly, his acting does not
       fulfill the promise of that tentative week at Cambridge....,"
       states Mr. Norton.

1351. "Paul Robeson as Othello," New York Times Magazine, October 3,
       1943, p. 15.

       This article states that Paul Robeson's much discussed inter-
       pretation of "Othello," produced on the road in London would come
       to Broadway under the auspices of the Theatre Guild. In the sup-
       porting cast would be Jose Ferrer as Iago and Uta Hagen as
       Desdemona. There are five photos of Paul Robeson as "Othello"
       in this article.

1352. Barnes, Howard. "Robeson is Othello," New York Herald Tribune,
      October 20, 1943.

      Mr. Barnes labeled Mr. Robeson's interpretation as "majestic."
      He continues:
           The Robeson performance is as triumphant as the setting
           and action in which it unfolds....he brings dignity,
           warmth and terror to a part which has eluded many
           great actors.... Robeson has the figure, the force
           and the voice to reflect every aspect of the ill-
           fated Moor....

1353. Morehouse, Ward. "'Othello' As Done By Guild....Provides Exciting
      Evening," New York Sun, October 20, 1943.

      The writer comments on Mr. Robeson's role as Othello. He con-
      cludes:
           Paul Robeson takes over a role which has been done by
           Booth and Barrett, by Salvini and Robert B. Mantell,
           and comparatively recently by such players as Walter
           Huston, Philip Marivale and Walter Hampden. Mr. Robeson
           played the Moor in London a dozen years ago and returned
           to the part, an immeasurably improved actor, for summer-
           theater presentations in Cambridge and Princeton. In
           his performance last evening at the Shubert he gave
           a portrayal of great resonance, vitality and fluency,
           and one surpassing any Othello within my experience.
           He brings majesty and power to the role, as well as
           pathos and terror....

1354. "Robeson Gives Vitality to Role," New York Sun, October 20, 1943.

      The article states, in part: "Paul Robeson, the first Negro of
      modern times to appear in a New York presentation, gives a giant's
      stature and remarkable clarity and vitality to his role. It was a
      glorious triumph for Robeson and for the American theater and for
      the grand tradition of Shakespeare, and for the human race, in
      general."

1355. Waldorf, Wilella. "Two on the Aisle: Paul Robeson a Striking
      'Othello' at the Schubert Theater," New York Post, October 20,
      1943, p. 36.

      The critic comments on Mr. Robeson's role as "Othello." The writer
      states that Margaret Webster and Paul Robeson, with the assistance
      of Jose Ferrer and Uta Hagen, a good cast and Robert Edmond Jones
      as designer, gave Broadway its finest production of "Othello" in
      years. With it the Theatre Guild opened its 26th subscription
      season in distinguished fashion at the Shubert Theatre. The critic
      states:
           What Mr. Robeson needed, apparently, was a director
           like Margaret Webster and time to grow into the part,
           for he is now a tremendously impressive embodiment
           of the famous Moor about whose countenance so many
           Shakespearean authorities have argued. Mr. Robeson
           has the physique, the dignity and the noble quality

(Waldorf, Wilella)

      the role demands, and, above all, a speaking voice
that does full justice to its poetry. His tortured
reaction to Iago's scheming is immeasurably more
affecting now than it was in London thirteen years
ago, when he did much more sweating and groaning....

1356. Gold, Mike. "Paul Robeson Restored Dignity to Stage," Daily
      Worker, October 21, 1943.

The reviewer declares: "Most Broadway first nights attract an
audience that almost makes a profession out of being seen at such
evenings. It is the carriage trade of New York, and it really
doesn't speak for the nation.... But Paul Robeson's first-night
audience consisted of universal humanity and its applause was not
that of a clique. This was the American people greeting Shakespeare. It reminded one of the great days in New York when the
people formed torchlight processions for Shakespearean actors like
Macready and Booth, dragged their carriages through the streets,
and fought bitter street battles over their respective merits.
Rubbing shoulders with the stock-market dukes and black-market
barons and their expensive ladies were accounting clerks and mer-
chant seamen, lady welders and housewives and well-known trade-
union leaders -- carpenters, house painters and hundreds of erect,
clean young men in army or navy uniform. A large delegation of
professors and students from Princeton sat together; many famous
actors, authors, musicians, painters and sculptors rubbed shoulders
with British sailors. Hindus and European refugees. There was a
certain millionaire sitting in the midst of some dark, handsome,
eager faces that came from Harlem.... With his singing, Robeson
had won a place in the cultural life of America. Now, with
'Othello' Robeson has restored dignity and power to the shabby
commercial stage," concludes Mr. Gold.

1357. Harris, Sydney J. "Robeson Rouses Broadway to Ovation with
      'Othello,'" Chicago Daily News, October 28, 1943.

The author declares that Robeson dominated the play "Othello" at
every turn. Physically impressive, towering above all others on
the stage, his portrayal of the tortured Moor was at once sensitive and dramatic, states Harris. He concludes:
      Only the incomparable authority of Robeson could
      have dwarfed the subtle performance of Jose Ferrer,
      who made Iago a credible villain, not the cringing,
      ratlike character we have seen in the past, but a
      ruthless, egocentric paranoid - one of Shakespeare's
      most skillful delineations come alive....

1358. "Critics Acclaim Paul Robeson's 'Othello,'" Pittsburgh Courier,
      October 30, 1943, p. 19.

Paul Robeson played the role of "Othello" at a Broadway theater
in New York City. He was hailed by critics as having given the
best interpretation of the role of the Moor, in the play.

1359. Marshall, Margaret. "Drama: Othello," Nation, Vol. 157, No. 18,
       October 30, 1943, pp. 507-508.

       The critic comments on Mr. Robeson's role in "Othello." She de-
       clares:
              Paul Robeson has an imposing figure and a powerful
              voice. But he performs rather than acts. Under Miss
              Webster's direction he performs passably well, but he
              creates no illusion. He speaks - often sings - Othello's
              lines, but he is not Othello in the sense that Mr. Ferrer
              is Iago. And he is not the Moor as Shakespeare con-
              ceived him. Both Mr. Robeson and Miss Webster have
              tried to prove that Othello is a Negro; they have
              attempted also to prove that "Othello" is a play
              about race. Both theories seem to me false and foolish.
              Fortunately Miss Webster's artistic sense is superior
              to her ideology, which has been confined to the
              public prints and does not appear in the play. There
              is no particular reason why a Negro should not play
              Othello or, for that matter, why a Negro should.
              Color aside, Robeson is simply not the type. The
              exotic quality is missing. Moreover, Shakespeare's
              Moor was surely a man of movement, as agile in his way
              as Iago. Robeson is monumental and inert. He makes
              no use whatever of his body, which becomes a dead
              weight. His voice does move, and it is fit to declaim
              such wonderful lines as "...when I love not thee,
              Chaos is come again." But even his voice gets out
              of character; it is too often reminiscent of Paul
              Robeson, singer of spirituals. Also its great volume
              is too often unstopped - some of Othello's "Oh's" are
              simply rushes of vast and shapeless sound.

1360. "Tneater: Man and Moor," Newsweek, Vol. 22, No. 18, November 1,
       1943, pp. 90, 93.

       The article discusses Paul Robeson in the role of "Othello." It
       states that Robeson is internationally noted not only as actor
       and singer but as a crusader deeply disturbed by the problems of
       his race. According to the writer in playing the role of Othello,
       Robeson feels that he is "talking for the Negroes in the way only
       Shakespeare can." This play is about the problem of minority
       groups - a Black Moor who tried to find equality among the whites.
       It's right up my alley, states Robeson. The reviewer concludes:
       "In addition to his assurance as an actor, Robeson brings to Othello
       a voice and physical presence that few contemporary actors can
       match."

1361. Young, Stark. "Othello," New Republic, Vol. 109, No. 18, November
       1, 1943, pp. 621-622.

       The writer discusses Mr. Robeson's role in "Othello." He declares
       that the fact that the actor in this case is a Negro has no direct
       bearing on the subject, since Othello was portrayed as black up
       to the nineteenth century when critical romanticism changed his
       color to the Arabian. The Italian original of the story uses the

(Young, Stark)

word negrazza to describe him, states Mr. Young. Mr. Robeson, a
singer of distinction, still lacks for this role the ultimate requirement, which is the fine tragic style. By virtue of true
feeling and intensity of soul he has its equivalent at times; and
then he is moving and deep, surmises the reviewer. He suggests
two things to Mr. Robeson: One is that he recast, as it were,
his first speeches in the play, and a number of others later on,
where he is too agressive vocally, has too much projection of the
tone, gives us the wearing sense of an overworked diaphragm where
only the relaxation of dignity and strength are required. In
the scenes that call for more emotion or decision his voice is
very fine, unrivaled on our stage. The other has to do with style,
the elusive matter of stage bearing, so important in this part, as
his acting often shows. In the scenes of despair he crumples up
into a defeat far too domestic, gentle and moving though it may be.
He must discover a style, remote but equally pathetic, for these
moments. Otherwise his performance is admirable, is noble, tender
and rich in scope. It has no little of the depth and stretch of
music. And underneath is constantly there is a kind of spiritual
humility that is akin to grandeur, concludes the critic.

1362.   "'Othello': Paul Robeson Gives a Magnificent Performance as the
        Moor of Venice," Life, November 22, 1943, pp. 87-88, 90.

        The article states that Paul Robeson gave a magnificent perfor-
        mance as the Moor of Venice in "Othello." It was pointed out
        that the role of the Moor has been played by some of the world's
        most accomplished actors. "But despite Shakespeare's intention
        that the part be played by a Negro, it remained for the present
        production to satisfy that condition on Broadway by casting Paul
        Robeson as the Moor," concludes the article. Robeson is seen in
        several scenes from the play.

1363.   Buchwald, Nathaniel. "Paul Robeson in Othello," The Worker,
        November 28, 1943, p. 7.

        The writer comments about Paul Robeson's role in "Othello." The
        writer declares that Robeson brings to the part of Othello both
        his Negro consciousness, his rich and profound personality and the
        consciousness of the actor's task. He argues that the special
        Robesonian quality which makes him particularly suited for the
        part of Othello predominates over his technique. Mr. Buchwald
        concludes, in part: "....You have the feeling that in this part
        Robeson is not the virtuoso actor, that this is not merely one
        of the greater roles in his repertory, but that it is the role of
        his life to which he has brought something all his own. Yes, the
        great, the original, the compelling, the revealing elements of
        Paul Robeson's Othello is Paul Robeson...."

1364. Gilder, Rosamond. "Othello and Venus," Theatre Arts, Vol. 27, No. 12, December, 1943, pp. 699-703.

The writer reviews the Broadway play "Othello," starring Paul Robeson. The reviewer declares that the arrival of "Othello" would be important on this score alone but with the added interest of Robeson's long heralded performance...it becomes a major event. The author argues that Paul Robeson brings to the role the nobility of his presence, his understanding of the role, his grave, deep, moving voice. His Othello is a massive creature, physically powerful with the gentleness that often accompanies great strength. He expresses well the simplicity, even the guilessness, that Shakespeare so clearly defines, surmises Gilder. The reviewer concludes that "Mr. Robeson's performance is forceful but he does not always achieve the dynamic fuison of his intellectual understanding of the parts and the raw material of its emotional contents. His Othello arouses admiration and pity but not quite the Aristotelian 'terror' that Shakespeare constantly demands of his interpreters."

1365. Gelders, Robert Van. "Robeson Remembers: An Interview with the Star of 'Othello' Partly About His Past," New York Times, January 16, 1944, Section 2, p. 1.

The actor discusses a number of topics including his football career at Rutgers. He states that he played in ninety-nine games out of a hundred with a smile on his face. There was one time, however, that he lost his temper and went out of his head with a rage. This one time was when he was a freshman trying to make the team when he lost his temper and floored the whole backfield of the team. He was about to smash one back on the ground when the coach yelled: "Robery, you're on the varsity." He also stated that his father was born into slavery in 1843 in North Carolina.

1366. "Ruth to Aid Bond Drive," New York Times, January 29, 1944, p. 165.

Babe Ruth appeared on the Fourth Base Loan radio show to help sell War Bonds. It was also stated that Paul Robeson, once great football player and greater now as actor and singer would participate.

1367. "Paul Robeson, as 'Othello,'" Opportunity, Vol. 22, No. 1, January-March, 1944, p. 27.

This article suggests that Paul Robeson's portrayal of Othello in the Theatre Guild presentation of the Shakespearean drama at the Shubert Theater was widely acclaimed by dramatic critics. The article declares that Paul Robeson played Othello twice before; in London in 1930 and more recently in summer theaters in this country. However, this is the first time on Broadway that a Negro actor has appeared in the role, surmises the writer. This Theatre Guild presentation of "Othello," directed by Margaret Webster, has surpassed the record run in America, concludes the article.

1368. Dreer, Herman. "The Negro in the Course of Study of the High
       School," Negro History Bulletin, Vol. 7, No. 7, April, 1944, p.
       165.

       The writer points out that in teaching Shakespeare's "Othello,"
       the instructor should mention Paul Robeson and Ira Aldridge,
       Negroes who were great interpreters of the little role.

1369. Putnam, Samuel. "Artist of the People," The Worker, April 16,
       1944, p. 10.

       The writer traces Paul Robeson's acting and singing beginning in
       1924 with his performance in "All God's Chillun Got Wings."
       Mr. Putnam declares that back in the glaring twenties, he was a
       disconcerting phenomenon. Robeson refused to be a mere enter-
       tainer. With an astonishing range of abilities and a rich
       cultural background, he might have made a success in any one of
       half a dozen careers, surmises the author. He said like Leonardo
       da Vinci, or a modern Picasso, Paul Robeson might have "done a
       little of everything" - and done it well. Instead, what he has
       lost in breadth he has gained in depth. Today, with each fresh
       appearance in the theater or concert hall his art has new and
       still more dazzling facets to show, and at the same time an ever
       new profundity of meaning and intensity of social passion. Mr.
       Putnam concludes:
               This I believe, is what really accounts for his
               present superb Othello, the greatest of our
               generation, one of the greatest ever. He is the
               Moor, the Moor of Venice as Shakespeare conceived
               him for his age; but he is also Paul Robeson, who
               puts into the part a passion that Shakespeare
               never knew, one that is of our own time, one that
               holds the hope of human brotherhood for the bright-
               dawning world of tomorrow.

1370. Beatty, Jerome. "America's No. 1. Negro," American Magazine,
       Vol. 137, No. 5, May, 1944, pp. 28-29, 142-144.

       The writer argues that Paul Robeson, playing "Othello" in 1944 in
       New York, not only broke all American boxoffice records for this
       Shakespearean tragedy, but established himself firmly as America's
       most distinguished living Negro. It was pointed out that when
       Robeson played professional football in 1921-1922 he received as
       much as $1,000 a game. The author states that at one time Robe-
       son was offered several hundred thousand dollars if he became a
       prize fighter and he turned it down because he wanted to be a
       lawyer. The writer said Robeson is a man of great charm, he
       possesses some sort of hypnotic magic, as though he were a genie
       out of a bottle, and whether he is talking about the Negro, Russia,
       "Othello," football, Chinese literature, Mrs. Robeson, his father,
       Eugene O'Neill, or Paul Robeson, Jr., you want him to keep on as
       fast as he can. Beatty concludes:
               Paul Robeson broke the back of prejudice to command
               recognition as a football star, lawyer, concert singer,
               and actor. Today he has won top triumphs by his
               magnificent portrayal of Shakespeare's "Othello."

(Beatty, Jerome)

> And all to prove to his people that they, too, can
> rise to the heights.

1371. Underwood, Mela. "Joe and Uta," Collier's, Vol. 113, May 20, 1944, p. 21.

The article is mainly about Joe Ferrer and his wife, Uta. There is some mentioning of Paul Robeson in this article. The author points out that the Ferrers' have become fast friends with Mr. Robeson, the distinguished Negro who is Uta's stage husband in "Othello," and when, as sometimes happens, Robeson becomes the object of race prejudice it burns them up. "The worst offenders are ignorant fools who are not worthy to shine Paul Robeson's shoes," Uta states. It was also pointed out that Paul Robeson would not play any Jim Crow theaters.

1372. Leonard, Claire. "The American Negro Theatre," Theatre Arts, July, 1944, pp. 421-423.

The writer declares that Paul Robeson along with other artists have tried to present a true conception of Black lives. He also states that the American Negro Theatre want to emulate the integrity and dignity of artists such as Paul Robeson and others, who reached out for the American Negro Theatre.

1373. Hutchens, John L. "Paul Robeson," Theatre Arts, October, 1944, pp. 579-585.

The author states that Paul Robeson is an actor - more than that, an artist - who had been moving steadily toward this Othello throughout his career, whether he realized it or not. In one sense this triumph is still mildly astonishing; a man who has never considered himself truly an actor does not just move into a great and demanding role and score the success of his life in it, even though it is a success within certain limitations. In another sense it was all but inevitable. From the first he had the commanding presence that is so decisive a physical and pictorial factor in the production: he looks the might Moor, the warrior, argues Hutchens. His voice, always a fine instrument, has grown richer and subtler through the years. And finally, and perhaps most important, he is a man of intellect, whose understanding of his world and his time has added vastly to his growth as an artist, states the writer. The author concludes:

> The obstacles facing the Negro artist are so great
> and so many that no one could truly say that Robeson's
> theatre future is of his own choosing. But no one
> could deny, either, that he has served the theatre
> well, and the ideals he brought to it. His race,
> and the American stage, have moved forward a little
> because of him.

1374. "Robeson Brings Fine Acting to Des Moines Audience," Iowa Bystander, December 14, 1944, p. 1.

This article states that the mighty and magnificent Paul Robeson in the Margaret Webster's production of William Shakespeare's play, "Othello," made the role of the Moor, the great and terrible figure of tragedy when an audience of 4,000 applauded him at the Shrine auditorium. The article continues that not only did the Negro actor receive an enthusiastic welcome as he portrayed the great role of the dark Moorish husband of the fair and lovely Desdemona, played by Uta Hagen, but he brought to Des Moines by his fine acting and his powerful resonant voice a deeper appreciation of the dignity of the Negro race which is hampered by racial prejudice.

1375. Casey, Robert J. "Add Robeson to 'Othello' and Bard Comes to Life," Chicago Daily News, April 11, 1945, p. 24.

The critic declares for his money, there is only one Paul Robeson and only he can play that role. He asserts that he was made to order for the role, and with his magnificent voice and diction he sticks out of a really remarkable cast like a tower.

1376. Murdock, Henry T. "'Othello' has Excitement, Dash - and Paul Robeson," Chicago Sun, April 11, 1945.

The writer suggests that Paul Robeson was a mighty ebony volcano as the wrong Othello and he fits the role with such bearing and such aptness for the text that the appearance of a Negro in the role is no longer novelty - it's convention to be obeyed in future versions.

1377. Pollack,Robert. "'Othello' Is All They Said about It in N.Y.," Chicago Sun, April 11, 1945.

The author contends that it is difficult to divorce, in one's own mind, Paul Robeson, an American leader of enormous potency and stature, from Paul Robeson, the Shakespearean actor. For the Theatre Guild to have cast him in the title role was an inspiration and he is always theatrically effective, states Mr. Pollack. His reading has resonance and dignity. His person is overpowering and his sincerity is indeniable. Yet he is not a great Othello, argues the critic. He went on to declare that you may go to this play because Robeson is in it but you probably remain afterwards to cheer Jose Ferrer.

1378. Stevens, Ashton. "Stevens Finds 'Othello' Spectacular, But-," Chicago Herald-American, April 11, 1945, p. 12.

The writer declares that "Othello" was on the whole more spectacular than emotional. He goes on to explain that Mr. Robeson's Othello, superbly pictured, deep-voiced and declamatory from the start, yet it seemed to him to have very little inner power. Stevens states that he had no doubt that Robeson was the most magnificently Morrish Moor in the picturial record of the tragedy. He then goes on to conclude that Robeson's imagination didn't

(Stevens, Ashton)

live up to his and he would be remembered by his Othello.

1379. Burns, Ben. "Robeson Writes History at Erlanger with Masterful
       Acting in 'Othello,'" Chicago Defender, April 21, 1945, p. 17.

       The critic argues that history was being written by the great Paul
       Robeson at the Erlanger theater in Chicago. It is more than
       theatrical history. It is epoc-making, precedent-shattering
       American history that is a happy omen of a new world acomin' in
       U.S. race relations. But Robeson's magnificent performance as
       "Othello" is important not only because it is an historic event.
       Its significance goes further than the simple fact that Robeson
       is the first Negro to play "Othello" on an American stage and
       kiss a white woman before a mixed audience. Mr. Burns declares,
       perhaps even more remarkable is Robeson's masterful ability to
       translate this great work of Shakespeare's into human terms, into
       thrilling, moving drama understandable to the everyday common man.
       "Othello," as played by Robeson and a splendid supporting cast,
       is not the heavy-handed Elizabethian drama of free verse that is
       crammed down the throats of unwilling students. The Erlanger
       production is as modern and up-to-date as a jazz concert. Mr.
       Burns concludes:
           ....But standing head and shoulders above all not only
           physically but as a brilliant actor is Paul Robeson,
           whose resonant voice and perfect diction make "Othello"
           the outstanding triumph of the theater in the past
           decade. His achievement in bringing "Othello" down
           to terms of today will live and be remembered for
           years to come. To miss Robeson in "Othello" is to
           miss history in the making.

1380. "'Othello' With Paul Robeson Returns to City Center May 22,"
       Daily Worker, May 1, 1945, p. 11.

       This short announcement declares that the Theatre Guild's record-
       holding Shakespearean presentation of the Margaret Webster pro-
       duction of "Othello," starring Paul Robeson, Jose Ferrer and Uta
       Hagen, will return from a triumphant transcontinental tour, for
       an engagement of two weeks only at the City Center.

1381. Morse, George Chester. "Broadway Re-Discovers the Negro," Negro
       History Bulletin, Vol. 9, No. 8, May, 1946, pp. 175-176, 189.

       The writer declares that Eugene O'Neill started a furore when he
       presented Paul Robeson in his play "All God's Chillun Got Wings"
       which depicted a then daring dramatic situation of intermarriage.
       Editorials in newspapers warned of the possibility of grave racial
       disturbances if the play was presented. Hysteria was rampant, but
       no riots occurred as was predicted. The author states that critics
       were lavish in their praise of Robeson's role as "Othello."

1381a. Washington, Fredi. "Open Letter to Paul Robeson," People's Voice,
       June 1, 1946, p. 14.

       The writer is the newspaper's theatrical Editor. She wrote an open
       letter to Paul Robeson asking him to play the part of Denmark Vesey
       in the movie version of his life. Vesey was a slave who planned
       a revolt to overthrow the slave system. The movie would be
       called "Set My People Free." Miss Washington wrote:
           It is not for that reason alone that "Set My People
           Free" is an important document, which all Americans
           should know about that, I, as many others who have
           read the script, implore you to lend your time and
           talents to it; but because it is an exciting drama.
           This is the kind of theatre vehicle that should by all
           means be produced, getting the best possible casting,
           direction and production. You might point to other
           actors of ability who could play the role. I have no
           doubt that that is so, though I don't know who they
           would be. But there is one thing you cannot deny,
           and that is there is no actor with your diversified
           ability who has consistently fought for and demanded
           an end to jimcrow in the theatre as well as outside
           the theatre. The fact that you were the first Negro
           to play the title role in Othello opposite a white
           "Desdemona" in the American commerical theatre to
           packed audiences throughout the country, proves that
           the success of plays dealing with Negro characters
           and life, good though they be in their own right,
           must not only have good and competent actors they
           must have in addition a name which has tremendous
           box office value.
       She also suggests: "Your name, Paul, carries that box office value.
       And that value carries with it a tremendous responsibility to the
       cause for which you have given unstintingly of your time, energy,
       abilities and finances. This is not the time nor the place to
       slacken the intense drive to bring to theatre goers better theatre,
       educational theatre, a more stimulating theatre, yes, and an
       artistic theatre which clasps hands with reality. Set My People
       Free has all of these things and more. It is a play which should
       and must reach Broadway next season...," concludes the author.

1382. "Robeson to Leave Stage," New York Times, January 27, 1947, p. 16.

       Paul Robeson announced in St. Louis, Missouri, that he intends to
       abandon the theatre and concert stage for the next two years to
       "talk up and down the nation against race hatred and prejudice."
       He declares: "Some of us will have to speak up and appeal to the
       people to respect the common rights of others.... It seems that
       I must raise my voice, but not by singing pretty songs."

1383. "Paul Robeson Plays Role of Emperor Again: Noted Actor Gives Ex-
       hibition in New Jersey," Philadelphia Tribune, August 15, 1948.

       According to this writer Paul Robeson played the role of "The
       Emperor Jones" at the McCarter Theatre in Princeton, New Jersey.
       The critic concludes: "Eugene O'Neill's delineation of the Pullman

(Philadelphia Tribune)

porter, who reverts to type when he no longer had the props of
civilization, was played magnificently by Robeson, whose huge
figure and rich voice served to heighten the effects in the
darkened scenes and faint backgrounds of the play. Despite the
fact that he had played the part many times, Robeson gave a performance which one critic describes as "fresh and vital as if he
had only now realized its possibilities."

26. UN-AMERICAN ACTIVITIES COMMITTEES

1384. "Says Negroes Shun Subversive Groups," New York Times, October 9,
1946, p. 24.

Edgar G. Brown, Director of the National Negro Council, testified
before the California Legislature's Committee on Un-American
Activities, and told it that he did not consider Paul Robeson as
a real spokesman or representative campaigner for Negroes. He
declares that the real leaders of the colored race were the
Ministers.

1385. "Paul Robeson Case," Washington (D.C.) Evening Star, June 1, 1948.

This article states how fortunate Robeson was to live in America
and that he had made achievements in this country that not many
Americans have been able to equal. Yet, contends the article,
Mr. Robeson pays homage to the Communists and to Russia, and
says that Russia has produced more freedom for the people than has
the United States. It concludes that in light of this expressed
opinion what difference does it make whether he actually is a Communist or not. He has said enough to show that he is wholly
biased and that in his testimony before the committee (The House
Un-American Activities Committee) he appeared, not as a witness,
but as a propagandist, declares the writer.

1386. Hall, Robert F. "Patterson Papers Try to Frighten Robeson,"
Daily Worker, June 8, 1948, p. 9.

The writer argues that the Patterson newspapers were in a blind
rage because Paul Robeson stated a few blunt truths about the
conditions of the Negro people when he testified before the Senate
Judiciary Committee. The editorial view was that Robeson had
fared very well in America. Therefore, how dare he suggest that
some things are better in Soviet Russia! Mr. Hall argues that not
only the Negro people but the human race can be proud of Paul
Robeson -- because he is the defender of the rights of the people.

1387. "Paris Parley Held Maneuver by Reds," New York Times, April 19, 1949, p. 6.

It was stated that Paul Robeson was reported by the House Un-American Activities and other organizations that the singer was affiliated "with from fifty-one to sixty Communist-front organizations."

1388. Editorial. "Drop That Gun, Jackie," Afro-American, July 16, 1949, p. 4.

The editor states, in part: Jackie Robinson says he is going down to Washington to appear before the House Un-American Activities Committee this week. He has been invited to call Paul Robeson a "liar." Robeson is the great American singer who said he loved the Russians and would refuse to fight a war against them. Robeson also said that he would much rather fight the Southern whites who are denying equal rights to colored people than the Russians who have not done anything to us at all. Jackie told the newspaper reporters that he and his teammate, Roy Campanella "would fight any agressor, the Russians or anybody else who wanted to take away the things I have gained...." Yes, we know Jackie will fight. He fought in the last war and he is a good American. And so is Paul Robeson a good American and despite the fact that Jackie is one of the finest athletes in the nation, he cannot begin to fill Paul Robeson's shoes. When Jackie Robinson talks about the things he has gained, he is thinking of himself. When Paul Robeson says he is not willing about himself. He is not thinking about Russia. He is thinking about millions of colored people in the South who can't vote, who are terrorized by mobs at the least provocation, and cannot get a decent job or a decent education. Our advice to Jackie Robinson, as much as we admire him, is that he put away his pop gun and put on his baseball uniform. He is more credit to us as a baseball player than a politican, concludes the editor.

1389. Editorial. "An Old Strategy," Daily Worker, July 21, 1949, p. 7.

The editor asserts that the House Un-American Activities Committee's strategy was divide and conquer. He concludes:
The Committee feared to hear Paul Robeson. That is because the issue is not "loyalty," not Robeson versus Robinson, but Negro liberation versus "white supremacy" and peace versus war. These issues they want to bury. But neither Negro leaders like Robeson, nor the Negro people, nor labor, nor the Communists will let them get away with their divisive tactics no matter how many "Yes men" they manage to get before their sneering committee.

1390. Editorial. "Where Real Probe is Needed," Afro-American, July 23, 1949, p. 4.

This editorial declares: "No editor from the AFRO-AMERICAN is going to appear before the House Un-American Activities Committee to testify to the loyalty of the colored race. We are Americans

(Afro-American)

like everybody else. Like Ivory Soap, our loyalty is 99 44/100
per cent pure, but we do not accept an invitation from Georgia's
Representative Wood to discuss with our patriotism with him. We
would much rather discuss with Congress Mr. Wood's Americanism,
Georgia is the home of the Ku Klux Klan and Governor Talmadge...."
He continues to assert:
    Mr. Wood and his colleagues have been considering
    whether to invite Paul Robeson to appear before the
    Un-American Activities Committee and ask him whether
    he is a Communist or not. Well, let's suppose Mr.
    Robeson is a Communist -- so what? There are a lot
    of Communists in this country, colored and white.
    Every colored person who has to live in Mr. Wood's
    state has incentive enough to turn to Communism.
    We are greatly surprised that more of them have not.
    If anybody asks us, Paul Robeson's eye is on Georgia,
    not Russia. He is using Communism as a vehicle to
    get relief from jim crow. Georgia uses the Ku Klux
    Klan as a vehicle to maintain white supremacy. Mr.
    Robeson's politics and Representative Wood's politics
    are different, but they are both politics.

1391. Graves, Lem, Jr.   "Jackie Flays Bias in Army," Pittsburgh Courier,
       July 23, 1949, pp. 1, 4.

       Jackie Robinson appeared before the House Un-American Activities
       Committee and is reported to have made the following comments:
       With regard to Paul Robeson's statement, on which he had been
       asked to comment, Robinson said: "It sounds very silly to me.
       But he has a right to his personal views and if he wants to sound
       silly when he expresses them in public that's his business and
       not mine. He's still a famous ex-athlete and a great singer and
       actor." Robinson is also reported to have said: "The white public
       should start toward real understanding by appreciating that every
       single Negro who is worth his salt is going to resent any kind
       of slur and discrimination because of his race and is going to use
       every bit of intelligence he has to stop it. This has absolutely
       nothing to do with what Communists may or may not be trying to do.
       And white people must realize that the more a Negro hates communism
       because it opposes democracy, the more he is going to hate any
       other influence that kills off democracy in this country - and
       that goes for racial discrimination in the Army, and segregation
       on trains and buses and job discrimination...."

1392. "Robinson Hits U.S. Bigots: Hearing on Robeson Proves Boomerang,"
       Afro-American, July 23, 1949, pp. 1, 2.

       According to this article what was intended to be a frontal attack
       on Paul Robeson boomeranged against the House Un-American Activi-
       ties Committee. Instead of hearing tirades against Robeson, the
       Committee was told that lynchers are the real enemies of this
       country and that the lawmakers should and must work to make the
       ideal of democracy real, states the article. Jackie Robinson was
       invited to appear before the House Committee to refute a recent

(Afro-American)

statement Paul Robeson is alleged to have made in Paris that "colored people will not fight in a war against Russia." The Brooklyn Dodgers stellar second baseman used his time to point out what is really wrong with America and what the white public should do to correct it.

1393. Reid, Clyde. "Paul Says Jackie Was Used as a Political Tool by Committee," New York Age, July 30, 1949, p. 3.

The writer reports that in a closed press conference at the Hotel Theresa, Paul Robeson gave "his" side of the current Robeson versus Everybody and Everybody versus Robeson quabble. Robeson was quoted as saying:
How dare the House Un-American Activities Committee ask Jackie Robinson or anyone else to testify as to the loyalty of the American Negro. Have they invited Joe DiMaggio down to testify about Italian loyalty? Has anyone testified about the loyalty of the French, Spanish or other nationalities? These hearings are just steps in the white supremacy move to further intimidate the Negro? There is no argument between Jackie and myself, it has to do with Negro people. It is an attempt on the part of those behind the committee - American capitalists - that one percent of the nation that commands the rest, to terrorize the Negro - show him up so that he will not get his rights. My main concern is to get at this Un-American Activities Committee. It's headed by a man who calls the Ku Klux Klan an American Institute, and is on its way to try and beat the Negro back into enslavement. I'm willing to appear before the committee at any time, I only hope that Wood (committee chairman) will be there.

1394. Editorial. "What America Fears Most," Afro-American, August 6, 1949, p. 4.

According to the editor, all this hullabaloo in the Un-American Activities Committee, headed by Representative Wood of Georgia, has a psychological foundation in fear. Everybody knows that Communism comes in only when the existing governments work excessive hardships on their citizens. These hardships may keep them poor, ignorant and starving as in Europe at present, or as in the far Southern States. The exploited and the oppressed everywhere are fully ripe for Communistic propaganda. The sharecroppers in the Delta region of Louisiana, or the laborers in the turpentine camps in Florida, who are deprived of their vote, who are subject to the terror of the Ku Klux Klan and the lynching by mobs, may not seem ripe for revolution yet.... There is no question about the fact that the stage is all set for a revolution of the oppressed some day unless this government in Washington compels the States to treat all citizens alike. Paul Robeson may be a voice crying in the wilderness today, but what will happen when there are ten thousand Paul Robesons or two million or ten million? All any

(Afro-American)

oppressed masses need is leadership and the House Un-American
Activities Committee is simply fearful that Mr. Robeson represents that type of leadership, concludes the editor.

27. WORLD WAR II

1395. "4,000 Hear Robeson, Pearl Buck Play Bias," Baltimore Afro-
       American, April 18, 1942, p. 1.

       This article states that Paul Robeson discusses the purpose of
       World War Two. He is reported to have said: "If the American
       people really want to see that this is a free America, they must
       see in this struggle that their freedom is tied up with the
       freedom, not only of the European peoples, but of the colonial
       peoples everywhere....not only of the 15,000,000 colored Ameri-
       cans, but with the freedom of millions of other colored peoples,
       and certainly of the 160,000,000 Africans who might stand be-
       tween Hitler and Dakar, between Hitler and South America, between
       Hitler and New York." Miss Pearl S. Buck asserts that war unity
       required the elimination of distrust.

1396. "Paul Robeson Raps Bias as a Delay to Victory," Pittsburgh Courier,
       November 27, 1943, p. 20.

       Paul Robeson spoke in New York City at the Herald Tribune Forum.
       He told the audience that victory for all Americans in the war
       (World War Two) was delayed by economic discrimination against
       the Negro people, by the segregation and inferior status assigned
       to Negroes in the armed services and by the Southern poll tax
       system. The singer argues that the Negro people's yearning for
       democratic freedom pre-dated Fascism, and that ever since the
       Fascist attack on Ethiopia the Negro people have seen the con-
       nection between their own interests and the struggles of all
       oppressed peoples.

1397. "Orphan Asylum Renamed," New York Times, April 7, 1944, p. 17.

       Fitz Harvey, 15 years old, received from Mayor La Guardia a $25
       war bond donated by Paul Robeson, to the winner of a city-wide con-
       test for a new name for the Colored Orphan Asylum at Riverdale
       Children's Association. Mr. Robeson introduced the boy to the
       Mayor and said that the change of name was "fraught with signi-
       ficance" as a symbol of the constant strengthening of unity among
       all peoples and races in the city. The new name, effective
       immediately, marked the beginning of a policy of admitting chil-
       dren to the institution, regardless of race.

1398. Anderson, Trezzvant W. "Robeson at Berchtesgaden." No name, no date. Newspaper article found in Moorland - Spingarn Research Center, Howard University.

This article was written by an ex-Army private. He asserts that he heard Paul Robeson sing in August 1945 and a group of Black soldiers met Mr. Robeson and the singer told them how things were in America, and what they were to expect when they returned to the states. Mr. Anderson concludes:
> And then he looked over our battle records, and told
> us the satisfaction which he felt over what we had done
> in those 183 grueling frontline days, and then we really
> felt like human beings who were a real part of the big
> scheme of things back at home. Yes, indeed, he made
> us feel that all those sacrifices, and battle risks,
> were really worth it. That was our first contact
> with anybody from America since we left its shores
> many months ago. And it was really good for us. And
> when he said that he'd tell the folks back home about
> us, then we really did feel great! And that night
> we heard a tall robust Negro sing at Berchtesgaden.
> It was Paul Robeson! We had met an American hero, and
> that American hero had met some other American heros.
> Everybody was happy!

E. 1950-1959

1. ACTOR

1399. "Robeson Film Wins Annual English Prize," Journal and Guide,
       January 11, 1956, p. 1.

       "Sanders of the River," the British-made film starring Paul Robeson
       and Nina Mae McKinney, which is reported as receiving only in-
       different success in its American showings, was awarded the annual
       gold medal presented by the Institute of Amateur Cinematographers
       for the most significant talking picture of 1935. The film was
       produced by Alexander Korda's London Film Company. The in-
       stitute's gold medal is comparable to that of Hollywood's Academy
       of Motion Picture, Arts and Sciences' award, and is the most
       coveted trophy of English producers.

2. AFRICA

1400. "National Church Confers Title on Paul Robeson," West African
       Pilot (Aba, Nigeria), February 8, 1950, p. 1.

       According to this article, the National Church of Nigeria granted
       Paul Robeson the title, "Champion of African Freedom." This award
       given amidst "deafening applause" was granted for selfless service
       to Africa," concludes the article.

1401. "Heads of 11 Million Africans Thank Robeson for U.S. Aid," Daily
       Worker, March 31, 1952, pp. 1, 6.

       A cablegram signed by Dr. J.S. Moroka, President-General of the

(Daily Worker)

South African National Congress, and Y.M. Dadoo, Chairman of the
South African Indian Congress stated that eleven million non-
white South Africans greatly elected and inspired by news of
American expressions of sympathy and support for their struggle
against radicalism and Malan fascism....

1402.   "Africans Rally for Freedom to Robeson's Songs," Daily Worker,
        April 13, 1952, p. 2.

        According to this article Paul Robeson's bass voice roared for
        freedom in Johannesburg and Harlem as 11,000,000 non-white South
        Africans began their epic struggle to be citizens of their native
        land. Thousands of Africans marched to the voice of Robeson
        pouring from loudspeakers in the Fordsburg Square in Johannesburg
        where speakers, led by Dr. J.S. Moroka, President of the African
        National Congress (ANC), urged them to refuse to obey the Apar-
        theid (total Jimcrow) laws of the fascist Malan government.
        Following the meetings held in Johannesburg,Durban, Capetown and
        other centers, plans of the ANC, the South African Indian Congress
        and the Franchise Action Committee, "representing the Cape Co-
        loreds," were worked out for defying the law setting aside special
        bus and train seats, living areas, park benches and amusement
        places for non-whites. The African Freedom movement was supported
        by the Council on African Affairs, headed by Paul Robeson. During
        some three hours on the corner of Harlem's Lenox Avenue and 126th
        Street, at least 5,000 persons heard a number of speakers explain
        what the Africans were fighting for and were urged to support
        them. Robeson spoke at the rally and asserts: "....The fight
        in Africa is a challenge to us Negroes from the Africans, who
        are saying to us, 'How long are you going to take it?'.... If
        the South Africans win some freedom we will win some here,
        too...."

1403.   Shields, Art. "Nkrumah Organ Hits Ban on DuBois Trip to Ghana,"
        Daily Worker, May 2, 1957, pp. 1, 7.

        The U.S. State Department denied Dr. W.E.B. DuBois a passport to
        attend the Ghana Republic's independence celebration. Prime
        Minister Nkrumah's official party newspaper, the Ghana Evening
        News called the denial "a slap in the face" of Africa. Paul
        Robeson called for a big campaign to permit DuBois to accept
        Nkrumah's invitation. He said that we can help our African brot-
        hers best by winning our freedom here. "A big step to Negro
        freedom," he said "would be taken when Negro people assemble in
        Washington by the thousands in the great pilgrimage gathering on
        May 17." Robeson also remarks: "Another step for Negro freedom
        will be taken when Dr. DuBois wins the rights to stand on the
        soil of Ghana. That will inspire the colored peoples here and
        abroad, for Dr. DuBois is the father of the Ghana Republic."

3. ANTI-PAUL ROBESON

1404. Rorty, James and Winifred Raushenbush, "The Lessons of the Peek-
       skill Riots," Commentary, Vol. 10, No. 4, October, 1950, pp. 309-
       353.

       The authors hold Robeson reponsible for the Peekskill riots. They
       call Robeson a top-flight Communist spokesman. The writer con-
       stantly refer to supporters of Paul Robeson as "Robesonites."
       The authors conclude: "The Peekskill riots provide us with a
       shocking example of how not to deal with Communist fomentation of
       racial and religious tension and conflict. Their sequels also pro-
       vide us with a dismaying example of the intellectual confusion and
       tactical ineptitude of many of our professional liberals. Whether
       we have learned enough soon enough, from these experiences will be
       demonstrated during the weeks and months immediately ahead.

1405. "Dixie Messiah (Colored) Raises Self in Wrath Against Robeson,"
       Philadelphia Tribune, November 14, 1950.

       This article is about a Negro, James T. (Popeye) Bellafont, from
       Montgomery, Alabama, who organized an anti-Paul Robeson drive.
       Mr. Bellafont claimed to be the national president of the Mutual
       Association of Colored People. He watned Negroes throughout the
       South to sign a petition to stop Paul Robeson speaking for the
       Negro. Bellafont also wanted 17 governors of Southern and border
       states to approve his campaign and write letters recommending his
       program. He expresses his philosophy and campaign as follows:
       "I am tired of Paul Robeson running off his mouth and making it
       hard for me and other Negroes like me." He blamed Robeson and
       "outsiders" for all the troubles of the South, particularly the
       recent trouble in his home town. Why does he want to see Robeson?
       He calls Robeson an aggitator and wanted him to stop his talking.
       He said: "In the first place, Robeson doesn't have any business
       saying if war with Russia comes, the Negro won't fight. Robeson
       may not fight, but he can't speak for me, or any other Negro but
       himself," according to the article.

1406. Raushenbush, Winifred. "Paul Robeson: Messiah of Color," Freeman,
       Vol. 1, November 13, 1950, pp. 111, 114.

       This is a critical and anti-Robeson article. The essence of the
       article is that Paul Robeson was a tool of the Communist Party.
       The writer states:
              Today the great Paul Robeson sits in his Connecticut
              house, waiting to be used. He is one of the most
              valuable assets the Kremlin has ever acquired. For
              he is the voice of America as the Politburo wants the
              people of Asia to hear it; the Messiah who, they hope,
              will lead the colored peoples of the world into the
              strong sunlight of communism's unclouded future....
              The Party would be even smarter, however, it is
              smuggled Paul Robeson out of the country and shipped
              him to Asia to persuade Asiatics, by his lies and his

(Raushenbush, Winifred)

songs, that the United States is a weak, vile and
divided country, in which revolution is imminent.
He is admirably fitted for this role. He claims
to know fifteen languages, and to have learned
Norwegian in a day. His stature, his amiability,
his powerful, calm, resonant voice are still magic
to audiences anywhere. But Robeson has about come
to the end of his string. Instead of grappling with
himself and deciding what he wanted to do with his
much better than average intelligence and gifts, he
has coasted, letting life make all the decisions for
him. But he is still Pastor John Drew Robeson's son.
He would like, finally, to do something great, perhaps even something difficult. If he can believe in
his mission, that will save him - at least in his
own eyes. But if he is aware that he is only a
tool, he will suffer, and his suffering may destroy
him.... The possibility that Robeson might break
with the Communist Party, to which he has never
given allegiance publicly, is remote, according to
top-flight Negro intellectuals. They believe he is
too deeply involved and that the Party has too much
on him. Paul Robeson's father was a slave until the
age of fifteen. Today the son is not his own man;
he has not been his own man for many years. From
slavery to slavery in two generations is much too
short a span for American stock as good as that of
the Robesons.

1407.   "Salt from Sugar Ray," Newsweek, Vol. 137, No. 3, January 15, 1951,
         p. 23.

The article states that like another man of the same name (Jackie
Robinson), Sugar Ray Robinson had some words to say to the world
about the Negro question. Returning from a triumphant tour of
Europe, the world welterweight champion angrily answered charges
of American discrimination against Negroes which he had repeatedly
heard abroad. "They were capitalizing on statements made by Paul
Robeson," he said, blaming the Communists for spreading the
charges. "Mr. Robeson speaks for himself and not for the American
Negro. He certainly doesn't speak for my race. If the things the
Communists say were true, I'd never be in the position I'm in
today. America provides opportunity for everyone, regardless of
race, creed, or color," states the article.

4. AUTOBIOGRAPHICAL BOOK

1408. Cassio, Lewis. "Word-of-Mouth Spurs Sale of Robeson Book," The Worker, March 16, 1958, p. 2.

According to this writer Paul Robeson's new book, Here I Stand, will be a big best-seller of 1958. The publisher reported sales of 2,000 per week since the book was published on February 14, 1958. He also points out that the book was ignored by the columns of the daily press, but because of a word-of-mouth campaign, it met with snowballing orders. Several Negro newspapers, such as the New York Amsterdam News, Pittsburgh Courier, and Baltimore Afro-American reviewed the book.

1409. "New Edition (Of Here I Stand)," The Worker, April 20, 1958, p. 12.

This short article states that the first edition of 10,000 copies of Here I Stand, by Paul Robeson, was sold out six weeks after publication. It was also pointed out that a new edition of 25,000 copies was now coming off the press. The new paperbound edition sold for $1.00, a reduction of 50¢ from the first printing. The price of the hardcover edition remained at $2.50.

1410. "Paul Robeson Book is Sought by Many," Pittsburgh Courier, May 17, 1958, Magazine Section, p. 7.

Readers from four cities wrote letters to the Editor saying that Paul Robeson's book, Here I Stand, was not sold in their cities and they wanted to know where they could purchase it. Apparently most bookstores were "Blacklisting" the book. The cities mentioned in the article were: Cleveland, Ohio; Washington, D.C.; Miami, Florida; and Atlanta, Georgia.

5. BIRTHDAYS

1411. Berry, Abner. "He Spoke for Me When I had No Tongue," Daily Worker, May 11, 1952, pp. 1, 6.

This article refers to a celebration held in New York City for Paul Robeson on his 54th birthday. The title of the article was taken from a poem that was written especially for Robeson which states in part: "Paul Robeson how proudly your name flourishes on my tongue. Who spoke and acted for me when I had no tongue."

1412. "Robeson Jubilee to Highlight Negro Culture," Daily Worker, May 11, 1953, Section 2, p. 2.

The article states that Paul Robeson's 54th birthday would be marked, in Chicago, by a "Jubilee for Peace and Freedom," drama-tizing the development of the culture of the Negro people of which

(Daily Worker)

Robeson himself is such an important part. The article also states that Paul Robeson was regarded as the "Frederick Douglass" of modern times and acclaimed throughout Europe, Asia and Africa as one of the greatest living Americans.

1413. "India Plans to Honor Robeson at 60; Nehru Cites 'Cause of Human Dignity,'" New York Times, March 21, 1958, p. 4.

The article states that Prime Minister Jawaharlal Nehru of India and his daughter, Mrs. Indira Gandhi, are giving warm support to a nationwide campaign to honor Paul Robeson, American singer. Mr. Nehru termed Mr. Robeson a sufferer in the "cause of human dignity." The Prime Minister in a letter to the all-India Committee organizing the celebration, wrote:
> This is an occasion which deserves celebration not only because Mr. Robeson is one of the greatest artists of our generation, but also because he has represented and suffered for a cause which should be dear to all of us - the cause of human dignity. Celebration of his birthday is something more than a tribute to a great individual. It is also a tribute to that cause for which he has stood and suffered.

1414. "India Honours Mr. Robeson: Plans for Birthday Celebrations," London Times, March 26, 1958, p. 9.

According to this article Mr. Nehru, Prime Minister of India, welcomed proposals to hold celebrations in India's main cities to mark the sixtieth birthday anniversary of Mr. Paul Robeson. The Prime Minister declares:
> This is an occasion which deserves celebration not only because Paul Robeson is one of the greatest artists of our generation but also because he has represented and suffered for a cause which should be dear to all of us - the cause of human dignity. The celebration of his birthday is something more than a tribute to a great individual; it is also a tribute to that cause for which he has stood and suffered.

1415. "Assail Manhattan Center Ban on Robeson Rally," Daily Worker, April 29, 1952, p. 8.

This article states that in announcing a public celebration of Paul Robeson's 54th birthday, to be held May 8 at Rockland Palace, 155th Street and Eighth Avenue, the United-Freedom Fund revealed that the management of Manhattan Center had broken an oral agreement to rent the hall for another celebration on the same night. A delegation of Negro, union and cultural representatives was refused an interview with the Manhattan Center management. On the delegation were Dr. Alpheus Hunton, secretary of the Council on African Affairs; Bert Aldes, business manager of Robeson's paper, "Freedom," and Leon Strauss, executive secretary of the Furriers

(Daily Worker)

Joint Board. The United-Freedom Fund also called on all New
Yorkers to protest Manhattan Center's action. Despite the agreement made with Bery Alves, Business Manager of the fund, Manhattan
Center's manager Al Shapiro, refused to rent the hall. It was
noted that Robeson spoke at Manhattan Center last week as a guest
on another program. Mrs. Pearl Lawes, spokesman, declares:
"Let protests to Manhattan Center be followed by block-buying of
tickets for the Rockland Palace concert, so that Paul Robeson's
great voice can bring inspiration to us all."

1416. Belfrange, Cedric. "Robeson Birthday Parties set in 27 Countries,"
       National Guardian, April 7, 1958, p. 7.

       This article declares that 27 countries from around the world would
       celebrate Paul Robeson's 60th birthday. It was pointed out that
       in Mexico City, 20 top figures in music, art, dance, movie, trade
       union and farm organizations were reported sponsoring a concert;
       in Aleppo, Syria, a committee of lawyers and teachers headed by
       an Economic Ministry official; in Peking, a joint group of literary,
       art, peace, music, and cultural relations committees. Hungary
       planned concerts "throughout the country," and Bulgaria in Plovdiv,
       Russe and Verna as well as Sofia, according to this writer. In
       London distinguished sponsors of the Robeson Committee are throwing
       a big birthday party to launch the campaign on what it hopes will
       be the final lap. The publisher Dennis Dobson announced the forth
       coming appearance of a new Robeson biography by Marie Seton, the
       biographer of Eisenstein, and of Robeson's own book Here I Stand.
       An introduction to the biography has been written by Britain's
       most eminent living historian, Sir Arthur Bryant, author of The
       Turn of the Tide based on the war diaries of Viscount Alan Brooke,
       concludes the article.

1417. "Nehru Soft Pedals Words on Robeson," New York Times, April 9,
       1958, p. 4.

       According to this article, Prime Minister Jawaharlal Nehru made a
       careful attempt to remove political implications from his support
       for celebrations marking the sixtieth birthday of Paul Robeson.
       Mr. Nehru said Mr. Robeson represented "the cause of human dignity."
       He added that the celebrations would be a "tribute to that cause
       for which he has stood and suffered."

1418. "Robeson Thanks Chinese," New York Times, April 20, 1958, p. 2.

       According to this article Mr. Robeson sent a message to the
       Chinese people saying "one day I hope to greet you on Chinese
       soil." The message thanked the Chinese people for celebrating
       Mr. Robeson's sixiteth birthday and continued: "And thanks be
       to your brave leaders and to all the Chinese people for their
       Socialist contribution and their defense of peace."

1419. "Celebrations in Bulgaria," The Worker, April 27, 1958, p. 7.

This article declares that the biggest concert hall in Bulgaria was filled at the concert honoring Paul Robeson on his sixtieth birthday April 9. Peoples' Artist, Mikhail Popov, well-known basso of the Sofia National Opera said: "Paul Robeson has devoted his art to the triumph of peace and friendship among people." George Pirinsky, vice president of the Bulgarian Peace Committee spoke on significant moments of Robeson's life in the fight for peace and democracy. Pirinsky declares: "Today when in London and New Delhi, Moscow, Berlin, Sofia and Prague men in all walks of life and professions celebrate Robeson's 60th anniversary, the Bulgaria peace fighters appreciate his contribution to the fight for peace, democracy and social progress. Robeson's name and voice have spread the world over, inspiring crusaders against racist discrimination." Robeson's birthday was also honored in other Bulgarian cities like Plovdiv, Rousse. Many messages were sent to the great American artist.

1420. Robeson, Eslanda. "How World Greeted Paul Robeson," The Worker, April 27, 1958, pp. 6-7.

The wife of Paul Robeson declares that throughout seven long years of persecution Paul Robeson has been sustained by the knowledge that many people in many places, near and far, have continued to respect him and remain steadfastly loyal to him as an artist and as a man. These people, whose number runs into hundreds of millions, have assured Paul from time to time that they consider him a great artist and a courageous human being. They have been indignant because the U.S. Department of State continues to deny him his right to travel, preventing them from hearing him sing and act. They have, upon occasion, arranged trans-Atlantic telephone concerts in order to hear his "live" voice, states the author. This year, friends, neighbors, colleagues and admirers all over the world decided to honor Paul Robeson by celebrating his 60th birthday (April 9). Formal and informal Paul Robeson Birthday Committees were organized in Australia, Bulgaria, Ceylon, China, Ecuador, England, France, Germany, Hungary, India, Japan, Mexico, Norway, Poland, Sweden, Switzerland, the USSR and the USA. She concludes:

Paul is deeply moved by this extraordinary manifestation of friendship, concern and support. It is our plan to preserve these messages in a special 60th Birthday Album. He warmly thanks all those who have so thoughtfully and generously made his 60th birthday such a memorable occasion. His family is deeply grateful, etc. In order that you know at once how happy you have made us - this is our personal Thank You to each and every one of you....

1421. "The Triumph of Paul Robeson," New Times, No. 16, April, 1958, p. 2.

This editorial declares: "Paul Robeson's sixtieth birthday had world-wide reverberations. The great Negro singer and champion of peace and democracy was honoured in many countries. In about

<u>(New Times)</u>

thirty, Robeson Birthday Committees were formed, with the participation of prominent public personalities, including some who do
not share Robeson's political views.... The international homage
paid Robeson on his sixtieth birthday is fresh evidence that the
world public does not share the Washington conception of 'subversive activities,' which has been the excuse for persecuting
Robeson. The celebration of his birthday was a triumph for Paul
Robeson, a victory for justice over tyranny, of progress over
reaction," concludes the article.

1422. "Robeson Careers Revival Stirs U.S.,Foreign Press," <u>Pittsburgh
Press</u>, May 3, 1958, p. 21.

This article states that the long dormant career of singer Paul
Robeson became a matter of international interest in recent months
as he re-entered the field of public entertainment. Meanwhile,
it was pointed out, that India, Russia, and Germany celebrated
the singer's 60th birthday.

1423. "Honors for Paul Robeson in India," <u>Christian Century</u>, Vol. 75,
June 4, 1958, pp. 676-677.

The 60th birthday of Paul Robeson was celebrated in India's chief
cities. Addressing a public meeting in Bombay, Chief Justice
M.C. Chagla of the Bombay High Court cited reasons for the celebration: "Robeson is the first of all a great artist to whom
God has given a divine voice; he has become famous for his singing
of songs, especially Negro spirituals, which express the struggles
and aspirations of the people of the world; he has used his art
as a weapon against oppression and inequality."

1424. Shapiro, Sidney. "Peking Letter on Paul Robeson," <u>The Worker</u>,
June 15, 1958, p. 6.

This writer states in this letter from Peking, China, that Paul
Robeson's 60th birthday was celebrated in China as an event of
major international significance. For two days preceding his
birthday and on the day itself the National radio network played
recordings of his songs. On April 9th, the entire cultural page
of China's leading newspaper, <u>The People's Daily</u> was devoted to
articles about Paul. Mr. Shapiro suggests that although Paul's
glory shines brighter than ever, the Eisenhower Doctrine has become an object of hatred and contempt.

6. CITY COLLEGE OF NEW YORK AFFAIR

1425. Maged, Mark. "The Robeson Incident," The Campus (Undergraduate
       Newspaper of the City College of New York), November 16, 1951,
       p. 2.

       This was an editorial in the student newspaper. The editor states
       that why Mr. Paul Robeson has been denied the use of the Great
       Hall raises a disturbing question. Was it, as one faculty member
       maintained, that the SFCSA feared that Mr. Robeson would not
       draw a large enough audience? We hardly think so. Nor do we think
       that Mr. Robeson is not of sufficient stature or importance to
       justify his appearance. He concludes:
           Why Mr. Robeson was turned down still is not clear,
           although we have our own opinions. We are certain,
           however, that the choice of who shall appear in the
           Great Hall should not, in the final analysis, be
           left up to the SFCSA. We believe that the Student
           Council should be empowered to override such decisions
           of the SFCSA by a two-thirds vote. Only through such
           a method can the problem of who can be heard in the
           Great Hall be placed where it belongs - in the hands
           of the students themselves.

1426. "Student Council Condemns SFCSA Action in Barring Robeson From
       Great Hall," The Campus (Undergraduate Newspaper of The City
       College of New York), November 16, 1951, p. 1.

       This article states that the Student Council vigorously condemned
       the action of the Student Faculty Committee on Student Activities
       in refusing to allow Paul Robeson to speak in the Great Hall. By
       a vote of 28-4, with two abstentions, SC expressed "extreme dis-
       approval of the committee's action, terming it 'an abridgement of
       academic freedom.' At its meeting, the SFCSA, voting 6-3-1, ap-
       proved a motion stating that 'the use of the Great Hall should not
       be extended to the Young Progressives of America for the appearance
       of Mr. Paul Robeson.'" Mr. Robeson was asked to speak at the
       College, Thursday, January 10 from 12-2. The invitation was ex-
       tended by the Young Progressives of America and the Non-Partisan
       Student Committee to Call Upon Paul Robeson, states the article.

1427. "Robeson Ban Stirs City College Row: Protests Over Refusal to
       Let Singer Use Hall May Bring Recommendation Today," New York
       Times, November 19, 1951, p. 25.

       The City College Student-Faculty Committee on Student Affairs
       denied Paul Robeson permission to speak in the college's main
       auditorium and the college's elected student Council, protested
       the committee's decision, calling it an "abridgement of academic
       freedom." Robeson had been invited to speak by the college
       chapter of the Young Progressives of America and by a student
       committee set up to arrange his appearances. Prof. Samuel Hender,
       Chairman of the Faculty Academic Freedom Committee, said that al-
       though he disagreed with Robeson's views, anyone at the college

should be allowed to do so. "We should not imitate the totalitarian methods of eliminating freedom of speech and education,"
he said.

1427.   Fischer, Jay. "Council Seeks Withdrawal of Robeson Ban," The
Campus (Undergraduate Newspaper of the City College of New York),
November 21, 1951, pp. 1, 4.

According to this reporter the Student Council sent a letter to the
General Faculty Committee on Student Activities, and appealed the
decision of the SA barring singer Paul Robeson appearing in the
Great Hall.... The letter states: "the Student Council does not
endorse the views of Mr. Robeson. However, it is the feeling of
the Student Council that when a recognized student organization
invites a well known guest, that organization should be allowed
full use of college facilities...." According to Fischer the group
indicated that the recommendation was made in recognition of
the large number of students, "who, although opposed to the views
of Mr. Robeson, are in favor of permitting his appearance in the
Great Hall."

1428.   Maged, Mark. "L'Affaire Robeson," The Campus (Undergraduate Newspaper of City College of New York), November 21, 1951, p. 2.

This was an editorial in The Campus. He wrote, in part: "Fwxeh
jexlbn nsrtal imenst glbst srasnck pascnek iklgn.... This is just
what we see in the SFCSA's explanation of how and why Paul Robeson
was banned from the Great Hall. First, individual members of the
committee said politics was not a factor in the group's decision.
They said the issue was over the definition of the word 'co-
sponsorship.' Dean Engler went ever further, and stated that any
one of three regulations governing speaker's policy could have been
invoked in the denial to Robeson...." Mr. Maged concludes:
          Frankly, from what we have observed, it all seems
          like just so much political double talk, to disguise
          the fact that the College is trying to bar a man, who,
          as one person remarked at yesterday's meeting "will
          cause the school a good deal of trouble." It appears
          that the verbal knots in which the SFCSA is tieing
          itself, are serving no purpose, except to further
          the aims of the very good they are designed to
          supress....

1429.   Clark, Kenneth B. and James S. Peace, "Explains SFCSA Vote,"
The Campus (Undergraduate Newspaper of the City College of New
York), November 30, 1951, p. 8-9.

Clark, a Black man and Chairman of the Student Faculty Committee
on Student Activities (SFCSA) and Peace, Secretary of SFCSA, wrote
a letter to the Editor of The Campus explaining the SFCSA position
on the use of the Great Hall for an appearance by Paul Robeson.
They wrote, in part:
          According to the reports appearing in the students'
          newspaper and the metropolitan press there are some

(Clark, Kenneth B. and James S. Peace)

> fundamental distortions and confusions concerning the
> action of the City College Uptown, Day Session,
> Student-Faculty Committee on Student Activities, in
> reference to the request of YPA for the use of the
> Great Hall for its program on January 10th, 1952....
> They pointed out that the majority of the SFCSA re-
> jected as wholly inadequate the unprecedented verbali-
> zation of "technical" co-sponsorship as interpreted
> by the President of the Student Council. No other
> student group was presented as a co-sponsor of this
> program. The non-partisan Student Committee to call
> upon Paul Robeson was not presented as a co-sponor at
> that time. This non-partisan Student Committee is
> not a legitimate chartered student organization....
> The SFCSA took no action barring Paul Robesom from
> the college campus. The decision of the SFCSA is
> not an "abridgement of academic freedom." The YPA
> is held to the same regulations which govern all
> other recognized student organizations. The YPA
> should not be granted any special privileges and
> immunities any more than it should be subject to
> arbitrary restrictions because of its political
> point of view.

1430. "College and BHE Attacked by Critics for Rules Restricting Outside Speakers," The Campus (Undergraduate Newspaper of the City
College of New York), November 30, 1951, p. 4-S.

This article declares that to organizations at the College had been
granted complete freedom in selecting speakers and topics for
their meetings, except under certain circumstances covered by
College and Board of Higher Education (BHE) regulations. According to the article the controversy over the rights of Paul Robeson
to speak in the Great Hall does not stem from any stated regulations. According to SFCSA members, there is no question that
Mr. Robeson has a right to speak at the College. The dispute
centers solely about the use of the Great Hall. The majority of
SFCSA feel that co-sponsorship of Mr. Robeson, which is necessary
under existing regulations, involves active support of the man.
One of the committee members, expressing the views of at least
several of the majority, declared his disapproval of granting
college facilities to a man "of Robeson's ilk," concludes the
article.

1431. Executive Committee, YPA. "YPA Defends Its Invitation of Robeson
to Great Hall," The Campus (Undergraduate Newspaper of the City
College of New York), November 30, 1951, p. 8.

The writer declares, in part, in a letter to the Editor of The
Campus:

> ....We of the YPA face neither paradoxes nor dilemmas
> insofar the storm rages around the action of SFCSA.
> When we originally considered extending an invitation
> to Mr. Robeson, we wouldn't imagine that use of the

(Executive Committee, YPA)

> Great Hall would be denied him. We felt his ap-
> pearance would bring honor to our College. We
> felt that as the most renowned leader of the Negro
> people's struggle for equality, and as one of the
> international personalities most active in the quest
> for world peace and co-operation, as one who is
> perhaps more popular with the people of the world
> than any other single man alive, Paul Robeson would
> be welcomed by everyone at City College. Save for
> the issue of academic freedom raised since we con-
> sidered the invitation, an object lesson in morality
> itself, the reasons for requesting the Great Hall
> remain unchanged. They were originally sound.
> Application for the Hall conformed to every written
> requirement and was at no time legally defective.
> The grounds for denial rest on some apparently un-
> written laws conceived at will by certain members of
> SFCSA. It is the validity of such misconception that
> we contest....

1432. Goldman, Louis and Manny Sternlicht. "No Abridement," The Campus
(Undergraduate Newspaper of the City College of New York),
November 30, 1951, p. 8.

This is a letter to the Editor of The Campus. The writers declare:
> There is no abridgement of academic freedom involved
> (in the Robeson issue), as the Communists and their
> fellow lackeys in the Student Council would have you
> believe. The speaker in question has been allowed to
> speak at City College. It was assumed by the Communist
> Party (for no decision of this sort can be made without
> the expressed knowledge and approval of certain key
> Communist Chieftains) that Paul Robeson would not be
> granted permission to use the Great Hall. Thus, an
> incident would be created which they would utilize
> for their own ends. It is a well-known fact that the
> privilege of speaking in the Great Hall is only re-
> served for outstanding Americans: to equate Paul
> Robeson with Eleanor Roosevelt and Bernard Baruch
> is to commit a travesty over the dead bodies of
> American soldiers in Korea....

1433. Main, Day. "Urges SFCSA to Reconsider," The Campus (Undergraduate
Newspaper of the City College of New York), November 30, 1951,
p. 8.

The writer, a member of the NAACP, wrote a letter to the Editor
of The Campus. He declares:
> We support your stand on the issue of denying the
> Great Hall to YPA for Paul Robeson's appearance. We
> want to point out that Mr. Robeson has spoken and sung
> at the College previously. His political opinions and
> convictions were no different then. They were as

(Main, Day)

controversial and as subject to criticism as they are
now. The only change has been the increased pressure
against academic freedom and the development of the
tendency to silence individuals and groups who speak
against government policy in foreign affairs and controversial domestic issues....

1434. Muste, A.J. "Defends Right of Free Speech and Discussion," The
Campus (Undergraduate Newspaper of the City College of New York),
November 30, 1951, p. 8.

This was a letter written to the Editor of The Campus. The
writer declares:
It was heartening to read in a recent issue of the
New York Times the quotation from your editorial in
which you protested against denying the use of the
Great Hall at City College for a meeting at which Paul
Robeson was to speak. The Fellowship of Reconciliation
is uncompromisingly opposed to all war and violence
and consequently to Communism and any form of totali-
tarianism. Furthermore, the Fellowship has throughout
the several decades of its existence maintained a
policy of not engaging in any kind of organization
collaborating with the Communist Party or "fronts"
or peace movements which leave themselves open to
penetration by Communists or totalitarians of any
sort. Consequently, we disagree with many of Mr.
Robeson's views. This is precisely the reason why
non-Communists should intransigently defend the right
of persons like Mr. Robeson to speak freely....

1435. Richman, Sy. "SFCSA Ruling Supported by Sr. President," The Campus
(Undergraduate Newspaper of the City College of New York), November
30, 1951, p. 8-S.

This was a letter written to the Editor of The Campus by Sy
Richamn, Senior Class President. He asserts:
I have avidly read "The Campus" and I think I understand Mr. Walpin's voluble arguments for the appearance
of Robeson in the Great Hall. It is interesting to
note that my position has never been sought by the
representatives of a "fair and competent" press. If
the forty-odd students who have waylaid me in order
to hear by "deviationist" stand are any indication, I think that other students and perhaps "The
Campus" too should know my stand as well as one minor
fact in the issue.... It really doesn't take much
from my point of view to question Robeson's right to
the Great Hall. Special club facilities at the Hall
are given to organizations not to replace Madison
Square Garden or Columbus Circle but as a rational
attempt to make available a tool in the educational
process. College, Student Council, student organizations, and YPA do not exist for any other reason

(Richman, Sy)

> than they are educational tools in the eyes of our
> turstees and ourselves. I for one fail to see such
> a functional use in Robeson's appearance. It isn't
> because I disagree with his views. I would vote
> for Robeson's appearance if it would be at a forum
> type of meeting or series where there is an obvious
> attempt of the sponsors to present views and counter-
> views, opinions, and refutations. But I refuse to go
> along on an invitation and program which reflects
> no attempt whatsoever to mirror the purposes and
> and ends of the institution providing the facilities.
> The institution's only ends are educational.

1436.   Walpin, Gerald."SC President Calls Ban An Abridgment," The Campus
        (Undergraduate Newspaper of the City College of New York),
        November 30, 1959, p. 8-S.

> The President of the Student Council wrote a letter to the
> Editor of The Campus. He argues:
> With all the rationalization by the majority of the
> SGCSA that the only reason Paul Robeson was not allowed
> to use the Great Hall was due to the regulations in-
> volved, the incident is in reality a breach of academic
> freedom. Suddenly the regulations have been inter-
> preted to the letter of the law. When Mrs. Roosevelt
> spoke in the Great Hall only one student organization
> sponsored the meeting. Yet today the SFCSA has stated
> that Paul Robeson cannot speak in the Great Hall
> because only one organization invited him.... It
> is not a question of agreeing or disagreeing with
> Robeson. I for example, (and I believe 98% of the
> student body) disagree vehemently with him, and
> believe him to be a traitor to this country and the
> United Nations. It is rather a question of allowing
> all opinions to be presented to those who wish to
> hear them.

1437.   Fischer, Jay. "Robeson Great Hall Speech Approved if Part of
        Forum," The Campus (Undergraduate Newspaper of the City College of
        New York), December 6, 1951, p. I.

According to the writer, Paul Robeson could appear in the Great
Hall only if he spoke in a forum program, the Student Faculty
Committee on Student Affairs voted. The committee, by a vote of
5-1-3, approved a motion by Student Council President Gerald
Walpin suggesting that all interested parties involved in the Paul
Robeson affair consider a forum program in which the singer would
speak on one side of the issue, "Peace in Relation to American
Foreign Policy." A day after the SFCSA motion, the General Faculty
Committee on Student Activities voted unanimously to uphold the
original decision of the SFCSA denying Mr. Robeson use of the
Great Hall. The committee held that the SFCSA had acted with its
powers, states the reporter. This vote altered the original
SFCSA decision not to sponsor the controversial singer under any

(Fischer, Jay)

circumstances. The SFCSA resolution further pointed out that any
plans for Mr. Robeson's appearance would have to be submitted to
them for consideration. Following its former decision to deny
Mr. Robeson use of the Great Hall, the SFCSA denied that this
action constituted an abridgement of "academic freedom" as charged
by several groups. The committee held that all of the regulations
pertaining to the use of the Great Hall had not been fulfilled,
and that their action merely upheld these regulations ...,
declares Fischer.

7. COMMUNISM

1438. "Imbrie Withdraws Aid to Communists," New York Times, August 27,
       1949, p. 68.

       James Imbrie, Progressive Party candidate for Governor of New
       Jersey, resigned from the "National Non-Partisan Committee for the
       Defense of the Rights of the Twelve Communists" in protest against
       organized attempts to influence Federal Judge Harold R. Medina in
       his ruling. He sent a letter and telegram to Paul Robeson stating
       in detail his reasons for resigning. Robeson had presided at the
       committee meeting of the Progressive Party along with Mr. Imbrie.
       The article pointed out that Mr. Robeson had long been identified
       with Communist-front activities and organizations. His latest
       activities, according to the article, was the sending of a message
       to the International Youth Festival in Budapest, in which he
       called for the "complete liquidation of fascism the world over and
       the establishment of lasting peace and cooperation with the
       countries of the peoples of the Soviet Union."

1439. "Paul Robeson: Right or Wrong, Right, Says W.E.B. DuBois, Wrong,
       Says Walter White," Negro Digest, March, 1950, pp. 8-18.

       Both writers state their case for and against Robeson's statement
       that Negroes would not fight against the Soviets in any war.
       Dr. DuBois concludes:
           ....We ought to know that Communism is Socialism with
           more extreme methods and more immediate goals, but that
           the Russia of the Czars could have been rescued from
           utter collpase by no other method. If America and
           other lands can reform their industry and social ills
           by methods other than Communism, Russia has never
           tried to force them to do otherwise. The only area
           where Russia has actively supported Communism is in
           the countries on her border where western Europe re-
           peatedly and by elaborate spying and intrigue, tried
           to make Poland, Esthonia, Latvia, Lithuania, Czecho-
           slovakia, Finland and the Balkans, jumping off places
           to reconquer Russia and East Europe, for the cause of
           high profits based on ignorance and cheap labor. This

(Negro Review)

       is the reason that certain powerful elements in
America do not want Socialism or Communism even discussed, and will call any Progressive Party or movement "subversive." Paul Robeson stands for Peace and
Free Speech to fight War and Poverty....
Mr. White disagreed with Dr. DuBois. He concludes:
    ....Paul Robeson is wrong in giving consent by silence
to a political way of life whose strategy is amoral
and subject to reversal whenever it suits the whims or
fears of a tiny group of men in the Kremlin. Minorities
like the Negro are mere pawns in the global chess game
being played by Russia as was demonstrated so clearly
when Stalin and Hitler signed their inexplicable and
infamous pact on August 22, 1939. The amorality of
the U.S.S.R. was made ever more clear when Hitler's
armies invaded Russia in 1941.... Paul Robeson may
believe it is justifiable to practice consistency and
integrity only on alternate Thursdays. I don't agree.
Russia's eloquent and perfervid denunciation of
colonialism and race prejudice has been singularly
meaningless to me ever since she sold oil to Italy
to crush Ethiopia and her shameless switch of policy
on the Negro question when the Stalin-Hitler honeymoon
ended abruptly.

1440. Raymond, Harry. "Mass Action for Freedom Urgent, Robeson Tells
Rally," Daily Worker, April 14, 1950, pp. 2, 8.

The writer states that Paul Robeson addressed 3,000 men and women
at a rally at Manhattan Center in New York City and told them:
"I am disturbed not only for the freedom of leaders of the
American workingclass but the freedom of all American liberals."
Robeson recalls that a million votes were cast for the Progressive Party and Henry Wallace in 1948. "Where are those million votes?" he demands. "Where are the 500,000 who should be in
Washington today? Where are the 50,000 who should be marching
in every city today?" "But the rank and file of the American
people," Robeson declares, "stand ready to fight." "The Communists," he said, "are the first to say 'I am ready to sacrifice
for American freedom.' That is why I am standing side by side
with the Communist leaders."

1441. Editorial. "Mr. Ferrer and Mr. Chaplin," Nation, Vol. 176, No. 5,
January 31, 1953, p. 90.

This article points out that Jose Ferrer, a friend of Paul Robeson,
a few days later after he wired the American Legion National Commander that he would join in the veterans' "fight against communism,"
issues a statement denouncing Paul Robeson for having accepted the
Stalin Peace Prize.

1442.   "Robeson Urges Struggle to Defeat 'Double Jeopardy,'" Daily Worker,
        March 10, 1954, p. 6.

        Robeson urged a fight on behalf of the Communist leaders and Smith
        Act victims, released from federal penitentiary and subsequently
        rearrested as being members of the party under the Smith Act
        clause. The singer declares: "So a tremendous fight must be waged
        to see that there will be no double jeopardy, to see that the de-
        cision in the Claude Lightfoot case is reversed and to see that
        freedom of opinion and ideas is still a part of our heritage."

1443.   "Robeson Bars Query in London on Red Lie," New York Times, July
        12, 1958, p. 5.

        Paul Robeson twice refused to say whether he was a member of the
        Communist Party when reporters in London asked him if he were a
        member of the Communist Party. He told them the question was
        ridiculous and the reporters had no right to ask it. About 200
        people welcomed Paul and Eslanda Robeson at the London Airport.
        He sang "Swing Low, Sweet Chariot" for the television cameras,
        states the article.

                            8. FAMILY

1444.   Walls, William J. "Comment on Rev. Benjamin C. Robeson's Ap-
        praisement of His Brother,Paul," Quarterly Reivew of Higher Edu-
        cation Among Negroes, Vol. 22, No. 4, October, 1954, pp. 163-164.

        The writer states that Benjamin Robeson's article on his brother,
        Paul, was well written and inspiring. Bishop Walls also surmises
        that as for Paul Robeson, when the cold war is spent and ideologies
        have found each its sphere and lines of understanding and useful-
        ness out from isolated intolerance and mutual fear, Paul will still
        stand as a peoples' hope, the embodiment of a people's character
        and of American courageous conviction. He concludes that Robeson
        will stand forth as one who believes in linking together the good
        of both the United States and Russia for one united and redirected
        human race looking toward social salvation and permanent political
        peace.

1445.   Robeson, Paul, Jr. "My Dad," New Challenge, February, 1955, pp.
        16-18.

        The son states that Paul Robeson was his Dad, and to him, the most
        wonderful thing that he had learned about his father was that he
        belonged to millions of people throughout the world. They think
        of him as their own.... The younger Robeson declares that his
        father never wavered from his principles. Paul Jr. concludes,
        in part:
                He has devoted his life and talent to the struggle
                of people everywhere for freedom, life. I can recall
                that whenever I brought a problem to him, he would in

(Robeson, Paul, Jr.)

> his own way -- with a question or by an example --
> convey to me the idea: "Find the right principle
> first. Then the path is clear, and never step
> aside from it."

9. FASCISM

1446. "Robeson Sees Rise of Fascism in U.S.," New York Times, August 4,
1959, p. 5.

Paul Robeson attended a meeting of the World Youth Festival in
Vienna and declares that the American people can not "talk of
giving full freedom and democracy to Africa when 18,000,000 of us
do not have full freedom in the United States." The article states
that Mr. Robeson charged that United States foreign policy was
being infiltrated by "fascism." The report asserts that Mr. Robeson suggests that Mr. Nixon's trip to the Soviet Union and Poland
would demonstrate to the Vice President that the people who live
in those countries really want peace. The article declares that
delegates to the festival who tried to question or criticize
Mr. Robeson's statements were shouted down or ruled out of order
by the Communists, who controled the program.

10. HONORS

1447. "Lvov Honors Robeson," New York Times, October 8, 1950, p. 19.

The Town Council of Lvov in Southern Poland named a street after
Paul Robeson, the singer, according to this article.

1448. "Soviet Street Named Robeson," New York Times, April 3, 1955,
p. 173.

According to this article, Tass, the Soviet news agency, reported
that a main street in a new state farm settlement in the Soviet
"waterlands" had been named for Paul Robeson, American singer.

1449. "Soviet School Cites Robeson," New York Times, September 14, 1958,
p. 30.

This article states that Paul Robeson was made an honorary professor of the Moscow State Conservatory of Music.

11. HOUSE COMMITTEE ON UN-AMERICAN ACTIVITIES

1450. "Paul Robeson is Called: House Unit is Investigating Passport Irregularities," New York Times, May 28, 1956, p. 6.

The House Committee on Un-American Activities announced that it had summoned Paul Robeson to testify in its investigation of alleged passport irregularities by Communist sympathizers. According to the article, Mr. Robeson, left-wing basso, has travelled as an honored guest in the Soviet Union.

1451. "Un-American Probers Cite Paul Robeson for Contempt of Congress," Washington Daily News, June 12, 1956, p. 1.

According to this article the House Committee on Un-American Activities voted unanimously to cite Paul Robeson for contempt of Congress. The action came after Mr. Robeson refused to say whether he was a communist. He shouted at committee members: "You are the non-patriots and you are the un-Americans and you ought to be ashamed of yourselves." Committee Chairman Francis E. Walter (D., Pa.) immediately banged his gavel and announced the hearing adjourned. "I think it should be," Mr. Robeson commented. "I've stood just about as much of this as I can," Rep. Walter said. "You should adjourn this forever," Mr. Robeson snapped over his shoulder as he left the witness stand. Rep. Walter huddled with other members and they voted unanimously to recommend that Robeson be cited for contempt. The singer was the first witness as the committee resumed hearings into charges that communists have obtained American passports to travel abroad to promote Soviet propaganda, concludes the article.

1452. "House Group Favors Citing Paul Robeson," New York Times, June 13, 1956, p. 1, 25.

This article states that contempt of Congress proceedings were begun against Paul Robeson as the upshot of a shouting, table-thumping and gavel-banging hearing at the Capitol. The contempt action was voted by a sub-committee of the House Committee on Un-American Activities after the singer had clashed repeatedly with the chairman, Representative Francis E. Walter. Mr. Walter said this was based on Mr. Robeson's "general conduct" at the hearing, "personal attacks" on the committee and "the smear" of Senator James O. Eastland of Mississippi. According to this article, Mr. Robeson brought a stormy morning session to a sudden close by raising his resonant bass voice to shouting pitch and asserting: "You are the non-patriots and you are the Un-Americans and you ought to be ashamed of yourselves."

1453. "Builder Relates Red China Visit," New York Times, June 14, 1956,
       p. 16.

       This article was not specifically about Paul Robeson. It did,
       however, mention that the House Un-American Activities Committee
       did formally vote 7-0 to start contempt of Congress proceedings
       against Paul Robeson, who refused to say whether he was a Com-
       munist.

1454. Editorial. "Paul Robeson Is Right," California Voice (Oakland),
       June 22, 1956.

       Paul Robeson appeared before the House Un-American Activities
       Committee and this Black newspaper had this to say, in part:
       Robeson embodies the unrestrained and righteous rage
       that has broken bonds. His is the furious spirit
       wearied with tedious checker playing that stretches
       through nearly a hundred years in order to gain the
       rights guaranteed one hundred years ago. Robeson's
       cry is for justice, happiness and freedom here and
       now, while we live, not in some far away time in the
       future. His is the voice...that shouts down the
       promises of by-and-by and bellows "No! Now!" A
       sensitive, tormented soul, he is that Other Self,
       the Alter Ego that a million Negroes try in self
       defense to disown. His protest is the authentic
       Protest of the Negro.... And when Paul Robeson
       says, "I don't think a Negro will fight for an
       Eastland," Robeson is right....

1455. "The House Un-American Activities Committee Fiasco," Charlottes-
       ville-Albemarle (Virginia) Tribune, June 22, 1956, p. 1.

       This Black newspaper declares, in part:
       Paul Robeson is a great artist and a deeply sympathetic
       human being. His own success did not blind him to the
       wrongs suffered by his race.... Robeson's cry is for
       justice, happiness and freedom here and now, while we
       live, not in some far away time in the future. His
       is the voice...that shouts down the promises of by-
       and-by and bellows "No! Now!" A sensitive, tormented
       soul, he is that Other Self, the Alter Ego that a
       million colored people try in self defense to disown.
       His protest is the authentic protest of the colored
       man.... And when Paul Robeson says, "I don't think a
       colored man will fight for an Eastland," Robeson is
       right.

1456. Dunnigan, Alice A. "Paul Robeson Roars: U.S. Needs to Clean Up
       Mississippi, Alabama!," Pittsburgh Courier, June 23, 1956, p. 3.

       Paul Robeson appeared before the House Committee on Un-American
       Activities and told the committee that what this Government needs
       to do is to go down in Mississippi and Alabama and clean up that
       situation there. The Committee voted 7-0 in recommending contempt
       of Congress proceedings against Paul Robeson. The singer also

(Pittsburgh Courier)

told the group that "it is unthinkable to me, that anybody will take up arms in the name of (Senator) 'Eastland' against Russia," states the writer.

1457. Editorial. "Paul Robeson Right," Afro-American, June 23, 1956, p. 1.

This Black newspaper supported the position that Paul Robeson took before the House Un-American Activities Committee. The editor asserts, in part:
....We agree with Mr. Robeson that its (HUAC's) members could more profitably spend their time passing civil rights measures and bringing in for questioning such un-American elements as those white supremacists and manifesto signers who have pledged themselves to defy and evade the very constitution they had previously sworn to uphold and maintain....

1458. Fleming, Thomas. "Paul Robeson is the Conscience of US," San Francisco Sun Reporter, June 23, 1956, p. 1.

This reporter comments on Paul Robeson's stand before the House Un-American Activities Committee. He argues, in part:
...Robeson in as far as most Negroes are concerned occupies a unique position in the United States or the world for that matter. Whites hate and fear him simply because he is the conscience of the United States in the field of color relations. Those Negroes who earn their living by the sweat of their brows and a few intellectuals almost idolize the man. He says the things which all of them wish to say about color relations and the manner in which he says these things attracts the eye of the press of the world....

12. KOREAN WAR

1459. "Davis Sees U.S. Reds Refusing to Register," New York Times, September 10, 1950, p. 47.

Benjamin J. Davis, Jr., former New York City Councilman and con- victed Communist declares at a rally in New York City that his party would never register, "no matter how many bills they pass requiring us to do so." At the meeting Davis protested the State Department revoking Paul Robeson's passport. Paul Robeson attended the rally and predicted that the Korean War would "logically end in the emergence of the former colonial areas as full-fledged peoples' Socialist democracies like that in Eastern Europe and China. Robeson declared that he was "politely imprisoner," and was prevented the State Department from "doing my life work," The singer urged the Negro people to join their "true friends,"

(New York Times)

the Communist party, in a drive to prevent American intervention in Korea.

1460. "Robeson, Mann Join New 'Peace Crusade,'" New York Times, February 1, 1951, p. 11.

A new organization called "American Peace Crusade," sponsored by a group including Thomas Mann, the writer and Paul Robeson, singer, urged a "Peace Pilgrimage" to Washington. This organization called for withdrawal of American troops from Korea, an end to war in the Far East and recognition of the "Chinese People's Republic" to representation in the United Nations.

13. LABOR MOVEMENTS

1461. "Robeson to Speak at Peace Rally at U.S. - Canada Line," Daily Worker, April 29, 1952, p. 8.

According to this report an appeal to all people's organizations to make the Paul Robeson rally at Peace Arch Park, May 18, "a gathering of international significance" for peace and freedom was issued by the Mine, Mill & Smelter Workers Union (MMSWU). The union sponsored the affair as a benefit for the United Freedom Fund. Peace Arch Park, on the U.S. Canadian border near Blaine, Washington, has long been symbolic of international good will, states the article. Ted Ward, of the Mine, Mill Committee, in a letter publicizing the event, expressed the hope that "as many individuals and family groups as possible will gather at the Peace Arch not only to hear the greatest living voice sing and speak for us," but to express indignation over the State Department's refusal to permit Robeson to leave the U.S. Plans for the border meeting were formulated after the Truman Administration banned Robeson and Vincent Hallinan from going to Canada as guests of the MMSWU Canadian convention in Vancouver, B.C., in February.

1462. "Leftists Observe an Early May Day," New York Times, April 30, 1955, p. 3.

Paul Robeson along with several other speakers spoke at the Provisional Workers and Peoples Committee May Day rally in New York City. This meeting was held two days ahead of the international holiday that would officially be celebrated in Russia. It was pointed out "By far the biggest hand of the rally went to speak briefly." More than 2,500 people showed up for the rally. The meeting was peaceful and no violence occurred.

14. LEADERSHIP

1463. Cox, Oliver C. "The New Crisis in Leadership Among Negroes,"
       Journal of Negro Education, Vol. 19, No. 4, Fall, 1950, pp. 459-
       465.

       The writer declares that Paul Robeson was a Negro socialist leader,
       because he was nurtured, so to speak, in the socialist tradition,
       and ripened without equivocation into a convinced advocate of
       socialism. He goes on to point out that in the United States his
       prestige probably outranks that of any socialist leader, regard-
       less of color.

1464. Davis, Benjamin J. "The Negro People in the Fight for Peace and
       Freedom," Political Affairs, Vol. 29, May, 1950, pp. 101-114.

       Various references are made to Paul Robeson throughout this
       article. It was surmised that Paul Robeson, along with several
       other Blacks, are the true leaders of the Negro people. Robeson
       is also discussed as Head of the Council on African Affairs and
       his relations with the Soviet Union. Some attention is devoted
       to the Peekskill riots and Robeson's concert there. He concludes
       that tens of thousands of Negro workers and their families turned
       out at Peekskill to greet Robeson on his subsequent national tour.

1465. Miers, Earl Schenck. "Paul Robeson - Made in America," Nation,
       Vol. 170, May 27, 1950, pp. 523-524.

       The author asserts that Robeson's tragedy is that he does not see
       that the age and the atmosphere which produced him have already
       lost much of their hold upon the future. Jackie Robinson,
       testifying before a Congressional committee, made the change
       clear. Any difference of opinion between Robeson and Robinson
       is basically not one between two prominent members of the Negro
       race or between men of conflicting ideologies; it is a difference
       in the philosophical attitudes of two generations. In the long
       run only Westbrook Pegler and his tribe will be unable to com-
       prehend this distinction, but, then, about all Pegler has ever
       taught us is that no one perspires so profersed as the man beating
       a dead horse, asserts the writer. "America's security can be
       little endangered by Robeson, no matter how violent his statements.
       As an artist he is a unique product of his time; as an emotionally
       impeded, intellectually confused American he is not. So he must
       carry on his struggle sustained by half-truths and scorned by
       those who should understand him best," concludes the author.

1466. Miers, Earl Schenck. "Paul Robeson: Made by America," Negro
       Digest, Vol. 7, No. 12, October, 1950, pp. 21-24.

       This article was reprinted from the Nation magazine. The writer
       concludes that essentially Paul Robeson revolts against the com-
       placency of a generation that fails to understand much of the world
       around it. He argues that America's security can be little en-
       dangered by Robeson, no matter how violent his statements. Miers

(Miers, Earl Schenck)

concludes: "As an artist he is a unique product of his time; as
an emotionally impeded, intellectually confused American he is not.
So he must carry on his struggle sustained by half-truths and
scorned by those who should understand him best."

1467. Editorial. "The Not So Strange Case of Paul Robeson," California
Eagle, April 5, 1951, p. 5.

The editor asserts that Paul Robeson is always busy learning the
music and languages of different peoples, studying their ways of
life, so that he may understand them better. One heartening result of this work is that many people in many countries - including
Russia and China - know and love Paul Robeson, for the human normal reason that he has taken the trouble to learn their difficult
languages, their music, something about their very different ways-
of-life, and to be friendly with them. That's the stuff that diplomats are made of - or should be. In all the years Robeson was
learning the music and languages of peoples, everybody seemed to
think he was brilliant and wonderful; it wasn't until he went on
to learn about them socially, economically and politically, that
he ran into trouble, states the writer. She declares: "I
certainly do not agree that there is anything strange about the
case of Paul Robeson. Unless you consider it strange that he, a
Negro-American, lifted up his voice and said a big NO! around
the world to the people and Governments who are pushing him, his
People, Colonial Peoples, and other Minorities around. There is
something very strange about the case of the Negro leaders, who
are so frantically opposing him for this. Considering the behavior
of some of these "Leaders," maybe there is something strange about
Robeson, at that. Whoever thought a Negro would have the nerve to
publicly - very publicly - denounce the foreign and domestic
policies of the Administration, when he believes them to be Un-
American, dangerous and wrong? ....The editor concludes:
    Leaders come in many different varieties: some are
    self-appointed, some are appointed by others, and some
    just emerge. The appointed leaders are usually
    highly paid, and usually have to keep their leadership
    by force - naked force with guns, soldiers and police,
    or concealed force with political, economic and social
    pressure; the leader who emerges usually achieves and
    keeps his leadership by keeping in step with the
    people he leads, by expressing what is on the minds
    and hearts of the people. This is in the final analysis,
    the most powerful kind of leader. You can abuse or
    even kill, but he emerges an even greater leader. I
    believe Paul Robeson is that kind of leader and that
    is why it is taking such an unprecedented mobilization
    of strength to try to put him down. The State
    Department, the Administration, the concert theatre
    and film industries, the press and radio, and some
    of the Negro "Leaders" have combined to try to im-
    mobilize him to divorce him from the Negro people,
    and from his fabulous career. But Paul Robeson is
    awful big, and there he stands, like a giant oak,

(California Eagle)

        like a mountain - solid. I do not believe that
        they can unroot him, nor blast him down.

1468. Pittman, John. "Mister Freedom, Himself," Daily Worker,Magazine
       Section, April 15, 1951, pp. 1, 6.

       According to the writer, at the age of 52, Paul Robeson is a man
       who knows what the Negro people want, who has made the attainment
       of their needs his supreme task, and is sure he will accomplish it.
       What is this task?, asks Mr. Pittman. To speak out and fight for
       full, unconditional economic, political and social citizenship of
       every Negro man, woman and child. How will it be accompliahed?
       Robeson sees it as the product of a victorious struggle by a power-
       ful coalition of Negroes and whites, mainly working men and women.
       He sees the south as a major area of struggle, and speaks in
       defense of the interests of both the Negroes and poor whites of
       that region. He believes the Negro trade unionists hold the key
       to the organization of the Negro people in such a coalition, and
       he has come to reply on the white trade unionists as the section
       among U.S. whites most willing and able to join the Negro people
       in their struggle for complete liberation, argues the author.
       Mr. Pittman surmises that Robeson was keenly aware of the power
       of the international labor movement, and believes the Chinese,
       Soviet, African, West Indian and working classes of other European
       and Asian and Latin American countries are today allies of the
       Negro people because they have the same interests. The writer
       suggests that his belief causes Robeson to place the issue of
       peace in the forefront of all his present activities. Because,
       as he says, "we can't win freedom without peace. The present war
       drive has brought out of the sewer all of our white supremacist
       enemies and placed them in positions of power. By imposing peace
       on the war-makers, we will strike a mortal blow at the racists."
       And even now, amidst the current war-hysteria, Robeson thinks
       this coalition of Negro and white people in the United States can
       impose peace. Such is the essence of his confidence, asserts
       Pittman. Many peoples have honored Robeson. The Soviet peoples
       have named a mountain peak for him. Numerous songs, cantatas and
       ballads have been dedicated to him. The great poets of Turkey,
       China and Latin America have sung his praises in rhyme. The
       African peoples have appropriated him as their own spokesman. And
       Pietro Nenni, the Italian Socialist leader, in awarding Robeson
       and Picasso the prizes for foremost services in the cause of peace,
       honored him as "man and artist." For us, the two are inseparable,
       states Pittman. He concludes:
              But the honor Robeson appreciates most, I think, is
              the description given him by a Negro woman who sent
              in a subscription to Freedom. "I think of Paul Robeson,"
              she said, "as Old Man Freedom himself."

1469. "Robeson's Peace Stand Landed by Cleveland Editor," The Worker,
       May 30, 1952, p. 8.

       According to this article in attacking U.S. government foreign
       policy and white supremacist ideology, Paul Robeson "echoes the

(The Worker)

feelings of every Negro who has sense enough to get in out of the
rain," Charles H. Loeb, editorial staff member of the Black newspaper, Cleveland Call & Post, declares in his May 3rd column,
"World on View."

1470. McGowan, Edward D. "Step the Foes of Negro Freedom," Freedom,
July, 1953, p. 4.

McGowan was a minister and Chairman of the Committee to Defend
Negro Leadership. He made a speech before the National Fraternal
Council of Churches, U.S.A., Inc., April 30, 1953. Rev. McGowan
declares:
     ....I must defend Paul Robeson, the greatest artist
     of this century. Paul Robeson has interpreted the
     classics for me in a way that no other person could.
     When he sings I am thrilled as no other person can
     thrill me. I know Paul Robeson personally, and he has
     talked to me from the depths of his heart and I will
     come to my own conclusions about Paul Robeson. No
     one else can tell me what I must think or believe
     about this great leader of the Negro people.

1471. Pittman, John. "Magazine Sponsors Cultural Tribute to the
Robesons," Daily Worker, October 20, 1954, p. 7.

The tribute was sponsored by New World Review. This annual banquet was held in New York City. Both Paul and Eslanda Robeson
were honored. Dr. Harry F. Ward spoke for all the 500-odd guests
when he asserts: "Paul Robeson's voice will go on when the little
people in Washington are forgotten and the big people behind them
are remembered only as traitors to humanity."

1472. Longstreet, Hester. "What Robeson Said," Afro-American, June 30,
1956, p. 4.

This was a letter written to the Editor. He declares, in part:
"The House Un-American Committee needs to investigate the Communist editors of the AFRO. Any publication that would print a
picture of Paul Robeson and play him up as a hero should be barred
from the mails." The Editor replied and stated: "No editor nor
member of the AFRO staff belongs to the Communist Party."

1473. McDaniel, Mrs. Rachel. "What Robeson Said," Afro-American, June
30, 1956, p. 4.

This was a letter to the Editor. The reader surmises, in part:
"The AFRO's front page editorial 'Mr. Robeson is Right' was a
masterpiece. Such is the climate for conformity in America today
that I can think of no other publication but the AFRO which would
have the courage to make that statement." She concluded: "I
congratulate and salute a valiant newspaper which refuses to be
cowed or intimidated. Unfortunately, your kind is all too few
these days."

1474. Patterson, William L. "In Support of Paul Robeson's Rights,"
       Pittsburgh Courier, December 1, 1956, p. 10.

       This was a letter to the Editor of this newspaper. Mr. Patterson
       asserts that Paul Robeson has been informed by the Supreme Court
       that it will not support his demand for a State Department hearing
       in his fight for a passport and the right to travel. Robeson's
       complaint is not alone that Mr. Dulles has denied him a passport;
       Paul Robeson is the only living American against whom an order
       has been issued directing immigration authorities not to permit
       him to leave the continental confines of the United States, de-
       clares the reader. He concludes: "The issue is one of freedom of
       speech, the right to earn a living, and as the Universal Declara-
       tion prescribes, the right of every law-abiding citizen to freely
       leave his country if he so desires. The weight of enlightened
       and progressive public opinion is stronger than an edict of the
       State Department. Support Paul Robeson's right to travel."

1475. Robeson, Flora. "Paul Robeson," London Times, May 4, 1957, p. 7.

       This was a letter to the Editor of The Times. The writer states
       that the British Actors' Equity Association lived up to the best
       traditions of the English stage in carrying a motion to support the
       efforts to enable Mr. Paul Robeson to sing in England.... She
       concludes: "There must be many like myself who have no sympathy
       for Paul Robeson's politics, but nevertheless would love to hear
       his voice, the most beautiful natural voice of this century, and
       see the play Othello...."

1476. Wilson, J. Dover. "Paul Robeson," The Times, May 10, 1957, p. 13.

       This was a letter to the Editor of The Times. The reader declares
       that for some reason or other, the Government of the United States
       refuses to allow Mr. Paul Robeson to pass the Statue of Liberty
       and cross the Atlantic. If it is afraid he may in some way conta-
       minate the politics of the most conservative-minded people in the
       world, its fears are groundless states the writer. The letter
       goes on to assert "we should not give Mr. Robeson time or breath
       to waste upon such trivialities." We want his breath for
       spirituals and other songs; we long to hear it speak the glorious
       poetry that Shakespeare spoke through the mouth of Othello, con-
       cluded Mr. Wilson. He also declares: "In the name of Shakespeare
       we appeal to Washington: let him loose upon us!"

1477. Editorial. "Paul Robeson," Los Angeles Herald-Dispatch, July 4,
       1957, Editorial Page.

       The editor asserts that the Herald-Dispatch hails Paul Robeson as
       the man best fitted by virtue of sincerity, integrity and courage,
       to give leadership to the Negro people in this day. He asserts,
       in part:
               Our people need Paul Robeson. And Paul Robeson needs
               us. In Paul Robeson we have a leader whose courage and
               endurance in the good fight has been tested in the
               fires of hell, who rather than betray his principles
               had defied the fascists in the State Department, bodily

(Los Angeles Herald-Dispatch)
    proclaiming his devotion to the cause of the Negro
    and colonial freedom....

1478. Patterson, William. "A Hero of His Time," The Worker, April 6,
       1958, pp. 8-9, 11.

       The writer argues that Paul Robeson is a "Citizen of the World."
       His affinity with mankind flows from his love of liberty. Not
       gold, not prestige, not the homage of men and women drives Paul
       Robeson. He is animated by his love of liberty, suggests Mr.
       Patterson. He concludes:
            The road traversed by Robeson is one of consistent
            struggle. He sees in the march of socialism the
            greatest force making for Negro liberation. He
            sees in the liberation struggle of the Asian, African
            people's great allies for his own people, progressive
            America. We say "Hail and Long Life!" to Paul Robeson,
            singer of the people's songs, actor, author and
            citizen of the world of freedomseeking mankind.

                    15. LETTERS TO THE EDITOR

1479. Hughes, George. "What Robeson Said," Afro-American, June 30, 1956,
       p. 4.

       This was a letter written to the Editor. He observes, in part:
       "You certainly performed a real service by printing a detailed
       account of Mr. Robeson's testimony before the House Committee on
       Un-American Activities. The daily newspapers carried stories of
       his citation for contempt, without stating a single thing he had
       done to earn it. After reading Robeson's hard-hitting replies
       to the committee's questions, I can understand why a group of
       white men would hold any colored man who answered as he did to be
       sassy and impertinent."

1480. Henderson, W.A. "What Robeson Said," Afro-American, June 30, 1956,
       p. 4.

       This was a letter written to the Editor. The reader declares, in
       part: "I was amazed to see the AFRO give such a big headline and
       picture treatment to Paul Robeson. He has done more to hurt our
       cause than anybody. And for the AFRO to argue editorially that
       he is right was just too much for a red-blooded American like me
       to take. I say he should be deported to Russia."

1481. Johnson, P.H. "What Robeson Said," Afro-American, June 30, 1956,
       p. 4.

       This was a letter to the Editor. The reader declares, in part,
       that he "hopes a jury puts Paul Robeson behind the bars where he

(Johnson, P.H.)

should have been years ago."

1482.   Keemer, Edgar B.   "He's Not Yellow," <u>Afro-American,</u> June 30, 1956,
p. 4.

This was a letter written to the Editor. The author, a medical
doctor, declares, in part: "Hurrah, for Paul Robeson who called
it like it is when he testified before the House Un-American
Activities Committee. We need more of this same type of direct
palaver and less high-toned, diplomatic dallying in this hard
fight to batter down that artificial but persistent American
barrier - skin color. Furthermore, I'll bet 99 percent of colored
people will say 'amen' to Mr. Robeson's timely blast. The Committee knows this too.... Knowing this man's versatile talents
and realizing the many sacrifices he has had to make in order to
defend his principles we can only say: 'He may be "red," we don't
know. In fact, his personal beliefs are none of our business.
But this much we do know - he certainly isn't "yellow"!'" concludes the reader.

1483.   Patterson, William L.   "Paul Robeson's Latest Success," <u>New Times,</u>
No. 20, May, 1959, p. 31.

This was a letter written to the <u>New Times</u>. He states, in part:
"Much has been written about the excellence of the Shakespeare
Memorial Theatre's 100th anniversary of 'Othello' with Paul
Robeson in the title role. But all of the praise cannot be given
to the talents of its great star. That dramatic characterization
had more than its technically artistic side. Art it was, art of
voice and gesture and mine, superb artistry. But tribute was
paid by that audience that historic night to Paul Robeson the
man. For Paul Robeson, the road that led to Stratford-on-Avon
was a long and torturous highway. Yet Don Cook, political reporter turned dramatic critic for the screening, who reviews the
plays in the <u>New York Herald-Tribune</u> for April 12, asked us to:
'Forget Paul Robeson's politics for the moment and consider instead the whole complex emotional background against which this
eminent Negro faced the opening night....' What does Mr. Cook
want? Is the 'eminent Negro' to lose his eminence if his politics
are found distasteful to Mr. Cook or his press? Politics is precisely what is not forgotten as the <u>Herald-Tribune</u> so hastily
concerts Mr. Cook into a dramatic critic.... The artistry of that
performance expressed that art which reflects man's irresistible
drive for human dignity, mankind's struggle for freedom, progress,
peace. Stratford-on-Avon was an historical point on the road
Paul Robeson chose to follow."

16. LETTER TO ROBESON

1484. Nazvanov, Mikhail. "Open Letter to Robeson From a Soviet Actor,"
       The Worker,Magazine Section, July 6, 1952, p. 7.

       For the past several months the Pushkin Dramatic Theatre of Moscow
       was presenting a play entitled "John - Soldier of Peace" written
       by the young Soviet playwright, Yuri Krotkov. The play which
       centers around "John Robertson, talented Negro singer and gallant
       soldier of the many-million strong army of peace," was dedicated
       to Paul Robeson. The "Open Letter " to Robeson was sent to the
       actor-singer by Soviet actor M. Nazvanov who plays the part of
       "John Robertson" in the play. The Soviet actor declares: "I
       should like to conclude my letter with wishes of good health, new
       achievements in your art and further success in the lofty struggle
       for the victory of peace and democracy. I shall be supremely
       happy if I should ever have the occasion to meet you personally and
       to press your courageous hand."

17. NBC AFFAIR

1485. Raymond, Harry. "NBC Refuses to Reveal Who Got Robeson Banned
       From TV," Daily Worker, March 15, 1950, pp. 1, 2, 9.

       The National Broadcasting Company maintained strict silence when
       asked by the Daily Worker to identify persons whose protests led
       to barring Paul Robeson from appearing on Mrs. Franklin D. Roose-
       velt's television program next Sunday afternoon. NBC vice-
       president Sidney Eiges told Mr. Raymond in his office at Rocke-
       feller Center he had "no way of knowing" the identity of the 30
       persons who telephoned the network protesting Robeson's scheduled
       TV appearance. "We try to get the names and addresses of the
       persons who call," Eiges said, "but we don't always get them."
       The reporter asked if 30 annonymous telephone calls to NBC would
       cause cancellation of appearance of such an outstanding artist as
       Robeson. "Well, there were 119 calls," the NBC vice-president
       replied, "and some of them represented large organizations. I
       think the thing is washed up." Could you name any of the persons
       whom you say represent large organizations?, the writer asked.
       "I cannot," Eiges replied. Eiges assured him he considered
       Robeson a "great artist," states Mr. Raymond.

1486. Pittman, John. "Wall Street Fears Robeson," Daily Worker, March
       16, 1950, p. 6.

       The writer argues that the decision to cancel Paul Robeson's
       participation in Mrs. Eleanor Roosevelt's television forum on
       "The Negro's Position in Politics Today" was made by Monopoly
       Incorporated by Wall Street itself. Mr. Pittman contends that it
       was easy for the NBC management to ban Robeson and issue a state-

(Pittman, John)

ment spelling over with arrogant white supremacy. It was also
surmised that the barring of Robeson was far from being only a
"Robeson problem" or even a "Negro matter." It was a matter of
the American people against the Trusts. The author concludes:
    Robeson can be proud that he so....speaks the Negro
    people's mind and so shakes the rotten props of
    American capitalism that Wall Street singles him
    out as a spread target. But what can be said of the
    liberals, of the white artists and musicians, of
    trade unions in the communications industry and
    outside of it, of all the decent democratic white
    Americans who pooh-pooh the ban on Robeson and ob-
    jectly conform to a diκtat aimed at controlling their
    own thoughts?

1487. "Dorothy Parker Protests NBC Ban on Paul Robeson," Daily Worker,
       March 19, 1950, p. 2.

       The article suggests that Miss Dorothy Parker, Chairman of the
       Voice of Freedom Committee sent a telegram of protest to NBC's
       vice-president Sidney Eiges. She declares, in part:
           On behalf of its 3,000 monitors throughout the nation
           the Voice of Freedom Committee vigorously protests
           radio's latest crime against freedom of the air. All
           freedom-loving and fair-minded listeners are shocked
           at NBC's high handed cancellation of Mrs. Roosevelt's
           March 19th TV show because Paul Robeson was one of the
           scheduled participants. We are horrified that NBC
           permits the Journal-American to dictate who shall or
           shall not be heard on its network as a public service
           feature, especially so since NBC itself invited
           Mr. Robeson to speak as vice-chairman of the Pro-
           gressive Party. Mr. Robeson is eminently qualified
           to discuss the question, "The Negro in American
           Political Life," both as an outstanding leader of
           the Negro people and one of the foremost Americans
           of our time. Millions of listeners would like the
           privilege of hearing Mr. Robeson's views on the
           subject. We urge that you remember that the air
           still belongs to the people and is only leased to
           the broadcaster. We demand a rescheduling of the
           original show including Mr. Robeson, or we shall be
           obliged to petition the FCC.

1488. "Pickets Continue Vigil at NBC to Protest Ban on Robeson," Daily
       Worker, March 19, 1950, p. 2.

       The article states that for the second day pickets marched during
       the noon hour Friday at Radio City protesting the National Broad-
       casting Company's banning of Paul Robeson from Mrs. Franklin D.
       Roosevelt's Sunday TV program. Ferdinand Smith, executive secre-
       tary of the Harlem Trade Union Council, leader of the picket
       line, announced he would head a delegation Monday to lodge the
       protest directly with Charles R. Denny, NBC executive vice-

(Daily Worker)

president. The Harlem Trade Union Council, Smith said, is presenting Robeson as a featured speaker at a rally entitled, "Labor
Salutes the Negro People," Thursday, 8 p.m., at Golden Gate Ball
Room, 142nd Street and Lenox Avenue. Rep. Adam C. Powell, scheduled
to appear with Robeson on the censored TV program will be a speaker
at the Golden Gate rally. Mr. Smith concludes:
> We are going to demand that Denny reschedule the
> television show with Mr. Paul Robeson on the
> program. Denny cannot ignore the public wish to
> view this program. Denny must give our delegation
> a positive answer or the Harlem Trade Union Council
> will continue to picket in front of NBC until he
> does....

1489.   "Trade Deplores 'Circus Liberalism,' Feels Sincere Guys Take Rap,
Too," Variety, March 22, 1950, p. 24.

This article points out that the Voice of Freedom Committee sent
a wire to the National Broadcasting Company (NBC) declaring:
"All freedom loving and fairminded listeners are shocked at NBC's
high-handed cancellation of Mrs. Roosevelt's March 19 NBC show
because Paul Robeson was one of the scheduled participants. We
are horrified that NBC permits the Journal-American to dictate
who shall or shall not be heard on its network as a public service
feature, especially so since NBC itself invited Mr. Robeson to
speak as vice-chairman of the Progressive Party."

1490.   "Charge Personal Bias Caused Robeson Ban," Daily Worker, March 23,
1950, p. 4.

According to this report, Charles R. Denny, Vice-President of the
National Broadcasting Company, was accused of being guided by
his "personal prejudices" when he banned Paul Robeson from appearing
last Sunday on Mrs. Franklin D. Roosevelt's TV program. The ac-
cusation was contained in a letter presented to Denny's secretary
at Radio City by a delegation from the Harlem Trade Union Council,
stated the article. Signed by Ferdinand Smith, executive secretary
of the Council, the letter protested Denny's "continued refusal"
to meet with representatives of Harlem and other areas on Robeson's
censorship. The letter was delivered to Denny's office by Kelly
Woolley, Mrs. Rosalie Pinkney and Marcus McGroom, spokesmen for
the Harlem Trade Union Council, concluded the article.

1491.   Burley, Dan. "Clothesline," New York Age, March 25, 1950, p. 14.

The writer comments on the banning of Paul Robeson from NBC television. He declares, in part:
> NBC Television barring of Paul Robeson from Mrs. FDR's
> broadcast was one of the most vicious examples of un-
> Americanism on record. The television outfit takes an
> impossible position in refusing to grant an American
> the right to present an opinion, a viewpoint of his
> attitude because he is being criticized and condemned
> by his natural enemies - the cracker block in Congress

(Burley, Dan)

> and the vicious anti-Negro elements that would make
> good publicity available only to the most tried and
> true Uncle Toms. Which, thank God, Robeson ain't!

1492. Jones, Ralph. "Editorial On Paul Robeson," Philadelphia Independent, March 25, 1950.

> The editor asserts: "Mrs. Eleanor Roosevelt still has the
> biggest soul that endears her to millions of people throughout
> the world. This was demonstrated as she extended an invitation to
> Paul Robeson to appear on her television show that is carried on
> a national hookup. Her generous show of friendship for Mr.
> Robeson, however, could not offset the public distaste against
> Paul's pro-Soviet public utterances. So great was the reaction
> that Mr. Robeson's appearance was indefinitely cancelled."

1494. Editorial. "Fear of Truth," Boston Chronicle, March 25, 1950,
       Editorial Page.

> The editor declares: "There is nothing more un-American than the
> suppression of the individual's innate right to freedom of speech.
> Nevertheless, many men and women in our nation are currently
> engaging in trying to suppress - in some instance, with force and
> violence, as the Peekskill riots of last summer are perennial re-
> minders - a fellow American's right to express opinions with which
> they disagree and reject...." He declares: "The most outrageous
> suppression which occurred last week was the cancellation of Paul
> Robeson's scheduled appearance on Mrs. Eleanor Roosevelt's tele-
> vision program over the National Broadcasting Company's network.
> Such an act was indefensible, whether or not one agrees with Mr.
> Robeson. It leads intelligent people to wonder if Mr. Robeson
> has something to say which the owners of NBC are fearful of having
> listeners hear. Moreover, the program was precisely devoted
> to airing trends of political thinking among the Negro people....
> No well-informed person can deny that Mr. Robeson, who was to re-
> present the Progressive Party, stands for an important trend in
> Negro political thought, despite the numerical paucity of its
> avowed adherents.... Were the suppressors afraid that Mr. Robeson's
> views, declared with his customary vigor and persuasiveness, might
> overweigh the others, because he is a greater man than either?...."

1494. Robinson, M.T. "Paul Robeson and the NBC Affair," Philadelphia
       Independent, March 25, 1950.

> Mr. Robinson comments on the banning of Paul Robeson from NBC
> television. He declares, in part: "....Such is free enterprise.
> It can stop and start things in a jiffy. Five thousand people
> and perhaps a million telegrams at considerable expense failed to
> convince Congress that a national FEPC was urgent. 'An flux' of
> telephone protests caused NBC to cancel Paul Robeson's appearance
> on Mrs. Roosevelt's program. Nobody knows the number of people
> involved in this influx. The public only knows that Paul did
> not and will not appear. Thus the voice of a great American on be-
> half of civil rights for his people was silenced."

1495. "Bergen Record Rips T.V. Ban on Robeson," Daily Worker, March 26,
       1950, p. 3.

       According to this article the conservative Bergen Evening Record
       scored NBC suppression of Paul Robeson's television discussion of
       Negro rights as "a savage and cynical denial of at least one of
       those rights." In an editorial titled "A Voice is Stilled,"
       the Record reminded its readers of its opposition to Robeson and
       the Progressive Party, but declares: "The National Broadcasting
       Company is urgently petitioned to re-examine without delay its
       cencellation of Paul Robeson's scheduled appearance on Mrs.
       Roosevelt's television show. The Progressive Party has charged
       that the network's action amounts to censorship. The charge is
       obviously substantiated...." The Record concludes by asserting:
            N.B.C. says no good purpose could have been served
            by allowing Mr. Robeson to speak on the issue of Negro
            political life. How does it know? Who says so? We
            in the Western world hold that truth is approached
            through free competition among ideas; we have not yet,
            begun subscribing to the surface when opposing views
            are liquidated is the truth.

1496. Edel, Leon. "Robeson Keeps Rolling Along," Sunday Compass,
       March 28, 1950.

       The writer interviewed Mr. Robeson concerning NBC banning him from
       appearing on its television program. Mr. Edel observed that Paul
       Robeson leaned back in his chair, his massive frame relaxed; the
       big voice, capable of thunderous accents, was modulated and soft.
       There was no bitterness in what he said, no touch of irony.
       "Artists," he said, "cannot be denied their audience," states the
       reporter. He said he wanted to bring music within the reach of
       all, to "those who normally never get near the concert halls, whose
       only chance of hearing Anderson or Heifetz is when they are on
       the air or when a few of them struggle into the balconies....,"
       concludes Mr. Edel.

1497. Cooper, Ruth. "Protests Can Force NBC to Drop Ban, Robeson Says,"
       Daily Worker, March 21, 1951, p. 4.

       The author reported that Robeson declares: "I am convinced that
       the banned for this shameful episode rest entirely on NBC. The
       program is a sustaining one and whatever pressure there was came
       from the network itself. There is no question that the mounting
       protests can mean that the program will be held at a later time.
       I hope that Mrs. Roosevelt and Elliott Roosevelt will struggle, as
       I am sure they will, for the civil rights of everyone to be
       heard." Robeson described the ban "as approaching the point of
       absurdity": "I have been on NBC and other networks any number of
       times," he declares. Robeson mentioned appearances with the
       Philadelphia Symphony Orchestra, the dramatization of Othello and
       his presentation of Ballad for Americans. "I am confident that if
       people everywhere speak out against this violation of free speech,
       I will be on." The singer declares: "I cannot and will not accept
       the notion that because someone is accused of being a Communist
       or a 'Communist sympathizer' that he has no right to speak. This

(Cooper, Rudy)

is absurd in a world where there are tens of mliions of Communists."
He adds: "We can only speak of peace in the world with them,
and not without them. There is no question of my attitude to the
Soviet Union and the peoples democracies of Europe and Asia. My
feelings to them are the same as Lafayette's feelings as a Frenchman toward America in his time."

1498.   "TV Ban on Robeson Hit by Negro Press," Daily Worker, March 30,
        1950, p. 11.

The article states that several Negroes' newspapers such as the
Boston Chronicle, New York Age, Philadelphia Independent, and
Baltimore Afro-American, spoke out against the banning of Paul
Robeson from NBC television. The essence of the articles was that
it was un-American to suppress one's freedom of speech.

1499.   Berry, Abner W. "But Robeson's Voice Got Through," Daily Worker,
        February 24, 1952, Section 2, p. 2.

United States Government officials stopped Paul Robeson from
crossing the border to Canada to address a union meeting. But
the Canadian unionists heard him anyway. With the aid of a union
on the United States' side of the line Robeson talked and sang to
the gathering by telephone. The writer concludes that it was
the America of the plain people that Robeson was defending at the
border and went on to defend over the telephone and which his great
voice continues to defend against those in whose interest the
border guard acted. Robeson's passport was cancelled and he could
not travel - even to Canada.

                        18. OTHELLO

1500.   Cook, Don. "Robeson's Othello at the Home Park," New York Herald
        Tribune, April 12, 1959, Section 4, pp. 1, 3.

The writer declares that one should forget Paul Robeosn's politics
for the moment, and consider instead the whole complex emotional
bakcground against which this eminent Negro faced the opening
night of the Shakespeare Memorial Theater's 100th season in the
role of "Othello." He asserts that by any standards it had to be
more than just the opening of another Shakespeare season at
Stratford - or even of the Memorial Theater's centenary season.
It was also, a climactic occasion in the complex life of a great
artist. The unique opportunity to seize upon Robeson's presence
in England again, at last, and the undoubted sympathy which his
American passport and political troubles have engendered for him
in Britain, certainly was not lost on the Memorial Theater directors,
he surmised. He concludes:
        Robeson's voice, Robeson's magnificent stage presence,
        Robeson's authority and personality dominate. The

(Cook, Don)

> chances are it will have even greater integration
> and power after the cast has settled in on the pro-
> duction and learned its strengths and weaknesses....For
> Paul Robeson, the road that led to Stratford-on-Avon
> was a long and torturous highway.... The artistry of
> that performance expressed that art which reflects
> man's irrestible drives for human dignity, mankind's
> struggle for freedom, progress, peace, Stratford-on-
> Avon was an historical point on the road Paul Robeson
> chose to follow....

1501. "Mr. Paul Robeson Very Ill: To Miss 'Othello'," London Times, January 31, 1959, p. 6.

This article states that Mr. Paul Robeson was seriously ill according to a statement from the Shakespeare Memorial Theatre,
Stratford-on-Avon in England. Because of his illness, Mr. Robeson
could not fulfill his engagement to play the title role in
"Othello" which would open in April.

1502. "Robeson Will Perform as Othello in England," New York Times, February 11, 1959, p. 49.

This article states that Paul Robeson will be able to undertake
the title role in "Othello" at the Shakespeare Memorial Theatre,
Stratford-on-Avon, England, in mid-March. Robeson previously
could not undertake the role because of illness. According to
reported sources he was suffering from bronchitis and exhaustion
when he was taken to a Moscow hospital.

1503. "Robeson in Britain for 'Othello'," New York Times, March 10, 1959, p. 11.

Paul Robeson arrived in London, by air from Moscow, after having
recovered from an illness in a Kremlin hospital. He was there to
play the title role in "Othello" at the Shakespeare Memorial
Theatre at Stratford-on-Avon.

1504. Darlington, W.A. "2 U.S. Actors Star on British Stage: Robeson
and Wanamaker in 'Othello'," New York Times, April 8, 1959, p. 41.

Paul Robeson and Sam Wanamaker appeared in the chief parts as
Othello and Iago, respectively, and both distinguished themselves
greatly, states Darlington. The reviewer contends about Robeson
as Othello: "He has that authority now among the best I have ever
seen - perhaps, second only to the magnificent performance of
Godfrey Tearle...."

1505. "Miscasting Handicaps Robeson's 'Othello'," London Times, April 8, 1959, p. 14.

The critic argues that when Mr. Paul Robeson last played "Othello"
in England, he was handicapped by a freakish production and a
grotesquely maimed text. He has greater stage assurance now than

<u>(London Times)</u>

he had in 1930, states the writer, but no greater command of
Shakespearian verse, and again he is sadly handicapped by an
over-clever production.   He continues to suggest that the impression of inaudibility is quite irrestible in the present case,
for Mr. Sam Wanamaker and Miss Mary Ure, the Iago and the Desdemona, have not Mr. Robeson's magnificent voice and they cannot
speak verse even as well as he mananged to do so. He concludes:
"The miscasting of both these actors (Wanamaker and Ure) robs
Mr. Robeson of his best chance of making something memorable of
the part.... His performance is occasionally exciting if hardly
ever touches the heart."

1506.   "Robeson as Othello," <u>Herald-Tribune</u> (Paris Edition), April 9,
1959, Entertainment Section.

Paul Robeson was 60 years old when he returned to England for his
last major theatrical performance. The reviewer surmises, in
part:
....Mr. Robeson turned in an amazing performance.
He seemed to give everything, realizing perhaps that
a great many people in many parts of the world were
wondering how he would handle "Othello" after all
these years....many....came to see if Mr. Robeson's
deep bass voice had lost any of its vigor. It hadn't....

1507.   Wallace, Philip Hope. "Paul Robeson in Othello," <u>Manchester
Guardian Weekly</u>, April 9, 1959, p. 11.

The writer comments on Robeson's role in "Othello." He states:
....Paul Robeson, returning after nearly a quarter of
a century to the stage in England, slightly cheated our
memories of that long-ago powerful Othello of his at the
Savoy. True, he still has the volume, the imposing
stature, the sonority, and the generosity. His rage
looks dangerous, and at the end he excites the pity due
to a noble animal at bay; but tonight he was also stiff
and monotonous and, though there was richness of
tone and feeling, there was no richness in the phrasing
of his delivery. He is an instinctively noble Othello
who, in spite of the magnificence of his voice,
curiously fails to get the best out of the wonderful
words in which Shakespeare portrayed the character.

1508.   Darlington, W.A. "Robeson's Performance in 'Othello' Hailed by
Stratford Playgoers," <u>New York Times</u>, April 12, 1959, Section 2,
p. 3.

The reviewer declares that he placed Paul Robeson's performance as
Othello the second best Othello of all that he had seen, second
only to the performance given by Godfrey Tearle. He states that
Mr. Robeson had all of the qualities that go to make an ideal
Othello - all but one. According to Darlington, Robeson lacks
the ability to deliver Shakespeare's verse so that it touches the
heart. Other critics, however, state Robeson as Othello as "Strong

(Darlington, W.A.)

and stately...a superman of a general." "Nobly spoken," said
another. "Superb," added a third.

1509. "Shakespeare Meant for Othello to be a Black Man," Hue, June, 1959,
pp. 38, 48.

According to this short article:
Although Shakespeare meant his tragic hero, Othello,
to be an African, Paul Robeson's role as an authentic
"bronze Colossus" was the first in the history of
Stratford-on-Avon. After kissing his stage wife,
Desdemona (actress Mary Ure), six times and acting
the part of a Moor crumbling under jealousy, Robeson
stepped forward before a wildy cheering audience.
Then, responding spontaneously, he applauded the
audience. So overwhelmed was he that when the
curtain finally came down he was standing in the
wrong place - and it landed on his head.... "I'm
very happy. That was a wonderful audience."
Robeson received a record of 15 curtain calls....

1510. Tunan, Kenneth. "The Theatre Abroad: England," New Yorker,
Vol. 35, No. 32, September 26, 1959, pp. 112, 113, 114, 116, 117.

Mr. Tunan comments on Paul Robeson's role in "Othello." He
suggests that Mr. Robeson had very little Shakespearean experience.
The critic concludes:
....In more appropriate company, I am sure, Mr. Robeson
would rise to greater heights than he does. As things
are, he seems to be murdering a butterfly on the
advice of a gossip columnist. His voice, of course,
is incomparable -- a foundation -- shaking boom. It
may, however, be too resonant, too musically arti-
culated for the very finest acting. The greatest
players -- Kean and Irving, for example -- have
seldom been singers as well. Their voices were
human and imperfect, whereas the noise made by
Mr. Robeson is so nearly perfect as to be nearly
inhuman....

1511. "Paul Robeson's Othello at Shakespeare Memorial Theatre a Splendid
Success," Shakespeare Newsletter (New York), Vol. 9, No. 2, April,
1959, p. 9.

It was pointed out that Paul Robeson and Sam Wanamaker, gave the
Shakespeare Memorial Theatre at Stratford-on-Avon one of the most
distinguished premiere performances it has had in years. Both
actors captured the fancy of the public, states the article.
Robeson played Othello and Wanamaker played Iago. Robeson did not
start rehearsing until March 16th although the play opened on
April 7th. Robeson had done Othello many times, including breaking
records in New York City.

1512. "Stratford Memorial Theatre Ends 100th Season," Shakespeare News-
       letter (New York), Vol. 9, No. 5, November, 1959, p. 33.

       It was brought out in this article that Paul Robeson was hailed
       by critics as "the second best" Othello in the history of the
       theatre.

                          19. PASSPORT AFFAIR

1513. "Robeson Asks Court to Lift Passport Ban," New York Times, December
       20, 1950, p. 28.

       Paul Robeson filed suit against Secretary of State Dean Acheson
       in an effort to prevent cancellation of his passport, which he
       needed for a European concert tour. Papers filed by the singer in
       Federal District court described the baritone as one who "has
       deservedly won for himself respect and recognition throughout
       the world, not only as one of the great living Americans, but
       also as one of the world's leading personalities." Robeson states
       that he had a "property right" guaranteed under the Constitution
       to engage in his profession outside of the United States and asked
       the court to force a lifting of the State Department's ban.

1514. "Robeson's Plea," Newsweek, Vol. 37, No. 1, January 1, 1951, pp.
       13-14.

       The article states that Paul Robeson filed a suit in Washington
       Federal Court against Secretary of State Dean Acheson, asking the
       court to lift the passport ban. His plea described him as a man
       who "has deservedly won for himself respect and recognition
       through out the world, not only as one of the great living
       Americans but also as one of the world's leading personalities....
       a spokesman for the working men and women of America." He had
       a "property right" to the passport, Robeson said. The court,
       applying the democratic code to which Robeson objected, would
       decide, concludes the article.

1515. "Robeson Loses Passport Suit," New York Times, April 13, 1951,
       p. 12.

       Federal Judge Walter M. Bastian dismissed a suit filed by Paul
       Robeson, to compel the Government to grant him a passport. Mr.
       Robeson filed the suit in December, 1950. He announced that he
       wanted the passport to make a European tour. The State Department
       denied it on grounds that his planned travels were not "in the
       best interest of the country." Judge Bastian ruled the State
       Department was within its "discretion" in turning down the
       application.

1516. "Miners' Invitation to Mr. Paul Robeson," London Times, August 15,
       1951, p. 4.

       According to this article the executives of the Scottish area of
       the National Union of Mineworkers meeting in Edinburgh, England,
       agreed to invite Mr. Paul Robeson to give a series of recitals
       throughout the Scottish coal fields. Since Mr. Robeson's pass-
       port was cancelled by the United States Department of State, the
       executive would ask the American Ambassador in London to issue
       the necessary permit for the Scottish tour.

1517. "Robeson Passport Ban Protested," New York Times, October 29, 1951,
       p. 12.

       The delegation to the Negro Labor Council that was meeting in
       Cincinnati, shouted vigorous protests against the State Department's
       refusal to issue a passport for Paul Robeson to travel in Europe.
       Mr. Robeson heard two hours of speeches devoted to the denial of
       his passport. Speaking of Mr. Robeson, Mr. William R. Hood,
       President of the Council, declares: "We shall use all the power
       of this convention to see that Paul Robeson will have the right
       to move about like other citizens."

1517a. Gordon, A.J. "U.S. Cancels Robeson's Passport after He Refuses to
       Surrender It," New York Times, August 4, 1950, pp. 1, 22.

       The writer states that the State Department asked Paul Robeson,
       a native American, a noted singer and leader of left-wing move-
       ments, to surrender his passport. He refused to give it up.
       Local and national officials of the Immigration and Customs services
       and the Federal Bureau of Investigation were ordered to stop
       Robeson if he tried to leave the country. Gordon delcares that it
       was learned that Robeson's activities in left-wing movements
       and his outspoken criticism of this country's international dealings
       had much to do with the revocation of the passport. Government
       officials said it was an uncommon practice to "pick up" a passport,
       particularly if issued to a native born person. It was pointed out
       that Robeson on his return from his trip to Russia, spent con-
       siderable time and made a number of addresses in which he praised
       the Soviets. According to Mr. Gordon, at the same time, Robeson
       disparaged what was being done by the United States Government.

1518. "Robeson Adamant and Keeps Passport," New York Times, August 5,
       1950, p. 16.

       Paul Robeson said he would not surrender his passport until the
       State Department, which demanded its return, gives him an adequate
       reason for its actions. Nathan Witt, counsel for Robeson declares
       that Robeson is a native born American, and one of his inalienable
       rights is to travel freely, subject only to those reasonable re-
       strictions which apply to all citizens. He concludes:
            Until we are shown to the contrary, it is also clear
            to us that the administration seeks to deprive Mr.
            Robeson of these rights as part of its efforts to
            deprive him of inalienable rights to freedom of
            thought and expression. We are sure that the people

(New York Times)

of the world will hear Mr. Robeson whether he
speaks here or abroad.

1519. Editorial. "Paul Robeson's Passport," New York Herald-Tribune,
August 6, 1950.

The editor declares, in part:
The State Department acts correctly in cancelling Paul
Robeson's passport.... The question is whether the
issuance of the passport with the implication of guarantee, is in the best national interests. And in
Mr. Robeson's case, the State Department is simply
stating in full authority that his projected travels
are not to the best American interests. Mr. Robeson
will have to stay at home. Paul Robeson's record as
an agitator...is well known. His plans call for an
extensive series of appearances at European "peace"
rallies, followed by ideological traipsings through
Africa and Australia.... That is something this
country can well be spared. The State Department
has acted effectively, and is disinclined to debate
the matter with Mr. Robeson or his lawyer. Discreation
has been ably exercised: this is not the sort of un-
official ambassador we want roaming the world under an
American passport.... Paul Robeson need not think that
he can have his citizenship both ways. The State
Department's realism will be acclaimed by every firm-
minded American.

1520. Editorial. "The Robeson Passport," Afro-American, August 8, 1950,
p. 2.

The editor states, in part:
The action of the U.S. State Department in cancelling
the passport of Paul Robeson strikes us at first glance,
as an unnecessary and unreasonable blunder. While we
hold no brief for Mr. Robeson's beliefs or utterances,
we cannot see how the State Department, in justice,
can deprive one citizen of his rights while, at the
same time, permitting others to move about freely without penalty. Some of the things that Mr. Robeson has
said about the U.S. may not have been palatable, but
no one has yet come forward with an official denial of
them, declares the writer. He continues to suggest
that on the other hand, countless White Americans have
been permitted to travel the world over with State
Department sanction, spewing their venomous views on
racial relations wherever they saw fit. Haven't such
persons actually done the cause of democracy more harm
than can ever be done by a score of Robesons? Keeping
Robeson at home won't stop him from thinking, talking
and writing. We dislike the idea of seeing anyone
gagged, especially when the basis for such gagging is
not clearly based upon proven charges. There are many

(Afro-American)

> others far more dnagerous than Paul. What about
> them?

1521. "Robeson Plans Australian Trip," New York Times, August 9, 1950,
      p. 34.

Paul Robeson, whose passport was cancelled by the United States
Government Department of State, accepted an invitation to visit
Australia in September. The secretary of the Democratic Rights
Council said Robeson had stated he would attend the Australian
Peoples' Assembly for Human Rights Congress.

1522. Civil Rights Congress. "About Robeson's Passport," The Union
      (Cincinnati, Ohio), August 10, 1950, p. 1.

This article states:
> Mr. Robeson is a native-born American and one of his
> inalienable rights is the right to travel freely,
> subject only to those reasonable restrictiong which
> apply to all citizens. In this connection, it is
> important to note that Mr. Robeson's ability to earn
> a living is conditioned on his right to travel
> abroad. He has invitations to concerts in European
> countries, in Israel, in the Caribbean, in Australia
> and elsewhere. The action of the State Department
> arbitrarily cuts off the right of this American
> citizen to earn a living. Until we are shown to the
> contrary, it is also clear to us that the admin-
> istration seeks to deprive Mr. Robeson of these
> rights as part of its effort to deprive him of his
> inalienable right to freedom of thought and expression.
> This incident forms part of the rapidly developing
> pattern of repression and of arbitrary deprivation of
> the rights of the American people. We are sure that
> the people of the world will hear Mr. Robeson whether
> he speaks here or abroad.

1523. "Robeson Passport Loss Protested," New York Times, August 10, 1950,
      p. 23.

Nine women and a man called at the State Department to protest re-
vocation of the passport of Paul Robeson. Mrs. Christina Staneslow,
who said she represented the People's Party of Connecticut, said
cancelling Mr. Robeson's passport is tantamount to taking away
the singer's means of livelihood. The passport was revoked on the
grounds that Mr. Robeson's travels were "not in the interests
of the United States."

1524. "Journey's End," Time, Vol. 56, No. 7, August 14, 1950, p. 12.

    According to this article:
        As one of the world's highest paid musicians, Paul
        Robeson had traveled far from the house in Princeton,
        N.J. where he was born the son of a runaway slave.
        But he wasn't satisfied with his progress in the U.S.;
        16 years ago, he went all the way for Moscow and de-
        cided that Negroes had a better chance of advancing
        under the Commies. For the last three years, in
        London, Moscow, Paris, Manhattan, he had faithfully
        slandered the Atlantic Pact, the Marshall Plan, the
        U.S. defense of Korea -- shouting, all the while for
        Soviet-style "peace." Robeson would have to stay
        put a while in the land that has seemed to him, at
        various times, fascist, imperialistics, bourgeois
        and warmongering. To the State Department, Robeson's
        statements did not seem in the best interests of the
        U.S., or representatives of the U.S. people. A
        sample: "It is unthinkable that (American Negroes)
        would go to war on behalf of those who have oppressed
        us for generations," against a country (U.S.S.R.)
        "which in one generation has raised our people to
        the full dignity of mankind." Said a State Depart-
        ment spokesman: "We won't give a passport to anybody
        else...up to the same thing."

1525. "They Didn't Rally Round," Collier's, Vol. 126, October 28, 1950,
      p. 86.

    The article declares, in part:
        Paul Robeson held a rally for "peace, freedom and
        jobs" not long ago on a street corner in New York's
        Harlem. He told his listeners that he planned to sue
        the State Department for revoking his passport because
        his projected trip abroad was "not in the interests
        of the United States." We think that the department's
        decision, on the record of Mr. Robeson's past per-
        formances, was unassailably right. And we rather
        imagine that the majority of American Negroes, for
        whom he professes to speak, don't think his spouting-
        off represents the country's best interests or their
        own. At least the turnout at his rally would indicate
        as much. An acquaintance of ours happened to pass
        this Harlem street corner while Mr. Robeson was in
        the midst of his speech. He generously estimated the
        crowd at 200. Harlem's population is at least 350,000.
        We think the figures speak for themselves.

1526. Moos, Elizabeth. "Free Paul Robeson!," Masses and Mainstream,
      Vol. 4, No. 10, October, 1951, pp. 8-10.

This article discusses the United States State Department denial
of his passport to travel to foreign countries. Miss Moos asserts
that unless the decision of the State Department is reversed and
Mr. Robeson receives his passport, he cannot fill his engagements.

(Moos, Elizabeth)

Not only are out anti-cultural officials depriving men and women
abroad of the longed-for pleasure of hearing this great artist,
they are attempting to destroy his livelihood as well, she declares. Miss Moos concludes:
> More than any other American artist, Paul Robeson
> is a world figure. He has mastered many languages
> and devoted years to studying the arts of other
> lands. He has sung to the Chinese and to the Slavic
> peoples in their own tongues; his name is widely
> known in Africa.... It is more than a world renowned
> artist that we must defend. It is a noble human
> being, a great-hearted man, passionately devoted to
> the cause of peace and freedom - freedom for his own
> people, the Negro people, and for the oppressed every-
> where. Let men and women, the youth of America now -
> today - take up the fight to free Paul Robeson so that
> his voice may ring out over all the earth.

1527. Spencer, Rudolph J. "Robeson Says He Will Defeat State Dept. in
its Effort to Prevent Him from Traveling Abroad," Black Dispatch,
February 23, 1952, p. 1.

This article declares that Paul Robeson was denied permission by
United States immigration authorities to cross the border into
Canada when he was scheduled to speak to a convention of British
Columbia members of the Mine, Mill and Smelters Workers Union.
He was stopped at Blane, Washington when his automobile arrived
at the immigration and custom officers, handed a written order
prohibiting his entry and informed that if he proceeded to
Vancouver, B.C., upon his return he would be subject to prosecution
and imprisonment. Condemning the government's action as an out-
rageous violation of his civil rights and indicative of police
intimidation he returned to Seattle, Washington, declares the
writer. He predicted that he would defeat the State Department's
efforts to restrict his travels. With concrete facts at hand he
enumerated the many un-democratic evils and injustices and
violations of civil rights of the Negro people committed by those
sworn to uphold the Constitution. Robeson reminded these listeners
that Negroes are a working people and thousands on both coasts have
memberships in democratic practicing maritime labor unions and because these organizations demand a living wage, decent housing,
and full democracy for all regardless of race, creed and color,
many Negro workers have been screened off their jobs and denied
future employment. For his critics who had been at odds with him
for his pro-Russia friendship and who had urged him to leave this
country he said that he was not going anywhere. "This is my home,"
he said. It is the writer's opinion that in the years to come
Paul Robeson's name will be placed alongside Fred Douglass' for
their careers, turbulent and controversial, bear resemblances.
Douglass was born a slave, Robeson's parents were slaves. Douglass
fought for physical and civil freedom; Robeson is fighting for
first class citizenship rights, concludes Mr. Spencer.

1528. Berry, Abner W. "The Government Confesses in Answering Paul Robeson," The Worker, April 13, 1952, p. 2.

The writer surmises that the United States Government finally confessed in open court that Paul Robeson's passport was withdrawn because of his activity in "behalf of the colonial peoples of Africa." And in the same confession, the government admitted that it considered Robeson "a spokesman for large sections of Negro Americans" and "disproved....(Robeson) political activities and associations abroad." The author was referring to an obscure footnote to the government's legal brief in answer to Robeson's suit in Federal Court for the return of his passport. The answer the government usually gave to questions as to why Paul Robeson's passport was cancelled was: "Robeson's foreign travel was 'not in the best interest' of the United States."

1529. Loeb, Charles H. "World on View - Paul Robeson," Cleveland Call & Post, May 3, 1952.

Writing in his May 3 column before a scheduled Robeson concert in Cleveland was to take place, Loeb declares: "If there had ever been any doubt that our present State Department is committed to a policy of imperialism for its most powerful allies, it was removed in the State Department action last August 7, 1950, of refusing to Robeson a passport to travel abroad." The Negro columnist then quoted the State Department's admission that it moved against Robeson because "he has been extremely active in behalf of independence of the colonial peoples of Africa..." Referring to the artist as "the great Robeson," Loeb took issue with his statement that Negro Americans would not fight against the socialist Soviet Union, then added, "But on the basic issues of foreign policy, in his attacks on the U.S. policy of playing footsie to the imperialist designs of England and France, and in his castigation of the continuing white supremacy ideology of the American government, Robeson, even in his untouchablity, echoes the feelings of every Negro who has sense enough to get in out of the rain."

1530. "A.M.E. Zion Church Conference Hits State Dept. Ban on Robeson's Travel," The Worker, May 21, 1952, pp. 3, 6.

According to this report the right of Paul Robeson to have back his passport was supported by the 34th quadrennial national conference of the powerful African Methodist Episcopal Zion Church at the Brooklyn A.M.E. Zion Church. The A.M.E. Zion Church has 600,000 members. Paul Robeson attended the conference and addressed the delegates. Senior Bishop William J. Walls addressed the conference and declared:
    Tonight we have had a son of Zion here to sing. His father was a pastor in our church and also a fighter. I will tell you why the State Department has refused Paul Robeson a passport. The reason he is barred from going abroad is that Paul Robeson advocates independence for the colonial people.

1531. "Curb on Robeson Stands," New York Times, August 8, 1952, p. 5.

The suit by Paul Robeson to have the State Department revalidate
his passport was ordered thrown out of court. The United States
Court of Appeals sent the issue back to the District Court with
instructions that it be dismissed, since, it held, nothing concrete remained of the case. The court reasoned that, since the
passport expired January 25, 1951, and no application for renewal
was shown to have been made, there was nothing left at issue.

1532. "Court Weights Robeson Appeal," New York Times, March 17, 1952,
p. 8.

The United States Circuit Court of Appeals took under advisement
an appeal from Paul Robeson who is trying to force the State
Department to issue him a passport. He lost in district court on
April 13, 1951, in his effort to get the court to order the department to let him have one, and arguments on his appeal to the
circuit court were heard last week.

1533. "Robeson Trip Unlikely," New York Times, December 27, 1952, p. 11.

The State Department indicated that a passport would not be granted
to Paul Robeson for travel to the Soviet Union to recieve the
Stalin Peace Prize. Michael J. McDermot, press officer for the
State Department asserts: "The last time he applied, he was refused. We see nothing to indicate that his attitude has changed."

1534. "Robeson Asks for Passport," New York Times, August 1, 1953, p. 8.

Paul Robeson applied for his passport to appear in the title role
in a London production of "Othello," under the sponsorship of
Leslie Linder. Mr. Robeson, since his last appearance abroad in
the Spring of 1950, was twice denied a renewal of his passport
by the State Department. It was pointed out that Mr. Linder
requested a work permit for Mr. Robeson from British Actors'
Equity Association, the union's general secretary, Gordon Sandison,
replied:
          It was the unanimous opinion of the council that
          Mr. Robeson's status is such that we cannot raise
          any objection to his appearing in this country. Indeed,
          the council expressed its satisfaction at the prospect
          of seeing Mr. Robeson play this part, in which he has
          previously made so striking an appearance. We would
          welcome his appearance in this country.

1535. "Passport Refused to Mr. Paul Robeson," London Times, September
16, 1953, p. 5.

This article states that the South Wales Miners' Executive
announced that Mr. Paul Robeson, who recently accepted the Miners'
invitation to be their guest at their annual eisteddfod at Portcawl
had been refused the restoration of his passport by the United
States State Department.

1536. "U.S. Bars Robeson Trip to Wales," New York Times, September 16, 1953, pp. 2, 5.

The United States State Department refused to allow Paul Robeson to attend a Welsh coal miners' song festival, according to the South Wales Miners' Executive Committee.

1537. "'Robeson Salute' Will Open Fight for Travel Right," Daily Worker, May 11, 1954, p. 8.

A cultural salute to Paul Robeson was to be held on May 26 at the Renaissance Casino in Harlem, New York. This would be the opening event in a national campaign to restore the artist's right to travel abroad.

1538. Strong, Augusta. "Seek Passport for Envoy of The People," Daily Worker, May 16, 1954, pp. 6, 11.

The State Department denied Robeson a passport because the government lawyers cited Robeson's "frank admission that he has been for years extremely active politically in behalf of the independence of the colonial peoples of Africa...the diplomatic embarrassment that could arise from the presence abroad of such a political meddler traveling under the protection of an American passport is easily imaginable...." This was the government case. The author concludes:
> Far from being a source of "embarrassment" to the American people abroad, Robeson has helped to preserve abroad respect and love for the America which rejects Dulles as its spokesman, or military bases that dot the world as symbols of our culture, and the atom and H-bomb explosions as the best expressions of our great minds.

1539. "Phila. Tribune Urges Passport for Robeson," Daily Worker, July 23, 1954, p. 8.

According to this article, The Philadelphia Tribune, the leading local Black newspaper, editorially called upon the U.S. State Department to re-issue the passport of Paul Robeson. The editorial titled "Paul Robeson's Passport" said: "The right to work is basic. One of the great minds of the early Christian era laid down the dictum, 'He who will not work, neither shall he eat.' To deny a man the right to work at the kind of work for which he is best fitted is heartless and inhuman." Robeson had invitations to sing and act overseas that would have enabled him to make a livelihood for six months. He should not be denied the right to work. The State Department should give this American his passport, states the Daily Worker.

1540. Williamson, John. "Britain -- Right to Left Cries 'Let Robeson Come'," The Worker, October 23, 1954, pp. 8, 10.

The author points out that all in London, with few exceptions, are in agreement that Robeson should be granted a passport by the State Department, and allowed to visit England, Scotland and Wales.

(The Worker)

The London Cooperative Party sent an article to 130 trade union
newspapers that had the following message as its lead paragraph:
Paul Robeson, American Negro and world famous concert
and opera singer, whose voice is beloved in all lands,
has many times been described as a giant. This is
appropriate in many ways - a giant of songs, a giant
of opera, and a giant of man. I am sure that while
Americans know that Paul sprang from and belongs to
them, and has a love and devotion for the true values
of America, as he so movingly sings in "What Is
America to Me," that they also appreciate the contributions of the British Labor Movement in making the
American Paul Robeson, the Giant of the World that
he is today.

1541.   "State Department Bans Robeson Visit to Soviet Writers," Daily
Worker, November 30, 1954, p. 8.

Robeson was invited by the Congress of Soviet Writers to the
Congress. His application for a passport from the United States
Passport Office was denied. It was denied on the grounds that he
did not meet the procedure outlined in Section 51.137 of the
Passport Regulations. The regulations referred to require an
applicant to "prove" that his views do not deviate from those
of the State Department as a prerequisite for receiving a passport.
Robeson challenged the State Department's right to deny him on
the grounds that it's refusal to grant him a passport deprives him
of his constitutional rights of freedom of speech, thought and
assembly, and freedom to earn a living guaranteed by the First
and Fifth Amendments of the Constitution.

1542.   "Robeson Seeks Passport Again," New York Times, January 14, 1955,
p. 11.

According to this article, Paul Robeson said he was a "loyal,
native born American citizen," asked the Federal District Court
to direct the State Department to grant him a passport. He also
asked the court to allow him to visit Canada, Mexico and other
Western Hemisphere countries on travel not requiring a passport.
The article also declares that he had been identified with
leftist causes for a long time.

1543.   "Robeson Offered 'Othello' Role in Soviet Film: Again Applies
to State Dep't for Passport," Daily Worker, May 16, 1955, p. 3.

Robeson was offered the role of "Othello," by Sergei Yutkevich,
Director of the Mosfilm Studio of the Soviet Union. The director
wrote Robeson saying "knowing you as a magnificent portrayer of this
role, we would be very happy if you would agree to play Othello
in our film, in either English or Russian, whichever language you
would prefer." Robeson, after accepting the offer, applied, once
again, for a passport from the State Department. The actor saw
the offer as "a wonderful opportunity to participate in a major
artistic work." He also states this part was the most important

(Daily Worker)

screen role he has ever afforded.

1544. "Mr. Robeson Claims Rights to Travel: Denial of Passport," London
       Times, July 19, 1955, p. 6.

       This article states that Mr. Paul Robeson referred to a recent
       court decision in passport cases as an indication that the State
       Department had acted "arbitrarily and unlawfully" in denying him
       a passport for the past five years. Mr. Robeson said he wished
       to obtain a passport to go to London to act in a stage production
       of "Othello" and also to make a film of the play in Moscow.

1545. "Mr. Paul Robeson's Right to Travel," London Times, July 20, 1955,
       p. 7.

       The article reports that the State Department announced that it
       was easing travel restrictions on Mr. Paul Robeson, who has been
       identified with left-wing groups and who had been refused per-
       mission for five years to travel outside the continental limits
       of the United States. The State Department stated that it would
       permit him to fulfill engagements in Canada, to enter which he
       does not require a passport.

1546. "Robeson May Travel - But Not in Europe!," Daily Worker, July 20,
       1955, pp. 1, 7.

       The State Department rescinded the special order restricting Paul
       Robeson's right to travel to the continental limits of the United
       States. The order in effect against Robeson since 1952, prevented
       his traveling to Canada, Mexico, the West Indies, Hawaii, Jamaica,
       Trinidad and British Guiana, places where in general no passport
       is required.

1547. "Robeson Asks Passport as Both a 'Natural' and 'Equal' Right,"
       Daily Worker, July 19, 1955.

       Robeson and his attorneys met with the State Department and asked
       that the actor's passport to be restored.Robeson argues: "The
       right to travel is not only a 'natural right,' as the Supreme
       Court has said, but also an 'equal right.' That is the way the
       Negro citizens of this country see it. Indeed colored peoples
       all over the world will see here a basic test of democratic
       principles." He said that the many offers he has received for
       "concert stage and film appearances in other lands" are "great
       importance" to him as an artist. They afforded him an opportunity
       to earn a livelihood in the practice of his profession, he said.

1548. Editorial. "Robeson's Passport," Daily Worker, July 20, 1955,
       p. 5.

       The editor states that.it is ironic that one of the principal
       reasons for the denial of a passport to Paul Robeson was to pre-
       vent his speaking and acting for just such a meeting for peace as
       is now under way in Geneva. State Department functionaries now

(Daily Worker)

say that they will give "careful and prompt attention" to Robeson's request, declares the editor. He concludes that "however, the only proper attention to be given is the granting of a passport, a step which will raise our country's prestige."

1549. "Robeson May Enter Canada, U.S. Rules," New York Times, July 20, 1955, p. 12.

The State Department gave permission for Paul Robeson to travel to Canada. The article states that Mr. Robeson could travel to and from Canada as often as he liked. The State Department declared that the restriction confining Mr. Robeson to the continental limits of the United States had been applied on the basis of wartime travel control regulations.

1550. "Robeson Wins Limited Right to Travel; Seeks Full Right Without Signing Oath," National Guardian, August 1, 1955, p. 12.

The United States State Department lifted the orders restricting Paul Robeson's rights to travel to the continental limits of the United States. Before this time Robeson could not travel to such countries as Canada, Mexico, the West Indies and Jamaica. Usually no passport was necessary to travel to those countries.

1551. Berry, Abner W. "Once There Was a Man," Daily Worker, August 4, 1955, p. 5.

The writer points out that Paul Robeson was one of the best loved Americans abroad: Africa, England, South Africa and several Scandinavian countries. In fact, many of those countries invited him to become a citizen of their countries. Berry concludes that when he thinks of British farmers and all the others to whom Robeson is considered, along with Franklin D. Roosevelt, he wonders what they think of the Americanism of the Department of State in refusing Robeson a passport.

1552. "Mr. Paul Robeson's Passport Plea: State Department to Contest Issue," London Times, August 5, 1955, p. 8.

This article states that the State Department had decided, after consultation with the Department of Justice, to continue the fight against giving a passport to Mr. Paul Robeson. It was also pointed out that the Belfast Trades Council decided to ask Mr. Paul Robeson to visit Belfast for a cultural function under their auspices if his passport for Europe was renewed.

1553. "Robeson Passport: U.S. to Fight Singer's Efforts to Leave the Country," New York Times, August 5, 1955, p. 42.

The State Department decided to fight the effort of Paul Robeson, to force it to give him a passport. Early in 1955 the singer filed suit in Federal District Court to require John Foster Dulles, Secretary of State, to give him a passport. The Justice Department countered that the singer had not used up all the administrative

(New York Times)

means of getting a passport.

1554. "Paul Robeson's Passport Case," Roman Catholic Weekly Tablet
(London), August 13, 1955.

This Roman Catholic newspaper supported Paul Robeson's rights to
a passport. It states, in part:
We think the American government is making a wrong
decision.... He can be an effective figure on the
platform or radio, and it is tempting to stop him -
but the price is too high if it prevents the Western
world pointing proudly to one of its decisive
superiorities over the Communist world, that in the
Western world men are free to move about, to with-
draw from a community and enter another, and are not
held prisoners against their will....

1555. "Court Rules Robeson's Passport Suit Premature," Daily Worker,
August 17, 1955, p. 3.

Federal Judge Burmita S. Matthews refused to order the State Department to grant a passport to Paul Robeson because Robeson
should first follow through on the administrative procedures set
up by the State Department for handling disputed passport cases
before applying to the courts for relief, asserts the article.
The judge said she could not find that Secretary of State John
Foster Dulles "has abused his discretion or has acted arbitrarily
in Robeson's case." The State Department demanded that Robeson
sign a non-Communist affidavit in order to get a passport.
Robeson told reporters: "Of course I won't sign it. I consider
it an invasion of every constitutional liberty I have."

1556. Dunie, Morrey. "Robeson's Court Plea for Passport Rejected,"
Washington Post, August 17, 1955, p. 16.

According to Mr. Dunie, District Court Judge Burnita S. Matthews
refused to order the State Department to issue a passport to
Paul Robeson. After listening to arguments by Robeson's lawyer,
Leonard B. Boudin, of New York, and United States Attorney Leo A.
Rover, the jurist ruled that Robeson has no standing in court
until he exhausts his administrative remedies at the State Department. Before his application could be considered, Robeson
was told he would have to file a non-Communist affidavit. The
singer-actor has refused to file the document and came to court
in an effort to force the issuance of the passport.

1557. "Mr. Robeson's Plea Rejected: Federal Court Ruling on Passport,"
London Times, August 17, 1955, p. 6.

This article states that Judge Burmita Matthews of the Federal
District Court rejected an application by Mr. Paul Robeson for a
court order requiring the State Department to grant him a passport. Judge Matthews declared that Mr. Robeson must "follow
through" the administrative procedures of the department's

(London Times)

passport division before applying to the courts for release. The judge also argued that she did not find that the Secretary of State had abused his discretion or acted arbitrarily in the case.

1558. "Case of Paul Robeson: Why Some Americans Can't Get Passports," U.S. News and World Report, Vol. 39, August 26, 1955, pp. 79, 80, 81.

On August 16, 1955, in the United States District Court for the District of Columbia, a hearing was held on Paul Robeson's motion for an injunction to compel the State Department to issue him a passport. This article gives extracts from the official transcript of the hearing. The State Department withheld Robeson's passport when he refused to sign an affidavit that he was not a Communist. The court found no abuse of "discretion" in such a procedure.

1559. "3 Negro Papers Support Robeson's Passport Fight," Daily Worker, September 1, 1955, p. 8.

The three Negro newspapers that supported Robeson's passport fight were: the Los Angeles Herald-Dispatch, the San Diego Lighthouse, and the Pittsburgh Courier. All of the papers pointed out that Robeson was denied a passport by the State Department because of his color. The Herald-Dispatch was the most vocal of all and ran a front page editorial and stated that it is to the eternal credit of Robeson that he has unhesitatingly rejected all treacherous deals with the State Department for him to keep silent when he travels abroad.

1560. "Britons Appeal for Robeson," New York Times, September 10, 1955, p. 11.

Delegates at the Trade Union Congress meeting at Southport, England, appealed to President Dwight D. Eisenhower to allow Paul Robeson a passport to come to Britain. The singer was refused a passport because he was identified with Communist causes.

1561. Belfrage, Cedric. "They Want the Cadillac Curtain, Lowered for Paul Robeson," National Guardian, September 26, 1955, p. 3.

"The British Workers and people are anxious again to hear this great son of America." Those words concluded a cable from Southport, England, to the White House, Washington, on September 9. The cable was a plea to Eisenhower to release Paul Robeson from behind the Cadillac Curtain in the spirit of Ike's post-Geneva suggestion that "all curtains should begin to come down." It was a sample of the windy weather over here which -- as U.S. diplomats have no doubt already reported -- threatens to attain gale force if Robeson is much longer denied a passport, states the reporter. The cable was signed by almost 300 people at the annual trades Union Congress meeting, 249 of whom were delegates. Five of the signers were MP's, including Weavers and Chemical Workers secretaries, Ernest Thorton and Robert Edwards. Five

(National Guardian)

were TUC General Council members: Textile, Boilermakers and
Railwaymen, secys., Alfred Roberts E.J. Hill and James Campbell,
and Engineers pres. Openshaw and Mineworkers vice-pres. Ted
Jones. Among British workers the fight to liberate Robeson is
taking on a new emphasis, as the central symbolic expression of
their concern over American thought-control. In the past few
weeks alone, three union bodies - the Belfast Trades & Labor
Council and the Scottish and S. Wales branches of the Miners -
have renewed invitations to Robeson to come and sing for them.
They all consider him not merely a "great son of America" but a
towering man whom workers everywhere are proud to call Comrade,
concludes Mr. Belfrage.

1562. "Powell in Europe Queried Everywhere about Robeson," Daily Worker,
       October 4, 1955, p. 4.

       Rep. Adam Clayton Powell told how everywhere in Europe that he
       visited, he was asked about the denial of a passport to Paul
       Robeson. He traveled to Germany, England, France, Italy, and
       Austria and in all those countries he was asked the same
       question about Robeson.

1563. "Mr. Paul Robeson's Passport," London Times, January 6, 1955, p. 4.

       This article states that the Scottish Labour M.P.s and trade
       unionists are among those sponsoring a petition to be presented
       to the United States Government through its Glasgow consulate
       for the restoration of Mr. Paul Robeson's passport. The peti-
       tion was addressed to President Dwight D. Eisenhower, whom it
       urged to restore Mr. Robeson's passport "in the spirit of your
       declaration that all curtains, whether in guns or of regulation,
       would begin to come down."

1564. "Scots Give Support: Seeking Robeson's Passport," Pittsburgh
       Courier, January 28, 1956, p. 26.

       This article states that four leading public figures in Glasgow,
       Scotland, joined with members of the British Parliament and leading
       figures of the stage and signed a petition calling for the re-
       storation of Paul Robeson's passport.

1565. "British Musicians Plead for Robeson," Daily Worker, February 2,
       1956, p. 2.

       This article points out distinguished British composers and
       musicians wrote to President Dwight D. Eisenhower asking him to
       give Paul Robeson his passport back. They said in their letter:
           As participants in the cultural life of Britain we
           admire him as a singer and feel that there should be
           no artifical barriers to cultural exchange between
           peoples and nations. We are confident that most
           Britons yearn for the opportunity of hearing
           again this great golden voice of America that has
           brought joy and comfort to millions of people.

1566.   "Robeson Continues Passport Appeal," New York Times, February 7, 1956, p. 18.

        Paul Robeson's attorneys presented an argument before the United States Court of Appeals stating that the United States State Department had no right to make would-be travelers swear to a non-Communist oath. The United States Government's position has been that in refusing to swear the required oath, Mr. Robeson in effect did not complete his application. It therefore contends that he has not exhausted his administrative remedies and has no right to file suit at this point, states the article.

1567.   Gardner, Lew. "A Londoner Spoke to Robeson by Telephone," Daily Worker, February 16, 1956, p. 7.

        The author spoke to Paul Robeson over the telephone from London. Robeson states that he had received many letters from the people of Britain wishing him well and supporting him in his campaign to win back his passport. The singer also asserts that he hoped that he would soon win his passport back and be able to sing at the Welsh miners' Eisteddfod in October.

1568.   "Appeal on Behalf of Mr. Paul Robeson," London Times, May 7, 1956, p. 6.

        This article states that Mr. Roy Mason, Labour M.P. had written to Mr. Selwyn Lloyd, the Foreign Secretary, asking if the Minister could initiate discussions that would allow Mr. Paul Robeson to make a summer tour in England. Mr. Robeson had been invited by Yorkshire miners and other industrial organizations to sing at their annual galas.

1569.   "Appeal Court Bars Robeson's Passport," New York Times, June 8, 1956, p. 32.

        The Federal Court of Appeals refused unanimously to order the State Department to issue a passport to Paul Robeson. Mr. Robeson, the court held, had failed to exhaust administrative remedies open to him. He twice refused to participate in informal hearings offered by the State Department. He also declined to execute an affidavit concerning past or present membership in the Communist Party.

1570.   Cayton, Horace R. "World at Large: Paul Robeson," Pittsburgh Courier, July 7, 1956, p. 10.

        This columnist argues that to deny Paul Robeson a passport is to deny an American citizen of one of his fundamental rights. There is no doubt that Robeson is unhappy with many conditions in the United States, especially the treatment of Negroes, "but that seems to me," states Mr. Cayton, "to be a position which he has a right to take and is shared by many others." He went on to surmise that he agreed with Robeson that one's political opinions are one's right. He concludes: "I probably would not agree with things Robeson might say. But I am anxious for the exercise of his American right to say them."

1571. "Robbed of His Rights as an Artist," Pittsburgh Courier, July 7, 1956.

The newspaper states, in part:
There is a great fear that he would embarrass the U.S. abroad in regard to the Negro question. This is sheer foolishness. The world is well aware of the treatment which America accords its Negro population. The foreign press on occasion gives more space to these events than the American press.... The Till case, the Authorine Lucy case and other such events are world property. What on earth could Robeson say that has not already been said about these sad affairs?... This denial is robbing him of some of the most important years of his life.

1572. "Court Hears Robeson Passport Case," Daily Worker, March 9, 1956, p. 3.

The government argued that Robeson had not exhausted his "administrative remedies" and that the State Department had given only a "tentative denial" and no "final decision" to grant him a passport. The case was heard in a U.S. Court of Appeals. It made no decision, but took the case under advisement.

1573. "Passport Called 'A Natural Right': Boudin Argues for Robeson and Has Counsel Present Own Case on Appeal," New York Times, March 9, 1956, p. 8.

Leonard B. Boudin, attorney for Paul Robeson argued in the Federal Court of Appeals that the right to travel abroad belongs to every American and could not be abridged by the State Department. Mr. Boudin also was denied a passport and he was represented by Attorney Harry I. Rand. Mr. Robeson had applied for a passport to attend meetings in Rome and elsewhere under communist auspices.

1574. "Manchester Appeal for Paul Robeson: Message to President Eisenhower," London Times, March 12, 1956, p. 6.

According to this report over 400 people in the Free Trade Hall in Manchester, England, passed a resolution asking the President of the United States to "intercede with the departments involved to secure for Mr. Paul Robeson a passport so that once more we may hear this great American singer." The article went on to assert that although other meetings have been held protesting against Mr. Robeson's "captivity" in America, this one was generally regarded as inaugurating a national campaign to apply pressure on the United States.

1575. "Accept Notables' Brief on Robeson Passport," Daily Worker, March 16, 1956, p. 8.

The U.S. Court of Appeals accepted a brief and accompanying amici curiae brief appealing the government's arbitrary denial of passport to Paul Robeson. The amici curiae brief was signed by Dr. W.E.B. DuBois, Dr. Alphaeus Hunton, Dr. Herbert Aptheker,

(Daily Worker)

Eslanda Goode Robeson, Rev. Charles Hill, Dr. Samuel Sillen and others. The brief states, in part:
To make issuance of a passport to Paul Robeson conditional on his silence would deprive the Negro people of an important means of struggle against oppression.... Mr. Robeson is one of America's finest citizens, a credit to his country and his race, and beloved of millions all over the world. The Secretary of State would serve the United States best by granting Mr. Robeson's passport and enabling him more effectively to win and hold for us the friendship of the world's peoples.

1576. "Robeson to Sing in Canada," New York Times, March 23, 1956, p. 21.

Paul Robeson, singer, who was refused exit from the United States into Canada in 1952, will make a country-wide tour of Canada in April and May, it was announced. His Canadian agents said Robeson, who gave a concert in Toronto last month, would encounter no border-crossing difficulties for the proposed tour of at least fourteen Canadian cities.

1577. Belfrage, Cedric. "Big Rally in England Demands Robeson Get Right to Travel," National Guardian, March 26, 1956, p. 3.

According to this reporter, there was a "Let Paul Robeson Sing" public meeting held at the Lesser Free Trade Hall on March 11, 1956, in Manchester, England. The writer declares that the United States State Department was going to hear louder and louder noises from this part of the world until it releases Robeson. In Scotland, a broad committee was gathering petition signatures by the thousands. In the Manchester area a mass petition drive was announced at the meeting by Len Johnson, Negro ex-middle weight champion of the British Empire. The South Wales Miners Federation has for the fourth time invited Robeson as honor guest at its annual musical Eisteddfod (which this year will have an essay contest on the theme: "Does the popular press help to promote international understanding?" and "The role of the agitator today"). One of the two miners' delegates sent to the Manchester meeting by the SWMF said: "Our executive was unanimous in deciding to send delegates. We are accused of sometimes not being in step with the rank and file, but on this we know we have the complete approbation of 100,000 miners in S. Wales," states Mr. Belfrage.

1578. "Robeson Pushes Appeal: Asks Supreme Court to Act in Fight for Passport," New York Times, September 6, 1956, p. 7.

Paul Robeson asked the United States Supreme Court to intervene in his three-year passport controversy with the State Department. The United States Court of Appeals unheld a lower court's dismissal of the suit. The lower court said it could not "assume the invalidity of a hearing which has not been held or the illegality of questions which have not been asked."

1579. "High Court Denies Hearing to Robeson," Daily Worker, November 6, 1956, p. 2.

The United States Supreme Court denied a hearing to Paul Robeson in his fight to force the State Department to grant him a passport.

1580. "Robeson Loses Appeal," New York Times, November 6, 1956, p. 32.

Paul Robeson lost an attempt in the Supreme Court to compel the Secretary of State to issue him a passport. A Federal District Court ruled that it did not have jurisdiction, since Mr. Robeson had not requested a hearing or followed other administrative procedures provided for in the State Department's regulations. The effect of the Supreme Court's rejection of his appeal is to leave standing the lower court's ruling.

1581. Editorial. "The Robeson Decision," Daily Worker, November 7, 1956, p. 5.

The editorial states that the Supreme Court's denial to act on Paul Robeson's passport case means that he is under house arrest. The editor declares:
     Thus one of America's finest and most famous sons, renowned in the four corners of the earth, is kept virtually a house prisoner status, his elementary rights to travel as a free man taken away from him. What a disgrace! Three quarters of the world will see this petty official tyranny as a racist act against a Negro who was a prioneer critic of the jimcrow system and is an uncompromising foe of colonialism.

1582. "Mr. Robeson Fills the Stage: Equity Critics of 'Political Stunt'," London Times, April 29, 1957, p. 6.

This article states that the British Actors' Equity Association passed a resolution to support efforts being made to enable Mr. Paul Robeson to sing in London. One member of the Association, Miss Helena Gloag, disagreed with the resolution and argued that the resolutions were a political stunt, "not from a political party but from an international subversive movement, Communism." She suggested that Mr. Robeson's course, if he wished to leave the United States, was the single one of renouncing his citizenship. "Surely, any valid person who makes such a statement that we are above politics is a fool, a coward, or a Communist," she concludes. Mr. Felix Aylmer, president of the Association stated that the resolution was a request by artists to be abled to hear, and work with a great international artist.

1583. "British Actors Union Votes Support for Paul Robeson," Daily Worker, May 3, 1957, p. 7.

At the annual meeting of Equity, organization of British actors in London, passed a resolution demanding that the American Government grant Mr. Robeson a passport so that he could appear in London. Gus Verney, actor and producer states that the British

(Daily Worker)

theatre was very much the poorer by denial of the opportunity either
to work with him or to see him work. Verney also remarks that
"neither our theatre nor the theatre of the world could afford,
to waste talent such as Paul Robeson's 'for irrelevant reasons.'"
All of the actors at the meeting, however, did not agree with the
resolution. Some believed that the resolution was a "political
stunt." One of the persons that was in opposition of the resolution declared "it is a stunt, not springing from a political
party but from an international subversive movement, Communism."

1584. "Laborities at London Rally Hit Robeson Ban," Daily Worker, May
        30, 1957, p. 2.

        Representatives of 1,750,000 Londoners urged the American Govern-
        ment to let Paul Robeson have a passport so that he could come and
        sing in Europe. Robeson sang to the rally through a telephone
        hookup that was transmitted across the Atlantic. Speaker after
        speaker praised the actor. Arthur Horner, the miners' leader,
        said Paul Robeson was an expression of the freedom of culture
        everywhere and was a great man who had "dared to stake his own
        destiny on the right to have an opinion and to express it."
        Another speaker stated that "nothing Paul Robeson would do or say
        over here would result in any anti-American feeling such as is
        being whipped up by the Suez group."

1585. "Robeson May Get Passport," Pittsburgh Courier, January 25, 1958,
        p. 22.

        This article states that Paul Robeson may soon be issued a pass-
        port to travel abroad after being denied one for several years.
        This supposition was based on the premise that Robeson accepted
        invitations to appear on British commercial TV and make a nation-
        wide concert tour in England.

1586. Gelb, Arthur. "Robeson Appeals Passport Denial," New York Times,
        February 4, 1958, p. 32.

        Paul Robeson asked the State Department for a "limited" passport
        to appear in the summer with one of England's most celebrated
        companies, the Shakespeare Memorial Theatre at Stratford-on-Avon.
        The State Department Passport Office deemed it necessary that
        Mr. Robeson "answer the questions with respect to Community party
        membership before consideration can be given to his request for
        passport facilities," according to the reporter.

1587. "Asks 'Limited' Passport OK," Variety, February 5, 1958, p. 2.

        Paul Robeson who's been denied a passport to travel abroad since
        1950, asked the U.S. State Department to reconsider its position
        in order that he may appear in the Shakespeare Memorial Theatre at
        Stratford-on-Avon, England. Although Robeson was seeking only a
        "limited" passport, the Government would not issue such a document
        until the singer-actor "answered questions in respect to Communist
        party membership."

1588.   "Robeson Gets Invite to British TV," The Worker, February 9, 1958, p. 3.

This article states that Paul Robeson was invited by Associated Television Ltd., a leading British TV firm to appear personally on April 6th program and other future programs. Robeson had not been allowed to leave the United States for a number of years and he did not know if the United States Government would allow him to travel to London to accept the invitation.

1589.   "Robeson Asks Limited Passport to England," Pittsburgh Courier, February 15, 1958, p. 22.

Paul Robeson was appearing at the Oakland (California) Auditorium. While he was on the west coast he made a number of appearances in California churches. The singer was awaiting news from the State Department regarding his request for a limited passport to appear with the Shakespeare Memorial Theatre at Stratford-on-Avon, England.

1590.   "Robeson Sues for Passport," New York Times, March 1, 1958, p. 2.

Paul Robeson filed a new Federal Court suit seeking a passport so he could go to England to play in a Shakespearean comedy. According to the article, the singer, a long-time admirer of the Soviet Union, charged that the State Department's refusal since 1953 to give him a passport violated his constitutional rights.

1591.   "Actors Equity Requested to Assist Paul Robeson in Getting Limited Visa," New York Times, April 1, 1958, p. 34.

Actors' Equity was requested by Black Actor Ossie Davis, to assist Paul Robeson in getting a limited visa from the State Department to act in "Pericles," which will be revived at the Shakespeare Memorial Theatre, Stratford-on-Avon, England. The plea was the subject of a resolution introduced by Ossie Davis and adopted by a vote of 111 to 75 at Equity's meeting on the past Friday. The union's governing board will consider the recommendation.

1592.   DuBois, W.E.B. "The Real Reason Behind Robeson's Persecution," National Guardian, Vol. 10, No. 25, April 7, 1958, p. 6.

The writer suggests that the real reason behind Robeson's persecution was that the United States Government wanted to silence him because of his activities on behalf of the colonial peoples of Africa. The Government also recognized that Mr. Robeson had a worldwide audience that would listen to what he had to say.

1593.   Lewis, Anthony. "Robeson is Allowed Hemisphere Travel," New York Times, April 30, 1958, p. 1.

The United States State Department relaxed its restrictions on foreign travel by Paul Robeson. It informed the singer and actor that he was free to travel in the Western Hemisphere, where no passport was required. But he still was unable to go to Europe or elsewhere because he could not obtain a passport.

1594. Anderson David. "Robeson and Lamont Passports Received After 7-
       Year Fight," New York Times, June 27, 1958, p. 16.

       Paul Robeson and Corliss Lamont received their passport after
       struggles that had been going on since 1950. The United States
       Supreme Court ruled that passports could not be withheld because
       of a citizen's "beliefs or associations." Mr. Robeson said: "I
       wish to thank Mr. (Leonard) Boudin, and of course, the Supreme
       Court for what has happened, and also the thousands and thousands
       of people of all races and creeds who have been my passport."
       Mr. Lamont, a partner in the J.P. Morgan & Co., also a crusader
       for left-wing causes, according to Anderson, also issued a state-
       ment. He stated, in part: "I am happy that my court battle has
       been vindicated by the Supreme Court decision...."

1595. "Mr. Paul Robeson Gets His Passport," London Times, June 28, 1958,
       p. 5.

       This article states that the United States State Department did
       not wait for court orders based on the U.S. Supreme Court's recent
       passport decision to reach it, but immediately issued a passport
       to Paul Robeson and others who had been refused because of their
       alleged Communist association. It was also surmised that Mr.
       Robeson planned to fly to London immediately for a series of stage
       and television performances.

1596. "Robeson Happy, Off to London!," Pittsburgh Courier, July 5, 1958,
       p. 3.

       After having refused a passport by the U.S. State Department, it
       was forced to comply with a ruling by the U.S. Supreme Court to
       grant Mr. Robeson his passport. Mr. Robeson almost immediately
       traveled to London to fulfill some concert engagements. The
       article states that he would be given a hero's welcome when he
       goes overseas.

1597. "Robeson, Lamont Passport," National Guardian, July 7, 1958, p. 1.

       This article declares that after an eight year legal battle the
       United States Supreme Court ruled that passports could not be
       withheld because of a citizen's "beliefs or associations." Both
       Paul Robeson and Corliss Lamont received their passports.

1598. "U.S. State Department Issues Paul Robeson a Passport After Refusing
       for Eight Years," Jet, July 10, 1958, p. 5.

       The United States State Department finally issued Paul Robeson a
       passport after refusing him one for eight years. The State
       Department did not wait for court orders based on the Supreme
       Court's recent passport decision, instead it immediately issued
       Robeson a passport.

1599. North, Joseph. "Out There Millions Await Him," The Worker, July
       13, 1958, pp. 8-9.

       The author declares that millions of people in Britain await Paul
       Robeson's presence there and that he would be allowed to travel
       there by the United States Government, who had cancelled his pass-
       port. Robeson also received offers for concerts from all parts
       of the world.

1600. Editorial. "Mr. Robeson Takes a Trip," Wall Street Journal, July
       14, 1958, p. 8.

       This newspaper declares that the baritone is on his way because the
       Supreme Court decided recently that the State Department didn't
       have the right to deny a man a passport just because the Govern-
       ment didn't like a man's views about this country or about Com-
       munism. He declares, in part:
            We thought the Supreme Court right then, and we think the
            President is wrong now to ask Congress to pass a law re-
            turning that power to the State Department. Such a
            law, we think, would be wrong for several reasons.
            For one thing, we can see no reason why a man free to
            travel in any of the 48 states should be barred from
            travelling overseas. If a man is a danger to the
            country, then the man should be tried and convicted,
            he should be put in jail. A great many have. But
            if a man is not a danger within the country, we can't
            see how he can suddenly endanger the country once out-
            side its borders. Paul Robeson is a man with whose
            opinions about this country we completely disagree.
            But can a radical baritone's voice drown out Mr. Dulles?
            Can his views threaten N.A.T.O., or nullify all the
            billions of dollars we've spent on foreign aid to
            make friends and influence other nations? If so, we
            have built a foreign policy that is insecure, indeed;
            and we might be the better off for knowing about it.
            The fact is that Paul Robeson can't possibly do those
            things. He will be acclaimed in London, perhaps, for
            his artistry and acclaimed in Moscow for his political
            views. But what off-key remarks can Robeson make over-
            seas that he hasn't said right here at home? And what
            has he said here that hasn't got overseas? Our Govern-
            ment and private agencies have spent millions upon
            millions of dollars to strengthen the image of America
            as the land of the free. But will other people in
            other places not think of us as the land of the fearful
            if we deny the right to travel to our own critics?

1601. Editorial. "Beliefs and Passports," Manchester Weekly Guardian,
       July 17, 1958.

       The editor argues that Paul Robeson was in London as the first
       beneficiary of the Supreme Court's ruling that the State Depart-
       ment has no power at law to deny a man a passport because of his
       "beliefs and associations." He argues, in part:
            He need never have been prevented from coming; the

(Manchester Weekly Guardian)

> State Department has itself to blame if he is now
> made to look like a victim rescued after eight years.
> But the Supreme Court ruling has naturally upset
> Congress and the Administration.... It makes the
> enjoyment of a passport a right which may be cur-
> tailed only by statute. At least that is the hopeful
> interpretation put upon it by Mr. Dulles and Congress,
> who are hastening to plug the gap by putting through
> a new statute; it may be that when it comes to the
> point the Court will say that the right to travel is
> an implicit constitutional right and cannot be nibbed
> away (except in criminal cases) by amending the law.
> The issue is different from anything we have known,
> because here   the power to grant or withhold pass-
> ports is discretionary.

1602.   "Protest at Export Cars in Parade," London Times, May 4, 1959,
         p. 7.

Paul Robeson participated in the May Day parade in Birmingham,
England. At the town rally after the parade, Mr. Robeson reportedly told a crowd of 1,500: "It's wonderful that I am again
participating freely in a May Day celebration. At home (United
States) that could be the cause for passport restrictions."

1603.   "Robeson to Defy Curb," New York Times, August 23, 1959, p. 58.

According to this article, Paul Robeson declares that he would ignore United States' passport restrictions and visit Communist
China and Hungary to give concerts. Mr. Robeson, who passed through
Budapest on his way to Rumania, told the Hungarian Communist paper,
Nepszabadsag: "For ten years I have been a prisoner in my own
country. I was not allowed to go abroad and I was prevented from
meeting the European soldiers of the world peace movement."

20. PEEKSKILL

1604.   "Peekskill Jury Puts Blame for Riot Last Summer on Robeson's
         Followers," New York Age, June 24, 1950, p. 4.

This article surmises that the supporters of Paul Robeson were responsible for the riots of Peekskill last fall, according to the
controversial report of the Westchester County Grand Jury which was
issued after months of testimony. According to this article, the
report had already been branded a "white-wash" by many observers.
It contrasted strongly with a survey of the riots made by the
American Civil Liberties Union and issued earlier this year. The
ACLU found that the riots were caused by a traditional anti-Semitic
attitude in the Peekskill area and specifically charged the local
Peekskill newspaper with agitating the violence which occured at

(New York Age)

the two concerts. Concerning this newspaper, the grand jury report admitted that an editorial in the paper just before the riots
"intensified" local feeling against Robeson and his supporters
but concluded, "there is no evidence that this publicity was
intended to incite disorders...." The grand jury also absolved
police from any blame in handling the concert-goers, again contra-
dicting the ACLU survey..., concludes the article.

1605. "Robeson, 20 Others Lose Damage Suit," New York Times, January 24,
       1952, p. 10.

       Federal Judge Sylvester Ryan dismissed the $2,100,000 damage suit
       brought by Paul Robeson, and twenty-nine others, against West-
       chester County officials and two veterans organizations as a result
       of two Peekskill riots in 1949. The disturbances occured in August
       and September, 1949, when Mr. Robeson attempted to give concerts
       in Peekskill. The plaintiffs, among them Howard Fast, writer,
       asked for amounts ranging from $10,000 to $200,000 for personal in-
       juries, assault, and deprivation of civil rights.

                           21. PERSONAL LIFE

1606. "Robeson Home is Sold," New York Times, July 21, 1953, p. 18.

       It was pointed out that the twelve-room home that Paul Robeson
       owned in Enfield, Connecticut, since 1941, was sold. Although
       the asking price was $35,000., no sale price was disclosed. The
       property included a recreation building containing a billiard
       room, bowling alley and swimming pool.

1607. "Robeson to Sell Home: Left-Wing Singer Plans to Move to be Nearer
       New York," New York Times, September 21, 1950, p. 14.

       Mrs. Paul Robeson announced that she and her husband put their
       fifteen-room house up for sale in Enfield, Connecticut and will
       build one in South Norwalk, Connecticut so that they could be near
       New York. She said living in South Norwalk would enable them to
       commute to New York. In recent years they have occupied the
       Enfield house only a few months each year, according to the
       article.

1608. "Paul Robeson to Live in London," London Times, September 22, 1958,
       p. 6.

       According to this article Paul Robeson began a British concert tour
       in Blackpool and said that he would make his home in London. The
       singer is reported to have declared: "I find the British people
       very warm and I have lived here before. London will be my centre
       as Hollywood is the centre for some British film stars. I don't
       want any overtones or suggestions that I am deserting the country

(London Times)

of my birth. If I have a concert in New York I will go there and
return to London."

1609. "Robeson Intends to Live in London," New York Times, September 22,
1958, p. 26.

Robeson said he would make his future home in London. He declares:
"I find the British people very warm and I have lived there before.
London will be my center, as Hollywood is the center for some
British film stars. I don't want any overtones or suggestions
that I am deserting the country of my birth.... If I have a concert in New York, I will go there and return to London." It was
pointed out that Paul Robeson has never made a secret of his
bitterness over racial discrimination in this country.

1610. Kearns, L.J. "The Midnight of Jose Ferrer," Confidential Magazine,
September, 1955, pp. 258-261.

The writer states that Jose Ferrer had private detectives follow
his wife and they found her and Paul Robeson rehearsing a private
love scene off stage. Mr. Ferrer's wife, Uta, played the part of
Desdemona in Othello, which starred Paul Robeson as well as
Ferrer. The article states that Uta offered to ditch Robeson
if Jose would get rid of his playmate Phyliss Hill, whom Ferrer
later married. Uta also hired detectives to follow Ferrer. It
was at midnight that Ferrer and the detectives broke in Uta's
bedroom during her private "love scene" with Paul Robeson,
according to this article.

22. POLITICS

1611. Editorial. "Of Peace, Dignity, and Error," Winston-Salem (N.C.)
Journal, April 18, 1950, p. 6.

The editor comments on the speech that Paul Robeson made at the
funeral of Mrs. Morando S. Smith in Winston-Salem, North Carolina.
The writer declares: "No intelligent, fair-minded person can
quarrel with the objective outlined in Robeson's words here. It
is the aim of all men of honesty and good will to help bring into
existence a world in which 'all people can walk in full human
dignity' - a world in which every man, woman and child can have
enough to eat, enough clothes to wear, decent housing, proper
recreational, educational and employment opportunities....'"

1612.   Fiske, Mel. "Robeson and Benson Lead FEPC Vigil," Daily Worker,
        May 25, 1950, p. 1.

        Elmer Benson and Paul Robeson, co-chairman of the Progressive
        Party, led the vigil for FEPC as it began in front of the White
        House. Back of them were trade union leaders, civil organization
        officials, and church representatives bearing placards urging
        President Truman to put the heat on Congress to adopt FEPC. Robe-
        son, Benson and Rep. Vito Marcantonia (ALP-NY), emphasized that the
        vigil was being conducted to arouse the "conscience of the Ameri-
        can people" behind passage of FEPC and the anti-polltax bill,
        according to Fiske. Robeson, who returned recently from a tour
        of the nation, said he found that "people everywhere feel deeply"
        about FEPC and Congressional efforts to kill it. "They'll come
        from everywhere to support this vigil," he predicted.

1613.   "Boston Museum Officials Hit Ban On Robeson Portrait," Daily
        Worker, October 19, 1950, p. 4.

        According to Mr. William G. Dooley, Director of Education at the
        Boston Museum of Fine Arts, Boston Mayor Hynes barred Paul Robe-
        son's portrait from exhibition in public buildings. Mayor Hynes
        declares: "I am not going to glorify any avowed Communist
        whether white, Negro or yellow." Florence H. Lucomb, Progressive
        Party candidate for Congress argues: "Besides being one of the
        world's greatest artists, who by his songs and acting has delighted
        millions, Paul Robeson is one of the world's greatest fighters
        for the advancement of all people, white as well as colored. Mayor
        Hynes brings shame upon Boston, not upon Paul Robeson." It was
        also pointed out that Robeson, Chairman of the Council on African
        Affairs charged: "A combination of politicans and gangsters have
        united to fleece the people officially through high taxes and
        frozen wages, and unofficially through graft and corruption."
        She declares:
            They hide their deeds behind a thin hysterical screen
            of anti-Communism and obviously would risk atom-bomb
            war rather than exposure. But the people will not
            long be deceived. They will fight for peace, for
            friendship with the Soviet Union, with Peoples'
            China, for a free Africa and for a truly democratic
            America which extends full civil rights to the Negro
            people. While Mayor Hynes spends his time tearing down
            pictures I feel obliged to continue taking this message
            to the American people. I remain confident of their
            judgment.

1614.   "Robeson Backers May Picket Garden in Protest Against the Ban on
        Meeting," New York Times, September 2, 1950, p. 6.

        Mass picketing of Madison Square Garden was threatened by the
        Council on African Affairs because the Garden refused to rent the
        premises to a Council meeting on September 14th. The Civil Rights
        Congress, the American Labor Party, the Progressive Party and cer-
        tain labor unions would join in the protest. Paul Robeson de-
        nounced the Garden's action as a denial of free speech and the
        right of assembly. According to this report, Mr. Robeson echoed

(New York Times)

the Communist party belief that all the world's trouble could be
settled in peace.

1615.   Editorial. "Paul Robeson and John Derrick," Daily Worker,
         December 19, 1950, p. 2.

         This article is about Paul Robeson's denial by the Concourse Plaza
         Hotel, in the Bronx, New York, for the use of it to give a speech
         that was sponsored by the American Labor Party. The editor also
         discusses the killing of John Derrick, a young Negro soldier, by a
         New York City policeman. The writer declares that Robeson speaks
         for the John Derricks of America, for his oppressed brothers, as
         he speaks for the nation as a whole. He concludes: "In making a
         virtual prisoner of Robeson in his own country, the enemies of the
         people merely confirm the truth and power of his words. They are
         foolish indeed if they think they can stop this truth. The killers
         of John Derrick should be brought to trial. The men who gag Robeson
         should be challenged by every citizen who values his own freedom."

1616.   "Robeson Exit Barred," New York Times, February 1, 1952, p. 14.

         Robeson was stopped by United States Immigration officials from
         crossing over into Canada. He was going to Vancouver, B.C., to
         speak to a meeting of the Mine, Mills and Smelter Workers Union.
         If he left the United States, it would be defiance of the law
         that bars such departure for "the best interests of the Govern-
         ment."

1617.   Howard, Milton. "The Noose of Silence Around Paul Robeson," The
         Worker,Magazine Section, December 7, 1952, p. 7.

         The author argues: "The boycott of organized silence rims around
         Robeson's creative art like a noose. It is a boycott which robs
         America of its greatest national artist...no less than the great
         songs of the world. It robs the nation of its creative contact
         with the nation-within-a-nation, the Negro people's national
         culture would simply be unrecognizable, enfeebled, without pulse
         or blood." So that when they rim organized silence around Robeson
         they are not merely trying to stifle that Niagara voice of his which
         frightens them so; they are also stabbing at the musical art of
         the whole of America and of the Negro nation within it,argues
         Mr. Howard. He concludes:
                And with such a non-Robesonian academic attitude to
                art, we shall become imitators, sterile snobs, buyers
                of the classic heritage as if it were a museum piece
                imported for a Hearst, not the fountainhead of new art
                growing out of the classic as the oak grows out of
                the soil.

1618.   "Double Play: Chaplin to Robeson to Malenkov," Saturday Evening
         Post, Vol. 227, September 4, 1954, pp. 10, 12.

         The article concludes that on the same day when Chaplin's acceptance
         of the communist "peace" prize was announced, a cablegram from

(Saturday Evening Post)

Chaplin was read to an audience of thousands at a large gathering in New York, billed as a "Cultural Salute to Paul Robeson." The purpose of the affair, as the Community Party explained, was "to launch the campaign for his right as an artist to travel abroad." What this really means is the alleged right of a nominal American citizen, who at heart is a Soviet subject, to go abroad in what is practically wartime in order to help our enemy, asserts the article.

1619. "Paul Robeson and the UAAC," San Francisco Sun-Reporter, June 23, 1956, p. 1.

This Black newspaper comments on Robeson's testimony before the House Committee on Un-American Activities. It declares, in part:
Robeson as far as most colored people are concerned occupies a unique position in the U.S., or the world, for that matter. White hate and fear him simply because he is the conscience of the U.S. in the field of color relations. Those colored people who earn their living by the sweat of their brows and a few intellectuals idolize the man. He says the things which all of them wish to say about color relations, and the manner in which he says these things attract the eye of the press of the world....

1620. "T.V. Ban on Robeson: Big Hit in Pittsburgh," Pittsburgh Courier, May 3, 1958, p. 3.

This article states that Mr. Robeson's appearance on ABC-TV Chicago station WBKB was cancelled. The Vice President of WBKB was quoted as saying: "Robeson is a free citizen. Let him hire a hall if he wants to make a speech. But I'll have no part of it." Mr. Robeson, however, was receiving unprecedented acceptance in all of his appearances along his triumphant coast to coast journey. In Pittsburgh, Robeson was forced to sing before 2,000 avid listeners on the Central Baptist Church and met with unprecented acclaim from the audience after he had been denied the use of the Soldiers and Sailors Memorial Hall, concludes the article.

1621. "Robeson Contradicted," New York Times, August 5, 1959, p. 9.

According to this article, a group of United States Negro delegates to the World Youth Festival accused Paul Robeson of "giving a dishonest and distorted picture of the United States racial problem." Robeson stated the day before that Negroes in the United States did not have full freedom and democracy, concludes the article.

23. RUSSIA

1622. "Soviet Invents Relatives Singer Robeson," New York Times, June 2, 1950, p. 10.

The Literary Gazett of Moscow stated that Paul Robeson's grand-children were studying in a Moscow school. Robeson declared that he had no grandchildren. His only son, Paul, Jr., had been married about a year and he and his new bride were living in New York. Robeson surmises that perhaps the Literary Gazett has spoken of his "grandchildren," because "I feel like a grandfather and pro-tector of all children."

1623. "Moscow Scores U.S. on Robeson," New York Times, August 6, 1950, p. 9.

Moscow's two leading newspapers, Pravda and Izvestia, called can-cellation of American singer Paul Robeson's passport by the United States State Department "persecution." It was also reported that the Communist International Union of Students had protested against the cancellation.

1624. "Personalities - Paul Robeson Among Guests at the Soviet Embassy's Reception in Washington, D.C.," New York Times, November 19, 1950, Section 6, p. 66.

Paul Robeson was among guests at the Soviet Embassy's reception in Washington, D.C., celebrating the thirty-third anniversary of the revolution in Russia. There is a photo of Robeson at the reception. A picture of Joseph Stalin is seen in the background of the photo of the gathering.

1625. "Fund Deception on $3,500,000 Laid to 3 Groups Linked to Reds," New York Times, February 25, 1955, p. 9.

Three alleged Communist-front organizations were charged with de-ception in the collection and spending of $3,500,000 in the last twelve years. The three organizations were The American Committee For The Proestion of the Foreign Born, the Joint Anti-Fascist Re-fugee Committee and the Civil Rights Congress. Paul Robeson was National Director of the Civil Rights Congress and testified on its behalf. He states according to the article, he had no idea how much money the Congress raised. Mr. Robeson told the court: "I sing for Hadassah, and the Sons of Israel and any number of worthwhile causes and no one asks me how much money they raised." The committee chairman reminded Mr. Robeson that there was a difference between singing for a cause and accepting the re-sponsibility of chairmanship.

1626. "Mr. Robeson is Right," <u>Afro-American</u>, June 23, 1956, pp. 1, 2.

This editorial declares: "If he stands up before a Congressional committee and tells its members what colored people are saying all over the nation with reference to segregation, disfranchise- ment and discrimination on account of color, he's only doing in Washington what's being done in the rest of the U.S. by red- blooded Americans, white and colored...." The article also states:

> We agree with Mr. Robeson that its (the committee's) members could more profitably spend their time.... bringing in for questioning such un-American elements as those white supremacists and manifesto signers who have pledged themselves to defy and evade the very Constitution they had previously sworn to uphold and maintain.... We are not Communists, nor do we follow the Communist line. Moreover, we do not approve of some of the activities and statements attributed to Mr. Robeson. But we do contend that if Mr. Eastland and Mr. Walters and members of the White Citizens Councils are entitled to freedom of speech, so is Mr. Robeson. The first Amendment as well as the Fifth Amendment should apply with equal force to everybody.

1627. White, Walter. "The Strange Case of Paul Robeson," <u>Ebony</u>, Vol. 6, No. 4, February, 1951, pp. 78-84.

The author, Secretary of the NAACP, called Paul Robeson the No. 1 U.S. Negro spokesman of Russia. Mr. White argues that despite Robeson's inconsistence, there can be little doubt of the sin- cerity of his convictions, whatever one may think of the sound- ness of them, regarding of the triumph of communism over capitalism. The writer argues:

> One of the puzzling aspects of Robeson's thinking during recent years is his inability to see through opportunism of Soviet domestic and foreign policy. But no honest American, white or Negro, can sit in judgment on a man like Robeson unless and until he has sacrificed time, talent, money and popularity in doing the utmost to root out the racial and economic evils which in- furiate men like Robeson. He is an ominous portent to white democracy in the United States, Europe, the Union of South Africa and Australia of what other colored men may turn to in frustration and despair. If there be a lesson in the political career of Paul Robeson as well as an explanation of his behavior, it could be simply stated in this fashion: It would be wise for the white world, instead of querying Negroes on their attitude towards Robeson, rather to take stock of themselves. White America is more fortunate than it deserves to be in that there are so few Robesons as far as political beliefs are concerned. The extraordinary truth is that the overwhelming majority of Negroes have been wise enough to see Russia's faults as well as those of the United States and to

(White, Walter)

>choose to fight for freedom in a faulty democracy
>instead of surrendering their fates to a totalitarian
>philosophy.

1628. "Russian Robeson," Newsweek, Vol. 37, No. 10, March 5, 1951, p. 42.

There is a photo of a White (whose face is painted black) actor
cast as an American Negro singer named John Robertson (modeled
upon Paul Robeson) and he tells a group of "American workers"
about his trip to Russia in a scene from a Soviet play called
"John - The Soldier of Peace."

1629. Alan, Robert. "Paul Robeson - The Lost Shepherd," Crisis, Vol. 58,
No. 9, November, 1951, pp. 569-573.

In this article the author reflects on the factors which changed
a popular singer and actor into an American commissar. The
writer contends that Robeson was a Kremlin Stooge. He suggests:
>The "Peekskill Riot" of 1949 was perhaps the highwater
>mark of his career as Communism's No. 1 Negro spokes-
>man in America. The publicity attached to that un-
>fortunate incident was relished by the Communists.
>But, much to the Communists' dislike, Americans learned
>anew at Peekskill the foolishness of playing into the
>hands of the Communists.... Now we find Paul Robeson
>still singing and ranting the Communist "line" from
>time to time, but he does so before small gatherings,
>where he receives little attention....

1630. "Nikita Hosts the Robesons," Pittsburgh Courier, December 13, 1953,
p. 1.

It was stated that Mr. Nikita Khrushchev, Premier of the Soviet
Union, played host at a party held in Yalta, The Crimea, for
Mr. and Mrs. Paul Robeson. It was during their European tour.

1631. "Portrait," Time, Vol. 62, No.   , October 5, 1953, p. 42.

This article reported "For outstanding services in the struggle
against warmongers and for the strengthening of peace," Baritone
Paul Robeson received the International Stalin Peace Prize for
1952 (complete with diploma showing a picture of Joe Stalin) in
ceremonies in Manhattan. The award, good for $25,000 in cash, would
have been tendered in Moscow if the State Department had let
Robeson make the journey. The substitute presentation of what
author Howard Fast called "the highest award which the human race
can bestow upon one of its members" was described by the Daily
Worker: "....There was a hush as the medal, with Stalin's likeness on one side, was pinned on. Then came the misty eyes as
Fast embraced the guest of honor, tiptoeing to kiss him on both
cheeks." Robeson, "in a voice shakey as few have heard it," said:
"I have always been, I am, and I always will be, a friend of the
Soviet Union," concludes the article.

1632.   "From the Soviet Actor who Portrayed Robeson," The Worker,
        January 10, 1954, p. 8.

        Mikhail Nazvanov, the Soviet Actor who portrayed Robeson in the
        stage play, "John - Solider of Peace," had this to say to Robeson:
        "I can only admire the consistent, high-minded fight for peace
        and the strengthening of friendship among different peoples which
        Paul Robeson is conducting with so much courage. His inspiring
        songs and passionate public speeches carry equal appeal and con-
        viction for unbiased people wherever they might have lived. Be-
        cause of this, the presentation of the Stalin Peace Prize he has
        so well merited was a signal event indeed." The Soviet actor also
        declared that the most significant trait of Paul Robeson, the
        artist and fighter, is in his opinion, was Robeson's genuine and
        deep humanism.

1633.   "Pickets Harass Pro-Soviet Rally," New York Times, November 14,
        1956, p. 18.

        About 200 people, mostly Hungarians and Hungarian-Americans,
        jeered and threw eggs, tomatoes, ammonia-filled bottles and sticks
        at Paul Robeson and others that were attending a meeting of the
        National Council of The American-Soviet Friendship Association
        that was held in New York City. Mr. Robeson was flanked by police-
        men as he arrived and departed. He was shepherded for a block on
        leaving and boarded a taxi on Broadway still harrassed by a number
        of pickets. Mr. Robeson did not arrive until the last half hour
        of the meeting. He spoke and hailed the achievements of the Soviet
        Union and credited many of the social gains of Negroes in the
        United States to the influence of Soviet examples and pressure,
        according to the article.

1634.   "Soviet Amity Group Hails Paul Robeson," New York Times, April
        10, 1958, p. 9.

        Paul Robeson was the guest of honor at a meeting sponsored by the
        Chicago Council on American-Soviet Relations. The meeting marked
        his sixtieth birthday. Mr. Robeson's birthday was also celebrated
        in the Soviet Union, Communist China, India and Albania. It was
        also stated in this article that the Actors' Equity governing board
        turned down a recommendation that it intercede with the State
        Department to obtain a limited passport for Mr. Robeson. The
        council turned down the request because it was felt that it was
        not a proper Equity function.

1635.   Kushner, Sam. "Chicago Fete Cheer World's Greetings to Robeson,"
        The World, April 20, 1958, p. 12.

        The Chicago Council for American-Soviet Friendship gave Paul
        Robeson a birthday party on his 60th birthday. More than 750
        people attended the gathering. He told the audience that "America
        would not be what it is today - without the contributions of the
        left." He proudly hailed the contributions of the American left
        to the progress of mankind, states Mr. Kushner.

1636.   "Soviet Plans Film on Robeson," New York Times, February 25, 1958,
        p. 23.

        According to this article, the Soviet Union would make a movie
        about Paul Robeson, actor and singer. It was stated that the
        central documentary film studios had started production of
        movies about "Outstanding Peace Partisans." The movie of Mr.
        Robeson would be released later this year (1958), states the
        article.

1637.   Bulst, Vincent. "Moscow Crowd Hails Paul Robeson's Return,"
        Washington Post, August 16, 1958.

        Robeson visited Moscow, Russia and received a widely-enthusiastic
        welcome upon his arrival by air for a two-week visit. Smiling and
        undisturbed by the swaying crowd at the foot of the Soviet jet air-
        liner which brought him from Brussels, Robeson spoke a few words
        of Russian into a forest of microphones, states Mr. Bulst. He
        said: "Greetings friends...greetings...I am very happy to be
        here again." Culture Minister N. A. Mikhailov, chief Soviet
        greeter, tried desperately to clear a path for Robeson and his
        wife from the plane to a waiting limousine. The exuberant ad-
        mirers waved large bunches of gladioli and tried to push their way
        through to Robeson to present their bouquets in person. Among
        the officials and unofficial greeters were singers from the Bolshoi
        Theater, poets, composers and other representatives of Soviet
        cultural life, concludes the writer.

1638.   "Robeson in Moscow," New York Times, August 16, 1958, p. 10.

        Paul Robeson and his wife, Eslanda, were greeted at the Vnukovo
        Airport in Moscow by Moscow friends, leaders of the Soviet Peace
        Defenders Committee, artists, musicians and journalists. He was
        welcomed by Nikolai A. Mikhailov. Robeson was there to give
        several concerts.

1639.   "Robeson on Moscow TV," New York Times, August 17, 1958, p. 33.

        Paul Robeson sang "Water Boy" and a song in Russian for Moscow TV
        viewers. He appeared on a program that introduced him with films
        showing chain-gang prisoners in the United States. But in a live
        interview, Mr. Robeson told his audience "things are going along
        much better now in the United States." He told his viewers
        "there is a great concern for a better life in the United States"
        and said millions of Americans supported the Supreme Court's
        freedom of travel decision, according to this article.

1640.   "Fight for Freedom, Robeson Tells Reds," Washington Post, August
        18, 1958.

        Paul Robeson gave a concert in the Soviet Union and 12,000 fans
        packed Moscow's Sports Palace to hear him. He was introduced
        as the Soviet Union's great and dear friend "and as a fighter for
        peace and friendship throughout the world." Robeson also spoke
        to the crowd and declares, in part: "When I read in America about
        the sputnik, my thoughts went out to my friends, the peoples of

(Washington Post)

the Soviet Union whose minds and hands have created this miracle,
opening up to mankind the boundless expanse of the cosmos.... I
am here because you helped my family and gave us strength. The
fight for freedom goes on. A new world is coming. I know no
other land where people breathe so free...." His recital included
Negro spirituals, Russian folk songs and "John Brown's Body."
He told the audience John Brown was an American martyr who fought
for his (Robeson's) father's freedom from slavery, states the
article.

1641. "Khrushchev Receives Robeson," New York Times, August 31, 1958,
       p. 2.

       This is a large photo of Khrushkchev and Robeson at the top of
       the page. Under it reads: "Nikita S. Khrushchev, the Soviet
       Premier, with Paul Robeson, the American singer, at Black Sea re-
       sort near Yalta, where the Soviet leader is vacationing. Mr.
       Robeson is on public appearance tour of Britain and Europe."

1642. "Robeson to Tour in Germany," New York Times, September 17, 1958,
       p. 7.

       This article states that Paul Robeson plans to tour East Germany
       next spring, the East Berlin newspaper Neues Deuschland reported.
       It also states that Robeson would return to Russia to complete
       two films. One of the Soviet films deal with his own life story.

1643. "Paul Robeson is in Moscow," New York Times, December 31, 1958,
       p. 12.

       This article states that Paul Robeson and his wife were in Moscow
       and would stay there for a month's visit.

1644. "Khrushchev Hails 58," New York Times, January 1, 1959, p. 37.

       Nikita S. Khrushchev welcomed the New Year with a statement that
       1958 had been such a good year "I hate to see it end." He made
       the statement to nearly 700 guests, including diplmats, who saw
       the old year out and greeted 1959 at the traditional Kremlin
       (Moscow) Ball. Paul Robeson sang at a reception and also parti-
       cipated in the ball.

1645. "Paul Robeson in Moscow Hospital," New York Times, January 13,
       1959, p. 28.

       Paul Robeson entered a Moscow hospital, but his acquaintances,
       according to the article, said nothing was seriously wrong. They
       said he had been suffering from a cold and was overtired, states
       the article.

1646. "Mikoyan's Statement in Moscow on His U.S. Visit," New York Times, January 25, 1959, p. 3.

Anastas I. Mikoyan, a First Deputy Premier of the Soviet Union held a news conference on his visit to the United States in which he cited Paul Robeson. He said Paul Robeson, the singer, who was visiting the Soviet Union with his wife, was "also a voice of America and he is pleasing to our ears."

1647. "Robeson Ill in Moscow," New York Times, January 31, 1959, p. 12.

According to this article, Paul Robeson was seriously ill in Moscow and was unable to play the title role in the English theatre production of "Othello." The 60-year-old singer entered a Moscow hospital January 12th. Mrs. Robeson is reported to have declared: "Paul is heartbroken. This (the play, Othello) was to have been the peak of his career."

1648. "Robeson is 'Quite Well,'" New York Times, February 1, 1959, p. 41.

According to this report, Paul Robeson, who was in a Moscow hospital for three weeks with bronchitis was doing "quite well." A Soviet official said Mr. Robeson, who is 60 years old, would have to rest for some time and that his period of convalencence would depend on the health of his wife, Eslanda, who underwent treatment for an unspecified illness. Mr. and Mrs. Robeson were in the Kremlin Hospital, reserved for Government officials and distinguished foreign guests.

1649. "Soviet Filming Robeson's Life," New York Times, February 4, 1959, p. 29.

According to this article, Soviet film-makers have nearly completed a movie on the life of Paul Robeson, showing the American singer as an "unbending peace champion." Tass, the Soviet news agency, said Mr. and Mrs. Robeson, "helped greatly" in the work, to be completed this month. The Robesons have been visiting Moscow. He had been under treatment in a Soviet hospital for a respiratory illness, states the article.

1650. "Robeson at Moscow Meeting," New York Times, February 22, 1959, p. 73.

Paul Robeson made a public appearance in Moscow for the first time since he was a patient in the Kremlin Hospital. The newspaper, Evening Moscow,said the singer had appeared at a World Peace Council bureau meeting.

1651.   Granam, Shirley. "Robeson Brought Moscow Christmas Cheer!,"
        Pittsburgh Courier, February 7, 1959, Magazine Section, pp. 1, 2,
        3.

        The writer asserts that there was a new Father Frost (Santa Claus)
        in Moscow this winter. His name is Pavel Vasilyevich, which is
        Russian familiar and endearing name for Paul Robeson: Paul, son
        of William. She said that Christmas in Moscow extended from our
        Christmas, Dec. 25, to January 6, the old Russian Christmas by the
        Greek Orthodox calendar. During that period children are the most
        important, most evident, most entertained citizens of Moscow.
        Everything, including the Krelmin, is turned over to them. Paul
        Robeson arrived in Moscow from London the evening of Dec. 28,
        just in time for the huge Christmas Festival in Moscow's Sports
        Stadium, an edifice about twice the size of Madison Square Garden.
        The writer surmises children of all ages were crowded to the roof,
        watching a delightful performance in the ring below them. Suddenly
        the giant fur tree in the middle of the ring winked, and there,
        in a pool of flood lights stood Paul Robeson. Miss Graham de-
        clared that it would seem impossible to contain the screams of
        joy, cheers and applause which rocked the crowd. Children rushed
        down the aisles, threw themselves on him, tugger at his legs.
        When quiet was finally restored, Paul sang and the children fairly
        rolled with delight, states the reporter. Paul Robeson gave a
        recital in the concert Hall of the Bolshol Theatre. The writer
        declared that the place was packed to the roof. She concludes:
               Paul Robeson is a great artist because of the sum
               total of all his talents. His extraordinary per-
               ceptions, fine mind and delicate sensitivity enable
               him to communicate himself to his audience with all
               his deep compassion and love for humanity....

1652.   "Robeson in Soviet Amity Unit," New York Times, May 11, 1959, p. 5.

        Paul Robeson was elected a vice-president of the British-Soviet
        Friendship society at a conference of the organization, it was
        announced by the organization. The society's president is the
        Rev. Hewlett Johnson, Dean of Canterbury, known as "The Red Dean."

                             24. SINGER

1653.   "Concert by Robeson is New Project," Daily Worker, March 19, 1950,
        p. 1A.

        This article declares that an exciting new idea lies behind the
        concert appearance of Paul Robeson and Ray Lev at the Cleveland
        Music Hall. The reporter states that born from a long standing
        dream of Mr. Robeson's, this concert is one of six which the two
        artists are giving in major American cities. Mr. Robeson hopes
        that his present tour with Miss Lev will create the beginnings
        of an independent concert circuit, one which will not discriminate
        against Negro singers, which will help all younger artists establish

(Daily Worker)

national reputations, and which will bring the best in the musical
world to people who cannot afford to take their families : to
high proces concert halls. The present concert was under the
auspices of the Progressive Party.

1654.   "1,500 Cheer Robeson: Artist Packs Baptist Church," Daily Worker,
        March 26, 1950, p. 1A.

        According to this report once again the South Side community de-
        monstrated its support for Paul Robeson, when it packed the
        Tabernacle Baptist Church to hear him in concert. The close re-
        lationship that the audience felt for the singer and what he
        stands for was evident by the prolonged applause when Robeson
        announced his intention to keep on fighting and speaking for his
        people, concludes the article.

1655.   "Paul Robeson Sings at Shoulder-to-Shoulder Concert for Peekskill
        Victim Tonight," Daily Worker, March 28, 1950, p. 10.

        Paul Robeson was scheduled to sing at the Manhattan Center to help
        raise money to finance the two-million dollar law suit against
        New York State and Westchester County officials by Robeson and the
        victims of the mob violence at Peekskill last summer.

1656.   "Paul Robeson Concert Draws Enthusiastic Thousands," California
        Eagle, May 18, 1950, p. 1.

        According to this article cheers and applause that fairly raised
        the roof greeted Paul Robeson, great American leader of all the
        oppressed, when he came on the stage at the Elks auditorium last
        Friday evening in a concert given under the auspices of The
        California Eagle and the 14th Congressional District IPP. Robeson,
        his eyes shining with joy at the spontaneous greeting, remarks, in
        part: "This is the part of America that I love. I don't like the
        Rankins or the oil interests. I won't have my boy die for their
        benefit. This is the America I love, and this is the America I
        would fight for and die for. The reactionaries are afraid of the
        Negro people. They have reason to be. There is a deep thing
        stirring from below. Among all the people who are oppressed, among
        the hungary and suffering, among the working people. The millions
        who have built this land are beginning to understand, and they will
        not let it be stolen from them to benefit only the rich. We
        fought and died for this country in Alabama, in Mississippi, and
        Tennessee. We fought for our freedom. And we are going to have
        it. We are being joined by 150,000,000 people in Africa, who are
        crying out, 'We, too, want to be free. We want to be free like
        China....' My people are under great stress. It may be that
        American Fascists will try to do to us what Hitler did to the
        Jews. But if they do, I'm sure they will not win...."

1657. "Robeson Flies to Peace Meeting," New York Times, May 29, 1950,
       p. 11.

       This article states that Paul Robeson announced that he was flying
       to London to attend a series of peace meetings. He states that
       he planned to speak at one of the meetings and to return to the
       United States for a concert in Boston.

1658. "Hotel Sustained in Barring A.L.P.," New York Times, December 21,
       1951, p. 16.

       Supreme Court Justice Samuel Dickstein sustained the Concourse
       Plaza Hotel in the Bronx in its refusal to rent a ballroom to the
       American Labor Party for a meeting to honor Paul Robeson. Accord-
       ing to the article, Mr. Robeson, a leading proponent of left-wing
       causes, was to have received at the hotel the Second World Peace
       Congress international award voted to him in Warsaw. Robeson
       received the award at the Hunts Point Palace. About 500 people
       attended the ceremony. The actual award was still in the mail,
       states the writer.

1659. Shields, Art. "Robeson Hails Peace Fight in Latin America," The
       Worker, April 20, 1952, pp. 3, 6.

       Paul Robeson and the returning peace delegates from the Monte-
       video conference hailed the millions of fighters for peace in Latin
       America at a meeting at the Yugoslav-American Home. Novelist
       Howard Fast presided. Robeson declares: "The Latin American
       people are wonderful peace allies. They are not confused about
       Korea. They remember how the American Government seized Texas
       and Cuba. These Latin American allies, however, must know we
       are with them. They are persecuted by the same forces that
       brought my people - the Negro people, from Africa, the people
       are not oppressed by a Malan but by the American imperialists who
       own their tin, their silver, and their fruit."

1660. "Paul Robeson is Barred by Oakland Auditorium," New York Times,
       April 26, 1952, p. 18.

       The director of Oakland's Municipal Auditorium cancelled permis-
       sion for singer Paul Robeson to give a concert in the hall on
       May 23rd. City Manager John F. Hassler of Oakland stated that
       refusal to allow Robeson to use the auditorium "has nothing to
       do whatsoever with politics."

1661. "Mr. Robeson Banned," London Times, April 30, 1952, p. 5.

       This article surmises that Mr. Robeson was refused permission to
       sing at the San Francisco War Memorial Opera House, where the
       United Nations Charter and the Japanese Peace Treaty were signed.
       The Board of Trustees said they had banned Mr. Robeson because he
       was considered a pro-Communist, unfit to appear within a memorial
       to war dead.

1662. "Robeson Denied Hall in Chicago; Sings to 5,000," Atlanta Daily World, June 6, 1952, p. 5.

Because no local hall could be secured to give a concert in Chicago, Paul Robeson gave a free concert in the public park. The huge crowd was enthusiastic over Robeson's singing, but did not respond as readily when it came to petitions seeking the return of Robeson's passport, now denied him by the U.S. State Department, and the signing of peace petitions, according to this report. Official sponsors of Robeson's Chicago appearance were The Committee for the Negro in the Arts and the Greater Chicago Negro Labor Council, a left wing group. Robeson sang also under the blessings of the Washington Park Forum, a group that usually meets in the spot at which he held his recital. The Forum meeting proper was held immediately after the Robeson program ended, states the article.

1663. Hamburg, Alice S. "Berkeley's Example: Paul Robeson Concert," Nation, Vol. 174, June 7, 1952, p. 536.

The writer states that Robeson was denied the use of a public auditorium in San Francisco and Oakland. On May 6 the board met to vote on the request. Mrs. Eileen Ready, chairman, and member, A.K. Sackett voted "no" on the grounds that to permit the noted singer to appear in the school auditorium would be "giving into communism which we are fighting in Korea." But three members of the board voted "yes": Mayor Laurence L. Cross, who is also minister of a local community church; Mrs. Mildred Brown, and David P. Smith, active Republican, who laid down the sole condition - which the Negro Labor Council was glad to meet - that no political speeches be made at the concert, according to the writer. Mr. Smith told the audience: "....Why then are the Russians winning this battle for the hearts and minds of people? One of the major factors is that although we preach freedom regardless of race, color, or creed, unfortunately we do not always practice it.... If we turn down this noted singer, the action would be proof to the people of India and Indo-China, even to minority groups here, that Paul Robeson was denied a place to sing because he is a Negro. I beseech you...to prove to the world by example that democracy does work."

1664. "40,000 Attend Robeson Concert: Singers Voice in Pristine Resonance and Glory," Manchester (England) Guardian, June 7, 1952, p. 3.

According to this article forty thousand persons heard Paul Robeson sing at the International Peace Arch in the State of Washington on the Canadian border, recently,his audience about evenly divided between Americans and Canadians. Later in Oakland and San Francisco, civic auditoriums were denied Robeson on grounds that he is a left-winger. Nevertheless, he sang in San Francisco in a dual concert in two halls the same evening, in Macedonia Baptist Church, and the following evening he appeared in Berkeley's Community Center Theatre, where the board had voted 3 to 2 in his favor. One Pacific Coast city went so far as to pass a law to bar him, states the reporter. Ever since the beginning of Robeson's

Articles about Robeson   589

(Manchester Guardian)

concert tour of 30 states on April 1, opposition to him on the part of civil authorities have waxed intense and acrimonious. Much of the opposition is an afthermath of the 1949 Peekskill riots, precipitated by veterans and race baiters, after which Robeson brought a damage suit of two million dollars. Robeson's very presence seems to arouse a hysterical fear in those who oppose his political views. Not since Frederick Douglass' time have white Americans so greatly feared a colored American, concludes the writer.

1665. "400 Hear Paul Robeson Sing in Pittsburgh (Pa.)," The Worker, June 29, 1952, p. 8.

According to this article despite last minute obstacles raised by the city building department and the attempt of the Pittsburgh Press to block the concert, Paul Robeson sang in Pittsburgh on June 20th to an audience of 400 people. The reporter quotes Robeson as saying: "No matter how much I want to travel - and I do - I'm staying here in America until my people are much freer!" This evoked one of the many demonstrations of the love and respect with which he is regarded by all progressive-minded people. "My loyalty," he declares, "is to the great traditions of the struggle for freedom in this country." The writer asserts that Robeson blasted the demands of the leaders of the government for loyalty to their policies of supporting the exploiters of the Negro people in Africa - "support of Malan in South Africa where oppression is worse than in Mississippi, of the Belgian exploiters of the Congo, which region rightly belongs to my (the Negro) people." Applause greeted a resolution demanding that the State Department restore his passport to Robeson. Following the concert a banquet was held in his honor at one of the hotels in the area, concludes the article.

1666. Jones, John Hudson. "Robeson Tour a Triumph for the Artist and People," The Worker, July 6, 1952, Section 1, pp. 1, 8.

The singer gave 15 concerts in as many cities before nearly 75,000 people and in his own words "enjoyed" it more than at any other time of his illustrious career spanning over a quarter of a century. The tour honored his 54th birthday. Robeson's concerts were distinguished by the appearance of young local talent. This has become a feature of all great artist's work today (1952) - the encouragement of young Black talent as well as that of others. The tour was sponsored by the United Freedom Fund, states the author.

1667. "Robeson Recital Stands: Hartford Education Board Again Refuses to Cancel Permit," New York Times, November 14, 1952, p. 25.

The Board of Education refused for the second time to rescind its action in granting to the People's Party of Connecticut the use of Weaver High School Auditorium for a recital by Paul Robeson. The Board held a special meeting to act on a resolution approved by the City Council demanding that the Board refuse to permit

(New York Times)

Mr. Robeson to sing in the hall.

1668. Berry, Abner. "Denounce Scheme to Circulate Unauthorized Robeson Records," Daily Worker, December 16, 1952, p. 7.

The article mentions that three unauthorized Paul Robeson records were in circulation. The label on the records carried the announcement: "For private use only. Not for resale." The records, however, were sold in stores. An official of the Othello Record Co., which is now (1952) preparing a special subscribers edition of a new authorized Robeson record album declares: "Every unauthorized record sold is a swindle of Paul Robeson and of those who want to hear his voice on records. This swindle was made possible because the big companies no longer promoted or issued Robeson's recordings."

1669. "Recital by Robeson Opposed in Hartford," New York Times, November 11, 1952, p. 17.

The Hartford Board of Education voted to allow Paul Robeson to give a recital in the Weaver High School auditorium, although the Board received opposition from veteran groups and from city councilman John F. Mahon. Lewis Fox, President of the Board of Education said that "freedom of speech and freedom of assembly are two of the most cherished rights granted by the American Constitution."

1670. "Rift Over Robeson Grows," New York Times, November 12, 1952, p. 17.

The City Council of Hartford, Connecticut, adopted a resolution urging the Hartford Board of Education to call a Special meeting to reconsider its agreement to allow Paul Robeson to give a recital in Weaver High School Auditorium. Dr. John Marsalka of New Haven, Executive Vice Chairman of the People's Party in the state, said that to deny Mr. Robeson use of the school hall would mean a rejection of "his constitutional rights that will lead to the denial of these rights to all people."

1671. "Hartford Pays $4,000 for Policing Robeson," New York Times, November 18, 1952, p. 33.

City officials state that it cost Hartford almost $4,000 in overtime pay for about 250 policemen who were called out to prevent any disturbance at a concert by Paul Robeson. The concert was in the Weaver High School Auditorium over protests of the City Council. No incidents were reported at the concert, which drew about 600 persons. The police who did overtime were led personally by Police Chief Michael J. Godfrey.

1672. Keeler, Ellen. "Robeson's Popularity Greater Than Even Concert Tour Shows," Daily Worker, September 6, 1955, p. 6.

Robeson held concerts in Oakland, San Francisco, San Diego, Berkeley, California. He spoke and sang to trade unions, churches, fraternal organizations, women's groups and youth groups. He told the different groups: "I speak for peace, for equality for my people, and for an end to colonialism. When the leaders of the dark races gathered at Bandung they called for these very same things. When the leaders of the Big Four met in Geneva they asked for peace. It is perhaps for these reasons my people have turned to me with warm, friendly greetings."

1673. "Robeson Ready to Sing: Recovered from Surgery, He Awaits Passport Decision," New York Times, January 21, 1956, p. 14.

Paul Robeson underwent an operation last October for an abdominal obstruction. He announced that he was returning to "public activity." "My plans for resuming my career as an artist are bound up, of course, with the matter of getting a passport; and I hope that soon this issue will be favorably resolved so that I will be able to accept the many offers that have come for concert, stage, and film engagements in other lands," he argues. The Robeson passport case was before the United States Court of Appeals.

1674. Terris, Nicholas. "Robeson Greeted by 2,700 in Toronto," Daily Worker, February 13, 1956, pp. 1, 8.

The writer surmises that the ovations that Robeson received in Toronto, Canada, were not only for the artist but for Robeson the fighter for peace and Negro liberation. Robeson told the crowd: "I can not tell you how wonderful it is to be free a few days from house arrest and avail myself of the opportunity of meeting again so many of my friends in Canada."

1675. "Canadians Acclaim Robeson on Concert Stage, Radio, TV," The Worker, February 26, 1956, p. 10.

Robeson performed in Toronto, Canada, in the Massey Hall, Toronto's biggest music center. A crowd of 2,800 attended the concert. Through his songs he told of love and struggle; of peace and of freedom; of life and of death and the spirituals of his own people. Paul Robeson was also heard by thousands of others in Toronto during a 15-minute radio broadcast. He also appeared on CBC television.

1676. "News in Brief," London Times, February 28, 1956, p. 5.

This article states that the Executive Committee of the Scottish Area National Union of Mineworkers decided to invite Mr. Paul Robeson to sing at the Scottish miners May Day gala in Edinburgh.

1677. "Canada Bars Paul Robeson," New York Times, April 11, 1956, p. 5.

       The Federal Immigration Department of Canada denied Paul Robeson
       a visa, annoucning simply that "He will not be admitted under pre-
       sent auspices." The sponsor of the seventeen concert tours was
       the Labor Progressive (Communist) Party.

1678. "Mr. Robeson's Canada Tour Cancelled," London Times, April 11,
       1956, p. 9.

       This article states that Mr. Paul Robeson had to cancel a concert
       tour of Canada. An Immigration Department spokesman in Ottawa,
       Canada, states that Mr. Robeson "will not be admitted under present
       auspices." The singer had been booked to appear in some 17
       Canadian cities where tickets had already been sold.

1679. "Paul Robeson in Toronto," Musical Courier, Vol. 56, No. 6, April,
       1956, p. 38.

       A reviewer had this to say about Robeson's performance. He reports,
       in part:
           ....His voice has lost much of its old richness, and
           vocal technique seemed stale, one assumes due to a
           recent illness and very limited concert activity.
           But the Robeson smile, the ability to make words
           mean something through song, are powers he has not
           lost. Whether one agrees or not with Robeson's point
           of view on the world in general only the listener can
           deny that he is still a great artist....

1680. Orday, David. "Paul Robeson Sings to 10,000 on the West Coast,"
       Daily Worker, August 15, 1957, pp. 6, 7.

       Robeson appeared five times in California in August and sang to
       10,000 people in Los Angeles and San Francisco. Speaking before
       the crowd the singer told them "my labors in the future will re-
       main the same as they have been in the past." "They will be based
       on my whole experience - in the anti-fascist struggle that saw its
       finest expression in Spain, in the worldwide struggle of working
       people against their oppressors." He also asserts:
           This struggle is going on and has reached a new height.
           Not only abroad - where the colonial peoples are
           leading the fight and where three-quarters of the
           human race has refused to be kicked around any
           longer - but also here in my own United States,
           where the Negro people of the South - who are also
           a semi-colonial people - are leading the fight.

1681. "Robeson Accepts British Bid," New York Times, January 15, 1958,
       p. 59.

       Paul Robeson accepted a bid to sing on British television. Assoc-
       iated Television said Mr. Robeson accepted an invitation to appeal
       on its "Sunday Night at the London Palladium." It said he would
       make a concert tour of Britain after the program.

1682.   Editorial. "Paul Robeson Invited to Appear on TV," London Daily
         Worker, January 16, 1958.

         The editor declares that the invitation to Paul Robeson to appear
         on commercial television will have the support of the immense
         majority of the British people. He also asserts that surely no
         one in America or elsewhere can suspect Associated Television
         Ltd. of engaging in a political stunt. It simply knows that
         among all sections of the British people, quite irrespective of
         their politics, there is a keen desire to see and hear Paul
         Robeson. He concludes: "So Associated Television is out to give
         the public what it wants in a big way...."

1683.   "Paul Robeson Hopes Booking Ban Ending," Variety, February 15,
         1958, pp. 2, 79.

         Paul Robeson was giving concerts in California churches because
         the concert halls were closed to him. The Oakland Auditorium,
         however, allowed him to give a concert there on February 9, 1958.
         Robeson surmises that he soon hopes that he will be able to
         appear in other major concert halls.

1684.   "Robeson Sings on Coast," New York Times, February 10, 1958, p. 26.

         According to this article, Mr. Robeson made a successful comeback
         to the concert stage. A capacity crowd of 2,000 persons jammed
         a hall in Oakland, California, to hear the singer in his first
         performance before a large gathering in several years. The
         article states that Mr. Robeson said that he considered the con-
         cert a success, but added that he did not intend to continue giving
         concerts.

1685.   Hentoff, Nat. "Paul Robeson Makes a New Album," Reporter, April
         17, 1958, pp. 34-35.

         This was the first time in ten years that Robeson had been engaged
         to sing for an "established" record label. He was signed for a
         series of sessions for Vanguard Records. When Robeson made the
         recording, he was sixty years old. During the recording session,
         the singer was interviewed by Mr. Hentoff. He relates that
         Robeson declared that "ninety percent of all spirituals are penta-
         tonic.... There is also a pentatonic harmony in folk music that
         several composers of this and the last century have found in-
         spiration in...." Robeson states that he would no longer give
         the more formal recitals of primarily "art songs," he prefers an
         informal context that would enable him to demonstrate his penta-
         tonic bridges with examples in several languages.

1686.   "Robeson Concert Off: Pittsburgh Memorial Hall Cancels April 21
         Program," New York Times, April 2, 1958, p. 35.

         The Superintendent of Soldiers and Sailors Memorial Hall said that
         Paul Robeson's concert, scheduled for April 21, was cancelled
         because it would not be consistent "with the memorial character of
         the building." The official said the promoter of the concert had
         made no mention of Mr. Robeson's appearance when he engaged the hall.

1687.   "Paul Has Big Voice...Will Sing," Pittsburgh Courier, April 12,
        1958, p. 2.

        Mr. Robeson was scheduled to appear in concert in Pittsburgh, how-
        ever, he could not secure a large enough hall. Therefore, he
        sought the largest church in the city to give his concert.

1688.   "Robeson WILL Sing: Churches Rallying to Artist," Pittsburgh
        Courier, April 19, 1958, p. 3.

        Robeson was scheduled to appear in concert at the Soldiers and
        Sailors Memorial Hall in Pittsburgh. However, the hall cancelled
        his appearance. Two Black Churches, Central Baptist Church,
        Wesley Centre A.M.E. Zion and St. Matthews A.M.E. Zion Church
        offered him their facilities to be used for his concert.

1689.   Schonberg, Harold C. "Paul Robeson Sings, Lectures in First City
        Recital in 11 Years," New York Times, May 10, 1958, p. 19.

        Mr. Robeson appeared in Carnegie Hall in New York City. He sang
        in several languages - English, German, Russian, Hebrew, Yiddish
        and Chinese. The author states that as a lecturer Mr. Robeson
        was superb - frequently witty, sonorous, completely uninhibited.
        He gave the audience a lecture on the relationship between African
        and Chinese music, saying he wanted to relate the music of his
        own people - the music of all the music. Schonberg declares:
              The most musical vocalism of all came not in the singing
              but in the brief "Othello" excerpt. Mr. Robeson's
              shading, his magnificent diction, and his effective
              use of pauses and the sheer color of his speaking
              voice showed more art and vocal resource than any-
              thing heard during the musical portion of the program.

1690.   North, Joseph. "Robeson Triumphs Here; World Says: Come On!,"
        The Worker, May 18, 1958, p. 16.

        This article discusses Paul Robeson's recent concert in Carnegie
        Hall in New York City. He declares that at the concert one readily
        understood why this American is honored today like no other of his
        time, or perhaps of any time - for most of mankinds' two and
        a half billions displayed its love for him upon his sixtieth
        birthday on April 9th. Mr. North concludes:
              The man is a unique phenomenon of the Twentieth
              Century, embodying its might and suffering its woe.
              More than any other artist, of today or of yesterday,
              he belongs to the people for whom he battles relent-
              lessly and for whom he sings like an angel.

1691.   "Return of Paul Robeson," Newsweek, Vol. 51, No. 20, May 19, 1958,
        p. 95.

        The writer states that to the dismay of those who had admired him
        as a singer and actor, Paul Robeson gave up his career a decade or
        more ago to become one of the most controversial figures of a
        generation. In 1958 Paul Robeson gave a concert at Carnegie Hall
        at age 59. The critic concludes:

(Newsweek)

He sang a program made up principally of folk songs,
and it was hard to assess the condition of his voice,
for he used a microphone. Visibly restrained at
first, he warmed up as the concert progressed and
traces of the old and eloquent Robeson voice flashed
through. It seemed sad that he was at his most persuasive in those numbers which had long outworn
political overtones - like the union song, "Joe
Hill" or the spiritual "We Are Climbing Jacob's
Ladder," in which he changed "Soldiers of the
Cross" to "Soldiers in this Fight."

1692. "Robeson at Carnegie Hall," New York Times, May 24, 1958, p. 19.

This article states that Paul Robeson made his second appearance
of the season in Carnegie Hall in New York City. According to
this article, his program of traditional melodies and folk songs
included a group of Negro Spirituals, a Hassidic chant, and songs
of China and other countries.

1693. Cunningham, Evelyn. "Thunderous Applause for Paul Robeson: His
Second New York Recital is Tremendous Hit," Pittsburgh Courier,
May 31, 1958, p. 21.

Paul Robeson gave a recital at Carnegie Hall in New York City.
This was his second appearance in the hall in a month. The reviewer states that strangely Robeson was weakest in his spirituals
and at his best in the folk songs. He was particularly delightful
when he compared Chinese and African dialects, vividly demonstrating
through tonal quality and body motion how one differed from the
other, reports Miss Cunningham. She concludes that the audience
loved every moment of the concert. He received thunderous applause from the audience.

1694. "Paul Robeson," Musical America, Vol. 58, No. 7, June, 1958, p. 16.

This article states, in part:
....From the standing ovation at Mr. Robeson's entrance,
to his final encore, the recitation of "The Rail
Splitter," the evening proceeded comme it faut....
Mr. Robeson was of course in full command of the
evening. Never have I seen an artist, who, by his
sheer personality, can hold such complete interest
and attention of a public, young and old, intellectual
and ignorant. And yet, he did not "push" - remained
always in good taste, natural, easy going, humorous,
and serious.

1695. "Robeson Still Compels, But Concert Slow," New York Age, June 7, 1958, p. 1.

According to this article, Paul Robeson came to Harlem and presented a concert to about 1,000. The writer states that the concert was one half hour late, contained a 35 minute intermission and was too long - two hours and fifteen minutes. But few if any of the people that attended the poorly publicized concert, went away in total disappointment. Only a talent the calibre of Mr. Robeson's could have accomplished this under the circumstances, concludes the article.

1696. Calta, Louis. "Robeson to Leave for Britain Soon," New York Times, June 26, 1958, p. 22.

Paul Robeson, who for the last eight years has been denied a passport, will be able to leave for London within a few days to fulfill stage, concert and television commitments there. A recent United States Supreme Court decision voided State Department regulations denying passports to persons of allegedly doubtful loyalty.

1697. J.F.S. "Mr. Robeson Returns," Musical America, Vol. 58, No. 7, June, 1958, p. 16.

One critic described Mr. Robeson's return to the concert stage. He asserts, in part: "From the standing ovation at Mr. Robeson's entrance, to his final encore, the recitation of "The Rail Splitter," the evening proceeded comme it faut.... Mr. Robeson was of course in full command of the evening. Never have I seen an artist, who, by his sheer personality, can hold such complete interest and attention of a public, young and old, intellectual and ignorant. And yet, he did not "push," remained always in good taste, natural, easy going, humorous, and serious."

1698. Robeson Off to Europe After an 8-Year Battle," New York Times, July 11, 1958, p. 8.

Paul Robeson, who had been barred for eight years from leaving the United States because he refused to sign a non-Communist affidavit for a passport left for London to start a series of concerts. Mr. Robeson was asked if he planned to stay abroad. He replied, according to this article: "This is my land. My grandfather and father were born here, too, and I don't plan to leave it."

1699. "British TV Signs Robeson," New York Times, July 14, 1958, p. 41.

According to this article British Commercial television signed Paul Robeson for a series of concerts starting July 26.

1700. "Mr. Paul Robeson's Rectial: Folk Songs of Many Lands," London
       Times, July 28, 1958, p. 5.

       This artical reports on Paul Robeson's British television appearance.
       The reviewer declares that he found with relief that Mr. Robeson
       is one of those whose age showed no signs of withering and that he
       still sang with a huge delight in his songs. He sang folk songs
       from China, Russia, France, Wales, and Mexico, a spiritual and a
       Bach chorale. The writer concludes: "This was a half hour with
       a fine and thoughtful artist."

1701. "Paul Robeson Sings in Wales," New York Times, August 4, 1958,
       p. 12.

       Paul Robeson shared a platform with Aneurin Bevan, Laborite leader,
       at a curtain-raiser to the National Esiteddfod (Music Festival in
       Ebbw Vale, Wales). Mr. Bevan opened the festival as member of
       Parliament for Eddw Vale. Mr. Robeson sang several folksongs.

1702. "Rich Tone at 60," Daily Telegraph and Morning Post (London),
       August 10, 1958.

       The newspaper reviewed Robeson's concert at Albert Hall in London.
       It wrote, in part: "A crowded Albert Hall cheering and shouting
       for its special favorites, welcomed Paul Robeson back to London
       last night. Ole Man River has flowed under many bridges (and
       been checked by various dams) since that famous voice was last
       heard here, and though Robeson is now 60, it remains a magnificent
       instrument."

1703. "Warm Welcome for Mr. Paul Robeson: A Feast for the Ear," London
       Times, August 11, 1958, p. 2.

       Paul Robeson gave a concert at the Albert Hall in London, England.
       The reviewer asserts that the splendour of Mr. Paul Robeson's voice
       was nowhere more apparent than when to make his farewell to the
       envormous audience who would not let him go, he recited an ideali-
       stic poem about peace and brotherhood by a Chilean poet as a grand
       finale. He surmises:
              His depth, richness and resonance of tone were a
              feast for the ear, while the genuine fervour behind
              it all suggested that in speech he can find just as
              great an outlet for his powers of expression as in
              song. With Mr. Robeson it is the actual voice it-
              self, rather more than what he is singing about, that
              provides our thrills, and still today his tone (in so
              far as the microphone allowed us to judge) seems totally
              unimpaired by the passing of time; both full out and in
              falsetto it is a sound as glorious as it is unique.

1704.   "British TV Spotlights Paul Robeson," Pittsburgh Courier, August
        16, 1958, p. 23.

        According to this article Paul Robeson, whose return to Britain was
        comparable to a conquering hero's added more laurels to his credit
        with his first of these scheduled concerts for Associated Tele-
        vision. His initial stint for a TV was a 30 minute recital,
        screened without any breaks for commercials, titled "Paul Robeson
        Sings." A TV, whose presenter of Robeson scored a major coup,
        gave the singer top rated treatment worthy of his artistic talents,
        states the writer.

1705.   Dunbar, Rudolph. "Belafonte vs. Robeson!: Did Harry Outshine
        Paul?," London Chronicle, August 23, 1958, p. 24.

        This article centers on Robeson and Belafonte, who were performing
        simultaneously in London. The British press made a great ado
        about which one was the "greatest." The London Chronicle declares:
        For 20 years Paul Robeson has symbolized the art of his race. But
        it would seem now that 31-year old Harry Belafonte, the slim six-
        footer from Harlem, has displaced him...."

1706.   Graham, Shirley. "Robeson, Belafonte, Du Bois Make London Town
        Sparkle," Pittsburgh Courier, September 6, 1958, p. 23.

        The writer states that both Robeson and Belafonte received good
        reviews by the British presses. She argues that although Bela-
        fonte created somewhat of a sensation on his first appearance in
        Britain, obviously commercial attempts to play the young Belafonte
        against Robeson fell very flat. Miss Graham also points out after
        a 13-year absence, England warmly welcomed Dr. Du Bois.

1707.   "Mr. Paul Robeson to Sing in St. Paul's," London Times, September
        27, 1958, p. 8.

        This article states that Mr. Paul Robeson would sing at the evening
        service in St. Paul's Cathedral on October 12. Mr. Robeson was
        scheduled to sing for about half an hour. It was also stated
        that there would be a collection for the defense and aid fund
        established by Christian Action for the treason trials in South
        Africa.

1708.   "Paul Robeson at Memorial Theatre," Shakespeare Newsletter (New
        York), Vol. 8, No. 2, September, 1958, p. 28.

        This brief article states that Paul Robeson whose memorable role
        in "Othello" was widely heralded in 1943 and 1945 will repeat the
        role at the Stratford-on-Avon Memorial Theatre, in Londin, in
        the 1959 season.

1709.   "Paul Robeson in Wales," Evening Post (South Wales), October 6,
        1958.

        This article concerns Paul Robeson's appearance at the autumn
        Eisteddfod in Wales. President of the South Wales area, Mr. William
        Paynter, told the big audience that they were honoring a great man

(Evening Post)

and a great artist. Dr. D.D. Evans, the Area General Secretary, presented Paul Robeson with a minature miner's lamp. Printed on the base of the lamp is the following inscription: "Greetings to Paul Robeson From the South Wales Miners, October, 1958." The singer had a great ovation from the miners and the members of their families, states the writer.

1710.   "Robeson Brings the Rafters Down," Heath Guardian (Wales), October 10, 1958.

In October of 1958, Paul Robeson was the guest artist at the autumn Eisteddfod in Wales. The program notes recall the historic occasion has been the custom of the singing country of Wales to invite Paul Robeson to be a guest of honor at the National Eisteddfod, their famous musical event. Paul made a beautiful film about the lives and work and music of the Welsh miners, many years ago, called "Proud Valley"; and they have never forgotten him. When he appeared on the stage, surrounded by the choir of Welsh children, the mighty audience joined the children in singing "We'll Keep a Welcome in the Valley for Him," states the article.

1711.   "Mr. Robeson Sings at St. Paul's Cathedral," Yorkshire Post (Leeds), October 13, 1958.

One of Mr. Robeson's most successful concert tours, when he visited England, was given at St. Paul's Cathedral in London. One observer declared, in part: "...He entered a few minutes before the choir. He sat in the front row on the north side of the dome.... The choir in white surplices, followed by the clergy, came in pro- cession from the south choir aisle, wheeling around to enter the choir itself. The congregation stood up. Above all other heads could be seen the square cut, heavy black features of the singer they had all come to hear.... With words of the Negro spirituals, "We are Climbing Jacob's ladder" (sic), his powerful bass.... burth forth tremendous volume and then, a minute later, as he leaned forward on the lectern, so emptied the church of sound that he had the vast congregation learning forward tensely to catch the words of the whispered melody...."

1712.   "Paul Robeson," The Yorkshire Post (Leeds, England), October 13, 1958.

This article states, in part, about Paul Robeson's appearance in the Cathedral, in London: "....He entered a few minutes before the choir. He sat in the front row on the north side of the dome.... The choir in white surplices, followed by the clergy, came in procession from the south choir aisle, wheeling around to enter the choir itself. The congregation stood up. Above all other heads could be seen the square cut, heavy black features of the singer they had all come to hear.... With words of the Negro spiritual, "We are Climbing Jacob's ladder" (sic), his powerful bass...burst forth tremendous volume and then, a minute later, as he leaned forward on the lectern, so emptied the church of sound that he had the vast congregation leaning forward tensely

(The Yorkshire Post)

to catch the words of the whispered melody...."

1713. "St. Paul's Crowded for Mr. Robeson's Recital," London Times,
       October 13, 1958, p. 5.

       This article asserts that Mr. Paul Robeson gave a recital at the
       St. Paul's Cathedral in London to help the South African Treason
       Trial Fund established by Christian Action. Ticket holders occupied
       every seat, and many people stood at the back of the cathedral.
       After the first part of the recital, Canon L.J. Collins said that
       they were all grateful for this "unique experience of hearing
       Mr. Robeson giving his voice to the glory of God and the service
       of his fellow-men."

1714. "Robeson Sings in Cathedral," New York Times, October 13, 1958,
       p. 4.

       Paul Robeson sang spirituals before 4,000 persons in St. Paul's
       Cathedral in London. The service, organized by the Church of
       England's Christian Action Movement, was to raise funds for ninety
       persons waiting trial on charges of subversive activities in South
       Africa. The American singer also read a lesson at the end of the
       service.

1715. Middleton, Peggy. "Go Down, Moses, Tell Old Pharaoh, Let My
       People Go!," National Guardian, October 20, 1958, p. 12.

       This article states that Paul Robeson sang a number of spirituals
       in the St. Paul's Cathedral in London, England, on October 12,
       1958, before 4,000 persons....

1716. "Robeson Triumphs for 4,000 in London," Pittsburgh Courier, October
       25, 1958, p. 23.

       Paul Robeson sang before an audience of 4,000 white and Black
       people in the St. Paul's Cathedral in London. The article states
       that the rich, melodious voice of the singer soared into the
       regions of space in the church. During the service, a collection
       was taken for the South African treason trial fund. The writer
       concludes: "It was a triumph for Paul Robeson."

1717. "Afro-Asian Film Festival Welcomes Robeson," Bulletin of the World
       Council of Peace, October, 1958, p. 1.

       The article states that on August 20th, a huge crowd at Taskent
       attended the opening ceremony of the Afro-Asian Film festival,
       held in the Lenin Square, where the torch of the festival was lit
       and the festival flag hoisted. N. Mikhailov, USSR Minister of
       Culture conveyed greetings from the Soviet workers in the field
       of culture to the delegates. Mr. Harjots, leading the Indonesian
       delegation, spoke for the Asian countries and Mr. Hussein Sidky,
       leader of the UAR delegation for the African Countries. Paul
       Robeson, the guest of honour, received a great ovation; he spoke
       briefly and sang for the delegation. The 15-day festival, was

(Bulletin of the World Council of Peace)

organized to help film workers in Asian and African countries to
learn about each other's films and establish friendly contacts.

1718.   "Mr. Paul Robeson at Albert Hall," London Times, December 1, 1958,
         p. 14.

         This article states that Mr. Paul Robeson gave a song recital in
         the Albert Hall in London. The reviewer asserted:
                Needless to say Mr. Robeson sang beautifully, even
                when dragging "Schubert's Cradle Song" along at some-
                thing like half its proper speed. Nursing his voice
                unobtrusively, he went tirelessly on with a clarity of
                enunciation that made the lavish programme notes an
                expensive luxury, and occasionally dropping to a
                pianissimo that was an object lesson to any would-be
                singer present. Fundamentally, of course, what Mr.
                Robeson sings is immaterial; all his songs are sung
                with complete sincerity and are his way of making
                friends with an audience. There is abundant artistry
                in all his proceedings but it aims at creating a
                fellowship with his listeners. It is all simple,
                rather sad - our friendship with Mr. Robeson is a
                community of suffering and aspiration - but it is
                always, after two hours of simple music, a remarkably
                real experience.

1719.   "Paul Robeson Sings at Trafalgar Square," London Times, June 29,
         1959, p. 6.

         This is a photo of Paul Robeson singing at the base of Nelson's
         Column in Trafalgar Square in England during a demonstration
         against nuclear armament organized by the British Peace Committee.

                                25. SPORTS

1720.   House, J.C. "There He Stands - In Sports History," The Worker,
         April 6, 1958, p. 11.

         The writer argues that Paul Robeson is best known to the younger
         generation as a magnificent baritone, actor and people's spokesman,
         but he was also an All-American football player. Mr. House dis-
         cusses Mr. Robeson's accomplishments as an athlete while at
         Rutgers University. He also points out that Robeson's name dis-
         appeared from sport history books, even those of Rutgers' "Hall
         of Fame."

26. STALIN PEACE PRIZE

1721. "Robeson Accepts Stalin Prize on Behalf of U.S. Peace Fighters,"
       Daily Worker, December 24, 1952, p. 3.

       Paul Robeson accepted the Stalin Peace Prize "not as an individual,
       but as a part of the growing peace movement in the United States."
       He declares, in part:
               For the peace fighters in America, this award has
               the greatest significance. Already the prize has
               called forth profound gratification and pride among
               many sections of the Negro people and the progressive
               forces of our land. For me personally, it is a moving
               experience - a great award and honor which I shall
               cherish all my life.

1722. Foster, William Z. "Robeson's Stalin Peace Prize Shows World-Wide
       Prestige," Daily Worker, December 29, 1952, p. 5.

       The writer surmises that politicans such as Truman, Acheson,
       Eisenhower, Dulles, McCarran cannot possibly hold down a great
       figure like Paul Robeson. Foster states, in part:
               His golden message of peace, in spite of everything
               they can do to prevent it, soars above all their
               persecutions, and spreads to the four corners of
               the earth. The Stalin Peace Prize awarded him is a
               fitting symbol of the prestige and honor which Paul
               Robeson enjoys among the poor and oppressed in all
               parts of the world.

1723. "Stalin Prize Presented: Robeson Gets 'Peace' Award From Howard
       Fast," New York Times, September 24, 1953, p. 38.

       The gold Medal and inscribed citation of an international Stalin
       Peace Prize for 1952 were presented to Paul Robeson at a gathering
       of 300 persons in New York City. A $25,000 cash award goes with
       the prize. The singer, unable to obtain a passport from the State
       Department, could not go to Moscow to accept his prize. In pre-
       senting the prize to Mr. Robeson, Mr. Fast called the Stalin
       Prize the highest that "the human race can bestow on any one of
       its members."

1724. North, Joseph. "Robeson Receives 'Highest Award Humanity Can
       Bestow'," The Worker, October 11, 1953, Section 1, p. 7.

       The author is referring to the Stalin Peace Prize that was awarded
       to Paul Robeson. In receiving the honor Robeson repeated what he
       has always maintained: He is, has been and always will be a friend
       to the Soviet Union and he told why, for there he had seen, with
       his own eyes, the equality men and women of all races and he had
       seen the works they had achieved in their brotherhood. Robeson
       was not allowed to go to Russia to receive the award in person.
       He was given the award in New York City. Robeson declares: "It
       is not a sacrifice, it is an honor, the highest honor, to take the

(North, Joseph)

blows for one's people."

1725. "Robeson Wins Stalin Peace Prize, Hailed as Leader of Negro People," Daily Worker, December 22, 1953, p. 3.

Robeson was one of seven people to win the Stalin Peace Prize. The prize carried an award of $25,000. The prizes were awarded by a special international committee. Robeson was hailed as "the standard bearer of the oppressed Negro people." The prizes for "strengthening peace among nations" were established on Stalin's 70th birthday.

1726. "No U.S. Tax on Stalin Peace Prize," London Times, February 5, 1959, p. 9.

This article states that Mr. Paul Robeson would not have to pay income tax on the $25,000 he was awarded in 1953 for the Stalin Peace Prize. The United States Internal Revenue Service had claimed $9,655 of the award, but then accepted Mr. Robeson's argument that no tax was due, since he had performed no services for the Soviet Union and made no effort to win the prize.

1727. "Robeson Wins Tax Suit," New York Times, February 5, 1959, p. 25.

Paul Robeson won a five-year fight to escape taxation on the $25,000 Stalin Peace Prize he received in 1953. The Internal Revenue Service announced it was abandoning its claim to $9,655 in taxes on the award. It took the position that the prize, the highest Soviet award of its kind, was in the same tax-exempt category as the Nobel and Pulitzer prizes.

F. 1960-1969

1. ANTI- AND PRO-ROBESON

1728. Sokolsky, George E. "These Days....Paul Robeson Speaks," Washington Post, December 6, 1960.

This columnist writes a critical assessment of Paul Robeson's
views. He states:
Paul Robeson is a singer. He is also a Negro and an
ardent Communist supporter. There are many singers and
many Negroes, but they do not go all over the world
making speeches against the United States. Paul
Robeson chooses to spew hate against his own country.
That is, of course, his right. Anyone may hate the
United States who chooses to do so, but what does the
United States do about it? Apparently, the Government of the United States takes no notice, although
we do maintain an agency, the USIA, to give this country
a good name. The fact that Paul Robeson can sing "Ol''
Man River" better than anyone else can, does not warrant
his going down to Australia and saying this: If
there was a war between Russia and America he would
be on the side of the Soviet Union, "who could win -
and should win." This seems to me to be pretty close
to treason. Everywhere I go I tell people - "Over
there is the United States - and there is a lie and
Paul Robeson is a liar." But he is also an artist.
Is an artist warranted to be a liar? There was a time
when the State Department with greater wisdom than the
Supreme Court, refused to give Robeson a passport to
travel the earth doing damage to this country. This
country is spending a fortune in an effort to establish
a favorable image throughout the world. This man,
knowing that people will listen to his nonsense because

(Sokolsky, George E.)

> they want to hear him sing, was unable to leave this
> country. Then the Supreme Court made it possible for
> any Communist or America-hater to travel on American
> passports and Congress has failed to pass an adequate
> act defining the passport and stating who is entitled
> to one....

1729. Spivack, Robert G. "A Voice is Silenced," New York Herald Tribune,
September 15, 1963, Section 2, p. 4.

The writer states that Paul Robeson was one of the great Negro
singers of our time. Like many of his race he felt frustrated
and unhappy but, unlike other Negroes, he hitched his wagon to a
red star, moved his family to Moscow and began to sing the praises
of the Soviet Union.... He went on to surmise last spring the
Parisian newspaper, Figaro, disclosed Robeson's whereabouts. It
ran a story quoting him as totally disillusioned about Russia and
communism. According to the Figaro report, Robeson said he had
long believed that minorities in the Soviet Union had "complete
freedom" and could live "without the least restrictions." But, he
acknowledged, that experience had taught him "this wasn't the
case at all," according to Mr. Spivack. The author states that
Robeson declares: "They had to adopt Soviet customs. They were
told that their culture was inferior to the new culture coming
from the Soviet state. The only great writers were Soviet.
Western art was decadent, Western music scandalous. I am disillusioned because I found a different form of oppression which is
all the more dangerous because it operates in the name of a bogus
liberation." Robeson had for years been Moscow's favorite Negro.
But once this story appeared things began to happen to Mr. Robeson
and, so far as it is known, are still happening to him, argues
Mr. Spivack.... One friend, Edric Connor, a West Indian actor,
seems to accept the validity of the Figaro account, and this may
be the explanation of what happened to Robeson, asserts the author.
He quotes Connor as declaring: Paul is a tired man. "This is a
man who has made history. Getting the Stalin Peace Prize meant
an awful lot to him. Then Khrushchev came into power, and you
know what happened, not only to things and people connected with
Stalin, but to Stalin himself. Paul has never been the same man
since." Mr. Spivack concludes: "For now - and perhaps forever -
the magnificent voice of Paul Robeson is silent."

2. AWARD

1730. "Telegrams in Brief," London Times, October 7, 1960, p. 12.

This report states that Humbolt University, in East Berlin, conferred an honorary degree of Doctor of Philosophy on Mr. Paul
Robeson for his "services in the great struggle for peace."

3. BIRTHDAY

1731. Patterson, William L. "Paul Robeson: A Giant Among Men," Political
Affairs, Vol. 47, No. 5, May, 1968, pp. 17-21.

This aritcle was a salute to Paul Robeson on his 70th birthday.
The author quotes much of Robeson's philosophy from the actor-
singer's book, Here I Stand. Patterson states that Robeson has
never seen his contributions to the fight "to root out the racial
and economic evils of his country" as a sacrifice. "Three score
and ten years most of them spent in the greatest cause in all the
world - the freedom of mankind!," asserts the author. He concludes:
> We salute Paul Robeson, Afro-American, American, citizen
> of the world and one of its greatest humanists. Millions
> of American youths will find in the life of Paul Robeson
> heroic deeds to emulate. He has helped to make history
> at a moment when the demand was for grants. Our
> country has produced few that are his peer.

1732. "Paul Robeson Celebrates 71st Birthday on April 9," New York Amsterdam News, April 12, 1969, p. 2.

This article points out that Paul Robeson was 71 years old on
April 9. His alma mater, Rutgers University, in New Brunswick,
dedicated a music and arts lounge honoring him. It was a student-
initiated project. Robeson, now living in Philadelphia, was a
1919 Phi Beta grad of Rutgers and an All-American football player.
He later received a law degree from Columbia before becoming an
opera performer and actor, concludes the article.

1733. Patterson, William L. "In Honor of Paul Robeson," Political
Affairs, Vol. 48, No. 5, May, 1969, pp. 17-22.

This article was made at a meeting in tribute to Paul Robeson's
71st birthday in Chicago, Illinois, April 13, 1969. He declares:
> Today we have gathered to celebrate the 71st birthday
> of Paul Leroy Robeson. He is with us although he is
> ill. His spirit deminates this meeting. His fight
> is for our dignity as human beings - our constitutional
> rights - for the salvation of our country from those who
> would do here what the bloody Hitler and and his
> creators did in Germany - make a police state of our
> land. Every fight we black men wage to eliminate the
> ghetto, to get full employment, decent housing,
> schools where our children are really educated, is
> a fight for our country and all who battle for
> national liberation. The militant voices today
> echo Paul Robeson's call to action. He is a great
> pioneer who will take his stand beside the deathless
> Frederick Douglass and the immortal W.E.B. DuBois....
> It is proven by the treatment accorded Paul Robeson
> and W.E.B. DuBois, by the murder of Dr. Martin Luther
> King and Malcolm X, and the attempts to behead the

(Patterson, William L.)

militant organizations of today. As Paul wrote, our
battle for national liberation has become linked with
every existing struggle for human progress whether
in Africa, Asia, Latin America or Europe. We have
learned vital lessons from Paul. We salute him. We
salute him as one of our foremost leaders, one of the
great men of the world, a resident of the United States
and a citizen of the world.

4. COMMUNISM

1734.   "Robeson Dispute with Communists Denied by His Son," New York
Times, September 15, 1963, p. 73.

Published reports that Paul Robeson had become disillusioned
with Communism and was being held in East Berlin against his will
were described by his son as "lies out of the whole cloth."
Paul Robeson, Jr., his son, declares that his father's recent
flight to East Berlin had "no political overtones." The son
says his father had been suffering from "exhaustion" for several
years and was planning to take a long rest.

5. FILMS

1735.   Cripps, Thomas R. "Movies in The Ghetto Before Poitier," Negro
Digest, Vol. 18, No. 4, February, 1969, pp. 21-27, 45-48.

Paul Robeson is mentioned throughout this article. The writer
points out that the greatest coup of Black film maker Oscar
Micheaux was the signing of Paul Robeson to do "Body and Soul."
Cripps declares that "Body and Soul" was sophisticated for its
day (1924), yet it went unnoticed outside of the ghetto theatres.
The author argues that the most striking instance of White awakening to the box office power of Black themes was Paul Robeson
starring in "The Emperor Jones," which did surprising business
and helped persuade Hollywood to reexamine its racial policies.

6. FREEDOM FIGHTER

1736. Patterson, William L. "Man Among Men," Daily Worker, April 5,
       1960.

       The writer asserts that Paul Robeson belongs to the history of
       the Black man wherever you find them. He belongs to the un-
       written history of this United States which when written in keeping
       with reality will reveal the bond that separably united black and
       white Americans in the fight to deepen and enrich their heritage
       of freedom and destroy the heritage of slavery, states the writer.
       Patterson surmises that Paul Robeson was "Made in America." The
       corruption of this society left this man no choice - as a man -
       but to fight back. His life is an example worthy of emulation
       so far as the struggle for human freedom is concerned, by every
       American youth, black and white, states the author. He concludes:
            Paul Robeson, great black man, great American, great
            human being, for all for whom I am privileged to
            speak I say: The people's victory will be won.
            Those who tremble at your voice are aware of that.
            Millions of youth have learned from you. Salute!

1737. Dodd, Martha. "Paul Robeson," Mainstream, Vol. 16, No. 5, May,
       1963, pp. 53-56.

       The writer discusses Paul Robeson through several stages: "Moti-
       vation," "Discrimination," "Whole Man." Miss Dodd best summed
       up Robeson in her section on him as a "Whole Man." She argues:
            Paul Robeson is a whole man, all of one piece, above
            all an American and a Negro-American. Everything fell
            into place in his life, once he had fully understood the
            reasons for war and exploitation of man by man. He
            did not waste time searching his soul in fruitless,
            egoistic arguments or indecision. He knew what he
            had to do. To serve the people was the noblest aim
            of man. For this he must train himself not only in
            singing - after all a human voice can only endure a
            certain span of years - but in speaking, thinking,
            writing, organizing, taking action. Unconsciously
            he was preparing himself for the life of a revolutionary.
            "I have overcome by fear of death.... I know how hard
            it's going to be in America," "Our freedom is going to
            see the end of the struggle." But what he did know
            and said repeatedly was that "We must fight to the
            death for peace and freedom." "I am only a folk-
            singer." Yes, he is a folk singer, but a folk-singer
            for and of the world, a giant of a man in soul,
            intellect, voice and purpose! It does not matter
            if he is 65, 35, or 80. He is ageless: a towering
            mountain, a wide and lovely valley, the tallest tree
            in our American forest. Our friend, and the friend
            and brother of the human race, once said, "I always
            knew from my youth....that my life, would never be a
            very personal one....I have the greatest feeling of

(Dodd, Martha)

> belonging to people everywhere. They have given
> me everything....

1738. Kihss, Peter. "Paul Robeson Ends Self-Exile," New York Times,
December 23, 1963, p. 1, 26.

Mr. and Mrs. Paul Robeson returned to the United States after five
years and five months abroad. At Idlewild Airport in New York
City one reporter asked Paul Robeson if he planned to take part
in the civil rights movement in the United States. He replied:
"Yes, I've been part of it all my life."

1739. "Paul Robeson: Disillusioned Native Son," New York Times, December
23, 1963, p. 26.

According to this article, Paul Robeson's own talents, first as
scholar and college athlete, then as singer and actor, permitted
him to surmount most of the handicaps of his race. But he has
always been a militant fighter against racial discrimination, and
it was this, declares the writer, he has explained, that led him
to Marxism and positions indistinguishable from the Communist
party line. The writer asserts that his career traced a mounting
curve of success - in concerts, motion pictures and the theatre
in America and Europe. Abroad and particularly in Russia which
he visited first in 1934, he said he found relief from Jim Crowism
he experienced in this country.

1740. Flynn, Elizabeth Gurley. "Voice of Paul Robeson," The Worker,
April 19, 1964, p. 7.

The writer declares that the treatment accorded Paul Robeson is
one of the most shameful and scandalous chapters of many in this
disgraceful period of the 1950's.... But Paul Robeson's "crimes"
endeared him instead of isolating him from thousands of people....
She suggests that since Paul Robeson has returned to America,
after being absent for a number of years, he will contribute
now, as ever before, to the full limit of his strength.

1741. Editorial. "Welcome Home, Paul Robeson," Freedomways, Vol. 4,
First Quarter, Winter, 1964, pp. 6-7.

The editor declares that although Paul Robeson was a Phi Beta Kappa
scholar, All-American athlete and Spingarn Medalist, he was above
all a sterling fighter in the cause of Freedom, Human Dignity and
World Peace - the noblest ideals of man - Paul Robeson was the inspiration and idol of a whole generation of Negro youth, who grew
to adulthood in the early struggles of the CIO (Congress of Industrial Organization) and New Deal. Robeson had been in Europe
for the past five years and returned to his native country.

1742.   Stevens, Hope R.   "Paul Robeson - Democracy's Most Powerful Voice,"
        Freedomways, Third Quarter, Summer, 1965, pp. 365-368.

        The author, a long-time friend of Robeson, points out that in the
        decade of the nineteen thirties, the name and voice of Paul
        Robeson became synonymous with protests for the working people it
        condemned injustice, long hours, low wages; for the Black man, it
        demanded equality, dignity and the end of segregated living and
        discrimination. Robeson sang the songs of freedom, of love, of
        piety, of hope, with a new meaning for all oppressed and dispos-
        sessed people -- but particularly for Black people, states Stevens.
        The songs of protest and solace that the Black people of America
        have composed and sung to noteless music for over three centuries,
        he dignified and glorified by presenting them with pride and con-
        fidence everywhere he went, states the author. He asserts:
            I wanted to pay tribute to one who has long since been
            called to his place in the Hall of Fame by the lovers
            of freedom and the fighters for peace and justice all
            over the world. His has been appropriately called
            democracy's most powerful voice. Nature endowed him
            with a magnificent talent, housed it in a massive,
            robust, rugged and most attractive frame; provided a
            winsome and congenial personality to go along with it;
            instilled in him a quality of courage in direct ratio
            to his enormous physique; and topped it off by
            saturating this extraordinary man with boundless love
            for his fellows and an uncompromising hatred of in-
            justice and oppression in all their ugly forms. He,
            on his part, accepted these gifts as tools with which
            to work. He invested them, developed them, applied
            them and continues to exhaust them. He has probably
            personally addressed, in speech and in song, without
            the aid of television, more people on the earth, than
            any other living human being. I am, of course,
            referring to Paul Robeson.

1743.   "'Recognize Robeson,' is Demand at Rutgers," Daily Worker, March
        14, 1969, p. 9.

        According to this article, a demand for recognition by Rutgers
        University of one of its most famous alumni, Paul Robeson, is
        growing among its students and faculty. William Decker Clarke,
        deputy commissioner of finance of New York City and eastern vice-
        president of the fraternity Alpha Phi Alpha, said in a speech at an
        installation ceremony last week that the University had a duty to
        "re-establish" recognition of the great singer withdrawn because
        of his activities as a fighter for peace and his partisanship for
        the Socialist Soviet Union where he lived for a number of years....

7. HONORS

1744. Smith, Jessica. "Paul Robeson Honored in GDR," New World Review,
       Vol. 35, No. 6, June, 1967, p. 63.

       The author declares that in early April Paul Robeson's 69th birth-
       day was marked at a special ceremony in East Berlin's Museum of
       German History. The audience included leading personalities from
       the arts, sciences and other fields. Everyone present received a
       booklet giving a brief illustrated account of Paul Robeson's life
       and work. The ceremonies opened with a short documentary film
       about his visit to the GDR in October, 1960, at which time he re-
       ceived an honorary doctorate from Berlin Humboldt University,
       and the Order of the Star of International Friendship from the GDR
       government. The film "Native Land" produced by Frontier Films in
       1940-42, was also shown. Narrated by Paul Robeson, it shows the
       US people's struggles of the '30's, and features songs by Robeson
       and Pete Seeger. The leading address was given by Professor Kpeler,
       Knepler, Director of College of Music. He told of the great love
       and esteem in which Paul Robeson is held in the GDR as in all the
       socialist countries, both as an artist and a fighter for the rights
       of his own and all people, and read a telegram of greeting to
       Mr. Robeson. A number of Robeson records have been released in
       GDR, the latest entitled "The Other America," featuring Earl
       Robinson as well. A number of books about Paul Robeson have been
       published in the GDR. In addition there is a Paul Robeson Archive
       attached to the Academy of Arts.

8. ILLNESS

1745. "Mr. Paul Robeson Ill in Moscow," London Times, April 15, 1961,
       p. 8.

       This report declares that Mr. Paul Robeson, who was to have sung
       at the "Africa Freedom Day" concert at the Festival Hall in London
       was in the hospital in Moscow. He was suffering from exhaustion
       and had to cancel all engagements for several months. The announce-
       ment was made by the London Movement for Colonial Freedom.

1746. Farnsworth, Clyde H. "Robeson to Rest in East Germany," New York
       Times, August 26, 1963, p. 2.

       The reporter asserts that Paul Robeson boarded a Polish Airline
       from London, where he was convalescing, and flew to the German
       Democratic Republic and would have a general medical checkup fol-
       lowed by a holiday in one of that country's beautiful spas.
       According to the article, the flight came after the (London) Sunday
       Telegraph reported it had received a suggestion that an attempt
       would be made to "smuggle" the 65-year-old-singer to a Soviet-bloc
       Capital "to keep him quiet" because he had "broken with Moscow."

(New York Times)

A friend of Mr. Robeson's called that allegation "sheer nonsense."

1747. "Paul Robeson in East Berlin: Flight with Wife From London,"
       London Times, August 26, 1963, p. 8.

       This article asserts that Mr. Paul Robeson flew, with his wife,
       Eslanda Goode Robeson, into East Berlin from London. His where-
       abouts were kept secret and only his family and close friends had
       been permitted to see him. Mr. Robeson's agent, Mr. Harold Davison,
       said in London that the singer had gone to an East German spa to
       convalesce and after a good rest he was expected back in London
       for some recordings.

1748. "Robeson Undergoes Check-Up in Berlin," New York Times, August 27,
       1963, p. 26.

       This article asserts that Paul Robeson would undergo medical tests
       in an East Berlin hospital and that he would enter a nursing home
       there. His wife states that Mr. Robeson was suffering from cir-
       culatory trouble. Mr. Robeson, according to this article, was
       sending his countrymen "a message of greetings and best wishes for
       the civil rights march on Washington to take place on Wednesday."

1749. "Paul Robeson Injured in New York: Found Lying on Waste Ground,"
       London Times, October 19, 1965, p. 12.

       This article states that Paul Robeson, the Negro singer and cham-
       pion of Civil Rights, was found injured and semi-conscious on some
       waste land in New York. It was reported that he was taken to a
       hospital and released after treatment for cuts on the forehead and
       right eye and injuries to an ankle and hip. Mrs. Robeson reported
       her husband missing and stated he suffered from an illness which
       caused him to lose his balance.

1750. "Paul Robeson, 67, is Found Injured: Singer Lying in Vacant Lot --
       Condition Termed Fair," New York Times, October 19, 1965, p. 35.

       Paul Robeson was found lying in a semi-conscious condition in a
       clump of weeds near 169th Street and Highbridge Park in New York
       City. He was taken to Vanderbilt Clinic for treatment of facial
       lacerations and injuries to his left ankle and right hip. His
       wife told police that he had been ill and occasionally suffered
       lose of balance and dizzy spells. Mr. Robeson told police that
       he did not know he was injured or how he came to be in the lot.

1751. "Paul Robeson in the Hospital," New York Times, August 6, 1969,
       p. 294.

       This article states that Paul Robeson underwent treatment for a
       heart ailment at the University hospital in Philadelphia. The re-
       port states that he had been in ill health since 1961 when he
       suffered a physical breakdown while playing in Europe.

9. LECTURESHIP

1752. "Paul Robeson Offered Lectureship," London Times, May 16, 1962,
p. 11.

This article states that Mr. Paul Robeson, the American Negro
singer, was offered a post as lecturer at Ghana University's Institute of African Studies.

1753. "Robeson Weighs Ghana Offer," New York Times, May 17, 1962, p. 3.

According to this report, Paul Robeson was offered a lectureship
to teach at the University of Ghana in Africa. The article declares that Robeson was "thinking about accepting" the position.
It was also pointed out that Mr. Robeson was "delighted and
honored" at the offer to teach in the University's new School of
Music and Drama.

10. MRS. ESLANDA ROBESON

1754. "Eslanda Goode Robeson is Dead; Writer and Wife of Singer, 68,"
New York Times, December 14, 1965, p. 43.

This article not only discusses her own accomplishments but also
the influence that she had on her husband, Paul Robeson. It was
pointed out that she encouraged her husband to enter the theater
since she felt there was strong racial prejudice against Negro
lawyers. According to this article, Mrs. Robeson persuaded her
husband to participate in a Young Men's Christian Association
pageant as Simon The Cyrenean in the early 1920's. This led to
the Provincetown Players, an association with Eugene O'Neill and
parts in the O'Neill plays, "All God's Chillun God Wings," "The
Hairy Ape," and his most famous role "The Emperor Jones."

1755. Smith, Jessica. "Eslanda Robeson - 1895-1965," New World Review,
Vol. 34, No. 1, January, 1966, pp. 8-13.

Various references are made to Paul Robeson throughout this article. The editor states that both Paul and Eslanda Robeson were
among their most treasured contributors to the New World Review
It was also pointed out that Paul and his wife traveled widely and
at huge concerts and gatherings in many countries the people of
the socialist countries and other parts of the world expressed
their love and admiration for them. The editor declares that
Paul Robeson on a number of occasions told of this deep gratitude
to his wife for her influence in determining his course as a singer;
and for her great and manysided contributions to his development
as an artist and as a human being. He also spoke of his wife's
lifelong work for full equality for the Negro people, for human
advancement and peace.

11. PAUL ROBESON ARCHIVE

1756. "Paul Robeson Archive in the GDR," Information From the Peace
Movement of the German Democratic Republic, May, 1965, p. 1.

This news release states that the name of Paul Robeson, the famous
Negro singer, has been synonymous with all the great struggles for
peace and progress over the past thirty years or more. Whether
from the political or the concert platform, Paul Robeson has never
failed to move and inspire his audience for the great human ideals.
Friends and admirers of Paul Robeson's work will be pleased to
learn that with the consent of Paul and Eslanda Robeson; an archive
has been established to collect and preserve the many documents,
records, tape recordings, photos, newspaper cuttings, etc., connected with his life and work. The Paul Robeson Archive will be
at the Academy of Arts in Berlin, the capital of the GDR. The
Paul Robeson Committee of the GDR, composed of leading personalities, many of whom have been associated with Paul Robeson, such
as Prof. Ernest Herman Meyer, Prof. Albert Norden, Prof. George
Knepler and Dr. Franz Loeser, held a press conference to announce
the establishment of the Paul Robeson Archive on April 10th.
Prof. Meyer, one of German's leading composers, appealing for
support for the archive presented a valuable record of Paul
Robeson speaking and singing for the Aid to Spain Movement, recorded in London in 1936. The committee states further that Paul
Robeson's work belonged to the whole of progressive humanity and
with this in mind the committee invited support from all parts
of the world, concludes the article.

12. POLITICS

1757. Cotton, Lettie Jo. "The Negro in the American Theatre," Negro
History Bulletin, Vol. 23, No. 8, May, 1960, p. 175.

The writer declares that Paul Robeson can only be described in
superlative terms. It was argued that Robeson is a symbol of Negro
advancement on the implacable stallion of talent. "His career
stands in the annals of history as a great giant step in the long
process of gaining respect for the Negro as a performer, as artist,
and as an individual," surmises Cotton. The author concludes:
      Perhaps the society that turned so successful a man
      toward another economic ideology ought to survey itself
      for the seeds of discontent. America closed her door
      to a brilliant artist, for Negro and Red are two colors
      which constitute the untouchable.

1758. "When You Love Your Country, Duty is to Point Out Its Faults,"
       Pittsburgh Courier, November 12, 1960, p. 23.

       This article decalres that while Paul Robeson was on tour in New
       Zealand he states: "When you love your country it is your duty
       to point out its faults." The article also asserts that the singer
       told reporters that he still considered himself a "true American."
       He went on to say that he had refused to answer questions from the
       Un-American Activities Committee because the chairman had been a
       Senator from Mississippi. "It would have been like being judged
       by Dr. Verwoerd...and speaking of Dr. Verwoerd....he'd better get
       out of South Africa damned quick." Mr. Robeson told his ques-
       tioners that his life as an artist "was over" and that he was no
       longer interested in making money or in being important. "But
       my life as a scholar is just beginning. I want to know one langu-
       age as well as that of those who were my oppressors," states the
       writer.

                              13. RETIREMENT

1759. Feron, James. "Robeson Will Return to U.S. Monday to Retire,"
       New York Times, December 20, 1963, p. 10.

       The writer states that Paul Robeson would return to the United
       States and retire, at the request of his doctors, from performing
       professionally, because of poor health. Mr. and Mrs. Robeson
       had been living in Europe since 1958. Harold Davison, Mr. Robeson's
       agent, said that the singer was returning to the United States
       "because it's his home." He said the singer's politics were be-
       hind him. Mr. Davison also declares: "He's quite thrilled with
       the prospect of his seeing his family in New York. He hasn't seen
       his son or his two grandchildren for quite some time."

1760. "Paul Robeson to Retire," London Times, December 20, 1963, p. 5.

       According to this article, Paul Robeson, the singer, arrived in
       London from East Germany and stated that he would retire from
       singing, according to Mr. Harold Davison, his London agent. He
       had been out of the United States for five years and for the past
       four months had been receiving treatment at a hospital in East
       Berlin. The singer stated that he would stay in London and rest
       for awhile before going to see his family in America.

14. RUSSIA

1761. "Robeson Talks in Moscow," New York Times, January 24, 1960, p. 26.

It was reported by the news agency, Tass, that Paul Robeson addressed workers at a ball-bearing plant in Moscow and also sang
American folksongs for them. Tass said the singer received an
enthusiastic ovation. He praised the recently announced Soviet
troop reduction program and the disarmament plan presented by
Premier Khrushchev last fall, states the article.

1762. "Robeson Sits with Khrushchev," New York Times, January 30, 1960,
p. 7.

According to this article, Premier Khrushchev and Paul Robeson
sat together in a box at the Bolshoi Theatre at a presentation of
scenes from the plays of Anton Chekhov in honor of the 100th
anniversary of his birth. It was also reported that Mr. Robeson
was called on stage and sang some songs in Russian.

1763. "Robeson Ill in Moscow," New York Times, April 15, 1961, p. 15.

According to this report Paul Robeson was in a Moscow hospital
suffering from exhaustion. He was to have starred at an "African
Freedom Day" concert at London's Royal Festival Hall on April 21st.
The Movement for Colonial Freedom, the concert sponsors, announced
that Mr. Robeson was ill.

1764. "Paul Robeson Movie Announced by Russians," Jet, Vol. 13, March
13, 1965, p. 65.

A movie about actor-singer Paul Robeson will be made by the Soviet
Union and released later this year, Moscow radio reported. Production of movies about "outstanding peace partisans," including
Robeson and Dr. Hewlett Johnson, the "Red Dean of Canterbury,"
has been undertaken by the central documentary film studios, it
was reported.

15. RUTGERS DAYS

1765. "Of People and Things," New Brunswick (N.J.) Sunday Times, October
16, 1966.

This article is about James M. Burke, then editor and publisher
of the New Jersey Legislative News, Trenton. Robeson helped
save his life. The writer declares:
    Burke was given up for dead when he plunged off the
    bank of the Raritan Canal and landed unconscious in
    the stream 50 feet below.... He was on his way to
    Neilson Field from the dressing quarters in Baltimore

(New Brunswick Sunday Times)

Gym when the accident happened and if it hadn't been
for Paul Robeson and Cliff Baker, Rutgers Teamates,
he would surely have perished.... "Big Robey raced
down in football gear, plunged into the water and
hauled me out. Baker was at his side and they
quickly revived me. I had been up for a goner by
others who had witnessed my plunge from the cliff....
I always said I owe my life to Robey and Baker,"
Burke after declared.

1766.   Fishman, George. "Paul Robeson's Student Days and the Fight
Against Racism at Rutgers," Freedomways, Vol. 9, No. 3, Third
Quarter, 1969, pp. 221-229.

The writer discusses how Robeson was discriminated against from
the time he entered Rutgers in 1915 on a state scholarship. Most
of this article centers on Paul Robeson's football days at Rutgers
and how he was discriminated against on the football field. Although Robeson was a two time All-American at Rutgers and received
over 14 varsity letters his picture was missing from the gallery
of football players in the Rutgers gym. The writer concludes:
"....The student upsurge has led to the inclusion of Robeson's
picture in the Rutgers gym, the opening of the Paul Robeson Music
and Arts Lounge, and the recognition by Professor Richard Mc-
Cormick, Chairman of the History Department, speaking for the
University, of the need for a Rutgers Paul Robeson archives and
center. This 'lifting of the corner of the curtain' on Paul
Robeson is part of a larger accomodation to the needs and just
demands of the Black students of the Camden, New Brunswick and
Newark campuses of Rutgers. History does move forward!" The
author also includes three documents in this article: 1. James
Carr (first Black to graduate from Rutgers in 1892) protests
Jim Crow treatment of Paul Robeson, 2. Recognition of Paul Robeson
by the New York Times in 1919, 3. Speech Robeson made to the New
Brunswick, New Jersey, YMCA, in 1919, entitled, "The Future of
the Negro in America."

16. SINGER

1767.   "Mr. Paul Robeson Sings," Nottingham Evening News (England), April
27, 1960.

When Mr. Robeson toured England one observer submitted that although he was over 60 years old, he still held complete mastery
over his audiences. He declares:
It was that intimacy of contact that always makes his
recitals so different from anybody else's.... As always
there is the exciting sense of improvisation in his performances, the anticipation that he will bring from the
pile of papers and song sheets on the piano the song we

(Nottingham Evening News)

　　　particularly want to hear....

1768.　"Paul Robeson at May Day Celebration," Daily Record (Scotland),
　　　May 6, 1960.

　　　Paul Robeson participated in the May Day celebrations in Scotland.
　　　According to this article...."The magic of Paul Robeson gave
　　　Scotland one of its biggest May Day demonstrations for years...."
　　　At the end of the program, the miners honored Robeson by pre-
　　　senting him with a miniature miner's lamp. Printed on the base
　　　was the inscription...."From The Scottish Miners to Paul Robeson,
　　　2-5-1960."

1769.　Jensen, Owen.　"Robeson, A Legend Comes True," The Evening Post
　　　(Wellington, New Zealand), October 21, 1960.

　　　Paul Robeson gave a concert and was ecstatically received by the
　　　audience.　One writer noted Robeson's informal attitude on stage.
　　　He observes, in part:
　　　　　....Last night at the Town Hall, a big ungainly man
　　　　　came on the platform, almost awkwardly; he felt in
　　　　　one pocket for his glasses, in another for a pro-
　　　　　gramme, in the process dropping his handkerchief
　　　　　from still another pocket and taking time off to
　　　　　pick it up again; he acknowledged the tremendous
　　　　　applause from the tremendous audience by himself
　　　　　clapping back to them, and then he smiled; and then
　　　　　he sang; and a legend has come true....

17. TRIBUTES

1770.　Pittman, John.　"Mount Paul," New World Review, Vol. 30, No. 2,
　　　February, 1962, pp. 24-28.

　　　The writer discusses why a Soviet mountain peak bears the name of
　　　Paul Robeson.　Pittman states that the Soviet people named a
　　　mountain peak after Robeson as a truly great human being, a world
　　　champion of peace and of all oppressed peoples, they attribute
　　　to him the qualities of a great internationalist.　He also declares
　　　that a man's activities in behalf of peace, the extent to which
　　　he fights war and the causes of war between the Great powers -
　　　this is the determining yardstick for the Soviet people of Paul
　　　Robeson's role and work in today's world.　Pittman concludes:
　　　"....now when our century still has a third of its course to
　　　run, for a majority of the people on our planet, Paul Robeson, son
　　　of a Negro slave, is the most loved and honored living American."

1771. Archer, Doug. "2,000 Hail Paul Robeson at Freedomways Tribute,"
       Worker, May 2, 1965, pp. 3, 5.

       According to this reporter roaring applause greeted Paul Robeson
       as he welcomed an overflow audience of 2,000 friends and admirers
       at the Americana Hotel last week. Robeson stood in the center
       of the Albert Ballroom, his massive frame radiant in floodlight
       beams, and applauded the audience in return. Thunderous applause
       burst forth from the standing crowd and lasted several minutes.
       "It was a mighty time," said Ossie Davis, master of ceremonies.
       "It was a moment in the presence of greatness." This was the
       salute by "Freedomways," to Paul Robeson on his 67th birthday.

1772. North, Joseph. "A Prophet in His Own Time," Daily World, May 2,
       1965, pp. 3, 12.

       The author comments on the Welcome Home Celebration that Freedom-
       ways had honoring Paul Robeson at the Hotel Americana in New York
       City. Mr. North observes: "....The man who is said to be the best-
       known American in the world, and I dare say the most beloved re-
       ceived the homage of some 2,000 representative citizens who see
       him as the embodiment of the universal dream - that one man is the
       brother to all others equal in stature, in rights and in dignity.
       They came, and inspired by the man and the occasion, were trans-
       figured into a shining assembly of brotherhood; many came down
       from the United Nations, so there is no question that all races
       were here. Which was as it should be, in fact as you expected it
       to be. They came to honor Robeson safely home after his five year
       stay abroad. It was an evening of jubilation - a jubilee," states
       the author. He concludes:
            ....for the celebration came as vast events swept
            across our nation - the Negro freedom movement rolling
            grandly on, this cause for which he has pioneered and
            is giving boundlessly of his own life. He had suffered
            grievously for this cause, barred for years from the
            stage which he graced, and deprived for years from his
            right to travel to other lands where audiences were
            awaiting him. He was safely home now....

1773. Editorial. "Salute to Robeson," Freedomways, Vol. 5, No. 3, Third
       Quarter, 1965, pp. 363-365.

       The Editor declares, in part:
            On April 22 last, Freedomways held a "Salute to Paul
            Robeson" as a tribute and welcome home to this great
            artist and pioneer in the struggle for human rights in
            our country. It will be remembered that Freedomways was
            the first national magazine to editorially welcome
            Mr. Robeson back to America (Feb. 1964). However, many
            of our readers felt that, in addition, there should be
            some occasion of public acclaim for a man so greatly
            admired. How right they were! The response to Freedom-
            ways initial announcement of the Salute was overwhelming....

(Freedomways)

> For weeks the names kept pouring in, right up to the
> very day of the affair. As people packed into the Albert
> Hall of the Hotel Americana that Thursday evening, there
> wasn't even "standing room," remaining. Old friends
> flew in from Chicago, Detroit, Washington, D.C., and as
> far west as California. People "who hadn't seen each
> other in years" were there. Many among those present
> had earned the honor of being called old-timers, for
> they had stood with the man they affectionately called "Paul"
> at the Battle of Peekskill more than 15 years ago, when
> the dark clouds of McCarthyism were just beginning
> to envelop this country, and Mr. Robeson was singled out
> as one of the first targets of that infamous period of
> persecution. Together with these "old-timers" were
> young people from the Southern battle-front and Northern
> campus movements of today, a new generation of freedom
> fighters, many of whom were seeing Paul Robeson for the
> first time in person. Many from the Harlem and Bedford-
> Stuyvesant communities of New York came out because (as
> several expressed it) they felt "our freedom movement has
> now caught up with many of the things Paul Robeson
> fought for all these years; it's time we openly ack-
> nowledged his contribution."

1774. Lewis, John. "Paul Robeson - Inspirer of Youth," Freedomways,
Third Quarter, Summer, 1965, pp. 369-372.

> The speaker told the guests at this "Salute to Paul Robeson":
> We salute more than a man, we salute a cause. We
> salute the dreams and aspirations and the hopes of
> an oppressed people whether they be in Salem,
> Alabama, in Jackson, Mississippi, or in Vietnam....
> We of the SNCC (Student Non-Violent Coordinating
> Committee) are Paul Robeson's spiritual children
> because they, too, have rejected gradualism and
> moderation.

1775. Segal, Edith. "Tribute to Paul Robeson," New World Review, Vol.
35, No. 2, February, 1967, p. 61.

> The writer states that Paul Robeson was in Leningrad, Russia, and
> while there attended a circus. Even at the circus, according to
> Segal, Paul Robeson was proclaimed as a "prominent cultural
> figure." When his name was called the audience, which packed the
> theatre immediately burst into smashing applause. It was the name
> they... knew and loved, concludes the author.

1776. Hatcher, Richard Gordon. "Which is the Path of Change?," The
Worker, June 9, 1968.

The author was the Mayor of Gary, Indiana. He was the first Black
mayor of that city. The mayor addressed a gathering of the N.A.A.
C.P. Legal Defense Fund, in May, 1968. In this speech he assessed
what he saw as the "forces of change" in the United States society;
the Black and White liberals; Black power advocates; and White
radicals. In his remarks, he declares:

> When Paul Robeson, who had thrilled the black middle
> class as actor and singer, turned his magnificent bass-
> baritone to more profound issues, he too was scorned.
> In the words of one of his own songs, "They scandalized
> his name." In 1949, when Robeson said in Paris, "Hell
> no, we won't go," he was saying what Black young men are
> chanting today in Harlem and Watts and on college cam-
> puses up and down the land. And when he wrote the
> following in 1958, he was a decade ahead of his time.
> He said, in his book Here I Stand: "I am not
> suggesting, of course, that the Negro people should
> take law enforcement into their own hands, but we
> have the right, and above all, we have the duty, to
> bring the strength and support of our entire community
> to defend the lives and property of each individual
> family. Indeed, the law itself will move a hundred
> times quicker whenever it is apparent that the power
> of our numbers has been called forth. The time has
> come for the great Negro communities throughout the
> land -- Chicago, Detroit, New York, Birmingham and
> all the rest -- to demonstrate that they will no
> longer tolerate mob violence against one of their
> own." The liberals helped to silence Robeson's voice,
> helped hound him out of the country, under the guise
> of helping to protect the country against the Com-
> munist menace. What, in fact, liberalism, Black and
> white, did was to help silence voice after voice of
> protest out of a mistaken notion that the way to pro-
> gress was to agree with white power structure on
> everything -- its foreign policy, its ethics, its
> witch hunting, and its paranoid anti-Communism. How
> they damaged white militancy! How they dampened the
> spirit of black men!....

G. 1970-1979

1. AFRICA

1777.   Guma, Alex La. "Paul Robeson and Africa," African Communist, No.
46, Third Quarter, 1971, pp. 113-119.

Alex La Guma, the South African writer, read the paper printed
here at a symposium on "Paul Robeson and the Afro-American Strug-
gle," held April 13-14, 1971, at the Academy of Arts, Berlin,
German Democratic Republic. The essence of the article was that
Paul Robeson spent his whole life fighting for the freedom of
Africa from European colonialism on that continent. He also
mentioned Paul Robeson's role as Chairman of the Council of
African Affairs.

1778.   "Anti-Imperialists Must Defend Africa," Black Liberation Journal,
Vol. 1, Winter, 1976, pp. 2-4.

This was an abridged version of a speech made by Robeson at a
meeting in Madison Square Garden, New York City, on June 6, 1946.
The meeting was sponsored by the Council on African Affairs, an
organization that Robeson helped to found and was Chairperson of
it throughout its existence. The editor of the Black Liberation
Journal called Paul Robeson a titanic fighter for world peace and
freedom for all workers and oppressed peoples from all forms of
exploitation and oppression. He also asserts: "We feel that
these remarks are a fitting introduction to this issue of the
Black Liberation Journal, for they place in a historical context
current developments in Africa, especially with respect to the
People's Republic of Angloa...."

1779. Stuckey, Sterling. "I Want to be African: Paul Robeson and the
       Ends of Nationalist Theory and Practice, 1914-1945," Massachusetts
       Review, Vol. 17, No. 1, Spring, 1976, pp. 81-138.

       The writer points out that perhaps Robeson's first public state-
       ment of nationalism, of affirmation of the need for Afro-Americans
       to assume responsibility for their own liberation, was his com-
       mencement speech at Rutgers in 1918. According to Dr. Stuckey,
       for nearly fifty years Paul Robeson's devotion to people of African
       descent mounting even as his interest in other peoples gained
       ground, was the motives power behind his political and intellectual
       endeavors. Dr. Stuckey concludes:
           As cold war fever and hysteria enveloped America,
           Robeson's philosophy and activities inspired unusual
           fear and hatred in government circles. The multi-
           faceted genius had compared the post-war era with that
           breakdown of medievalism which pre-aged the Renaissance.
           He foresaw a similar "shattering of a universe"
           because entrapped, pent-up forces of color, for
           centuries subjected to European **suzerainty, were**
           beginning to break loose, threatening to make the
           European vision of itself sadly unrealizable, the
           Eurocenter focus of world power soon irretrievable.
           The day was not too distant when the most incandescent
           dreams of nationalists from the early nineteenth
           century to Robeson himself would achieve, however
           uncertain the workings of the human will, the
           tangibility of freedom. It was, after all, that
           goal to which Robeson had devoted his life.

                              2. BIRTHDAYS

1780. "Paul Robeson on Cover of Black World," Black World, Vol. 20,
       No. 6, April, 1971, p. 49.

       Paul Robeson was on the cover of this magazine. His appearance
       on the cover commemorated his 73rd birthday. This write up de-
       clares that he was "one of the finest singers in the world and
       an actor of singular power and attractiveness...." It also
       states that Mr. Robeson found himself villified and boycotted by
       the entertainment industry because of his defiant stance against
       American racism and hypocrisy. A calculated campaign sought to
       destroy his career and to create in the nation's mind an image
       of him as a subversive and an enemy of the state, concludes the
       article.

1781. "Robeson Celebration in German Democratic Republic (GDR),"
      Muhammad Speaks, July 16, 1971, pp. 8-9.

      Robeson's 73rd birthday was celebrated in the German Democratic
      Republic. The two-day international symposium and a large
      solidarity meeting was called together by the Paul Robeson Com-
      mittee in the United States, the Trade Union Federation, the Peace
      Council, the Humboldt University of Berlin, and the Academy of
      Arts and the Afro-Asian Solidarity Committee. A large delegation
      from the United States was present as well as peoples from other
      countries. According to this article some of the speakers and
      shorter contributions recalled Paul Robeson's efforts at estab-
      lishing a Black culture to its full rights in the U.S.A. and making
      it loved and respected around the world. They followed the story
      up to the present day, giving the GDR listeners an idea of new
      developments in the USA today, asserts the article. The author
      concludes: "Paul Robeson's age and health have prevented him
      from singing or speaking up in recent years the way he used to.
      But he and his spirit are still alive, and his words - calling
      freedom and for people in all countries to join in fighting
      racism, war and the hateful men of fold - were recalled and re-
      peated in Berlin...."

1782. "Honors to Paul Robeson on His 74th Birthday," Freedomways, Vol.
      12, No. 1, First Quarter, 1972, p. 67.

      This was an announcement by this magazine that states: "Freedom-
      ways welcomes the naming of the new student center at Rutgers
      University, Newark Campus, for Paul Robeson. This action was
      voted by the Board of Governors of Rutgers University in time
      for Robeson's birthday, April 9th."

1783. "Robeson Birthday Celebrated by Du Sable Museum," Black World,
      Vol. 21, No. 10, August, 1972, pp. 80-81.

      The 74th birthday of Paul Robeson was celebrated by the Du Sable
      Museum of African American History in Chicago, in a program at
      the Paul Lawrence Dunbar High School. Lloyd Brown, author of
      the novel "Iron City," was featured speaker at the celebration.
      Charles and Margaret Burroughs, founder and curator, respectively,
      of the Museum, designated April 16, Mr. Robeson's birthday, as the
      date for an annual cultural and benefit event for the Museum.

1784. Editorial. "Salute to Paul Robeson," Daily World, April 10, 1973,
      p. 7.

      The editor asserts that the lesson of Paul Robeson's seventy-fifth
      birthday is that where the people's struggle was, there was Paul
      Robeson. His enormous talent, passion and devotion were given
      unhesitating to the great movements for peace and democracy,
      against war and racism and fascism, surmises the writer. He con-
      cludes, in part:
           Robeson's humanism, his passion for the people, found
           expression in the historic movements of our times. He
           understood that the working class movement was the
           heart and soul of the struggle against exploitation

(Daily World)

and reaction. That was the basis of his efforts for
Blacks and White working class unity: for the alliance
of the Black liberation movement with the working
class movement: for the alliance of the national
liberation struggles with the world working class
movement: for socialism.... That has been the
essence of his political being. It was expressed
in his contributions to the organization and struggles
of the trade unions....

1785. Johnston, Laurie. "Robeson, at 75, is Feted in Absentia," New
York Times, April 16, 1973, p. 48.

This article discusses the cultural celebration of Paul Robeson's
75th birthday that was held on April 15th at Carnegie Hall. Mr.
Robeson was ill and could not attend the meeting. He sent a tape
message. It said, in part:
I want you to know that I am the same Paul, dedicated
as ever to the worldwide cause of humanity for freedom,
peace and brotherhood.... My heart is with the continuing struggles of my own people....(for) not only
equal rights but an equal share.... I rejoice together with the partisans of peace - the peoples of
the Socialist countries and the progressive elements
of all other countries...that the movement for peaceful co-existence has made important gains and that the
advocates to retreat.

1786. Murray, Alex. "Salute to Paul Robeson," Antillean Caribbean Echo,
April 28, 1973, p. 16.

The writer comments on the birthday party given at Carnegie Hall
on Paul Robeson's 75th birthday. Mr. Murray asserts that it is no
accident that the best piece written on Paul Robeson recently was
by a white man, Pete Hamill in the New York Post, and that the
well-dressed and racially mixed audience at Carnegie Hall who
attended his 75th birthday celebrations greeted Angela Davis'
remarks that he was revolutionary, "with light applause." However
they made up for this with a tumult of applause for his rendition
(via the movie tapes) of "Ol' Man River." That MUST mean something.... The writer declares that the man who gave up a career,
his very life in the interests of Blacks, whose moving voice and
scholarship were placed on the line for Black emancipation was
allowed to rot in New York during the sixties, and no Black militant of that turbulent period even remembered him. When the
history of the Black man is written, wherever it is written, the
omission of Paul Robeson from Page 1 will be slap on the face of
every Black in the world, states the author. Let any militant of
today read his "Here I Stand" and realize how small his efforts
are when compared with Robeson's. When Harry Truman died, he was
remembered as the man who dropped the Atom bomb, not as the man
who crucified Paul Robeson in a far more inhuman manner than the
way the Christ was crucified, an event commemorated only last
week, according to the writer. He concludes:

(Murray, Alex)

But it isn't Truman who is on trial as far as I am
concerned. It's the complacent Blacks, the sell-outs,
the easily bought loud mouths who pretend to go all the
way back to the days of slavery to honor heroes, and
who neglected to honor a real live hero in their midst.
For those who remember him, and honor him, and consider
themselves unworthy to lick his boots, he is still a
vivid memory and inspiration. We, and I know that
there are many, would prefer to use that memory to
uplift our souls, our spirits in our determination
to be men and women. He did not need a gun. We do
not....

1787. Lumer, Hyman (Editorial Comment). "Paul Robeson's 75th Birthday,"
Political Affairs, Vol. 52, No. 4, April, 1973, pp. 1-3, 52.

The writer declares that in vain have the ruling-class forces of
reaction in this country tried to silence Paul Robeson, to erase
his name from people's minds. "Today his music is heard by
growing numbers and his stature grows ever greater in the eyes
of our people, both Black and White," states Lumer. This article
also reviews Robeson's accomplishments. The author suggests that
although Mr. Robeson's activities were cut short by illness, his
influence is nevertheless increasingly felt. He concludes: "It
is with deep feelings of love and reverence that we join with the
countless others, in this country and abroad, who are saying:
'Happy Birthday, Paul.'"

1788. "Paul Robeson Honored at Carnegie Hall," Crisis, Vol. 80, No. 7,
August-September, 1973, p. 250.

Nearly 3,000 persons gathered at Carnegie Hall in New York City
on April 15th and paid tribute to Paul Robeson on his 75th birthday. Paul Robeson was not present at the celebration being confined to his home in Philadelphia where he continues to suffer a
circulatory ailment which has plagued him for many years. He
was represented by his son, Paul Robeson, Jr., who brought along
a taped message from his father in which he said, in part:
....Though I have not been able to be active for
years, I want you to know that I am the same Paul,
dedicated as ever to the worldwide cause of humanity
for freedom, peace and brotherhood....

1789. Johnson, Robert E. "Ailing Lonely Paul Robeson Observes his 76th
Birthday," Jet, Vol. 46, No. 3, April 11, 1974, pp. 10-17.

The writer points out that as Robeson faces his final curtain in
life's drama in his sister's home in Philadelphia, where love embraces and enrapts him and his memories on his 76th birthday,
Robeson can take heart at his defense when it is said by most
whites - and some few Blacks - that he had shown himself to be ungrateful to the good white folks of America who had given him
wealth and fame and that he should have nothing to complain about,
states Johnson. It is, perhaps, because of Robeson's immense power

(Johnson, Robert E.)

and gentleness that he is now allowed to spend his last days away
from the tumult and confrontation. When his home address was published in a white daily newspaper, a neighbor made this observation to <u>Jet</u>: "Since his (Robeson) address is known, his home is
the most respected and protected, the most hallowed and historic
site in all of Philadelphia. The graffiti (writing and paintings
on walls and buildings) is noticeably absent in this area and the
little that has been on the home of Mr. Robeson has been removed."
There is still some hope that America may yet recognize the contributions which Robeson made that helped make America great, concludes the writer.

1790. Berliner, David. "A Night for Remembering A Magnificent Giant,"
       <u>Washington Post</u>, October 20, 1976, p. 1.

       This article discusses a benefit that was held in Paul Robeson's
       honor at Carnegie Hall in New York City. Sidney Poiter summed
       up the feelings of the audience when he proclaimed: "When Paul
       Robeson died, it marked the passing of a magnificent giant whose
       presence among us conferred nobility upon us all....a dedicated
       humanist....our debt to Paul." The benefit was to raise money
       for the Robeson Archives that would document his activities.

1791. Anekwe, Simon. "Post Editor Tells Why She Wrote Book on Robeson,"
       <u>New York Amsterdam News</u>, February 25, 1978, p. 7.

       This article concerns Dorothy Bulter Gilliam who wrote the book,
       <u>Paul Robeson, All-American</u>. She states that she wrote the book
       after attending a "Salute to Robeson" at Carnegie Hall to honor
       his 75th birthday. She declares that the discovery of the true
       Robeson during that coverage of the Salute, filled her with a
       certain "fury" that this "gigantic man had been taken from us" by
       those who contrived to bury his achievements under the rubble of
       racism, the Cold War and McCarthyism.

1792. "UN Hails Robeson," <u>New York Amsterdam News</u>, April 15, 1978, p.
       D1, D4.

       This article was portion of a speech delivered by Lloyd L. Brown
       at the United Nations in a session of the UN's Special Committee
       Against Apartheid held to commemorate the 80th birthday year of
       the late singer, actor and political activist, Paul Robeson.
       Mr. Brown declares that if ever there was a man who might be said
       to personify the UN's ideal of universality, it was that great
       Afro-American who, as artist and man, dedicated his life to the
       principle he so often referred to as "the oneness of mankind."
       And if the UN is the perfect setting for this celebration, it
       might be noted too that equally appropriate is that sponsorship
       by the Special Committee Against Apartheid, states Brown.

3. BLACK HISTORY

1793. Cameron, Gledhill. "Paul Robeson: The Forgotten Man," Times
       Advertiser (Trenton, N.J.), February 13, 1972, Magazine Section,
       pp. 1-5.

       This article marked the 1972 National Black History Week Cele-
       bration. The author points out the contributions that Paul
       Robeson made to Black history in America and the world. He re-
       viewed Mr. Robeson's many accomplishments on and off the stage and
       in the movies. The author suggests that although Robeson was a
       pioneer for human rights, he has been overlooked by the history
       books including Black History books.

1794. "In Memory of Paul Robeson: A Great Name in Black History," New
       Observer (Washington, D.C.), May 15, 1976, p. 11.

       The editor asserts that the magnificent voice of the great Paul
       Robeson had been stilled, but the inspiration of his words and
       deeds in the fight against racism, fascism and for peace and an
       end to the exploitation of humanity will live forever. He also
       declares: "Early in his life, through experience, study and dis-
       cussion of political affairs, Robeson came to understand and ap-
       preciate the inseparable relationship of the liberation struggle
       of his people with those of the masses of Africa, Asia, Latin
       America and the Caribbean area...."

4. CHINA

1795. Yeakey, Lamont H. and Robert Glassman. "Friendship Has a History:
       Paul Robeson," New China, Vol. 1, No. 1, Spring, 1975, pp. 38-39.

       The writers point out that Paul Robeson, the famous Black singer
       and actor, has been an active friend of the Chinese people for
       most of his 76 years. Beginning in the late 1920s and 30s, Robe-
       son became deeply interested in China and its people. He read
       books on Chinese culture and history and, as with an impressive
       number of other languages, learned to read, write, speak, and
       sing in Chinese. When the Japanese invaded China, he gave several
       popular concerts in Europe and the United States to raise support
       and funds for China Relief. In 1941, he recorded a benefit album
       with a Chinese chorus; the title song was Chee Lai!, Chinese for
       "Arise!", declare the authors. In her introduction to that album,
       Mme. Sun Yat-sen (Soong Ching Ling) wrote: "Some of the finest
       songs (of the Chinese mass movement) are being made available to
       Americans in the recordings of Paul Robeson, voice of the people
       of all lands." After World War II, Paul Robeson championed the
       Chinese Revolution as the only way for China to develop free to
       exploitation and foreign domination. Confident that "the Chinese
       people have their freedom and are going to keep it," he saw the

(Yeakey, Lamont H., and Robert Glassman)

Korean War as an attempt to renew Western control of China and
insisted from the start that "the new and real China be seated in
the UN," state the writers. They conclude: "Although he was
denied an opportunity to visit China while he was still in good
health, Robeson maintained, 'I have for a long time felt a close
kinship with the Chinese people.'" He believed that "a new
strength like that of gallant China will add its decisive weight
to insuring a world where all men can be free and equal."

1796. Childress, Alice. "Salute to Paul Robeson, Friend of China,"
New China, Vol. 2, No. 1, June, 1976, p. 40.

The writer argues that Paul Robeson was not the man to sit down to
a full bowl while his brothers and sisters went hungry. Constantly
under attack, because of his unrelenting fight against racism and
inhuman treatment of the masses, he shouted his protests when
others whispered theirs or remained silent. He so loved the
American people that he dedicated his life to building a better
society. Most of his time was spent in resistance against the
genocidal persecution of his race as they suffered in the grasp
of the first aftermath of bondage, legalized "Jim Crow," states
Miss Childress. In a concert at Carnegie Hall in New York City,
Robeson once spoke of the similarities he had discovered in Chinese
and African languages, how their inflections so musically changed
the meaning of one word into many others. He demonstrated by
reciting in Mandarin and African tongues, and ended by saying that
such cultural patterns held in common proved the kinship of humankind. He later made an album of Chinese people's revolutionary
music titled "Chee Lai," accompanied by a Chinese chorus conducted
by Liu Liang-mo, states the writer. She concludes: "Today he
is universally remembered through books, films, sculpture, tape,
records, and the praises of the people. In 1952 he received the
Stalin Peace Award. A lofty mountain in the Ala-tor chain in the
Soviet Union is named "Robeson" in his honor. He lived to see
the day when the People's Republic of China clasped hands with
the African nations of Tanzania and Zambia, helping them finance
and build a great railroad which further builds friendship, peace,
and progress between two continents." She continues: "Paul
Robeson's greatest dream - a world at peace, the hungry fed, and
an end to racism - is left for us to achieve. Farewell to Paul
Robeson, alive forever!"

5. COLD WAR

1797. Cheng, Charles W. "The Cold War: Its Impact on the Black
Liberation Struggle Within the United States," Freedomways, Vol.
14, No. 4, Fourth Quarter, Part II, 1973, pp. 281-293.

Almost half of this article is devoted to Paul Robeson and his
struggle against the United States Cold War of the late 1940s

(Cheng, Charles W.)

and 1950s. The writer feels that it was the following remarks
made before the House Un-American Activities in June, 1956, that
led to the federal government's withdrawal of Robeson's passport.
He said: "What should happen would be that this U.S. Government
should go down to Mississippi and protect my people." Cheng
concludes:
> Now it would be misleading to conclude that Blacks
> were in any way behind the persecution of Robeson.
> As Robeson himself has written, "white folk on top"
> were responsible for the witch hunt and the repression
> he was subjected to. It need only be noted that the
> atmosphere of the country had reached such a state
> of red frenzie that some Black citizens also became
> "dupes" of the Cold War philosophy.

6. COMMUNISM

1798. James, C.L.R. "Paul Robeson: Black Star," Black World, November,
1970, pp. 106-115.

The author, a friend of Robeson, writes about his recollections of
him. The writer met Robeson while both were living in London.
James points out that if Paul Robeson wanted to he could have
build a movement in the natural successor to the Garvey Movement.
Robeson did not want to start a movement that would evolve around
him. Also Robeson felt himself committed to the doctrines and
the policies of the Communist Party, asserts James.

1799. Slattery, William J. "The Robeson Confusion," Encore, Vol. 1,
Spring, 1972, pp. 70-74.

The author states that the White community is confused about Paul
Robeson, what he stood for and what he did in his lifetime because
a fearful government silenced him and a cowardly white press corps
let the government get away with it. He points out that the Black
community is not in the least confused about Robeson. During the
time the establishment press pretended Robeson did not exist, the
Black press kept its readers informed of his activities almost
on a daily basis. Slattery argues:
> It was thought during the 1940's and 1950's that the
> Russians were using Robeson. According to biographer
> Brown, Paul, Howard Fast and others, this is not true.
> Communist-dominated organizations could always be
> counted upon to give Robeson a platform during these
> years of blackout. Robeson needed to gain respect for
> his people. So in the final analysis, Robeson was
> using the Communists. Robeson, the American hero,
> irritated his countrymen with his friendship for the
> Russians, frightened them when he spoke of Black Power
> and finally enraged them to action when he announced

(Slattery, William J.)

that Black Americans would not take up arms against
Red Russians. By 1949 the war between Black Paul
Robeson and white America was on.

1800. Farrakhan, Minister Louis. "The Propaganda Machine of White
America," Black Nation Information Bulletin, Vol. 1, No. 5, March,
1973, p. 2.

There is one section entitled, "Black People Made to Hate Paul
Robeson." The essence of this article was that the White news
media tried to discredit Robeson in the eye sight of Black people,
because they could not break him. Because he stood up to them
that spread the lie about him being a communist.

1801. "Jet Bureau Chief Bares Mail-Tampering Complaint Sparked by Paul
Robeson," Jet, Vol. 49, No. 6, November 20, 1975, p. 9.

Simeon Booker, Jet Washington Bureau Chief, received a letter from
the United States Supreme Court Justice William Orville Douglas
that had been opened and was delivered to Booker more than six
months after it had been written. Booker in turn wrote Douglas:
"I don't know what to make of it. But someone opened your letter
despite your rank as an U.S. Supreme Court justice, and there is
no way to find out how widespread has been the distribution, especially since you mentioned the name of the most hated Black, probably, of this century. At least, I want you to know that there
is a strange entanglement connected with all of this. Perhaps a
mentioning of the name, Robeson, has engulfed us in 'a communist
threat.' And somebody or group has been carrying on a crusade."
Justice Douglas responded by mail: "The story you tell does not
amaze me although it makes me rather sad. It doesn't amaze me
because the mail that I sent to my office from the state of
Washington in September, 1973, finally reached the office in
August, 1974. Moreover, in June of this year when in the West,
I wrote a memo to the court on the famous Nixon case and sent it
airmail from Yakima, Washington, and it took nearly a month for
it to get there, so how many read it I do not know."

1802. Bernheimer, Martin. "All Hats Off to Robey, Man....," Los Angeles
Times, February 1, 1976, Calendar Section, pp. 1, 58.

The writer declares that it wasn't just the voice that made Paul
Robeson a unique artist. The voice was just the foundation.
Robeson sang with degrees of emotional fervor, with honesty and
intelligence that made even the simplest folk song a thing of
eloquence. He had everything: imagination, taste, resource,
passion. The writer asked the question, Was he really a Communist?
Robeson responded to the question himself in 1947. The city council
of Peoria, Illinois, had just banned the appearance of "any speaker
or artist who is an avowed or active propagandist for un-American
ideology." "Whether I am or am not a Communist or a Communist
sympathizer is irrelevant," he said. "The question is whether
American citizens, regardless of their political beliefs or
sympathies, may enjoy their constitutional rights." Mr. Bernheimer

(Bernheimer, Martin)

concludes: "Some people admired Robeson's art but resented his insistence on mixing that art with politics. Such people could
never understand Robeson. They could not understand that Robeson's
ideals - and idealism - affected everything he did. Everything."

1803.   "Paul Robeson: Singer, Actor and Foe of Racism was Victim of
Communist Witchhunt," Globe and Mail (Toronto, Canada), January
24, 1976, p. 30.

This article gives an overview of Paul Robeson's life. The reporter declares that besides being a great singer who made Negro
spirituals beloved by audiences frequently hostile to members of
his race, Robeson was a powerful actor whose performances as
"Othello" and "The Emperor Jones" were among the most stirring
of his time. He concludes by asserting: "In his last years, he...
lived as a recluse or, as in the title of America's most famous
book about the black experience in America, as an invisible man."

7. CULTURAL PHILOSOPHER

1804.   Stuckey, Sterling. "The Cultural Philosophy of Paul Robeson,"
Paul Robeson: The Great Forerunner. Editors of Freedomways.
New York: Dodd, Mead & Co., 1978, pp. 50-64.

The writer argues that though very few scholars are aware of it,
few people in this country's history have taken as serious an interest in cultural questions as Robeson. The 1930s was the period
of his most profound insights in to the nature of the black past
and present, the time of his deepest reflections on the state of
world cultural groupings. His philosophy of cultural philosophy
was projected in that decade in a series of brilliant essays and in
newspaper interviews. Robeson penetrated to the foundations
of Black culture, exposed the chief dangers of the culture of the
larger society and accurately identified the essential ingredients
of world cultures while calling for the synthesis that would save
mankind, states Stuckey. The author argues that on the basis of
what is now known about Robeson's scholarship, it seems not unreasonable to advance the view that he has easily earned a place
high on that select list of major commentators on American culture,
a list that includes W.E.B. DuBois, Sterling Brown, Constance
Rourke, F.S.C. Northrop, Ralph Ellison and Melville Herskovits.
Before long, it should not be possible to conduct a serious discussion of black culture or to relate American culture to the main
value systems of the world, without giving respectful attention to
the cultural philosophy of Robeson, suggests the author. He concludes that there is much irony here, for his enduring and profound influence, despite all of the efforts to silence the man and
to blot his example from our minds, will very likely be a result of
his heretofore largely unknown intellectual achievements.

8. EULOGY

1805. Holing, Gary. "The Death of Paul Robeson," New York Times, January
       25, 1976, p. 7.

       The writer states that Paul Robeson was an actor, singer, athlete,
       scholar, social philosopher, political activist, and more, and his
       talents in several fields were not merely adequate but at the
       highest levels of accomplishment. He declares: "Yet his refusal
       to separate any of his callings from his political beliefs and
       perceptions of himself as a Black subjected him to severe political
       persecution." Holing concludes: "...Though he did not seek it,
       he also received the wrath of many Americans because he fought
       racial discrimination when most Blacks did not and because he
       was a Socialist...."

1806. Brown, Lloyd. "Paul Robeson's Eulogy," New York Amsterdam News,
       January 31, 1976, p. 4.

       The author, a writer who for many years was a close friend and
       collaborator of Paul Robeson, was in 1982 writing a Robeson
       biography (that has yet, in 1981, to be published). Mr. Brown
       declares: "The tallest tree in our forest has fallen. Along
       with the countless persons here and around the world who mourn
       his loss, I think that Nature herself must feel that with the
       passing of Paul Robeson something uniquely wonderful has departed
       from the earth. Surely Nature must have smiled to see the arrival
       on this planet of the seventh and last child born to Maria Louisa
       Robeson and the Reverend William Drew Robeson in Princeton, New
       Jersey, on April 9, 1898." Brown contends that over the years
       that cosmic smile of pleasure glistened on a myriad of faces as
       Paul's audiences were touched by the human grandeur of this
       Afro-American who stood before them like Shakespeare's noblest
       Roman: "the elements so mix'd in him that Nature might stand
       up and say to all the world: This was a man!," states the author.
       He concludes: "...How fortunate we were to have had Paul Robeson
       walk the earth among us! As artist and man, he was a prophetic
       vision of how wondrously beautiful the human race may yet become.
       Now he belongs to the future...."

1807. Brown, Lloyd L. "Paul Robeson: Now He Belongs to the Future,"
       Freedomways, Vol. 16, No.1, First Quarter, 1976, pp. 11-14.

       This speech was delivered by his close friend and collaborator
       at Paul Robeson's funeral on January 27, 1976. The speaker declares
       that only the serious breakdown of Paul Robeson's health could
       sideline him from his dedicated efforts to make a better world;
       and that happened in 1965 when he was forced to retire from public
       life. He wanted to live in complete seclusion and so he con-
       sistently declined to be interviewed. According to Brown, quite
       naturally, Robeson keenly regretted the fact that while he was the
       same man in spirit, he could no longer, "hear the burden in the heat
       of the day." A song bird who can no longer sing, an eagle who can
       no longer soar, a Joshua too weak for any more battles - of course,

(Brown, Lloyd L.)

there was for him that kind of sadness, argues the author. He
concludes: "How fortunate we were to have had Paul Robeson walk
the earth among us! As artist and man he was a prophetic vision
of how wondrously beautiful the human race may yet become. Now
he belongs to the future."

1808.   Editorial. "Free At Last! Paul Robeson, 1898-1976," New York
Amsterdam News, January 31, 1976, p. A-4.

The editorial begins by stating that there is a certain type of
Black man in these United States with whom America's inperfected
Democracy has not yet learned how to deal. The type of man we
refer to is a Black man of great ability and great emotions, who,
unlike a Sidney Carton, is capable of their directed exercise and
who would rather walk tall in the darkness than to shuffle through
life in sunlight and safety. White America has never found it
difficult to recognize, and at times honor, Black men who are
willing to bow, scrape, and shuffle through life even though they
possessed talents which made this unnecessary. But white America
had steadfastly refused to give full credit and recognition to a
Black man who demands recognition on the basis of his performance
alone, states the editor. He continues to argue, such a man was
Paul Robeson, Phi Beta Kappa scholar, one of the world's greatest
bassos, two times all-American football player, a talented lawyer,
a world statesman - and more than all that - a charismatic leader
of Black people all over the world. White Americans couldn't locate
Robeson's Achilles heel, if he had one, so they invented one.
They branded him as a disloyal American and they used that to keep
him "in his place." But sophisticated Blacks knew, and have always
known, that the real reason whites would never pay full tribute to
Robeson was the fact that Paul would never bend, bow or scrape
to anybody. He just went on walking tall.... The editor also
compared Louis Armstrong to Paul Robeson and declared: "Yet while
Black people loved and admired the talents and artistry of Louis
Armstrong, they also knew that when it came to being the whole
man, Armstrong couldn't carry the brief case of Paul Robeson. But
Paul wouldn't shuffle for whites and so Armstrong was toasted
while Robeson was roasted...."

1809.   Hoggard, J. Clinton. "Don't Mourn for Me - But Live for Freedom's
Cause," Freedomways, Vol. 16, No. 1, First Quarter, 1976, pp. 15-
18.

The speaker, Presiding Prelate, Sixty Episcopal District of the
A.M.E. Zion Church, was a childhood friend of Paul Robeson. He
delivered the eulogy. This article presents excerpts from it.
He declares that Paul Robeson, singer, actor, peacemaker, human
rights activist and minority peoples' friend has joined the
immortals. The Bishop surmises that since in one's patience,
one possesses one's own soul, it can be truly said that Paul
learned how to be patient in adversity. He lived a long active
life until harrassment began to take its toll on his physical frame;
even so, he was comforted by words of long ago from his all-
famous performance of "Othello": "Good name in man or woman,

(Hoggard, J. Clinton)

dear, my lord, is the immediate jewel of their souls: Who steals
my purse, steal trash; 'tis something, nothing...."

1810. Howard, Juanita R. "Sadness in Dark Old Men," New York Amsterdam
News, January 28, 1978, p. D-11.

The writer discusses the views of her 81 year old grandfather and
other elderly Black men who knew or hear Paul Robeson. They along
with the author, mourned his death. These senior citizens silently
identified with Paul Robeson's agony - those who had so many
times been inspired by his courage - upon hearing of that great
man's death, might also be "feeling kind of lonely," argues the
writer.

1811. Jones, L. Clayton. "Let's Be Grateful that We Lived in His Time,"
New York Amsterdam News, January 31, 1976, pp. 1, 2.

The writer declares one watches with restrained anger as a nation
of hypocrites grudgingly acknowledges the passing of a twentieth
century phenomenon. Paul Robeson, All American athlete, Shakespearean actor, basso profundo, linguist, scholar, lawyer, activist.
He was all these things and more. I suspect, however, that the
essential Paul Robeson is to be found in the uses to which he
put his massive intellect. At bottom, he was an intellectual
activist possessed of impeccable academic credentials, declares
the writer. Mr. Jones surmises that Paul Robeson was a great
artist is indisputable. While the depth of his talents assured
his pre-eminence as an artist, it was the breadth of his commitment to the poor and disadvantaged of the world and the quality
of mind and character brought to bear on that commitment that
assures his stature as one of the few great men of our time. He
continues:
        Despite the opprobrium of a hysterical nation in the
        1950's, Paul Robeson never bowed. He knew exactly who
        he was and understood that his vision was too keen
        and far too broad for the minds of the parochial
        midgets who sought to cripple him. While most of us
        were seeing a Communist threat behind every closed
        door, Paul Robeson was viewing the world as an inter-
        dependent whole. He was twenty-five years ahead of
        us in advocating detente with the Soviet Union and
        lost his passport for it. He campaigned for a free
        and independent Africa and was stoned by a white mob
        in Peekskill. He protested the idiocy of American
        racism throughout the world and watched his income
        dwindle....

1812. Clarke, John Henrik. "Paul Robeson," Africa: International
Business, Economic and Political Magazine, No. 55, March, 1976,
pp. 68-69.

The writer declares that Paul Robeson was indeed more than an
artist, activist and freedom fighter: "The dimensions of his
talent made him our Renaissance man. He was the first American

(Clarke, John Henrik)

artist, Black or White, to realize that the role of the artist extends far beyond the stage and the concert hall. Early in his
life he became conscious of the plight of his people, stubbornly
surviving in a racist society. This was his window on the world.
From this vantage point he saw how the plight of his people related to the rest of humanity. He realized that the artist had
the power, and the responsibility to change the society in which
he lived," declares Clarke. The writer gives a biographical overview of Robeson's life. He concludes:
    Next to W.E.B. DuBois, Paul Robeson was the best
    example of an intellect who was active in his peoples'
    freedom struggle. Through this struggle both men
    committed themselves to the struggle to improve the
    lot of all mankind. Paul Robeson's thoughts in this
    matter is summed up in his book, Here I Stand....

1813. Wilmeth, Don B. "Paul Robeson: A Career Dedicated to the Human
       Spirit," Intellect, Vol. 104, No. 2375, May-June, 1976, p. 589.

The writer comments on the death of Paul Robeson. He declares that
Robeson possessed an overwhelming love of humanity and strong, un-
shakable convictions at a time when such beliefs from a Black
artist led to ostracism from Establishment quarters. He was misquoted and misinterpreted repeatedly and all but forgotten as a
speical talent and fighter for men's rights. His own profession
has assured that his memory will live on through the establishment
of the yearly Paul Robeson Citation. Robeson should be remembered
by all as more than a consummate artist. It was pointed out
"....Robeson was one of those 'who brought selflessness and brotherhood to fellow black men and women' and demonstrated a rare courage
of conviction as an example to all people."

9. FEDERAL BUREAU OF INVESTIGATION

1814. Johnson, J.J. "Was FBI Involved in Attempts to Kill Paul Robeson?,"
       Daily World, October 25, 1979, p. 11.

The author states that Paul Robeson was the object of intense
harrassment by the FBI, CIA, U.S. State Department and other government agencies for 36 years. He declares that circumstantial
evidence suggests that the FBI had full knowledge of several
attempts to take the life of Paul Robeson. It was pointed out
in this article by Paul Robeson, Jr., that after going over about
3,500 documents from the FBI, he found that there were at least
four occasions, 1946, 1955, and twice in 1958, when cars in which
his father was being transported were sabotaged. Both the cars and
drivers in each case were under FBI surveillance, suggests
Mr. Johnson.

10. FILMS

1815. Cripps, Thomas R. "The Myth of the Southern Box Office: A Factor
       in Racial Sterotyping in American Movies, 1920-1940," The Black
       Experience in America: Selected Essays. Austin: University
       of Texas Press, 1970, pp. 120, 125, 129, 134, 136, 143.

       Various references are made to Robeson throughout this article.
       It was pointed out that such famous individual Blacks as Paul
       Robeson took up the cause against state laws allowing theatre
       segregation by swing them, night clubs and other facilities for
       racial indignities while whites joined in. The author also states
       that Paul Robeson drew praise from the white trade papers for
       his role in "Body and Soul."

1816. Cripps, Thomas. "Paul Robeson and Black Identity in American
       Movies," Massachusetts Reviews, Vol. 11, Summer, 1970, pp. 468-
       485.

       The author argues that more than any other single figure, Paul
       Robeson accepted as a personal responsibility the problem of
       bridging the gap between the "race movies" of the ghettos and
       the commercial movies of Hollywood. In a dozen films, most
       of them produced outside of Hollywood, he attempted to create
       strong Black characters who provided important elements of plots
       rather than merely backgrounds for predominant white stories.
       That he eventually failed is a testament to the intransigence of
       the system of commercial movies rather than a sign of his own
       lack of will or effort, states Cripps. He also declares:
           If any black man should have been capable of such
           a feat it must be Robeson. Unlike any other black
           performer, he came to the medium "pre-sold." He
           had been an All-American football player at Rutgers,
           and following his graduation from Columbia Law School,
           had embarked upon a glamorous apprenticeship with
           Eugene O'Neill's Provincetown Players. His formidable
           credentials from other media gave Robeson the inde-
           pendence that should have allowed some freedom of
           choice. No other Negro actor could say the same.
           What mark has Robeson's career left? His intended
           bridge between "race movies," experimental cinema, and
           Hollywood was a failure, but it was the monopolistic
           studios' failure -- not Robeson's. His career was an
           experiment whose results have only recently led to
           change. He demonstrated that the most poorly con-
           trived low-budget black "race movie" created black
           characters that blind, rigid, Hollywoodians have
           yet to see. In a day when little else was possible
           his focus on the black psyche at least kept alive the
           possibility of an eventual black cinema. He also
           helped open the way, even in his own day, to better
           roles for less controversial figures such as Clarence
           Muse, Joel Fluellen, and Rex Ingram. And he provided
           living proof that athletes and stars from other media

(Cripps, Thomas)

might be used to introduce Negroes to the screen.
Athletes such as Joe Louis, Kenny Washington, and
Woody Strode and singers such as Harry Belafonte and
Sammy Davis owed part of their beginnings to Robeson.
He also kept alive the willingness to experiment
that has led finally to such efforts as the filming
of Leroi Jones' "The Dutchman," like Robeson's films,
shot in England and outside of the major studios;
and Gordon Parks' "The Learning Tree."

1817.   Kagan, Norman. "The Return of 'The Emperor Jones," Negro History
Bulletin, Vol. 34, No. 7, November, 1971, pp. 160-162.

The author discusses the movie "The Emperor Jones" and the role
Paul Robeson played in it. The writer points out that when Robeson made "The Emperor Jones" he was "still hopeful that he could
help his people with his films." Several reviews in this article
praised Robeson's acting ability in the film.

1818.   Bogle, Donald. "Transcending Racist Trash: A Legacy of The First
Black Movie Stars," Saturday Review of the Arts, Vol. 1, No. 2,
February 2, 1973, p. 25.

The writer declares that Paul Robeson was one of the greatest
American actors. He suggests that Robeson was the only American
Black star of the 1930's to work in foreign pictures, in which
he thought he could escape type-casting. The foreign movies,
however, like his Hollywood feature films ("Show Boat" and "Tales
of Manhattan" among others), seldom met with his approval. Robeson accepted a picture always with the hope that it would
"elevate" the state of his people: after completing a role, he
would discover that, if anything, his talents had been exploited,
states Bogle. The writer concludes:
    Robeson's greatest contribution to Black film history --
    and the aspect of his work that most disturbed white
    American movie-goers -- is his proudly defiant port-
    rait of the Black man in "The Emperor Jones," his
    best-known film. Robeson portrays Brutus Jones, a
    Black man who refuses to be subservient. An arrogant,
    strong-willed braggart, he rises from Pullman porter
    to autocrat. In one particularly effective scene on
    a railroad car Robeson goes through the stock "Yes,
    sirs" and "No, sirs" with his white employers, but
    he is so full of energy and self-mockery that his be-
    havior is not at all self-demeaning. Later, when he
    mocks his white employer for the benefit of his
    Black woman, Robeson epitomizes a Black man asserting
    himself, consciously cutting the Man down to size.
    Today, as we sit in theaters and watch Jim Brown or
    James Earl Jones or Poitier walking tall with eyes
    straight forward, we think of the young Robeson. Now
    seventy-four (in 1973) and an invalid, he, too, must
    know that his influence on other Black actors has been
    incalculable.

1819. "Briefs on The Arts: 2 Robeson Films Off Festival List," <u>New</u>
       <u>York Times</u>, April 7, 1973, p. 38.

       According to this article, two films starring Paul Robeson joined
       the list of motion pictures withdrawn from the American Film In-
       stitude festival, in protest of its cancellation of Constantin
       Costa-Gavras' "State of Seige." George Stevens, Jr., the Film
       Institute's director said he would bow to the wishes of Paul
       Robeson, Jr., who represented his father, in withdrawing "The
       Emperor Jones," and "Song of Freedom." Mr. Stevens said that the
       Robeson films had been scheduled at the Kennedy Center in
       Washington as a birthday tribute to the actor and singer, who
       would be 75, the day the films were to be shown. The director
       said "it would not be appropriate to show them against his wishes."

1820. Weaver, Harold D., Jr. "Paul Robeson and Film: Racism and Anti-
       Racism in Communications," <u>Negro History Bulletin</u>, Vol. 37, No. 1,
       January, 1974, pp. 204-206.

       The author divided this article into two parts. The first gives a
       general examination of his multi-faceted life and serves to in-
       troduce the reader to some of his contributions and achievements.
       The second major subdivision, the bulk of this presentation,
       examined the relationship of Robeson's involvement in film and
       with other interests of his life. Major attention was given to
       film (1) as an expression of Robeson's anti-colonial efforts and
       (2) as a catalyst to Robeson's initial exposure to the Soviet
       Union, an exposure which was to have a significant impact on
       Robeson as a man and as a public figure. The writer declares that
       it might be appropriate to mention two widespread, but false,
       myths that exist about Robeson and the USSR: (1) <u>He has never</u>
       <u>been a member of the Communist Party</u>, joining only one political
       organization his entire life, the Council of African Affairs
       (which he co-funded and which concerned itself with African
       liberation from colonialism and imperialism before being politically
       smeared into oblivion); (2) <u>He did not exile himself to the USSR</u>,
       but was, in fact, kept from leaving the United States for eight
       years;his extended residence abroad was in England. In con-
       clusion, "The essence of Robeson's evolution as a man can be seen
       in his changing the lyrics of Oscar Hammerstein's 'Ol' Man River.'
       Early in his artistic career Robeson was to sing it as written:
       You get a little drunk and you lands in jail, I gets weary and
       sick of tryin', I'm scared of livin' and feared of dyin'. His
       later message to the world's oppressed, with whom he identified
       and to the oppressor, for whom he had scorn, is summed up by the
       significant changes: You show a little grit and you'll land in
       jail. I must keep fightin' until I'm dyin'. He dared assert
       his manhood and that of his people. That is how Robeson responded
       to racism, whether it be in the classroom, on the football field,
       in the political arena, on the stage, in the concert hall, or on
       the screen," declares Weaver.

1821. Murray, Jim. "Paul Robeson's Film Career," New York Amsterdam
       News, January 31, 1976, pp. 1, 2.

       The writer states that Paul Robeson was involved in the film in-
       dustry for some 12 years, between 1930 and 1942 and as much as he
       was acclaimed as an actor, he also became equally respected as
       one who made his feelings about the persistent injustices known
       to the world. Robeson was an actor who participated reluctantly,
       and while he is perhaps guilty of accepting at least one demeaning
       role ("Tales of Manhattan"), he has to be credited for the many
       others which he rejected outright, states Mr. Murray. A second
       significant fact about his career is reflected in the artist's
       fame overseas. Robeson was able to work in the British film in-
       dustry with far greater success than he ever did in the United
       States. Mr. Murray concludes: "...To his credit, Paul Robeson
       lived another 36 years, but 'Tales of Manhattan' was the last time
       he ever had anything to do with Hollywood."

1822. Harrell, Alfred D. "Film's Early Black Auteurs," Encore, Vol. 6,
       No. 17, September 12, 1977, p. 36.

       The writer states that the University of Pennsylvania's Annenbury
       Center, in a special program headed by Oliver Franklin, sponsored
       the annual comprehensive Paul Robeson International Film Festival,
       a Showcase for independent American Black filmmakers. He also
       surmises that Oscar Micheaux, a newspaper writer and novelist,
       introduced Paul Robeson in "Body and Soul" (1925), not a fore-
       runner of the 1947 boxing film, states the writer.

1823. Johnson, Helen Armstead. "Paul Robeson: On Stage," First World,
       Vol. 2, No. 1, Spring, 1978.

       The writer declares that even a brief consideration of Robeson the
       performer should touch upon the following things: His entrance
       into and the highlights of the world of entertainment and theatre;
       his attitudes toward his work and himself; Black perceptions of
       the relationship between his theatrical roles and race; and,
       finally, the universal man. She discusses those things in this
       article. The author concludes:
           In retrospect Robeson's dramatic roles seem to have
           been linked randomly by theme: the Black leader -
           usually tribal - and a white love interest. This was
           certainly true from the beginning and the end: "Taboo"
           and "Othello." Although Robeson seemed to confirm the
           myth that Blacks are natural-born actors, he rose
           majestically above both myth and technique. On stage,
           with great personal dignity and a keenly sensed sin-
           cerity of spirit, he made people "hear the whisperings
           in their buried memories." Moreover, he undeniably
           played "thrillingly upon the nerves and knocked at the
           hearts of people everywhere." Whenever Paul Robeson
           stood before a mirror, he saw the universal man in
           whom he beieved so deeply.

1824. Schlosser, Anatol. "Paul Robeson in Film: An Iconoclast's
       Quest for a Role," Paul Robeson: The Great Forerunner. Editors of
       Freedomways. New York: Dodd, Mead & Co., 1978, pp. 72-86.

The writer argues: "The story of Paul Robeson as an actor in
motion pictures is the story of a quest; a quest for roles in which
he could portray the culture and the humanness of his people.
The story is one of struggle to maintain his dignity as a Negro
and his integrity as a Negro artist. To reach these objectives
he had to overcome an American film industry that pereptuated a
racial stereotype of the Negro, and a British film industry that
promulgated a colonial vision of Africa," states the author. The
author suggests that Robeson as an actor in theatre and film
was confronted with the choice that faced all Negro performers.
Is the choice to play a role that one considers less than worthy
a private or a public one? For years the Negro performer was
content to get any role, much less a starring one. But somewhere
along the way, Robeson, and many other artists, came to understand
that the choice involved a responsibility to himself, not only as
an artist, but to himself as a Negro, and to his people, states
the author. Schlosser concludes: "Robeson made the choice, one
that helped him grow as a person, as an artist, and one that
helped his people."

1825. Edelman, Rob. "Paul Robeson: A Forgotten Renaissance Man,"
       Films in Review, Vol. 30, No. 6, June/July, 1979, pp. 321-331.

The writer asserts: "Paul Robeson is a legendary American, one
of the few true Renaissance men of the 20th century. An actor,
singer, scholar, athlete, and political activist, Robeson could
dominate a stage or concert hall like the sun radiating its rays
across the land on a hot summer day. His rich baritone voice
was resonant and melodic. He enraptured his audiences with his
talent -- despite the color of his skin." Mr. Edelman argues, in
part:
       Had Robeson been born white, or had he been born in a
       more tolerant era, every school child in America
       would speak his name along with Muhammad Ali's and
       Martin Luther King's. But he was a Black man who
       reached his maturity at a time when Negroes were con-
       signed to the back of the bus, third-class citizens
       in a white-dominated society. He was once asked if
       those of his race should ignore the brutality that
       was inherent to racial prejudice. 'If someone hit me
       on the cheek," he defiantly responded, "I'd try to
       tear his head off before he could hit me on the other
       one." Many considered Paul Robeson too "uppity"; he
       was doomed to be stifled by the climate of his times.
There are several photos of Robeson from several of his movies as
well as a "Paul Robeson Filmography." In addition to the 11 films
listed there are 3 documentaries that Robeson narrated and recorded
the prologue and the films' theme songs.

11. FREEDOM FIGHTER

1826. McBrown, Gertrude Parthenia. "Paul Robeson: World Renowned
       Actor, Singer and Scholar," Negro History Bulletin, Vol. 33, No. 5,
       May, 1970, pp. 128-129.

       The author declares: "Although we are often prone to dwell on the
       contributions of Paul Robeson as Actor, Singer, Scholar and
       Athlete, the actual strength of the man as a great human being
       centers around his basic principles of justice for all mankind
       and particularly a shift from the stand he took at the beginning
       of his career. I can hear him saying over and over, 'With all
       the energy at my command, I fight for the rights of the Negro
       people and other oppressed labor-driven Americans to have a decent
       home, decent job and the dignity that belongs to every human being."
       Paul Robeson is the symbol of dignity, always looking up with his
       head high. I remember him quoting a verse at playwright Lorraine
       Hansberry's funeral, a part of which reads - 'Sometimes I feel
       like an eagle in the air; an eagle in the air.' He concludes with
       'As Lorraine says farewell, she bids up keep our heads high and
       to hold on to our strength and powers to soar like an eagle.'"
       She concludes: "Paul Robeson holds his head high and soars like
       the eagle. This is his right. He says when questioned about
       living under the unfair American system, 'I'm staying here be-
       cause my father was a slave and my people died to build this
       country and I'm going to stay here and have a part of it just
       like you.' Yes, Paul Robeson, great soul that you are, you and
       your parents are part of our PROUD HERITAGE."

1827. "Robeson Did Most to Herald Black Plight, Says Sociologist," Jet,
       June 3, 1971, p. 49.

       Speaking at the Rutgers University Student Center, Joyce Ladner,
       noted Black sociologist declares that most Black intellectuals
       step to a different drummer, but that none had called the plight
       of the Negro to the attention of America as Paul Robeson. She
       suggests that Robeson cried for justice, freedom and happiness,
       which is the authentic protest of the Negro. Dr. Ladner concludes
       that men like Robeson give so much to their beliefs to change
       society, but are destroyed because others fail to heed their call.

1828. Editorial. "Paul Robeson: The Great Forerunner," Freedomways,
       Vol. II, No. 1, First Quarter, 1971, p. 5.

       The editors state that Paul Robeson, the man, has become a legend
       in his own time. Yet his personal Odyssey is inseparable from the
       life and struggles of the Afro-American community and the monu-
       mental changes which have taken place in the world over the last
       half-century. They declare that Robeson's experiences and his
       contributions need to be seriously studied for the rich meaning
       they hold for the present period. As the racist military adventure
       in Southeast Asia spreads and the casualties mount once again
       pushing the world dangerously close to a nuclear third world war,
       we are reminded that it was Paul Robeson, as an internationally

(Freedomways)

recognized champion of world peace among the nations, whose voice
was raised to "bring the troops home from Korea two decades ago,"
declares the writer. They conclude:
As our Movement gathers strength to turn back the
Nixon-Agnew repression, we are reminded that Robeson
was an early target of McCarthyism and a symbol of
the fight back spirit, the right to hold "controversial" opinions, during the Eisenhower-Nixon years.
And as the rank and file of labor go to battle in
the strike struggles ahead, among the longshoremen,
western ore miners and others in the basic industries
there are many who remember Paul as concert artist
who identified with and inspired them by his presence
on the picket lines and in the union halls.

1829.   Mitchell, Loften.   "Time to Break the Silence Surrounding Paul
Robeson," New York Times, August 6, 1972, Arts and Leisure Section,
pp. 1, 7.

The writer states that Robeson was one of those who brought selflessness and brotherhood to fellow Black men and women. Mitchell
concludes: "This amazing man, this great intellect, this magnificent genius with his overwhelming love of humanity is a devas-
tating challenge to a society built on hypocrisy, greed and profit-
seeking at the expense of common humanity. A curtain of silence
had to be brought down on him. He had to be kept off TV, maligned
and omitted from the history books. Perhaps if we begin to lift
the curtain of silence surrounding the accomplishments of Paul
Robeson, we may begin to walk down the road toward nationhood
and equality."

1830.   Audrey, James.   "The Real Forerunner in Civil Rights," National
Scene Magazine, Supplement. Vol. 1, No. 13, November-December,
1972, pp. 3-4

The essence of this article was that although many Blacks and
Whites have not heard of Paul Robeson, he was a forerunner in
the civil rights for Blacks and others before most modern civil
rights leaders were even born. Many believe that it is only
during recent times that Black leaders have marched and protested
for Blacks' rights. Yet, Robeson was leading the fight and
marching for Blacks' Civil Rights in the 1930s, 1940s, and 1950s.

1831.   Lewis, Claude.   "Salute to a Man They Couldn't Put Down," Philadelphia Sunday Bulletin, April 15, 1973, pp. 1, 7.

The writer points out that Paul Robeson's name is still (1973)
important in England where he is revered as one of the greatest
performers of all time. And in Russia, where he is still (1973)
recognized today for his artistry and his humanity, and in France
for his intellect, and in Germany for his courage and commitment
to his ideals. He surmises that it is at home in America that
he is recognized more for his "rabble-rousing and troublemaking"
than for his massive talents. Mr. Claude observes: "He is being

(Lewis, Claude)

honored more for his outspokenness on behalf of black people for three decades than for his competence and ability as a performer." He concludes: "Paul Robeson is a name from the distant past. A past tainted by a national effort to dishonor and contain him. It was an effort that almost succeeded but that is finally doomed to failure because of those who remember, and because of those who refuse to condemn him for speaking out against the grim and evil practices of his own nation...."

1832. Editorial. "Lest We Forget...," New York Amsterdam News, April 21, 1973, p. A-4.

The editor declares that Paul Robeson was the only athlete designated as a college All-American for two consecutive years who has not been admitted to the college football hall of fame. He was a Phi Beta Kappa scholar from Rutgers University; a lawyer, a graduate of Columbia Law School. Paul Robeson's son has said that it is time to lift the curtain of silence surrounding his father. We agree, states the editor. Too many of us may have forgotten that for almost eight years Robeson was under virtual house arrest in this country. The United States government had cancelled his passport. Booking agencies and managers and owners of concert halls tried to impose a black-out on Robeson's performing artistry, declares the writer. He concludes:
> The time has come for Black Americans to define Paul Robeson on their terms within the context of both the current and historical Black experience. On this basis, it could be said that Paul Robeson is our living Nat Turner. Like a rebellious slave he defied the chains and shackles which American racism tried to place upon him....

1833. Killens, John O. "Wanted: Some Black Long Distance Runners," Black Scholar, Vol. 5, No. 3, November, 1973, pp. 2-7.

He states that Paul Robeson was a great long distance runner of this century. Killens told Robeson, "Brother Paul, to every black artist with a heart or memory, you are the Big Daddy...." "And yet some of our young folk do not know Big Paul, the athletic, intellectual, artistic, masculine giant and genius of the Twentieth Century. We need our heroes desparately," concludes the author.

1834. Cheng, Charles W. "The Cold War: Its Impact on the Black Liberation Struggle Within the United States," Freedomways, Vol. 13, No. 3, Third Quarter, 1973, Part I, pp. 184-199.

Various references are made to Paul Robeson. There is an excerpt from Robeson's book, Here I Stand: "Indeed, before the 'cold war' brought about a different atmosphere, those broader interests of mine were considered by many Negroes to be quite admirable; and when in 1944, I was honored by the NAACP with the Spingarn Medal my activities on behalf of 'freedom for all men' were said to be a special contribution I had made." The writer also declares that the positions of the CIO, the NAACP, leaders like Randolph, and

(Cheng, Charles W.)

the defeat of Benjamin Davis, as a city Councilman in New York
City, represented a temper of the times. He concludes: "A
temper that did much to promote the persecution of two of the
giants in the black liberation struggle, Paul Robeson and W.E.B.
DuBois...."

1835. Crockett, George W. "Paul Robeson: True Revolutionary," Freedomways, Vol. 13, No. 3, First Quarter, 1973, pp. 10-13.

The writer declares that Paul Robeson's Americanism will long out-
live the lies and slanders of those evil men who feared the people.
Because Paul Robeson was of the people. He worked with them, performed for them and fought for them. All of them, all over the
world. "Especially the people, especially the people," he sang,
"that's America to me." He argues: "...But history does not
apologize for its unspeakable crimes, nor does it make amends for
its mindless cruelties. It is for us, the inheritors, to inscribe
in the pages of history for all to see the full truth of the full
meaning of Paul Robeson. Robeson -- the revolutionary." Judge
Crockett also declares: "Yes, a revolutionary in the true sense
of the word. He was appalled by the status quo. He exposed the
sins of our times. He struggled for change. He gave his boundless energies and his superb gifts freely, but most of all to
those who were fighting for change -- to the unions, to the anti-
fascist, to the youth and to the struggle for black power. May his
revolutionary fervor live on. Each of us, in our own life, in
our own heart, in our own yearning has a special place and a
special gratitude for the man we honor tonight. I know what the
richness of his presence has meant to me. I know hundreds of
people in the city in which I live who remember, who are grateful
to him, and who love him."

1836. Editorial. "Paul Robeson," Freedomways, Vol. 13, No. 1, First
Quarter, 1973, pp. 5-7.

The editors state: "Given the personal magnetism and achievements
of Paul Robeson; the talented individual, it is possible to overlook or underrate the significance of Paul Robeson the historical
figure, the activist Robeson with a vision of human society and its
development. The special significance of Paul Robeson, the
historical figure, is that he clearly understood the epoch in which
we live. It is the epoch in which the Socialist world community,
its ideals and examples of material and cultural progress is the
ascendant influence in the lives of the majority of the world's
peoples." In his book, Here I Stand, published in 1958, Robeson
wrote: "My deep conviction is that for all mankind a socialist
society represents and advances to a higher stage of life that
it is a form of society which is economically, socially, culturally,
and ethnically superior to a system based upon production for private profit." The editorial concludes:
          Robeson, the man and historical figure, was not only
          Black, gifted and militant, a tact admirably expressed
          by the venerable Black educator Mary McLeod Bethune when
          she called him "the tallest tree in our forest." More

(Freedomways)

than this, Paul Robeson was one of a mere handful of
prominent public personalities who deeply understood
and fully identified with the revolutionary changes
taking place in the world. It is a source of much
happiness for us that Paul Robeson has lived to see
the day that his perspective of 1958 is increasingly
becoming an important part of the scientific social
thought of the Freedom Movement in these troubled
times. We proudly and affectionately salute him as
the greatest living American."

1837.   "For Paul Robeson on his 75th Birthday," New World Review, Vol. 41,
No. 2, Second Quarter, 1973, pp. 44-46, 50-52.

The editorial declares, in part: "The editors and staff of New
World Review join the many thousands of people throughout the world
expressing homage and love to you, dear Paul, in this period of
celebration. We salute you for that glorious voice which has
sounded the tocsin of the freedom struggle everywhere, and brought
beauty and joy wherever it rang out. We salute you for your warm
humanity, for your enduring contributions to the cause of the
liberation of the Black people, of all the oppressed and exploited,
of all the world's people. We ourselves feel special gratitude
for the help you have given our magazine over the years, expressing
in our pages your unswerving support for the socialist lands,
deepening understanding of their role in the world through your
own experiences, your often repeated statements such as 'I was,
I am and always will be a true friend of the Soviet people and
the Union of Soviet Socialist Republics' and 'Here, for the first
time, I walked in human dignity.' Your life and work have helped
create that better world for which we strive. You have enriched
our lives of generations to come. Your impact on these times
will endure forever....'"

1838.   Crowley, James. "Witch Hunters Haunted Paul Robeson...And Robbed
America of a Great Talent," Philadelphia Inquirer, January 27,
1974, pp. 8-I, 12-I.

The writer declares that Paul Robeson was destroyed not because
he is Paul Robeson, the singer of songs, the toast of the whole
civilized world, the theatre's greatest "Emperor Jones" and the
star of other Broadway and Hollywood hits, but in spite of this.
He was destroyed because he is a symbol and most threatening of
all, an articulate symbol. He was an articulate symbol of all
races and all creeds struggling for some of the rights and
privileges of the unoppressed. Mr. Crowley concludes: "He was
and is a symbol, moreover, and a black one at that, who would
not let his own great material rewards blind him to the material
and spiritual privation of others. And this was his worst
'crime.'"

1839. Neal, Steven. "The Resurrection of Paul Robeson," Philadelphia
       Inquirer, March 10, 1974, pp. 10-12, 14, 16, 18.

       The article declares that Paul Robeson was now living with his
       sister behind the drawn curtains of a dingy West Philadelphia row-
       house. He called Paul Robeson a great man who fought for the
       equality of all men and especially Black people for more than forty
       years. Mr. Neal recalls that part of Robeson's decline was
       virtually anit-Communist attacks on him. Inspite of those attacks,
       surmises Mr. Neal, Paul Robeson did his share to help better con-
       ditions for mankind. He also gives an overview of Robeson's career.
       The reporter suggests that it is past time for people to know of
       Robeson's contributions to mankind.

1840. Stone, Chuck. "Paul Robeson, 76 a T. tan," Philadelphia Daily
       News, April, 1974.

       The writer points out that Paul Robeson was 76 years old on April
       9th. The essence of this tribute was that although Robeson is
       no longer active on the stage or in the movies, or in the civil
       and political rights movements, he "paid his dues." He spoke
       out against injustices in the world and especially in the United
       States long before it was popular.

1841. Editorial. "Paul Robeson," Chicago Defender, January 26, 1976,
       p. 12.

       The editor declares that few men or women have contributed more
       to the cause of freedom than Paul Robeson. His was a multi-
       faced crusade in which he lifted his voice in songs, in speeches,
       against the ceaseless tide of oppression and systematic denial
       of political options. For fully a quarter of a century, Robeson's
       name was a household word. His ingenuity was reflected in many
       dimensions. His brilliant performance in Shakespeare's stirring
       tragedy, Othello, heightened his reputation as a man of many
       talents. But it was in the arena of the struggle for racial
       justice and equity where Robeson stood as a towering figure against
       the landscape of social injustice. His crusading zeal extended
       far beyond local geography. He remained throughout his life a
       strict and impassioned advocate of human rights, surmises the
       writer. He concludes:
             Robeson was virtually stripped of his citizenship for
             his amity with the Soviet Union where he was hailed
             as a hero and a great humanitarian. Because he was a
             dissenter who had the courage to state his convictions
             openly and forthrightly, Robeson was driven into
             isolation and sepulchral silence. Now that he is dead,
             white America is singing his praise as a great American
             whose "voice enriched the culture from which it grew
             and the lives of all who heard it." Of course, Robeson
             was a great American. To praise him at his graveside
             is a post-mortem recognition that exposes a congenital
             myopia which has stunted America's intellectual growth.
             Be that as it may, Paul Robeson now belongs to history and
             his soul, like that of John Brown's goes marching on....

1842. Davis, Ossie. "Paul Robeson - A Power That Bigots Feared," New
       York Amsterdam News, January 31, 1976, pp. A-1, A-2.

       The actor surmises: "...Paul knew and said a simple truth which
       is at once the key to our freedom and the explanation of why we
       are still unfree: white power is built to a great degree in this
       country and in the world on the absence of Black power - the two
       go together - they fit like hand in glove. It is therefore ab-
       solutely essential if white European-American capitalist power is
       to preserve its place on the top of the heap that Blacks and Reds
       and Yellow people be kept as much as possible in a continuing
       position of powerlessness." Mr. Davis asserts that Paul saw this
       and fought against it with all his might. He called for and ex-
       emplified Black folks, Yellow folks, Red folks, poor folks and
       working folks to rise up and take power. He was a walking,
       talking, one-man revolution and the fear in the hearts of the
       white establishment was that if Black people were to begin lis-
       tening to Paul Robeson they might begin also insisting on their
       own Black share of world resources, our share of living space,
       of jobs, and of security in America. And, to the white power
       structure that is impossible - in their view, there simply isn't
       enough to go around, surmises Mr. Davis. The writer concludes:
           ....It is as impossible to keep an idea in jail as
           it is to put music in a bottle - to think that because
           Robeson is in a coffin that he is dead. Not so, my
           man! Robeson is in our hearts as well as our dreams.
           The world has not yet heard the last of this big Black
           man, and will not until what he fought for - a world
           where everybody has an equal chance to be judged
           according to his talent....

1843. Walker, William O. "Paul Robeson: A Martyr for a Cause," Call
       and Post, January 31, 1976, pp. 1, 4.

       The publisher of this newspaper asserts that the death announce-
       ment of Paul, will have little if any meaning to the young people
       whose musical taste and style includes none of the superb musical
       talents of this man. Neither will his passing cast much of a
       ripple in the world of present day college and professional foot-
       ball players, although Paul Robeson was a pioneer in this sport.
       Many actors will pay scant attention to Robeson's death notice,
       yet, no Black actor on the scene today has equaled the heights
       attained on the American or European stage that Robeson did.
       The civil rights movement with its roots in the fifties and sixties,
       does not record the name of Paul Robeson along with that of Martin
       Luther King, Whitney Young and Malcolm X and others, but Paul was
       paving the way for them when the risk and danger was much greater
       because the battle lines within the race had not then been formed
       or identified. Paul Robeson, by any standards of measurement
       on any facet of racial struggle, was a great man, states the
       publisher. The publisher declares:
           While I was visiting the Paul Robeson Junior High
           School in East Berlin, Germany, last May, a girl
           student was asked what did she want to be when she
           grew up. She readily replied: "like Paul Robeson."
           I think this is the greatest tribute any person can

(Walker, William O.)

pay to the sainted memory of Paul Robeson. What
Paul Robeson was trying to do 25 years ago in
establishing friendship with Russia, U.S. Secretary of
State Henry Kissinger is now bending his every effort
to achieve. Yet Paul was condemned, while Kissinger
is praised. Through most of his life, the thinking
and deeds of Paul Robeson were much ahead of his
time....

1844. Weusi, Msemaji. "Paul Robeson: A Giant Among Men," Black News,
Vol. 3, No. 6, January, 1976, p. 22.

The writer states that if any of their readers are under thirty
years of age, the chances are that they have never heard of Paul
Robeson. That is because the power structure and white news media
did a monumental job of applying the "silent treatment" as the
best and possibly only way of stilling the powerful enticing
voice of this courageous Black man who was the forerunner to
Malcolm, King, Rap and Muhammad. Not having a Black/Afrikan
Nationalist publication in those days to "teach hard" about our
warriors and heroes, the racist white press' "silent treatment"
(the omission of any and all news about this outspoken and most
active Brother) certainly accomplished its task. As a consequence,
much of the Brother's verbal indictment of this country's brutal
treatment of Black people and his varied efforts to mobilize
Black people were unknown by many of us. The writer states:
"We at BLACK NEWS pledge that such a sabatoge will never happen
again! Our pages will be used to describe the activities and ex-
tol the virtues of every Brother or Sister on the planet earth
who's making an outstanding contribution to the Black man's
struggle for complete liberation and self-determination! "
According to the writer, although Paul Robeson had "made it" and
could have remained famous, very wealthy and allowed himself to
be the token negro, he refused to keep silent in the face of
genocide treatment of Black people by this country and raised his
mighty voice, all around the stages of the world to denounce such
treatment....

1845. Johnson, Robert E. "Paul Robeson: Fearless Foe of White Racism,"
Jet, Vol. 49, No. 9, February 12, 1976, pp. 16-20.

In this article, the author attempts to close the information gap
that exists between Robeson's generation and today's Black youth.
The writer states that for his words and his deeds, America -
especially Black America - is better off, and everyone knows it.
It was also stated that Robeson refused to let his extraordinary
success be used to explain away the oppression of millions of
Black Americans. More than that, declares Paul Robeson, Jr., he
used his success and his immense prestige and talents as weapons
in an all-out struggle against that oppression....

1846. "Paul Robeson: A Man Before His Time," Philadelphia Tribune,
       February 14, 1976, p. 11.

       This article states that Paul Robeson was a man before his time.
       He recognized the evil of racism, he began early to speak out
       against Jim Crow and racial oppression even during his recitals.
       It was also asserted that was great primarily because of his un-
       deviating integrity and wide range of talents. When he died, the
       world lost a great citizen, concludes the article.

1847. Weusi, Kasisi Jitu. "Paul Robeson: The Giant," Black News, Vol.
       3, No. 7, February, 1976, pp. 7-8.

       The writer argues that while a lot of our folks were still sound
       asleep listening to Amos & Andy, Beulah, and gang fighting, Paul
       Robeson was standing tall, a Black man being an international
       image of our struggle. He was an outstanding singer and per-
       forming artist. He had superior mentality. He understood that
       being an African, born and reared in the wilderness of racist,
       capitalist, America that these attributes were not enough unless
       he was first politically a man. So Paul stood tall and told it
       like it was and called the U.S. what it actually was for his
       peoples. For this he paid the price, states the writer....
       He also surmises:
           We can only really and truly admire Paul Robeson when
           we measure his position against the modern day Black
           stars. Look at Wilt Chamberlain, Kareem Abdul
           Jabbar, Sammy Davis, Harry Belafonte or Sidney
           Poitier. Here are 5 internationally known Blacks who
           are constantly in the spotlight as a result of their
           prowess in sports and entertainment. But when have
           you heard any of them speak about the conditions of
           racism and exploitation that ravage our people, young
           and old even today. They are afriad and so they keep
           their mouths shut, make money and allow "the man" to
           continue to castrate them in the process. Paul
           Robeson not only spoke out but also made it quite
           clear that he would not retract his statement "not
           even one thousandth of an inch...."

1848. "Guest Editorials: 'Paul Robeson,' January 23, 1976," Crisis,
       Vol. 83, No. 3, March, 1976, pp. 77-78.

       Three editorials from the pages of the Washington Post, New York
       Amsterdam News and New York Times are included as guests. All
       three newspapers praised Paul Robeson and said in essence, that
       he was a Black man that stood up for his principles and walked
       tall.

1849. Smith, Jessica. New World Review, Vol. 44, No. 2, March-April,
       1976, pp. 3-4.

       The writer states that Paul Robeson's whole life was a great song
       of liberation that will ring out until all the peoples of the
       earth are free. All of Paul's energies, his art, his love of
       people and hatred of their exploiters, his whole passionate being -

(Smith, Jessica)

all were utterly devoted to the liberation of the Black and colored peoples, of the working class, of the repressed and wretched of the earth, of people everywhere striving toward the sun, argues Smith. She concludes: "In Paul's beloved name, let us pledge ourselves anew to find (US-USSR Detente) that way!"

1850. Bassett, Ted. "Paul Robeson: A Giant Among Giants," Political Affairs, Vol. 55, No. 4, April, 1976, pp. 26-31.

The author states that the life and struggles of the late Paul Robeson, towering giant among giants and pre-eminent citizen of the United States and the world, has left an indelible mark on the cause of progressive humankind. Bassett discusses Robeson's accomplishments. He concludes: "Robeson is gone but his legacy remains. His marching songs are deathless. They will echo in the hearts of humanity through the ages."

1851. "Be Like Robeson - Trudeau," Canadian Tribune, June 7, 1976.

Trudeau, Canadian Prime Minister sent a message to the Fourth Annual Nation Black Awards Presentation. He urged Black Canadians "to follow in the tradition of Paul Robeson who...is best known for his dedication to the improvement of society and his loyalty to his convictions."

1852. Patterson, William L. "Paul Robeson - There He Stood," New World Review, Vol. 44, No. 6, November-December, 1976, pp. 10-13.

The writer declares: "There he stood together with other makers of history, actively, tirelessly and fearlessly proclaiming his credo, his unalterable belief in the revolutionary termination of progressive mankind's struggle to end for all time 'man's exploitation and repression of his fellow man and woman.' He was an inseparable part of that struggle in all its ramifications. He was an artist, an artist of social revolution and an artist seeking a profound, and lasting change in the order of society, one of the seekers of and for peace - world peace," surmises Patterson. He concludes:
    In the United Nations all Soviet Union and other
    socialist countries and all the progressive forces
    are making a determined fight against racism and for
    peace. Paul Robeson has departed but millions of
    youth of every creed and color will take his stand
    for peace and an end to racism. These are historic
    tasks. Blacks will play no bit part on this historic
    stage....

1853. Pope, Marcella. "Paul Robeson," New World Review, Vol. 44, No. 6, November-December, 1976, p. 12.

This was an excerpt from her address to the Paul Robeson Memorial Meeting, held in Washington, D.C., April 30, 1976. She declares: "Paul Robeson the athlete, the scholar, the artist, the leader, the victim, the inspiration, was a man for all ages." She states

(Pope, Marcella)

that Paul Robeson came to Washington, D.C., in 1948, at his own
expense and in a concert he lifted that magnificent, big booming
voice in songs of free people, in songs of working people in
struggle, in songs which told of his unwavering love for all
humanity, in songs which cried out against injustice and exploitation. The author concludes:
>   And he did it all in love, and for a small group of
>   low-paid Black workers that they might walk in dignity
>   and sit down at a table and bargain for a living wage....
>   He also contributed $5,000 himself to help restaurant
>   workers who were on strike in Washington, D.C., in
>   1948....

1854.   Francis, Elman V. "Paul Robeson: A Man Before his Time," Afro-
American, February 5, 1977, p. 13.

The writer asserts that few people who reached the pinnacle of
success have cast down all the comforts and glory to fight against
inequality and oppression without ever thinking of their own
safety and security. As a great athlete, a gifted actor, and above
all, a soul-stirring singer, Paul Robeson captured the minds of
millions all over the world. But the sad plight of his own
people and that of the suppressed millions in Africa and Asia dis-
comforted him, declares Dr. Francis. He concludes:
>   Fearlessly, without ever shrinking from facing ad-
>   verse situations, Paul Robeson pushed his way forward
>   and showed his people through his own life and
>   political philosophy how they should march toward
>   freedom and equality. Anyone interested in learning
>   about Paul Robeson's contribution to Black America
>   must devote his attention to Robeson's autobiography,
>   Here I Stand.

1855.   Peters, Ida. "Casals and Remembering Paul Robeson," Afro-American,
January 2-7, 1978, p. 10.

The writer asserts that the most poignant "Christmas card"to pass
her desk was the greeting from 91 year old Eva Jessye, the famed
teacher, choir director, keeper of the George Gershwin "Porgy and
Bess" score - now living at U. of Michigan, Ann Arbor. She is
pictured in two circles, "so much to tell...." "So little time."
Included with the card is a copy of a Creed she feels should be
adopted by all artists. It's from Pablo Casals as follows:
"....I am a man first, an artist second. As a man, my first obligation is to the welfare of my fellow men. I will endeavor to
meet this obligation through music - the means which God has given
me - since it transcends language, politics and national boundaries.
My contributions to world peace may be small, but at least I will
have given all I can to an ideal I hold sacred." The author said
on another insert included with her card, the courageous director
and world traveler for the first "Porgy and Bess" and for all the
revivals and the movie, sent a flyer headed, CASALS. On the bottom
she wrote....Remember Paul Robeson? On the flyer Casal expresses
a view we hope our readers will take with them into 1978 while we

(Peters, Ida)

reflect on the merits of James Earl Jones and Paul Robeson. He writes: An affront to human dignity is an affort to me, and to protest injustice is a matter of conscience. Are human rights of less importance to an artist than to other men? Does being an artist exempt one from his obligations as a man? If anything, the artist has a particular responsibility, because he has been granted special sensitivities and perceptions, and because his voice may be heard when others are not. Who, indeed, should be more concerned than the artist with the defense of liberty and free inquiry, which are essential to his very creativity?"

1856. Clarke, John Henrik. "Paul Robeson: The Great Fore-Runner," First World, Vol. 2, No. 1, Spring, 1978, pp. 25-27.

The writer asserts that Paul Robeson was indeed more than an artist, activist and freedom fighter. The dimensions of his talent made him our Renaissance man. He was the first American artist, Black or white, to realize that the role of the artist extends far beyond the stage and the concert hall. Dr. Clarke argues, in part:
Early in his life he became conscious of the plight
of his people, stubbornly surviving in a racist
society. This was his window on the world. From
this vantage point he saw how the plight of his people
related to the rest of humanity. He realized that
the artist had the power, and the responsibility, to
change the society in which he lived. He learned
that art and culture are weapons in a people's struggle
to exist with dignity, and in peace. Life offered
him many options and he never chose the easiest one.
For most of his life he was a man walking against the
wind. An understanding of his beginning, and how he
developed artistically and politically, will reveal
the nature of his mission and the importance of the
legacy of participation in struggles that we have
inherited from him.

1857. Clarke, John Henrik. "Paul Robeson: The Artist as Activist and Social Thinker," Paul Robeson: The Great Forerunner. Editors of Freedomways. New York: Dodd, Mead, and Co., 1978, pp. 189-201.

The author states that Paul Robeson was indeed more than an artist, activist and freedom fighter. The dimensions of his talent made him our Renaissance man. He was one of the first American artists, Black or white, to realize that the role of the artist extends far beyond the stage and the concert hall. Early in his life he became conscious of the plight of his people, stubbornly surviving in a racist society. This was his window on the world, states Prof. Clarke. He argues:
From this vangate point he saw how the plight of his
people related to the rest of humanity. He realized
that the artist had the power, and the responsibility,
to change the society in which he lived. He learned
that art and culture are weapons in a people's struggle

(Clarke, John Henrik)

to exist with dignity, and in peace. Life offered
him many options and he never chose the easiest one.
Robeson is the archetype of the Black American who
uncompromisingly insists on total liberation. His
example and his fate strike to the very heart of
American racism. For the nation to confront him
honestly would mean that it confronts itself - to
begin at last the process of reclamation of the
national soul.

1858. Edwards, Harry. "Paul Robeson: His Politics Legacy to the
Twentieth-Century Gladiator," Paul Robeson: The Great Forerunner.
The Editors of Freedomways. New York: Dodd, Mead, and Co., 1978,
pp. 17-25.

The author contends that the legacy of Paul Robeson was that he
openly and staunchly stood up for his convictions. According to
Edwards, Paul Robeson was not only an intellect, but a man of
great passions as well. In his athletic career - as in all other
sectors of his life - he never lost sight of the fact that intellectuality devoid of passion results in tecynocratic sterility,
while passion divorced from intellectuality inevitably leads to
chaos. Therefore, concludes the writer, any portrayal of Paul
Robeson and the significance of his deeds that did not encompass
both would be to separate the shadow from the act, to emphasize
the words while ignoring what is being said.

1859. Hine, Darlene Clark. "Paul Robeson's Impact on History," Paul
Robeson: The Great Forerunner. Editors of Freedomways. New York:
Dodd, Mead and Co., 1978, pp. 142-149.

The author declares that the striking and invaluable legacy Robeson left to Black and White America - and thus his impact on
history - is a dual one. One side of the legacy was the lesson
derived from his individual struggle for freedom, which was embodied in his pursuit of the passport and the right to travel.
This one aspect of his life clearly reveals the extent to which
white government officials were willing to go in order to nullify
the Constitution and suspend the rights of American citizens who
strayed from the beaten path of exploitation of the masses for the
private gain of a few. Hines asserts that Robeson's activities
and statements in behalf of liberation for all oppressed peoples
and his analysis of the role the American government plays in the
perpetration and continuation of national and international oppression of colored people throughout the world comprise the other
side of his legacy. "From him we can learn, develop and sharpen
our own commitment and resolve to participate in and support the
collective international struggle for peace and freedom," concludes
the writer.

12. HIGH SCHOOL CLASSMATES

1860. Jardin, Ed. "Paul Robeson - Not Forgotten," Courier-News (N.J.),
       April 20, 1973, p. 11.

       This article states that Paul Robeson was not forgotten by his
       white childhood friends in Westfield, Somerville, New Brunswick,
       and Princeton, N.J. They recall how he was a friend and the most
       outstanding athlete at Somerville High School. There is a photo-
       graph of Paul Robeson in a baseball uniform along with members of
       the 1914 team.

1861. Perry, Bernice. "Norfolk's Winston Douglas Recalls School Days
       with Paul Robeson," Journal and Guide, January 31, 1976, p. 2.

       The writer reports on one of Paul Robeson's high school classmates,
       Winston Douglas. "I commuted nine miles to Somerville High School
       and on some days when I didn't feel like going home I spent the
       night at the Robeson's," Douglas remembers. "There was one parti-
       cular night that I had stayed over; Paul and I had a pillow fight.
       We were jumping on the bed and the slat came out and underneath
       the bed was a chamber pot. Paul's sister, Marian, who was the
       woman of the house because their mother was dead, came in quietly
       to clean up the mess and left...." Douglas recollects that
       Robeson was always cheerful and Douglas sometimes called him the
       man with the built-in smile. "He hated racism and he never played
       before a segregated audience; Paul also liked being out doors,"
       states Douglas.

13. HOLLYWOOD'S WALK OF FAME

1862. Krebs, Abin. "Notes on People: Paul Robeson in the 'Hollywood
       Walk of Fame'," New York Times, July 15, 1978, p. 15.

       The Actors Equity and the Screen, Actors Guild submitted Paul
       Robeson's name for the "Walk of Fame," a strip of pavement on
       Hollywood Boulevard and the Hollywood Chamber of Commerce refused
       to place his name on the pavement because of his leftist activities.
       Tom Bradley, the Black Mayor of Los Angeles protested the ex-
       clusion and said he was "disturbed and saddened" by the rebuff, to
       the memory of the athlete, singer and actor.

1863. "Robeson Missed Hollywood Star, But Gained Friends as Fame Battle
       Continues," Jet, Vol. 54, No. 20, August 3, 1978, pp. 54-55.

       According to this article, an impressive coalition of actors'
       union officials, actors, city officials and laymen came together
       to protest Hollywood Chamber of Commerce's decision not to im-
       plant a star on the tourist-trap Walk of Fame pavement in honor
       of the late Paul Robeson. The late singer-actor received support

(Jet)

from Mayor Tom Bradley of Los Angeles, Jackie Cooper, Lena Horne, Edward Weston, Warren Hollier, Paul Robeson, Jr. The son states that his father rejected Hollywood because it is run by big racists money. He rejected the cultural values of Hollywood and said that as far as Black images were concerned, Hollywood wasn't realistic. But while I'm not campaigning for honors for dad, he was a pioneer in films and if a star should be placed in his honor then it should be there, concludes his son.

1864.   Sansweet, Stephen J. "The Birth of A Star in Hollywood Today Ends a Controversy: Activist Singer Paul Robeson is Finally Judged Worthy of a Plaque in The Sidewalk," Wall Street Journal, April 7, 1979, pp. 1, 22.

The article states that the Hollywood Chamber of Commerce reversed itself to allow Paul Robeson's name to be added to "The Walk of Fame." Originally the Chamber of Commerce was deluged with criticism from Los Angeles Mayor Tom Bradley, Jackie Cooper, Lena Horne, Actors' Equity and The Screen, Actors Guild and the First Unitarian Church of Los Angeles. The selection committee later reversed itself, saying it had received added information about Mr. Robeson's career as an entertainer.

1865.   "Hollywood Hindsight," New York Times, April 11, 1979, p. 24.

This article comments on Paul Robeson's name being embedded into Hollywood Boulevard. The writer wanted to know why did it take so long for Robeson's name to go down in cement. He concludes: "If the three-mile strip known as the Hollywood Walk of Fame were meant to confirm various notions, of political purity, or even wise allegiances, Mr. Robeson's name would have no place there. But if, as we always assumed, the measure of the honor is talent, then this powerful singer and actor should never have been denied."

1866.   Qualles, Paris H. "What Price a Star?: Paul Robeson vs. Holly-wood Chamber of Commerce," Crisis, Vol. 86, No. 7, August/September, 1979, pp. 297, 300, 301.

This article concerns the Hollywood Chamber of Commerce denial of Paul Robeson's star in Hollywood's Walk of Fame. After much popular outcry from Mayor Tom Bradley, Jackie Cooper, Ben Vereen, Lena Horne, KNXT-TV, LATA, SAG, Actors' Equity and others, the Chamber of Commerce reversed their decision after claiming to have received "additional information needed to fairly evaluate the artist's qualifications."

14. HONORS

1867. Shepard, Richard F. "Going Out Guide," New York Times, February
       16, 1973, p. 20.

       This article mentions a Paul Robeson celebration in his honor at
       Carnegie Hall. Mr. Robeson received a tribute at the W.E.B. Du
       Bois Cultural Evening, sponsored by Freedomways magazine. He
       was ill and did not attend the event.

1868. Grossman, Victor. "A Paul Robeson Public School in the GDR,"
       Panorama, March 3, 1973.

       The writer points out that a public school in the eastern section
       of Berlin, capital of the German Democratic Republic (GDR) named
       its building after Paul Robeson. Mr. Grossman declares that Robe-
       son had visited Germany in 1960 and was a friend of the working
       class of people in the GDR.

1869. "Establish Paul Robeson Scholarship Fund," The Sphinx, Vol. 59,
       No. 2, May-June, 1973, p. 34.

       The NU Chapter of Alpha Phi Alpha Fraternity at Lincoln University
       in Pennsylvania established a Scholarship in honor of Paul Robeson,
       who was a member of that organization.

1870. "Rutgers Honors Paul Robeson," Black Panther, June 9, 1973, p. 5.

       This article states that Rutgers University awarded Robeson an
       honorary Doctor of Humane Letters degree.

1871. "William Marshall Named to Robeson Awards Committee," Jet, Vol. 45,
       October 14, 1973, p. 86.

       William Marshall, was appointed to the Paul Robeson Annual Awards
       Committee to Actors' Equity, the national professional actors'
       organization. The newly-formed committee commissioned sculptor
       Richmond Barthe to create a bust of Paul Robeson, which will be
       on permanent display at the committee's headquarters in New York
       City. A metal replica of the bust and a 4,000 dollar cash grant
       will be awarded to an outstanding person in the arts and humanities.

1872. Perkins, Thelma Dale. "A Letter to Paul Robeson on Our Visit to
       Mt. Robeson," New World Review, Vol. 41, No. 4, Fourth Quarter,
       1973, pp. 52-58.

       The author writes of her impressions of the Soviet Union on her
       first trip there in the form of a letter to Paul Robeson. The
       zenith of the trip was the visit to Mt. Robeson in the Soviet
       Socialist Republic of Kirghizia. She along with other Afro-
       American delegates on the trip thanked the Kirghizia people for
       perpetuating the memory of Paul Robeson by naming the highest
       peak in the Ala-Tau mountains after him.

1873. "Sculptor Olga Manuilova," New World Review, Vol. 43, No. 2, March-
       April, 1974, p. 9.

       There is a photo of a bust of Paul Robeson and its sculptor Olga
       Manuilova, which she produced for the dedication of Mt. Paul
       Robeson in Kirghizia, U.S.S.R. The photo was taken at the foot
       of Mt. Robeson.

1874. Braden, Carl. "The German Democratic Republic After Twenty Five
       Years," New World Review, Vol. 42, No. 6, November-December, 1974,
       pp. 16-17.

       The writer points out that Paul Robeson and other Black people
       in the United States are highly honored and greatly esteemed in the
       German Democratic Republic. It was also stated that there is a
       Paul Robeson Archives at the Academy of Art in Berlin, and Robeson
       has received high praises at celebrations in his honor in that
       city.

1875. "Miss Dee and Davis Get Robeson Prize," New York Times, June 2,
       1975, p. 36.

       Ruby Dee and Ossie Davis, the husband and wife acting team, were
       named the recipients of the Paul Robeson Citation "for outstanding
       creative contributions both in performing arts and in society at
       large." The award was established by the Actors' Equity Association
       as a tribute to the actor-singer for his lifelong efforts in the
       cause of freedom, of equality, and his concern for humanity. The
       first citation went to Mr. Robeson last year (1974).

1876. "Paul Robeson Players," Black World, Vol. 25, No. 6, April, 1976,
       p. 88.

       The Paul Robeson Players was founded in 1971, in Compton, Cali-
       fornia. During the summer of 1975, the Robeson Players went to the
       community to select some 40 youths to perform in a Bicentennial
       production, "From Kings and Queens to Who Knows What," by Vel
       Trass. Because of this production the Paul Robeson Players has,
       according to this article, probably received more public praise
       and written endorsements from elected officials throughout the
       State than any other Black arts group. More essentially, the
       Robeson Players are receiving considerable financial support
       from the Compton City government, states the article.

1877. "The Day They Named the School for Paul Robeson," New York Amster-
       dam News, June 19, 1976, p. B-1.

       Public School 191, an elementary school in Brownsville in Brooklyn,
       New York, was named Paul Robeson Public School in June, 1976.

1878. "Honoring Robeson," Princeton Packet (N.J.), October 16, 1976.

       This article mentions that Abalon Place and a part of Walnut Street
       was renamed as Paul Robeson Place in the Town of Princeton, New
       Jersey.

1879.   "N.Y. Law School Establishes Paul Robeson Scholarship," Jet, Vol.
        51, No. 22, February 17, 1977, p. 29.

        A Paul Robeson scholarship fund for minority and legal studies was
        established by Black students at the Columbia University Law
        School. The scholarship will be awarded to second-year law students
        who have achieved an outstanding academic record and have demon-
        strated an interest and commitment to the study of legal issues
        emerging from the affairs of minority groups.

1880.   "Detroit Prepares for 'Paul Robeson Day'," Bilalian News, December
        8, 1977, p. 2.

        According to this article a week-long program commemorating the
        birthday of the acclaimed actor, artist, scholar, athlete and
        human rights fighter was being planned in Detroit, Michigan.
        Mayor Colman A. Young served as Honorary Chairman for the Robeson
        80th Birthday Week, issued a call for sponsorship and participation,
        adding, "We are inviting actors, singers, academicians and others
        to appear at our planned seminars and programs. Many of those,
        after all, have been helped in gaining public acceptance because
        of the self sacrifices made by Paul Robeson in his life-long
        struggle against discrimination and racism." This article also
        reported on some comment that Sidney Poitier asserted:
            I found him to be overwhelming in his knowledge,
            formidable in his commitment. He had phenomenal
            clarity.... In thos days you pursued black rights
            and equality for minorities within a prescribed set
            of circumstances outlined by the establishment....
            which is something he couldn't live with.... He
            was concerned about Harry (Balefonte) and myself.
            He used to tell us not to be too radical because he
            never wanted us to lose our credibility. He used to
            outline for us our responsibilities within the con-
            fines of being artists.... He had an impact on every
            selection I've ever made as an actor.

                15. HOUSE COMMITTEE ON UN-AMERICAN ACTIVITIES

1881.   "History Brought to Life - 'You're the Un-Americans!'," Daily
        World, March 17, 1977, p. 8.

        This is a review of the play, "Point of Order: An Inside Look at
        the Backside of the Front," in which Paul Robeson's testimony be-
        fore the United States House Committee on Un-American Activities
        in 1956 is the climax of the play. The play was performed in
        Minneapolis, Minnesota at the Dudley Riggs' ETC Theater in March,
        1977.

16. HUMANITARIAN

1882. Gilliam, Dorothy. "Paul Robeson: Renaissance Man of the Arts, Social Activist," Washington Post, January 24, 1976, p. B5.

This biographer states that Robeson was more than a concert artist, stage and screen actor, athlete and scholar; he was a passionate humanitarian. She surmises that Robeson's personal odyssey was inseparable from the life and struggle of Black Americans and Common people around the globe to whom he felt closest. The writer declares from the statement Robeson issues in 1964, it appears simple that the times have caught up with his ideas: "The power of Negro action of which I (Paul Robeson) wrote in my book (Here I Stand) has changed from an idea to reality.... The concept of mass militancy, or mass action, is no longer deemed 'too radical in Negro life,'" states Robeson.

17. ILLNESS

1883. Johnston, Louire. "Paul Robeson is Ill," New York Times, January 13, 1976, p. 66.

It was reported that Paul Robeson was in Philadelphia's Pennsylvania Medical Center in "fair condition" with an undisclosed illness. The 77-year-old singer was diagnosed as having a circulatory ailment in 1963.

18. LEADERSHIP

1884. "Ten Greats of Black History," Ebony, August, 1972, pp. 35-42.

Paul Robeson is included in this list. The other nine are: Richard Allen, Nat Turner, Frederick Douglass, Booker T. Washington, W.E.B. DuBois, Marcus Garvey, Martin Luther King, Jr., Malcolm X and Thurgood Marshall. The article gave a short biographical sketch of each man. It was pointed out of Paul Robeson that "one of the most multi-faceted genuises of recorded history for nearly a half century, Paul Robeson, dedicated himself totally to the cause of the liberation of all oppressed people irrespective of color." The article concludes: "...no black man has ever had more to give -- or has given more -- to his people than Robeson. His enormous gifts and his incontestable humanity should easily earn him a place on any list of great men."

1885. Weaver, Harold D., Jr. "Paul Robeson: Beleagured Leader," Black
       Scholar, Vol. 5, No. 4, December, 1973-January, 1974, pp. 24-32.

       The author argues that despite Robeson's international fame in the
       concert halls, in the theatre, and on the screen, it is significant
       that this artist-activist never allowed his personal success to
       explain away what happened to his people. Dr. Weaver concludes
       that he dared assert his manhood and that of his people. That is
       how the beleagured Robeson responded to racism, whether it be in
       the classroom, on the football field, in the political arena, on
       the stage, in the concert hall, or on the screen, states the
       writer.

1886. Rollins, Bryant. "What Would They Do Today?," New York Amsterdam
       News, January 21, 1978, p. 6.

       The writer wanted to know what would King and Robeson be doing if
       they were living in 1978. He suggests Dr. King would have thousands
       of people in the streets protesting, agitating, organizing, mobi-
       lizing. He would be running national economic boycotts, not to
       accomodate major industries, but to confront them and to force them
       to change their policies, states Mr. Rollins. He declares that
       Robeson, though not the street activist and organizer that King
       was, clearly would support with his words, his songs, his dramatic
       capabilities, any such effort. While he was active, Robeson gave
       unstintingly of his time and talents to political movements and
       organizations trying to mobilize poor people for radical change.
       The writer asserts that we badly need leaders today of the mold
       of a Robeson or a King. Independent, creative men and women with
       integrity, gut, honesty and a deep caring and concern for
       ordinary people...

1887. O'Dell, J.H. "A Rock in a Weary Lan': Paul Robeson's Leadership
       and 'The Movement' in the Decade Before Montgomery," Paul Robeson:
       The Great Forerunner. Editors of Freedomways. New York: Dodd,
       Mead, and Co., 1978, pp. 119-129.

       The writer states that contemporary writers and publishers of Black
       history texts and social studies materials who leave brother Paul
       out of the story are not writing our history. Let us be abundantly
       clear on that point. Nor was he just a singer and actor deserving
       a few lines of passing reference as some of the "better" Black
       Studies materials would have us believe, declares the author. He
       asserts that this enormously talented and dedicated freedom fighter
       was the central rally figure and chrismatic personality of the
       movement during a certain period. This is a role and responsibility
       only a mere handful of giant personalities in our history have
       successfully fulfilled. We are reminded that following Robeson
       that role was filled by Dr. Martin Luther King, Jr. It is a
       role which has been invested with honor, sacrifice and the highest
       integrity. So it is not to be dismissed or rendered inconsequential
       by falsifiers who claimed to be writing history. He concludes:
       "A Negro spiritual, that musical art form which he did so much to
       make widely known and appreciated throughout the world, perhaps
       best describes Paul Robeson's significance for the Freedom Move-
       ment in the decade before the Montgomery bus protest. He was, in

(O'Dell, J.H.)

in the words of that ancestral song, 'A Rock in a Weary Lan'.'"

19. LETTERS TO EDITORS

1888.   "Drama Mailbag," New York Times, September 10, 1972, Arts and
Leisure Section, pp. 12, 16.

Three letters were written to the editor concerning Paul Robeson
and also comments on Loften Mitchell's article, "Time to Break
the Silence Surrounding Paul Robeson." One letter was from Bing-
hamton, N.Y., another one from a student at Rutgers University
and the third letter from a Princeton, N.J., resident.

1889.   "Sports Editor's Mailbox: Paul Robeson," New York Times, October
5, 1975, Sports Section 5, p. 2.

This is a letter to the Sports Editor about Paul Robeson. The
writer states that he saw Robeson play football in 1918 at Ebbets
Field in Brooklyn, New York. The game versus Rutgers against the
Great Lakes Naval Training Station. According to the writer
Robeson put on a performance that made the All-Americans look like
amateurs. He called Robeson: "The greatest football player of
his time or any other time."

1890.   Hammer, Nina. "The Death of Paul Robeson," Los Angeles Times,
February 1, 1976, Part 8, p. 1.

This was a letter to The Times. The reader asserts, in part:
"....I never missed an opportunity to hear and see Paul Robeson,
as I had the unforgettable pleasure in 1945 to see Paul Robeson
in 'Othello' at the then Biltmore Theater. Now with this glorious
voice and noble man stilled forever, I feel sorry for those who
never heard and saw this great artist, and shied away because of
misguided propaganda. America committed an unforgivable misdeed
toward itself. I am deeply grieved over this great loss to the
people of the world."

1891.   Pine, Edith and Seymour Pine. "The Death of Paul Robeson," Los
Angeles Times, February 1, 1976, Part 8, p. 1.

This was a letter to The Times. The readers declare: "Congratulations to The Times for its recognition of a great American. It
saddens me that his contributions to the civil rights movement
have gone unnoticed these many years. His sin in the eyes of
America was not so much what he said, but rather that he said it
decades before the country was able to listen. Had this not been
so, he might have lived the life of a Nobel Peace laureate instead
of a reviled exile. There is still a great deal to accomplish in
achieving civil rights, and as our spokesmen praise Dr. Martin
Luther King, they should also speak of Paul Robeson.

1892. Phillips, James T. "The Death of Paul Robeson," Los Angeles
       Times, February 1, 1976, Part 8, p. 1.

       This was a letter written to The Times by a reader. He asserts,
       in part: "I hasten to express my appreciation of the eloquently
       sincere and reasoned assessment of the late Paul Robeson by Sidney
       P. Anderson. I think that the article, as a remarkably succinct
       statement in commemoration of the passing of Robeson, was as
       nearly befitting of him as his admirers might hope for."

1893. Rhenshog, Patricia. "The Death of Paul Robeson," Los Angeles
       Times, February 1, 1976, Part 8, p. 1.

       Miss Rhenshog wrote a letter to The Times concerning Paul Robeson's
       death. She states: "Long before Paul Robeson's death I was one
       of the few young people familiar with his name, let alone appre-
       ciative of his extraordinary singing voice. After his death I was
       surprised to read of his many other gifts and disappointed to
       learn of his associations with communism. My disappointment is
       now replaced with understanding and regret. I read Anderson's
       article, which shed a light on Paul Robeson, the human being. I
       thank Anderson and rise with him to applaud Paul Robeson."

1894. Siegal, Sidney. "The Death of Paul Robeson," Los Angeles Times,
       February 1, 1976, Part 8, p. 1.

       This was a letter written to The Times. The writer states, in part:
       "I am what many would call a 'bleeding-heart liberal,' so it gives
       me pleasure to read the opinions of a fair-minded man who is a
       'card-carrying conservative.' Would that all communication be-
       tween people of opposing viewpoints were on such a high level of
       fairness and reason. It is all too rare. The Times deserves a
       lot of credit for providing a forum for the expression of all shades
       of opinion from its readers.... Thank you for publishing Sidney
       P. Anderson's great article (Editorial Page 5, January 27) about
       Paul Robeson. I admire the integrity that Anderson exhibited by
       writing a tribute to a great man with whom he strongly disagreed
       on a political level."

1895. Tannenbaum, Dick. "The Death of Paul Robeson," Los Angeles Times,
       February 1, 1976, Part 8, p. 1.

       This was a letter to The Times. The writer declares, in part:
       "....He wasn't mentioned in history books like Nathan Hale. He
       wasn't mentioned on football game broadcasts like Red Grange. He
       wasn't mentioned in dramatic reviews, like Barrymore. He wasn't
       mentioned by opera critics like Caruso. The man who was never
       mentioned despite the fact that he truly excelled, not in one of
       the above fields but in all of them. Now, as the fires that raged
       in him cool and he is put lifeless into the ground we mention and
       accept the fact that he lived. Now, safely silenced, he is suddenly
       mentioned as a 'great American' and newspapers write editorials
       about him and soon halls of fame and history books will doubtless
       find a place for him and we can pat ourselves on our bicentennial
       backs for living in a country where even the dissident can be a
       hero, once he is dead...."

1896. Ebner, Michael H. "Robeson's Patriotism," New York Times, February 3, 1976, p. 30.

This was a letter written to the editor of the New York Times. The writer commented on the Times editorial memoralizing Paul Robeson upon his death. Ebner suggests that in refusing to perform for his fellow citizens, Paul Robeson rendered a noble generation which hear his voice that, whatever the strengths of democracy it harbors certain fundamental weaknesses. And if Robeson himself became confused about the merits of these two concepts, perhaps it was the inherent weaknesses of democracy, amid its often noted strengths which mistakenly led him to see solance in Communism. The author concludes: "His voice was missed while he still lived and now is gone, but his message will live, one hopes, forever. And democracy has been strengthened by his studied silence."

1897. Guice, Pamelad. "To A Soviet Admirer," New Orleans Times Picayune, February 8, 1976, p. 14.

This was a letter to the editor of The Times Picayune. The reader wrote: I wonder how the late Paul Robeson (The Times-Picayune, January 24) would have fared as the son of a runaway slave in Russia, the country that considers him 'one of the USSR's fondest friends.' It also occurs to me that very many talented black people have won the recognition and plaudits they deserve -- without turning on the United States."

1898. Todres, Albert F. "Robeson/College Ideals," New York Times, February 15, 1976, Section 5, p. 2.

This was a letter written by Albert F. Todres to the Sports Editor of the New York Times. The writer questioned the National Football Foundation and Hall of Fame and asked it why Paul Robeson was omitted from its membership. He was informed that Robeson was left out because of his views on Communism. The chairman of the Foundation, Chester J. La Roche, said he would welcome evidence that Robeson was a citizen in good standing as specified by the foundation's by-laws. Mr. Todres stated that Paul Robeson was in the fore-front of the struggle for human and civil rights long before it was fashionable. He concluded: "He was dedicated to the dignity of the human race. What more worthy cause can an individual have?"

1899. Graham, Lorenz. "Paul Robeson," Ebony, Vol. 31, No. 6, April, 1976, p. 17.

This was a letter to the editor. The writer concludes: ".... Robeson was not so viciously attacked because he had communist ties. They wanted to silence him because they hated and feared this strong man who was using his abundant talents to cry his bitter protests and his prophetic warnings."

1900. Jenkins, Timothy L. "Perspective on Paul Robeson," Washington
       Post, December 20, 1977.

       This was a letter to the editor of the Post. The writer states
       that the play "Paul Robeson" was an acute embarrassment. He
       declares that for those who hold the deepest respect for the legacy
       and legend of the man Robeson, the controversy surrounding the play
       about him, this controbersy comes not as a source of embarrass-
       ment, but rather as a way of hope. According to Mr. Jenkins, the
       hope is that this figure, obscured by the most plastic personality
       manufactured by the media, should once again become a standard of
       measurement in politics, in art, athletic excellence and intel-
       lectual integrity.

1901. Shreve, Porter G. "Perspective on Paul Robeson," Washington Post,
       December 20, 1977.

       This was a letter to the Editor of the Washington Post, concerning
       Paul Robeson. The writer, who was white, declares that he was
       sympathetic to Paul Robeson, Jr., who sought to preserve his
       father's integrity. He was referring to the play "Paul Robeson,"
       that was playing at the National Theatre in Washington, D.C.
       Mr. Shreve declares: "We need our past heroes - the Paul Robesons
       and the Martin Luther Kings, but it is not helpful to resurrect
       and deify the dead to fight our battles. One hopes they have in--
       spired the leadership that is in each of us to carry on the
       struggle in our own time.... 'Paul Robeson' may be an imperfect
       production, but it obviously has touched some of us who may re-
       cognize the need to assert ourselves in our own right, but who
       may feel inadequate without an ideal."

1902. Britton, Mariah A. "A View of Paul Robeson," New York Amsterdam
       News, January 28, 1978, p. 10.

       This was a letter written to the editor of this newspaper. The
       reader comments on the play "Paul Robeson," starring James Earl
       Jones. Britton surmises that the protest against the play was
       misplaced. It should be at the U.S. Government, the College Hall
       of Fame and in our everyday lives. She concludes: "Paul Robeson
       was a great man. There is no stage wide enough nor monologue
       long enough to address itself to the essence of what he stood
       for...."

1903. Blackwell, Elsena. "The Robeson Controversy," New York Amsterdam
       News, February 18, 1978, p. 6.

       This was a letter written to the editor of this newspaper. The
       reader comments on the play, "Paul Robeson," starring James Earl
       Jones. She states that she agrees with Pete Hamill that Paul
       Robeson had "a voice too big for the concert hall." Since he was
       a many faceted personality, with so many different dimensions,
       it would be almost impossible to capture the complete essence of
       the man in 2½ hours on stage, suggests Blackwell. She concludes:
       "I think the play does not detract from the stature of the man,
       and James Earl Jones gives a magnificent portrayal. I say to all
       of those who object, put your money where your mouth is."

1904. Bently, Eric. "Playwrights' Protest: The Right to Deplore,"
       New York Times, June 8, 1978, p. 26.

       This was a letter written to the Editor of the New York Times.
       Bentley contends that the people who considered the Paul Robeson
       play pernicious not only had the right to say so - in paid ads,
       in private letters, in all peaceful and normal channels - they had
       an obligation to Paul Robeson as they saw him and obligation to our
       society as they understand it. He concludes: "Yes, the 33
       (playwrights) have the same rights to deplore such action, the
       same obligation to deplore it."

                        20. MUSIC

1905. Reasons, George and Sam Patrick. "Paul Robeson - Baritone of
       Distinction," Washington (D.C.) Evening Star, May 2, 1970.

       The authors argue that the rich deep baritone voice of Paul Robe-
       son made him one of the greatest singers of his day. He was known
       and acclaimed on both sides of the Atlantic for his consummate
       artistry. But Robeson's political views cast a deep and somber
       shadow over his life and over his career. He was an open admirer
       of the Soviet Union, a position which led his homeland to reject
       him, state Reasons and Patrick. They also assert that during the
       cold war, Robeson's views came under violent criticism. He was
       called before the House Committee on Un-American Activities and
       identified as a "Communist sympathizer." He was picketed at
       practically every performance. The writers conclude: "Even so,
       Robeson did not waver in his views. In 1952, he accepted the
       Stalin Peace Prize from the Soviet Union...."

1906. Novak, Benjamin J. "Opening Doors in Music," Negro History
       Bulletin, Vol. 34, No. 1, January, 1971, p. 10.

       The article states that Paul Robeson used his superb resonant bass
       in recitals before turning his major energies to the stage. The
       author concludes that it can only be conjectured whether in a more
       favorable climate, Paul Robeson might have concentrated upon grand
       opera. Robeson's vigor and resolution are such, however, that if
       the medium had fired his imagination he doubtless would have pur-
       sued such a goal, states Novak.

1907. Barnett, Etta Moten. "Paul Robeson: The Musician," First World,
       Vol. 2, No. 1, Spring, 1978, pp. 30-31.

       The writer states that Paul Robeson came to Kansas City for a con-
       cert in 1930 when she was at the University of Kansas preparing
       for my senior voice recital. She was also researching a paper on
       "Afro-American Songs." Robeson was guest in the home of friends
       of hers on 24th Street where most Black visiting artists stayed
       because of hotel discrimination. She came home from Lawrence,
       Kansas, that weekend as usual. Mrs. Barnett requested and was

(Barnett, Etta Moten)

granted an audience with Mr. Robeson. She states that she had
been advised by the Dean of the School of Fine Arts to "go to
New York after graduation and try your luck." Paul Robeson represented New York to her. She took her music along. He did want
to hear her voice. She sang songs from her program - early Italian,
French art songs, German Leider, an aria from "Samson and Delilah,"
ending with a group of Negro spirituals (all Black singers ended
recital programs with a group of Negro spirituals in those days).
Robeson was extremely polite. The comments he made that day
opened my eyes to a new approach to folk music in general and to
Afro-American music in particular. I must tell you how happy I
was to have Lawrence Brown, Robeson's own accompanist play for me.
Both of them commented on my pronunciation of the Italian, French
and German texts, emphasizing my phrasing and "flavor" in the
Negro spirituals. The two of us laughingly decided that being
"PKs" (Preacher's kids) might have helped us, states the author.
The writer declares: "I have wished many times that I could have
documented a few of the theories which Robeson touched upon that
memorable day." She concludes: "....Today we are flowing back
into the mainstream of world music, which includes the music of
Asia, Africa, Europe, and the Americas, with a future potential
of immense richness -- all taking from each other wonderful banks
of music. To my mind, Paul Robeson is an important depositor."

1908. Schlosser, Anatol, I. "Paul Robeson's Mission in Music," Paul
        Robeson: The Great Forerunner. Editors of Freedomways. New York:
        Dodd, Mead & Co., 1978, pp. 87-93.

The writer contends that in Paul Robeson's tripartite world of performance -- theatre, film and music was the one in which he discovered that he could best realize his personal ambitions and
political vision. In his native ante-bellum New Jersey, he was
schooled in the ways of white America and his place as a Negro.
It became apparent to him that in spite of a scholarship to and a
degree from Rutgers University, in spite of being named an All-
American football star, in spite of a law degree from Columbia
University, the barriers of racial prejudices would stand between
him and his ability to fulfill himself in his chosen field of law.
He returned to the stage, where he found that "whether singing or
acting, race and color prejudices are forgotten. Art is one form
against which such barriers do not stand." The author states that
in 1958 Robeson was granted a passport and he departed on a long
overdue tour of Europe, Australia and New Zealand. While abroad
he has asked why he kept his American citizenship. The singer who
had given years of his life, art, time, money and talents to a
nation that in part rejected him and attempted to imprison his
voice, responded to that question: "Because I have a right to it,
through the sweat, toil, and blood that were taken from my people."
After five and a half years abroad, earning the acclaim of all who
heard him, Paul Robeson, American citizen, son of an escaped slave,
man with a mission, returned to his native land to rest, concludes
the author.

1909. Abdul, Raoul. "Robeson, The Artist," <u>New York Amsterdam News</u>,
       January 31, 1979, p. 2.

       The writer was music critic of the <u>Amsterdam News</u>. He writes it
       was very difficult for the professional music critic to evaluate
       the singing of the late Paul Robeson. He possessed one of the
       most beautiful vocal instruments ever produced by this country.
       But, in matters of technique, musicianship and style, he never
       became a complete master. As he stated to the press many times,
       Robeson wanted only to be an artist of the people. With the ex-
       ception of a few art songs by Schubert and Mussorgasky and an
       occasional operatic aria, he devoted his programs to the folk-
       songs of the world's people, states Mr. Abdul. He was one of the
       first concert artists to present an entire program of Black Ameri-
       can folkmusic. The historical event took place on Sunday, April
       19, 1925, at the Greenwich Village Theatre with Lawrence Brown
       at the piano. Public and critics alike found it an overwhelming
       experience. He concludes: "Last Saturday afternoon, the Metro-
       politan Opera presented 'Boris Godunov.' After the performance I
       listened to my recording of Robeson both reciting the text and
       singing an excerpt from this opera. It was indeed a great loss
       to the operatic world that we never heard him in this role
       onstage."

                         21. PAUL ROBESON ARCHIVES

1910. Scarupa, Harriet Jackson. "The Paul Robeson Archives: Legacy of
       Courage," <u>Essence</u>, Vol. 8, No. 6, October, 1977, pp. 60-61, 84,
       86, 88, 91.

       This article discusses the Paul Robeson Archives. The writer inter-
       viewed Paul Robeson, Jr. The son states that the Archives material
       consists of some 50,000 items; letters, speeches, press state-
       ments, articles, records, tapes, sheet music, scripts, posters,
       programs, awards, photographs, Robeson's own personal library,
       African artifacts and a few costumes. At least 90 percent of
       it was owned by the Robeson family, the rest was acquired and
       was still (in 1977) being acquired from England, the Soviet Union
       and elsewhere. The author concludes that Paul Robeson's story -
       its triumphs and its trials - is movingly documented in the
       archives.

1911. Scarupa, Harriet Jackson. "The Paul Robeson Archives: Legacy of
       Courage," <u>Paul Robeson: The Great Forerunner</u>. New York: Dodd,
       Mead & Co., 1978, pp. 202-210.

       The writer points out that Paul Robeson, Jr., and the Board of the
       Paul Robeson Ardhives are in advanced states of negotiations with
       the Moorland-Spingarn Research Center of Howard University for
       the purpose of donating the entire Paul Robeson and Eslanda Goode
       Robeson Collection to them. Placing the collection at the Moor-
       land-Spingarn Research Center, a repository for a vast amount of

(Scarupa, Harriet Jackson)

material documenting the history and culture of Black people
throughout the world, will ensure that Robeson's remarkable achievements will assume their rightful place as a permanent part of
this nation's historical record. Following the transfer of the
collection to its permanent repository, the Robeson family will
continue to ensure that copies of the materials will be made
available to interested individuals, libraries and educational
institutions throughout the world, states Scarupa. She asserts:
"The documents that tell the Paul Robeson story will soon be released to the world. Let them serve as a powerful reminder. A
reminder that what happened to Paul Robeson because his views
happened to offend the powers-that-be -- what one writer termed
that 'attempt to blot from history a man's meaning' -- must never
happen again. Never."

22. PAUL ROBESON, JR.

1912. "Robeson Jr. Sets Record Straight," Daily Worker, April 24, 1970,
       p. 8.

       In a "Tribute to Paul Robeson," his son clears up some miscon-
       ceptions about his father, when the eastern region of the Alpha Phi
       Alpha Fraternity met at Rutgers. Among the many corrections
       pointed out by Robeson, Jr., was that although his father was
       named the leading football player on Walter Camp's list of foot-
       ball greats for two years, the senior Robeson has never been named
       to the Football Hall of Fame. Another was that Paul Robeson, Sr.,
       was never declared a Communist, although he lived in Russia for a
       number of years, states Paul Jr.

1913. Robeson, Paul Jr. "A Son's Tribute to His Father," New York Am-
       sterdam News, April 21, 1973, p. 11-C.

       Paul Robeson's son, Paul Jr., discusses how certain powers in
       America attempted to silence his father and distort what he stood
       for. Yet, they could not. The son recalls his father's appearance
       before the House Committee on Un-American Activities, the Peekskill
       riots, and the singer passport being revoked between 1950 and
       1958. He declares that the most unique and important things
       about his father was his personality - the man himself. The son
       concludes:
           My father is one of the very few people who has
           always cast light and warmth on those near to him -
           never a shadow. It is because of his personal
           qualities that one has to see and hear him in order
           to appreciate him in his full dimension. The sight
           and sound of this Black warrior in his prime was
           truly something no one would ever forget.

1914. Robeson, Paul Jr. "A Son's Stirring Tribute to His Father," New
       York Amsterdam News, April 21, 1973, Part II, p. D-1.

       This is the concluding part of a reprint of an earlier article,
       "Paul Robeson: Black Warrior," that appeared in a 1971 issue of
       Freedomways. The son attempts to "set the record straight" about
       his father's accomplishments.

1915. "Notes on People: Paul Robeson's Estate," New York Times, February
       4, 1976, p. 65.

       It was pointed out that Paul Robeson left three-fourths of his
       $150,000 estate to his son, Paul Robeson, Jr., and the rest to
       his sister, Marion Forsythe of Philadelphia, with whom he lived
       during the declining years of his life.

1916. "Paul Robeson Estate Valued at $150,000," Los Angeles Times,
       February 4, 1976, Section 1, p. 10.

       This article reported that Paul Robeson who died January 23, at
       the age of 77, left an estate estimated at $150,000, it was dis-
       closed in Manhattan Surrogate Court Tuesday.   Under a will made
       January 15, 1973, Robeson left three-quarters of his estate to his
       son, Paul Robeson, Jr., of New York, and the remainder to a sister,
       Mrs. Marion Forsythe, states the article.

1917. "Paul Robeson's Estate Valued at $150,000," Jet, Vol. 19, No.21,
       February 19, 1976, p. 57.

       When Paul Robeson died on January 23, 1976, he left an estate
       values at $150,000, consisting mostly of liquid assets and se-
       curities. According to executorial attorney Martin Rober, the
       international freedom fighter left three quarters of the estate
       to his son, Paul Jr., and the rest to his sister, Mrs. Marion
       Forsythe. According to the article that Robeson left an estate
       of that size is remarkable considering that he had not worked
       at any of his chosen professions for up to 10 years before his
       death. The value of the estate does not include Robeson's price-
       less library of books, speeches and tapes. These will be turned
       over to the Paul Robeson Archives in New York.

1918. "Robeson's Son Won't Cooperate on Film," Jet, Vol. 50, April 1,
       1976, p. 51.

       Paul Robeson, Jr., declares that he would not cooperate in any way
       with Universal-TV and NBC-TV, who have announced plans to present
       a three-hour special on his famous father's life. He concludes:
           I intend to oppose vigorously any attempt to cynical
           exploitation of my father's death by those shamelessly
           denied him access to the television medium during his
           active career. I sincerely hope that actors asked by
           Universal-TV and NBC-TV to play the part of Paul
           Robeson will refuse to do so.

1919. Robeson, Paul Jr. "Paul Robeson: A Home in That Rock," Freedom-
       ways, Vol. 16, No. 1, First Quarter, 1976, pp. 8-10.

       This speech was delivered by his son at Paul Robeson's funeral on
       January 27, 1976. His son declares his father never regretted
       the stand he took, because almost 40 years ago, in 1937, he made
       his basic choice. He said then: "The artist must elect to fight
       for freedom or for slavery. I have made my choice. I had no
       alternative." According to the speaker, Paul Robeson felt a deep
       responsibility to the people who loved him and to all to whom he
       was a symbol. He concludes:
            When he felt that he could no longer live up to their
            expectations, he chose to retire completely. When he
            could no longer raise his voice in song to inspire and
            to comfort, he chose silence; because Paul Robeson's
            view, his work, his artistry, his life, were all of one
            piece....

1920. Cannon, Terry. "Slander With A State Department Label," Daily
       World, October 13, 1977, p. 8.

       According to this article, Paul Robeson Jr.'s freedom of infor-
       mation suit released a memorandum, "The Robeson Story," by Vice
       Consul Roger P. Ross, to the United States State Department calling
       for a slanderous article about Paul Robeson to be written and placed
       in a United States magazine, then later reprinted and distributed
       in Africa. The reprinted article was written and placed in the
       NAACP's Crisis Magazine for its November, 1951, issue. It was en-
       titled "Paul Robeson - the Lost Shepherd" and written under the
       pseydonym, Robert Alan. Mr. Cannon suggests that the editorial
       in the New York Times in 1951 and the Walter White article at-
       tacking Robeson in the February, 1951, issue of Ebony magazine
       were also a part of the United States Government's inspired or
       planted pieces designed to discredit Robeson....

1921. Robeson, Paul Jr. "Paul Robeson: Black Warrior," Paul Robeson:
       The Great Forerunner. The Editors of Freedomways. New York:
       Dodd, Mead & Co., 1978, pp. 3-16.

       This article was written by his son. The son argues that not only
       have a web of lies and falsifications been institutionalized, but
       his father's entire record of achievements have been all but
       eradicated in the United States. The writer contends that the
       historical record clearly and indisputably shows three essential
       things; first, his father's achievements in several different
       fields were extraordinary taken individually: taken all together
       there were unprecedented. Second, he challenged the racism of this
       country to its foundation and linked the liberation struggles of
       Black people in America to those of all oppressed peoples every-
       where. In the Black Warrior tradition Paul Robeson told it like
       it was -- told it for the whole world to hear. Third, he withstood
       the full weight of a massive campaign by the government and the
       mass media of the white establishment to silence him. The essence
       of this article is that Paul Robeson, Jr., attempts to "set the
       record straight" about his father. He concludes: "My father was
       one of the very few people who always cast light and warmth on

(Robeson, Paul Jr.)

those near him - never a shadow. It is because of his personal
qualities that one had to see and hear him in order to appreciate
him in his full dimension."

1922.   Robeson, Paul Jr. "Tribute to Paul Robeson," Paul Robeson: The
Great Forerunner. Editors of Freedomways. New York: Dodd, Mead
& Co., 1978, pp. 308-310.

The author's son delivered the speech at his father's funeral on
January 27, 1976. He states his father knew the price he would
have to pay and he paid it, unbowed and unflinching. He knew that
he might have to give his life, so he was not surprised that he
lost his professional career. He was often called a Communist,
but he always considered that name to be an honorable one, declares the son. He concludes: "....Paul Robeson felt a deep
responsibility to the people who loved him and to all those to
whom he was a symbol. When he felt that he would no longer live
up to their expectations, he chose to retire completely. When he
could no longer raise his voice in song to inspire and to comfort,
he chose silence; because Paul Robeson's views, his work, his
artistry, his life, were all of one piece...." He also argues that
his father's legacy belongs also to all those who decide to follow
the principles by which he lived. It belongs to his own people
and to other oppressed peoples everywhere. It belongs to those
of us who knew him best and to the younger generation that will
experience the joy of discovering him, asserts Paul Robeson, Jr.

1922a.   "Notes on People: Robeson's Son Says Father was Under Surveillance," New York Times, October 1, 1979, Section 2, p. 4.

Paul Robeson, Jr., states that his father, Paul Robeson, Sr., was
under United States Government surveillance. The son declares
that he obtained government documents through the Freedom of Information Act soon after his father's death in 1976, which pointed
to a pattern of wiretapping, mail interception and even sabotage.
"For example," Mr. Robeson said, "documents show that the government had informants who monitored doctors' reports at every hospital where he was treated.

23. PAUL ROBESON -- THE PLAY

1923.   Bond, Jean Carey. "Robeson Play Protest Grows," New York Amsterdam News, January 14, 1975, pp. A-1, B-6.

This writer asserts that the controversy which has been stalking
out-of-town appearances of "Paul Robeson," the play based on the
life of the famed singer/actor and starring James Earl Jones,
escalated on Wednesday with the publication of a two-page advertisement in Variety magazine condemning the production on the

(Bond, Jean Carey)

threshold of its January 19 premiere in New York. Although the statement praises "the magnificent acting of James Earl Jones (which) elevates the portrait to sympathetic and commanding levels," it goes on to point out that "There will be many persons, unknowing of the true dimensions of Robeson or the full extent of what was done to him, who may be grateful for what is given. But it is precisely here that the greatest danger lies. For we in the Black community have repeatedly seen the giants among us reduced from revolutionary heroic dimensions to manageable, sentimentalized size."

1924. "James Earl Jones Is in Rehearsal for One-Character 'Paul Robeson,'" New York Times, August 13, 1977, p. 12.

The article states that James Earl Jones would return to Broadway in a one-character play based on the life of reowned actor and singer, Paul Robeson. Don Gregory, who produced "Paul Robeson," plans a long pre-Broadway tour, in Louisville, KY; St. Louis; Philadelphia; Boston; Cleveland; Milwaukee; Chicago and Washington, D.C., before the Broadway engagement, according to this article.

1925. Lindsey, Robert. "James Jones Gives Robeson Part Life," New York Times, August 31, 1977, p. C-20.

The writer states that James Earl Jones was bringing life to the character of Paul Robeson, a Black man with a curiously paradoxical place in American history. Lindsey surmises that for decades after World War II, Mr. Robeson was all but a pariah in the mainstream of white America and even among parts of Black society. It was pointed out that the new Robeson play was likely to raise anew the controversy surrounding the son of a former slave who seemed to do so many things so well. James Earl Jones declares: "His life was and is a tragedy, and so will the play although we are having great deals of fun and humor with it, as he did with life. But it was a tragedy." Don Gregory, the producer of the play, states that he thought there was a great sense of National guilt about Robeson.

1926. Bentley,Eric. "Robeson's Life," New York Times, September 28, 1977, Section 3, p. 6.

Mr. Bentley wrote a letter to the New York Times, stating that there were several errors in the article on Paul Robeson ("James Jones Gives Robeson Part Life," August 31) that appeared in that newspaper. Bentley states at least four errors, including that Robeson lived abroad especially in England not so much out of anger, rather "he was offered very attractive contracts and engagements in England."

1927. White, Jean M. "The 'Paul Robeson Dispute': A Dramatic Clash
       Over the Play's Portrait," Washington Post, December 7, 1977,
       pp. B-1, B-13.

       The article discusses the stage play "Paul Robeson," starring James
       Earl Jones that was playing at the National Theater, in Washington,
       D.C. Critics of the play, that was written by Black playwright
       and producer, Phillip Hayes Dean, declared that the play was a
       "pernicious perversion of the essence of Paul Robeson." They
       also protested the portrayal of Robeson as a "naive, ignoble giant,"
       and said the members of the Black community "have repeatedly seen
       the giants among us reduced from revolutionary heroic dimensions
       to manageable sentimentalized size." The protests followed the
       play from Louisville to Chicago to Philadelphia to Washington,
       D.C.

1928. "Open Letter to the Citizens of Washington: A Statement of Con-
       science Concerning the Theatrical Production 'Paul Robeson',"
       Daily World, December 9, 1977, p. 8.

       The play opened in Washington, D.C. on December 5, 1977. This
       statement, signed by many prominent Black leaders, writers, and
       actors condemns the play as a pernicious perversion of the essence
       of Paul Robeson.

1929. "Blacks Protest 'Robeson'," New York Times, January 11, 1978,
       Section 3, p. 15.

       Fifty-six Black writers, artists, educators and religious and
       political leaders protested James Earl Jones' one-man show,
       "Paul Robeson," as a "pernicious perversion of the essence of
       Paul Robeson." The protest was printed as a two-page advertise-
       ment in Variety. The statement attacked the play as "a tissue of
       invention and distortion ranging from the most elementary facts
       of the man's youth, aspirations, and development; of the role of
       his brothers, his wife; to the chronological events of his life
       and career -- all presumably in the effort to create 'acceptable'
       motivation to soften the genuine ones." According to the letter,
       the signer had either "seen the production or read versions in
       progress." Don Gregory, producer of "Paul Robeson," declares
       that most of the signers had seen the revised play. He
       declares "....Let them come and see it, and then take ads."

1930. "Open Letter to the Entertainment Industry: 'A Statement of Con-
       science'," Variety, January 11, 1978, pp. 133, 134.

       This ad was placed in this newspaper and was signed by 56 "pro-
       minent" Black Americans protesting the play "Paul Robeson." This
       ad was sponsored by The National Ad Hoc Committee to End the Crimes
       against Paul Robeson. It states, in part: "We the undersigned
       members of the Black community, having seen the production or
       read versions in progress, regretfully feel compelled to take the
       extraordinary step of alerting all concerned citizens to what we
       believe to be however unintended, a pernicious perversion of the
       essence of Paul Robeson...."

1931. Bond, Jean Carey. "Robeson Play Protest Grows," New York Amster-
       dam News, January 14, 1978, pp. A-1, B-6.

       This article discusses the play, "Paul Robeson," starring James
       Earl Jones. She comments on an advertisement that appeared in
       Variety and signed by 56 "prominent" Black Americans protesting
       the play as "a pernicious perversion of the essence of Paul
       Robeson." Mrs. Bond declares that the current controversy is
       evidence that even in death the legendary figure of Paul Robeson
       can still inspire passionate emotions in Americans just as his
       artistic offerings and political activities did in life.

1932. "Challenged Play on Robeson Debuts," New York Amsterdam News,
       January 14, 1978, p. D-7.

       This article announces that the play, "Paul Robeson," starring
       James Earl Jones would open on January 19th, at the Lunt-Fontanne
       Theater for a limited engagement. It also gives a short summation
       of Paul Robeson's life and states that in addition to being a
       world reowned concert singer, Broadway star, motion picture star
       and recording star, he was also the toast of international society.

1933. Editorial. "Paul Robeson's Legacy," New York Amsterdam News,
       January 21, 1978, p. 6.

       The editor states that his newspaper joins the 56 prominent Blacks
       that signed a two-page ad in Variety protesting the play "Paul
       Robeson." Although the editor had not seen the play, he said he
       respected the opinions of those 56 individuals who had. He then
       argues that any effort to diminish the hugeness of Robeson's in-
       tellect, fiery political independence, strength of character or
       finely-honed talent is an insult on all Black Americans. The
       writer advises that before anyone goes to see the play, he should
       first read Robeson's autobiography, Here I Stand. He concludes:
       "Then go see the play, if you want, and be aware of the trickery
       involved. Robeson in real life was so much greater than Robeson
       on Broadway that we cannot imagine why anyone would want to bother
       with the inferior version."

1934. Eder, Richard. "Stage: James Earl Jones is Robeson," New York
       Times, January 20, 1978, Section 3, p. 3.

       This was a review of the Broadway theatrical play "Paul Robeson,"
       starring James Earl Jones. The reviewer contends that the play
       is essentially an acted out narrative, a kind of travelogue through
       Mr. Robeson's biography. Eder surmises that the play does not
       show the unique human character of the man sufficiently to be able
       to sense what is happening to him as he trudges through history
       like a left-wing March of Time. His scholarship is alluded to,
       but there is little he says that shows us the mind of a thinker,
       or even the heart of a hero, concludes the reviewer.

1935. Editorial. "A Correllary to Robeson," New York Amsterdam News,
       January 21, 1978, p. 6.

       The editor declares that the controversy over the play "Paul
       Robeson" raises another difficult issue, that of cultural racism.
       He asserts that he doubts that white would have backed a play that
       accurately depicted Paul Robeson as the revolutionary that he was.
       The writer asked the question, when will our money-rich Black
       athletes and our money-rich Black singers, dancers, TV and movie
       stars, join together and collectively begin to finance works that
       accurately depict Black life in America?

1936. Brewster, Townsend. "'Robeson' Play is a Mixed Bag," New York Am-
       sterdam News, January 28, 1978, p. D-11.

       The writer discusses the play "Paul Robeson," starring James Earl
       Jones. He declares that except for the exchanges with Lawrence
       Brown and for the HUAC scene, in which Mr. Wallace plays Committee
       Chairman Walters, the evening is a monologue that requires James
       Earl Jones to create not only Paul Robeson but also the more than
       thirty subordinate characters, including the Peekskill mob, who
       carry on the action of the play. The burden on the star, who,
       on opening night, moreover, was ill, was perhaps excessive. And,
       unfortunately, the text exacted of him more emulation of Robeson
       the actor, though Mr. Jones; proficiency lies in approximating the
       latter rather than the former, states Mr. Brewster. He concludes:
       "Nevertheless, though the long evening was not without longueurs,
       this artist, as might be expected, performed with power and
       brilliance. The author and the director, Lloyd Richards, joined
       him on stage for the standing ovation he received, and the set
       designed, H.R. Poindexter, might have done as well. But has the
       controversy ended?"

1937. Kerr, Walker. "The Actor Vs. The Legend - Who Should Win?,"
       New York Times, January 29, 1978, Section 2, p. 3.

       The author reviews the play "Paul Robeson," starring James Earl
       Jones. He contends that in the contest between actor and subject,
       it is here the actor will win. Kerr concludes: "Mr. Jones is so
       original a performer and possessed of so much idiosyncratic energy,
       that his presence on the stage is simply stronger than our memory
       of Mr. Robeson. Wishing to honor a legend, he dominates it."

1938. Brown, Lloyd L. "Robeson Play is 'Entertainment for the Phili-
       stines'," New York Amsterdam News, February 18, 1978, p. D-6.

       The writer comments on the play, "Paul Robeson," starring James
       Earl Jones. He argues that the play that uses his name is not
       Paul Robeson. It is a feeble caricature of that Black artistic
       genius whom the Philistines banned from Broadway for many years.
       Just as Samson's enemies would not have gone to see him had he not
       been in chains, so in this case the white theater goers were not
       to be scared away by a truthful depiction of Robeson as a Black
       revolutionary hero, states Mr. Brown. He concludes: "Clearly
       then, it is a sin and a shame that the incomparable real-life
       Robeson, who for years was prevented from speaking for himself,

(Brown, Lloyd L.)

is now misrepresented on Broadway by the words of a counterfeit Robeson."

1939. Lask, Thomas. "Robeson to Re-open on 'Colored Girls' Bill," New York Times, March 2, 1978, p. C-17.

This article states that the play "Paul Robeson" would be in the same theatre, but on different days, with "For Colored Girls." The latter play gave five performances each week and the Robeson play four a week. Joseph Papp reopened the play after it was closed for a week after only 45 performances. Mr. Papp states that he was reopening the play because of his great admiration both for the late singer-actor and for James Earl Jones, whom he characterized as "one of the finest actors in the country." He also declares that "There must be thousands who knew nothing of Paul Robeson. This will give them a chance to be inspired by this man's life."

1940. Lewis, Barbara. "Lloyd Richards on Paul Robeson," New York Amsterdam News, March 4, 1978, pp. D-6, D-7.

Mr. Lloyd Richards directed the play, "Paul Robeson," starring James Earl Jones. He said when he saw the play out of town, it had problems, and it needed work. He decided to direct it after the work played in Philadelphia. The desire to widen the sphere of knowledge about Robeson was a prime factor in Richard's decision to direct the play.

1941. "Papp Reopening 'Robeson' at Booth Theater," New York Amsterdam News, March 4, 1978, p. D-6.

Producer Joseph Papp announced that although the play "Paul Robeson" closed at the Lunt-Fontanne Theatre, it would reopen at the Booth Theatre. Papp describes the late Paul Robeson as one of his childhood heroes, whose name should be in lights on Broadway as long as possible. He also praised the acting of James Earl Jones, who stars in "Paul Robeson."

1942. Wadud, Ali. "Closing of 'Robeson' a 'Senseless Tragedy'," New York Amsterdam News, March 4, 1978, p. D-6.

The writer contends that the closing of the play "Paul Robeson," starring James Earl Jones, was a sad and senseless tragedy. He declares that the play filled him with inspiration and awe and based on everything he read and heard about Mr. Robeson, he must say that if we did not get the essence of him on that stage, he does not know whom else it could have been. Mr. Wadud said there were no distortions in the play.

1943.   Washington, Sam.   "TV Report Fans 'Robeson' Fire," <u>New York Am-</u>
<u>sterdam News</u>, March 4, 1978, p. D-6.

This article discusses Carl Stokes' program "Urban Journal" that
was seen on NBC television in New York City. Mr. Stokes states
that many of the signers of the "Statement of Conscience" concerning the play, "Paul Robeson," starring James Earl Jones, had
not seen the play and signed the protest because of friendship.
Some of the signers protested to NBC and objected to Mr. Stokes'
assertions.

1944.   O'Connor, John J.   "Carl Stokes Takes on 'Paul Robeson'," <u>New</u>
<u>York Times</u>, March 12, 1978, Art and Leisure, Section 2, p. 29.

In this article Carl Stokes reacts to "a statement of conscience"
that appeared in <u>Variety</u> that was signed by 56 distinguished representatives of the Black establishment objecting to the play
"Paul Robeson." Stokes declares: "This is a play Americans need
to see, not because an actor rises to superlative heights in his
portrayal of a character, which Jones does, but because this play
reintroduces Paul Robeson to the American public and causes white
and Black Americans to confront atrocious treatment they accorded
this remarkable man."

1945.   Goldstein, Richard.   "For Colored Folks Who Have Considered Censorship," <u>Village Voice</u>, March 13, 1978, p. 44.

The writer discusses the events surrounding the producing of the
play "Paul Robeson" starring James Earl Jones that closed in
March, 1978, after 45 performances, in New York City. Goldstein
surmises "Paul Robeson," the play, was a brainchild of the
National Broadcasting Company and Universal Studios who acted
against the wishes of its subject. Many hands shaped its script
not all of them Black, concludes the author. Goldstein tended to
agree with Joseph Papp, producer of the play when Papp declared:
"There must be thousands who know nothing of Paul Robeson. This
(the play) will give them a chance to be inspired by the man's
life."

1946.   Gresham, Jewell Handy.   "Paul Robeson: Another View," <u>New York</u>
<u>Amsterdam News</u>, March 18, 1978, p. A-6.

The writer was (in 1978) Executive Director of the Coalition of
Concerned Black Americans. She comments on Carl Stokes' observation on his NBC-TV "news" reports. She declares that Mr. Stokes
had no right to make inaccurate statements about the 56 signers
of the "Statement of Conscience" concerning the play, "Paul
Robeson," starring James Earl Jones, without first contacting
most of the signers.

1947.   Guinier, Ewart. "The Paul Robeson That I Knew," Black Scholar,
        Vol. 9, No. 6, March, 1978, pp. 45-46.

        The writer discusses Paul Robeson as he knew, observed, listened
        to and saw between 1929 and 1953. He states that after seeing
        James Earl Jones portray Robeson in the play, "Paul Robeson," he
        saw a disfigured Paul Robeson. Dr. Guinier suggests that there
        were numerous factual errors in the play. It was also pointed
        out that there was no account in the play of Robeson's exertions
        over the years (and particularly from 1947) on behalf of workers,
        White as well as Black, struggling to better their economic and
        general social conditions.

1948.   Bassett, Ted. "The Real Robeson," Daily World, April 8, 1978,
        pp. 13, 16, 17.

        The writer comments on the play "Paul Robeson" and declares that
        it distorts the life of the man. He surmises that it presents a
        false image of the real Robeson, is highly fictionalized, larded
        with trivia, and marred by racism and anti-communism. Mr. Bassett
        asserts that the U.S. monopoly ruling class tried to make the
        living Robeson a non-person, but failed miserably. Now that he
        is dead they are trying to prevent his memory. The play serves
        this purpose, concludes the writer.

1949.   Cannon, Terry. "Open Forum on''Robeson': Packaging Greatness,"
        Daily World, May 5, 1978, p. 8.

        This article states that now that the play "Paul Robeson" has
        closed - hopefully never to be resurrected - a perhaps more im-
        portant issue than the play's Classic Comics treatment of Robeson
        has come to the fore. This is the issue of how the criticisms
        of the play were treated by the mass media, states Cannon. To
        examine these issues, which will continue long after the closing
        of the play, the Coalition of Concerned Black Americans presented
        an open forum, "Paul Robeson: The Play, the Protest, the Legacy
        and the Lessons" at Hunter College. The members of the forum were
        James Baldwin, Julian Bond, Paul Robeson, Jr., Clayton Riley,
        Jewell Handy Gresham and Gil Noble.

1950.   "Controversy Over Robeson Play Continues in Forum on His Image,"
        New York Times, May 14, 1978, p. 49.

        There was a panel held at Hunter College in New York on "Paul
        Robeson - The Play, the Protest, the Legacy and the Lessons."
        The members included James Baldwin, Ossie Davis, Paul Robeson, Jr.,
        Clayton Riley, and Dr. Jewell Handy. The focus of the symposium
        was on what was the image of the late singer, actor, and athlete
        in the play by Philip Hayes Dean. Baldwin told the audience when
        it came to Black heroes the "popular culture wanted a chocolate
        John Wayne." The play, Mr. Baldwin said, portrayed Robeson as a
        "misguided, tragic hero." Davis states that in the play Robeson
        could not be made a socialist, "that's dangerous." "What this
        country needs," he said, "is a hero who is Black and a Socialist."
        Paul Robeson, Jr., declares that the play about his father should
        portray him in a true light.

1951. Fraser, C. Gerald. "33 Playwrights Protest 'Censure' of
'Robeson'," New York Times, May 18, 1978, p. C-20.

In response to recent protests against the play "Paul Robeson,"
33 prominent playwrights, members of the executive council of the
Dramatists Guild, issued a statement deploring attempts "to influence critics and audiences againat a play." It also stated
that a playwright must be prepared to accept criticism no matter
how bitter or even unfair, from critics and other individuals who
disagree with opinions he or she expresses. Some of the signers
of the letters included Edward Albee, Ed Bullins, Richard Rogers,
Lillian Hellman, Mary Rogers, Paddy Chayefsky, Jay Lerner, Sidney
Kingsley, and James Goldman.

1952. Campbell, Colin. "Robeson's Return," Horizon, Vol. 21, May, 1978,
pp. 35-37.

This article concerns the play "Paul Robeson." The author argues
that the uproar has been a remarkable, if unintended, tribute to
Paul Robeson, who remains a towering figure in the minds of politically conscious Black Americans. He has turned out to be as
controversial, although in another way, after death as he was
during his turbulent lifetime. A complex and extraordinary man,
Robeson often seemed larger than life to his contemporaries.
Today many of his admirers argue that he is too big to be captured
on stage, states Campbell. The author concludes:
What the controversy has demonstrated is that
Robeson is still too lively to allow even the most
muscular and crafty biographer to pin him down without
a fight. He is too lively in another way - an accessible and attractive character again, after decades
as a nonperson - to allow careful biographers and
intense political factions to keep the man all to
themselves. He was a large man, and will be a long
time before most people fully comprehend him.

1953. O'Connor, John J. "TV: James Earl Jones Portrays Paul Robeson
on WNET," New York Times, October 8, 1979, Section 3, p. 20.

This article states that James Earl Jones portrayed Paul Robeson
in the play of the same name on WNET, Channel 13, that "the portrait is hardly without flaws. This ia a middle-class interpretation of Paul Robeson...." In the end, though the audience
is confronted with the reality of Paul Robeson as an exceptional
person. This much is made clear, no matter what objections might
be triggered by Mr. Phillip Hayes Dean's script, states O'Connor.
He concludes: "He (James Earl Jones) is intense, incredibly
moving and thoroughly convincing."

24. PEEKSKILL

1954. Anekwe, Simon. "Robeson Defies Peekskill Crowd Performs Concert
Amidst Violence," New York Amsterdam News, January 31, 1971, p. 5.

According to this author, the crowd at Peekskill, where violence
erupted wanted to lynch Paul Robeson. This incident was brought
on, partly by the Peekskill Evening Star, states Mr. Anekwe. The
Star had "heralded" the concert in words like these: "It appears
that Peekskill is to be treated to another concert visit by Paul
Robeson, renowned Negro baritone. Time was when the honor would
have been ours -- all ours. As things stand, like most folks who
put America first, we're a little doubtful of that honor." Some
supporters discovered sharp shooters armed with rifles on trees
outside the grounds. The organizers then tried to persuade
Robeson not to expose himself by leaving his car and going to the
platform to sing. But Robeson's mind was made up. He had come
to sing for the people and he did, out in the open, on the stage.
The writer went on to assert that no incidents occurred during the
concert. But when it was over and the concert goers drove home-
wards, they fell into ambush after ambush on all three roads
leading from the site. He declares what's more, there were troopers
standing by the attackers, apparently to dissuade anyone who
attempted to fight back. But hardly anyone was in a position to
do so; for those being assaulted were trapped in their cars or
busses. Thus it was on the road and in the night that the real
slaughter of Peekskill took place, stated Mr. Anekwe. He argues:
"The hospitals were filling up. All over Westchester the hospitals were filling up with the blinded, the bleeding and the
wounded, the cut, the lacerated faces, the fractured skulls, the
infants with glass in their eyes, the men, women trambled and
beaten, the Negroes beaten and mutiliated, all the terribly hurt
who had come to listen to music. The music of Paul Robeson. He
had defied the men with hate and the rifles with telescopic lenses.
He had a right to sing and those who wanted to hear him sing had
a right to listen. Such was the drama that marked Robeson's
life."

1955. Wright, Charles H. "Paul Robeson at Peekskill," Paul Robeson:
The Great Forerunner. Editors of Freedomways. New York: Dodd,
Mead & Co., 1978, pp. 130-141.

The writer states that Robeson's position paper, on the Peekskill
affair enraged his enemies more than ever, and spurred them on to
more imaginative acts of violence against him. His prophecy and
plea, out of tune with the times, were ignored. Peekskill's first
anniversary was more than two months away when the United States
military forces entered the Korean phase of our Southeast Asian
misadventure that would eventually waste millions of lives,
trillions of dollars and accelerate our headlong plunge into financial and moral bankruptcy. Before a year had elapsed, the dis-
ruptive fissure within the CIO became an unabridgeable chasm, as
the latter-day saints, then in power, began to exorcise the militant demons of the left. Guardians of the status quo in

(Wright, Charles H.)

Birmingham, Bogalusa and Selma were instructed and encouraged by the permissiveness of Peekskill. They bided their time and kept their powder dry, argues Wright. He also declares that in less than a year, Robeson's passport was cancelled by a punative State Department. Denied the opportunity to make a living at home and unable to travel abroad, he was sentenced to a slow death by economic strangulation and political repression. Robeson, as usual, would not cooperate with his enemies. Not only did he refuse to die, he lived to see all of his unpopular causes become a part of the everyday American way of life, argues Wright. The author concludes:

> Despite the vindications of time and circumstance, Robeson remains a prophet without honor in his own land. One of the most glaring evidences of this dishonor is Robeson's absence from the College Football's Hall of Fame. He is the only two-time All-American so ignored. A reversal of this decision, long overdue, could signal the start of a timely re-evaluation of this controversial American, and, perhaps, a change in his outrageous fortune.

25.   ROBESON'S MURAL

1956.   Gellert, Hugo. "Hugo Gellert - Style and Tenacity," Daily World, May 19, 1973, Magazine Section, pp. 5-7.

This article discusses Gellert's successful struggle to get Robeson into his mural for Hillcrest High School in Queens, New York. The writer points out that he met bitter resistence by some people to exclude Robeson from the mural. There was also some discussion about Gellert's print of Robeson exhibited at the New York World's Fair of 1939-1940 and later given to the library of Birmingham, Alabama.

26.   RUSSIA

1957.   Murphy, George B, Jr. "Black Delegation Visits the USSR," New World Review, Vol. 39, No. 4, Fall, 1971, pp. 41, 45, 46.

The author, a Black American, along with several other Blacks, visited the U.S.S.R. and gave his impressions of their visit. He states Soviet writers deeply appreciated the writings of Paul Robeson and other writers of the Black older generation such as W.E.B. DuBois and Langston Hughes. Mr. Murphy also reports that he and the delegation presented two large frame prints of Paul Robeson, done by Bert Phillips, a Black artist in Chicago to

(Murphy, George B., Jr.)

them and Dushambe, capital of Tadzhikistan.

1958.   Murphy, George B., Jr.   "Paul Robeson Immortalized by Soviet
Citizens," Afro-American, July 22, 1972, p. 5.

An American delegation presented a drawing of Paul Robeson done by
Black artist Bert Phillips to the Uzbek Friendship Society in
Tashkent, Russia. The following statement was also made during
the presentation. It states, in part:
    In the ceaseless struggle of nations and peoples to
    develop everlastingly self-fulfilling lives, great
    art harmonizes in diversity, the rich cultures of
    working people flowing from their struggles to harness
    and appropriate for themselves the boundiful life-
    giving resources of mother earth. The practitioners
    of great art in every age of world history have
    come to know and understand this through their im-
    mersion of themselves and their art, in the struggles
    of the people, the common people, the working people.
    "That is why Paul Robeson is a great artist, who
    stands on the stage of world history, the greatest
    American artist of this century. It is in this
    spirit that we present this drawing to the Uzbek
    Friendship Society, by Bert Phillips, an Afro-
    American artist, on behalf of this delegation, and
    as a symbol of the affection of Afro-Americans and
    all progressive Americans for the people of the
    Uzbek Soviet Socialist Republic, in the name of
    friendship and peace."
In a warm response to the presentation, the deputy chairman of the
society said, "Robeson evokes deep affection in the hearts and
minds of our people."

1959.   Murphy, George B., Jr.   "Friendship Visit: USSR, 1972," New World
Review, Vol. 41, No. 1, First Quarter, 1973, p. 21.

The world traveler points out that in 1949 the people in the Soviet
Socialist Republic of Kirghizia honored Paul Robeson for his great
national and international contributions as artist and anti-
imperialist fighter for peace, justice and brotherhood, when
they named one of the Tien Shan mountain peaks in their country
"Mt. Paul Robeson."

1960.   "US-USSR Friendship Societies - The People's Role in Closer Ties,"
New World Review, Vol. 41, No. 4, Fourth Quarter, 1973, p. 38.

In 1973, the Chicago Committee of American-Soviet Friendship
proudly dedicated the Anniversary observance to Mr. Paul Robeson,
whose magnificent and profound artistry illumined the path of
American-Soviet friendship, according to the article.

1961.   "Professor Paints Portrait of Paul Robeson for U.S.S.R.," Jet,
        No. 45, No. 8, November 15, 1973, p. 36.

        Bertrand Phillips, a Black Northwestern University Assistant Pro-
        fessor, was asked by the Soviet Union, to paint a portrait of Paul
        Robeson for the rededication ceremony of Mt. Paul Robeson. The
        USSR named the mountain in the entertainer's honor in 1949.

1962.   Murphy, Madeline W. "Destination: Mt. Paul Robeson," The World
        Magazine, December 1, 1973, pp. M10-M11.

        The writer, a Black American, reports on her trip to Mt. Paul
        Robeson in the Soviet Union. She concludes:
            Our three-day stay in Frunze was jampacked with tours
            of the residential and commercial areas, the parks and
            official buildings of the Presidium. We were on a
            hectic pace with visits to a coat factory, a state
            farm in the country, the studio of Gapar Aytiyev, a
            post-revolutionary Kirghizian artist, to a news con-
            ference with the working press; and, most importantly,
            to visit and rededicate Mt. Paul Robeson in the Tien
            Shan mountains.

1963.   "Paul Robeson's Letters Given to Howard U," Philadelphia Tribune,
        November 30, 1974.

        According to this article letters of tribute to Paul Robeson from
        Soviet citizens poured into Moscow radio and television stations
        in response to a national celebration of the singer-actor's 75th
        birthday on April 9, 1973, because "the people don't know the
        address of Paul Robeson...." The letters were given to the Moor-
        land-Spingarn Research Center at Howard University. All but one
        of the 200 letters to Robeson was in Russian. Dr. Michael R.
        Winston, Director of the Moorland-Spingarn Research Center, said
        the letters will be translated into English, indexed and made
        available for use by scholars. As of 1981 the letters had not
        been translated.

1964.   Golden, Lily. "Black People in the Soviet Union," New World Review,
        Vol. 43, No. 5, September-October, 1975, pp. 17, 18, 20.

        The author states that Paul Robeson visited the Soviet Union many
        times, performing for large and enthusiastic audiences. She also
        points out that Robeson states in his book, Here I Stand, his
        assessment of the Soviet Union when he declared: "....I came to
        believe that the experiences of the many peoples and races in the
        Soviet Union...would be of great value for other peoples of the
        East in catching up with the modern world...."

1965.   Butler, Josephine. "Report on the Paul Robeson Friendship Society,"
        New World Review, Vol. 45, No. 4, July-August, 1977, p. 23.

        The Paul Robeson Friendship Society was organized in July, 1976,
        in Washington, D.C. The complete name of this group is "Hands
        Around the World - Paul Robeson Friendship Society." Internation-
        ally the society has been involved in spreading information in all

(Butler, Josephine)

D.C. schools about the youth program of the National Council of American-Soviet Friendship, including invitations to participate in the International Children's Festival at Camp Artek and the Summer High School Camp and Travel Program.

1966. Kudrov, Konstantin. "My Meeting with Paul Robeson," New World Review, Vol. 41, No. 2, Second Quarter, 1973, pp. 52-54.

The Russian jouranlist declares: "And we, Soviet people are deeply proud of our unbreakable friendship with Paul Robeson; we value and honor this wonderful man." He asserts: "As a precious souvenir I preserve an autographed copy of a photo I took of Robeson in the Crimea. I am happy that my work as a journalist led to my acquaintance with Robeson, to our friendship. I have been enriched by this friendship and knowledge of his life and work. I fully agree with the words expressed in the early fifties by Pablo Neruda, the noted Chilean poet and public leader: 'Robeson is a splendid example for the world of the indivisible unity of a man of art and a class-conscious fighter.'" The writer concludes:
We, Soviet people, have loved and love him for this, and on the occasion of the 75th birthday of this fine man, I extend my very best greetings and congratulations. May the warmth of millions of hearts of people of goodwill everywhere on the globe, who know and remember Robeson, the singer and fighter, give him strength and health.

1967. Kudrov, Konstantin. "Paul Robeson: A Russian Remembrance," Rutgers Alumni Magazine, Vol. 53, No. 3, Winter, 1974, pp. 26-27.

The writer discusses his many years of friendship with Robeson beginning with his first meeting with him in Moscow in 1934. He last saw him in the Crimea in 1958. He asserts:
I am happy that my work as a journalist led to my acquaintance with Robeson, to our friendship. I was enriched by a study of his life, and I fully agree with the words expressed in the early Fifties by Pablo Neruda, the noted Chilean poet and public leader: 'Robeson is a fine man, a splendid example for the world of the indivisible unity of a man of art and a class-conscious fighter.' The Soviet people love him for this, and on the occasion of the 76th birthday (April 9) of this fine man, I extend my very best greetings and congratulations and bow to him, in the Russian custom. I wish him to bravely endure his ailment. May the warmth of millions of hearts of people of goodwill everywhere on the globe, who know and remember Paul Robeson, the singer and fighter, give him strength.

1968. "USSR Names 40,000-Ton Tanker for Paul Robeson," <u>Jet</u>, Vol. 53, No. 20, February 2, 1978, p. 26.

The Soviet Union in honor of Paul Robeson named a new 40,000-ton tanker after him. Robeson was the first of his race to be so honored. Throughout his life Robeson consistently spoke of his deep admiration for the Russian people.

1969. Tynes, Slava. "Paul Robeson: Great Friend of the Soviet People," <u>Paul Robeson: The Great Forerunner</u>. Editors of <u>Freedomways</u>. New York: Dodd, Mead & Co., 1978, pp. 94-99.

The writer states that "Pavel Vasilyevich," that is how Paul Robeson, the great American actor and singer, asked to be called after the Russian manner when he visited the Soviet Union. In this way he stressed that in the USSR he had found not only friends, but also a land of socialism for which he went on fighting so bravely at home, in the United States of America. He also states that every time when Paul Robeson came to the USSR again paragraphs appeared in the Soviet press with warm words addressed to the dear and welcomed friend. Every time he was embraced by the Soviet people who greatly respected and admired his unbending heroic character, who are proud of him, who hold him up as an example for their children and have written books about him in order to commemorate for the generations to come the image of this extremely humane man. Paul Robeson has become a character in some plays by Soviet playwrights, while a mountain summit in the western Tyran-Shan and Trans-Ili Ala-Tau mountains in Central Asia has been named after him. Paul Robeson is very near and dear to Soviet people, concludes Tynes.

27. RUTGERS UNIVERSITY

1970. "Rutgers Names Arts Music Lounge for Robeson," <u>Jet</u>, Vol. 38, April 30, 1970, p. 60.

Rutgers University paid homage to its most distinguished Black alumnus, Paul Robeson, the actor, scholar and lawyer. The ceremonies, which marked the first such tribute paid by the New Brunswick, N.J., university in 35 years, were highlighted by the dedication of the Paul Robeson Arts and Music Lounge in the school's student center. University President Mason Gross and Paul Robeson, Jr., were among the speakers. Robeson, who lives in Philadelphia, was unable to attend the ceremonies because of ill health. He graduated from Rutgers in 1919 and became a controversial figure when he visited the Soviet Union in the late '30s and returned home extolling its virtues. "Here for the first time I walk in full human dignity," Robeson had said of his experience there. Paul Jr. said his father was not referring to communism as a way of life, but was talking about the general attitude toward Blacks in the Soviet Union. Gross said Robeson suffered from being ahead of him time, and added that "New Jersey has not yet

(Jet)

distinguished itself on those Robeson standards."

1971. "Portrait of Robeson Given to Rutgers," The Sphinx, Vol. 56, No. 6, October, 1970, pp. 25-28.

The Eastern Region of the Alpha Phi Alpha Fraternity presented a portrait of Paul Robeson to Rutgers University, New Brunswick, New Jersey. It was painted by artist Alvin C. Hollingsworth. Paul Robeson was a member of that fraternity.

1972. Robeson, Paul, Jr. "Rutgers Salutes Paul Robeson," Freedomways, Vol. 10, No. 3, Third Quarter, 1970, pp. 237-241.

This speech was delivered at Rutgers University in April, 1970, at an affair sponsored by Eastern Region of Alpha Phi Alpha Fraternity and the Rutgers Student Center. He states, in part: "In the Rutgers library you will find a letter from a white Rutgers alumnus which in the most strident racist tones calls for Paul Robeson's execution in the electric chair for the remarks he made in 1949 at a World Peace Conference when he said American Negroes should not fight against the Soviet Union on behalf of the United States. It was in this atmosphere that the campaign to silence my father was launched - a campaign that resulted in confiscation of his passport for eight years." He concludes:
There are those who seek to lessen Paul Robeson's stature by creating the false image of a tragic, misled figure, victimized by the times. Nothing could be further from the truth. Paul Robeson was way ahead of his time - a trailblazer. He knew full well the price he would have to pay and he paid it - unbowed and unflinching. There is sadness now in the fact that today he is in retirement and in poor health. But he can rejoice in the countless others who march along the broad trail he blazed. He bore the burden in the heat of the day, he survived the fiercest repression and he remained unvanquished - in this there is majestic triumph.

1973. Gelder, Lawrence Van. "Notes on People: Paul Robeson," New York Times, February 12, 1972, p. 19.

It was pointed out that the Board of Governors of Rutgers University voted to name the student center on the university's Newark campus for Paul Robeson. Mr. Robeson had a distinguished career at Rutgers, where he was an All-American football player, Phi Beta Kappa scholar and Valedictorian of the class of 1919.

1974. "Rutgers Honors Robeson," New York Times, April 10, 1972, p. 39.

Ceremonies dedicating the student center of the Newark's campus of Rutgers University as the Paul Robeson Student Center were held at the campus. Robeson was an All-American football player and Valedictorian of the Rutgers Class of 1919.

1975. Walker, Joe. "Rarely Appreciated Voice for Peace and Justice:
       Garland About Robeson's Noble Head, the Twilight of His Day,"
       Muhammad Speaks, June 30, 1972, p. 4.

       The writer states that the Board of Governors of Rutgers University
       voted to name the new student center at its Newark Campus after
       the school's most illustrious alumnus - Paul Robeson. Walker
       travelled to Africa, Asia, Europe and Latin America and declares
       that he learned of the tremendous world respect for this Black
       artist. The author surmises: "In East Germany I discovered the
       Paul Robeson Archives (in 1969) with displays highlighting
       Robeson's academic, sports and artistic achievements, his life-
       long close association with the ordinary folk of this world and
       his conviction that the rights of man are a class issue. I was
       stunned when I realized that no comparable tribute to or record
       of Robeson's life and contributions existed in the United
       States...."

1976. Bloustein, Edward J. "Robeson Dedicated Speech," Negro History
       Bulletin, Vol. 35, No. 6, October, 1972, p. 141.

       This is a speech made by Dr. Edward J. Bloustein, President of
       Rutgers University on the dedication of the Paul Robeson campus
       center at Newark-Rutgers. He states: "Today after a period of
       neglect by this University of which I am ashamed, we return to
       Paul Robeson some small portion of that honor he brought to us."
       Dr. Bloustein declares that Robeson transcended his time, his
       race and his own person to join that select group of souls who
       speak for all humanity. The speaker concludes: "Paul Robeson is
       a great humanist, a man who helps to bring us all together, helps
       us, amidst differences in which we can and should take great
       pride, to find, nourish and glory in our common humanity."

1977. Fishman, George M. "History Does Move Ahead," American Dialog,
       Vol. 7, No. 1, Winter, 1972, pp. 32-35.

       The writer states that there is a letter in an exhibit from the
       University Archives of Rutgers University that revealed official
       Rutgers University racism towards Paul Robeson during his under-
       graduate years at the university. New developments on the
       Rutgers, New Brunswick, scene are related to movement and demands
       by the Black students. They are related in the naming of a
       Paul Robeson Lounge on the New Brunswick campus and in the Paul
       Robeson Commemorations, 1969-1970, concludes Mr. Fishman.

1978. "Rutgers Program to Honor Robeson," New York Times, April 8, 1973,
       p. 111.

       The article states Paul Robeson's Alma Mater, Rutgers University
       also disowned and ignored him in the 1940s because of his political
       activities. However, beginning on April 8, 1973, in a week-long
       program the university would present a series of events commemo-
       rating Mr. Robeson's accomplishments on the stage and screen, in
       scholarship and on the athletic field. Mr. Robeson was very ill
       and would not be able to attend the ceremonies. Standing in for
       his father was Paul Robeson, Jr., an engineer. The program was

(New York Times)

funded by the University and a $10,000 matching grant from the
National Endowment for the Arts.

1979. "Paul Robeson at Rutgers," Rutgers Daily Targum, April 10, 1973,
       12 pp.

       This was a special issue of the university's newspaper. It recapped
       Paul Robeson's accomplishments at Rutgers University. Some at-
       tention is also devoted to other facets of Robeson's life. This
       tribute to Paul Robeson by his alma mater finally shows that at
       least the students recognize his contributions to the world.

1980. "Paul Robeson at Rutgers," Black Voice, April 24, 1973.

       This Black students' newspaper at Rutgers University, New Bruns-
       wick, New Jersey, devoted a great part to Paul Robeson. It
       characterized his accomplishments at Rutgers University during
       his university days there. Some attention was devoted to his many
       accomplishments as a freedom fighter. There was also a long re-
       view of Robeson's second edition of Here I Stand by Professor
       Harold D. Weaver, Jr. An article on the Paul Robeson Black Arts
       Ensemble, a student group at Rutgers, and its performance there of
       Broadway music, was also discussed.

1981. "Rutgers University Pays Tribute to Paul Robeson at Last," Jet,
       Vol. 44, April 26, 1973, p. 16.

       According to this article Rutgers University, in New Brunswick,
       New Jersey, which for several years has kept Paul Robeson in its
       alumni closet, finally honored him in absentia. The state uni-
       versity which awarded Robeson a bachelor's degree in 1919 -- the
       third Black man to be graduated from the school, gave him an
       honorary doctorate on his 75th birthday as part of a recent pro-
       gram marking Robeson's accomplishments in the arts, scholarship
       and on the athletic playing field. The Rutgers program, financed
       with the help of the National Endowment for the Arts which contri-
       buted a $10,000 matching grant, detailed Robeson's accomplishments,
       using records, films, photographs and lectures presented by
       Robeson's friends and scholars who have studied Robeson's life.

1982. "Robeson Given Honorary Doctorate by Rutgers University," Black
       World, Vol. 22, No. 9, July, 1973, p. 89.

       Robeson was awarded the honorary degree of Doctor of Humane Letters.
       Robeson was ill and could not receive the degree in person. It
       was accepted by his son, Paul Robeson, Jr.

1983. "Rutgers to Show Robeson Series," New York Times, November 4, 1973,
       p. 83.

       A retrospective of most of Paul Robeson's movies were shown, re-
       portedly the first ever, at Rutgers University, November 4th
       through the 19th. The program was coordinated by Professor Harold
       D. Weaver of Rutgers African Studies Department. Some of the

690   A Paul Robeson Research Guide

(New York Times)

films include: "Show Boat," "Emperor Jones," "Proud Valley,"
"Big Fella," "Dark Sands," and "King Solomon's Mines."

1984. Yeakey, Lamont H. "A Student Without Peer: The Undergraduate
College Years of Paul Robeson," Journal of Negro Education,
Vol. 42, No. 4, Fall, 1973, pp. 489-503.

The author, a graduate student at Columbia University, read this
paper at the 56th Annual Meeting of the Association for the Study
of Afro-American Life and History that was held in October, 1971,
in Philadelphia. Much of this article is devoted to Robeson as
an athlete. He surmises that although Paul Robeson's sports-
manship was a masterful demonstration of superior athletic prowess
unparalleled by any student yet to attend Rutgers, his scholarship was equally, if not more, impressive. The writer argues:
"In retrospect, one can say that Paul Robeson, demonstrating that
he was not just equal to, but in fact superior to the vast majority
of whites, atheletically and academically, attacked the prevailing
myth of white superiority. With this he singlehandedly demonstrated the absurdity of the belief in black inferiority. Subsequently, his trailblazing somewhat eroded white resistance to
black students attending white college. Unfortunately, his impact
did little to lessen the restraints imposed on black students in
those years. Nevertheless, Robeson's performance stimulated intercollegiate athletics, brought new life to the games, and helped
to foster a new understanding among some black and white students,"
states Yeakey.

1985. White, Gordon S., Jr., "Rutgers Seeks to Get Paul Robeson in Hall
of Fame," New York Times, September 23, 1975, p. 44.

Rutgers University opened a campaign to have Paul Robeson, one
of the finest football players in the university's history, elected
to the National Football Foundation Hall of Fame. Dr. Edward
Bloustein, President of Rutgers University, led the drive and
declares that Robeson was kept out of the Hall of Fame because of
his political sympathies. The college president declares: "He
has been neglected because he had a political flirtation with the
Soviet Union. He happens to be one of the great scholar-athletes
in the nation and also a great artist. I'm looking forward to
arousing interest in this across the nation." Paul Robeson, Jr.,
declares that his father has never publicly or privately expressed
his feelings on election to the Hall of Fame. The younger Robeson also states: "It is a disgrace to the Hall of Fame that he
is not in it. It is a reflection on the Hall of Fame and not on
my father that he is not in (it)."

1986. "Paul Robeson," Newsweek, Vol. 86, No. 14, October 6, 1975, pp.
       58-59.

       The article contends that Robeson once declared: "American demo-
       cracy is Hitler Fascism." The article also states that Robeson,
       ailing and 77, has passed word that he wants to be named to
       college football's Hall of Fame. His alma mater, Rutgers Univer-
       sity, is leading the fight to get him into the Hall of Fame.
       Dr. Edward J. Bloustein, President of Rutgers, declares: "He is
       truly one of the heroic figures of our culture and yet we have
       neglected him because he had a political flirtation with the
       Soviet Union."

1987. "A College Named for Robeson?," New York Times, October 29, 1975,
       p. 88.

       Forty members of the faculty of Livingston College is Piscataway
       submitted a petition to their faculty chamber asking that the name
       of the school be changed to Paul Robeson College in honor of the
       singer and actor who graduated from Rutgers University in 1919.
       The 275 member chamber had to vote on the change and if it ap-
       proved of it, it would then have to go to the Rutgers University
       Board of Governors for final approval.

1988. "Livingston Split over a New Name, Change of Rutgers to Paul
       Robeson College," New York Times, November 19, 1975, p. 92.

       The Livingston College community appeared to be equally divided
       over the proposal to rename the school Paul Robeson College in
       honor of the singer and actor, who was a 1919 alumnus of Rutgers
       University. Some that opposed the name change stated that since
       Mr. Robeson was identified very prominently as a leftist and a
       Communist a name change honoring him would also identify Living-
       ston as a leftist institution. Those who supported the name
       change argued Livingston College is committee to democratic and
       progressive education, and these are things Paul Robeson stood
       for and fought for all of his life. They also declared: "It
       would be an honor to us to name our college after him."

1989. "Livingston College Balks to Name Shift," New York Times, December
       4, 1975, p. 87.

       The faculty of Livingston College at Piscataway defeated a move
       to change the name of the institution to Paul Robeson college to
       honor the Black Rutgers University All-American football player
       and actor and singer. The faculty chamber refused to bring change
       resolution to a vote, instead, it approved a proposal to find some
       other means of honoring Mr. Robeson.

1990. "Rutgers Memorial Service Pays Homage to Robeson," New York Times,
       February 6, 1976, p. 32.

       It was reported that twelve members of the Rutgers University
       community spoke at a memorial service in honor of Paul Robeson.
       Speaking of several ways that Mr. Robeson could best be remembered,
       Norman Epting, senior editor of the university's Black and Puerto

(New York Times)

Rican student newspaper, said: "If you feel you are oppressed,
and you will not let oppression stop you then the spirit of Paul
Robeson is with you." Several poems about the actor, winter
athlete, scholar and political activist were read as well.

1991. Robinson, Eugene H. "A Distant Image: Paul Robeson and Rutgers'
Students Today," Paul Robeson: The Great Forerunner. Editors of
Freedomways. New York: Dodd, Mead & Co., 1978, pp. 178-188.

The writer declares that with Paul Robeson, a giant oak whom
America attempted to cut down with McCarthyite axes in his prime
for his progressive beliefs and radical actions. Professor Harold
Weaver, director of the Rutgers College (New Brunswick) Afro-
American Studies Program, estimated that at least 75 per cent of
the Black students at Rutgers don't know who Paul Robeson was or
is. With the numerous "special" programs in the New Brunswick
area, Black students number approximately 1,500 or 10 per cent of
the total enrollment; so, perhaps, 1,100 are not aware of Paul
Robeson's accomplishments. The white student awareness is probably very, very significantly lower. How, then, to write
honestly under the suggested title for this essay, "Paul Robeson
Inspires Rutgers' Students Today"? Answer: it can't be done,
states Robinson. He argues that an annual event with nationwide,
if not international publicity, which honors Robeson the Man in
life, love, laughter, word, and deed; this should be sponsored
by SAS, Alpha Phi Alpha, Black alumni and possibly Freedomways.
The same sponsors should raise funds for Paul Robeson Scholarships
for Black scholar-activists selected by leaders and members of
Rutgers' Black student organizations. Then, and only, then can
we say fully, as has been said partially, that "Paul Robeson inspired Rutgers' students today," concludes the writer.

28. SPORTS

1992. Edwards, Harry. "Paul Robeson: The Embodiment of The Athlete's
True Heritage," Freedomways, Vol. II, No. 1, First Quarter, 1971,
pp. 74-77.

The writer declares that Robeson, in his intellectual brilliance
and political awareness, must have known the probably outcomes of
his convictions. And even if he did not foresee these, there were
certainly ample signposts along his chosen route to point them
up to him. But he chose to travel on, to stand firm on his convictions. Herein lies an important part of his legacy to those who
are now or who are desirous of becoming athletes. For not once
did Paul Robeson allow the glitter, the newspaper print, and the
athletic recognition to deter him from expressing those ideals
and political attitudes which he held as a matter of conscience.
In today's world, the environment of the athlete is fraught with
pressures to conform to the archaic, reactionary and racist

(Edwards, Harry)

character of the athletic sphere, often under threat of dismissal
from sports participation, loss of educational support, or by
threat of issuing negative references on the athlete as a person
with a "bad attitude." In this long-overdue time of turbulence in
sports, all athletes and aspirants would do well to note carefully
Robeson's example, asserts the author. It is the nature of the
convictions that is important and the fervor with which a person
hastens to channel his feet and actions in the same direction as
his words and conscience. The price of such audacity can be high,
but never so high as the price of condescension and hypocrisy,
particularly American style, argues Dr. Edwards. He concludes:

> This then is part of the athletic legacy of Paul
> Robeson. By persecuting him and attempting to wipe
> even his memory from the athletic world, America has
> only succeeded in his further glorification, a glori-
> fication which has and will continue to light the way
> for other people, especially athletes. When the lies
> and myths supporting the "house-of-cards" social and
> political structures known as American society are
> finally erased and when, among other things, the whole
> story is told about the athletes who really lived up
> to the ideals of sports, there is little doubt in
> my mind that the name and deeds of Paul Robeson will
> figure prominently in that chapter of post-Babylon
> history....

1993. Jay, Mike. "The View from Left Field: Fame Vote Slights
Robeson," Daily World, February 22, 1972.

The author surmises that the 12 men who decide who gets into the
National Football Foundation's College Hall of Fame at Rutgers
have again bypassed selecting Paul Robeson, one of the greatest
college gridders of all time. The Hall of Fame selectors barred
him because of a clause stating that to be elected a player "must
have proved his worth as a citizen carrying the ideals forward
into his relations with his community and his fellow man." The
selection committee did not believe Robeson proved his worth. It
thought the football player was ungrateful for all of the opportunities he received in this country. The writer suggests that
Robeson never allowed the personal successes he achieved, in sports
in his career as an entertainer, to deter him from the struggle
against the oppression of his people.

1994. "38 Athletes Named to Black Hall of Fame," New York Times, June
29, 1973, p. 33.

Paul Robeson was among the 39 Black Athletes named to the Black
Hall of Fame by the editors of Black Sports magazine.

1995.   "Effort Launched to Put Versatile Robeson in Hall," Jet,   Vol. 49,
        No. 6, October 30, 1975, p. 48.

        The author contends that there is currently a move underway to
        have the former brawny lineman to become enshrined into the
        prestigious National Football Foundation and Hall of Fame where
        he would join other college football greats. Because of the com-
        plex nature of Robeson's life, some members of the two groups are
        nervous about Robeson's nomination. Many think that he is a
        Communist and therefore unfit for their shrine. The two groups
        are hesitant about bestowing their honors on Robeson until they
        obtain "some more information."

1996.   "Robeson: The Hard Way!," Long Island Press, January 24, 1976,
        p. 20.

        This is an article appearing in the Sports section of this news-
        paper. It states that Paul Robeson, the concert artist, All-
        American football player and multi-sport star at Rutgers who died
        yesterday, made the school's all-white football squad in 1916
        which was no easy chore. This article discusses the events sur-
        rounding how Robeson made the football team.

1997.   Israel, David. "It's Far Too Late to Honor Robeson," Washington
        Star, January 25, 1976.

        The author said that the television networks that would not offer
        Paul Robeson work two decades ago are paying tribute to him. The
        newspapers, including The Star, that castigated him editorially
        for having the courage to be right before his time are praising
        him now. All these men who would have had him in chains are
        mourning him. Paul Robeson can be forgiven for his indiscretions.
        He is dead. The writer declares, that yes, Paul Robeson can be
        forgiven but those who sincerely cherish his memory, those who
        knew him to be a great man during the vibrant years of his life,
        should never forgive or forget the people who tried to destroy
        him, who tried to break his will and wreck his career. He sur-
        mises that this is a small matter, but there is something those
        of us in sports can do for Robeson's memory. We can remember
        forever that the men who run the National Football Foundation and
        its Hall of Fame were among the small and the powerful and the
        hating who refused justice to Robeson because he dared to exercise
        his Constitutional rights. Jimmy McDowell, an official of the
        National Football Foundation Hall of Fame and a good old boy from
        Tennessee, has explained in the past that Paul Robeson was not a
        member, though he might deserve to be there more than any other
        man, because his induction would cause controversy. After all,
        Robeson was a militant,he was involved in "Communist" activities.
        He was political. This is an organization that sponsors affairs
        where they exalt George Murphy and Bob Hope and the memory of Ike
        and J. Edgar, great Americans all, over cheap meals and rotten
        jokes while the expensive hookers lounge upstairs in the hotel
        rooms, asserts Mr. Israel. He concludes:
            It is better this way, then, keeping out Paul Robeson.
            He would not want to be a part of their affair anyway.
            He would not want to become part of all they represent.

(Israel, David)

> So keep Paul Robeson out, keep him out forever. That
> Hall of Fame is not worthy of being graced by his
> greatness.

1998. Isaacs, Stan. "Paul Robeson Comes Homes," Newsday, January 29,
       1976, Part 2, p. 3.

The writer points out that Paul Robeson was ahead of his time.
His admirers and detractors might agree on that. What Robeson
said about injustice in the 1930's and 1940's are commonplace
utterances today. But he was out in front by himself then, and
at a time when dissent was equated with Communism. Robeson was
villified. He was, as much as any victim of a shooting war, a
casualty of the Cold War, argues Mr. Isaacs. He concludes:
> In any historical roll call of American Black
> athletic titans, the list would start with Jack
> Johnson, continue with Robeson, Jesse Owens, Joe
> Louis, Jackie Robinson, Bill Russell and Jim Brown to
> Muhammad Ali, and it should be recorded that all but
> Owen and Louis would come to be marked as militants
> who frequently incurred the wrath of many Americans....

1999. Barron, Allan P. "Paul Robeson," Black Sports, Vol. 5, No. 8,
       February, 1976, p. 4.

The publisher of Black Sports compares the life of Muhammid Ali
with Paul Robeson. He states that both were profiles in courage.
He also compares Ali's book, The Greatest, to Robeson's work,
Here I Stand. Barron argues that Ali's fight was against the
Vietnam conflict. Robeson's fight was against the strident anti-
Communist fervor of the McCarthy era, and on the side of an
individual's right to express his political beliefs. He concludes:
"Here I Stand is about a man of honor and pride taking a defiant
stand. Every word of it is true, the book says, and if you don't
like it, tough."

2000. "Black Hall of Fame Adds 21 More to its Inductees," Jet, Vol. 50,
       No. 3, April 8, 1976, p. 54.

Paul Robeson was among the 21 athletes inducted in the Black
Athletes Hall of Fame (BAHF). The BAHF was formed in 1975 to pay
tribute to those Blacks and White Atheltes and Officials who
helped Blacks progress in amateur and professional athletics.

29. STATE DEPARTMENT

2001. Kahan, Albert E. "We Embrace Our Friends: 'The Enemy'," American
Dialog, Vol. 6, No. 1, Autumn, 1971, pp. 26-32.

The writer gives a short comparison of Louis Armstrong to Paul
Robeson. He states in essence that if Mr. Armstrong spoke out
like Robeson, he, too, would have been blacklisted. Robeson was
not invited to make United States State Department tours like
Armstrong because Robeson would have spoken out to expose United
States imperialism and racism. Mr. Kahn concludes:
> He (Armstrong) left a legacy of incredible music for
> all peoples to enjoy far into the future. He made a
> lot of people happy for a long time and that's no
> small achievement. Needless to say Paul Robeson's
> achievements were far greater than Louis Armstrong's --
> at least as it affected Black peoples of the world....

2002. Ellison, W. James. "Paul Robeson and the State Department,"
Crisis, Vol. 84, May, 1977, pp. 184-189.

The author declares that the Truman Administration used the government's coercive power to silence Robeson. However, the extent to
which it did so has not heretofore been examined. That the
government used illegal and unconstitutional tactics in its campaign against Robeson is not an abnormality attributable to the
Cold War era of the 1950s. Ellison went on to state that the
State Department files reveal that it not only manifested the
government's disapproval of Robeson's political activities by revoking his passport and forbidding him to leave the continental
United States from 1950 to 1957, but also that Washington made
diplomatic threats to discourage another government from honoring
Robeson as a great humanitarian and activist for human rights.
The files further reveal that as late as 1962, Washington attempted
to prevent Robeson's employment abroad in a non-political area and
that the government sought to undermine Robeson's political impact
by issuing timely anti-Robeson news releases, argues Ellison. He
also surmises: "Robeson fared no better with the State Department
under the Kennedy Administration than he had when Truman and Eisenhower were President. Four years after the Supreme Court forced
the return of his passport, the feeling of the State Department
that he was a source of embarrassment generally and more specifically a threat to America's interest in Africa and Asia had not
changed one iota. The Department was determined to destroy
Robeson politically and economically by undermining his international prominence and rendering him politically impotent." He
concludes:
> Ultimately, the Supreme Court provides the only
> realizable means of keeping "the government off the
> backs of the people." The justice Robeson won he won
> through the Court. But the justice was not only for
> himself. It was also for the millions of Americans on
> whose behalf he stood up and suffered. Freedom is
> never free.

30. TRIBUTES

2003. "Paul Robeson Receives Ira Aldridge Award from Black History Association," Negro History Bulletin, Vol. 33, No. 5, May, 1970, p. 128.

Paul Robeson received an award at the 33rd annual meeting of the New York Chapter of the Association for the Study of Negro Life and History recently when he was presented its top honor. As more than 1,200 people looked on at a luncheon at the Waldorf-Astoria, Paul Robeson, Jr., received the coveted Ira Aldridge Award for his father from Frederick O'Neal, chairman of Actor's Equity and a national vice president of the AFL-CIO. The award states, in part: "To Paul Robeson for the pride he gave Afro-Americans as an artist, scholar and athlete." In responding to the presentation the younger Robeson said the award had special meaning to his father because of the "personal inspiration he has derived from the historical achievement and great dignity of Ira Aldridge." He suggests: "Those who run this country, the establishment, have suppressed the truth about Paul Robeson's achievements. They have done so because, at the very height of his achievement, he refused to let his personal success be used to explain away the injustices of the millions of his people in America. He told it like it was for the whole world to hear. The curtain of silence has been drawn around my father because the pride he has given to Black Americans is inseparably linked to his dignity and courage as a man. This award today draws aside a part of that curtain."

2004. "Black Academy Presents Award," New York Times, September 21, 1970, p. 54.

Paul Robeson was one of eight Black men and women inducted in the Black Academy of Arts and Letters for their "notable and sustained contributions to the arts and letters." Mr. Robeson could not attend the ceremony because of illness.

2005. "BAAL Gives Robeson Award," Black World, Vol. 20, No. 2, December, 1970, pp. 70, 125.

At its annual meeting in New York City, the Black Academy of Arts and Letters gave a special award to Paul Robeson...."for his in-estimable contribution to the understanding of the Black Ex-perience." Robeson was ailing and could not attend the meeting. His son accepted the award for the great baritone-actor.

2006. "Local 1199 Pays Tribute to Paul Robeson," 1199 News, January, 1971, pp. 14-15.

This report concerns a tribute to Paul Robeson that was held at Local 1199, Drug and Hospital Employees Union new headquarters in New York City on November, 1970. This was the union's 2nd annual tribute to the 73-year-old freedom fighter, singer and actor. Robeson was ill and could not attend the affairs.

2007.   "Display Exhibit on Paul Robeson at Black Museum," Jet, Vol. 40,
        No. 12, June 17, 1971, p. 20.

        An exhibit on Paul Robeson was shown at the Detroit International
        Afro-American Museum. The exhibit was called "The Life and Times
        of Paul Robeson." Dr. Charles H. Wright, chairman of the board
        of the Museum declares: "We feel Robeson was a forerunner of
        the civil rights movement. We believe his stand tended to focus
        public attention on injustices Blacks suffer and set the stage for
        changing. He could communicate with all people because he spoke
        24 languages and dialects."

2008.   "Tribute to Paul Robeson," Muhammad Speaks, November 26, 1971,
        p. 4.

        According to this article over 650 predominately U.S. Black and
        Spanish-Speaking Union members and friends packed the Martin
        Luther King, Jr., Labor Center of Local 1199 Drug and Hospital
        Union recently to pay tribute to Paul Robeson. It was the union's
        2nd annual tribute to the 73-year-old Black freedom fighter, singer,
        actor and athlete. Robeson was in ill health in Philadelphia
        and could not attend this affair that was held in New York City.

2009.   "Gillespie to Honor Robeson," New York Amsterdam News, December 4,
        1971, p. C-1.

        This article states that jazz trumpter Dizzy Gillespie would pre-
        sent a "Tribute to Paul Robeson and Black Culture," on Tuesday,
        December 7, in the Princeton University Chapel, Princeton, New
        Jersey. Gillespie, who has just returned from an overseas tour,
        will be accompanied by a choral group and will be joined in the
        tribute by Rev. Dr. Ernest Gordon, Dean of the University Chapel.
        The Chapel is hosting the program. Musician composer Gillespie,
        one of the leaders of the "bop" movement in modern jazz, has, like
        Robeson, toured the world many times, twice under sponsorship of
        the U.S. Department of State, states the article.

2010.   Davis, Ossie. "To Paul Robeson - Part I," Freedomways, Vol. II,
        No. 1, First Quarter, 1971, pp. 99-102.

        The writer declares: "Paul, to all the old gang of us who hung
        around him, was a reservoir, the sum of the Black man's capacities,
        a great national, Black phenomenon that all of us flocked to behold.
        A hero to all, gigantic and available. And as with all heroes
        the gift was one way. His vast bulk, warm and reassuring like a
        mother's breast, was more than adequate to all our infinite needs
        and hungers: Paul gave and gave, and gave; we took, and took, and
        took. Paul was a banquet, a feast for all hungers, and we raided
        him. All of us: Black folks, white folks, Communists, liberals,
        artists, politicians, race leaders, labor leaders -- we raided
        him. To us he was inexhaustible bounty from heaven, and we went
        to him as beggars go, never bothering to put anything back -- only
        to take, and take again, and never say thanks, fighting the world
        and each other for our inalienable right to consume Paul Robeson,
        and consume his we did," argues Mr. Davis. He argues, in part:
            And Paul confirmed us in our impudent wasting by

(Davis, Ossie)

> never denying that he was air, or water to our every
> need. He was his own spendthrift, a most generous pro-
> vider of himself, open to one and all 24 hours a day.
> Yet Paul was no fool. He gave because he had to.
> Because he loved us, and knew better than we the
> bottomlessness of our needs and desperations....
> Now it is over. Paul who like the provident father
> lived beyond his means in order to feed us, is spent
> and exhausted. Age is upon him, and illness has
> killed, not the man, but our capacity to feed upon
> the Man! The larder is empty, and we who never learned
> to forage for ourselves are baffled. We cannot accept
> the fact that there is no more Paul, and whine and
> wonder who is going to feed us now. And those of us
> who count ourselves insiders, the experts and the
> devotees, are not sure of our calling....

2011. Davis, Ossie. "To Paul Robeson - Part II," _Freedomways_, Vol. II,
       No. 2, Second Quarter, 1971, pp. 192-197.

This is a continuation of a previous article that appeared in the
First Quarter of _Freedomways_. Mr. Davis asserts that Paul was no
dupe, and even less a traitor. Black he was, through and through,
in feeling, thought,act; maintaining by choice, at whatsoever the
cost, his position, his far forward position, in the struggle for
Black liberation - a struggle which had long ago become the
central fact in his existence, and for which he had a strategy -
a Black strategy. Paul concluded, after much seeking and searching
that Black liberation would never come to his people short of
socialism...that socialism, and socialism alone was our hope and
our salvation. It was this conviction that governed all his
choices. Paul was as ardent in his defense of socialism as Imamu
Baraka is in defense of black nationalism - and both for the same
reason! Each man sees his philosophy as the indispensable vehicle
for black liberation! And each, in his own way, is right! Paul
believed in socialism and he said so, but unlike Imamu he did not
proselytize, he sought no converts, suggests the writer.... He
concludes:

> Paul spoke 25 languages, not as an exercise in expertise,
> but as a source through which he could absorb the many
> cultures into which he had not been born, but to which
> he was instinctively determined to belong. He con-
> sumed a language for the cultural essences it con-
> tained, and became in practice, in custom, and in habit,
> a loyal member of all the groups whose songs he sang.
> He had studied many life styles till they became his
> by second nature, was himself transfigured by what he
> learned, and became by accident what socialist societies
> are meant to produce by design. It just may be that
> Paul is _Socialist Man!_....

2012. Patterson, William L. "A German Tribute to Paul Robeson," American
       Dialog, Vol. 6, No. 1, Autumn, 1971, pp. 15-16.

       It was pointed out that Paul Robeson, one of the world's greatest
       revolutionaries, was honored at a two day International Symposium
       in April of this year on his 73rd birthday in the city of Berlin,
       capital of the German Democratic Republic. The honored guest could
       not attend because of illness. Mr. Patterson argues that the sym-
       posium honoring this Black freedom fighter took place in Berlin,
       intended as the capital of a Hitlerian Third Reich which was to
       dominate a world of genocidal racism. The people of Berlin and the
       entire G.D.R. paid homage to a Black man, an outstanding national
       liberation fighter, an internationalist who saw and taught the
       relationship of the struggles of all people for freedom, states
       the author. He concludes: "In honoring Paul Robeson, the people
       of the G.D.R. delivered a powerful blow against racism on an in-
       ternational scale."

2013. "Robeson Gets Tribute from Alpha at Rutgers," New York Amsterdam
       News, April 18, 1972, p. 42.

       This report states that Paul Robeson, barred for years from the
       campus of Rutgers University despite the fame he brought there in
       spirit on April 5, when the Eastern regional section of Alpha Phi
       Alpha Fraternity paid him tribute. Robeson, athlete, singer, actor,
       and lawyer lies ill in a Philadelphia sanitarium, but was re-
       presented by his son, Paul, Jr., who received a huge oil painting
       of his father that will now hand in the newly dedicated Paul
       Robeson Music Room on the campus. The auditorium of the Student
       Center rang with oratory during the tribute, with ABC Network's
       Mal Goode the main speaker, and Rutgers' President Dr. Mason W.
       Gross and other dignitaries on the platform. Goode recalled the
       glories of Robeson's Rutgers career and dramatized the fate of
       him and other graduates of major colleges whose degrees meant
       nothing in this nation, before integration. It was also pointed
       out in this article that Robeson Jr., made specific corrections
       in the published article on Robeson's career. One was the fact
       that the actor was named leading football player on Walter Camp's
       list of football greats for two years, yet Robeson was never been
       named to the Football Hall of Fame. Another was that he was never
       a declared Communist, although he lived in Russia for a number of
       years....

2014. "Robeson Given Solomon Carter Fuller Award," Black World, Vol. 21,
       No. 9, July, 1972, p. 80.

       Paul Robeson was presented the Solomon Carter Fuller Award of the
       Black Psychiatrists of America for "demonstrating the qualities
       of community leadership, compassion and selflessness so emphasized
       by America's first Black psychiatrist, and for the forthright
       furtherance of the mental health of Black people." The award was
       presented at the 125th anniversary of the American Psychiatric
       Association in Dallas, Texas, by Dr. J. Alfred Cannon, Chairman
       of the Black Psychiatrists of America.

2015.   "Robeson Will Receive Whitney Young Award," New York Times,
        September 7, 1972, p. 87.

        The article states that Paul Robeson, former actor, singer and
        pioneer activist in the civil rights movement was named the re-
        cipient of the second annual Whitney M. Young, Jr., Award. The
        award was presented at Yankee Stadium during the half-time of the
        Whitney M. Young, Jr., Memorial Football Classic between Grambling
        and Morgan State.

2016.   Wilson, John S.   "30 Musicians Get Ellington Medal at Yale,"
        New York Times, October 9, 1972, p. 36.

        Paul Robeson was of the 30 musicians chosen to receive the Duke
        Ellington Medal at Yale University. Robeson was ill and could
        not be present.

2017.   "Paul Robeson Gets Special Image Award from the NAACP," Jet, Vol.
        43, No. 12, December 14, 1972, pp. 56-57.

        Paul Robeson received a special Image Award of the NAACP Hollywood
        Chapter for his "eminence as an Artist and a fighter for human
        justice." Because of poor health the singer-actor could not attend
        the banquet.

2018.   Goldenberg, (Miss) B.   "Robeson Tribute," Sunday Times, February
        1, 1973, p. 13.

        The reader comments on an article about Paul Robeson by Harold
        Hobson. She declares: "I must protest against Harold Hobson's
        so called 'tribute' to Paul Robeson (Arts, last week). His opinion
        of Robeson's Othello is by no means general. Paul Robeson un-
        fortunately lived in a time when he could get very few parts worthy
        of him either on stage or screen." Miss Goldenberg concludes:
        "Nevertheless he gave great pleasure to millions who remember
        him with affection for his personality as well as his singing.
        Even if we disagreed with his opinions, his dignity and integrity
        were respected."

2019.   "Lincoln Vets Honor Robeson," Daily Worker, February 13, 1973,
        p. 11.

        The Veterans of the Abraham Lincoln Brigade who fought in Spain
        against Francisco Franco, celebrated their 36th anniversary at a
        dinner where they presented a plaque to Paul Robeson on his 75th
        birthday for his contributions to the anti-Franco cause and to
        freedom of all people. Robeson visited Spain in 1937 and enter-
        tained the Spanish Loyalist Government. He sang for the Brigade
        and gave it the moral support that it needed. Robeson was ill and
        did not attend the dinner. He was represented by Lloyd Brown who
        accepted the plaque on Robeson's behalf, states the writer.

2020. Walker, Joe. "State Paul Robeson Birthday Tribute," Muhammad
       Speaks, March 23, 1973, p. 6.

       The author points out that a cultural salute honoring Paul Robeson
       would be held at Carnegie Hall on April 15th. Robeson would be
       75 years old on April 19th and the tribute would mark his contri-
       butions as an athlete, scholar, actor, singer and passionate
       fighter for the cause of Black and other oppressed people during
       an active career that spanned nearly half a century, surmises
       Mr. Walker. The writer calls Robeson, "one of the greatest bass
       baritones of musical history." He also suggests that he was a
       fighter for his people, a supporter of labor's struggles and a
       world-wide voice for freedom, peace and justice.

2021. "Belafonte, Others Plan April 15, Robeson Tribute," Jet, Vol. 44,
       No. 2, April 5, 1973, p. 54.

       Plans were revealed for a birthday celebration honoring retired
       singer-actor, Paul Robeson, who would be 75 years old on April
       15th. In line with Robeson's birthday, Local 1199, the Drug and
       Hospital Union, planned a portrait and sculpture exhibition of
       the famous Black American.

2022. "A Tribute to Paul Robeson," Daily World, April 9, 1973, p. M-5.

       This is an excerpt from a speech made by Judge George W. Crockett
       at Freedomways' tribute to Paul Robeson, February 16, 1973. The
       full speech was published in the Spring 1973 issue of Freedomways.

2023. Freeman, Muriel. "Somerville Alma Mater Plans Hometown Tribute
       to Robeson," Somerset (N.J.) Messenger Gazette, April 19, 1973,
       p. 15.

       This article discusses Somerville High School's reunion. Robeson
       was on the 1915 Somerville High School's football team. One of
       the six photographs of this full page article shows four of
       Robeson's white High School friends standing beisde him. This
       article points out that Robeson was the most illustrious alumunus
       to ever graduate from Somerville High School.

2024. "German Capital Names School for Robeson, 75," Jet, Vol. 44, No.
       4, April 19, 1973, p. 15.

       Berlin, the capital of the German Democratic Republic, named one
       of its public schools for him on his 75th birthday, April 9th.
       Although schools in the Republic are not generally named after
       living persons, an exception was made to honor Robeson.

2025. Shepard, Richard F. "Going Out Guide," New York Times, April 19,
       1973, p. 50.

       It was pointed out that "Robeson Revisited: The Story of Paul
       Robeson," was told by nearly 60 photographs, posters, drawings,
       paintings, and sculptures, located in the union labor headquarters
       of the Martin Luther King, Jr., Labor Center, 310 West 43rd Street,
       New York City. The exhibition in honor of the singer's 75th

(Shepard, Richard F.)

birthday, traces his life from 1917 to his activities on behalf
of the leftist politics he espoused. Shepard concludes that this
exhibition is not so much a history as a particular feeling for
the man that the exhibition strives for and achieves, recalling
his magnificent "Ol' Man River," and his appearance at demonstrations.

2026. "3,000 Honor Robeson in Carnegie Hall Tribute," Jet, Vol. 44, No.
6, May 3, 1973, p. 63.

More than 3,000 fans and friends of Robeson got together at New
York's Carnegie Hall to honor the Black giant on his 75th birthday. Dizzy Gillespie lauded Robeson as "my personal champion,"
and Sidney Poiter said that "before no Black man or woman had
been portrayed in American movies as anything but a sterotype."
Angela Davis termed Robeson as being "a partisan of the socialist
world" and "above all, a revolutionary." He was represented by
his son, Paul Robeson, Jr.

2027. "Tribute to a Black Man: Paul Robeson," Black World, Vol. 22, No.
9, July, 1973, pp. 88-89.

In April, more than 2,000 people assembled in Carnegie Hall in
New York City to pay their respects to Paul Robeson. The tribute
was organized by singer Harry Belafonte and architect Ralph
Aswang. Paul Robeson was in ill health and could not attend. In
a taped message, Mr. Robeson said: "Though I have not been able
to be active for years, I want you to know that I am the same
Paul, dedicated as ever to the worldwide cause of humanity for
freedom, peace, and brotherhood." For the occasion, excerpts
from his films and plays were shown, and portions of his speeches
broadcast.

2028. "Robeson Given Honorary Doctorate by Rutgers," Black World, Vol.
22, No. 9, July, 1973, p. 89.

The citation accompanying the honorary degree read as follows:
    Grandson of slaves, Benjamin and Saba, and son of
    an escaped slave, William, you have been called "the
    tallest tree in our forest," and your voice "the
    finest musical instrument wrought by nature in our
    time." We celebrate today your abundant gifts, not
    the least of which is the humane and heroic quality of
    your life. After a period of neglect too long contri-
    buted to and countenanced by the University, we return
    to you with this degree some small portion of that great
    honor you have brought to us. Scholar, athlete, man
    of letters, artist, political leader, you have illumined
    and ennobled each of these areas of human experience,
    setting thereby a measure of worth for all men and all
    time. By songs, deed and word you have touched men's
    minds, no less than their hearts. You have given the
    common man of all races and all lands a new vision of
    himself. Now, therefore, because you have sung the

(Black World)

song of freedom and human worth for all the world to
hear, under the authority vested in me (President Edward J.
Bloustein) by the Board of Governors of Rutgers, the
State University of New Jersey, I hereby confer upon
you the degree of Doctor of Humane Letters, honoris
causa, with all the rights, privileges and immunities
pertaining thereunto, here and elsewhere.

2029.   Giocondo, Mike. "Actors Union in Tribute: Robeson Ideal Honored--
State Dept. Bars the Way," Daily World, January 13, 1974, p. 8.

According to this writer the Actors' Equity Association, AFL-CIO,
honored Paul Robeson, world famous Black athlete, actor/singer,
by naming him first recipient of an annual award named for him.
The award was accepted by Paul Robeson, Jr., on behalf of his
ailing father. The award was given "in grateful recognition of
distinguished contributions to the performing arts and for commitment to the struggle for a decent world in which all men can live
in dignity and peace."

2030.   "John Henry Memorial Jubilee for Paul Robeson," Daily World,
August 15, 1974, p. 8.

This was the Second Annual John Henry Memorial Authentic Blues and
Gospel Jubilee on Labor Day weekend, 1974, near Beckley, West
Virginia, dedicated to Paul Robeson because he has the same qualities as John Henry who died at Talcott, West Virginia, while
working and completing with the steam drill in the Big Bend tunnel
for the C & O Railroad. In 1939 Paul Robeson played the role of
"John Henry" in the stage play. It opened in December in Philadelphia in 1939.

2031.   Editorial. "Robeson Profile on 'Interface'," New York Amsterdam
News, June 4, 1975, p. B-10.

This editor comments on a profile on Paul Robeson's life on the
television program "Interface." The writer states that Robeson
was an outstanding athlete who was twice elected All-American, but
not admitted to the Football Hall of Fame. He was a linguist,
fluent in 20 foreign languages. He was an attorney, a concert
performer of international renown. He was an actor whose interpretation of Shakespeare's "Othello" has yet to be equalled. He
was a trailblazer, a Black activist forty-years ago. He spoke out
for human rights at a time when Blacks who thought like he did
were not allowed to speak out. The editor concludes: "His name,
Robeson, Paul Robeson. For the first time on National Television,
Interface - in a special one-hour edition - will present the truth
about the one Black man who could not, be silenced or assassinated
in "A Profile of Paul Robeson" airing Tuesday, June 3rd at 10 P.M.
on Channel 13. The multiple careers of Paul Robeson -- as an
actor, singer and political activist are focused on, with rare film
interviews enabling the viewer to look at the real Robeson.
Robeson appears in costume as "Othello" while he talks about the
meaning of the role to a Black man...."

2032.   Editorial. "Robeson Benefit Sunday," New York Amsterdam News,
        July 1, 1975, p. D-13.

        The editor discusses the "Salute to Paul Robeson" on his 75th
        birthday. It was held at Carnegie Hall in New York City. The
        Salute Committee felt strongly that, in view of decades of virtual
        exclusion of Robeson's name from reference books and the films of
        the mass media in the United States, it was essential that there
        be a center in this country that would assemble, preserve and make
        available to scholars and the interested public, a complete re-
        cord of his life and work. Hence, the proceeds of the "Salute"
        were to establish the Paul Robeson Archives, states the article.

2033.   Jordan, Vernon. "Vernon Jordan Tribute," New York Amsterdam News,
        January 31, 1976, p. 2.

        The Executive Director of the National Urban League, Vernon
        Jordan declares: "The nobleness of Paul Robeson marked him as
        one of those rare individuals who deserve the accolade 'Immortal.'
        He strode across his time like a giant, fearless and ever willing
        to do and speak those things that he believed in. He was a
        study in courage, a man of vast dignity and understanding who
        will long be remembered and revered."

2034.   Sutton, Percy E. "Sutton Tribute to Robeson," New York Amsterdam
        News, January 31, 1976, p. 2.

        The author tells how he remembers Paul Robeson. He contends that
        while the death of Paul Robeson did not come as a shock, it did
        come with a heavy weight of loss. The loss of Paul Robeson will
        not be limited to the Blacks of this world who saw in him a giant
        of a man who spoke words of courage and acted out his convictions.
        He declares: "But, Paul Robeson's death is a loss to every free-
        dom loving person who saw in him the embodiment of the free
        spirit, strength, intellect, and a strong conscience with stronger
        convictions. His death means the loss of a giant of an advocate
        for the downtrodden and beleaguered." The writer remembers Paul
        Robeson as a man who refused to crawl and stood up and walked
        tall when lesser men, maimed and injured by the hostility of the
        environment, stopped and surrendered under the oppressive burden.
        But most of all, Mr. Sutton remembers Paul Robeson with pride.
        The author concludes:
                Even in death, Paul Robeson stands as a monumental
                reminder that it is possible to find within oneself
                a purpose, and then to relentlessly and bravely pur-
                sue that purpose. Paul Robeson's purpose was to be
                a man. All who looked at the life of Paul Robeson
                know that he did, in fact, live and die as a man.
                The words, "Paul Robeson," can now be printed in our
                dictionary of synonyms as the word "man." To say
                "Paul Robeson," is to say it all.

2035.   Jarrett, Vernon. "Inspiring Tribute to a Universal Man," Chicago
        Tribune, February 1, 1976, Section 2, p. 5.

        The writer states that they brought Robeson's body "back home to
        the ghetto in the heart of Harlem" last week when 4,000 mourners
        paid him their final respects at old Mother Zion Church, the
        famous African Methodist Episcopal Zion Church on East 137th
        Street near Lenox Avenue. All day New York-area radio stations
        announced that the funeral was a private affair. But the crowds
        came, 300 standing outside in the rain throughout the ceremony....
        One had to weep a little while listening to Robeson's recorded
        voice saying "we are climbing Jacob's ladder" - which the church
        choir sang later - and while singing spirituals and folk music
        from around the world. One song was "Old Man River," which Robe-
        son made famous 40 years ago, asserts the author. But the remorse
        seemed to disappear as speakers traced this man's life from his
        birth on April 9, 1893, in Princeton, New Jersey, to his death on
        January 23 in Philadelphia. This is the first funeral where I
        heard people applaud eulogizers, including the clergy, states
        Mr. Jarrett. He continues, "maybe that's the way Robeson would
        have wanted it - an inspired audience."

2036.   Belt, Byron. "A Tribute to Robeson," Long Island Press, February
        1, 1976, Section 6, pp. 1, 16.

        The author declares that America has produced few who gained such
        delight of artistic achievement and acclaim, yet who died reviled
        by many, and forgotten by more, as Paul Robeson. He was a man of
        magnificent musical, dramatic and human stature. His passing
        brought many tributes, almost all meeting the anguished and
        brightening the glory, states Mr. Belt.... He concludes: "Paul
        Robeson's last great triumph came...in the 1958 production of
        'Othello'. It was the final time the great man, his art and his
        public were truly one. His death should challenge the conscience
        of America to restore the good name of one of her most noble sons."

2037.   "Blacks Honored at Hall of Fame Awards," Jet, Vol. 49, No. 24,
        March 11, 1976, pp. 60-61.

        At the Third Annual Black Film-Makers Hall of Fame ceremonies there
        were a number of glowing verbal tributes to the late Paul Robeson
        and a respected silence was observed in the memory of the singer-
        actor. Robeson was inducted into the Black Film-makers Hall of
        Fame at its first ceremonies in 1974.

2038.   Roberts, Milt. "Paul Robeson - A Tribute," Black Sports, Vol. 5,
        March, 1976, pp. 8, 10, 58.

        The writer discusses Robeson's greatness as an athlete, enter-
        tainer and humanist. He states that Robeson, athlete and actor,
        performed with an eloquence and grace that earned him recognition
        as Othello of the stage and All-American honors on the gridiron.
        Mr. Roberts surmises that it may not have been possible for Paul
        Robeson, a truly complex man, to separate the two Othellos - the
        Othello of battle - for he was both. Perhaps his pride compelled
        him to strife his love for his native land, not out of hatred,

(Roberts, Milt)

but for the dignity of his personal honor. He concludes: "And so, if Robeson's niche of honor inside the Nation's College Football Hall of Fame has thus been forefeited, his formidable tower of honors will ever continue to loom in loneliness nearby, casting a huge shadow over the gridiron shrine."

2039. Wheeler, Tim. "World Homage to the Great Paul Robeson," Daily World, May 14, 1976, p. 8.

This was a tribute given to Paul Robeson at Shiloh Baptist Church in Washington, D.C., on April 30, 1976. Representatives from Ghana, Nigeria, India, USSR, Jamaica, German Democratic Republic, World Federation of Trade Unions, Panama, Black Women Restaurant Workers' Local in Washington, D.C., the Paul Robeson Multimedia Center, Washington, D.C., and several other outstanding Blacks were present.

2040. "Concert Tribute to Robeson," Daily World, May 20, 1976, p. 8.

This concert was given at the McMillan Auditorium at Columbia University, New York City, on May 16, 1976. The following persons performed: Beatrice Rippy, soprano; Carroll Hollister, accompanist; Antar S.K. Mberi, poet.

2041. "Tribute to Robeson at Carnegie, October 8," New York Times, September 29, 1976, p. 27.

It was announced that "An Artists' Tribute to The Life of Paul Robeson" would be held at Carnegie Hall on October 8th to memotialize the well known singer, actor, and Black activist. The program would be sponsored by the Friends of the Paul Robeson Archives. The archives are a program to gather and catalogue the extensive materials relating to the life and career of the singer. The proceeds from the concert would go to the archives.

2042. "Renaming of Airport for Robeson Is Urged," New York Times, August 14, 1977, Section 11, p. 23.

Phillip Zeidenberg, of Teaneck, New Jersey, in a letter to the New Jersey Edition of the New York Times, suggests that Newark International Airport be renamed Robeson International Airport; because Robeson traveled the entire world championing the cause of the downtrodden. A legend in his time, and someone who should never be forgotten.... The name change did not occur.

2043. "Central State Art Center Named After Paul Robeson," Jet, Vol. 53, No. 12, December 8, 1977, p. 15.

Central State University named its new $6 million cultural and performing arts building after Paul Robeson. Dr. Art Thomas, Vice President for Academic Affairs, declares: "The new center is one of the show places of the campus, therefore, we decided to name it after one of Black America's proudest Black men."

2044. "Seeger Wins Robeson Award," New York Times, January 17, 1978, p. 11.

Actors' Equity Association gave its 1977 Paul Robeson Award to folk singer Pete Seeger, who was blacklisted in the 1950s along with the late Mr. Robeson by the entertainment industry over political beliefs. In accepting the award, Mr. Seeger said it was appropriate to sing an African and a Russian folk song, two forms of music that, he said, deeply touched Paul Robeson.

2045. Richardson, Amadeo. "World Leaders in Tribute to Robeson at UN," Daily World, April 13, 1978, p. 3.

This writer suggests that Paul Robeson whose name and spirit are present wherever there is a battle for human freedom against racism and oppression, was honored at the United Nations in April. The UN Special Committee Against Apartheid celebrated his memory as representatives of governments, labor leaders and fighters for Black freedom in the United States and Africa rose to salute Robeson on the 80th anniversary of his birth.

2046. Ericson, Raymond. "Tribute to Paul Robeson at Fisher Hall," New York Times, June 9, 1978, Section 3, p. 13.

This article discusses a fund raising program at Fisher Hall in New York City for the Paul Robeson Archives. When Robeson died in 1976 he left behind some 50,000 items related to his life ranging from clippings about his theatre and film performances to unpublished writings. Sidney Poiter, one of the sponsors of the program along with Lena Horne, John Hammond and Arthur Krim, made film greetings for the occasion, as did Prime Minister Michael Manley of Jamaica. A reception was held after the program that was hosted by several United Nations ambassadors including Andrew Young of the United States and representatives from Nigeria, Tanzania, Zambia, Jamaica, Mozambique, Guinea-Bissar, Guyana and the Organization of African Unity.

2047. Bloustein, Edward J. "Tribute to Paul Robeson," Paul Robeson: The Great Forerunner. Editors of Freedomways. New York: Dodd, Mead & Co., 1978, pp. 257-258.

The speaker states: "Robeson was a scholar. He graduated from Rutgers College as class Valedictorian; Paul Robeson is a man of intellect. An athlete, he won twelve varsity letters and achieved All-American status twice; Paul Robeson provides a model of physical grace, strength and prowess. That prowess, it is my hope, will soon be recognized by membership in the Football Hall of Fame. An artist, he established himself as one of the greatest American singers and actors of this century; Paul Robeson is universally acclaimed for his professional preeminence. A voice of his people, he spoke and lived Black pride before it became politically acceptable in the white community; Paul Robeson is a model of Black political activism," states Bloustein. He concludes: "Thus, crowning all else, Paul Robeson is a great humanist, a man who helps to bring us all together, helps us, amid differences in which we can and should take great pride, to find,

(Bloustein, Edward J.)

nourish and glory in our common humanity."

2048. Boegelsack, Brigitte. "Tribute to Paul Robeson," Paul Robeson:
The Great Forerunner. Editors of Freedomways. New York: Dodd,
Mead & Co., 1978, pp. 259-262.

The writer states: "What is being collected in our Archives (in
the German Democratic Republic) are not only testimonials to his
high art as actor and singer, but proofs of his fight for human
rights as well. Thus the Archives contain recordings, tapes,
books and biographies, his addresses and articles, photographs
and films, correspondence and documents, newspaper articles,
which appeared in many countries about his art and his fight, radio
and television appearances, posters, program notes."

2049. Brown, Lloyd L. "Tribute to Paul Robeson," Paul Robeson: The
Great Forerunner. Editors of Freedomways. New York: Dodd, Mead
& Co., 1978, pp. 263-266.

The author states: "Who can doubt that the man who went to Spain
in the thirties to sing for the antifascist troops would in the
sixties have gone to Vietnam to sing for their liberation army?
Indeed, knowing Paul's genius for languages, we can be sure that
he would have sung their freedom songs in the purest Vietnamese.
And Africa -- so dear to his heart for all these years -- how he
would have welcomed the chance to stand with the liberation movements there!" He concludes:
But despite those regrets, this you should know:
during the years of his illness Paul Robeson felt
safe and secure in the bosom of his family. While
his son, Paul Jr., devotedly took care of his affairs,
Paul lived with his sister, Marion, in Philadelphia.
All of us who knew and loved Paul Robeson should rejoice in knowing that throughout his last years he
was sustained and comforted by the loving devotion of
Marion. Just as in his boyhood Paul grew up in the
sheltering love of his father, during his declining
years -- thanks to that miracle of love named Marion --
he was able to find once again "a home in that rock."

2050. Browne, Robert S. "Tribute to Paul Robeson," Paul Robeson: The
Great Forerunner. Editors of Freedomways. New York: Dodd, Mead
& Co., 1978, pp. 267-268.

The writer concludes: "We should all be grateful that this giant,
who like so many other great men found his thinking to be too far
ahead of his people's has lived to see his life's work vindicated
and his name publicly restored to the position of eminence from
which it never slipped in the minds of some of us. Thank you,
Paul, for brining me insights and perspectives that have meant
so much to me in later life."

2051. Burroughs, Margaret. "Tribute to Paul Robeson," Paul Robeson:
       The Great Forerunner. Editors of Freedomways. New York: Dodd,
       Mead & Co., 1978, pp. 269-271.

       The writer declares: "I am thinking of Paul Robeson now and I am
       thinking of myself. I am thinking that had it not been for Paul
       Robeson, for what he is, for what he believed, for what he stood
       and fought for, for what he sacrificed for, that I myself, might
       not be, to a great degree, what I am, how I am, stand, fight for
       or hold the beliefs that I hold today. Perhaps I might not be
       imbued with certain ideals which are tremendously important to
       me. I am filled with gratitude as I think of how Paul Robeson,
       this so humane human, this beautiful man, this splendid son of
       the African peoples, this great American inspired me and certainly
       countless untold others like me. For years, Paul Robeson has
       been my barometer, a system of checks and balances to measure how
       much my life, our lives, have been involved with concern for
       people and the liberation of our own black people, of oppressed
       peoples all over the world."

2052. Childress, Alice. "Tribute to Paul Robeson," Paul Robeson: The
       Great Forerunner. Editors of Freedomways. New York: Dodd, Mead
       & Co., 1978, pp. 272-273.

       Paul Robeson's newspaper, Freedom, was once located nearby at 53
       West 125th Street, states the writer. The year she remembers was
       1951. The same address housed the Council On African Affairs, with
       offices occupies by Dr. Alphaeus Hunton and Dr. W.E.B. DuBois.
       Louis Burnham was the editor of Freedom and served it with under-
       standing dedication. John Gray frequently dropped in and contri-
       buted his services of organization and fund raising. Robeson was
       seldom able to enter the building without stopping outside to have
       a chat with some of the people who lived or worked on that block.
       Even Harlemites just passing by were not shy about talking to him.
       Attitudes, more than words, conveyed brotherly and sisterly
       feelings toward him, states the author. "Hey there, excuse me,
       Mr. Robeson, I just wanta say I'm in agreement with you and would
       like to take this opportunity to shake your hand." I see Paul
       taking visitors to the offices of DuBois and Hunton, laughing and
       chatting, greetings and well-wishing...followed by deep and earnest
       conversations about Africa, and at a time when too many of us
       thought it strange that some of us found so much identification
       with that continent. Lorraine Hansberry was typing a paper for
       Robeson. Actors and writers and musicians dropping in because...
       "I want to ask Paul something." If Paul was there...never a
       refusal, concludes Childress.

2053. Conyers, John. "Tribute to Paul Robeson," Paul Robeson: The
       Forerunner. Editors of Freedomways. New York: Dodd, Mead & Co.,
       1978, p. 274.

       This was a tribute to Paul Robeson that was held in the U.S. House
       of Representatives on January 28, 1976. The Congressman declares,
       in part:
            Paul Robeson stands as a monument to the capacity of
            the human spirit to achieve excellence in the fact of

(Conyers, John)

adversity. His talent and courage fused to manifest personal greatness despite the conditions under which he lived. Mr. Robeson gave of himself, whether on the concert stage or the picket line. He sang, struggled, suffered and died for the cause of human dignity. We could ask no more of him.

2054. Crockett, George W. "Tribute to Paul Robeson," Paul Robeson: The Great Forerunner. Editors of Freedomways. New York: Dodd, Mead & Co., 1978, pp. 275-279.

The writer declares: "We join to pay tribute tonight to the greatest American of us all: Paul Robeson. His voice, his talents, his genius, all art part of the magnificent heritage left to us and to the world despite the brutal and desperate efforts to silence that voice, to stifle that talent and to bury that genius. They would erase the legacy of Paul Robeson. They would forget his works, obliterate his gifts and expunge his thoughts. They would still his sounds and cloak his name and his greatness in a suffocating miasma of empty nothing. They would make of him, as they have tried to make so many others, an invisible man, states the writer. He also declares:
But kings will not be dethroned by fools. Giants will not be toppled by pygmies. And the people's heroes will survive even the mightiest onslaughts of the mightest imperialists. Along with Frederick Douglass and W.E.B. DuBois, Paul Robeson is one of the greatest of these people's heroes. His life is an inspiration - one without parallel today. He has confidence in the people. He is fully committed to the fight against the evils of war, poverty and racism. His loyalties and his friendships are inviolable. And he believes in America.

2055. Dent, Tom. "Tribute to Paul Robeson," Paul Robeson: The Great Forerunner. Editors of Freedomways. New York: Dodd, Mead & Co., 1978, pp. 280-283.

The writer contends that his decision to become more than an artist by enlisting his body and mind in the fight for freedom of our people against oppression, Robeson became a prophet of the Black Arts Movement of the sixties and seventies. A prophet because it is this very concept of the Black artist as community mover-builder in a political as well as cultural sense that dominates our movement today, states Dent. He argues that the artist has as much obligation to join the fight against racism as anyone else. Both are sides of the same coin. The author concludes:
And this is the legacy of Robeson's lesson. That any success achieved at the expense of our people or at the cost of ignoring our condition in America is worthless. That the Black artist cannot isolate himself in an Ellisonian cocoon, no matter how important he thinks his work is. That it is senseless to talk about Black artistic development unless we have a

(Dent, Tom)

concomitant community development (and vice versa).
To the furtherance of these ideas and images Paul
Robeson gave us the commitment of his life. He
was far, far ahead of his time. For those of us
working in the South today, we see him, in our
mature vision, as an indelible source of Black
strength, Black talent, Black wisdom.

2056.   DuBois, Shirley Graham. "Tribute to Paul Robeson," Paul Robeson:
The Great Forerunner. Editors of Freedomways. New York: Dodd,
Mead & Co., 1978, p. 284.

The writer declares: "Paul Robeson -- Tallest tree in the forest--
High as the Mountains," they said of him in Europe. And BIG!
That big smile embracing everybody in sight - and beyond; the
big Voice speaking or singing. All-American, unexcelled at a
people's rally, on stage, or in the concert hall." She concludes:
I never heard Paul say that Black is beautiful - he
simply lived beautifully. Paul Robeson - Symbol
of Manhood, of Courage, of Loyalty to the Best,
the Unbowed and Undefeated: Paul Robeson -
Beautiful! With sincere gratitude for his being.

2057.   Gregory, Dick. "Tribute to Paul Robeson," Paul Robeson: The
Great Forerunner. Editors of Freedomways. New York: Dodd,
Mead, & So., 1978, p. 285.

The activist declares that Paul Robeson is both a prototype and
an inspiration to the new Black attitude which is shared by the
pure spirits in America today of all ages and colors. His life
tells us all that a man does not have to buckle under and give in
to an oppressive, racist, insane social and political system.
Paul Robeson is truly a man and the system has never been able to
alter, change or subdue him, asserts Gregory. He concludes:
Those who share the vision of a liberated society owe
a great debt to Paul Robeson; for his life has embodied
the reminder of Tom Paine, what we obtain too cheap, we
esteem too lightly. To stand up for the right demands
courage and commitment and Paul Robeson has shown us
that one man who truly possesses such qualities can
expose evil and oppression for what they are.

2058.   Hoggard, J. Clinton. "Tribute to Paul Robeson," Paul Robeson:
The Great Forerunner. Editors of Freedomways. New York: Dodd,
Mead, & Co., 1978, pp. 286-289.

The author declares that Paul Robeson, singer, actor, peacemaker,
human rights activist and minority peoples' friend, has joined the
immortals. Born in a parsonage, reared in a Christian family
home, surrounded by culture and courage inherited from his mother
and his father, Paul Robeson was fitted for the battle of life both
physically and mentally, states Hoggard. He went on to say that
as Paul Robeson saw more of the world and compared life in countries other than the United States, he invoked hostility,

(Hoggard, J. Clinton)

governmental vindictiveness which led to the lifting of his passport, and personal harassment during the McCarthy years which
subjected him to inquisition and interrogations. But the course
of his ex-slave father, who ran to freedom, spurred Paul on to no
compromise with any man on the matter of conscience, human rights,
civil rights or personal dignity, asserts the writer. He concludes:
> The legacy of a good name is bequeathed Paul Jr. and
> his family; his sister, Mrs. Marion Forsythe, her
> daughter, the nieces, the nephews, the grandnieces,
> the grandnephews - keep it good for justice and
> freedom, for character and culture, for racial
> pride and religious commitment.

2059. Horne, Lena. "Tribute to Paul Robeson," Paul Robeson: The Great
Forerunner. Editors of Freedomways, New York: Dodd, Mead, & Co.,
1978, p. 290.

The author said, in part: "...You are honoring tonight the third
great black hero of my life, Paul Robeson. I came to know him as
a young woman, alone, trying to find myself, trying to know why
I reacted to the outside world as I did, why my pride was so
fierce and so bleak, and what had created this pride. Paul Robeson
told me about my heritage, my grandmother, my forebears, about
black people everywhere. He told me about my black self. He
seemed to me to become the repository of the information that dictated my life style...."

2060. Koinage, Mbiyu. "Tribute to Paul Robeson," Paul Robeson: The
Great Forerunner. Editors of Freedomways. New York: Dodd, Mead,
& Co., 1978, p. 291.

The writer sent the actor-singer a letter on behalf of the President of Kenya, Jomo Kenyatta. He told Robeson that his name would
not be forgotten by the people of Africa, let alone in the world.

2061. Murphy, George B., Jr. "Tribute to Paul Robeson," Paul Robeson:
The Great Forerunner. New York: Dodd, Mead & Co., 1978, pp. 296-
299.

The writer states in the caseless struggle of nations and peoples
to develop everlasting self-fulfilling lives, great art harmonizes
in diversity, the rich cultures of working people flowing from
their struggles to harness and appropriate for themselves, the
bountiful, life-giving resources of mother earth. The practitioners
of great art in every age of the world history have come to know
and understand this through their immersion of themselves and
their art in the struggles of the people. According to the
writer, that is why Paul Robeson is a great artist, who stands on
the stage of world history, the greatest American artist of this
century. He concludes:
> The heritage of Robeson's strength and courage lives
> on in the national and world struggle now mounted to
> free from prison the young brilliant, black communist,

(Murphy, George B., Jr.)

> Angela Davis, leaders of the Black Panther Party, and
> hundreds of black and white youth struggling against
> murder and repression at home, and the genocidal
> policy of our government against the heroic people
> of Indo-China, South Africa, North Korea and the
> Arab countries of the Middle East.

2062.   Nenru, Jawaharlal. "Tribute to Paul Robeson," Paul Robeson:
         The Great Forerunner. Editors of Freedomways. New York: Dodd,
         Mead, & Co., 1978, p. 300.

         The writer was Prime Minister of India from 1946-1964. He states,
         in part: "I am happy to know that an All-India Committee has
         been formed under the distinguished chairmanship of Chief Justice
         Chagla, to celebrate the sixtieth birthday of Paul Robeson. This
         is an occasion which deserves celebration not only because Paul
         Robeson is one of the greatest artists of our generation, but
         also because he has represented and suffered for a cause which
         should be dear to all of us - the cause of human dignity."

2063.   Patterson, William L. "Tribute to Paul Robeson," Paul Robeson:
         The Great Forerunner. Editors of Freedomways. New York: Dodd,
         Mead and Co., 1978, pp. 301-303.

         The writer declares that Paul Robeson was one of the first to sign
         the indictment that charged the Government with Genocide. He
         gave thought and study to its contents. He led the delegation
         which carried this historic document to the secretariat of the U.N.
         while the general secretary of the CRC presented an identical
         petition to the delegates of the General Assembly in Paris, France.
         Patterson asserts that Paul Robeson's action was unique. He was
         already a celebrated internationally known concert artist, a
         noted actor of stage and screen. His future was secure if he
         stuck to his own affairs. But his concern was for the poor and
         oppressed of the world. He believed that there was security for
         none if not for all. Life had taught this lesson. Paul's ex-
         periences with segregation in the ghetto, his knowledge of the
         trials and tribulations of other citizens of color were lessons
         he could not forget. He made of his art a weapon for the people.
         He was ready to charge genocide against those who had butchered
         Filipinos in the Philippines, Cubans in Cuba and nationals of
         color in the U.S.A., states Patterson. The author concludes:
> He charged genocide. So too did the world of pro-
> gressive mankind. The crime remains a policy of
> governments. Vietnam reveals racism as an exportable
> crime; a people's court will one day try the guilty.
> It is even now in process of being created as more and
> more people take the cry into the streets. Those who
> charge genocide against the rulers of the USA will
> bring the criminals to book. Paul Robeson's name
> will be among them. It holds a special place among
> those who give priority to human freedom.

2064. Perkins, Thelma Dale. "Tribute to Paul Robeson," Paul Robeson: The Great Forerunner. Editors of Freedomway. New York: Dodd, Mead & Co., 1978, pp. 304-307.

The writer suggests: "To know and understand the roles of Paul and Eslanda Robeson in this period should be instructive to our present younger generation in their search for identity. The Robesons, like Douglass and W.E.B. DuBois and many others, are part of a long and proud heritage of Blacks who have lent their talents, their energies and sometimes their lives to the struggles for freedom. The social studies and history books touch only lightly if at all on what role the Robesons and other Blacks have played in the freedom struggles of this country and the world. Black and white children are led to believe, as a well-meaning friend said recently that "Blacks have finally taken the initiative for their own freedom." That is not the fact. Not only have Blacks fought for their own freedom throughout history, but consistently they have been responsible in no small part for enabling our society now as in the past to enjoy human freedom to the relative measure it exists today," concludes the author.

2065. Seeger, Peter. "Tribute to Paul Robeson," Paul Robeson: The Great Forerunner. Editors of Freedomways. New York: Dodd, Mead & Co., 1978, pp. 311-312.

The writer states: "For me, Paul Robeson will live forever. His strength made us stronger; his artistry inspired us to be better artists. The day will come when the hard-working people of the world will put an end to class exploitation, an end to racism, and militarism, and poverty, and I am glad that this book will remind our sons and daughters how another step on Jacob's Ladder was brought closer and sooner by this giant of the twentieth century, Paul Robeson."

H. 1980-1981

A SELECTED LIST

1. HOLLYWOOD'S WALK OF FAME

2066. Qualles, Paris H. "What Price A Star?: Paul Robeson Vs. Hollywood Chamber of Commerce, A Postscript," Crisis, Vol. 87, No. 1,
January, 1980, p. 26.

This postscript to the original article points out that following
the tumultuous uproar induced by the Hollywood Chamber of Commerce's denial of Paul Robeson's star in the Walk of Fame, an
embarrassed selection committee reversed their decision and granted
Robeson his star. Mr. Qualles concludes: "The sixties will never
again return, but the eighties are just about upon us. Few of us
may possess the vocal qualities of a Paul Robeson, but in the final
analysis, what he was saying is infinitely more important than
how it was said...."

2. FREEDOM FIGHTER

2067. Editorial. "Paul Robeson," Winston Salem (N.C.) Chronicle, April
25, 1981, p. 4.

The editor declares that this article's purpose is simply to pay
homage to one of the greatest men to ever walk this earth: Paul
Robeson, a transplanted North Carolinian who became a "citizen
of the world!" Paul Robeson...Phi Beta Kappa, "All-American"
athlete, Shakespearian Actor, Concert Singer, Linguist, Lawyer,
and Human Rights Activist...Paul Robeson - perhaps the only true

(Winston Salem Chronicle)

"Renaissance man" this nation ever produced! He continues, yet,
despite his great talents, Robeson never appeared on network
television, nor received the recognition he so richly deserved
from the print media. Why, you ask? Simply because Mr. Robeson
took a stand against injustice and oppression in America and
throughout the world. The fact that he was a noted artist was of
little concern to him, argues the editor. The editor concludes:
"By speaking out against racism at home and imperialism abroad,
Mr. Robeson forsook what could have been a lucrative career in
music and theater. But the America of the 1930's and 1940's did
not want its 'colored' actors to be so political. Thus, Mr.
Robeson was in effect, 'silenced' by the entertainment industry,
as well as certain governmental forces." He further asserts:
> Time and space will not permit me to go into the
> depth necessary to give you the true meaning/im-
> portance of Paul Robeson to the struggle for justice
> and equality in this world. But, in recognition of
> the 83rd anniversary of his birthdate (April 9) it
> is only fitting that this brief tribute be made. It
> is important that our children be made aware of a
> true hero - a man who excelled at everything he
> attempted: scholar, athlete, artist, lawyer - truly
> a man for all seasons! So let us remember the courage,
> the sacrifices, the contributions of Mr. Robeson.
> But more than that, let us use his life as a measuring
> rod for us; for only then can we insure that his work
> will not be in vain.

3. FILM

2068. "Warfield Still in Demand for Fame 'Showboat' Role," Winston-
Salem Journal, July 5, 1981, Section C, p. 6.

William Warfield played the role of Joe in the 1951 movie version
of "Show Boat." He gave a strong singing rendition of "Ol' Man
River." He said he was greatly influenced by the great singer
Paul Robeson. Robeson played the role of Joe and sang "Ol' Man
River" in the 1935 film version of "Showboat."

4. HAROLD CRUSE'S VIEWS OF ROBESON

2069. Cruse, Harold. "A Review of The Paul Robeson Controversy," Part
II, First World, Vol. 2, No. 4, 1980, pp. 26-32, 62.

Mr. Cruse continues his response to the earlier article, "Reflections on Reflections About the Black Intellectual," by

(Cruse, Harold)

Sterling Stuckey and Joshua Lesile. The author states that it
is the essentially evolutionary process of Robeson's development
that the Robeson admirers distort for ideological, partisan and
political reasons. "Stuckey's work on Robeson is amateurship
hagiology. It is the kind of intellectual obfuscation on world
expert from a following of a historical, uncritical hero worshippers. Sterling Stuckey's position paper on Robeson, 'I Want
to be African: The Ends of Nationalist Theory and Practice, 1919-
1945,' reads like the work of an advanced graduate student anxious
to win the approval of a biased clique of academic peers or thesis
advisors," surmises the writer. He quotes not one single item
from Eslanda Robeson's first book about her husband (1930), but
only from her book, <u>African Journey</u> (1945). The Robeson admirers
would, naturally, consider it "impertinent" to dare ask the
question why it was Eslanda who went to Black Africa but not
Robeson himself (since it was he who wanted to be African). Was
it not, indeed, obligatory that Robeson take the time to visit
Black Africa at least once in his career? Is it "impertinent"
to ask the question as to how it happened that a <u>major</u> Black
singer and actor never performed in a <u>minor</u> play, opera, oratorio,
cantata, etc., by an accomplished (I don't say 'major') Black
playwright, composer or libretist?, states Cruse. The author
concludes:

> In the case of Robeson studies, what is required to
> devise a closer scrutiny of the actual, the <u>real</u>
> evolutionary factors in the hero's rise to inter-
> national fame? Upon close examination, these factors
> reveal that Robeson's views on music, art, politics,
> Africa, etc., went through an evolution (just like
> everybody else's) and that, during the 1920's, at
> least, his "consciousness" was neither below nor
> above any other contemporary "Negro" college graduate
> of his generation. He was exceptional only because
> he was more gifted, but his understanding of how to
> use these gifts was no more advanced than many others.
> His path to international fame was paved and cultivated
> by others (mostly white), and he was not the only
> Black artist propelled to Europe in search of broadened
> "opportunities." In fact, Josephine Baker emigrated
> to France and became a "household" word in Paris long
> before Robeson became an exceptional Black in Moscow.
> Robeson was to later claim that because of <u>his</u> acceptance
> and celebrity in Russia, it was demonstrated that the
> Russians were "free" of race prejudice. Josephine
> Baker had every right to claim that the French were
> also "free" of racism because of <u>her</u> universal accep-
> tance, but everybody knows that the French, as one of
> the main imperialistic nations in Africa, was no model
> of racial idealism.

Mr. Cruse points out that a careful reading of Philip Foner's book
on Robeson reveals that, well into the 1930's Robeson was no less
confused on the question of American Blacks' relationship to Africa
than any other "Negro" in the United States who never had the opportunity to leave home for intellectual "broadening" of horizons.

5. LEADERSHIP

2070. Jardin, Edward A. "Great Sayings," New York Times, April 19, 1980.

The writer suggests that Robeson's espousal of left-wing causes made the distinguished actor-singer highly unpopular with many Americans, Blacks as well as whites, at the height of the Cold War. He concludes: "Today, however, it is widely recognized that his unflagging fight against racism earned for him a lasting place in the pantheon of Black American heroes that includes Frederick Douglass, W.E.B. DuBois, Malcolm X and Martin Luther King."

6. ROBESON NOT LOVER

2071. "Lady Mountbatten Love Affairs Bared; Robeson, Hutchinson in New Book," Jet, Vol. 59, No. 1, September 18, 1980, p. 44.

This article states that a recently printed biography by Richard Hough, entitled, Mountbatten: Hero of Our Time, claims that the wife of the British war hero carried on a love affair with the popular Black entertainer Leslie Hutchinson and recalled that the Mountbattens sued a newspaper because it alleged that she has an affair with world famous Paul Robeson; a Black American who won wide acclaim in London for his stage roles and popular concert appearances.

XV
Book Reviews

On many occasions I have publicly expressed my belief in the principles of scientific socialism, my deep conviction that for all mankind a socialist society represents an advance to a higher stage of life—that it is a form of society which is economically, socially, culturally, and ethically superior to a system based upon production for private profit.

Paul Robeson

1. BOOKS BY PAUL ROBESON

A SELECTED LIST

2072. Keith, Harold L. Here I Stand By Paul Robeson. New York: Othello
       Associates, 1958. 128 pp. Pittsburgh Courier, February 22, 1958,
       Magazine Section, p. 1.

       The writer reviews Robeson's book, Here I Stand. Mr. Keith asserts
       that "Mr. Robeson is now deep into the third act of his neatly
       real-life role with his latest book, Here I Stand, shining
       forth as his soliloquy." He goes on to surmise that in taking
       his stand, Mr. Robeson covers every aspect of a running feud he
       has carried on the United States Government. Robeson defends his
       friendship with the convicted Communist, states Mr. Keith. The
       reviewer concludes: "But, regardless of one's personal views,
       Mr. Robeson has stated his case in plain language for everyone
       to read. The tragic Moor, consumed by his suspicion of his be-
       loved Desdemona, now awaits the daggers of Iagos."

2073. Editorial. Here I Stand By Paul Robeson. Chicago Crusader,
       March 8, 1958.

       This book was reviewed under the caption "Paul Robeson: A Man."
       The editor states: "The other day it was announced that Paul
       Robeson's long awaited autobiography, Here I Stand, had gone on
       sale. We here at the new Crusader were vitally interested because
       we have thought all along that great singer, athlete and lawyer
       as well as freedom fighter, has been cruelly maligned, falsely
       accused and persecuted because he wouldn't bow down to the white
       folks." He declares that Paul Robeson has been one of the
       mightiest of all Negro Voices raised against world oppression of
       people based on race, color, national origin and religion. He is
       known, wherever there are people, as a champion of the rights of
       mankind. Yet, in his own country, when his friendship for the

(Chicago Crusader)

Soviets came under fire of the Dies Committee on Un-American
Activities in Congress, the persecution went so far that his marvelous achievement in becoming one of Walter Camp's all-time All-
American football selections was dropped by most newspapers. The
fact that he was a top singer, a Phi Beta Kappa at Rutgers University, a Spingarn medal winner and foremost interpreter of
Shakespeare on the dramatic stage was all conveniently forgotten
as Negro newspapers with the exception of three - New York Amsterdam News, the Crusader and the Afro-American - joined the
chorus of white papers in pillorying this great American. Other
Negro editors, scared that Washington might send FBI agents to
check on them, took to their heels whenever the name Robeson was
mentioned, states the reviewer. The editor concludes, in part:
"We wanted him (Robeson) at the side of Martin Luther King in
Montgomery. We wanted him on the campus of the University of Alabama when Autherine Lucy was humiliated. We wanted and needed
him at Little Rock and at Calumet Party in Chicago where Negro
leaders hid until it was safe to come out while the little Negroes
were out there trading bricks with the cracker whites. There are
times in our struggle for full equality when words won't do the
trick. There are times when stalwart men like Robeson, carved in
the heroic mould of Cudjo, Fred Douglass, Jack Johnson, Dr. Ossian
Sweet of Detroit and Oscar DePriest of Chicago, are needed for the
physical example. This is the kind of leadership that Paul
Robeson lives and sings about that will get Negroes off their
knees where they are being executed daily before the firing squad
of racial prejudice, discrimination, Jim Crow and anti-Negro
terrorism, onto their own two legs on which they must stand like
men and fight this thing out toe to toe. White folks are scared
of this type of Negro leadership...."

2074. Redding, Saunders. Here I Stand By Paul Robeson. Afro-American,
        March 15, 1958, p. 2.

The reviewer declares that two things are made crystal clear in
Here I Stand. The first is that Paul Robeson is inheritor of a
family tradition that goes back through our generations and for
nearly 2 hundred years. It is a tradition that is as vital in him
as it was in his great-great-grandfather - that Cyrus Bustill who
played a part in the American Revolution and who was one of the
founders of the first mutual aid society of colored people. The
second thing that is made clear is that Paul Robeson has been persecuted for living up to his heritage, to his responsibility.
Redding suggests that Here I Stand is not a complaint, and most
certainly it is not a complaint of a personal kind. Simple and
sincere, it is primarily a statement of principles and convictions.
According to Redding, Here I Stand is a program of action for
colored Americans. It is a program based on the postulate that
"Freedom can be ours, here and now: the long-sought goal of full
citizenship under the Constitution is now within our reach." It
is a program designed to operate on three levels: The Moral level,
which involves not only the moral pressure that the American creed
exerts, but also the pressure exerted by America's assumption of
the moral leadership of the world: The economic level, which

(Redding, Saunders)

stipulates a recognition of the fact that there is a powerful body
of white Americans who realize that their basic economic interests -
more and more dependent on good relations with a world three-
fifths "colored" - are further jeopardized by every instance of
prejudice and discrimination: - the political level, which presumes
a recognition of the "power of organization" and which, in order to
utilize that power would temporarily erase all superficial differences (of party, of economic background, of social class) and
"place the interests of our people, and the struggle for those
interests, above all else," argues Redding. He concludes: "It
is a program of 'common action for colored Americans.' But no
American of whatever color can really quarrel with Robeson's
principles and his program. Undoubtedly though many Americans
will quarrel - and especially those who will hear about and not
read his book. Here I Stand is not a book for those who are un-
converted or only half converted to the American ethic. It is a
challenge to the wholly converted to implement that ethic. It is
a challenge to 'fulfill the American dream.'"

2075. Here I Stand By Paul Robeson. Crisis, March,1958, pp. 187-188.

This author of a very critical review suggests that the book is
Mr. Robeson's apoligia for his political beliefs and public actions
during the past seventeen years. He uses a prologue, five
chapters, an epilogue, and five appendixes in an attempt to explain
where he now stands with respect to Negro advancement and Soviet
Russia. His explanations,however, are disorderly and confusing and
what comes through is the blurred picture of a man with a large
sense of mission but with no practicable plan for its achievement,
states the reviewer. He argues that at no time since Robeson's
return to the States in 1939 could he be dubbed a Negro leader.
In fact, he had little to do with Negroes and he always lent his
talents to the Communist and Russian cause. Mixed and all-white
left-wing groups could always get Mr. Robeson's support, but
ordinary Negroes and their organizations could not even get a
reply to a letter. He has mostly sentimental roots among American
Negroes. Negroes admired him as an athlete and concert singer and
applauded his frequent outbursts against the degradation of his
people, but they never regarded him as a leader, nor did they
admire him for strict adherence to the Communist Party line,
declares the critic. He concludes: "Mr. Robeson is still naive
and unaware of present-day realities. He imagines his misfortunes
to stem, not from his own bungling, but from the persecution of
'white folks on top'...."

2076. Here I Stand By Paul Robeson. Blitz (India), April 5, 1958.

This book was reviewed under the caption, "Black Voice of God."
The editor felt that the book not only merited attention but
called for action as well. He surmises: "...we must take Robeson's
slogan, THE TIME IS NOW and arrange mass demonstrations to show
that we completely and solidly support the cause of the American
Negro...."

2077. Lonesome, Buddy. <u>Here I Stand</u> By Paul Robeson. <u>St. Louis Argus</u>,
       April 25, 1958.

       The reviewer quoted several passages from Chapter 4, "The Time Is
       Now," and Chapter 5, "The Power of Negro Action." He suggests
       that those chapters were "particularly pertinent" to understanding
       Robeson. Mr. Lonesome states: "....The author gives an example
       of a Negro family huddling in their newly purchased home while a
       mob of howling bigots mills around the house. Robeson then
       candidly asks, 'Where are the other Negroes?' There I differ
       with him, for it certainly wouldn't be right for Negroes to rush
       to arms, thereby creating another mob, to still the howls of the
       indignant white bigots. But then I remember the indulgent smirks
       of Americans around the country when Indians in Lumbee, N.C.,
       grabbed rifles to rout a klavern of white-sheeted Ku Kluxers, and
       I pause for deep reflection...."

2078. Davis, Benjamin. <u>Here I Stand</u> By Paul Robeson. <u>Political Affairs</u>,
       Vol. 36, No. 4, April, 1958, pp. 1-8.

       Mr. Davis declares that with the publication of <u>Here I Stand</u>, a
       new dimension is added to the massive array of Robeson's contri-
       butions to the goal of human dignity. Beautifully, simply and
       movingly written, bold in conception, sound in content, broad in
       approach, it cuts through the welter of lies, slanders and con-
       fusions - which have surrounded the convictions of this man. In
       the first place, it sets the record straight, states the reviewer.
       He also suggests that plainly, it is addressed to the Negro
       people; but it abounds in solid meat for the labor movement of
       the country, and for all democratic white Americans. Viewing the
       Negro people's movement in all its complexity, totality and
       unity, it brings forward a people's program of action which, if
       seized upon by the Negro people and their allies, could not fail
       to have the most profound positive effects upon the present
       struggles of the Negro for dignity and full citizenship. This,
       undoubtedly, is why the hierarchy of bourgeois literary authorities
       in which the <u>New York Times</u> ranks high, did not even find the
       space to list <u>Here I Stand</u> among the new publications, much less
       review it. This conspiracy of muteness on the part of the mono-
       poly press -- at least in New York -- is itself a significant
       tribute to the book, surmises the writer. The reviewer suggests:
            <u>Here I Stand</u> is Robeson's first book; and everyone
            who reads it will earnestly hope that it will not be
            his last. Obviously, it is not the definitive catalog
            of his countless and extraordinary experiences. That
            would take volumes, and one can only wish that, in
            the not too distant future, they will be written.
            But into the 128 living pages of this book the author
            manages to compress enough truth and inspiration to
            leave the reader amply rewarded.

2079. Bonosky, Phillip. <u>Here I Stand</u> By Paul Robeson. <u>Daily Worker</u>,
       May 4, 1958, pp. 9, 11.

The title of this book review was "The Education of Paul Robeson."
The reviewer surmises that the publication of Paul Robeson's
<u>Here I Stand</u> is a political event of the greatest importance. Not
only does it make a profound contribution to the struggle for
Negro rights, it also helps to deepen the struggle for peace and
democracy both here and all over the world. Few Americans, states
the reviewer, are in the unique position of Robeson. He stands
now, at 60, surveying a lifetime remarkably rich in experience
and thought. He began life - as the son of a one-time slave -
in Princeton, New Jersey, a little bit of the South in the North,
as he points out. Paul Robeson's education had two parts: one
was the formal academic sector of schools, lectures and tests, in
which he excelled. The other was more austere, more real; it
centered around the great question: what is the hope of the Negro
people in America and in this world? THE ANSWER TO IT took him
at first outside America to England, where he came to know another
kind of country, a country of a genteel ruling class that seemed
to love culture. It seemed to him for awhile that here, where he
was appreciated as an artist and a cultured man, he would live
the rest of his days. Why come back to the America of Jim Crow,
of daily insults, and even worse, of the blantant worship of money
in all things, declares the writer. Mr. Bonosky states that his
living education led him to Africa, which he, son of Africans,
now "discovered." There he understood more profoundly the terrible
struggle the world was beginning against the forces of fascism and
enslavement.... The reviewer concludes: "THIS BOOK is therefore
both a rallying cry and inspiring call to action. It aims to
reforge the iron of struggle in the Negro people. It calls upon
the Negro people to chart a program. It points out to all white
men and women of good will the ways and means in which they can
help push forward the struggle. It tells the exploited colored
peoples of the world, in Africa, in Asia, in the islands of the
Caribbeans, that this son of America, bound to them too by indis-
soluble bonds of brotherhood, is on their side -- the side of
full freedom of Negro people here in the USA, and just as much
the world over! Thus, this book, written so beautifully, with
such warmth and instinct with the poetic idiom of the Negro folk
singer and preacher, takes its place in the range of political
works which simultaneously become works of art. No person
reading it can fail to respond to its passion, a passion which,
taken as their own by millions of people will become an irresistible force. Every club should take bundle orders of <u>Here I Stand</u>.
It must be sold everywhere."

2080. Taylor, William C. <u>Here I Stand</u> By Paul Robeson. <u>Los Angeles
       Herald-Dispatch</u>, May 8, 1958.

The reviewer discusses mainly Chapter 5, "The Power of Negro
Action." He declares that this chapter by itself makes this book
a "must" on every reading list. Mr. Taylor concludes, in part:
"While strongly advocating unity of Negro and White. Robeson
warns of a 'rising resentment against the control of our affairs
by white people, regardless of whether that domination is expressed

(Taylor, William C.)

by the blunt orders of political bosses or more discreetly by the
advice of white liberals which must be heeded or else.' Along
with his insistence that the liberation movement must be led by
an independent black leadership, Robeson had stressed that another
quality was also needed: 'To live in freedom one must be prepared
to die to achieve it... He who is not prepared to face the trials
of battle will never lead to a triumph.'" To the Los Angeles reviewer Robeson's ideas on this subject were "right down the alley,"
and he quoted the following passage on page 110 of Here I Stand,
as being especially meaningful: "The primary quality that Negro
leadership must possess, as I see it, is a single-minded dedication
to their people's welfare.... For the true leader all else must
be subordinated to the interests of those whom he is leading."

2081.   Here I Stand By Paul Robeson. Jewish Current, Vol. 27, No. 6,
        June, 1958.

        The reviewer observes that the book is a moving document. He
        surmises that the first edition of 10,000 was sold in two months
        and a new printing of 25,000 is being enthusiastically received.
        "I am a Negro," the book begins. He is a part of the Harlem
        community, of the "church where on Sunday mornings I am united
        with the fellowship of thousands of my people...." Winning a
        scholarship to Rutgers was "the decisive point of my life" because
        "I knew I was not inferior." He traces the expansion of his
        horizons. "This belief in the oneness of human kind...has existed
        within me side by side with my deep attachment to the cause of
        my own race." His "stand" has two elements; for the world, the
        principles of Bandung; for the Negro in the United States" "Freedom
        can be ours, here and now," and "Negro action can be decisive."
        He proposes an all-inclusive "national conference of Negro lead-
        ership," to lead Negro action for Freedom Now, states the writer.
        He concludes: "Progressive Jews have a passion for Robeson,
        vividly expressed at many a Morning Freiheit concert. Robeson
        knows this, for he speaks of "the Jewish people with whom I have
        been especially close." Believing in the right of all people every-
        where to travel and migrate as they wish, I find the State De-
        partment's restricting his right to travel only in the Western
        Hemisphere particularly offensive. He should be heard every-
        where. I wish he could go to England to play Othello again, or
        to the Soviet Union to sing the songs of many peoples in many
        languages, including his unforgettable rendition of the Yiddish
        song about Reb Levi Yitzhok of Berdiehev's lawsuit against God
        himself."

2082.   Perry, Thelma D. Here I Stand By Paul Robeson. Boston: Beacon
        Press, 1971, 121 pp. Negro History Bulletin, Vol. 34, No. 7,
        November, 1971, p. 67.

        The reviewer declares that this book, first published in 1958, is
        Robeson's account of the beliefs he held; how he came to hold them;
        his controversial associations and activities; and the restrictions
        imposed against him by the U.S. Government, which virtually
        wrecked his career. World-wide, Paul Robeson was in demand as a

(Perry, Thelma)

first rate artist and performer, but he was also a political
activist on behalf of independence of the colonial peoples of
Africa. He believed and stated that racial prejudices were at a
minimum in the communist nations as distinguished from the white
supremacy complex of his own country. It was his opinion that
scientific socialism could project a program which would be more
effective in improving the quality of life for all people than an
imperialistic capitalism. Such "heresy" was anathema to the U.S.
Government, and the State Department denied him a passport, thus
grounding him from 1950 to 1958. He states that he was not even
allowed to go to countries such as Canada, for which an American
passport was not required, argues Mrs. Perry. She concludes, in
part: "Many things in this book are interesting, not the least
the Appendix section. Appendix D is omitted, though it is cited
(p. 57), but Appendix E is a 1964 statement by the author, a
fitting postulude. Regrettably, space limitations prevent a full
recital and summarization of the author's experiences, attitudes,
and his salient details. Suffice it to note that anyone concerned with the broad patterns of change in the past generation,
and the operational political forces that now shape black and
white and global relationships, will find here rewarding, perhaps
invaluable reading. This is so whether or not they share Paul
Robeson's outlook.

2083.   Weaver, Harold D. Here I Stand By Paul Robeson. Boston: Beacon
Press, 1972, Black World, Vol. 21, No. 9, July 1972, pp. 85-86.

The reviewer contends that with the reissuing of Paul Robeson's
major political statement, Here I Stand (originally published in
1958), he has emerged from non-person to person. That this
extraordinarily productive man is known and admired throughout
the world, and yet virtually unknown to American youth, reflects
the mistreatment meted out to political heretics by the Establishment media. That he was Black - and, in addition, a threatening
male - intensified his reduction from superhuman to non-person,
states Mr. Weaver. He concludes: "...The book is the culminating
political statement of a courageous, humane, and pioneering hero -
extraordinarily productive in the interpretive arts, politics,
athletics, and scholarship - who dared assert his manhood and
that of his people."

2084.   Shappes, Morris A. Here I Stand By Paul Robeson. New York:
Othello Associates, 1958, Jewish Current, Vol. 27, No. 2, February,
1973, p. 22.

The reviewer argues that when this book first appeared in 1958, it
went into three editions and sold 50,000 copies despite a total
boycott by the white commercial presses, as Paul Robeson's collaborator, Lloyd L. Brown, notes in his Introduction to the new
edition (Beacon: Boston, 1971). Shappes surmises: "We were
among those who hailed the volume then (June, 1958), as did the
Morgan Freiheit, although Brown omits these reviews from his
survey. For Robeson's reference to "the Jewish people, with whom
I have been especially close" (p. 4) was based on an unusual

(Shappes, Morris)

relationship he had with the Jewish People as a whole and progressive Jews in particular. It was not only that Robeson was
popular among Jews, as he was among others, as a great singer
and actor. Progressive Jews responded to him because as an
artist he expressed his solidarity with Jews by singing our folk
songs and our hymns of struggle, not only here but all over the
world, including the Soviet Union. To progressive Jews he was
also a leader in social action, especially in the struggle for
unity of Black and White, of Black and Jew." Mr. Shappes points
out that it is therefore appropriate that the current revival of
interest in and appreciation of Robeson, which has expressed itself in public tributes, in reissues of his recordings, in radio
and TV programs, should also lead to reissue of this memorable
book, part instructive and moving autobiography of his first 17
years, largely an outline of the evolution of his political beliefs
and a statement of his program and strategy for Black liberation.
For Robeson is both, as Lloyd Brown calls him, 'the Great Forerunner of his people's liberation movement, and at present still a
Great Frontrunner.' Black people and would-be White allies of the
Black movement - have much to learn from Paul Robeson's life-
style and principles, states the editor. He concludes: "....
Robeson's book is more than the sum of its ideas. It is written
with warmth, humor, passion, dignity and a sense of Black history
that has a special impact. Although illness has kept Robeson
out of all public life for years, his presence is with us and is
growing as he approaches his 75th birthday, April 9."

2085. Stuckey, Sterling. "Paul Robeson Revisited," New York Times Book
Review, October 21, 1973, pp. 40-41.

This is a review of Paul Robeson's reissued autobiography, Here I
Stand. This book was first published in 1958. This review is
as much a historical commentary on Robeson as it is a review of
his book. The reviewer argues that while the autobiography is
of lesser literary quality than Robeson's previously published
works, the book has advantages: until those earlier essays,
interviews and speeches are published, nowhere else will one find
his position on so many critical issues better represented than
in its pages. Dr. Stuckey concludes: "Until he is restored to
his rightful place in the land of his birth, his treatment will
represent in the future, as it has in the past, the single most
striking example in our time of America's vulnerability on the
question of human freedom."

2086. Butterfield, Stephen. Black Autobiography in America. Amherst,
Mass.: University of Massachusetts Press, 1974, pp. 5, 103-106,
225-226.

The author discusses Robeson's book, Here I Stand, and how it was
received by both Black and White news media. He called Robeson
a communist as well as actor, singer, Pan-Africanist, and champion
of freedom for all oppressed people. Dr. Butterfield, once again
erroneously makes statements about Black autobiographies when he
declares: "The need to write about his life, therefore, as in all

(Butterfield, Stephen)

black autobiography, is political." Obviously that assertion is
not correct. He concludes: "But it was the 'ominous drumbeat
of history' that forced him to stand among the masses whose songs
he had adopted."

2. BOOKS ABOUT PAUL ROBESON

A SELECTED LIST

A. PAUL ROBESON, NEGRO BY ESLANDA GOODE ROBESON

2087. O'Neill, Eugene. "Introduction" to Paul Robeson, Negro by Eslanda
Goode Robeson. London: Harper & Brothers, 1930, 178 pp.

Mr. O'Neill declares: "In gratitude to Paul Robeson in whose
interpretation of Brutus Jones, I have found the most complete
satisfaction any author can get - that of seeing his creation
born into flesh and blood, and in whose creation of Jim Harris
in my 'All God's Chillun Got Wings' I have found not only complete
fidelity to my intent under trying circumstances, but beyond that,
true understanding and racial integrity."

2088. Paul Robeson, Negro By Eslanda Goode Robeson, London Times, May
20, 1930, p. 10.

This was a review of Paul Robeson, Negro, by his wife, Eslanda
Goode Robeson. The reviewer surmises that the implications of
the title of the book are obvious enough in a sense. He asserts
that the chapter on Harlem (N.Y.) develops them, and there are
further sidelights on the position of the Negro, educated or un-
educated, in the account of Mr. Robeson's early experiences as a
concert singer, in the course of which he was often debarred by
color from getting any sort of hotel accommodation even of the
most modest kind. A Negro, even if he happens to be a great
artist, is still regarded primarily as a Negro in the United
States, and as such he is a lesser creature than the white man,
states the writer. He concludes that the racial pride and the
enthusiasm for Negro culture of both the writer of this book and
the subject of it are very clearly expressed. The writer also
called Mr. Robeson an interpreter of the Negro mind.

2089. Paul Robeson, Negro by Eslanda Goode Robeson. London: Victor
Gollancz, 1930, 153 pp. The London Times Literary Supplement,
May 22, 1930, p. 432.

The reviewer states that the work was written in an artless but
quite attractive strain, this biographical record illuminates many
aspects of Negro life and character which are not strickly relevant to the main narrative. It would be foolish, of course, to
attempt to generalize about the Negro on the strength of a personal
sketch of this kind, but there is a strong temptation to do so
in view of the position Mr. Paul Robeson occupies as an interpreter

(London Times Literary Supplement)

of the negro mind and sensibility, argues the writer. As an actor
and a singer of negro spritiuals he has charmed and impressed us
more than any other contemporary negro artist. The sketch of his
career and personality which his wife provides in this book
emphasizes - quite unconsciously for the most part - two characteristics, vitality and adaptability. These, allied to a native
artistic talent, have enabled him to achieve the sort of distinction that is only rarely possible for the negro in the United
States, but that would appear to be much more often within the
reach of the negro population in general or at any rate of the
educated negroes in the East, than "colour" restrictions and handicaps allow at the present, argues the critic. The reviewer concludes: "Mrs. Robeson's record, as the illuminating chapter on
Harlem goes to show, is written for English readers. It is a
simple and unpretentious narrative, which leaves a very pleasant
impression of both the subject and the writer of the book."

2090.   Paul Robeson, Negro by Eslanda Goode Robeson, The World, June 22,
         1930.

The reviewer asserts that the saga of the new Negro, the recently
published life of Paul Robeson as told by his wife, Eslands, is
that rare romance, the story of a college hero who really
amounted to something afterward. Robeson has succeeded equally in
scholarship, athletics, law, acting and singing. But the bar
sinister of a dark completion did make it hard sledding sometimes,
according to this wife's testimony, states the writer. He surmises
that Mrs. Robeson quotes with pride the critics' verdict on his
performance in the leading role of "The Emperor Jones," and in
"All God's Chillun Got Wings." Extraordinarily versatile, he was
able to earn a living later with his fine singing voice giving
Negro spiritual concerts, when Negro acting parts proved scarce.
Moving in a prescribed circle in "the Village," the friend of
Eugene, Carl Van Vechten, Glenway Westcott, the Cooks, and so on,
many of the race barriers tumbled. Robeson, through his wife,
pays tribute where it is due. But Harlem was the only unreservedly
friendly country. From her vantage point in a London suburb where
she declares race prejudice to be comparatively negligible, Mrs.
Robeson scores her countrymen for their "Jim Crow" practices,
bitter at the eternal banishment from hotels, and restaurants and
sleeping cars, according to the critic. That Paul should act
"Othello" in London was her supreme ambition, and she set about
cunningly to make it his, declares the reviewer. He states that
Robeson said, "When I do Othello they'll all expect a crusted
American accent. I'll fool 'em," boasted Paul. "I'll do the
role in good honest English, as pure as I can make it, because pure
English will bring out the music of the text. Why, I might as
well sing the Negro dialect of the spirituals with a correct
Boston accent, as do Othello in 'American.'" He concludes: "That
Robeson accomplished this appears to be amply attested to be the
critics' eulogistic accounts of his performance."

2091. Gannett, Lewis. Paul Robeson, Negro By Eslanda Goode Robeson,
       New York Herald, June 26, 1930.

       The reviewer asserts that of so intimate a book one can hardly
       speak except in first names. Simple and naive, it is a proud
       wife's account of her husband's success. Mr. Gannett suggests
       that any one who has seen Paul act or heard him sing knows that
       the man instinctively and profoundly touches universal chords.
       Even so, Paul was always a Negro. We are proud in New York, and
       with some reason, of the relative equality of opportunities which
       Negroes enjoy here. Essie writes with warm passion of Negro Har-
       lem, not the night clubs dressed up for white patronage, but the
       living, pulsing capital of the black American world, states the
       critic. But even in New York, when Paul was stranded between
       Greenwich Village and Harlem, the color bar silently lifted it-
       self -- "he could get a good meal in any good restaurant or
       hotel -- except the Pennsylvania - from Tenth Street to 130th
       Street: at none of the innumerable first-class eating places
       could he be served as a Negro guest." In traveling it was
       difficult to obtain Pullman accommodations or hotel rooms. Life
       in London was simpler. Mr. Gannett concludes: "Essie's book
       about Paul, sincere, affectionate, almost naively intimate, is a
       unique and very winning portrait of a great American."

2092. Hughes, Langston. Paul Robeson, Negro By Eslanda Goode Robeson,
       New York Tribune, Book Section, June 29, 1930, pp. 1, 2.

       The writer entitles his review "Ambassador to The World." He says
       that Paul Robeson was a famous man. In Vienna, Paris, Berlin,
       London, New York, Chicago, people who knew anything at all knew
       his name, had heard him sing or seen him act in the theater. Mr.
       Hughes suggests that Mrs. Robeson had "written a chatty, informing
       and naively intimate book that couldn't have been bettered by the
       best press agent." In it one learns as much about Mrs. Robeson
       as one does about Paul - and a good deal about them together.
       The reviewer declares: "At the beginning there's a chapter on
       the Negro church and, near the middle, some sound and sensible
       pages on Harlem and the Negro problem. Paul's life in two worlds
       is pictured - uptown and down, black and white - and many of his
       current friends are named, most of them celebrities in one way
       or another. The book is dotted with Glenways and Genes and Hughs
       and folks like that whose last names are Westcott and O'Neill and
       Walpole and so on - names that the big world knows, but that,
       most certainly, the poor dark members of the little churches in
       Jersey wouldn't recognize at all. But their Paul belongs to this
       big world now. Sometimes his old friends in these north Jersey
       congregations read about him in the Negro weeklies, and they are
       very proud. They were proud when he lived among them. They were
       proud twelve years ago when his conduct on the football field put
       his name into the headlines where few Negro names had been before.
       Now when his deep racial voice sings "I don't feel no ways tired"
       in Vienna and Prague and Berlin, and the press of Central Europe
       is loud in its acclaim, his old friends who still walk humbly are
       mightly glad. Millions of colored people all over the country
       are glad, too. When his magnificent black body moves across the
       stage these days in a London theater revivifying Shakespeare's

(Hughes, Langston)

Moor, every dark workman and servant in America can feel "He's one of us," and they know that, from their estate, a noble representative has risen. He concludes: "Paul Robeson is their ambassador to the world."

2093.   Paul Robeson, Negro By Eslanda Goode Robeson, Times, Vol. 25, No. 26, June 30, 1930, p. 55.

The critic declares that Paul Robeson, Negro is partly biography, partly propaganda for the "new," educated Negro, partly a paean of press clippings. The reviewer also gives a short overview of Paul Robeson's accomplishments as well as some background of his college life at Rutgers University. The writer suggests Biographer Eslands thinks white people "astonishingly ignorant about Negroes." Says she: "The Negro problem is not so much of a problem as America would have the world believe. The Negro is a problem because he is described as a citizen of the U.S. by the Federal Constitution, and yet in some individual states he is placed in the impossible position of being a full citizen, but enjoying none of the rights of citizenship," concludes the reviewer.

2094.   Feld, Rose C.   Paul Robeson, Negro By Eslanda Goode Robeson, New York Times Book Reviews, July 13, 1930.

According to this reviewer Paul Robeson's triumph on the English stage as Othello makes this biography of him by his wife an extremely timely one. Robeson, as he himself believes, was undoubtedly born under a lucky star. Disappointment and disillusionment he probably has had in his life, but his triumphs overshadow these by far. Feld declares this book is compelling by its simplicity and naivete. Mrs. Robeson is frankly enamored of her husband and proud of his achievement as an artist and a Negro. She sees his faults as an individual, as a husband, as a father, and speaks with most disarming truth about them, but she speaks with the affection of a mother for a spoiled but brilliant child. Not that she believes that Paul Robeson has been spoiled by his successes; over and over again she repeats how kind and unaffected and charming he is, but at the same time she wishes he were less lazy, less procrastinating, more devoted to the business of fatherhood. She scolds him fondly in the pages of the book as doubtless she does in the privacy of her home, states the writer. The reviewer asserts that Mrs. Robeson is no mental lightweight. She has a chapter on Harlem and the Negro which is penetrating and thought-provoking. As far as this reviewer is concerned it is the best thing in the book. "One wishes there were more of it; it gives frankly and interestingly the psychology of the Negro in his relationship to white people and the expressions of escape which his race consciousness gives him. That the cultured Negro is happier in Europe than in America she makes clear; at the same time she points out, America is home to him, and a nostalgia for familiar scenes makes his return emotionally imperative. In the light of literature this book will not cast lengthy shadows but as a homely picture of colorful individuals it has much to recommend

(Feld, Rose)

it," concludes the reviewer.

2095. Paul Robeson, Negro By Eslanda Goode Robeson, The Interstate
Tattler, July 18, 1930.

The reviewer asserts that the book is an interesting biography
Essie Robeson has written about her husband. One feels her sincere
admiration for him all through it. He is her great hero. Paul
Robeson's life has been a succession of triumphs. Unlike many
others who have achieved great things, he has had few difficulties
and handicaps. Although others may consider being a Negro a handicap, he has never worried about the color of his skin. In high
school he was a brilliant student; at Rutger's University he was
a "four letter" man in sports and elected to Phi Beta Kappa; he
was a successful law student at Columbia University; he won name
for himself in two of Eugene O'Neill's plays; he has been a sensation on two continents with his concepts of Negro spirituals;
and now when he is less than thirty-five he has successfully
played "Othello" in the London theatre, states the reviewer. There
is a certain naivete and simplicity to this book that makes it
very charming. There are intimate scenes between husband and wife:
when she scolds him about his laziness, and for neglecting his
child. But always there is her great love and admiration for him
as her husband, an artist and a Negro, declares the writer. The
critic declares: "I enjoyed greatly the chapter on Harlem. It
is one of the most interesting pieces of writing about this community one will find any place. I only wish there had been more
of it. Of course many of the things she has written about here
most Negroes are acquainted with. But it will be an eye-opener
for many white readers. It is a charmingly affectionate book,
and you will close it with a pleasant and almost thrilled feeling."

2096. Paul Robeson, Negro By Eslanda Goode Robeson, Boston Herald, July
26, 1930.

The writer declares that Mrs. Robeson writes with remarkable de-
tachment in this biography of her famous husband. The reviewer
asserts that Mrs. Robeson makes his life story very vivid and
readable, presenting him, very happily, both as artist and as a
man who is equally at home in two alien racial worlds.

2097. Young, Stark. Paul Robeson, Negro By Eslanda Goode Robeson, New
Republic, August 6, 1930, pp. 345-346.

The author gives a very, very poor review of this book. He states:
"We need only remember all that to regret this biography and to
think what a book might be written about him." Young concluces:
"The whole case of this book is most regrettable. Its mediocrity
spoils the fine material it attempts; its trite, and sometimes
specious, plausibility invites a certain approval that is only another kind of condescension."

2098. DuBois, W.E.B. Paul Robeson, Negro By Eslanda Goode Robeson,
       Crisis, Vol. 37, No. 9, September, 1930, p. 313.

       Dr. DuBois asserts: "I suggest that all of our readers should buy
       and read the Biography of Paul Robeson written by his wife. The
       story of Paul Robeson's life is fascinating. It is well written,
       well printed, and illustrated with many interesting portraits.
       The only criticism is voiced in the tenth chapter of the book it-
       self." Paul Robeson is pictured as saying: "She thinks I'm a
       little tin angel with no faults at all, and so, of course, the
       book is stupid, uninteresting, and untrue. Marion looked at
       Essie with twinkling eyes. Perhaps you're not the one to write
       it, then, she said comfortingly." The hero is made a little too
       perfect, but with all that, the evident triumph of a fine black
       man makes fascinating reading and something unusual in these days
       when everything black in literature has to come from the slums,
       wallow in Harlem, and go to Hell.

2099. Paul Robeson, Negro By Eslanda Goode Robeson, Abbot's Monthly
       Review, April, 1931.

       According to this reviewer a book on the life of Paul Robeson is
       naturally an easy assignment. The only danger is that the person
       attempting the job might not do full justice to it. Certainly
       there is no chance to fall down from the point of view of the
       interest such a book would contain, for the Paul Robesons do not
       come every day -- they are the persons who can be classes as "one-
       in-a-million" and "one to an age." It would be difficult to find
       another person whose life, in the few short years Robeson has
       lived, crammed with experiences appealing to the biographer as is
       true in the case of this athlete, student, singer, actor and
       philosopher. Rarely can we find a person whose excellence in any
       one of these fields merits for him a biography before he has
       reached twoscore years, states the writer. He concludes:
       "....One is apt to ramble a bit when trying to discuss a character
       with as many facets as Paul Robeson possesses. Added to this, a
       wife who has chosen as her life's work the achieving of the various
       aims mapped out by her husband, there can hardly be room for doubt
       as to the ultimate success of the pair. And you have such a com-
       bination in Mr. and Mrs. Paul Robeson, all of which is pointed
       out in this most remarkable book. The most I can say for it is
       that it should be read, and widely, by young and old of the
       Negro race as well as of all other races. In saying this, I only
       endorse what other critics have said with an unanimity that is
       almost startling. If you want to know what a black man can do
       and has done in what the Nordic likes to call his world, read
       Paul Robeson, Negro by his wife. You'll be surprised!,"
       concludes the reviewer.

B. BIG BEN BY EARL SCHENCK MIERS

2100.   "New Novel Based on Trials, Triumphs of Paul Robeson," Baltimore
        Afro-American, February 28, 1942, p. 5.

        This is a review of a novel entitled, Big Ben (Philadelphia:
        Westminster Press, 1942, 238 pp.). It was written by Earl
        Schenck Miers. The reviewer argues that based on the story of
        Paul Robeson's career from the beginning of his college career
        to his first triumph as a concert singer, Big Ben represents the
        avowed attempt of its white author to plead for a minority group
        that "dignity" of treatment that is due to all human beings. He
        continues to surmise that from the point of view of its general
        reading public, the book should attain much success. The tribu-
        lations and triumphs of Big Ben have been woven into a fascinating
        story, which should commend to a more sympathetic understanding
        of the efforts of the colored man seeking a higher goal in a pre-
        judiced white world. The reviewer also suggests that nevertheless,
        like all white authors, Mr. Miers suffers from an inability to
        grasp the true psychology of the colored man. Big Ben's innocuous
        reactions to the barriers of racial prejudice are, in reality,
        not those of the colored man but what the misunderstanding white
        man thinks they would be. He concludes: "Moreover, the book
        suffers from the repeated use of the epithet n____. While that
        in itself is inexcusable, it is impossible to forgive the author
        for committing the heinous crime of depicting the educated Big
        Ben as thinking of himself as a n____. Mr. Miers is to be
        commended, however, for bringing before the reading public a type
        of colored person - intelligent and educated - which is so con-
        sistently ignored by novelists in portrayal of life of colored
        people."

        C. PAUL ROBESON: CITIZEN OF THE WORLD BY SHIRLEY GRAHAM

2101.   Baker, Blanch M. Theater and Allied Arts: A Guide to Books
        Dealing with the History, Criticism, and Teaching of the Drama
        and Theater and Related Co. New York: Wilson, 1952, pp. 264-265.

        There is a review of Shirley Graham's Paul Robeson: Citizen of
        the World (New York: Julian Messner, 1946, 264 pp.) book. The
        compiler called this biography a sympathetic account of Robeson's
        life, and the difficulties and the triumphs of his career as
        singer and actor. It was also pointed out that Robeson scored
        a success as Othello.

D. PAUL ROBESON BY MARIE SETON

2102.   Paul Robeson By Marie Seton. London: Dennis Dobson, 1958, 254
pp., London Times, August 14, 1958, p. 11.

The writer surmises that Miss Seton adds much interesting material
about Paul Robeson's early life and development as an actor and
singer. He concludes: "Her book is written in the awed style
of the lives of the saints. Robeson does everything except float
on a millstone. If this reverential attitude is common among
friends, it is easy to see why he has remained politically a
Bourbon."

E. PAUL ROBESON: THE AMERICAN OTHELLO BY EDWIN P. HOYT

2103.   Paul Robeson: The American Othello. By Edwin P. Hoyt. New York:
World, 1967, 228 pp. New York Times, November 12, 1967, Section
7, pp. 28, 30.

The reviewer contends that the rise and fall of Paul Robeson are
set down here in clinical detail by the seasoned biographer who
lets the facts speak for themselves. According to this review,
with his striking personal endowments, his triumphs on the concert and musical stages, Robeson established himself as one of
the finest singers of his time. After his tour-de-force interpretation of Othello midway in World War II, he might also have
become one of the finest actors. Instead, there followed his
quest for racial equality, his long exile in the Soviet Union, the
sad return to his homeland and the oblivion of his old age. This
thoughtful book, states the reviewer, demonstrates that it is
too simple to call Robeson his own worst enemy, suggests the
reviewer. He concludes: "He was not the first artist whose career
was destroyed by his convictions in our present climate, he will
not, unfortunately, be the last."

2104.   Lubasch, Arnold. Paul Robeson: The American Othello By Edwin P.
Hoyt, New York Times, December 21, 1967, p. 35.

This reviewer argues that tragedy is a theme in his biography of
Paul Robeson. It is a tragedy of a great artist deprived of the
freedom to travel and the opportunity to perform because he advocated unpopular views in an intolerant era. It is also the
tragedy of a Negro fighter for civil rights so far ahead of his
time that his influence was dissipated in controversy before
civil rights became fashionable, asserts the critic. Mr. Lubasch
declares: "Hoyt has written a well intentioned introduction to a
most remarkable human being. The writing is simple and clear, but
the results seem second hand and oversimplified. The authentic
voice of Paul Robeson remains to be heard."

F. PAUL ROBESON: THE LIFE AND TIMES OF A FREE BLACK MAN

BY VIRGINIA HAMILTON

2105. Laudau, Elaine. Paul Robeson: The Life and Times of A Free
       Black Man By Virginia Hamilton. New York: Harper & Row, 1974,
       217 pp. New York Times, December 22, 1974, Section 7, p. 8. A
       book written for ages 12 and up.

       The reviewer states: "The story is told in a rich historical con-
       text, Miss Hamilton's readable explanation of political indeologies
       prevalent during the Second World War and McCarthy era enables
       young readers to identify with Robeson's actions, as well as
       grasp the complexities of the times. Unlike most young-adult bio-
       graphies, the text remains unfictionalized and acquires chilling
       authenticity as each incident is fully documented by Senate testi-
       mony, newspaper and magazine quotes, Robeson's autobiography or
       texts by his wife and close friends. Yet Virginia Hamilton's
       magical ability to conjure up vivid images is still present in
       parts of the book, especially in her portrayal of Robeson's near-
       lynching in Berlin," states Miss Landau. The reviewer concludes:
       "Virginia Hamilton's book is far more than a compelling story of
       banished blacks; it is a vivid chronicle of dignity and deter-
       mination with which all young people can identify."

G. PAUL ROBESON: ALL-AMERICAN BY DOROTHY BUTLER GILLIAM

2106. "Paul Robeson's Neglected Side Depicted in New Book," Jet, Vol.
       51, No. 24, March 3, 1976, p. 10.

       This is a brief review of Dorothy Butler Gilliam's book, Paul
       Robeson, All-American. According to this review, Mrs. Gilliam
       gathered bits of information in the United States, England and
       Germany and put together a fast-moving, well documented, complete
       look at Robeson and where he stood throughout his life.

2107. Engs, Robert F. Paul Robeson: All American By Dorothy Butler
       Gilliam. Washington, D.C.: New Republic, 1976, 216 pp. Chroni-
       cle of Higher Education, April 11, 1977, p. 16.

       The reviewer declares that Dorothy Butler Gilliam's Paul Robeson:
       All-American is a biography of one of the 20th century America's
       most important, but least understood, Black figures. As an athlete,
       actor, singer, and political activist, Paul Robeson influenced
       many thousands of lives, black and white, in the United States
       and abroad. His "exorcism" from the American body politic and
       American consciousness by the governmental paranoia of the 1940's
       and 1950's is a crime for which our nation has yet to admit guilt.
       The consequence has been that the present generation of Americans
       has little sense of who or what this magnificent man was, argues

(Engs, Robert F.)

the writer. Mr. Engs states that Mrs. Gilliam is to be commended
for her determination and energy in seeking to end this neglect
of Robeson. But to deal justly with Mrs. Gilliam's book, the
reader must taken two points into consideration. First, hers is
an "unauthorized" study, written with neither the cooperation nor
hindrance of the Robeson family. As a consequence, certain necessary information was unavailable to her. Second, Mrs. Gilliam
addresses herself to a general audience, not to professional
historians or biographers. They will certainly find serious fault
with her book, but that is merely to say that she has not written
the book they wanted. The writer also surmises that Mrs. Gilliam
has not written a very good book. Its basic deficiency stems from
the author's conception of her task. Mrs. Gilliam wants to restore
Robeson to his place among the pantheon of 20th-century Black
leaders. Certainly Robeson has been denied his rightful place within that group. On the other hand, these leaders do not all come
from the same mold, nor can they be readily fitted into the same
category during their public lives. Paul Robeson was different -
proud, defiantly so. Any biographer who fails to explain that
does Robeson and the people he sought to influence a disservice.
Unfortunately, Mrs. Gilliam does just that, states Professor Engs.
He concludes: "Mrs. Gilliam has given us a timely reminder that
we need to know Paul Robeson and to understand the trials to which
he was subjected. It remains for future authors, however, to discover the answers to the questions Mrs. Gilliam does not realize
she has raised."

2108. Willingham, Alex. Paul Robeson: All-American By Dorothy Gilliam,
        First World, Vol. 2, No. 1, Spring, 1978, pp. 45-47.

The reviewer suggests that the evaluation of this book ought to be
addressed in two distinct but closely related areas which reflect
the state of Black biography just now. First, the temptation,
perhaps instrinsic to biographical work, to over emphasize the
individual at the expense of other factors. Gilliam does this,
though I am less concerned about her personalism as such than I
am about the limited analytical level at which she works, which
leads her now to near apology for her man's foibles and then to
be vaguely non-committal where there would appear to be obvious
grounds for criticism. The other broad area is the need for increased attention to Black biography of the period covered by
Robeson's life. This project is particularly important because
it now seems to be necessary to any reliable explanation of the
decline of the activism of the 1960's especially when the focus
is on the transformation of that activism into the twin corruptions
of radical (usually, but not exclusively, Marxian) sectarianism
on the one hand and enbourgeoisment on the other, states Professor
Willingham. He concludes: "Dorothy Gilliam's Paul Robeson is commended because it is a fresh source of material sympathetic to an
important Afro-American and written in a style accessible to the
average reader. It serves to suggest again the tremendous research
responsibilities, and it affirms that study of the middle period
is significant for political activity in the post-Civil Rights
era."

2109. Suggs, Henry Lewis. Paul Robeson: All-American By Dorothy Butler
       Gilliam, Negro History Bulletin, Vol. 41, No. 5, September-
       October, 1978, p. 893.

       The writer declares that Gilliam's treatment of Robeson's assoc-
       iation with the American Communist Party lacks literary depth and
       scholarship. Her analysis of the key elements of Robeson's public
       life as well as his political philosophy is bland and amateurish.
       Dr. Suggs goes on to declare: "This book is not only a biography
       of a great artist but a narrative which crystalizes the social,
       artistic movements of the Harlem Renaissance, the allied solidarity
       of World War II, and the hysterical backlash of McCarthyism. But
       the book falls short of clearing the controversy over Robeson's
       life. Nor does it obliterate the clouds of obscurity and ignorance
       that surrounded him during most of his adult life."

XVI
Obituaries

. . . London was the center of the British Empire and it was there that I
"discovered" Africa. That discovery, which has influenced my life ever
since, made it clear that I would not live out my life as an adopted English-
man, and I came to consider that I was African.

Paul Robeson

A. COUNTRIES

A SELECTED LIST

1. CANADA

2110. "Singer, Actor and Foe of Racism Was Victim of Communist Witch-
       hunt," Globe and Mail (Toronto, Canada), January 24, 1976, p. 30.

       The writer suggests that Paul Robeson possessed of the country's
       great voices and became the first full-fledged Black star. But
       his increasing involvement in the civil rights movement and left
       wing causes led to him being branded a Communist. The author
       observes that besides being a great singer who made Negro spirituals
       beloved by audiences frequently hostile to members of his race,
       Robeson was a powerful actor whose performances as "Othello"
       and "The Emperor Jones" were among the most stirring of his time.
       The writer concludes: "In his last years, he refused requests
       for interviews and lived as a recluse or, as in the title of one
       of America's most famous books about the Black experience in
       America, as an invisible man."

2111. Editorial. "Death of Paul Robeson," Montreal (Canada) Star,
       January 27, 1976.

       The editorial states that Robeson was talking in a militant manner
       at a time when there was no Black vote to speak of when the Black
       consciousness had barely surfaced. It was a time when a great
       many people could not see beyond the thickets of ideology. The
       late Jawaharlal Nehru summed up Paul Robeson's unique stature when
       he called him "one of the greatest artists of our generation (who)
       reminds us that art and human dignity are above all differences
       of race, nationality and color." The editor concludes: "And we
       are not so far gone in virtue that we can afford to take those
       words for granted just yet."

2112. Weisburd, Abe. "Paul Robeson: Revolutionary Artist," Guardian,
       Vol. 28, No. 17, February 4, 1976, p. 3.

       Mr. Weisburd declares: "....In 1949, at the height of the U.S.
       cold war against its former ally, the Soviet Union, with the
       attendant anticommunist McCarthite hysteria preparing Americans
       for a war against the war-weakened country, Robeson committed a
       cardinal sin against the U.S. ruling class. At the World Peace
       Congress in Paris, Robeson said: 'It is unthinkable that American
       Negroes could go to war on behalf of those who oppressed
       them for generations against the Soviet Union, which in one gene-
       ration has raised our people to human dignity.' In that sentence
       Robeson articulated the deep feelings of the Black masses about
       their oppression by the white racist ruling class. He did more.
       He raised in the sharpest terms the question of why the oppressed
       Black masses should even consider taking up arms in behalf of
       their oppressors, in imperialist wars, against liberation movements
       or against a socialist country that had wiped out racism. Robeson
       had great influence in the Black community, where he was respected
       and trusted,"states the writer. "Robeson's statement - and the
       positive reaction to it from Black people - shook the ruling class
       to the core. The media had built up his prestige in order to show
       in a token way that Blacks could achieve success; Robeson turned
       out to be not only a dangerous red, but also a dangerous Black,"
       according to Mr. Weisburd. The ruling class decided that Robeson
       had to be completely suppressed. He became a major target. He
       concludes: "Robeson was a Marxist-Leninist. He wrote in his book,
       Here I Stand: 'On many occasions I have publicly expressed my
       belief in the principles of scientific socialism, my deep conviction
       that for all mankind a socialist society represents an advance to
       a higher stage of life -- that it is the form of society which is
       economically, socially, culturally and ethically superior to a
       system based on production for private profit.'"

                           2. ENGLAND

2113. "Mr. Paul Robeson: Distinguished Singer and Actor," London Times,
       January 24, 1976, p. 14.

       The editor declares that it will no doubt be as a singer that he
       will chiefly be remembered, yet Robeson, in his time, played many
       parts. He was a lawyer, film star, actor, lecturer, philanth-
       ropist, an ardent social reformer in the Negro cause, and an ad-
       mirer of the Russian way of life. He might have achieved many
       things in his life, but his acting ability and his voice led him
       inevitably into the world of entertainment, and his early associ-
       ation with the playwright, Eugene O'Neill, and through him with
       the Provincetown Players theatrical group in New York in the early
       twenties, led to a career in the theatre but ultimately to one
       in films, states the writer. He continues to assert that Holly-
       wood accepted him only gradually and with caution, alarmed by the
       impact that an outstanding Negro personality might have in the

(London Times)

cinema. For Robeson dedicated himself to the cause of the Negro. He felt within him an immense pity for the Negro slaves of the past, and this pity he expressed in songs such as "Sometimes I Feel Like a Motherless Child," "Water Boy," and "Weepin' Mary," states the writer. He concludes: "He was possessed of exceptional talent, a tremendous physique, and a vital personality. Nature had created him on heroic lines and there was an heroic quality about much that he achieved both as an entertainer and as a spokesman for his race."

2114. "Paul Robeson," Manchester (England) Guardian Weekly, February 1, 1976, p. 7.

The article mentions the death of Robeson. The writer, Philip Hope-Wallace states: "Robeson was in every way a big fellow, used as a willing stalking horse by left-wingers on whom he wasted a lot of talent and time."

3.   FRANCE

2115. "Paul Robeson Est Mort," L'Humanite (Paris), January 24, 1976, p. 6.

The article states that Paul Robeson died at age 77. It gives a historical sketch of his life and includes most of his major accomplishments. This Paris, France, newspaper declares that Paul Robeson was an international spokesman for human rights.

4.   INDIA

2116. "Paul Robeson Dead," Hindustar Times (New Delhi, India), January 24, 1976, p. 7.

According to this article Paul Robeson was America's first full-fledged Black star. But the career was virtually destroyed in anti-Communist witchhunts of the 1940's and 50's and he became an "invisible" man in a country which ironically had come to accept many of his ideas on racial justice and equality. As well as being a great singer who made Negro spirituals beloved by audiences frequently hostile to members of his race, Robeson was a powerful actor whose performances as "Othello" and "The Emperor Jones" were among the most stirring of his time, states the newspaper.

5. JAMAICA

2117. "Robeson 77, Dies After Stroke," Daily Gleaner (Kingston, Jamaica),
       January 24, 1976, p. 1.

       The author states that Paul Robeson who drew bravos for his rich
       voice and was vilified for his associations with communism died
       Friday in a Philadelphia hospital. He was 77. The actor, singer,
       athlete and outspoken critic of American racism, was the son of
       a runaway slave. He had lived in self-imposed seclusion at his
       sister's home in West Philadelphia for more than a decade, seeing
       only family members and a few friends. Robeson's biting state-
       ment about racism, combined with his praise for the Soviet Union
       and friendship with U.S. Communist party members, served to
       ostracize him in the 40s and 50s, concludes the author.

B. STATES

A SELECTED LIST

1. ALABAMA

2118. "Paul Robeson: Freedom Fighter," Tuskegee (Ala.) Times, February
       4, 1976, p. 1.

       According to this article, Paul Robeson was in the minds of many,
       an illustrious Black American simply born several more decades
       before Mr. Robeson's time would come, it would take a Paul Robeson
       to make such a time come to pass, states the article. The writer
       states that it was his passionate zeal for human life that
       brought him into the greatest world renown and to official dis-
       grace and a living martyrdom at the hands of his own countrymen.
       He concludes: "In this latter sense, he was a true messiah
       figure 'giving his life as a ransom for many.' During the 1940's
       he became the most heroic, perhaps of all the contemporary Black
       activists. Supported directly and indirectly by countless numbers,
       he personified or represented in his own majestic presence the
       determination of Black Americans to be free, whatever 'freedom'
       in American might come to mean."

2. CALIFORNIA

2119. "Paul Robeson, Singer, Dies at 77," Los Angeles Times, January 24, 1976, Section 1, pp. 1, 6.

The article states that Paul Robeson who drew bravos for his rich bass baritone voice and was vilified for his associations with communism, died Friday in a Philadelphia hospital. He was 77. The actor, singer, athlete and outspoken critic of American racism was the son of a runaway slave. He had lived in self-imposed seclusion at his sister's home in West Philadelphia for more than a decade, seeing only family members and a few close friends. Robeson's biting statements about racism, combined with his praise of the Soviet Union and friendship with U.S. Communist party members, brought him ostracism in the 1940's and 1950's, states the article.

2120. Editorial. "Paul Robeson Is Dead," Sacramento Bee, January 26, 1976.

The editor declares that Paul Robeson was an exceptionally talented man with a sense of justice that came not from mindless exhileration at some rally but from a powerful, sustained love of mankind and an abiding belief in equality.... He concludes: "His outspoken criticism of the treatment of Blacks in America and his friendliness with the Communists in the 40s and 50s made him a target of Red hunters in the United States. He was questioned by the House Un-American Activities Committee but through it all he maintained tne special dignity and majesty that he gave to the causes he espoused. Robeson used his talents and his position to proclaim that the most fundamental tenet of democracy is equality. In doing so, he brought this country closer to the ideals it proclaims for itself."

2121. Anderson, Sidney P. "The Two Different Lives of Paul Robeson: Assessed by a Card-Carrying Conservative," Los Angeles Times, January 27, 1976, Section 11, p. 5.

The author surmises that tragically, many young Americans had only the faintest inkling of Paul Robeson, 77, until headlines recounted his death last week in a Philadelphia hospital. Even people in their early 40s may only dimly recall that he popularized "Ol' Man River" both on Broadway and, four years later, in the 1936 film version of "Show Boat." But perhaps their most vivid memory of Robeson is the way he espoused Communist doctrine in the 50s, even winning a Stalin Peace Prize for his proselytizing. I have no intention of writing an apologia for Paul Robeson. He does not need it, and he would not have wanted it. Rather, what is called for is a reassessment of Robeson, the artist, and Robeson, the man, according to current social and political tenets, states Mr. Anderson. The author asks the question, did Robeson really desire the totalitarian excess of Soviet Communism to be visited upon his fellow Americans? He thinks not. To him it is realistic to assume that Robeson was infatuated with the social

(Anderson, Sidney P.)

gospel of Soviet life, particularly as it preached the total and unqualified absence of racial discrimination. In my view, Robeson's turn to communism simply reflected his unquenchable thirst for Black dignity, states the writer....

2122. Gilliam, Dorothy. "Robeson's People Say Their Goodbyes: Funeral in Harlem," Los Angeles Times, January 29, 1976, Section I, p. 7.

The writer states that Robeson died at the age of 77 in Philadelphia. An All-American football star who later became known internationally for such songs as "Ballad for Americans" and "Ol' Man River," and film roles such as "The Emperor Jones," was silenced during the Cold War for his outspokenness on behalf of Blacks and the poor, and for his friendly sentiments toward the Soviet Union. The funeral was held at Mother AME Zion Church in Harlem, one of the oldest Black churches in America. An estimated 5,000 persons jammed inside and several hundred were turned away. A night funeral is not unusual among Blacks, so working people can attend, states Miss Gilliam.

2123. "In Memorian: Paul Robeson, 1898-1976," Black Scholar, Vol. 7, No. 5, January-February, 1976, pp. 1, 42, 48.

There is a drawing of Paul Robeson on the cover of this journal. The topic for this issue is "Black Popular Culture." On page 42 there is a poem by Jon Eckles, entitled "I Heard That," that referred to Robeson. It states Paul chose Red, Malcolm was X'ed.... Also in this issue on page 48 it announced that there will be a National Conference on Paul Robeson that would be held April 21-23, 1976, at Purdue University.

2124. Editorial. "Paul Robeson is Dead," Sun Reporter (San Francisco, California), February 7, 1976.

The editor surmises that Death as it comes to all men has finally claimed Paul Robeson. While Robeson's physical presence has been removed, his legacy will grow with the span of time.... The editor concludes: "There are five Blacks in the 20th century whose struggles in humanity's cause figuratively respond to the inscription on the dome of the California State Capitol. 'Bring me men to match my mountain': W.E.B. DuBois, Paul Robeson, Malcolm X, Martin Luther King, and Mary McLeod Bethune. Of these five none suffered more, yet always kept the faith than Robeson. Robeson was indeed a man for all seasons. As humanity continues its long enduring struggle against all forms of tyranny, Robeson will be judged as one of the great warriors in this crusade by generations yet unborn....."

3. GEORGIA

2125. Editorial. "Paul Robeson's Challenge," <u>Atlanta Constitution</u>, January 28, 1976, p. 4A.

The editor declares, in part: "Actor, Singer, Athlete, Scholar, Exile. Paul Robeson. After 17 years he has given up the fight. He had struggled against racism, making strong statements that, along with his praise of the Soviet Union, caused him to be ostracized in the 1940s and 50s. And during the McCarthy spy hunt in 1950, Robeson had his passport revoked. Through it all he was praised for his singing and acting ability. Probably his most famous performances were in the role of Shakespeare's "Othello," when his rich bass voice made the character live on stage in Europe, as well as Broadway...." He concludes: "Our challenge is to continue his struggle."

2126. Ross, Hubert B. "In Memoriam: Paul Robeson (April 9, 1898 - January 23, 1976)," <u>Phylon</u>, Vol. 37, No. 1, March, 1976, pp. 5-6.

The editorial declares that in the seventy-seventh year of his illustrious life, Paul Robeson, perhaps the most charismatic Black personality of his generation, has at last "laid down (his) heavy load." He concludes: "But even the successes of Paul Robeson were not attained without hardship, humilitation, constant struggle to assert both his manhood and his humanity. Particularly as he employed his energies in political activism was he reveiled, 'buked' and 'scorned.' He remained steadfast, however, in allegiance to his beliefs and values. We must honor him not only for what he did to entertain us, but also for what he did to inspire us, and because he exemplified in the model of his own life's career and experience 'the fatherhood of God and the brotherhood of man'."

4. ILLINOIS

2127. "Singer Paul Robeson Is Dead: 'Man Without a Country' in '50s,' <u>Chicago Tribune</u>, January 24, 1976, Section N1, p. 3.

This article declares that Paul Robeson who enchanted world concert audiences with his rich bass voice and shocked many Americans with his close ties to Russia, died Friday. He was 77. Robeson, a Black, was an outspoken critic of American racism, lacing his stage performances with biting freedom songs and commentary about the injustice heaped on his Black brothers. He frequently sang the praises of the Soviet Union, a country he visited frequently and eventually fell in love with. Back home he openly admitted close friendships with members of the Communist Party. It was also pointed out that in Moscow, the official Soviet news agency Tass paid tribute to Robeson as an "outstanding Negro singer and

(Chicago Tribune)

prominent public leader of the United States." Tass, providing
unusually quick notice of the death, said: "The persistent struggle
for Negro civil rights and for stronger world peace won him recognition not only in the United States but also outside it."

2128. Editorial. "Paul Robeson," Chicago Defender, January 26, 1976.

The editor declares that few men or women have contributed more to
the cause of freedom than Paul Robeson. His was a multi-faced
crusade in which he lifted his voice in songs, in speeches,
against the ceaseless tide of oppression and systematic denial of
political options. For fully a quarter of a century, Robeson's
name was a household word. His ingenuity was reflected in many
dimensions. His brilliant performance in Shakespeare's stirring
tragedy, Othello, heightened his reputation as a man of many
talents. But it was in the arena of the struggle for racial justice and equity where Robeson stood as a towering figure, against
the landscape of social injustice. His crusading zeal extended
far beyond local geography. He remained throughout his life a
strict and impassioned advocate of human rights, surmises the
writer. He concludes: "....Robeson was virtually stripped of his
citizenship for his amity with the Soviet Union where he was hailed
as a hero and a great humanitarian. Because he was a dissenter
who had the courage to state his conviction openly and forthrightly,
Robeson was driven into isolation and sepulchral silence. Now
that he is dead, while America is singing his praise as a great
American whose 'voice enriched the culture from which it grew
and the lives of all who heard it.' Of course Robeson was a great
American. To praise him at his graveside is a post-mortem recognition that exposes a congenital myopia which has stunted
America's intellectual growth. Be that as it may. Paul Robeson
now belongs to history and his soul, like that of John Brown's,
goes marching on."

2129. Editorial. "Paul Robeson Is Dead," Morning Star (Rockford,
Illinois), January 27, 1976.

The editor asserts that Paul Robeson who died last week at the age
of 77, was a unique American. His controversial contributions
to his country and its culture won him both criticism and applause.
His athletic and singing successes provided him with a public
platform and he began to use it to speak out on the subject of
racism and the need for freedom for his fellow Black men, states
the writer. He concludes: "....It is ironic that the bitterness
of the reaction that surrounded Robeson's words of two decades
would have been almost non-existent if he were saying many of them
today."

2130. Thompson, M. Cordell. "Harlem Bids Robeson Goodbye In the Rain,"
       Jet, Vol. 49, No. 20, February 12, 1976, pp. 14-15.

       The writer discusses Paul Robeson's funeral in New York City. He
       calls Robeson a model of a renaissance man. It was also pointed
       out in the article that during Paul Robeson's life time, he in-
       vested scrupulously both in and outside of this country. He
       invested in his own name and in the name of close friends and
       associates because he seemed to have the firesight about the tactics
       that might be tried against him, asserts Thompson. In the same
       article, Lloyd Brown, Paul Robeson's biographer states that many
       people thought Robeson went to live with his sister because he
       was destitute. "That's a lie," declares Brown. "He went there
       because she was his last surviving sister out of a family of
       seven brothers and sisters. He was not enormously wealthy but he
       was quite comfortably well off," concludes his biographer.

2131. "Freedom Seeker Passes with Humor: Thousands Bid Final Farewell
       to Paul Robeson," Bilalian News, February 20, 1976, pp. 3, 7.

       This article states that an overflow crowd of over 5,000 people
       filled the Mother African Methodist Episcopal Zion Church for the
       funeral of the great Bilalian freedom fighter, artist, athlete
       and statesman, Paul Robeson. It declares that the service was
       dignified, short and simple. It included tributes from several
       long-time friends. The article surmises that for Paul Robeson,
       the concert hall, screen and stage were always platforms from
       which to challenge Jim Crow and human exploitation.... According
       to this report, he immortalized many songs, including "Ole Man
       River" from "Show Boat" and many Bilalian spirituals, labor and
       folk songs. The article concludes: "Robeson will also be re-
       membered for defying racist terror and direct physical threats
       on his life and giving two memorable open-air concerts in Peeks-
       kill, N.Y. Robeson travelled widely, and everywhere he spoke
       out sgainst racial, religious and political discrimination. The
       world hailed him as an outstanding fighter for human rights...."

2132. Douglas, Carlyle. "Paul Robeson: Farewell to a Fighter," Ebony,
       Vol. 31, No. 6, April, 1976, pp. 33-42.

       Much of this article is about his funeral in Harlem, New York.
       The writer also gives an historical overview of Robeson's life.
       Several photos of Paul Robeson are also included in this article.
       The article declares that a large segment of the American public
       was outraged when he accepted the Stalin Peace Prize in 1952.
       Robeson made his last tour, to Australia and New Zealand in 1960.
       In 1961, according to this article, arteriosclerosis caused his
       retirement from the stage. He made his last public appearance
       at the Freedomways Magazine salute to him in New York, in 1965.

5. INDIANA

2133. Editorial. "Paul Robeson Is Dead," Post-Tribune (Gary, Indiana), January 28, 1976.

The editor asserts that had Paul Robeson been known only for his great bass voice and his athletic skills, his death last week quite likely would have invoked outpourings of nostalgic appreciation. But Paul Robeson chose also to be an outspoken advocate, and in the process he became one of the more controversial characters of those post-World War II years and saw the beginnings of the Cold War.... He concludes: "By the time of his death, Robeson had been forgotten by many and the voice that won him fame as Othello and in making 'Ol' Man River' the hit it became was gone. He died in relative obscurity to which he did not seem greatly to object. But Robeson should be remembered not only for his sports skills which won him All-American football honors and for his great voice, but also for that part of his advocacy that pointed up the unfairness to his bretheren when he had reached pinnacles of fame. We still think Robeson was wrong on communism, but it should not be forgotten that he was right on much and had the courage to speak out."

2134. Editorial. "Paul Robeson Is Dead," Indianapolis News (Indiana), January 29, 1976.

The editor surmises "Paul Robeson, who rose far above the crowd and won admiration for his talents as a singer and actor, became a symbol of alienation from America, the land that bore him and honored him...." He concludes: "Paul Robeson turned in his hurt and anguish to Communism, and the Soviet Union made him into an instrument of propaganda which gave him a pride and role that many regard as false because he championed Freedom in a system where freedom, for most people, barely exists if at all. He returned to the United States, and here a few days ago he died, old and weak, still wearing the emotional tatters of alienation, yet still remembered and respected for his talent and his individuality and manhood by the society he rejected because he believed it had rejected him."

6. IOWA

2135. Editorial. "Paul Robeson Is Dead," Des Moines (Iowa) Register, January 27, 1976.

The editor declares from 1927 to 1963, Paul Robeson was a magnificent singer, actor, and rights crusader. His renown was worldwide. He had to win fame abroad before he was widely recognized at home. After 1963 his health was poor, and he died the other day at 77. He was a great American, states the editor. He went

(Des Moines, Iowa, Register)

on to assert that: "....Robeson's Communist sympathies led to
harrassment by congressional committees, denial of a U.S. passport in 1950 and until the Supreme Court ordered one granted in
1958. Honors once granted were revoked. He spent many years
abroad, but always returned home, always thought of himself as an
American. Long before his death, honors begans to return." He
concludes: "His story needs to be remembered. Anyone who ever
heard him sing 'Old Man River' or play 'Othello' will never forget
it. Fortunately much of his magnificent singing is preserved on
records."

7. KENTUCKY

2136. "Singer, Black Activist Paul Robeson Dies at 77," Courier-Journal
(Louisville, Kentucky), January 24, 1976.

According to this article: "One of the nation's greatest men, an
individual whose time on earth has been spent in the pursuit of
justice for all human beings and toward the enlightenment of men
and women the world over." Such was the description of Paul
Robeson, the singer, actor and Black liberationist, ill and all but
forgotten in his 75th year, by Clayton Riley, the American cultural
historian. Robeson, who drew bravos for his rich bass voice and
was vilified for his associations with communism, died yesterday
in a Philadelphia hospital at 77. One of the most influential
performers and political figures to emerge from Black America,
Robeson was under a cloud in his native land during the Cold War
as a political dissenter and an outspoken admirer of the Soviet
Union, which gave him the Stalin Prize in 1952...., asserts
the article.

8. LOUISIANA

2137. Roberts, Chris. "Paul Robeson, Racism Fighter, Dead," New Orleans
Times Picayune, January 24, 1976, p. 16.

The author states that Paul Robeson, who drew bravos for his rich
bass voice and was vilified for his associations with communism,
died Friday in a Philadelphia hospital. He was 77. The actor,
singer, athlete and outspoken critic of American racism was the
son of a runaway slave. He had lived in self-imposed seclusion at
his sister's home in West Philadelphia for more than a decade,
seeing only family members and a few close friends. Robeson's
bitting statements about racism combined with his praise of the
Soviet Union and friendships with U.S. Communist party members,

(Roberts, Chris)

served to ostracize him in the 40s and 50s, states Roberts. His
passport was revoked in 1950 at the height of Senator Joseph
McCarthy's inquisition into suspected Red activities in the United
States. Other Blacks shunned him because of his political views.
Toward the end, the honors were returning, although Robeson ignored
them. Rutgers University, where Robeson starred in football,
named a student center in his honor. A chapter of the National
Football Foundation nominated him for induction into the Hall of
Fame. And his life was the subject of an hour-long documentary
on national television last year...., concludes the author.

9. MARYLAND

2138. Editorial. "Robeson Is Dead," The Sun (Baltimore, Maryland),
       January 25, 1976.

The editor argues that anyone believing that Black achievement,
civil rights struggles and tangled loyalties are recent phenomena,
the career of Robeson is instructive.... He concludes: "Paul
Robeson was a majestic figure, large, powerful and dignified, as
a scholar, an athlete, an artist and a man. As controversialist,
he could be powerfully right, and powerfully wrong. But this is
a big nation, so big it need never have feared even a Robeson,
big enough to have admitted that its imperfections led to his
alienation. At his death at 77 he can be remembered as one of
the great athletes, singers, and actors of the century. And in
the public controversies which prematurely buried his talent, he
can be remembered as a powerful, flawed symbol of problems that
this country is still striving to overcome."

2139. Editorial. "Paul Robeson Is Dead," News American (Baltimore,
       Maryland), January 28, 1976.

According to this assessment, Paul Robeson, the American bass-
baritone singer and actor, demands attention here on the event of
his death last Friday from a stroke at the age of 77.... His was
a magnificent talent which inevitably brought the house down in
thunderous approval -- a tremendous talent sadly wasted because
of intellectual distractions and a certain personal fury which
raged within him...., states the editor. He also asserts that
Robeson turned to communism, praising it as the only solution to
the terrible racial pain which tortured him. His attitude won
him the 1952 Stalin Peace Prize -- and subsequently destroyed his
career as a great artist. It was a terrible mistake he made,
and the result was a terrible artistic loss because of the cloud
he created about himself in his native land, argues the editor.
He concludes: "Pro-communists are not ordinarily given accolades
in this space. Paul Robeson, brilliant but misguided, should have
kept singing and acting his magic without polemics. If he had, he
would have helped his race and the injustices admittedly afflicted

(News American)

upon it here for so many years far more effectively than in any
other way. The way he chose was a tragic mistake -- both for him
and for the world which was deprived of his towering talent for
so many years. Sad, sad we feel at the passing of Paul Robeson.
Sad, sad it is how many people can delude themselves into thinking
that miseries somehow can be solved by tyranny rather than through
the imperfect but single real hope of humanity -- insistence on
personal expression through democracy. We mourn the passing of
Paul Robeson and his confused genius, even more, we mourn a world
where genius of any kind if not universally recognized and
applauded."

2140. "Paul Robeson Bade Farewell," Afro-American, January 31, 1976, pp.
1, 2.

This article gives an overview of Paul Robeson's accomplishments.
It states that his outspoken political views made him the target
of Communist hunters in later life. The article also pointed
out that Robeson used his prestige and talents in an attempt to
ease the sufferings of other Black Americans and drew the wrath
of racist hate groups....

2141. Editorial. "Paul Robeson," Afro-American, February 7, 1976, p. 4.

The editor declares that Paul Robeson was far more than just a
great baritone singer who could act with the best of them. He
was an outraged Black man who refused to bow and scrape in the
face of brutal racial degradation heaped on his people. He expressed interest in Communism in the 1930s after a concert tour
of the Soviet Union, and gave critics a new weapon with which to
batter and hound him. But Paul Robeson never surrendered his right
to speak as a man against the racial discrimination perpetrated
by white Americans. His voluntary exile for five years could be
interpreted as part of his protest. His decision to return to the
U.S. in December, 1963, was in no way a sign of relenting. This
was his country, and like others who were not pleased with its
imperfections, he came home as any citizen has a right to do,
states the editor. He concludes: "....There was great pain and
sadness in Paul Robeson's life. There also was great happiness,
achievement, valor and inspiration. No matter what mission Paul
Robeson might have aimed to accomplish, his life tells a story of
America's beauty and opportunities, its racial discrimination and
distortion, its acceptances and rejections that provides a lesson
from which most of us could profit greatly."

10. MICHIGAN

2142.   "Athlete, Singer, Social Critic: Paul Robeson Is Dead at 77,"
        Detroit Free Press, January 24, 1976, pp. 1A, 5A.

        According to this article Paul Robeson, who drew bravos for his
        rich bass voice and was vilified for his associations with com-
        munism, died Friday in a Philadelphia hospital. He was 77. The
        actor, singer, athlete and outspoken critic of American racism
        was the son of a runaway slave. He had lived in self-imposed se-
        clusion at his sister's home in West Philadelphia since 1963,
        seeing only family members and a few close friends. He was ad-
        mitted to Presbyterian Medical Center on December 28, after suf-
        fering a stroke. Robeson's biting statements about racism, com-
        bined with his praise of the Soviet Union and friendships with
        U.S. Communist party members, ostracized him in the 40s and 50s.
        His passport was revoked by President Truman in 1950, during a
        period when anti-communism in America was at its height. Other
        Blacks shunned him because of his political views. Robeson as
        a performer, was probably best known for his portrayal of Othello,
        the noble Moor of Venice. He drew 20 curtain calls for the role
        at the Savoy in London in 1930.

2143.   "Paul Robeson: April 9, 1898 - January 23, 1976," INNA (The
        Afrikan History Club #2 Newsletter), April 9, 1976. Memorial
        Issue.

        The articles in this issue were written by children in grades 4-6
        and Special Education at McFarlane Elementary School, Detroit,
        Michigan. It discusses Robeson's heritage, family, studies, law
        degree, songs, movies, recordings, ability as a linguist, his
        wife, sister, son, Paul and Jackie Robinson, Lawrence Brown, and
        W.E.B. DuBois, etc.

11. NEW YORK

2144.   Editorial. "Paul Robeson," New York Times, January 24, 1976, p.
        24.

        The editor declares, in part: "The magnificent voice in its prime
        filled the concert hall; it spoke in dramatic power and in passion;
        it spoke of gentleness and the warmth of humankind. Whether con-
        veying the tragedy of Othello or the compassion of the spiritual,
        the voice of Paul Robeson enriched the culture from which it grew
        and the lives of all who heard it. The tragedy of Paul Robeson,
        like that of Othello, was stark; virtue and misjudgment were
        sharply juxtaposed. Anger at the injustice of racial discrimination
        led him to advocate a political system that would serve neither
        his race nor his own ideals of justice. Ultimately, he chose
        politics over art, and the world lost a source of inspiration.

(New York Times)

Ailing and embittered through the last years of his life, even
after returning to his homeland from self-imposed exile, Mr.
Robeson shunned the efforts of a new generation to offer him the
respect so fully due his artictic genius. For reasons of politics,
his native country had abruptly and callously turned its back on
him long ago; yet Paul Robeson, like Othello on his deathbed,
could honestly say, 'I have done the state some service, and
they know it.'"

2145.   Grossberger, Lewis. "Paul Robeson: Every Kind of Mourner But
the Young," New York Post, January 27, 1976, p. 1.

The writer states that Paul Robeson was in Harlem (New York) making
his last public appearance. He was referring to his funeral.
About 5,000 people showed up for it. It was pointed out that
there was a whole generation of Black people who never heard of
him. The article reports: "In years to come, he will be considered as great a man, if not greater - as a symbol of Black
people - as Martin Luther King."

2146.   Hunter, Charlayne. "Mourners, At the Chapel, 'Go Tell It' to
Robeson," New York Times, January 27, 1976, p. 34.

This article is about the people who came to Benta's Funeral Home
in Harlem, New York, to pay their last respects to Paul Robeson.
There were tapes of Robeson singing "Amazing Grace," and "Ol' Man
River," and "Go Tell It To The Mountain," being played at the
funeral home. The reporter gives many instances of some of the
people that visited the funeral home that knew Robeson.

2147.   "Paul Robeson," Variety, January 28, 1976, p. 77.

A short sketch of his life depicting his accomplishments on and
off the stage and in films. The article called him a Black singer
and one time pro-Soviet political activist.

2148.   Missick, Victoria. "5,000 Pay Final Respects to Robeson," Daily
World, January 29, 1976, pp. 1, 9.

This article reports on Paul Robeson's funeral. It was pointed
out that more than 5,000 people attended.

2149.   Adams, Julius J. "The Legacy of Paul Robeson," New York Amsterdam
News, January 31, 1976, p. A-4.

The writer surmises that Paul Robeson, who died in Philadelphia,
on January 23, at the age of 77, has already been heralded in
America and throughout the world for his excellence as a scholar,
athlete, concert artist and dramatic actor. But his contribution
as a political activist, to the advancement of the Black man in
his native land is yet to be properly and adequately assessed.
Mr. Adams declares that while Robeson lost favor with a wide segment of white Americans, including the white press, and frightened
a number of Congressmen by a speech he made in Paris in April,

(Adams, Julius J.)

1949, his devotion to the fight for justice and equality for Black communities was never questioned. He also believes that Paul Robeson had charted his own course in the fight for equal treatment of Black Americans, and he obviously felt that he was making "a substantial contribution" toward this end. And, while he might have made himself expendable, there are many who now believe that what Robeson did in the 1940s paved the way for what Thurgood Marshall of the NAACP and others were able to do in the 1950s, and what Martin Luther King and his followers were able to achieve in the 1960s, asserts Adams. The writer suggests that whether Robeson really believed that Blacks in general would desert their country is a moot question. His subsequent expression of his own feelings for his country would suggest that his controversial statement could have been a result of momentary pique. Or, drawing upon his skill as a lawyer, he might have made the statement as a strategic move, sensing that the shock might bring the country to its senses. It appears, in fact, that it did. He concludes: "In any event, Blacks in particular, and the nation in general, owe an everlasting 'thank you' to Paul Robeson for being willing to expose himself as an expendable, leaving the battle for others to carry on in their own way consistent with the times, needs and circumstances."

2150.   Jones, L. Clayton. "Goodbye, Paul: Let's Be Grateful That We Lived in His Time!," New York Amsterdam, January 31, 1976, pp. A-1, 2.

The author states that one watches with restrained anger as a nation of hypocrites grudgingly acknowledges the passing of a twentieth century phenomenon. He suspects that the essential Paul Robeson is to be found in the uses to which he put his massive intellect. Mr. Jones surmises that while the depth of his talents assured his pre-eminence as an artist, it was the breadth of his commitment to the poor and disadvantaged of the world and the quality of mind and character brought to bear on that commitment that assures of his stature as one of the few great men of our times.

2151.   "Paul Robeson's Funeral," New York Amsterdam News, January 31, 1976, p. 5.

The article states that Paul Robeson, veteran soldier of Black manhood was eulogized Tuesday night during the funeral service held at Mother A.M.E. Zion Church where mourners filled the 2,500 capacity sanctuary and the autidorium below. On Wednesday morning his body was taken to Frankcliff Cemetery in Hartsdale, New York, and created at a private funeral. By 7:30 p.m. Tuesday night, people who braved the cold and wet weather were being directed away from the Sanctuary doors to the basement, where they followed the service through loud speakers. From the balcony of the church, one could see the people almost evenly Black and white, states the writer. Before the pulpit lay Robeson's body in a casket draped in black with red roses on top. On either end were wreaths and behind these on the left side stood a cross

(New York Amsterdam News)

of white flowers. At either side also stood six pall bearers:
while above and to the rear the 22-voice Cathedral Choir contrasted with the assorted colors in the church as the men and
women gleamed in white. Here are some of the statements made by
persons attending Paul Robeson's funeral as reported in the
Amsterdam News: Uta Hagen, Actress, played Desdemona in the
Broadway production of Othello: "It was a great privilege to have
worked with him. He was a great artist and a wonderful human
being."; Mr. and Mrs. Marion Cumbo, Director of Triad Presenta-
tions and Concert Cellist: "We have followed his career right on
from the very early days and he has been a source of great inspiration to us,"; Leontyne Price, Soprano, Metropolitan Opera:
"A great man, a great friend, a great leader and a profound
artist,"; Dick Campbell: "He was one of the great performers of
our time, but more than that, he was a great person in that he
never compromised his art for his position in society and as a
fighter for human rights. Further, he would never in his late
years, accept an engagement where he offered his talent free
unless they permitted him to express an opinion with respect to
human rights. He was way ahead of his times in terms of all the
people who were his contemporaries,"; Eubie Blake, Composer-
Pianist: "I admired Paul Robeson for his courage to be outspoken
when it was not acceptable for a Negro to protest against the
establishment. His motto, 'We are America, too!' stands us in
good stead today when there still exists a rift. I am proud to
have had a hand in launching his career also,"; Count Basie,
Band Leader: "One of the great thrills of my career is that he
made a record with me."

2152.   Tyler, Andrew. "Paul Robeson Is Dead - Paul Robeson Lives On,"
New York Amsterdam News, January 31, 1976, pp. 1, 2.

The writer is a Justice of New York State's Supreme Court. He
declares that Paul Robeson is dead. And there will be no Mount
Rushmore built for him. Paul Robeson is dead, and there is no
pyramid being constructed to house his remains. Paul Robeson is
dead, and there are no bronze plaques to mark his steps or the
places where he stood. There are no monuments of steel or stone
for this great Black man, yet there are monuments. The paradox
in the statement becomes clear when we realize that this Black
man's monument was his life, constructed with the brick and mortar
of his own deeds and fabulous talents. This Black man's monument
was the legacy of his life, his career, his courage, and the inspiration which he kindled in the hearts and souls of every Black
man, woman and child who knew him or knew of him. He continues to
say Paul Robeson is dead. This much we can be sure of. Judge
Tyler concludes: "....But we can also be sure that as long as
there are Black men and women who demand that freedom be more than
a lyric from the National Anthem, as long as there are Black men
and women who demand that the shining star of liberty and the
pursuit of happiness be seen by brown eyes as well as blue, Paul
Robeson will indeed live on...."

2153. "Paul Robeson," Time, Vol. 107, No. 5, February 2, 1976, p. 55.

The article states in part: "Paul Robeson, 77, superbly talented and ultimately tragic singer, actor and civil rights leader who won a world fame known to few blacks of his generation and spent his last years sick, half-forgotten and in Coretta Scott King's words, 'buried alive'; following a stroke (died) in Philadelphia." It also declares that in the 1940's and 1950's he was an out-spoken champion of civil rights.

2154. Saal, Hubert. "(Paul Robeson) Tragic Hero," Newsweek, Vol. 87, No. 5, February 2, 1976, p. 73.

The writer asserts that Paul Robeson, the son of a run-away slave, once summed up his unprecedented achievements by writing: "'As I went out into life, one thing loomed above all else: I was my father's son, a Negro in America.' That was the challenge that led him to the pinnacle of success - and to the deepest despair. Last week this monumental American died at the age of 77." Mr. Saal suggests when Robeson was in the United States he became a vigorous opponent of racism, picketing the White House, refusing to sing before segregated audiences, starting a crusade against lynching and urging Congress to outlaw racial bars in baseball. But his outspoken admiration for the Soviet Union, which culminated in his acceptance of a Stalin Peace Prize in 1952, inflamed public opinion during the cold war and eventually wiped out his career. Summoned before House and Senate committees, he refused to say whether or not he was a Communist (privately he maintained he was not), and called his inquisitors *Fascist-minded.' It was also pointed out that in 1950, the State Department revoked his passport and Robeson became virtually a prisoner in America. He was black-listed by concert managers - his income, which has been $104,000 in 1947, fell to $2,000 - and he was removed from the list of All-Americans. Enraged, his resonant voice turned shrill in denunciation of the 'princes of privilege'...." He concludes: "Paul Robeson went early, if naively, into the battle for black freedom. He could have sat back on the 50-yard line, rich and famous. But he chose to stand up and be counted - risking everything. Robeson was a genuine tragic hero - 'one that loved not wisely, but too well.'"

2155. Smith, Dennis and Dan Posen. "Paul Robeson, 1898-1976: A Story of Struggle and Tragedy," Workers' Power, February 2, 1976, p. 11.

The writers argue with Robeson's death has come a parade of feature articles and editorials in the capitalist press. Twenty years after they smeared and tried to silence him, they are praising him and pointing out how unfairly he was treated. It is a characteristic of the capitalist press that it constantly attacks injustice - twenty years too late. And the truth is too much for them to admit. The truth is that Paul Robeson spent the last eleven years of his life a broken and defeated person. He was the victim of a system that tried to destroy all who attempted to fight its exploitation and oppression. They assert that many ordinary people, not as well-known as Robeson, suffered for their political beliefs in this country even worse than he did. But

(Smith, Dennis and Dan Posen)

many other pro-Communist Party intellectuals, far less talented
and courageous than Robeson, simply hid or sold out. Robeson did
not. The American ruling class went all-out to destroy him because he would not renounce his opposition to their system. There
are still millions of people who remember Robeson's singing of
working class ballads of struggle like "Joe Hill." Or how he
turned black spirituals into powerful songs for freedom and liberation from slavery and racism. They deserve to be re-issued
and played over and over, according to the author. They conclude:
"The message Robeson wanted us to hear, and even some of his art,
was distorted by the complete dead end of the politics he supported.
That is a cruel fact. But still, much of the message will be long
remembered."

2156.   Gornick, Vivian. "Harlem Bids Farewell to Paul Robeson," Village
        Voice, February 9, 1976, pp. 73,75

        The writer asserts that Paul Robeson was part of the progressive
        world, a man who had come to political consciousness through
        Marxist vision, a man who sang at our rallies, marched in our
        parade, made common cause with the Soviet Union, and at all times
        supported the American Left. She argues that it was through
        the Left that Robeson had been raised up and it was because of
        the Left that he had been hurled down. He was, according to
        Gornick, a tragic hero -- of the Left. She surmises: "Robeson
        had never been 'made' by the Left, he had been 'made' by being
        Black. Robeson had brought to the Left not his need, but his
        fulfillment; not his Black frustration, but his Black wholeness."
        Gornick concludes: "...He had cleaved to the Left as had many men
        and women of large and talented spirit coming of age in those
        magnetic and terrible decades between the world wars; and the Left
        had been for him - as it had been for so many - yet another great
        theatre in which to play out the vivid drama of his soul. But the
        defining talents, the integration of spirit, the emotional den-
        sity that had made the man who entered the Left -- that was all
        rooted here in this valuted space, in the structure of this black
        life. The human wealth had been Robeson's gift to the Left.
        What the Left had done was to accept the gift: thereby enriching
        both itself and then, in turn, the man who made the gift...."

2157.   "Paul Robeson," Nation, Vol. 222, No. 5, February 7, 1976, pp.
        132-133.

        The editor declares the death of the great actor and singer Paul
        Robeson is an occasion to remind ourselves of what he was -- and
        what he might have been. His career on the stage was successful,
        even triumphant, but the story of what he went through, here and
        abroad, tells much about how hard and humiliating was the life of
        even a talented American Black man in the last three-quarters of
        a century. The writer also points out that even on the stage, his
        greatest triumphs were not in his own country but in Europe. That
        is not to say he was unappreciated at home, but his success in
        America was largely as a singer of spirituals, a traditional role
        for Blacks and one that the culture could comfortably accept.

(Nation)

"What always seemed too much for Paul," a high school classmate
recalls, "was that in this country they always wanted him to sing
spirituals -- especially that sentimental Broadway version of the
spiritual, 'Ol' Man River.'" No wonder he felt more at home in
countries that accepted him as a man and artist, without the
American cultural deformation, argues the writer. According to
the author, what Robeson experienced and saw all around him radi-
calized his views. In the 1930's that usually meant great sympathy for post-revolutionary Russia and a certain unwillingness to
see the country or Lenin and Stalin as it really was. Naturally,
Robeson became a prime target for the witch hunters of the cold
war, suggests the author. He also asserts that late in his life,
American society began making amends to Paul Robeson. Rutgers
gave him an honorary degree and its president, Edward J. Bloustein, did his best to get him admitted to the Football Hall of
Fame (where the same kind of political considerations that caused
boxing scandalously to block the career of Muhammad Ali was undoubtedly at work). At a tribute to him in Carnegie Hall in New
York on his 75th birthday, Coretta King said that Robeson had been
"buried alive" because he had "tapped the same wells of latent
militancy" as had her husband. Paul Robeson was not there to hear
these words of praise and expiation. "He was old and ill and
living as a recluse in Philadelphia, alone with a justified pride.
Extreme suffering makes for extreme politics, which is not to pre-
sume to offer an apology for the views of his extraordinary man.
Abroad, Paul Robeson was seen as a great American. At home, he
was an American black, however famous," concludes the editor.

2158. Cohen, Bart. "Remembering Paul Robeson: All American Scholarly
        Singer, Fighter for Freedom," Public Employee Press, February 13
        1976.

The author discusses how he met Paul Robeson. He declares that
Robeson maintained a deep commitment to the poor and disadvantaged
of the world, to peace and freedom for all people. For this he
was persecuted for decades, and most Americans were deprived of
his vast talent. Now Paul Robeson is dead, states Cohen.

2159. Wilkins, Roy. "Remembering Robeson," Long Island Press, February
        14, 1981.

Mr. Wilkins surmises that any man has the right to arrange himself
on the side which seems to get the goal in good shape. He concludes: "Robeson proudly and consistently paid the price for his
beliefs. That is why we salute him. That is why he is great."

2160. Goodman, Mark. "Final Tribute to Paul Robeson," New Times, Vol.
        6, No. 4, February 20, 1976, p. 68.

The writer argues that Robeson was a moody and complex figure as
passionate and full of rage as Othello, as vainglorious as Emperor
Jones. He roamed the world as a sort of Black Philip Nolan, a
self-imposed exile from a land that howled in fury when he refused
to be a Credit To His Race. That idiotic condescension might have

(Goodman, Mark)

stuck nicely to Joe Louis and Mantan Moreland and Nat King Cole,
but Paul Robeson swatted it off his giant shoulder as if it were
a sickly caterpillar, states the writer. He roared, he fumed,
he dared to say that in the Soviet Union he "walked with dignity
for the first time," and he was predictably vilified in return.
But if you listened to him, you heard that all he really wanted
was captured in those two lines of his legendary rendition of
"Ol' Man River"; he just wanted the white boss off his broad,
Black back, surmises Goodman. The writer declares that Robeson
also spoke out for Black pride when Stokely Carmichael was a pup,
and taught himself such difficult African dialects as Yoruba and
Efik. It's good that he could thus occupy himself, because his
employability (an emerging term) in the U.S. plummeted drastically -
especially after he took the Fifth before the McCarthy Committee.
He left America to live in London, but later came home to live in
rigorous seclusion with his sister in Philadelphia, argues Mr.
Goodman. He concludes: "Robeson had too subtle and sensitive a
mind not to have noted the irony of his private embattlement v.
the battlements of the flaming Sixties. But nothing lured him out
to speak; his fight was done. Young blacks scarcely knew who he
was; older whites agreed that he was born before his time. That
might do for Ingrid Bergman and Lenny Bruce, but not for Paul
Robeson - his banishment from society was nothing short of a
national disgrace. He died in near obscurity at the age of 77,
surely tired of livin;, and just as surely too bitter to be
scared of dyin'."

2161. "On the Death of Paul Robeson: An Immortal Legacy," Freedomway,
       Vol. 16, No. 4, Fourth Quarter, 1976, p. 304.

       This memoriam was written immediately after Robeson died on
       January 23, 1976. The article concludes: "Racial bias will con-
       tinue to speak of Robeson as one of the 'greatest Black figures'
       in history - but the majority of humankind will recall a greatness
       that far transcends any color line. His life record stands as
       a testimony to the fact that people of every race and nationality
       can and indeed must be united to insure a world-wide victory for
       peace and progress."

2162. Graves, Earl G. "The Publisher's Pages," Black Enterprise, Vol.
       6, No. 8, March, 1976, p. 5.

       About a third of this page is devoted to Paul Robeson. He points
       out that times have changed in America because of the unselfish
       efforts of great persons, many of whom epitomize the way in which
       this country, in all too many instances uses and abuses its greatest
       natural resources - its people. This sad fact was made all too
       clear with Paul Robeson's recent death, declares the publisher.
       He also states why Paul Robeson would be remembered: "He will be
       remembered for his heroic stand.... He will be remembered for his
       steadfast adherence to principle when the times, the 'Cold War'
       times called for expediency. He will be remembered for not bowing
       when others crumbled. He will be remembered for foregoing per-
       sonal wealth because he insisted upon all people having a fair

(Graves, Earl)

share of the wealth...." Graves concludes: "....we should occasionally take the time to reflect upon those qualities of Paul
Robeson's that made him truly heroic. Hopefully, it will serve
to make us, too, a more valuable resource for our people and our
nation."

2163. "Paul Robeson: April 9, 1898 - January 23, 1976," Crisis, Vol.
83, No. 3, March, 1976, pp. 79-70.

This was an article by Reuters (News Service) on the life and times
of Paul Robeson. It declares that Paul Robeson, one of America's
truly great singers, was also the country's first fullfledged
Black star - until his career was destroyed by a backlash caused
by his fight against racism. The article states that Robeson's
problem was simple. "He refused to remain quiet about the plight
of his people and he compounded this error in the eyes of much
of the establishment by turning to left-wing politics in his fight.
He devoted himself to the civil rights struggle a generation
before the massive demonstrations of his fellow Blacks in the
1950s and 1960s," concludes the author.

2164. "Paul Robeson: Fallen Warrior," CORE Magazine, March, 1976, p. 25.

The editor declares, in part: "Several generations of Blacks loved
and idolized him. His sonorous, powerful baritone captivated them;
his legendary athletic prowess enthralled them; and his academic
brilliance inspired them. When he put all his accomplishments on
the line to fight for his people, they did not give beans about
his politics; they only knew that he was for THEM, for HIS people.
Whites condemned him for his political ideology during all those
years when Blacks had precious few of their own to look up to....
to emulate. Paul Robeson stood out like a shining star that
guided a people who needed hope so badly...."

2165. "Paul Robeson," Opera News, Vol. 40, No. 22, May, 1976, p. 46.

This obituary states that this towering bass was esteemed in the
concert field for the expressive power he brought to lieder and
spirituals. Politically, he proved controversial for his sympathy with leftist causes. Grandson of a slave, he won unusual
acclaim as an actor both onstage and in movies; among his triumphs, he did O'Neill's "Emperor Jones" on film, Shakespeare's
"Othello" on Broadway. Many have felt a loss that his unique
vocal and dramatic talents were never united in opera, for he
might have been an ideal Boris Godunov, King Marke, Sarastro or
Fiesco; had he been born a quarter-century later, Robeson would
doubtless have made opera an important aspect of his work, concludes the writer.

2166.   Current, Gloster B. "Paul Robeson (1898-1976)," Black Perspective in Music, Vol. 4, Fall, 1976, pp. 302-306.

The author states that Paul Robeson will go down in the annals of history as one of the greatest fighters for freedom of expression in a long line of Black heroes who strove and were martyred for their assaults on prejudice and injustice. Mr. Current surmises that Robeson struggled and suffered as a result of his views and died respected as a man of tremendous strength and pride, although misunderstood and often pilloried. The author declares: "He was uncompromising, provocative; he sacrificed a prosperous career, but his noble efforts, nonetheless, will always serve as a highwater mark of the fight for freedom in these United States...."

2167.   "In Memory of Paul Robeson," Black Liberation Journal, Vol. 1, No. 1, Winter, 1976, p. 1.

The article declares that the magnificent voice of the great Paul Robeson has been stilled, but the inspiration of his words and deeds in the fight against racism, fascism and for peace and an end to the exploitation of humanity will live forever. Early in his life, through experience, study and discussion of political affairs, Robeson came to understand and appreciate the inseparable relationship of the liberation struggle of his people with those of the masses of Africa, Asia, Latin America and the Caribbean area. His outlook became universal, states the writer.... He concludes: "The thought and ideas of Robeson are part and parcel of the armory of those who seek liberation the world over."

12. OHIO

2168.   Editorial. "Paul Robeson Dies at 77," Akron (Ohio) Beacon Journal, January 27, 1976.

The editor suggests that it should be enough for any man to have been a great actor. Or a great singer. Or a great athlete. Paul Robeson, who died Friday at 77, was all of those things. And much more. His enormous talents, from the playing fields at Rutgers where he was twice an All-American end in football to the Broadway stage where his performance as Othello set records for a Shakespearean play, may have been overshadowed by his role as a social critic... The editorial concludes: "His 'sins' of a generation ago are today official policy of the United States. Add to the list of Robeson's talents the ability to be 25 years or more ahead of his time. It is not incidental to Paul Robeson's career that he was Black. His status as part of a persecuted minority no doubt directed much of his thinking and much of his criticism. But race is incidental to greatness. He was not a great Black man; he was a great man who happened to be Black."

2169. Editorial. "Paul Robeson Is Dead," Cincinnati (Ohio) Post,
       January 31, 1976.

       The editor declares that without question, Robeson's accomplish-
       ments as an All-American football player, Phi Beta Kappa, debating
       champion and valedictorian at Rutgers and later as an actor,
       singer and crusader for human rights earn him high rank among
       Black Americans of the 20th century. "The tragedy, of course, is
       that Robeson's persistent and sometimes gullible praise for the
       Soviet Union and his scathing denunciation of racism in the United
       States damaged his career and made Robeson a target of anti-
       Communists during the late 1940s and early 1950s," states the
       editor. He concludes: "Looking back, there's a temptation to
       think of Robeson as a saint, a martyr, a dupe or a fool, depending
       on your political predilections and your view of history. We
       prefer to think of Paul Robeson as an enormously gifted man whose
       contributions to his race - and whose bittersweet love affair with
       his country - will not be soon forgotten."

2170. "Paul Robeson Dies at 77," Call and Post, January 31, 1976, p. 4.

       The article asserts that Paul Robeson, the famous Black baritone
       and actor whose admiration for individual liberty brought him con-
       tempt from the American public during the 1950's died at age 77,
       Friday, January 23, in Philadelphia. "Robeson is little known to
       many young Blacks today, but in his heyday he stood as a symbol
       for Black people because of his singing and acting success, and
       willingness to stand up and fight for his rights and those of the
       Negro race," concludes the article.

13. PENNSYLVANIA

2171. "Paul Robeson, 78, Dies," Pittsburgh Press, January 23, 1976, p. 5.

       This short article announced Paul Robeson's death. It called him
       a one-time All-American football star at Rutgers University in
       1917, who became a famous actor, singer and "outspoken anti-
       capitalist."

2172. Neal, Steve. "P. Robeson, Singer, Activist Dies," Philadelphia
       Inquirer, January 24, 1976, pp. 1, 6.

       The writer declares that Paul Robeson fit the Renaissance model
       of the universal man. He sang folk songs and spirituals in more
       than 20 languages. Before he started his artistic career, he dis-
       tinguished himself as an All-American football player. Later in
       life, he made contributions as a political activist and cultural
       theorist. Mr. Neal concludes: "During the 1930's, Mr. Robeson
       was the best known Black figure in the United States. With his
       diverse talents and rich, booming voice, he also cultivated an
       enormous international following...."

14. TENNESSEE

2173. Editorial. "Paul Robeson Is Dead," Commercial Appeal (Memphis,
       Tennessee), January 27, 1976.

       The editor states that almost everyone can agree now that Paul
       Robeson, who died last week at age 77, was a great artist. He
       proved that early in his career, in his appearance as Brutus Jones
       in "The Emperor Jones" and in singing such songs as "Ol' Man
       River" in "Showboat." Even in his late years when he returned to
       Carnegie Hall after a long absence he again was greeted with a
       long standing ovation by a sold-out house. It was his advocacy of
       civil rights very early in that movement and then his refusal to
       say under oath whether he was a Communist that brought down upon
       him the wrath of many Americans. His civil rights activities in
       retrospect certainly were not unreasonable. Organized baseball
       did eventually drop its racial barriers as he had urged, and Blacks
       in the South did win the right to vote freely and to eat and sleep
       in public accommodations. It was difficult for some Americans to
       understand why he was such a "Radical" in such matters, but should
       not have been, according to this editorial. He concludes: "....
       He was, after all, himself, a victim of the nation's segregation
       policies accepted as an artist. But not as a person...."

2174. "People....In the News: Singer Paul Robeson Dies at 77," Nashville
       Banner, January 24, 1976, p. 6.

       Reported from UPI news service, states that Paul Robeson, inter-
       nationally known baritone singer, actor, football star and Black
       activist died at a Philadelphia local hospital. He was 77. It
       was also pointed out that Robeson's outspoken political views
       including remarks favoring the Soviet Union, made him the target
       of Communist hunters in later life and alienated many admirers.

15. VIRGINIA

2175. "Victim of Racism Mourned: Paul Robeson's 'Ol' Man River' Thrilled
       Nation," Journal and Guide, January 31, 1976, p. 2.

       It was stated that Paul Robeson, a grandson of American slaves,
       whose booming baritone rendition of "Ol' Man River" brought him
       fame around the world, died January 23rd at the age of 77. A
       spokesman of Presbyterian University Hospital said Robeson, who
       had been living in seclusion in West Philadelphia for 11 years, was
       admitted to the hospital December 28th for treatment of a stroke.
       Tests showed he was suffering from a severe cerebral vascular dis-
       order. His condition became worse and doctors had held out little
       chance for recovery, states the article. An All-American Football
       player who turned to singing and acting on the stage and screen,
       "Robeson's outspoken political views made him the target of

(Journal and Guide)

Communist hunters in later years. He also used his prestige and talents in an attempt to ease the sufferings of other black Americans and drew the wrath of racist hate groups....," states the writer.

2176.   "Brother Paul," Journal and Guide, February 7, 1976, p. 8.

This article declares: "The World Of Poverty, Sickness and Despair lost a loyal friend in the death of Paul Robeson, January 23, in a Philadelphia hospital. In 77 years the famous baritone singer and football star laid his life on the line and sacrificed more personally than the average civil rights leader of this generation in his crusade for Black Americans...."

16.   WASHINGTON, D.C.

2177.   "Paul Robeson," Washington Star, January 28, 1976.

This editorial declares throughout his acclaimed artistic career, Paul Robeson did not lend himself to a clear perception by the American public. Mr. Robeson defied racial and political stereotypes in years when to do so was not congenial to vast numbers of Americans. Mr. Robeson, who died Friday in Philadelphia, at the age of 77, however, might well have claimed Othello's own epitaph - "I have done the state some service....," states the writer. The editor continues: "Mr. Robeson's difficulties came in large measure because his conception of 'the state' was wider than national boundaries would encompass. Yet during the anti-Red phobia of the 1950s, when he was assailed for his favorable comments about the Soviet Union and his socialistic beliefs, Mr. Robeson eloquently asserted his place, as a Black, in the American experience. Asked by a member of the House Un-American Activities Committee why, if he had felt free in Russia, he had not stayed there, Mr. Robeson replied: "Because my father was a slave, and my people died to build this country, and I am going to stay right here and have a part of it, just like you...." Mr. Robeson long denied he was a Communist; he never denied his priorities, never muted his assertions for racial and personal dignity. He paid a price, states the editor. He concludes: "It was a different America, a dramatically different nation in many ways, that presented itself to Mr. Robeson's last years. It is now a better America, we choose to believe, in the terms that formed his goals and his beliefs. He was part of the transition."

2178. Gilliam, Dorothy. "Last Goodbye to Paul Robeson: 'He's Free at
        Last'," Washington Post, January 29, 1976, pp. G1, G15.

        This article concerns Paul Robeson's funeral. The writer points
        out that most of Robeson's mourners were ordinary people - not
        the rich or the famous or even politicians. But they passed a
        steady stream gazing with tenderness - not idle curiosity, states
        Miss Gilliam. The funeral services were held at Mother A.M.E.
        Zion Church, in Harlem, New York. Over 5,000 people jammed in-
        side; several hundred were turned away. The funeral was held at
        night so working people could attend.

2179. Lynch, Acklyn R. "Paul Robeson: His Dreams Know No Frontiers,"
        Journal of Negro Education, Vol. 45, No. 3, Summer, 1976, pp. 225-
        234.

        The author argues that Paul Robeson's death marked the passing of
        perhaps the most important American cultural and political figure
        in the twentieth century. Mr. Robeson was a man whose versatility
        has been unparalleled in American history as scholar, linguist,
        actor, singer, athlete, humanitarian, and whose striving for ex-
        cellence in every undertaking was embroidered by a deep humility
        which endeared him to the hearts of millions of people around the
        world, states Mr. Lynch. The writer asserts that Paul Robeson
        remained steadfast in his criticism of fascism, racism, colonialism,
        and imperialism. He concludes: "Today (1976), as a result of
        the bitter and traumatic experiences of the sixties and seventies,
        we have come to realize the significance of Paul Robeson's 'stand'
        and his clarity of thought on the dangers of contemporary
        American society."

Part Two
Appendices

A
Discography

A. SINGLE RECORDS[*]

A Selected List

1. 1925

		LABEL
Records:	Bye and Bye	Vic 19743
	Were You There?	Vic 19742
	Steal Away	HMV B-2187
	Joshua Fit De Battle of Jericho	Vic 19743
	Water Boy	Vic 19824
	Swing Low, Sweet Chariot	Vic 20068
	Sometimes I Feel Like A Motherless Child	Vic 20013

2. 1926

Records:	Li'l Gal	Vic 19824
	Nobody Knows De Trouble I've Seen	Vic 20068
	On Ma Journey	Vic 20013

*
Many of these records can be found at the Rogers and Hammerstein
Archives of Recorded Sound of the New York Public Library and at the
Library of Congress. The sheet music for many of these records is
located in the Lawrence Brown Collection at the Schomburg Center on
Black History and Culture.

3. 1927

Records:	Hear De Lam's A-Cryin'	Vic 20604
	Ezekiel Saw De Wheel	Vic 20604
	I'm Goin' To Tell God All O' My Troubles	Vic 20793
	I Got A Home In Dat Rock	Vic 21109
	Deep River	Vic 20793
	Witness	Vic 21109

4. 1928

Records:	Ol' Man River	Vic 35912
	Seem Lak' To Me	HMV B-2777
	Down De Lovers' Lane	HMV B-2777
	Scandalize My Name	HMV B-2771
	Sinner, Please Doan' Let Dis Harves'	HMV B-2771
	Weepin' Mary, I Want To Be Ready	Vic 22225
	My Lord What A Mornin'	HMV B-2897
	De Li'l Pickaninny's Gone To Sleep	HMV B-2948
	Git On Board, Li'l Children	Vic 22225
	Early In The Morning	HMV C-1585
	Carry Me Back To Old Virginia	HMV C-1585
	Old Folks At Home	HMV C-1585
	Goodnight, Ladies	HMV C-1585
	Down South In Dixie	HMV C-1585
	Oh! Rock Me, Julie	HMV B-3033
	Oh, Didn't It Rain	HMV B-3033
	Mammy	HMV C-1591
	Roll Away, Clouds	HMV C-1591

5. 1929

Records:	Sonny Boy	HMV B-2948
	Little Pal	HMV B-3146
	Lonesome Road	HMV B-3146
	Just Keepin' On	HMV B-3199
	Mighty Lak' A Rose	HMV B-9110
	Mammy Is Gone	HMV B-3663

6. 1930

Records:	Hail De Crown	HMV B-3409
	Exhortation	HMV B-3409
	I Stood On De Ribber	HMV B-3381
	Peter, Go Ring Dem Bells	HMV B-3381
	High Water	HMV B-3663
	Swanee River	HMV B-3664
	Poor Old Joe	HMV B-3664
	My Old Kentucky Home	HMV B-3653
	Ol' Man River	HMV B-3653

7. 1931

Records:	River Stay 'Way From My Door	Vic 22889
	Rockin' Chair	Vic 22889
	I'm A Rolling and Singing	HMV C-2287
	Hail De Crown	HMV C-2287
	Joshua Fit De Battle of Jericho	HMV C-2287
	I Got A Robe	HMV C-2287
	Oh Lord I Done	HMV C-2287
	De Gospel Train	HMV C-2287
	Black Sheep	HMV C-2287
	Heav'n Bells Are Ringin'	HMV C-2887

I'll Hear De Triumpet Sound	HMV C-2887
Swing Low	HMV C-2287
Walk Together, Children	HMV C-2887
My Heart Is Where The Mohawk Flows Tonight	HMV B-4052
The Folks I Used To Know	HMV B-4052
Mary Had A Baby	HMV B-4336
Li'il Gal	HMV B-4093
Bear De Burden	HMV B-4336
All God's Chillun Got Wings	HMV B-4436
That's Why Darkies Were Born	HMV B-4058
When It's Sleepy-Time Down South	HMV B-4058
Seekin'	HMV B-4093

8. 1932

Records:

Ol' Man River	Col 55004
Nearer, My God, To Thee	HMV C-2517
Mah Lindy Lou	HMV B-4309
Ma Curly-Headed Baby	HMV B-4309
Pilgrim's Song	HMV B-4421
Roll The Chariot Along	HMV B-4421
Since You Went Away	HMV B-4396
Wid De Moon, Moon, Moon	HMV B-4396
Got The South In My Soul	HMV B-4354
Hush-a-Bye Lullaby	HMV B-4354

9. 1933

Records:

Round The Bend Of The Road	Vic 24318
Take Me Away From The River	Vic 24318
Swing Low, Sweet Chariot	Vic 25547
Oh Mah Journey	Vic 25547

Bye and Bye	HMV B-4480
Were You There?	HMV B-4480
Swing Aong	HMV B-8018
Piccaninny Shoes	HMV B-4499
In A Narrow Street	HMV B-4499
Carry Me Back To Green Pastures	HMV B-8081
Lazy Bones	HMV B-8010
Blue Prelude	HMV B-8018
Roll De Ole Chariot	HMV C-2621
Mary Had A Baby	HMV C-2621
Swing Low	HMV C-2621
Heav'n, Heav'n	HMV C-2621
Carry Me Back	HMV C-2621
Mighty Lak' A Rose	HMV C-2621
Round The Bend Of The Road	HMV C-2621
River, Stay 'Way From My Door	HMV C-2621
Ol' Man River	HMV C-2621
Fat Li'l Feller Wid His Mammy's Eyes	HMV B-8066
Short'nin' Bread	HMV B-8060
Water Boy	HMV B-8103
Doan You Cry, Ma Honey	HMV B-8156
Steal Away	HMV B-8103

10. 1934

Records:

Scarecrow	HMV B-8132
Wagon Wheel	Vic 24635
So Shy	HMV B-8132
Piccaninny Slumber Song	HMV B-8156
St. Louis Blues	Vic 24635

Mammy's Little Kinky-Headed Boy	HMV B-8135
Little Man, You've Had A Busy Day	HMV B-8202
I Ain't Lazy, I'm Just Dreamin'	HMV B-8202
The Banjo Song	HMV B-8219
Lazy Bones	HMV C-2708
Scarecrow	HMV C-2708
Fat Li'l Feller	HMV C02708
Wagon Wheels	HMV C-2708
Deep River	HMV C-2708
Ma Curly-Headed Baby	HMV C-2708
Carry Me Back To Green Pastures	HMV C-2708
Old Folks At Home	HMV C-2708

11. 1935

Records:	Shenandoah	Vic 27438
	Jes' Mah Song	Vic 26289
	De Ole Ark's A-Movering	HMV B-8478
	Ezekiel Saw De Wheel	HMV B-8478
	Joshua Fit De Battle of Jericho	HMV B-8478

12. 1936

Records:	Honey Dat's All	Vic 25362
	Gloomy Sunday	Vic 25362

13. 1937

Records:	Mam'selle Marie	HMV B-8550
	Dere's No Hidin' Place	HMV B-8550
	Oh! No John	HMV B-8541
	Passing By	HMV B-8541
	Hammer Song	HMV B-8550
	Li'l David	HMV B-8550

I Don't Know What's Wrong	HMV B-8591
Sometimes I Feel Like A Motherless Child	HMV B-8604
The Wanderer	HMV B-8604
Dere's A Man Goin' Roun' Takin' Names	Vic 26289
No More	Vic 25889
Work All De Summer	Vic 25809
Didn't My Lord Deliver Daniel	Vic 25809
Still Night, Holy Night	HMV B-8668
All Through The Night	HMV B-9021
Solitude	HMV B-8664
Mood Indigo	HMV B-8664

14. 1938

Records:	Summertime	Vic 26359
	It Take A Long Pull To Get There	Vic 26359
	It Ain't Necessarily So	Vic 26358
	A Woman Is A Sometime Thing	Vic 26358
	Just A-Wearin' For You	Vic 25873
	At Dawning	Vic 25873
	Song Of The Volga Boatman	HMV B-8750
	An Eriskay Love Lilt	HMV B-8750
	Encantadora Maria	HMV B-8781
	Goin' To Ride Up In De Chariot	Vic 26251
	Every Time I Feel De Spirit	Vic 26251
	Lay Down Late	Vic 26251
	After The Battle	HMV B-9149
	David Of The White Rock	HMV B-9149
	Trees	Vic 26168
	Songs My Mother Taught Me	HMV B-8830

Loch Lomond	Vic 27227
Drink To Me Only With Thine Eyes	Vic 27430

15. 1939

Records:	Down De Lovers' Lane	Vic 2674
	Lullaby	Vic 26409
	Night	Vic 26409
	The Little Black Boy	HMV B-8918
	Dear Old Southland	Vic 26741
	Jerusalem	Vic 27348
	The Blind Ploughman	Vic 26651
	The Cobbler's Song	HMV B-8977
	Oh, Could I But Express In Song	Vic 26651
	Love At My Heart	HMV B-9281
	Nothin'	Vic 26741
	The Rosary	Vic 26498
	A Perfect Day	Vic 26498
	Absent	Vic 27366
	Black Eyes	Vic 26651
	Oh, Promise Me	HMV B-9059
	Plaisir d'amour	HMV B-9059
	Sylvia	Vic 27366
	She Is Far From The Land	HMV B-9010
	Thora	HMV B-9037
	Now Sleeps The Crimson Petal	HMV B-9281
	Sea Fever	HMV B-9257

16. 1940

Records:	Deep River	HMV B-9024
	Lord God Of Abraham	HMV B-9024

Ballad For Americans - Part 1	Vic 26516
Ballad For Americans - Part 2	Vic 26516
Ballad For Americans - Part 3	Vic 26517
Ballad For Americans - Part 4	Vic 26517

17. 1941

Records: King Joe - Part 1   Col C-516

            King Joe - Part 2   Col C-516

18. 1960*

Records: Sanders Of The River (Selections   7EG.8185
            From Films)

Canoe Song
Long Song
Congo Lullaby
The Killing Song

There Is A Green Hill   7EG.8386
Nearer My God To Thee
Jerusalem
Stille Nacht, Heilige Nacht

Negro Spirituals   7EG.8422

Water Boy
Were You There
Steal Away
Joshua Fit De Battle Of Jericho

Song Of Freedom   7EG.8431

Song Of Freedom
The Black Emperor
Sleepy River
Lonely Road

Negro Lullabies   7EG.8449

Ma Curly-Headed Baby
Mah Lindy Lou
Mightly Lak' A Rose
Fat Li' Feller Wid His Mammy's Eyes

*
NOTE: All records are recorded under EMI label.

Best Love Songs   7EG.8486

Just A Wearyin' For You
Ol' Man River
Trees
Deep River

Porgy And Bess   7EG.8510

Highlights
Summertime
A Woman Is A Sometime Thing
It Ain't Necessarily So
It Takes A Long Pull To Get There

Paul Robeson Medley   7P.226

Lazy Bones
Fat Li'l Feller
Scarecrow
Wagon Wheels
Deep River
Ma Curly-Headed Baby
Carry Me Back To Green Pastures
Old Folks At Home

B. SINGLE RECORDS FROM FILMS

A Selected List

1. 1928

Ol' Man River ("Show Boat")   HMV C-1505

2. 1930

Ol' Man River ("Show Boat")   HMV B-3653

3. 1932

Ol' Man River ("Show Boat")   Col 55004

4. 1935

Long Song ("Sanders Of The River")   Vic 25107

Congo Lullaby ("Sanders Of The River")   Vic 25106

Canoe Song ("Sanders Of The River")   Vic 25106

Killing Song ("Sanders Of The River")   Vic 25107

5. 1936

Sleepy River ("Song Of Freedom")   HMV B-8482

Ol' Man River ("Show Boat")   Vic 25376

Lonely Road ("Song Of Freedom")   HMV B-8483

Song Of Freedom ("Song Of Freedom")   HMV B-8482

The Black Emperor ("Song Of Freedom")   HMV B-8483

6. 1937

My Way ("Jericho")	JMV B-8572
Golden River ("Jericho")	HMV B-8572
Ho! Ho! ("King Solomon's Mines")	HMV B-8586
Climbing Up ("King Solomon's Mines")	HMV B-8586
Lazin' ("Big Fella")	HMV B-8607
Roll Up, Sailorman ("Big Fella")	HMV B-8607
You Didn't Oughta Do Such Things ("Big Fella")	HMV B-8607
Deep Desert ("Jericho")	Vic 25743

7. 1939

Ebenezer ("Proud Valley")	HMV B-9020
Land Of My Fathers ("Proud Valley")	Vic 27227

C. ALBUMS

A Selected List*

Ballad For Americans
Date: 1939
Label: RCA Victor
Songs: Ballad For Americans
        Joe Hill
        Four Insurgent Generals
        Peat Bog Soldiers
        Meadowland

Chee Lai: Songs Of New China
Date: 194?
Label: Keynote K520/2
Songs: Chee Lai
        Work As One
        Feng Yang
        Chinese Farmer's Song
        Chinese Soldier's Song
        Riding The Dragon
        Song Of The Guerrillas

Song Of Free Men
Date: 1942
Label: Columbia MM534
Songs: From Border To Border
        Oh, How Proud Our Quiet Don
        The Purest Kind Of A Guy
        Joe Hill
        The Peat-Bog Soldiers
        The Four Insurgent Generals

*There were a number of albums that Paul Robeson made that I could not
 locate. Therefore, this is ONLY a selected list of his most available
 albums.

Native Land
Song Of The Plains

Paul Robeson: Spirituals
Date: 1949
Label: Columbia ML 4105
Songs: Go Down, Moses
          Balm in Gilead
          By An' By
          Sometimes I Feel Like A Motherless Child
          John Henry
          Water Boy
          Nobody Knows De Trouble I've Seen
          Joshua Fit De Battle Of Jericho

Swing Low, Sweet Chariot
Date: 195?
Label: Columbia ML 2038
Songs: Swing Low, Sweet Chariot
          Ev'ry Time I Feel De Spirit
          I Got A Home In Dat Rock
          O, Gimme Your Han'
          No More Auction Block
          Great Gittin' Up Mornin'
          Hear De Lam's A-Cryin'
          Goin' To Ride Up In De Chariot
          I'll Hear De Trumpet
          Ezekial Saw De Wheel
          Poor Wayfarin' Strangers
          Hammer Song
          Dere's A Man Goin' Round
          I Know De Lord
          Git On Board, Little Children
          Li'l David

Paul Robeson - Spirituals
Date: 195?
Label: Columbia ML54105
Songs: Go Down Moses
          Balm In Gilead
          By An' By
          Sometimes I Feel Like A Motherless Child
          John Henry
          Water Boy
          Nobody Knows De Trouble I've Seen
          Joshua Fit De Battle Of Jericho
          Also Popular Favorites

Othello/Shakespeare
Date: 1953
Label: Columbia SL 153

Robeson Sings
Date: 1953
Label: Othello Records R-101
Songs: The Four Rivers
        Wanderin'
        Witness
        Hassidic Chant
        My Curly-Headed Baby
        Night (Sung in English and Russian)

A Robeson Recital of Popular Favorities
Date: 1954
Label: Columbia ML 54105
Songs: Ol' Man River
        I Still Suit Me
        Ma Curly-Headed Baby
        Mah Lindy Lou
        The House I Live In
        Wagon Wheels
        Sylvia
        It Ain't Necessarily So
        Spirituals

Solid Rock: Favorite Hymns of My People
Date: 1954?
Label: Othello Records R-201A-F
Songs: Jacob's Ladder
        Someday He'll Make It Plain
        Balm
        Amazing Grace
        End Of My Journey
        The Solid Rock

Paul Robeson
Date: 1958
Label: Vanguard VSD 2015
Principally Negro Spirituals

Paul Robeson
Date: 1958
Label: Vanguard VRS-9037
Songs: Waterboy
        Shenandoah
        Deep River
        John Brown's Body
        Jerusalem
        Londonderry Air (Danny Boy)
        Sometimes I Feel Like A Motherless Child
        Get On Board, Little Children
        The House I Live In
        Loch Lomond
        Drink To Me Only With Thine Eyes
        Joshua Fought The Battle Of Jericho
        All Through The Night

Encore Robeson!
Date: 1959
Label: Monitor MP-581
Songs: Skye Boat Song
         Shlof Mein Kind
         Now Sleeps The Crimson Petal
         Dans Le Printemps
         Passing By
         Little Gal
         Mistress Mine
         Kevin Barry
         Zvornost
         No More Auction
         Some Day He'll Make It
         Plain To Me
         Didn't My Lord Deliver Daniel
         Bear The Burden In The Heat Of Day
         Mount Zion
         I'm Gonna Let It Shine
         Let Us Break Bread Together On Our Knees
         Amazing Grace

Paul Robeson At Carnegie Hall: May 9, 1958
Date: 1959 Vol. 1
Label: Vanguard VRS-9051
Songs: Every Time I Feel The Spirit
         Balm in Bilead
         Volga Boat Song
         Monologue From Shakespeare's Othello
         O Thou Silent Night
         Chinese Song
         My Curly-Headed Baby
         Old Man River
         Going Home
         Monologue From Boris Godunov
         The Orphan
         Christ Lay In Todesbanden
         Didn't My Lord Deliver Daniel
         Lullaby
         O No, John
         Joe Hill
         Jacob's Ladder

Paul Robeson: Favorite Songs
Date: 1959, Vol. 1
Label: Monitor MPS 58
Songs: Hammer Song
         Water Me From The Lime Rock
         Scandalize My Name
         Jacob's Ladder
         Witness
         Stand Still
         Jordan
         Takin' Names
         Swing Low, Sweet Chariot
         Hassidic Chant - Kaddish

Wanderer
Songs My Mother Taught Me
Vi Azoi Lebt Der Kaiser
The Minstrel Boy
The Orphan
Zog Nit Keymol
Joe Hill

Favorite Songs
Date: 1959-1961, Vol. 2
Label: Monitor MP-580
Songs: Hammer Song
         Water Me From The Lime Rock
         Scandalize My Name
         Jacob's Ladder
         Witness
         Stand Still Jordan
         Takin' Names
         Swing Low, Sweet Chariot
         Hassidic Chant: Kaddish
         Wanderer
         Sons My Mother Taught Me
         Vi Azoi Lebt Der Keyser
         The Minstrel Boy
         The Orphan
         Zog Nit Keynmol
         Joe Hill

Emperor Of Song
Date: 1960
Label: EMI DLP.1/65
Songs: Ma Curly Headed Baby
         Carry Me Back To Green Pastures
         I Still Suit Me
         Just A-Wearyin' For You
         Swing Low, Sweet Chariot
         My Old Kentucky Home
         Fat Li'l Feller Wid His Mammy's Eyes
         Shortn'nin Bread
         Song Of The Volga Boatman
         Wagon Wheels
         My Way

Incomparable Voice
Date: 1960
Label: Odeon 1155
Songs: Ol' Man River
         Trees
         Songs My Mother Taught Me
         Night
         The Rosary
         Solitude
         St. Louis Blues
         Mighty Lak' A Rose
         Mood Indigo
         Deep River

Paul Robeson
Date: 1960
Label: Verve MGV-4044 (Import)
Songs: Some Enchanted Evening
         Mah Lindy Lou
         The Skye Boat Song
         The Riddle Song
         Down De Lover's Lane
         Land Of My Fathers
         I'll Walk Beside You
         Ma Curly Headed Baby
         Trees
         Castle Of Dromore
         Just A' Wearying For You
         Climbing Up De Mountain

Paul Robeson Song Recital
Date: 1961?
Label: Supraphon SHA 10062
Songs: Ein Feste Burg
         Christ Lag in Todesbanden
         Sarastro's Aria
         All Men Are Brothers
         Cradle Song
         The Orphan
         Quilter Now Sleeps
         We Are Climbing Jacob's Ladder
         Song Of Freedom
         Songs My Mother Taught Me
         By The Waters Of Babylon
         Going Home
         Love Song
         Deep River
         Water Boy
         Sometimes I Feel Like A Motherless Child

Paul Robeson: Ballad For Americans And Carnegie Hall Concert
Date: 1965, Vol. 2
Label: Vanguard VSD-79193
Songs: Ballad For Americans
         Go Down Moses
         On My Journey
         Patterns Of Folk Song
         Hassidic Chant Of Levi Issac
         Freedom
         The Minstrel Boy
         O Grieve You Now My Mother
         Eriskay Love Lilt
         This Is The Hammer
         Scandalize My Name
         Now Sleeps The Crimson Petal
         The Four Rivers
         Mexican Lullaby
         All Men Are Brothers

Songs of Free Men/Spirituals
Date: 1968
Label: Odyssey 32160268
Songs: Songs of Free Men (recorded in 1942)
        From Border to Border
        Oh, How Proud Our Quiet Don
        The Purest Kind of a Guy
        Joe Hill
        The Peat-Bog Soldiers
        The Four Insurgent Generals
        Native Land
        Song of the Plains

Songs: Spirituals (recorded in 1942)
        Go Down Moses
        Balm in Gilead
        By an' By
        Sometimes I Feel Like A Motherless Child
        John Henry
        Water Boy
        Nobody Knows de Trouble I've Seen
        Joshua Fit de Battle of Jericho

The Best of Paul Robeson
Date: 1970 Vol. 2
Label: EMI SRS 5127
Songs: Summertime
        I Still Suits Me
        Short'nin Bread
        It Ain't Necessarily So
        Swing Low, Sweet Chariot
        Rockin' Chair
        Killing Song
        Sleepy River
        Lonesome Road
        Cobbler's Song
        Carry Me Back to Green Pastures
        Steel Away
        Deep River
        Long Song

The Best of Paul Robeson
Date: 1970 Vol. 3
Label: Starline-EMI SRS 5193
Songs: The Black Emperor
        My Old Kentucky Home
        Black Eyes
        Shenandoh
        Fit Li'l Feller Wid His Mammy's Eyes
        At Dawning
        Jerusalem, Night
        Dear Old Southland
        Song of the Volga Boatmen
        A Woman is a Sometimes Thing
        Land of My Father
        Were You There

Song of Freedom
Solitude
Lonely Road

Paul Robeson - A Man and His Music
Date: 1971
Label: Everest 3291
Songs: Mammy
        Nothin'
        The Blind Ploughman
        Snowball
        Old Folks at Home
        Poor Old Joe
        Lonesome Road
        Dear Old Southland
        Sleepy Time Down South
        Loch Lomand

Paul Robeson: In Live Performance
Date: 1971
Label: Columbia M-30424
Songs: Every Time I Feel the Spirit
        Ezekiel Saw the Wheel
        I'll Hear the Trumpet Sound
        Get On Board Little Children
        L'Amour de Moi
        Volga Boatmen
        Joe Hill
        Ol' Man River
        Swing Low, Sweet Chariot
        No More Auction Block
        Water Boy
        Chinese Children's Song
        The House I Live In
        Sometimes I Feel Like A Motherless Child
        We Are Climbing Jacob's Ladder

An Evening With Paul Robeson
Date: 1971
Label: Afro-American Museum of Detroit, Michigan
        (Record made from tapes of Robeson's concerts in the early
        1950s).
Songs: No More Auction Block
        Brother Sing Your Country's Anthem
        From Boris Gudunov
        Letters to Marine
        Cooks & Stewards Unions
        Kaddish
        Water Boy

Songs of My People
Date: 1972
Label: RCA Victor LM 3292
Songs: Git On Board
        Li'l Children
        Were You There?
        Dere's No Hidin' Place
        Deep River
        Witness
        Water Boy
        On Ma Journey
        Swing Low, Sweet Chariot
        Ezekiel Saw de Well
        Nobody Knows de Trouble's I've Seen
        I Want To Be Ready
        Sometimes I Feel Like A Motherless Child
        Joshua Fit de Battle of Jericho
        Hear de Lam's A-Cryin'
        Bye and Bye
        Weepin' Mary
        Steal Away
        I'm Goin' to Tell God All O' My Trouble
        Li'l Gal
        I Got A Home-in-a-Dat Rock

The Essential Paul Robeson
Date: 1974 (two records)
Label: Vanguard VSD57-58
Songs: Everytime I Feel The Spirit
        Balm of Gilead
        Volga Boat Song
        Monologue from Othello
        O, Thou Silent Night
        Chinese Children's Song
        My Curly Headed Baby
        Old Man River
        Going Home
        Monologue from Boris Gudunov
        The Orphan
        Christ Lag in Todesbaden
        Didn't My Lord Deliver Daniel
        Lullaby
        O, No John
        Joe Hill
        Jacob's Ladder
        Ballad for Americans
        Deep River
        John Brown's Body
        Jerusalem
        Londonderry Air
        Water Boy
        Shenandoah
        Sometimes I Feel Like A Motherless Child
        Get On Board Little Children
        The House I Live In
        Loch Lomond

          Drink to Me Only with Thine Eyes
          Joshua Fought The Battle of Jericho
          All Through the Night

Paul Robeson
Date: 197?
Label: Pathe EMI C054-05219
Songs: Ol' Man River
         Trees
         The Rosary
         Solitude
         St. Louis Blues
         Mood Indigo
         Deep River
         Joshua Fit The Battle of Jericho
         Just A Wearyin' for You
         My Way
         My Old Kentucky Home
         Nearer My God To Thee
         Song of the Volga Boatmen
         Still Night, Holy Night

Paul Robeson, Ol' Man River
Date: 1976?
Label: EMI C054-05219
Songs: Ol' Man River
         Trees
         The Rosary
         Solitude
         Saint-Louis Blues
         Mood Indigo
         Deep River
         Joshua Fit the Battle of Jericho
         Just A Wearyin' For You
         My Way
         My Old Kentucky Home
         Nearer, My God, To Thee
         Song of the Volga Boatmen
         Still Night, Holy Night

When I Have Sung My Songs: The American Art Song, 1900-1940
Date: 1976
Label: New World Records NW 247
Songs: Li'l Gal
         Deep River

Paul Robeson: Scandalize My Name
Date: 1976
Label: The Classics Record Library
Songs: Scandalize My Name
         Water Boy
         My Lindy Lou
         Ol' Man River
         Get On Board Little Children
         Monologue from Boris Gudunov
         The Orphan

King Joe
I Got A Home In That Rock
Balm In Gilead
Chinese Children's Song
Joe Hill
The Peat Bog Soldiers
Song of the Plains
My Curly Headed Baby
By and By
Nobody Knows the Trouble I've Seen
Joshua Fit De Battle of Jericho
Little David Play On Your Harp
I Know The Lord
Every Time I Feel The Spirit
Going Home
Sometimes I Feel Like A Motherless Child
Patterns of Folk Song and Hassidic Chant
Monologue from Othello
Volga Boat Song
Jerusalem
The Minstrel Boy
Didn't My Deliver Daniel
Deep River
The House I Live In
Londonderry Air
O Thou Silent Autumn Night
John Brown's Body
Swing Low, Sweet Chariot
No More Auction Block
We Are Climbing Jacob's Ladder

Historic Paul Robeson
Date: 1981
Label: Everest
Songs: Christ Lag in Todesbanden
        Cradle Song
        Orphan
        Now Sleeps The Crimson Petal
        Jacob's Ladder
        Song of Freedom
        Songs My Mother Taught Me
        By the Water of Baby-Lon
        Going Home
        Erisksay Love Lilt
        Deep River
        Water Boy
        Sometimes I Feel Like A Motherless Child
        Ein Feste Burg
        O Isis and Osiris
        All Men Are Brothers

B
Unpublished Recordings

NCP 1176   Paul Robeson Sings 3 Negro Spirituals

Cassette 11632   His Life and Career Discussed by Pete Seeger and Ossie Davis (Center for Cassette Studies 26672)

T 8668   Citation By Actors' Equity (1-7")

LW05554
6/29/43   Labor For Victory

T5855 9B1
6/29/41   Calm As The Night,and Deep River (Coca-Cola Programs)

T5855 12B2
10/12/41   Ezekiel Saw De Wheel, and All Through the Night

LW05554
6/27/43   Labor For Victory Program Entitled "John Henry" Broadcast 6/27/43. Copy from Office of War Information DISC E5386

LW07749
no date   Paul Robeson and Company in Final Scene From "Othello"

T5833
6/15/43   Speech At Atlanta University, Atlanta, Georgia

LWO-5078   Appeared on "The Pursuit of Happiness" Program, November 5, 1939

NCP2531/2532   CBS Forecast Series, "All God's Children," Broadcast 8/26/48.

*
Located in Recorded Sound Division of The Library of Congress.

LWO12240

Answering You, Office of War Information Recording E6075, Recording No. C2376A, New York, (date unknown)

RXA169

Paul Robeson Talks About His Life, 1958. Pacific Tape BB053 (31')

OWI Acetate

Guest Spot on "Show Of Yesterday, Today and Tomorrow," May 17, 1942

C
Filmography

1.   BODY AND SOUL (1924)
     Cast: Paul Robeson, Mercedes Gilbert, Julia Russell
     Director: Oscar Micheaux
     Country: Filmed in the United States
     Time: ca. 75 minutes (Silent Film)

2.   BORDERLINE (1929)
     Cast: Paul Robeson, Eslanda Robeson, Hilda Doolittle
     Director: Kenneth MacPherson
     Country: Switzerland
     Time: ca. 80 minutes

3.   EMPEROR JONES (1933)
     Cast: Paul Robeson, Rex Ingram, Ruby Elzy, Fredi Washington,
            Dudley Diggs, Frank Wilson, Gordon Taylor, Grandon Evans,
            Blueboy O'Connor, Jackie Mayble
     Director: Dudley Murphy
     Country: United States
     Time: 73 minutes

4.   SANDERS OF THE RIVER (1935)
     Cast: Paul Robeson, Nina McKinney, Robert Cochrane, Robert
            Walker, Leslie Banks, Toto Ware
     Director: Zoltan Korda
     Country: England
     Time: 88 minutes

5.   SHOW BOAT (1936)
     Cast: Paul Robeson, Irene Dunne, Allan Jones, Hattie McDaniel,
            Charles Winninger, Helen Morgan, Clarence Muse, Eddie
            Anderson, George Reed
     Director: James Whale
     Country: United States
     Time: 113 minutes

6. SONG OF FREEDOM (1937)
    Cast: Paul Robeson, Elizabeth Welch, Robert Adams, Toto Ware,
           Orlando Martins, James Solomon
    Director: J. Elder Wills
    Country: England
    Time: 70 minutes

7. KING SOLOMON'S MINES (1937)
    Cast: Paul Robeson, Cedric Hardwick, Anna Lee, Roland Young,
           John Loder, Robert Adams, Makubalo Hlubi, Ecco Homo Toto,
           Sydney Fairbrother, Frederick Leister
    Director: Robert Stevenson
    Country: England
    Time: 80 minutes

8. JERICHO (1937)
    Cast: Paul Robeson, Henry Wilcoxen, Princess Koyka, Lawrence
           Brown, Wallace Ford, Eslanda Robeson, James Carew, Ike
           Hatch, Rufus Fennel, Orlando Martins
    Director: Thornton Freedland
    Country: Egypt and England
    Time: 75 minutes

9. BIG FELLA (1938)
    Cast: Paul Robeson, Elizabeth Welch, Roy Emerton, Lawrence Brown,
           Eslanda Robeson, James Hayter
    Director: J. Elder Wills
    Country: England
    Time: ca. 80 minutes

10. PROUD VALLEY (1939)
    Cast: Paul Robeson, Edward Chapman, Simon Lach, Rachel Thomas,
           Edward Rigby, Janet Johnson, Charles Williams, Jack Jones,
           Dilys Davies, Edward Lexy
    Director: Pen Tennyson
    Country: England
    Time: 77 minutes

11. TALES OF MANHATTAN (1943)
    Cast: Charles Boyer, Rita Hayworth, Edward G. Robinson, Paul
           Robeson, Ethel Waters, Clarence Muse, Eddie Anderson,
           George Reed, Cordell Hickman
    Director: Julien Duvivier
    Country: United States
    Time: 118 minutes

B. DOCUMENTARIES

1. MY SONG GOES FORTH (1936)

   Paul Robeson does not appear in this film, however, he recorded
   the Prologue and the theme song for this work about Johannesburg,
   South Africa, and how it grew from a mining town to a modern
   city over a fifty-year period.

2. NATIVE LAND (1942)

   Mr. Robeson does not appear in this film, however, he narrated
   and sang the musical score for this work about a Senate investigation of racial discrimination in the South.

3. SONG OF THE RIVERS (1954)

   Paul Robeson does not appear in this film, however, he narrated
   and sang the musical score for this documentary about people
   working along the banks of four great rivers: Mississippi
   (United States), Nile (Egypt), Ganges (India), and Volga (Russia).

4. PAUL ROBESON, THE TALLEST TREE IN OUR FOREST (1975)

   This 90 minute film was Produced, Written and Reported by Gil
   Nobel. Photographs, filmclips, interviews, sound recordings and
   newspaper clippings document the life of Paul Robeson.

5. PAUL ROBESON - A CELEBRATION (1976?)

   This 25 minute film was made by Barbara Jamison (27 Constantine
   Place, Summit, New Jersey 07901). Live film, still photographs,
   sound recordings and tapes document the life and times of Paul
   Robeson. Available from Barbara Jamison in both super-8 and
   16 mm.

D
States and Cities in Which Robeson Performed

ALABAMA

   Tuskegee

ARIZONA

   Phoenix

CALIFORNIA

   Barkerfield
   Berkeley
   Burbank
   Fresno
   Hollywood
   Long Beach
   Los Angeles
   Marysville
   Oakland
   Palo Alto
   Pasadena
   Pueblo
   Redlands
   Sacramento
   San Diego
   San Francisco
   San Jose
   San Quentin
   Stockton

COLORADO

>   Boulder
>   Denver
>   Pueblo

CONNECTICUT

>   Bridgeport
>   Hartford
>   Norwalk

DELAWARE

>   Wilmington

DISTRICT OF COLUMBIA

FLORIDA

>   St. Petersburg

GEORGIA

>   Atlanta
>   Macon
>   Savannah

HAWAII

>   Honolulu

IDAHO

>   Boise

ILLINOIS

    Chicago
    Evanston
    Great Lakes
    Oak Park
    Springfield
    Urbana

INDIANA

    Bloomington
    Fort Wayne
    Gary
    Indianapolis
    Terre Haute

IOWA

    Davenport
    Des Moines
    Fairfield
    Oskaloosa
    Ottumma

KANSAS

    Topeka
    Waterloo
    Wichita

KENTUCKY

    Louisville

LOUISIANA

    New Orleans

MAINE

    Portland

MARYLAND

  Baltimore

MASSACHUSETTS

  Amherst
  Boston
  Brookline
  Cambridge
  Dennis
  Roxbury
  Springfield
  Wellesley
  Worchester

MICHIGAN

  Alma
  Ann Arbor
  Benton Harbor
  Detroit
  East Lansing
  Escanaba
  Ishpemping
  Kalamazoo

MINNESOTA

  Duluth
  Mesabi
  Minneapolis

MISSISSIPPI

  Jackson

MISSOURI

  Columbia
  East St. Louis
  Jefferson City
  Kansas City
  St. Louis

MONTANA

    Butte
    Helena
    Kalispell
    Missoula

NEBRASKA

    Hastings
    Lincoln
    Omaha

NEVADA

    Reno

NEW HAMPSHIRE

    Nashua

NEW JERSEY

    Elizabeth
    Montclair
    New Brunswick
    Newark
    Paterson
    Princeton
    Somerville
    Trenton
    Westfield

NEW YORK

    Albany
    Binghamton
    Brooklyn
    Bronx
    Buffalo
    Clinton
    Corona
    Huntington
    Ithaca
    Oneonta

Peekskill
Rochester
Schenectady
White Plains

NORTH CAROLINA

Durham
Greensboro
Ralaigh
Salisburg
Winston-Salem

NORTH DAKOTA

Fargo
Grand Forks
Minot

OHIO

Cincinnati
Cleveland
Columbus
Dayton
Toledo

OREGON

Klamath Fall
Portland
Salem

PENNSYLVANIA

Beaver
Bethlehem
Carlisle
Erie
Grennsburg
Harrisburgh
Philadelphia
Pittsburgh
State College
Swarthmore

SOUTH CAROLINA

    Charleston
    Columbia

SOUTH DAKOTA

    Rapid City

TENNESSEE

    Johnson City
    Knoxville
    Memphis

TEXAS

    Dallas

UTAH

    Ogden
    Salt Lake City

VERMONT

    St. Albans

VIRGINIA

    Norfolk
    Richmond

WASHINGTON

    Blaine
    Bremerton
    Seattle
    Spokane
    Tacoma

WISCONSIN

   Madison
   Milwaukee

WYOMING

   Laramie

E
Countries and Cities
in Which Robeson
Performed

A SELECTED LIST

AUSTRALIA

Adelaide
Brisbane
Hobart
Melbourne
Perth
Sydney

AUSTRIA

Vienna

CANADA

Calgary
Edmonton
Montreal
Nanaimo
Ontario
Quebec
Sudbury
Toronto
Vancouver
Victoria
Windsor
Winnipeg

CZECHOSLOVAKIA

Prague

DENMARK

Copenhagen

EGYPT

Cairo

ENGLAND

Bath
Beaconsfield
Birmingham
Blackbourn
Bournemouth
Brighton
Bristol
Buxton
Cambridge
Carlisle
Cheltenham
Coventry
Derby
Douglas
Ealing
Eastbourne
Folkstone
Gateshead
Great Yarmouth
Hammersmith
Hampstead
Harrogate
Hastings
Huddersfield
Hull
Ipswich
Kent
Lancastershire
Leeds
Leicester
Liverpool
London
Lowestoft
Manchester
Margate
Montreal

Norwich
Oxford
Preston
Scarborough
Sheffield
Southampton
Suffolk
Swindon
Torquay
Tynbridge Wells
Wolverhampton
Worthing
Yarmouth
Yorkshire

FRANCE

Marseilles
Paris

GERMANY

Berchtesgaden
Berlin
Dachau
Dresden
Hamburgh
Munich
Nuremburg

HUNGARY

Budapest

IRELAND

Belfast
Cork
Dublin
Limerick
Londonderry

ITALY

Turin

JAMAICA

Kingston

NEW ZEALAND

Auckland
Christchurch
Wellington

NORWAY

Oslo

PANAMA

Colon
Panama City

POLAND

Warsaw

RUMANIA

Bucharest

RUSSIA

Kiev
Leningrad
Moscow
Odessa
Sevastopol
Stalingrad
Tiflis
Uzbek
Yalta

SCOTLAND

Aberdeenshire

Clydebank
Dundee
Edinburgh
Glasglow
Hebrides
Kilmarnock
Perth

SPAIN

Barcelonia
Madrid
Tarragona
Valencia

SWEDEN

Stockholm

TRINIDAD

WALES

Caernarvon
Cardiff
Ebbw Vale
Llandudno
Newcastle
Rhyl
Swansea

F
Theaters, Plays, and Cities in Which Robeson Performed

A SELECTED LIST

THEATERS	PLAYS	CITIES	DATES
Lafayette	"Simon the Cyrenian"	New York	1921
Sam H. Harris	"Taboo"	New York	1922
Opera House	"The Voodoo"	Blackpool, England	1922
Provincetown	"All God's Chillun Got Wings"	New York	1924
Fifty-Second Street	"The Emperor Jones"	New York	1925
Ambassadors	"The Emperor Jones"	London, England	1925
The Comedy	"Black Boy"	New York	1926
The Republic	"Porgy"	New York	1928
Drury Lane	"Show Boat"	London, England	1928
Kunstler	"The Emperor Jones"	Berlin, Germany	1930
Savoy	"Othello"	London, England	1930
Ambassadors	"The Hairy Ape"	London, England	1931
Casino	"Show Boat" (Revival)	New York	1932
Embassy	"All God's Chillun Got Wings"	London, England	1933

Arts	"Basalik"	London, England	1935
Embassy	"Stevedore"	London, England	1935
Westminster	"Toussaint L'Ouverture"	London, England	1936
Unity	"Planet in the Sun"	London, England	1936
Forty-Fourth Street	"John Henry"	New York	1940
Philharmonic Auditorium	"Show Boat" (Revival)	Los Angeles	1940
Westport	"The Emperor Jones" (Revival)	Westport, Connecticut	1940
Battle Hall	"Othello"	Cambridge, Massachusetts	1942
*Shubert	"Othello"	New York	1943
Shakespeare Memorial	"Othello"	Stratford-on-Avon, England	1959

*Played Othello 295 times, the longest run on record for a
Shakespearean production.

G
Languages or Dialects
Spoken by Robeson

A SELECTED LIST

LANGUAGES OR DIALECTS	COUNTRIES
Ashanti	Ghana
Benin	Nigeria
Edo	Nigeria
Efik	Nigeria
Egyptian	Egypt
Ibo	Nigeria
Mande	French West Africa, Sierra Leone, Liberia
Swahili	Zanzibar and East Africa
Yoruba	Guinea, Ghana, Dahomey, Nigeria
Zulu	Natal
Hindustani	India
Arabic	Arabia, Jordan, Lebanon, Syria, Iraq, Egypt, Northern Africa
Chinese	China
Japanese	Japan
Czechoslovakian	Czechoslovakia

Greek	Greece
French	France
German	Germany
Hebrew	Israel
Hungarian	Hungary
Italian	Italy
Persian	Persia
Russian	Russia
Basque	Bay of Biscay
Yiddish	Germany
Yugoslavian	Yugoslavia
Finnish	Finland, Sweden, Norway
Danish	Denmark
Norwegian	Norway
Polish	Poland

H
Monuments and Memorials Named for Paul Robeson

A SELECTED LIST

Mount Robeson. A mountain named after Paul Robeson in the Soviet Republic of Kirghizia. One of the highest peaks of the Tien Shan mountains was the one named after him in 1949.

Paul Robeson Street. The Town Council of Lvov, in Southern Poland named a street after Paul Robeson in 1958.

Paul Robeson Choir. Established in Berlin, German Democratic Republic in 1963.

Paul Robeson Archives. Established in Berlin, German Democratic Republic in 1965.

Paul Robeson International Symposium. This was a two-day symposium held in Berlin, German Democratic Republic, April 13-14, 1971.

Paul Robeson Players. This group was founded in Compton, California, by Robert Browning in 1971.

The Paul Robeson Exhibit. This exhibit was sponsored by and shown at the Detroit International Afro-American Museum in 1971.

Paul Robeson Campus Center. Established on the Newark campus of Rutgers University in March, 1972.

Paul Robeson Lounge. Established at Rutgers University in April, 1972.

"Paul Robeson." A one-character play based on Paul Robeson's life, starring James Earl Jones. Play opened on Broadway in New York City in August, 1973.

Paul Robeson Public School. A school in the eastern borough of Berlin, capital of the German Democratic Republic named in April, 1973.

Paul Robeson Scholarship Fund. This fund was established by the Alpha Phi Alpha Fraternity at Lincoln University, Pennsylvania, in 1973.

Paul Robeson Lecture Series. This program was established at the University of Massachusetts, Amherst, for 1973-1974.

Paul Robeson Actors' Equity Award. Robeson was the first recipient of this award. This award was given in June, 1974.

Paul Robeson Humanitarian Award. This award is given annually by the Alpha Phi Alpha National fraternity. The award was first given in December, 1975.

Paul Robeson Audio-Visual Room. Moorland-Spingarn Research Center, Howard University, Washington, D.C. established in 1976 (?).

National Conference on Paul Robeson. The African Studies and Research Center of Purdue University hosted the meeting in April, 1976.

Paul Robeson Friendship Society was organized in Washington, D.C., in 1976.

Paul Robeson Public School 191. This elementary school in Brownsville, Brooklyn, New York, was named in Paul Robeson's honor in June, 1976.

Paul Robeson Street. This street, located in Princeton, New Jersey, was named in Robeson's honor. It was named on July 8th and September 14, 1976.

The Storefront Museum, Paul Robeson Theatre, Jamaica, New York. Established in 1976 (?).

Paul Robeson Cultural Center. This center was established at Pennsylvania State University, University Park, in 1977.

Paul Robeson Cultural and Performing Arts Center. This $6 million building was named after Mr. Robeson at Central State University, Wilberforce, Ohio, in 1977.

Paul Robeson International Film Festival. This was an annual event begun at the University of Pennsylvania in 1977.

Paul Robeson Medal of Distinction. This award was started in 1977 by the Black Filmmakers Hall of Fame. In February, 1977, Alice Childress received this award.

Paul Robeson Scholarship. This fund was established in 1977 by the Black students at the Columbia University Law School for minority and legal studies.

The Paul Robeson. In 1978, the Soviet Union named a 40,000 ton tanker in honor of Paul Robeson.

Paul Robeson Lecture Series. This meeting was established at Medgar Evans College, City University of New York, Brooklyn, New York, in February, 1978.

Robeson Commemorative Week was held in Detroit, Michigan, April 9-16, 1978. This week-long celebration commemorated his 80th birthday.

I
Countries That
"Officially and Unofficially"
Celebrated Paul Robeson's
Sixtieth Birthday on
April 9, 1958

A SELECTED LIST*

Australia

British Guiana

Bulgaria

Ceylon

China

Czechoslovakia

Denmark

Ecuador

Egypt

England

Ghana

France

Germany

Hungary

India

*This list is significant because this was the period that Paul Robeson's passport was revoked and he could not travel abroad. These countries showed the United States Government how much respect they had for Paul Robeson. To them, he was "A Citizen of the World."

Ireland

Israel

Jamaica

Japan

Mexico

New Zealand

Nigeria

Norway

Pakistan

Poland

Scotland

South Africa

Spain

Sweden

Switzerland

Soviet Union

Syria

United States

Wales

J
Poetry Inspired
by Paul Robeson

A SELECTED LIST

Jean F. Brierre. "To Paul Robeson." Translated from the French by Frances Waldman. Negro Quarterly, Vol. 1, No. 4, Winter-Spring, 1943, pp. 363-364.

Dorothy Littlewort. "Paul Robeson." Opportunity, Vol. 24, No. 2, April, 1946, p. 81

Nazim Hikmet. "To Paul Robeson." Written in October, 1949, by the late Turkish poet while in prison. Poems by Nazim Hikmet, 1954, p. 55.

Beulah Richardson. "Paul Robeson." Freedom. June, 1951, p. 7.

Peter Blackman. "My Song Is For All Men." Daily Worker, November, 1951, p. 7.

Binem Heller. "Zog Nisht Kaynmol....To Paul Robeson." Jewish Life, Vol. 6, No. 7, 1952, p. 17.

Dora Titlbom. "To Robeson." Translated from the Yiddish by Martha Millet. The Worker, May 31, 1953, p. 8.

"To Paul Robeson." Daily Worker. Writer was from Brooklyn, New York. September 12, 1955, p. 7.

"To Paul Robeson on His 60th Birthday." Daily Worker, April 27, 1958, p. 7.

Fred Field. "Paul Robeson (1960)." The Forerunner and Other Selected Poems, 1914-1970. 1970, p. 38.

Percy Edward Johnston. "To Paul Robeson." Sixes and Sevens. Paul Bremen, Editor. London: Paul Bremen Publisher, 1962, pp. 85-88.

Sarah E. Wright. "Until They Have Stopped." Freedomways, Vol. 5, No. 3, Third Quarter, 1965, pp. 378-379.

Henri Percikow. "For Paul Robeson." Freedomways, Vol. 5, No. 3, Third Quarter, 1965, p. 411.

Edith Segal. "For Paul Robeson." Take My Hand, Poems and Song for Loves and Rebels. Introduction by Ossie Davis. New York: Dialog Publications, 1969, p. 96.

Sarah Fell Yellin. "Brother Paul." Flower Children and Other Poems, by Sarah Fell Yellin, 1969, pp. 28-29.

Percy Edward Johnston. "To Paul Robeson, Opus No. 3." From the magazine Dasein: A Journal of Aesthetics, Literature and Philosophy, edited by Johnston. Reprinted in Cavalcade: Negro Writing From 1760 to the Present, 1971. Arthur P. Davis and Saunders Redding. Boston: Houghton Mifflin Company, 1971, pp. 771-772.

Gwendolyn Brooks. "Paul Robeson." Family Pictures,by Gwendolyn Brooks. Detroit: Broadside Press, 1971, p. 19.

Vernon-Turner Kitabu. "Paul Robeson." Freedomways, Vol. 11, No. 4, Fourth Quarter, 1971, pp. 370-371.

Pablo Neruda. "Ode to Paul Robeson." Translated by Jill Booty. Salute to Paul Robeson: A Cultural Celebration of His 75th Birthday, April 15, 1973. New York City, 1973. Also in Freedomways, Vol. 16, No. 1, First Quarter, 1976, pp. 19-24.

Jon Eckels. "I Heard That." Black Scholar, Vol. 7, No. 5, January-February, 1972, p. 42.

Edith Segal. "When Robeson Sings." Daily Worker, April 9, 1973, p. 8.

Tal James. "Our Tree." Salute to Paul Robeson: A Tribute to A Forgotten Freedom Fighter. Detroit: McFarlane Men's Club and Afrikan History Clubs, No. 2 and No. 3, 1975, p. 4.

Tal James. "A Lesson From Paul." Salute to Paul Robeson: A Tribute to A Forgotten Freedom Fighter. Detroit: McFarlane Men's Club and Afrikan History Clubs, No. 2 and No. 3, 1975, p. 13.

David Cumberland. "Paul Robeson: We Are Now His Home." Daily World, February 11, 1976, p. 8.

Evelyn O. Chisley. "Declaration (The North or Polar Star Shall Be Called Paul's Star After January 23, 1976)." Daily World, February 11, 1976, p. 8.

Susan Kling. "Tribute: To Paul Robeson." Daily World Magazine, February 14, 1976, p. M-7.

Antar Sudan Katara Mberi. "Suite of the Singing Mountain." Daily World, May 14, 1976, p. 8.

James Brown. "Paul Robeson." Freedomways, Vol. 16, No. 3, Third Quarter, 1976, p. 178.

Willie J. Magruder. "Too Tall, Paul, Too Tall That's All." Freedomways, Vol. 17, No. 1, First Quarter, 1977, p. 19.

Michael S. Harper. "Paul Robeson." Black Scholar, Vol. 8, No. 8, April, 1977, p. 34.

Ann Sadowski. "A Home in This Rock." To Live Like Paul Robeson. New York: Young Workers Liberation League, 1977, p. 24.

Gwendolyn Brooks. "Paul Robeson." Paul Robeson: The Great Forerunner, by The Editors of Freedomways. New York: Dodd, Mead and Company, 1978, p. 235.

Richard Davidson. "For Paul Robeson." Paul Robeson: The Great Forerunner, by The Editors of Freedomways. New York: Dodd, Mead and Company, 1978, pp. 236-237.

Nikki Giovanni. "The Lion in Daniel's Den." Paul Robeson: The Great Forerunner, by The Editors of Freedomways. New York: Dodd, Mead and Company, 1978, p. 238.

Edward Royce. "To Paul Robeson." Paul Robeson: The Great Forerunner, by The Editors of Freedomways. New York: Dodd, Mead and Company, 1978, p. 251.

Joseph Mason Andrew Cox. "Homage to Paul Robeson." New and Selected Poems, 1966-1978, by J.M.A. Cox. Bronx, N.Y.: The Blue Diamond Press, 1978, pp. 114-115.

Lenwood G. Davis. "A Beautiful Human Being." Unpublished, 1981.

_____. "A Man of Understanding." Unpublished, 1981.

_____. "A Twentieth Century Phenomenon." Unpublished, 1981.

_____. "All The World Has Gone Mad." Unpublished, 1981.

_____. "Always in My Heart." Unpublished, 1981.

_____. "America Does Not Mean Paul Robeson." Unpublished, 1981.

_____. "April Is His Month." Unpublished, 1981.

_____. "April Is The Month." Unpublished, 1981.

_____. "Black He Was." Unpublished, 1981.

_____. "But Not in America." Unpublished, 1981.

_____. "Citizen of The World." Unpublished, 1981.

_____. "Freedom Fighter #1." Unpublished, 1981.

_____. "Freedom Fighter #2." Unpublished, 1981.

_____. "He Did His Own Thing." Unpublished, 1981.

_____. "He Did It All." Unpublished, 1981.

_____. "He Did Not Want to Die." Unpublished, 1981.

_____. "He Fought for Changes." Unpublished, 1981.

_____. "He Knew He Would Last." Unpublished, 1981.

_____. "He Loved His America." Unpublished, 1981.

_____. "He Loved Humanity." Unpublished, 1981.

_____. "He Too Was Not Assassinated." Unpublished,
1981.

_____. "He Understood." Unpublished, 1981.

_____. "He Used His Pen As A Weapon." Unpublished,
1981.

_____. "He Wanted to Be Himself." Unpublished, 1981.

_____. "He Was A Man #1." Unpublished, 1981.

_____. "He Was A Man #2." Unpublished, 1981.

_____. "He Was A Man #3." Unpublished, 1981.

_____. "He Was A Man #4." Unpublished, 1981.

_____. "He Was a New Yorker." Unpublished, 1981.

_____. "He Was His Own Man." Unpublished, 1981.

_____. "He Was Just Paul." Unpublished, 1981.

_____. "He Was Not Free." Unpublished, 1981.

_____. "He Was One of Them." Unpublished, 1981.

_____. "He Was Not An Uncle Tom." Unpublished, 1981.

_____. "He Was the Drummer Major." Unpublished, 1981.

_____. "He Worked for Freedom." Unpublished, 1981.

_____. He Would Be Remembered." Unpublished, 1981.

_____. "He Would See." Unpublished, 1981.

_____. "Here I Stand." Unpublished, 1981.

_____. "His Dreams Became Realities." Unpublished,
1981.

_____. "His Dreams Came True." Unpublished, 1981.

_____. "His Gut Feeling." Unpublished, 1981.

_____. "His Name is Paul Robeson." Unpublished, 1981.

_____. "His Smile, His Friendliness, His Concerns."
Unpublished, 1981.

_____. "His Son Will." Unpublished, 1981.

_____. "His Song As A Weapon." Unpublished, 1981.

_____. "How Beautiful It Would Be." Unpublished,
1981.

_____. "How Not To Be A Leader In Europe." Unpub-
lished, 1981.

_____. "How To Be A Klansman." Unpublished, 1981.

_____. "How To Be A Leader in America." Unpublished,
1981.

_____. "I Think of Paul Robeson." Unpublished, 1981.

_____. "I Wish Tatia Had Known Paul Robeson." Unpub-
lished, 1981.

_____. "Is The Political Robeson Dead?" Unpublished,
1981.

_____. "Life Held the Key." Unpublished, 1981.

_____. "Light in the Person of Paul Robeson." Unpub-
lished, 1981.

_____. "Mr. Human Rights." Unpublished, 1981.

_____. "Mr. Universal." Unpublished, 1981.

_____. "Music Is Universal." Unpublished, 1981.

_____. "One of A Kind." Unpublished, 1981.

_____. "Othello Is Paul Robeson." Unpublished, 1981.

_____. "Paul and Pauls." Unpublished, 1981.

_____. "Paul Knew African History." Unpublished, 1981.

_____. "Paul Robeson." Unpublished, 1981.

_____. "Paul Robeson: A Man of The Human Race." Unpublished, 1981.

_____. "Paul Robeson: A Renaissance Man." Unpublished, 1981.

_____. "Paul Robeson Had Many Titles." Unpublished, 1981.

_____. "Paul Robeson Knew Black History." Unpublished, 1981.

_____. "Paul Robeson Loved Harlem." Unpublished, 1981.

_____. "Paul Robeson The Working Man's Friend." Unpublished, 1981.

_____. "Paul Wanted...." Unpublished, 1981.

_____. "Robeson, The Peacemaker." Unpublished, 1981.

_____. "September Is the Month...." Unpublished, 1981.

_____. "Thanks to Paul Robeson." Unpublished, 1981.

_____. "The Greatest." Unpublished, 1981.

_____. "The Ku Klux Klan and Paul Robeson." Unpublished, 1981.

_____. "The Meaning of Paul Robeson, #1." Unpublished, 1981.

_____. "The Meaning of Paul Robeson, #2." Unpublished, 1981.

_____. "The Meaning of Paul Robeson, #3." Unpublished, 1981.

_____. "The Month of His Death." Unpublished, 1981.

_____. "The Somebodies and the Nobodies." Unpublished, 1981.

_____. "The Tallest Tree." Unpublished, 1981.

_____. "They Do Not Remember Him." Unpublished, 1981.

_____. "They Respected Him." Unpublished, 1981.

_____. "They Were As Much of a Prisoner as He Was."
Unpublished, 1981.

_____. "They Were Friends." Unpublished, 1981.

_____. "To Be Paul Robeson." Unpublished, 1981.

_____. "We Live As Men, We Die As Men." Unpublished,
1981.

_____. "We Owe Him So Much." Unpublished, 1981.

_____. "Who Will Remember Paul Robeson." Unpublished,
1981.

_____. "You Have Written The Truth." Unpublished,
1981.

_____. "You Were Always There." Unpublished, 1981.

K
Archival and Manuscript
Materials

A SELECTED LIST

Afro-American Historical and Cultural Museum, Philadelphia, Pennsylvania. Selected photographs, letters and memorabilia of Paul Robeson, multi-talented athlete, artist, and political activist.

Amistad Research Center, New Orleans, Louisiana. This center has a Verticle File of newspaper clippings on Paul Robeson.

Atlanta University, Trevor Arnett Library, Atlanta, Georgia. In the Paul Robeson Papers, there are a series of circular letters (usually mimeographed with rubber-stamped signature) (1942-1959) sent out by Paul Robeson as Chairman of the Council on African Affairs, soliciting moral and financial support for Africans in their mobilization against the Axis powers and for freedom from imperialism. The Eslanda Goode Robeson Papers are also located at Atlanta University. Mrs. Robeson, in a series of undated letters describes her husband's concert tours (1930-1931?) in England and on the Continent and a Russian tour in 1936.

British Library, Department of Manuscripts, London, England. The Assistant Keeper of Manuscripts reports that the library has no manuscripts of or relating to Paul Robeson.

Columbia University, Rare Books and Manuscripts, New York City. There are two letters written by Paul Robeson. One is in the National Emergency Civil Liberties Committee Papers and the other is in the Council on Religion and International Affairs Papers. Materials can also be found in the Alexander Gumby Collection at Columbia University.

Detroit Public Library, Detroit, Michigan. In the E. Azalia Hackley Collection there are four verticle file folders containing clippings, one folder of photographs, one folder of programs, fourteen recordings, and two posters.

Federal Bureau of Investigation, Washington, D.C. This agency has several thousand (between four and five) "documents" on Paul Robeson that it collected between the 1940's and 1960's. These materials can be acquired through the Freedom of Information Act.

Fisk University Library, Nashville, Tennessee. This library has Verticle Files of newspaper clippings on Paul Robeson.

Hampton Institute Library, Hampton, Virginia. This library has a Verticle File of newspaper clippings on Paul Robeson.

Harvard University, the Houghton Library, Cambridge, Massachusetts. There are three letters written by Robeson. One is to E.E. Cummings (no date); the other two are to Alexander Woollcott: a letter dated February 14, 1931, and a telegram (copy) dated June 3, 1931.

Howard University, Moorland-Spingarn Research Center, Washington, D.C. There are two boxes of newspaper clippings. The Manuscript Division is processing Paul Robeson's personal papers and they are scheduled for completion in 1985. This nearly 50,000 piece collection includes unpublished manuscripts, letters, business correspondence, documents, handbills, programs, scrapbooks, pamphlets, personal papers, unfinished manuscripts, scripts, press releases, scenarios, etc.

Library of Congress, Manuscript Division, Washington, D.C. The Manuscript Division does not hold a collection of Paul Robeson papers per se; material to, from, or about him may be found in a number of sources, including the Nannie Helen Burroughs and Margaret Webster Papers, the National Association for the Advancement of Colored People Records and the National Urban League Papers.

New York University, Elmer Holmes Bobst Library, Tamiment Collection, New York City. Vertical File ephemera including pamphlets and miscellaneous biographical items.

Paul Robeson Archives, German Democratic Republic, Berlin, Germany. This archives was established in 1965. It consists of tapes, records, photographs, posters, announcements, invitations, programs, leaflets, newspaper clippings, books, articles, brochures, speeches, statements, interviews, reviews, correspondences, letters, recollections, etc. Most of this collection is in German and has not been catalogued.

Princeton University Library, Princeton, New Jersey. The Theatre Collection includes several souvenirs, autographed programs, scripts, plays, posters, etc.

Rutgers University, New Brunswick, New Jersey. The University Archives has a number of pieces of material on Paul Robeson, such as his Senior Thesis, Yearbooks, newspaper clippings, and other materials pertaining to Robeson's undergraduate days at Rutgers University. There is some material on Robeson in the American Labor Party papers, which are located in the Special Collections Department at Rutgers.

Schomburg Center for Research in Black Culture, New York City. The
Paul Robeson collection includes books, pamphlets, programs, magazine
articles, scrapbooks, newspaper clippings on microfiche and in folders,
albums of phonograph records and some personal papers. The Lawrence
Brown Papers are also at the Schomburg Center. They contain two scrapbooks (1925-1960) of clippings and telegrams covering the Robeson-Brown
concert years.

Southern Illinois University, Carbondale, Illinois. The Herbert Marshall
Collection of Paul Robeson consists largely of playscripts and screen-
plays including "Show Boat," "Stevedore," "John Henry," and "Porgy," in
which Robeson played leading roles. The scripts have been arranged alphabetically by author and fill two and one half manuscript boxes. There
are also two musical scores in the collection, one of which is for "Show
Boat." Also included is one folder of correspondence, two manuscripts
concerning Robeson, a playbill from Plant in the Sun, and a publicity
poster from The Proud Valley. Photographs and newsclippings complete
the boxed material. Robeson's personal library comprising seventy-three
volumes has been shelved at the end of the collection as free-standing
volumes. They are arranged, for the most part, alphabetically by author.
Included in his library is an autographed copy of Othello and many of
the books bear his or his wife's signature.

Tuskegee Institute, Hollis Burke Frissell Library, Tuskegee Institute,
Alabama. Tuskegee Institute has no manuscripts of Mr. Robeson as such,
but it does have a massive clippings file. Many of the clippings come
from Black newspapers that are now defunct.

United States Department of State, Washington, D.C. It has one box
of Documents related to the Communist-oriented activities of Paul
Robeson for 1946-1962.

University of California at Berkeley, California. The Bancroft Library
has: three telegrams to Noel Sullivan, 1931; form letter with facsimile
signature, September 6, 1949, written on behalf of the Civil Rights
Congress (in papers of Professor R.T. Birge); telegram, May 4, 1946, to
Robert W. Kenny, Attorney General of California, enclosing statement on
Spain adopted at a meeting of the National Committee to Win the Peace;
two letters from Mrs. Robeson to Noel Sullivan, 1931 and n.d.; photocopy
of Margaret Cardozo Holmes' interview prepared for the Schlesinger
Library Black Women Oral History Project, Radcliffe College, in which she
comments on Robeson; photographs of Mr. and Mrs. Robeson.

Wake Forest University Library, Winston-Salem, North Carolina. This
library has two Verticle File Folders on Paul Robeson. Most of the
clippings come from the major newspapers, such as the New York Times,
Washington Post and Christian Science Monitor for the 1940s and 1950s.

Winston-Salem State University, O'Kelly Library, Winston-Salem, North
Carolina. This library has Verticle File Folders of newspaper clippings
from Black newspapers.

Yale University, The Beinecker Rare Book and Manuscript Library, New
Haven, Connecticut. There are: two letters to James Weldon Johnson,
two autographed letters signed and one autographed note signed to
Gertrude Stein, five autographed letters signed, seven autographed post-
cards signed, five telegrams, two letters to Carl Van Vechten and one
telegram to Richard Wright. The Department of Manuscripts and Archives
in the Sterling Library at Yale University has one letter from Paul
Robeson to Victor Jerome, and two letters from Jerome to Robeson. There
is also the James Weldon Johnson Collection at Yale University. One box
is devoted to Paul Robeson material. It contains over seventy-five
photographs and over thirty programs of plays and concerts signed by
Mr. Robeson, occasionally with explanatory notes; pamphlets and leaflets,
over forty leaves of clippings, articles about Mr. Robeson and other
items.

Index

ABOUT THE COMPILER

LENWOOD G. DAVIS is Associate Professor of History at Winston-Salem State University. He received both his B.A. and M.A. degrees in history from North Carolina Central University, Durham, North Carolina, and a doctorate in history from Carnegie-Mellon University. Dr. Davis has compiled more than seventy bibliographies. He is the author of eight books, *I Have a Dream: The Life and Times of Martin Luther King, Jr.* (1973), *The Black Woman in American Society: A Selected Annotated Bibliography* (1975), *The Black Family in the United States: A Selected Bibliography of Annotated Books, Articles, and Dissertations on Black Families in America* (1978), *Sickle Cell Anemia: A Selected Annotated Bibliography* (1978), *Black Artists in the United States: An Annotated Bibliography*, coauthored with Janet L. Sims (1980), *Marcus Garvey: An Annotated Bibliography*, coauthored with Janet L. Sims (1980), *Black Aged in the United States* (1980), and *Black Athletes in the United States: A Bibliography* (1981), coauthored with Belinda S. Daniels. He also has four additional bibliographies forthcoming from Greenwood Press in 1983 and 1984.